THE ROUTLEDGE COMPANION TO WOMEN AND MUSICAL LEADERSHIP

The Routledge Companion to Women and Musical Leadership: The Nineteenth Century and Beyond provides a comprehensive exploration of women's participation in musical leadership from the nineteenth century to the present. Global in scope, with contributors from over thirty countries, this book reveals the wide range of ways in which women have taken leadership roles across musical genres and contexts, uncovers new histories, and considers the challenges that women continue to face.

The volume addresses timely issues in the era of movements such as #MeToo, digital feminisms, and the resurgent global feminist movements. Its multidisciplinary chapters represent a wide range of methodologies, with historical musicology, models drawn from ethnomusicology, analysis, philosophy, cultural studies, and practice research all informing the book. Including almost fifty chapters written by both researchers and practitioners in the field, it covers themes including:

- Historical Perspectives
- Conductors and Impresarios
- Women's Practices in Music Education
- Performance and the Music Industries
- Faith and Spirituality: Worship and Sacred Musical Practices
- Advocacy: Collectives and Grass-Roots Activism

The Routledge Companion to Women and Musical Leadership: The Nineteenth Century and Beyond draws together both new perspectives from early career researchers and contributions from established world-leading scholars. It promotes academic-practitioner dialogue by bringing contributions from both fields together, represents alternative models of women in musical leadership, celebrates the work done by women leaders, and shows how women challenge accepted notions of gendered roles. Offering a comprehensive overview of the varied forms of women's musical leadership, this volume is a vital resource for all scholars of women in music, as well as professionals in the music industries and music education today.

Laura Hamer is Senior Lecturer in Music at The Open University.

Helen Julia Minors is Professor and Head of the School of the Arts at York St John University.

The Routledge Companion to Women and Musical Leadership brings a fresh perspective to the growing body of research about women and music through its focus on leadership, and in fact it is the first volume of research dedicated to this topic. This spotlight on leadership allows the authors to articulate the broader effects of strategies to remedy the underrepresentation of women in many areas of musical activity and to examine these issues at an institutional level. This edited collection looks at women exercising leadership in many areas of music and from many different angles. The volume is strengthened by its wide-ranging dimensions, from the sixty-nine authors coming from throughout Europe as well as North and South America, Australia, and South Asia to the diversity of topics as well as varied methodologies utilized. The issues addressed move well beyond those most frequently addressed, e.g., composers, conductors, and performers, to include women in faith and spiritual leadership roles (Jewish, Anglican, and different strands of spiritual music in India) and to advocacy and activism in music. From my outlook as both a musicologist and conductor – someone who has endeavored throughout my career to let each facet inform the other aspect of my work – this collection pays generous attention to both lived experiences and theoretical foundations. As someone who was intrigued by the conference which fostered this volume, I look forward to its publication and to reading these new, fresh ideas.

J. Michele Edwards, *Professor Emerita of Music,*
Macalester College, St. Paul, MN, USA

ROUTLEDGE MUSIC COMPANIONS

Routledge Music Companions offer thorough, high-quality surveys and assessments of major topics in the study of music. All entries in each companion are specially commissioned and written by leading scholars in the field. Clear, accessible, and cutting-edge, these companions are the ideal resource for advanced undergraduates, postgraduate students, and researchers alike.

THE ROUTLEDGE COMPANION TO MUSIC AND MODERN LITERATURE
Edited by Rachael Durkin, Peter Dayan, Axel Englund, Katharina Clausius

THE ROUTLEDGE COMPANION TO ETHICS AND RESEARCH IN ETHNOMUSICOLOGY
Edited by Jonathan P.J. Stock and Beverley Diamond

THE ROUTLEDGE COMPANION TO CREATIVITIES IN MUSIC EDUCATION
Edited by Clint Randles, Pamela Burnard

THE ROUTLEDGE COMPANION TO APPLIED MUSICOLOGY
Edited by Chris Dromey

THE ROUTLEDGE COMPANION TO TEACHING MUSIC COMPOSITION IN SCHOOLS: INTERNATIONAL PERSPECTIVES
Edited by Kirsty Devaney, Martin Fautley, Joana Grow and Annette Ziegenmeyer

THE ROUTLEDGE COMPANION TO GLOBAL FILM MUSIC IN THE EARLY SOUND ERA
Edited by Jeremy Barham

THE ROUTLEDGE COMPANION TO WOMEN AND MUSICAL LEADERSHIP
Edited by Laura Hamer and Helen Julia Minors

More information about this series can be found at www.routledge.com/series/RACL

THE ROUTLEDGE COMPANION TO WOMEN AND MUSICAL LEADERSHIP

The Nineteenth Century and Beyond

Edited by Laura Hamer and Helen Julia Minors

NEW YORK AND LONDON

Designed cover image: suteishi (iStock/Getty Images Plus Collection)

First published 2025
by Routledge
605 Third Avenue, New York, NY 10158

and by Routledge
4 Park Square, Milton Park, Abingdon, Oxon, OX14 4RN

Routledge is an imprint of the Taylor & Francis Group, an informa business

© 2025 Taylor & Francis

The right of **Laura Hamer** and **Helen Julia Minors** to be identified as the authors of the editorial material, and of the authors for their individual chapters, has been asserted in accordance with sections 77 and 78 of the Copyright, Designs and Patents Act 1988.

All rights reserved. No part of this book may be reprinted or reproduced or utilised in any form or by any electronic, mechanical, or other means, now known or hereafter invented, including photocopying and recording, or in any information storage or retrieval system, without permission in writing from the publishers.

Trademark notice: Product or corporate names may be trademarks or registered trademarks, and are used only for identification and explanation without intent to infringe.

ISBN: 978-0-367-45676-4 (hbk)
ISBN: 978-1-032-81220-5 (pbk)
ISBN: 978-1-003-02476-7 (ebk)

DOI: 10.4324/9781003024767

Typeset in Sabon
by Apex CoVantage, LLC

CONTENTS

List of Music Examples   xiii
List of Figures   xiv
List of Tables   xvi
Contributor Biographies   xvii
List of Abbreviations   xxvi
Dedication and Acknowledgements   xxix

1 Defining, Surveying and Interrogating Women in Musical Leadership   1
Laura Hamer and Helen Julia Minors

PART I
Historical Perspectives: Historical Perspectives: An Introduction   13
Laura Hamer and Helen Julia Minors

2 Augusta Hervey: Lady of 'The Ladies' Guitar and Mandoline Band'   15
Sarah Clarke

3 Examining the Birth of Guitar Societies in America: From Women Guitarists' Advocacy to Philanthropy   26
Kathy Acosta Zavala

4 'Scatter[ing] All Prejudices to the Winds': Wilma Norman-Neruda and Camilla Urso as Leaders of the Nineteenth-Century String Quartet   38
Bella Powell

5   Surviving the Everyday: Gendered Violence, Patriarchal Power
    Structures, and Strategies of Resistance in Late Nineteenth-Century
    Ladies' Orchestras   51
    Nuppu Koivisto-Kaasik

6   Sites of Empowerment: *Fin-de-Siècle* Salon Culture and the Music of
    Cécile Chaminade   65
    Ann Grindley

7   'Une Belle Manifestation Féministe': The Formation of the Union des
    Femmes Professeurs et Compositeurs de Musique   79
    Laura Hamer

8   The Forgotten Woman: Joan Trimble (1915–2000) and the Canon of
    Twentieth-Century Irish Art Song   92
    Orla Shannon

9   'There is No Gate, No Lock, No Bolt That You Can Set Upon
    the Freedom of My Mind': Being a Woman in Franco's Prisons:
    A Glimpse Through Music   107
    Elsa Calero-Carramolino

PART II
Conductors and *Impresarios*: Conductors and *Impresarios*: An Introduction   125
Laura Hamer and Helen Julia Minors

10 Lilian Baylis: The Visionary Impresario   127
    Kenneth Baird, with Laura Hamer

11 Musical Ghosts: Re-Instating Elsie April in Historical Narratives
    of the British Musical   141
    Arianne Johnson Quinn and Sarah K. Whitfield

12 'She is a Degenerate Cocaine Addict': Emma Carelli, A *Diva-
    Impresario* Facing Her Opponents   153
    Matteo Paoletti

13 Henriette Renié as a Harp Ensemble Leader, Choral and Orchestral
    Conductor, and *Impresario* in the Light of Archival Sources   167
    Temina Cadi Sulumuna

14 An American Female Violinist and Conductor in Paris: "La Kazanova
    et Ses Tziganes" (1933–1938)   183
    Jean-Christophe Branger
    Translation: Kiefer Oakley

15	Edis de Philippe, the Israel National Opera (INO), and the Politics of Music *Kira Alvarez*	195
16	Odaline de la Martinez – Conductor, Composer, Entrepreneur, Leader *Carola Darwin*	206

PART III
Women's Practices in Music Education: Women's Practices in Music Education: An Introduction
Laura Hamer and Helen Julia Minors 219

17	Embodying the Rhythm of Self in Leadership *Judith Francois*	223
18	Learning to Coach, Coaching to Lead *Jane Booth and Jane Cook*	235
19	The Work that (Irish) Women Do: Reframing Leadership in a British University Ceílí Band *Anne-Marie Beaumont*	248
20	'It's Not About Me!': The Life and Leadership of Cathi Leibinger *Margaret J. Flood*	261
21	Addressing Cyclic Gender Constructs in Music and Music Education in the UK *Abigail Bruce and Chamari Wedamulla*	274
22	Pipeline to the Podium: Can Gender Differentiated Pedagogical Approaches Address the Underrepresentation of Women Conductors? *Katherine Hanckel*	290
23	Women Leading Change in Assessment Calibration *Michelle Phillips*	300
24	Innovation and Leadership in Group Teaching Across the Lifespan: Three Case Studies *Cynthia Stephens-Himonides, Margaret Young, and Melanie Bowes*	309
25	Training Early Career Women Teachers in Choral Leadership: Building a Community of Practice *Rebecca Berkley*	321

PART IV
Performance and the Music Industries: Performance and the Music Industries: An Introduction   333
Laura Hamer and Helen Julia Minors

26 Women's Musical Leadership in Music Industries and Education   335
    Laura Hamer and Helen Julia Minors, with Alice Farnham, Katy Hamilton, Emma Haughton, Jessy McCabe, Sarah MacDonald, Davina Vencatasamy and Eleanor Wilson

27 Preparing Women for Musical Leadership: Student and Faculty Voices   358
    Allison Gurland, Elizabeth Markow, Rebekah E. Moore, and Shannon Pires

28 Women Leading Opera in the UK: An Ethnographic Study of Innovation   374
    Elizabeth Etches Jones

29 Diversity in Italian Music Programming: Symphonic and Chamber Music Programming in Milan   386
    Valentina Bertolani and Luisa Santacesaria

30 Beyond Music Workshops: A Composer and a Community   401
    Jenni Roditi

PART V
Faith and Spirituality: Worship and Sacred Musical Practices: Faith and Spirituality: Worship and Sacred Musical Practices: An Introduction   437
Laura Hamer and Helen Julia Minors

31 Leading the Way: Victorian Premonitions for the Female Voice in Anglo-Jewish Music   439
    Danielle Padley

32 Sisters in Song: Women Cantors and Musical Creativity in Progressive Jewish Worship   451
    Rachel Adelstein

33 Maruja Hinestrosa: Faith and Introspection in a Colombian Composer   464
    Luis Gabriel Mesa Martínez

34 Undoing Sanctity: Imee Ooi's Popular Contemporary Buddhist Music   483
    Fung Ying Loo and Fung Chiat Loo

35 The Female Role in Sacred Musical Practices in *Shīʿah* Rituals in Iraq   495
    Ahmed Al-Badr

36 A Muslim in a Baptist Church: Discovering My Calling as a Sacred
    Musician   509
    Theresa Parvin Steward

37 Power, Pop, and Performance   520
    Major John Martin

38 'No Lady Need Apply': Women and Girls in Cathedral
    Musical Leadership   541
    Enya HL Doyle and Katherine Dienes-Williams

39 Unsuitable for Evensong: Examining Exclusion and Diversity in the
    Repertoire of Oxford Collegiate Anglican Choirs   550
    Caroline Lesemann-Elliott

PART VI
Advocacy: Advocacy: Collectives, and Grassroots Activism: An Introduction   563
Laura Hamer and Helen Julia Minors

40 Power, Care and the Paradox of Leadership: A Kabbalistic Enquiry   567
    Nicky Gluch

41 Toppling Systemic Exclusion: Women's Roles in a Century of Jazz   579
    Tahira Clayton, Amanda Ekery, and Hannah Grantham

42 Mapping the Boundaries: Encountering Women's Creativity in the Salon   590
    Briony Cox-Williams

43 Women's Leadership Within Latin American Musicians' Unions:
    Opportunities and Challenges   600
    Ananay Aguilar

44 From 'Women's Revolutions Per Minute' Through 'Taking Race Live'
    to Co-Founding 'Equality, Diversity and Inclusion in Music Studies
    Network': Supporting, Developing and Establishing Collaborative
    Networks for Change   612
    Helen Julia Minors

45 Women's Revolutions Per Minute: Access to, Distribution,
    and Recognition of Music by Women   622
    Hilary Friend and Helen Julia Minors

46 Gender Relations in New Music (GRiNM) and Yorkshire Sound
    Women Network (YSWN): Case Studies in Activism
    and Organisation for Change   636
    Stellan Veloce, Brandon Farnsworth, Rosanna Lovell, Heidi Johnson,
       Abi Bliss, and Eddie Dobson

47 Sounding the Feminists: Campaigning for Institutional Change to
    Support Women in Music in Contemporary Ireland   649
    Laura Watson

Index   663

MUSIC EXAMPLES

8.1	Joan Trimble, 'Girl's Song', bb. 17–18	97
8.2	Joan Trimble, 'Girl's Song', bb. 39–41	97
8.3	Herbert Howells, 'Girl's Song', bb. 46–48	98
8.4	Joan Trimble, 'Girl's Song', bb. 3–5	99
8.5	Joan Trimble, 'Girl's Song', bb. 12–16	99
8.6	Joan Trimble, 'Girl's Song', bb. 18–21	99
8.7	Herbert Howells, 'Girl's Song', bb. 21–25	100
8.8	Joan Trimble, 'Girl's Song', b. 27	100
8.9	Joan Trimble, 'Girl's Song', bb. 1–3	101
8.10	Herbert Howells, 'Girl's Song', bb. 1–4	101
8.11	Joan Trimble, 'Girl's Song', bb. 41–42	102
8.12	Joan Trimble, 'Girl's Song', b. 12	102
8.13	Joan Trimble, 'Girl's Song', bb. 37–38	103
33.1	Transcription of the first stanza of Maruja Hinestrosa's *Yaguarcocha*	470
33.2	Maruja Hinestrosa, *Reproche*, Final Stanza	471
33.3	Maruja Hinestrosa, *Eco lejano*	472
33.4	Maruja Hinestrosa, *Todos llevamos una cruz*	472
33.5	Excerpt from Franz Schubert's *Ellens dritter Gesang*. Breitkopf & Härtel edition (1895)	475
33.6	Excerpt from Maruja Hinestrosa's *Ave Maria*. Luis Gabriel Mesa Martínez's edition (2014)	476
33.7	Bars 20–30 from Mesa Martínez's edition of Maruja Hinestrosa's *Ave Maria*	476
35.1	Transcription of the *Itha terdoon* ('If you wish') *Leṭmeye*	501
35.2	Transcription of *dish imbellileh* ('I enter the shrine wet') *Leṭmeyeh*	505
37.1	Evangeline Booth, 'I Bring Thee All'	525
37.2	The Joystrings, 'A Starry Night'	529
37.3	Dorothy Gates, *Hope* (2009), bars 1–4	534

FIGURES

10.1	*The Drawing of a Great Lady*, Lilian Baylis by Sir William Rothenstein (1922)	128
18.1	OSCAR	238
20.1	Cathi Leibinger and her mentor, Colonel Arnold Gabriel	267
29.1	Overview of the quantitative data, seasons 2018–2019	389
30.1	John Cage 4'33" score, given to Jenni and signed by the composer following her involvement in the Almeida Theatre schools workshops based around their production of Cage's Europeras 3 and 4 in 1990 (personal collection)	403
30.2	*September Boxes for Orchestra*, source material for my 1985 Guildhall School Symphony Orchestra finals undergraduate piece, taking a playful music workshop approach into composition: 'what does this size box and its position on the page suggest to you, musically? Sketch in some ideas.' A starting point posed to me by Peter Wiegold. From this I composed a notated orchestral score	404
30.3	Composition lesson with Peter Wiegold, 1982/83, my notes	405
30.4	The Loft: Jenni talking to people gathered around at The Improvisers' Choir 'Land Mass' album launch (11 May 2019)	414
30.5	Jenni conducting The Improvisers' Choir, at the first in a three-concert 'Club Vocalé' series held at the Earl Haig Hall, Crouch End, 26th September 2016	418
30.6	Jenni performing Vocal Tai Chi at Inspiral Lounge, Camden Town, London. April 2012	418
30.7	The Improvisers' Choir (TIC) with Jenni conducting. Koç University, Istanbul, Turkey. December 2016	421
30.8	Conduction, basic signals handout for Wellcome Trust reading room public workshops on 22nd September 2018 and 28th February 2019, led by Jenni, with members of The Open Choir for Improvisers (TOCFI) present to support the public	422
30.9	Jenni with TIC, TOCFI, and special guest Cleveland Watkiss MBE at Earl Haig Hall, Crouch End, London. Concert on 25th November 2016	423

Figures

30.10	In 2019 TIC were funded by PRS Foundation, with generous matching funds from a private donor, to record an album. The result, completed in 2021, is a thirteen-track odyssey through the landscape of the choir's vocal reaches and enriched with visual interpretations of the journey, from the roots to the heavens	424
33.1	Maruja Hinestrosa (c. 1930)	466
33.2	Sanctuary of Las Lajas. Roman Catholic Basilica church built on a cliff, overlooking the Guáitara River in the outskirts of Ipiales (Nariño)	474
35.1	Period of holding rituals during the months of *Muḥarram* and *Ṣufer*	499
35.2	The *Almullayeh*, Umm Noor, wearing the *bwima* and the black *Hashemi* decorated with religious texts	500
35.3	*Almullayeh*, Umm Hawra, performing the *Alnaʿi*. She appears in the picture holding a notebook in her left hand while placing her right hand on her right cheek and closing her right ear so that she can hear herself clearly	502
35.4	A bird's-eye view of the *Alleṭum wuqufen* activity	504
35.5	The standard structure of the *Muḥarram*, *ʿashura*, and *Arbiʿineyeh* Rituals	506
37.1	Evangeline Booth	522
37.2	The Joystrings on the Steps of St. Paul's Cathedral, London, 1964	527
37.3	The Joystrings, publicity photograph (1964)	528
37.4	Dorothy Gates	530
37.5	Dorothy Gates conducting the Greater New York Youth Band, Montclair, NJ, USA	533
40.1	The *sefirot* mapped onto the human form	574
43.1	Practices that unions around the world implement to promote gender equality in their structure	606
43.2	Achievements observed by those unions that have implemented some of the activities	606
43.3	Responses to event feedback questionnaire	609

TABLES

3.1	American Guild of Banjoists, Mandolinists and Guitarists Organising Committee	28
3.2	List of the American Guild of Banjoists, Mandolinists and Guitarists' 1902 Governing Body	28
3.3	List of Members of Miller's American Guitar Society (1906)	30
3.4	Founding Members of the American Guitar Society	32
5.1	The Members of Wiener Damen-Capelle Maiglöckchen (1895)	53
9.1	Catalogue of Songs Composed by Female Inmates in Spanish Prisons from 1938 to 1948	114
11.1	Elsie April's Compositions and Musical Arrangements (selected)	149
17.1	Authentic Leadership Constructs	226
23.1	The Percentage Marks Arrived at by Each Group of 4–5 Delegates for Each of the Four Performances	305
23.2	Delegate Responses to Two Questionnaire Items	305
26.1	Initial Questions to Spark Debate	337
28.1	The Participants and Their Respective Organisations	375
29.1	Institutions and Number of Events in the 2018–2019 Concert Season	387
33.1	List of Maruja Hinestrosa's Compositions	467
33.2	Some National Recordings of Maruja Hinestrosa's *Cafetero*	477
42.1	Modes of Audience Experience, Abercrombie and Longhurst	595

CONTRIBUTOR BIOGRAPHIES

Kathy Acosta Zavala has a musicology PhD from the University of Arizona. Her dissertation revealed Vadhah Olcott-Bickford's crucial role in the construction of the modern American guitar landscape. Her other research interests include the soundscapes of protests in the USA in American symphonic commissions during WWII. She is Young Musicians Unite's Operation Manager in Miami and an adjunct music professor at MDC-Kendall campus. She is an active guitarist.

Rachel Adelstein is an ethnomusicologist and Hebrew tutor based in New Haven, Connecticut. She received her PhD from the University of Chicago in 2013, with a dissertation entitled "Braided Voices: Women Cantors in Non-Orthodox Judaism." Between 2014 and 2017, she was the Gaylord and Dorothy Donnelley Junior Research Fellow at Corpus Christi College, University of Cambridge. Her published and forthcoming work addresses women's music and agency in Jewish sacred spaces, the music of British Reform, Liberal, and Masorti synagogues, and the history and meaning of congregational melodies in Jewish life.

Ananay Aguilar is an affiliated researcher at the faculty of music at the University of Cambridge, having completed two externally funded projects there. She is also the head of TENU, a tech transfer company. Her research interests lie in the interface between music business and policy and its impact on the everyday lives and creative skills of talented musicians. Her book on legal rights is forthcoming with Palgrave.

Ahmed Al-Badr is a professional musician working in Iraq.

Kira Alvarez, PhD, is a researcher at Freie Universität Berlin working at the intersection of history, music, politics, and religion. She holds a PhD in history from Freie Universität Berlin, funded by the German Research Foundation, and received fully-funded degrees from Stanford University (MA in history and MA in music), Hebrew University (MA in religion), and Swarthmore College (BA in religion and history). Kira has taught and published her work throughout the U.S. and Europe.

Contributor Biographies

Kenneth Baird is Managing Director of the European Opera Centre based at Liverpool Hope University.

Anne-Marie Beaumont was formerly Subject Leader for two undergraduate degrees at the University of Wolverhampton and has over twenty years' experience in HE in Ireland and the UK. As a Senior Fellow of the Higher Education Academy, she is particularly interested in curriculum development and a broadening of the traditional conceptions of what a music degree should contain. She is currently Music Development Officer for Music Generation in Wicklow, Ireland.

Rebecca Berkley is Associate Professor of Music Education at the University of Reading. She is Artistic Director of Universal Voices and Postgraduate Director of taught programmes at the university. Her work focuses on the importance of musical literacy in creative classroom practice and musical cognition and the development of musical knowledge in music teachers and students. She is a highly experienced choral director with a wide-ranging professional practice, including conducting children's, youth, and adult choirs, music theatre, and operatic repertoire.

Valentina Bertolani is a musicologist specialising in cultural diplomacy, collective improvisation, and electronic music. She co-edited *Live-Electronic Music: Composition, Performance, Study* (Routledge 2018). She is currently working on a project titled 'ARPOEXMUS – Archiving post-1960s experimental music: Exploring the ontology of music beyond the score-performance dichotomy', funded by the European Commission.

Building on 30 years as a clarinetist with orchestras internationally, **Jane Booth** now applies her ensemble skills, creativity, and vision to the world of communication. A Master Coach and Organisational Consultant, Jane facilitates Leadership and Systems development work. Ignite's *Leaders on and off Stage* is underpinned by research into leadership in the creative industries.

Jean-Christophe Branger, Professor of Musicology at the Université Lumière Lyon 2, has devoted most of his work to the history of music in France during the Third Republic, especially Massenet and Debussy. He is the author of monographs and numerous symposiums or essays on music, musicians, or composers of this period.

Abigail Bruce received her Masters by Research in Music from Kingston University. She has worked with schools and colleges, supporting young people to make informed decisions about education progression. As part of the government's National Collaborative Outreach programmes, her work aims to address demographic underrepresentation in HE. She currently works at Decent Music PR and Future Hits Radio. She is an active singer-songwriter.

Elsa Calero-Carramolino is a Doctor Cum Laude (University of Granada, 2021) in History and Arts (Musicology). Since 2014 she has worked in the area of music and punishment during Franco's regime. The results of her research have been published in both Spanish and English, in publishers such as Brepols, British Forum for Ethnomusicology, Fondo de Cultura Económica, and Routledge. She recently published the book *Sonidos al otro lado del muro. Música y otras prácticas sonoras en las cárceles de Franco (1938–1948)* (Granada: Universidad de Granada, 2023), in which she analyses the impact of musical practice in the post-war prison context.

Contributor Biographies

Sarah Clarke is a classical guitarist who has taught the instrument for many years. Her research interests centre on the guitar in nineteenth-century England, and she has completed her doctorate at the Open University.

Tahira Clayton is a vocalist, activist, songwriter, and educator based in New York City. She currently serves as Vice President of Women in Jazz Organization. More information can be found at www.tahiraclayton.com.

Jane Cook holds a BA (Philosophy), a PGCE, Diploma in Coaching, and is a Master Practitioner and Coaching supervisor with the EMCC. She has a broad international client base as a coach and coach trainer. She is the founding director of Linden Learning and the senior coaching advisor for Guildhall Ignite.

Briony Cox-Williams is a pianist and researcher. She has given concerts with a particular concentration on Lieder and neglected piano repertoire of the nineteenth century. As a scholar, she has published articles on women composers and on nineteenth-century performance practice in song. Currently a Lecturer at the Royal Academy of Music, London, she is working on a book about the nineteenth-century salon.

Carola Darwin lectures in History of Music at the Royal College of Music and performs as an opera and concert singer. Her work on Johanna Müller-Hermann was part of BBC R3's *Five Women Composers* Project. In October 2019, she premièred *Endless Forms Most Beautiful*, by Cheryl Frances-Hoad, commissioned with funds from the Arts Council.

Katherine Dienes-Williams was appointed Organist and Master of the Choristers at Guildford Cathedral in January 2008 following six years as Director of Music at the Collegiate Church of St Mary, Warwick. She was the first-ever female member to be elected to the Cathedral Organists' Association, and on her appointment to Guildford, became the first-ever woman to hold such a post in the Church of England.

Enya HL Doyle completed her doctorate on gender diversity and inclusion in music-making, which reflects her commitment to scrutinising the often-subtle and underlying forms of exclusion which are embedded in practice, policy, and organisational culture. As a trained classical singer (DipLCM), a Fellow of the Royal Society of Arts, and Associate Fellow of the Higher Education Academy, Dr Doyle's inclusion consultancy work largely orbits around Higher Education and the Arts and culture sectors in the UK and Ireland. She is currently the Diversity, Equity, Accessibility, and Inclusion advisor at the Royal Irish Academy of Music.

Amanda Ekery is a multi-instrumentalist/composer. She has been praised by *Downbeat Magazine*, Chamber Music America, and New Music USA. She is the founder of El Paso Jazz Girls, Assistant Director of Academic Affairs at The New School, and teaching artist for the Met Opera and Jazz at Lincoln Center. Learn more at www.amandaekery.com.

Alice Farnham is a British conductor and author of *In Good Hands – The Making of a Modern Conductor*, published by Faber Books. She trained at the St. Petersburg Conservatoire with the legendary pedagogue Ilya Musin. Guest conducting includes the Royal Opera House Covent Garden (The Fireworkmaker's Daughter), Mariinsky Theatre (The Rape of Lucretia), Calgary Opara (Norma, 50th Jubilee Gala), Folkoperan (Turandot, Satyagraha, Carmen),

Wermlands Opera (Bernstein on Broadway), Grange Park Opera (Falstaff, I Capuleti e i Montecchi), Teatru Manoel Valetta (Dido & Aeneas).

Margaret J. Flood is Instructor of Music and the Coordinator of Music Education at Florida Southern College in Lakeland. She is a Ph.D. Candidate in Music Education at the Frost School of Music – University of Miami and founder of the Frost Young Women Conductors' Symposium and Virtual Web Series.

Judith Francois is Senior Lecturer in the faculty of health, science, social care, and education with a particular focus on Leadership and Management in Nursing. Current roles include teaching across a range of pre- and post-registration modules, including Foundation, Pre-registration, and MSc programmes. She is Associate Dean for Access and Participation for the Joint Faculty of St Georges and Kingston Universities, as well as the lead for the Admissions for the Nursing Associate Foundation Degree.

Hilary Friend is a composer and activist for women in music. She was the director of WRPM, Women's Revolutions Per Minute.

Nicky Gluch is a conductor and writer based in Sydney, Australia. In 2018, she commenced a PhD at the Sydney Conservatorium of Music exploring the role of empathy in conducting leadership. She also regularly programmes and presents for Fine Music Sydney radio station.

Hannah Grantham is an interdisciplinary music researcher with interests in museums, musical instruments, jazz, folk music, and the material culture of music. She has worked with collections at the Smithsonian, the University of South Dakota's National Music Museum, and the Music Library at the University of North Texas.

Ann Grindley is a PhD candidate at the Open University, where her funded doctoral studies include working with DONNE Women in Music. She has presented widely on women in music and works in university administration.

GRiNM (Gender Relations in New Music) is an autonomous, heterogeneous collective working on issues of gender and diversity in New Music. It generates statistics and promotes discussion on issues of equality and inclusion through institutional platforms such as festivals and conferences, as well as artistic methods of protest and intervention. Members included in this volume are **Stellan Veloce, Brandon Farnsworth,** and **Rosanna Lovell.**

Allison Gurland completed her music industry major and business administration minor degree at Northeastern University. She completed two internships with Concerted Effort and The John F. Kennedy Center for the Performing Arts. She is Senior Coordinator, Event Presentation – New York Rangers, at Madison Square Garden Sports Corp.

Laura Hamer is a Senior Lecturer in Music at the Open University. She is a Feminist Musicologist. Her monograph, *Female Composers, Conductors, Performers: Musiciennes of Interwar France*, 1919–1939, was published by Routledge in 2018 (paperback edition, 2020). She is editor of The Cambridge Companion to Women in Music since 1900 (Cambridge University Press, 2021). Between 2022 and 2024, she was Principal Investigator of the AHRC-funded Women's Musical Leadership Online Network.

Contributor Biographies

Katy Hamilton is a freelance researcher, writer, and presenter on music. Her area of specialisation is the music of Johannes Brahms and his contemporaries, and she has also been involved in projects covering subjects as diverse as the history of the Edinburgh Festival, the role of émigré musicians in post-1945 British musical life, and variety shows at the Wigmore Hall in the early twentieth century. She is a regular presenter at the National Gallery and has also provided notes and concert introductions for the Victoria & Albert Museum, Royal College of Music, Wigmore Hall, University of Nottingham, and St George's, Bristol. She has taught at the Royal College of Music and the University of Nottingham, published and assisted on projects focussing on nineteenth-century vocal music, and is an active chamber accompanist and repetiteur, having worked with instrumentalists, singers, and choirs in England, Ireland, Spain, and Germany.

Katherine Hanckel is the associate band director at the Potomac School in McLean, Virginia. She joined the faculty as a return to her Northern Virginia roots after having taught previously in North Carolina and the District of Columbia.

Emma Haughton is an AHRC-funded doctoral candidate at Kingston University, under the supervision of Professor Helen Julia Minors and Professor Sarah Upstone. Her work explores the female symphonists of the 20th century, notably Ruth Gipps, Florence B. Price, and Ina Boyle. She is an educator and a freelance woodwind player, actively performing in the North West of England.

Elizabeth Etches Jones is a PhD candidate at Royal Holloway, University of London. Her research explores organisational culture, innovation, and risk in the UK opera industry. She holds an MMus (Distinction) from Royal Holloway and a First Class BA in Music from the University of Oxford.

Nuppu Koivisto-Kaasik is a postdoctoral researcher currently affiliated with the Uniarts History Forum, Helsinki. Her research interests include (but are not limited to) musical life in nineteenth-century Eastern Europe, women musicians, urban history, and transnational cultural exchanges. She completed her PhD at the University of Helsinki.

Caroline Lesemann-Elliott completed her PhD at Royal Holloway, specialising in Early Modern English convent music. She has a master's degree from Royal Holloway and a bachelor's in music (first-class with honours) from the University of Edinburgh. She is Visting Fellow in Music at the Bodleian. Caroline's research revolves around the music of 17th- and early 18th-century English convents in exile. She has featured as a singer-scholar in multiple concert projects featuring her research at Christ Church Cathedral Oxford, such as The Life of St Frideswide (October 2019, in collaboration with Korrigan Consort and lutenist Liz Kenny) and 'To Play King': Baroque Music of Court and Cloister (August 2021 in collaboration with Sub Rosa). She has also co-led multiple projects at Oxford University, including The Gentlewomen (an opera collage exploring femicide, music, and the 16th-century Ferrarese ensemble the Concerto delle Donne, funded by TORCH, February of 2020) and the mini-documentary Doors, Dwellings, and Devotion: Recreating an Anchoritic Rite of Enclosure (funded by the John Fell OUP fund in collaboration with the Oxford University Music Faculty, August 2021). She has recently started a historically informed ensemble dedicated to exploring the lives of English Christian women religious called the Basilinda Consort.

Contributor Biographies

Fung Chiat Loo is based at the University of Malaysia in the department of music. She completed her PhD at the University of Sheffield and her master's at the Royal Welsh College of Music and Drama. Recent publications include: 'Birdsongs, Structure and Harmonic colour of Non-birdsong Subjects in Olivier Messiaen's 'La bouscarle' from Catalogue d'oiseaux' in *Revista Música Hodie*, 21 (2021).

Fung Ying Loo is an associate professor of music in the music department, within the faculty of creative arts, at the University of Malaya. She teaches ethnomusicology and research methodology. After obtaining her Fellowship (Trinity College of London) and Bachelor of Music (Hons) in piano performance (Universiti Putra Malaysia), she furthered her music study at the Royal Welsh College of Music and Drama, where she received her Master of Music in Piano Performance with distinction. She studied piano under Michael Schreider, Barno Khaknazarov, Larisa Rakhmanova, and Lillian Joseph, and had master classes conducted by Artur Pizzaro, Boris Berman, Irina Osipova, Julian Jacobson, Richard MacMahon, Olga Malissova, and Ng Chong Lim. As a pianist, her performances locally and abroad included the first piano concertos of Beethoven and Tchaikovsky under the baton of Zakhid Khaknazarov, recitals at St. John's Smith Square and St. Martin-in-the-Fields, and a recording for Ceri Richard's Themes and Variations published by National Museums and Galleries of Wales, UK. She completed her PhD at the University of Sheffield, UK in 2009. Her work has appeared in International Review of the Aesthetics and Sociology of Music, Muzikološki Zbornik, Revista Música Hodie, Asian Theatre Journal, International Journal of Music Education, IEEE Multimedia, Media Watch, and other publications.

Sarah MacDonald is a Canadian-born conductor, organist, pianist, and composer living in the UK, and she holds the positions of Fellow and Director of Music at Selwyn College, Cambridge, and Director of Ely Cathedral's Girl Choristers. She has been at Selwyn since 1999, and was the first woman to hold such a post in an Oxbridge Chapel. Sarah came to the UK from Canada in 1992 as Organ Scholar of Robinson College, Cambridge after studying piano, organ, and conducting at The Royal Conservatory of Music's Glenn Gould School in Toronto with Leon Fleisher, Marek Jablonski, and John Tuttle. She has made over 35 recordings, variously in the guises of pianist, organist, conductor, and producer, and currently works most frequently with Regent Records. Her first solo disc, a recording of Bach's Goldberg Variations on the Steinway-D in Ely Cathedral will be released in 2023.

Elizabeth Markow is currently a manager at YouTube at BMG – The New Music Company. She completed her degree with a music industry major and a recording minor at Northeastern University in Boston. During that time she completed an internship with Glassnote Records in New York and Warner Bros. Records in Los Angeles.

Major John Martin is a major in the Salvation Army. He completed his PhD under the direction of Professor Helen Julia Minors in 2023 at Kingston University, London. He is an active conductor, composer, and performer, and with the Salvation Army has travelled the world with music, performing and creating with other Salvation Army members globally. John's music is published by the Salvation Army.

Luis Gabriel Mesa Martínez is Associate Professor and Director of the Master of Music program at Pontificia Universidad Javeriana (Colombia). He has a Doctor of Philosophy in Musicology from the University of Granada (Spain).

Contributor Biographies

Jessy McCabe is a special education needs and disability teacher in the UK. She led the petition in 2015 to bring women into the Music GCSE curriculum in high schools, which gained much press and had success in making that change happen. She is an advocate for equality in education.

Helen Julia Minors is Professor and Head of the School of Arts at York St John University, where she co-leads on the university's anti-racist pedagogy working group. She is also a visiting professor at Lulea University of Technology in Sweden. She was founded and first co-chair of EDI Music Studies UKI and former chair of MusicHE. She is a broadcaster and performer. Her recent publications include: *Music, Dance and Translation* (Bloomsbury 2023); *Teaching Music Performance in Higher Education: exploring the potential of artistic research* (forthcoming Open Books, 2024), co-edited with Stefan Östersjö, Gilvano Dalagna, and Jorge Salgado Correia; *Artistic Research in Performance through Collaboration*, co-authored and co-edited with Martin Blain (Palgrave 2020); as well as a range of articles and chapters, including recent articles in *Tibon* (2021) and *The London Review of Education* (2019), and chapters in *Routledge Companion to Applied Musicology* (2023) and *Intersemiotic Perspectives on Emotions: Translating across Signs, Bodies and Values* (2023).

Rebekah E. Moore is an assistant professor at Northeastern University. Her teaching and research are driven by a commitment to showing how musicians and artists are essential workers who empower us to make meaning, find connection and community, and imagine – and thus activate – our way to better futures. To do this, she builds on ethnomusicological approaches to music as social life, pursued through the ethnographic methodology of participatory action research, and communicated with an interpretive lens that combines emergence and agency theories and transformative justice principles. She has published academic articles in the Asian Journal of Communication, Asian Music, Collaborative Anthropologies, and Inside Indonesia, and her work will appear in the forthcoming anthologies *At the Crossroads of Music and Social Justice* (Indiana University Press) and *Sounding Out the State of Indonesian Music* (Cornell University Press).

Matteo Paoletti is Lecturer in Theatre Studies at the University of Genoa. He was awarded the Carlo Terron Prize (2012) and the Galileo Galilei Prize (2019). In 2020, Cambridge University Press published his monograph on the development of musical theatre economics between Europe and South America in the early 1900s.

Michelle Phillips is Senior Lecturer and Head of Enterprise at the Royal Northern College of Music. She undertakes research on music perception and obtained her PhD from the Centre of Music and Science at the University of Cambridge. Michelle is the outgoing Chair of MusicHE. Her research explores music and the perception of time, music and maths, audience response to live and recorded music, music and entrepreneurship, and music and Parkinson's. Her edited collection entitled *Music and Time: Philosophy, Psychology and Practice*, co-edited by Michelle and Dr Matthew Sergeant, was published by Boydell & Brewer in June 2022.

Shannon Pires graduated from Northeastern University with a degree in the Music Industry. She is Associate Manager, Artist & Label Relations at Vevo, previously being Grammy U Campus Ambassador at The Recording Academy.

Contributor Biographies

Bella Powell completed her PhD at the University of York, supervised by Aine Sheil and supported by a Sir Jack Lyons Scholarship. Her PhD research investigated the informal prohibition or 'ban' on women playing the violin in England during the eighteenth and nineteenth centuries. She is a keen viola player and music educator.

Arianne Johnson Quinn is on the faculty at Florida State University's Honours Programme, and is Research and Archival Associate for the Noël Coward Archive Trust. She focuses on the cultural, political, and musical intersections between American and British musicals in London from 1920–1960. She is writing a monograph on the Theatre Royal, Drury Lane.

Jenni Roditi (née Jennifer Rodd) attended Guildhall School of Music for her undergraduate studies in composition and piano. She then spent twelve years as composer-in-residence with Lontano. Alongside her composing, Jenni has evolved a music leadership practice based on her passion for creative singing.

Luisa Santacesaria is Adjunct Professor of Music and Production, at the Università degli Studi di Firenze, Italy. She was previously editor at musicael ettronica.

Orla Shannon is Government of Ireland Postgraduate Research Scholar studying at Dublin City University. Her current research explores the area of gender disparity in the canon of twentieth-century Irish art song and is endorsed by the Contemporary Music Centre, Ireland, where she was appointed the inaugural scholar-in-residence.

Cynthia Stephens-Himonides is a senior lecturer in music at Kingston University, where she is course leader for the master's degrees in performance and music education. She is a pianist and gained her doctorate at The University of Texas at Austin. Her background in higher education teaching has been as a teacher educator and researcher specialising in instrumental music teaching and learning. A recent chapter was published in *Leadership of pedagogy and curriculum in higher education* (Routledge 2019).

Theresa Parvin Steward is a Muslim sacred musician who works in communities of faith at Trietsch Memorial United Methodist Church. She has a doctorate of music from the University of Nevada, Las Vegas. She is the owner of Stewart Academy of Music and a consultant for Denton Independent School District, as well as adjunct professor at Tarrant County College.

Temina Cadi Sulumuna is a concert harpist and musicologist. She completed her PhD in music arts (2015). She works at the Fryderyk Chopin University of Music in Warsaw. She has presented her research at national conferences in Warsaw and Bydgoszcz, as well as at international conferences in Aveiro, Budapest, Dublin, Glasgow, Karlsruhe, London, Lucca, Manchester, Nottingham, Rzeszów, Saint Petersburg, and Vilnius.

Davina Vencatasamy is a music therapist, EMDR therapist, EDIB advocate, and educator. She is an assistant lecturer at the University of Derby. She is also currently a doctoral candidate at Lesley University in the USA. She has been working in SEN and mental health settings with a wide range of client groups

Laura Watson is the associate professor of music and deputy head of the department of music at Maynooth University, Ireland. She is sole author of the monograph, *Paul Dukas: Composer*

and Critic, and is co-editor of two volumes: with Helen Julia Minors, *Paul Dukas: Legacies of a French Musician* (Routledge 2019) and with Jennifer O'Connor-Madsen and Ita Beausang, *Women and Music in Ireland* (Boydell & Brewer 2022). She is an active co-leader of Sounding the Feminist.

Chamari Wedamulla is a postdoctoral researcher in music education from Sri Lanka, currently working on an Arts Council project at Birmingham City University. She completed her PhD in 2023 under the supervision of Helen Julia Minors, at Kingston University, London. As a music teacher she has worked in special needs schools in the UK and overseas, and she has taught on a postgraduate master's programme in music education. Her research focuses on interdisciplinary and inclusive music teaching practices.

Sarah K. Whitfield is a music and theatre historian, researcher, and practitioner. She is Doctoral Programmes Coordinator at the Royal College of Music. She uses digital humanities methods alongside traditional archival research to challenge established narratives, focusing on uncovering the work that under-represented and minoritised figures do and have done in the arts. She most recently co-authored *An Inconvenient Black History of British Musical Theatre 1900–1950* with Sean Mayes, and edited the collection *Reframing the Musical: Race, Culture and Identity* (2019).

Eleanor Wilson is Creative Director at NMC Recordings Ltd. She is an active composer and violinist, with her most recent album released in 2023 with Bigo and Twigetti. Before joining a long career at NMC, she was previously in Production & Licensing at Hyperion Records.

YSWN (Yorkshire Sound Women Network) works to address gender and other inequalities in audio through education, advocacy, and inspiring and enabling women, girls, and minority genders to explore sound and music technology. Founded in 2015 as an informal group, YSWN became a non-profit Community Interest Company in 2018. YSWN colleagues contributing to this book are **Eddie Dobson**, **Abi Bliss**, and **Heidi Johnson**.

ABBREVIATIONS

ABC	American Band College (US)
ACE	Arts Council England (UK)
AEC	Association Européenne des Conservatoire (Europe)
AGS	American Guitar Society (US)
AHRC	Arts and Humanities Research Council (UK)
ARC	Abortion Rights Campaign (Ireland)
AUDEM	Asociación Uruguaya de Músicos, Uruguayan Association of Musicians (Uruguay)
BAME	Black and Minority Ethnicities (UK)
BBC	British Broadcasting Corporation (UK)
BECAL	*Programa Nacional de Becas de Posgrados en el Exterior Carlos Antonio López* (National Scholarship Program for Postgraduate studies Abroad, Paraguay)
BIPOC	Black, Indigenous, and People of Colour
BMG	Banjo, Mandolin, and Guitar (Movement, US)
CBC	Canadian Broadcasting Corporation (Canada)
CCM	Contemporary Classical Music (used specifically in Chapter 54, GRiNM and YWSN)
CEMA	Council for the Encouragement of Music and the Arts (UK)
CIC	Community Interest Company (UK)
CMC	Contemporary Music Centre (Republic of Ireland)
COMA	Contemporary Music for All (UK)
CTRPW	Central Trust for the Redemption of Penalties by Work (Central de Nuestra Señora de la Merced para la Redención de Penas por el Trabajo, Spain)
CUK	Conservatoires UK (UK)
EDI	Equality, Diversity and Inclusion (UK)
ENO	English National Opera (UK)
FBA	Florida Bandmasters' Association (US)
FIM	International Federation of Musicians (Fédération Internationale des Musiciens) (France)
FUDEM	Federación Uruguaya de Músicos, Uruguayan Federation of Musicians (Uruguay)

Abbreviations

GRID	Gender Research in Darmstadt (Germany)
GRiNM	Gender Relations in New Music (Germany)
GRL!	Girls Rock London (UK)
HEI	Higher Education Institution (UK)
HMUK	Help Musicians (UK)
IBO	Irish Baroque Orchestra (Republic of Ireland)
IGRA	International Guitar Research Archive (US)
IGV	Internationale Guitarristische Vereinigung
IMRO	Irish Music Rights Organisation (Republic of Ireland)
INO	Irish National Opera (Republic of Ireland)
INO	Israel National Opera (Israel)
IPO	Israel Philharmonic Orchestra (Israel)
JC	*The Jewish Chronicle* (UK)
KPIs	Key Performance Indicators (UK)
MCR	Music Commission Report (UK)
MMN	Music Mentor Network (US)
MPA	Music Performance Assessments (US)
MTNA	Music Teachers' National Association (US)
NAfME	National Association for Music Education (US)
NCH	National Concert Hall (Republic of Ireland)
NLI	National Library of Ireland (Republic of Ireland)
NMC	New Music Company (UK)
NSOS	National Student Opera Society (UK)
OfS	Office for Students (UK)
OdlM	Odile de la Martinez (Cuban-American composer-conductor, b.1949)
OFSTED	The Office for Standards in Education (UK)
OSCAR	Outcome, Situation, Choices, Actions, Review (UK/US)
PGCE	Postgraduate Certificate of Education (UK)
PRS	Performance Rights Society (UK)
RAM	Royal Academy of Music (London, UK)
RCM	Royal College of Music (London, UK)
RIAM	Royal Irish Academy of Music (Dublin, Republic of Ireland)
RMM	Recreational Music Making (US)
ROH	Royal Opera House (London, UK)
RNCM	Royal Northern College of Music (UK)
RTÉ	Raidió Teilifís Éireann (Radio & Television of Ireland, Republic of Ireland)
SADEM	Sindicato Argentino de Músicos, Argentinian Musicians' Union (Argentina)
SEDA	Staff and Educational Development Association (UK)
SEND	Special Educational Needs and Disabilities (UK)
SIMCCAP	Sindicato de Músicos, Compositores y Cantantes del Perú, Union of Musicians, Composers and Singers of Peru (Peru)
SINDMUSI	Sindicato dos Músicos Profissionais do Estado do Rio de Janeiro, Union of Professional Musicians of the State of Rio de Janeiro (Brazil)
SRPW	System of Redemption of Penalties by Work (*Sistema de Redención de Penas por el Trabajo*, Spain)
STEM	Science, Technology, Engineering and Maths (UK)
STIN	*Società Teatrale Internazionale* (Walter Mocchi's theatrical company)

Abbreviations

STF	Sounding the Feminists (Ireland)
SUTM	Sindicato Único de Trabajadores de la Música, Union of Music Workers (Mexico)
TCD	Trinity College Dublin (Dublin, Republic of Ireland)
TIC	The Improviser's Choir
TOCfi	The Open Choir for Improvisers
U.F.P.C.	Union des Femmes Professeurs et Compositeurs de Musique (Union of Women Music Teachers and Composers, France)
UNEAC	Unión de Escritores y Artistas de Cuba, Union of Writers and Artists of Cuba (Cuba)
UNESCO	United Nations Educational, Scientific and Cultural Organization
USO	United Service Organization (US)
USP	Unique Selling Point
UTM	Unión de Trabajadores de la Música, Guild of Music Workers (Costa Rica)
VUCA	Volatile, uncertain, complex and ambiguous leadership environment (UK)
WCN	Women Cantors' Network (US)
WLMW	Women's Liberation Music Workshop (UK)
WRPM	Women's Revolutions Per Minute (UK)
YSWN	Yorkshire Sound Women Network (UK)

DEDICATION AND ACKNOWLEDGEMENTS

Dedication

We dedicate this book to our women role models, musical leaders and mentors, without whom we would both not be in our respective positions in Higher Education. Notable thanks to our early-career mentors, including:

Professor Susan Wollenbury, Laura's tutor at the University of Oxford; Composer Margaret Lucy Wilkins, Helen's lecturer and initial introduction to the issues of women in music; Hilary Friend, Helen's mentor and manager from Women's Revolutions Per Minute.

Moreover, we must mention the two women who guided our doctoral research and supported us in starting our own careers: Dr. Caroline Rae (Cardiff University) and Professor Deborah Mawer (Royal Birmingham Conservatoire).

Acknowledgements

Many relatives, friends and colleagues have supported and encouraged us through the gestation of this project, and there are many people we would like to thank. Firstly, our thanks go to all of our authors, who worked on this throughout the very challenging period of the global Covid19 pandemic. Secondly, our thanks go to Genevieve Aoki at Routledge, who has been an exceptionally supportive and diligent editor. We are grateful to The Open University for funding towards the initial conference which sparked our work upon this project and for support towards interview transcription costs. We are also grateful to The Open University for providing further financial support which enabled us to run the Women's Musical Leadership Online Project throughout 2021, which then became the Women's Musical Leadership Online Network – funded by the AHRC – from 2022.[34] We thank the Royal Musical Association and the Institute of Musical Research, who also provided funding for the First International Conference on Women and/in Musical Leadership. Special thanks are due to all of our many friends and colleagues who talked about the nature of women's musical leadership with us and helped to bounce ideas around as we worked on this book. We also extend our gratitude to our institutional colleagues at The Open University, Kingston University, and York St John University for all of their support.

1
DEFINING, SURVEYING AND INTERROGATING WOMEN IN MUSICAL LEADERSHIP

Laura Hamer and Helen Julia Minors

Throughout our careers in music education, we have both benefitted from three significant experiences which have led us to co-edit this book. Firstly, we have both had significant support, guidance, and mentorship from women in the music industries who had broken part of the glass ceiling, who had advocated for change, and who made efforts to facilitate us within the early twenty-first century to enable us to become autonomous, individual thinkers within our fields. Secondly, we both were given the opportunity to become managers in Higher Education and specifically to lead music departments unusually early (28–30) in our careers, rising to the position where our choices and decisions impacted entire student cohorts and teams of staff. Thirdly, we have both developed our research to encompass our passions, and at the same time this has developed our interests in making change for the better, to support wider access to music education, to ensure we facilitate the diversification of curricula, and so diversify the pipeline into the music industries. Our careers have been in different institutions, though we both chose to volunteer for the National Association of Music in Higher Education (now called MusicHE), and both have been trained as coaches and mentors. These activities have helped us to consider the subject within a national and global context in relation to policy and regulatory changes, and from this macro level, consider the wellbeing and needs of the staff we have had the good fortune to lead and to support, to collaborate with, and to explore the possibilities of our subject. This personal experience, the 'I' of our positionality, made us acutely aware of the barriers facing people across the music industries, both historically and currently. We wanted to explore this in more detail. We are very aware that many voices bring many experiences, and together, we can share examples of good practice, share stories and experience to help others, and also give voices to composers, musicians, artists, and craftspeople who perhaps have been marginalised. To this end, this book has been a labour of love for us. We chose to start this journey with launching a conference, the International Women and/in Musical Leadership Conference, which we hosted in London between 7–9 March 2019 with the aim, as the conference website notes, to challenge and explore musical leadership:

> Musical leadership remains ones of the most male-dominated musical areas. As late as 2013, female conductors achieved a significant first, when Marin Alsop became the first woman to direct the Last Night of the Proms. Although female composers, songwriters, and performers have attracted significant scholarly attention, the issue of women's

musical leadership remains intriguingly under researched. This conference – timed to coincide with International Women's Day 2019 – seeks both to redress this by focusing upon the participation of women in musical leadership (understood in the broadest possible sense) and to promote academic-practitioner dialogue.[1]

The conference brought together over 70 colleagues from more than 20 countries. The reach, the interest, and the relevance were global. Moreover, the urgency of the issues – to tackle inequalities, to give voice to underrepresented women, and to readdress industry disparities in programming, commissioning, renumeration, and in leadership – was stark. As such, this volume is extensive in bringing together many voices from an open call for contributions. Across its 48 chapters and 70 authors, collated into 6 parts, we have contributions and examples from Argentina, Australia, Austria, Brazil, Columbia, Costa Rica, Cuba, England, Finland, France, Germany, Iraq, Ireland, Israel, Italy, Malaysia, Malaya, Mexico, New Zealand, Norway, Paraguay, Peru, Poland, Scotland, Spain, Sri Lanka, UK, Uruguay, USA, and Wales.

This book is much needed! In fact, we think it is urgent that we reassess, present, and facilitate the voices of women in leadership to support all the grassroots work, the national collectives and charities (many included as examples in this book), to ensure we amplify these voices to make the change we advocate for. We advocate for equity in the music industries (in the broadest sense of the music field as an eco-system from education throughout one's musical life). But what, broadly, are we advocating for? Equity throughout education (equity of representation in the curriculum); equity throughout the professional music industries (to support different career types, carer, maternity/shared parental/adoption and menopause support, wellbeing support); equity in archiving and the presentation of historical facts; as well as a more diverse understanding of our lived experiences at home, to ensure equity of presentation and access (radio/TV programming), and faith settings (music in ritual and celebration); as well as equity of funding and commissioning opportunities. In what follows all these issues recur in different settings.

Women, Leadership, and Women's Musical Leadership

What is musical leadership? Why focus on women in leadership within the music industries and music education in particular? We use leadership to refer to those people who lead activities at various levels in institutions, organisations, charities, and within music education. Musical leadership, as we have commented elsewhere, however:

> is often construed as residing in male authority figures, quintessentially exemplified in classical music through the figure of the maestro conductor. This 'maestro myth', as Norman Lebrecht has characterized it, has been perpetuated since the mid-nineteenth century through the 'maestro-writing tradition' of male conductors from Berlioz and Wagner, through Stokowski, Furtwängler and Boult, to Boulez. The maestro tradition was so powerful for so long that it actively and effectively marginalized other voices within musical leadership, including those of women.[2]

This volume seeks consciously to confront and contend the long-embedded tradition of the 'maestro myth', by not only showcasing a range of women who have been active within the conductor's role but in also expanding the notion of musical leadership far beyond the podium itself and covering a wide range of musical leadership activities.

Defining and Interrogating Women in Musical Leadership

As is reflected across the volume, a leader does not have to also be a manager. A leader is someone who advocates for others, who makes changes in consultation with the needs of the sector and context, who facilitates others and leads, where possible, by example. A leader might also become a role model. A leader sets a collective unified path for the journey our teams are taking. The chapters that follow define different forms of leadership and refer to a wide range of literature and research. These skills and attributes are our overview of how we set out the project. We aspire as leaders to be adaptive, to facilitate, to guide, but also to set a direction, to use where possible collective and distributed approaches, and to recognise that a leader is also accountable for the final decision making. Consultation, listening, hearing others, and seeking contextual data, facts, and evidence are core parts of such a role. As such, we see musical leadership in broad terms spanning all genres, all cultures, countries and languages, and all peoples. We have defined musical leadership elsewhere as:

> a concept which incorporates the roles musicians, in practice, take not only as conductors and musical directors, rather encompassing all leadership activity, all musicking activity, from project managing events, to leading workshops and lessons, to managing charities and networks, to leading change on the ground in small-scale projects, to leading instrumental ensembles, to leading sales and marketing, outreach work, to leading advocacy and activism activity.[3]

This book acknowledges that leadership is within institutions, organisations, and charities; however, it is not only at the upper echelons of companies on an executive board. The book embraces both individual and collective women's musical leadership.

Although since its emergence in the later decades of the twentieth century Feminist Musicology has now developed into an established field of music scholarship, and works upon individual and groups of women musicians abound, studies of women's musical leadership are less common.[4] In offering a volume dedicated to women's musical leadership, we hope to develop recent work which has sought to progress Feminist Musicology beyond a focus upon hidden/compensatory history and gender studies, and instead further considers women's musical work through the lens of leadership.

As Deborah L. Rhode asserts in her exposé of women's leadership in education, business, law, and politics: 'Women need advocates, not simply advisors, and this kind of support cannot be mandated'.[5] These are people who speak when they/we are not present, people who chose to be mentors, who chose to diversify leadership, who support them/us in facilitating their/our agency. As Alverson and Billing recognised and asserted just before the millennium:

> An interesting possibility of broadening the impact of gender reflection in the study of leadership would be to go beyond (or beside) the somewhat unproductive comparisons of male and female leadership and the normalizing position of men and instead study specific examples of leadership processes.[6]

Indeed, in response to their work, Máirtín Mac An Ghaill and Chris Haywood have explored what contemporary gender experiences mean in our culture and society, remarking that there remains a 'relative absence of women in managerial positions', while recognising 'women's different styles of leadership [and] the social and cultural barriers operating against females in managerial posts'.[7] Notably, throughout this book, they call for institutions to consider processes and policies and their impact on the different genders.

Literature in the field of popular music has been identifying the need for resilience for those working in the industry, and at the same time, Higher Education institutions are referring to resilience as a desirable skill for industry. Robin James tackles this notion head on in her engaging book on popular music, feminism, and neoliberalism. She notes that: 'resilience is the new means of production', after contextualising resilience as an 'upgrade on modernist notions of coherence and deconstruction'.[8] Resilience has however been critiqued in many contexts, as it can often be used as a response in situations where bullying or abuse have been reported. We do not wish to equate resilience with toughness. Resilience is not an excuse to avoid empathy. This is significant, as like Rhode, Ghaill, and Haywood, they all identify that the emphasis for change has historically been laid at the door of those who have not historically had access, in other words at the feet of women. But now, the policy and research literature all attest to the benefit of diversifying leadership and recognising the benefit of different ways of doing things. Although our demographic identity might now have been specifically named in policies, 'race and gender are *regulatory* mechanisms: they determine to whom and to what extent specific laws apply'.[9] This is important: as noted here, the book is intersectional, and being aware of policies which cross different demographic criteria is helpful to ensuring we reach beyond our own positionality. It is because of this that we need to challenge these barriers, to remove them, and to broaden definitions and representations of leadership. To do this, organisations, institutions, and charities, or rather *the management* need to be held accountable to making changes. Or as James has already said, we need not fight resilience in itself; it can be a useful quality, but it should not be the only quality. To come out the other side that doesn't require 'anarchic destruction' of the individual, we need an 'intensified regularity and orderliness'.[10]

Creating new policies, new regulations, does not need to come from government. Institutions set their own strategies and have their own ability to create change. In doing so they need to heed the warning of philosopher Janet Radcliff Richards, who in the '80s recognised that feminism might seek to make equal opportunities but that it might in fact reinforce gender performance and stereotypes: 'Women, in the expectation of leadership, independence, strength, chivalry and all the rest in men, put men under pressure to keep to these traditional masculine ideals, whether or not the men themselves feel inclined to do so'.[11] In short, the changes need to be co-constructed and done so in an open, inclusive manner. As editors, we are both based in the UK, in Wales and England respectively, as such we do refer to UK policies and procedures in parts of the book to share our positionality and experiences in the field. For example, in the UK, the Equality Act of 2010 includes 9 characteristics which it is against the law to discriminate against. These 9 are: age, disability, gender reassignment, marriage and civil partnership, pregnancy and maternity, race, religion or belief, sex, sexual orientation.[12] What this means is that all employers must abide by this law. Change becomes incentivised in order to maintain a legally operating business.

Any approach to looking at women's musical leadership therefore needs to be recognised in an intersectional context. Defined by Kimberlé Crenshaw in 1989, intersectionality recognises the need to consider the whole individual and all aspects of their identity.[13] Although we focus on women specifically to tackle the problem of representation, we do not ignore the other demographic criteria of our identity: it is because these issues need to be intersectional that the volume is so expansive in length and has so many contributors. We wish to ensure that lived experience sits alongside research and other forms of evidence in the volume and in the other work we are doing with the Women's Musical Leadership Online Network.[14]

In this book, we use women, and woman, in the broadest sense of the words, to refer to anyone identifying as a woman, and anyone historically identified in the extant material as 'women', a 'woman', 'her', 'she', 'mother', 'sister', 'daughter', or 'wife'. As the book covers the nineteenth century and much archival material, as well as currently lived experience, clarification is needed. When we use the word female, we use it either in quotations from other sources, or as recognition of gender specified medically and not in terms of lived experience and personal identity. When 'feminism' is used, it is used in quotations, or is defined for the context and wave of feminism referred to.[15] We do so because the data in many reports shows us that it is people other than those identifying as men who suffer from a lack of representation in programming, or in broadcasting, and it shows in the leaky pipeline women have in the music industries, with few reaching the top positions.[16] We do not use one word in order to exclude anyone. Our authors make every effort to be careful of language, and the context of the author and the example(s) covered in their chapters impacts how language has been used, in such a way that is relevant and appropriate to the setting of what is being discussed and where the author/artist is situated. In a book with a wide global and historical reach, the language does vary by necessity. Our priority has been to ensure the authors can be authentic and present their examples and experiences in such an authentic way. This openness to using different words, and to questioning women/woman is an approach which speaks to Diane Elam's challenge, that: 'We do not yet know what women can do'.[17] She says this as she rightly notes that it 'remains uncertain what it would mean to be a woman . . . just as it remains uncertain what precisely would constitute knowledge of women'.[18] She does this to challenge an almost-existential question about putting limits, criteria, and terminology on identity and lived experience. In other words, there is potential of women untapped, there are activities and happenings already done which we are unaware of, and reassessments and retellings that are needed. Sometimes the language varies; sometimes women are absent, censored or deleted; sometimes, we need to focus on an individual's intersectionality and not only on this one criterion.

Mentoring, Role Modelling, and Allyship

Without role models, one cannot see oneself represented, and so it is very difficult to imagine oneself in such positions. Moreover, in seeing one kind of person, one gender, one class, one ethnicity, it becomes potentially difficult to consider other ways of doing things for organisations that are accustomed to particular management styles. As Averil Leimon calls out: 'Many of the available models of leadership are predominantly male constructed, rooted in male design and run organizational theories and approaches'.[19] Many volumes, including new editions of this cited book, have begun to develop new models and new approaches, but overall there are three essential things we all need: 1. More awareness of what women have achieved and done historically, without editing them out of the history books; 2. Role models in a variety of industries, at the board tables, and in positions of power; 3. The choice of having a mentor or coach to facilitate one's own agency.

As cited here, Rhode notes that women need advocates, but we also want, need, and benefit from mentors. As we have previously stated:

> There is a will for leadership amongst women, but that appetite is often limited due to the many barriers which are actual and perceived. By speaking of women in the broadest sense (fully inclusive of transgender women), and by focusing on the intersectional context, we aim to support discussion of the different forms of leadership, the different ways in which training might take place, and the varied ways in which we can develop a peer- and co-mentoring scheme to facilitate individual development and opportunity of individual experiences.[20]

Goldman, in her survey of women and punk, refers to the 2016 list of top DJs – perhaps not surprisingly, it featured only one woman. Goldman calls through this book for women to question how we can sound like us and be ourselves even without it being role modelled or shown to us first.[21] She draws on the work of Stacey Smith who, as the head of the Inclusion Initiative at the University of Southern California, looked at the percentages of women in the pop music industry since 2012 to 2017. The results were stark: 'women had composed a mere 12.3 percent and performed few[er] than 25 percent'.[22] Smith's conclusion was stark but very real, and one which recent researchers looking at national and regional radio pop broadcasts have shared: 'The voices of women are missing from popular music'.[23]

More recently, women have taken this lack of representation into their own hands. Through a number of collective and activist groups, reports analysing data for concert programming, festivals, and broadcasting – i.e. the cold hard data facts – are being presented. There are many, but 3 to mention here: 1. Gabriel Di Laccio established DONNE Women in Music to support the representation of women composers in the classical music industry. Since 2018, she has been preparing an annual report analysing the programming data of top orchestras. The report for 2021–2022 – reporting on the top 111 orchestras – was her largest yet. It found that 76.4% of all music programmed was written by dead white men.[24] Specifically, in total, 92.3% of all works programmed were by men and 87.7% were white men. Only 7.7.% were by women, and only 2.1% were by global majority women.[25] 27.5% of works performed were written by only 10 dead white men, including Beethoven (4.8% of everything programmed), Mozart (4.6%) and Tchaikovsky (3.3%). Therefore, singularly, each of these men is performed more than the entirety of the global majority women.

Similar reports have been done in other parts of the sector. Lynda Coogan Byrne has been doing excellent work with the Why Not Her? Collective. They have released reports charting the programming of popular music in the UK and Ireland. Looking at the latest UK report for 2022–2023, the figures are as stark as those from the classical industry. Of the UK artists in the top 100 Airplay, only 24% were women, with 20% gender collaboration.[26] The overarching data looks at gender and ethnicity. It also looks at 27 UK radio stations, which for some stations show improvement in the last year, though concerns are raised by the Why Not Her? Collective, which has older reports that show improvements tend to last a year and disappear again. In 2022–2023, BBC Radio 1 aired 45% music by men, down from 85% the previous year, and 25% music by women, up from 15%, with 30% of the music now being by gender collaboration (e.g. multiple songwriters), in comparison to none the previous year.[27] The importance of the report shows that radio stations are clustered by who owns them, and the link to the main music companies releasing music is clear. Those releasing music want it heard on the radio, and the radio plays the releases, so stasis rather than change has been the staple activity. Some stations still hardly play women: for example, KissFresh, a Bauer radio station, played 85% men, and only 10% women and 5% collaboration, compared to no women the previous year. Of the global-owned radio stations, Capital played 60% men, up from 40% the previous year. More shockingly, Planet Rock and Absolute Radio, in the test period, only played white artists for their top 20 playlist, in other words the most played bands/groups/artists. Others, including Vick Bain who is a leading consultant in this field and director of the F-List,[28] has released reports counting the data in the industry, with the aim of industry change and providing hard data to support the issues for which we are advocating.[29]

There is a growing body of work in this area and many chapters in the book draw on such reports, from many countries and sectors of the music industries. The range of material which is available, both from recent research into programming and representation, to archival material, to education syllabi, and personal experience is vast. This book cannot possibly be all-encompassing, but it presents a range of themes to support the sharing of stories, experiences, data, examples, and change, to feedback into research yes, but also to support those trying to make change, to provide examples which can be referred to as precedents and to bring multiple voices together in one place for the first time on this topic.

Overview of the Book Structure

Due to the range of issues impacting women's musical leadership, we have divided this book into 6 significant parts, each of which has its own sub-themes and its own bespoke introduction. In Part I, Historical Perspectives, authors present specific historical case studies of women musical leaders who have either been marginalised from the history books, not recognised until now, or who were known perhaps in one capacity but had another role as a musical leader which has not been presented to date. Women have always been involved in music and leading it, but it is little documented. Back in the 1980s, Jane Bowers and Judith Tick, in their groundbreaking volume *Women Making Music*, made clear that women were leading music in churches, as nuns, and in salons.[30] This part of the book expands this field. The examples include three chapters dedicated to strings: Augusta Hervey and the Guitar and Mandoline Band, Vahdah Olcott-Bickford and the American Guitar Society, and Wilma Norman-Neruda and Camilla Urso and the All-Male String Quartets of the nineteenth century. Then chapters move to women's leadership via women's orchestras, women leading salon activity, and women establishing organisations, here in the form of the Union des Femmes Professeurs et Compositors de Musique (U.F.P.C.) in France. Specific examples are then taken from the Irish Joan Trimble to women's musical resistance in Franco's prisons. The topics are varied. The opening chapter of the part outlines the specific themes, but of importance here is that these figures are being accessed through archival materials, press reports, documentary evidence in programme notes, flyers, reports, letters, and such like. Most have not been explored in detail in research, and so this part offers a crucial reassessment of some aspects of history to reassert women's place as musical leaders.

In Part II, Conductors and Impresarios, we continue some of this historical discourse alongside the contemporary, with a focus on the traditional notion of the leader, that of the conductor who, standing at the front of the orchestra, looks all commanding and imposing. The chapters in this part follow specific women, such as Lilian Baylis, through to genre examples in British Musical Theatre with Elsie April, to impresarios including Emma Carelli and Henriette Renié. Those women leading ensembles from their instrument, such as Helen Erdberg (*la Kazanova*), or those women leading large opera institutions, such as Edis de Philippe receive attention next. The part closes with a detailed exposé of Odaline de la Martinez as a leader in many musical settings, including conducting, although she does not restrict herself to that. Ultimately in Part II, these authors reappropriate the notion that the work of a conductor or impresario is analogous to business leadership, and assert the skills, the unique activities, and roles these women held, mostly in a time and/or place where their presence at the front of the group (as conductor) or leading behind the scenes (as impresario) would have been culturally revolutionary,

In Part III, Women's Practices in Music Education, we present a wide range of examples to ensure we do not forget one of the key areas which feeds the future music industries. Although the music education space has often been considered to be appropriate for women, with valued careers as schoolteachers and piano teachers existing for centuries, here we look more in detail at what women have done to develop music education, how they've done it, and why. The authors themselves work (or have worked) in music education and many include examples from their own practice as well as from research. As mentoring and coaching is so central to the book, we start this part with chapters dedicated to the issues, situated broadly then within a specific music conservatoire, before moving to examples of musical cultures and national/regional musics being introduced in settings other than their original, raising questions of identity for the teachers/lecturers. The data of women in music is then used to look at syllabi, policy, representation, and impact on education. Education which focuses on conducting is also explored, as well as assessment calibration, piano group tuition, and choral direction.

In Part IV, Performance and the Music Industries, we look to specific examples and to multi voices to share experiences in an autoethnographic manner. As such, the chapters brought together in this part of the volume look different; they are fewer but longer, starting with two co-authored multi-voiced chapters (presenting the experiences of 13 women) exploring the music industries and education systems in the UK and USA, with contributors presenting from the recording industry, event management, conducting, broadcasting, music therapy, education, copyright, and music business. Then four specific examples of leadership are shown, from the opera industry to programming festivals, specific cultural challenges, and a long life as a creative woman artist changing focus and developing from a composer to a performer. The 'I' is strong throughout this part, and evidence is drawn both from personal experience and examples of practice.

It is important to hear these women. As Goldman has commented, women have not always been heard:

> What is women's music? I haven't heard enough of it, sadly, to be able to lay many handy guidelines, but it might have something to do with the way the Raincoats organize themselves and their instruments, no lead singers or players, a conscious change from the top-dog/underdog pattern set up by the patriarchal structure.[31]

Presenting the first person, insider, voice from a variety of experiences is important to establishing role models and fostering confidence in others to become mentors.

In Part V, Faith and Spirituality: Worship and Sacred Musical Practices, we include a wide range of faiths and people to share how music is used in such local community and faith-based settings. The range of faiths includes Judaism, Islam, Buddhism, and Christianity (including Baptist, Anglican, Salvation Army, and Roman Catholic voices). The authors of several of the chapters are also worship leaders or musical leaders within religious settings, as well as researchers themselves, and their own authentic, lived experience informs some of their discussion. As with Part IV, the insider I is often strong and intentional. The chapters balance data and research evidence alongside personal experience over some time. What music means in faith and what musical leadership is in these settings is questioned. But importantly, women do not always have, have not always had, and might not be able to have, a place of leadership in faith practices, but their roles within the musical aspect of faith celebration, commitment, and ritual is shown to be strong among these chapters.

The final part, Part VI, Advocacy: Collectives and Grass-Roots Activism, moves towards current issues whereby women are leading change through establishing new charities, collectives, organisations, and practices where they have felt something needed to be done and nothing was happening. The examples of advocacy vary and come from faith-based settings, education, business, unions, collectives, and charities. The examples cover Ireland, Germany, Spain, and span Latin America as well as the UK and USA. As such, the theme here might be advocacy, though the topics cross and intersect with the rest of the book. It is because of the historical place of women that such work is needed, and that work continues to span the performance setting, music business, faith settings, education, and institutional leadership. As in the punk context, these women would recognise this call: 'women had been paying the price of systemic powerlessness, domestically disenfranchised, publicly and professionally mocked, or rendered invisible. One way of the other, en route to the bright future, as usual, women were bound to bleed'.[32]

Many of the people (not only those identifying as women) writing in this volume are working in contexts where a women's right to lead, to choose, to have the right to her body, is not a legal right. Many could not access the Covid19 vaccine during the writing of the book during the global pandemic. Our experiences vary widely due to nationality and country of work, faith, sexuality, disability/neurodiversity and health, caring responsibilities, and the context of the law and political policy we live and work under. Preparations for the book started in the autumn of 2019, and continued throughout and beyond the lockdown periods of the global Covid19 pandemic. All of the authors' lives were touched by the virus, with some suffering severe illness themselves or within their families and, sadly, also some experiencing bereavements. It is important that all the chapters are read with sensitivity to this.

This volume shows that women's leadership is different, and women's musical leadership is different. It calls for new models and presents models and examples for others. To again quote Goldman, as a model for change:

> We must make a place in a market manipulated to pander to the cliched male gaze; find a voice four for our feelings when we've never heard anyone sound the way we hear in our head; break generations of our family's female mode of being; construct new forms of family and effective motherhood; position ourselves within newly possible flexing of gender experimentation and fight for the right to do so.[33]

What Goldman says here for punk can be translated and adapted for any genre. We hope readers of this book will be inspired to think more about the intersectional identities of the people working in music education and across the music industries and be ready to challenge preconceptions and instilled institutional bias. As the book is so varied, rather than present a single bibliography at the end, we present each chapter's bibliography after it. The bibliography here presents our core references, but we also present a few texts per part which we suggest as material for when readers are thinking of expanding their knowledge. No list will be conclusive and all-encompassing, so rather than try to do that, we offer texts we know have helped ourselves, our students, friends, and colleagues in expanding their awareness. We do this in good faith.

Notes

1. The conference call was shared on both our institutional websites: International Women and/in Musical Leadership Conference, accessed August 12, 2023, https://fass.open.ac.uk/iwmlc and accessed August 12, 2023, www.kingston.ac.uk/events/item/3183/07-mar-2019-international-women-andin-musical-leadership-conference/.
2. Laura Hamer and Helen Julia Minors, "Introducing WMLON: Women's Musical Leadership Online Network," in *Women's Leadership in Music: Modes, Legacies, Alliances*, edited by Iva Nenić and Linda Cimardi (Bielefeld: transcript Verlag, 2023), 142. For an excellent study of von Karajan and hypermasculinity on the podium, see Adam Behan, "Reading Creativity Forwards and Backwards: Process and Product Revisited with Herbert von Karajan's Legato Aesthetic and Hypermasculinity," *Music and Letters* 103, no. 4 (November 2022): 708–28.

3. Hamer and Minors, "Introducing WMLON," 141.
4. For two recent studies of women's musical leadership, see Iva Nenić and Linda Cimardi, eds., *Women's Leadership in Music: Modes, Legacies, Alliances* (Bielefeld: Transcript Verlag, 2023); and Helen Rusak, *Women, Music and Leadership* (New York: Routledge, 2023). See also, Part V – "Opportunities and Leadership in the Music Professions," in *The Routledge Handbook of Women's Work in Music*, edited by Rhiannon Mathias (Abingdon and New York: Routledge, 2022).
5. Deborah L. Rhode, *Women and Leadership* (Oxford: Oxford University Press, 2017).
6. Mats Alvesson and Yvonne D. Billing, *Understanding Gender and Organizations* (London: Sage, 1997), 211.
7. Máirtin Mac An Ghaill and Chris Haywood, *Gender, Culture and Society: Contemporary Femininities and Masculinities* (New York: Palgrave MacMillan, 2007), 87.
8. Robin James, *Resilience and Melancholy: Pop Music, Feminism, Neoliberalism* (Winchester: Zero Books, 2015), 4.
9. Ibid., 15.
10. Ibid., 48.
11. Janet Radcliffe Richards, *The Sceptical Feminist: A Philosophical Enquiry* (London: Routledge and Kegan Paul, 1980), 146.
12. See, accessed August 12, 2023, www.equalityhumanrights.com/en/equality-act/protected-characteristics.
13. Kimberlé Crenshaw, *On Intersectionality: The Essential Writings of Kimberlé Crenshaw* (New York: New Press, 2014).
14. Hamer and Minors, "Introducing WMLON," 146.
15. For a more detailed overview of the waves of feminism and the impact on women in music, see Hamer and Minors, "Introducing WMLON," 145–47.
16. "Equality & Diversity in Global Repertoire | 111 ORCHESTRAS | 2021/2022 Season," DONNE – Women in Music, accessed August 12, 2023, https://donne-uk.org/research-new/; "Why Not Her? Collective, "Gender and Racial Disparity Data Report on UK Radio 2022–2023," accessed August 12, 2023, www.canva.com/design/DAFftZl9-HI/ymwZ2rr091OJYeCzyNOrUA/view?utm_content=DAFftZl9-HI&utm_campaign=designshare&utm_medium=link&utm_source=publishsharelink; Vick Bain, "Counting the Industry – Report," accessed August 12, 2023, https://vbain.co.uk/research/.
17. Diane Elam, *Feminism and Deconstruction* (London: Routledge, 1994), 27.
18. Ibid.
19. Averil Leimon, François Moscovici, and Helen Goodier, *Coaching Women to Lead* (London: Routledge, 2011), 146.
20. Hamer and Minors, "Introducing WMLON," 146.
21. Vivien Goldman, *Revenge of the She-Punks: A Feminist Music History From Poly Styrene to Pussy Riot* (Austin: University of Texas Press, 2019), 22.
22. Goldman, *Revenge of the She-Punks*, 22.
23. Ibid.
24. "Equality & Diversity in Global Repertoire | 111 ORCHESTRAS | 2021/2022 Season," DONNE – Women in Music, accessed August 12, 2023, https://donne-uk.org/research-new/.
25. Ibid.
26. Why Not Her? Collective, "Gender and Racial Disparity Data Report on UK Radio 2022–2023," accessed August 12, 2023, www.canva.com/design/DAFftZl9-HI/ymwZ2rr091OJYeCzyNOrUA/view?utm_content=DAFftZl9-HI&utm_campaign=designshare&utm_medium=link&utm_source=publishsharelink.
27. Ibid.
28. See, *Search for Musicians – The F-List Directory of UK Female+ Musicians*, accessed August 21, 2023, thef-listmusic.uk.
29. See Vick Bain, "Counting the Industry – Report," accessed August 12, 2023, https://vbain.co.uk/research/.
30. Jane Bowers and Judith Tick, eds., *Women Making Music: The Western Art Tradition, 1150–1950* (Urbana: University of Illinois Press, 1987), see pp. 20–22, 201, and 232–33.
31. Vivien Goldman, *Melody Maker* (December 1, 1979), cited in, Goldman, *Revenge of the She-Punks*, 17.
32. Goldman, *Revenge of the She-Punks*, 18.
33. Goldman, *Revenge of the She-Punks*, 53.

Bibliography

Alvesson, Mats, and Yvonne D. Billing. *Understanding Gender and Organizations*. London: Sage, 1997.
Bain, Vick. "Counting the Industry – Report." Accessed August 12, 2023. https://vbain.co.uk/research/.
Bowers, Jane, and Judith Tick, eds. *Women Making Music: The Western Art Tradition, 1150–1950*. Urbana: University of Illinois Press, 1987.
Crenshaw, Kimberlé. *On Intersectionality: The Essential Writings of Kimberlé Crenshaw*. New York: New Press, 2014.
DONNE – Women in Music. "Equality & Diversity in Global Repertoire | 111 ORCHESTRAS | 2021/2022 Season." Accessed August 12, 2023. https://donne-uk.org/research-new/.
Elam, Diane. *Feminism and Deconstruction*. London: Routledge, 1994.
Equality and Human Rights. Accessed August 12, 2023. www.equalityhumanrights.com/en/equality-act/protected-characteristics.
Ghaill, Máirtín Mac An, and Chris Haywood. *Gender, Culture and Society: Contemporary Femininities and Masculinities*. New York: Palgrave MacMillan, 2007.
Goldman, Vivien. *Revenge of the She-Punks: A Feminist Music History from Poly Styrene to Pussy Riot*. Austin: University of Texas Press, 2019.
Hamer, Laura, and Helen Julia Minors. "Introducing WMLON: Women's Musical Leadership Online Network." In *Women's Leadership in Music: Modes, Legacies, Alliances*, edited by Iva Nenic and Linda Cimardi, 141–52. Bielefeld: Transcript Verlag, 2023.
"International Women and/in Musical Leadership Conference." Accessed August 12, 2023. https://fass.open.ac.uk/iwmlc and www.kingston.ac.uk/events/item/3183/07-mar-2019-international-women-andin-musical-leadership-conference/.
James, Robin. *Resilience and Melancholy: Pop Music, Feminism, Neoliberalism*. Winchester: Zero Books, 2015.
Leimon, Averil, François Moscovici, and Helen Goodier. *Coaching Women to Lead*. London: Routledge, 2011.
Radcliffe Richards, Janet. *The Sceptical Feminist: A Philosophical Enquiry*. London: Routledge and Kegan Paul, 1980.
Rhode, Deborah L. *Women and Leadership*. Oxford: Oxford University Press, 2017.
Why Not Her? Collective. "Gender and Racial Disparity Data Report on UK Radio 2022–2023." Accessed August 12, 2023. www.canva.com/design/DAFftZl9-HI/ymwZ2rr091OJYeCzyNOrUA/view?utm_content=DAFftZl9-HI&utm_campaign=designshare&utm_medium=link&utm_source=publishsharelink.

Suggested Reading

Part I

Bowers, Jane, and Judith Tick, eds. *Women Making Music: The Western Art Tradition, 1150–1950*. Urbana: University of Illinois Press, 1987.
Hamer, Laura. *Female Composers, Conductors, Performers: Musiciennes of Interwar France, 1919–1939*. London: Routledge, 2018.
O'Connor-Madsen, Jennifer, Laura Watson, and Ita Beausang, eds. *Women and Music in Ireland*. London: Woodbridge: Boydell & Brewer, 2022.
Seddon, Laura. *British Women Composers and Instrumental Chamber Music in the Early Twentieth Century*. London and New York: Routledge, 2016.

Part II

Brooks, Jeanice. "Noble et grande servant de la musique: Telling the Story of Nadia Boulanger's Conducting Career." *Journal of Musicology* 14, no. 1 (1996): 92–116.
Edwards, J. Michele. "Women on the Podium." In *The Cambridge Companion to Conducting*, edited by José Bowen. Cambridge: Cambridge University Press, 2003.
Farnham, Alice. *In Good Hands: The Making of a Modern Conductor*. London: Faber & Faber, 2023.

Part III

Hess, Juliet. *Music Education for Social Change: Constructing an Activist Music Education*. London and New York: Routledge, 2019.
McPhearson, Gary E., and Graham F. Welch. *Music and Music Education in People's Lives: An Oxford Handbook of Music Education, Volume 1*. Oxford: Oxford University Press, 2018.
Talbot, Brent C., ed. *Marginalized Voices in Music Education*. London and New York: Routledge, 2018.
Wieland Howe, Sondra. *Women Music Educators in The United States*. New York: Scarecrow Press, 2014.

Part IV

Caust, Josephine. *Arts Leadership in Contemporary Contexts*. London and New York: Routledge, 2018.
Cooper, Rae, Amanda Coles, and Sally Hanna-Osbourne. *Skipping a Beat: Assessing the State of Gender Equality in the Australian Music Industry*. Sydney: The University of Sydney, 2017. Accessed August 12, 2023. https://ses.library.usyd.edu.au/handle/2123/21257.
Powers, Ann. *Good Booty; Love and Sex, Black and White, Body and Soul in American Music*. New York: William Morrow, 2017.

Part V

Boyce-Timan, June. *Unconventional Wisdom – Gender, Theology and Spirituality*. London: Taylor & Francis Ltd, 2008.
_____. *In Tune With Heaven Or Not: Women in Christian Liturgical Music – Music and Spirituality 1*. London: Peter Lang, 2014.
Redmond, Layne. *When the Drummers Were Women: A Spiritual History of Rhythm*. New York: Echo Point Books, 2021.

Part VI

DONNE – Women in Music. "Equality & Diversity in Global Repertoire | 111 ORCHESTRAS | 2021/2022 Season." Accessed August 12, 2023. https://donne-uk.org/research-new/.
International Alliance for Women in Music. Accessed August 12, 2023. https://iawm.org/.
Scottish Women Inventing Music. Accessed August 12, 2023. www.scottishwomeninventingmusic.com/.
Sounding the Feminist. Accessed August 12, 2023. www.soundingthefeminists.com/.
The F-List. Accessed August 12, 2023. https://thef-listmusic.uk/.
Why Not Her? Collective. "Gender and Racial Disparity Data Report on UK Radio 2022–2023." Accessed August 12, 2023. www.canva.com/design/DAFftZl9-HI/ymwZ2rr091OJYeCzyNOrUA/view?utm_content=DAFftZl9-HI&utm_campaign=designshare&utm_medium=link&utm_source=publishsharelink.
Yorkshire Sound Women Network. Accessed August 12, 2023. https://yorkshiresoundwomen.com/.

General

Hamer, Laura, ed. *The Cambridge Companion to Women in Music since 1900*. Cambridge: Cambridge University Press, 2021.
Jones, Judie. *Succeeding as a Woman in Music Leadership*. London: Creative Arts Development, 1983.
Mathias, Rhiannon. *Lutyens, Maconchy, Williams and Twentieth-Century British Music: A Blest Trio of Sirens*. Farnham: Ashgate, 2012.
_____, ed. *The Routledge Handbook of Women's Work in Music*. London: Routledge, 2022.
Nenić, Iva, and Linda Cimardi, eds. *Women's Leadership in Music: Modes, Legacies, Alliances*. Bielefeld: Transcript Verlag, 2023.
Rusak, Helen. *Women, Music and Leadership*. New York: Routledge, 2023.

PART I

Historical Perspectives

Historical Perspectives: An Introduction

Laura Hamer and Helen Julia Minors

Part I examines a broad range of historical perspectives on women's musical leadership. Largely focused upon Europe and North America, the chapters consider women's musical leadership within both the private musical sphere of contemporary salon culture and the public musical world of the concert hall. The chapters cover examples drawn from both the classical and popular music industries, encompassing a wide variety of women's musical work, following performers, composers, pedagogues, and musical campaigners. The part offers detailed case studies of individual women composers, including Cécile Chaminade and Joan Trimble; considerations of women's leadership roles within chamber music ensembles, including Augusta Hervey, Getrude Miller, Vahdah Olcott-Bickford, Wilma Norman-Neruda, and Camilla Urso; and historical studies of women's collective musical activism and group resistance, including considerations of the Maiglöckchen Ladies' Orchestra, the *Union des Femmes Professeurs et Compositeurs de Musique* (U.F.P.C.), and resistance amongst women political prison inmates within Franco's Spain. All of the chapters presented within Part I draw upon extensive archival research, whilst Orla Shannon's chapter ('The Forgotten Woman: Joan Trimble (1915–2000) and the Canon of Twentieth-Century Irish Art Song') also uses musical analysis, and Elsa Calero-Carramolino's chapter ('"There is no gate, no lock, no bolt that you can set upon the freedom of my mind": Being a woman in Franco's prisons: A Glimpse through Music') is further enriched by her detailed ethnographic study.

To provide an overview of the individual chapters, in Chapter Two Sarah Clarke situates the performance and teaching activities of Augusta Hervey and her 'Ladies Guitar and Mandoline Band' within the context of aristocratic women's amateur and philanthropic music-making activities in Victorian England. Speaking in dialogue with Clarke in Chapter Three, 'Examining the Birth of Guitar Societies in America: From Women Guitarists' Advocacy to Philanthropy', Kathy Acosta Zavala explores the role which women's philanthropy and voluntary labour played in establishing guitar societies in the US in the early decades of the twentieth century, with particular reference paid to the pioneering guitarists Gertrude Miller and Vahdah Olcott-Bickford. Shifting to a consideration of women's musical leadership within the realm of chamber music, in Chapter Four Bella Powell considers the roles which the violinists Wilma Norman-Neruda and Camilla Urso played in normalising women leading otherwise all-male string quartets in the later nineteenth century.

DOI: 10.4324/9781003024767-2

Attention moves from nineteenth-century chamber ensembles to nineteenth-century ladies' orchestras in Chapter Five, where Nuppu Koivisto-Kaasik offers a compelling reading of patriarchal power structures and women's strategies of resistance within the gendered (and sometimes violent) world of the later nineteenth-century Central European entertainment industry. In Chapter Six, Ann Grindley moves the spotlight onto women's participation in *fin-de-siècle* salon culture and provides a persuasive case study of Cécile Chaminade's musical leadership within this site, with particular attention paid to her activities and reception within the Anglophone world. In Chapter Seven, Laura Hamer considers the U.F.P.C. (*Union des Femmes Professeurs et Compositeurs de Musique*/Union of Women Music Teachers and Composers), a feminist union of women musicians which was founded in Paris in 1904 to defend the collective interests of women musicians and to provide their membership with professional opportunities.

Moving further into the twentieth century in the final four chapters within Part I, in Chapter Eight Orla Shannon offers a compelling reassessment of Irish composer Joan Trimble, with special attention paid to her song output and reasons for her exclusion from the canon of twentieth-century Irish art music. In Chapter Nine, Elsa Calero-Carramolino offers an insightful and innovative study of collective musical resistance amongst women prisoners in Franco's Spain.

Many of the issues introduced within Part I – particularly the importance of both individual and collective women's musical leadership, activism, philanthropy, groups and networks, and advocacy – act as historical precedents for wider themes explored throughout the volume. In particular, the collective resistance, activism, and advocacy of the Maiglöckchen Ladies' Orchestra, U.F.P.C., and amongst women political prison inmates in Franco's Spain form striking historical parallels for the case studies of contemporary women's collective musical leadership explored in depth within Part VI, 'Advocacy: Collectives and Grass-Roots Activism'.

2
AUGUSTA HERVEY
Lady of 'The Ladies' Guitar and Mandoline Band'[1]

Sarah Clarke

As amateur music making flourished in Victorian England, one amateur ensemble comprised a group of aristocratic women and was called the 'The Ladies' Guitar and Mandoline Band'. Augusta Hervey (1846–1927) was one of the main instigators of the ensemble and played with it throughout its existence. This group and others like it were largely overlooked by historians until Paul Sparks researched it in 2012 and revealed some of its intriguing activities.[2] The band, however, was only part of Augusta's long career.

Early Life

Augusta was from an aristocratic English family; she was the granddaughter of the fifth Earl and First Marquess of Bristol, whose country residence was Ickworth House in Suffolk. Her parents were Lord William Hervey (1805–1850), the third son of the Marquess and Cecilia Hervey, née. Fremantle (1809–1871).[3] Little is known about Augusta's education; it is unlikely that she went to school and was most probably educated by her mother and governesses at home. She was a pianist and would certainly have had encouragement and informal piano lessons when very young from her mother or her maternal grandmother, Betsey Fremantle. Betsey's diaries, which have nearly all survived, give fascinating insights and show that music was important to her. It can safely be assumed that she was an accomplished keyboard player.[4] The diaries also make it clear how very important her grandchildren were to her later on. After the premature death in 1850 of Lord William Hervey, Betsey spent most of the subsequent five years with her daughter Cecilia and Cecilia's three small children and older stepdaughter. Music would have been part of their everyday lives, and Augusta would have been much influenced by her grandmother. On 4 May 1851 Betsey wrote about her granddaughter:

> This was little Gussey's birth day [*sic*], just 5, she has learnt several tunes on the piano and plays them very nicely. I gave her a locket with my hair and the dear child was . . . highly delighted with all her little presents.[5]

When she was older, this tuition was supplemented with lessons from private music masters rather than at an institution such as the Royal Academy of Music (as was common for upper-class women of the time).[6] It is known that she studied with Jacob Blumenthal in the 1870s; she wrote in a diary on 2 May 1878 that she had 'worked hard with Blumenthal'.[7]

As was typical for young women of her class, Augusta was presented at court as a debutante to the Princess of Wales, deputising for Queen Victoria, at Saint James's Palace on 16 May 1863. Some two thousand of the nobility and gentry attended, and among the five hundred debutantes was another member of the Hervey family, Lady Mary Hervey (1845–1928), who was Augusta's first cousin and just one year older.[8] As adults, they shared much music together.

The first newspaper report so far found of Augusta playing the piano in public dates from May 1876.[9] The writer noted that the efforts of amateur performers such as Augusta were exempt from criticism but nevertheless praised her ability, as did other reports that followed.[10] A later performance in particular indicates what an accomplished player she must have been. In 1880 a charity concert was organised by her contemporary and friend, Lady Folkestone.[11] It took place in Saint James's Hall with amateur performers who included Henry Leslie's choir as well as Augusta, and there can be no doubt that only skilled players would have taken part. The highlight of this event was a performance in the middle of the evening of Romberg's Toy Symphony, for which Lady Folkestone enlisted the help of several leading musicians of the day; in particular, Arthur Chappell played the woodpecker; Joseph Barnby the nightingale; Charles Hallé the quail, and Arthur Sullivan the cuckoo.[12] Royalty were among the audience, and *The Daily Telegraph* noted how 'Saint James's Hall burst into smiles; the smiles soon became laughter, the laughter ended in applause'.[13]

The Band

In addition to the piano, Augusta played and performed in public on the guitar. In 1884, she used it to accompany three Neapolitan songs performed by Lady Folkestone.[14] The titles were listed in a review and two of them, 'Fuor di Parigi' and 'Tiri Tomba', were probably arrangements by the prominent Victorian guitarist Catharina Pratten.[15] However, it was the guitar band that Augusta founded with her cousin Lady Mary in approximately 1885 that is of particular interest to historians of the guitar. Paul Sparks has described the inspirations that probably led to the forming of this group.[16] The first was a 'Viennese Lady Orchestra', conducted by Madame Schipek, which was performing at the Albert Palace in Battersea in 1885.[17] The second influence also came from abroad and was a troupe of so-called Spanish students. Several such groups visited London in this period, but the one that had impact on this occasion was probably the *Granados*, a group of guitar and mandolin players who played at the Alhambra Music Hall.[18]

It is interesting to consider how a group of aristocratic women who were undoubtedly bound by the class conventions of the day could have been so influenced by these ensembles. Women were certainly enjoying much greater freedom than they had in earlier times, not least by riding bicycles, but for the Herveys and their circle, careers as professional musicians remained out of the question.[19] In contrast, the Viennese women were professional and, although respectable, would have been from musician families of a so-called lower-middle artisan class, as defined by Margaret Myers.[20] In an interview, conductor Madame Schipek even mentioned exactly how much her leading players received, with the others getting less.[21] Likewise the Spanish students were professional players in their performances as the *Granados* at the Alhambra, where they played to urban working and lower-/middle-class audiences in a music hall that would not have been regarded as respectable by many.[22]

As Philip Rudd has put it in his thesis about Lady Folkestone, the crucial difference for the aristocratic women was the function of music; for them music was not a livelihood but an entertainment to be enjoyed on a firmly amateur basis.[23] Nevertheless, it was a big step forward for these lady amateurs to take their music in large ensembles out of their homes into public spaces, which was such a contrast to the music-making of Augusta's grandmother, Betsey, who only performed at private occasions.[24] The person who helped make these public performances acceptable was Lady Folkestone. She was without doubt a pioneer, as not only was she unusually the first woman to regularly conduct a British orchestra in public,[25] but the activities of amateurs like her were a crucial prelude for the performances of the professional women's groups in Britain that followed.[26] With characteristic panache she founded an amateur Ladies' String Band, which gave its first performance with a Ladies' Choir in 1882.[27] Such was the ostentation of the occasion that the acceptability of an ensemble of aristocratic women could not be questioned.[28] She herself conducted: the band had twenty-eight players, of whom seven ladies had titles, and in addition there was a choir of thirty-one singers which included six countesses.[29] The venue chosen for their first performance was Stafford House, one of the greatest mansions in London,. The room they performed in was the magnificent picture gallery and royalty were present. The occasion was a glittering one in more ways than one; it was reported that many of the performers wore 'masses of diamonds'[30] and, in addition, this was the first occasion on which the Duke of Sutherland used electric light in the gallery.[31]

Following this lead, Augusta and Lady Mary started their band around 1885 and continued to perform until at least 1900. There have been some challenges in researching this ensemble. One difficulty came from the lack of visibility of the group during the twentieth century. There were several reasons for this. As Philip Rudd has noted, the significance of both amateurs and so-called popular music, of which the band's repertoire consisted, have suffered neglect from musicologists until recently.[32] In addition, as Margaret Myers described in her research into women's orchestras, a similar lack of interest and devaluation has been applied to women instrumentalists.[33] These ensembles were marginalised and viewed merely as yet another example of upper-class women's accomplishments.

Guitar researchers in particular have missed many of the activities of guitar and mandolin groups like this because little mention is made of them in the instrument-specific periodicals of the time. The first of these periodicals was the *Banjo World* of 1893, produced by Essex and Cammeyer, a company run by two banjo players, both men.[34] As one would expect, their periodical showed significantly more interest in groups that included their instrument. A correspondent complained in 1898 that the guitar and mandolin were being neglected by the journal, to which the editor robustly retorted that the fault lay with the players of those instruments for not sending in material.[35] The editor at that time was Home Gordon, another male banjo player.[36]

A further difficulty has come from the problem of identifying the band. From the late 1880s and into the 1890s several similar groups existed, and when newspaper reports mention 'The Ladies' Guitar and Mandoline Band' one cannot be certain to whom they are referring. In addition, the few references to the Hervey group that have been found which list the players make it clear that membership was flexible and must have been adjusted according to who was available and what was required. A report in 1892 in the *Queen* newspaper noted that there were then between thirty and forty members 'on the books',[37] and this membership no doubt changed over time. To add to the confusion it is also possible that some of the players played in more than one group, as Augusta herself did. For example, she led the 'Phoenix Green Amateur Mandoline and Guitar Ladies' Band' in 1900.[38]

Nevertheless, it has been possible to piece together some details of the band's activities. Its early years were described in the *Queen* newspaper: founded by Miss Augusta Hervey, 'the well known pianist' and her cousin, the group started in a small way rehearsing at Lady Mary's London residence, number six Saint James's Square. By 1892, it was being run by a committee with Maud Sullivan as secretary, and rehearsals were held at her residence in Grosvenor Square. Initially only guitarists were included, and Catharina Pratten conducted.[39] Some of the women were inspired to take up the mandolin after hearing the Spanish students and these instruments were added to the band, at which point Pratten stepped aside and leadership passed to various of the leading mandolin players in London at the time, all men who supposedly came from Italy or Spain. Each conductor made a mark on the band's repertoire. Their early pieces would have included arrangements by Pratten, which she also published, and they reflected a clear interest in music relating to Mediterranean countries. They included *Bolero, Addio a Napoli, Il Gondolira,* and *Zapateado*.[40] Surviving copies of other pieces have not been found, although commentaries suggest that they were well written and suited to the medium. Cristofaro, the famous Italian mandolinist who briefly conducted the group before his early death in 1890, wrote a 'Serenade for solo voice and chorus with accompaniment of mandolins and guitars', which was probably performed when he conducted the group in the Steinway Hall in 1889.[41] Philip Bone described the work as both original, novel, and 'exceedingly effective', noting in 1914 that the autograph manuscript was kept by the band.[42] Zerega, an American who posed as a Spaniard, was with the group for about four years and added a *Potpourri Espagnol* to their repertoire.[43] Francia, the Italian mandolin virtuoso, conducted the group from 1895 until 1898, and in his last year the band took part in a concert playing 'with delightful verve, steady time, and beautiful gradations of light and shade'. The highlight was a performance of Francia's own *Characteristic Fantasia* during which a mandolin duet was played by Lady Clayton and Miss Slade followed by a coda which the band attacked 'with a vivacity which was rewarded by prolonged applause'.[44]

It has been possible with reasonable certainty to identify from the players named many occasions when the Hervey band probably performed. It usually took part in charity events which were in keeping with women's well-established philanthropic activities;[45] most were concerts, and there were a few occasions when it provided incidental music at bazaars or sales. Two events have been found that took place at the houses of members of the group. In May 1890, the band played during a National Silk Exhibition at number seven, Saint James's Square, the London residence of Lord Egerton and next door to the Hervey household. His daughter, Lady Beatrice Egerton, was a member of the group.[46] On another occasion, in 1897, they played during a sale of the Working Ladies' Guild at number one, Belgrave Square, the London home of Reuben Sassoon, who was a close confidant of the Prince of Wales.[47] His two daughters, Rachel and Flora, were in the band.[48]

The question remains as to whether Augusta's activities were those traditionally expected of women or whether she was, like many New Women of her time, exploring newfound freedoms. Two pieces of her writing may indicate whether she believed marriage and motherhood remained the true vocation of women. The first is a manuscript of a story in three short sections which may have been intended for serialisation in a journal. In it the heroine, Cynthia, a talented amateur pianist, fails to take up an opportunity of studying music in Leipzig, the place to which many music students (including Ethel Smyth) aspired at that time, and instead accepts a woman's supposed true vocation and marries the Baron after performing the solo part of his concerto in a concert in Prince's Hall.[49] The second has a similar theme and is a short story in which the heroine, Gladys, fails to secure any professional singing engagement in London and returns home to Wales for an apparently more appropriate engagement to a young man.[50] It is uncertain if Augusta's work reflected her own beliefs. It may be that she regarded the stories of Cynthia and Gladys in the same light as another of her novels (*The Last*

Day of her Life), which she published in 1894 and which she dismissed in a letter as a 'shilling dreadful about to adorn the railway bookstalls'.[51]

Whatever the case, the reality was that when Augusta's band started, she was thirty-nine and hope of the ideal of marriage would have been receding by then; she never did marry. In the absence of marriage, she put her energy into the ensemble, with musical performances occupying much of her time. However, all the indications are that with these she continued to maintain an accepted amateur role, never crossing the line to become professional. It is even noticeable that members of her band paid lip service to established gender roles of the time by largely employing male professional musicians to conduct after Pratten's departure, and thus not disturbing the established gender hierarchy. Although Augusta did conduct twice, in 1891 and 1899, and Maud Sullivan 'led' the band in 1892, these were almost certainly stopgap arrangements, as noted by a commentator describing the event of 1891.[52] This was in contrast to Lady Folkestone, who always conducted her Ladies' Band herself. Remaining as an amateur had two sides to it; Augusta would not have been sharpening her skills in response to the criticism that was usually levelled at professionals.[53] On the other hand, as Sterndale Bennett reputably pointed out, she would not have been a servant of a public that sought surprise as well as enjoyment but instead could play as she wished and thought best.[54]

Teaching and Publishing

Performing on piano and guitar were not the only musical activities Augusta undertook. She published a few pieces of music and in addition gave piano lessons advertising these for 'a limited number of pupils' with terms of ten shillings and sixpence for one hour in the 1880s.[55] In the 1911 census, she listed her occupation as music teacher. With these activities it could be construed that she was professional, although this would depend on a definition of 'professional'; something contemporaries themselves struggled to identify. In 1896, the question was raised in the journal *The Troubadour* and various suggestions were offered. However, the only consensus reached by the correspondents was that defining the term was difficult. Mr. J. E. Newell called for some regulation in the profession to guard the public from 'quacks' and 'charlatans'; a sentiment shared by many musicians at the time. Maude Evans, a singer and mandolin player, considered that someone was professional if they devoted their whole life to music to the exclusion of all other occupations. Charles Thomas brought the issue of money into the discussion, suggesting that anyone who was paid a proper fee, as opposed to a nominal sum or expenses, was a professional.[56] Fred Hawes agreed, noting that the fee was the key to the issue and a professional musician could work some of the time in other occupations, provided his musical activities attracted a professional fee.[57] Earlier in 1888, Henry Fisher in Blackpool published a book *The Musical Profession*, that extended the definition further by suggesting that to be professional a musician must depend on his or her fees for his or her livelihood.[58] This view was echoed by another writer in 1896 who commented: 'a professional performs for his living and expects remuneration on every occasion. By some peculiar freak of nature it is ordained that he requires bodily nourishment like other men, hence his inability to work for nothing'.[59]

Without a clear definition it is difficult to conclude whether Augusta was professional in some of her activities. She did not devote all her working time to music. However, her ten shilling and sixpence fee for piano lessons was the same as the average charge for piano lessons at the Guildhall School of Music in the same period; according to the School's prospectuses the mid-point of the fees was two guineas for twelve twenty-minute lessons, or three guineas for twelve half-hour lessons. These figures were the equivalent of Augusta's ten shillings and sixpence per hour, which could therefore be regarded as a professional fee.[60] The question of whether she needed the money is a difficult one to answer without full knowledge of her income and without establishing what constituted 'need'. She inherited from her mother, who died in 1871, an annual income of two hundred and sixty pounds.[61] Housekeeping accounts in Mrs Beeton's *Every-day Cookery* of the 1890s suggest that an annual income of two hundred pounds would not include any servants, and an income of three hundred pounds would include only one.[62] For someone of Augusta's class, domestic staff would have been seen as essential, in which case the inheritance from her mother would have been insufficient if that was all she had. There are indications that she felt it necessary to earn money; in a letter of 1894 she mentioned that she had moved house from Milner Terrace to Moore Street in Chelsea and described her new residences as having 'various advantages of which economy is not the least!'[63] In addition, a letter in the archives from a friend in 1900 outlines which journals would pay her best for an article suggesting that this issue was a concern.[64] Whatever her situation, her addresses do establish that she was considerably less well-off than her cousin; the streets she lived in were described in 1902 as being ones that were passed through in order to get to the aristocratic part of Chelsea in neighbouring Lennox Gardens.[65] In contrast, when in London in the 1880s, Lady Mary resided in the Hervey residence in Saint James's Square, a house which the family had owned since it was first built in 1677,[66] and which the 1851 census recorded as having twenty-seven resident servants.[67] Lady Mary would have been aware of her cousin's situation and, touchingly, in her will left Augusta a life annuity of two hundred pounds. In the event, however, Augusta died first and never benefitted from it.[68]

Augusta's Achievement

Regardless of whether her teaching was to be regarded as professional work, most of Augusta's activities remained within traditional boundaries; teaching had long been seen as an acceptable occupation for women, and the giving of public performances as an amateur for philanthropic purposes was seen as beyond reproach by even the most conservative of critics. However, the fact remained that her ladies' band was the first of its sort and many such groups followed in the 1890s.[69] In this sense she was, like Lady Folkestone, a pioneering leader.

There is little doubt that the girl who was described as 'very forward for her age' at the age of eight by her grandmother[70] grew to be an intelligent and articulate woman, as evidenced by the invitations she received from Lady Waldegrave of Strawberry Hill in Twickenham in the 1860s and 1870s.[71] Lady Waldegrave was renowned for her entertaining; invitations were highly valued and never given 'on account of wealth or title'. Strawberry Hill was described as:

> the Mecca towards which the eyes of the ambitious turned . . . Around [Lady Waldegrave] crowded the men and women who were making the history of the time . . . women on account of their wit, or beauty or wisdom.[72]

As regards the band, Augusta's writing shows how much straightforward enjoyment she took in making music with others. In the archives is her undated manuscript with the title 'Amateur bands'. She wrote:

> There is a joy in Concerted Music that is not found in mere solo playing. It is a delight to bear a part in producing the great . . . works that have roused echoes in every corner of the globe.[73]

Notes

1. I am grateful to Paul Sparks for comments on this research. For an earlier version of this chapter, see Sarah Clarke, "An Instrument in Comparative Oblivion? Women and the Guitar in Victorian London" (Unpublished doctoral diss., The Open University, 2021).
2. Paul Sparks, "'A Considerable Attraction for Both Ears and Eyes:' Ladies' Guitar and Mandoline Bands in Late Victorian London," *Soundboard* 38, no. 4 (2012): 36–44. At this time 'mandolin' was often spelt 'mandoline'.
3. For the Hervey family tree, see Michael De-la-Noy, *The House of Hervey* (London: Constable, 2001), vii.
4. Betsey's diaries spanned 1789–1857. An edited version covering the years 1789–1820 was published in three volumes in the 1930s. A planned fourth volume was not published. Elizabeth Wynne Fremantle, *The Wynne Diaries*, with contributions from Eugenia Wynne, edited by Anne Fremantle, 3 vols. (London: Oxford University Press, 1935–1940). Elaine Chalus noted that Betsey and her sister Eugenia were competent artists and skilled musicians. See E. H. Chalus, "Fremantle [née Wynne], Elizabeth [Betsey], Lady Fremantle (1778–1857), diarist," *Oxford Dictionary of National Biography*, October 4, 2007, accessed March 29, 2017, www.oxforddnb.com/view/10.1093/ref:odnb/9780198614128.001.0001/odnb-9780198614128-e-92613.
5. Aylesbury Centre for Buckinghamshire Studies, Lady Elizabeth (Betsey) Fremantle, Journals, D/FR/D/6/39, entry for May 4, 1851. 'Gussey' was Augusta's family name.
6. I am grateful to Adam Taylor of the Royal Academy of Music Library for confirming that Augusta did not attend the Academy. Personal communication, February 6, 2019.
7. Bury St. Edmunds, Suffolk Record Office, Hervey Family Archives, Literary MSS. and other papers, 941/62/8, Diary of Augusta Hervey, entry for May 2, 1878. A review of a concert in which she performed noted that she was a pupil of Blumenthal. See Anonymous, "Oswestry, Lady Harlech's Concerts," *Shrewsbury Chronicle*, November 7, 1884, 7. Blumenthal was a German composer and pianist who had settled in England in 1848. See James Brown, *Biographical Dictionary of Musicians* (London: Alexander Gardner, 1886), 101. It is not known who taught Augusta the guitar.
8. Anonymous, "Last Saturday's Presentations at St James's Palace to HRH the Princess of Wales," *Court Journal*, Supplement to 1792, May 23, 1863, 2. Lady Mary was the daughter of Lord William Hervey's eldest brother, the second Marquess of Bristol.
9. Anonymous, "Trained Nurses' Annuity Fund," *London Evening Standard*, May 13, 1876, 3.
10. Twentieth-century research suggests that good amateurs, as distinct from 'dabblers,' could be better than some professionals. See Robert Stebbins, *Amateurs, Professionals and Serious Leisure* (Montreal: McGill-Queen's University Press, 1992), 38. If similar research for Augusta's period were to be undertaken, it is likely that the findings would be similar. A 'dabbler' takes only a slight interest in something.
11. Born Helen Matilda Chaplin in 1846, she married William Pleydell-Bouverie in 1866, who succeeded to the title of Lord Folkestone in 1869 and the title of Lord Radnor in 1889. For simplicity Helen Matilda will be referred to as Lady Folkestone here. She was an accomplished amateur musician.
12. The event was described in Lady Folkestone's autobiography. See Helen Pleydell-Bouverie, Countess of Radnor, *From a Great-Grandmother's Armchair* (London: Marshall Press, 1927), 108–10. Augusta was listed the previous day among the performers. See Anonymous, "Advertisements," *The Times*, May 13, 1880, 1.
13. Anonymous, "St. James's Hall," *The Daily Telegraph*, May 15, 1880, 3.
14. Anonymous, "Macuynlleth, The Marchioness of Londonderry's Evening Concert," *Montgomeryshire Express*, November 4, 1884, 5.
15. C. Pratten, *Songs of All Nations 5 Tiri Tomba* (London: Lonsdale, n.d.); C. Pratten, *Songs of All Nations 10 Neapolitan Air* (London: Lonsdale, n.d.). Catharina Pratten, née Pelzer, (1824–1895), who styled herself Madame Sidney Pratten after her marriage in 1854, was an important guitarist in London. Her pupils included Princess Louise and other women of nobility. See Frank Mott Harrison, *Reminiscences of Madame Sidney Pratten* (Bournemouth: Barnes and Mullins, 1899).
16. Sparks, "A Considerable Attraction for Both Ears and Eyes," 36.
17. Pleydell-Bouverie, *From a Great-Grandmother's Armchair*, 111.
18. Anonymous, "Alhambra Theatre," *Globe*, March 17, 1886, 6.

19. For upper-class women, music was seen as an accomplishment needed for the 'marriage market' and later as a domestic pastime.
20. Margaret Myers, "Searching for Data about European Ladies' Orchestras, 1870–1950," in *Music and Gender*, edited by Pirkko Moisala and Beverley Diamond (Urbana: University of Illinois Press, 2000), 189–213, (190).
21. Anonymous, "An Orchestra of Women," *Pall Mall Gazette*, October 13, 1885, 11.
22. Dagmar Höher, "The Composition of Music Hall Audiences, 1850–1900," in *Music Hall: The Business of Pleasure*, edited by Peter Bailey (Milton Keynes: Open University Press, 1986), 73–92 (75).
23. Philip Rudd, "Countess, Conductor, Pioneer: Lady Radnor and the Phenomenon of the Victorian Ladies' Orchestra" (Unpublished doctoral diss., University of Iowa, 2017), 118.
24. Betsey recorded in her diary her dismay when she discovered in 1798 that her cousin, Augusta Correr, who used the stage name Angelleli, had become a professional musician. She wrote on January 22: 'Mde Angelleli made her first appearance, to my no small surprise and vexation' and on January 27 wrote: 'I would give my world that she had not chosen London to expose herself'. See Fremantle II, 200–01.
25. Rudd, "Countess, Conductor, Pioneer," 155.
26. Derek Scott has noted that the first British ladies' orchestras were amateur. See Derek Scott, *Sounds of the Metropolis* (Oxford: Oxford University Press, 2008), 22.
27. A newspaper report confirmed the year. See "Royal College of Music," *The Times* (July 3, 1882), 5. Lady Folkestone gave the incorrect year of 1881 in her autobiography. See Pleydell-Bouverie, *From a Great-Grandmother's Armchair*, 111.
28. Paula Gillett has noted how Lady Folkestone's activities 'contributed significantly to a climate of greater acceptance of public performance by respectable – and even married – women'. See Paula Gillett, "Entrepreneurial Women Musicians in Britain from the 1790s to the Early 1900s," in *The Musician as Entrepreneur 1700–1914*, edited by William Weber (Bloomington: Indiana University Press, 2004), 198–220 (211).
29. Anonymous, "Viscountess Folkestone's Concert," *Bristol Mercury*, July 8, 1882, 5.
30. Anonymous, "Concerts," *World*, July 5, 1882, 13.
31. Pleydell-Bouverie, *From a Great-Grandmother's Armchair*, 111. Stafford House was renamed Lancaster House in the early twentieth century.
32. Rudd, "Countess, Conductor, Pioneer," 2, 16. Rudd notes that the term 'popular' was not always clearly defined.
33. Myers, "Searching for Data about European Ladies' Orchestras, 1870–1950," 205.
34. The firm Essex and Cammeyer was established by the two banjo players Clifford Essex and Alfred Cammeyer in 1892 at 59 Piccadilly where they had a banjo studio. See Richard Ineson and Anthony Peabody, *A Short Biography of the Unique Joe Morley* (Fakenham: Clifford Essex Music Company, 2017), 6–7.
35. Anonymous, "Notes and Comments," *Banjo World* (August 1898), 117.
36. The editor was not named in the edition of the journal; reference to his role was made later. See Anonymous, "Notes and Comments," *Banjo World* (December 1900), 18.
37. Anonymous, "Ladies' Bands," *Queen* (March 19, 1892), 464.
38. Anonymous, "Hartley Wintney," *Hants and Berks Gazette and Middlesex and Surrey Journal* (April 28, 1900), 7.
39. "Ladies' Bands."
40. The exotic repertoire was accompanied in one concert by the 'picturesque Spanish costumes' worn by the players. See 'Musical Note," *Shoreditch Observer*, March 24, 1893. Such costumes were probably also used on other occasions.
41. "Signor Di Cristofaro's Annual Morning Concert," *Le Follet* (August 1, 1889), 200.
42. Philip Bone, *The Guitar and Mandolin* (London: Schott, 1914), 81.
43. This was performed on December 18, 1893, the first concert found at which Guerra conducted. See Anonymous, "Morning Concert at the Pavilion," *Brighton Gazette* (December 21, 1893), 5. The first concert found at which Zerega conducted was on March 3, 1891 and the last found was on July 12, 1893. See "Advertisements," *Morning Post*, February 25, 1891, 1; "At the Prince of Wales's Club," *Pall Mall Gazette*, July 13, 1893, 8. Zerega's real name was Edgar E. Hill, and he was from Columbus, Indiana. See "Zerega and Hill are One," *New York Journal*, September 28, 1896, 7.
44. Anonymous, "Signor Francia's Mandoline Recital," *Banjo World*, April 1898, 58. Francia's first appearance found was on May 21, 1895, and his last found was on May 12, 1898. See Anonymous,

"Advertisements," *Morning Post*, May 13, 1895, 1; "Advertisements," *Morning Post*, April 18, 1898, 1.
45. The band performed at three of the conductor's own concerts, those by Cristofaro, Zerega, and Francia. It is unclear if these events were technically for charity. Nevertheless, the amateur status of the band was never in question. For Cristofaro's concert see "Signor Di Cristofaro's Annual Morning Concert," *Le Follet*, August 1, 1889, 200. For Zerega's concert see "Advertisements," *Morning Post*, February 25, 1891, 1. For Francia's concert see Anonymous, "Advertisements," *Morning Post*, May 13, 1895, 1.
46. "Arrangements for the Day," *Morning Post*, May 14, 1890, 7. A report of Lady Beatrice's wedding gifts, which included a diamond brooch from members of the band, confirmed her membership. See "The Coming Marriage of Mr. Kemp, M.P. and Lady Beatrice Egerton," *Heywood's Advertiser*, July 31, 1896, 5.
47. Cecil Roth, "The Court Jews of Edwardian England," *Jewish Social Studies* 5 (1943), 355–66 (361).
48. "The Grand Concert," *South Bucks Standard*, July 15, 1892, 5.
49. Hervey Family Archives, Literary MSS. and other papers, 941/62/8.
50. Augusta Hervey, "Getting an Engagement," *Good Words*, December 1905, 65–70.
51. Augusta Hervey, *The Last Day of Her Life* (London: Skeffington & Sons, 1894). Augusta referred to the book in a letter to the father of a pupil, Mr Arkwright. See Hereford, Herefordshire Archive and Record Centre, Hampton Court Estate, Letters from Augusta Hervey, A63/IV/21/12. Letter to Mr Arkwright dated 15 February [1894]. A 'shilling dreadful' was a short sensational novel costing one shilling.
52. Augusta conducted in 1891. See "Ladies' Bands." She also conducted in 1899. See Anonymous, "Arrangements for this Day," *Morning Post*, May 6, 1899, 7. Maud led in 1892. See, "The Grand Concert."
53. For a discussion of this see Nancy B. Reich, "Women as Musicians: A Question of Class," in *Musicology and Difference* (Berkeley: University of California Press, 1993), 125–46 (126).
54. Bettina Walker, *My Musical Experiences* (London: Novello, Ewer & Co., 1892), 21.
55. Advertisements were placed in the *Morning Post* between April 29, 1887 and May 4, 1887.
56. See "Troubadours" Table Talk, What Is a Professional Musician?," *Troubadour* (October 1896), 200–01. All the contributors would have seen themselves as professional. J. E. Newell was an organist who also published music for mandolin and guitar. See James Brown and Stephen Stratton, *British Musical Biography* (London: William Reeves, 1897), 295–96. Maude Evans was a contralto singer and played mandolin and banjo. See Anonymous, "Miss Maude Evans," *Gentleman's Journal and Gentlewoman's Court Review*, March 16, 1896, 1371. Charles Thomas was a banjo player. See Anonymous, "Biographical Sketches, Mr. Charles Thomas," *Troubadour*, January 1897, 249.
57. "Correspondence, What Is a Professional Musician?," *Troubadour*, December 1896, 240. Fred Hawes was a banjo player who performed with the Black Crow Minstrels. See "Metropolitan Notes," *Troubadour*, March 1898, 38.
58. Henry Fisher, *The Musical Profession* (London: J. Curwen & Sons, 1888), 119. Fisher was an organist and teacher in Blackpool. See Cyril Ehrlich, *The Music Profession in Britain* (Oxford: Clarendon Press, 1985), 121.
59. Anonymous, "Amateur, Pro-amateur and Professional," *Troubadour*, June 1896, 199. These issues continue to be debated today. See Rosemary Golding, "Introduction," in *The Music Profession in Britain 1780–1920*, edited by Rosemary Golding (Abingdon: Routledge, 2018), 1–11 (1–3). For a description of the founding of associations for musicians such as the Incorporated Society of Musicians see Ehrlich, *The Music Profession in Britain*, 126–41.
60. London, London Metropolitan Archive, Guildhall School of Music and Drama Archive, General Prospectuses, CLA/056/AD/02/001. The fees quoted in the late 1880s varied. For twelve twenty-minute lessons they could be £1 10s; £2 2s; or £3 3s. For twelve half-hour lessons they could be £2 4s; £3 3s; or £4 14s 6d.
61. An undated document of Cecilia's gives this figure, which comprised one hundred and sixty pounds interest on capital Cecilia had inherited, and would leave in addition an annuity of one hundred pounds for Augusta until she married. See Hervey Family Archive, Miscellaneous papers, 941/62/5. £260 in 1890 would be roughly equivalent to £35,500 today.
62. Anon, *Beeton's Every-day Cookery and Housekeeping Book*, Entirely New ed. (London: Ward, Lock & Co., [1898?]), xxv.
63. Letters from Augusta Hervey, A63/IV/21/12. Letter to Mr Arkwright dated 8 February [1894].

64. Hervey Family Archive, Literary MSS., and other papers, 941/62/8. Letter from G Stiegil. December 12, 1900.
65. G. E. Mitton, *Chelsea* (London: Adam & Charles Black, 1902), 664.
66. Arthur Dasent, *The History of St. James's Square* (London: Macmillan, 1895), 209.
67. Public Record Office 1851 census for 6, St. James's Square, Westminster, St. James, H.O. 107/1484. The Marquess of Bristol was resident for this census. The family were absent for later censuses in the century when only a skeleton staff were listed.
68. Will of the Right Honourable Mary Katherine Isabella Hervey, Probate, London, October 13, 1928.
69. Paul Sparks notes that the Hervey Band was the original one and that there were many imitators. See Sparks, "A Considerable Attraction for Both Ears and Eyes," 43.
70. Lady Elizabeth (Betsey) Fremantle, Journals, D/FR/D/6/40, entry for May 4, 1854.
71. For Augusta's visits to Strawberry Hill see Anonymous, "Fashionable World," *Morning Post*, April 7, 1866, 5; Anonymous, "Fashionable World," *Morning Post*, July 21, 1868, 5; Anonymous, "Fashionable World," *Morning Post*, July 22, 1874, 5; Anonymous, "Fashionable World," *Morning Post*, July 25, 1876, 5. For her visit to Lady Waldegrave's house at Carlton Gardens. See Anonymous, "Fashionable World," *Morning Post*, February 24, 1873, 5. For her visit to Lady Waldegrave at Chewton Mendip. See "Lord Carlingford and Frances Countess Waldegrave," *London Evening Standard*, October 24, 1874, 3.
72. "Court and Club," *Graphic*, February 5, 1898, 162.
73. Hervey Family Archives, Literary MSS. and other papers, 941/62/8.

Bibliography

Archives

Aylesbury, Centre for Buckinghamshire Studies, Lady Elizabeth (Betsey) Fremantle, Journals.
Bury St. Edmunds, Suffolk Record Office, Hervey Family Archives.
Hereford, Herefordshire Archive and Record Centre, Hampton Court Estate, Letters from Augusta Hervey.
London, London Metropolitan Archive, Guildhall School of Music and Drama Archive.

Published Sources

Bone, Philip. *The Guitar and Mandolin*. London: Schott, 1914.
Brown, James. *Biographical Dictionary of Musicians*. London: Alexander Gardner, 1886.
_____, and Stephen Stratton. *British Musical Biography*. London: William Reeves, 1897.
Dassent, Arthur. *The History of St. James's Square*. London: Macmillan, 1895.
De-la-Noy, Michael. *The House of Hervey*. London: Constable, 2001.
Ehrlich, Cyril. *The Music Profession in Britain*. Oxford: Clarendon Press, 1985.
Fisher, Henry. *The Musical Profession*. London: J. Curwen & Sons, 1888.
Gillett, Paula. "Entrepreneurial Women Musicians in Britain from the 1790s to the Early 1900s." In *The Musician as Entrepreneur 1700–1914*, edited by William Weber, 198–220. Bloomington: Indiana University Press, 2004.
Golding, Rosemary. "Introduction." In *The Music Profession in Britain 1780–1920*, edited by Rosemary Golding, 1–11. Abingdon: Routledge, 2018.
Harrison, Frank Mott. *Reminiscences of Madame Sidney Pratten*. Bournemouth: Barnes & Mullins, 1899.
Hervey, Augusta. *The Last Day of Her Life*. London: Skeffington & Son, 1894.
_____. "Getting an Engagement." *Good Words*, December 1905, 65–70.
Höher, Dagmar. "The Composition of Music Hall Audiences, 1850–1900." In *The Business of Pleasure*, edited by Peter Bailey, 73–92. Milton Keynes: Open University Press, 1986.
Ineson, Richard, and Anthony Peabody. *A Short Biography of the Unique Joe Morley*. Fakenham: Clifford Essex Music Company, 2017.
Mary, Isabella, and Mayson Beeton. *Mrs. Beeton's Every-day Cookery and Housekeeping Book*. Entirely New ed. London: Ward, Lock & Co., 1898.
Mitton, Geraldine Edith. *Chelsea*. London: Adam & Charles Black, 1902.

Myers, Margaret. "Searching for Data about European Ladies' Orchestras, 1870–1950." In *Music and Gender*, edited by Pirkko Moisala and Beverley Diamond, 189–213. Urbana: University of Illinois Press, 2000.
Pleydell-Bouverie, Helen. *Countess of Radnor, From a Great-Grandmother's Armchair*. London: Marshall Press, 1927.
Pratten, Catharina. *Songs of all Nations*. 5 Tiri Tomba. London: Lonsdale, n.d.
_____. *Songs of all Nations*. 10 Neapolitan Airs. London: Lonsdale, n.d.
Reich, Nancy B. "Women as Musicians: A Question of Class." In *Musicology and Difference*, edited by Ruth Solie, 125–46. Berkely: University of California Press, 1993.
Roth, Cecil. "The Court Jews of Edwardian England." *Jewish Social Studies* 5 (1943): 355–66.
Rudd, Philip. "Countess, Conductor, Pioneer: Lady Radnor and the Phenomenon of the Victorian Ladies' Orchestra." Unpublished doctoral thesis, University of Iowa, 2017.
Scott, Derek, *Sounds of the Metropolis*. Oxford: Oxford University Press, 2008.
Sparks, Paul. "'A Considerable Attraction for Both Ears and Eyes.' Ladies' Guitar and Mandoline Bands in Late Victorian London." *Soundboard* 38, no. 4 (2012): 36–44.
Stebbins, Robert. *Amateurs, Professionals and Serious Leisure*. Montreal: McGill-Queen's University Press, 1992.
Walker, Bettina. *My Musical Experiences*. London: Novello, Ewer & Co., 1892.
Wynne Fremantle, Elizabeth. *The Wynne Diaries, with Contributions from Eugenia Wynne*, edited by Anne Fremantle, 3 vols. London: Oxford University Press, 1935–1940.

3
EXAMINING THE BIRTH OF GUITAR SOCIETIES IN AMERICA
From Women Guitarists' Advocacy to Philanthropy

Kathy Acosta Zavala

Across the United States, there are sixty registered guitar societies and clubs, which shape the American guitar-specific institutional landscape.[1] Each of these organisations promotes the classical guitar through presenting concert series, sponsoring educational projects, and forming local guitar ensembles. Guitar societies are, in their majority, small non-profits funded by local guitar enthusiasts and professional guitarists.[2] While these organisations have become ubiquitous in the twenty-first century, they were non-existent at the turn of the twentieth century, and the history surrounding their creation is not a well-researched subject. To fill this musicological void, this chapter aims to address how guitar societies first came to America and to unveil the primary actors who mobilised to form guitar-specific organisations: women from the Banjo, Mandolin, and Guitar (hereafter BMG) movement.

Women's philanthropy is embodied in the history of the plucked and plectral instruments. Although the phrase 'nation's cultural custodians' has been used to describe women's philanthropic endeavours in the arts, scholars such as Kathleen D. McCarthy have challenged this notion by detailing the limited power these women held within art institutions.[3] Furthermore, according to McCarthy, 'far from assuming a custodial role', American women philanthropists in the arts were 'inveterate pioneers'.[4] The study of the history of the institutionalisation of the classical guitar reveals that, as primary actors, women guitarists of the BMG movement were indeed pioneers who successfully lobbied for and established American guitar societies in which they could hold power and maintain cultural and artistic control. Furthermore, the central creative products of Western Art music are usually understood to be compositions in a canon that is dominated by white males, but the activities of pioneers such as American guitarist Vahdah Olcott-Bickford (born Ethel Lucretia Olcott, 1885–1980) invite us to continue to rethink how we define creative activity and how these pioneers shaped important cultural enterprises. The establishment of these instrument-specific organisations can also be contextualised in direct contrast with the all-male organisations that were established by BMG advocates at the turn of the twentieth century, such as the American Guild of Banjoists, Mandolinists, and Guitarists.

The creation of American guitar societies was a by-product of women guitarists' entrance into the workforce as teachers, performers, and artists, and of the long-standing tradition of women's philanthropy and volunteerism in the arts. Although the first American guitar society, the Los Angeles Guitar Society (which became the American Guitar Society in 1924),

DOI: 10.4324/9781003024767-4

was founded in 1923, articles published in American BMG journals along with documents found at the International Guitar Research Archive (IGRA) show that BMG women guitarists mobilised to form guitar societies as early as 1905.

Between the 1890s and the 1930s the classical guitar was one of the plectral and plucked instruments promoted by the BMG movement, and it is within the backdrop of this movement that professional women guitarists began to emerge.[5] During this period, the adjective 'classical' was not used in America to describe the guitar; the gut/nylon six-string European instrument that derived from the modified five-string baroque guitar. This adjective was adopted in the 1920s and 1930s when guitar advocates wanted to clearly distinguish their European nineteenth-century playing tradition from the plectrum tradition that was being used to play 'steel-strung' guitars.[6] The adjectives 'classical' and 'steel-strung' also became associated with genre divisions, and the steel-strung guitar was directly linked to jazz and popular music.[7]

Women's presence in the early days of the BMG movement was sparse but crucial because it established precedents that helped smooth the entrance of a newer generation of women instrumentalists. Guitarists such as Meta Bischoff-Henning (b. 1867–?) and Dominga Lynch (dates unknown) were the pioneers who opened the door to concertising and composing for women guitarists emerging in the first decades of the twentieth century, such as Gertrude Miller (1879–?), Jennie Durkee (1877–1941), and Vahdah Olcott-Bickford.[8] As members of the BMG movement, this new generation of women guitarists became key players in the formation of American organisations that would solely champion the classical guitar at a time when all plectral instruments were promoted under one label – BMG – and instrumental independence was not encouraged.

Among these group of women, Vahdah Olcott-Bickford stands out as the most influential figure. Olcott-Bickford was an established guitar *virtuosa* and a prominent writer and contributor to plucked-stringed journals, such as *Cadenza* and *Crescendo*. She was one of the founders of the first American guitar society and its sole musical and operations director from 1923 until the 1970s. Olcott-Bickford's legacy as an institutional pioneer converges as the consummation of BMG women's years of advocacy on behalf of the classical guitar and the propeller for the formation of similar guitar-specific organisations across America.

The BMG Guild: Women in a Man's World

At the turn of the twentieth century, the BMG movement was flourishing in America as instrument manufacturers and owners of music printing businesses continued to grow their customer base by publishing journals such as *Crescendo* and *Cadenza*. In 1895, the plectral and plucked instruments community began exploring the possibility of organising a national gathering.[9] And that same year, Clarence L. Partee, the editor and owner of *Cadenza*, suggested the formation of 'an association of the profession similar to the Music Teachers' National Association [MTNA], with a President, Secretary, Treasurer, etc.' in an article published in his journal.[10] Although letters published in *Cadenza* indicate that Partee's suggestion was initially welcomed among his readers, the establishment of such an organisation was delayed until 1902.[11]

The first national organisation established to champion plucked and plectral instruments in the United States was the American Guild of Banjoists, Mandolinsists, and Guitarists, hereafter referred to as the BMG Guild. Its formation was led by several BMG magazine editors, Charles Morris and Clarence Partee in particular, who after an intense two-year advocacy and marketing campaign established their guild on Wednesday 22 January 1902, in Boston, MA.[12]

From its planning stages, which were officially announced in *Cadenza*'s October 1900 issue, the BMG Guild was led by men and, although women were welcomed as members, none held power. As Table 3.1 shows, women were not invited to be a part of the organising committee. This committee was formed by BMG magazine owners and editors, which automatically excluded women's participation because within the BMG movement no business was owned by a woman. Furthermore, as Table 3.2 shows, in Boston, women were not elected to the inaugural board of directors and, according to historical records, women were not even present at the Boston meeting.[13]

The lack of women's presence in the formation of the BMG Guild may be connected to the fact that district secretaries had more traditional values and adhered to cultural boundaries that normalised the presence of boards segregated by gender. As Linda Whitesitt reports, in the nineteenth century and the first half of the twentieth all-male boards were the public faces of musical institutions, while women served in all-women committees or clubs.[14] While it is unclear what personal views each member of the BMG Guild's inaugural governing body held regarding women's public roles, there is no record documenting any efforts made to include women's input or to invite them to serve in positions of leadership until 1909. A report published in *Crescendo* in that year details that outgoing president George L. Lansing asked his colleagues during the election of officers to strongly consider nominating 'a lady' to the

Table 3.1 American Guild of Banjoists, Mandolinists and Guitarists Organising Committee

Name	BMG Journal	Guild Organising Committee Role
Charles Morris	Stewart's Journal, Director and Editor	District Secretary
Clarence L. Partee	Cadenza, Editor	District Secretary
C. C. Adams	The Concerto, Editor	District Secretary
F. L. Keates	Stewart's Journal, Associate Director & The Major, Editor	Assistant District Secretary
Fred C. Meyer	The Tempo, Editor	Assistant District Secretary
Otto H. Albrecht	The Enterprise, Editor	Assistant District Secretary
Charles F. Graeber	The Reveille, Editor	Assistant District Secretary

Source: Data from 'The American Guild of Banjoists, Mandolinists and Guitarists: Organizing Work', *Cadenza* 7.2 (October 1900), 21.

Table 3.2 List of the American Guild of Banjoists, Mandolinists and Guitarists' 1902 Governing Body

Name	Officer Position
Ira H. Odell	President
Charles Morris	Vice-president
Clarence L. Partee	Secretary and treasurer
A. A. Farland	Executive Committee Member
Samuel Siegel	Executive Committee Member
W. J. Kitchener	Executive Committee Member
George L. Lansing	Executive Committee Member
H. F. Odell	Executive Committee Member

Source: Data from 'The Guild is Formed: Representative Members of the Banjo, Mandolin and Guitar Industries, with Teachers and Publishers of Music Get Together in a Practical Way', *Cadenza* 8.7 (March 1902), 14–15.

executive board, arguing that in his experience women were 'the best workers'.[15] Both Mrs. Alma J. Morse and Miss Cora L. Butler were elected to serve on the BMG Guild's executive board, becoming the first women to hold any power within this organisation.

Although women did not serve as officers, records show that some of them, such as guitarists Vahdah Olcott-Bickford and Jennie Durkee and banjoist Fannie Heinline, were active members, presenting papers and playing concerts at annual conventions.[16] Indeed, the BMG Guild's annual conventions featured selected women instrumentalists throughout its concerts and facilitated networking. In 1904, Heinline was the first woman ever engaged to co-headline the BMG Guild's annual convention's main concert, which was held in Carnegie Hall that year.[17] Also, concert reviews published in *Cadenza* and Olcott-Bickford's testimony reveal that she performed at the BMG Guild annual conventions that were held in Cleveland, OH (1914); Providence, RI (1915); Washington, DC (1916); Boston, MA (1917); Atlanta, GA (1920); Los Angeles, CA (1921); and New York City, NY (1922).[18] In 1922, Durkee was also in attendance at the BMG Guild's twenty-first annual convention, performing an arrangement of selections from *Il trovatore* on her ukulele during the last day's banquet.[19] As Olcott-Bickford was also a performer and attendee at this convention, this event is the earliest documented face-to-face meeting between both women guitarists.[20]

Gertrude Miller's First Efforts to Form an American Guitar Society

Gertrude Miller was the first American guitarist to organise and mobilise to make the formation of guitar societies in America a reality. Miller was one of the women guitarists who emerged as a concert artist and teacher at the turn of the twentieth century. She was known in the BMG community for her position as the editor of *The Ladies of the Banjo, Mandolin, and Guitar Realm* between 1902 and 1903, and other articles she wrote for *S.S. Stewart's Banjo and Guitar Journal*. In 1902, Miller was enthusiastic about the formation of the BMG Guild, hoping its organisation would 'do much in [sic] behalf of the guitar'.[21] Nevertheless, there is no record of her involvement with the organisation.

Miller wrote two articles that paved the way for the formation of the first American guitar society. Both articles were titled 'The American Guitar Society' and were published in the November 1905 and the June 1906 issues of *Cadenza*.[22] In them, Miller urged fellow American guitarists to join her in forming a guitar society that would be – as specifically stated in the article – the American analogue of the *Internationale Guitarristische Vereinigung* (IGV, International Guitar-Players Association).[23] Miller's call to action, although not logistically innovative, was visionary and driven by nationalistic tones. It proposed to unify the American classical guitar tradition through formal organisation and to provide institutional support for contemporary American guitar composers.[24] This type of instrument specialisation was not uncommon in America, as there was the precedent of the American Guild of Organists (founded in 1896), but Miller's proposal was in direct competition with the BMG Guild and the BMG movement's tradition of promoting all plucked and plectral instruments under the same label.

The response from the BMG community to Miller's call to action was slow and lacked momentum, but initial membership rosters foreground women's desire to be involved with such an organisation. By November 1905, there were some guitarists who were supportive, although there were very few of them. Among the nine members who had replied to Miller, three were women, and Miller's colleague, Jennie M. Durkee, was one of them.

By June 1906, Miller received twenty more membership applications, but not enough to 'formally organize', so she followed up with a second request to get the American Guitar Society up and running.[25] Her second article informed the guitar community that there was still time to sign up.[26] It also included an updated list of members, which featured the names Ethel Lucretia Olcott and Myron A. Bickford (Olcott-Bickford's future husband and renowned mandolinsist). Table 3.3 lists the 1906 members; notably, the membership continued to be centred in the Midwest, with Olcott-Bickford as one of only two California members, illustrating the mostly regional reach of this early attempt at an American guitar organisation.

This list is evidence of the fact that emerging women guitarists such as Miller, Olcott-Bickford, and Durkee were interested in the formation of the first American guitar society as early as 1905 and supported the push to create an instrument-specific organisation that would solely champion the classical guitar.

Jeffrey J. Noonan's research concludes that Miller's organisation was centred on the upper Midwest and was short-lived and unsuccessful.[27] There is no evidence in BMG journals that contradicts his conclusion; furthermore, Miller disappeared from the pages of BMG journals after 1906. However, although it was unsuccessful, Miller's efforts to form the first American Guitar Society had ripple effects, inspiring one of her young woman colleagues,

Table 3.3 List of Members of Miller's American Guitar Society (1906)

Name	Region
Philip J. Bone	Luton, England
Myron A. Bickford	Springfield, Massachusetts
Jennie M. Durkee	Denver, Colorado
Salvatore Tomaso	Chicago, Illinois
Ethel Lucretia Olcott	Los Angeles, California
Johnston Bane	-
C. F. Jansen	Chicago, Illinois
Gertrude Miller	Vinton, Iowa
Helen Decker Edwards	Denver, Colorado
Mr. Newcombe	Chicago, Illinois
I.X. Linn	Denver, Colorado
Everett McNeil	Denver, Colorado
Mr. Mouratt	Chicago, Illinois
Mr. Eckdall	Chicago, Illinois
G. E. Willey	Chicago
E. C. Root	Portage, Wisconsin
George B. Durkee	Chicago, Illinois
John Santschi	South Bend, Indiana
Henry Hapke	Moline, Illinois
J. M. Sheppard	New York, New York
G. W. Darling	Greensburg, Pennsylvania
T. J. Kugler	Chicago, Illinois
Harry Ferry	Kent, Ohio
G. A. Graeber	Lawrence, Kansas
William Sherman	Orillia, Canada
Thomas Tyler	Mason City, Iowa
G. W. Robinson	Providence, Rode Island
Florence Boyle	Alameda, California
Charles Ford	Mansfield, Ohio

Source: Data from Miller, 'The American Guitar Society', *Cadenza* 12.3 (November 1905), 12–13 (p. 13).

Olcott-Bickford, to take action and advocate for the formation of an American guitar society in the following decades.

Olcott-Bickford never forgot Miller's pioneering role and the lasting effects this first campaign had on her. In an article she wrote for *Guitar Review* in 1956 about the history of the classical guitar in America, she acknowledged Miller as the first American guitarist who tried to form a guitar society in America and described the impact Miller's actions had on her:

> A little town in Iowa nurtured three guitarists, probably never heard of elsewhere. However, I deeply feel that I must pay them tribute for the part they played in my work for the guitar . . . These three were J. Miller, the father, and Gertrude Miller and Emily Miller Burton, his daughters. Mr. Miller taught his daughters to become excellent guitarist-performers [*sic*]. Gertrude Miller was the first person to ever try to start a guitar society in America. Though the child died aborning, she gave me the 'seed' and the earnest desire to try again to persevere and succeed in such an undertaking. It led me to organize *The American Guitar Society* in Los Angeles in 1923, which at present is the oldest guitar society uninterruptedly in existence in the entire world.[28]

Almost two decades after the first attempt was made at unifying the American guitar community, Miller's dream came to fruition at a gathering at the Los Angeles Stock Exchange Building. This meeting changed the institutional landscape of the classical guitar in America for decades to come.

Olcott-Bickford and the First American Guitar Society

On the evening of 27 September 1923, Los Angeles classical guitar enthusiasts and professionals came together to form the first American guitar society. On that day, the Los Angeles Guitar Society – later to be known as the American Guitar Society (AGS) – was born.

The meeting began at 8 p.m. and took place at the office of J. A. Larralde located in the Los Angles Stock Exchange Building.[29] It was organised by Larralde, a Los Angeles guitar amateur and enthusiast who was interested in forming a local guitar club and who wanted to meet the famous guitarist by the name of Vahdah Olcott-Bickford who had recently arrived in Los Angeles from New York City. According to Olcott-Bickford's appointment book, she arrived in Los Angeles with her husband, Zarh Myron Bickford, on 28 June 1923.[30] The historic meeting was very productive and, after a long discussion, the Los Angeles Guitar Society was founded, officers and members of the executive board were elected, and a committee was formed to re-write the society's Constitution and By-laws based on the outline Larralde provided at the gathering.[31]

Contrary to the formation of the BMG Guild and the German guitar societies two decades prior, and reflecting a wider post-World-War-One context, women guitarists were deeply involved in the formation of the first American guitar society. They were invited to the historic meeting and were elected as officers and executive board members. Among the eight women who attended this first meeting were four well-regarded professional guitarists: Jennie M. Durkee, Adele Ferrer Wightman, Lillian Weller Kemp (1883–1925), and Olcott-Bickford (the guest of honour). Durkee and Weller Kemp were two of Olcott-Bickford's contemporaries. They were featured in *Cadenza* in the 1900s and their activities were published in biographical sketches and concert notices. Adela Ferrer Wightman was considered California guitar royalty as the daughter of Manuel Y. Ferrer and was a close friend of Olcott-Bickford. At AGS's inaugural meeting, Olcott-Bickford and N. K. Russill were elected executive board members and Olcott-Bickford was elected Musical Director. On 7 January 1924, Weller Kemp joined

Olcott-Bickford and Russill as a member of the Executive Board after H. C. Allen resigned the post.[32] Weller Kemp's involvement with AGS was cut short by her premature death in 1925, but while she was alive, she was very invested in the organisation, serving on the executive board and playing as a member of the AGS guitar ensemble. Ferrer Wightman's biographical information is unknown and there is limited record of her involvement with the AGS after 1923.

AGS's founding members were a mixture of professional musicians, amateur classical guitarists, professional guitar players, and a local BMG store owner. Olcott-Bickford, Jennie M. Durkee, and Adele Ferrer Wightman were professional guitarists with active private teaching studios. George C. Lindsey was a local BMG businessowner, and in the 1900s he was the leader of his own BMG club. Zarh Myron Bickford was a professional musician who had a longstanding career as a BMG multi-instrumentalist, playing the classical guitar quite well although his primary BMG instrument was the mandolin, and he was a conductor, including of BMG ensembles. Among the amateur guitarists were Roy E. Poehler, J. A. Larralde, and Lillian Weller Kemp, who had retired from her professional career as a concert guitarist after marriage. This diverse roster resembled IGV's membership roster, which Karl Huber reports as featuring professional orchestral musicians, private guitar teachers, instrument makers and music publishers, and amateur players.[33] Table 3.4 shows AGS's full list of founding members and indicates the members elected to serve as officers and Executive Board members.

The formation of AGS was Olcott-Bickford's dream come true, and her work on behalf of this organisation was a labour of love and artistic fulfilment. As records published in BMG journals and letters show, Olcott-Bickford had longed for the formation of a guitar society in America for decades and was willing and prepared to step up as a leader regardless of whether the labour was paid or unpaid. In 1906, she had been one of the guitarists to answer Miller's call to action; in 1915, she wrote an article that very much resembled Miller's 1905 and 1906 articles. Found in her archives, it is an article entitled 'Guitarists' Society of America'.[34] In this unpublished call to action, Olcott-Bickford volunteered to become the society's secretary and a member of the publication committee that would determine which compositions met the standards for release.[35]

At the time Olcott-Bickford agreed to become the AGS's musical director in 1923, it was agreed that she would receive a salary for her work.[36] Unfortunately, the AGS was a very small organisation, with only eighteen members in its first year, and membership dues were

Table 3.4 Founding Members of the American Guitar Society

Women	Men
Adela Ferrer Wightman	George C. Lindsey (President)*
Vahdah Olcott-Bickford* (Musical Director)	Zarh Myron Bickford (Vice President)*
Jennie M. Durkee	H. C. Allen*
N. K. Russill*	Dr. J. H. Cleaver
R. W. Manahan	Edward Philbrook
Lillian Weller Kemp	Roy E. Poehler
Dorothy A. Freeman	E. A. Johnson
Ruth Elledge	Frank M. Vogt
	Hugo H. Possner
	J. A. Larralde (Secretary and Treasurer)

Source: Data from 'Minutes of Meeting of September 27, 1923', series V, box 152, Vahdah Olcott-Bickford Collection, International Guitar Research Archives, Special Collections, CSUN University Library, Northridge, CA.

Note: *Members of the Executive Board

allocated to other expenses, such as stationery, postage, and rent for the group's office in Los Angeles.[37] The organisation's economic situation did not improve or deteriorate during the following years, but with such tight budgets it became impossible to pay Olcott-Bickford for her time, expertise, and resources.

Even though Olcott-Bickford never received economic remuneration and primarily relied on her teaching, performing, and music publishing incomes, she served the AGS willingly and with dedication for more than fifty years, maintaining artistic control over the organisation's music publications and its concert programming. Her conviction to serve her community and profession was rooted in her understanding of the importance of philanthropy and its impact on the arts. Having grown up in Los Angeles, she was well aware of women's commitment to preserving and promoting the arts through her early involvement with women's clubs, and in 1912, she wrote candidly about this situation, critiquing *Cadenza* for excluding women's work on behalf of the development of music in America in one of its editorials.[38] The *Cadenza* editorial's assertion that businessmen were active in Boston's musical scene as amateur performers in local opera choruses and contributed financially to the upkeep of musical institutions was not untrue. Nevertheless, it singled out men's contributions without any acknowledgement of the arduous labour of women living on the East Coast. As a Los Angeles resident who had witnessed first-hand the activism of Angelenas on behalf of the arts, Olcott-Bickford took issue with the editorial's claims and wrote that in her opinion, women, not men, were the ones who continued to support this art form through their philanthropic endeavors and volunteerism.

Conclusion

During the BMG movement, American organisations established to champion the plectral and plucked instruments, such as the American Guild of Banjoists, Mandolinists, and Guitarists, were male-dominated. Women guitarists were not elected to serve as officers or members of executive committees, and their participation was limited to being active members. As a young performer emerging at the turn of the twentieth century, in 1905, Gertrude Miller became the first American guitarist to advocate for the formation of a guitar-specific organisation. Her attempts to challenge the power imbalance and to forge leadership roles for American women guitarists were supported by her women colleagues, but ultimately, they were unsuccessful. Inspired by Miller's vision, Vahdah Olcott-Bickford revived this idea in the 1920s, building a non-profit model that granted women like herself artistic and administrative control while establishing an independent institutional path for the classical guitar.

Olcott-Bickford's work on behalf of the AGS fundamentally changed the American classical guitar landscape. The AGS's formation inspired the establishment of other local guitar societies across America, such as the New York Society of the Classical Guitar in 1936. Her philanthropic endeavors preserved the classical guitar society tradition in Los Angeles through concert programming, lecture-recitals, and publications. And, in the last decade of her life, she counseled and helped younger classical guitarists who were leading the establishment of guitar programmes in Los Angeles universities, such as Ronald Purcell (1932–2011), and those who were intending to form a new type of national guitar organisation, such as Thomas Heck (1943–2021).

Nowadays, a few women follow in the footsteps of Olcott-Bickford and lead American guitar societies. Martha Masters is the president of the Guitar Foundation of America, Asgerdur Sigurdardottir is the president of the Baltimore Classical Guitar Society, and Julia Pernet has been the president of the Tucson Guitar Society for much of the twenty-first century. Furthermore, the present author served the Tucson guitar community as the Tucson Guitar Society's operations director from 2013 until 2019 and as its president during the 2019–2020 season. Although we represent the minority of classical guitar society leaders, it is important to highlight that women have always been involved in guitar society boards and held officer roles. Gender equity in modern guitar society boards and leadership roles is outside of the scope of this study, but the question of why women's presence in these roles has not increased since Olcott-Bickford's time certainly raises an important research question that I hope will be addressed in future scholarship.

Notes

1. *Find a Guitar Society*, accessed August 20, 2020, www.guitarfoundation.org/page/Societies. This list was compiled by the Guitar Foundation of America a while ago and is currently outdated. Guitar societies included in this list that do not have working websites have been removed from the official count.
2. Guitar Societies such as the Austin Classical Guitar Society (ACGS) and the Cleveland Guitar Society (CGS) have adopted extensive growth strategies by implementing education initiatives and partnering with local schools. *About AGS*, accessed August 21, 2020, www.austinclassicalguitar.org/about/, and *About the Cleveland Classical Guitar Society*, accessed August 21, 2020, https://cleguitar.org/about-ccgs/.
3. Kathleen D. McCarthy, *Women's Culture: American Philanthropy and Art, 1830–1930* (Chicago, IL: University of Chicago Press, 1993), xi.
4. Ibid., xiv.
5. Jeffrey J. Noonan, *The Guitar in America: Victoria Era to Jazz* (Jackson: University Press of Mississippi, 2007), 21–22. Noonan notes that the name of this movement was a label that businessmen used around the first years of the twentieth century to identify 'themselves, their customers, and others devoted to the plectral instruments'. Noonan, *The Guitar in America*, 21. Noonan specifies that the BMG movement was active from the late 1890s to the 1920s, but that BMG magazines were published until the 1930s.
6. Noonan, *The Guitar in America*, 155.
7. Ibid.
8. Noonan provides short biographical sketches of pioneering women guitarists such as Meta Bischoff-Henning and Dominga Lynch, and young women guitarists who followed in their steps. See Noonan, *The Guitar in America*, 64–68. The second chapter of the author's dissertation expands on Noonan's research and provides more biographical and professional information about these women. See Kathy Acosta Zavala, "Toward a History of the Institutionalization of the Classical Guitar: Vahdah Olcott Bickford (1885–1980) and the Shaping of Classical Guitar Culture in Twentieth-Century America" (The University of Arizona, PhD diss., 2020), 66–116.
9. Clarence L. Partee, "The Proposed Convention of Banjoists," *Cadenza* 1, no. 6 (July–August 1895): 4. According to Partee, in 1895, banjoist Frank B. Converse suggested holding a national convention of banjo teachers and players in order to 'settle at once and forever all disputed points in regard to correct fingering, general method of teaching, and other important issues.' Partee, "The Proposed Convention of Banjoists," 4. Frank Buchanan Converse has been referred to as 'the father of the banjo'. For more information about Converse's writings, see *A History of the Banjo: Frank Converse's Banjo Reminiscences*, edited by Paul Heller (Charleston, SC: Createspace Independent Publishing Platform, 2011).
10. Partee, "The Proposed Convention of Banjoists," 4.
11. Letters supporting Partee's suggested association were published in *Cadenza*. For a full transcript, see "Correspondence," *Cadenza* 2, no. 1 (September–October 1895): 14.
12. The official formation of the much-expected guild was reported by both *S.S. Stewart's Banjo and Guitar Journal* and *Cadenza* in their February issues. See Charles Morris, "A Memorable Day for Boston: The Launching of the Guild and the Holding of a Festival," *S.S. Stewart's Banjo and Guitar Journal* 19, no. 2 (February 1902): 2–4; and Clarence L. Partee, "The American Guild of Banjoists, Mandolinists and Guitarists: A Report on the Preliminary Work Accomplished and Prospectus of the Future Work to be Undertaken by the Guild," *Cadenza* 8, no. 6 (February 1902): 10–12.
13. Morris, "A Memorable Day for Boston," 2. Present at this historical meeting were thirty-seven member applicants and one journalist: C. L. Partee, Charles Morris, Walter Jacobs, D. L. Day, G.

L. Lansing, B. E. Shattuck, A. A. Babb, A. C. Robinson, W. P. Hovey, H. F. Odell, Giuseppe Pettine, Samuel Siegel, Thos. J. Armstrong, O. H. Albrecht, Frank Perry, Harry N. Davis, Daniel H. Day, Frank X. Audet, A. E. Squier, Myron A. Bickford, Fred J. Bacon, A. C. Crashaw, R. M. Northrop, C. C. Williams, Ernest H. Swaney, W. A. Cole, Peter W. Foley, John E. Russell, J. J. Derwin, Edward J. Hussey, Fred C. Martin, Thomas R. Lincoln, James J. McKerman, R. T. Hall (of the *Boston Herald*), Charles J. Dorn, H. M. Bronson, A. C. Burnham, Harry Wolff.

14. Linda Whitesitt, "Women as 'Keepers of Culture': Music Clubs, Community Concert Series, and Symphony Orchestras," in *Cultivating Music in America*, edited by Ralph P. Locke and Cyrilla Barr (Berkeley: University of California Press, 1997), 73–78.
15. "Guild Bulletin," *Crescendo* 1, no. 11 (May 1909): 6–8.
16. During the BMG Guild's 1917 annual convention, several women presented papers, among them Olcott-Bickford. The subjects ranged from 'The Chapter–A Community Asset', which was presented by Mrs. Hilton, to 'The Guild's Opportunity in the South', which was presented by Mrs. L'Ella Griffith-Bedard. For more information about these papers, see "The Chapter Day Program," *Cadenza* 23, no. 12 (June 1917): 7.
17. Clarence L. Partee, "Editorial: The New York Mandolin, Guitar and Banjo Concert a Great Success," *Cadenza* 10, no. 6 (February 1904): 22.
18. Vahdah Olcott Bickford, "Vahdah Olcott-Bickford: About Myself," *Rosette* (July–August 1975), transcript published on the American Guitar Society website, accessed July 18, 2020, https://web.archive.org/web/20081120185352/www.americanguitarsociety.org/printarticles.html.
19. Anonymous, "The Story of the Twenty-First Annual Convention and Concert," *Cadenza* 29, no. 6 (June 1922): 8–11 (10).
20. Anonymous, "The Story of the Twenty-First Annual Convention and Concert," 8. Olcott Bickford performed on Tuesday evening at a recital in Wurlitzer Hall.
21. Gertrude Miller, "Notes by a Keen Observer," in *The Ladies of the Banjo, Mandolin, and Guitar Realm*, edited by Elsie Tooker, *S.S. Stewart's Banjo and Guitar Journal* 19, no. 4 (May 1902): 5.
22. Gertrude Miller, "The American Guitar Society," *Cadenza* 12, no. 3 (November 1905): 12–13; and Gertrude Miller, "The American Guitar Society," *Cadenza* 12, no. 10 (June 1906): 15–16.
23. Guitar clubs were a feature of the German guitaristic environment since the formation of *Leipziger Gitarre Club* (Leipzig Guitar Club) in 1879, but news of their activities did not reach the American BMG community until 1900. To see one of the earliest mentions of a German guitar society in American BMG journals, see "The International League of Guitarists," translated by Maurice Jacobi, *Cadenza* 6, no. 6 (July-August 1900): 19. This article provided preliminary information about the IGV, which had been founded in Germany in 1899.
24. Miller, "The American Guitar Society" (1905), 12–13.
25. Miller, "The American Guitar Society" (June 1906), 15–16 (16).
26. Ibid., 15–16.
27. Noonan, *The Guitar in America*, 16.
28. Vahdah Olcott-Bickford, "The Guitar in America," *Guitar Review* 23 (June 1959): 17–19 (18).
29. Larralde sent out invitation letters detailing the meeting time and place to fellow guitar amateurs, teachers, and students in anticipation of the meeting. A template of this letter survives in Olcott-Bickford's collection, see 'Meeting #1. Form Letter #1," series V, box 152, Vahdah Olcott-Bickford Collection, International Guitar Research Archives, Special Collections, CSUN University Library, Northridge, CA.
30. Olcott-Bickford 1923 Appointment Book, series VI, box 164, Vahdah Olcott-Bickford Collection, International Guitar Research Archives, Special Collections, CSUN University Library, Northridge, CA. Her appointment book documents that a crew began packing their New York residence on June 20 and they left for California on June 24.
31. "Minutes of Meeting of September 26, 1923," series V, box 152, Vahdah Olcott-Bickford Collection, International Guitar Research Archives, Special Collections, CSUN University Library, Northridge, CA.
32. "Meeting Minutes, January 7, 1924," series V, box 152, folder 11, Vahdah Olcott-Bickford Collection, International Guitar Research Archives, Special Collections, CSUN University Library, Northridge, CA. Allen submitted his letter of resignation on January 3, 1924, citing his desires to take on another hobby and needing to leave his responsibilities with AGS to dedicate his time to this new hobby. Allen's resignation survives in AGS's archives; see H. C. Allen to J. A. Larralde, AGS

Secretary, January 3, 1924, series V, box 149, folder 1, Vahdah Olcott-Bickford Collection, International Guitar Research Archives, Special Collections, CSUN University Library, Northridge, CA.
33. Karl Huber, *Die Wiederbelebung des künstlerischen Gitarrespiels um 1900: Untersuchungen zur Sozialgeschichte des Laienmusikwesens und zur Tradition der klassischen Gitarre* (Ausburg: Lisardo, 1995), 61; Luiz Carlos Mantovani Junior, "Ferdinand Rebay and the Reinvention of Guitar Chamber Music" (PhD diss., Royal College of Music, 2019), 24–25.
34. "Guitarists' Society of America," series V, box 166, folder 9, Vahdah Olcott-Bickford Collection, International Guitar Research Archives, Special Collections, CSUN University Library, Northridge, CA. The article states that 'those who send in their names before January 1, 1915 will be charter members of the society'. This line is critical in determining when Olcott-Bickford may have written this article. I have searched throughout BMG journals published between 1914 and January 1915 to no avail. Since Olcott-Bickford was a columnist for *Crescendo* during that time, it would be most logical for her to have published this article with that journal. The fact that this is not the case leads me to believe that this article was never published.
35. Although some of Olcott-Bickford's writings have been previously discussed by scholars, this article was first referenced by the author in her dissertation. The article's existence was unknown until 2020. For a full transcript of this article and more details about it, see Zavala, "Toward a History of the Institutionalization of the Classical Guitar," 189–91 and 317–18.
36. Vahdah Olcott-Bickford to Sophocles T. Papas, January 10, 1927, CSUN's Library Digital Collections, accessed November 18, 2020, https://digital-collections.csun.edu/digital/collection/VOBCorr/id/427/rec/1.
37. Cover, *Crescendo* 17, no. 6 (December 1924), 1.
38. Ethel Lucretia Olcott, "A Reply," *Crescendo* 5, no. 3 (September 1912): 23. For more information about women's contribution to the development of music culture in Los Angeles, see Kenneth H. Marcus, *Musical Metropolis: Los Angeles and the Creation of a Music Culture, 1880–1940* (New York: Palgrave MacMillan, 2004) and Catherine Parsons Smith, *Making Music in Los Angeles: Transforming the Popular* (Los Angeles: University of California Press, 2007). For more information about Olcott Bickford and her early involvement with women's clubs in Los Angeles, see Zavala, "Toward a History of the Institutionalization of the Classical Guitar," 99–102.

Bibliography

About AGS. Accessed August 21, 2020. www.austinclassicalguitar.org/about/.
About the Cleveland Classical Guitar Society. Accessed August 21, 2020. https://cleguitar.org/about-ccgs/.
Acosta Zavala, Kathy. "Toward a History of the Institutionalization of the Classical Guitar: Vahdah Olcott Bickford (1885–1980) and the Shaping of Classical Guitar Culture in Twentieth-Century America." PhD diss., The University of Arizona, 2020.
"Correspondence." *Cadenza* 2, no. 1 (September–October 1895): 14.
Find a Guitar Society. Accessed August 20, 2020. www.guitarfoundation.org/page/Societies.
"Guild Bulletin." *Crescendo* 1, no. 11 (May 1909): 6–8.
Heller, Paul, ed. *A History of the Banjo: Frank Converse's Banjo Reminiscences*. Charleston, SC: Createspace Independent Publishing Platform, 2011.
Huber, Karl. *Die Wiederbelebung des künstlerischen Gitarrespiels um 1900: Untersuchungen zur Sozialgeschichte des Laienmusikwesens und zur Tradition der klassischen Gitarre*. Ausburg: Lisardo, 1995.
Mantovani Junior, Luiz Carlos. "Ferdinand Rebay and the Reinvention of Guitar Chamber Music." PhD diss., Royal College of Music, 2019.
Marcus, Kenneth H. *Musical Metropolis: Los Angeles and the Creation of a Music Culture, 1880–1940*. New York: Palgrave MacMillan, 2004.
McCarthy, Kathleen D. *Women's Culture: American Philanthropy and Art, 1830–1930*. Chicago, IL: University of Chicago Press, 1993.
Miller, Gertrude. "Notes by a Keen Observer," in "The Ladies of the Banjo, Mandolin, and Guitar Realm," edited by Elsie Tooker." *S.S. Stewart's Banjo and Guitar Journal* 19, no. 4 (May 1902): 5.
———. "The American Guitar Society." *Cadenza* 12, no. 3 (November 1905): 12–13.
———. "The American Guitar Society." *Cadenza* 12, no. 10 (June 1906): 15–16.
Morris, Charles. "A Memorable Day for Boston: The Launching of the Guild and the Holding of a Festival." *S.S. Stewart's Banjo and Guitar Journal* 19, no. 2 (February 1902): 2–4.

Noonan, Jeffrey J. *The Guitar in America: Victoria Era to Jazz.* Jackson: University Press of Mississippi, 2007.

Olcott, Ethel Lucretia. "A Reply." *Crescendo* 5, no. 3 (September 1912): 23.

Olcott Bickford, Vahdah. "The Guitar in America." *Guitar Review*, June 23, 1959, 17–19: 18.

———. "Vahdah Olcott-Bickford: About Myself." *Rosette*, July–August 1975. transcript published on the American Guitar Society website. Accessed July 18, 2020. https://web.archive.org/web/20081120185352/www.americanguitarsociety.org/printarticles.html.

Parsons Smith, Catherine. *Making Music in Los Angeles: Transforming the Popular.* Los Angeles: University of California Press, 2007.

Partee, Clarence L. "The Proposed Convention of Banjoists." *Cadenza* 1, no. 6 (July–August 1895): 4.

———. "The American Guild of Banjoists, Mandolinists and Guitarists: A Report on the Preliminary Work Accomplished and Prospectus of the Future Work to be Undertaken by the Guild." *Cadenza* 8, no. 6 (February 1902): 10–12.

———. "Editorial: The New York Mandolin, Guitar and Banjo Concert a Great Success." *Cadenza* 10, no. 6 (February 1904): 22.

"The American Guild of Banjoists Mandolinists and Guitarists: Organizing Work." *Cadenza* 7, no. 2 (October 1900): 21.

"The Chapter Day Program." *Cadenza* 23, no. 12 (June 1917): 7.

"The Guild Is Formed: Representative Members of the Banjo, Mandolin and Guitar Industries, with Teachers and Publishers of Music Get Together in a Practical Way." *Cadenza* 8, no. 7 (March 1902): 14–15.

"The International League of Guitarists." Translated by Maurice Jacobi. *Cadenza* 6, no. 6 (July–August 1900): 19.

The Lullaby Project. Accessed August 21, 2020. www.austinclassicalguitar.org/the-lullaby-project/.

"The Story of the Twenty-First Annual Convention and Concert." *Cadenza* 29, no. 6 (June 1922): 10.

Whitesitt, Linda. "Women as "Keepers of Culture": Music Clubs, Community Concert Series, and Symphony Orchestras." In *Cultivating Music in America*, edited by Ralph P. Locke and Cyrilla Barr, 73–78. Berkeley: University of California Press, 1997.

Bibliography

About AGS. Accessed August 21, 2020. www.austinclassicalguitar.org/about/.

About the Cleveland Classical Guitar Society. Accessed August 21, 2020. https://cleguitar.org/about-ccgs/.

"Correspondence." *Cadenza* 2, no. 1 (September–October 1895): 14.

Find a Guitar Society. Accessed August 20, 2020. www.guitarfoundation.org/page/Societies.

"Guild Bulletin." *Crescendo* 1, no. 11 (May 1909): 6–8.

"The American Guild of Banjoists Mandolinists and Guitarists: Organizing Work." *Cadenza* 7, no. 2 (October 1900): 21.

"The Chapter Day Program." *Cadenza* 23, no. 12 (June 1917): 7.

"The Guild Is Formed: Representative Members of the Banjo, Mandolin and Guitar Industries, with Teachers and Publishers of Music Get Together in a Practical Way." *Cadenza* 8, no. 7 (March 1902): 14–15.

"The International League of Guitarists." Translated by Maurice Jacobi. *Cadenza* 6, no. 6 (July-August 1900): 19.

The Lullaby Project. Accessed August 21, 2020. www.austinclassicalguitar.org/the-lullaby-project/.

"The Story of the Twenty-First Annual Convention and Concert." *Cadenza* 29, no. 6 (June 1922): 10.

4

'SCATTER[ING] ALL PREJUDICES TO THE WINDS'

Wilma Norman-Neruda and Camilla Urso as Leaders of the Nineteenth-Century String Quartet

Bella Powell

During the first half of the nineteenth century, women's music-making in England took place within the confines of strict social parameters. Instrument options for women were limited; aside from singing, their musical life echoed the social roles they were expected to play: they took a subservient role to male musicians, predominantly playing accompanying instruments such as the harp and piano. For most women of the upper- and middle classes, music-making was learned as an 'accomplishment', for the purposes of providing suitable domestic entertainment within the private sphere of the home and attracting potential suitors. Despite its potential for chamber music, they were effectively barred from playing the violin, although contemporary sources generally spoke of a 'prejudice' rather than an overt 'ban'.[1] This informal prohibition only started to ease during the 1860s–70s, with the first women violinists admitted to the Royal Academy of Music in 1872. However, during these decades, two of the most successful female continental *virtuosa* violinists, the Moravian Wilma Norman-Neruda (1838–1911) and the French-born, American-based Camilla Urso (c. 1840–1902), were active as chamber musicians, and successfully combined their solo careers with leading chamber ensemble performances in London (the other members of these ensembles being almost exclusively male, aside from the occasional female pianist).[2]

Norman-Neruda and Urso both feature in much of the modern scholarship on nineteenth-century female violinists, but while reviews of their quartet performances often feature in broader discussions of their reception, there has been little analysis of the reception and reviews of their performances specifically as chamber musicians.[3] Further examination is therefore useful in establishing the significance of these women performing chamber music publicly, on socially prohibited instruments, while fulfilling the musically authoritative role of leader. This chapter explores what contemporary reviews of chamber performances by Wilma Norman-Neruda and Camilla Urso might reveal about attitudes towards women's music-making in the nineteenth century, particularly in the context of women in positions of musical authority.

The 'Prejudice' Against Women Violinists and Barriers to Chamber Music

During the first half of the nineteenth century, women's musical opportunities were limited. As instrumentalists, they were mainly confined to the harp and piano. Rita Steblin has argued that 'this rigid gender division between instruments reflected the roles of the sexes in society: the men (soloists or leaders) held the positions of power while the women (accompanists or followers) did as they were told – were subservient.'[4] Consequently, playing an instrument outside those allotted to one's gender not only transgressed musical norms, but also implicitly challenged social conventions. This is particularly important to consider in the context of women quartet leaders, as it is vital in understanding the gendered and politicised undercurrents of critical reactions.

In the first half of the century, aside from the prejudice against female violinists, women faced multiple barriers in accessing chamber music, both in the public and private realm, and particularly as string players. Although chamber music was a popular form of entertainment, women did not typically play string instruments even within the realm of the home. Christina Bashford's work on chamber music during the period explains that 'serious musicking was a regular recreation in many country houses and functioned alongside the better-known gentlefolk pursuits of hunting, shooting, and fishing.'[5] String quartets were particularly popular, and culture enabled fluid movement across class boundaries, with groups often comprising a combination of upper-class amateurs and working professional musicians. However, this fluidity did not transcend gender; women were not invited to participate, other than as pianists, where they might join for occasional piano trios or quartets. Although women did not take part in string quartets, as Bashford has noted, they nevertheless found alternative means to engage with the repertoire, such as playing piano transcriptions.[6]

Female string players were generally barred from attending conservatoires and therefore faced challenges in accessing instrumental tuition and opportunities for formal training in chamber music. Even if a woman violinist managed to access this training and gain ensemble experience, she then faced the challenge of chamber music politics; for a woman to take part in a string quartet, she firstly had to make the right social or musical contacts to be invited to play. In addition, the male players would need to regard her as an equal or, in the case of her leading, be willing to accept her in an authoritative role.

However, English attitudes towards women violinists gradually relaxed over the course of the century. While the handful who performed in England during the first half of the century were almost exclusively from continental Europe, by its closing decades, female players were admitted to conservatoires and often forged careers as chamber musicians after graduating. Although women were (usually) barred from joining professional orchestras until the early twentieth century, these chamber music activities marked an important step towards their eventual inclusion.

By the close of the nineteenth century, chamber music performance offered significant opportunities for women to establish performing careers beyond the role of soloist. This was particularly important since the demands of a solo performing career and touring schedule often conflicted with societal expectations around female roles in marriage and family life. In contrast, chamber music, being more closely aligned with the domestic sphere, may have offered the potential for a less contentious avenue for female performance. The combination of this with the high level of visibility of artists like Wilma Norman-Neruda, whose quartet played in regular chamber concert series in London, may have resulted in a perception of chamber music as offering more fixed performance opportunities, circumventing some of the objections around a career exclusively as a soloist. Chamber music therefore represented a potential career in music performance for women violinists and gave increased visibility to women who successfully carved out careers for themselves as professional string players. As female pioneers in this genre, Wilma Norman-Neruda and Camilla Urso are therefore particularly important, as their success in the early 1870s appears to have inspired the generation of women who pursued careers as chamber musicians in subsequent decades. In some ways, it is therefore perhaps surprising that two professional solo violinists chose to delve into the world of quartet playing, not only challenging the *status quo* by playing the violin, but also breaking into an exclusively male domain, and assuming a musically authoritative role.

Wilma Norman-Neruda and Camilla Urso

The lives of Camilla Urso and Wilma Norman-Neruda share a striking number of similarities. Like most women violinists before them, both were born into families of professional musicians and started playing the violin at an early age. A handful of female violinists had performed across Europe and visited England with relative success before Urso and Norman-Neruda. Most notable among these were Maddelana Lombardini-Sirmen (1745–1818) and Louise Gautherot (1763–1808) in the late seventeenth century, and the Milanollo sisters Teresa (1827–1904) and Maria (1832–1848) in the 1840s.

Wilma Norman-Neruda and Camilla Urso were not the first women to play in quartets; Maria and Teresa Milanollo included occasional quartet-playing as part of their concert activities. There are few mentions of this in surviving English source materials, but at least one English obituary referred to Maria also having played in a string quartet.[7] Teresa played at least once as part of a quartet during the sisters' time in London in 1845, at the Beethoven Quartet Society, leading the quartet in A major Op.18, No.5, before being replaced for the rest of the programme by Sivori and Sainton, who alternated leadership for the final two pieces.[8] Although the *Musical World* reviewed the concert, Teresa was barely mentioned.[9] The impact of the Milanollo sisters as chamber musicians therefore seems to have been rather limited, with their quartet performances taking the form of occasional appearances, presenting little challenge to the *status quo*.

These earlier female players typically started their careers as successful child prodigies but seem to have struggled to maintain their careers as adults, often ceasing their performing activities when they married. It seems likely that the demands of a performing career conflicted with ideas about appropriately fulfilling the role of wife and mother. Meanwhile, their novelty value as child prodigies would have diminished as they approached adulthood, and while audiences might have tolerated young girls playing socially unconventional instruments, this tolerance would not readily have extended to adult women performers.

Norman-Neruda and Urso initially fitted this model; both women married at a young age and ceased performing around this time. However, they both subsequently resumed their careers as touring violinists: Norman-Neruda after she left her first husband in 1869, and Urso after being widowed around 1860.[10] Both women later remarried to second husbands who were actively involved with their careers. In Urso's case, this was her manager, and in Norman-Neruda's, her long-time musical collaborator, Charles Hallé. Most importantly though, they seem to have occupied parallel positions in Europe and America as pivotal figures in overcoming the prohibition and earning the acceptance of women as violinists.

Wilma Norman-Neruda

Wilhelmina Norman-Neruda was born in 1838 in Moravia to a musical family.[11] Although she was expected to play the piano, she taught herself to play her brother's violin in secret, before taking lessons with Leopold Jansa. Norman-Neruda's father acted as a manager for his children and toured them around Europe and Russia as a troupe of child prodigies. Wilma Norman-Neruda performed in public for the first time at the age of seven, and regularly appeared with her siblings throughout German-speaking Europe, often playing trios or quartets alongside solo items. She first performed in England in 1849, at the age of eleven, and she continued to tour Europe as part of the family troupe until she married conductor Ludwig Norman in 1864, when she started a family and ceased publicly performing.

After separating from Ludwig Norman, Wilma resumed touring again, and from 1869, she made annual visits to London for the winter and spring seasons. She quickly made her mark on the London music scene, performing a large number of concerts to great acclaim, both as a soloist and a chamber player. She was favourably compared with the leading male players of the day, particularly Joseph Joachim. Such parallels were exemplified by *The Strad* in 1894:

> What Joachim is to the sterner sex as a violinist, just the same is Lady Halle [*sic*] to the gentler. These two names will be handed down to posterity as belonging to two of the very greatest artists that the world has ever seen.[12]

Comparisons were also drawn to other male contemporaries, with *The Musical Times* remarking in 1887 that 'The most accomplished of lady violinists is doing something to atone for the gap caused by the absence this season of Mr. Sarasate.'[13] Meanwhile, in 1893, *The Sewanee Review* commented that her 'profound classical style compares quite favourably with that of Wilhelmj.'[14] Norman-Neruda settled in England, continuing to perform well into the 1890s and touring extensively across the continent, America, and Australia, often with Charles Hallé, whom she eventually married in 1888.

Norman-Neruda was regarded as being particularly influential in overturning the 'ban' on women playing the violin, with one nineteenth-century commentator remarking that 'Madame Neruda, like a musical St. George, has gone forth, violin and bow in hand, to fight the dragon of prejudice.'[15] Though the casting of Neruda in the role of masculine hero may seem unexpected, such an analogy is less surprising in the context of the association between violinists and heroic themes in the nineteenth-century imagination, as well as its reflection of a broader critical language intrinsically bound up with masculine performance idioms.[16] However, unusually for a woman performer, reviews of Norman-Neruda's solo playing contained very few mentions of her physical appearance or references to 'feminine' aspects of her playing. She appears to have been regarded as a serious artist rather than a novelty, and accepted as a performer equal to her male counterparts.

Camilla Urso

Camilla Urso was a contemporary of Norman-Neruda's, born in Nantes into a family of professional musicians in 1840. She started violin lessons at six and studied with Massart at the Paris Conservatoire from the age of seven. Nineteenth-century sources often claimed Urso to be the institution's first female student, but this has been contested in more recent scholarship.[17] One of the many benefits of this training was the opportunity to play string quartets. An early biography claimed that 'Massart advised Camilla to join a quartette in order to perfect herself in reading music at sight. Once a week she spent an hour or two in playing with three others at the Conservatory.'[18] One of these regular collaborators was the virtuoso-composer Wieniawski, a contemporary of Urso's at the institution. Sightreading as part of a string quartet also formed part of the Conservatoire examinations.[19]

On completing her studies, Urso was lured to the United States with the offer of a lucrative three-year tour. The tour never materialised and Urso was left stranded, but nevertheless managed to launch a career, making her New York debut aged ten. She took a career break from 1855 to '63, during which time she moved to Nashville with her parents and shortly afterwards married her first husband, had three children, and was then widowed. In 1863, she returned to performing and married Frédéric Luère, who later became her manager. Urso's motivations for returning to performing are not known but may have been triggered by financial necessity. Alternatively, it is possible that Urso's second marriage provided a more supportive environment for her to recommence a performing career if domestic demands or spousal opposition had formed obstacles to this during her first marriage. Urso forged a successful career for herself in the United States, combining chamber music with appearances as a soloist alongside many of the country's leading orchestras. She was well received by the American press and made tours across the United States, Australia and New Zealand, South Africa, and Europe, including performances in England between 1871–72. For many of these, she had her own concert troupe, managed by her husband, and she often played chamber music, such as string quartets and trios, in her concerts alongside solo items.

When Urso arrived in the United States, female violinists were rare, and both nineteenth-century and modern writers refer to her as being pivotal in the acceptance there of the violin as an instrument for girls, casting her in a role similar to that of Norman-Neruda in England.[20] Later in her life, Urso was particularly significant for being outspoken about life as a woman violinist. Most female players up until this point (including Norman-Neruda) had diplomatically avoided being drawn on the subject, but Urso was one of the first to speak and write frankly about the issues faced by women violinists. She particularly advocated for the inclusion of women in orchestras, one of her most notable contributions being the delivery of her article 'Women and the Violin: Women as Performers in the Orchestra' as a speech at the Woman's Musical Congress in Chicago in 1893. In this, Urso argued the case for women as orchestral violinists and for equality of pay, asserting that female violinists were equally as talented as their male counterparts, and that in her experience, their playing was more expressive, and they were more diligent and reliable than male players.

It is worth considering what enabled these women to be in a position where they could partake in public ensemble playing, especially in a leading role. I suggest that the early musical education of both artists was significant in this respect, as for both Norman-Neruda and Urso, quartet and chamber playing was normalised in their formative years. Both women had access to opportunities that were not available more generally to women musicians, which enabled them to incorporate chamber music as part of their careers. Norman-Neruda benefitted from the advantage of growing up in a large musical family which functioned as a ready-made chamber training ensemble. Meanwhile, Urso, as a rare female student of the violin at the Paris Conservatoire, gained access to ensemble training that was otherwise denied to women. By the mid-1850s, women were increasingly taking part in chamber music as pianists, and combined with Norman-Neruda and Urso's existing quartet experience, it seems likely that this created a climate in which quartet performances seemed a logical addition to their concerts.

The English Performances and Reception of Norman-Neruda and Urso

Norman-Neruda first performed in England in April 1849 at the age of eleven. She returned as an adult in May 1869, and by the November of the same year had appeared as the leader in a variety of quartet concerts. She subsequently made annual visits to London for the winter and spring seasons, and most notably spent many years playing regularly and leading quartets in the Monday and Saturday 'Pops' Concerts at St James's Hall.[21] The 'Pops' formed part of a broader trend of increased chamber music concerts in the mid-nineteenth century, but were particularly significant as the proximity of St. James' Hall to the West End rendered them accessible to, as Bashford observes, 'people ever further down the social scale'.[22] Indeed the critic George Bernard Shaw described them as having 'contributed, more than any other cause, perhaps, to the spread and enlightenment of musical taste and culture in England.'[23] Neruda played at the invitation of Joachim – she took on the role of first violin in the 'Pops' quartet during the winter season, while Joachim took a counterpart role during the spring season. Norman-Neruda and Joachim developed a friendly relationship, and the two players were often compared, including by Joachim himself, who remarked that 'when people have given her a fair hearing, they will think more of her and less of me.'[24] This public endorsement and support of Norman-Neruda by Joachim may have been a significant factor in acceptance of her as a quartet leader.

The reception of Norman-Neruda and Urso's performances in London offer some valuable insights into public attitudes towards women in quartets. Reviews of Norman-Neruda's first appearances as a quartet player were predominantly positive, but it was clear that her role as woman leader was a source of curiosity for London audiences. *The Musical World* reported:

> There was a startling novelty in the performance. The quartet party was led by a woman; and the leader played with such power, force, dignity and fire as few indeed of the most gifted men are endowed withal . . . in a single eight-bar phrase Mdme. Norman-Neruda scattered all prejudices to the winds . . . the bare white arms of the gifted lady were as full of power as of grace; that the tone produced was surprisingly round, rich, and pure; that the intonation was never at fault; and that every individual passage was delivered with unfaltering skill, and masterly decision . . . Madame Neruda, we must hasten to explain, needs no special consideration on account of her sex.[25]

The Orchestra took a similar tone:

> Strange as, despite many instances of female proficiency, a violin always looks in the hands of a woman, the mastery of Madame Neruda over her instrument proclaims her the thorough artist. Her tone is rich and full, her bowing free, her phrasing excellent, her capability of managing the pianissimi and fortissimi unexceptionable. All the works undertaken by her betrayed not only a perfect conception of the composer's meaning but also a power and ease scarcely to be looked in the bare white arms which so rivetted [*sic*] the attention of the audience.[26]

Many reviews such as these, dating from the first few months of Norman-Neruda's appearances leading quartets, took a positive approach, and seem to have engaged with her playing in artistic terms, even if this was undermined by the discussion of female proficiency and the eroticised undertones in the description of her performance; both these aspects were recurring themes in reviews of female violinists, particularly in the latter half of the nineteenth century. She also seems to have avoided much of the criticism often directed at solo women violinists, who frequently encountered accusations of lacking the 'vigour', tonal strength, or intellectual understanding to play substantial works, while facing disparaging remarks about playing 'trifles' when they performed smaller-scale works.

However, this was not the case in all reviews, with both Norman-Neruda's tone and intellectual capacity criticised in a small number of critical responses, such as in *The Observer*:

> It is rare to see a lady violinist of such skill. Her execution is peculiarly neat and highly-finished, and her shake surpasses almost anything we ever heard . . . The only objection

we could find to her playing is a want of tone. The violin in her hands is a softened and
subdued instrument, and has something of the effect produced by the use of the mute;
but her command over the mechanical requisites of her art cannot be questioned. The
unpleasant effect caused by the ungraceful attitude, with the head thrown back in a defi-
ant style, and the rapid evolutions of the large bow are quite lost sight of in the agreeable
sound produced from the strings.[27]

Meanwhile, *The Musical World* also criticised Norman-Neruda's tone as being inferior to that of Joachim, asserting that this 'is where, on such an instrument as the fiddle, a woman must inevitably fall short of a man'.[28] More interestingly though, the same piece also included a discussion concerning her capacity as an interpreter, which remarked on her playing of Beethoven that

The ripe productions of the greatest of musicians are out of her intellectual reach . . .
in Mendelssohn she is showy and brilliant; but in the larger and profounder works of
Beethoven she is somewhat out of her depth.[29]

This ties into broader nineteenth-century ideas about the limits of female intellect and a critical dialogue evident in parts of the press, which allowed women to succeed in surface-level technique, while insisting that they lacked the intellectual capacity to understand the intention of larger-scale works by 'great' composers such as Beethoven. While Norman-Neruda usually managed to escape such judgements, this review offers a rare example of the criticism levelled at her.

Although reviews indicate that both critics and audiences found Norman-Neruda's leading rather a novelty, the majority of reviews were overwhelmingly positive. The handful of reviews which found fault with her playing appear to have relied on typical criticisms of female players relating to tone and musical intellect. However, none of the critical responses seem to have indicated any explicit criticism of her as a leader, or any suggestion that this might have been an unsuitable role for a woman.

By the time of her first appearances in England, Norman-Neruda had already made a name for herself on the continent as a serious soloist and was also well-connected within European musical circles, counting friendships and musical collaborations with Joachim, Vieuxtemps, and Hallé among others. The endorsement and respect of these eminent (male) performers may well have aided in positively influencing the attitudes of the press and the public towards her. Perhaps most tellingly, after the first few months of initial press interest subsided, much of the critical reception of Norman-Neruda's playing was indistinguishable from that of her male counterparts. Reviews were fleeting, and those which were longer predominantly focused on aspects of the music rather than including extended discussions of the players; she seems to have been accepted genuinely as an equal. While Norman-Neruda set an important precedent for women leading string quartets, Camilla Urso's performances were also important in paving the way for female violinists in chamber music, although rather less is known about her performances. Urso visited England between December 1871 and September 1872; between March and June 1872, she led quartet performances in a number of concerts, often in addition to solo items.

Although Urso's English quartet appearances were few in number, reviews of these provide valuable further insights regarding the reception of performances by women leaders. Urso played in string quartets in her United States performances, and awareness of this reached the European press at an early stage; in 1863, well before Norman-Neruda's appearances, on hearing that Urso intended to tour Europe, the *Musical World* speculated, 'May we hope, then, to hear Mdlle. Urso leading the quartets at the Monday Popular Concerts?'[30] Although it took another nine years for this to come to fruition, it is nonetheless significant that Urso was well-known enough in England for it to be suggested she lead at the Monday concerts, and that the London music establishment was apparently receptive to this idea.

Camilla Urso's first London appearances took place in 1871, when she gave a handful of solo performances of the Mendelssohn violin concerto, including at the Crystal Palace and Philharmonic Concerts series, followed in 1872 by a variety of solo and chamber ensemble performances. Urso's first appearance as a quartet player in England seems to have been in March 1872 at St. George's Hall. An advertisement stated that she would play 'the first violin part in Schubert's Quartet in D minor, in Mendelssohn's Trio in the same key, and in Hummel's Quintet in E flat minor' at 'Mr Ganz's concert'.[31] Urso's reputation clearly preceded her; in advance of this first performance, *The Times* described her as 'the distinguished violinist from Paris'.[32] She played in a range of flexible chamber music ensembles, performing quartets by Schubert, Beethoven, Mendelssohn, and Haydn; string and piano trios by Mendelssohn, Hummel, Beethoven, Mendelssohn, Jansa, Schubert, Onslow, and Schumann, as well as piano quartets by Schumann and Mozart, and quintets by Hummel and Dussek.

Although it is not clear who organised Urso's appearances in London in 1872, it is likely that a link with the violinist and conductor Wilhelm Ganz was significant. Urso played in several of a six-week series of chamber music concerts at St George's Hall in the spring of 1872, directed by Ganz, as well as several soirées and chamber concerts of the New Philharmonic Society, an organisation which Ganz was heavily involved with (he later become co-conductor and then director). However, as Jennifer Schiller's work on Urso notes, 'most of her appearances were private concerts at private homes'.[33] Consequently, it is harder to glean details about these performances and their reception.[34] Other appearances included quartets at piano recital concerts and 'musical mornings' of her quartet colleagues and musical collaborators.

Reviews of Urso's playing contained significantly more references to her gender than were typically found in reviews of Norman-Neruda, and critical reactions were rather more mixed. While Norman-Neruda's reviews were almost unanimously positive, many of Urso's contained outright criticism or implied pejoratives relating to gender. Urso's reviews are, therefore, rather more useful in ascertaining a broader spectrum of responses to women performers.

A typical example can be found in a review of one of Wilhelm Ganz's Saturday Evening Concerts, published in *The Era*, which described Camilla Urso as 'the great feature of the evening', and remarked that:

> Madame Urso is certainly one of the finest players we have heard for a long time . . . There was none of the weakness we are accustomed to associate with feminine playing, the bold opening movement of Schubert's being led off with as much vigour as any masculine player, save and except Herr Joachim, is capable of infusing. Madame Urso's bowing is wonderfully energetic and animated, her tone is large, full, and brilliant, and her execution most masterly . . . She plays her composer with a genuine reverence for his ideas rather than her own, and in more than one instance sacrificed opportunities for display in rigidly adhering to the text.[35]

Despite the superficially positive tone, the discussions of expected subservience of the female artist to the male composer and allusions to stereotypically 'weak' female playing again betray the perceptions of women players that Urso and Norman-Neruda still faced.

While Norman-Neruda often seemed to escape the typical criticism of women violinists lacking tone or vigour, tonal strength was a common theme in reviews of many nineteenth-century female players, including Urso. For example, *The Musical Standard* remarked of Ganz's third Saturday concert that:

> Our sense of gallantry, as well as the prescriptive right of custom, demands that we should first notice the *primo violino*, Madame Camilla Urso . . . that she is a gifted musician is at once evidenced by the fact of her so ably rendering some of the most difficult music the masters of the art ever wrote; in all those feminine qualities which may aptly be applied to the violin–viz., the refinement, softness, expression, she is most successful; but for fire and energy, and breadth of tone, we will not compare her with her masculine rivals.[36]

While acknowledging Urso's musicianship, the message appears to be that she might be considered successful in the more 'feminine' aspects of playing, but she could never truly hope to be considered as a player of equal stature to her male colleagues. Meanwhile, the benevolent 'gallantry' of the reviewer, which set the tone for much of the review, serves to further undermine Urso's credibility.

Similarly, the same publication remarked of Urso's appearance at the fourth Ganz concert that:

> Though Madame Urso led the Mendelssohn quartet with all the ease and polish of a practised quartet player, we were not quite satisfied; her tone though full and round seemed dull, wanted the ringing silvery brightness of tone which should form one of the greatest charms of a fine solo player.[37]

This critique of Urso's lack of power or tone is particularly interesting in light of other reviews which praised this aspect of her playing. A review in *The Musical World* reporting on the fourth Ganz evening concert highlighted Urso's tone and musicianship alongside the 'feminine' traits: 'In broadness of style, fulness of tone, and mode of phrasing she vies with the most renowned classical violists of the day, and adds the charms of refinement and elegance.'[38] Meanwhile, critical response to the third Ganz concert, published in *The Orchestra*, was similarly positive:

> The Third of Mr. Ganz's series of Saturday Evening Concerts again brought forward the admirable artistic capacity of Mdme. Camilla Urso, who has approved herself a violinist of rare order. Nothing better could be imagined that the sustenance of her part of the first of Beethoven's Rasoumowski set of quartets – that in F, which she led with a breadth, freedom, and accuracy which stamp her among the first artists of her school.[39]

Although reviews were few and brief, Urso generally appears to have been regarded in equal standing with her male collaborators, with *The Observer* remarking of one concert that 'The names of the *artistes* who took part in these several choice pieces are in themselves satisfactory guarantees that they were done full justice to; and so they were.'[40] Interestingly, there seems to have been little comparison made between Urso and Norman-Neruda as quartet players, despite them both performing in London in 1872.[41]

Although Urso only visited England once, reviews of her performances are nonetheless useful to measure against those of Norman-Neruda as a barometer of critical responses and attitudes. Urso's reviews reveal a more complex dialogue around female performance. Although no direct criticism of her as leader seems evident, her authority as a player was undermined in numerous reviews by the criticisms levelled at her regarding tone and power. Meanwhile, the repeated emphasis on 'feminine' traits of Urso's playing simultaneously seem to mark an acceptance of her playing with a new, feminised critical language emerging in response to the success of female players, while also functioning as an implicit criticism in some reviews.

Concluding Thoughts

Urso and Norman-Neruda's performances need to be considered in the context of broader mid- to late nineteenth-century socio-musical culture. Changing socio-politics in the nineteenth-century musical world created new opportunities for women violinists in the realm of chamber music. Christina Bashford's work on the nineteenth-century string quartet notes that 'at some concerts, particularly in the second half of the century, "star" violinists were habitually slotted above three local players.'[42] These visitors were typically virtuosi who visited England while touring Europe, and Urso (and to some extent, Norman-Neruda) fits this model. Simultaneously, Tully Potter suggests that a changing musical dynamic, shifting from the first violin-driven style of the earlier part of the century to a more even distribution of musical roles, was a factor in 'the players in professional quartets gradually [becoming] more equal.'[43] This is particularly significant for female players, as an increasing democratisation within chamber music may well have created a musical environment more conducive to their participation, and consequently increased the opportunities available to them.

Although neither Norman-Neruda nor Urso seems to have explicitly encountered criticism for *leading* string quartets, both experienced issues in their reception which related to the broader issues encountered by women violinists. For Norman-Neruda, there appears to have been an initial element of novelty and sexualisation, which she seems to have overcome. Urso found that despite the precedence set by Norman-Neruda, she encountered more criticism for her 'feminine style' and perceived lack of tone. However, the broadly positive critical reactions to both players perhaps indicate that the London press and audiences may have been slightly more open-minded towards women in positions of musical authority in the nineteenth century than we might expect. In addition to the critical and public reactions, the inclusion of female players such as Norman-Neruda and Urso in chamber music, especially in first violin roles, suggests a growing acceptance of female players by their male contemporaries.

Some research has been undertaken on the careers of women violinists during the nineteenth century, but much of this focuses on their careers as soloists, with little space given to discussing the scope or significance of their work as chamber musicians. Norman-Neruda and Urso were both hugely influential in making the violin more acceptable for female players. In the closing decades of the nineteenth century, following the admittance of women violinists to conservatoires, a number of all-female string quartets appeared in London, a precursor to their gradual admittance to the professional orchestral world during the course of the twentieth century. There is still much to be explored in the lives and careers of women string players as ensemble participants in the late nineteenth and early twentieth centuries; gaining a better understanding of the reception of earlier performances by figures such as Norman-Neruda and Urso can inform and help to shape the critical-historical narrative of emerging female roles within ensemble performance.

Notes

1. Typical examples are illustrated by *John Bull*, which referred to a 'prejudice against female violinists' in 1845, and the *Illustrated Review* in 1870, which described a 'prejudice that prevents English

ladies from taking up the instrument.' Unsigned, "Theatres and Music," *John Bull*, June 14, 1845, 375 and Unsigned, "Dramatic and Musical Criticisms," *The Illustrated Review: A Fortnightly Journal of Literature, Science and Art* 1, no. 3 (1870), 121. See also Bella Powell, "Notions of Virtuosity, Female Accomplishment, and the Violin as Forbidden Instrument in Early-Mid Nineteenth-Century England," in *The Routledge Handbook on Women's Work in Music*, edited by Rhiannon Mathias (Abingdon, Oxon and New York: Routledge, 2021), 241–49.

2. There is some debate over Urso's exact date of birth. Most sources give the date as 1842, while Schiller's doctoral thesis on Urso argues the case for 1840. Schiller cites a birth certificate with this date, and suggests 'the incorrect birth year seems to have originated from Urso herself, and presumably was used in order to make her more marketable and remarkable as a child prodigy.' Jennifer Schiller, "Camilla Urso: Pioneer Violinist (1840–1902)" (DMA, College of Fine Arts at the University of Kentucky, 2006), 6.
3. For example, both women feature throughout Paula Gillett's *Musical Women in England, 1870–1914: "Encroaching on All Man's Privileges"* (Houndmills: Macmillan, 2000) and Tatjana Goldberg's *Pioneer Violin Virtuose in the Early Twentieth Century: Maud Powell, Marie Hall, and Alma Moodie: A Gendered Re-Evaluation* (Oxon: Routledge, 2019). Meanwhile, Simon McVeigh's chapter "'As the Sand on the Sea Shore': Women Violinists in London's Concert Life around 1900," in *Essays on the History of English Music in Honour of John Caldwell*, edited by Emma Hornby and David Maw (Woodbridge: Boydell & Brewer, 2010), 232–58 highlights the importance of chamber music as part of Norman-Neruda's career and image.
4. Rita Steblin, "The Gender Stereotyping of Musical Instruments in the Western Tradition," *Canadian University Music Review* 16, no. 1 (1995), 8–44: 39.
5. Christina Bashford, "Historiography and Invisible Musics: Domestic Chamber Music in Nineteenth-Century Britain," *Journal of the American Musicological Society*, 63, no. 1 (2010), 291–360: 311.
6. Ibid., 309.
7. [Unsigned] "Maria Milanollo," *The Musical World*, 23, no. 46 (1848): 721.
8. J. W. D., "The Beethoven Quartet Society," *The Musical World* 20, no. 25 (1845): 289–90.
9. Ibid., 289.
10. Little biographical information exists about this period of Urso's life; however, Jennifer Schiller's research suggests that Urso's first husband, George M. Taylor, "Died Before Camilla Was Yet 20 Years Old." Schiller, "Camilla Urso," 23.
11. She generally gave her name as 'Wilma', and this is therefore the version of her name which will be used throughout this chapter.
12. ['Bass Viol'] "Wilhelmine Maria Franziska Neruda (Lady Hallé)," *The Strad* 5, no. 52 (August 1894), 105–07: 107.
13. [Unsigned] "Madame Néruda's Orchestral Concerts," *The Musical Times and Singing Class Circular* 28, no. 532 (1887): 344.
14. T. L. Krebs, "Women as Musicians," *The Sewanee Review* 2, no. 1 (1893): 76–87: 81.
15. Lady Blanche Lindsay, "How to Play the Violin," *The Girl's Own Paper* 15 (1880): 232.
16. For more in-depth discussion of the violin's militaristic associations during the nineteenth century, see Maiko Kawabata, "Virtuoso Codes of Violin Performance: Power, Military Heroism, and Gender (1789–1830),"*19th Century Music* 28, no. 2 (2004): 89–107.
17. Freia Hoffman has identified Félicité Lebrun as having studied at the conservatoire from 1799. Freia Hoffman, "*Urso, Camilla*': Europäische Instrumentalistinnen des 18. und 19. Jahrhunderts (2010), accessed February 20, 2021, www.sophie-drinker-institut.de/urso-camilla.
18. Charles Barnard, *Camilla: A Tale of a Violin. Being the Artist Life of Camilla Urso* (Boston, MA: Loring, 1874), 57.
19. Ibid., 58.
20. For example, Freia Hoffmann argues that 'Her meteoric career triggered a similar wave of successors in the US, as was the case with the sisters Milanollo on mainland Europe and Wilma Norman-Neruda in England.' Hoffman, *Urso, Camilla*.
21. Yvonne Amthor, '*Neruda, Nerudová, Wilma, Wilhelmine, Vilemína, Vilhelmina (Maria, Marie, Franziska, Františka), verh. Norman-Néruda, verh. Hallé.*' Europäische Instrumentalistinnen des 18. und 19. Jahrhunderts (Undated), accessed February 21, 2021, www.sophie-drinker-institut.de/cms/index.php/neruda-wilma.
22. Christina Bashford, "Historiography and Invisible Musics: Domestic Chamber Music in Nineteenth-Century Britain," *Journal of the American Musicological Society* 63, no. 2 (2010), 291–360: 315.

23. George Bernard Shaw and Dan H. Laurence, *Shaw's Music: The Complete Musical Criticism*, edited by Dan H. Laurence, 3 vols., 2nd rev. ed. (London: Bodley Head, 1989), i, 907.
24. Baroness Von Zedlitz, "A Chat with Lady Hallé," *Cassell's Family Magazine* (1894), 779–84: 783.
25. [Unsigned] "Monday Popular Concerts," *The Musical World* 47, no. 47 (1869): 797.
26. [Unsigned] "Concerts," *The Orchestra* 13, no. 320 (1869): 116–17: 116.
27. [Unsigned] "Monday Popular Concerts," *The Observer*, November 14, 1869, 6.
28. [Unsigned] "Monday Popular Concerts," *The Musical World* 48, no. 5 (1870): 71–72.
29. Ibid.
30. [Unsigned] "Dinorah at Zurich," *The Musical World* 41, no. 14 (1863): 214.
31. [Unsigned] "Waifs," *The Musical World* 50, no. 9 (1872): 145–46: 145.
32. [Advertisement] *The Times*, March 2, 1872, 1.
33. Schiller, "Camilla Urso," 42.
34. Ibid.
35. [Unsigned] "Our Contemporaries," *The Musical World* 50, no. 17 (1872): 269.
36. [Unsigned] "St. George's Hall," *Musical Standard* 2, no. 398 (1872): 135.
37. [Unsigned] "St. George's Hall," *Musical Standard* 2, no. 399 (1872): 152.
38. [Unsigned] "Concerts Various," *The Musical World* 50, no. 13 (1872): 206.
39. [Unsigned] "Concerts," *The Orchestra* 17, no. 442 (1872): 371–72 (372).
40. [Unsigned] "Mr. Ganz's Saturday Evening Concerts," *The Observer*, March 17, 1872, 3.
41. It is not clear whether Urso and Neruda were acquainted, although it seems likely that their paths would have crossed while they were both performing in London in 1872.
42. Christina Bashford, "The String Quartet and Society," in *The Cambridge Companion to the String Quartet*, edited by Robin Stowell (Cambridge: Cambridge University Press, 2003), 1–18: 9–10.
43. Tully Potter, "From Chamber to Concert Hall," in *The Cambridge Companion to the String Quartet*, edited by Robin Stowell (Cambridge: Cambridge University Press, 2003), 39–59: 42.

Bibliography

[Advertisement]. *The Times*, March 2, 1872, 1.
Amthor, Yvonne. "*Neruda, Nerudová, Wilma, Wilhelmine, Vilemína, Vilhelmina (Maria, Marie, Franziska, Františka), verh. Norman-Néruda, verh. Hallé.*' *Europäische Instrumentalistinnen des 18. und 19. Jahrhunderts* (Undated). Accessed February 21, 2021. www.sophie-drinker-institut.de/cms/index.php/neruda-wilma.
Barnard, Charles. *Camilla: A Tale of a Violin. Being the Artist Life of Camilla Urso*. Boston, MA: Loring, 1874.
Bashford, Christina. "The String Quartet and Society." In *The Cambridge Companion to the String Quartet*, edited by Robin Stowell, 1–18. Cambridge: Cambridge University Press, 2003.
———. "Historiography and Invisible Musics: Domestic Chamber Music in Nineteenth-Century Britain." *Journal of the American Musicological Society* 63, no. 2 (2010): 291–360.
['Bass Viol'] "Wilhelmine Maria Franziska Neruda (Lady Halle)." *The Strad* 5, no. 52 (August 1894): 105-7.
Davison, James William (Signed 'J.W.D.'). "The Beethoven Quartet Society." *The Musical World* 20, no. 25 (1845): 289–90.
Gillett, Paula. *Musical Women in England, 1870–1914: "Encroaching on All Man's Privileges."* Basingstoke: Macmillan, 2000.
Goldberg, Tatjana. *Pioneer Violin Virtuose in the Early Twentieth Century: Maud Powell, Marie Hall, and Alma Moodie: A Gendered Re-Evaluation*. Oxon: Routledge, 2019.
Hoffmann, Freia. "Urso, Camilla.' *Europäische Instrumentalistinnen des 18. und 19. Jahrhunderts*. 2010. Accessed August 30, 2020. www.sophie-drinker-institut.de/urso-camilla.
Kawabata, Maiko. "Virtuoso Codes of Violin Performance: Power, Military Heroism, and Gender (1789–1830)." *19th Century Music* 28, no. 2 (2004): 89–107.
Krebs, T. L. "Women as Musicians." *The Sewanee Review* 2, no. 1 (1893): 76–87.
Lindsay, Lady Blanche. "How to Play the Violin." *The Girl's Own Paper*, April 10, 1880, 15.
McVeigh, Simon. "'As the Sand on the Sea Shore': Women Violinists in London's Concert Life around 1900." In *Essays on the History of English Music in Honour of John Caldwell*, edited by Emma Hornby and David Maw, 232–58. Woodbridge: Boydell & Brewer, 2010.

Potter, Tully. "From Chamber to Concert Hall." In *The Cambridge Companion to the String Quartet*, edited by Robin Stowell, 39–59. Cambridge: Cambridge University Press, 2003.

Powell, Bella. "Notions of Virtuosity, Female Accomplishment, and the Violin as Forbidden Instrument in Early-Mid Nineteenth-Century England." In *The Routledge Handbook on Women's Work in Music*, edited by Rhiannon Mathias, 241–49. Abingdon, Oxon and New York: Routledge, 2021.

Schiller, Jennifer. "Camilla Urso: Pioneer Violinist (1840–1902)." DMA, University of Kentucky, 2006.

Shaw, George Bernard, and Dan H. Laurence. *Shaw's Music: The Complete Musical Criticism*, edited by Dan H. Laurence, 3 vols., 2nd rev. ed. London: Bodley Head, 1989.

Steblin, Rita. "The Gender Stereotyping of Musical Instruments in the Western Tradition." *Canadian University Music Review* 16, no. 1 (1995): 128–44.

[Unsigned] "Concerts." *The Orchestra* 13, no. 320 (1869): 116–17.

[Unsigned] "Concerts." *The Orchestra* 17, no. 442 (1872): 371–72.

[Unsigned] "Concerts Various." *The Musical World* 50, no. 13 (1872): 206.

[Unsigned] "Dinorah at Zurich." *The Musical World* 41, no. 14 (1863): 214.

[Unsigned] "Dramatic and Musical Criticisms." *The Illustrated Review: A Fortnightly Journal of Literature, Science and Art* 1, no. 3 (1870): 121.

[Unsigned] "Madame Néruda's Orchestral Concerts." *The Musical Times and Singing Class Circular* 28, no. 532 (1887): 344.

[Unsigned] "Maria Milanollo." *The Musical World* 23, no. 46 (1848): 721.

[Unsigned] "Monday Popular Concerts." *The Musical World* 47, no. 47 (1869a): 797.

[Unsigned] "Monday Popular Concerts." *The Observer*, November 14, 1869b, 6.

[Unsigned] "Monday Popular Concerts." *The Musical World* 48, no. 5 (1870): 71–72.

[Unsigned] "Mr. Ganz's Saturday Evening Concerts." *The Observer*, March 17, 1872, 3.

[Unsigned] "Our Contemporaries." *The Musical World* 50, no. 17 (1872): 269.

[Unsigned] "St. George's Hall." *Musical Standard* 2, no. 398 (1872a): 135.

[Unsigned] "St. George's Hall." *Musical Standard* 2, no. 399 (1872b): 152.

[Unsigned] "Theatres and Music." *John Bull*, June 14, 1845, 375.

[Unsigned] "Waifs." *The Musical World* 50, no. 9 (1872): 145–46.

Von Zedlitz. "A Chat with Lady Hallé." *Cassell's Family Magazine*, 1894, 779–84.

5
SURVIVING THE EVERYDAY
Gendered Violence, Patriarchal Power Structures, and Strategies of Resistance in Late Nineteenth-Century Ladies' Orchestras

Nuppu Koivisto-Kaasik

Dear parents! Please forgive me for having always written you letters in which I told you that I was doing well. I am in no way to blame for this, since the director [of the *Maiglögckchen* ladies' orchestra] always dictated these letters to me. Now I need no longer fear him, since he and his wife [Josephine Preissig] are being held in pre-trial detention . . . My dear parents, the letter you wrote to the director in Leipzig, asking him to send me home at once, caused me many sufferings . . . The other girls were even worse off, the director tied them tightly to chairs and hit them . . . One time, when his cane broke, the director bought a dog whip and told us we would be getting it in the neck when he took us to Russia. We are all happy that the trip came to nothing.[1]

This is how sixteen-year-old aspiring musician Caroline Fonda described her everyday life in the ladies' salon orchestra *Erste Wiener Damen-Capelle Maiglöckchen*, led by bandmaster Julius Onczay, in October 1895.[2] The ensemble had toured Central Europe for some years before Onczay's violent and abusive behaviours were revealed in the press, leading to a scandalous court case.[3] By late 1895, the news had spread all over the world, resulting in a public debate on working conditions in ladies' salon orchestras.[4] In this chapter, I analyse the forms of gender-based violence experienced by the members of the Maiglöckchen orchestra. How and why did abuse become a part of their everyday lives? Were there similar features in other late nineteenth-century ladies' orchestras; and, if so, what does it tell us about the gendered power hierarchies of the *belle époque* entertainment industry? Special attention is paid to the musicians' strategies of resistance.

Following the traditions of feminist musicology, this chapter aims to consider the gendered power hierarchies of late nineteenth-century musical life from a wider perspective, through the prism of the Maiglöckchen case.[5] This feminist analysis is backed up by presenting socio-historical data on the band members. However, discussing the sensitive themes of abuse and violence requires more specific theoretical attention. Art historian Griselda Pollock has, in my opinion, successfully analysed the role of domestic abuse in the life and career of the artist Charlotte Salomon (1917–1943). Salomon has become widely known for her magnum opus *Leben? oder Theater*, which draws on elements from the artist's own family history as well as European societies and cultures in general, combining watercolours, literary elements, and musical references. Pollock has suggested that instead of concentrating solely on large-scale historical tragedies such as the Holocaust, attention should be paid to the way in which Salomon's work portrays feminine subjectivities, their strategies of navigating a heavily gendered system of institutional and social norms, as well as the recurring, intimate violence they might have faced. Psychoanalytic close readings are Pollock's main tools for mapping out the tension between these two dimensions, 'the Event and the Everyday, the exceptional and the mundane', as she calls them.[6]

Pollock's method is not directly applicable in this case, since we are dealing with radically different historical circumstances. Furthermore, similar issues and methods of analysis have been widely discussed in the fields of microhistory and the history of violence, although from a slightly different perspective.[7] Nevertheless, I argue that the conceptual interplay between the Event and the Everyday is a useful tool for constructing feminist analyses of domestic and gender-based violence.[8] In this case study, Julius Onczay's trial becomes the historical Event, from the shadow of which we need to trace the abusive Everyday as experienced by the orchestra members.

In analysing historical patterns of violence, ethical issues of anonymisation need to be carefully thought out. After thorough consideration, I have decided to include the full names of everyone involved. As Kirsi Vainio-Korhonen has pointed out, this can serve to promote the agency of marginalised historical actors and emphasise their active resistance against the oppressor.[9] Furthermore, the Event took place almost 130 years ago, and historical newspaper articles available on the Internet state the full names of everyone involved. However, in accordance with the basic ethical principles of historical research, I have avoided any unnecessary dwelling on sensationalist details.[10]

Unfortunately, first-hand sources on the Maiglöckchen orchestra are scarce. Although judiciary proceedings of the trial in Hamburg must have existed, the city's archives are only partially preserved, and were not consultable at the time of research.[11] Thus, my source material consists mainly of German and Austrian newspaper articles as well as the Dusseldorf-based *Der Artist*, the main weekly paper for entertainment artistes.[12] Nevertheless, newspaper evidence needs to be handled with caution, as it was written in order to attract readers. To back up my analysis, I have used a variety of first-hand sources such as birth and marriage records as well as judiciary documents when tracing the lives and careers of the musicians.[13]

In general, ladies' salon orchestras have remained a neglected part of the Western musical past. The ensembles have mainly been studied by Dorothea Kaufmann (1997) and Margaret Myers (1993). Although the Onczay scandal was widely publicised during the heyday of ladies' orchestras, it has received no attention whatsoever in music historiography. The social problems regarding ladies' orchestras have, however, been discussed by Kaufmann and Nancy M. Wingfield (2017).[14] Furthermore, music sociologists Anna Bull, Christina Scharff, and Anna Ramstedt, among others, have conducted ground-breaking studies on sexual misconduct and structures of gendered abuse in the modern-day classical music industries. Thus, this chapter aims to contribute to a historical contextualisation of the phenomena studied by these scholars. This chapter examines the background of the Maiglöckchen orchestra, before focusing on the Event, i.e., Onczay's trial. Finally, the forms of resistance and rebellion expressed by the orchestra members are analysed in detail.

In Search of the *Maiglöckchen* Orchestra

The term 'ladies' orchestra' may refer to many different sorts of historical bands. In this chapter, it is used to denote a certain type of late nineteenth-century salon or restaurant orchestra, known as *Damenkapelle or Damenorchester*, which literally translate to 'ladies' band' or 'ladies' orchestra'. As *Damenkapellen* were an extremely popular phenomenon all around

Europe before the Great War, we are talking about hundreds of orchestras and thousands of professional musicians.[15] Although late nineteenth-century ladies' orchestras ranged from brass bands to small family ensembles, they shared certain common features.[16] These orchestras of ten to fifteen musicians usually led an itinerant lifestyle, taking up engagements in cafés and restaurants. Their members – mostly young women – were rarely conservatory-trained: rather, they came from so-called *Musikstädte*, rural towns with significant musician communities in Central Europe.[17] A typical ladies' orchestra included at least one man, normally serving as the director. The musicians were usually dressed in white frocks with colourful sashes to enhance their youth and good looks.[18]

In many respects, the Maiglöckchen orchestra fits well into the stereotypical mould of a late nineteenth-century ladies' orchestra. The *Hamburger Anzeiger* stated that it consisted of eight women and two men, a standard distribution by gender in these ensembles.[19] Apart from Caroline Fonda, a musician's daughter from Vienna, all the members came from Bohemia or Moravia (see Table 5.1). This was not unusual: most of the women working in ladies' orchestras came from the Habsburg Empire – which resulted in the popularity of 'Viennese' or 'Austrian' bands.[20] Like many other ladies' salon orchestras, the *Maiglöckchen* ensemble adopted the practice of white dresses with ornamental sashes.[21] Even the orchestra's name – literally, 'lilies-of-the-valley' – blended in: different flower names such as Edelweiss or Blauveilchen ('pansies') were popular among the ensembles.[22] In terms of line-up, little information has survived. Based on the size of the orchestra, it seems that it was a typical, piano-trio-based salon ensemble.[23] As customary, the ensemble was led by a violinist, Josephine Ernestine Preissig, who was older and more experienced than the other band members. Apparently, Preissig also served as a music teacher for her younger colleagues. As for Julius Onczay, he acted as the orchestra's impresario rather than its conductor.[24]

The musicians were young indeed; at the time of Onczay's arrest and trial, their ages ranged from 13 up to 18 years (see Table 5.1).[25] Late nineteenth-century newspapers, of course, tended to exaggerate their stories for shock value. However, based on a comparison with parish registers, it seems that the information about the musicians' ages and hometowns provided by the press was surprisingly accurate.[26] In general, the presence of teenage girls was not uncommon in ladies' orchestras, as the trade was learned on the go rather than through a separate music school system. It was hinted that some of Maiglöckchen's string players only pretended to perform, their bows having been treated with soap; a well-known trick of the trade in the entertainment industry.[27] Some reporters even noted that Onczay had lured the

Table 5.1 The Members of Wiener Damen-Capelle Maiglöckchen (1895)[30]

Name	Age	Hometown	Father's occupation
Marie Mischkowska	18	Prague	Higher functionary (at a sugar mill)[31]
Wilhelmine Reth	17	Prague	[–]
Ida Nosswitz	17	Brno	[–]
Lola [Aloisia] Frey	16	Modřice	[State official][32]
Caroline Fonda	16	Vienna	Musician
Julie Faltinek [Faltynek][33]	15	Židlochovice	[–]
Hedvig Schwab	14	Brno	Professor [Private instructor]
Marie Böhm	13	Jirkov	[Confectioner]
[Eduard Czajanek][34]	21	Frýdek-Místek	Conductor [Music teacher]
[Hermine Doležal][35]	[13]	[Olomouc]	[Conductor]

young girls into his orchestra by promising to send them to 'a music school in Leipzig'.[28] Since Leipzig with its prestigious conservatory was one of the leading music cities in late nineteenth-century Europe, it is no wonder that this promise sounded appealing.[29]

The orchestra members' social backgrounds were varied. As has been suggested elsewhere, ladies' orchestras were typically family enterprises originating from small, rural towns specialising in music-making.[36] Most of the young women came from relatively modest backgrounds, families of craftspeople or musicians – a strongly hereditary profession in the nineteenth century.[37] Thus, at least three of the Maiglöckchen orchestra's members were daughters or sons of musicians and conductors. What catches the researcher's eye, however, is the relatively high social status of some of the orchestra members. Marie Mischkowska and Lola Frey came from the family of state officials and business functionaries, and Hedwig Schwab's father was a private instructor.[38] As middle-class and well-off women flooded European conservatories in the late nineteenth century to become music teachers and musicians, it is likely that Mischkowska, Frey, Schwab, and the other orchestra members were hoping to pursue this career path to financial independence. This must have made Onczay's promises about Leipzig especially alluring. Another important feature is that, apart from Caroline Fonda, the young women were recruited from different parts of Bohemia and Moravia, not only from the north-western parts of the kingdom, which formed a veritable hub of the whole ladies' orchestra phenomenon. Considering the brutality of Onczay's behaviour, it might have been a conscious tactic not to hire too many mutually acquainted musicians. If this was the case, his plan backfired, uniting young women of different circumstances and regional backgrounds to rebel against patriarchal violence.

Many ladies' orchestras toured for years on end.[39] The Maiglöckchen orchestra, in contrast, only existed for a couple of years. The ensemble started its work around 1893 or 1894, at a time when ladies' orchestras were rapidly gaining popularity throughout Europe.[40] Onczay founded his ensemble in the Austrian Empire, the centre of the booming ladies' orchestra culture.[41] Later, the orchestra took on a tour in Central Europe, travelling from Brno to Silesia via Saxony, continuing to Belgium via Aachen.[42] At this point, the orchestra's traces vanish, after Onczay found out that one of the musicians had managed to send a secret postcard to her worried parents, alerting them about the bandleader's violent behaviour.[43] In October 1895, the orchestra could at last be traced to Hamburg, where Onczay was taken into custody by the police. The rest of the ensemble continued their journey to Lübeck, where they had secured an engagement for the upcoming weeks.[44] After a few days, Josephine Preissig was detained as Onczay's mistress and partner in crime.[45]

The amount of power Onczay possessed in the Maiglöckchen orchestra needs to be emphasised. As Dorothea Kaufmann has shown, a late nineteenth-century ladies' salon orchestra was by no means an equal or democratic community.[46] In fact, it could be described as a hierarchical, family-like body of musicians, the head of which was the director or conductor. This is not to imply that every bandmaster was an abuser, but to point out that musicians working in ladies' orchestras were at the mercy of their director. Legal supervision for potential mistreatments was rendered problematic due to the itinerant nature of the orchestras.[47] There was no labour union for women musicians, and activists in women's and temperance movements were not especially interested in visiting musicians from abroad.[48] All in all, it is important to keep in mind that the Maiglöckchen orchestra was rather a typical ladies' salon orchestra of its time. Since the orchestra's tours concentrated on the German and Austrian Empires and since the victims were white, European women, Onczay's violence was happening in the heart of Europe. This will help us explain the extraordinary proportions of the international scandal surrounding the Event of this study, Onczay's trial, which in turn is indicative of the underlying imperialist and racist thinking prevalent in the European middle classes and press at the time.

The Event: Julius Onczay's Trial

Six months after his arrest, in March 1896, Julius Onczay appeared before the Hamburg Circuit Court. He was accused of 'deprivation of liberty', 'assault', as well as 'moral crimes'. The trial was public – except for the 'moral' charges, referring to sexual misconduct and violence and therefore handled behind shut doors. The event was, of course, closely followed by local reporters.[49] Onczay's violence had taken both physical and psychological forms. Not only had he caused severe bodily harm to the young women,[50] he had also taken total control of their contacts with the outside world.[51] Some of the women had been slandered and sexually assaulted.[52] Based on this evidence, Onczay was convicted to a penitentiary for eighteen months for slander and acts of violence. He disputed all accusations, claiming that the court case had been staged by professional rivals.[53] His complaints continued months after the incarceration.[54]

The Event of 1896 was not the first time Onczay appeared before a court of law. It is therefore necessary to take a look at his personal history. According to the trial reports, Julius Onczay had been born into the family of an attorney in 1854 in the town of Kaschau (Košice).[55] In his youth, he had worked for a railway company and for the Ministry of Communications as a revenue officer and clerk, settling in Pest.[56] By the beginning of the 1880s, however, Onczay had been fired from both jobs for forging train tickets and official documents.[57] Onczay's illegal activities were not limited to his professional life. In 1881, he tried to resolve his financial problems by marrying a country girl with a sizeable dowry and luring her to Pest to take care of a café he had bought.[58] Once the couple had settled in, it turned out Onczay had committed bigamy.[59] Threatened with legal consequences, he decided to make a run for it, stealing some money and his wife's trinkets.[60] After a few weeks, Onczay was found and convicted to prison for eighteen months.[61]

Although Onczay had managed a café in the early 1880s, it was only after this first prison sentence that he fully started his career as an *impresario*. His professional reputation had now been tarnished, which probably increased the attraction of a career change in his eyes. In fact, one of Onczay's first enterprises was a ladies' orchestra of sixteen musicians, performing in Prague and Budapest in 1885.[62] The project quickly fell through, and Onczay was again soon held in custody for theft.[63] By 1887 he had moved to Saint Petersburg, trying to make a living as a circus *impresario* in the Russian Empire.[64] His name turns up again in Austria with the founding of the Maiglöckchen orchestra in 1893.

It is deceptively easy to write Onczay's biography as the stereotyped story of a vicious scoundrel, descending from petty crime to inhuman cruelty. Such simplifications should, however, be avoided in order to properly understand and do justice to the structural and institutional nature of misogynist practices and gender-based violence in late nineteenth-century Europe. Although Onczay's violent behaviour took shocking forms, he was by no means the only abusive man in the industry. On some occasions, ladies' orchestras could be used as fronts for trafficking young women. As the number of ladies' orchestras grew during the 1890s, newspapers started to get wind of agents and *impresarios* coaxing young women into sex work with promises of a musical career. In 1898, for example, a ladies' orchestra director called Jakob Ehrlich was tried in Krakow for trafficking teenage girls to Thessaloniki, forcing them to work as prostitutes.[65] Unfortunately, we do not have enough quantitative data on how widespread human trafficking was in late nineteenth-century ladies' orchestras. Nevertheless, public debates on the issue were animated. Warnings of so-called 'girl trafficking' in the entertainment business remained a standard feature in the Austrian press well into the 1910s. They were especially common in the Eastern parts of the Empire, such as Bukowina – where Onczay had tried to recruit musicians – and Galicia, which were considered the worst areas for human trafficking in Eastern Europe.[66] The articles often contained racist and antisemitic undertones, especially against (Hungarian) Jews. Certain regions abroad, such as Buenos Aires or Russian cities, also enjoyed a questionable reputation.[67] The problem was thus 'externalised' to the Eastern parts of Europe, as well as the neighbouring Ottoman and Russian Empires by the German-language press, which diverted attention from the abuse and violence happening at the core regions. In the late 1890s, the problems of *Mädchenhandel* were taken up in *Der Artist*, advocating for the foundation of a labour union for ladies' orchestras.[68]

Thus, the Maiglöckchen ensemble became a typical example of the social problems associated with ladies' orchestras; in short, of their austere Everyday. One reporter for *Reichspost* even commented that Onczay's abominable actions demonstrated 'how profoundly the spectator has been misled when he assumes that he could find happy, high-spirited creatures behind the white-clad maidens in "ladies' orchestras"'.[69] Although Onczay was not accused of procuring *per se*, his behaviour ticked all the boxes for 'girl trafficking' in the eyes of his contemporaries. The shock value of the Event, therefore, was to be found mostly in the fact that everything had happened at least partly in Western and Central European towns and, more importantly, right under the noses of German and Austrian authorities, who had been incapable of tracking Onczay's movements.

By the time of Onczay's trial, the Maiglöckchen orchestra had already been disbanded. After the director's and Josephine Preissig's arrests, the rest of the ensemble had been permitted to continue performing in Lübeck under the direction of Eduard Czajanek.[70] However, this arrangement soon turned out to be impossible, as the public flocked to gawp at the musicians 'who had been treated like animals'.[71] Subsequently, the orchestra broke up and the members were told to return to their hometowns, after having given their testimonies.[72] It is now time to give the floor to them.

Resistance and Rebellion: Surviving Violence in the Everyday

Evidently, Julius Onczay's goal had been to recruit adolescent girls, who were easier to subjugate than adult musicians. Nevertheless, the orchestra members rebelled – it seems that Onczay seriously underestimated them in this respect. Their testimonies include several instances of active physical resistance. In July 1895, Julie Faltynek had even managed a brief escape in Hamburg.[73] Another musician, Hermine Doležal, had succeeded in securing a position in another orchestra, which had allowed her to leave the Maiglöckchen ensemble before Onczay's arrest.[74] The resistance had taken verbal forms as well. Several witnesses stated that the musicians had openly complained about Onczay's behaviour to outsiders, but since no physical evidence such as wounds had been shown, nobody had intervened.[75]

In most cases, the orchestra members backed up each other in their acts of resistance. This is not surprising in terms of the close-knit Everyday they intensely shared. As was customary in ladies' orchestras, the musicians shared their rooms and spent every day together under the supervision of the bandmaster and Josephine Preissig.[76] Their austere domestic circumstances were described at length by the *Hamburger Anzeiger*'s reporter who visited and interviewed the band in October 1895:

> [In the second floor], in a room 3 meters long and 1 ½ meters wide, lives Onczay's ladies' orchestra. A cupboard, a three-legged table, a chair which utters groaning sounds when sat on, a washing table wholly without legs, and three wide beds, there is the wretched equipment of this ladies' orchestra's lodgings.[77]

Curiously enough, the musicians' feelings of compassion extended to Josephine Preissig. Although she had taken part in punishing the musicians by depriving them of food or money, the orchestra members lamented that 'it had always been disheartening for them to see "Madam Conductor" beaten'.[78] She was seen as a fellow victim, and the fact that she had been responsible for all actual music-making probably made her more approachable. Unlike Onczay, who 'could not distinguish an oboe from a double bass', Preissig had performed alongside the musicians and taught them their instruments.[79]

In the violent Everyday of the Maiglöckchen orchestra, it was not easy to maintain this network of solidarity. Julie Faltynek had, after her escape, appealed to the local police forces in Hamburg-Stankt Pauli, informing them of the orchestra's whereabouts. When interviewed by the officers, however, the musicians had denied any accusations against their bandleader. Later, the musicians testified that Onczay had in fact forced them to lie by threatening and intimidating them beforehand.[80] This incident serves as an excellent illustration of why abusive and violent behaviour was so difficult to track in late nineteenth-century ladies' orchestras. Young, unprotected women were in a legally weak position to press any charges on their own, especially if they did not have a reliable male guardian at hand.[81] Furthermore, abuse was easily hidden behind the private realm of everyday life. Domestic violence was not universally condemned or criminalised to the extent it is now in most countries.[82] Even the forms of social and financial control exerted by Onczay, although taken to extreme measures, were not unusual in ladies' orchestras. Young women musicians on tour were dependent on the orchestra's director. If a musician wished to go out, she needed a chaperone just to maintain her reputation.[83] The bandmaster often had total authority over the musicians' meals and pay checks.[84] Working in restaurants, where their audience mostly consisted of more or less drunken men, the orchestra members were used to dealing with what we call sexual harassment, even assault.[85]

Considering these power hierarchies, the Maiglöckchen orchestra starts to seem more and more like the tip of the iceberg. One cannot help but ask how many cases went unreported. For this reason, it is important to emphasise the active, mutual resistance expressed by the band members. This has crucial implications for our theoretical dynamic of the Event and the Everyday. Instead of the dramatic press-narrative of a deranged monster and his pitiable victims, we are offered a glimpse of daily life overshadowed by patriarchal power structures as experienced by the musicians themselves.

One crucial question remains: what became of the Maiglöckchen orchestra members after the Event? Information on the musicians is not easy to track down, but parish registers, newspapers, and other sources shed some light on their later careers. At least some of the musicians managed to continue their professional careers. Hedwig Schwab, for instance, returned to her hometown of Brno, where she is listed as a piano teacher, at least until marrying a state official in 1912. Schwab appears to have pursued contacts with the variety show industry even in Brno, as her marriage contract was witnessed by the owners of a local café and a music hall.[86] The Brno parish registers also hint at Julie Faltynek's marriage in 1909, although not much else about her later life is known.[87]

In the early 1900s, the name of a new and popular operetta and variety singer, Hermine Doležal Ferry, pops up in the Viennese press.[88] It is not entirely clear whether she was the same person or merely a namesake of the Maiglöckchen Doležal. However, given the entertainment industry and music context, a connection between the two would seem plausible.[89] The singer-Hermine, furthermore, mostly performed as Hermine Ferry – a choice which might reflect a wish to distance oneself from past events and sensationalist press coverage, although stage names were a common phenomenon in the early twentieth-century entertainment industry.

In any case, Hermine Doležal Ferry managed to forge a notably successful and long career in various soubrette roles, becoming somewhat of a local celebrity and eventually marrying into a refined Viennese middle-class family, the Nathanskys.[90]

Conclusions

I suggest that the most fruitful outcome from this case study is not to be found in the source material *per se* – rather, it may be read between the lines. Undeniably, documentation on the Maiglöckchen orchestra remains elusive and fragmented. When contextualised within contemporary discussion of human trafficking as well as the orchestra's standard profile, the anomaly of the Event becomes questionable. This serves to shift attention from the monstrosities committed by Julius Onczay to the bandmembers' agency, from an isolated incident to gendered power hierarchies – in short, from the Event to the Everyday.

Despite the shock value of newspaper articles, I argue that the Maiglöckchen case should be understood as an indicator rather than an exception. This is not to undermine the radical nature of Onczay's abusive behaviour, nor am I claiming that all ladies' orchestras were identical in terms of social problems and rigid hierarchies. If anything, the public uproar caused by Onczay's case can be interpreted as a wake-up call; abuse was not only happening in the overseas entertainment industry, but in the heart of Europe. Although there is no direct link, the Onczay scandal seems to have significantly contributed to the budding 'girl trafficking' discussion within the late nineteenth-century entertainment industry, increasing public debate and ultimately leading to attempts of creating a labour union specifically for ladies' orchestras. On the other hand, the Maiglöckchen case also invites us to consider critically the uproar caused specifically by the fact that the victims were white, Christian, and European. Thus, a detailed, intersectional analysis of whiteness and structural racism would greatly profit the studies of late nineteenth-century *Mädchenhandel* in the future.

In the contemporary press, the prevalent narrative of the 'case Onczay' culminated in what I have been calling the Event: his trial and conviction. Even for a historian, it would be all too easy to play the righteous judge and present the narrative as 'a rake's progress' of its kind. This, however, would draw the reader's attention solely to the abuser's personality and biography, making him the anti-hero of the story. In addition, it could serve to divert focus from a large-scale structural problem, creating a false impression of a few 'bad apples' in the industry. Since the aim in feminist research is to emphasise the women's perspective, this approach does not serve our purpose. By tracing recurring patterns of violence on the one hand and resistance on the other, another tale starts to take shape, focusing on psychological dynamics and social hierarchies as experienced by Hermine Doležal, Julie Faltynek, and others. This flash of the Everyday in ladies' orchestras helps us discern underlying patriarchal power structures – such as the male directors' position of authority and the family-like patterns of daily life – in the late nineteenth-century entertainment industry. Furthermore, the counter-story created by the musicians' strategies of resistance and survival stories serves to highlight active rebellion against patriarchal norms rather than positioning them as passive victims of gendered violence.

Notes

1. "Liebe Eltern! Ihr müsst mir schon verzeihen, dass ich Euch immer Briefe schrieb, in welchen ich meldete, dass es mir gut gehe. Ich bin keineswegs daran schuld, da mir der Director immer diese Briefe dictirte. Jetzt brauche ich keine Angst mehr vor ihm zu haben, denn er und seine Frau sind in Untersuchungshaft genommen worden. . . . Ihr Brief, liebe Eltern, den Sie dem Director nach Leipzig schrieben, er möge mich sofort nach Hause schicken, hat mir viel Leid gebracht. . . . Anderen Mädchen ist

es noch schlechter gegangen, er hat sie an Stühle fest angebunden und . . . geschlagen. Als einmal der Stock zerbrach, kaufte er sich eine Hundspeitsche und sagte uns, wir würden ihn erst kennen lernen, wenn er mit uns nach Russland reisen werde. Wir sind alle glücklich, dass es nicht dazu gekommen ist. "Entführte Mädchen," *Prager Tagblatt*, October 19, 1895, 8; see also "In den Geheimnissen der Damenkapellen," *Hamburger Anzeiger*, October 22, 1895, 2. All translations are by the author unless otherwise indicated. Josephine Preissig was not officially Onczay's wife, but his mistress.
2. "Eine Bestie," *Arbeiter-Zeitung*, March 15, 1896, 6.
3. "Verschwundene Mädchen," *Hamburger Anzeiger*, October 8, 1895, 9.
4. See, e.g., "En damorkesters roman," *Hufvudstadsbladet*, November 1, 1895 (no 297), 2.
5. Marcia J. Citron, *Gender and the Musical Canon*, 2nd ed. (Urbana and Chicago: University of Illinois Press, 2000); Susan McClary, *Feminine Endings: Music, Gender and Sexuality* (Minnesota and Oxford: University of Minnesota Press, 1991).
6. Griselda Pollock, *Charlotte Salomon and the Theatre of Memory* (New Haven, CT: Yale University Press, 2018), 14.
7. See, e.g., Kaisa Vehkalahti, "Se virallinen tarina? Lastensuojeluarkistojen hiljaisuuksia," in *Salattu, hävetty, vaiettu: miten tutkia piilossa olevia ilmiöitä*, edited by Antti Häkkinen and Mikko Salasuo (Tampere: Vastapaino, 2015), 234–63; Antti Häkkinen and Mikko Salasuo, "Johdanto," in *Salattu, hävetty, vaiettu: miten tutkia piilossa olevia ilmiöitä*, edited by Antti Häkkinen and Mikko Salasuo (Tampere: Vastapaino, 2015), 13.
8. Pollock, *Charlotte Salomon and the Theatre of Memory*, 480. Even though this chapter focuses on violence and misconduct in a professional, i.e., orchestra setting, I have deliberately chosen to use the term 'domestic violence' along with 'gender-based violence/abuse', in order to underline the family-like, patriarchal hierarchies in late-nineteenth-century ladies' orchestras. On terminology, see also Satu Lidman, *Väkivaltakulttuurin perintö: sukupuoli, asenteet ja historia* (Helsinki: Gaudeamus, 2015), 18–20.
9. Kirsi Vainio-Korhonen, "Historiantutkimus, vastuullisuus ja tietosuoja," *Tieteessä Tapahtuu* 36, no. 4 (2018): 4–7.
10. Pirita Frigrén, "Tirkistelyä vai ymmärryksen lisäämistä? Historioitsija arkaluontoisista asioista kirjoittamassa," in *Historiantutkimuksen etiikka*, edited by Satu Lidman et al. (Helsinki: Gaudeamus, 2017), 80–89.
11. The Onczay case was handled in the Hamburg *Landesgericht* tribunal, and most of its archival material from the nineteenth century has been lost; see the online inventories of Staatsarchiv Hamburg, accessed April 26, 2020, www.hamburg.de/bkm/online-findmittel/. I was planning to visit the archive in March 2020, but the plan fell through due to the COVID-19 pandemic. The archival personnel, however, have confirmed to me via e-mail (April 29, 2022) that there are indeed no surviving documents on the Onczay case available.
12. The material has been mostly gathered from the following databases: Europeana Newspaper Library, accessed April 26, 2020, www.europeana.eu/en/collections/topic/18-newspapers, and from ANNO, the digitized newspaper collection of Österreichisches Nationalbibliothek, accessed April 26, 2020, http://anno.onb.ac.at/. *Der Artist* is only available on microfilm (1885–1887, Universitätsbibliothek Johann Christian Senckenberg, Frankfurt am Main, sig. MF 24261; 1892–1896, Bibliothek, Carl-von-Ossietzky Universität Oldenburg, sig. F 61 mus 545 VT 0076).
13. Litoměřice, The State Regional Archives of Litoměřice, sig. 70/29, Jirkov baptismal registers 1877–1883, accessed April 11, 2022, http://vademecum.soalitomerice.cz/; Brno, Moravian Regional Archives, Brno–Neposkvrněné početí P. Marie na Křenové baptismal registers 1877–1881 (17083), Brno-sv. Jakub marriage registers 1907–1920 (16897), Modřice baptismal registers 1865–1879 (1360), Židlochovice baptismal registers 1871–1881 (2197), accessed April 11, 2022, www.mza.cz/actapublica/; Budapest, The Budapest City Archives, HU BFL VII.106, Documents of the Royal Prison of Budapest, Register of convicted prisoners (1881, no. 0875); Registers of prisoners on remand (1881, no. 825; 1885, no. 1998), accessed April 26, 2020, www.eleveltar.hu/; Opava, Opava Regional Archives, Místek census records 1890, NAD 825/489, accessed April 11, 2022, https://digi.archives.cz/da/.
14. See also Dorothea Kaufmann, "*. . . routinierte Trommlerin gesucht*". *Musikerin in einer Damenkapelle zum Bild eines vergessenen Frauenberufes aus der Kaiserzeit* (Karben: CODA Verlag, 1997), 102–04. Risto Pekka Pennanen is currently doing research on human trafficking in late-nineteenth century Central European musical life.
15. Kaufmann, "*. . . routinierte Trommlerin gesucht*", 30, table 1; Nuppu Koivisto, "Sähkövaloa, shampanjaa ja Wiener Damenkapelle: naisten salonkiorkesterit ja varieteealan transnationaaliset

verkostot 1877–1916" (PhD thesis, The Finnish Musicological Society/University of Helsinki, 2019), 305–15, appendix 2.
16. Kaufmann, "... *routinierte Trommlerin gesucht*", 59–78.
17. Annkatrin Babbe, "Von Ort zu Ort: Reisenden Damenkapellen in der ersten Hälfte des 19. Jahrhunderts," in *Populares und Popularität in der Musik, XLII Wissenschaftliche Arbeitstagung Michaelstein, 6. bis 8. Mai 2016*, edited by Christina Philipsen and Ute Omonsky (Michaelstein: Augsburg & Blankenburg, 2017), 305–06; Kaufmann, "... *routinierte Trommlerin gesucht*", 21–25.
18. Maren Bagge, ""am besten, wie Sie sehn, tut uns die Pfeife stehn": Werbung und Inszenierungsstrategien von Damenensembles um 1900 auf Postkarten," in *Wege: Festschrift für Susanne Rode-Breymann*, edited by Annette Kreutziger-Herr et al. (Hildesheim: Georg Olms Verlag, 2018), 5–29; Margaret Myers, "Blowing Her Own Trumpet: European Ladies' Orchestras & Other Woman Musicians 1870–1950 in Sweden" (PhD diss., Göteborgs Universitet, 1993), 150–51; Kaufmann, "... *routinierte Trommlerin gesucht*", 154–56.
19. "Verschwundene Mädchen," 9; "Aus den Geheimnissen der Damenkapellen," *Hamburger Anzeiger*, October 20, 1895, 2. For comparison, see, e.g., Koivisto, 150 (table 5).
20. Koivisto, 44–49.
21. "Aus den Geheimnissen der Damenkapellen," 2.
22. Bagge, "am besten, wie Sie sehn, tut uns die Pfeife stehn," 17 and 22.
23. "Verschwundene Mädchen," 9; "In den Geheimnissen der Damenkapellen," 2.
24. "Entführte Mädchen," 8; "Zum Fall des Musikdirektors Onczay," *Hamburger Anzeiger*, October 16, 1895, 2; "Nochmals der Fall Onczay," *Hamburger Anzeiger*, October 17, 1895, 2; "Der Fall Onczay," *Hamburger Anzeiger*, March 10, 1896, 5.
25. The information is based on *Hamburger Anzeiger*'s articles ("Verschwundene Mädchen," 9; "Aus den Geheimnissen der Damenkapellen," 2).
26. Litoměřice, 70/29, fol. 155; Brno, 17083, fol, 646; 16897, fol. 205; 1360, fol. 273; 2197, fol. 227.
27. "Der Fall Onczay," 5.
28. "Aus den Geheimnissen der Damenkapellen," 2.
29. On the Leipzig conservatory, see Yvonne Wasserloos, *Das Leipziger Konservatorium der Musik im 19. Jahrhundert: Anziehungs- und Ausstrahlungskraft eines musikpädagogischen Modells auf das internationale Musikleben* (Hildesheim: Georg Olms Verlag, 2004).
30. I have provided additional or corrected information derived from church books (available for Lola Frey, Julie Faltynek, Marie Böhm, Hedwig Schwab, and Eduard Czajanek) in square brackets. For the sake of clarity, I have chosen to use the correct family name forms indicated in original documents instead of systematic misspellings in the press (Faltynek instead of Faltinek, Doležal instead of Dolézal).
31. Austrian newspapers tell us that K. Mischkowsky owned a sugar mill in Bečváry, situated in the Kolín district near Prague ("Fremdenliste," *Prager Tagblatt*, April 28, 1877, 7). However, I have not been successful in finding any information on Marie Mischkowska in local birth record registers so far.
32. The birth records state Frey's father's profession as *Rathausaufseher*, which literally translates to 'town hall overseer' and thus indicates a rather high-ranking position. Brno, 1360, fol. 273.
33. Faltynek's father's profession is unclear due to faded ink and the author's poor proficiency in Czech. However, both her mother and father came from families of shoemakers (*obuvník*), i.e. craftspeople. It is also worth stressing that Faltynek's birth record is written in Czech in a bilingual church book, which might indicate that Czech was her mother tongue. Brno, 2197, fol. 227.
34. "Aus den Geheimnissen der Damenkapellen," 2. It is not entirely clear whether Czajanek was working in the orchestra before Onczay's arrest. Czajanek was referred to as a conductor's son in the press, but local census records from Místek list his father as a music teacher (*Musiklehrer*); see Opava, NAD 825/489, 1007–12.
35. On Hermine Doležal, see p. 13.
36. Koivisto, 76–80. See also Babbe.
37. Koivisto, 77 (table 1). See also Myers, 145; Babbe, 316.
38. *Privatlehrer*; Brno, 17083, fol, 646; 16897, fol. 205. In the newspapers, he is – apparently erroneously – referred to as a university professor.
39. See, e.g., Monika Kornberger, *Grünner (Grüner), Familie* (2019), in Oesterreichisches Musiklexikon online, accessed April 26, 2020, www.musiklexikon.ac.at/ml/musik_G/Gruenner_Familie.xml.
40. "Damy muzykalne," *Kurjer Lwowski*, January 14, 1894, 6.

41. During 1893 and 1894, Onczay stayed in Graz ("Fremden-Liste," *Grazer Tagblatt*, October 27, 1893, 7) and in Bukowina ("Im Glaspavillon des 'Hotel Weiss'," *Bukowinaer Post*, April 12, 1894, 6).
42. "Verschwundene Mädchen," 9; "Zum Fall des Musikdirektors Onczay," 2.
43. "Verschwundene Mädchen," 9; "Ein verhafteter Musikdirektor," *Hamburger Anzeiger*, October 12, 1895, 2.
44. "Zum Fall des Musikdirektors Onczay," 2.
45. Ibid.; "Nochmals der Fall Onczay," 2.
46. Kaufmann, "... *routinierte Trommlerin gesucht*", 92.
47. Koivisto, 201.
48. Koivisto, 194–210.
49. "Der Fall Onczay," 5. Onczay's case received attention in *Der Artist* as well: see "Ein Mann Namens Julius Onczay," *Der Artist*, October 20, 1895, 12; "Wie bereits gemeldet," *Der Artist*, October 27, 1895, 12–13; "Die Capelle des verhafteten Capellmeisters Julius Onczay," *Der Artist*, November 3, 1895, 14; "Process Onczay," *Der Artist*, March 15, 1896, 13–14.
50. "Aus den Geheimnissen der Damenkapellen," 2.
51. "Kunstproletariat," *Arbeiterinnen-Zeitung*, November 7, 1895, 8; "Entführte Mädchen," 8.
52. "Der Fall Onczay," 5.
53. Ibid.
54. "Etwas vom 'Musikdirektor' Onczay," *Hamburger Anzeiger*, October 28, 1896, 2.
55. "Nochmals der Fall Onczay," 2; "Der Fall Onczay," 5; "Bigamie," *Die Presse*, July 1, 1881, 9. Onczay's mother tongue was Hungarian, although he spoke Slovak and German; see HU BFL VII.106, Register of convicted prisoners (1881, no 0875); Registers of prisoners on remand (1881, no 825; 1885, no 1998).
56. "Der Fall Onczay," 5.
57. "Bigamie," 9.
58. Ibid.
59. "Zweifache Ehe," *Neuigkeits-Welt-Blatt*, November 5, 1881, 9; "Der Fall Onczay," 5.
60. "Bigamie," 9.
61. "Zweifache Ehe," 9.
62. "Während der Durchreise," *Prager Tagblatt*, April 19, 1885, 14; "Damen, musikalisch," *Prager Abendblatt*, May 23, 1885, 6; "Damen, musikalisch," *Prager Abendblatt*, September 21, 1885, 7.
63. HU BFL VII.106, Register of prisoners on remand (1885, no 1998).
64. "Jules Onczay," *Der Artist*, July 17, 1887, 16; "Мѣстный отдѣлъ," *Лифляндские губернские вѣдомости*, March 18, 1888, 2; "Matkustavaisia," *Hämäläinen*, June 25, 1890, 4.
65. "Der Impresario einer Krakauer Damen-Capelle vor Gericht," *Der Artist*, April 24, 1898, 16–17.
66. See, e.g., "Oesterreichische Liga zur Bekämpfung des Mädchenhandels," *Czernowitzer Allgemeine Zeitung*, March 22, 1908, 5. See also Nancy M. Wingfield, *The World of Prostitution in Late Imperial Austria* (Oxford: Oxford University Press, 2017), 199. This phenomenon was also referred to as 'white slave trade' (*weiße Sklaverei*) in the Press.
67. Wingfield, *The World of Prostitution in Late Imperial Austria*, 176, 241–43; Kaufmann, "... *routinierte Trommlerin gesucht*", 102–05.
68. Kaufmann, "... *routinierte Trommlerin gesucht*", 175–77.
69. "wie sehr man getäuscht ist, wenn man hinter den weissgekleideten Mädchen einer 'Damencapelle' glückliche, lebensfrohe Geschöpfe vermuthet." "Ein musikalischer Sclavenhalter," *Reichspost*, October 24, 1895, 9.
70. "Das letzte Kapitel," *Hamburger Anzeiger*, October 27, 1895, 2.
71. "Die gleich Thieren behandelt ... wurden." "Das letzte Kapitel," 2.
72. "Zum Falle Onczay," *Hamburger Nachrichten*, October 26, 1895, 15.
73. "Entführte Mädchen," 8.
74. "Kunstproletariat," 8.
75. "Der Fall Onczay," 5.
76. Kaufmann, "... *routinierte Trommlerin gesucht*", 100.
77. "Dort haust in einem nur kleinen, etwa 3 Meter langen und 1½ Meter breiten Zimmer die Onczay'sche Damenkapelle. Ein Schrank, ein dreibeniger Tisch, ein Stuhl, der ächzende Töne von sich giebt, wenn man sich auf denselben niederläßt, ein Waschtisch, fast ganz ohne Füße, und drei

breite Betten, das ist die armselige Ausstattung der Wohnung dieser Damenkapelle." "Aus den Geheimnissen der Damenkapellen," 2.
78. "doch hat es ihnen . . . immer leid gethan, wenn die 'Frau Direktor' Schläge erhielt." "Aus den Geheimnissen der Damenkapellen," 2.
79. "kaum eine Oboe von einer Bassgeige unterscheiden kann." *Arbeter Zeitung* March 15, 1896 (no. 74), 6.
80. "Der Fall Onczay," 5.
81. There were, of course, differences in women's legal position in different states. On the situation in Germany around 1900, see Marion Röwekamp, "Women's Admission to the Legal Profession in Germany between 1900 and 1933," in *Women in Law and Lawmaking in Nineteenth and Twentieth-Century Europe*, edited by Eva Schandevyl (New York: Routledge, 2016), 77.
82. Rachel G. Fuchs and Victoria E. Thompson, *Women in Nineteenth-Century Europe* (Basingstoke: Palgrave Macmillan, 2004), 39.
83. See, e.g., Marie Stütz, "Mitteilungen über reisende Musiker im Erzgebirge," in *Marie Stütz: Aufzeichnungen einer reisenden Musikerin: Quellentexte und Kommentare*, edited by Monika Tibbe (Oldenburg: BIS Verlag, 2012), 89.
84. Kaufmann, ". . . *routinierte Trommlerin gesucht*", 92.
85. Myers, 178–84; 238–174; Kaufmann, ". . . *routinierte Trommlerin gesucht*", 108–12.
86. Brno, 17083, fol, 646; 16897, fol. 205.
87. Brno, 2197, fol. 227.
88. See, e.g., "Theater an der Wien," *Neues Wiener Journal*, November 21, 1902, 10; [Untitled], *Curliste Carlsbad*, July 16, 1912, 6.
89. Late nineteenth-century birth records of the town of Olomouc, sadly, seem not to have survived – although the indexes are consultable on site – and tracing Doležal's family history would thus require more substantial archival work in the Czech Republic.
90. On Doležal Ferry, see, e.g., her obituary ("Hermine Ferry gestorben," *Neues Wiener Tageblatt*, April 6, 1922, 29).

Bibliography

Archival Sources

Brno, Moravian Regional Archives [Moravský zemský archiv v Brně] <https://www.mza.cz/actapublica/> [accessed 11 April 2022]
17083 Brno–Neposkvrněné početí P. Marie na Křenové baptismal registers 1877–1881
16897 Brno–sv. Jakub marriage registers 1907–1920
1360 Modřice baptismal registers 1865–1879
2197 Židlochovice baptismal registers 1871–1881
Budapest, The Budapest City Archives
HU BFL VII.106, Documents of the Royal Prison in Budapest <https://www.eleveltar.hu/> [accessed 26 April 2020]
Register of convicted prisoners (1881, no 0875)
Registers of prisoners on remand (1881, no 825; 1885, no 1998)
Litoměřice, The State Regional Archives of Litoměřice [Státní oblastní archiv v Litoměřicích] <http://vademecum.soalitomerice.cz/> [accessed 11 April 2022]
Sig. 70/29, Jirkov baptismal registers 1877–1883
Opava, Opava Regional Archives
< https://digi.archives.cz/da/> [accessed 11 April 2022]
NAD 825/489, Místek census records 1890

Newspapers

"Aus den Geheimnissen der Damenkapellen." *Hamburger Anzeiger*, October 20, 1895, 2.
"Bigamie." *Die Presse*, July 1, 1881, 9.
"Damen, musikalisch." *Prager Abendblatt*, May 23, 1885a, 6.
"Damen, musikalisch." *Prager Abendblatt*, September 21, 1885b, 7.

"Damy muzykalne." *Kurjer Lwowski*, January 14, 1894, 6.
"Das letzte Kapitel." *Hamburger Anzeiger*, October 27, 1895, 2.
"Der Fall Onczay." *Hamburger Anzeiger*, March 10, 1896, 5.
"Der Impresario einer Krakauer Damen-Capelle vor Gericht." *Der Artist*, April 24, 1898, 16–17.
"Die Capelle des verhafteten Capellmeisters Julius Onczay." *Der Artist*, November 3, 1895, 14.
"Ein Mann Namens Julius Onczay." *Der Artist*, October 20, 1895a, 12.
"Ein musikalischer Sclavenhalter." *Reichspost*, October 24, 1895b, 9.
"Ein verhafteter Musikdirektor." *Hamburger Anzeiger*, October 12, 1895c, 2.
"Eine Bestie." *Arbeiter-Zeitung*, March 15, 1896, 6.
"En damorkesters roman." *Hufvudstadsbladet*, November 1, 1895 (no. 297), 2.
"Entführte Mädchen." *Prager Tagblatt*, October 19, 1895, 8.
"Etwas vom 'Musikdirektor' Onczay." *Hamburger Anzeiger*, October 28, 1896, 2.
"Fremden-Liste." *Grazer Tagblatt*, October 27, 1893, 7.
"Fremdenliste." *Prager Tagblatt*, April 28, 1877, 7.
"Hermine Ferry gestorben." *Neues Wiener Tageblatt*, April 6, 1922, 29.
"Im Glaspavillon des 'Hotel Weiss'." *Bukowinaer Post*, April 12, 1894, 6.
"In den Geheimnissen der Damenkapellen." *Hamburger Anzeiger*, October 22, 1895, 2.
"Jules Onczay." *Der Artist*, July 17, 1887, 16.
"Kunstproletariat." *Arbeiterinnen-Zeitung*, November 7, 1895, 8.
"Matkustavaisia." *Hämäläinen*, June 25, 1890, 4.
"Мѣстный отдѣлъ." *Лифляндские губернские ведомости*, March 18, 1888, 2.
"Nochmals der Fall Onczay." *Hamburger Anzeiger*, October 17, 1895, 2.
"Oesterreichische Liga zur Bekämpfung des Mädchenhandels." *Czernowitzer Allgemeine Zeitung*, March 22, 1908, 5.
"Process Onczay." *Der Artist*, March 15, 1896, 13–14.
"Theater an der Wien." *Neues Wiener Journal*, November 21, 1902, 10.
"Verschwundene Mädchen." *Hamburger Anzeiger*, October 8, 1895, 9.
"Während der Durchreise." *Prager Tagblatt*, April 19, 1885, 14.
"Wie bereits gemeldet." *Der Artist*, October 27, 1895, 12–13.
"Zum Fall des Musikdirektors Onczay." *Hamburger Anzeiger*, October 16, 1895, 2.
"Zum Falle Onczay." *Hamburger Nachrichten*, October 26, 1895, 15.
"Zweifache Ehe." *Neuigkeits-Welt-Blatt*, November 5, 1881, 9.
[Untitled]. *Curliste Carlsbad*, July 16, 1912, 6.

Other Printed Sources

Stütz, Marie. "Mitteilungen über reisende Musiker im Erzgebirge." In *Marie Stütz: Aufzeichnungen einer reisenden Musikerin: Quellentexte und Kommentare*, edited by Monika Tibbe, 88–90. Oldenburg: BIS Verlag, 2012.

Internet Sources

Monika Kornberger. *Grünner (Grüner), Familie* (2019), in Oesterreichisches Musiklexikon online. Accessed April 26, 2020. www.musiklexikon.ac.at/ml/musik_G/Gruenner_Familie.xml.
Staatsarchiv Hamburg. *Online-Findmittel*. Accessed April 26, 2020. www.hamburg.de/bkm/online-findmittel/.

Bibliography

Babbe, Annkatrin. "Von Ort zu Ort: Reisenden Damenkapellen in der ersten Hälfte des 19. Jahrhunderts." In *Populares und Popularität in der Musik, XLII Wissenschaftliche Arbeitstagung Michaelstein, 6. bis 8. Mai 2016*, edited by Christina Philipsen and Ute Omonsky, 303–17. Michaelstein: Augsburg & Blankenburg, 2017.

Bagge, Maren. '"am besten, wie Sie sehn, tut uns die Pfeife stehn": Werbung und Inszenierungsstrategien von Damenensembles um 1900 auf Postkarten." In *Wege: Festschrift für Susanne Rode-Breymann*, edited by Annette Kreutziger-Herr et al., 5–29. Hildesheim: Georg Olms Verlag, 2018.

Bull, Anna. *Class, Control, and Classical Music*. Oxford: Oxford University Press, 2019.

Citron, Marcia J. *Gender and the Musical Canon*, 2nd ed. Urbana and Chicago: University of Illinois Press, 2000.

Frigrén, Pirita. "Tirkistelyä vai ymmärryksen lisäämistä? Historioitsija arkaluontoisista asioista kirjoittamassa." In *Historiantutkimuksen etiikka*, edited by Satu Lidman et al., 51–70. Helsinki: Gaudeamus, 2017.

Fuchs, Rachel G., and Victoria E. Thompson. *Women in Nineteenth-Century Europe*. Basingstoke: Palgrave Macmillan, 2004.

Häkkinen, Antti, and Mikko Salasuo. "Johdanto." In *Salattu, hävetty, vaiettu: miten tutkia piilossa olevia ilmiöitä*, edited by Antti Häkkinen and Mikko Salasuo. Tampere: Vastapaino, 2015.

Kaufmann, Dorothea. "*. . . routinierte Trommlerin gesucht"*. *Musikerin in einer Damenkapelle zum Bild eines vergessenen Frauenberufes aus der Kaiserzeit*. Karben: CODA Verlag, 1997.

Koivisto, Nuppu. "Sähkövaloa, shampanjaa ja Wiener Damenkapelle: naisten salonkiorkesterit ja varieteealan transnationaaliset verkostot 1877–1916." PhD diss., The Finnish Musicological Society/ University of Helsinki, 2019.

Lidman, Satu. *Väkivaltakulttuurin perintö: sukupuoli, asenteet ja historia*. Helsinki: Gaudeamus, 2015.

McClary, Susan. *Feminine Endings: Music, Gender and Sexuality*. Minneapolis and Oxford: University of Minnesota Press, 1991.

Myers, Margaret. "Blowing Her Own Trumpet: European Ladies' Orchestras & Other Woman Musicians 1870–1950 in Sweden." PhD diss., Göteborgs Universitet, 1993.

Page, Tiffany, Anna Bull, and Emma Chapman. "Making Power Visible: 'Slow Activism' to Address Staff Sexual Misconduct in Higher Education." *Violence Against Women* 25, no. 11 (2019): 1309–30.

Pollock, Griselda. *Charlotte Salomon and the Theatre of Memory*. New Haven, CT: Yale University Press, 2018.

Ramstedt, Anna. "'You just had to learn to live with it': Gendered and Sexual Misconduct in Classical Music Culture in Finland." *Musiikkikasvatus* 26, no. 2 (2023): 40–55.

Röwekamp, Marion. "Women's Admission to the Legal Profession in Germany between 1900 and 1933." In *Women in Law and Lawmaking in Nineteenth and Twentieth-Century Europe*, edited by Eva Schandevyl, 75–102. New York: Routledge, 2016.

Scharff, Christina. *Gender, Subjectivity, and Cultural Work: The Classical Music Profession*. London: Routledge, 2017.

Vainio-Korhonen, Kirsi. "Historiantutkimus, vastuullisuus ja tietosuoja." *Tieteessä Tapahtuu* 36, no. 4 (2018): 4–7.

Vehkalahti, Kaisa. "Se virallinen tarina? Lastensuojeluarkistojen hiljaisuuksia." In *Salattu, hävetty, vaiettu: miten tutkia piilossa olevia ilmiöitä*, edited by Antti Häkkinen and Mikko Salasuo, 234–63. Tampere: Vastapaino, 2015.

Wasserloos, Yvonne. *Das Leipziger Konservatorium der Musik im 19. Jahrhundert: Anziehungs- und Ausstrahlungskraft eines musikpädagogischen Modells auf das internationale Musikleben*. Hildesheim: Georg Olms Verlag, 2004.

Wingfield, Nancy M. *The World of Prostitution in Late Imperial Austria*. Oxford: Oxford University Press, 2017.

6
SITES OF EMPOWERMENT
Fin-de-Siècle Salon Culture and the Music of Cécile Chaminade

Ann Grindley

Marcia J. Citron, the leading Chaminade scholar, argues that many women composers who were active during the 1900s and across the *fin-de-siècle* period have been linked negatively to the salons and salon culture. She argues that Cécile Chaminade provides a case in point.[1] Cécile Chaminade (1857–1944) was a pianist and composer active in *fin-de-siècle* Paris. She completed around 400 compositions (many of them piano works), of which nearly all were published. In 1913 she received the honour of becoming the first female composer to be awarded the Légion d'Honneur.[2] Beyond France, Chaminade was popular in Britain, where she toured annually and performed for Queen Victoria,[3] and in the US, where she conducted an extensive tour and where many Chaminade Clubs were formed by enthusiasts for her music around 1900.[4] Citron argues, however, that although Chaminade was extremely popular through 1910, her reputation was tarnished through mere association with the salon.[5] Citron cites *The New Grove Dictionary* from 1980, as perpetuating this perspective by including Gustave Ferrari's entry from *Grove's Dictionary of Music and Musicians*, 2nd edition, from 1911, which states that Chaminade's music is intended for the drawing room.[6] She also writes that Nicolas Slonimsky has deployed the salon as a sign of trivial music in his definition of 'pseudo-music' in *Music Since 1900*, 4th edition, from 1971.[7] Citron states:

> These accounts typify the pervasive twentieth-century association of women with the salon, and the salon with marginal artistic activity. The social and stylistic democratization in the salon has reinforced negative gender associations.[8]

She suggests that the reason for this is that the salons have been denigrated as feminised spaces and were therefore not beneficial to those who participated in them. She goes on to explain that much of this denigration can be attributed to 'male society' beginning to 'fear the *salon* as a site of female power', and she asserts that a deliberate suppression of women was conducted through 'discreditation: denigration of the mixing of the personal and the artistic within the home'.[9]

This is a valid argument to make and there is evidence to support this. Chaminade's career was intrinsically linked with salon culture, and following the popularity of her compositions and performances during her career and lifetime, she has faded into the background and remained largely out of focus for the duration of the late twentieth century until the present. The late 1970s and early 1980s saw a small resurgence of interest in Chaminade and her works. For example, Danielle Laval recorded a selection of her piano works in 1980, including *Arabesque*, Op. 61, and *Automne*, Op. 35, No. 2. This recording included a commentary for the sleeve by French composer and music critic Gérard Condé.[10] Although Condé claims to have 'rediscovered' Chaminade, Citron's books and a focused French-language study by Cécile Tardif have brought Chaminade's life and career into more focus.[11] This alone, however, has not reignited fresh interest in Chaminade within musicology or the public performance repertoire, and familiarity with her name is often associated with a small number of her compositions which have been added to music exam board syllabi, due to the complexity of her works and the technical ability required to play them.[12] Her omission from the Western musical canon of works performed in concert halls, recorded, taught in classrooms, and played on the radio has largely obscured her from music historiography, but revisiting these predominantly biographical studies and combining the resurgence of interest in musical women with the more recent revisionist research into salon culture has prompted this research, which aims to provide a timely reappraisal of Chaminade's reception and career.

Academics such as Anja Bunzel, Natasha Loges, Jeanice Brooks, Sylvia Kahan, Aisling Kenny, Susan Wollenberg, Susan McClary, Jann Pasler, and Karin Pendle have recently provided revisionist studies of salon culture and the work of musical women within these sites. Such revisionist work has focussed not only on women composers, but also on the many forms of work in which women have participated as a contribution to musical society, such as teaching, performance, and patronage. The resurgence of research on women's work in music over the last decade, which has included salon reappraisal, has examined and demonstrated wider musical activity and musical culture away from traditional patriarchal models. An example of such revisionist work can be found in Sylvia Kahan's study of Winnaretta Singer, the Princesse de Polignac. According to Kahan, Singer-Polignac 'commissioned over twenty pieces of new music, providing important opportunities to composers such as Chabrier, Fauré, Stravinsky, Satie, Falla, and Poulenc at critical junctures in their careers',[13] and she also supported women composers, such as Tailleferre and Nadia Boulanger, by commissioning works[14] and introducing them to her influential circle.[15] Many of these works were showcased at her salon, a renowned site, rich in opportunity and publicity.[16] Revisionist studies of women's work in music, like Kahan's, demonstrates the significance and impact women's work as *salonnières* had on musical society. Although this developing body of revisionist research on salon culture has appeared over the last decade, it has not yet considered Chaminade. This chapter is therefore intended to contribute to this work. Citron's *Bio-Bibliography* on Chaminade concludes with an explanation that the volume should act as a catalyst for further analysis and research on Chaminade, and so this chapter also aims to build upon the academic foundations laid by Citron to re-examine her relationship with the salons and further trace and examine Chaminade's reception and career.[17]

Musical Salon Culture

With beginnings in the symposia of Ancient Greece, Anja Bunzel and Natasha Loges describe salons throughout history as an evolving social practice.[18] Citron states that 'the term itself came from seventeenth-century France, when large rooms in palatial settings began to be called *salons*', and that by the end of the century, 'particularly at Versailles, the term also connoted musical performances in such rooms'.[19] In its smallest construct, European salon culture witnessed a gathering of artists and intellectuals in the drawing-room of a home.

A grandiose example of the same cultural setting could be witnessed most famously in the Paris Salon, which housed the annual exhibition of the Académie des Beaux-Arts.[20] Musical, artistic, and literary salons operated as sites for participants to share ideas, debate, share new works, and participate in critical discourse, but unlike more formal professional, educational, and public sites, which shared some of these characteristics, salons operated under a cloak of culture and sociability.[21] Bunzel and Loges clarify that the seventeenth century is Western scholarship's most ardent era of the salons; however, the nineteenth century experienced something of a reinvention and modernisation of salon culture,[22] which Citron supports by suggesting that their rise in popularity during this century stems from both musical activity moving away from the church and the court, and the aristocracy's desire to maintain its elitist privileges.[23]

Citron discusses the salon as an important site of female culture, and although she briefly discusses France and Vienna, she focuses on Germany in her analysis. According to Citron, towards the end of the eighteenth century, several Jewish women in Germany developed the role of the host of private gatherings among the upper-middle class, featuring leading artists of the time, and began a two-hundred-year tradition of women's leadership within the salon.[24] Citron's assertion that this offered an intellectual and artistic outlet for women is suggestive of the salon acting as a site of empowerment for women. Indeed, she states that 'the *salon* afforded a unique vehicle for the expression of their minds and hearts', an opportunity unavailable to women through any alternative outlet, and describes salon activity as 'a sparkling showcase for the considerable talents of some brilliant women', referring to Fanny Arnstein, Henriette Herz, Rahel Levin, and Fanny Hensel.[25] Citron focuses on Hensel, claiming that the salon offered Hensel opportunities to conduct, perform, and compose, and enabled her to act as organiser, chronicler, and contractor, activities which, in the public domain, would not have been accessible to Hensel. Indeed, despite publication of works and public performance being largely prohibited to her, Hensel composed over 400 works due to her involvement with the salon.[26] This type of revisionist research reflects on salon culture and re-evaluates how women operated and thrived in these environments.

Lorraine Byrne Bodley discusses Hensel's Sunday *musicales*, which were functioning from at least as early as 1831, according to Hensel's diary.[27] These *musicales* witnessed performances between 11 in the morning and 2 in the afternoon, with Saturday evenings devoted to rehearsals.[28] These private performances soon became extremely popular and eventually attracted audiences of up to 200 people.[29] Byrne Bodley states that despite the cultural restrictions on women during this period, 'her [Hensel's] "salon" became one of the most important centres of music making in Berlin musical life, for hearing unusual repertoire superbly performed, and bordering on professional concert life'.[30] This suggests evidence that the salon was operating as a site of serious musical performances. Furthermore, the salons acted as educational sites:

> For intellectually and artistically gifted women such institutions were of immense importance, providing them with a space in which to create their own 'universities', where they could exchange ideas and advance their own learning.[31]

This revisionist analysis of Hensel's salon life and salon leadership helps to establish the levels of professionalism these sites operated on, the parameters of their influence and their significance in public musical life. According to Citron, 'for women active in the *salon*, the site afforded rich opportunity for creative artistry and a place where professional identity could be expressed according to different standards.'[32]

Jeanice Brooks reiterates Citron's analysis through her work on Nadia Boulanger and how she operated professionally through use of the salon:

> While this kind of salon performance might be considered a largely irrelevant remnant of an earlier era – a nostalgic attempt to revive a world definitively destroyed by the Great War – it has long been recognized that in Parisian avant-garde musical circles, aristocratic patrons such as the Beaumonts were a major force throughout the interwar period. Private concerts could be part of a suite of activities that included organizations or subvention of public institutions, and other contributions to wider concert culture.[33]

Salon audiences were predominantly made up of members of high society, well-known artists, and impresarios, who brought with them their prestige within society, their valuable contacts, their access to commerciality within the music industry, and money. Kahan explains that the elite members of society during the late nineteenth century were like the celebrities of today and that similarly, members of the general public wanted access to them. The newspapers devised what Kahan refers to as an 'inspired marketing ploy' and by reporting on salon activity – sharing gossip and intimate details about the gatherings, guests, and *salonnières* – they satisfied the demands of their readers, and also increased their own sales.[34] The benefit to musicians was that this provided copious amounts of exposure.

Fin-de-Siècle Musical Salon Culture

Revisionist research on salon culture is a crucial development in understanding the significance of these sites, particularly within the field of feminist musicology. Citron explores the denigration of the salon and how this has damaged the reputation of many women by association. As discussed, and as Citron has argued, Chaminade's reputation appears to have been tarnished by association with the salon. An important element in understanding the denigration of salon culture and women's activities is the wider political situation at the time. The *fin-de-siècle* period witnessed an important cultural shift within France. Jann Pasler details this, noting that the Prussian victory and the aftermath of the Franco-Prussian War left France in political and cultural turmoil, which Pasler explains created a paradox.[35] Indeed, according to Pasler, 1870 generated a united ambition throughout France, and across all political persuasions, towards pride in itself as a nation and within its own French culture.[36] Whilst wanting to reaffirm their own identity, they also wanted to strengthen their image: an emphasis was placed on being seen as strong, masculine, and modern, which ran contrary to the popularised Romanticism and feminised bourgeois salon culture.[37] Salon culture came to be viewed as exemplifying the supposedly weak culture of Second Empire France, which was constructed as complicit in France's military defeat by the Franco-Prussians.

> In the context of close relationships with the rest of Europe, reinventing themselves as a nation entailed not only looking back to past glories, whether under kings, emperors, or revolutionaries, but also taking stock of present accomplishments and promoting hope in the future. With defeat to Prussia, French conservatives and progressives alike looked to the arts rather than the military to revive national pride and respect ... Central to the country's regeneration and its future glory, progress in French music – particularly new orchestral sounds reinforcing its sensual immediacy – served as a metaphor for French pride both at home and abroad.[38]

This cultural modernisation and masculinisation were also heavily influenced by both the performance of lots of German music in France over many years, as well as the complicated love-hate relationship with and influence of Wagner.[39] This shift provided numerous complications for Chaminade. Having forged a professional career which stemmed from the salon, and by producing music very much associated with salon performance, any widespread denigration of salon culture would have a negative impact on her career and reception within France. This explains, at least in part, Chaminade's motives in developing a career outside of France and within the Anglophone world. Wagner's influence can be very much linked with the denigration of salon culture. Returning to Byrne Bodley's research, she describes Wagner's 'pejorative linkage of the Jewish with the feminine in salon culture' as directly affecting the reception of Hensel and her music.[40] Indeed, she engages with Leon Botstein's writing on music, femininity, Jewish identity, and salon culture to emphasise the impact of this denigration. This quote from Botstein, reiterated in Bryne Bodley's work demonstrates the derogatory nature of Wagner's cultural impact:

> By 1900, for many musicians influenced by Wagnerian ideology . . . the traditions and repertoire of the salon and nineteenth-century domestic music-making reeked of a repugnant, feminized culture . . . The greatness of Wagner, in the judgement of Friedrich Nietzsche . . . lay in the composer's attempt to redeem music from the philistine, bourgeois, and superficial, understood as a species of the feminine . . . A rift developed between the construct of the feminine and Jewish on one hand and true German culture and musicality on the other.[41]

There are two important strands here. The first is that the German influence in France and France's drive towards a more masculine cultural identity was in some part influenced by this ideology. Secondly, by relating this to Citron's writing on reception and intertextuality, there is evidence of the word 'feminine' alone connoting 'lesser'.[42] Similarities can be drawn between the denigration of women and the feminine salon culture and the denigration of women's music and the feminised language of critical reviews, often used to damage the reception and reputation of *musiciennes*; such as the case with Marguerite Canal, as discussed in Laura Hamer's work.[43]

The culture of the time was one which provided a struggle for women, particularly those who wanted to reach professional standards. Heir of the sewing machine wealth, Singer-Polignac used her wealth and status to enhance the musical world in which she lived, becoming a patron of the arts and *salonnière*. As discussed, and as Kahan has argued, Singer-Polignac supported artists and showcased new works at her salon. In describing Singer's initial accomplishments in the first two months of activity, although lauded by guests and press, her role as a *salonnière* was still unfairly associated with 'women's work', aspiring and succeeding, but only in the private domain.[44] Kahan states:

> Women could aspire, if they wished, to careers as soloists, taking the full course of training at the Conservatoire, but upon receiving their diplomas they had to confront a disdainful battalion of (male) concert organizers, conductors, colleagues, competitors. And although some orchestras did admit women to their ranks, most were inaccessible, as a professional venue even to the most talented women instrumentalists. Women composers had the slightest chance of all to succeed, given, admittedly, how difficult it was for any composer to succeed.[45]

This misogyny permeated the reputation of salon culture, salon activities, and musicians active within these sites. Kahan's work provides a broad narrative of the period and a complex and detailed account of salon culture in France during this period.

Returning to Brooks's work, she describes Boulanger's salon leadership as building upon the foundations created by other female-led sites:

> Although shared with men whose background allowed them to function in this environment, the salon milieu accorded women far greater agency than did most state institutions, and provided an arena for effective action under the cloak of sociability. Building on these possibilities, Nadia created her own educational institution in the Boulangers' Haussmannian apartment at 36, rue Ballu.[46]

Boulanger's salon was predominantly an educational site, where she taught groups of between 30 and 50 students a range of musical topics, including harmony, accompaniment, and sight-reading, as well as teaching individual private lessons.[47] Boulanger's reputation led to her friendship and collaboration with Winnaretta Singer, Princesse de Polignac, whom Brooks describes as 'one of the most powerful women on the early twentieth-century Parisian musical scene'.[48] According to Brooks, by 1925 Boulanger was renowned enough to tour in the US, following in the footsteps of Chaminade, who toured the US in 1908. As well as performing at various public venues, Boulanger also performed in music clubs and private homes, replicating aspects of her European salon performances and pedagogical salon activity.[49]

According to Adrienne Fried Block and Nancy Stewart, in America, the complex relationship between the private and public, and amateur and professional within the musical world mirrored that of Europe.[50] What they refer to as the Music Club Movement began with the Rossini Club established in Portland, Maine, in 1868, which was set up to 'provide members a place outside the home where they could share their music'.[51] These educational sites where amateur musicians could perform for their peers and for audiences quickly grew in momentum and 'by 1893 there were forty-two women's amateur musical clubs, thirty-five of which sent representatives to the National Convention of Women's Amateur Musical Clubs'.[52] The fact that there was such a convention is a testament to their cultural significance and the popularity of these sites, which appear to stem from the salon. These clubs offered women the chance to enhance their skills, further their education, develop their professional portfolio, and connect with audiences and peers, much like the European salons. Citron confirms as much by stating that by 1900, in the US, the parlor 'functioned as a great musical equalizer'.[53] According to Brooks, during her time in America, Boulanger replicated aspects of her European salon performances and pedagogical salon activity in music clubs and private homes.[54] This suggests a strong correlation between the activities of American Clubs and European salon culture, perhaps previously initiated by Chaminade's influence on American salon culture and her strong reception in the US.

Cécile Chaminade

Although the majority of Chaminade's compositions consist of piano miniatures and *mélodies*, she spent a number of years during her early career developing her skills and experimenting with large-scale works, including *Callirhoë*, Op. 37, her Ballet Symphonique, and *Concertstück* for Piano and Orchestra, Op. 40. Both compositions did enter the public sphere and were premiered on 16 March 1888 at the Grand-Théâtre in Marseille, and on 18 April 1888 at the Cercle Catholique; Société de Musique in Anvers [Antwerp], Belgium, respectively.

However, for women composers active during this period, there was little opportunity to write many large-scale works due to lack of commissions, opportunities for repeat performances, and few opportunities for such works to be published.[55] Indeed, Laura Hamer writes that throughout the late nineteenth century, for those women who had managed to establish careers as composers, there was a trend for composing small-scale genres, such as Chaminade's miniatures and *mélodies*. If we apply this to Chaminade, this explains that her move from focusing on large-scale genres during her early career to small marketable works was very much a practical decision.

Chaminade's definitive foray into salon performance of exclusively her own compositions began at the home of Le Couppey on 25 April 1878,[56] and continued on to a successful recital of her first published chamber work, *Trio* No. 1, Op. 11 alongside several of her piano miniatures and *mélodies* on 8 February 1880 at the Salle Erard.[57] According to Citron, the April 1878 salon performance programme became a model for her recital and repertoire style throughout her career.[58] Chaminade received a generous amount of positive reviews and media attention for this performance, including one such review in *La Revue Théatrale Illustrée* published on 28 April 1878 which describes her compositions as 'fresh inspirations revealing a talent that is serious and in full possession of itself'.[59] Her recital at the Salle Erard prompted a review in *Le Ménestrel* published on 15 February 1880 describing her *Trio* as 'written with a hand already firm and assured and reveals a skill that is profound and serious'.[60] Such an early career-defining moment involving salon performance provides an initial example of how Chaminade benefited from the salon environment and gives some insight into her reception in France during this period; however, her reception in the Anglophone world, particularly in England and America, was where Chaminade found great success. For example, the composer's tours in England beginning in June of 1892 became an almost annual event, and developed into a relationship between Chaminade and the British public that Citron refers to as 'a special mutual affection'.[61] Indeed, Britain provided Chaminade with a level of attention and praise which far outshone her reception in France. Chaminade would spend several months in England, performing her compositions at various large-scale public venues, such as St. James's Hall in London, and it was also in Britain that she recorded her piano rolls for the Aeolian Company, including a live duet performance with her own piano rolls as her accompanying partner at the Aeolian Hall.[62] According to Citron, Chaminade found favour with Queen Victoria. Chaminade was invited to perform at Windsor Castle and dedicated her song *Reste* to Princess Beatrice. The composer also attended the Diamond Jubilee celebrations and was awarded a Jubilee medal. Citron also states that Chaminade's organ *Prélude*, Op. 78, was performed at Queen Victoria's funeral in 1901.[63] Citron alludes to a plethora of critical reviews of Chaminade during her touring in Britain, but only investigates two undated reviews from Manchester, estimated to be from 1894.[64] One of these, from *The Manchester Courier*, describes Chaminade as possessing 'gifts that are closely allied with genius'.[65] Chaminade's British reception has remained somewhat underexplored, but these references to critical reviews of prominent moments in her career begin to provide an insight into the extent of her career in England.

Chaminade's career and reception in the US has been given slightly more academic attention in recent years. Citron's research on Chaminade's American career focuses on the Chaminade Clubs and her American tour in 1908. The Chaminade Clubs, of which there were at least 100, were what Citron describes as something of a unique phenomenon.[66] Citron describes them as socially acceptable outlets for women and amateur musicians with diverse performance opportunities to meet and perform.[67] There is certainly some scope here for a comparison of these clubs with European salon culture. Both sites were predominantly run by women and gave women opportunities to pursue music in a way which was not necessarily available to them through the formal and mainstream avenues, both educationally and professionally, and both were constructed under a guise of sociability. Citron's discussion of Chaminade's American tour has been explored further in other academic work, including that of Michele Mai Aichele. According to Aichele, many of the Chaminade Clubs in the 1920s took part in National Music Week events, engaged in community projects, and the ones still active now promote guest artists, host young musicians' competitions, and provide scholarship funding.[68] Aichele provides further information on how the clubs of the early 1900s ran parallel with Chaminade's career, for example: Chaminade's second Philadelphia concert was sponsored by the Chaminade Club of that city.[69] Other clubs wrote and performed 'odes' to Chaminade to reiterate the goals and ambitions of the clubs.[70] Aichele asserts that women utilised the Chaminade Clubs as a means of entering the public sphere and developing their music practice away from the domestic sphere.[71] This not only further reiterates the influence Chaminade had on women and musical culture, but also provides a template of American Chaminade Clubs through which to draw comparisons with European salon culture and gauge how influential the salons were on these American clubs.

Susan McClary describes Diamanda Galas, Janika Vandervelde, Laurie Anderson, and Madonna as contemporary women musicians who have each carved out a niche for themselves in response to their awareness of musical traditions and its oppressive conventions.[72] McClary discusses this awareness as, at the very least, an intuitive one. Chaminade publicly demonstrated an awareness of the limitations of her gender as a professional woman composer due to musical traditions and the social and cultural constraints of her time, and Citron includes a quote by Chaminade in her *Bio-Bibliography*, indicating as much. This statement was published in an interview with the composer in *The Washington Post* in 1908:

> I do not believe that the few women who have achieved greatness in creative work are the exception, but I think that life has been hard on women; it has not given them opportunity; it has not made them convincing . . . Woman has not been considered a working force in the world and the work that her sex and conditions impose upon her has not been so adjusted as to give her a little fuller scope for the development of her best self. She has been handicapped, and only the few, through force of circumstances or inherent strength, have been able to get the better of that handicap. There is no sex in art. Genius is an independent quality. The woman of the future, with her broader outlook, her greater opportunities, will go far, I believe, in creative work of every description.[73]

This articulate commentary of how Chaminade regarded the societal limitations imposed upon her gender demonstrates a very conscious awareness and understanding. In a similar way to McClary's case studies, Chaminade also created her own niche opportunities to function as a musician, although instead of directly challenging stereotypes she employed and exploited aspects of traditional ideas of femininity on a commercial level within her professional career.

Richard Langham Smith explores this further in a 1994 article for *The Musical Times*.[74] According to Langham Smith, Chaminade had a box of Morny soaps named after her. 'You could buy her smell, in a nice tidy box with her signature and a snippet of her music alongside Magnolia, French Fern'.[75] Indeed, upon further research these were not the only products associated with the composer. Whilst Langham Smith captures the scope of the marketing employed by Chaminade, including the use of floral, traditionally feminine Art Nouveau decorations on the sheet music, which were popular at the time of her publications, he asserts that these tactics could not have helped her reputation as a serious composer.[76] Although this aligns in some ways to her denigration as a composer of women's salon music, there is an alternative perspective here. It seems that she could have been consciously playing upon feminine tropes for her own commercial ends. She also seems to have been a very shrewd businesswoman. This kind of promotion would have enabled Chaminade to increase her reputation amongst her target audience, allowed her to earn more money, and would have empowered her as a working woman in the world. Indeed, this kind of activity can be compared to the modern trend of celebrity influencers, which allows individuals to act as self-promoting agents, gaining publicity and financial accolades for associating themselves with commercial goods. This self-promotion would have contributed to enabling Chaminade to act as a full professional agent within her social, economic, and cultural spheres.

Sandra Crawshaw suggests that although the products Chaminade represented were unconnected to the musical world of her profession, they were emblematic of what she as a public figure represented: 'a successful, attractive and sophisticated French woman'.[77] Crawshaw supports this by discussing the Morny perfume named Chaminade (Song of the Road), which was released worldwide in 1910. According to Crawshaw, the dedication was by special permission of the composer. This suggests that Morny and Chaminade saw a mutually beneficial relationship through the selling of these products and supports the view that not only was Chaminade a popular public figure for women at this time, but that she was also happy to perpetuate gendered tropes and be associated with feminine products. Much like the soaps, the perfume also included a snippet of Chaminade's music, along with her signature, and, according to Crawshaw, the perfume was a top selling product for Morny that later became a product line, which included lotions, talc, and bath salts featuring the same 'Chaminade' scent, and continued to sell for more than two decades into the 1930s, implying the longevity of both the demand for these products and the reputation of the composer.[78]

Amanda Harris provides some analysis on Chaminade's reception, particularly in regard to feminism and ideas surrounding the New Woman. Harris's definition of feminism encompasses a revisionist and broader range of activities by women which contributed towards their freedom and equal rights. Her argument supports that of Karen Offen, whom Harris quotes as saying, 'Feminism is the name given to a comprehensive critical response to the deliberate and systematic subordination of women as a group by men as a group within a given cultural setting'.[79] Harris asserts that the term 'feminist' originated in France in the 1880s and was principally concerned with legal and economic equality.[80] A cultural setting, as mentioned in Offen's quote, could apply to the salon environment, and Harris supports this idea by drawing on Chaminade's use of this site. According to Harris, the French feminist publication *La Française* published an article in their 7 August 1909 edition, which 'supported the idea that women musicians were advancing the cause of feminism'. Harris states that in the regular 'Musique' section of the paper, there was a report on the most recent Friday salons held in conjunction with the paper by an anonymous author who quotes extensively from Armand Silvestre's writing on Cécile Chaminade from 1901:

> The works of a woman artist, as admirably talented and marvellously hard-working as Mme. Cécile Chaminade do more for the real emancipation of women and are more threatening to the lengthy autonomy of men than all the talking about it.[81]

According to Harris, the quote was printed without commentary on the author's own opinion, which Harris suggests implies a complete agreement with Silvestre's views. The only opinion supplied by the author was an assertion that if Silvestre's commentary was written today, his views would probably be bolder still.[82] There are two important strands here. The first is that Chaminade's own musical activity was received as feminist by definition of the fact that it advanced the equality of women. Indeed, Hamer asserts that although many *musiciennes* did not publicly declare any allegiance to the feminist movement, the very act of pursuing professional public careers was, in itself, a serious disregard of societal norms.[83] The second is that her activities in the salon, and the salon as a site itself, were empowering and beneficial to women within and outside of the musical world. Harris later discusses the British Society of Women Musicians, which was founded in 1911 and 'was formed as a means of providing support networks to women musicians and composers'.[84] Ethel Smyth, an English composer and active member of the women's suffrage movement, was an honorary committee member during its first two years of activity, during which period the composers Liza Lehmann and Cécile Chaminade successively held the office of president, according to the society archives held at the Royal College of Music Library, London and accessed by Harris.[85] This suggests that Chaminade had affiliations with active feminists during this period and was involved in cultural activities to support women, enable women to develop professionally, and offer women an opportunity for more freedom.

In relation to Chaminade's reception in the US, Aichele discusses her representation as both 'New Woman' and 'True Woman'. According to Aichele, this analysis of her public persona and representation is crucial in terms of tracing Chaminade's reception and helps to explain the contradictions in her reputation: that is, both the portrayal of her as a traditional woman working within the acceptable private sphere and domestic setting, closely aligned with 'True Woman', and the reality of her as a professional composer, supporting herself financially and travelling to other countries, and therefore more aligned with 'New Woman'.[86] 'New Woman' was representative of a progressive, independent woman, who was engaged professionally outside of the home, whereas 'True Woman' was representative of a more traditional female ideal, and was closely associated with women who remained within the domestic sphere, were married, and raised children.[87] Aichele asserts that biographers, critics and advertisers shaped Chaminade's image to fit their agenda; however, she predominantly discusses the dual representation of 'True Woman' and 'New Woman' through her inclusion in popular fictional literature of the time.[88] According to Aichele, Chaminade and her music were included in many fictional stories, including three of newspaper reporter Harold MacGrath's (1871–1932) novels, *The Million Dollar Mystery*, *The Man on the Box*, and *The Princess Elopes*. Aichele explains that all three novels feature strong female leads who are intelligent, wealthy, and accomplished.[89] Aichele suggests that Chaminade's portrayal in these three novels as well as others mentioned in her thesis are symbolic and representative of several 'types of women'. Chaminade often represents women with careers and presents the 'New Woman' in a positive light; she also represents women of wealth, status, and intelligence who play only within the private domain and are categorised as 'True', demonstrating societal limitations; and finally, her music was often associated with suspect, shady, and unhappy characters. Aichele asserts that this demonstrates the fluidity of her representation and reception within culture and is also indicative of her popularity and 'ubiquitous status as the leading composer of her sex'; it was unusual for a female composer and her music to be utilised in fiction in this way.[90]

Indeed, Harris confirms that 'la Femme Nouvelle', the 'New Woman', an Anglo-American cultural import was obsessively discussed and gained increasing currency in France from the 1890s onwards.[91] This 'educated woman who travelled independently and engaged in feminist conferences', and who was 'closely associated with theatre, literature and journalism', could easily be applied to the model of Chaminade as a highly talented and professional French composer who toured England and America and who was associated with salons, the Musical Club Movement, and Chaminade Clubs, a cultural setting for women to engage in education and music.[92]

Conclusion

Revisionist work on salon culture and women's work in music is doing much to reshape the historical narrative of negative feminised connotations and dismissal and provides a fresh perspective on both the significance of these sites and the significance of women's work in musical history. Salons offered women a professional and educational site and a platform for a career otherwise unavailable to them in traditional, mainstream, and public spheres. Chaminade, who has been unfairly ignored within musical history and dismissed as a composer of drawing-room music, is a crucial case-study in reappraising these sites and understanding how they offered women an opportunity for a professional career. Chaminade utilised salons to promote her works, develop a commercial presence, and was fundamental in the American adoption of European salon culture and the formation of Music Clubs.

Notes

1. Marcia J. Citron, *Gender and the Musical Canon*, revised ed. (Urbana and Chicago: University of Illinois Press, 2000), 108.
2. Marcia J. Citron, *Cécile Chaminade, a Bio-Bibliography* (New York; Westport, CT and London: Greenwood Press, 1988), 17.
3. Ibid., 11.
4. Ibid., 15.
5. Citron, *Gender and the Musical Canon*, 108.
6. Ibid., 108.
7. Ibid.
8. Ibid.
9. Ibid.
10. Danielle Laval, *Cécile Chaminade: Pièces Pour Piano* (Paris: Pathé Marconi, EMI, 1980) [on vinyl].
11. Cécile Tardif, *Portrait de Cécile Chaminade*. (Montréal: Louise Courteau, 1993).
12. The ABRSM lists Chaminade's *Scarf Dance*, Op. 37 No. 3, as an option for students completing Grade 8 Piano in their 2019/20 syllabus, and Chaminade's *Concertino in D*, Op. 107 complete, as an option for students completing DipABRSM in Flute in their Music Performance Diploma syllabus.
13. Sylvia Kahan, *Music's Modern Muse: A Life of Winnaretta Singer, princesse de Polignac*, Vol. 22. (Rochester: University of Rochester Press, 2010), xvii.
14. Ibid., 232.
15. Ibid., 234.
16. Ibid., xvii.
17. Citron, *Cécile Chaminade*, 26.
18. Anja Bunzel and Natasha Loges, eds., *Musical Salon Culture in the Long Nineteenth Century* (Woodbridge: Boydell & Brewer, 2019), 1.
19. Citron, *Gender and the Musical Canon*, 104.
20. Bunzel and Loges, eds., *Musical Salon Culture in the Long Nineteenth Century*, 1.
21. Ibid., 2.
22. Ibid.
23. Citron, *Gender and the Musical Canon*, 104–05.
24. Ibid., 105.
25. Ibid., 105–06.
26. Ibid., 106.
27. Lorraine Byrne Bodley, "Fanny Hensel's 'Musical Salon'," in *Women and the Nineteenth-Century Lied*, edited by A. Kenny and S. Wollenberg (Surrey and Burlington: Ashgate, 2015), 53.
28. Ibid.
29. Ibid., 54.
30. Ibid., 55–56.
31. Ibid., 45–59.
32. Citron, *Gender and the Musical Canon*, 108.

33. Jeanice Brooks., *The Musical Works of Nadia Boulanger: Performing Past and Future Between the Wars* (Cambridge: Cambridge University Press, 2013), 1.
34. Kahan, *Music's Modern Muse*, 84.
35. Jann Pasler, *Composing the Citizen: Music as Public Utility in Third Republic France* (Berkeley; Los Angeles; London: University of California Press, 2009).
36. Ibid., 20.
37. Ibid., 234.
38. Ibid., 234–35.
39. Ibid., 231–357.
40. Byrne Bodley, "Fanny Hensel's 'Musical Salon'," 58.
41. Leon Botstein, "Music, Femininity, and Jewish Identity: The Tradition and Legacy of the Salon', in *Jewish Women and their Salons*, edited by Bilski and Braun, 162.
42. Citron, *Gender and the Musical Canon*, 179.
43. Laura Hamer, *Female Composers, Conductors, Performers: Musiciennes of Interwar France, 1919–1939* (Abingdon and New York: Routledge, 2018), 69.
44. Ibid., 90.
45. Ibid.
46. Brooks, *The Musical Works of Nadia Boulanger*, 27.
47. Ibid.
48. Ibid., 32–33.
49. Ibid., 29.
50. Adrienne Fried Block and Nancy Stewart, "Women in American Music, 1800–1918," in *Women and Music: A History*, edited by Karin Pendle, rev. ed. (Bloomington: Indiana University Press, 2001), 203.
51. Ibid.
52. Ibid., 203–04.
53. Citron, *Gender and the Musical Canon*, 107.
54. Brooks, *The Musical Works of Nadia Boulanger*, 29.
55. Hamer, *Female Composers, Conductors, Performers*, 34.
56. Citron, *Cécile Chaminade*, 4.
57. Ibid., 5.
58. Ibid., 4.
59. Ibid., 112.
60. Ibid., 113.
61. Ibid., 11.
62. Ibid.
63. Citron, *Cécile Chaminade*, 11.
64. Ibid., 11.
65. Ibid., 151–52.
66. Ibid., 15.
67. Ibid.
68. Ibid., 103–04.
69. Ibid., 109.
70. Ibid., 113–14.
71. Ibid., 114.
72. Susan McClary, *Feminine Endings: Music, Gender, and Sexuality* (Minneapolis and London: University of Minnesota Press, 2002), 34.
73. Citron, *Cécile Chaminade*, 24.
74. Richard Langham Smith, "Sister of Perpetual Indulgence. On the 50th Anniversary of Her Death," *The Musical Times* 135, no. 1822 (December 1994).
75. Ibid., 740.
76. Ibid.
77. Sandra Crawshaw, "The Reception of the Music of Cécile Chaminade in Colonial New Zealand (1894–1934): Contexts and Institutions," (MA thesis, University of Otago, 2015), 7.
78. Ibid.
79. Amanda Harris, "Composing Women and Feminism at the Turn of the Twentieth Century in England, France and Germany," (PhD diss., The University of New South Wales, 2008), 12.

80. Ibid., 11.
81. Ibid., 209.
82. Ibid., 208–09.
83. Hamer, *Female Composers, Conductors, Performers*, 20.
84. Ibid., 237.
85. Ibid.
86. Aichele, Cécile Chaminade as a symbol, iv–4.
87. Ibid., 13.
88. Ibid., 4.
89. Ibid., 5.
90. Ibid., 98–99.
91. Harris, *Composing Women and Feminism*, 12–13.
92. Ibid., 12–13.

Bibliography

Aichele, Michele Mai. "Cécile Chaminade as a Symbol for American Women, 1890–1920." Doctoral thesis, University of Iowa, 2019.

Briscoe, James, ed. *New Historical Anthology of Music by Women*. Bloomington and Indianapolis: Indiana University Press, 2004.

Brooks, Jeanice. *The Musical Works of Nadia Boulanger: Performing Past and Future between the Wars*. Cambridge: Cambridge University Press, 2013.

Bunzel, Anja, and Natasha Loges, eds. *Musical Salon Culture in the Long Nineteenth Century*. Woodbridge: The Boydell Press, 2019.

Citron, Marcia J. *Cécile Chaminade, a Bio-Bibliography*. New York, Westport, CT and London: Greenwood Press, 1988.

———. *Gender and the Musical Canon*. Rev. ed. Urbana and Chicago: University of Illinois Press, 2000.

Cook, Susan C., and Judy S. Tsou, eds. *Cecilia Reclaimed: Feminist Perspectives on Gender and Music*. Urbana and Chicago: University of Illinois Press, 1994.

Crawshaw, Sandra N. "The Reception of the Music of Cécile Chaminade in Colonial New Zealand (1894–1934): Contexts and Institutions." Doctoral thesis, University of Otago, 2015.

Hamer, Laura. *Female Composers, Conductors, Performers: Musiciennes of Interwar France, 1919–1939*. Abingdon and New York: Routledge, 2018.

Harris, Amanda. "Composing Women and Feminism at the Turn of the Twentieth Century in England, France and Germany." Doctoral thesis, The University of New South Wales, 2008.

Kahan, Sylvia. *Music's Modern Muse: A life of Winnaretta Singer, princesse de Polignac*. Vol. 22. Rochester: University of Rochester Press, 2010.

Kenny, Aisling, and Susan Wollenberg, eds. *Women and the Nineteenth-Century Lied*. Surrey and Burlington: Ashgate, 2015.

Laval, Danielle. *Cécile Chaminade: Pièces Pour Piano*. Paris: Pathé Marconi, EMI, 1980 [on vinyl].

Magner, Candace. "The Songs of Cécile Chaminade." *Journal of Singing – The Official Journal of the National Association of Teachers of Singing* 57, no. 4 (2001): 23–35.

Mawer, Deborah, ed. *Historical Interplay in French Music and Culture, 1860–1960*. London and New York: Routledge, 2018.

McCann, Karen J. H. "Cécile Chaminade: A Composer at Work." Doctoral thesis, University of British Columbia, 2003.

McClary, Susan. *Feminine Endings: Music, Gender, and Sexuality*. Minneapolis and London: University of Minnesota Press, 2002.

Op den Kamp, Claudy, and Dan Hunter, eds. *A History of Intellectual Property in 50 Objects*. Cambridge and New York: Cambridge University Press, 2019.

Pasler, Jann. *Composing the Citizen: Music as Public Utility in Third Republic France*. Berkeley, Los Angeles and London: University of California Press, 2009.

Pendle, Karin, ed. *Women & Music: A History*, 2nd ed. Bloomington and Indianapolis: Indiana University Press, 2001.

Phillips, Peter. "Piano Rolls and Contemporary Player Pianos: The Catalogues, Technologies, Archiving and Accessibility." Doctoral thesis, University of Sydney, 2016.
Scott, Derek B. *Sounds of the Metropolis: The 19th Century Popular Music Revolution in London, New York, Paris, and Vienna*. New York: Oxford University Press, 2008.
Smith, Richard L. "Sister of Perpetual Indulgence." *The Musical Times* 135, no. 1822 (1994): 740–44.
_____, and Caroline Potter, eds. *French Music Since Berlioz*. London and New York: Routledge, 2006.
Smith, Robin R. J. "The mélodies of Cécile Chaminade: Hidden Treasures for Vocal Performance and Pedagogy." Doctoral thesis, Indiana University, 2012.
Tardif, Cécile. *Portrait de Cécile Chaminade*. Montréal: Louise Courteau, 1993.

7
'UNE BELLE MANIFESTATION FÉMINISTE'

The Formation of the Union des Femmes Professeurs et Compositeurs de Musique

Laura Hamer

Writing in *Gil Blas* in December 1911, René Simon described the formation of France's first all-woman orchestra by the Union des Femmes Professeurs et Compositeurs de Musique (Union of Women Music Teachers and Composers, hereafter U.F.P.C.[1]) as 'a beautiful feminist demonstration' ('une belle manifestation féministe').[2] Given the *fin-de-siècle* French press's tendency to describe all public, professional activity amongst women as acts of feminism – regardless of whether or not the individual women concerned were actually aligned with the feminist movement – it is not surprising that Simon chose to characterise the Orchestra of the U.F.P.C. in this way. In the case of the U.F.P.C., however, the 'feminist' label was indeed apt, as it was a pro-suffrage and feminist organisation. Although by the outbreak of the First World War the U.F.P.C. counted around 800 members and was one of the most active music societies in Paris, it has now become an extremely obscure organisation. It has been very under-researched and, beyond a few passing references, is virtually absent from even the scholarship on women musicians in *fin-de-siècle* France.[3] This chapter seeks to redress this by throwing fresh light upon the U.F.P.C., questioning the motivation for its formation, and surveying its activities throughout the early years of its existence (from 1904 to the outbreak of the First World War). Why so many women musicians felt the need to join an organisation designed to protect their interests is considered through a discussion of the institutionalised discrimination they tended to face. The establishment of the U.F.P.C. is also contextualised within both the development of *fin-de-siècle* French feminism and the concomitant emergence of 'femmes nouvelles' ('new women'), which many of the individual members seemed to embody. That so many women musicians participated in the significant work of this avowedly feminist trade union constitutes a greater involvement in feminist politics than has previously been acknowledged.

Motivation, Formation, 'Unionisation'

The U.F.P.C. was founded in Paris in 1904.[4] Its aims were to defend the collective interests of women musicians – incorporating composers, performers, and teachers – to support and facilitate their professional activities, and to encourage solidarity amongst them.[5] The U.F.P.C. was established by the music teacher, critic, and sociologist Marie Daubresse (who is also known by the male pseudonym Michel Daubresse, which she used for her music criticism).[6] In 1914

Daubresse published a book about the conditions of professional musicians in contemporary society, *Le Musicien dans la société moderne* (*The Musician in Modern Society*).[7] In this book – which reveals her strong political commitments to both feminism and trade unionism – she discussed her motivation for establishing the society. Daubresse considered the situation of single, middle-class women who had received a thorough musical education and needed to use this to support themselves. She claimed that:

> Spurred on by an urgent need, women have become teachers, performers, even composers. They have taught the piano – how many they are, O gods! – the harmonium and even the organ, the harp, the violin, the cello, the guitar, the mandolin . . . and the double-bass.[8]

As music formed such a fundamental part of middle- and upper-class women's education, teaching, as Florence Launay has also noted, 'could turn out to be a life saver for women from bourgeois and aristocratic backgrounds touched by a reversal of fortunes.'[9] Alone, such women, according to Daubresse, were often taken advantage of financially, and generally struggled to make ends meet. Therefore, she resolved to form a union of women musicians:

> Woman musician myself, I thought first and foremost of other women musicians. Why not take women from amongst the great family of female artists by the hand? [In France there are around 400 professional women musicians.] Why not substitute amongst them, instead of the spirit of animosity, that rightly or wrongly they are accused of, a warmer welcome? . . . If they were in agreement, they would help each other . . . But, under what guise? . . . Trade-union guise was suggested. – But . . . what was that? – We had to inform ourselves: [women] musicians being more familiar with the notes on a stave than with the statutes of a professional organisation.[10]

In an article that Daubresse wrote for *La Revue musicale SIM* in 1911 entitled 'How to Form A Union of Women Musicians', she commented that the prospect of forming a union was extremely frightening for many of the middle-class women who were initially involved with the U.F.P.C.: 'I know from experience, that the term "union" literally terrifies lots of well brought-up women; they pronounce it with difficulty; those three syllables ["syn-di-cat"] smell of the labour exchanges, the communist, the revolutionary.'[11] Daubresse's comments highlight how daunting the idea of organising themselves into a union initially was for many (largely middle-class) women musicians; such an association at the time would connect them with the far left, which was often viewed as dangerous and radical. However, she was fully persuaded that 'union form was the one that offered the most advantages to its members.'[12] She claimed that forming a union was necessary, as employers were inclined to take advantage of female musicians by paying them less than male colleagues and expecting long hours of unpaid overtime.[13] She counselled other (presumably female) readers of *La Revue musicale SIM* that 'it is not very difficult to found a union; a few administrative formalities, that it is easy to become conversant with, are sufficient.'[14] Daubresse recalled how many professional women musicians were active in France, and reminded these of the strength that came through union: 'if those 4,000 women got along with each other, joined forces, *united* together, they would be a force'.[15]

The inaugural meeting of the U.F.P.C. took place on 1 March 1904. From an initial ten women, the U.F.P.C. quickly developed into a fully-fledged union, with Daubresse acting as its first president.[16] Together they took advice from the prominent (male) trade unionist,

M. Perrin, in order to understand the legal requirements for forming such an organisation. They instituted monthly meetings, drew up rules and a statute, set up an organising committee, established an office for their headquarters,[17] obtained official permission for the society, and registered its existence with the appropriate authorities. They became, as Daubresse declared in *Le Musicien dans la société moderne*, 'unionised'.[18]

The U.F.P.C. agreed on a comprehensive statute which laid out (in 34 articles) the exact aims, rules, and regulations of the union.[19] This statute specified the U.F.P.C.'s goals as:

1. To facilitate, by all the means at its disposal, the members in exercising their profession;
2. To take the initiative in everything that could contribute to the moral, material, and intellectual well-being of its members;
3. To establish a benevolence fund for members who are unable to work through sickness, accident, or retirement;
4. The defense of the entire professional interests of all the members.[20]

In order to join the U.F.P.C., prospective members had to be nominated by two current members in good standing, to be in agreement with the society's goals, and not already be members of any similar organisation. (Interestingly, admission was not restricted to women, although they did make up the majority of the membership.) Members were liable to pay an annual subscription of 10 francs, which was payable either quarterly or once a year.[21] The U.F.P.C. was administered by a general assembly, an executive committee, and a control commission. The executive committee, which met at least once a month, was made up of an elected president, two vice-presidents, a secretary, a treasurer, an executive manager,[22] and at least three ordinary members. Committee posts were tenable for one year, and post-holders were eligible for reelection. All society activities were discussed and voted upon at open meetings.[23] In keeping with France's contemporary drive towards secularity, the final article of the U.F.P.C.'s statute decreed that: 'All political and religious discussion during meetings is forbidden'.[24]

The Need for a Union of Women Musicians: Professional Disputes and Institutionalised Sexism

An article appeared in *Le Ménestrel* in November 1906 praising the initiative of the founders of the U.F.P.C. for forming an organisation dedicated to campaigning for and championing the rights of women musicians, and highlighting the unequal professional playing field which they confronted:

> Amongst the numerous professional societies which are founded every day, we will allow ourselves to highlight one of the most assuredly useful and interesting, the Union des Femmes Professeurs et Compositeurs de Musique, which . . . dates to 1904 and is in full operation. It would be almost useless to indicate the goal of this artistic group. We know what a delicate and difficult situation a woman has in today's society. Perhaps that of a woman artist is even more delicate and even more difficult than that of others . . . The idea of the society . . . is due to several women artists whose initiative is based on the known axiom: unity through strength. It is by that union, and by the collective effort that it will naturally bring about, that they have conceived the hope of progressively improving the situation of women musicians. There, where a single will remains powerless, several wills united can triumph over many difficulties, can level out many obstacles.[25]

The very existence of a union dedicated to defending and promoting the professional rights of women musicians emphasises the fact that alone, as Daubresse highlighted in *Le Musicien dans la société moderne*, they tended to face institutionalised discrimination. Although there were large numbers of women who earned their livings through music in *fin-de-siècle* France – from famous concert artists, such as Marguerite Long or Blanche Selva, to the hundreds of female music teachers – the vast majority faced systematic, gender-based discrimination on a regular basis, which particularly affected their educational and professional opportunities.

Although the Paris Conservatoire had been open to women since it opened in 1795, women could not access an equal education to men. Until the First World War, Conservatoire classes were segregated according to sex, and differences often existed between the curriculums prescribed for men's and women's classes. In 1904, Joseph Chaumié, Minister of Public Instruction, in agreement with the Conservatoire, legislated to limit the number of women in each string class to a maximum of four. This decision was motivated because, as Launay has noted, 'it seemed scandalous that [female] students who were not able to envisage an orchestral career were taking the places of [male] students for whom such study could lead to work as an orchestral musician.'[26] Commenting on this, Daubresse observed in *Le Musicien dans la société moderne* that: 'At the moment, women instrumentalists, who every day are becoming more numerous, seek to use their talent other than through teaching . . . from the sidelines, they eye symphony and even theatre orchestras.'[27] Although women orchestral players remained rare, largely confined to the seconds, and generally paid less than their male colleagues, by the early years of the twentieth century some women had become members of professional orchestras. The Orchestre Colonne, for instance, employed women amongst the second violins, violas, and cellos.[28]

Women composers were also beginning to demand greater access to a wider range of professional activities during the *fin de siècle*.[29] As Annegret Fauser has elegantly chronicled in a seminal article on the subject, women composers' struggles for greater official recognition against an often hostile professional and institutional environment are clearly seen in their entry to the Prix de Rome competition in 1903.[30] Lili Boulanger's success in winning the Premier Grand Prix de Rome in 1913 marked a very important milestone in women's greater access to the professional world of composition.

A Wider Mirror for the U.F.P.C.: 'Femmes Nouvelles' and Feminists

The alarm felt by some critics and members of the musical establishment by the emergence of a greater number of professional women musicians – and crucially, ones that were beginning to demand equal access to all areas of the profession – in *fin-de-siècle* France directly mirrors a much wider contemporary gender battle. In particular, many commentators were concerned by the emergence of what they termed 'femmes nouvelles' ('new women'). Mary Louise Roberts has defined the phenomenon of the 'femme nouvelle' as:

> A group of primarily urban, middle-class French women [who] became the object of intensive public scrutiny. Some remained single; some entered non-traditional marriages; some were prominent feminist activists; some took up the professions of medicine and law, journalism and teaching. Despite their differences, all of these women challenged the regulatory norms of gender by living unconventional lives and by doing work outside the home that was coded masculine in French culture.[31]

Another characteristic of the 'femme nouvelle' was that she was highly educated. Following the Camille Sée Law (1880), which established Lycées for girls, secular secondary and higher education became increasingly accessible to women. Thus, as Robert notes, 'by the end of the century ... there existed a sizeable group of educated women in France who yearned for work and a life beyond the parlor.'[32] These 'femmes nouvelles' were regarded by many with alarm, who viewed them as a threat to the traditional balance between the sexes. As Roberts has further commented:

> French print culture treated the New Woman obsessively. In the 1880s and 1890s, readers ... were exposed almost daily to articles, surveys, and editorials concerning the unruly "femme nouvelle" ... Underlying such widespread interest seemed to be the anxiety that, preoccupied with her career, the New Woman would not fulfill her domestic destiny.[33]

Daubresse embodied the figure of the 'femme nouvelle'. She was single, highly educated, practised a range of white-collar professions which had recently opened up to women, including journalism and teaching, as well as being a professionally trained musician and a feminist activist.

The struggles of 'femmes nouvelles' to gain greater professional recognition in *fin-de-siècle* France were accompanied by the concomitant development of French feminism, within which many 'femmes nouvelles' were active. French feminism had developed steadily throughout the later nineteenth century, although it remained largely the concern of educated, middle-class, urban women concentrated in the Paris region.[34] Several feminist associations were established to protect and promote the rights of particular groups of women. The membership of the *Société pour l'amélioration du sort de la femme et la revendication de ses droits* (more commonly referred to as *Amélioration*), for example, was largely made up of professional women (particularly doctors and lawyers), and principally concerned with improving their working conditions. As I have previously noted, the U.F.P.C. – whose membership was made up exclusively of women musicians and whose aims were all geared towards promoting and protecting their rights – may also be seen as fitting within this wider political trend of the establishment of specific feminist organisations to cater for particular groups of women.[35]

Activities and Members

As Simon-Pierre Perret and Harry Halbreich have commented, the U.F.P.C. corresponded to 'a real need' and consequently 'enjoyed a remarkable development'.[36] Within the first few years of its existence the U.F.P.C. established very wide-ranging professional activities. In June 1904 they established a pension fund, with the composer Isabelle Delâge-Prat acting as its first president. At the same time they also founded a benevolence fund to support unemployed female musicians who were unable to work through sickness or accident. From February 1905, the U.F.P.C. published their own monthly newsletter (*Bulletin Mensuel*). They also established a music lending library and organised regular talks and seminars for their membership. They envisaged even greater plans, including two *Maisons des Musiciennes* (Women Musicians' Homes). One was an effective almshouse for elderly, widowed, unwell, and/or impoverished women musicians who were no longer able to support themselves; the other for still-active women musicians were they could work free from domestic cares and worries.[37] Additionally, as Daubresse recalled in *Le Musicien dans la société moderne*, after the official business of each monthly meeting was concluded, the members 'exchanged projects: the organization of classes, musical performances; they arranged meetings, hours for rehearsals.'[38] She characterised the camaraderie which developed at these occasions thus: 'An ambiance of warm sympathy and open cordiality animated them, it enfolded them and certain members, who had arrived tired and sad, became lighter, a little consoled, hoping in the better days that their sisterly union would assure them.'[39]

The U.F.P.C. organised several ensembles. In December 1905 they formed a Choral Society. This was initially under the direction of the male organist M. Stolz, and then taken over by a M. Bernard.[40] A glowing review appeared in *Le Monde artiste* in March 1906 which highlights the calibre of performers who participated in their concerts:

> The concert organised by the U.F.P.C. has won, thanks to the tireless activity of the president, Mme Daubresse, a great success; on the programme, choruses by Chaminade and de Pierné, performed by the U.F.P.C.'s Choir, made up exclusively of the lady members, under the skilful direction of the excellent musician, M. Bernard; Mlle Hélène de Fleury, Prix de Rome, was particularly celebrated in her own piano works; the talented harpist, Mlle Marguerite Achard, was strongly applauded.[41]

Starting on 21 March 1907, the U.F.P.C. also organised regular chamber music concerts at the Salle Gaveau.

Beyond the activities specifically designed to benefit their membership, the U.F.P.C also organised modestly priced concerts of classical music for working-class audiences. An anonymous article published in *Le tout-théâtre* in 1905 outlined this initiative thus:

> The aim of this exclusively French union is to assist women [music] teachers and performers in procuring classes or concerts.[42] It also intends to organise popular concerts at reduced rates, thereby giving women musicians the means to be heard and offering the working classes the opportunity to hear good music.[43]

These early concerts highlight two characteristics that would come to define the U.F.P.C.: enterprise and philanthropy.[44]

One of the most striking features of the U.F.P.C. was the remarkable professional democracy amongst its membership, as the organisation included both famous concert artists alongside hundreds of women teachers who struggled to make a living working mainly with children and amateurs. As a letter sent on behalf of (then president) Madame Auguste Chapuis in June 1932 noted, 'artists of great renown and talent feature amongst the active members.'[45] During the *fin de siècle*, such active celebrity members included Marguerite Long, Hélène Fleury, Henriette Renié, Jane Bathori, Lucie Caffaret, and Lily Laskine. In sharp contrast to other concerts they appeared at, for U.F.P.C. events such high-profile performers shared platforms with much less high-profile female musicians. Long's biographer Cecilia Dunoyer has commented on the pianist's eagerness for the U.F.P.C., noting that 'Long was not afraid to encourage competent female initiatives'.[46] Enthusiasm to collaborate with the U.F.P.C. was not limited to high-profile female musicians. Perret and Halbreich have commented on the composer Albéric Magnard's zeal to work with them: 'Magnard was immediately in total agreement with an association whose goals satisfied his social ideals and affirmed his hope to see, through effective means, his feminist theories develop and finally materialise.'[47]

Intriguingly, given her well-known and decidedly chilly later attitudes towards feminism, Nadia Boulanger also participated in the U.F.P.C.'s concerts. Commenting on Nadia Boulanger giving the premier performance of her own *Pièce pour orgue sur des airs populaires flamands* at a U.F.P.C. concert on 22 March 1915, Caroline Potter has observed that 'this connection reveals that Boulanger did occasionally ally herself with women's organisations, though in later years she refused to identify herself with the feminist cause'.[48]

Indeed, the extent to which well-known women musicians – especially performers – engaged with the society (of which they were also often members themselves) – indicates that many more French women musicians actively espoused the contemporary feminist cause than has hitherto been acknowledged.

A Platform for Female Instrumentalists: The Orchestra of the U.F.P.C.

Building upon the success that their Choral Society and chamber-music concerts had achieved and the rapid expansion of their membership during the first few years of their existence, the U.F.P.C. decided to form an orchestra in the autumn of 1911. As Perret and Halbreich have observed:

> By the end of the year 1911, the association was 800 members strong and counted enough qualified members to enable the creation of a symphony orchestra. Around 50 instrumentalists, 52 exactly, were selected. They claimed the desks of the strings and some of the winds but, in order to fill the brass and percussion parts, the reinforcement of robust musicians from the Orchestra Hasselmans proved to be necessary.[49]

I have discussed the activities and reception of the Orchestra of the U.F.P.C. immediately prior to and during the First World War in detail elsewhere.[50] However, it is vital to highlight briefly the importance of this all-woman (pro-feminist) orchestra here. As noted, the Orchestra of the U.F.P.C. was the first all-woman orchestra to be established in France, although numerous all-woman orchestras already existed in other parts of Europe (particularly in the German-speaking regions) as well as North America.[51]

The Orchestra of the U.F.P.C. had several resemblances to other all-woman orchestras. Firstly, the majority of the members of the Orchestra of the U.F.P.C. had received a conservatoire education. Most of the women had trained at the Paris Conservatoire, and many had been awarded a *premier prix* in their discipline. Secondly, the orchestra provided professional female instrumentalists with their own dedicated ensemble. Although women had been making some headway joining French orchestras since the later nineteenth century, they tended to face discrimination (whether unconscious or institutionalised) when auditioning for male-dominated professional orchestras. Thirdly, at a time when few female wind, brass, or percussion players existed – due to the contemporary social taboo over women playing these instruments – the orchestra had to decide whether or not to hire men so that they could form a full symphony orchestra.[52] As Perret and Halbreich indicate in somewhat gendered terms in the quote cited earlier, male wind, brass, and percussion players from the Orchestra Hasselmans joined the Orchestra of the U.F.P.C. to fill these parts.[53]

Whilst the majority of all-woman orchestras active during the *fin de siècle* had women conductors, the Orchestra of the U.F.P.C. did not work with a female director until 1917, when composer Marguerite Canal led the orchestra at a series of wartime charity concerts at the Trocadéro.[54] Although, as was the case with their Choral Society, it could appear puzzling that the Orchestra of the feminist U.F.P.C. chose to work with male conductors rather than drawing a female leader from amongst their membership, they were not reluctant to work with men, particularly in areas – such as conducting – that women often lacked access to. Launay and Perret and Halbreich have suggested that the pianist Charlotte Bérillon acted as 'second chef' for the Orchestra of the U.F.P.C. around 1912.[55] Extant concert announcements and reviews, however, suggest that she did not actually conduct them in public.[56]

The Orchestra of the U.F.P.C.'s first concert, as part of a series of four, took place on 11 December 1911 at the Salle Gaveau.[57] They presented an eclectic programme which brought together Schubert's First Symphony, Corelli's Concerto Grosso in G Minor, Magnard's *Hymne à la justice*, Borodin's 'Polovtsian March' from *Prince Igor*, a selection of *mélodies* by Mozart and Huon de Saint-Quentin (performed by Marianne Nicot-Vauchelet), the prelude to Saint-Saëns's *Andromaque*, an orchestration of Ravel's *Pavane pour une infant défunte*, and Liszt's Piano Concerto in E Flat, performed by Marguerite Long. The gendered nature of the criticism which women musicians tended to receive during the *fin de siècle* was evident in reviews of this first performance. Although reviews tended to be positive overall, as Dunoyer has commented, 'critics consistently expressed their surprise at the high level of the [inaugural] performance'.[58] This is also apparent in the honest review which appeared in *La Liberté*:

> I confess with humility that I was not going without some apprehension . . . This distrust proved unjustified. First, the U.F.P.C. proves with utmost simplicity how easy it is to compose a delightfully new programme simply by using old works that other orchestras neglect to perform. Second, these ladies . . . form the best string section in Paris, except for the Société des Concerts du Conservatoire.[59]

This surprise at the quality of the orchestra was also evident in a review by Pierre Lalo which appeared in *Le Temps*:

> I have to admit that at the first concert . . . I was not without doubts. What was a women's orchestra . . . going to produce while so many male orchestras . . . remain so far from perfect? Those doubts were in vain, and the female instrumentalists gave me . . . a very happy surprise.[60]

These reviews illustrate the incredulity with which many critics first viewed the U.F.P.C., which tended to transform into a genuine admiration and respect for the women after witnessing what they had come together to achieve. The Orchestra of the U.F.P.C. continued to give concerts in Paris in the years directly preceding the First World War, and then continued to give regular charity concerts in aid of the wounded throughout the First World War.[61]

Conclusion: Fighting for Better Conditions for Women Musicians

The U.F.P.C. was one of the largest and most active music societies in *fin-de-siècle* France. Its membership was diverse, counting both hundreds of otherwise unknown music teachers alongside famous concert artists. Given that the U.F.P.C. defined itself as a feminist union, the sheer number of women who joined confirms that musicians were far more involved in feminist politics than has been previously acknowledged. This is intriguing on a number of levels. As discussed earlier, feminists were widely denigrated in *fin-de-siècle* France. Thus, it often took considerable courage for individual women to identify publicly as feminists. As Daubresse commented in *Le Musicien dans la société modern*, the prospect of identifying with unionism – which was also widely vilified – was also often initially intimidating for many middle-class female musicians. That so many women were willing to overcome any reservations that they might have felt at joining a feminist union affirms that they were prepared to band together to demand better professional conditions. Secondly, despite this, it is equally captivating that the U.F.P.C. has been virtually obliterated from both French music history and women's history.

Notes

1. The Union des Femmes Professeurs et Compositeurs de Musique themselves adopted the acronym U.F.P.C.; thus I have chosen to retain it.
2. René Simon, "Informations musicales: Les Concerts: Premier Concert de l'Union des Femmes Professeurs et Compositeurs de Musique," *Gil Blas*, December 13, 1911, 5.
3. Florence Launay has currently given the most attention to the U.F.P.C. The U.F.P.C. is given a short consideration in her monograph, *Les Compositrices en France au XIX siècle* (Paris: Fayard, 2006). She also briefly considers it in her two shorter studies: Florence Launay, "Les Musiciennes: de la pionnière adulée à la concurrente redoutée," *Travail, genre et sociétés*, no. 19 (2008): 41–63; and Florence Launay, "L'éducation musicale des femmes au XIXe siècle en France: Entre art d'agrément, accès officiel à un enseignement supérieur et professionnalisation," in *Genre & Éducation: Former, se former, être formée au féminin*, edited by Bernard Bodinier, Martine Gest, Marie-Françoise Lemmonier-Delpy, and Paul Pasteur (Mont-Saint-Aignon: Publications des universités de Rouen et du Havre, 2009), 203–10.
4. The U.F.P.C. continues to exist, though under the name 'Association Femmes et Musique': Association femmes et musique (accessed August 24, 2022).
5. A number of women musicians' societies had already been established prior to the U.F.P.C. The Association des femmes artistes et professeurs (Association of Women Artists and Professors) was founded by Pauline Thys in 1877; the Association pour l'enseignement du piano pour les femmes (Association of Women Piano Teachers) was founded by Hortense Parent in1893; and the Association mutuelle des femmes artistes de Paris (Paris Mutual Association of Women Artists), which incorporated women painters, sculptors, engravers, writers, and musicians, in 1894. Additionally, the Union des femmes artistes musiciennes (Union of Women Musician Artists) was founded in 1910. Launay, *Les Compositrices en France au XIX siècle*, 156–57.
6. Under the professional name Michel Daubresse, Daubresse published music journalism in a range of journals, including *La Revue musicale*, *Le Courrier musical*, and *Le Guide musical*.
7. Marie Daubresse, *Le Musicien dans la société moderne* (Paris: Le Monde musical, 1914).
8. 'Aiguillonnées par un pressant besoin, les femmes sont devenues professeurs, virtuoses, voire compositeurs. Elles ont appris le piano – quelle quantité sont-elles, ô dieux! – l'harmonium et même le grand orgue, la harpe, le violon, le violoncelle, la guitare, la mandoline etc . . . la contrebasse.' Daubresse, *Le Musicien dans la société moderne*, 80. All translations from the original French, unless otherwise stated, are by the author.
9. 'la musique se révéler une bouée de sauvetage pour les femmes de milieu bourgeois et aristocratique touchées par des revers de fortune.' Florence Launay, "L'éducation musicale des femmes au XIXe siècle en France," 208.
10. 'Musicienne, je pensais d'abord aux musiciennes. Pourquoi, dans la grande famille des femmes artistes, celles-là, ne se tendraient-elles pas la main? . . . [Il y a en France, environ 4.000 femmes vivant de la musique.] Pourquoi ne substitueraient-elles pas, à l'esprit d'animosité qu'à tort ou à raison on leur reproche, un accueil plus amène? . . . Si elles sympathisaient, elles s'aideraient . . . Mais, sous quelle forme? . . . – La forme syndicale fut suggérée. – Mais . . . qu'était-cela? . . . – Il fallait s'en instruire: les musiciennes étant plus familières avec les points sur portée de cinq lignes qu'avec les statuts d'une association professionnelle.' Daubresse, *Le Musicien dans la société moderne*, 99.
11. 'Je sais par expérience, que ce terme: 'syndicat' épouvante littéralement beaucoup de femmes bien élevées; elles le prononcent difficilement; ces trois syllabes sentent les Bourses du Travail, le communiste, le révolutionnaire.' Michel [Marie] Daubresse, "Comment fonder des syndicats de musiciennes," *La Revue musicale SIM* (15 July 1911), 98.
12. '. . . l'association syndicale est celle qui offre à ses membres le plus d'avantages.' Daubresse, "Comment fonder des syndicats de musiciennes," 98.
13. This gender pay gap was not unique to the music profession as, at best, employed women in *fin-de-siècle* France received two-thirds of a male colleague's salary for the same work. Expecting women to undertake unpaid overtime was another common problem. See Susan K. Foley, *Women in France since 1789: The Meanings of Difference* (Basingstoke and New York, Palgrave Macmillan, 2005), 186–88.
14. 'Il n'est pas très difficile de fonder un syndicat; quelques formalités administratives, qu'il est facile de connaître sont suffisantes.' Daubresse, "Comment fonder des syndicats de musiciennes," 100.
15. 'si ces 4000 femmes s'entendaient, s'unissaient, se *syndiquaient*, elles seraient une force.' Daubresse, "Comment fonder des syndicats de musiciennes," 99–100.

16. Simon-Pierre Perret and Harry Halbreich specify that Daubresse acted as president of the U.F.P.C. until January 1907, when she was forced to step down due to ill health. Simon-Pierre Perret and Harry Halbreich, *Albéric Magnard* (Paris: Fayard, 2001), 322. This information is reproduced under the history section of the U.F.P.C.'s website, accessed July 13, 2018, www.ufpc.info/spip.php?article5. However, a letter sent on behalf of Madame Auguste Chapuis to the librarian of the Bibliothèque Marguerite Durand, in response to a request for information about the U.F.P.C., in June 1932, states that Daubresse acted as president until 1919, when she stepped down on grounds of ill health. (The post was then taken over by Chapuis, wife of the composer Auguste Chapuis.) Letter sent on behalf of Madame Auguste Chapuis to the Bibliothèque Marguerite Durand (June 18, 1932); Bibliothèque Marguerite Durand, Paris.
17. The headquarters of the U.F.P.C. were originally situated at 13 rue de l'Arc-de-Triomphe, Paris. Anonymous, "Paris et départements," *Le Ménestrel*, November 10, 1906, 355.
18. Daubresse, *Le Musicien dans la société moderne*, 100.
19. Union des Femmes Professeurs et Compositeur de Musique, *Statutes*; archival copy held at the Bibliothèque Marguerite Durand, Paris.
20. '1° De faciliter, par tous les moyens dont il peut disposer, l'exercice de la profession des syndiquées; 2° De prendre l'initiative de tout ce qui peut contribuer au bien-être moral, matériel et intellectuel de ses membres; 3° De constituer une caisse de prêts gratuits en cas de maladie, d'accident, de repos forcé et de retraite pour les syndiquées; 4° La défense des intérêts généraux professionnels de toutes ses adhérentes.' Union des Femmes Professeurs et Compositeur de Musique, *Statutes*, 3.
21. Union des Femmes Professeurs et Compositeur de Musique, *Statutes*, 4.
22. The executive manager took special responsibility for advertising and responding to offers of employment, communicating with the membership, and undertaking all the processes that were necessary to the smooth running of the society.
23. All members in good standing were entitled to vote. Union des Femmes Professeurs et Compositeur de Musique, *Statutes*, 7–9.
24. 'Toute discussion politique ou religieuse est interdite au cours des réunions.' Union des Femmes Professeurs et Compositeur de Musique, *Statutes*, 10. The first law requiring the separation of state and church in France, and declaring France to be a secular Republic, came into force in 1905.
25. 'Parmi les nombreuses associations professionnelles qui se fondent chaque jour, on nous permettra de signaler l'une des plus utiles assurément et des plus intéressantes, l'Union des femmes professeurs, et compositeurs de musique, qui date . . . de 1904 et qui est en plein fonctionnement. Il serait presque inutile d'indiquer le but de ce groupement artistique. On sait quelle est la situation délicate et difficile de la femme dans la société actuelle. Plus délicate peut-être et plus difficile que toute autre est celle de la femme artiste . . . L'idée de l'association . . . est due à quelques femmes artistes dont l'initiative s'est appuyée sur l'axiome connu: L'union fait la force. C'est par cette union, et par l'effort collectif qu'elle amènera naturellement, qu'elles ont conçu l'espoir d'améliorer progressivement la situation des femmes musiciennes. Là où une volonté unique, reste impuissante, plusieurs volontés réunie peuvent triompher de beaucoup de difficultés, aplanir beaucoup d'obstacles.' The article concluded by reminding readers that the U.F.P.C. was not rich, and beseeching 'friends of the society' ('amis de l'association') to send donations to their headquarters. Anonymous, "Paris et départements," 355.
26. 'Il semblait scandaleux que des étudiantes qui ne pouvaient envisager de carrière à l'orchestre prennent la place d'étudiants pour lesquels les études devaient déboucher sur une activité de musicien d'orchestre.' Florence Launay, "Les Musiciennes: de la pionnière adulée à la concurrente redoutée," 52.
27. 'Actuellement, les femmes instrumentistes, devenues chaque jour plus nombreuses, cherchent l'utilisation de leur talent ailleurs que dans le professorat . . . elles regardent du côté des orchestres de concert et même de théâtre.' Daubresse, *Le Musicien dans la société moderne*, 80–1.
28. For *Le Musicien dans la société moderne*, Daubresse interviewed a number of prominent male conductors about their views on female instrumentalists. Interestingly, both André Messager and Vincent d'Indy insisted that women should be paid the same salaries as men and lamented the fact that they often were not. Daubresse, *Le Musicien dans la société moderne*, 82 and 84.
29. For an authoritative study of women composers in nineteenth-century France, see Launay, *Les Compositrices en France au XIXe siècle*.
30. Annegret Fauser, "*La Guerre en dentelles*: Women and the Prix de Rome in French Cultural Politics," *Journal of the American Musicological Society* 51 (1998): 83–129.
31. Mary Louise Roberts, *Disruptive Acts: The New Woman in Fin-de-Siècle France* (Chicago, IL and London: University of Chicago Press, 2002), 3.

32. Roberts, *Disruptive Acts: The New Woman in Fin-de-Siècle France*, 6.
33. Ibid.
34. For a detailed study of the development of feminism in later nineteenth-century France, see Steven C. Hause with Anne R. Kenney, *Women's Suffrage and Social Politics in the French Third Republic* (Princeton, NJ: Princeton University Press, 1984).
35. Laura Hamer, *Female Composers, Conductors, Performers: Musiciennes of Interwar France, 1919–1939* (Abingdon and New York: Routledge, 2018), 17–18.
36. 'Correspondant à un réel besoin, l'Union connaît un développement spectaculaire.' Perret and Halbreich, *Albéric Magnard*, 323.
37. Daubresse, *Le Musicien dans la société moderne*, 103–05.
38. '. . . échangent des projets: organisation de cours, de séances musicales; elles prennent des rendez-vous, conviennent des heures de répétitions.' Daubresse, *Le Musicien dans la société moderne*, 102.
39. 'Une ambiance de chaude sympathie et de franche cordialité les anime, les enveloppe et certaines d'entre elles, venues fatiguées et tristes, s'en vont plus légères, un peu consolées, espérant dans les jours meilleurs que leur assurera leur fraternelle union.' Daubresse, *Le Musicien dans la société moderne*, 102–03.
40. In her *Le Musicien dans la société moderne*, Daubresse specified that Stoltz voluntarily devoted a lot of his time (in old age) to working with the U.F.P.C.'s Choral Society. Daubresse, *Le Musicien dans la société moderne*, 103.
41. 'Le concert organisé par l'Union des femmes Professeurs et compositeurs de musique a remporté, grâce à l'activité inlassable de la présidente, Mme Daubresse, un fort beau succès; au programme, des chœurs de Chaminade, de Pierné, par la chorale de l'Union, composée exclusivement des dames sociétaires, sous l'habile direction de l'excellent musicien, M. Bernard; particulièrement fêtée, Mlle Hélène de Fleury, prix de Rome, dans ses œuvres pour piano; Mlle Marguerite Achard, la harpiste si goûtée, fort applaudie', Anonymous, "Courrier de la Semaine," *Le Monde artiste*, March 11, 1906, 158.
42. The statutes of the U.F.P.C. did not specify that membership was restricted to those of French nationality. At least one Swiss musician (the composer-harpsichordist Marguerite Rœsgen-Champion) became a prominent member after the First World War.
43. 'Cette union, exclusivement française, a pour but de venir en aide aux femmes professeurs ou exécutantes en leur procurant des leçons ou des concerts. Elle se propose aussi d'organiser des concerts populaires à prix réduits, en donnant ainsi aux femmes musiciennes le moyen de se faire entendre et d'offrir aux classes populaires l'occasion d'écouter de la bonne musique.' Anonymous, "Union des Femmes Professeurs et Compositeurs de Musique," *Le tout-théâtre: les spectacles en France et à l'étranger: auteurs, compositeurs, actrices, programmes* (1905): 186.
44. Organising cheap concerts of classical music for working-class audiences was not unique to the U.F.P.C., but fits into a much broader contemporary trend of musicians and musical societies offering such concerts, as a form of social justice. For a detailed consideration of the social role of music in Third Republic France, see Jann Pasler, *Composing the Citizen: Music as Public Utility in Third Republic France* (Berkeley; London: University of California Press, 2009).
45. 'Parmi ses membres actifs figurant des artistes de haute notoriété et du plus sur talent.' Letter sent on behalf of Madame Auguste Chapuis to the Bibliothèque Marguerite Durand (18 June 1932); Bibliothèque Marguerite Durand, Paris.
46. Cecilia Dunoyer, *Marguerite Long: A Life in French Music* (Bloomington and Indianapolis: Indiana University Press, 1993), 55. Long's support of the U.F.P.C.'s goals are not hard to understand, given that she had herself personally experienced institutionalized discrimination at the Paris Conservatoire. She had been passed over for promotion to teach one of the advanced piano classes on account of her sex twice (in both 1907 and 1913). Long eventually became the first woman to teach an advanced performance class at the Paris Conservatoire in 1920.
47. 'Magnard est d'emblée totale communion avec une association dont les objectifs comblent son idéal social et fortifient son espoir de voir, grâce à des moyens efficaces, ses thèses féministes se développer et se concrétiser enfin.' Perret and Halbreich, *Albéric Magnard*, 323.
48. Caroline Potter, *Nadia and Lili Boulanger* (Aldershot: Ashgate, 2006), 78. Léonie Rosenstiel has indicated that Nadia Boulanger also participated in concerts organisés by the Ligue Française pour le Droit des Femmes (another French feminist society) during the early months of 1921. Léonie Rosenstiel, *Nadia Boulanger: A Life in Music* (New York and London: W.W. Norton & Company, 1982), 152. Commenting on her later career, Kimberly A. Francis has suggested that 'Boulanger denounced left-wing feminism and supported instead French Catholic feminist thought.' Kimberly

A. Francis, *"Teaching Stravinsky: Nadia Boulanger and the Consecration of a Modernist Icon* (Oxford and New York: Oxford University Press, 2015), 68.

49. 'À la fin de l'année 1911, l'association est forte de huit cents adhérents et compte suffisamment d'éléments qualifiés pour permettre la création d'un orchestre symphonique. Une cinquantaine d'instrumentistes, cinquante-deux exactement, sont choisies. Elles s'approprient les pupitres des cordes et quelques-uns des bois mais, afin de pouvoir les postes des cuivres et des percussions, le renfort de robustes musiciens de l'orchestre Hasselmans se révèle nécessaire.' Perret and Halbreich, *Albéric Magnard*, 323.
50. Hamer, *Female Composers, Conductors, Performers: Musiciennes of Interwar France, 1919–1939*, 163–68.
51. On the development of all-woman orchestras and the emergence of women conductors, see J. Michele Edwards, "Women on the Podium," in *The Cambridge Companion to Conducting*, edited by José Bowen (Cambridge: Cambridge University Press, 2003), 220–36; and Carol Neuls-Bates, "Women Orchestras in the United States, 1925–45," in *Women Making Music: The Western Art Tradition, 1150–1950*, edited by Jane Bowers and Judith Tick (Urbana and Chicago: University of Illinois Press, 1986), 349–69.
52. The slightly later all-woman French orchestra, the Orchestre féminin de Paris (founded by violinist and conductor Jane Evrard in Paris in 1930), decided to become a string orchestra precisely because of the difficulty over finding professional female wind and brass players (although the composer Yvonne Desportes occasionally joined the ensemble on percussion). On the Orchestre féminin de Paris, see Laura Hamer, "On the Conductor's Podium: Jane Evrard and the Orchestre féminin de Paris," *The Musical Times* 152, no. 1916 (Autumn 2011): 81–100; and Hamer, *Female Composers, Conductors, Performers: Musiciennes of Interwar France, 1919–1939*, 168–75.
53. As quoted, Perret and Halbreich have claimed that the Orchestra of the U.F.P.C. did include a few female wind-players. Perret and Halbreich, *Albéric Magnard*, 323. A number of contemporary critics, however, stated that all of the wind parts (along with those of the brass and percussion) were taken by men. See, in particular, René Simon, "Informations musicales: Les Concerts: Premier Concert de l'Union des Femmes Professeurs et Compositeurs de Musique," 5; and Pierre Lalo, "La Musique," *Le Temps*, March 5, 1912, 3.
54. For a discussion of Canal's work conducting the Orchestra of the U.F.P.C. during the First World War, see Laura Hamer, "Paths to the Podium," Review-Article of Jeanice Brooks, *The Musical Work of Nadia Boulanger: Performing Past and Future Between the Wars* (Cambridge: Cambridge University Press, 2013); for *Journal of the Royal Musical Association* 141, no. 2 (Autumn 2016): 501–03.
55. Florence Launay, "Les Musiciennes: de la pionnière adulée à la concurrente redoutée," 55; and Perret and Halbreich, *Albéric Magnard*, 324.
56. On the emergence of women conductors in fin-de-siècle France, see Laura Hamer, *Musiciennes of Interwar France, 1919–1939*, 161–63.
57. Anonymous, "L'orchestre de l'Union des Femmes Professeurs et Compositeurs de Musique," *Le Ménestrel*, December 9, 1911, 391.
58. Dunoyer, *Marguerite Long: A Life in French Music*, 55.
59. Anonymous, *La Liberté*, December 19, 1911; cited from Dunoyer, *Marguerite Long: A Life in French Music*, 55–56. Translation by Dunoyer.
60. 'Je dois convenir qu'au premier concert donné par la société je n'étais point dépourvu de crainte. Qu'allait produire un orchestre de femmes . . . lorsque tant d'orchestres d'hommes . . . demeurent fort loin de la perfection? Cette crainte était vaine, et les instrumentistes féminins m'ont causé . . . une fort heureuse surprise.' Pierre Lalo, "La Musique," *Le Temps*, March 5, 1912, 3.
61. The U.F.P.C. also continued to arrange regular concerts after World War One. For a discussion of their activities during the interwar period, see Hamer, *Female Composers, Conductors, Performers: Musiciennes of Interwar France, 1919–1939*, 17–20.

Bibliography

Archival Sources

Fonds U.F.P.C. Bibliothèque Marguerite Durand, Paris (France).

Published Sources

Anonymous. "Union des Femmes Professeurs et Compositeurs de Musique." *Le tout-théâtre: les spectacles en France et à l'étranger: auteurs, compositeurs, actrices, programmes* (1905): 186.
Anonymous. "Courrier de la Semaine." *Le Monde artiste*, March 11, 1906a, 158.
Anonymous. "Paris et départements." *Le Ménestrel*, November 10, 1906b, 355.
Anonymous. "L'orchestre de l'Union des Femmes Professeurs et Compositeurs de Musique." *Le Ménestrel*, December 9, 1911, 391.
Daubresse, Michel [Marie]. "Comment fonder des syndicats de musiciennes." *La Revue musicale SIM*, July 15, 1911, 98.
_____. *Le Musicien dans la société moderne*. Paris: Le Monde musical, 1914.
Dunoyer, Cecilia. *Marguerite Long: A Life in French Music*. Bloomington and Indianapolis: Indiana University Press, 1993.
Edwards, J. Michele. "Women on the Podium." In *The Cambridge Companion to Conducting*, edited by José Bowen, 220–36. Cambridge: Cambridge University Press, 2003.
Fauser, Annegret. "*La Guerre en dentelles*: Women and the Prix de Rome in French Cultural Politics." *Journal of the American Musicological Society* 51 (1998): 83–129.
Foley, Susan K. *Women in France since 1789: The Meanings of Difference*. Basingstoke and New York: Palgrave Macmillan, 2005.
Francis, Kimberly A. *Teaching Stravinsky: Nadia Boulanger and the Consecration of a Modernist Icon*. Oxford and New York: Oxford University Press.
Hamer, Laura. "On the Conductor's Podium: Jane Evrard and the Orchestre féminin de Paris." *The Musical Times* 152, No. 1916 (Autumn 2011): 81–100.
_____. "Paths to the Podium." Review-Article of Jeanice Brooks, *The Musical Work of Nadia Boulanger: Performing Past and Future Between the Wars* (Cambridge: Cambridge University Press, 2013); for *Journal of the Royal Musical Association* 141, No. 2 (Autumn 2016): 501–3.
_____. *Female Composer, Conductors, Performers: Musiciennes of Interwar France, 1919–1939*. Abingdon and New York: Routledge, 2018.
Hause, Steven C., with Anne R. Kenney. *Women's Suffrage and Social Politics in the French Third Republic*. Princeton, NJ: Princeton University Press, 1984.
Lalo, Pierre. "La Musique." *Le Temps*, March 5, 1912, 3.
Launay, Florence. *Les Compositrices en France au XIX siècle*. Paris: Fayard, 2006.
_____. "Les Musiciennes: de la pionnière adulée à la concurrente redoutée." *Travail, genre et sociétés*, No. 19 (2008): 41–63.
_____. "L'éducation musicale des femmes au XIXe siècle en France: Entre art d'agrément, accès officiel à un enseignement supérieur et professionnalisation." In *Genre & Éducation: Former, se former, être formée au féminin*, edited by Bernard Bodinier et al., 203–10. Mont-Saint-Aignon: Publications des universités de Rouen et du Havre, 2009.
Neuls-Bates, Carol. "Women Orchestras in the United States, 1925–45." In *Women Making Music: The Western Art Tradition, 1150–1950*, edited by Jane Bowers and Judith Tick, 349–69. Urbana and Chicago: University of Illinois Press, 1986.
Pasler, Jann. *Composing the Citizen: Music as Public Utility in Third Republic France*. Berkeley, CA and London: University of California Press, 2009.
Perret, Simon-Pierre, and Harry Halbreich. *Albéric Magnard*. Paris: Fayard, 2001.
Potter, Caroline. *Nadia and Lili Boulanger*. Aldershot: Ashgate, 2006.
Roberts, Mary Louise. *Disruptive Acts: The New Woman in Fin-de-Siècle France*. Chicago, IL and London: University of Chicago Press, 2002.
Rosenstiel, Léonie. *Nadia Boulanger: A Life in Music*. New York and London: W.W. Norton & Company, 1982.
Simon, René. "Informations musicales: Les Concerts: Premier Concert de l'Union des Femmes Professeurs et Compositeurs de Musique." *Gil Blas*, December 13, 1911, 5.

8

THE FORGOTTEN WOMAN

Joan Trimble (1915–2000) and the Canon of Twentieth-Century Irish Art Song

Orla Shannon

Joan Trimble (1915–2000) was born into a family of Anglo-Irish roots to parents Marie Dowse (1887–1968) and William Egbert Trimble (1882–1967).[1] Both parents had musical backgrounds: her mother was an accomplished violinist from South Dublin and her father was a bass-baritone and collector of folk songs from Co. Fermanagh (in what is now Northern Ireland).[2] The composer noted the encouraging natures of her parents in her memoirs: 'They didn't mind what we played as long as we *did* play'.[3]

Following in her mother's footsteps, the teenage Trimble travelled to Dublin for violin and piano lessons at the Royal Irish Academy of Music (hereafter RIAM) with her sister, Valerie, who studied cello and piano.[4] Her professor of composition at the time, John Larchet (1884–1967), had an interest in Irish traditional music, which became a distinct feature of her writing style. Idiomatic references to this genre enveloped the critical reception of her compositional output to the extent that she attempted to redefine her musical identity, albeit unsuccessfully, with *Sonatina*, a work for two pianos (1940): 'The sonatina, I had hoped, would turn out to be some-thing new. Formalised, dissonant as far as possible, uncompromising. But it did not quite work out that way!'[5]

Trimble's third-level education commenced in 1932 with an academic scholarship to study at Trinity College Dublin (hereafter TCD). Here, she graduated with a Bachelor of Arts degree in 1936 and a year later became the first woman to obtain a BMus degree from the university.[6] She completed the latter whilst studying at the Royal College of Music (hereafter RCM) in London for further musical training. Her decision to emigrate had been influenced by renowned tenor Count John McCormack, who had invited her to perform the piano solos as part of his farewell tour of Ireland in 1936.[7]

As a student at the RCM, Trimble received compositional training from Herbert Howells and Ralph Vaughan Williams, and went on to win the Sullivan Prize for composition and the Cobbett Prize for her chamber work, *Phantasy Trio* (1940). She also took piano lessons with Arthur Benjamin, who encouraged the pursuit of a career as a piano duettist with her sister. This led to a busy career of concert performances, touring, and frequent broadcasts on the BBC, including lunchtime concerts at the National Gallery in London during the Second World War and weekly broadcasts with the BBC Concert Orchestra as part of the popular series, 'Tuesday Serenade', between the 1940s and 1950s. Arguably, her most significant achievement took place in 1957 when she became the first woman to be commissioned by the BBC to write an opera for television called *Blind Raftery*. She returned to the RCM to pursue a longstanding post as professor of accompaniment and general musicianship which she held from 1959 to 1977.

The composer enjoyed a renewed appreciation for her music in her later years. She was awarded an honorary Masters from Queen's University, Belfast in 1983, an honorary fellowship from the RIAM in 1985, and was later appointed the vice president of the RIAM in 1997. A further resurgence of interest in her compositional output emerged following a coincidental unearthing of her *Ulster Airs* by a researcher at the BBC Northern Ireland Archives in preparation for a St. Patrick's Day concert in 1989.[8] The rediscovery prompted a revival for the composer with commissions offered by BBC Northern Ireland for her 75th and 80th birthdays respectively, as well as a letter from RTÉ to compose a large-scale orchestral work in 1998.[9]

Despite these achievements, Trimble's music is little performed today and commentary on her musical identity or analytical studies of her compositions are exceedingly limited, warranting scholarly attention.[10] Given the marginal extent to which her musical narrative is represented in discourse, it is clear that Trimble's posthumous reception does not reflect the recognition that she gained during her lifetime. This realisation that her later reception did not match that of the early years of her career was also stated in her obituary announcement: 'The best of her music, attractive and always beautifully crafted, deserves the appreciation that she won early in her career.'[11]

This opening contextualisation of Trimble's life and background forms the basis from which her musical legacy is reappraised. This chapter assesses her critical reception as derived from primary source material and posits that her relatively small output, compared to that of her male counterparts, has been detrimental to her representation in the canon of twentieth-century art music. Attention is then focused upon her early composition, 'Girl's Song' (1938). Through a detailed analysis of this song, it is argued that a re-examination of Trimble, with a view to including her within the canon, is timely.

Obstacles

The previous biographical overview outlines the success Trimble attained both as a composer and a performer throughout her life and highlights that her compositional oeuvre and achievements were primarily concentrated in her early years. It also sheds light on a revival in her later years that did not prevail posthumously. In this section, four factors are proposed to have impeded the development of Trimble's compositional career and subsequent posthumous reception: identity, the Second World War, gender, and family commitments. Each factor is assessed with consideration for the cultural attitudes, gender-normative roles, and socio-political upheavals of the twentieth century in Ireland and the UK.

The first factor explores the complex relationship between politics and identity with regards to nationalist and unionist ideologies at the turn of the twentieth century in Ireland. For the most part, Trimble's corpus of work was published by companies in London or transpired as a result of UK-based commissions. In fact, her music has yet to be published in Ireland.[12] It is, therefore, important to evaluate the appreciation of her critical reception within the context of her island of birth, probing questions as to why demand for her music was tenuous and performances of her music seldom during her early career.

The political circumstances and ensuing rise of patriotic outlooks during a period of post-colonial rule in the first half of the twentieth century in Ireland gave way to a more hostile reception for art music. Axel Klein contextualises these cultural nuances and surmises that, although select Protestant names – Yeats, Beckett, Wilde – were reclaimed as Irish in poetry, this was not the case in music.[13] Several key developments attest to the emergence of such an 'art-ethnic' divide regarding the appreciation of Irish traditional music compared with Irish art music.

One such example is the establishment of the Dublin *Feis Ceoil* in 1897 by Annie Patterson (1869–1934). Although it was a stimulus for musical studies in Ireland, its stated aims highlighted a growing stylistic divergence: 'to promote the study of Irish music, to encourage the cultivation of music in Ireland, to hold an annual music festival and to collect and publish Irish traditional music'.[14] The influence of the Gaelic Revival also strengthened this evolving perception of a national sound.[15] It brought about a renewal of interest in historical Irish texts and folklore that prompted a reappraisal of the definition of 'Irish music'.[16] For *Taoiseach* (Prime Minister) Eamonn de Valera in 1933, this definition constituted compositional practices of 'the Celtic nations' that conformed to the characteristics of Irish traditional music:

> Ireland's music is of singular beauty . . . It stands pre-eminent amongst the music of the Celtic nations. It is characterised by perfection of form and variety of melodic content . . . Equal in rhythmic variety are our dance tunes – spirited and energetic, in keeping with the temperament of our people.[17]

These brief examples demonstrate the cultural weight placed on an identity of pan-Celticism, as well as the restrictive standards to which a composer had to conform to be appreciated as *Irish*. It is important to consider the trajectory of Trimble's compositional career within this historical context. Although born in Northern Ireland, the perception of her identity as an authentically *Irish* composer was ambivalent for three reasons: to further her musical education she had emigrated to England in search of reputable publishers and recording companies and settled in London; she held British citizenship following the partition of Ireland in 1921; and she was born to parents from both sides of the border.[18]

However, Trimble's compositional voice largely encompassed traits borrowed from Irish traditional music despite living in London during her most active compositional period. While she maintained this awareness of her Irish heritage in her creative output, it may be argued that her identity did not conform to such cultural perceptions of *Irishness* – exacerbated by the fact that she no longer resided in the country – and thus inhibited a full acceptance of her music in Ireland. This postulation was also raised in an Irish newspaper article in her later years:

> It was of Ireland and was Irish, but there were too many hyphens there for simplicity, too much of a sense of separateness from the majority of the people on this island, too great a sense of kinship with the people of Britain and the world, for normal categories of identity to apply.[19]

While these considerations contextualise the complexities surrounding the reception of Trimble's music in Ireland, it is also important to note briefly the positive impact of her identity as a British citizen which enabled the composition of select works. These included *Phantasy Trio* for the Cobbett competition at the RCM, which required entrants to hold British citizenship, as well as *Érin go Bragh*, and *Blind Raftery*, both of which were commissions by the BBC open exclusively to British citizens. In this way, Trimble's identity could be understood as paradoxical, given that she both conformed to and diverged from temporal understandings of British and Irish nationality to varying degrees, which in turn resulted in mixed opportunities for the dissemination of her music.

The Second World War also affected Trimble's compositional career. In the lead-up to the war, the composer noted that the quantity of her compositional output had already been compromised due to 'part-time work of all kinds outside the RCM'.[20] During the final year of her degree at the conservatoire, for example, her studies were disrupted by the London Blitz (1940–41), and her time to compose further hampered when she and her sister, Valerie, took on full-time positions as voluntary nurses with the Red Cross in response to the bombing.[21] As noted by the composer, the role involved 'An eight-hour shift, six days a week, always on call.'[22] Consequently, Trimble rarely composed without the catalyst of a commission.

From the post-war years emerged a wave of new European musical trends, as evidenced by a rise in harmonic experimentation. Select examples of such procedures included atonality, increased dissonance, and serialism. By comparison, Trimble's compositional voice remained reliant on a distinctive blend of tropes borrowed from Irish traditional music, neo-classicism, and French impressionism. She noted: 'I could never conform to the new scene and there was no room in it for me or anyone else like me'.[23] This quote and her aforementioned work for two pianos, *Sonatina*, reflect her awareness of these stylistic developments and her incapacity to incorporate such radicalised compositional procedures into her music. When situated within the context of prevailing trends, one may question the extent to which these circumstances account for the diminished quantity in Trimble's output following the Second World War and, by consequence, whether her innate compositional style proved detrimental to her critical reception.

A third factor to have impacted the trajectory of her compositional career is gender, most notably in relation to her role as a wife and mother. Trimble once stated in article that 'composition is a man's world' and turned to the words of H.G. Wells to describe the impact that gender had played on her compositional career: 'No one expects [a man] to deal with the next meal, or the child's measles'.[24] In 1942, Trimble married an English medical practitioner, Dr John Greenwood Gant (1917–2000), whose busy career restricted her time for compositional engagements. It became incumbent upon her to carry out the domestic tasks of the household in London and to raise their three children with little to no help: 'I had a large house to run, a husband and children to look after – the minimum of help – and a busy professional career. It was getting harder than ever to find time to write music.'[25]

Alongside these multitudinous domestic obligations, Trimble maintained a busy performance career writing and arranging music as a touring piano duo with her sister. She additionally held secretarial duties answering the phone for her husband's practice, further reducing her time to compose. She stated: 'If I had married another musician, as my sister did, instead of a medical doctor, life could have been much simpler, and working conditions less chaotic.'[26]

The chaotic conditions to which she refers apply to the composition of her opera for television, *Blind Raftery* (1957). The thirty-year hiatus following this opera affirms the extent to which the demands of mother- and wifehood hampered her output. In fact, she produced only two works during this period: a duet for two harps, *Introduction and Air* (1969), and a chamber work for wind quintet, *Three Divisions* (1990). Arguably, this gap in her compositional career may be understood as a cultural by-product arising from the societal and patriarchal position of women in twentieth-century Britain and Ireland.

The final factor is the composer's commitments to her family newspaper, *The Impartial Reporter*. Following her father's death in 1967, she inherited this newspaper, as well as a new role as its proprietor, hindering her time for composition. Her responsibilities included bi-weekly commutes from London to Enniskillen to attend editorial meetings at a time when the Northern Ireland Conflict (1968–98) was beginning to escalate.[27] As per its title, the newspaper was renowned for reporting events in a tone devoid of political leanings:

> Regardless of the frowns of the party and the smiles of power, we shall state our own convictions . . . we shall defend the Protestant when we consider him in the right, and the Roman Catholic may expect similar treatment.[28]

The composer's initial attempts to run the paper whilst living in London proved too difficult. This resulted in her permanent return to the family home residence in Enniskillen, Co. Fermanagh in 1977, as well as her subsequent resignation from her professorship at the RCM. During this time, she also acted as primary carer for her husband, who had developed an incapacitating neurological disease. As a direct consequence, Trimble lacked the time to expand upon the strides she made in her early compositional career. These commitments further contextualise the circumstances that contributed to the composer's limited creative output in later life.

Leading such a busy life greatly affected Trimble's compositional career to the extent that she described herself as an 'occasional' composer.[29] The aforementioned factors shed light not only on the challenges faced by the composer but additionally on a culture which facilitated the emergence of gender disparity within the canon of art song today. This contextualisation rationalises the chapter's reappraisal of Trimble's compositional identity as well as the need for increased critical retrospection on the representation of women composers within musicological discourse more generally. Although limited in quantity, Trimble's music offers unique and innovative stylistic developments within the genre of art song, as argued through the following musicological analysis.

Analysis

The critical examination in this section aims to contribute to the growing body of scholarship committed to analysis of music by women composers. Its analytical study of 'Girl's Song' serves to reappraise one of Trimble's earliest vocal works with special consideration for her text-setting techniques.[30] Central to the evaluation is a comparison between the composer's setting of the vocal work and that of her first teacher at the RCM, Herbert Howells.[31] While myriad compositional features are examined, the analysis especially focuses on musico-poetic associations, offering new findings to the existing literature. From this analysis, the idiosyncratic nuances of Trimble's writing style as a composer of art song are uncovered, and a new appreciation for her music realised.

Trimble's first three compositions were written between the ages of sixteen and seventeen whilst studying under Howells at the RCM. She recalled: 'I asked if I could write a song because words are so important to me and I love poetry.'[32] Together they formed an untitled song trilogy for mezzo-soprano and piano that was premiered at the RCM on 1 March 1938 in a performance by Diana Herring with accompaniment by the composer.[33] The first, 'My Grief on the Sea' (1937), was published upon its second draft by Winthrop Rogers along with the second, 'Green Rain' (1937). Although 'Girl's Song' was written to complete the trilogy, it still awaits publication. A probable explanation for its unpublished status may be attributed to its absence from the Dublin *Feis Ceoil*,[34] where the first two works initially gained propitious adjudication and exposure at this acclaimed platform in 1938.[35]

For 'Girl's Song', Trimble turns to the poetry of Wilfrid Wilson Gibson (1878–1962), a British poet from Hexhem, Northumberland whose artistic reputation attained the epithet 'The People's Poet'.[36] Her choice of text was likely inspired by her teacher Howells, who also set the text as the final song of his collection, Four Songs Op. 22 (1916), for female voice and piano. Identically titled, the poem of 1914 was first published in an issue of *New Numbers* magazine. It showcases the poet's associations with folk anecdotes and narrative text in its depiction of a pastoral scene. The central character, doubling as narrator, is a young woman who spectates as pigs are brought to the fair and, through a humorous *volta*, reveals that her interest lies not with the pigs, but rather in the man steering the cart.[37]

Structurally, the poem is two stanzas in length, comprising eight lines respectively. Each contains a definite rhyme scheme of alternate and single rhyme: abccabab abccabab. Trimble reflects this poetic layout through regular piano interludes which are interjected every four lines to mirror the patterns in the rhyme scheme. Although largely faithful to the original words, the setting contrasts 'My Grief on the Sea' and 'Green Rain' in its inclusion of two textual deviations. The first explicitly imitates Howells' setting in its repetition of the word 'hiding' at bb. 17–18 (Example 8.1) which accentuates the humorous actions of the woman as described in the poem. Trimble elevates this whimsical characterisation through use of a higher *tessitura* on the repeated word (e"), use of melisma within an otherwise syllabic phrase, and a rising dynamic.

The second textual deviation occurs at bb. 39–40 (Example 8.2) and closely imitates Howells' setting in its dramatic portrayal of the concluding clause at bb. 46–48 (Example 8.3). In both settings, the word 'throbbing' appears three times in succession, generating a sense of momentum towards the climatic final word, 'heart'. The development of dynamics to *forte* and position of this word as the apex of each phrase – g" in Trimble's setting and an e" appoggiatura onto d" in Howells' setting – demonstrate the considerable extent to which the excerpts compare in their vivacious settings of the climax.

Additional similarities may be seen when comparing the rhythm in the vocal line of these same examples. Although Trimble's syncopated ascending motif contrasts the *tenuto*-marked

Example 8.1 Joan Trimble, 'Girl's Song', bb. 17–18.
Source: Courtesy of the National Library of Ireland.

Example 8.2 Joan Trimble, 'Girl's Song', bb. 39–41.
Source: Courtesy of the National Library of Ireland.

Example 8.3 Herbert Howells, 'Girl's Song', bb. 46–48.
Source: Reproduced with permission of the Herbert Howells Trust.

repeated quavers in Howells' setting, her phrase includes an array of characteristic rhythmic conventions borrowed from her teacher's excerpt: the subdivisions of a halfway point within measures, the placement of the first syllable on stronger downbeats, and motivic repetition. Given the time signature difference of simple quadruple and simple duple meter, Trimble's treatment of this textual deviation may be construed as a reimagined version of her teacher's setting in augmentation. Despite these connections, her setting demonstrates originality in its employment of a syncopated scotch snap rhythm and rising melodic contour to symbolise the woman's beating heart in the form of word painting. In this way, Trimble evokes a more expressively nuanced representation of the concluding lines and, by consequence, offers an elevated adaption of Howells' setting.

Trimble's faithfulness to the poetic metre is the next feature assessed. The poem is primarily composed of stanzas in iambic trimeter, with intermittent anapaestic foot, and deviations to tetrameter, utilised as a means of illuminating the two instances of single rhyme (lines 3–4 and 11–12).[38] From the onset, the text-setting parallels the iambic trimeter in the opening line:

⏑ ´ ⏑ ´ ⏑ ´ ⏑
I saw three black pigs riding

Trimble's sensitivity to the poetic metre is evident in the placement of stressed syllables on the stronger beats of the bars. This conventional approach to the text-setting heightens the unaccented–accented syllabic pattern, as Example 8.4 illustrates.

Another example may be seen at bb. 12–16. Here, Trimble draws on specific rhythmic values to parallel a temporary shift to the anapaest feet at the beginning of lines 5 and 6:

⏑ ⏑ ´ ⏑ ´ ⏑ ´ ⏑
But it wasn't black pigs riding

⏑ ⏑ ´ ⏑ ´ ⏑ ´
In a gay and gaudy cart

In both lines, she employs quavers as anacruses to denote the two unstressed syllables ('but it' and 'in a') which effectively pre-empt the downbeats upon which the accented syllables

The Forgotten Woman

Example 8.4 Joan Trimble, 'Girl's Song', bb. 3–5.
Source: Courtesy of the National Library of Ireland.

of the anapaests fall ('was'-nt' and 'gay'). The similarities between these lines function as a form of emphasis to enhance this change in poetic metre, as displayed by the paradigmatic illustration (Example 8.5). The example also exhibits Trimble's sensitivity to the literary effect of alliteration between 'gay' and 'gaudy', as displayed by the pitch repetition on g'♯ at b. 15. These compositional devices demonstrate the exhaustive degree to which the composer places the intelligibility of the text to the fore of her setting.

Example 8.6 (bb. 18–20) offers a contrasting example where the text-setting and poetic metre do not align. In this excerpt, a rhythmic motif of a quaver followed by a dotted crotchet contradicts the structure of the anapaest, 'flutter'. The ensuing effect of syncopation

Example 8.5 Joan Trimble, 'Girl's Song', bb. 12–16.
Source: Courtesy of the National Library of Ireland.

Example 8.6 Joan Trimble, 'Girl's Song', bb. 18–21.
Source: Courtesy of the National Library of Ireland.

deliberately disrupts the poetic metre, representative of the word's meaning. Trimble accentuates the symbolism through use of the rising piano motif which follows, and hence establishes a compelling example of unification between the music and text.

In turning to Howells' setting, the same rhythmic idiosyncrasy may be seen in diminution as a semi-quaver and dotted quaver (b. 22, Example 8.7). It highlights both composers' prioritisation of the meaning of the word over the poetic metre, as well as the extent to which Trimble drew influence from her teacher. Moreover, the reliance on his treatment of the rhythm, albeit brief, could offer insight as to why Trimble's work was never published. This is persuasive in noting that both Howells' setting and the first two songs of her trilogy were published by Winthrop Rogers. While speculative, it is also important to balance this consideration against the fact that Trimble was a teenager with student status at the time of its composition, thus negating such postulated perceptions of the work lacking originality.

In fact, there are many examples where Trimble's text-setting is innovative in its treatment of Gibson's poetry. One such may be seen at b.27, where her use of pitch repetition in the vocal line effectively elevates the literary technique of onomatopoeia. In setting four rhythmically equal quavers as a repeated a' and c", Trimble illuminates the binary architecture of the phrase and strengthens the sound associations of the words 'jolting, jingling' in a vocal style indicative of declamation. She additionally enhances the alliteration between these two words through her placement of the word 'jolting' on the downbeat of the bar, and use of a minor-third ascent directly on 'jingling'. Example 8.8 illustrates these musico-poetic associations.

Next evaluated are the stylistic features that evoke an ambience of pastoralism in Trimble's setting. In turning to Patterson's analysis of the characteristics of traditional Irish music,[39] a multiplicity of idiomatic references to this genre are identified as devices through which the composer conveys the poetic theme of idyllic ruralism. These include modal harmonies, the

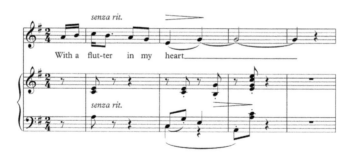

Example 8.7   Herbert Howells, 'Girl's Song', bb. 21–25.

Source: Reproduced with permission of the Herbert Howells Trust.

Example 8.8   Joan Trimble, 'Girl's Song', b. 27.

Source: Courtesy of the National Library of Ireland.

reiteration of the key note, ornamentation in the form of triplets and passing notes, lowered sevenths, and passages of ascending and descending quintuplets, sextuplets, septuplets, and scalic demi-semi quavers imitative of harp textures. The employment of a vamp-like chordal accompaniment throughout the setting also epitomises this compositional flavour of 'Irishness'. Its ensuing sense of buoyancy fittingly characterises the comedic poetic content and thus asserts the role of the piano as one of mimetic importance.

Although these elements combine to distinguish Trimble's iconic writing style, the stylistic parametres of Howells' setting are also governed by similar features of Irish traditional music. Specific comparisons may be seen in the exclusive use of triplets in rising auxiliary form, the treatment of harp textures as ascending arpeggiated sextuplets, and the inclusion of quasi-folk elements in both piano openings. Examples 8.9 and 8.10 demonstrate the specific features of quaver movement, off-beat chordal vamping, and staccato articulation that attest to such stylistic similitude between the two introductions.

Despite the various parallelisms to her teacher's setting, Trimble displays distinct originality in her idiosyncratic treatment of the harmony. She devises an eclectic compositional voice that combines modal tonalities and harmonic conventions derived from *fin-de-siècle* French sound worlds. The former may be seen in the opening lines where a gradation of harmonic modes from Irish traditional music are presented through transitions between Dorian (bb. 3–7) and Lydian (bb. 8–11) modes on C. These modes reappear in various guises throughout and shape the cyclic harmonic trajectory of the work in its final return to the opening Dorian mode on C. The harmony is also imbued with chromaticism and a prevailing sense of harmonic ambivalence, reminiscent of Debussy and Ravel. These features are evoked through chord extensions, tonal ambiguity, tertiary relationships between chordal progressions, and remote accidentals.

Trimble employs this unique harmonic context as a platform for rhetorical expression. Bb. 41–42 of the piano coda (Example 8.11) provides an example. In turning to the final quaver

Example 8.9 Joan Trimble, 'Girl's Song', bb. 1–3.
Source: Courtesy of the National Library of Ireland.

Example 8.10 Herbert Howells, 'Girl's Song', bb. 1–4.
Source: Reproduced with permission of the Herbert Howells Trust.

Example 8.11 Joan Trimble, 'Girl's Song', bb. 41–42.
Source: Courtesy of the National Library of Ireland.

beats of these bars, a distinct instance of bitonality is established between the B-major triad in the right hand of the piano against the open fifth on A♭ in the left. The ensuing dissonance is obfuscated by the enharmonic spelling of d"♯/d'♯ in the right hand against e♭ in the left. This unusual notation may be understood symbolically as a representation for 'burning blood', where both the woman's feelings and remote accidentals are portrayed as unfamiliar entities. In this way, Trimble's experimentation with bitonality offers an inventive dimension through which she expresses textual meaning and harmonic interest alike.

Trimble's esoteric treatment of the harmony is also evident at b.12 (Example 8.12), where a semitone clash functions as word painting. Set as passing notes, the b' and d"♯ quavers of the right-hand piano are presented against the c"♯ in the vocal line, giving rise to a temporal discord from which the following A-major dyad resolves. Although brief, the dissonance is purposeful in its alignment with the word 'but' and is therefore effective in symbolising the contradictory nature of the text. The technique offers a more detailed approach of unification between the music and text.

Trimble's programmatic treatment of the accompaniment is the final feature assessed. As mentioned, the piano line is largely constructed of vamp-like chords with select passages influenced by harp textures. Throughout her setting, the composer utilises this line as a medium for the establishment of musico-poetic associations. Bb.37–38 (Example 8.13) present a select example where a combination of ascending and descending arpeggiated sextuplets, septuplets, and demi-semi-quavers are employed as audible representations for the woman's 'hot blood'. Through smooth transitions between the treble and bass clef, Trimble creates a musical continuum in the piano line that evokes a movement indicative of blood flow. Furthermore, the physicality of hand-crossing as a performative technique further enhances this musical symbolism and thus offers another medium through which Trimble conveys the intelligibility of the text.

Example 8.12 Joan Trimble, 'Girl's Song', b. 12.
Source: Courtesy of the National Library of Ireland.

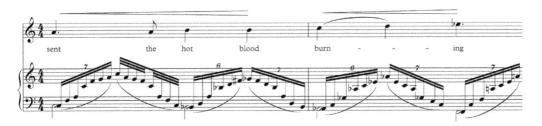

Example 8.13 Joan Trimble, 'Girl's Song', bb. 37–38.
Source: Courtesy of the National Library of Ireland.

Conclusion

This chapter presented a revaluation of Trimble's critical and posthumous reception and offered a musicological analysis of one of her few unpublished works, 'Girl's Song', to give a reappraisal of the composer's musical legacy. By using primary source materials, it provided an overview of her main achievements and proposed four factors that impeded the development of her compositional career: identity, the Second World War, wifehood and motherhood, and family commitments. Each of these factors were considered detrimental to the composer's reception history. They contributed to the challenging historical context within which the dissemination and, in turn, the longevity of her music was hampered. By situating the composer's career trajectory within these circumstances, the chapter shed light on the various obstacles that Trimble overcame to produce her limited compositional output and, moreover, to attain appreciation for her music in the face of political upheavals, gendered agency, and cultural attitudes. It therefore posits her merit as a foremost Anglo-Irish composer of the twentieth century, especially in noting the promise she showed in her early years against the external forces that restricted Trimble's capacity to progress her compositional career thereafter.

Also presented in this chapter was the first comparative analysis between Trimble's setting of 'Girl's Song' and that of her teacher, Howells. With its focus on text-setting techniques, the findings exposed select examples of musical conventions derived from her teacher's vocal work such as the employment of a strophic setting, identical textual deviations, rhythmic motifs, and an indebtedness to an Irish idiom. While these features demonstrated a stylistic similitude between the two songs, the analysis also uncovered myriad examples of innovative compositional tropes in Trimble's setting that demonstrated her artistry as a vocal composer, notwithstanding her student status. Leading examples included her sensitivity to the rhyme scheme and poetic metre, elevation of literary devices, her unique harmonic framework fusing disparate references to the sound worlds of French and Irish music, a programmatic treatment of the accompaniment, and an idiosyncratic approach to the harmony as a medium for rhetorical expression.

In equating the work as a combination of borrowed and original material, the chapter asserts that Trimble offers an elevated version of Howells' setting. She accomplishes a sense of increased exuberance and familiarity in her setting, justifiable in its function as the final song of her trilogy and comedic poetic themes. Consequently, the work may be appreciated for its establishment of a temporal stylistic aesthetic best suited to the structure of a 'programme finisher', and thus warrants recognition as an innovative contribution to the development of art song. The chapter subsequently concludes by arguing the need for such a multifaceted reappraisal of Trimble's critical reception and cautions its importance as a contextual lens through which the achievements, musical legacy, and canonical value of Trimble, and indeed other women composers, might be fully realised. It is hoped that through this evaluation, further analysis might emerge on music by women composers hitherto unexplored and that its findings might prompt increased critical debate regarding the position of women composers in contemporary canonical structures beyond the academic sphere.

Notes

1. Her father owned a signed copy of the Ulster Solemn League and Covenant.
2. "Accomplished Composer and Newspaper Owner," *Irish Times*, August 12, 2000, accessed October 4, 2020, www.irishtimes.com/news/accomplished-composer-and-newspaper-owner-1.302223.
3. Unpublished notes for a memoir retrieved from uncatalogued materials at the NLI, MSS 5796, 5950, 6916.
4. Joan Trimble, "Intermezzo: Joan Trimble," *To Talent Alone: The Royal Irish Academy of Music 1848–1998* (Dublin: Gill & Macmillan, 1998), 393–95.
5. Joan Trimble, "Joan Trimble," *Contemporary Music Review* 11, no. 1 (1994): 277–84 (280).
6. 'Entrance Books/Matriculation Registers," *Student Records*, Trinity College Dublin Archives, TCD MUN V23/8.
7. Michael Fisher, "The Green Bough," *Nationwide*, June 13, 1995. Programme excerpt retrieved with permission from RTÉ archives, Programme ID: TY0151013. https://www.rte.ie/archives/2016/0824/811624-joan-trimble-pianist/.
8. Kevin Myers, "An Irishman's Diary," *Irish Times*, September 13, 1989. Uncatalogued materials, NLI, MS 5796.
9. Uncatalogued letter, NLI, MS 5796, box 2 of 3.
10. Select secondary sources include: Sarah Burn, "Trimble, Joan," *Grove Music Online* (January 20, 2001), accessed February 20, 2020, https://doi-org.dcu.idm.oclc.org/10.1093/gmo/9781561592630.article.43088; Alasdair Jamieson, *Music in Northern Ireland: Two Major Figures* (Surrey: Grosvenor House Publishing, 2017); Lisa McCarroll, *The Celtic Twilight as Reflected in the Two-Piano Works of Joan Trimble (1915–2000)* (unpublished PhD thesis, University of Houston, 2013); Ruth Stanley, *Joan Trimble (1915–2000) and the Issue of Her 'Irish' Musical Identity*, (unpublished Master's thesis, University of Limerick, 2012).
11. "Pianist and Composer Who Lost Confidence but Found Her Voice again – Clear and Distinctive – at the Age of 75," *Irish Times*, August 7, 2000. Uncatalogued materials, NLI, MS 6919.
12. Hand-written scores of select unpublished works are available at CMC Ireland, accessed November 20, 2020, www.cmc.ie/composers/joan-trimble.
13. Axel Klein, "No State for Music," *The Invisible Art: A Century of Music in Ireland 1916–2016*, edited by Michael Dervan (Dublin: New Island, 2016), 47–68 (49).
14. Records of the *Feis Ceoil* Association, NLI, Acc. 5555.
15. For context on the impact of the Gaelic Revival in Ireland see: Lorraine Byrne-Bodley, "Part Two: Music in Ireland," in *Music Preferred: Essays in Musicology, Cultural History and Analysis in Honour of Harry White* (Vienna: Hollitzer, 2018); John Hutchinson, *The Dynamics of Cultural Nationalism: The Gaelic Revival and the Creation of the Irish Nation State* (London: Awin & Unwin, 1987); Philip O'Leary, *The Prose Literature of the Gaelic Revival, 1881–1921: Ideology and Innovation* (Pennsylvania: Penn State University Press, 1994).
16. For more on the position of art music in the early to mid-twentieth-century Ireland see: Mark Fitzgerald and John O'Flynn, *Music and Identity in Ireland and Beyond* (Farnham: Ashgate, 2014); David Hammond, "The Popular Tradition in Ireland Today," in *Four Centuries of Music in Ireland*, edited by Brian Boydell (London: Four Court Press, 1976); Axel Klein, "No State for Music," in *The Invisible Art: A Century of Music in Ireland 1916–2016*, edited by Michael Dervan (Dublin: New Island, 2016), 47–68; Joseph Ryan, "Before the Beginning," in *The Invisible Art: A Century of Music in Ireland 1916–2016*, edited by Michael Dervan (Dublin: New Island, 2016), 1–32; Harry White, *Music and the Irish Literary Imagination* (Oxford: OUP, 2008); Harry White, "Nationalism, Colonialism and the Cultural Stasis of Music in Ireland," in *Musical Constructions of Nationalism: Essays on the History and Ideology of European Musical Culture, 1800–1945*, edited by Michael

17. Eamonn de Velera, *Athlone Station and Transmitter Officially Opened*, Radio Eireann, February 6, 1933 (Original identifier: 1999/026) cited in Klein, *The Invisible Art*, 61.
18. Robert Lynch, "Unravelling Ireland," in *The Partition of Ireland: 1918–1925* (Cambridge: Cambridge University Press, 2019), 115.
19. Kevin Myers, "An Irishman's Diary," *Irish Times*, September 13, 1989. Uncatalogued materials, NLI, MS 5796.
20. Trimble, *Contemporary Review*, 277.
21. Bombing raids against London and other cities by Nazi Germany during the Second World War.
22. Trimble, *Contemporary Review*, 279.
23. Ibid., 282.
24. Ibid., 281.
25. Ibid.
26. Ibid.
27. A period of political conflict commonly referred to as 'The Troubles' in Northern Ireland, involving republican and loyalist paramilitaries, the British forces, and civil rights groups.
28. An excerpt from the first editorial letter by William Trimble cited in Gary Grattan, "Impartial Still Making News 175 Years On," *Belfast Telegraph*, July 5, 2008, accessed October 10, 2020, www.belfasttelegraph.co.uk/imported/impartial-still-making-news-175-years-on-28270062.html.
29. "Accomplished Composer and Newspaper Owner," *Irish Times*, August 12, 2000, accessed November 10, 2018, www.irishtimes.com/news/accomplished-composer-and-newspaper-owner-1.302223
30. With grateful acknowledgement to the NLI for permission to reproduce copyright materials: Joan Trimble, "Girl's Song," *Untitled Trilogy*, NLI MS 5796, box 2.
31. With grateful acknowledgement to the Herbert Howells Trust (registered charity No. 1121065) for permission to reproduce copyright materials: Herbert Howells, "Girl's Song," *Four Songs with Piano*, Op. 22 (London: Winthrop Rodgers, 1919).
32. Joan Trimble, interview by Philip Hammond, "Woman of Parts," *Soundpost*, 23 (December 1984 – January 1985), 24–27, (25).
33. Unpublished ephemera, NLI MS 5950.
34. Classical music festival in Ireland, established in 1897.
35. Adjudicated by English composer Armstrong Gibbs (1889–1960).
36. R.H. Hogg, *Wilfrid Wilson Gibson: People's Poet; a Critical and Biographical Study of WW Gibson 1878–1962* (unpublished PhD thesis, Newcastle University, 1989), 4.
37. A rhetorical or dramatic shift in thought or emotion which occurs towards the latter section of a poem.
38. Iambic trimeter refers to a poetic meter consisting of three iambic units per line where each unit comprises an unaccented syllable followed by an accented syllable; Anapaestic foot refers to a syllabic pattern containing two short or unstressed syllables followed by a longer accented syllable; Tetrameter refers to a line of poetry comprising four metrical feet.
39. Annie Patterson, "The Characteristic Traits of Irish Music," *Proceedings of the Musical Association*, 23rd sess. (1896–1897), 97–103.

Bibliography

Primary Sources

"Entrance Books/Matriculation Registers." *Student Records*, Trinity College Dublin Archives (TCD), MUN V 23/8.
Fisher, Michael. "The Green Bough." *Nationwide*, June 13, 1995. https://www.rte.ie/archives/2016/0824/811624-joan-trimble-pianist/.
Howells, Herbert. "Girl's Song." *Four Songs with Piano*, Op. 22. London: Winthrop Rodgers, 1919.
Myers, Kevin. "An Irishman's Diary." *Irish Times*, September 13, 1989. Uncatalogued materials, National Library of Ireland (NLI), MS 5796.
"Pianist and Composer Who Lost Confidence but Found Her Voice again – Clear and Distinctive – at the Age of 75." *Irish Times*, August 7, 2000. Uncatalogued materials, NLI, MS 6919.

Records of the *Feis Ceoil* Association, NLI, Acc. 5555.
Trimble, Joan. "Girl's Song." *Untitled Trilogy*, NLI, MS 5796, box 2.
Unpublished materials, NLI, MSS 5796, 5950, 6916.

Secondary Sources

"Accomplished Composer and Newspaper Owner." *Irish Times*, August 12, 2000. Accessed October 4, 2020. www.irishtimes.com/news/accomplished-composer-and-newspaper-owner-1.302223.

Burn, Sarah. "Trimble, Joan." *Grove Music Online*, January 20, 2001. Accessed February 20, 2020. https://doi-org.dcu.idm.oclc.org/10.1093/gmo/9781561592630.article.43088.

Grattan, Gary. "Impartial Still Making News 175 Years on." *Belfast Telegraph*, July 5, 2008. Accessed October 10, 2020. www.belfasttelegraph.co.uk/imported/impartial-still-making-news-175-years-on-28270062.html.

Hogg, Roger. "Wilfrid Wilson Gibson: People's Poet; A Critical and Biographical Study of WW Gibson 1878–1962." Unpublished PhD thesis, Newcastle University, 1989.

Jamieson, Alasdair. *Music in Northern Ireland: Two Major Figures*. Surrey: Grosvenor House Publishing, 2017.

Klein, Axel. "No State for Music." In *The Invisible Art: A Century of Music in Ireland 1916–2016*, edited by Michael Dervan, 47–68. Dublin: New Island, 2016.

Lynch, Robert. "Unravelling Ireland." *The Partition of Ireland: 1918–1925*. Cambridge: Cambridge University Press, 2019.

McCarroll, Lisa. "The Celtic Twilight as Reflected in the Two-Piano Works of Joan Trimble (1915–2000)." Unpublished PhD thesis, University of Houston, 2013.

Patterson, Annie. "The Characteristic Traits of Irish Music." *Proceedings of the Musical Association* 23, no. 1 (1896–97): 97–103.

Stanley, Ruth. "Joan Trimble (1915–2000) and the Issue of her 'Irish' Musical Identity." Unpublished Masters thesis, University of Limerick, 2012.

Trimble, Joan. Interview by Philip Hammond. "Woman of Parts." *Soundpost* 23 (December 1984–January 1985): 24–27.

⎯⎯⎯. "Joan Trimble." *Contemporary Music Review* 11, no. 1 (1994): 277–84.

⎯⎯⎯. "Intermezzo: Joan Trimble." In *To Talent Alone: The Royal Irish Academy of Music 1848–1998*. Dublin: Gill & Macmillan, 1998.

9

'THERE IS NO GATE, NO LOCK, NO BOLT THAT YOU CAN SET UPON THE FREEDOM OF MY MIND'[1]

Being a Woman in Franco's Prisons: A Glimpse Through Music

Elsa Calero-Carramolino

The Second Spanish Republic, which was established on 14 April 1931, considered women to be civilians on the same level and with the same rights as men. However, while they were considered equal to men in terms of the law, Spain's conservative powers never accepted these political ideas. These changes were seen as a threat by the conservative powers, especially the Roman Catholic Church, who supported the Fascist soldiers, the landowners, and the right-leaning soldiers.[2] Nevertheless, during this period, women could buy and sell properties, attend university classes, vote, have the right to an abortion, and get divorced. They also were allowed to apply for jobs, open their own bank accounts, and even get involved in politics. Thus, they could access government and take part in public institutions. In the area of music, in addition to opportunities as performers (not only as singers but as soloists and orchestral players), women could become and receive recognition as composers and conductors.

The list of women composers and conductors during these years is quite large, although regrettably most of these women were forced to abandon their positions once Franco came to power. I would like to recall here the names of composers Amparo Barayón Miguel (1904–1936) and Blanca Brissac Vázquez (1910–1939), both shot by the rebel soldiers;[3] Lluisa Casagemas I Coll (1873–?), Emma Chacón Lasauca (1866–1972), Eloísa d'Herbil Silva (1847–1944), Onia Farga Pellicer (1882–1938), María del Carmen Figueirido Torija 'Gueritorgy' (1904–1988), Rosa García Ascot (1902–2002), Carme Karr de Alfonsetti (1855–1934), María Teresa Oller Benlloch (1920–2018), María de Pablos Cerezo (1904–1990), Julia Parody (1890–1973), María Teresa Pelegrí Marimón (1907–1995), María Luisa Ponsa (1878–1919), María Teresa Prieto Fernández de Llana (1896–1962), María Rodrigo Bellido (1888–1967), and Matilde Salvador Segarra (1918–2009), among others. In the field of the baton, some of the women who stood out were Aurea Rosa Clavé (1856–1940) and Emiliana de Zubeldía (1888–1987), both choir conductors; Elena Romero Barbosa, an orchestral conductor; and Emma Martínez de la Torre Shelton (1889–1980), who worked as a stage manager.[4]

The army, headed by a group of Fascist soldiers, promoted a *coup d'état* on 18 July 1936, which turned into a war that ran from 1936 to 1939. During the Spanish Civil War, and despite their political differences, left-wing women (including socialists, communists, and anarchists) all subscribed to the struggle against Fascism and collaborated over many different tasks both at the front and in the background. Following Franco's victory, women were expected to represent the values promoted by Fascism: submission, obedience, tradition, and religion. Consequently, women lost every right they had achieved in the previous years. They were not allowed to think or act for themselves. Women musicians could not create or be recognised as creators.[5] Prior to the Second Spanish Republic, and afterwards during the Dictatorship, women attended classes at the conservatoires without any ambition of developing careers in music. Although it was very common to see women teachers at musical schools, they were never in high-responsibility pedagogical or administrative positions.[6] All of them were regarded as worthless civilians, regardless of whether they had previously endorsed left-wing politics or not. Moreover, they were considered dangerous as they could spread the 'communist gene' if they were not educated according to the official discourse.[7]

Scholarship on Francoism and Sources on Franco's Prisons

Over the past twenty years, Francoism has been approached from multiple scholarly perspectives, and a noticeable number of publications have been produced dedicated to this problematic period of Spain's history. Some of the investigations published in recent years constitute an essential bibliographical corpus for an understanding of the use made of music during Francoism. Good starting points have dealt with the study of the everyday life of the population during the dictatorship, such as the work of José Ángel Ascunce,[8] the studies of Mirta Núñez about the repressive methods employed by the government,[9] and the research of Aurore Ducellier,[10] who has been the first to address political resistance through artistic creation in Spanish prisons. In terms of the approach to musical policies and the musical institutions established by Franco's regime, it is essential to mention the works of Professors Gemma Pérez-Zalduondo, Germán Gan-Quesada, and Javier Suárez-Pajares.[11] Jo Labanyi and Beatriz Martínez del Fresno have both produced general overviews of the cultural exchanges between Fascist Italy, Germany, and Spain.[12] To complete this summary of scholarship dedicated to the manipulative sonic environment of Francoism, it is essential to refer to the wider studies of music and its political meanings in the totalitarianism. I refer here to the works of such authors as Roberto Illiano, Massimiliano Sala, and Erik Levi.[13]

By taking into account the arguments of Domingo Rodríguez[14] in relation to the penitentiary system of Francoism, I have pushed the boundaries of this research field through recovering a lot of valuable data which has been published in a considerable number of articles under the keywords: music, prisons, and Francoism. The primary sources that underpin the basis of this chapter include a diversity of documents related to the prisoners' musical daily life. This covers official documents coming from the government, such as laws and regulations; the General Office of Prisons, including Memoranda and Bulletins; and judicial proceedings, press cuttings, inmates' files, photographs, diaries, correspondence, and even a limited number of songbooks and scores. The primary bibliography, which includes the testimonies from the prisoners themselves – most of them published during the 1980s after Franco's death – is also considered. Through a detailed examination of these documents, it is possible to determine the different kinds of musical practices performed by women in prisons during the Dictatorship, the impact these policies had on them, and the means through which the regime developed such cultural programmes. The first part of the following chapter analyses the institutions created by the state to re-educate women in prisons, musically speaking, and the tasks, means, and methods established by the regime to accomplish these objectives. Secondly, the reactions of women prisoners to these propaganda programmes and how they resisted the regime by introducing their ideas of freedom by making use of the same institutions that Francoism had designed to suppress them are explored.

'Femininity' Against 'Feminism': Redefining Gender Roles Through Music in Franco's Prisons

Once the war was over on 1 April 1939, the concepts of 'woman' and 'femininity' were re-signified through opposition to feminism. Thus, the left-wing ideas represented by the so-called 'red ones' were forbidden and persecuted.[15] During this period, all women had to deal with their submission to men, regardless of whether they had left or right political leanings. Despite male chauvinism,[16] women were accused of persuading men to follow their political ideas, recalling how Eve supposedly got to Adam when she invited him to bite the forbidden fruit. Inspired by the Nazi racial-purity discourse, the regime charged Spanish psychiatrist Antonio Vallejo-Nájera with developing a medical explanation for the reasons why the Communists were humans of lower quality than those who supported right-leanings. In answer to this commitment, the Falangist psychiatrist based its study on the assumption that women were the lowest-class humans as they possessed the 'red gene'. This 'medical condition' could be transferred from mothers to babies. According to this theory, the government justified its re-education policies against women as a measure of prevention, as well as the kidnapping of newborns and death sentences. It was all considered a sanitisation of the country to preserve the Spanish race.[17]

The Feminine Section of Falange and the Role of Housework-Schools in the Development of Musical Programmes in Prisons

Franco's antifeminist politics reduced women, whether they were imprisoned or not, through their confinement to housekeeping and private tasks. They were not allowed to take part in public life. Women could be at the foreground and recognised for their actions only if they assumed that they existed to be subservient to men. However, if they had already been incarcerated, women were merely servants to the authorities.[18]

In this part of the chapter, I will focus on the specific punishment policies adopted by Francoism to re-educate female political prisoners. The first aspect that the regime introduced to achieve women's submission was to deny them the status of political prisoners. Although most of the women arrested were accused of political action, unlike men they were never recognised as political prisoners; as such, they were not eligible to apply for the sentence reductions available to male prisoners. Of course, not all incarcerated women were political prisoners; there were also women accused of prostitution or stealing, both consequences of the deprivation policies exercised against women, who were not allowed to work. However, this feminisation process was applied both to political and non-political prisoners, with special regard to the first group as they were the ones who spent the most time behind bars.

As part of the prison's re-education programme, the state developed a model with subjects related to women's 'well-being'. This issue became the main purpose of the Feminine Section of the Falange: the women's branch of the Fascist Spanish Party, which lasted from 1934 to 1977. Led by Pilar Primo de Rivera, from 1937 onwards it became the official institution of the single party of Franco's government in charge of dealing with women's political issues. Central was the control and censorship of the activities and cultural products consumed by women: music, literature, cinema, radio broadcasts, and the press. For instance, musical practices appeared to the regime as a re-educational instrument through which to instil National-Catholic values in women to recover them for the nation's interests. This was deemed particularly important, because as women they were destined to re-populate a country which had been devastated by war. However, they were encouraged to fulfil their reproductive task by accepting their ideological gender roles and sexual submission.[19] In this sense, musical practices were used to teach them how. Song lyrics, for instance, were full of these behavioural patterns, while their performance was used to illustrate the appropriate body language.

Although the re-education process in prisons during Francoism did not appear on the official legislation until 1944 when the Penal Code was approved, by then the government had already developed a firm political framework through the publication of a substantial number of legal statutes. As a matter of fact, this was all part of the inmate's musical education, as state propaganda was addressed specifically to political prisoners, even though they were not considered as such in legal terms.[20]

As part of the education programmes in women's prisons during Francoism, the Female Section of Falange developed several workshops in which women prisoners were taught gender-based tasks, such as sewing skills, cookery, household tasks, children's care, and, last but not least, music, which had a significant presence to train women how to be subservient to men. For instance, as is evidenced in the subsequent regulations about musical practices in prisons, music was an additional way of discriminating against women based on gender prejudices. For that reason, the repertoires, musical ensembles, and the means arranged by the state to develop musical performances in prisons were different for male and female inmate populations.

The central reasons for introducing music in prisons were, on the one hand, to present the prisoners with up-to-date initiatives in terms of cultural propaganda; whilst, on the other hand, it was to provide the state with an explanation to justify the prisoners' release in order to unfreeze the overcrowded prisons during the period of European isolation against Spain. On the whole, this assumption was named the *Sistema de Redención de Penas por el Trabajo* (System of Redemption of Penalties by Work, hereafter SRPW), a punitive and economic measure based on the Roman Catholic precept of the redemption of sins through prayer and physical effort.[21]

The SRPW had been regulated since 1937, two years before the end of the Civil War, by a Decree which was targeted for use in the territories that had already succumbed to Franco's Army.[22] Once the war had finished, the Government built up the *Patronato Central de Nuestra Señora de la Merced para la Redención de Penas por el Trabajo* (Central Trust for the Redemption of Penalties by Work, hereafter CTRPW). This institution was in charge of every duty related to the inmate's life, including the musical programmes and its functions.

Official musical practices in prisons were both a form of indoctrination of Fascist precepts and a weapon to demoralise the inmates. For instance, the prisoners were forbidden to sing left-wing songs, marches, or anthems, whilst they were forced to perform the Fascist ones and punished if they dared to reject them. The main purpose of the musical and cultural propaganda was to turn enemies into allies and thus turn them into messengers of the nation's duties.

The Gendering of Punishment Through Music in Prisons

Whilst male prisoners were rewarded with sentence reductions for joining the musical activities organised by the regime, as well as being able to participate in prison music-making as instrumental players, conductors, or composers, women did not have this possibility as they were not considered political prisoners. As I stressed earlier, most of the arguments advanced by Francoism to justify women's submission relied on women's intellectual inferiority. The regime denied women's capacity to decide by themselves their political affiliation, which should be specified by the closest man in their social environment: a father, a husband, a brother, or a priest. In this particular context, the state was the one who played the masculine role. The law was a masculine product and women should obey it without regret. Paradoxically, Francoism perpetuated Eve's biblical imagery as the one born from Adam's rib, but at the same time blamed her for having persuaded Adam to try the forbidden fruit. However, Spanish National-Catholicism never argued how it was possible to persuade a man from this lower intellectual position. The state limited itself to blaming women and to punishing them in accordance with these theories.

Additionally, as music was deemed natural for the female gender, women were considered instinctively musically gifted. This belief was neither new nor limited to Spain; it has a long history across diverse cultures, particularly in the case of vocal music, which was used in Francoist prisons to express the greatness of the Nation. In contrast, men were believed to have to make a hard musical effort, for which they should be rewarded.

Thus, women were not allowed to participate as instrumental players, conductors, or composers; rather, they were confined to performing vocal works composed by men. Whereas the musical repertoire in male prisons was mostly based on instrumental and often symphonic music, in female institutions Nationalist and Roman Catholic anthems were performed together with folksongs.[23] For women, music programmes in prisons were disseminated in accordance with the trilogy: God, Motherland, Home. This educational pattern in the Francoist disposal of culture has already been considered by several authors in the field of gender studies.[24]

As a result, the concepts of Fatherland/Motherland themselves acquired different meanings which had a great impact on prison musical practices. The rhetoric of vocal work within men's institutions was saturated with verbs such as 'conquer' and images of 'warriors' who should protect and sacrifice their lives for the Motherland; women, as the Motherland themselves, were expected to remain patient, fragile, delicate, and receptive to the males' legacy. By implication, they were relegated to vocal performance and denied self-expression in music.

Owing to the issues described here, the structures put in place by the dictatorship for the development of musical practices among male and female inmates were not only different but gendered. That is to say, while men's prisons were furnished with instruments and scores, as well as other essential equipment to accomplish musical tasks,[25] women's prisons were never provided with musical instruments; neither were women prisoners allowed their own. On the contrary, they were required to create everything needed for their performances and to undertake everything from stage design to costumes.

The clothing used during these events is quite important. Women were not only allowed to make costumes for prison performances; they were forced by the authorities to make them. The making and wearing of accessories were considered part of the re-education programme in feminine tasks; at the same time it humiliated female prisoners even further by forcing them to wear these costumes when they did not have enough cloth to get dressed properly in their day-to-day life. Women's performances were subjected to wearing what was deemed to be appropriate clothing. That is, 'modest' clothing which did suggest any overt sexuality. Paradoxically, in a society where women were relegated to a secondary sexual role as objects of desire, they weren't allowed to act in a provocative way, either in the context of musical performance or more widely in their daily lives, due to Roman Catholic ideas of pureness and chastity. The state was the owner of their bodies, not them.

By imposing a vocal repertoire on them, not only did Francoism deny them the possibility of playing instruments but also the opportunity to learn how to play them. As I have studied in previous works, even male prisoners with no previous experience were given the chance to enrol in musical activities in prison and learn not only how to play instruments or to sing, but also to write music.[26] Furthermore, male musical participation within prisons was focused on interpretation and composition, with concerns about leadership and the idea of having someone to head their orchestras, choirs, and wind bands. On the contrary, female prisoners had to learn how to co-operate due to the diversity of tasks with which they were charged. Co-operation in women's institutions was not only a matter of musical development, but also a requirement for survival.

During this period, death rates in Spanish prisons were unusually high.[27] All too often, numberless inmates ended their days dying of starvation, suffering diseases, ill treatments, and physical and sexual abuses, as well as executions ordered by the martial courts. These extreme conditions were harder for women, as many of them were incarcerated whilst pregnant or with their babies. Furthermore, countless women were raped in prison. None of them were provided with fundamental hygiene facilities, such as sanitary towels, underwear, or nappies for their children. Inevitably this enhanced a feeling of communal suffering amongst female inmates, strengthening their moral and physical reserves. As prisoners' sons and daughters were not registered, there are no official records of the births in prison during these years. Oral testimonies explain that mothers were not only incarcerated whilst pregnant, but that they also went to prison with their children if after their sentencing there was no one who could take care of the child. Children were allowed to remain in prison with their mothers until they were two years old. Afterwards, they were sent to the nearest relative or one of the many children's care institutions spread all over the country, until reaching the age of twenty-one. Other common practices were to steal the child from the mother's hands once the recommended breast-feeding period ceased in order to execute the mother, or just to sell the child to a rich family faithful to the regime.[28]

Nonetheless, most of the children who were born in prison died due to starvation, illnesses, or because of the freezing temperatures of the institutions. This was another ring of the women's penalty chain, as they suffered from anxiety and depression, as well as other mental issues, due to these hard conditions.[29] This enforced sense of community helped to preserve their identities, whilst at the same time giving them the ability to resist the restrictions imposed upon them by the government by pretending to accept the gender roles assigned to them.

The Role of Women in the Musical Resistance Against the Dictatorship in Prisons

In 2006, Fernando Hernández-Holgado interviewed Manolita del Arco.[30] Accused of having taking part in the actions of the clandestine Communist Party after the war, she was one of the women who served the longest sentences. She was imprisoned for nearly twenty years. When Manolita was asked about her experience in taking part in clandestine cultural leisure during her imprisonment, she pointed out:

> To celebrate the first of May [International Worker's Day or Labour Day],[31] or . . . there were always dates for celebrating. However, we had to do it without being noticed . . . The theatre plays used to take place in the toilets. Some of them were written by us and then we used to perform them there. Once we performed one about the Republic, so there was one girl dressed like that, another dressed as a communist, another was a socialist . . . of course no-one wanted to play the role of the Fascist.[32]

The first evidence of musical resistance among women in prisons in the early post-war era was opposition to having to perform the Falangist marches, songs, and hymns. Female inmates hit back not only by changing the meanings of the lyrics but also by distorting how they were performed. For instance, the Fascist anthem: *'Cara al sol'* ('Face to sun') became *'Cara al suelo'* ('Face to ground'), whilst *'Cara al sol te pondrás morena'* ('Face to sun, you'll sunbathe') became *'Cara al sol que me pongo enferma'* ('Face to sun so I get ill'). Not only were the lyrics changed, but the way of singing the songs was important, too. Other examples are the Fascist statements *'España. Una. España Grande. España. Libre'* ('Spain One, Spain Great, Spain Free)' where the word *'libre'* ('free') used to be shouted fiercely, while the 'one' and 'great' were barely audible.[33] The Spanish philosopher and anthropologist Alberto Sucasas posits the idea of these practices as a form of 'adaptation as a priority of the individuals',[34] who were constantly fighting to keep their humanity in an environment whose main purpose was to achieve their dehumanisation.

Changing the lyrics of the Fascist songs was one of the methods by which women recovered their political identity in prisons through music, but it was not the only one. In addition, they wrote their own pieces. The following table collects a list of twenty-five musical pieces composed by women in prisons between 1938 and 1948. To complete the records shown here, I relied on the field research I undertook as part of my PhD (2017–2021).[35] This provided me with a wide range of oral testimonies as well as diaries, notebooks, and biographies written by the prisoners, some of them even published after Franco's death. Investigation made by other researchers in previous works about female prisoners' living conditions have also been useful.[36]

The pieces, which are different forms of songs from satirical hymns to lullabies or protest songs, have survived in the memories of the women who used to sing them. No musical scores have been left, as they never existed. Women did not have paper to write. A great number of them even did not know how to write, so musical notation was useless within the prison context. For that reason, it is difficult to speculate how these songs would have sounded, as most of the melodies have been lost. The texts and the oral memories have become the main evidence of the existence of the practice.

As can be discerned from the table, there is an appreciable degree of variety in the nature of these compositions, even if they often subscribe to the same ideals. Yet despite their diversity, they all share some common characteristics. Firstly, it should be noticed that most of these works date from the period of 1938–1949, although the Dictatorship lasted until 1975. This does not mean that there were no further women prisoners held on political grounds later in the Dictatorship. However, by then most women had started to be released from prisons or had already been killed, so the extent to which the collective activity reduced is difficult to trace. On the other hand, musical programmes in prisons were considerably affected by the post-war era, as the Spanish government used its penitentiary policy to extend its diplomatic discourse to Europe and Latin America. In the same line, clandestine activities strengthened their networks to subvert the prison's policies, and this had an impact on the priorities of prisoners' resistance, which focussed instead on asking for their freedom by sending letters to different national and international organisations. In other words, music was understood to be part of leisure and it was not until the 1960s that it was revived as a tool for political action.

Secondly, as I explained, no scores of these works have survived. As these songs were part of the unofficial and subversive activities that women prisoners undertook to resist the regime, its survival was inevitably linked to the absence of physical evidence. Female inmates had no alternative other than to sing the entire repertoire by heart. In other words, these songs survived thanks to the fact that they continued to be sung in the private space, years after women had been released. The songs were orally transmitted from mothers to daughters.

Table 9.1 Catalogue of Songs Composed by Female Inmates in Spanish Prisons from 1938 to 1948[37]

Title	Author			Prison and year of composition
Cárcel de ventas	13 Roses			Female Central Prison of Ventas (Madrid), 1939
Musical genre	**Topic**	**Length**		**Recovered the first time by...**
Song	Description of life in prison	23 lines		Tomasa Cuevas, 1985
Title	**Author**			**Prison and year of composition**
A «trece flores caídas»	Ángeles Ortega García-Madrid			Female Central Prison of Ventas (Madrid), 1939
Musical genre	**Topic**	**Length**		**Recovered the first time by...**
Song	Death	14 lines		Femando Hernández Holgado, 2003
Title	**Author**			**Prison and year of composition**
Pasacalles en Ventas en el año 39	Unknown			Female Central Prison of Ventas (Madrid). 1939
Musical genre	**Topic**	**Length**		**Recovered the first time by...**
Song	Freedom	31 lines		Tomasa Cuevas (Cuevas, 1985: 728–730)
Title	**Author**			**Prison and year of composition**
Vuelan por encima del convento	Unknown			Female Provincial Prison of Durango, 1939
Musical genre	**Topic**	**Length**		**Recovered the first time by...**
Song	Description of life in prison.— Freedom	17 lines		Tomasa Cuevas, 1985
Title	**Author**			**Prison and year of composition**
[Saludo Durango]	Unknown			Female Provincial Prison of Durango, 1939
Musical genre	**Topic**	**Length**		**Recovered the first time by...**
Song	Freedom	5 lines (incomplete)		Tomasa Cuevas (Cuevas, 1985: 732)
Title	**Author**			**Prison and year of composition**
El cura de Ocaña	Unknown			Female Reformatory of Ocaña, 1940
Musical genre	**Topic**	**Length**		**Recovered the first time by...**
Song	Description of life in prison	52 lines		Tomasa Cuevas, 1985

(*Continued*)

Table 9.1 (Continued)

Title	Author		Prison and year of composition
[Cuando tocan las campanas]	Unknown		Female Provincial Prison of Durango, 1940
Musical genre	**Topic**	**Length**	**Recovered the first time by...**
Song	Description of life in prison.-- Freedom	18 lines	Tomasa Cuevas, 1985
Title	**Author**		**Prison and year of composition**
Amigo Chimpancé	Unknown		Female Detention Centre of Orue, 1941
Musical genre	**Topic**	**Length**	**Recovered the first time by...**
Song	Description of life in prison	220 lines	Tomasa Cuevas, 1985
Title	**Author**		**Prison and year of composition**
Coplas por la Victoria de los aliados en la II Guerra Mundial	Julia Vigre and Carmen Caamaño		Female Central Prison of Ventas (Madrid), 1945
Musical genre	**Topic**	**Length**	**Recovered the first time by...**
Spanish song	World War	18 lines	Fernando Hernández, 2006
Title	**Author**		**Prison and year of composition**
Copias de la huelga de hambre	Unknown		Female Central Prison of Ventas (Madrid), 1945
Musical genre	**Topic**	**Length**	**Recovered the first time by...**
Spanish song	Description of life in prison	24 lines	Fernando Hernández, 2006
Title	**Author**		**Prison and year of composition**
Canción de los guerrilleros	Maria Dolores Pérez Enciso		Detention camp of Toulouse, 1947
Musical genre	**Topic**	**Length**	**Recovered the first time by...**
Song	Lucha armada	28 lines	Fernando Hernández, 2003
Title	**Author**		**Prison and year of composition**
Canción de la Pepa	Unknown		Female Central Prison of Ventas (Madrid), 1945

(*Continued*)

Table 9.1 (Continued)

Title	Author	Prison and year of composition
Musical genre	**Topic**	**Length**	**Recovered the first time by...**
Song	Description of life in prison;- Death	32 lines	Fernando Hernández, 2003

Title	Author	Prison and year of composition
La ventana	Anónima	Female Central Prison of Ventas (Madrid), 1945
Musical genre	**Topic**	**Length**	**Recovered the first time by...**
Song	Description of life in prison.– Freedom	26 lines	Tomasa Cuevas. 1985

Title	Author	Prison and year of composition
Lumita	Unknown	Female Central Prison of Ventas (Madrid), 1945
Musical genre	**Topic**	**Length**	**Recovered the first time by...**
Lullaby	Freedom	20 lines	Tomasa Cuevas, 1985

Title	Author	Prison and year of composition
Pueblo de España	Unknown	Female Central Prison of Ventas (Madrid), 1947
Musical genre	**Topic**	**Length**	**Recovered the first time by...**
Song	Description of life in prison	6 lines (uncomplete)	Tomasa Cuevas, 1985

Title	Author	Prison and year of composition
Las 13 rosas	Unknown	Female Provincial Prison of Durango, ca. 1939
Musical genre	**Topic**	**Length**	**Recovered the first time by...**
Song	Death	28 lines	José Gabriel González, 2013

Title	Author	Prison and year of composition
La Cárcel de Ventas de Madrid	Victoria Molinete Gómez	Female Central Prison of Ventas (Madrid), ca. 1939
Musical genre	**Topic**	**Length**	**Recovered the first time by...**
Song	Description of life in prison	24 lines	José Gabriel González, 2013

(*Continued*)

Table 9.1 (Continued)

Title	Author		Prison and year of composition
Title	**Author**		**Prison and year of composition**
Somos las presas del 39	Les dones del 36		Female Central Prison of Ventas (Madrid), ca. 1939
Musical genre	**Topic**	**Length**	**Recovered the first time by...**
Song	Description of life in prison	14 lines	José Gabriel González, 2013
Title	**Author**		**Prison and year of composition**
El pasodoble de la cárcel	Julia Vigre and Carmen Caamaño		Female Central Prison of Ventas (Madrid), ca. 1939
Musical genre	**Topic**	**Length**	**Recovered the first time by...**
Pasodoble	Description of life in prison.– Freedom	18 lines	Rosa Zaragoza, 1988
Title	**Author**		**Prison and year of composition**
Sardinas frescas	La ferina de Puerto Chico		Female Convent-Prison of the Oblatas (Santander), 1945
Musical genre	**Topic**	**Length**	**Recovered the first time by...**
Couplet	Description of life in prison	16 lines	Ana R. Cañil, 2008
Title	**Author**		**Prison and year of composition**
¿De dónde vienes morena?	Unknown		Female Central Prison of Barcelona, ca. 1939
Musical genre	**Topic**	**Length**	**Recovered the first time by...**
Chotis	Prisoner's women (wives, sisters, etc.)	7 lines (incomplete)	Elsa Calero-Carramolino, 2016
Title	**Author**		**Prison and year of composition**
En la calle del pez	Unknown		Female Central Prison of Ventas (Madrid), ca. 1940
Musical genre	**Topic**	**Length**	**Recovered the first time by...**
Couplet	Pornography	18 lines	Javi Larráuri, 2010

This provides us with an explanation for why the repertoire was based on the popular composition model of the songs of that period. As they were all well-known by the prisoners, it facilitated the memorising process. Learning by heart allowed this repertoire to survive beyond its physical boundaries once the prison period was over.

As this repertoire formed part of the individual memories of the inmates, its study is limited by their capacity to remember and to transmit them, as well as the knowledge of their families about this untold past, as most of them have passed away in recent years. These songs were often changed by the prisoners, to facilitate memorisation and also to add their own performative interpretations. When analysing these pieces, the researcher must be aware of all of these difficulties. This discloses both the liveliness of such a repertoire and the presence of music as an inseparable part of the women's self-identity.

Another caveat that should be emphasised is the recurrent anonymity of the pieces. While it is possible to identify straightforwardly the composers of male clandestine songs, as they used to sign their scores and lyrics, this is not the case with the women's pieces. Women were aware of how risky these political actions were in the prison context, especially the women who were incarcerated with their babies; they took care not to incur further punishment for being discovered actively resisting the regime.

What has remained from this kind of musical production are the bonds between the pieces and the penitentiary institution in which they were written. This correlation between the music and the prison space allows us to understand the repertoire as a collective manifestation rather than an individual one. In fact, this seems reflective of the wider trend of women's tendency towards community, rather than individuality, in the forms in which they practice political activism.

Additionally, it should be pointed out that, although the length of the pieces does not subscribe to a common pattern, they are all based on representative structures of Spanish poetry. Special attention was paid to characteristic folklore patterns: romances and seguidillas. The main topics developed by these compositions tended to explore abstract rather than exclusive subjects: death, loneliness, political fight, descriptions of living in prison, and freedom. The tone in which these songs were written moves from the satirical to the gloomy. In sharp contrast to their male comrades, women did not address their songs to anyone. Even when singing about love or deeper emotions, they weave their messages in abstract terms. They prioritised the idea rather than the addressee or themselves as speakers or creators. Women remained in the background of their creations as authors, but also as the subjects, even if the lyrics often explored their own experiences.

Thanks to the field work and the recordings undertaken by some of the researchers mentioned earlier, there are some pieces whose sound has been preserved. This is the case of songs such as '*El pasodoble de la cárcel*', '*Cárcel de Venta*', and '*Somos las presas del 39*', which were all re-recorded by the activist-singer Rosa Zaragoza in 1988.[38] In addition, '*En la calle del Pez*' was recorded by Javi Larráuri in 2010,[39] and '*¿De dónde vienes morena?*', one of my first contributions to this area in 2016.

Conclusion

In conclusion, this chapter has explored the musical practices employed as a means of re-education for political prisoners in women's prisons in Spain and the women inmates' patterns of resistance against this in the period directly following the Spanish Civil War. It can be asserted that the imposition of the Fascist soundscape in prisons provoked in the inmates several reactions. Women prisoners tried to recover their gendered and sexual political identities by pretending to accept the background and passive role imposed by the dictatorship. By using the same institutions created by the regime (i.e., songs) specifically to undermine them, they resisted the system and introduced their own left-wing ideas. Women as creators and performers, as well as stage designers and costume makers, became the guardians of the musical repertoire in prisons, whether officially or unofficially. For that reason, they acquired a key role in the recollection of such practices developed by the victims of Franco's reprisal.

Through detailed examination of the testimonies of survivors, I have been able to identify that the non-leading attitude adopted by women eases the recollection of their musical experience. They learnt to co-operate, thereby avoiding individual recognition. The women interviewed were more open-minded – and sometimes this means that they expressed themselves more sincerely – when they were asked about their musical experiences in prisons, whereas male prisoners tended to avoid mentioning music in their testimonies. Sometimes men even denied its existence or their involvement in musical practices. This attitude may be interpreted in many ways, but it is probable that the sense of shame experienced by male inmates for their musical participation was prompted as a form of survivor's guilt that they had not suffered as much pain during their confinements as their comrades who were executed or were tortured to death. The trace left by the musical punishment imposed by Francoism had consequences for male and female prison populations. For women, this violent use of music was especially hard considering they were reduced to mere vessels of the repertoire; expected to play, sing, and move as the masculine authority of the state wanted them to play, sing, and move. In this sense their bodies were used to fulfil the nation's indoctrination purposes. Music was used to punish, but also to penetrate women's bodies with the symbolic discourse of Francoism.

Notes

1. Virginia Woolf, *A Room of One's Own*, New ed., edited by David Bradshaw and Stuart N. Clarke (Stratford-on-Avon: Shakespeare Head Press, 2015), 63. This work was supported by the Spanish National Agency of Research [FJC2021-046775-I] in collaboration with the Autonomous University of Barcelona.
2. Ángel Viñas, *¿Quién quiso la guerra civil?. Historia de una conspiración* (España: Editorial Crítica, 2019).
3. Elsa Calero-Carramolino, "Represión, supervivencia y preservación de la cultura musical en las presas del franquismo", in *Afinando ideas: aportaciones multidisciplinares de la joven musicología española*, edited by Consuelo Pérez-Colodrero and Candela Tormo-Valpuesta (Granada: Universidad de Granada, 2018), 289–318.
4. Compositoras españolas. *La creación musical femenina desde la Edad Media hasta la actualidad* (Madrid: CDMD, 2008).
5. Antonio Vallejo-Nájera, *Política racial del nuevo estado* (San Sebastián: Editorial Española, 1938), 6.
6. Desiré García-Gil and Consuelo Pérez-Colodrero, "Mujer y educación musical (escuela, conservatorio y universidad): dos historias de vida en la encrucijada del siglo XX español," *Dedica: revista de educaçao e humanidades* 6 (2014): 175–76.
7. Antonio Vallejo-Nájera, *Eugenesia de la hispanidad y regeneración de la raza* (Burgos: Editorial Española, 1937).
8. José Ángel Ascunce, *Sociología cultural del franquismo (1936–1975). La cultura del nacional-socialismo* (Madrid: Editorial Biblioteca Nueva, 2015).
9. Mirta Núñez, "Propaganda oficial para adornar el mundo carcelario en la posguerra. Historia y comunicación social," *Historia y Comunicación Social* 4 (1999): 135–54. Also from the same author: Mirta Núñez, "La cárcel tras los muros: El trabajo de los presos en la España de Franco," in *El republicanismo español: raíces y perspectivas de future*, edited by Ángeles Egido and Mirta Núñez (Madrid: Biblioteca Nueva, 2001), 143–74; Mirta Núñez, *La gran represión* (Madrid: Flor del Viento, 2009).

10. Aurore Ducellier, *Le voix résilientes. La poésie carcérale sous le premier franquisme* (Paris: Université Sorbonne Nouvelle, 2016).
11. Gemma Pérez-Zalduondo, *La música en España durante el franquismo a través de la legislación (1936–1951)* (Granada: Universidad de Granada, 2001). Javier Suárez-Pajares, *Joaquín Rodrigo y la música española de los años cuarenta* (Valladolid: Glares, 2005). Also from the same author as continuation of his previous work: Javier Suárez-Pajares, *Joaquín Rodrigo y la música española de los años cincuenta* (Valladolid: Glares, 2008).
12. Jo Labanyi, *Constructing Identity in Contemporary Spain. Theoretical Debates and Cultural Practices* (Oxford: Oxford University Press, 2000). Beatriz Martínez del Fresno, "Realidades y máscaras en la música de la posguerra," in *Actas del congreso Dos décadas de cultura artística en el franquismo (1936–1956)*, edited by Gemma Pérez-Zalduondo y María Isabel Cabrera-García (Granada: Universidad de Granada, 2000), 31–82.
13. Roberto Illiano, *Music and Dictatorship in Europea in Latin America* (Luca: Brepols, 2009). Also from the same publisher and year: Gemma Pérez-Zalduondo and Germán Gan-Quesada, *Music and Francoism* (Luca: Brepols, 2009). Massimiliano Sala, *Music and Propaganda in the Short Twentieth Century* (Luca: Brepols, 2014).
14. Domingo Rodríguez, "Configuración y evolución del sistema penitenciario franquista (1936–1945)," *Hispania Nova: Revista de Historia Contemporánea* 7 (2007), supplement. Also from the same author: Domingo Rodríguez, "La redención de penas a través del esfuerzo intelectual: educación, proselitismo y adoctrinamiento en las cárceles franquistas," *Revista de Investigación en Educación* 11, no. 1 (2013): 58–78.
15. The Francoist government considered dissident ideas all the same, and so to frame them it referred to them as 'red' ideas. The colour red was associated in Spanish politics with the Communist Party, but it was used to define all political opposition to Fascism, as Anarchists and Socialists also participated in acts of resistance. Even Monarchists and some Catholic Sectors were against the regime. Antonio Vallejo-Nájera, *Eugenesia de la hispanidad y regeneración de la raza* (Burgos: Editorial Española, 1937).
16. I propose this concept to analyse discrimination against women during Francoism according to the definition given by Hannah Arendt about the narcissism of societies or groups from a society and the sense of responsibility developed over the 'backward people," as this was how women were looked at by men. Hannah Arendt, "Imperial, Nationalism, Chauvinism," *The Review of Politics* 7, no. 4 (1945): 441–63: 457.
17. Vallejo-Nájera, 1937.
18. Pilar Primo de Rivera, *Cuatro discursos* (Burgos: Editora Nacional, 1939), Chapter 1.
19. In this sense, during the dictatorship several books and leaflets were published which were specifically addressed to women in order to instruct them about how they had to behave in their marital relationships, from the housework to the sexual field. These behavioural patterns were also spread through the cultural propaganda, especially magazines, films, and theatre plays. This aspect of the sexual and gender education through texts has been analysed by Carme Molinero and more recently by Francisco Canes: Carme Molinero, "Mujer, franquismo, fascismo. La clausura forzada en un 'mundo pequeño'," *Historia Social* 30 (1998): 97–117; and Francisco Canes, "Los libros de texto de la Sección Femenina de FET de las JONS," in *La Constitución de Cádiz: genealogía y desarrollo del sistema educativo liberal / XVI Coloquio Nacional de Historia de la Educación*, edited by M. Gloria Espigado et al. (Cádiz: Universidad de Cádiz, 2013), 597–610.
20. Ricardo Vinyes, "El universo penitenciario durante el franquismo," in *Una inmensa prisión*, edited by Jaume Sobrequés, Carmen Molinero, and Margarida Sala (Barcelona: Crítica, 2003), 55–176.
21. José Agustín Pérez del Pulgar, *La solución que España da al problema de sus presos políticos* (Valladolid: Lib. Santarem, 1939), 50.
22. 'Decreto número 281'. *Boletín Oficial del Estado*, 224 (June 1, 1937), 1698–99.
23. PCRPT, *La obra de la Redención de Penas. La doctrina – La práctica – La legislación* (Alcalá de Henares: Talleres Penitenciarios de Alcalá de Henares, 1942), 130.
24. Teresa González, "Dios, Patria y Hogar. La trilogía en la educación de las mujeres," *Hispania Sacra* LXVI 133 (2014): 337–63 (pp. 347–48).
25. PCRPT, 130.

26. Elsa Calero-Carramolino, "Regenerados y redimidos: perfiles de músicos en las cárceles franquistas (1939–1975)," in *Música y represión política, de la Alemania Nazi a la España Franquista*, edited by Enrique Téllez Cenzano (Valencia: Edictoràlia, 2020), 79–112.
27. The numbers of repression in Spain during Francoism are a critical point as the Spanish Government has never provided any information in relation to this, so the most up-to-date information has been provided by different researchers from the 1980s until now. For instance, Hugh Thomas estimates that 100,000 people were killed by the Francoists during the Civil War (1936–1939). Another historian, Michal Richards, defends that taking into account people killed during the war and the ones who were died in prison from 1939 to 1945, the number of deaths increases to 400,000; from that number, according to Guy Hermet, 192,000 would correspond to the prisoners executed after the martial law. Hugh Thomas, *La guerre d'Espagne* (Paris: Robert Laffont, 2009), 209–71; Michael Richards, *A Time of Silence: Civil War and the Culture of Repression in Franco's Spain, 1936–1945* (Cambridge: Cambridge University Press, 1998), 11; Guy Hermet, *La guerre d'Espagne* (Paris: Seuil, 1984), 10.

    On the other hand, the Report of the Working Group on Enforced or Involuntary Disappearances of the United Nations estimates that 114,000 were kidnapped by the dictatorship. From that number, 30,000 would be prisoner's children who were separated from their mothers while they were in prisons: Ginebra, United Nations, Report of the Working Group on Enforced or Involuntary Disappearances – Mission to Spain, A/HRC/27/49/Add.1.
28. Mirta Núñez Díaz-Balart, "La infancia "redimida": el último eslabón del sistema penitenciario franquista," *Historia y Comunicación Social* 6 (2001): 137–48.
29. Fernando Dualde Beltrán, "La profilaxis de la enfermedad mental en la psiquiatría franquista: esquizofrenia, eugenesia y consejo matrimonial," *Revista de la Asociación Española de Neuropsiquiatría* 92 (2004), accessed February 10, 2022, https://scielo.isciii.es/scielo.php?script=sci_arttext&pid=S0211-57352004000400008#back.
30. Ricard Vinyes was one of the first Spanish researchers to analyse women's experiences in Franco's prisons.
31. This date was chosen after the Marxist International Conference of 1889, during which a resolution to support the working class was adopted. Since then, the date has been important in the remembrance of working-class rights.
32. Fernando Hernández, "Manolita del Arco Palacio (1920–2006)," *Hispania Nova. Revista de Historia Contemporánea* 6 (2006), supplement.
33. Hernández, supplement.
34. Alberto Sucasas, "Fenomenología de lo inmundo. Imre Kertész y la memoria de Auschwitz," in *Las víctimas como precio necesario*, edited by José Antonio Zamora Zaragoza, Manuel Reyes Mate Rupérez and Jordi Maisó Blasco (Barcelona: Trotta, 2016), 35–50.
35. Elsa Calero-Carramolino, *Prácticas musicales del ecosistema sonoro penitenciario franquista (1938–1948): propaganda, contrapropaganda y clandestinidad* (Granada: Universidad de Granada, 2021). This research has been recently published: Elsa Calero-Carramolino, *Sonidos al otro lado del muro. Música y otras prácticas sonoras en las cárceles de Franco (1938–1948)* (Granada: Universidad de Granada, 2023).
36. See the references quoted in this chapter.
37. Updated for the final time in February 2022. There might be changes while the research process progresses further.
38. *Dones del 36*, dir. by Rosa Zaragoza (Tecnosaga, 1988).
39. *Mujeres republicanas*, dir. by Javi Larráuri (Javi Larráuri, 2010).

Bibliography

Arendt, Hannah. "Imperial, Nationalism, Chauvinism." *The Review of Politics* 7, no. 4 (1995): 441–63.

Ascunce, José Ángel. *Sociología cultural del franquismo (1936–1975). La cultura del nacional-socialismo*. Madrid: Editorial Biblioteca Nueva, 2015.

Calero-Carramolino, Elsa. "Represión, supervivencia y preservación de la cultura musical en las presas del franquismo." In *Afinando ideas: aportaciones multidisciplinares de la joven musicología española*, edited by Consuelo Pérez-Colodrero and Candela Tormo Valpuesta, 289–318. Granada: Universidad de Granada, 2018.

———. "Regenerados y redimidos: perfiles de músicos en las cárceles franquistas (1939–1975)." In *Música y represión política, de la Alemania Nazi a la España Franquista*, edited by Enrique Téllez Cenzano, 79–112. Valencia: Edictoràlia, 2020.

Canes, Francisco. "Los libros de texto de la Sección Femenina de FET de las JONS." In *La Constitución de Cádiz: genealogía y desarrollo del sistema educativo liberal/XVI Coloquio Nacional de Historia de la Educación*, edited by M. Gloria Espigado et al., 597–610. Cádiz: Universidad de Cádiz, 2013.

Compositoras españolas. *La creación musical femenina desde la Edad Media hasta la actualidad*. Madrid: CDMD, 2008.

Dualde Beltrán, Fernando. "La profilaxis de la enfermedad mental en la psiquiatría franquista: esquizofrenia, eugenesia y consejo matrimonial." *Revista de la Asociación Española de Neuropsiquiatría* 92 (2004). Accessed February 10, 2022. https://scielo.isciii.es/scielo.php?script=sci_arttext&pid=S0211-57352004000400008#back.

Ducellier, Aurore. *Le voix résilientes. La poésie carcérale sous le premier franquisme*. Paris: Université Sorbonne Nouvelle, 2016.

García-Gil, Desiré, and Consuelo Pérez Colodrero. "Mujer y educación musical (escuela, conservatorio y universidad): dos historias de vida en la encrucijada del siglo XX español." *Dedica: revista de educaçao e humanidades* 6 (2014): 171–86.

Ginebra, United Nations, Report of the Working Group on Enforced or Involuntary Dissappeareances – Mission to Spain, A/HRC/27/49/Add.1.

González, Teresa. "Dios, Patria y Hogar. La trilogía en la educación de las mujeres." *Hispania Sacra* LXVI 133 (2014): 337–63.

Hermet, Guy. *La guerre dEspagnee*. Paris: Seuil, 1984.

Hernández, Fernando. "Manolita del Arco Palacio (1920–2006)." *Hispania Nova. Revista de Historia Contemporánea* 6 (2006): 1–15.

Illiano, Roberto. *Music and Dictatorship in Europea in Latin America*. Luca: Brepols, 2009.

Labanyi, Jo. *Constructing Identity in Contemporary Spain. Theoretical Debates and Cultural Practices*. Oxford: Oxford University Press, 2000.

Levi, Érik. *Mozart and the Nazis: How the Third Reich Abused a Musical Icon*. London: Yale University Press, 2010.

Martínez del Fresno, Beatriz. "Realidades y máscaras en la música de la posguerra." In *Actas del congreso Dos décadas de cultura artística en el franquismo (1936–1956)*, edited by Gemma Pérez-Zalduondo and María Isabel Cabrera-García, 31–82. Granada: Universidad de Granada, 2000.

Molinero, Carme. "Mujer, franquismo, fascismo. La clausura forzada en un "mundo pequeño"." *Historia Social* 30 (1998): 97–117.

Núñez Díaz-Balart, Mirta. "La infancia "redimida": el último eslabón del sistema penitenciario franquista." *Historia y Comunicación Social* 6 (2001a): 137–48.

———. "La cárcel tras los muros: El trabajo de los presos en la España de Franco." In *El republicanismo español: raíces y perspectiva de futuro*, edited by Ángeles Egido and Mirta Núñez, 143–74. Madrid: Biblioteca Nueva, 2001b.

———. *La gran represión*. Madrid: Flor del Viento, 2009.

Pagés, Joan. *Les dones del 36*. Barcelona: Insitut d'Educació de l'Ajuntament de Barcelona, 2010.

PCRPT. *La obra de la Redención de Penas. La doctrina – La práctica – La legislación*. Alcalá de Henares: Talleres Penitenciarios de Alcalá de Henares, 1939–1949.

Pérez del Pulgar, José Agustín. *La solución que España da al problema de sus presos políticos*. Valladolid: Lib. Santarem, 1939.

Pérez-Zalduondo, Gemma. *La música en España durante el franquismo a través de la legislación (1936–1951)*. Granada: Universidad de Granada, 2001.

———, and Germán Gan-Quesada. *Music and Francoism*. Turnhout: Brepols, 2009.

Primo de Rivera, Pilar. *Cuatro discursos*. Burgos: Editora Nacional, 1939.

Richards, Michael. *A Time of Silence: Civil War and the Culture of Repression in Franco's Spain, 1936–1945*. Cambridge: Cambridge University Press, 1998.

Sala, Massimiliano. *Music and Propaganda in the Short Twentieth Century*. Turnhout: Brepols, 2014.

Suárez-Pajares, Javier. *Joaquín Rodrigo y la música española de los años cuarenta*. Valladolid: Glares, 2005.

———. *Joaquín Rodrigo y la música española de los años cincuenta*. Valladolid: Glares, 2008.

Sucasas, Alberto. "Fenomenología de lo inmundo. Imre Kertész y la memoria de Auschwitz." In *Las víctimas como precio necesario*, edited by José Antonio Zamora Zaragoza, Manuel Reyes Mate Rupérez, and Jordi Maiso Blasco, 33–50. Barcelona: Trotta, 2016.

Thomas, Hugh. *La guerre d'Espagne*. Paris: Robert Laffont, 2009.

Vallejo-Nájera, Antonio. *Eugenesia de la hispanidad y regeneración de la raza*. Burgos: Editorial Española, 1937.

_____. *Política racial del nuevo estado*. San Sebastián: Editorial Española, 1938.

Viñas, Ángel. *¿Quién quiso la guerra civil?. Historia de una conspiración*. España: Editorial Crítica, 2019.

Vinyes, Ricardo. "El universo penitenciario durante el franquismo." In *Una inmensa prisión*, edited by Jaume Sobrequés, Carmen Molinero, and Margarida Sala, 155–76. Barcelona: Crítica, 2003.

Woolf, Virginia. *A Room of One's Own*. New ed., edited by David Bradshaw and Stuart N. Clarke. Chichester, UK: John Wiley & Sons Ltd., 2015.

PART II

Conductors and *Impresarios*

Conductors and *Impresarios*: An Introduction

Laura Hamer and Helen Julia Minors

Part II – 'Conductors and *Impresarios*' – considers a range of women active in some of the most male-dominated roles within the music industries, functioning in extremely male-dominated spaces and working in very public genres. Unlike other parts of the current volume, and although they often collaborated closely with others, the case studies gathered here represent examples of individual (rather than collective) women's musical leadership. Part II covers women working as conductors, *impresarios*, and within other roles in music theatre, the opera, or concert life. The part includes case studies of women working within the theatre, including Lilian Baylis and Elsie April; detailed considerations of individual women *impresarios*, covering Baylis, Emma Carelli, Henriette Renié, and Edis de Philippe; and portraits of individual women conductors Renié, Helen Erdberg (known as *la Kazanova*), and Odaline de la Martinez. Many of these women pursued multi-faceted musical careers: pianist April, harpist Renié, and violinist *la Kazanova* were all well-known as performers, as were Carelli and de Philippe, who both pursued high-profile careers as operatic sopranos before they became *impresarios*, whilst de la Martinez is an internationally acclaimed composer.

Although women conductors have attracted an increased amount of scholarly recognition in recent years,[1] and several historical figures – such as Nadia Boulanger and Ethel Leginska – are now relatively established within music-historical narratives of the first half of the twentieth century,[2] the women considered here, Renié, *la Kazanova*, and de la Martinez, have not yet been included, and these chapters add significantly to studies of earlier twentieth-century conductors. Women *impresarios*, however, have been much well less researched to date. The studies included here, of Baylis, Carelli, Renié, and de Philipe, make important contributions and help bring a greater sense of gender equity to the historical overviews of earlier twentieth-century *impresarios*.[3] The majority of the chapters within Part II are based upon painstaking archival research, whilst Carola Darwin's draws upon an extensive ethnographic study, which enables us to hear the voice of de la Martinez, and those of her other participants, sounding through the text very clearly.

Chapters 10–12 all consider women's roles within theatre management in the first half of the twentieth century. In Chapter 10, Kenneth Baird considers the remarkable career of *impresario* Lilian Baylis (1874–1937), who played a foundational role in establishing several major British stage-based arts organisations, including the National Theatre, English National Opera, The Royal Ballet, and Birmingham Royal Ballet. In Chapter 11, Arianne Johnson

Quinn and Sarah K. Whitfield consider the substantial (yet often unacknowledged) contributions made to the development of the earlier twentieth-century British musical by the pianist, accompanist, and arranger Elsie April (1884–1950), notably through her artistic partnerships and collaborations with Charles B. Cochran and Noël Coward. In Chapter 12, Matteo Paoletti discusses the second career of the renowned Italian operatic soprano Emma Carelli (1877–1928) as an *impresario*, through a detailed consideration of her work managing the Teatro Costanzi in Rome in the early decades of the twentieth century.

In Chapter 13, Temina Cadi Sulumuna shines a penetrating light upon the musical leadership activities of the celebrated French harpist Henriette Renié (1875–1956) through considering her work as an ensemble leader – of her own renowned harp ensembles the *Sextuor Renié* and *Septuor Renié* – an occasional choral and orchestral conductor, and an *impresario*, most notably in relation to concerts intended to raise funds for her own musicians' benevolence fund, the *Petite Caisse des Artistes* (Little Fund for Artists). Retaining the focus on France, in Chapter 14, Jean-Christophe Branger considers the remarkable career which the American violinist and conductor Helen Victoria Rubin Erdberg (1907–1978, better known as *la Kazanova*) pursued in Paris during the 1930s as the violinist-leader of an otherwise all-male *tzigane* orchestra in the music halls. In Chapter 15, Kira Alvarez uncovers the career of the American operatic soprano turned *impresario* Edis de Philippe (1918–1978), who established the Israel National Opera (INO, founded 1947), which she ran – despite significant financial, political, and gender- and nationality-based barriers – until her death. In the final chapter within this part, Carola Darwin presents a compelling consideration of the conducting work of the Cuban American composer-conductor Odaline de la Martinez (b.1949), with particular attention paid to her work with her own ensemble, Lontano.

All the case studies of strong individual women leaders working within male-dominated musical roles and spaces brought together within Part II speak directly to the volume's central theme of women musicians confronting and confounding the *maestro* myth and tradition, as outlined in the Preface.

Notes

1. See, for example, Michele J. Edwards, "Women on the Podium," in *The Cambridge Companion to Conducting*, edited by José Bowen (Cambridge: Cambridge University Press, 2003), 220–36; and Laura Hamer, "On the Podium: Women Conductors," in *The Cambridge Companion to Women in Music Since 1900*, edited by Laura Hamer (Cambridge: Cambridge University Press, 2021), 64–79.
2. On Nadia Boulanger, see Jeanice Brooks, " 'Noble et grande servant de la musique': Telling the Story of Nadia Boulanger's Conducting Career," *Journal of Musicology* 14, no. 1 (Winter 1996): 92–116; and Jeanice Brooks, *The Musical Work of Nadia Boulanger: Performing Past and Future Between the Wars* (Cambridge: Cambridge University Press, 2013).
3. For another important study of Carelli, see Susan Rutherford, "The Prima Donna as Opera Impresario. Emma Carelli and the Teatro Costanzi, 1911–1926," in *The Arts of the Prima Donna in the Long Nineteenth Century*, edited by Rachel Cowgill and Hilary Poriss (Oxford: Oxford University Press, 2012), 272–89.

10
LILIAN BAYLIS
The Visionary Impresario

Kenneth Baird, with Laura Hamer

Lilian Baylis (1874–1937) was one of the most influential *impresarios* in the history of the performing arts in Britain. We assert that through her work over the first decades of the twentieth century she was the architect for the creation of some of the UK's most important performing companies. Baylis died on 25 November 1937. In an appreciation the following day, *The Manchester Guardian* was clear about her contribution:

> Miss Lilian Baylis . . . has left the most enduring memory. She made the Old Vic almost the one theatre in Britain to which an Englishman of cultivated tastes could go without first looking to see what was being played there – though not without first booking his seat. Her productions of Shakespeare did more than anything else to rescue our greatest dramatist from the hands of the unscrupulous actor-managers and to save him from the uncomfortable pedestal on which bardolaters had set him. It is significant that when this year controversy arose on the proposal to build a national theatre not only did Miss Baylis claim that she and her company were the national theatre but that many eminent authorities were ready to agree with her. Her work for opera was equally valiant, though its success was limited by the greater difficulties which surrounded it; the production of opera is an expensive pleasure, for which the English have always been unwilling to pay. Though Miss Baylis's name will always be connected with the Old Vic and Sadler's Wells theatres in London, she did not forget that London was not England. She sent a company to dance the ballets in the Northern cities and this year made it possible for Buxton to stage a dramatic festival of the highest quality. If she had lived longer this practical missionary of the theatre might have brought light into many dark places.[1]

In this chapter, we trace Baylis' career, paying particular attention to her ground-breaking innovations at the Old Vic and Sadler's Wells Theatres and role in establishing British ballet, and argue that her work laid the foundations for the creation of the National Theatre, English National Opera, The Royal Ballet, and Birmingham Royal Ballet.

Kenneth Baird, with Laura Hamer

Family Background and Apprenticeship with Emma Cons

Lilian Mary Baylis was born into a family of musicians and entertainers in London in 1874. At the age of seventeen, she emigrated with her family to South Africa. *The Gypsy Revellers* – the family's ensemble – set out to build on the success of their British concert presentations. Baylis was by now an accomplished musician, with the violin as her first study. The tour met financial difficulties, however; there were obvious tensions between the Dutch and British settlers drifting towards a Second Boer War and Baylis became seriously unwell.[2] Six years after her arrival, Baylis returned to London to assist her aunt, Emma Cons, who ran the Old Vic Theatre. Although this was initially planned as a short-term arrangement allowing Baylis to convalesce, the Old Vic was to become her operational base until her death in 1937.[3]

The Old Vic Theatre had originally opened in 1818 as the Royal Coburg Theatre. It gained its colloquial name of the 'Old Vic' after it was formally renamed the 'Royal Victoria Theatre' in the 1830s, and a rebuild in the early 1870s when it became the 'Royal Victoria Palace'. In 1880, the new lessee, Cons, oversaw a further change to the 'Royal Victoria Coffee and Music Hall'. Although Waterloo Bridge had opened this part of South London to the more affluent North, it was not an especially attractive area. The opening of Waterloo Station in the 1840s

Figure 10.1 *The Drawing of a Great Lady*, Lilian Baylis by Sir William Rothenstein (1922).
Source: reproduced with permission of the Lambeth Archives

had certainly swelled the potential audience, but not necessarily for the type of programme Cons had in mind.[4] As Edwin Fagg has commented:

> the district not only grew, but grew worse. In the 'seventies and 'eighties [1870s and 1880s], and even later, the neighbourhood of Stamford Street housed not only ordinarily unsavoury, but even infamous and notorious criminals, the two street levels near the bridge possibly favouring pickpockets and thieves of the meaner sort.[5]

Although in its history the theatre had attracted performers of distinction – such as Grimaldi, Kean, and Paganini – it had been built to present melodrama and popular entertainment, including pantomime and circus, and this largely remained its profile when Cons took over.

A talented artist, Cons had worked for distinguished London glassmaker James Powell & Sons, before taking over the lease of the Old Vic. She was part of a group of socially aware and dedicated women – sometimes referred to as 'New Women' (see also Chapter 7 ' "Une belle manifestation féministe: The Formation of the Union des Femmes Professeurs et Compositeurs de Musique' for a discussion of 'New Women'/'*femmes nouvelles*' in contemporary France) – who emerged in Britain at the end of the nineteenth century. Cons believed that women should pursue careers and favoured women's suffrage, identifying as a moderate suffragist (rather than a suffragette). She became the first woman Alderman of the London County Council in 1889 and was a friend of Octavia Hill, one of the three founders of the National Trust. Both were interested in the reform of social housing. Cons's vision for the Old Vic fitted with ease into this socially progressive and philanthropic ambition, retaining elements of the music hall, while introducing more educational offerings – 'concerts of "good music" . . . rather elementary opera . . . lectures'.[6] Three years after taking on the theatre, the Royal Victoria Coffee and Music Hall offered 'wholesome and cheerful recreation for the working classes of London'.[7] Soup, beef, cheese, currant cake, coffee, a return bus or tram ticket, and 'entrance to capital entertainment' could be had for one shilling and tuppence.[8] In spite of Cons' dedication, skills as a fundraiser for social causes, and the assistance of a series of professional theatre managers, the programme only made small shifts from what had gone before, consisting mainly of ballad concerts (comprising Victorian popular songs with some operatic arias). Although oratorio was introduced and opera concerts were given in tableau form to avoid infringing music-hall licencing regulations,[9] the big shift in programming and financial viability unquestionably came with Baylis' arrival in 1898.

Baylis was tactful over the role she played in taking over from her aunt, referring to herself as 'Acting Manager'. With characteristic self-effacement, Baylis later claimed to have stepped in 'to allow her [Cons] more time for her housing and other works for the public good'.[10] Even after Cons' death in 1912, Baylis as Lessee and Manager would continue to credit Cons' contribution in print – 'Royal Victoria Hall, founded by the late Miss Emma Cons in 1880' – and this practice continued into the 1930s. In reality, Baylis was the sole manager of the Old Vic from 1898, taking on this challenging task in her mid-twenties. In common with other very successful women leaders of the time, she developed a style of claiming expertise in nothing, putting her success down to enlisting 'the service of really first-class people',[11] rather than her own agency and talents.

Baylis developed a reputation as a particularly shrewd financial manager; demands considered unrealistic were routinely brushed aside with a quip. It is important to remember that she was developing a theatre before the existence of public subsidies for the arts. Although she would later be proved to be an astute risk-taker over big decisions, day-to-day finances had to be controlled. Her management style and prudent financial decision-making became widely known, and throughout her career this assisted in the purpose she intended: to limit demands, especially financial. There has been a tendency for Baylis' reputation to rest on stories and anecdotes relating to individual occurrences, many to do with money; but *impresarios* must develop strategies to tackle the less palatable, in part simply to cope with daily pressures. The quips and the claims not to be expert in anything were all part of this, while the longer-term vision continued to be pursued with complete determination. Baylis was particularly judicious in her ability to foresee potential challenges. For example, when offering Jane Vowles the title role in Holst's *Savitri* in 1935, Baylis made it absolutely clear that the fee was 'to cover your expenses for all performances and rehearsals', adding, 'I think it will almost certainly be broadcast on the 26th [October] but there is nothing extra for our artists in this!'[12] The tight budgetary regime at the Old Vic, and later at Sadler's Wells, became the stuff of anecdote; but the Old Vic had had an uncertain financial history when she took it on, and without financial stringency Baylis could not have succeeded in her longer-term ambitions.

Baylis' Vision for the Old Vic

Baylis had two targets for the development of the Old Vic: Shakespeare and opera. This was a radical change from what had gone before. She did not claim any credit in forming a strategy, rather citing public taste: 'Gradually the desire for ballad concerts became less and operas grew in favour.'[13] This is Baylis being self-effacing: aiming to create a repertory house based on the presentation of Shakespeare's plays and a wide range of operatic repertoire was a bold step, especially given the UK arts environment of the time, and it formed part of Baylis' vision for the development of the performing arts in the UK. There had been no Shakespeare under the Cons/Baylis regime until 1914, and within ten years every play in the First Folio had been performed.[14] Before Shakespeare, Baylis had turned the Old Vic into one of the two earliest picture houses in London (Alexandra Palace being the other). This proved immensely lucrative: admission of 1d [1 pence] and 2d [2 pence] made £2,000 in a couple of years, 'which I afterwards spent and lost on symphony concerts.'[15] Films were abandoned – supposedly because of difficulty in finding 'clean' films – in reality, however, probably because of growing competition. Alongside 'good' plays,[16] opera was given twice a week. There were also travel talks, and the work of Morley College – physically part of the building and established under Cons' lessee-ship – provided adult education courses with expert teachers. In 1914, Mendelssohn's oratorio *Elijah* was staged. By the Shakespeare Birthday Festival in spring 1918, the Royal Victoria Hall – now described as the 'People's Opera, Play and Lecture House' – had presented 200 performances of over two dozen plays (mainly Shakespeare) and 80 opera performances. Baylis achieved her goal of attracting a cross-section of society and the audience was similar in profile to a description of the opera chorus of 1920: 'clerks ... shop assistants ... telephone operators (and one member with the piquant profession of horse-coper)'.[17] The novelist Sir Hugh Walpole later observed that much of the audience for Sadler's Wells was 'for the most part from neighbouring districts'. He summarised Baylis' contribution to audience-building thus: 'She has made everybody feel that the Arts of acting and dancing and singing need every kind of hard work for their perfection but are in their performance simple and easy and belong to everybody.'[18]

Baylis' skill in developing the programme so rapidly lay in her ability to build a series of performing companies with key people in crucial positions. It is quite clear that she had the capability both to recruit with great discernment and to retain people for extended periods. There is the sense that those working at the Old Vic had great affection for their leader. After some success in presenting Shakespeare with the husband-and-wife team Matheson Lang and Hutin Britton, Baylis invited Ben Greet, an actor-manager who had experience in running his own companies, to join the Old Vic. Greet was an experienced Shakespearian. As well as directing, he could step in to play small roles or indeed leading characters: Malvolio in *Twelfth Night* or Prospero in *The Tempest*, for example. Baylis typically gave warm acknowledgement to the leading figures in her companies. As she recollected in a recording made in 1937:

> In 1914, Matheson Lang and his wife really put my feet on the right road for Shakespeare … I owe a tremendous lot to the Langs … Sir Philip Ben Greet produced for me for four years. Since then, I've had the most excellent producers.[19]

One of Bayliss' other important innovations during this time was the introduction of matinee performances for schools. These were supported by the London County Council.

The Old Vic attracted a remarkable group of actors between the two World Wars. Peggy Ashcroft, George Devine, Edith Evans, John Gielgud, Alec Guinness, Charles Laughton (viewed by Baylis as one of her more spectacular catches), Vivien Leigh, Laurence Olivier, Anthony Quayle, Michael Redgrave, Ralph Richardson, Flora Robson, Sybil Thorndike, and Harcourt Williams are some of the more familiar names from the Baylis years. It is estimated that more than 1200 actors were engaged by the Old Vic Company between 1914 and the end of the 1940s.[20] Actors tended to be engaged for a season, and a substantial proportion returned repeatedly and were given the opportunity to take roles which they would often not have secured elsewhere. Thus, the Old Vic became the most remarkable training ground for British theatre and the emerging British film industry.

In opera, Baylis' key collaborator was unquestionably Charles Corri. Corri, whom Baylis inherited from the Cons years, came from a long line of musicians and was clearly immensely skilled as an orchestrator and arranger. From the outset, there seems to have been little consideration of opera performances with piano accompaniment, which would have suited financial stringencies: instead, a small instrumental ensemble was used not only for opera, but also for the incidental music included in Shakespeare performances.[21] The policy was to present opera in English, which also accommodated Baylis' ambition to encourage English opera. As the well-known conductor Lawrance Collingwood observed, 'In 1922 she decided to mount an English opera and thereupon embarked on her policy of promotion of contemporary English works. Her choice was Ethel Smyth's *The Boatswain's Mate*'.[22]

Collingwood, who would later become a key figure in the Sadler's Wells Opera Company, was recruited by Baylis in 1920 to assist Corri as a *repetiteur*. Reflecting contemporary social views on gender, Collingwood openly admitted his amazement on his first visit to the Old Vic 'at finding a woman at the head of affairs there.'[23] He went on to give a precise description of the musical set-up in the company:

> The Shakespeare orchestra … consisted of: 2 violins, 1 viola, 1 'cello, a cornet, flute, clarinet and piano. Charles Corri played the 'cello, his brother the viola, and his son led the violins. This small band played at all the Shakespeare performances and was the nucleus of the enlarged orchestra which played at the opera. This latter consisted of: 4 first violins, 2 seconds, 1 viola, 1 'cello, 1 bass, 1 flute, 1 oboe, 2 clarinets, 1 bassoon, 2 trumpets, 2 horns, 1 trombone and timpani. This enlarged orchestra was further augmented on Wagner nights when there would be 4 horns, and 3 trombones … Gradually the standard of performance rose and soon Corri deemed it desirable to add *Tristan and Isolde* to the repertoire and we worked very intensely in preparation for it. The orchestra grew still further in size until it reached the large number of 28. Miss Baylis watched us working with eager impatience, following with interest every detail of the work.[24]

Now that performances of opera in reduced orchestrations have again become more widespread – both for economic reasons and to extend the range of venues which can be used – there can be greater appreciation for what Corri achieved. Although singers – notably including the soprano Joan Cross (who joined the Old Vic Company in 1923) – did not always find Corri's conducting sympathetic, he made a huge contribution to the tradition of opera performances in English. Corri moved with the opera company to Sadler's Wells in 1931, and on his retirement in 1935 he was one of the few members to be given a pension (no doubt reflecting the high regard in which Baylis held him).

Move to the Sadler's Wells Theatre

With the growing success of both the Shakespeare and the Opera companies, the limitation of space at the Old Vic was becoming a restriction to both. This was despite Morley College's move out of the building and refurbishment of the Old Vic itself. So, from the mid-1920s, Baylis planned her biggest gamble: the acquisition of the derelict Sadler's Wells Theatre. The new Sadler's Wells reopened under Baylis' management on 6 January 1931 with a production of *Twelfth Night*. The production was well received by the press. *The Daily Herald* reported the next day that:

> Sadler's Wells Theatre, the Old Vic of North London, was opened [. . .] last night, Mr J R Clynes, the Home Secretary, being in the audience [. . .] 'I declare Sadler's Wells open' Sir Johnston Forbes-Robertson [the distinguished actor] looked with pride round the crowded house [. . .] On the stage were mayors and councillors, wearing their badges of office [. . .] In her University robes sat Miss Lilian Baylis, whose undaunted spirit had created this new home for Shakespeare and opera.[25]

After a few months of an expanded programme, it seemed possible that Sadler's Wells would have to close. *The Old Vic and Sadler's Wells Magazine* for the start of the 1931/1932 season records that 'the Vic owes some £5,000, and the Wells some £22,000.'[26] Yet it was not the capital deficit which caused the main concern (although it was about £1.5 million in today's terms); rather the worldwide financial depression and its impact on ticket sales. Baylis writes in the Magazine that:

> The first Shakespeare season at the Vic started with the Great War. I feel it is a good omen that our first complete season commences with our country again at war, not thank God, with our brothers across the North Sea but at war with financial difficulties – our millions of unemployed and other national problems.'[27]

With characteristic openness, Baylis presented a number of pragmatic suggestions to address this:

> Perhaps in the face of national economies the man who must sit in a stall can't pay 14/6 for it; but he can perhaps pay 5/-. The man who usually spends a shilling cannot afford that any longer; but he can pay 6d. It is indeed for a People's Theatre a time of emergency; it is also a time of great opportunity. It is true that we have extraordinary difficulties before us; but we also have an extraordinary chance to bring into our net many who in the ordinary way would not dream of sampling Shakespeare or opera in English unless they could get it as cheaply as the nearest cinema entertainment. On these two notes therefore – determination and hope – the new season opens.[28]

It is typical of Baylis' leadership to place her overriding mission above excessive financial caution.

Collaboration with Ninette de Valois: Building a British Ballet Company

There had been various attempts by Baylis to introduce dance as the third element in the Old Vic programme, mainly within opera performances, when in 1926 Ninette de Valois – who had danced with one of the Diaghilev companies and had her own dance school in London – approached her. De Valois had a longstanding ambition to create a ballet company, initially within a repertory theatre, but had received several rejections from well-established enterprises. Baylis engaged de Valois, initially as essentially a movement coach, but also providing some opportunities to choreograph the dances in Shakespeare productions. Opera ballets and short stand-alone works followed; for instance, there were ten short 'curtain-raisers' in the 1929/1930 season. So, by the time of the acquisition of Sadler's Wells, it can be said there was already a small dance company (the Vic-Wells ballet) in place ready to move from the Old Vic. Baylis herself recounted that:

> I believe we are on the threshold of a great renaissance of ballet in England: and that this renaissance will be characterized by the fact that English dancers . . . will be acknowledged here, as they have long been abroad, as truly fine exponents of the most difficult and comprehensive of all the arts. When I was a young woman, I dreamed of a great temple where the three theatrical arts, drama, opera and dancing, could be housed. Some nine years ago Ninette de Valois came to me and revealed that she had been dreaming a very similar dream; she wanted to create an English school of ballet, attached to a theatre, where the dancers could have real and constant stage experience. At that time our Shakespeare and Opera companies were crowding each other out of the shabby Old Vic. But there was a movement on foot to acquire and rebuild the derelict Sadler's Wells and hand it over to our management. What was an impossibility in one ordinary building might be feasible in two under the same control. Ninette de Valois bided her time. She devised the dances in our operas and plays, with a scratch company rehearsed in odd corners, in bars and dressing-rooms, and drew up her big scheme. When it was certain that we would open Sadler's Wells in 1931 she persuaded me to give one whole evening each fortnight to ballet performances. Frankly I confess I did not believe these could be anything but an artistic success. I was wrong. There was, apparently, a public in London that had been waiting for just this experiment.[29]

By the time of Baylis' death in 1937, the Vic-Wells Ballet Company had grown to 32 dancers, two resident choreographers, a resident conductor, and a school of some 40 students.[30] (De Valois had moved her own school to be resident at Sadler's Wells). The majority of the new company members came from the school. The repertoire included Tchaikovsky's ballets alongside other classics such as *Carnaval*, *Coppelia*, *Giselle*, *Les Sylphides*, and an impressive list of new works created by the company. The latter included *Job* (Vaughan Williams, 1931), *Checkmate* (Bliss, 1937), *Façade* (Walton, 1922), and works set to the music of the resident conductor, Constant Lambert. Designers included Cecil Beaton, Vanessa Bell, Edward Burra, Edmund Dulac, Duncan Grant, and Rex Whistler. Dancers included Alicia Markova, Margot Fonteyn (who came from the theatre school), Robert Helpmann, and Anton Dolin. In 1935, Frederick Ashton joined de Valois as joint principal choreographer. De Valois followed Baylis' policy of encouraging British artists.

In an interview two months before her death, Baylis credited the success of the ballet company to de Valois who 'has had the inspiration all through', but also felt that Constant Lambert and Frederick Ashton were crucial members of the team.[31] The Sadler's Wells production of *The Sleeping Beauty* – in preparation at the time of Baylis' death – opened at the theatre in February 1939 with Margot Fonteyn as Princess Aurora and Robert Helpmann as the lead Prince. It was the revival of this Sadler's Wells production – again with Fonteyn and Helpmann – which reopened the Royal Opera House, Covent Garden, on 20 February 1946. New cast members included Beryl Grey, Moira Shearer, and Michael Somes; and there were new designs by Oliver Messel, who had designed productions for the Old Vic. So, while Baylis might well have been cautious over the re-emergence of what she could have felt was a rival institution, it was very much her team who had been engaged for the re-opening and who sustained and developed the early years.

Baylis' and de Valois' collaboration laid the foundations for the creation of not just one but two major British ballet companies: The Royal Ballet and the Birmingham Royal Ballet, both of which developed from the Royal Opera House. The Royal Opera House had had an uneven history in the 1930s. There had been an attempt to provide subsidies, but this was not sustained, and during the Second World War the theatre was used as a dance hall. After the war, there were plans to create a national lyric theatre, with support provided by the newly established Arts Council of Great Britain,[32] chaired by economist John Maynard Keynes. Keynes died shortly before the Arts Council was formally constituted, but his influence was felt through his chairing of the wartime Committee for the Encouragement of Music and the Arts (hereafter CEMA), which was established by Royal Charter in 1940. The 1944 CEMA report states that the Council planned 'to reclaim the Royal Opera House, Covent Garden, as the national centre for opera and ballet'.[33] Keynes was married to the Russian ballerina Lydia Lopokova, who had occasionally appeared with the Vic-Wells companies. He was also – with Lopokova – a founding member of the Camargo Society – established in 1929 to support British dance, and which had been associated with several of the Sadler's Wells productions. Keynes's brother Geoffrey, meanwhile, had developed the scenario for Vaughan Williams' *Job* from William Blake's *Illustrations of the Book of Job*.[34] Thus, Keynes knew the Vic-Wells operation and Baylis well.

The Sadler's Wells ballet company had toured extensively during the Second World War. Just before the reopening of the Royal Opera House, the Company had ended a gruelling year performing in London, the regions, and abroad, including performances in Germany. Six weeks of rehearsal at the Opera House was accompanied by constant building work. Tolerating the frustrations proved worthwhile: the Royal Opera House would become the Company's new home. Sadler's Wells Ballet retained its name at the Royal Opera House until 1956, when, to mark the 25th anniversary of its move in 1931 as the Vic-Wells Ballet to Sadler's Wells Theatre, it became The Royal Ballet. A new company sprang up at Sadler's Wells Theatre – the Sadler's Wells Theatre Ballet – continuing the tradition of touring. In 1990, the successor to this company moved to Birmingham to become the Birmingham Royal Ballet.

De Valois died in 2001 at the age of 102. She had directed The Royal Ballet until 1963, and The Royal Ballet School until 1970. Although her role in the development of British ballet is well-known, knowledge of Baylis' part has faded; indeed, it might be said that it has been written out. The Royal Opera House itself now states:

> The Royal Ballet owes its existence to the vision of Dame Ninette de Valois, dancer, choreographer and entrepreneur, who assembled a small company and school, the Vic-Wells Ballet, and, in 1931, persuaded Lilian Baylis to provide it with a home at the Sadler's Wells Theatre in North London.[35]

Lilian Baylis

Thus, the establishment of The Royal Ballet is attributed wholly to de Valois, and the crucial role also played by Baylis is unacknowledged. In a television interview in 1979, de Valois herself dismissed the years before the move to Covent Garden as 'fringe'.[36] Perhaps she felt her legacy would best be served by focusing on her work from 1945. There are occasional hints that Baylis was keen to keep de Valois's view of her own status in check, reflecting some animosity between the two women. For instance, Baylis spoke about finding dancers at the end of piers (even de Valois herself admitted that the first place that she danced professionally was the Old [West] Pier in Brighton). Furthermore, in the foreword to a 1934 study of de Valois, Baylis was quoted making reference to English dancers 'no longer hiding under foreign pseudonyms'.[37] De Valois was, of course, born Edris Stannus.

Assessing Baylis' Legacy

So how best to assess the quality and impact of Baylis' work? One of the criticisms often levied against her is that she failed to encourage new work. It is perhaps a rather harsh accusation, given that she was introducing work to a new audience unfamiliar with the core repertoire. The criticism certainly does not hold up when examining her work in dance, although in both theatre and opera there were also efforts to extend the repertoire. George Bernard Shaw was introduced from 1930 by Harcourt Williams, with Shaw visiting to read *Arms and the Man* to the Company. Ibsen's *Peer Gynt* was given its first performance in Britain in 1922, revived in 1935, and later joined by *An Enemy of the People* and *Ghosts* – one of the three plays taken to Buxton to establish a drama festival there. Chekhov appeared from the 1933/1934 season with *The Cherry Orchard* and was followed by a wartime production of *Uncle Vanya*. Pinero's *Trelawny of the Wells* first appeared in 1925, perhaps a wry hint of Baylis' ambitions for a second theatre.[38]

In opera, there was a commitment to new work and to British composers from the outset at Sadler's Wells. At the Old Vic there had been attempts to introduce new operas: Ethel Smyth's *Fête Galante* and *The Boatswain's Mate*, and two operas by the now largely forgotten Yorkshire composer Nicholas Gatty. In the 1930s, Sadler's Wells showed a strong commitment to British repertoire with operas – some entirely new – by Arthur Benjamin, a further opera by Nicholas Gatty, Gustav Holst (*Savitri*), a revival of Smyth's *The Boatswain's Mate*, followed by *The Wreckers*, Stanford's *The Travelling Companion*, Vaughan Williams' *Hugh the Drover*, and a treatment of *Macbeth* by Lawrence Collingwood. As further additions to the repertoire, Mussorgsky's *Boris Godunov* in its 1869 version was performed at Sadler's Wells in 1935 – the first performances of the original outside Russia – and two years earlier, Rimsky-Korsakov's *The Snow Maiden* was given its British premiere. Joan Cross described Baylis' contribution in opera thus:

> In my humble opinion, this briefly-told story is the picture of a foundation-stone of opera in England. From the end of the first war to the beginning of the second, Baylis had been responsible for building an opera company almost out of nothing into something which counted in musical circles in London and elsewhere. Most important of all, she had created a taste for opera in a not inconsiderable audience.[39]

Immediately after World War Two, Sadler's Wells Opera published a booklet on *Opera in English*.[40] As well as recording the Company's wartime service, the contributors – Tyrone Guthrie, Edwin Evans, Cross, Edward J Dent, and de Valois – aspired to the creation of a new kind of opera in the English language. 'If we are to create a really native type of opera we must strike out in new directions' was musicologist Edward J Dent's view. (Dent had himself made an important contribution to opera in English by his own first-rate translations for the Company.) Within weeks, the aspiration had been fulfilled. On 7 June 1945, largely through the insistence of Cross, who had run the wartime Company, Sadler's Wells Opera gave the first performance of Britten's *Peter Grimes*. There was immediate realisation that this was, indeed, the new direction that had been sought; the fortunes of opera in English were transformed. Baylis' work in building up a company which invariably sang in English, and in attracting a growing audience which appreciated opera in English, played a key part in this transformation. Writing about *Peter Grimes*, Britten admitted, 'the qualities of the Opera Company have considerably influenced both the shape and characterisation of the opera.'[41]

The Baylis companies were also among the first to tour abroad. As early as 1921, the theatre company performed at the Théâtre Royal du Parc in Brussels at the invitation of the Belgian Ministry of Fine Arts. In 1937, *Hamlet*, with Laurence Olivier in the title role and Vivien Leigh as Ophelia, was taken to Elsinore, although the Danish weather prevented outside performances. (Olivier later wrote: 'It was at Elsinore that I personally saw Lilian at the truest and best, when she would sit solidly through the age-long exterior rehearsals in the drenching rain, encouraging us with very rough pats on the back'.)[42] In the same year, the British Council chose the Sadler's Wells Ballet as the British contribution to the Paris Exhibition; they gave six performances at the Théâtre de Champs-Elysées.

All of this was achieved in the days before the general availability of public subsidy of the arts. Despite occasional hints of snobbery towards her – for example, de Valois somewhat cruelly opined in her memoir that 'mentally, she [Baylis] was not unlike a sincere, shrewd, devout peasant'[43] – Baylis was able to move within the top circles of society. She was an extremely skilled fundraiser. The fundraising committee established in 1925 to enable the purchase and refurbishment of Sadler's Wells included the Prime Minister (Stanley Baldwin), two former Prime Ministers (Arthur Balfour and H.H. Asquith), Sir Thomas Beecham, Lady Cunard, G K Chesterton, Winston Churchill, and John Galsworthy.[44] Shortly before, the move of Morley College and the improvements of the Old Vic required by the licensing authority were made possible by a gift of £30,000 from Sir George Dance. Baylis seems to have been able to attract funds from society figures from the outset: supporters of her first appeal in 1898 included Beecham, the composer Edward German, and Sir.[45] One of the annual fundraising events was the Costume Ball, which proved so successful that it moved to the Royal Albert Hall in the 1930s. The Coronation Year Ball of 1937 included an appeal by Laurence Olivier, who presented prizes for the Fancy Dress Parade with Edith Evans. The judges were the theatrical impresario Charles B Cochran, the actor Leslie Banks, Henry Wood, and Ivor Novello.

In 1993, Sir John Drummond interviewed the theatre designer Tanya Moiseiwitsch – who had learnt her craft in part at the Old Vic – and asked about her view of standards there. Moiseiwitsch shared seeing 'absolutely magical things', going on to state that 'Gielgud . . . as King Lear was as great as I ever wish to see.'[46] In assessing Baylis' overall contribution, Moiseiwitsch showed great perception: 'she did lend herself to stories'.[47] Much of what has been recorded about Baylis constitutes stories and anecdotes. Certainly, she may well have built up a persona, particularly to enhance her reputation for stern financial dealings. Claiming ignorance about the professional arts was an effective tool in allowing the huge range of talented people she managed to attract – and who cannot always have been easy to handle – scope in developing their own practice, until she decided to intervene. Baylis was a good musician: at an Old Vic rehearsal for *Don Giovanni* she was asked, without warning, to play the mandolin obbligato for the aria *Deh, vieni alla finestra*, which she did from memory. She was made an external examiner by the Royal College of Music in 1925. As well as planning the repertory, she alone cast opera performances until four years before her death. As Collingwood writes:

> It was not until 1933 that she began to feel that her tremendous work was becoming too much for her and she arranged for the conductors and producers to meet regularly to help her fix the repertoire and casts; until then she had been completely autocratic.[48]

To mark the centenary of Baylis' arrival at the Old Vic, in 1998 author, playwright, and screenwriter Ronald Harwood hosted a radio celebration of Baylis' life. The account of her work and achievements was given by author Joy Melville. She concluded that Baylis' legacy either directly or through 'people who came out of the Vic' could be credited with the creation of Sadler's Wells Opera (now English National Opera, hereafter the ENO),[49] Sadler's Wells Ballet (now the Birmingham Royal Ballet), The Royal Ballet, the Royal Court, the Stratford Festival, the Shakespeare Memorial Theatre, and, ultimately, the Royal Shakespeare Company and the National Theatre. Yet today, even among those who work in the arts, knowledge of Baylis' work has faded.

In 1981, ENO unveiled a plaque in the London Coliseum (its new home) celebrating the 50th anniversary of the founding of Sadler's Wells Opera and commemorating Baylis in 'homage' to her. 'Homage' in English is a strong word and perhaps reflected the fact that members of the Company still knew her work first-hand. ENO continues to acknowledge Baylis' foundational work. In the 'History of ENO' section of their website, they include a prominent photograph of Baylis and explain that:

> English National Opera traces its roots back to 1931 when Lilian Baylis established the Sadler's Wells Opera Company at the newly re-opened the Sadler's Wells Theatre. Baylis had been presenting opera concerts and theatre in London since 1898 and was passionate about providing audiences with the best theatre and opera at affordable prices, a belief that remains today at the heart of ENO.[50]

ENO's impressive and extensive outreach and educational programme was also originally named after Baylis (ENO Baylis) when it was founded in 1985. While this further homage to her is positive, it is also possible to suggest that it perpetuates the view that Baylis' work was primarily about access, rather than raising standards and forming companies in the performing arts. Set against the wider context that much of the work of arts, including, opera outreach, and education, tends to be female-dominated, it can be seen as consigning women's work in the theatre and opera house to this traditionally female-dominated space. At the National Theatre and Old Vic respectively there is a terrace and a circle named after Baylis, as well as a studio at Sadler's Wells Theatre. In the introduction to the radio celebration in 1998, Ronald Harwood expressed his strongly held view that one of the stages at the National Theatre should have been named after her.

In her lifetime, Baylis' achievements were widely recognised. As Doris Westwood recorded in *These Players: A Diary of the Old Vic*:

> We have heard that a great honour is to be bestowed upon Miss Baylis. She has been notified that Oxford University intends to confer on her the honorary degree of Master of Arts. The only other woman in the world to hold such a degree is the Queen.[51]

Baylis was indeed awarded an honorary master's degree from Oxford in 1924; Birmingham University followed with an honorary Doctor of Laws; and in 1929, she was made a Companion of Honour for services to the nation. Baylis wore her cap and gown on first and last nights; presumably, in part, to add gravitas to her fundraising appeals from the stage, and styled herself Miss Lilian Baylis, CH, MA Oxon (Hon) LL.D Birm (Hon). Sadly, this recognition of her achievements is now fading and is in danger of being lost entirely. As other personalities involved with the performing arts in Britain in the twentieth century have come to the fore in her place, we hope this reassessment will play its part in keeping alive knowledge of Baylis' truly remarkable achievements.

Notes

1. Anonymous, "Lilian Baylis," *The Manchester Guardian*, November 26, 1937, 10.
2. The Second Boer War took place between October 11, 1899 and May 31, 1902.
3. For a full biography, see Elizabeth Schafer, *Lilian Baylis: A Biography* (Hatfield: University of Hertfordshire Press, 2006).
4. See Edwin Fagg, *The Old "Old Vic" A Glimpse of the Old Theatre, from Its Origins as "The Royal Coburg", First Managed by William Barrymore, to Its Revival Under Lilian Baylis* (London: Vic-Wells Association, 1936).
5. Ibid., 120.
6. Ivor Brown, "Lilian Baylis Old Vic Directress and Empressario," *Theatre Arts Monthly* (February 1938): 114.
7. Ibid., 112.
8. Paraphrased from 'The Royal Victoria Coffee and Music Hall, 1883', a cartoon image reproduced in Edwin Fagg, *The Old "Old Vic"*.
9. A mix of national legislation, local regulation, and copyright rules meant that music halls were only permitted to present a series of sketches and numbers, each of limited length. Operatic arias had to be performed with limited movement.
10. *Lilian Baylis talks on "The Old Vic" and "Sadler's Wells" theatres*. A recording made for the Vic-Wells Association (a subsidiary of HMV), 1936. Private Record JGS 8. Tanya Moiseiwitsch Collection. Held by the British Library; Call Number: CKEY6796929. This recording was originally produced for the Vic-Wells Association and sold in the two theatres.
11. Lilian Baylis, Ibid.
12. Letter from Lilian Baylis to Janes Vowles (September 13, 1935); held in the private collection of the first author.
13. *Lilian Baylis talks on "The Old Vic" and "Sadler's Wells" theatres*.
14. Brown, "Lilian Baylis Old Vic Directress and Empressario," 114.
15. *Lilian Baylis talks on "The Old Vic" and "Sadler's Wells" theatres*.
16. 'Good plays' – judging from the first seasons – meant Sheridan and Goldsmith alongside Shakespeare.
17. Irene Beeston, " Kaleidoscope 1920–25," in *Vic-Wells: The Work of Lilian Baylis*, edited by Harcourt Williams and Lilian Baylis with Angus McBean (Photographer) (London: Cobden-Sanderson, 1938), 51.
18. Sir Huge Walpole, "A First-Class Cockney," in Ibid., 6–7.
19. *Lilian Baylis talks on "The Old Vic" and "Sadler's Wells" theatres*.
20. Harcourt Williams, *Old Vic Saga* (London: Winchester Publications Limited, 1949), Appendix B.
21. In 1918, Shakespeare's *Henry VIII* had a vocal trio by Edward German. By the 1930s, much of the incidental music was composed by Herbert Menges (who also acted as Music Director), with others contributing specific numbers; for example, Maurice Jacobson's Music for the Mime in *Hamlet*.
22. Lawrance Collingwood cited from Williams, Baylis, and McBean, *Vic-Wells: The Work of Lilian Baylis*, 78.
23. Ibid., 77.
24. Ibid., 78.
25. Anonymous, "New 'Old Vic' Opened – Rally of Leading Ladies – £70,000 Triumph," *The Daily Herald*, January 7, 1931, 2.

26. Lilian Baylis, "Editorial," *The Old Vic and Sadler's Wells Magazine* 1, no. 5, September–October 1931, 1.
27. Ibid.
28. Ibid.
29. Lilian Baylis, "Preface," in *Ninette de Valois and the Vic-Wells Ballet*, edited by Kate Neatby and Edwin Evans (London: British Continental Press, 1934), 7.
30. Ninette de Valois, "The Vic-Wells Ballet," in Baylis Wiliams and McBeady, *The Work of Lilian Baylis*, 97.
31. *Lilian Baylis talks on "The Old Vic" and "Sadler's Wells" theatres*.
32. The Arts Council of Great Britain was established in 1946.
33. Anonymous, "The Fifth Year. The End of the Beginning," Annual Report on the Work of the CEMA (1944), 6.
34. Geoffrey Keynes, *Job and the Rake's Progress*, Sadler's Wells Ballet Books no. 2 (1949): 24–34.
35. History, accessed September 9, 2023, roh.org.uk.
36. Dame Ninette de Valois interview with David Dimbleby for BBC One (first broadcast July 26, 1979).
37. Baylis in Neatby and Evans (eds.), *Ninette de Valois and the Vic-Wells Ballet*, 7.
38. Ibid.
39. Joan Cross, "The Bad Old Days," in *Tribute to Benjamin on His Fiftieth Birthday*, edited by Benjamin Britten and Anthony Gishford (London: Faber and Faber, 1963), 183.
40. Eric Crozier (ed.), *Opera in English*, Sadler's Wells Opera Books No. 1, Published for the Governors of the Sadler's Wells Foundation (London: The Bodley Head, 1945).
41. Benjamin Britten quoted in Stephen Williams, "Opera in London," *Penguin Music Magazine*, no. 1 (1946): 102.
42. Ninette de Valois, "The Vic-Wells Ballet," 99.
43. Ninette de Valois, *Come Dance with Me* (Dublin: Lilliput Press, 1957), 80.
44. Richard Jarman, *A History of Sadler's Wells Opera and English National Opera: An Illustrated Booklet, Published to Mark 50 Years of the Company's Work* (London: English National Opera, 1981), 14.
45. Fagg, *The Old "Old Vic"*, 122.
46. Tanya Moiseiwitsch interview with Sir John Drummond for BBC Radio 3 (first broadcast 19 April 1993).
47. Tanya Moiseiwitsch interview with Sir John Drummond (1993).
48. Lawrance Collingwood cited from Williams, Baylis, and McBean, *Vic-Wells: The Work of Lilian Baylis*, 80.
49. Joy Melville, "A Centenary Celebration of Lilian Baylis'; held at the British Library Sound Archive, Call Number: C125/315.
50. History of ENO | English National Opera (accessed August 24, 2023).
51. Doris Westwood with a Foreword by Lilian Baylis, *These Players. A Diary of the "Old Vic"* (London: Heath Cranton Limited, 1924), 253.

Bibliography

Primary Sources

Original letters of Lilian Baylis (held by Kenneth Baird).
The British Library Sound Archive: Various original sound recordings and broadcasts.

Printed Sources

Anonymous. "New "Old Vic" Opened – Rally of Leading Ladies – £70,000 Triumph." *The Daily Herald*, January 7, 1931, 2.
Anonymous. "Lilian Baylis." *The Manchester Guardian*, November 26, 1937, 10.
Anonymous. "The Fifth Year. The End of the Beginning." Annual Report on the Work of the CEMA (1944).
Baylis, Lilian. "Editorial." *The Old Vic and Sadler's Wells Magazine* 1, no. 5, September–October 1931, 1.

_____. "Preface." In *Ninette de Valois and the Vic-Wells Ballet*, Kate Neatby and Edwin Evans, 7. London: British Continental Press, 1934.
Britten, Benjamin, and Anthony Gishford, eds. *Tribute to Benjamin Britten on His Fiftieth Birthday*. London: Faber and Faber, 1963.
Brown, Ivor. "Lilian Baylis *Old Vic Directress and Empressario*." *Theatre Arts Monthly*, February 1938, 114.
Crozier, Eric, ed. *Opera in English*, Sadler's Wells Opera Books No. 1, Published for the Governors of the Sadler's Wells Foundation. London: The Bodley Head, 1945.
de Valois, Ninette. "The Vic-Wells Ballet." In *The Work of Lilian Baylis*, photography Harcourt Williams and Lilian Baylis with Angus McBeady, 97. London: Cobden-Sanderson, 1938.
_____. *Come Dance With Me*. Dublin: Lilliput Press, 1957.
Fagg, Edwin. *The Old "Old Vic" A Glimpse of the old Theatre, from Its Origins as "The Royal Coburg", first managed by William Barrymore, to Its Revival under Lilian Baylis*. London: Vic-Wells Association, 1936.
Jarman, Richard. *A History of Sadler's Wells Opera and English National Opera: An Illustrated Booklet, Published to Mark 50 Years of the Company's Work*. London: English National Opera, 1981.
Keynes, Geoffrey. *Job and The Rake's Progress*, Sadler's Wells Ballet Books No. 2 (1949).
Schafer, Elizabeth. *Lilian Baylis: A Biography*. Hatfield: University of Hertfordshire Press, 2006.
Westwood, Doris, with a Foreword by Lilian Baylis. *These Players. A Diary of the "Old Vic"*. London: Heath Cranton Limited, 1924.
Williams, Harcourt. *Old Vic Saga*. London: Winchester Publications Limited, 1949.
_____, and Lilian Baylis, eds., with Angus McBean, Photographer. *Vic-Wells: The Work of Lilian Baylis*. London: Cobden-Sanderson, 1938.
Williams, Stephen. "Opera in London." *Penguin Music Magazine*, no. 1 (1946): 102.

11
MUSICAL GHOSTS
Re-Instating Elsie April in Historical Narratives of the British Musical

Arianne Johnson Quinn and Sarah K. Whitfield

At once a pianist, arranger, accompanist, and musical mastermind, Elsie April (1884–1950) has long been ignored by scholars. Despite her many collaborations with some of the most significant forces in the musical world of London's West End — spanning several decades from the 1920s onward — her contributions have been, at most, a footnote in historical accounts of musical theatre. She has been politely dismissed by Coward's biographers as 'an important assistant to his success', a statement clearly based on assumptions about the life of female musicians in British theatre.[1] Even a cursory search for compositions written under the name of Elsie April in such major archival repositories as the British Library's catalogues reveals the numerous songs she composed and copyrighted, beyond the published Coward arrangements. Somehow, the full scope of her working practices has never made it into the historical record, despite the high regard in which her contemporaries held her. As theatrical *impresario* Charles B. Cochran (1872–1951) once noted:

> If you got near enough to inspect a pair of twinkling eyes, in a very expressive face, and delicate hands, it *could be* her. If you stopped the bike, and found the rider carrying a great quantity of manuscript music, and wearing an *extraordinary hat*, it *must have* been our Elsie ... As a musician, she had few equals and her composers [i.e. those she worked with], orchestras, conductors, singers and arrangers bowed to her superiority ... it was always a source of wonderment to observe this small person, so mistress of her art.[2]

Given the recognition by Cochran, one of Britain's most influential producers, her absence in the historical record is puzzling. However, it speaks to common industry practices and mechanisms of gendered erasure. In 1932, Peter Burnup asked in the theatrical newspaper *The Era*, 'Why doesn't Elsie April get a credit on the programme? [She] contributes as much as any man to the success of Cochran shows ... is someone afraid of ghosts?'[3] His use of the term 'ghost' is telling; the answer to this lies in a complex cultural web of market forces, gender parity, and lack of attention to female creators.

Although we often only remember April's work today as a footnote alongside the enormous musical output of Noël Coward (1899–1973), her life and work provide an important glimpse into the world of British musical theatre. Stephen Banfield's claim that between 1890 and 1924 in British musical theatre women were almost entirely absent from the process of making music is inaccurate. It overlooks the contributions of women composers like Liza Lehman, Clare Kummer, Kittie Stuart; music directors like Nellie Chapman, Mabel Mercer, and Edna Willoughby; as well as many women performers. Banfield suggests that the only women in the pit during this period 'will have been the harpists, with the possible exception of a back-desk violinist', again compounded outdated notions of women's performance.[4] In 1916, during an industrial dispute with theatre *impresario* and producer Oswald Stoll, 180 women musicians were employed in his seven London theatres overnight.[5] Despite long-held scholarly assumptions to the contrary, women made sizeable contributions to British musical theatre life. As this chapter demonstrates, Elsie April was one of the most significant forces on the style and genre of the early-twentieth-century British musical, not only on the work of male songwriters such as Noël Coward.

Part of the reason for a gap in the historical narrative of April's life stems from the paucity of archival sources that relate to her early years and development – something we are addressing in this chapter by retracing both this and her early professional career. Until recently, her work with British *impresario* Charles B. Cochran in the 1920s and '30s was relatively unknown. To members of the British theatre community during the time, however, she was known and loved. As Sheridan Morley, Coward's principal biographer and godson, noted, April was 'a small, bird-like woman given to wearing remarkable hats', who, 'while refusing ever to compose anything herself, would solemnly transcribe any note Noël ever sang to her.'[6] Despite this somewhat dismissive characterisation of her compositional abilities, Morley points to her musical influence upon his godfather's work, noting: 'hers was a major influence on the harmony of Coward compositions.'[7] This was perhaps bolstered by the apocryphal accounts of Coward, who in a fit of inspiration would ring April and hum a new tune while she notated it over the telephone. Nevertheless, her lasting influence is evident.

Much like many figures of the era, Charles B. Cochran enabled April's career. Cochran was one of the most significant *impresarios* in Britain from 1920 to the mid-1940s, producing everything from rodeo to operetta to the intimate musical revue.[8] He routinely hired an exclusive group of theatre professionals including choreographers, orchestrators, actors, musicians, artists, and critics, thereby fostering a sense of community and an image of exclusivity and cultural elitism. Agnes de Mille, who worked with Cochran in the 1930s, offers a glimpse of April's working practices and illuminates the remarkable skill level which April possessed. She stated:

> One of the most expert musicians in the business, the liaison officer between Cochran and every musician who works for him, from tympanist [*sic*] to composer. Noel [*sic*] Coward will not do a show without her. She does all the actual music dictation. She is known the world over, calls herself unaccountably, Elsie April, and is mistress of enough theatre gossip to keep anyone open-mouthed.[9]

In a world in which theatre exchanges meant commercial gain and reputations were heavily guarded, April's musical abilities and her work were unlikely to be fully detailed. So, this role as 'mistress' of theatre gossip played an important role in establishing and maintaining her career; her actual contribution is masked behind this necessary front. Other figures in the West End theatre community held her in similar high regard for her evident abilities. Clarkson Rose noted the ways in which Coward, who collaborated with April on so many of the works which bear his authorship, was indebted to April. As he notes:

> Where does he get his talent? Well, his grandfather was a considerable organist and was one of the pioneers of the Glee Club movement. He himself is not much of a pianist and would be the first to admit how much he owes, musically, to Elsie April.[10]

That Coward admitted to using an assistant is seen as a sign of his strength, not a musical failing on Coward's part, but reflective of standard commercial practice in the era. Stephen Citron notes, 'he was not an egomaniac'; Coward 'could allow himself to take advice from accomplished professionals like Elsie April who could write down what he played and sang and arranged the chorus numbers as well.'[11] Coward's musical contemporaries, including Ivor Novello, Jerome Kern, Cole Porter, and others whose work achieved critical acclaim in 1920s and '30s London regularly collaborated with orchestrators and arrangers who provided the bulk of the musical labour. Due to the ephemeral nature of music composition for the British stage, almost none of these musical figures were identified, and little remains today. This specific identification speaks to April's professional notoriety that she was noted as a collaborator in a period when many women, and collaborators in general, were uncredited.

Re-Establishing a Biography: From the Slums to the West End

Uncovering Elsie April's biography for the first time reveals both a remarkable story, which may have contributed to the erasure of April's work and certainly shaped her experiences. April was born Sarah Doyle in Ancoats, a deprived industrial area of Manchester, on 14 December 1884, to Irish parents Mary and Patrick Doyle, both tailors. Elsie April's mother, Mary Kate Ryan, had lived in Manchester since she was a child, though she had been born in 1861 in Corfu, also to Irish parents, and her father served in the British army. Rather than return to a country ravaged by famine and migration, Mary Kate's mother, Catherine, had moved with her two children to Manchester. The transition was often difficult for Irish migrants: 'the culture shock and sense of dislocation . . . must have been profound indeed; especially as a significant number of them were Gaelic speakers.'[12] Manchester, then a booming industrial centre, had attracted many Irish immigrants faced with the dire conditions during *an Gorta Mór* (the Great Hunger, 1845–1849), who tried to build a life for themselves in the expanding city. In 1881, Mary married a Waterford man, Patrick Doyle (b. 1859) at a Roman Catholic church in Salford; both of them are logged in the 1891 census as tailor, living with their three children including Sarah (Elsie), in the long-since demolished terraces of Slater Street.[13] Theirs was a piecemeal trade, which Charles Kingsley had earlier described in 1850 as particularly bleak, noting 'the slavery, starvation, waste of life, year-long imprisonment . . . which goes on among thousands of free English clothes-makers at this day.'[14] How much had changed in the intervening years is unclear.

While we know little of April's childhood, her living situation could not have been an easy one: life in Ancoats was grim, yet she found the means to learn the piano. As the Industrial Revolution created unimaginable wealth for mill owners, a demand for workers to support this new mass industry led to huge population growth in Manchester in 1851.[15] This created horrific slum conditions for those working in the mills and the associated industries. In 1892, a novelist described Ancoats, where April grew up, as 'That teeming, squalid quarter . . . more squalid, more haphazard, more nakedly poor even than London.'[16] Somehow in the middle of this environment, perhaps at church, April managed to learn to play the piano. It is possible, if unlikely, that she had a piano at home, since by the 1880s it was feasible for working people to hire-purchase a piano, although 'the quality of the cheapest pianos was very poor.'[17] Nonetheless, she appears in July 1893 as being among those children who had successfully taken their Elementary Honours Pianoforte exam, under the instruction of one 'Mr Norton'.[18] If this is the same Sarah, she would have been 7 years old.

Ancoats had benefited from multiple kinds of Victorian philanthropy; the Manchester University Settlement was founded in 1895, bringing middle-class lecturers and their families to live in the area.[19] This, along with the Manchester Art Museum, was an attempt to bring education with culture to the very poorest inhabitants of Manchester. It is impossible to know how April left, but by the 1901 census, she had left Ancoats behind and was a visitor in the house of Marie Hoffman, the widow of a wool merchant, in Palatine Road in Didsbury, a genteel leafy suburb of Manchester. Marie, a widow, lived with her daughter, Fanny, and a servant — April is listed only as a guest. Although census data only captures one night, she was more than just a visitor to the family; the evidence suggests that April had found a patron. The family were in some way involved with April's attendance at the fee-paying Royal Northern College of Music (then the Royal Manchester College of Music). Her record card suggests that she arrived at 12 (though she was actually 15); and lists her father, then crossed out and replaced by 'Weiss Hoffman' of 'Palatine Road, West Didsbury'.[20] She attended the school for two years, and there is no information as to why she started or indeed left in July 1901, now 17. Much remains a mystery about this period.

Three years later, Elsie April married Cecil Davidson, a civil engineer, and the family moved to London via a brief foray to Buenos Aires. Her family life was marred by multiple tragedies: of their five children together, two died in infancy (Walter b. 1906–d. 1997; Cecil, b. 1907–d. 1908; Douglas Noel b. 1908–d. 1994; Kathleen b. 1910–d. 1991; Daphne b. 1911–d. 1916). Her marriage with Cecil appears to have come to an end before the loss of her youngest daughter; he began a new family in 1915, but there is no further information. Again, while we know so little about this period, it is clear that with three children under the age of seven, April was playing for a touring theatrical company by at least September 1913.[21]

'The Glad Idlers': April as Touring Pianist, Performer, and Composer

Before she began working in the West End, April had a substantial career with the leading concert party The Glad Idlers as a pianist (both accompanist and soloist).[22] It is unclear how this overlaps with her family life, but purely chronologically, it must have. The Glad Idlers were made up of April, Muriel George, Phyllis Beadon, Ernest Butcher, Hubert Kiver (who had trained at the Royal Academy of Music), and led by Max Cardiff. Concert parties were immensely popular in seaside resorts before the mid-1920s. Their performances had a two-part structure. The opening was reflective of the Harlequinade tradition, with performers in white clown costumes (with the distinctive black pompoms and hats), which contrasted with the second half of the event, done in evening dress.[23] Concert parties were similar to yet separate from music hall revues, but they were frequently reported in theatrical magazines and newspapers and understood as part of the industry. One advertisement from the period hints at the versatility of such acts: 'The Pier's Own' Concert Party, for the Grand Pavilion Colwyn Bay placed in 1919, calls for 'Comedians, Tenors, Baritones, Sopranos, Contraltos, Light Comedian Soubrettes & Dancer, Pianist Must be Artistes of ability. Nothing too big entertained.'[24] Muriel George, who was also in the Idlers, remembers that during the 1913 season April gained the stage name she would use during the rest of her professional life:

> [Elsie April] was not her real name — we gave it to her — and we lived together all that season and she remained my close friend till she died. She was a complete marvel at the piano – could transpose a song up or down and could prompt you with the words too if necessary.[25]

The name had appeared as a character in Arnold Bennett's theatrical novels, and later Bennett himself proudly wrote to his wife about their meeting, and confirmed April had taken her name from the books: 'I thought it was such a lovely name that I took it for myself & it's been a very lucky name for me.'[26] It is likely she was working under the earlier name Elsie English, as the Glad Idlers had a somewhat coincidentally named pianist in June: 'Miss Elsie English entertains well with her piano songs.'[27] If this was indeed her, she would have been playing with Wallis Arthur's company as early as 1908.[28]

According to this historical record, by this point, April was performing not only as a soloist and accompanist, but as a vocal performer and sometimes actor. Reviews of the Glad Idler's shows (often but not exclusively at beach locations) frequently single out April for tremendous praise, noting that her own compositions were already being played. In one review of the company at Devonshire Park Pavilion, April is described as a 'front rank artist':

> Her accompaniments greatly added to the success of the items, and she proved herself no less capable with her songs at the piano, 'Waltz Me Dearie' and 'Plain Jane' being evidently relished.'[29]

In May 1915, her skill as a 'brilliant pianist and most finished accompanist' is noted: 'we even spotted one or two original items of hers on the programme, which goes to prove what a clever lady she really is.'[30] April stayed with the company till around 1917, but the original cast fell apart as the men joined the troops; tragically Hubert Kiver died in 1917 at the age of 23. That year April performed in variety accompanying Muriel George.[31] She was also involved in entertaining injured troops in special concerts, such as a performance in a Blackpool convalescence hospital. She seems to have had some connection with Blackpool, a famous centre of entertainment for working-class audiences: John Luxton (her partner from around this period) performed her song, 'The Wayside Tramp' there in 1919, and they advertised as a double act.[32] In the early 1920s, she and Luxton seem to have been hired by Herman Darewski, as part of a resident company at the Happy Valley concert venue at Southend.[33] By 1921, she married Luxton and had another child, Peter Luxton, who became a journalist for the *Manchester Guardian* but died at 24.

The 1920s and 1930s: Professional Practice

A court case brought over a lost music score offers tantalising details about April's work in the early 1920s. Reportage reveals that having left concert parties as a player, she was engaged by music publisher Herman Darewski. Between 1921 and 1922, she 'played all likely manuscripts' for the publisher before he agreed to take them on.[34] Reporting on the case suggests she had her own office at Darewski's to work through the material to be published. She also arranged for other concert parties during this period.

For several decades, April was Cochran's chosen musical mistress, rehearsal pianist, accompanist, and confidante, providing insight into his theatrical endeavours, and in turn influencing the performance style of each show from inception to the first production.[35] Cochran's memoirs describe her as 'Elsie April, without whose assistance the compilation of an entertainment of a musical character would seem impossible to me, was of enormous assistance as well.' This designation, in reference to a song 'panorama' Cochran produced which showcased 70 years of the British musical, is indicative of the level of respect which Cochran held for April. Clearly April was adept at many things beyond mere musical direction, including composition, orchestration, arranging, accompanying, vocal coaching, and musical direction. Each of these facets made her invaluable to Cochran and established a sphere of influence beyond a single *impresario*. Her persona as hardworking and yet approachable proved useful for Cochran at several points, including the creation of Cole Porter's London production of *Nymph Errant* (1933). Cochran recalled her influence on Porter's musical style for this production, stating, 'It was the oddest sight to see her and Cole, sitting in a corner, like a couple of washerwomen, working out the links for *Nymph Errant* – except that they had a stop-watch',[36] which she used to instil fear in the singers around her.

April was one of several prominent women with whom Cochran surrounded himself; others included Agnes De Mille, American choreographer and ballet dancer, and Cissie Sewell, who served as Cochran's ballet mistress. These women ran most of the day-to-day operations in Cochran's theatre, and each held their own fascination for the theatrical public. Cochran's memoirs detail an account of Sewell and April's relationship in a description of one of Cochran's infamous First Night performances:

> In the stalls sat Noël Coward, Frank Collins and Cissie Sewell, the redheaded, smart ballet mistress for all Cockie's productions. She and Elsie April had a series of code signals which they exchanged at frequent intervals. Elsie, in particular, had her likes and dislikes for chorus girls and small-part actors and actresses, and could make or mar their auditions by the way she played the piano.[37]

These accounts reveal the considerable sway that April exercised over Cochran's theatre, and the reliance he had upon her skills, intuition, and musical resources from the audition stage to production.[38] Cochran relied on her expertise beyond her musical abilities, as noted by her son Peter who observed that she was involved in a decision to hire Larry Adler, demonstrating her considerable personal influence over Cochran's commercial decisions.[39]

'Mastering the Master': Noël Coward and Elsie April

Sir Noël Pierce Coward, playwright, author, actor, and songwriter, began his musical career composing individual songs that were interpolated into revues. Author of more than 80 works for stage and screen, including more than a dozen musical works, Coward was a pivotal figure in the West End and beyond. His first attempt at a commercial revue, *London Calling* (1923), was produced by André Charlot. Coward's most significant early works were those produced by Charles B. Cochran, such as *Words and Music* (1928) and *Cavalcade* (1931).[40] Coward's songs, which include 'This Is a Changing World', 'Mad About the Boy', and 'London Pride', were so popular with the British public that they can be considered symbols of national identity. Many of Coward's popular songs are similar in style to the work of other songwriters of his generation, including British songwriters Vivian Ellis and Ivor Novello, and Americans such as Jerome Kern and Cole Porter, although his operettas are largely examples of romantic pastiche. Coward himself stated: 'I was born into a generation that still took light music seriously', a view which influenced his musical development.[41] In addition to his plays, Coward crafted more than a dozen musical plays, operettas, and revues, each of which required the considerable skill of an arranger such as April.

Coward and April met during rehearsals for Coward's first staged debut for producer André Charlot, *London Calling* (1923). Coward described April in the following manner:

> a small sharp-eyed woman named Elsie April, whose mastery of musical technique was miraculous. She could transfer melody and harmony on to paper with the swiftness of an expert shorthand stenographer. Her physical endurance, too, was staggering. She

could sit at the piano through the longest rehearsals, the most tedious auditions, seldom, if ever, playing a wrong note.[42]

Coward's description highlights the perceived tenacity and dedication of April's work ethic, noting her remarkable musical ability and adaptability in a gruelling rehearsal setting. Coward scholar Barry Day chronicles the beginning of the working relationship between Coward and April, stating:

To help him with the music, he recruited a "Small sharp-eyed" chain-smoking lady called Elsie April. When asked why, with all her skills, she had never composed anything herself, she replied, "Well, dear, I never seem to have any time".[43]

This was perhaps true, although her own 17 published contributions contradict this statement.

April's relationship with Coward began as a result of their work on the Charlot revue *London Calling!* (1923) and was solidified with their mutual work for Cochran. *London Calling!* contained several of Coward's early hits, including 'Parisian Pierrot', and starred Gertrude Lawrence. Although the details are scarce in terms of labour division between the two, given Coward's scant musical ability in terms of scoring, April likely served as accompanist and arranger for Coward, as she did for several other productions in the 1920s. Coward was clearly taken with her music style and work ethic, and although he was the master of a memorable tune, he was, lacking when it came to his ability to notate music. He was thus reliant upon April, with whom he worked more closely than with anyone else in his career. She supplied accompanying lines for his songs and orchestration.

Coward continued to work with April even after his relationship with Cochran dissolved due to professional differences. Coward and his associates remembered the playful and somewhat eccentric attitude of April throughout the creative process and particularly in rehearsals and auditions. Cole Lesley notes, 'Elsie, if some wretched girl had too shrill a soprano, would hiss, "She's been at the birdseed, dear." '[44] While Coward's admiration was public, her actual contribution is a mystery. However, he dedicated the score for his 1929 operetta *Bitter Sweet* to her: 'in gratitude for all the unfailing help and encouragement you have given me in music.'[45] She likely again contributed much of the musical detail to the score, and almost certainly supplied the orchestrations for the large theatre orchestra required for an operetta.

April was one of several female collaborators with whom Coward worked, including designer Gladys Calthrop, choreographer Wendy Toye, and others. These women formed a significant part of Coward's working life and social world, a story that remains to be told. In addition to her continued practical work for Coward and Cochran, who produced *Bitter Sweet*, she seemed to serve in an advisory capacity. Cole Lesley notes that April also accompanied him and Cochran on their trip to the United States for the production of *Bitter Sweet*.[46] In a letter to his mother Violet, dated 6 November 6 1929, he described a recent trip to see the New York premiere of *Bitter Sweet*, recalling:

Tonight I took Cissie Sewell and Elsie April to see *Whoopee!* (they deserve a treat having worked like dogs) and Eddie Cantor stepped forward and said that he wanted to introduce the greatest Theatrical Genius alive today and they popped a spotlight on me and I had to stand up and bow to me great American Public![47]

Clearly for more reasons than her musical skill, April was indispensable for Coward, and we can speculate that she provided more than his musical framework for his songwriting ideas, shaping harmonic structures, melodic and phrase lines, and crafting orchestrations, to the extent that he insisted on only working with April.[48] Sheridan Morley notes Coward's telegram to Cochran from New York in September 1931 in which Coward provides details of his conditions for the production of *Cavalcade*: 'INDIVIDUALS NECESSARY . . . ELSIE APRIL MUSIC SUPERVISION.'[49]

Cavalcade opened at London's Theatre Royal, Drury Lane on 13 October 1931, starring Mary Clare and Edward Sinclair and a large supporting cast of several hundred. It was an epic stage production that brought to life three generations of Britain's history, framed with Coward's popular songs including 'Twentieth Century Blues', with diegetic insertions of British popular and folk songs. The orchestra was under the direction of Frank Collinson – though in one case, owing to the non-arrival of band parts, one of Miss Burke's numbers was accompanied at the piano by the indispensable Elsie April. As rehearsals had been going on within twenty minutes of the rise of the curtain, the smooth working of the production was in the circumstances remarkable and made unnecessary Mr. Cochran's preliminary plea for indulgence.[50] Although we can never know for sure, April likely arranged the musical numbers in addition to assisting Coward with other musical details. This nationalist production propelled Coward to lasting fame in the 1930s, and along with him, April for her contributions.

Composition

Between 1914–1942, April published over 20 compositions that bore her name as composer. This is in addition to her arrangements of Coward's many songs, which included just as many musical theatre works. Although little is known about performances of her work, we can speculate that they were published for amateur and domestic music performances. Some instrumental pieces are listed among her publications, including an intermezzo entitled *Meadow Sweet*, scored for piano (1921) and *The Village Green: A Country Suite*. Her works also display an affinity to the style of light music, including her pseudo-Latin American number *An Argentine Serenade* (1918), which is imitative of the style of American composer Ferde Grofé (1892–1972). Later published works include instrumental arrangements of Noël Coward's musical theatre works, including *Operette* (1938) and an arrangement of the film score for *In Which We Serve* (1942). Although some were arrangements for theatrical productions, such as the 1942 Cochran revue *Big Top*, many of these are individual songs. Other songs such as 'The Wayside Tramp', and 'Come Home' are reminiscent of the English folk tunes popularised in orchestral arrangements by Gerald Finzi (1901–1956) and Ralph Vaughan Williams (1872–1958).

April's unique compositional voice is heard across all her compositions, including her distinctive lilting melodic lines. The wide-ranging stylistic influences in her work are indicative of both her musical training and her ability to intuit and recreate musical styles around her. The style of these compositions is unique, supporting the idea that she was a functional composer who wrote for specific commercial purposes rather than for the pure luxury of composition. Moreover, her playful assertion that she lacked the time to compose further solo compositions is supported, given that most of her works appeared before she began her partnership with Cochran.

Conclusion

As this chapter demonstrates, although April is best known for her long working partnership with Coward, the scope of her working life is significant. Her career spans several waves of

Table 11.1 Elsie April's Compositions and Musical Arrangements (selected)

Year	Title	Description
1914	'Waltz Me Dearie' and 'Plain Jane'	Songs used in the Glad Idlers performances, score missing
1918	'Faded'	Song, words by John P. Harrington. London: H. Darewski Music Publishing Co, 1918.
	'An Argentine Serenade'	Song, words by Fred Allendale London: Faber Music. Ascherberg, Hopwood, and Crew, ltd.
1919	'The Wayside Tramp'	Song, words by John P. Harrington. London: H. Darewski Music Publishing Co, 1918.
	'Tinker Jim'	Performed by Sydney Moorhouse (Empire Theatre) and John Luxton (Blackpool).[51]
1920	'At the End of a Valley of Daydreams'	Song, lyrics by J. Milton Hayes. London: H. Darewski Music Publishing Co
	'Come Home'	Song, lyrics by M. Hayes. London: Boosey & Co
	'Merchandise! – The Song of the Overseas Trade'	Song, lyrics by M. Hayes London: Reynolds & Co
1921	*The Village Green: A Country Suite*	Piano Solo, London: Herman Darewski Music Publishing Co., c1921. Reprinted 1934.[52]
	Meadow Sweet	Intermezzo. London: Herman Darewski Music Publishing Co.
1922	'I'm a Lone Man'	Baritone song, recorded by Wilfred Essex,[53] recorded by Malcolm McEachern for Vocalion 1926[54]
1923	'Love Man'	Songs, details unknown
	'The Road that Leads to Love Land'	
1925	'The Melody Mummers'	Song arrangements for concert party, details unknown
1928	*Bitter Sweet*	Music by Noël Coward, arrangements and piano solo by Elsie April
1934	*The Village Green*	Revision of 1921 work
1938	*Operette*	Music by Noël Coward, arrangements by Elsie April
1939	Charles B. Cochran's *Nightlights*	Musical arrangements for nightclub revue[55]
1940	BBC 'Cock-a-Doodle-Doo'	Musical arrangements for series of broadcasts
1942	*In Which We Serve*	Music by Noël Coward, piano arrangements by April London, Chappell and Co
	[unknown elements of the Cochran revue *Big Top*]	Music by Geoffrey Wright, Nicholas Brodzsky, Elsie April, and Harry Parr Davis[56]
	[unknown additional music for *Wild Rose*]	Contributed musical elements, details unknown

key theatrical periods and practices, and technological processes that reshaped the British musical theatre and popular song. Her professional engagements included children's dance shows, concerts at local political parties, daytime shows on the beach, evening pavilion shows, concert parties at early theme parks and at Blackpool Tower, radio and TV broadcasts, charity concerts and fundraising, music hall, revues, West End revues and shows, publishing, song pushing, and West End musicals. She worked through two World Wars and was involved in charity and entertainment for the troops in both of them. By addressing her considerable career, we can challenge assumptions about the apparently limited role of women in British musical theatre during this period. Her career reflects the messy reality of professional working lives in the theatre, which resists what we might expect to see: we may rank venues with certain cultural values that equate to more or less 'success'. Her life demonstrates a fluidity in moving between spaces and kinds of musical and theatrical productions. Her professional practice further reveals the fact that women may have been largely invisible in the creation of musical theatre, and yet they were responsible for shaping the distinct sound and style of the British musical.

As we consider April's career, we not only reclaim narratives of her life and work, but we consider the many facets that her work encompasses, including composer, actor, performer, pianist, accompanist, collaborator, professional practitioner, and arranger. We find ourselves, like the anonymous gossip columnist in *The Era* in 1932, wondering what might the 'ghost' of Elsie April unsettle? It is apparent that her influence on Coward's songwriting and musical language was extensive, and beyond this, she inhabited a world of musical performance that highlights the myriad theatrical genres and styles in Musical Theatre. It is clear that Elsie April was not a ghost. Like many other women she was a tangible, substantive presence in the shaping of British musical theatre.

Notes

1. Sheridan Morley, *Coward Revue Sketches*, edited by Barry Day (London: Methuen, 1999), x.
2. Charles Graves, *The Cochran Story: A Biography of Sir Charles Blake Cochran* (London: W.H. Allen, 1951), 257–59.
3. Peter Burnup, "Thinking Aloud," *The Era*, April 13, 1932, 2.
4. Stephen Banfield, "English Musical Comedy, 1890–1924," in *The Oxford Handbook of the British Musical*, edited by Robert Gordon and Olaf Jubin, 117–42 (Oxford: Oxford University Press, 2017) (123).
5. "Women Orchestras," *The Era*, October 18, 1916, 15.
6. Sheridan Morley, *A Talent to Amuse: A Biography of Noël Coward* (Boston, MA: Little Brown, 1985), 71.
7. Ibid.
8. James Harding, *Cochran* (London: Methuen Publishing, 1988), 105. See also: Charles B. Cochran, "Rodeo Reminisces," *Everybody's Magazine* (1945). Charles B. Cochran Collection, Scrapbook 115, GB 71, THM/97/115, The Victoria and Albert Theatre Museum Archive.
9. Agnes de Mille, *Speak with Me: Dance with Me* (Boston, MA: Little Brown, 1973), 161.
10. Clarkson Ross, "Coward," *The Bystander*, August 14, 1934, 7.
11. Stephen Citron, *Noël and Cole: The Sophisticates* (New York: Hal Leonard, 2005), 114.
12. M. A. Busteed and R. I. Hodgson, "Irish Migrant Responses to Urban Life in Early Nineteenth-Century Manchester," *The Geographical Journal* 162, no. 2 (1996): 139–53.
13. Demolished as part of 1965 slum clearances, renamed Clarence Street.
14. Charles Kingsley, *Alton Locke, Tailor and Poet*, section: 'Cheap Clothes and Nasty' (Project Gutenberg: 1850), accessed July 15, 2018, www.gutenberg.org/cache/epub/8374/pg8374-images.html.
15. M. Nevell, "Legislation and Reality: The Archaeological Evidence for Sanitation and Housing Quality in Urban Workers' Housing in the Ancoats Area of Manchester Between 1800 and 1950," *Industrial Archaeology Review* 36, no. 1 (2014): 48–74: 49.
16. H. Ward, "Chapter XIV," *The History of David Grieve* (Project Gutenberg, 1892). [online] accessed July 12, 2018, www.gutenberg.org/files/8076/8076-h/8076-h.htm.
17. D. Russell, *Popular Music in England 1840–1914: A Social History* (Manchester: Manchester University Press, 1997), 177.
18. "London College of Music," *Manchester Courier and Lancashire General Advertiser* (August 26, 1893), 3.
19. Manchester Settlement, *Our History*, 2020, accessed June 28, 2020, www.manchestersettlement.org.uk/about-us/our-history/.
20. Royal Northern College of Music, Archives and personal correspondence.
21. "The Glad Idlers," *Eastbourne Gazette*, September 24, 1913, 8.

22. "The Glad Idlers," *Eastbourne Gazette*, August 27, 1913, 8.
23. For more on the style of pantomime and harlequinade see Millie Taylor, *British Pantomime Performance* (Bristol: Intellect, 2007).
24. "The Pier and Grand Pavilion," *The Stage*, Iss. 1977 (February 6, 1919), 20.
25. Muriel George, *I Was a Folly* (c.1957), accessed August 26, 2020, https://web.archive.org/web/20160403032818/www.murielgeorge.info/index/view/story/memoirs/id/13.
26. Arnold Bennett (Letter 27/02/1928 to Dorothy Cheston Bennett), edited by James Hepburn *Letters of Arnold Bennett*, vol IV (Oxford: Oxford University Press, 1966), 536–38: 537.
27. "Grand Theatre Croydon," *Dorking and Leatherhead Advertiser*, June 28, 1913, 5.
28. "Beach Concert Pavilion," *Hastings and St Leonards Observer*, July 18, 1908, 2.
29. "Glad Idlers at the Pavilion," *Derby Daily Telegraph*, December 28, 1914, 2.
30. "To Kill Care," *Thanet Advertiser*, May 1, 1915, 3.
31. "Southampton Palace with Muriel George," *The Stage*, May 10, 1917, 18.
32. "Miss Elsie April," *The Stage*, January 25, 1917, 18.
33. Clarkson Rose, "Peradventure," *The Stage*, July 20, 1939, 2.
34. "Cases in Court," *The Stage*, October 29, 1925, 23.
35. Claire Cochrane, *Twentieth-Century British Theatre: Industry, Art and Empire* (Cambridge: Cambridge University Press, 2011), 54.
36. Harding, *A Cochran Story*, 258–59.
37. Graves, *The Cochran Story*, 146.
38. Graves, *The Cochran Story*, 257–59. See also Harding, *Cochran*, 51.
39. "Royalty Captivated by the Mouth-Organ," *Smith's Weekly*, (Sydney, NSW) (September 19, 1942), 13. See for instance 'Charles B. Cochran discusses his plans and describes . . . Hollywood As I See It," *Continental Daily Mail*, August 24, 1937 (located in Cochran Collection, GB 71 THM/97/99, the Victoria and Albert Theatre Museum Archive).
40. Harding, *Cochran*, 51.
41. Milton Levin, *Noël Coward*, updated ed. (Boston, MA: Twayne Publishers, [1968] 1989), 31.
42. Raymond Mander, *Theatrical Companion to Coward: A Pictorial Record of the First Theatrical Performances of the Works of Noël Coward* (New York: Macmillan Company, 1957), 59.
43. Wright, *A Tanner's Worth*, 47.
44. Levin, *Noël Coward*, 31.
45. Cole Lesley, *Remembered Laughter: The Life of Noel Coward* (New York: Random House, 1976), 126–27.
46. Lesley, *Remembered Laughter*, 128.
47. Barry Day, *Letters of Coward* (London: Vintage, 2009), 263.
48. Day, *Letters*, 263.
49. Coward in Morley, *A Talent*, 153.
50. "Big Top: New Cochran Revue," *The Stage*, March 26, 1942, 5.
51. "The Pier and Grand Pavilion," *The Stage*, no. 1977, February 6, 1919, 20.
52. "Broadcasting," *Western Morning News*, November 9, 1934, 10.
53. "Hareman Darewski," *The Stage*, May 25, 1922, 17.
54. "New Vocalion Records," *Horfield and Bishopston Record and Montepelier & District Free Press*, June 4, 1926, 2.
55. "New Music Composed by Elsie April and Lorraine," *The Radio Times*, May 12, 1939, 15.
56. "His Majesty's," *The Stage*, May 14, 1942, 5.

Bibliography

Banfield, Stephen. "English Musical Comedy, 1890–1924." In *The Oxford Handbook of the British Musical*, edited by Robert Gordon and Olaf Jubin, 117–42. Oxford: Oxford University Press, 2017.
"Beach Concert Pavilion." *Hastings and St Leonards Observer*, July 18, 1908, 2.
Bennett, Arnold, (Letter 27/02/1928 to Dorothy Cheston Bennett). *Letters of Arnold Bennett*, edited by James Hepburn, iv, 536–38. Oxford: Oxford University Press, 1966.
"Big Top: New Cochran Revue." *The Stage*, March 26, 1942, 5.
"Broadcasting." *Western Morning News*, November 9, 1934, 10.
Burnup, Peter. "Thinking Aloud." *The Era*, April 13, 1932, 2.

Busteed, M. A., and R. I. Hodgson. "Irish Migrant Responses to Urban Life in Early Nineteenth-Century Manchester." *The Geographical Journal* 162, no. 2 (1996): 139–53.
"Cases in Court." *The Stage*, October 29, 1925, 23.
Citron, Stephen. *Noël and Cole: The Sophisticates*. New York: Hal Leonard, 2005.
Cochran, Charles B. "Rodeo Reminisces." *Everybody's Magazine*, 1945; (Charles B. Cochran Collection, Scrapbook 115, GB 71, THM/97/115, The Victoria and Albert Theatre Museum Archive).
Cochrane, Claire. *Twentieth-Century British Theatre: Industry, Art and Empire*. Cambridge: Cambridge University Press, 2011.
Day, Barry. *Letters of Coward*. London: Vintage, 2009.
de Mille, Agnes. *Speak with Me: Dance with Me*. Boston: Little Brown, 1973.
George, Muriel. *I Was a Folly* (c.1957). Accessed August 26, 2020. https://web.archive.org/web/20160403032818/www.murielgeorge.info/index/view/story/memoirs/id/13.
"Glad Idlers at the Pavilion." *Derby Daily Telegraph*, December 28, 1914, 2.
"Grand Theatre Croydon." *Dorking and Leatherhead Advertiser*, June 28, 1913, 5.
Graves, Charles. *The Cochran Story: A Biography of Sir Charles Blake Cochran*. London: W.H. Allen, 1951.
Harding, James. *Cochran*. London: Methuen Publishing, 1988.
"Hareman Darewski." *The Stage*, May 25, 1922, 17.
"His Majesty's." *The Stage*, May 14, 1942, 5.
Kingsley, Charles. *Alton Locke, Tailor and Poet* (Project Gutenberg: 1850). Accessed July 15, 2018. www.gutenberg.org/cache/epub/8374/pg8374-images.html.
Levin, Milton. *Noël Coward*, Updated ed. Boston, MA: Twayne Publishers, [1968] 1989.
"London College of Music." *Manchester Courier and Lancashire General Advertiser*, August 26, 1893, 3.
Mander, Raymond. *Theatrical Companion to Coward: A Pictorial Record of the First Theatrical Performances of the Works of Noël Coward*. New York: Macmillan Company, 1957.
Morley, Sheridan. *A Talent to Amuse: A Biography of Noël Coward*. Boston, MA: Little Brown, 1985.
_____. *Coward Revue Sketches*, edited by Barry Day, x. London: Methuen, 1999.
Nevell, M. "Legislation and Reality: The Archaeological Evidence for Sanitation and Housing Quality in Urban Workers' Housing in the Ancoats Area of Manchester Between 1800 and 1950." *Industrial Archaeology Review* 36, no. 1 (2014): 48–74.
"New Music Composed by Elsie April and Lorraine." *The Radio Times*, May 12, 1939, 15.
"New Vocalion Records." *Horfield and Bishopston Record and Montepelier & District Free Press*, June 4, 1926, 2.
Rose, Clarkson. "Peradventure." *The Stage*, July 20, 1939, 2.
Ross, Clarkson. "Coward." *The Bystander*, August 14, 1934, 7.
"Royalty Captivated By the Mouth-Organ." *Smith's Weekly* (Sydney, NSW), September 19, 1942, 13.
Russell, D. *Popular Music in England 1840–1914: A Social History*. Manchester: Manchester University Press, 1997.
"Southampton Palace with Muriel George." *The Stage*, May 10, 1917, 18.
Taylor, Millie. *British Pantomime Performance*. Bristol: Intellect, 2007.
"The Pier and Grand Pavilion." *The Stage*, no. 1977, February 6, 1919, 20.
"The Glad Idlers." *Eastbourne Gazette*, August 27, 1913a, 8.
"The Glad Idlers." *Eastbourne Gazette*, September 24, 1913b, 8.
"To Kill Care." *Thanet Advertiser*, May 1, 1915, 3.
Ward, H. *The History of David Grieve* (Project Gutenberg, 1892). Accessed July 12, 2018. www.gutenberg.org/files/8076/8076-h/8076-h.htm.

12
'SHE IS A DEGENERATE COCAINE ADDICT'

Emma Carelli, A *Diva-Impresario* Facing Her Opponents

Matteo Paoletti

The entrepreneurial career of the former *diva* Emma Carelli (Naples, 1877 – Montefiascone, 1928) at the Teatro Costanzi of Rome represents one of the better-known examples of female *impresarios*' activity in the history of music, making her – as Susan Rutherford has noted – one of 'the handful of women that achieved access to management in the major opera houses of Britain, Europe, and North America'.[1] A soprano of international renown, at the age of twenty-two Carelli was already performing opposite Caruso and Chaliapin at La Scala and by the turn of the century was an acclaimed *diva* in both Europe and South America. Starting from 1908, however, she gradually replaced the limelight with managerial activity. In the autumn of 1911 La Teatral, a company held by her husband Walter Mocchi (1870–1955), appointed her manager of the main opera house of the Italian capital city, Rome, which she ran until 1926.[2] At the Costanzi, Carelli organised memorable seasons that included premieres of works by Mascagni and Puccini, the first continuous Italian runs of Diagilev's *Ballets Russes*, and several Futurist nights and exhibitions, hosted in the foyers of her theatre.[3] The former singer had to cease her activity when the Costanzi was purchased by the Fascist Governor of Rome to create the current Teatro dell'Opera di Roma. Two years later, in 1928, Carelli died in a car accident at the wheel of her flaming red Lancia Lambda.

The tragic death, the unusual career, and the role of Fascism in her removal from theatre management contributed to making Carelli 'an unexpected protofeminist',[4] who – according to the epigraph by the poet Guido Guida – 'gave life to the lyrical art, and to modern Rome the beginning of a great Theatre'.[5] As historian Victoria De Grazia has observed, this was a period in which 'young women of all backgrounds coming of age . . . were [exposed to] a disconcerting experience of new opportunities and new repressions: they felt the enticement of things modern; they also sensed the drag of tradition.'[6]

Even though Carelli's contribution to the feminist cause is questionable – and as we are about to see, she did not seem interested in either politics or in the improvement of the female condition – the former *diva* certainly played a crucial role in the development of the main opera house of Rome, as was already recognised in the mid-twenties by the board of directors of the *Società Teatrale Internazionale* (STIN), the joint-stock company that held the Costanzi: 'Mrs Emma Carelli . . . combines the quality of an exquisite artist to the one of perfect manager of the main opera house of Rome', organising 'seasons of artistic perfection' without any 'fear of incurring losses nor losing her unfailing energies'.[7] However, when talking about an idiosyncratic figure such as Carelli, the risk of perpetuating an uncritical celebratory narrative is always present. Hitherto unpublished archival sources preserved in Rome and Milan (including the voluminous correspondence produced by Carelli and her partners) prompt us to rethink her activity and her role in the Italian theatrical system from a more complex and nuanced perspective. Up to now, Carelli's work has always been reconstructed using secondary and very partial sources, mostly based on the biography written in 1932 by Carelli's brother, the scene designer Augusto Carelli.[8] Written shortly after his sister's death, the book used some selected sources – such as private letters and press reviews – to shape an exemplary and distinctive portrait of a successful woman who fought against the male power system until she was tragically put aside by the rise of Fascism. Despite his fascinating and brilliant storytelling, Augusto Carelli – who was himself a supporter of Mussolini – produced a narrative which marginalised the contributions made by his sister's business partners and co-workers, who certainly played very important roles in her progress. Carelli was indeed a strong and successful theatre manager, but she did not achieve this all by herself; she was a relevant part of a complex system that involved several stakeholders, including her father (the musician and singing teacher Beniamino Carelli, who launched her singing career at a very young age), as well as prominent members of the Italian cultural, political, and economic infrastructure with whom she had to relate to get subsidies, agreements, and – notably – her chairing position.

A Powerful Marriage: Emma Carelli and Walter Mocchi

The most important of Carelli's business partners was certainly her husband Walter Mocchi (Turin, 1871 – Rio de Janeiro, 1955), former leader of the Socialist Party and future supporter of the Fascists, whom she married in 1898. A powerful theatrical agent, representative of the publisher Sonzogno, and *impresario* for the South American tours of Pietro Mascagni, for the first three decades of the twentieth century, Mocchi was a key protagonist of the trans-Atlantic musical trade. Through the companies he established in Italy, Argentina, and Brazil (such as the *Sociedad Teatral Ítalo-Argentina*, the *Società Teatrale Internazionale*, and *La Teatral*) the *impresario* formed a 'trust' that controlled the main venues in Italy and South America, including the Colón of Buenos Aires, thus deeply influencing the commerce of artists and scores between Europe and the rising South American market. A few months after the debut of Puccini's *La Fanciulla del West* at the Metropolitan Opera in New York (December 1910), in June of 1911, Mocchi organised at his Teatro Coliseo in Buenos Aires the lavish world premiere of Pietro Mascagni's *Isabeau*, making the Argentine capital city a metropolis able to compete with New York, London, and Milan.[9] Even though Mocchi officially became his wife's agent after abandoning politics (in 1904), he had supported Carelli's singing career since they married while simultaneously exploiting his political connections. To give one curious example from the archives, as reported by the secret police (who were always attentive to left-wing activity), during the 1902 South American tour Mocchi held revolutionary lectures in Buenos Aires while escorting his wife, and during her run at the Opera engaged some anarchists 'as an enthusiastic and zealous claque, that one night, with a wholly American exaggeration, after the show took the horses from Carelli's carriage and pulled her coach to the hotel'.[10] This exploit was certainly 'unnecessary', as the policeman pointed out, since the soprano was already an acclaimed *diva* who was accustomed to singing with the best performers of the time and often conducted by Toscanini. However, Mocchi – who had become one of the main editors of the socialist newspaper *Avanti!*, and instituted in his companies special funds for propaganda – managed to support his wife's performances with massive press coverage. As part of this media strategy, a special eight-page issue of the Brazilian magazine

Rua do Ouvidor was dedicated to Carelli during her 1903 run at the Teatro Lyrico of Rio de Janeiro, testifying to her international success through the reproduction of pictures and letters dedicated to the *diva* by Arrigo Boito, Umberto Giordano, Ruggero Leoncavallo, as well as many enthusiastic critics from her previous international tours.[11]

After the establishment of two joint-stock companies with large share capital (the *Sociedad Teatral Ítalo-Argentina*, founded in Buenos Aires in 1907, and the *Società Teatrale Internazionale*, established in Rome in 1908), Carelli and Mocchi became probably the most powerful couple in the interoceanic theatrical business. While Mocchi ran the most important venues overseas in Argentina and Brazil, Carelli travelled the ocean as an accclaimed *diva* to sing in the theatres managed by her husband's associates. When Mocchi was away, Carelli demonstrated her entrepreneurial artistic leadership through controlling Mocchi's business in the theatres in which she was engaged as singer. For instance, during the 1908 Carnival season at the Teatro Regio, the theatre administrator Carlo Körner protested:

> Mrs Carelli domineered in Turin. Besides calling and keeping the Administrator and the Deputy Director of the Theatre at her disposal almost all day, she was pleased to interfere, to give advice, to order on how to stage the shows, with what moral benefit, I leave to others to judge.[12]

Far from being (only) characteristic *diva* stereotypes, Carelli's behaviour testifies to her prominence in the productive process, sometimes being perceived as a proxy of her husband. The previous season, in Trieste, Carelli's performance of Leoncavallo's *Zazà* had to be stopped by the police and ended up with a fight between the choristers – who supported Carelli – and members of the audience who accused her of 'imposing the opera' and 'being the wife of a Socialist leader'.[13]

Carelli's business leadership was unusual during a period in which all Italian women were subject to the *autorizzazione maritale* (marital authorisation) that per the 1865 law stated: 'The wife cannot donate, dispose of immovable property, subject it to mortgage, contract mortgages, transfer or raise capital, establish security, or compromise or stand trial with respect to such acts, without the authorisation of the husband.'[14] Until the repeal of the law in 1919, the major acts of Carelli had to be accompanied by a document by Mocchi that stated the capacity of his wife to underwrite agreements and run the family business.[15] Minor acts and ordinary administration could be signed independently, as far as they did not interfere with 'the interest of the marital union and of the family of whom [the husband] is the head, the custodian, and the legitimate representative'.[16]

According to late nineteenth-century jurisprudence, in case of doubt on a contract signed by a woman, 'especially in the presence of children', the male position should prevail.[17] Despite the juridical framework, Carelli used to negotiate as the highest level all by herself, and Mocchi was sometimes described as a kept man,[18] especially during his political career. For instance, the classified reports of the police often pointed out that 'Walter Mocchi . . . is said to be the husband of the singer Emma Carelli, but he lives on her behalf only as a lover'.[19]

The letters written by the soprano during her singing career confirmed the temper of the future manager, as she always negotiated her contracts herself, often using provocative tones. For instance, in 1909 she telegrammed Alberto Marghieri:

> If you think that it might be bad paying me L. 40,000 for the whole Carnival season, consider this . . . in America that is what I earn in a single month, and next year I will be paid L. 60,000. I respectfully bid you goodbye and I quit.[20]

A very effective portrait of Carelli's character emerges in a classified report which the Fascist police filed in 1925 after an anonymous person accused her of insulting the Fascist leaders and even Mussolini himself in her private conversations. This document is especially important, because it testifies that Carelli had never taken part in any feminist or political movements, and underlines the deference that the Fascists seemed to have for her managerial role and expertise:

> Emma Carelli, owner of the Costanzi Theatre, is renowned for her authoritative character and for her language, which is excessively free and shows little deference to anybody who has to deal with her. She has already been a famed lyrical artist, who has always lived in the theatrical environment, in which she is especially famous and held in special consideration for her artistic competence. All these things contribute to form her independent character, that makes her assume an attitude of superiority towards everybody; this attitude makes her a hostile person for most people, especially in the artistic field, and for her employees, that depend on her and are afraid of her. Regarding the anonymous accusation, the investigation demonstrated that she uses her speeches in the premises of the theatre to attack members of the Fascist government, as well as the Prime Minister. However, she seems to talk that way because Carelli demanded from the government a grant to lighten the heavy expenses that she has to carry for the forthcoming lyrical season, and had not obtained it. Whoever listens to her accusations does not give them any credit, because everybody is aware of her attitude of backbiting and coarse language. Mrs Carelli does not have any political principles, because she does not care about politics at all. However, it is well known that she is the wife of Walter Mocchi, former Socialist.[21]

Carelli as *Impresario*

Carelli's managerial career officially started in the autumn of 1911, when *La Teatral* took control of the Costanzi and appointed her manager of the Italian branch of the family business. Since Mocchi, as Carelli's brother recalled, was 'engaged in America due to Mascagni's tour, and was not endowed, like Saint Anthony, with the gift of ubiquity, he had unceasingly solicited the personal involvement of Emma in the preparation of the first season of the Costanzi.'[22] Carelli's first act as theatre manager was to negotiate with the Municipality of Rome to obtain the 'yearly grant of L. 80,000 for the lyrical season'; this was justified by 'the usual practice of the main cities, including Rome', and by the 'difficult conditions of the operatic market'. In the same letter, the *diva* appointed by *La Teatral* explained that 'The new company has the project, and the necessity, of giving new and modern shows, to respect all the tastes of the audience and to encourage the artistic proposals of young composers'.[23] The left-wing mayor Ernesto Nathan seemed unwilling to award a grant to an opera house that was perceived as a luxury for the Roman upper class, but the difficulty was solved by Mocchi, who – back from South America – exploited his Socialist background to demand from the mayor 'not the mere subsidy of a patron, but the development of a regular agreement between [his] company and the Municipality, that could give in return the rights of a real business partnership'. Mocchi's letter continued: 'the theatrical grants, once considered unproductive or luxury liabilities, or even worse a facility for the rich classes' had now to be considered an aid for 'the economic development of the working classes and the establishment of performances at popular prices', in a country in which 'opera should be considered a real aesthetic education'.[24] The consummate experience of the former politician succeeded in financing Carelli's activity with the requested L. 80,000 yearly subsidy, accorded for the three years of 1912–14. In return, *La Teatral* had to extend the usual obligation of popular performances with moderate prices. Mocchi and Carelli consciously positioned their argument within the wider contemporary trend of opening up classical music to all classes,[25] and also enhancing working opportunities for local practitioners. According to the agreement, the company had to guarantee priority to Roman workers and to create an orchestra and a choir 'that will ensure their fortune including when the Costanzi is closed, providing for most of them a job in the South American tours'.[26] Carelli's season was planned in tight connection with the South American tours of Mocchi's companies. The archives are full of the telegrams and letters that Carelli and Mocchi exchanged across the Atlantic to coordinate their seasons, break down the brokerage costs, and engage leading artists and composers.

The 1912 season of the Costanzi was prepared and performed with the usual quickness, since *La Teatral* 'victoriously staged 4 operas and 10 runs in 15 days, thus eloquently proving the seriousness with which the season was planned and directed',[27] and hosted the international star Isadora Duncan, who performed *Dances and Choruses* from Gluck's *Iphigenie*. The most relevant event of the season was *Elektra*, staged from 7 February to 13 April 1912. This was the last appearance of Carelli in a continuous run in Italy. Her performance was described by the Italian critics as 'one of the most genius and complete in the theatrical world', and the *diva* 'seemed to be willing to forget she was a distinguished and gifted artist, and she had not sung for almost two years, dedicating all the fervour of her rich nature to the humble, ignored labour of theatrical management.'[28] It is common opinion that after the success of *Elektra*, Carelli was overwhelmed by her entrepreneurial role and thus forced to give up her singing career. Although the South American activity of Mocchi indeed pushed the *diva* to focus more on the family business, Carelli did not abandon the stage straight away. In 1912, she accepted the offer made by Gabriele d'Annunzio and Ildebrando Pizzetti to perform *Fedra*, the new opera produced by Lorenzo Sonzogno. The project was discussed in Paris in August, and during all of the autumn the soprano studied the score in her studio.[29] On 31 October 1912, Mocchi included the premiere of *Fedra* in the programme presented to the Municipality of Rome, with his wife in the leading role.[30] Shortly after, the elegant brochure given to the subscribers of the Costanzi advertised the premiere for mid-March.[31] However, the delay of Sonzogno, who at the beginning of March had not even delivered the sketches of the opera, forced *La Teatral* to renounce the production for reasons of *force majeure* 'and Carelli, in the absence of *Fedra*, could not perform'.[32] The opera debuted at La Scala on 20 March 1915, with Salomea Krusceniski (a soprano bound to Mocchi's agency) in the leading role. Thereafter, Carelli focused on her managerial career, but she did not give up singing. For example, she successfully performed in the leading role of *Elektra* in Mocchi's 1914 South American tour.

While the orchestra and the choir of the Costanzi were engaged overseas, in Rome Carelli kept her theatre closed, reopening the venue in October 1912 with a dramatic season that often involved the star Ermete Zacconi as a guest artist. Following the return of the company from South America, the Carnival season started again on 26 December with the Italian adaptation of Wagner's *Die Walküre*, also hosting some of the most successful South American titles, such as Mascagni's *Isabeau*, which, starting from 6 February 1913, had a run of nineteen nights. During the 1913 season, *La Teatral* also organised at the Costanzi an exhibition of Futurist painters and sculptors that culminated in a conference with a speech of Umberto Boccioni and in two 'Futurist nights'.

Following the South American productive rush, in Rome Carelli also increased the theatre's production to optimise personnel costs, as the orchestra and the choir were paid in lump sums. For example, between 26 December 1912 and 17 April 1913, Carelli staged the astonishing number of 98 nights, thereby even surpassing the record of 84 nights performed in 1909–10 during Mascagni's direction.[33] According to critical reception and box office revenues, quantity did not affect quality, and 'outstanding honours' ('*onori superlativi*')[34] were tributed to soprano Rosina Storchio. The productive routine did not find favour with the musicians, however, who addressed their complaints to the municipality:

> The victims of the orchestra protest against Mrs Carelli, [who] treats her employees as beasts, [and] shows no respect either for the elderly or for young people, that needing their job undergo her will and resignedly bear maltreatment and tortures.[35]

The Carnival season 1913–14 was the last one in which *La Teatral* directly ran the Costanzi. Starting from 1914, the company was replaced by the '*Impresa Teatro Costanzi*', a new enterprise specially created by Mocchi and Carelli to manage the Roman opera house, which was still formally property of the STIN. In 1914, Mocchi and his associate Faustino Da Rosa once again won the grant of the Colón of Buenos Aires,[36] which they ran exclusively until 1918,[37] with the reasoning that 'their offer guarantees the usage of a preventive artistic organisation of one of the main stages of Europe, that is the Costanzi, indisputable advantage that warrants the homogeneity of the company and its preparation.'[38] The last official Roman season of *La Teatral* was particularly important for two artistic events: the Italian premiere of Wagner's *Parsifal*, staged on 1 January 1914, and the Roman debut of Mascagni-d'Annunzio's *Parisina*, which was finally staged after several troubled years between Mocchi, Sonzogno, the composer, and the librettist.[39] The season confirmed the impressive productive rhythm of *La Teatral*: 100 nights in three and a half months, 22 of which were *Parsifal*. The Italian and South American activities were so deeply intertwined that the press wrote about a 'tour of the Teatro Costanzi to Buenos Ayres (*sic*)'.[40] Even during the troubled times of the First World War, the tight trans-Atlantic cooperation revealed itself as a winning strategy to keep the venues open. Although Italy remained neutral until 23 May 1915, the conflict immediately impacted the Italian theatrical world, causing a sudden shutdown of theatres and agencies.[41] Thanks to Carelli's work, the Costanzi managed to continue to organise its seasons during the conflict, due to an ingenious 'combination' of major international venues planned by Mocchi, that involved the Roman theatre, the Colón of Buenos Aires, La Scala in Milan, and the Opéra and Opéra Comique in Paris. Carelli's contribution to the achievement of this project is confirmed by the archival sources, that testify how the female manager worked strenuously to engage the artists through a rich exchange of telegrams with her husband across the Atlantic. For instance, 'La Scala obtained the orchestra at special conditions. On the other hand, the choir broke up', telegraphed Carelli to Mocchi during the organisation of the season. 'Engage the masses as I told you, and complete them in North America . . ., and you will avoid huge expenses and unbearable difficulties.'[42]

Post-World War One Success

Despite the harsh attacks of Toscanini on Mocchi's endeavours ('No, Mr. Walter Mocchi, you cannot create anything, but only destroy everything – you cannot reform anything, but only deform everything'),[43] even in the period following the First World War the support of Mocchi and Carelli seemed to be crucial for the musical success of new scores in Italy and South America, as confirmed by the letters of Giacomo Puccini and Giovacchino Forzano during the production of *Il Trittico*, whose Italian premiere was performed at the Costanzi in 1919. 'I would like everything to be done with exceptional care: scenery, artists, and the calm that is needed for everyone ... Would this be possible with Carelli?' asked a concerned Puccini after Ricordi's proposal.[44] 'If you had been in Rome you would have seen how ... exceptionally Mocchi had emphasised the extraordinary success of *Il Trittico*', replied the librettist Forzano after the premiere, explaining: 'Mocchi was working in his own self-interest and for Rome and ... thinking about America ... and Puccini could not be indifferent to that'.[45] The prominent role of the couple is also testified by other major composers of the time: 'I know that Carelli is in Milan to form the company of the Costanzi, where two Puccini, two Zandonai, and two Mascagni operas will be staged', protested Italo Montemezzi to Ricordi's manager Carlo Clausetti. 'Please propose *L'Amore dei tre re* to Carelli. That is an idea that Carelli may like'.[46]

The successful activity of Mocchi and Carelli was also sustained by their tight cooperation with the publisher Renzo Sonzogno, competitor of Ricordi, who provided new scores (such as Mascagni's or, as mentioned earlier, Pizzetti's *Fedra*), singing stars, and constant press coverage through the magazines he controlled. During her singing career, Carelli had been a beloved interpreter of Sonzogno's composers, the most remarkable being Leoncavallo and Cilea. As a manager, she always paid great attention to Renzo's proposals. Renzo was a shareholder of Mocchi's companies and the publisher of his most important client, Pietro Mascagni, who had been appointed manager of the Costanzi in 1909–10, right before Carelli's takeover. In a public protest during Carelli's production of his new opera, *Il Piccolo Marat*, Mascagni gave an accurate and ironic description of that partnership. Mocchi considered the work overly expensive compared to predictable box office results, while Sonzogno obviously sustained the initiative. In the end, Carelli produced the opera anyway, although the staging was considered slovenly and shabby by Mascagni. The composer publicly observed:

> Mrs Carelli ... tried an audacious stroke, thus demonstrating much more bravery than her husband .... I am experienced in publishers and editors and I especially know Mr Sonzogno, Walter Mocchi, and Mrs Carelli, and I don't trust them at all: every week they fight, and every seven days they make peace due to many mysterious interests, carried on through a hundred Limited Companies, fifty Federations and twenty-five Syndicates that are dizzily made and undone through games of million*s*, of which they talk about together as though as they were nickels.[47]

As Mascagni pointed out, Mocchi and Carelli – along with their business partners – built up a huge network of influence, which they manipulated for their own interests, thus making them a powerful but not uniformly well-liked couple in the theatrical world. In 1922, after a South American tour in which Mascagni was overshadowed by the Wiener Philarmoniker engaged by Mocchi, the Maestro denounced his *impresario* to the Fascists as the 'Buffalo Bill of the Italian *impresarios* abroad', who 'offends Italian art by preferring German artists and repertoire'.[48] The powerful Mocchi, who was also a supporter of Mussolini, managed to manipulate his personal disagreement with Mascagni into a large-scale debate in the press regarding the crisis of musical theatre, which led to the Conference for the Lyrical Theatre that took place in Rome in 1923. These were indeed years of great difficulties for the traditional performing arts as, in Italy as elsewhere, they could no longer withstand the competition from the cinema and new light genres (such as the successful '*varietà*'[49]), while in South America the European companies had to face increasing demand from their audiences for a new national repertoire 'that never asserted itself'.[50] These phenomena led to a general crisis for theatrical exports, and Mocchi and Carelli had to balance their overseas losses with the earnings of the Costanzi, thus causing a significant deficit in STIN's budget.[51]

Financial Difficulties and Fascist Disapproval

The financial crisis of the couple met the interests of Mussolini, 'that commanded and wants the rebirth of the theatre', as explained to '*Il Duce*' by the Governor of Rome Filippo Cremonesi.[52] Since their early days in power, in late October 1922, the Fascists had been seeking a solution to provide the capital city with a public opera house; by 1923, architect Marcello Piacentini – who transformed the Costanzi into the current Teatro dell'Opera di Roma – had proposed several solutions in a pamphlet dedicated to the forthcoming creation of the National Opera House.[53] Mocchi and Carelli took advantage of the situation, and proposed that the Governor of Rome acquire their majority shareholding in the STIN – the joint-stock company that still owned the Costanzi – as well as their debts.[54] The operation was painstakingly planned,[55] and after a long negotiation, in the summer of 1926 the Governor paid off Mocchi and Carelli's majority shareholding (376 shares out of 400) at the inflated price of L. 1.886.662,[56] which included an overrated estimate for scenery, props, furniture, and costumes.[57]

After its refurbishment in 1928, the grand opening of the Teatro Reale dell'Opera di Roma was entrusted to Ottavio Scotto, a competing *impresario* to Mocchi in the South American market. Although Augusto Carelli argued that his sister was put aside because the board of directors 'was trembling at the idea of working with Mrs Carelli', who was 'a manager of such competence' that she 'could never have run the theatre as a dependant,'[58] the Governor of Rome probably preferred a fresh start with a less compromised manager. There is no evidence that the Fascists excluded Carelli as a woman. As a matter of fact, during the early 1920s, rising Fascism had a controversial attitude towards women's role in Italian society: as Victoria De Grazia has observed, on the one hand 'Mussolini's regime stood for returning women to home and hearth, restoring patriarchal authority, and confining female destiny to bearing babies', but at the same time 'the fascist dictatorship celebrated the *Nuova italiana*, or "New Italian Woman"'.[59] The regime at first seemed to accept Carelli's leadership. It should be noted that right before Mussolini's rise to power, in January 1920, Carelli's leading position had been recognised by some future Fascist leaders through her appointment as member of the committee of the Ministry of the Economy and Finance that should reform theatrical taxation in Italy. In that three-member commission, Carelli was not only the only woman, but also the sole representative of theatre and opera managers.[60]

However, it is also true that some factions of Fascist supporters could not stand seeing a woman in a powerful role, and Carelli became the victim of several anonymous letters sent to discredit her managerial activity. In 1925, an anonymous letter denounced Carelli to the police for supposed anti-Fascist behaviours, thus causing an investigation that resulted in the report of Carelli's character by the Fascist police quoted earlier. Once the Costanzi was sold and Carelli no longer held the management of the Costanzi, some anonymous 'Fascist artists' ('*artisti del Fascio*') addressed a letter to the Governor of Rome to congratulate him on his decision:

> It was a real shame that a theatre of the highest importance was managed by a woman like Carelli, who is a true degenerate cocaine addict, that leaves the running [of the theatre] to her chauffeur – that is to her lover – and also to that Spanish bass, Sabat. These foreigners should be eliminated, because we Italians, who also have beautiful voices, are sadly unemployed. But these foreigners are intrusive, and find ways to seduce the faded *diva* Carelli, who is a mobster. We all support your Highness the Governor of Rome and applaud in unison the vigorous fact that now the Capital of Italy will have its theatre, properly run by people that will not have any second purpose but justice.[61]

It is interesting that the anonymous Fascists not only described Carelli's power and influence in terms of '*camorra*' (mob), but also denounced her moral unfitness to run the main opera house in Rome, casting aspersions on her sexual behaviour. There had long been rumours in the theatrical world regarding Mocchi's and Carelli's affairs, although their business partnership had survived their marriage: as divorce was illegal in Italy, they separated in 1924 but kept on working together until the Costanzi was sold. The loss of the opera house definitely split Mocchi and Carelli as a couple and broke up their relationship. Mocchi moved to Brazil to support the career of his new lover and future wife, the soprano Bidu Sayão, while Carelli tried to reinvent her managerial activity, unsuccessfully proposing herself for the management of the San Carlo of Naples, as well as for other theatres in Italy and abroad. Publishing some excerpts from his sister's letterbook (conserved in the Archive of the Teatro dell'Opera in the early 1930s but currently missing), Augusto Carelli gave an effective description of Emma Carelli's mood after the sale of the Costanzi:

> What is tormenting, entering into the heart of the correspondence of such a painful soul, is to find Mrs Carelli (who a few weeks earlier dictated the law to everyone, always raising her voice), to find her with extended hand asking so humbly for work . . . And all her friends in Milan, Florence, Trieste, Naples, Paris, New York, answered her with fine words, but either making empty promises or betraying her.[62]

Unable to find a new position, Carelli wandered Europe driving her flaming red car, until the tragic accident which occurred on 17 August 1928 which cut her life short at the age of 51. Augusto Carelli chose to conclude the reconstruction of his sister's last years with a note written by Carelli a few days before her death: 'Three passions I had in this world: Walter Mocchi, the Costanzi Theatre and this damned car, that someday will crush me'.[63]

Conclusion

The activity of Emma Carelli has been long described (and rightly so) as an outstanding example of female leadership in the theatrical world of the early twentieth century. However, only a thorough analysis of primary and secondary sources can frame this exceptional figure in her kaleidoscopic complexity. The documentation produced by the police, by her partners, and notably by her opponents, provides an effective portrait of woman who was crucial for Italian culture and its circulation worldwide in a period of deep social transformations. Composers like Mascagni and Puccini had to deal with the theatrical networks Carelli and her husband envisioned and created, while Toscanini denounced their shady connections and their prominence in international operatic commerce. Carelli's wide range of interests – from opera to dance, from operetta to the Futurist *avant-garde* – is proof of her brilliant mind and her business acumen. And the letters of her Fascist detractors, focusing on sexual behaviour and moral unfitness to run the main opera house in Rome, underline the regression of parts of the Italian society during Mussolini's regime.

Notes

1. Susan Rutherford, "The Prima Donna as Opera Impresario. Emma Carelli and the Teatro Costanzi, 1911–1926," in *The Arts of the Prima Donna in the Long Nineteenth Century*, edited by Rachel Cowgill and Hilary Poriss (Oxford: Oxford University Press, 2012), 273. Besides Emma Carelli, these women were Marguerite Brunet Montansier at the Théâtre Italien in Paris (1801–03), Angelica Catalani at the same theatre (1815–18), Lucia Vestris at Covent Garden in London (1839–42),

Cosima Wagner at the Festspielhaus in Bayreuth (1883–1908), and Mary Garden for the Chicago Opera Association (1921–22). Like Carelli, most of them were former singers that focused on management in the second stage of their careers.
2. For a biographical overview, see: Raoul Meloncelli, "Emma Carelli," in *Dizionario Biografico degli Italiani* (Rome: Istituto dell'Enciclopedia italiana, 1960-), vol. 20 (1977), https://www.treccani.it/enciclopedia/emma-carelli_%28Dizionario-Biografico%29/. For the history of the Costanzi during Mocchi and Carelli's exploitation, see: Matteo Paoletti, *Mascagni, Mocchi, Sonzogno. La Società Teatrale Internazionale (1908–1931) e i suoi protagonisti* (Bologna: Dipartimento delle Arti e ALMADL, 2015).
3. For a detailed reconstruction of the seasons managed by Emma Carelli, see: Vittorio Frajese, *Dal Costanzi all'Opera: cronache, recensioni e documenti in 4 volumi* (Rome: Capitolium, 1977), vol. 2, 56–180.
4. Sergio Lambiase, *Adriana. Cuore di luce* (Milano: Bompiani, 2018), 2.
5. Emma Carelli rests at the Cemetery Verano of Rome. The full epigraph is: 'A Emma Carelli / Passione d'ogni atto / Purezza alata di canto / Umanità fra le finzioni della scena / Che diede all'arte lirica ammaestramento di vita / E alla Roma moderna / L'inizio d'un grande Teatro'. All translations are the author's own, unless otherwise specified.
6. Victoria De Grazia, *How Fascism Ruled Women: Italy, 1922–1945* (Berkeley and Los Angeles: University of California Press, 1992), 1.
7. 'la signora Emma Carelli . . . unisce la qualità di squisita artista a quella di perfetta direttrice del massimo teatro di Roma . . . e non teme di subire perdite né di logorare le sue inesauribili energie.' Archivio Storico della Camera di Commercio di Roma, *Ex Tribunale Civile e Penale di Roma – Sezione Commerciale*, b. 710/1908, f. 26, Verbale dell'assemblea generale degli azionisti della Società Teatrale Internazionale, Roma (February 28, 1925).
8. Augusto Carelli, *Emma Carelli. Trent'anni di vita del teatro lirico* (Rome: Maglione, 1932).
9. Matteo Paoletti, *'A Huge Revolution of Theatrical Commerce'. Walter Mocchi and the Italian Musical Theatre Business in South America* (Cambridge: Cambridge University Press, 2020).
10. 'egli ha trovato in loro una claque entusiasta e zelante, che, con esagerazione tutta americana, giunse una sera, a fine di spettacolo, a togliere i cavalli dalla vettura della Carelli, per tirarla a braccia fino all'albergo'. Archivio Centrale dello Stato, *Casellario Politico Centrale*, b. 3321.
11. *Rua do Ouvidor*, VII (1903), 1 and 3 October.
12. Archivio Storico Capitolino, *Società Teatrale Internazionale*, b. 18, f. 2, Report of Carlo Körner to STIN's administration (April 3, 1909).
13. *La Stampa* (February 3, 1907).
14. 'La moglie non può donare, alienare beni immobili, sottoporli ad ipoteca, contrarre mutui, cedere o riscuotere capitali, costituirsi sicurtà, né transigere o stare in giudizio relativamente a tali atti, senza l'autorizzazione del marito'. Codice civile del Regno d'Italia, 1865, Book I, tit. V, art. 134.
15. Archivio Storico Capitolino, *Ripartizione X (Antichità e Belle Arti) 1907–1920*, b. 55.
16. 'gli interessi di quella unione conjugale, di quella famiglia di cui egli è capo, custode e legittimo rappresentante.' Enrico Rosmini, *Legislazione e giurisprudenza dei teatri* (Milan: Hoepli, 1893), 393.
17. Ivi, 395.
18. Even though Mocchi, as a left-wing politician, had been criticised more for his hypocritical attendance of sumptuous opera houses together with his wife, the 'husband of the prima donna' had long been a derisory figure. See Susan Rutherford, *The Prima Donna and Opera, 1815–1930* (Cambridge: Cambridge University Press, 2006), 149–60.
19. 'Walter Mocchi [è] insieme alla cantante Emma Carelli, di cui si dice marito ed a cui carico vive soltanto come amante'. Archivio Centrale dello Stato, *Casellario Politico Centrale*, b. 3321, Letter of the Legazione d'Italia of Petropolis (Brazil) to the Ministry of the Interior (September 2, 1903).
20. 'Giacché pensate possa fare cattiva impressione pagare quarantamila Carnevale Quaresima Emma Carelli che guadagnale al mese in America e che guadagnerà sessantamila anno venturo all'estero tira una bella riverenza all'Internazionale e vi saluta'. Archivio Storico Capitolino, *Società Teatrale Internazionale*, b. 4, f. 8, Telegram of Emma Carelli to Alberto Marghieri (April 22, 1909).
21. 'Emma Carelli, proprietaria del teatro Costanzi, è nota per il suo carattere autoritario, e per il suo linguaggio troppo libero, e poco deferente per chiunque abbia occasione di trattare con lei. Essa, che fu già rinomata artista lirica, ha vissuto sempre nell'ambiente teatrale, ove è notissima, e tenuta in speciale considerazione per la sua competenza artistica. Tutto ciò è valso a formare in lei un carattere indipendente che le fa assumere atteggiamenti di superiorità verso chicchessia, atteggiamenti

che hanno finito per renderla invisa alla maggioranza, specie nel ceto artistico, e nel personale, che da esse dipende, e dal quale è anche temuta. Circa quanto si addebita alla Signora Carelli con l'anonimo che restituisco, è risultato che veramente costei nei locali del teatro con i suoi discorsi attacca i componenti il Governo Fascista ed anche S.E. il Presidente del Consiglio. Si attribuisce tale contegno al fatto di aver la Carelli richiesto al Governo la sovvenzione per alleviare le forti spese che dovrà sostenere per la imminente stagione lirica, e di non averla ancora ottenuta. Chi la ascolta non dà però importanza al suo parlare, tenuto conto della sua spiccata proclività alla maldicenza, e al turpiloquio. La Carelli non può dirsi che abbia principi politici, perché di politica non si interessa. È noto però che è moglie di Walter Mocchi, ex socialista.' Archivio Centrale dello Stato, *Ministero dell'Interno. Direzione generale di pubblica sicurezza. Divisione polizia politica. Fascicoli personali*, b. 245, f. Carelli, Report of the Chief of Police (December 14, 1925).

22. '[Mocchi], che a causa della lunga permanenza in America quell'anno per la *tournée Mascagni*, non poteva come S. Antonio godere del dono dell'ubiquità, aveva incessantemente sollecitato il concorso personale di Emma alla preparazione della prima stagione al Costanzi'. Carelli, *Emma Carelli*, 162.
23. 'la nuova Impresa ha il progetto, e la necessità di dare spettacoli nuovi e moderni, per rispettare tutte le tendenze del pubblico ed incoraggiare le promesse artistiche dei giovani.' Archivio Storico Capitolino, *Ripartizione X (Antichità e Belle Arti) 1907–1920*, b. 55, f. 3, Letter of Emma Carelli to Ernesto Nathan (November 2, 1911).
24. 'non per ottenere una pura e semplice sovvenzione a titolo mecenatistico, ma per addivenire, fra il MUNICIPIO e la mia Società, che gestisce il Teatro COSTANZI, ad un regolare contratto mecenatistico, ma per addivenire, fra il MUNICIPIO e la mia Società . . . ad un regolare contratto, in cui i diritti derivanti al Comune, per la sua collaborazione finanziaria, siano ben chiariti e tutelati . . . . [Le] sovvenzioni teatrali, considerate come spese improduttive o di lusso o, peggio ancora, come facilitazione fatta alle classi ricche . . . . La sempre maggiore elevazione economica delle classi lavoratrici, da un lato, e l'istituzione delle recite a prezzi popolari dall'altro, hanno ormai abolito il privilegio delle classi ricche, in materia teatrale, e che ovunque lo spettacolo lirico è ormai considerato, non più come un semplice divertimento, ma come una vera educazione estetica.' Archivio Storico Capitolino, *Ripartizione X (Antichità e Belle Arti) 1907–1920*, b. 55, f. 3, Letter of Walter Mocchi to Ernesto Nathan (December 15, 1911).
25. Jann Pasler, *Composing the Citizen: Music as Public Utility in Third Republic France* (Berkeley: University of California Press, 2009); Carlotta Sorba, *Il melodramma della nazione. Politica e sentimenti nell'età del Risorgimento* (Roma-Bari: Laterza, 2015).
26. 'assicurerà anche la loro sorte nei mesi in cui il Costanzi non funziona, scritturandoli, per la maggior parte, nelle proprie tournée sud americane, fintanto che farà tali tournée'. Archivio Storico Capitolino, *Ripartizione X (Antichità e Belle Arti) 1907–1920*, b. 55, f. 3, *Verbale di deliberazione della Giunta Municipale di Roma – Seduta del 24 gennaio 1912*.
27. 'ha preparato e mandato in scena vittoriosamente 4 opere in 15 giorni e 10 rappresentazioni; e queste cifre sono la più eloquente prova della serietà con cui la stagione è stata organizzata e viene diretta.' 'La grande stagione lirica del Costanzi'. *Il Teatro Illustrato* (January 15, 1912).
28. 'Emma Carelli . . . sembra voglia far dimenticare a sé stessa di essere un'artista di doti veramente eccezionali, e da quasi due anni non canta più e dedica il fervore della sua ricca natura alle umili, ignorate fatiche dell'azienda teatrale.' *La Vita* (February 8, 1912). The quotation is from the press review published in Frajese, *Dal Costanzi all'Opera*, 62–63.
29. *Il Teatro Illustrato* (October 1, 1912 and November 1, 1912).
30. Archivio Storico Capitolino, *Ripartizione X (Antichità e Belle Arti) 1907–1920*, b. 55, f. 4, Letter of Walter Mocchi to Alberto Tonelli, (October 31, 191), 2.
31. Archivio Storico Capitolino, *Ripartizione X (Antichità e Belle Arti) 1907–1920*, b. 55, f. 4, Programme of the lyrical season 1912-13.
32. Archivio Storico Capitolino, *Ripartizione X (Antichità e Belle Arti) 1907–1920*, b. 55, f. 4, Letter of Walter Mocchi to the City Council of Rome (March 2, 1913).
33. These numbers are taken from an analysis of the financial statements, conserved in the Archivio Storico della Camera di Commercio of Rome. The comparison with Mascagni's direction confirms the substantial unreliability of Augusto's narrative when talking about numbers: '[Emma staged] fourteen titles whereas seven or eight had always been performed, and a season of four months with more than hundred nights, whereas the theatrical openings had never overcome sixty or seventy days and the number of nights the cypher of sixty'. Carelli, *Emma Carelli*, 164–65.

34. Frajese, *Dal Costanzi all'Opera*, vol. 2, 69.
35. Archivio Storico Capitolino, *Ripartizione X (Antichità e Belle Arti) 1907–1920*, b. 55, fasc. 4, Anonymous letter to the City Council of Rome [delivered on April 4, 1913].
36. *Il Teatro Illustrato* (December 15–31, 1914).
37. Roberto Caamaño, *La historia del Teatro Colón 1908–1968* (Buenos Aires: Cinetea, 1969), vol. III, 77–78.
38. Archivio Storico Capitolino, *Ripartizione X (Antichità e Belle Arti) 1907–1920*, b. 55, f. 3, Letter of Emma Carelli to Adolfo Apolloni, [24] February 1915.
39. Renzo Sonzogno wanted Mascagni to work with d'Annunzio, after Franchetti and Puccini refused *Parisina*. In April 1912, the composer accepted the task, and completed the first part of the opera in only four months, but then he was stopped by the excessive length of the libretto, which was cut with much controversy. After the premiere at La Scala (December 15, 1913), the opera was shortened and d'Annunzio threatened a trial, but a new version of *Parisina* debuted once again at the Costanzi (March 21, 1914). Sonzogno accused the composer of causing heavy losses to the company. See: Cesare Orselli, *Pietro Mascagni* (Palermo: L'Epos, 2011), 91–95, 269–83.
40. *Il Teatro Illustrato* (March 15–31, 1914).
41. Isabella Piazzoni, *Dal "Teatro dei palchettisti" all'Ente autonomo: la Scala, 1897–1920* (Firenze: La Nuova Italia, 1995), 196–200.
42. 'Scala ottenne orchestra condizioni intesa, invece rottura coro . . . formati masse così, completandole nordamerica facendole istruire prima, eviterai enormi spese, difficoltà insuperabili'. Archivio Visconti di Modrone, Milan, b. H71, f. 9, Telegram of Emma Carelli to Walter Mocchi (October 7, 1916).
43. Harvey Sachs, *Reflections on Toscanini* (Grove Weidenfeld, 1991), 56, Letter of Toscanini to Uberto Visconti di Modrone (1916).
44. 'Vorrei che le cose fossero fatte con cura eccezionale – sia scene sia artisti sia calma necessaria in tutti. . . . Sarà questo con la Carelli?' Archivio Ricordi, *Lettere*, Letter of Giacomo Puccini to Carlo Clausetti (November 16, 1918).
45. 'Se foste stato a Roma avreste veduto con quale attività, con quale affettuoso buon volere e con quale esito il Mocchi abbia dato risalto al grande successo del *Trittico*. . . . Il Mocchi lavorava nel suo interesse e per Roma e . . . pensando all'America . . . . Ora capirete che a tutto questo Puccini non può essere rimasto insensibile.' Archivio Ricordi, *Lettere*, Letter of Giovacchino Forzano to Carlo Clausetti (February 12, 1919).
46. 'Veda di proporre alla Carelli *L'Amore dei tre re*, io direttore. È un'idea che la Carelli può trovare buona.' Archivio Ricordi, *Lettere*, Letter of Italo Montemezzi to Renzo Valcarenghi (1925).
47. 'La signora Carelli . . . tentò il volo d'audacia, dimostrando più coraggio di suo marito . . . . Io, che ho pratica di editori e di impresari e che particolarmente conosco il sig. Sonzogno, Walter Mocchi e la signora Carelli, ogni settimana in lite ed ogni sette giorni in pace, in forza di tanti interessi misteriosi, in virtù di cento Società Anonime e cinquanta Federazioni e venticinque Consorzi, che tra loro si fanno e si disfanno vertiginosamente, attraverso alla ridda di milioni, di cui tutti insieme parlano come di nichelini, io (dicevo) non ci credo punto né poco.' *La Tribuna* (April 2, 1920).
48. *La Stampa* (March 15, 1923).
49. By 1905, the revenues of varietà star Leopoldo Fregoli alone doubled those of the most important drama companies in Italy. In the meantime, without subsidies, opera could no longer offset productive costs. For an overview, see: Livia Cavaglieri, *Il sistema teatrale. Storia dell'organizzazione, dell'economia e delle politiche del teatro in Italia* (Roma: Audino, 2021), 59.
50. Annibale Cetrangolo, *Dentro e fuori il teatro. Ventura degli italiani e del loro melodramma nel Rio de la Plata* (Isernia: Cosmo Iannone, 2018), 185.
51. The couple had obtained the majority shareholding in the early 1920s, through a shady turnaround of stocks. For the corporate evolution of STIN, see Paoletti, *Mascagni, Mocchi, Sonzogno*, 338–49.
52. Archivio Storico Capitolino, *Società Teatrale Internazionale – Appendice*, b. 1, f. 1, Letter to Benito Mussolini [June 1926].
53. Marcello Piacentini, *Studi per il Teatro Massimo di Roma* (Roma: Sansaini, 1923).
54. According to STIN's financial statements, the company had debts for L. 5,436,792, paid by the Governor of Rome through an installment schedule that lasted until 1935.
55. For a reconstruction of the ministerial debate, see: Emanuela Scarpellini, *Organizzazione teatrale e politica del teatro nell'Italia fascista – nuova edizione riveduta e aggiornata* (Milan: LED, 2004),

78–80; Gianfranco Pedullà, *Il teatro italiano nel tempo del fascismo* (Corazzano: Titivillus, 2009), 69–72.
56. Archivio Storico Capitolino, *Società Teatrale Internazionale – Appendice*, b. 1, f. 2, *Dal Verbale delle Deliberazioni del Governatore adottate il giorno 18 maggio 1926 – Acquisto delle azioni del Teatro Costanzi*.
57. The Governor's lawyer even suggested a lawsuit against Mocchi and Carelli, because inside the theatre there were 'neither costumes nor footwear property of STIN, except for an insignificant bunch of deteriorated and useless . . . consumed material'. Archivio Storico Capitolino, *Società Teatrale Internazionale – Appendice*, b. 1, f. 2, *Relazione sulla riconsegna del materiale in uso alla Società in Accomandita 'Impresa Teatro Costanzi'*.
58. 'tremavano al pensiero di dover lavorare avendo in sott'ordine la signora Carelli', 'si rendevano conto che una direttrice così competente come la signora Carelli, non avrebbe mai potuto dirigere in sott'ordine il Costanzi'. Carelli, *Emma Carelli*, 301–02.
59. De Grazia, *How Fascism Ruled Women*, 1–2.
60. The other two members were Marco Praga, representative of the Italian Society of Authors, and Franco Liberati, representative of the theatre owners, STIN shareholder, and future executive for the Fascists. The works were concluded by February 1921, when the new taxation scheme was approved (*L'Arte Drammatica*, January 15, 1921).
61. 'Era una vera vergogna che un teatro della massima importanza fosse gestito da una donna che è una vera degenerata da una cocainomane come è attualmente la Carelli, che lascia fare tutto al Chauffeur cioè l'amante – e quel basso Sabat spagnuolo idem. Questi stranieri vorrebbero eliminati, perché noi italiani siamo purtroppo in molti a spasso – e delle bellissime voci. Ma quelli stranieri che sono invadenti e trovano le vie per entrare nelle seducenti grazie della diva tramontata Carelli cammorrista. Noi tutti ci uniamo a Sua Eccellenza il Governatore di Roma ed applaudiamo all'unisono dell'energico fatto: ora la Capitale d'Italia avrà il suo teatro gestito bene e da persone che non avranno il secondo fine – ma la giustizia.' Archivio Storico Capitolino, *Società Teatrale Internazionale – Appendice*, b. 1, f. 3, *Lettera to Filippo Cremonesi*, [delivered on June 21, 1926].
62. 'Quello che strazia, entrando nel vivo della corrispondenza di un'anima così dolorante, è il ritrovare la signora Carelli (che poche settimane prima dettava la legge a tutti, alzando la voce sempre), il ritrovarla con la mano tesa a chiedere così umilmente lavoro . . . . E tutti i suoi amici di Milano, di Firenze, di Trieste, di Napoli, di Parigi, di Nuova York, le rispondevano con belle parole, ma o promettendo a vuoto o disingannandola.' Carelli, *Emma Carelli*, 309.
63. 'Tre passioni ho avuto al mondo: Walter Mocchi, il Teatro Costanzi e questa maledetta macchina che un giorno o l'altro mi schiaccerà.' Carelli, *Emma Carelli*, 317.

Bibliography

Carelli, Augusto. *Emma Carelli. Trent'anni di vita del teatro lirico*. Rome: Maglione, 1932.
Cavaglieri, Livia. *Il sistema teatrale. Storia dell'organizzazione, dell'economia e delle politiche del teatro in Italia*. Roma: Audino, 2021.
Cetrangolo, Annibale. *Dentro e fuori il teatro. Ventura degli italiani e del loro melodramma nel Rio de la Plata*. Isernia: Cosmo Iannone, 2018.
De Grazia, Victoria. *How Fascism Ruled Women: Italy, 1922–1945*. Berkeley and Los Angeles: University of California Press, 1992.
Frajese, Vittorio. *Dal Costanzi all'Opera: cronache, recensioni e documenti in 4 volumi*. Rome: Capitolium, 1977.
Lambiase, Sergio. *Adriana. Cuore di luce*. Milano: Bompiani, 2018.
Meloncelli, Raoul. "Emma Carelli." In *Dizionario Biografico degli Italiani*. Rome: Istituto dell'Enciclopedia italiana, 1960–), vol. 20 (1977), *ad vocem*. https://www.treccani.it/enciclopedia/emma-carelli_%28Dizionario-Biografico%29/.
Orselli, Cesare. *Pietro Mascagni*. Palermo: L'Epos, 2011.
Paoletti, Matteo. *Mascagni, Mocchi, Sonzogno. La Società Teatrale Internazionale (1908–1931) e i suoi protagonisti*. Bologna: Dipartimento delle Arti e ALMADL, 2015. https://doi.org/10.6092/unibo/amsacta/4235.
_____. *'A Huge Revolution of Theatrical Commerce' Walter Mocchi and the Italian Musical Theatre Business in South America*. Cambridge: Cambridge University Press, 2020.

Pasler, Jann. *Composing the Citizen: Music as Public Utility in Third Republic France*. Berkeley: University of California Press, 2009.
Pedullà, Gianfranco. *Il teatro italiano nel tempo del fascismo*. Corazzano: Titivillus, 2009.
Piacentini, Marcello. *Studi per il Teatro Massimo di Roma*. Roma: Sansaini, 1923.
Piazzoni, Isabella. *Dal "Teatro dei palchettisti" all'Ente autonomo: la Scala, 1897–1920*. Firenze: La Nuova Italia, 1995.
Rutherford, Susan. *The Prima Donna and Opera, 1815–1930*. Cambridge: Cambridge University Press, 2006.
———. "The Prima Donna as Opera Impresario. Emma Carelli and the Teatro Costanzi, 1911–1926." In *The Arts of the Prima Donna in the Long Nineteenth Century*, edited by Rachel Cowgill and Hilary Poriss, 272–89. Oxford: Oxford University Press, 2012.
Sachs, Harvey. *Reflections on Toscanini*. New York: Grove Weidenfeld, 1991.
Scarpellini, Emanuela. *Organizzazione teatrale e politica del teatro nell'Italia fascista – nuova edizione riveduta e aggiornata*. Milan: LED, 2004.
Sorba, Carlotta. *Il melodramma della nazione. Politica e sentimenti nell'età del Risorgimento*. Roma-Bari: Laterza, 2015.

13
HENRIETTE RENIÉ AS A HARP ENSEMBLE LEADER, CHORAL AND ORCHESTRAL CONDUCTOR, AND *IMPRESARIO* IN THE LIGHT OF ARCHIVAL SOURCES

Temina Cadi Sulumuna

Among the French musical milieu at the turn of and through the first half of the twentieth century, Henriette Renié (1875–1956), an independent woman of a strong personality and of equally rich spiritual life,[1] clearly stands out. There are several reasons for this. She was a *virtuosa* harpist who was praised by many leading musical figures, such as Camille Saint-Saëns and Albert Roussel, as evidenced by her prolific correspondence.[2] She was a composer, mainly of harp works, and was awarded both the *Première Médaille* by the *Salon des Musiciens Français* in 1914,[3] and two years later, the *Prix Chartier* by the Académie des Beaux-Arts for her compositions.[4] Renié was also highly regarded as a harp professor with an international reputation, to whom students came from many different parts of the world, including Argentina, Belgium, Brazil, Chile, England, Finland, Italy, Mexico, Peru, Puerto Rico, Romania, Switzerland, and the United States (as evidenced by Renié's innumerable letters and her students' memoirs).[5] In addition, she successfully led her own harp ensemble for forty years, proved herself to be an active *impresario*, and occasionally took the role of conductor with choirs and small orchestras, usually in performances of her own works. This chapter considers Renié's (as yet under-researched) activities as a musical leader, encompassing her work as a harp ensemble leader, an *impresario*, and a choral and orchestral conductor, in light of archival materials. These consist of her manuscript diaries and separately entitled notebooks, which she kept all her life and which total more than 18,000 pages; her extensive correspondence, which includes more than 8,000 letters; Renié's memoirs, as well as those of people who had close links with her; concert programmes; and pertinent press coverage. These are preserved at the International Harp Archives in the United States and at various institutions in France,[6] and were also stored in the private collection of Renié's former heiress, violinist Jacqueline Lesprit-Maupin (1933–2018), and previously owned by Françoise des Varennes (1919–2004), Renié's goddaughter and first heiress, a recognised poet and playwright in her own right.[7] It is hoped that this chapter will shed further light on Renié's achievements and legacy in both

Henriette Renié as Harp Ensemble Leader

It was in 1894 that the nineteen-year-old Renié – who had already been awarded, among other things, first prize in harp in 1887, second prize in harmony four years later, and who would be awarded the second prize in counterpoint and fugue in 1895 at the Paris Conservatoire[8] – began to plan chamber music classes for her students. From a letter to her father Jean-Émile Renié, a well-known opera singer and painter, one learns how the idea for these classes originated:

> The mother of a young student, Alice Delbos, asked me if I could come to lead the ensembles at her home. I go there on Tuesdays every other week, and I give a sort of ensemble lesson. The instruments that are at my disposal are: harp, piano, pump organ, mandolin, and monochord, which somehow replaces the violin. We make all kinds of arrangements for these five instruments, and this is very amusing. By the way, you know that I cherish more and more the idea of creating ensemble classes next year. I would have, for instance, two sessions a month, and we would play the harp and violin (Marie Linder would play the violin); harp and piano; harp, piano, and violin; or finally two, three, or four harps. It would be very interesting, and I think that it'd be successful, because – if I am not mistaken – nobody so far has come up with the idea of such classes with harp. That's why I do not talk about this with anyone so that no one can steal my idea![9]

Renié's chamber music classes, which in the beginning were for two harps, piano, and violin,[10] commenced the following year, as Renié recorded in a letter, dated 4-6 December 1922, to French musicologist and music critic Marc Pincherle.[11] These classes were Renié's private enterprise in which mainly her private French harp students (many of whom at the same time received a conservatoire education) participated. International harp students principally attended her chamber music classes during the summer months.

Renié observed in her memoirs that it was performing the oratorio *Les Sept Paroles du Christ*, by her former Paris Conservatoire composition professor Théodore Dubois, that finally gave her the necessary push to transcribe works for her ensemble, as she valued the composition so much that she couldn't resist transcribing it.[12] In the aforementioned letter to Pincherle, she also revealed why she had begun to make transcriptions and what she thought of them:

> I realised that the harp literature was insufficient to mould the taste and style of my students. Therefore, I have transcribed myself classical and contemporary music, from symphonies to tone poems, oratorios, a few operas, and some chamber music pieces, etc . . . Some of them had only modest value, like transcriptions for four hands or two pianos; others, which were very successful, were more elaborated.[13]

The music ensemble classes proved to be extremely important in Renié's life. Not only did they enable her students to learn discipline and therefore be prepared to play in orchestras (which was Renié's chief aim, being aware that they had practically no opportunity to prepare themselves for orchestral playing as part of their formal training), but also – and this must have been a huge surprise for Renié – the chamber music ensemble classes gave rise to her successful professional ensemble called the Sextuor Renié, which was composed of six harps, and which later on, for some time, became the Septuor Renié when Marcel Grandjany, the eminent harpist and her student, joined it. Her ensemble – in which she usually performed the first harp part – called by some music critics 'a genuine small orchestra',[14] gave regular concerts from 1899. Their principal performance venues were the prestigious Salle Érard, Salle des Quatuors of the Gaveau firm (commonly referred to as the Salle Gaveau), Salle Berlioz, Salle d'Iéna, Salle des Concerts du Conservatoire, and at her Parisian studio, 55 de Passy Street.[15] Although her ensemble was composed of very good harpists, even *virtuosi*, and the individual parts of the pieces she transcribed were usually relatively easy for her fellow performers – the majority of whom had taken harp lessons with her, and therefore knew what manner of performing she expected from them – Renié was a demanding ensemble leader and inexorable as to the duration of the rehearsals, as evidenced by her correspondence. In a letter dated 22 July 1935 to the Puerto Rican harpist Maria-Rosa Vidal, one reads:

> Then, departing over Easter, and on my return, one-month preparations for a big session of chamber music. Nine rehearsals which lasted for three or even four hours! The musical session took place on June 6th.[16]

Renié was known for requiring a large amount of time and great dedication from her fellow performers. It happened that some of the advanced harp students coming from the United States to take harp lessons with her to help them put the finishing touches to their solo repertoire, though flattered by her invitation to perform during their stays in France with the six-harp ensemble, refused to participate at the expense of the time destined for practising their solo programmes, as they knew that she would require from them a flawless execution of the ensemble parts. We read, for instance, in Renié's 7 March 1949 letter to Mildred Dilling (1894–1982), the great American harpist and her beloved harp student:

> Geraldine wrote to me that,[17] after much thought, she found it more reasonable to renounce the sextet, fearing that the time spent on learning the parts would harm her [solo] work. I feel sorry for her, because I think that it would have interested her greatly… But I can't blame her for this; the time needed for the work under my supervision, and five afternoons to rehearse: it would have been almost one month wasted.[18]

Renié wrote original compositions but mostly transcribed numerous baroque, classical, romantic, and contemporary works for her harp ensemble. Some composers were as pleased with her transcriptions of their pieces for the Sextuor Renié as with the ensemble's execution. In an undated letter to her from Jacques de La Presle, we read that her transcription of his *Jardin mouillé* was tuneful and wonderfully done: 'It gives a new value to my work, and its performance is worthy of admiration'.[19] Similarly, Gabriel Pierné's correspondence to Renié, dated 3 November 1936, proves his satisfaction with her transcription of his *Marche des petits soldats de plomb*:

> My dear friend,
> I can't resist the great pleasure of congratulating you, you and your students, on the splendid execution, yesterday evening, of my *Marche des petits soldats de plomb* transcribed by you for six harps. Never have I heard a better-done transcription, a more rhythmical translation, vigorous and full of juvenile energy; and I bow in reverence to your twelve feet (including your students), I, the satisfied author.
> Sh! Let me give you a hug.
> Gabriel Pierné[20]

Music critics also praised Renié for her transcriptions and her original pieces for six or seven harps, as well as her Sextuor or Septuor Renié for their performances. Favourable reviews appeared in widely read press, including *L'Art musical*, *Excelsior*, *Le Journal*, *Le Ménestrel*, and *Le Monde musical*. For instance, on 3 January 1936, a review published in *L'Art musical* proclaimed that:

> Her [Renié's] famous ensemble of six harps (Mademoiselle Renié, Madam Bacqueyrisse-Le Dentu, Mademoiselle Bernard, Mesdames de Montesquiou, Kahan-Franck and de Navacelle) obtained a tremendous success in *Barcarolle*, in the spiritual *Défilé lilliputien* (an enthusiastic encore), and in *Contemplation*.[21]

Given the success of her harp ensemble, it doesn't come as a surprise that it was Renié's intention to replicate it abroad. As her correspondence reveals, her wish came true in the United States. Mildred Dilling – who took harp lessons from Henriette Renié for over thirty years – wrote to her from New York City:

> The music ensemble classes began with due fanfare last Thursday with eight harpists and six harps. Tomorrow, we'll go to Lyon & Healy,[22] and be able to have seven harps if necessary. We play *Les Petits soldats de plomb* [by Gabriel Pierné] and *Dolly* [by Gabriel Fauré], and tomorrow I'll make them practise *Menuet en mi* by Mozart.[23]

Turning now to Renié's legacy, her six-harp ensemble, which performed together until her death in 1956, was so successful that her students decided to revive it, encouraged by the success of the concert organised at the Salle Gaveau in 1975 (on the 100th anniversary of Renié's birth) for which the sextet was reconstituted. Thus, Renié's legacy lived on under a changed name: Sextuor de Harpes de Paris, made up of Odette Le Dentu, the leader of the ensemble, Bertile Fournier, Odette de Montesquiou, Marie-Laure De Brye, Geneviève Lions, and Suzanne Cotelle. Over the years, several harpists (Anne-Claire Cazalet, Annette Abscheidt, Véronique Ghesquière) succeeded to replace Renié's former students before the Sextuor de Harpes de Paris was definitively formed: Bertile Fournier, the leader, Sabine Chefson, Agnès Kammerer, Marie Saint-Bonnet, Geneviève Lions, and Caroline Rempp Verrey.[24] The ensemble chiefly performed transcriptions made by Renié, adding to this repertoire new ones, mostly made by the members of the Sextuor themselves (Sabine Chefson, Caroline Rempp Verrey), as well as original pieces written specifically for this ensemble, like *Port-au-Prince* by Bernard Andrès or *Étude miroir* Op. 42 by Michel Merlet.[25] The sextet widely popularised Renié's transcriptions performing, *inter alia*, at the Salle Pleyel and Salle Gaveau in Paris, at the Château de Versailles, Château de Ville d'Avray, Château d'Esclimont, Château d'Artigny, Château d'Isenbourg, Château de Gilly; and abroad – in Belgium, Luxemburg, and Lebanon during the Al Bustan Festival. The World Harp Congress (in Vienna, Paris, Copenhagen, and Prague) also propagated Renié's work by the Sextuor de Harpes de Paris. The successful ensemble ceased its activities with Bertile Fournier's retirement in 2001. However, Renié's legacy was still perpetuated through the Sextuor-derived Quatuor de Harpes de Paris. This four-harp ensemble (composed of the former members of Sextuor de Harpes de Paris: Marie Saint-Bonnet, Sabine Chefson, Agnès Kammerer, and Caroline Rempp Verrey) concertised for ten years in France and abroad, further promoting Renié's work,[26] as well as performing new four-harp transcriptions made by the ensemble members themselves.[27]

Françoise des Varennes and Jacqueline Lesprit-Maupin, both delighted with the Sextuor de Harpes de Paris preserving Renié's legacy, would collect newspaper clippings with reviews of performances given by the ensemble. From one preserved in their collection, dated 3 February 1982, entitled 'Richesses et couleurs de la harpe' ['Richness and colours of the harp'] we learn:

> The Théâtre de l'Hôtel de Ville [of Le Havre] welcomed, within its walls, last Friday, the famous Sextuor de Harpes de Paris[28] . . . The many Le Havre music-lovers, who filled the hall, were not mistaken. They warmly acclaimed this ensemble of *virtuoso* performers, who have been awarded prestigious prizes. One may say that in one evening, the harp, a favourite instrument, succeeded in winning over new harp followers. What a refinement and delicacy this most marvelous concert had, which, without any doubt, will always be remembered.[29]

Similarly, other newspaper clippings from the aforementioned private collection – 'Au musée. Le Sextuor de Harpes de Paris: Bonheur total' ['At the museum. Sextuor de Harpes de Paris: sheer bliss'] dated 22 April 1983 and the undated 'Le Sextuor de Harpes de Paris: un espace sonore étonnant. . .' ['Sextuor de Harpes de Paris: an astonishing sound space. . .'] – also reveal considerable critical acclaim. Let me conclude this section by citing some chosen excerpts from these clippings praising the ensemble's sonorous opulence and diversity – the qualities which Renié had pursued with her own sextet – thus demonstrating that the Sextuor de Harpes de Paris proved a worthy successor to the Sextuor Renié:

> First of all, it offers to the audience a fascinating spectacle of these six harps arranged like a fan, before seducing it with a technical and sonorous richness of a captivating originality: this self-portrait of the Sextuor de Harpes de Paris is highly accurate.[30] . . . From the seventeenth century to ours, the Sextuor will make us follow its path in a state of constantly renewed happiness. . . . The concert of Sextuor de Harpes de Paris? To put it simply, two hours of sheer bliss.[31]
>
> Also let us admit that with the Sextuor de Paris the harp is wonderfully served. So is the music. The six musicians master the art of enlivening the scores by exposing such voice,[32] by letting arise – on one and then on another instrument – the main motifs emphasising the thickness of the musical composition in its layers, undercoats, and little phrases, which disengage from the depths. Six instruments suffice then to create an amazing impression of a sound space with a multi-layerness of subtle and distinct plans.[33]

Henriette Renié as a Choral and Orchestral Conductor

Occasionally, Renié took on the role of conductor of chamber orchestras and choirs (which were not her own ensembles) in public. Her mahogany baton is still preserved as part of the Renié family's private collection; Henriette Renié's other baton was given by Jacqueline Lesprit-Maupin to the present author as a token of her gratitude for the author's research into Renié's artistic life.[34] Renié mounted the conductor's podium to direct mostly her own original works for harp and orchestra and transcriptions for choir or choirs or for soloist and choirs (sometimes with accompanying instruments) of her pieces that were originally destined for a solo voice with harp or piano accompaniment. This is evidenced by a review which appeared in *L'Art musical* of a concert almost entirely dedicated to Renié's works,[35] which took place on 19 December 1935 at the Salle des Concerts du Conservatoire: 'Finally, Miss Renié took the baton to conduct her pure *Prière à la Vierge*, in which is reflected a beautiful feeling, sung by Mr [Georges] Jouatte and the choirs'.[36] According to the programme, for this performance *Prière à la Vierge* was transcribed for soloist, two choirs, and piano. Annette Clément played the piano part and Jouatte was a tenor. Another concert – which featured Renié as a harpist with her Sextuor Renié, a conductor, and a composer – which received highly favourable reviews, took place on 3 June 1937 at the Salle Érard. *L'Art musical* and *Le Ménestrel* informed their readers that different harpist-soloists were accompanied by a double quartet or a small orchestra under the direction of Renié; for instance, in a performance of the *Adagio* from her *Concerto en ut mineur* composed in the years 1896–1901.[37]

Renié's taking possession of a conductor's baton adds to the diversified profiles of women conductors of the time. Some of them had received training in this discipline and aspired to direct the large leading Parisian orchestras of the interwar period, such as international women conductors Eva Brunelli, Gertrud Herliczka, and Carmen Studer-Weingartner, who appeared as guest conductors with the *grandes phalanges parisiennes* (the Orchestre Pasdeloup and the Orchestre symphonique de Paris).[38] Others, such as Jane Evrard and Nadia Boulanger, were not formally trained as conductors but regularly took to the podium to direct concerts. Evrard emerged as the conductor of her own all-woman string orchestra, the Orchestre féminin de Paris in 1930, which consertised in France and more widely in Europe in the 1930s and into the Second World War.[39] Nadia Boulanger, meanwhile, shunned all-woman orchestras and appeared instead as a guest conductor with highly respected French and foreign orchestras, including the Boston Symphony, the National Symphony, the New York Philharmonic, the Philadelphia Orchestra, and the Royal Philharmonic Society.[40] Renié, who did not receive instruction in conducting, does not fit into any of the mentioned profiles, as she appeared mainly as a composer-conductor for her own works. Thus, her profile as a female conductor evokes that of women composer-conductors around the turn of the twentieth century in France, such as Armande de Polignac, who were sometimes asked to conduct their own compositions as a special gesture towards their status as composers. This situation was no longer the case by the 1930s, when several women conductors were active within Paris.

Renié avoided mentioning her conducting activities.[41] In the *Questionnaire for Biographees* that she filled in a few years before her death – which was used for the compilation of the Biographical Section of the Fifth Edition of the international *Who is Who in Music* – in the space regarding principal profession(s) or specialties, she wrote: 'Music artist (Harpist), *Virtuoso*, Composer, Professor'.[42] Her not mentioning her conducting activity with choirs and small orchestras could have resulted from two factors. Firstly, as indicated previously, she only occasionally took up the conductor's baton to direct these ensembles, and secondly, not having formal training in conducting must have made her consider this activity as less important within her multi-faceted professional musical career – all the more so since she strove to attain perfection in the disciplines in which she was confident precisely because of the regularity with which she performed a given activity (such as teaching) and the formal training she had received (in music composition and harp performance). Although it seems that Renié herself downplayed her taking the podium to conduct choirs and chamber orchestras in public, I deemed it necessary to carry out research into this activity of hers as it is an unexplored aspect of her career within both monographs devoted to her and wider literature on women conductors in contemporary France.[43]

Though conducting wasn't Renié's main activity, it did not stop her making remarks about conducting to some eminent conductors, including Camille Chevillard and Jules Colonne. Both situations are described by Françoise des Varennes in her book *Henriette Renié. Harpe Vivante*, although she does not provide any details of the sources she availed herself of to back up her claims (though she could have been recollecting stories Renié had told her). However, having compared her wording with pertinent sources that I examined during my seven-year-long research in the United States and France, I can assert that, in the case of Chevillard, Varennes made use of Renié's memoirs, an interview which she probably gave in Geneva in September 1955,[44] and manuscript notes made by Geneviève Jouve (née Regnier, the sister of Marie-Amélie Regnier who was Henriette Renié's student and Françoise des Varennes's mother) in the case of Colonne.[45]

Renié regarded Chevillard very highly, but having noticed that during the rehearsal of her *Concerto en ut mineur* for harp and orchestra in 1901 he didn't observe the seven tempo changes appearing on the last page of the first movement, *Allegro risoluto*, eventually she couldn't refrain from pointing it out to him, just fifteen minutes before the concert. He replied to her crudely that her first movement exhibited too many changes of tempo, adding that there existed some beautiful works in which the tempo did not change.[46] In this case, one can assert that Renié's reaction is understandable, as she was the work's composer. However, she also criticised a conductor about their interpretation of another's composer's work, in front of the composer. This happened two years later during a rehearsal of *Concertstück* for harp and orchestra by Pierné under the direction of Colonne. As Colonne did not keep the right tempo, she, as the soloist, began to beat time tapping her foot. Pierné – who valued both Renié and Colonne as colleagues – found himself in a difficult situation, but admitted, having been asked by Colonne, that it was Renié's tempo he desired. Even after Colonne's promise to follow from then on any tempo she wanted without her beating time, she replied that it was precisely because he didn't seem to be following her that she was beating time herself.[47] Some may consider Renié's reaction disproportionate,[48] but it was precisely due to her strong personality, coupled with her great musical skills that she succeeded as a *virtuosa* performer, a music ensemble leader, an *impresario*, and a composer in what her friend Louise Regnier described in a letter, dated 10 November 1912, as an 'unfavourable milieu for female composers'.[49] In this letter, we also learn that Charles-Marie Widor considered Henriette Renié a great composer.[50]

Henriette Renié as *Impresario*

As discussed, Renié distinguished herself as an independent woman of strong personality who earned her own living. Not wanting to risk being hindered in her artistic activities, she never married.[51] However, fear of patriarchal authority promoting the domestic sphere as an ideal environment for women in contemporary France was not the only reason that Renié was unwilling to marry. The other reason was that she felt her calling to the monastic life, though the love of art and her desire to pursue a multi-faceted professional musical career made her remain among the laity. Still, it was her deep Roman Catholic faith that nurtured her stance on musical activities which – in her belief – should serve to bring people closer to God;[52] a task for which she must have developed a tough character to act independently not to betray her ideals. The strong nature of her personality is evidenced by the memoirs of people close to her and the stories related to me by Renié's late heiress, Jacqueline Lesprit-Maupin.[53] Renié's strong character also emerges from her extensive correspondence, as well as other archival materials. One of them is the aforementioned *Questionnaire for Biographees*.[54] When asked in the questionnaire to give the name and exact address of her manager or agent, she responded: 'I have never wanted to have one! I acted all by myself'.[55] Likewise, in the blank concerning membership and any offices in clubs, organisations, associations, ensembles, lodges, and fraternities, she wrote: 'None. I always act alone (even when doing good!)'[56]

Bearing in mind this attitude, it doesn't come as a surprise that she acted as an *impresario* for her Sextuor Renié and organised innumerable concerts attended by large audiences in her Parisian studio, which was also a stage for other chamber music formations and solo performances. These music sessions, which enabled Renié to perform at her own venue, promote her former and current students as well as her original compositions and transcriptions for various performing forces,[57] were recorded by her on reel-to-reel audio tapes. These had been presented to Renié by Mildred Dilling, most likely in 1949.[58] The recordings – which I had the opportunity to listen to in the presence of Jacqueline Lesprit-Maupin while undertaking research in Paris – prove that her Sextuor's performances were highly acclaimed by the audience. They also give proof of Renié's activity as a soloist performer till the age of eighty.

Being an *impresario* for her Sextuor was important for Renié not only because the ensemble was dear to her heart, but also because its concert activity was one of the sources financing the humanitarian aid destined for fellow artists which she organised. In 1914, Renié founded her *Petite Caisse des Artistes* (Little Fund for Artists) in order to provide immediate and anonymous assistance to artists left destitute by war.[59] After Renié's death, the Little Fund for Artists was managed from Renié's Parisian studio by her friend and leading violinist Marie-Thérèse Ibos (1922–2011), the daughter of Geneviève Aubert (also Renié's friend) and of Jean Ibos, a cellist at the Opéra de Paris. Renié's extant notebooks reveal that she analysed every artist's personal situation and assigned them a number. To take an example, here is her entry about the aid provided by her fund in 1918, mostly thanks to the proceeds from the concerts given by her six-/seven-harp ensemble, which had already become nationally recognised:

43. A singer, getting a little on in years; her daughter may be affected by tuberculosis and can no longer work; she provides for her daughter-in-law who has two babies (the youngest is one year old), and her husband is kept a prisoner [of war] in Germany. This young woman with tuberculosis could be sent to a sanatorium, but it is necessary that the grandmother be able to provide for the two little mites. The youngest has to be left in the care of a wet nurse; for partial assistance during 10 months in order to pay for the wet nurse (from March till December) – 200 francs.[60]

Some cases were classified by Renié as demanding particular attention, and therefore written down under the section *Secours immédiat pour les cas spéciaux* (Immediate Aid for Special Cases). For instance, one – dated 1918, with the assigned number 2 – concerned a talented young female harpist, a mother of two, who was to have gone on a tour with the Société de concerts du Conservatoire, but because of the bombings had to cease concert activities; the Little Fund for Artists allotted her 400 francs.[61]

These entries clearly show that the assistance provided by Renié's fund was indispensable for those affected, and even more so because very often the needy artists could only rely on the charitable financial aid she provided. Therefore, giving performances with the Sextuor/Septuor was for Renié a matter of the utmost importance. Renié's concerts for the benefit of the Little Fund for Artists were announced in the press and advertised through her own broad networks in Paris. The concert activity of Renié's ensemble had to be continued regardless of the dangerous situations during the two world wars, as evidenced by Renié's manuscript memoirs and by the writings of Françoise des Varennes. For example, after a German shell was fired at the Church of Saint-Gervais in Paris at Easter 1918, a decree was issued banning all public gatherings, which meant that concert halls were closed. Since the revenue from the sale of tickets was destined for the Little Fund for Artists, Renié sought out a venue where the performance of her ensemble, scheduled for 3 June, could take place.[62] The boom of the so-called 'Paris Gun' (a German long-range siege gun) resonated in the capital every fifteen minutes – as Renié recalled in her memoirs – punctuating her rehearsals and causing the glass window panes to rattle.[63] Still, her decision was firm: 'I am giving the concert, and I do not want to hear of anything else!'⁶⁴ She was not disappointed, for the audience, knowing that this was a charity concert, came in large numbers (of at least 600) to the hall of a theatre in Beethoven Street. Her fellow performers, although willing to play, were very afraid. Just before coming onto the stage, they were talking about the dangerous situation they found themselves in, but when Renié approached them, knowing her strong character, they immediately changed the subject of the conversation to musical topics, as Renié recalled years later, adding: 'I was not naive, but I pretended to be so!'⁶⁵

Thus, Renié's great efforts as an *impresario* for her Sextuor/Septuor enabled it to give regular concerts and be greatly praised not only for the technical and musical skills of its members, but also for supporting the lofty aims of the Little Fund for Artists. Concert programmes, newspaper announcements, and reviews give proof of her ensemble's involvement in this charitable activity. Let me quote one such announcement from the issue of the daily *L'Écho de Paris* from 29 January 1937:

> Next Tuesday, 2 February, at 9 o'clock in the evening, at the Salle Érard, a beautiful artistic performance will take place, organised by the famous harpist Henriette Renié as part of her work for the 'Little Fund for Artists', which has been discreetly relieving the hidden miseries of poor musicians for nearly twenty-five years [*sic*].
>
> Apart from the remarkable artist, we'll applaud her Sextuor of harps composed of Mademoiselle D. Bernard, Mesdames de Chamberet, Kahan, O. Le Dentu, and G. de Navacelle, whose musical perfection and homogeneity create a unique ensemble.⁶⁶

Due to Renié's independence, as particularly evidenced by her earning her own living, and the fact that she was regarded as a resourceful *impresario*, some of her male counterparts treated her as if she were on an equal footing in terms of finance. This is illustrated by her letter, dated 1 October 1927, addressed to Pincherle,⁶⁷ in which she asked him for his help for Victoria Barrière, a good pianist. The situation described by her was as follows: Renié was convinced that it was always the Pleyel Company which was liable for the costs resulting from the transport of instruments in Paris and other places. However, it turned out that Pleyel required Madame Barrière, who was to perform three chamber music concerts in Versailles with the cellist Louis César Ruyssen and the violinist Léon Zighera, to pay 400 francs for the transport of a piano for each of the concerts.⁶⁸ Renié was seeking Pincherle's help to make Pleyel change its decision, explaining at the same time that she had already found herself compelled to intervene on Barrière's behalf the previous year and pay for her. When she had asked Pleyel's director, Gustave Lyon, to solve the problem, he had proposed that she pay half of Madame Barrière's debt, with the other half being settled by himself.⁶⁹ This situation described by Renié to Pincherle, as well as the previously mentioned efforts to ensure performances of her ensemble in wartime, speak volumes about her having to make hardheaded decisions and display the indispensable resourcefulness of a good *impresario*.

Conclusion

Archival sources clearly indicate Renié was aware that she was making history as an independent female performer, music ensemble leader, *impresario*, composer, and harp teacher. Renié's being active within every field of the musical profession allows one to draw an analogy between her and Nadia Boulanger, who also pursued a multi-faceted professional musical career. Both organised concerts dedicated to the presentation of early and contemporary repertoire. Thus, both made many early music pieces known to a larger audience than before. Renié's concert programmes reveal that her dual specialisation in both early and contemporary music must have influenced Boulanger, twelve years her junior, who greatly enjoyed Renié's performances for her virtuosity and musicality. 'Our father, a faithful friend of Henriette's father, wouldn't have missed even one of her recitals for anything in the world. We went to them guided by our hearts, and returned with our spirits overwhelmed with most undisputed admiration'[70] – Boulanger recalled enthusiastically after Renié's death. Both developed significant teaching careers and found the teaching role fulfilling; though Renié never held a senior teaching post as a professor of her own advanced harp classes at prestigious public or private institutions and she supported herself through private teaching. Differences can be noted as well as in their conducting activities and their attitudes towards undertaking solo engagements as instrumentalists. Renié, mounting the conductor's podium only on an occasional basis to direct choirs and small orchestras and not pursuing a conducting career internationally, was firmly established as one of the foremost concert harpists of international caliber. She did not harbour doubts about her ability as a *virtuosa* player, and her reception as a solo harpist was in line with her perception of her ability in this respect. Critics never denied her evident extraordinary skill, emphasising her unparalleled virtuosity.[71] Conversely, Boulanger, who developed an international conducting career, would acknowledge the limits of her ability as a keyboard player and lack of confidence with solo performances, which might have been triggered – as Jeanice Brooks has remarked – by the reviews of her performances with Raoul Pugno that stressed the difference in skill between them.[72] However, Boulanger the conductor bears one more similarity to Renié the conductor, apart from neither of them having been formally trained in conducting, as indicated earlier. Boulanger's and Renié's roads to the conductor's podium were similar: the beginnings of their conducting activities were entrenched in their occupation as teachers. Boulanger launched her conducting activities from her classes, coupling analysis of compositions with their vocal-instrumental performances. For Renié, it was mainly her previously mentioned ensemble classes that enabled her to train in directing purely instrumental music.

Renié was aware that the way had been paved for her by other courageous women from the French musical *milieu*, such as Augusta Holmès or Cécile Chaminade. She implied this during her concert which took place on 12 May 1946 at Mrs Henri Enjalbert-Denfert-Rochereau's home at 11 Charles Floquet Avenue in Paris.[73] Undoubtedly, Renié's persistence and success in her artistic activities resulted from her strong personality, enormous musical talent, and her firm and unhidden belief, as a devout Roman Catholic, that by performing, composing, and promoting good music she was aspiring to the lofty aim of praising God,[74] *Ad maiorem Dei gloriam*!

Notes

1. Renié was a devout Roman Catholic. Throughout her life, religion, Christian philosophy, and art merged and complemented each other.
2. See *Hommage à Henriette Renié. Wybór korespondencji kompozytorki* [*Hommage à Henriette Renié. A Selection of the Composer's Correspondence*], collection, translation, introduction, and comments by Temina Cadi Sulumuna, foreword by Wojciech Nowik (Warszawa: Chopin University Press, 2017).
3. "1911 Historique 1926," "Liste des Artistes reçus et joués au Salon des Musiciens Français," [Bulletin] *Salon des Musiciens Français. Historique 1911–1926*, 1–6: 5, 21–28: 27; *Le Guide musical* (June 21–22, 1914), 482.
4. Paris, Académie des Beaux-Arts, *Procès-verbaux des séances de l'Académie des Beaux-Arts de l'année 1913–1918*: 'Séance du samedi 27 mai 1916," 341, 2 E 23.
5. See *Hommage*.
6. I conducted research at such institutions as Académie des Beaux-Arts, Archives nationales, Bibliothèque nationale de France, Éditions Henry Lemoine, Éditions Musicales Alphonse Leduc, Éditions

musicales Enoch & Cie, Fonds Ancien et Local at the Médiathèque Jean Renoir, Médiathèque Hector Berlioz at the Conservatoire national supérieur de musique et de danse, and Médiathèque Musicale Mahler.
7. Henriette Renié, concerned for Françoise des Varennes's frail health, had asked Jacqueline Lesprit-Maupin to take care of Françoise. Indeed, after Renié's death, Lesprit-Maupin looked after Françoise until Françoise's death.
8. Pierrefitte-sur-Seine, Archives nationales, *Registres d'inscription des élèves de l'an V à 1920*, AJ/37/355/1.
9. Provo, International Harp Archives, Music Special Collections (hereinafter referred to as 'IHA'), Henriette Renié, manuscript letter to Jean-Émile Renié, 'mardi soir' ['Tuesday evening'], [1894], box 27, fd. 4. 'La mère d'une petite élève Alice Delbos m'a demandé si je pourrais venir diriger des ensembles chez elle; j'y vais le mardi tous les 15 jours, et j'y fais une espèce de cours d'ensemble; voici les instruments dont je dispose: harpe, piano, harmonium, mandoline, et monocorde qui remplace tant bien que mal le violon; nous faisons toutes sortes d'arrangements pour ces 5 instruments et c'est très amusant. À propos de cela, tu sais que j'ai de plus en plus l'idée de faire un cours d'ensmble l'année prochaine; j'aurais, par exemple deux séances par mois; et nous jouerions, harpe et violon (ce serait Marie Linder, qui ferait le violon), harpe et piano, harpe, piano et violon ou enfin 2, 3, ou 4 harpes; ce serait très intéressant, et je crois qu cela prendrait bien, car si je ne me trompe personne n'a encore eu l'idée de cela avec la harpe; aussi je n'en parle à personne pour qu'on ne me vole pas mon idée!'.
All the cited excerpts are my own translation.
10. Renié's transcriptions and programmes for concerts featuring students attending her classes enabled the present author to gather information on the composition of ensembles during these classes. The composition, at the core of which were harps, was variable over the years, but it included mostly: solely harps in number of 2 to 7; harps (usu. 4) and flute; harps (usu. 3 or 6) and oboe; harps (usu. 4 or 6), violin and cello; harps (usu. 4) and string quartet; harps, solo violin and double string quartet; harps (usu. 3 or 6) and double string quartet; harps (usu. 2), violin and piano; harps (usu. 2 or 4), violin, cello and piano. One harp coupled with other musical instruments – usually violin (or 2 violins) and cello – was rather a rarity in Renié's classes.
11. Paris, Bibliothèque nationale de France, Département de la Musique (hereinafter referred to as 'BnF-Mus'), Henriette Renié, manuscript letter to Marc Pincherle, December 4–6, 1922, 47 rue Nicolo [Paris], VM BOB-23244.
12. IHA, Françoise des Varennes, typescript, box 7, fd. 4.
13. Renié, manuscript letter to Marc Pincherle, December 4–6, 1922. 'Je me rendais compte que la littérature de harpe était insuffisante pour former le goût et le style de mes élèves; j'ai donc transcrit moi-même musique classique et moderne, depuis des symphonies, jusqu'à des poèmes symphoniques, oratorios, q.q. opéras et frag^{ts} de la musique de chambre, etc... Certaines de ces choses avaient la valeur relative du 4 mains ou 2 pianos; d'autres qui faisaient très bien, étaient travaillées plus à fond [...]'.
14. See, for instance, "Mlle Henriette Renié," *Le Monde musical* (February 3–4, 1924), 70.
15. Renié, manuscript letter to Marc Pincherle, December 4–6, 1922.
16. IHA, Henriette Renié, manuscript letter to Maria-Rosa Vidal, copy, July 22, 1935, Étretat, box 27, fd. 3. 'Après, le départ pour Pâques et au retour, en un mois la préparation de la grande séance d'ensemble: 9 cours et des cours durant aussi bien 3 ou 4 heures! Cette séance a eu lieu le 6 juin'.
17. The reference is to Geraldine Ruegg (1921–2016), American harpist who translated into English Renié's *Méthode complète de harpe* published by Éditions Musicales Alphonse Leduc in 1946.
18. IHA, Henriette Renié, letter to Mildred Dilling, March 7, 1949, Paris, typewritten by Françoise des Varennes, box 28, fd. 1B. 'Geraldine m'a écrit qu'après avoir bien réfléchi, elle trouvait plus raisonnable de renoncer au sextuor, craignant que le temps passé à apprendre des parties nuise à son travail. Je le regrette pour elle, car je crois que cela l'aurait énormément intéressée... Mais je ne peux pas l'en blâmer; le temps de travail – voir avec moi – et 5 après-midi à répéter, c'était presqu'un mois de perdu'.
19. IHA, Jacques de La Presle, letter to Henriette Renié, undated, typewritten by Françoise des Varennes, box 19, fd. 7. 'Il apporte un nouvel intérêt à mon œuvre, et l'exécution en est admirable'.
20. IHA, Gabriel Pierné, letter to Henriette Renié, November 3, 1936, typewritten by Françoise des Varennes, box 19, fd. 7. 'Ma chère amie,/ Je ne résiste pas au grand plaisir de vous féliciter, vous et vos élèves, pour l'éblouissante exécution d'hier soir de ma *Marche des petits soldats de plomb* transcrite par vous pour six harpes; jamais je n'ai entendu transcription mieux faite, traduction mieux rythmée, ardente et jeune, et je dépose à vos 12 pieds (y compris vos élèves) l'hommage respectueux d'un auteur satisfait./ Chut! On s'embrasse./ Gabriel Pierné'.

21. M.I., "Société d'Études Mozartiennes. – Mlle Henriete Renié," *L'Art musical*, 1.7 (January 3, 1936), 187–88: 188. 'D'autre part, son fameux ensemble de six harpes (Mlle Renié, Mme Bacqueyrisse-Le Dentu, Mlle Bernard, Mmes de Montesquiou, Kahan-Franck et de Navacelle) remporta un vif succès dans une *Barcarolle*, un spirituel *Défilé lilliputien* (bissé d'enthousiasme), et *Contemplation*'.
22. Musical instrument manufacturer with headquarters and manufacturing facility based in Chicago, concentrating exclusively on harp production and sale from the 1970s.
23. IHA, Mildred Dilling, manuscript letter to Henriette Renié, 'Commencé le 22 avril, fini le 27' ['Begun on the 22nd of April, finished on the 27th'], no year stated, 400 East 52nd Street New York City, box 38, fd. 2. 'Le cours d'ensemble a commencé avec beaucoup d'éclat jeudi dernier avec 8 harpistes et 6 harpes. Demain nous serons chez Lyon & Healy et nous pourrons avoir 7 harpes si nous avons besoin. On joue *Les Petits soldats de plomb* et *Dolly*, et demain je donnerai *Menuet en mi* de Mozart'.
24. I am grateful to Caroline Rempp Verrey – who from 1981 to 2001 was a member of Sextuor de Harpes de Paris – for providing me with information on the members of Sextuor de Harpes de Paris and their concert activities.
25. Part of the repertoire was recorded by Sextuor de Harpes de Paris on two discs released on record label Quantum in 1992 and 1995. I thank Caroline Rempp Verrey for this piece of information.
26. Henriette Renié also made transcriptions for four harps. See the catalogue *Renié's Transcriptions for Several Harps (3*=3 or 6 harps)* included in: Françoise des Varennes, *Henriette Renié. Living Harp*, transl. by S. Clavel, W. Kerner, J. Waggener, in collab. with S. Maxwell, under the direction of S. McDonald, 2nd ed. (Bloomington, IN: Music Works – Harp Editions, 1990), 133–37. The original book was published without this catalogue.
27. I extend my thanks to Caroline Rempp Verrey for providing me with information on Quatuor de Harpes de Paris as Sextuor de Harpes de Paris' legacy.
28. At the time Sextuor de Harpes de Paris was composed of Odette Le Dentu, Bertille Fournier-Huguet, Odette de Montesquiou, Marie-Laure de Brye, Geneviève Dupas and Suzanne Cotelle.
29. France, private collection of Renié's heiress, newspaper clipping dated February 3, 1982: S.L., 'Richesses et couleurs de la harpe'. 'Le Théâtre de l'Hôtel de Ville accueillait, en ses murs, vendredi dernier, le célèbre Sextuor de Harpes de Paris. . . . Les nombreux mélomanes havrais, qui remplissaient la salle, ne s'y sont pas trompés. Ils ont fait un chaleureux accueil à ce groupe de virtuoses au palmarès prestigieux. On peut dire qu'en une seule soirée, la harpe, cet instrument privilégié, a su faire de nouveaux adeptes. Raffinement et délicatesse pour le plus merveilleux des éblouissements d'un concert qui, sans nul doute, fera date'.
30. The ensemble composed of Bertille Fournier, Odette de Montesquiou, Marie-Laure de Brye, Geneviève Dupas, Caroline Rempp and Anne-Claire Cazalet.
31. France, private collection of Renié's heiress, newspaper clipping dated April 22, 1983: Pierre Rousseau, 'Au musée. Le Sextuor de Harpes de Paris: Bonheur total'. ' "Dès l'abord, il offre au public le fascinant spectacle de ces six harpes déployées en éventail. Avant de la conquérir par des richesses techniques et sonores d'une captivante originalité": cet autoportrait du Sextuor de Harpes de Paris est, à l'emphase près, exact. . . . Du XVIIe siècle au nôtre, le Sextuor nous entraînera dans son sillage avec un bonheur constamment renouvelé. . . . Le concert du Sextuor de Harpes de Paris? Deux heures de bonheur total. Tout simplement'.
32. The reference is to: Odette Le Dentu, Bertille Fournier-Huguet, Odette de Montesquiou, Marie-Laure de Brye, Geneviève Dupas and Suzanne Cotelle.
33. France, private collection of Renié's heiress, undated newspaper clipping: 'Le Sextuor de Harpes de Paris: un espace sonore étonnant. . .'. 'Reconnaissons aussi qu'avec le Sextuor de Paris la harpe est merveilleusement servie. Et la musique aussi. Les six musiciennes maîtrisent l'art de faire vivre une partition en faisant ressortir telle voix, en laissant surgir, d'un instrument à l'autre, les motifs principaux, en détaillant l'épaisseur de l'écriture musicale dans ses strates, ses sous-couches, ses petites phrases qui se dégagent des profondeurs. Six instruments suffisent alors pour créer une étonante impression d'espace sonore avec un étalement de plans, subtile et net'.
34. Poland, private archives of the author, Jacqueline Lesprit-Maupin, manuscript letter to Temina Cadi Sulumuna, 15 August 2016, Étretat.
35. Renié's occasional conducting activity was confirmed to me also by Jacqueline Lesprit-Maupin.
36. M.I., p. 188. 'Enfin, Mlle Renié prit la baguette pour conduire sa pure *Prière à la Vierge,* où s'exprime un beau sentiment, chantée par M. Jouatte et les chœurs'.

37. Maurice Imbert, *L'Art musical*, 2.60 (June 18, 1937), 800; *Le Ménestrel*, 99.24 (June 11, 1937), 181.
38. For a detailed consideration of Eva Brunelli's, Gertrud Herliczka's, and Carmen Studer-Weingartner's conducting activities in France, see Jean-Christophe Branger, "Être cheffe d'orchestre à Paris dans l'entre-deux-guerres. Les concerts symphoniques dirigés par Eva Brunelli, Carmen Studer-Weingartner et Getrud Herliczka," *Revue de Musicologie* 102, no. 2 (2016): 319–61.
39. For a detailed consideration of Jane Evrard's conducting activities with her Orchestre féminin de Paris, see Laura Hamer, *Female Composers, Conductors, Performers: Musiciennes of Interwar France, 1919–1939* (London and New York: Routledge, 2018), 168–73; and Laura Hamer, "On the Conductor's Podium: Jane Evrard and the Orchestre féminin de Paris," *The Musical Times* 152, no. 1916 (Autumn 2011): 81–100.
40. For a detailed consideration of Nadia Boulanger's conducting activities, see Jeanice Brooks, *The Musical Work of Nadia Boulanger: Performing Past and Future between the Wars* (Cambridge: Cambridge University Press, 2013); Jeanice Brooks, "Noble et grande servante de la musique: Telling the Story of Nadia Boulanger's Conducting Career," *The Journal of Musicology* 14, no. 1 (1996): 92–116.
41. Being the leader of her Sextuor Renié/Septuor Renié fell for her into the category 'music artist-harpist', as she was its member, usually performing – as discussed – the first harp part.
42. IHA, Henriette Renié, *Questionnaire for Biographees* for the Biographical Section of the Fifth Edition of the international *Who is Who in Music*, box 22, fd. 7. 'Artiste musicienne (Harpiste) Virtuose Compositeur Professeur'.
43. See, for instance, Landy Andriamboavonjy, "Henriette Renié: harpiste, compositeur, pedagogue," (Master's thesis, Faculté de Lettres de Lyon II, 1990); Branger, "Être cheffe d'orchestre à Paris dans l'entre-deux-guerres. Les concerts symphoniques dirigés par Eva Brunelli, Carmen Studer-Weingartner et Getrud Herliczka," 319–61; Brooks, *The Musical Work of Nadia Boulanger*; Brooks, "Noble et grande servante de la musique: Telling the Story of Nadia Boulanger's Conducting Career," 92–116; Jaymee Haefner, "Renié, Henriette (Gabrielle Marie Sophie)," in *Grove Music Online* (Oxford: Oxford University Press, published online: March 28, 2019), accessed September 2, 2020, https://doi.org/10.1093/omo/9781561592630.013.3000000241; Jaymee Haefner, *One Stone to the Building: Henriette Renié's Life Through Her Works for Harp* (Bloomington, IN: Author House, 2017); Laura Hamer, "Armande de Polignac: An Aristocratic *Compositrice* in *Fin-de-siècle* Paris," in *Women in the Arts in the Belle Epoque: Essays on Influential Artists, Writers and Performers*, edited by Paul Fryer (Jefferson, NC, and London: McFarland, 2012), 165–85; Hamer, *Female Composers, Conductors, Performers*; Hamer, "On the Conductor's Podium: Jane Evrard and the Orchestre féminin de Paris," 81–100; Odette de Montesquiou, *Henriette Renié et la harpe* (Paris: Éditions Josette Lyon, 1998); Odette de Montesquiou, *The Legend of Henriette Renié*, edited by Jaymee Haefner, trans. Robert Kilpatrick (Bloomington, IN: Author House, 2006); Constance Caroline Slaughter, "Henriette Renié: a Pioneer in the World of the Harp," (Master's thesis, Rice University, 1992); Françoise des Varennes, *Henriette Renié. Harpe Vivante* (Paris: Barre-Dayez Éditeurs, 1983); des Varennes, *Henriette Renié. Living Harp*.
44. IHA, Henriette Renié, manuscript memoirs, box 28, fd. 6; IHA, Henriette Renié, interview (no information as to the interlocutor), probably September 1955, Geneva, box 28, fd. 6. Cf. des Varennes, *Henriette Renié. Harpe Vivante*, p. 40.
45. France, private collection of Renié's heiress, Geneviève Jouve, manuscript notes. Cf. des Varennes, *Henriette Renié. Harpe Vivante*, 45–46.
46. Renié, manuscript memoirs; Renié, interview.
47. Jouve, manuscript notes.
48. According to Jacqueline Lesprit-Maupin's account, Henriette Renié's strong personality manifested itself in spontaneity, hence in the described situation Renié's reaction lacked a discreet remark.
49. Nevertheless, although women faced gender-specific career restrictions at the time they were successfully active within various fields of the musical profession, including composition. See Florence Launay, *Les Compositrices en France au XIXe siècle* (Paris: Fayard, 2006); Hamer, *Female Composers, Conductors, Performers*.
50. IHA, Louise Regnier, manuscript letter to Henriette Renié, November 10, 1912, 1 r. [rue] de Seine [Paris], box 12, fd. 1E.
51. On the opportunities Henriette Renié had that she didn't want to take to get married, see des Varennes, *Henriette Renié. Harpe Vivante*, 33–34; de Montesquiou, *Henriette*, 15–16.
52. IHA, Henriette Renié, manuscript diary, March 24, 1945, box 57, fd. 2.

53. I would stay, during my research in Paris in the years 2015–2018, at Jacqueline Lesprit-Maupin's place that previously had been Renié's studio.
54. Renié, *Questionnaire for Biographees*.
55. *Ibid*. 'Je n'ai jamais voulu en avoir! J'ai agi moi-même'.
56. *Ibid*. 'Néant. J'agis toujours en individuelle (même en faisant du bien..!)'.
57. This entrepreneurial activity of Renié fitted within a wider trend of enterprising high-profile female performers – who were also renowned teachers – organising concerts themselves (in which they usually took part) and at the same time ensuring very good publicity for their teaching abilities. For a consideration of Marguerite Canal's, Marguerite Long's, and Nadia Boulanger's entrepreneurial skills, see Brooks, *The Musical Work of Nadia Boulanger*; Hamer, *Female Composers, Conductors, Performers*, 33, 68–69, 71.
58. For Renié's correspondence with Mildred Dilling concerning the records made on this reel-to-reel audio tape recording, see *Hommage*, 97–99, 101–03, 113–14, and 118–19.
59. Entries made by Renié in her notebooks demonstrate that the assistance was provided mainly to performers (both instrumentalists and singers), music teachers and the families of dead music professionals (for instance, a widow of a composer). In some entries a person in need is characterised only as an *artiste* ('artist'), *grand artiste* ('great artist') or *artiste musicien* ('music artist') without further specification.
60. IHA, Henriette Renié, Petite Caisse des Artistes – notebook, box 28, fd. 3. '43. Chanteuse un peu agée; fille menacée de tuberculose ne peut plus travailler; b. fille à sa charge, avec 2 bébés (le dernier un an), le mari étant prisonnier en Allemagne. Cette jeune femme tuberculeuse a pu être envoyée dans un sanatorium, mais il faut que la grand mère pourvoie aux besoins des 2 petits: il a fallu mettre le petit en nourrice – aide frag^{re} pr 10 mois de nourrice: (mars X^{bre}) – 200 f'.
61. *Ibid*.
62. The needy artists counting on the assistance provided by the Little Fund for Artists was more than enough reason for the determined Henriette Renié to infringe the regulations.
63. Renié, manuscript memoirs.
64. *Ibid*. 'Je donne un concert, je ne veux rien savoir d'autre!'.
65. *Ibid*. 'Je n'étais pas dupe, mais je faisais comme si!'. For another description of the circumstances of Renié's 1918 concert, see des Varennes, *Henriette Renié. Harpe Vivante*, 62–63. Françoise des Varennes also drew upon Renié's memoirs (though without providing any details about the source), but these – in contrast to the version of Renié's memoirs of which the present author availed herself – did not include the account of reactions of Renié's fellow performers.
66. 'Cercles," *L'Écho de Paris* (January 29, 1937), 5. 'Mardi prochain 2 février, à 21 heures, salle Érard, aura lieu une belle manifestation artistique organisée par la célèbre harpiste Henriette Renié pour son œuvre "la Petite Caisse des Artistes" qui, depuis près de 25 ans, soulage discrètement les misères cachées de pauvres musiciens./ Outre la grande artiste on applaudira son sextuor de harpes composé de Mlle D. Bernard, Mmes de Chambéret, Kahan, O. Le Dentu et G. de Navacelle, dont la prefection musicale et l'homogénéité font un ensemble unique'.
67. BnF-Mus, Henriette Renié, manuscript letter to Marc Pincherle, October 1, 1927, VM BOB-23244.
68. As the Pleyel archives do not mention – according to Pierre François, Pleyel Public Relations Manager within the Pleyel Division of Algam, to whom I am grateful for the information – the applicable transport conditions at the time, one cannot state with certainty whether Henriette Renié's belief as to Pleyel's liability in this matter was justified. Still, it was acceptable that in exceptional cases putting pianos at pianists' disposal did not include them bearing transport or tuning expenses. It could be then that Victoria Barrière's case was an exceptional one.
69. For the entire letter see *Hommage*, 70–71.
70. IHA, Nadia Boulanger, typewritten letter to Françoise des Varennes, November 18, 1975, Paris, box 2, fd. 2. Cf. des Varennes, *Henriette Renié. Harpe Vivante*, 51–52; de Montesquiou, *Henriette*, 41. 'Notre père – fidèle ami du père d'Henriette – n'aurait pour rien au monde manqué un de ces récitals où nous allions guidés par le cœur et, d'où nous revenions, l'esprit dominé par la plus indiscutable admiration.'
71. Even if some aspects of her playing did not please some critics, these were only isolated cases at the beginning of Renié's solo performing career because of her being seduced by technical aspects, which she admitted later on and remedied by concert programming including pieces that were less technically demanding but enabled her to display her remarkable artistic sensitivity. See IHA, Françoise des Varennes, *Henriette Renié. This Living Harp 1875–1956*, talk by Françoise des Varennes

under the patronage of Paul Paray, Member of the Institut de France, English transl. by Nancy Fortescue, typescript, 1974, 16, box 1, fd. 1; des Varennes, *Henriette Renié. Harpe Vivante*, 64.
72. See Brooks, *The Musical Work of Nadia Boulanger*, 29.
73. IHA, Henriette Renié, *Commentaires du 12 mai 1946 par Henriette Renié au cours d'un concert*, typewritten by Françoise des Varennes, box 24, fd. 1.
74. For detailed information about the interpenetration of music and Christian philosophy in Henriette Renié's life see Temina Cadi Sulumuna, "Essence and Context: Exploring the Links Between Music and Philosophy in the Light of Henriette Renié's Reflections," in *Of Essence and Context – Between Music and Philosophy*, series: *Numanities: Arts and Humanities in Progress*, Vol. 7, edited by Rūta Stanevičiūtė, Nick Zangwill, and Rima Povilionienė (Cham: Springer Nature Switzerland AG, 2019), 245–54.

Bibliography

'1911 Historique 1926'. "Liste des Artistes reçus et joués au Salon des Musiciens Français." [Bulletin]. *Salon des Musiciens Français. Historique 1911–1926*, 1–6, 21–28.
Andriamboavonjy, Landy, *Henriette Renié: harpiste, compositeur, pédagogue* (master's thesis, Faculté de Lettres de Lyon II, 1990).
Branger, Jean-Christophe. "Etre cheffe d'orchestre à Paris dans l'entre-deux-guerres. Les concerts symphoniques dirigés par Eva Brunelli, Carmen Studer-Weingartner et Getrud Herliczka." *Revue de musicologie* 102, no. 2 (2016): 319–61.
Brooks, Jeanice. "*Noble et grande sevant de la musique*: Telling the Story of Nadia Boulanger's Conducting Career." *Journal of Musicology* 14, no. 1 (1996): 92–116.
_____. *The Musical Work of Nadia Boulanger: Performing Past and Future between the Wars*. Cambridge: Cambridge University Press, 2013.
"Cercles." *L'Écho de Paris*, January 29, 1937, 5.
France, Private Collection of Renié's Heiress, Geneviève Jouve, Manuscript Notes.
France, Private Collection of Renié's Heiress, Newspaper Clipping Dated 3 February 1982: S.L. "Richesses et couleurs de la harpe."
France, Private Collection of Renié's Heiress, Newspaper Clipping Dated 22 April 1983: Pierre Rousseau. "Au musée. Le Sextuor de Harpes de Paris: Bonheur total."
France, Private Collection of Renié's Heiress, Undated Newspaper Clipping: 'Le Sextuor de Harpes de Paris: un espace sonore étonnant . . .'.
Haefner, Jaymee, 'Renié, Henriette (Gabrielle Marie Sophie)', in *Grove Music Online* (Oxford University Press, published online: 28 March 2019), https://doi.org/10.1093/omo/9781561592630.013.300000 0241 (accessed: 2 September 2020).
Haefner, Jaymee, *One Stone to the Building: Henriette Renié's Life through her Works for Harp* (Bloomington: AuthorHouse, 2017).
Hamer, Laura. "On the Conductor's Podium: Jane Evard and the Orchestre féminin de Paris." *The Musical Times* 152, no. 1916 (Autumn 2011): 81–100.
_____. "Armande de Polignac: An Aristocratic *compositrice* in *fin-de-siècle* Paris." In *Women in the Arts in the Belle Epoque: Essays on Influential Artists, Writers and Performers*, edited by Paul Fryer, 165–85. Jefferson, NC and London: McFarland, 2012.
_____. *Female Composers, Conductors, Performers: Musiciennes of Interwar France, 1919–1939* (London and New York: Routledge, 2018).
Hommage à Henriette Renié. Wybór korespondencji kompozytorki [*Hommage à Henriette Renié. A Selection of the Composer's Correspondence*], collection, translation, introduction, and comments by Temina Cadi Sulumuna, foreword by Wojciech Nowik. Warszawa: Chopin University Press, 2017.
I. M. "Société d'Études Mozartiennes. – Mlle Henriete Renié." *L'Art musical* 1, no. 7 (January 3, 1936): 187–88.
Imbert Maurice. *L'Art musical* 2, no. 60 (June 18, 1937): 800.
Launay, Florence. *Les Compositrices en France au XIXe siècle*. Paris: Fayard, 2006.
Le Guide musical, June 21–22, 1914, 482.
Le Ménestrel 99, no. 24 (June 11, 1937): 181.
"Mlle Henriette Renié." *Le Monde musical* (February 3–4, 1924): 70.
Montesquiou, Odette de, *Henriette Renié et la harpe* (Paris: Éditions Josette Lyon, 1998).

Montesquiou, Odette de, *The Legend of Henriette Renié*, ed. Jaymee Haefner, transl. Robert Kilpatrick (Bloomington: AuthorHouse, 2006).

Paris, Académie des Beaux-Arts. *Procès-verbaux des séances de l'Académie des Beaux-Arts de l'année 1913–1918*: 'Séance du samedi 27 mai 1916." p. 341, 2 E 23.

Paris, Bibliothèque nationale de France, Département de la Musique, Henriette Renié, manuscript letter to Marc Pincherle, 4–6 December 1922, 47 rue Nicolo [Paris], VM BOB-23244.

Paris, Bibliothèque nationale de France, Département de la Musique, Henriette Renié, manuscript letter to Marc Pincherle, 1 October 1927, VM BOB-23244.

Pierrefitte-sur-Seine, Archives nationales, *Registres d'inscription des élèves de l'an V à 1920*, AJ/37/355/1.

Poland, private archives of the author, Jacqueline Lesprit-Maupin, manuscript letter to Temina Cadi Sulumuna, 15 August 2016, Étretat.

Provo, International Harp Archives, Music Special Collections, Françoise des Varennes, *Henriette Renié. This Living Harp 1875–1956*, talk by Françoise des Varennes under the patronage of Paul Paray, Member of the Institut de France, English transl. by Nancy Fortescue, typescript, 1974, p. 16, box 1, fd. 1.

Provo, International Harp Archives, Music Special Collections, Françoise des Varennes, typescript, box 7, fd. 4.

Provo, International Harp Archives, Music Special Collections, Gabriel Pierné, letter to Henriette Renié, 3 November 1936, typewritten by Françoise des Varennes, box 19, fd. 7.

Provo, International Harp Archives, Music Special Collections, Henriette Renié, *Commentaires du 12 mai 1946 par Henriette Renié au cours d'un concert*, typewritten by Françoise des Varennes, box 24, fd. 1.

Provo, International Harp Archives, Music Special Collections, Henriette Renié, interview (no information as to the interlocutor), probably September 1955, Geneva, box 28, fd. 6.

Provo, International Harp Archives, Music Special Collections, Henriette Renié, letter to Mildred Dilling, 7 March 1949, Paris, typewritten by Françoise des Varennes, box 28, fd. 1B.

Provo, International Harp Archives, Music Special Collections, Henriette Renié, manuscript diary, 24 March 1945, box 57, fd. 2.

Provo, International Harp Archives, Music Special Collections, Henriette Renié, manuscript letter to Jean-Émile Renié, 'mardi soir' ['Tuesday evening'], [1894], box 27, fd. 4.

Provo, International Harp Archives, Music Special Collections, Henriette Renié, manuscript letter to Maria-Rosa Vidal, copy, 22 July 1935, Étretat, box 27, fd. 3.

Provo, International Harp Archives, Music Special Collections, Henriette Renié, manuscript memoirs, box 28, fd. 6.

Provo, International Harp Archives, Music Special Collections, Henriette Renié, Petite Caisse des Artistes – notebook, box 28, fd. 3.

Provo, International Harp Archives, Music Special Collections, Henriette Renié, *Questionnaire for Biographees* for the Biographical Section of the Fifth Edition of the international *Who is Who in Music*, box 22, fd. 7.

Provo, International Harp Archives, Music Special Collections, Jacques de La Presle, letter to Henriette Renié, undated, typewritten by Françoise des Varennes, box 19, fd. 7.

Provo, International Harp Archives, Music Special Collections, Louise Regnier, manuscript letter to Henriette Renié, 10 November 1912, 1 r. [rue] de Seine [Paris], box 12, fd. 1E.

Provo, International Harp Archives, Music Special Collections, Mildred Dilling, manuscript letter to Henriette Renié, 'Commencé le 22 avril, fini le 27' ['Begun on the 22nd of April, finished on the 27th'], no year stated, 400 East 52nd Street New York City, box 38, fd. 2.

Provo, International Harp Archives, Music Special Collections, Nadia Boulanger, typewritten letter to Françoise des Varennes, 18 November 1975, Paris, box 2, fd. 2.

Slaughter, Constance Caroline, *Henriette Renié: a Pioneer in the World of the Harp* (master's thesis, Huston, Texas: Rice University, 1992).

Sulumuna, Temina Cadi. "Essence and Context: Exploring the Links Between Music and Philosophy in the Light of Henriette Renié's Reflections." In *Of Essence and Context – Between Music and Philosophy*, series: *Numanities: Arts and Humanities in Progress*, vol. 7, edited by Rūta Stanevičiūtė, Nick Zangwill, and Rima Povilionienė, 245–54. Cham: Springer Nature Switzerland AG, 2019.

Varennes, Françoise des, *Henriette Renié. Living Harp*, transl. by S. Clavel, W. Kerner, J. Waggener, in collab. with S. Maxwell, under the direction of S. McDonald, 2nd ed. (Bloomington: Music Works – Harp Editions, 1990).

Varennes, Françoise des. *Henriette Renié. Harpe Vivante*. Paris: Barre-Dayez Éditeurs, 1983.

14
AN AMERICAN FEMALE VIOLINIST AND CONDUCTOR IN PARIS

"La Kazanova et Ses Tziganes" (1933–1938)

Jean-Christophe Branger
Translation: Kiefer Oakley

During the interwar period, several women pursued careers as conductors; this includes Ethel Leginska, Antonia Brico, or Vítězslava Kaprálová, to name only the most famous ones. The remarkable careers of Nadia Boulanger and Jane Evrard, both in France and internationally, have already been researched.[1] Interwar Paris also hosted a number of lesser-known international conductors, including Eva Brunelli, Carmen Studer-Weingartner, and Gertrud Herliczka, who aroused curiosity, interest, and eventually the enthusiasm of the press and the public.[2] (For a discussion of the work of Henriette Renié as a music-ensemble leader, conductor, and *impresario* in *fin-de-siècle* to mid-twentieth-century France, see Chapter 15 in the current volume.) This phenomenon was also evident in the Parisian music halls, where Joséphine Baker,[3] Éliane de Creus, and Dominique Jeanès became well known as the leaders of small jazz ensembles, which were sometimes otherwise made up exclusively of men, testifying to a marked change in mentalities and a society in the throes of change.[4] Among the women active within this wider trend for female conductors, the largely unknown musician Helen Erdberg, who, under the pseudonym of Eliena Kazanova or *la Kazanova*, led a small and exclusively male formation dedicated to (what at the time was described as) *Tzigane* music during the same period. In this chapter, I seek to paint her portrait based on a study of her professional archives which, although incomplete, provide information on both her musical and human personality.[5] Many press articles also make it possible to gauge the reception of her performances in Paris, which she oversaw from their organisation to performance.

Helen Victoria Rubin Erdberg was born in Philadelphia on 22 September 1907,[6] to a father and mother of Ukrainian *émigré* origin (Philip and Miriam Rubin). She studied the violin in Oklahoma City. There, she learned how to play the violin and then married A. D. Erdberg, a lawyer with whom she settled in New York.[7] The young woman separated from her husband, however, and continued her studies with Franz Kneisel (1865–1926), a brilliant violinist and conductor who spent most of his career in the United States, where he notably mounted a performance of Brahms' Violin Concerto. Pedagogically sensitive, Kneisel was also 'a demanding teacher, requiring much in both technical ability and expressive insight'.[8] Erdberg then went on to perform as a *Tzigane* violinist under the pseudonym of Eliena Kazanova in a repertoire that she may have developed alongside Kneisel, himself born in Bucharest, Romania. Shortly afterwards, in 1932, Kazanova migrated to Europe, where she established her own *Tzigane* orchestra, which she conducted from her violin with increasing success. She made her first appearances in Paris in January 1933, probably at the Moulin-Rouge, then at Marseille,[9] before regularly performing in the main music-halls of the capital (such as L'Alhambra, Le Rex, and L'ABC), throughout the provinces (encompassing Deauville, Lyon, Biarritz, and Marseille), and elsewhere in Europe (including Belgium, the UK, the Netherlands, Spain, and Italy). She also toured the United States for over a year before returning to France during the summer of 1937.[10]

The year after, on 17 April 1938, Kazanova took her orchestra to the Théâtre des Bouffes-Parisiens for the Parisian premiere of the operetta *Rien qu'un baiser . . .* (1933), by the Hungarian composer Mihály Eisemann (1898–1966), in a French adaptation that ran for two months.[11] Her fame was such that she made several recordings of *Tzigane* songs, as well as works by Chopin, Strauss, and Lehár,[12] in arrangements thought to be by herself or by a certain Mariansky, whom she preferred to Nathan Milstein (Universal Edition, 1935) for a posthumous nocturne by Chopin.[13] She separated her arrangements for concert performance from those she made to record, where she reduced the arrangement to only a few musicians (4 violins, 1 cello, 1 clarinet and a cymbalist), as is evident from a recording planned for 1938.[14]

This continuous professional advancement was to be interrupted by the rise of Nazism. Due to her Jewish heritage, Kazanova was forced to return to the United States, where she died in 1978. Her son, violinist Lajos Kazanova (b. ?-1987) continued her memory by matching 'his hectic and obscure existence to the wildness of an expressionist style that was even more frantic than that of his mother', but without 'accomplishing a successful career as a jazz violinist',[15] remarkable though it was.

The dazzling development of Kazanova's career in Paris can be explained first by the well-established presence of *Tzigane* music in France since the nineteenth century, to which Liszt contributed both through his musical works and his literary writings.[16] Although the presence of Gypsy[17] musicians in Europe dates back to the end of the fifteenth century and developed mainly in Hungary, France only welcomed them around 1840. Berlioz, Mérimée, and Gauthier discovered their music firsthand during their trips to Russia and Hungary between 1846 and 1859. Similarly, the ballet *La Gipsy*, first performed at the Paris Opera in 1839,[18] and the 'Marche hongroise' in *La Damnation de Faust* (1846) bear witness to a marked infatuation with Gypsy music and culture from this period.[19] The genre's success is undeniable, particularly at the Universal Exhibitions of 1867, 1889, and 1900,[20] to the point of inspiring many French composers from Delibes to Massenet[21] to Ravel, who composed his well-known rhapsody for violin and lute (or orchestra), *Tzigane*, for Hungarian violinist Jelly d'Aranyi in 1924, 'a piece of virtuosity in the taste of a Hungarian rhapsody'.[22] At the start of the Second French Empire, *Tzigane* orchestras and musicians were active all over Europe, where they sometimes settled, like Boldi, the famous '*Tzigane Rouge*', who in *fin-de-siècle* Paris displayed a talent at the Café de la Paix that was praised by Jean Cocteau and Paul Morand.[23] The popularity of *Tzigane* music did not falter as, after the Russian Revolution of 1917, many exiled artists performed successfully in the Russian cabarets of Paris.[24]

As for Kazanova, she marks the emergence of what Alain Antonietto has described as a '*Tzigane* music for *grands spectacles*' in Parisian music-halls,[25] where her orchestra was able to entertain for a whole evening or for just a part of it. The repertoire Kazanova presented with her orchestra reflected the tradition established since the beginning of the twentieth century, which consisted of Hungarian, Romanian, and Russian dances, Viennese waltzes, and character pieces, which is what her music-hall audience expected to hear. Although described as '*Tzigane*', this was not authentic Romani music, but rather represented the Eastern European, Russian, and Romani 'Other' to urban Parisian audiences.[26] In response to an *impresario*'s demand, Kazanova herself referred to the hybrid nature of the genre by judging it '*Tzigane*, true to *Tzigane*, and diversified.'[27] She admitted that it was a 'difficult genre to describe' while clarifying her orchestra's fortes: 'To make people dance, it plays tangos and waltzes very well. Yet, I would not recommend it for jazz since there is no brass.'[28] To perform this repertoire, she had an orchestra composed mainly of strings, with a cymbalum, a pan flute, and one or more singers, often drawn from the musicians themselves. Her orchestra brought together at least 12 or even 14 musicians, because she did not wish to perform with a 'small brewery orchestra'.[29] She justified this requirement from a musical point of view: 'It is impossible for me to perform with a small orchestra to get the same effect I would have in a theatre.'[30] The visual aspect of performance was far from being of secondary importance to her. In addition to her own personality, she responded to an *impresario*'s demand by claiming to have 'young and beautiful musicians at her beck and call.'[31] Her writings also reveal the ethnic diversity of her musicians; in 1938, her orchestra included Romanian, Hungarian, Russian, Belgian, German, and American musicians.[32] A 1937 letter also indicates their religious diversity, to which Kazanova curiously does not attach any importance when she mentions that several of her musicians were Jewish, in relation to the prospect of a tour in Germany that probably never happened:

> I am of that [Jewish] origin myself and I have a few musicians in my orchestra who are Jewish. I do not know what the true conditions revolving around the matter are, only the gossip, and I don't believe much in gossip, because I've had several offers for Germany from serious conductors who didn't seem to care much about it.[33]

By 1938 or 1939, however, she acknowledged how dangerous her situation was and returned to the United States.

'More Than a Woman, She's a God': An Exceptional Musical Personality

The musical quality of Kazanova's interpretations, which is said to have aroused Ravel's enthusiasm,[34] was underlined as early as her very first concerts. As a critic writing in *Le Petit Marseillais* put it:

> We will rarely have the opportunity to applaud a violinist of her kind, because she draws all the finesse and passion from her instrument, and with her fingering and bow, where charm and technique compete, she obtains, with her virtuosity, combined effects ranging from the softest *andante* to the most frenzied *crescendo*.[35]

The plethora of nuances and the agogic flexibility of the tempos which characterised the repertoire she played were also admired by a critic at *Le Figaro*:

> From time to time, the rhythm languishes itself for Viennese musing, then it picks up again to take us, after this precious rest, into an amazing tornado of sounds ... But all of this is subtly and wonderfully balanced. An incredible singer intertwines his voice to these various harmonies; there is a remarkable flautist, and the dark Kazanova herself, uses her violin with an impressive dexterity.[36]

The critics mainly focused on the violinist's magnetic presence and the influence she exerted on her musicians, however. Even to the point of making her a deity: 'Kazanova is more than woman, she's a God', as one Belgian columnist exclaimed in a description reproduced in a promotional brochure which gathered numerous press extracts from French and international periodicals.[37] Habitually dressed in a long black dress, the violinist and conductor was the subject of long descriptions of her playing, her spectacular gestures, and her advantageous physique, the whole being undeniably coloured with a strong erotic charge, as exemplified in the following description written by André Warnod for *Le Figaro*:

> Kazanova . . . seems more than ever possessed by the god or demon of music. The devil rather, for she appears quite demonic, her mane in the wind, eyes of flame, moulded in a black dress, one with her violin, vibrating all over, fierce, hallucinated, twisting, tensing as if the bow were playing on her bare nerves, while her fingers, prodigiously agile, scratch and caress the strings. She communicates her flame to her musicians, who are also carried away by the music like a tornado; they can be seen standing up, crouching, ready to leap, the cellos spinning like spinning tops. Kazanova moves towards one, towards the other, threatening and charming. She looks like a tamer working her beasts. One of these musicians, who is bald and looks like a faun, draws bewitching accents from the panpipes and Kazanova listens to him. Suddenly motionless as if penetrated by the high and tender singing. And what an expression takes her face! We have never seen an orchestra conducted in such a spectacular way.[38]

Her performance, of course, was part of a tradition that goes back to Niccolò Paganini, whose playing elicited similar comments in the early nineteenth century.

The image of an 'unleashed Maenad, possessed by hell, breaking the hairs of her bow, writhing and twirling through the waves of sounds, performing a kind of frantic dance',[39] comes back once again under the pen of the critic of *Comœdia*; however, this critic and the critic of *La Rampe* acknowledge Kazanova's immense power of conviction both on the public and on her musicians:

> La Kazanova unsettles, bewilders, can irritate . . . But boring does not describe her. And her musicians, including the famous pan-flautist, are above all her musical partners, but do not disdain each other either and, from time to time, join the 'boss' in passionate unison. What must the sober Edith Lorand, and even the nervous Lili Gyenes think of this frenetic conduct? Alfred Rode himself is of a temperate nature, if one compares him with the Kazanova-style orchestral outburst.[40]

Kazanova's performances stand in stark contrast to those left to us by Hungarian violinists Lili Gyenes (1904–1997) and Edith Lorand (1898–1960), according to a few visual testimonies from these two now little-known personalities. Lorand gained acclaim during the Weimar Republic by conducting an otherwise all-male ensemble in Viennese waltzes from her violin,[41] while Gyenes conducted a woman's orchestra in '*Tzigane*-inspired' repertoire.[42] Their outfits and gestures displayed a restrained exuberance, however; especially in Lorand's case, who choose to dress in a style nostalgic of the Austro-Hungarian Empire:

> Ahead, and alone lit by light blue rays, Edith Lorand leads the orchestra with the sound of her violin. A regular figure, with passionate eyes, an energetic attitude, a beautiful body enhanced by a blue crinoline dress with mauve decorations.[43]

As original as they were, Kazanova's concerts were nevertheless comparable with those of Alfred Rode (1905–1979), to whom she was often compared in her early performances.[44] As Elie de Loches has commented, Kazanova had the 'same way of conducting her orchestra with her violin, [used the] same gestures to highlight her singer, her cello or her first violin.'[45] The performances of Kazanova and her orchestra consciously perpetuated the romantic *cliché* of *Tzigane* musicians, whose virtuosity was romantically culturally constructed as the result of an instinctive genius or even a pact with the devil.[46] As Pierre Varenne expressed in *Paris-soir*:

> Kazanova, a bohemian with eyes as dark as the night, seems to flog her *Tzigane* orchestra with a bow rattling like a whip. As soon as she plays her violin, she swoons with her mouth tensed and her eyelids shut. Over the top? And why? Drama must be the natural element of this romantic nomad, probably born on the road, in some trailer across Central Europe.[47]

The various descriptions of her performances are like those delivered by Liszt,[48] as well as by those written by the columnists of the 1867 Universal Exposition reporting the concerts of Ferenc Dudás' orchestra: 'These musicians not only play with their hands, but also with their entire body. Everything in them twitches as if their nerves answered to the bow's squeaking . . . Music that is equally bitter and sweet.'[49] André Schaeffner was not to be outdone when, in 1924, he finely commented on the Parisian creation of Ravel's *Tzigane* by its Hungarish dedicatee:

> [Jelly d'Aranyi] transfigured these few pages of virtuosity. She didn't, strictly speaking, play them in a musical way, but rather with her bow and her whole body, she *danced them*. Pressing and dragging languorously on the notes, expressing all the feline character of these sinuous melodic curves and jerky rhythms that seem capable of drawing us twice into the winding of a new and wilder waltz, Mlle Jelly d'Aranyi was for a few too brief moments the incarnation of this enigmatic race which, coming from the East, from the plains of Russia and Hungary to the coasts of Spain, introduced into our Western music an irremediable principle of chromatic dissolution, of metric distortion.[50]

The seduction deemed to be exuding from Kazanova also fits within the traditional imagery of *Tzigane* musicians whose 'myth of fierce seducers' is transmitted through operettas such as *Le Baron tzigane* (1885) by Johann Strauss, *L'Amour tzigane* (1911) by Franz Lehár, and *La Comtesse Maritza* (1924) by Emmerich Kálmán.[51] With Kazanova, the situation and the gender roles and relations were reversed – as in *Carmen* – for not only did a woman assume the soloist's part, but also that of the conductor leading an all-male orchestra. The role of the male seducer was also clearly evoked and reversed in her chosen stage name, *La Kazanova*. Her playing and conducting ended up giving rise to metaphors that evoke a strongly eroticised relationship of domination. This is well illustrated by the description which Jean-Richard Bloch included in a review for *Marianne*: 'We could say of her that she is beautiful, violent, and sensual, splitting through the hairs of her bow, whipping her musicians, embodying an image of a cabaret's Delilah.'[52] One of the rare negative criticisms of her recordings testifies to the awkwardness sometimes felt by others:

> It may be that the erotic delight experienced by the viewer's eye watching *la Kazanova*, whose frenetic images cover the walls, makes the ear complacent – though the convulsive and twitching postures the *Tzigane* violinist displays may shock the less worldly.

But the record undermines her by allowing the instrument alone to resonate (Pathé). It must be admitted that alone, deprived of the assistance of the long black dress, the dark hair, the daring chin, and the big naked arms, this violin seems inexistent.[53]

The image conveyed by the young artist is not inconsistent with her engagement to direct the production of Einsemann's operetta, *Rien qu'un baiser . . .* , at the Bouffes-Parisiens in 1938. On the contrary. In an interview granted to the press, the theatre's director, Albert Willemetz, confessed bluntly: ' "We've chosen a conductor whose name [Kazanova] matches our title" says Mr Albert Willemetz, pointing to a young brunette energetically conducting. She is la Kazanova.'[54] The libretto of the operetta was particularly audacious, as it focused on Janine, 'an honest woman who publicly admits to being sexually frustrated' and for this reason wishes to divorce her husband who is unable to offer her 'just a kiss'.[55] The score obeys the codes of musical comedy, but also includes a few instrumental and vocal pieces justifying the use of Kazanova and her musicians, as it includes a tango (No. 11), a *czardas* (No. 12), and several waltzes,[56] which all fitted well within the type of repertoire which Kazanova and her orchestra were best known for interpreting.

Critics, however, seemed less willing to accept what could be agreed upon in the specific and marginal context of *Tzigane* music. Misogynistic and sexist remarks abounded in the contemporary press coverage. For instance, the critic who covered *Rien qu'un baiser . . .* for *L'Intransigeant* commented that:

> What is most striking at first, is the back of the neck of the 'conductor'. Exquisitely thin, this neck, topped by beautiful black hair, whose line harmonises with that of the shoulders [. . .] By the way, know that the 'conductor' is a woman – a woman with irresistible dynamic effects who sometimes, plays the violin *Tzigane*-style facing the audience with her chest reversed and her face enraptured by the sound of her own instrument.[57]

Émile Vuillermoz, though usually supportive of female conductors,[58] expressed a strong and strict opinion:

> It is not enough to hire the most agitated and photogenic of lady conductors to create an effective musical dynamism. Indeed, the charming Kazanova has found, at her own expense, that it is easier to slash her violin with a frenetic bow in the halo of a spotlight than it is to follow singers whose studies of music theory have been somewhat neglected.[59]

As for Maurice Yvain, he strongly criticised Kazanova's performance, his judgement perhaps being induced by his visceral hostility towards the presence of foreign composers or musicians in the French theatres of Paris:[60] 'At the head of an orchestra whose musicians are dressed in picturesque costumes, a curious woman called *la Kazanova* shakes, swoons, and dives into a trance, one can only hope she will learn her role as a conductor.'[61] Although he judged the score severely, Darius Milhaud was more lenient towards Kazanova's interpretation of it:

> We would spend a better evening if the music of Mr. Michel Eisemann was less banal, more varied (the same melodies come back constantly), with a less dull orchestration, despite the paprika that the young conductor '*La Kazanova*', who is a talented violinist with a solid technique and a lively spirit, puts into it by her sometimes excessive gestures.[62]

This was also the opinion of Henri Gil-Marchex, a fine connoisseur of *Tzigane*-inspired music, as he played the piano part in the 1924 premiere of Ravel's *Tzigane* in London with Jelly d'Aranyi:[63]

> If the inspiration of the composer Michel Eisemann does not pretend to surprise by its originality, the lively Kazanova and her noisy musicians in Hungarian gilded tones capture the attention with their *Tzigane* verve: waltzes, bohemian tunes, and even rumbas recall the delectable atmosphere of Budapest's cafés.[64]

These few minor setbacks barely tarnished the remarkable reception and career of Kazanova, whom we can understand as an outstanding and iconic female figure of orchestral conducting in the Parisian music halls of the interwar period. She was the one who Monique Forestier described in an article for *Minerva* as 'the great female study that every intelligent woman should read.' On the emergence of conducting as a profession that was on the way to being totally accessible to women, she further observed: 'But the most extraordinary conductor of a music-hall orchestra certainly is la Kazanova, that bacchantic musical freak, dark as night '.[65] Kazanova's personality is doubly interesting. Apart from the little-known spot she occupies in the history of women musicians, her body language and her relationship with her musicians appear transgressive and perfectly assumed, judging by her eminently subversive pseudonym (as discussed earlier), even if we understand these as part of the evolution of gender identities that the First World War had triggered. The representations of virility and femininity became deeply altered in the interwar period,[66] when fashion and social dances from the Americas (following hot on the heels of the raised hemlines that had initially resulted from the limited availability of fabric during the First World War) freed women's bodies in both their appearance and mobility.[67]

Kazanova's brief Parisian and European career also attests to an evolution in the place given to women in musical circles between the two world wars. The faces of woman conductors appear multiple, varied, and of a long-unsuspected richness: multiple due to the increasing number of female performers who entered this profession, and varied by the personal representation they chose to give it. From Nadia Boulanger, who resembled a vestal virgin totally devoted to the service of her art,[68] to the androgynous figure or 'glamorous public image'[69] of the blonde Jane Evrard[70] and the sensual brunette Kazanova, these musicians defended both their right to control their appearance and their body and their desire to embrace a profession until then largely reserved for men. The destiny of these musicians bears witness to the great freedom that prevailed at the time and which the moral order of Vichy and the Second World War jeopardised with consequences and regressions that can still be felt to this day.[71]

Notes

1. Jeanice Brooks, *The Musical Work of Nadia Boulanger: Performing Past and Future between the Wars* (Cambridge and New York: Cambridge University Press, 2013) and Laura Hamer, "On the Conductor's Podium: Jane Evrard and the Orchestre féminin de Paris," *The Musical Times* 152, no. 1916 (2011): 81–100.
2. See Jean-Christophe Branger, "Être cheffe d'orchestre à Paris dans l'entre-deux-guerres: les concerts symphoniques dirigés par Eva Brunelli, Carmen Studer-Weingartner et Gertrud Herliczka," *Revue de musicologie* 102, no. 2 (2016): 319–61.
3. In the 1930s, Joséphine Baker (1906-1975), who had a solid musical background, formed her own group (the Sixteen Baker Boys) which accompanied her, under her direction, notably at the

magazine *La Joie de Paris*, created in December 1932 at the Casino de Paris. See Bennetta Jules-Rosette, *Josephine Baker in Art and Life* (Urbana and Chicago: University of Illinois Press, 2007), 54, 174.

4. Cabaret pianist and songwriter Dominique Jeanès (1907–1982) conducted the orchestra of the Théâtre des Variétés from her piano, while Éliane de Creus (1905–1997) led a jazz orchestra in Michel Emer's operetta *Loulou et ses Boys* (1933). See Branger, "Être cheffe d'orchestre à Paris dans l'entre-deux-guerres," 336.
5. Schlesinger Library (Radcliffe Institute, Harvard Library), Papers of Eliena Kazanova.
6. Draft of Kazanova's letter to the impresarios Rottenbourg et Goldwin, November 5, 1937. All quotes from Kazanova's letters that are quoted afterwards are stored at the Schlesinger Library (Radcliffe Institute, Harvard Library), Papers of Eliena Kazanova.
7. The bibliographical information presented in this paragraph comes from the website's notice: accessed March 15, 2020, http://id.lib.harvard.edu/alma/990123347960203941/catalog.
8. Steven Ledbetter, "Kneisel, Franz," *Grove Music Online*, accessed March 14, 2020, https://www-oxfordmusiconline-com.libezproxy.open.ac.uk/grovemusic/display/10.1093/gmo/9781561592630.001.0001/omo-9781561592630-e-0000046768?rskey=4KCemK&result=1.
9. See Anonymous, "Les Avant-premières," *Le Petit Marseillais*, January 27, 1933, 4 and Elie de Loches, "Tziganes," *L'Africain*, February 5, 1933, 33.
10. Draft of Kazanova's letter to Jean Chalando (impresario in Alger), Paris, August 15, 1937.
11. The adaptation was made by Georges Delance with lyrics by Charles-Louis Pothier and famous librettist Albert Willemetz (1887–1964), who also ran the theatre. See Jacques Gana, *Encyclopédie multimédia de la comédie musicale en France*, 1918–1944, accessed Mars 14, 2020, https://www2.biusante.parisdescartes.fr/cm/?for=fic&cleoeuvre=291. A recording of excerpts sung by Tania Doll (Paris: Pathé PA 1539, 1938), put online on the same site, has preserved the memory of the performances and another, kept at the Bibliothèque municipale de Lyon (F-LYm), gathers instrumental excerpts conducted by Kazanova and her orchestra (Paris: Pathé PA 1537, 1938).
12. France's National Library BNF (F-Pn) has preserved the following recordings: *Rendez-vous chez Lehar*, [Paris]: [Pathé PA 23], [1934]; *Viens dans le bois* (air populaire hongrois; Etoile: air populaire roumain; Danse roumaine: air populaire roumain), [Paris]: [Pathé PA 24], [1934]; Johann Strauss, *Accelerationen*, C. Codolban, *Romance*, [Paris]: [Pathé PA 296], [1934]; Chopin, *Tristesse, étude n° 3 op. 10*, Willy Schmidt-Gentner, *Czardas* du film *Symphonie inachevée* (1934) de Willi Forst, [Paris]: [Pathé PA 374], [1934]; *Romance et Doïna* (gardas; Alfred Rode, *Infocata*: danses roumaines, Barch), [Paris, Chatou]: [Pathé PA 1538], [1940]. Three excerpts from the latter disc are available in a remastered double-album featuring historical recordings of Tzigane instrumentalists from the interwar period (*Tziganes: Paris/Berlin/Budapest/1910–1935*, Paris: Frémeaux & Associés, 1993).
13. Draft from Kazanova's letter to F. Rieder, Paris, 21 March 1938. A Pathé recording (PA 1459), named *Roumaineska*, « Pot-pourri d'airs roumains » arranged by Mariansky and conducted by Kazanova went on sale on Ebay on March 2020.
14. Draft from Kazanova's letter to F. Rieder, Paris, January 30, 1938.
15. Alain Antonietto, "Histoire de la musique tsigane instrumentale d'Europe centrale," *Musiques!*, *Études tsiganes* 3/1 (1994): 104–33 (133).
16. In addition to his *Rapsodies hongroises*, which celebrate Tzigane music, Liszt published in French his work *Des Bohémiens et de leur musique en Hongrie* in Paris (1/1859), then in Leipzig (2/1881) in a revised version. See Serge Gut, *Liszt*, ([Paris]: de Fallois; [Lausanne]: L'Âge d'homme, 1989), 587. See Ralph Locke, *Musical Exoticism: Images and Reflections* (New York: Cambridge University Press, 2009), 135–49.
17. The term Gypsy is used here solely in historical terms.
18. Ballet-pantomine in three acts by Henri de Saint-Georges, music by François Benoist, Aurelio Marliani and Ambroise Thomas, with Fanny Elssler in the title role.
19. Antonietto, 4–133 et Vaux de Foletier, 139–52.
20. See Annegret Fauser, *Musical Encounters at the 1889 Paris World's Fair* (Rochester: Rochester University Press, 2005), 254–61.
21. The influence of *Tzigane* music on Delibes can be seen in his ballet *Coppelia* (1870) or in *Kassya*, a comic opera that the composer left unfinished when he died in 1891. Massenet, who completed it shortly afterwards, composed a *Marche héroïque de Szabadi* (1879) based on the theme of a Tzigane composer, Ignác Szabadi, whom he met during a trip to Hungary in January 1879. See

Jean-Christophe Branger, "Présences de Liszt dans la vie et les œuvres de Massenet," in *Liszt et la France: musique, culture et société dans l'Europe du XIXe siècle*, edited by Malou Haine and Nicolas Dufetel (Paris: Vrin, 2012), 275–94 (279–82; 284–85).

22. "morceau de virtuosité dans le goût d'une rhapsodie hongroise" Maurice Ravel, "Esquisse autobiographique," *L'Intégrale: correspondance (1895–1937) écrits et entretiens*, edited by Manuel Cornejo ([Paris:] Le Passeur éditeur, 2018), 1441.
23. Antonietto, "Histoire de la musique tsigane instrumentale d'Europe centrale," 126–27.
24. Antonietto, "Histoire de la musique tsigane instrumentale d'Europe centrale," 132–33.
25. Antonietto, "Histoire de la musique tsigane instrumentale d'Europe centrale," 133.
26. Antonietto, "Histoire de la musique tsigane instrumentale d'Europe centrale," 128. The complex question regarding the authenticity of Tzigane music, which cannot be answered here, was already a burning topic at the end of nineteenth century, notably during the Universal Exposition of 1889. See Fauser, *Musical Encounters at the 1889 Paris World's Fair*, 254–61. This genre, spread throughout nineteenth-century Europe sometimes by musicians of different origins, quickly lost its authenticity. It mainly became 'the romantic symbol of a nomadic ideal of musical freedom' (Antonietto, "Histoire de la musique tsigane instrumentale d'Europe centrale," 107) and a *couleur locale* among others whose musical (harmonic, rhythmic, melodic) and interpretative characteristics deviated from the codes of European music.
27. 'tzigane, classique à la tzigane, très varié' Draft of Kazanova's letter to A. R. van der Berghe Jr., Paris, March 3, 1938.
28. 'le genre est difficile à décrire . . . Pour faire danser, il joue très bien les valses et les tangos. Je ne le recommande pas pour le jazz, puisque je n'ai pas de cuivres.' Draft of Kazanova's letter to Charles Hastert, Paris, August 20, 1937.
29. Draft of Kazanova's letter to Charles Hastert (International Artistic Agency), Bruxelles, July 12, 1938.
30. "Il est impossible pour moi de me produire avec un petit orchestre pour obtenir l'effet que je dois obtenir dans un théâtre." Draft of Kazanova's letter to Emilio C. Jacobsen, Brussels, September 1, 1938.
31. "musiciens jeunes et beaux." Draft of Kazanova's letter to G. Piers, Brussels, October 3, 1938.
32. Draft of Kazanova's letter to C. Jacobsen, Brussels, August 16, 1938.
33. 'Je suis de cette origine moi-même et j'ai quelques musiciens dans mon orchestre qui le sont entièrement. Je ne sais pas les conditions véritables qui y existent à ce sujet, sauf les potins qui en courent, et dans ces derniers je crois peu, parce que j'ai eu plusieurs offres pour l'Allemagne des directions sérieuses qui n'avaient l'air de ne pas faire grand cas de ce point-là.' Draft of Kazanova's letter to Eugène Wendling (a German impresario in Hamburg), La Haye, November 15, 1937. A 1933 advertisement nevertheless mentions that she performed with 18 musicians at the Montmartre, 20 rue de Clichy, then directed by a certain J. Toultchine, an émigré 'of old Russian nobility.' See A., "La Vie parisienne: anniversaire du *Montmartre*," *Comœdia*, April 7, 1933, 1–2.
34. Antonietto, "Histoire de la musique tsigane instrumentale d'Europe centrale," 133.
35. 'Nous aurons rarement l'occasion d'applaudir une violoniste de son genre, car elle tire de son instrument toutes les finesses, toute la passion que l'on puisse en tirer, et douée d'un doigté et d'un archet où le charme le dispute à la technique, elle obtient, avec ses virtuoses, des effets combinés qui vont de l'*andante* le plus doux au *crescendo* le plus endiablé.' G.C., "À l'Odéon, la Kazanova à la scène," *Le Petit Marseillais*, June 10, 1933, 4.
36. 'De temps à autre, le rythme s'alanguit pour des rêveries viennoises, puis il reprend de plus belle pour nous entraîner, après cet indispensable repos, dans une hallucinante tornade de sons . . . . Mais tout cela est dosé à merveille. Un excellent chanteur mêle sa voix à ces diverses harmonies; il y a un flûtiste remarquable, et la noire Kazanova, elle-même, se sert de son violon avec une stupéfiante dextérité.' Robert Destez, "Cirque et music-hall [L'Alhambra]," *Le Figaro*, May 22, 1933, 4.
37. 'Kazanova est plus qu'une femme, c'est un Dieu' in: *La Kazanova et ses tziganes*, advertising brochure without a date [1938?], stored in the Papers of Eliena Kazanova, Schlesinger Library, Radcliffe Institute, Harvard University.
38. 'Kazanova . . . semble plus que jamais possédée par le dieu ou le démon de la musique. Le démon plutôt, car elle apparaît tout à fait démoniaque, la crinière au vent, des yeux de flammes, moulée dans une robe noire, ne faisant qu'un avec son violon, vibrant tout entière, farouche, hallucinée, se tordant, se crispant comme si l'archet jouait sur ses nerfs mis à vif, tandis que ses doigts, prodigieusement agiles, griffent et caressent les cordes. Elle communique sa flamme à ses musiciens,

emportés eux aussi par la musique comme par une tornade; on les voit se dresser, s'accroupir, prêts à bondir, les violoncelles tournent comme des toupies. Kazanova s'avance vers l'un, vers l'autre, menaçante et charmeuse. On dirait une dompteuse faisant travailler ses fauves. Un de ces musiciens, qui est chauve et ressemble à un faune, tire de la flûte de Pan des accents ensorceleurs et Kazanova l'écoute. Soudain immobile comme pénétrée par le chant aigu et tendre. Et quelle expression prend son visage! Nous n'avons jamais vu conduire un orchestre d'une façon aussi spectaculaire.' André Warnod, "Chronique du music-hall [l'ABC]," *Le Figaro*, December 8, 1937, 4.

39. 'Ménade déchaînée, possédée par l'enfer, cassant les crins de son archet, se tordant sous la rafale des sons, exécutant une sorte de danse frénétique.' Gustave Fréjaville, "Kazanova et son orchestre," *Comœdia*, May 24, 1933, 1.
40. 'La Kazanova déroute, déconcerte, peut agacer . . . mais elle n'ennuie pas une minute. Et ses musiciens, dont le fameux *flûtiste* de Pan sont ses partenaires musicaux surtout, mais ne dédaignent pas non plus, parfois, de se mettre à l'unisson passionné de la 'patronne'. Que doivent penser de cette conduite frénétique la sobre Edith Lorand, et même la nerveuse Lili Gyenes? Alfred Rode lui-même est un sage tempéré, si on le compare comme allure de déchaîneur d'orchestre à la Kazanova.' Legrand-Chabrier, "La rampe du Music-hall," *La Rampe*, June 1, 1933, 19, 30.
41. See Wikipedia, accessed March 26, 2020, https://de.wikipedia.org/wiki/Edith_Lorand.
42. René Bizet, « Music-Hall », *L'Intransigeant*, mai 30, 1932.
43. Pierre de Trévières, "Paris," *La Femme de France*, May 10, 1931. Extract of a concert filmed in 1931 on YouTube: accessed March 26, 2020, www.youtube.com/watch?v=zy_kDTvKu3Y.
44. Rode first made a name for himself as the violinist and conductor of a Tzigane ensemble, before embarking on a career in cinema as an actor and director of films, some of which, such as *Juanita* (1935) or *Le Danube bleu* (1938), were designed to 'play Tzigane tunes and even Liszt.' Jean-Pierre Liasu, "Un film charmant: *Juanita*," *Comœdia* (30 September 1935).
45. Loches, "Tziganes," 33.
46. See also Antonietto, "Histoire de la musique tsigane instrumentale d'Europe centrale," 127.
47. 'Kazanova, bohémienne aux yeux de nuit, semble flageller son orchestre tzigane d'un archet qui cingle comme un fouet. Dès qu'elle joue du violon, elle se pâme bouche tendue, paupières closes. Chiqué? Pourquoi? Le drame doit être l'élément naturel de cette nomade romantique, née sans doute sur la grand'route, dans quelque roulotte de l'Europe centrale.' Pierre Varenne, "À l'A.B.C.," *Paris-soir*, December 10, 1937, 9.
48. Liszt, *Des bohémiens*, 1881, 380–82.
49. Quoted by Antonietto, "Histoire de la musique tsigane instrumentale d'Europe centrale," 118.
50. '[Jelly d'Aranyi] transfigura ces quelques pages de virtuosité. Elle ne les joua pas au sens proprement musical du terme, mais de son archet, de tout son corps elle les *dansa*. Appuyant et traînant avec langueur sur les notes, exprimant tout le caractère félin de ces sinueuses courbes mélodiques et de ces rythmes saccadés qui semblent à deux reprises nous entraîner dans l'enroulement d'une valse nouvelle et plus sauvage, Mlle Jelly d'Aranyi fut pendant quelques trop brefs instants l'incarnation de cette race énigmatique qui, venue d'Orient, des plaines de la Russie et de la Hongrie jusque sur les côtes d'Espagne, introduisit dans notre musique occidentale un irrémédiable principe de dissolution chromatique, de déformation métrique.' André Schaeffner, "Concerts-Colonne," *Le Ménestrel* 86, no. 49 (December 5, 1924): 508.
51. Antonietto, "Histoire de la musique tsigane instrumentale d'Europe centrale," 128.
52. 'On pourrait dire d'elle, belle, violente et sensuelle, crevant les crins de son archet, cravachant ses musiciens, qu'elle apparaît comme une Dalila de cabaret.' Maurice Verne, "Un auteur célèbre à l'A.B.C.," *L'Intransigeant*, December 11, 1937, 7.
53. 'Il se peut que le ravissement érotique éprouvé par l'œil du spectateur devant la Kazanova, dont les images frénétiques couvrent les murs, rende l'oreille complaisante, – encore que les postures convulsives dont la violoniste tzigane fait sa publicité choquent les moins difficiles. Mais le disque la dessert en ne laissant plus sonner que l'instrument (Pathé). Il faut avouer qu'à lui seul, privé du secours de la longue robe noire, des cheveux de ténèbres, du menton audacieux et des grands bras nus, ce violon paraît mince.' Jean-Richard Bloch, "Disques," *Marianne* 2, no. 70 (February 21, 1934): 5.
54. Almaviva, "M. Albert Willemetz nous parle de *Rien qu'un baiser*," *Le Figaro*, April 16, 1938), 8.
55. Christophe Mirambeau, *Albert Willemetz, un regard dans le siècle* (Paris: La Rampe, 2005), 364.
56. Mirambeau, *Albert Willemetz, un regard dans le siècle*, 363.
57. 'Ce qui frappe tout d'abord, c'est la nuque du 'chef d'orchestre'. Adorablement fine, cette nuque, surmontée de beaux cheveux noirs, et dont la ligne s'harmonise avec celle des épaules . . . Au fait,

sachez tout de suite que le 'chef d'orchestre' est ici une femme – une femme aux irrésistibles effets dynamiques, et qui parfois joue du violon à la tzigane, face au public, le torse renversé, le visage exprimant la volupté de s'écouter.' I., "Théâtres," *L'Intransigeant*, April 22, 1938, 8.
58. See Hamer, "On the Conductor's Podium," 82 and Branger, "Être cheffe d'orchestre à Paris dans l'entre-deux-guerres," 342–43; 353–54.
59. 'Il ne suffit pas d'engager la plus agitée et la plus photogénique des dames-chefs-d'orchestre pour créer un dynamisme musical efficace. La charmante Kazanova a pu constater, en effet, à ses dépens, qu'il est plus facile de sabrer son violon d'un archet frénétique dans l'auréole d'un projecteur, que de suivre des chanteurs dont les études de solfège ont été un peu négligées.' Émile Vuillermoz, "Les premières," *Excelsior*, April 22, 1938, 4.
60. Mirambeau, *Albert Willemetz, un regard dans le siècle*, 524.
61. 'À la tête d'un orchestre dont les musiciens sont affublés de costumes simili-tziganes, se trémousse, se pâme, tombe en transe une femme curieuse appelée la Kazanova, à laquelle on ne peut souhaiter qu'une chose c'est d'apprendre son métier de chef.' Maurice Yvain, "Bouffes-Parisiens," *Le Jour*, April 23, 1938, 8.
62. 'On passerait une soirée meilleure si la musique de M. Michel Eisemann était moins banale, plus variée (les mêmes airs reviennent constamment), d'une orchestration moins terne, malgré le paprika qu'y met, par ses gestes parfois excessifs, la jeune chef d'orchestre 'La Kazanova' qui est une violoniste de talent possédant une technique solide et un entrain endiablé.' Darius Milhaud, "Aux Bouffes: *Rien qu'un baiser*," *Ce Soir*, April 30, 1938, 6.
63. Ravel, *L'Intégrale*, 48 et 995.
64. 'Si l'inspiration du compositeur Michel Eisemann ne prétend pas surprendre par son originalité, la pétulante Kazanova et ses bruyants musiciens chamarrés de dorures hongroises accaparent l'attention par leur verve tzigane: les valses, les airs bohémiens, et même les rumbas évoquent l'atmosphère délicieuse des cafés de Budapest.' Henri Gil-Marchex, "Aux Bouffes-parisiens: Rien qu'un baiser," *Paris-soir*, April 24, 1938; in Gana, *Encyclopédie multimédia de la comédie musicale en France, 1918–1944*.
65. Monique Forestier, "Quand la femme tient la baguette de chef d'orchestre," *Minerva*, September 19, 1937, coupure de presse, Paris, Bibliothèque Marguerite Durand, Dossier Jane Evrard, Doss EVR.
66. See Luc Capdevila, François Rouquet, Fabrice Virgili, and Danièle Voldman, *Sexes, genre et guerres (France, 1914–1945)* (Paris: Payot & Rivages, 2010).
67. Sophie Jacotot, *Danser à Paris dans l'entre-deux-guerres: lieux, pratiques et imaginaires des danses de société des Amériques, 1919–1939* (Paris: Nouveau monde éd., 2013), 369 and 385.
68. 'Boulanger is presented as a sort of Vestal Virgin, sacrificing her sexuality and renouncing personal ambition in order to serve the true master: music.' Jeanice Brooks, ""Noble et grande servante de la musique": Telling the Story of Nadia Boulanger's Conducting Career," *The Journal of Musicology* 14, no. 1 (Winter 1996), 92–116 (93).
69. Hamer, "On the Conductor's Podium," 97.
70. Branger, "Être cheffe d'orchestre à Paris dans l'entre-deux-guerres," 349.
71. In 2011, H. Ravet again rightly points out the ongoing difficulty for any woman wishing to conduct. For male conductors, "the body is supposed to signify a 'virile' authority. Female conductors are confronted with this and must define their identity as women in a profession devolved to men where authority is exercised over male and female musicians. They not only work their technique . . . but also their gestures, thus positioning themselves in relation to the "masculine" and the "feminine". These gestures, the gestures of direction and their whole body in representation on the podium cannot appear too "masculine" nor too "feminine". This concerns both their appearance on stage and in their clothing as well as the way they approach and communicate with the musicians.' Hyacinthe Ravet, *Musiciennes: Enquête sur les femmes et la musique* (Paris: Éd. Autrement, 2011), 61.

Bibliography

Archival Sources

Bibliothèque Marguerite Durand, Dossier Jane Evrard, Doss EVR.
Schlesinger Library (Radcliffe Institute, Harvard Library), Papers of Eliena Kazanova.

Published Sources

A. "La Vie parisienne: anniversaire du *Montmartre*." *Comœdia*, April 7, 1933, 1–2.
Almaviva. "M. Albert Willemetz nous parle de *Rien qu'un baiser*." *Le Figaro*, April 16, 1938, 8.
Anonymous. "Les Avant-premières." *Le Petit Marseillais*, January 27, 1933, 4.
Antonietto, Alain. "Histoire de la musique tsigane instrumentale d'Europe centrale." *Musiques!, Études tsiganes* 3, no. 1 (1994): 104–33.
Branger, Jean-Christophe. "Présences de Liszt dans la vie et les œuvres de Massenet." In *Liszt et la France: musique, culture et société dans l'Europe du XIXe siècle*, edited by Malou Haine and Nicolas Dufetel. Paris: Vrin, 2012.
———. "Être cheffe d'orchestre à Paris dans l'entre-deux-guerres: les concerts symphoniques dirigés par Eva Brunelli, Carmen Studer-Weingartner et Gertrud Herliczka." *Revue de musicologie* 102, no. 2 (2016): 319–61.
Brooks, Jeanice. ""Noble et grande servante de la musique": Telling the Story of Nadia Boulanger's Conducting Career." *The Journal of Musicology* 14, no. 1 (Winter 1996): 92–116.
———. *The Musical Work of Nadia Boulanger: Performing Past and Future Between the Wars*. Cambridge and New York: Cambridge University Press, 2013.
Capdevila, Luc, François Rouquet, Fabrice Virgili, and Danièle Voldman. *Sexes, genre et guerres (France, 1914–1945)*. Paris: Payot & Rivages, 2010.
de Loches, Elie. "Tziganes." *L'Africain*, February 5, 1933, 33.
Destez, Robert. "Cirque et music-hall [L'Alhambra]." *Le Figaro*, May 22, 1933, 4.
Fauser, Annegret. *Musical Encounters at the 1889 Paris World's Fair*. Rochester: Rochester University Press, 2005, 254–61.
Fréjaville, Gustave. "Kazanova et son orchestre." *Comœdia*, May 24, 1933, 1.
G. C. "À l'Odéon, la Kazanova à la scène." *Le Petit Marseillais*, June 10, 1933, 4.
Hamer, Laura. "On the Conductor's Podium: Jane Evrard and the Orchestre féminin de Paris." *The Musical Times* 152, no. 1916 (2011): 81–100.
I. "Théâtres." *L'Intransigeant*, April 22, 1938, 8.
Jacotot, Sophie. *Danser à Paris dans l'entre-deux-guerres: lieux, pratiques et imaginaires des danses de société des Amériques, 1919–1939*, 369 and 385. Paris: Nouveau monde éd., 2013.
Jules-Rosette, Bennetta. *Josephine Baker in Art and Life*. Urbana and Chicago: University of Illinois Press, 2007.
Ledbetter, Steven. "Kneisel, Franz." *Grove Music Online*. Accessed March 14, 2020. https://www-oxford musiconline-com.libezproxy.open.ac.uk/grovemusic/display/10.1093/gmo/9781561592630.001. 0001/omo-9781561592630-e-0000046768?rskey=4KCemK&result=1.
Legrand-Chabrier. "La rampe du Music-hall." *La Rampe* 19, June 1, 1933, 30.
Liasu, Jean-Pierre. "Un film charmant: *Juanita*." *Comœdia*, September 30, 1935, n.p.
Locke, Ralph. *Musical Exoticism: Images and reflections*. New York: Cambridge University Press, 2009.
Milhaud, Darius. "Aux Bouffes: *Rien qu'un baiser*." *Ce Soir*, April 30, 1938, 6.
Mirambeau, Christophe. *Albert Willemetz, un regard dans le siècle*. Paris: La Rampe, 2005, 364.
Ravet, Hyacinthe. *Musiciennes: Enquête sur les femmes et la musique*. Paris: Éd. Autrement, 2011, 61.
Schaeffner, André. "Concerts-Colonne." *Le Ménestrel* 86, no. 49 (December 5, 1924): 508.
Varenne, Pierre. "À l'A.B.C." *Paris-soir*, December 10, 1937, 9.
Verne, Maurice. "Un auteur célèbre à l'A.B.C." *L'Intransigeant*, December 11, 1937, 7.
Vuillermoz, Émile. "Les premières." *Excelsior*, April 22, 1938, 4.
Warnod, André. "Chronique du music-hall [l'ABC]." *Le Figaro*, December 8, 1937, 4.
Yvain, Maurice. "Bouffes-Parisiens." *Le Jour*, April 23, 1938, 8.

15
EDIS DE PHILIPPE, THE ISRAEL NATIONAL OPERA (INO), AND THE POLITICS OF MUSIC

Kira Alvarez

The story of the Israeli American *impresario* Edis de Philippe (1918–1978), the founder and long-time director of the Israel National Opera (1947–1982, hereafter INO) is the striking case of a woman who against all odds succeeded in a heavily male-dominated artistic world and managed to establish a national opera company in the 'middle of the desert'.[1] Her story is important to know, because, especially in opera, women leaders have always been the exception, and their histories have often been ignored.[2] How did Edis de Philippe manage to create and sustain an opera company in Israel for over three decades despite her gender, despite facing relentless criticism, and after a previous attempt by the well-established – and male – Ukrainian Jewish conductor Mordechai Golinkin (1875–1963) to establish an opera house in Mandatory Palestine failed?[3] In examining this question, I focus on three aspects from de Philippe's career that show the complex layers involved in its making. First, I show that despite her artistic and political visions for the opera, de Philippe's institution faced hostility from the internationally renowned Habima Theatre and was often unfairly compared to the Israel Philharmonic Orchestra, the country's leading musical institution. Second, I home in on the organisational challenges of running a newly established opera house that constantly loomed large for de Philippe. Of particular interest here is the question of how de Philippe used her identity and connections as an American to help propel her plans forward. Finally, I examine the negative 'social reception' that de Philippe experienced by focusing on the criticism she faced from the preeminent music critic and musicologist during this period, Peter Gradenwitz.

Previous Attempts to Establish Opera in Mandatory Palestine/Israel

Before de Phillipe's first arrival in Mandatory Palestine in 1945, there had been another significant attempt to create an opera house in Mandatory Palestine by the Ukrainian Jewish conductor and *émigré* Mordechai Golinkin. Born in the province of Kherson in 1875, Golinkin became conductor of the famed Mariinsky Theatre in Petrograd (today St. Petersburg) in 1918.[4] He immigrated to Palestine in 1923 to achieve his life-long dream of creating a Hebrew opera company. Like many Eastern European immigrants who arrived in Mandatory Palestine, Golinkin was eager to establish Western classical music institutions in Palestine.[5] In a 1918 essay entitled 'A Hebrew National Theatre in Palestine', Golinkin expressed excitement at the prospect of a Jewish nation-state and presented the opera house as a necessary accoutrement of the nation-state-to-be (1927).[6] Golinkin's Palestine Opera opened in 1923 in Tel Aviv. Between 1927 and 1929, he travelled to the United States in order to raise funds for the financially frail opera company. But his failure to secure significant American private donations was the main reason for the demise of his opera company by the 1940s.[7] Although Golinkin's opera company failed, he became a great mentor and supporter to de Philippe. But Golinkin's backing was a rare exception. Most others in the classical music establishment were perpetually critical of Edis' work.

The Protagonist: Edis de Philippe (1918–1978)

Edis de Philippe was born in 1918 in New York City. The daughter of Ukrainian Jewish immigrants, she began her musical education at the age of six, and later studied at New York University. In 1935, she made her successful opera debut as a soprano in Washington D.C. in the presence of President and Eleanor Roosevelt, performing selections from *La Traviata* in honor of the President's birthday.[8] Soon afterwards she began performing regularly in opera houses throughout the United States and in Mexico, where she appeared in concerts sponsored by Coca-Cola.[9] By the second half of the 1930s, she was performing in the Paris Opera, and there 'met many refugees from Germany – people who had been prominent in music' before the Nazi takeover drove them into exile.[10] At the beginning of World War Two, she returned to North America where she performed for a number of organisations, such as the United Service Organizations (USO), and continued performing in Mexico. Although de Philippe had a growing opera career, her devotion to the Israel National Opera meant that she could not continue cultivating her career.

De Philippe travelled to Mandatory Palestine in November 1945 as a guest of the Jewish Agency and gave a series of recitals, including a performance with the short-lived Palestine Folk Opera (1940–1945) founded by Marc Lavry.[11] Her husband at the time, Max Rabinoff (1877–1966), was an *impresario* who was instrumental in helping create several important U.S. cultural institutions, including the Chicago Opera Company.[12] De Philippe's tour of Mandatory Palestine was well documented in the Mandatory Palestinian press, which regarded her as an international celebrity. It was at this time that de Philippe developed the idea of creating an opera company in Mandatory Palestine, building off the previous work of Golinkin's company. In 1946, de Philippe was invited to the Zionist Congress in Basel to present her plans for a national opera in Mandatory Palestine.[13] By 1947, de Philippe was performing at the Paris Opera when 'officials of the new Israel government asked her to go to Israel and organize an opera there.'[14] Her life-changing decision to move to Mandatory Palestine diminished any future plans that she would continue her career as an internationally famous singer in Europe and the U.S., since Mandatory Palestine was then an unsuitable place for an international musical career. Instead, her move signaled the intention that she was dedicated to the creation of a Jewish nation-state. Most importantly, by creating an opera house that aspired to international recognition she would contribute her talents and connections.

De Philippe used most of her prior career earnings to support the opera financially. Circumstances were not easy, and sources described her as working 'under depressive circumstances, disregarding warnings at home and abroad that she wouldn't succeed and would suffer the fate of her predecessors.'[15] The opening gala performances of her opera began on 29 November 1947 and included selections from operas such as *The Barber of Seville*, *Carmen*, and *Manon*. The opera's first season began on 15 April 1948, with a performance of Massenet's *Thais* with de Philippe in the title role of Thais. De Philippe's predecessor, Mordechai Golinkin, assisted the opera during its early years by conducting the opera orchestra.

Edis de Philippe's Vision and Criticism

Edis de Philippe, like Golinkin before her, envisioned an opera that should promote overtly national goals. De Philippe did not publish any overriding vision for the Israel National Opera like Golinkin's previously mentioned 1918 manifesto. That does not mean her ambitions were any less lofty, however. Her aim was to create an opera company that would perform established European operas all in Hebrew, fifty weeks in a year, and promote operas composed by new Israeli composers. Recruiting many singers for these new operas was not easy, and de Philippe used her American connections to bring American singers to Israel. Although many praised de Philippe, numerous Israelis also criticised her decision to depend on talent from abroad, claiming that 'more could be done if all available local talent were suitably utilized'.[16]

In addition to these criticisms, the actions of the national theatre and orchestra made it clear that they did not welcome the addition of another new Israeli cultural institution. A longstanding feud emerged in Tel Aviv between the INO and the Habima Theatre, Israel's national theatre. The latter allowed the opera to rent their space for rehearsals and performances, but conflicts soon emerged over the agreement, and representatives from Habima eventually placed locks on the doors to prevent the opera from entering. The feud culminated in the autumn of 1953 when opera members 'were arrested on charges of breaking into the theatre illegally and of resisting police offers who asked them to vacate the hall.'[17] That the opera company did not have a proper rehearsal space is one matter. It was clear that the theatre did not want to help a competing institution in a climate where there were already minuscule resources.

To complicate matters further, a growing rivalry quickly developed between the opera and the famed Israel Philharmonic Orchestra (IPO), founded in 1936 by renowned Polish Jewish violinist Bronislaw Huberman. The orchestra refused to collaborate with or even acknowledge the importance of the new opera company. Israel-based and international music magazines and daily newspapers reporting on activities in Israel would also comment on the activities of the IPO, remarking on its cultural importance as it toured internationally.[18] This forced de Philippe to be on the defensive and required her in private letters and interviews in both Israel and the United States to argue continuously for the relevance of opera in Israel. Despite all her ambition and connections, de Philippe was never able to make the opera company as powerful or famous as Huberman did with the orchestra. This was due to several factors all working against the development of opera, including de Philippe's gender, lack of celebrity status, and an inability to create a compelling origin story on the same level as Huberman's orchestra.[19]

De Philippe frequently pointed out the opera's differing artistic goals in contrast to the IPO in letters and interviews. In one article, de Philippe complained that music critic Yohanan Boehm 'makes comparisons between Bronislaw Huberman and myself – stating that Huberman founded the Orchestra and retired, whereas I continued.'[20] Boehm criticised de Philippe's leadership, questioning why she did not retire, emphasising that Huberman had done so for the benefit of the orchestra.

De Philippe also noted that her company rejected the cooperative system used by the IPO where all musicians managed the orchestra through an appointed committee. For de Philippe, the cooperative system that the IPO and other Israeli theatres established was not suitable for her opera company. Although the opera company numbered some 120 individuals – including soloists, an orchestra, conductors, ballet, and technicians – de Philippe insisted that fresh talent and new people be brought in to replace other artists.[21] The majority of the members of her company were on fixed-term contracts. As she commented, 'I did not consider this principle [the cooperative system] suitable for art, since the cooperative system has a tendency to crystallise an ensemble by retaining members who may have outgrown their usefulness.'[22]

Although de Philippe saw the opera as distinct from the IPO, she believed that both institutions should be able to coexist and collaborate. Initially, she hoped that the IPO and the INO could recognise each other as institutions with similar artistic goals and thus be able to collaborate on occasion. But the IPO's leadership, which by 1947 had the American conductor Leonard Bernstein as its musical adviser, refused to see the opera as an equal partner from the beginning. De Philippe later wrote about her disappointment that she could not establish a formal partnership in an unpublished and unsent letter written sometime in the 1950s:

> when I founded the INO I had several meetings with the director of the IPO at that time for the purpose of negotiating a mutual agreement whereby the IPO would become the official orchestra of the Israel National Opera. The answer to this request was 'negative' – the I.P. orchestra will never go down to the pit to play for anyone, opera or any other art form.[23]

De Philippe accepted this explanation, assuming that the IPO regarded itself as an orchestral institution first and foremost and did not experiment with other musical endeavours. However, as the IPO developed as an institution, its position on cooperation with opera changed. In the 1960s, the IPO sought to collaborate with opera companies from the U.S. and Europe, much to de Philippe's chagrin. At the same time, the IPO continued to refuse to collaborate with the INO. There seem only two plausible interpretations for this refusal: the orchestra only wanted to collaborate with famous musicians from abroad, and it regarded the INO as mediocre. The INO regularly employed foreign opera singers from abroad but never invited a guest orchestra from abroad, as they had their own 'in-house' orchestra. De Philippe was rightfully hurt, and felt that the IPO brought 'opera groups to squelch our own company'.[24]

De Philippe felt that the IPO was not respecting her company. She firmly believed, however, that both institutions only stood to gain by supporting each other, given the broader circumstances in which the opera and the orchestra found themselves. 'The INO is not the greatest in the world. The IPO is also not the greatest. Let us both strive to be fine artistic institutions and let us all have a sense of ethics as well,' de Philippe wrote in an unpublished and unsent letter in the 1950s.[25] For de Philippe, cooperation between Israel's two leading musical institutions would promise to improve their musical level and reputation without intrigues. She was genuinely baffled by the orchestra's rejection and what she regarded as its lack of integrity. While she acknowledged there might be an artistic rivalry between the two groups, she could not understand why the orchestra planned to bring in opera singers from abroad: 'Why did they do that? They knew what my ambitions were.'[26]

Time and again, de Philippe fought explicitly and implicitly in private letters and published interviews against the image that she played second fiddle to the orchestra in Israel. De Philippe, moreover, never intended to attack the IPO's status as Israel's foremost musical institution. Ultimately, however, her dispute with the IPO and her statements about the orchestra did not impede her from pursuing her organisational plans and long-term goals for her opera company.

Edis de Philippe's Organisational Plans

Financial Support

Despite the financial and social advantages that her American connections gave her, de Philippe understood that in order for her to realise her artistic vision of an opera company of international standing in Israel she needed significant funding. When she first performed in Mandatory Palestine in 1945, there was not yet a state-supported cultural infrastructure to sustain her future company. De Philippe thus had to continuously solicit financial support for the new opera, writing letters to private donors in the United States for assistance and eventually asking the Israeli government for continued funding.

De Philippe's American background, therefore, potentially gave her better access to a wider range of music and business connections in the United States than her 'predecessor' Golinkin, who came to Mandatory Palestine from Soviet Russia. She constantly communicated with Jewish American donors, and travelled to the United States to raise adequate funds for her opera company. Although a great deal of initial funding apparently came from de Philippe's personal funds, private and public funding eventually came through. This included a number of Jewish philanthropic organisations, including 'the Friends of the Hebrew Opera, the Histadrut, the Jewish Agency, the Municipality of Tel Aviv, [and] the Norman Foundation in America'.[27]

In the post-war, post-Holocaust world of the late 1940s, de Philippe made her case for supporting the opera financially by nearly always framing its importance in national terms. Thus, her letters asking potential private donors for financial support were often written with a broad perspective in mind. They invoked the political situation as a sales pitch to get donors who might generally be unwilling to support a seemingly purely cultural cause to contribute, such as Israel's ten-year anniversary celebrations. In a letter dated 2 January 1958, de Philippe wrote to Meyer Weisgal (1894–1977), an important Jewish American artist, fundraiser, and Zionist activist who later served as president of Israel's Weizmann Institute of Science. She asked Weisgal to 'keep the opera in mind' while he was travelling in the United States to raise money for Israel's ten-year anniversary celebrations, and asked him to search not only for donors, but also for internationally famous singers who could perform.[28] In another letter, de Philippe contacted noted Jewish American philanthropist Samuel Rubin reminding him of the upcoming ten-year anniversary, asking him to 'do all in your power to see that the opera receives a fair budget to enable us to do the work we are so able to do.'[29] Despite her great efforts, de Philippe's goals for opera in Israel continuously faced financial limitations and she constantly had to write to potential donors for financial assistance.

De Philippe also connected with colleagues she had previously worked with outside of Israel, but these potential donors were often already committed to supporting the IPO financially. For example, de Philippe often wrote and maintained a regular correspondence with Michael Nyman, a British theatre director. She also asked him for help in raising money in Britain for Israel's ten-year anniversary: 'I do wish you could raise a real substantial amount so that we could be more liberal and do some wonderful performances', she wrote to Nyman in 1958.[30] Nyman informed de Philippe in an earlier 1957 letter that he had written to Lillie Schultz, head of the American Committee for Israel's Tenth Anniversary, but reveals that 'she wrote back to say that she could not undertake further work. A pity.'[31]. Nyman observed, 'The obvious people who could help me are already committed to help the Israel Philharmonic Orchestra. They're very well organised – but not to help us, unfortunately.'[32] De Philippe's grand vision for opera in Israel thus faced financial limitations as it proved a lengthy process to find donors, and at a time when her competitor, the IPO, seemed to have full control of benefactors.

De Philippe's constant financial struggle was clear when company members expressed frustration that the opera was not well managed and complained of not receiving enough payment. American tenor Paul Kiesgen (1941–2011), who later became a celebrated voice professor at Indiana University's Jacobs School of Music, was eager to move to Israel in 1967 in order to work at the company. However, he criticised de Philippe for the salary she offered, writing, 'I feel that you are very seriously underestimating our worth.'³³ American tenor James McCray (1938–2018) also expressed disappointment in the amount of compensation he would receive for performances.³⁴ The continuous complaints demonstrate that the INO was struggling financially. Furthermore, it suggests that those artists who decided to work at the INO did so not only for art's sake, but because they had a desire to support Israel.

The Search for Artists

De Philippe faced an unusual problem: there were only a few people available in Israel at this time who could staff and run a good opera, and she therefore had to search abroad for the theatre directors, artistic managers, conductors, and singers who helped form the opera company. The correspondence between de Philippe and the hundreds of musicians and opera-related people comprises literally thousands of letters, which are archived at Tel Aviv University. They provide an intimate portrait of a leader who ran the opera almost as a one-woman show. De Philippe's letters also provide a close-up view into understanding how she went about achieving her vision for the opera. Though often tedious in content, de Philippe's correspondence vividly demonstrates the vast amount of labour and patience needed to find and recruit the competent cast of singers and professionals needed for an opera company. In addition to artists, de Philippe maintained close contact with other professionals whom one would not immediately associate with opera companies, but who were nevertheless an essential component of the opera's infrastructure. These included music publishers, wig designers, and technicians. These additional sets of exchanges demonstrate further the enormous and multifaceted amount of labour that de Philippe devoted to creating the opera.³⁵

In their correspondence with de Philippe, American artists often expressed a desire to work for her new and evolving opera company, which was not yet hampered by organisational problems. For example, many letters were written during 1967 at the time of the Six-Day War.³⁶ Conductor Christofer Macatsoris, today the music director of the prestigious Academy of Vocal Arts in Philadelphia, wrote de Philippe about his great wish to work in Israel because of what he felt were artistic limitations in the United States: 'the type of repertory performed in the U.S. is a generally limited one. . . . The large companies lack a certain artistic direction.'³⁷ Like many artists writing to de Philippe, he believed that the new opera would allow more artistic opportunities. American Metropolitan Opera tenor William Olvis (1928–1998) wrote to de Philippe in 1967 to express his desire to perform a few times in Israel. At the time, Olvis was working and performing in Munich.³⁸ Letters like these indicate the attraction that the INO held for some Americans: an opera company in a new nation with a woman American director.

Edis de Philippe Faces the Music Critics

Edis de Philippe, like any opera director, faced both positive and negative reviews of the opera company in Israel and abroad. But a particularly negative review of the INO and de Philippe by the eminent German Israeli musicologist and music critic Peter Gradenwitz (1910–2001) stands out and resulted in a libel suit.³⁹ The review and de Philippe's fight for her reputation highlights the immense challenges de Philippe faced, not least through trying to keep her opera company intact as she tried to battle hostile critics. The review in question was published in August 1952 in *Commentary*, a magazine devoted to American politics and Jewish affairs.⁴⁰

In 'On the Horizon: Culture in Tel Aviv and Environs', Gradenwitz discussed the cultural landscape in Israel, focusing on the theatre, orchestra, and opera. He did not mince his words, criticising all three institutions for their own individual shortcomings. Although he praised the IPO for its high standard of playing, he bemoaned the lack of a permanent conductor. He commended the numerous theatres' attempts at high performances, but criticised the lack of decent theatre space. In his criticism of the INO, however, Gradenwitz stated that opera was 'a strange case'.[41] He acknowledged Golinkin's early role in bringing opera culture to Israel, but he claimed that de Philippe's subsequent company created an inhospitable environment. First, he bemoaned her musical skill, criticising her decision to perform works that were beyond her limited vocal range when she appeared as soloist at the INO during its initial years. In his description of the INO's production of *La Traviata* with de Philippe in the title role, he wrote:

> Israel then witnessed perhaps the strangest production of *La Traviata* that has ever been offered in an opera house, with a narrator in front of the curtain telling the story of the play in the omitted scenes ... and a solo violin replacing the protagonists in the famous arias.[42]

According to Gradenwitz, de Philippe 'simply did not have the high notes required [of] Violetta in the arias of these scenes.'[43] He also condemned that fact that she ruled the company alongside her second husband, Simcha Even-Zohar, a local politician who did not have any artistic background. For Gradenwitz, de Philippe led with 'a dictatorial policy, not to speak of the absence of any artistic enterprise.'[44]

That de Philippe became the target of Gradenwitz's attack, which went beyond any cogent cultural criticism, is for two reasons. First, it highlighted the tensions between the numerous influential immigrant groups in the new nation-state. Gradenwitz represented German Jewry at its finest, a student of eminent musicologist Curt Sachs. Based on his background and biography, it is easy to suspect that Gradenwitz could not imagine that an American figure with money, but without a 'great' German musical education, could successfully run an élite musical institution in Israel. Second, his harsh criticism perhaps reveals the underlying gender discrimination de Philippe constantly faced in the male-dominated classical music world, even if it was generally not explicitly articulated. Thus, de Philippe faced a double layer of bias from Gradenwitz: as both an American and a woman.

Grandenwitz's comments, although harsh, were not unusual. Besides his criticisms, media reporting on de Philippe reveals a woman who was often reminded of her second-class gender status, and that looks mattered more than brains. For example, newspaper articles, whether written by women or men, would sometimes focus on de Philippe's looks, describing the aging former opera singer in the late 1960s as a 'still beautiful woman'.[45] In another example, numerous unpublished letters to de Philippe would often address her as 'Mr. de Philippe' or 'Sir de Philippe' automatically assuming that, given the paucity of female opera directors, de Philippe would certainly be a man.[46] This occurred frequently, even when de Philippe had written to the correspondent first. Thus, although critics are an expected part of the music profession, it is not surprising to see that de Philippe faced more criticism given the pioneering nature of a woman opera leader in young Israel. Even at the time of her death, numerous obituaries acknowledged that de Philippe experienced too much criticism. For instance, Alexander Zvielli's obituary for *The Jerusalem Post* observed: 'She was criticized for being too good a singer, for being too good a stage manager and too good an actress to be a singer.'[47]

Conclusion

In his memoirs, James G. McDonald, recounted his delight when he attended one of the first productions by the INO in 1948. McDonald praised the American founder of the opera for her remarkable leadership: 'How Mme de Philippe managed to do so much and so well with such scanty means remains a wonder to me.'[48] McDonald, who served as America's first ambassador to Israel from 1948 to 1951, repeatedly mentioned the opera in his memoirs as his main form of entertainment in the young country. McDonald's comments highlight three points. First, he praises a fellow American who to his surprise – in part perhaps because she was a woman, in part presumably because it was in what seemed to be an 'operatic desert' – managed to put on an opera that artistically met or even exceeded his expectations. Second, he points to the difficult material situation in which the opera company had to operate. Third, his own visits indicate the kind of crowd that attended the INO's performances. As in leading opera houses in capital cities elsewhere, it attracted an audience in which diplomats and other dignitaries mingled and thus served as a cultural stage for local and international élites. The INO hence served in several ways as a potent national symbol of the new state, symbolising the aspirations of young Israel to be considered a member of the community of so-called 'cultured', 'respectable', and 'civilized' (i.e., Western) nation-states. These relations were very largely societal in nature, built and maintained by private citizens, but as Ambassador McDonald's testimony suggests, they were also taken note of, and appreciated by official representatives of the United States and Israel, such as diplomats and politicians.

McDonald's praise for de Philippe's work contrasts greatly to that of many music critics such as Gradenwitz. The latter was of course a musicologist, and thus applied different musical standards than McDonald. But this contrast demonstrates how criticism of de Philippe must be contextualised. The American ambassador was generous in his praise, partially because de Philippe was a fellow American who provided opera performances that served as an important source of soft power for the United States in Israel. On the other hand, Gradenwitz was influenced not only by his musical expertise, but perhaps also by the American cultural stereotypes he brought from Germany.

De Philippe really was a woman 'musical pioneer' in creating a new opera company. Her opera company lasted until 1982; a 34-year existence that lasted longer than Golinkin's opera, and that was quite remarkable given the opera's constant financial difficulties, criticism, and structural instability. De Philippe herself never returned permanently to the U.S., embracing Israel as her new home and dying there in 1978.[49] Despite the opera's end, her work as the INO's *impresario* is not just a story of difficulties and defeat. After all, she was for several decades at the head of Israel's national opera. In short, it was at least as much a success story, because she was able to stake out a position for herself in a location that some considered on the margins of the classical music world. Here, in Israel, the competition was not as intense, and here this hardworking and well-connected woman was able to succeed despite all the criticism.

Notes

1. The archives of the Israel National Opera (INO) are located at The Israeli Center for the Documentation of the Performing Arts (IDCPA) at Tel Aviv University.
2. Sarah Caldwell (1924–2006) of Missouri and Emma Carelli (1877–1928) of Italy were two other notable female opera impresarios. Susan Rutherford, "The Prima Donna as Opera Impresario: Emma Carelli and the Teatro Costanzi, 1911–1926," in *The Arts of the Prima Donna in the Long Nineteenth Century*, edited by Hilary Poriss and Rachel Cowgill (Oxford: Oxford University

Press, 2012), 272–89. On Carelli, see also Matteo Paoletti, "'She is a degenerate cocaine addict': Emma Carelli, A Diva-Impresaria Facing her Opponents" (Chapter 12 in the current volume).
3. Mandatory Palestine was a geopolitical region that existed between 1920 and 1948 in the Middle East. It was established by the League of Nations following the defeat of the Ottoman Empire in World War I, and was placed under British administration as a League of Nations mandate.
4. The Kherson oblast (province) was part of the Russian Empire when Golinkin was born.
5. In particular, he was interested in creating classical music institutions that were influenced by Russian institutions. See the work of James Loeffler for an understanding of music in Russian Jewish life: James B. Loeffler, *The Most Musical Nation: Jews and Culture in the Late Russian Empire* (New Haven, CT: Yale University Press, 2010).
6. Mordechai Golinkin, "A Hebrew National Theatre in Palestine," in *The Temple of Art Tel-Aviv* (Tel Aviv: Pro Opera Building, 1927), 9–27. Although first written in 1918, it was only later published in 1927 in Tel Aviv in Hebrew and English.
7. A second serious, albeit smaller, attempt to create a national opera house in Mandatory Palestine was made during World War Two by the Latvian-born, German-trained composer and conductor Marc Lavry (1903–1967) and Prague-born conductor George Singer (1908–1980). The 'Palestine Folk Opera' was founded in 1940 and in 1945, when de Philippe first came to Mandatory Palestine, the Folk Opera was about to shut down.
8. Anonymous, "A Gala Performance and a New Star," *The Washington Times*, January 30, 1936, 121.1.2, Tel Aviv University (TAU) Music Archives.
9. "Muy Suntuoso Programa COCA COLA los Martes en XEW," *Radiolandia: El Noticiero del Radio*, November 30, 1938, 121.1.8, TAU Music Archives.
10. Dora Sowden, "Opera in Israel," *Jewish Affairs*, July 1968, 27. 121.1.6, TAU Music Archives.
11. The Jewish Agency is a non-profit organisation established in 1929 with the purpose of supporting Jewish immigration to then-Mandatory Palestine and from 1948 to Israel.
12. Her second husband, Simcha Even-Zochar, was Secretary of the Executive Committee of the Histadrut, Israel's national trade union organisation.
13. Owen S. Rachleff, "Opera in the Promised Land," *Opera News*, June 1973, n.p.
14. Dorothy Townsend, "Soprano Here on Visit Tells of Founding Opera in Israel," *Los Angeles Times*, November 6, 1955, 6, 121.1.7, TAU Music Archives.
15. "Edis de Philippe: Founder and Directress of the INO," Undated and Unpublished Biographical Data, 2, 121.1.1, TAU Music Archives.
16. Ada Oren, "Inside Israel: Musical Culture in Israel," *The Sentinel*, March 9, 1950, 10.
17. Anonymous, "Habimah-Israel Opera Feud Still Continues," *The American Jewish World*, October 9, 1953, 8. The feud resolved, but by 1956 the INO was in search of a permanent home. In 1958, the INO moved into its permanent home at the Kessem Cinema building in Tel Aviv until the company folded.
18. Anonymous, "Israel Philharmonic Orchestra Coming to U.S. in January '51," *The American Jewish World*, January 27, 1950, 2; Anonymous, "Israel Philharmonic, Soviet Orchestra in Cultural Exchange," *Bnai Brith Messenger*, July 1, 1966, 12.
19. Most of the musicians in the then Palestine Orchestra's early years were musicians who had fled Nazi Germany.
20. Edis de Philippe, "National Opera Chief Replies to *Post* Critic: Charges Are 'Arrogant and Fantastic,'" Says Edis de Philippe," *The Jerusalem Post*, October 20, 1966, n.p.
21. Edis de Philippe, "Opera in Israel," *WIZO in Israel*, January/February 1949, n.p.
22. De Philippe, "Opera in Israel," *WIZO in Israel*.
23. Edis de Philippe, "Why the IPO Should Not Give (?) Opera," Undated Letter 1950s, Tel Aviv University Music Archives, 121.1.9.
24. Ibid.
25. Ibid.
26. Proteus, "Operatic Israel," *Midstream: A Monthly Jewish Review* XX, no. 6 (June/July 1974): 82.
27. Edis de Philippe, "Opera in Israel," *WIZO in Israel* II, no. 6 (January/February 1949): n.p.
28. Edis de Philippe, "Letter to Meyer Weisgal" (January 2, 1958), TAU Music Archives, 44.8.247.
29. Edis de Philippe, "Letter to Samuel Rubin" (November 5, 1957), TAU Archives, 44.8.247.
30. Edis de Philippe, "Letter to Michael Nyman" (January 12, 1958), TAU Archives, 44.8.247.
31. Michael Nyman, "Letter to Edis de Philippe" (December 20, 1957), TAU Archives, 44.8.247.
32. Michael Nyman, "Letter to Edis de Philippe" (December 4, 1957), TAU Archives, 44.8.247.

33. Paul Kiesgen, "Letter to Edis de Philippe" (August 10, 1967), TAU Archives, 44.8.247.
34. James McCray, "Letter to Edis de Philippe" (June 28, 1966), TAU Archives, 44.8.247.
35. Edis de Philippe, "Letter to Michael Nyman" (January 19, 1958), TAU Archives, 44.8.247. Despite having some administrative support, the archives show that de Philippe still took on a lot of administrative responsibilities.
36. The Six-Day War (also known as the June War) was a war between Israel and various Arab countries that lasted from June 5 to 10, 1967.
37. Christofer Macatsoris, "Letter to Edis de Philippe" (July 15, 1967), TAU Archives, 44.8.232.
38. William Olvis, "Letter to Edis de Philippe" (February 2, 1967), TAU Archives. 44.8.232.
39. Gradenwitz was a crucial figure in the cultural world of Israel who was influential in swaying the minds of those in Israel. He studied with the most renowned musicologists and composers in Freiburg and Berlin, but his forced emigration from Nazi Germany led him eventually to teach at the musicology department of Tel Aviv University. Despite his influence, there is to date no study on the life of this important figure.
40. *Commentary* was founded by the American Jewish Committee (AJC) in 1945. The AJC, founded in 1906, is a Jewish advocacy group devoted to human and civil rights.
41. Peter Gradenwitz, "On the Horizon Culture in Tel Aviv and Environs," *Commentary* 14, no. 2 (August 1, 1952): 172.
42. Ibid.
43. Ibid.
44. Gradenwitz, "On the Horizon Culture in Tel Aviv and Environs," 173.
45. Dora Sowden, "Opera in Israel," *Jewish Affairs* (July 1968): 27.
46. G. Shirmer Inc. NYC Publisher, "Letter to Edis de Philippe" (November 30, 1962), TAU Archives, 44.8.247.
47. Alexander Zvielli, "Edis de Philippe: Grande Dame of Israeli Opera," *The Jerusalem Post*, July 17, 1978, n.p.
48. James G. McDonald, *My Mission in Israel: 1948–1951* (London: Victor Gollancz Ltd., 1951), 148.
49. After de Philippe's death, Simcha Even-Zohar took over leadership of the INO until lack of funding caused it to close in 1982.

Bibliography

Primary Sources

"A Gala Performance and a New Star." *The Washington Times*, January 30, 1936, 121.1.2, TAU Music Archives.

de Philippe, Edis. "Opera in Israel." *WIZO in Israel* II, No. 6 (January/February 1949).

———. "Why the IPO Should Not Give (?) Opera." Undated Letter 1950s, Tel Aviv University (TAU) Music Archives, 121.1.9.

———. "Letter to Samuel Rubin." November 5, 1957, TAU Music Archives, 44.8.247.

———. "Letter to Meyer Weisgal." January 2, 1958a, TAU Music Archives, 44.8.247.

———. "Letter to Michael Nyman." January 12, 1958b, TAU Music Archives, 44.8.247.

———. "Letter to Michael Nyman." January 19, 1958c, TAU Music Archives, 44.8.247.

———. "National Opera Chief Replies to *Post* Critic: Charges Are 'Arrogant and Fantastic,' Says Edis de Philippe." *Jerusalem Post*, October 20, 1966, n.p.

"Edis de Philippe: Founder and Directress of the INO." Undated and Unpublished Biographical Data, pp. 1–4, 121.1.1, TAU Music Archives.

G. Shirmer Inc., NYC Publisher. "Letter to Edis de Philippe." November 30, 1962, TAU Music Archives, 44.8.247.

Golinkin, Mordecai. "A Hebrew National Theatre in Palestine." In *The Temple of Art Tel-Aviv*. Tel Aviv: Pro Opera Building, 1927.

Gradenwitz, Peter. "On the Horizon Culture in Tel Aviv and Environs." *Commentary* 14, no. 2 (August 1, 1952): 170–74.

"Habimah-Israel Opera Feud Still Continues." *The American Jewish World*, October 9, 1953, 8.

"Israel Philharmonic Orchestra Coming to U.S. in January '51." *The American Jewish World*, January 27, 1950, 2.

"Israel Philharmonic, Soviet Orchestra in Cultural Exchange." *Bnai Brith Messenger*, July 1, 1966, 12.
Kiesgen, Paul. "Letter to Edis de Philippe." August 10, 1967, TAU Music Archives, 44.8.247.
Macatsoris, Christofer. "Letter to Edis de Philippe." July 15, 1967, TAU Music Archives, 44.8.232.
McCray, James. "Letter to Edis de Philippe." June 28, 1966, TAU Music Archives, 44.8.247.
McDonald, James G. *My Mission in Israel: 1948–1951*. London: Victor Gollancz Ltd., 1951.
"Muy Suntuoso Programa COCA COLA los Martes en XEW." *Radiolandia: El Noticiero del Radio*, November 30, 1938, 121.1.8, TAU Music Archives.
Nyman, Michael. "Letter to Edis de Philippe." December 4, 1957a, TAU Music Archives, 44.8.247.
———. "Letter to Edis de Philippe." December 20, 1957b, TAU Music Archives, 44.8.247.
Olvis, William. "Letter to Edis de Philippe." February 2, 1967, TAU Music Archives, 44.8.232.
Oren, Ada. "Inside Israel: Musical Culture in Israel." *The Sentinel*, March 9, 1950, 10.
Proteus. "Operatic Israel." *Midstream: A Monthly Jewish Review* XX, no. 6 (June/July 1974): 80–84.
Rachleff, Owen S. "Opera in the Promised Land." *Opera News*, June 1973.
Sowden, Dora. "Opera in Israel." *Jewish Affairs*, July 1968, 27. 121.1.6, TAU Music Archives.
Townsend, Dorothy. "Soprano Here on Visit Tells of Founding Opera in Israel." *Los Angeles Times*, November 6, 1955, 6, 121.1.7, TAU Music Archives.
Zvielli, Alexander. "Edis de Philippe: Grande Dame of Israeli Opera." *The Jerusalem Post*, July 17, 1978, n.p.

Secondary Sources

Loeffler, James B. *The Most Musical Nation: Jews and Culture in the Late Russian Empire*. New Haven, CT: Yale University Press, 2010.
Rutherford, Susan. "The Prima Donna as Opera Impresario: Emma Carelli and the Teatro Costanzi, 1911–1926." In *The Arts of the Prima Donna in the Long Nineteenth Century*, edited by Hilary Poriss and Rachel Cowgill, 272–89. Oxford: Oxford University Press, 2012.

16
ODALINE DE LA MARTINEZ – CONDUCTOR, COMPOSER, ENTREPRENEUR, LEADER[1]

Carola Darwin

Leadership is a much-discussed concept. A brief internet search gives access to videos, podcasts, books, courses, and companies all vying for attention and claiming to support and inspire would-be leaders. Recently, there has also been a growing interest in the particular challenges faced by women as leaders, inspiring books such as Harvard Business Review's *On Women and Leadership* and Sheryl Sandberg's *Lean In*.[2] Conducting, meanwhile, is a peculiarly public form of leadership. Apart from politicians, few other leaders are expected to stand on a podium and exercise their leadership skills on a group of adults in full view of the public. Plenty of what a conductor does also takes place behind closed doors, of course: negotiating contracts, preparing scores, and rehearsing, for example. Nonetheless, conductors are uniquely judged on their ability to lead in public and in the moment. Even a politician is only partly judged by his or her speeches. Despite the huge literature on leadership in general, however, there is relatively little written on conducting as a form of leadership. Much of a conductor's training is done aurally and through example and experience,[3] and where conducting texts discuss leadership, it is generally in the context of 'rehearsal technique', which is, as will become clear, only a part of the way in which an influential conductor can lead.[4] What, then, can be learned about conducting, and about the challenges for female conductors, by considering conducting as a form of leadership?

To explore the question, this chapter focuses on the conducting career of Odaline de la Martinez (b.1949). As the founder and director of the ensemble Lontano, she is famous as the first woman ever to conduct a complete BBC Prom on 20th August 1984,[5] and has also had a significant career as a guest conductor for orchestras around the world. To understand her career, I held a series of interviews in 2019 with the conductor herself and several musicians who have worked with her, most of them for many years. These interviews focused on Martinez's qualities as a conductor and as a musical entrepreneur and collaborator and were given context by a search of reviews and interviews in the press and other journals. The preliminary interview with Martinez herself was followed up in 2020 with further discussion. This focused on the conductor as leader, drawing on ideas from well-established writers on leadership in business.[6]

After a brief description of Martinez's career, this chapter discusses three aspects of leadership that emerged from the interviews: communication, tenacity, and inspiration.[7] The section

DOI: 10.4324/9781003024767-18

on communication starts with the most central type of leadership for conductors: the ability to communicate musical ideas and decisions, both in discussion in rehearsal and through gesture during the actual playing of the music. It also considers the expectations and boundaries that a conductor needs to establish if performances are to be successful. Secondly, under tenacity, I consider the challenges to successful leadership that any conductor faces, and the personal qualities that can help to overcome them. This section also discusses the particular difficulties that Martinez has grappled with as a woman conductor. Finally, the section on inspiration looks at leadership in conducting on the larger and longer-term scale: the ability to inspire others with the conductor's own vision, the importance of building a team, and opportunities for mentoring and inspiring others.

Career

Odaline de la Martinez was born in Cuba in 1949, but was sent to the USA after the Bay of Pigs invasion in 1961.[8] She studied at Tulane University in New Orleans and in 1972 came to the Royal Academy of Music (RAM) in London,[9] where she studied composition with Paul Patterson.[10] While still a student at the RAM, she founded the ensemble Lontano, which she has conducted ever since. She describes how she immediately felt that conducting was for her: 'something inside me felt complete for the first time. It was like my body and my brain were really in sync.'[11]

Her work with Lontano led to her first opportunities with major orchestras. In an interview for the *Kapralova Society Journal*, she described it like this:

> on a Friday, while visiting Andrew Kurowski, then a young BBC producer, about putting together a program with Lontano for Radio 3, I received a phone call from David Byers, the producer of BBC Northern Ireland. Apparently, the senior conductor of the BBC Northern Ireland Symphony had become ill at the last minute and they were desperately looking for someone to replace him. Was I free the whole of the next week? Whether I was or not, I became free. The BBC Music Library in London delivered the scores to me and I spent the whole weekend learning them. I clearly recall studying between rehearsals, during my lunch hours and back in the hotel. As soon as the radio recordings came out, I was invited to work with all the BBC orchestras and then with other orchestras. I haven't looked back since.[12]

Since then, as well as that first Prom, she has conducted orchestras on five continents,[13] formed two other orchestras (the London Chamber Symphony and the European Women's Orchestra), and premiered many operas, including Nicola LeFanu's *Dream Hunter*[14] and Berthold Goldschmidt's *Beatrice Cenci*.[15] She has also organised a number of music festivals, including a festival of Latin-American music on the South Bank in London in 1989,[16] and a festival of American music at the Warehouse in Theed Street biennially since 2006.[17] She has received many awards, both as a composer and a conductor.[18]

Martinez's work with Lontano has been at the centre of her career from the beginning. Founded with the flautist Ingrid Culliford (a fellow RAM student) in 1976, Lontano's work was driven by its conductor's belief that there was good music that deserved to be heard and that wasn't being performed, particularly contemporary music, music of the Americas and, a little later, music by women.[19] A particular passion for Martinez has been the English composer Ethel Smyth, whose work she has edited, performed, and recorded.[20] As well as conducting a huge range of repertoire, she has also been responsible for many commissions by composers such as Silvina Milstein, Erika Fox, and Anthony Gilbert.[21] The composer Nicola LeFanu said: 'Several of my most important pieces owe their life to her. So, for example, she commissioned *The Old Woman of Beare*, which is probably my best work.'[22]

Communication

In an interview, Martinez described the essential qualities to bring to conducting as warmth, enthusiasm, and a belief in the music (OdlM 2020). She considers herself 'lucky' because, as a guest conductor, she has generally been asked to conduct music that she likes and believes in. She sees her most important task as understanding the music and the composer's style and then communicating her understanding to the orchestra. In order to develop this understanding, as well as studying the score, Martinez listens to recordings and reads widely and deeply.[23]

Rhythmic clarity is particularly important to Martinez as a conductor; for her 'rhythm . . . makes or breaks a piece of music' (OdlM 2020). In our conversations, she described how her childhood in Cuba exposed her to the Afro-Cuban tradition of drumming:

> I remember going to sleep many nights with the really hypnotic sound of this Afro-Cuban drumming playing and [then] waking up really early in the morning when it stopped. And I think this has helped me to develop a really good sense of rhythm.
>
> (OdlM 2020)

As an example of this sense, she pointed out that a triplet is much more rhythmic if you hear it against two quavers in your head, rather than just within one crochet.[24]

When I asked the musicians who had worked with Martinez what they felt her qualities as a conductor were, they commented particularly on the absolute clarity of her conducting and the accuracy of her musical ear. The composer Nicola LeFanu, who has a long-standing association with Lontano, said: 'She's got a wonderful ear for pitch, but she's [also] got a fantastic sense of rhythm. And I think that's very obvious in what she does.' Natalie Bleicher, a pianist and composer, said:[25]

> She's a fabulous conductor. There's absolutely never any question about where the beat is, or what the expression is. And it's a real pleasure to watch someone who is that good at conducting, because not all conductors are that good.[26]

Several members of Lontano have played in the group for more than 20 years, and that loyalty is reflected in comments about Martinez's ability to get the best out of the players. Andrew Sparling, longstanding clarinetist with Lontano, said: 'I like working with conductors who make me play better than I think I can, and she's like that.'[27]

Clarity and rigour are seen by Martinez as central to her style as a conductor. She described her rehearsals as 'really rigorous. I like to rehearse really intensely, clearly, and quickly, and I engage with the details. . . . I work the musicians really hard' (OdlM 2020). However, she also makes sure that her conducting doesn't seem arbitrary: 'I try to explain how I envisage the music with the particular demands that I make,' she said, and 'I try to inspire, rather than dictate' (OdlM 2020). She knows what she wants to achieve and is happy to stop once she feels the orchestra has got there. 'When [the musicians] have figured out how to do it, and we do it really well, they can often go home early.' (OdlM 2020)

These qualities have also been reflected, to a very large extent, by reviews of her performances and recordings. As so much of the repertoire that she conducts isn't well-known, many reviews of her work limit their comments on her conducting to a few words. These are almost invariably positive and tend to mention the precision and energy of her conducting:

Odaline de la Martinez conducted with assured precision and momentum, injected [*sic*] rhythmic verve into the folkish patterns of the second movement.
(Malcolm Miller, 'Lipkin's Oboe Concerto', Tempo, 1991)[28]

The BBC Philharmonic under Odaline de la Martinez has salt spray coursing through its veins. Conflicting passages surge menacingly, yet balance with the solo voices is exemplary (if occasionally hard on the Huddersfield Choral Society) so that words come across with fine clarity.
(Robert Anderson, 'Ethel Smyth: The Wreckers' (Review)
The Musical Times, 1995).[29]

Conductor Odaline de la Martinez has a long-established understanding of Nicola LeFanu's evocative sound world . . . There was an unmistakable air of authority in her interpretation of the score of *Dream Hunter*, and she drew out sensitive and atmospheric playing from the chamber ensemble of seven instrumental players from her new music group Lontano.
(Paul Conway, 'Arts Centre, Aberystwyth:
Nicola LeFanu's "Dream Hunter"', Tempo, 2012)[30]

Occasionally, though, Martinez's clarity has been seen as a problem:

Her metronomic stance was a barrier to communication and the players' engagement was visibly and audibly more dynamic without her.
(Rian Evans 'Lontano/De La Martinez',
The Guardian, 2010)[31]

Martinez herself is conscious that she can 'come across as very demanding' (OdlM 2020). She said:

I can be very determined and straightforward . . . and being a woman that determination can seem a bit autocratic. [But] musicians tell me they prefer to know where they stand. Every time I say, 'I hope I haven't been too demanding,' and they say, 'no, no, we like to know where we stand.' I have softened some over the years, but I'm the same person.'
(OdlM 2020)

Martinez expects her musicians to have tried out the music beforehand (which is by no means always expected of orchestral players) and is clear about correcting mistakes: 'If I hear the mistake once I leave it, but if I hear it twice, I say something' (OdlM 2020). However, if she does need to make a boundary clear, she tries to avoid doing it in public:

I expect . . . musicians in Lontano to have looked at the music before we rehearse. And it's really easy, from the very first, to hear who hasn't looked at it. And I let them know, not then and there but . . . later on, that they should go and look at the music . . . As a result, when my musicians come to the rehearsal, they've looked at it.
(OdlM 2020)

She is careful, too, to schedule plenty of time for rehearsals, so that everything can be covered properly (OdlM 2020).

The ability to communicate with the musicians you are conducting is clearly a crucial skill for conductors, whether it is through gesture during the music, or in words, as part of the rehearsal process. Martinez sees this as an essential part of her job. 'The psychology of talking to musicians is very important – if they like you, they will do much for you. If they don't like you then you've got an uphill battle' (OdlM 2019). Meanwhile, Nicola LeFanu commented on the challenge this can present: 'You're making music with human beings, and you've got to be able to connect, . . . not just with the famous first violin, but with the bolshy second trombone (or vice versa!).'[32]

Writing on leadership focuses on a variety of communication skills as central to successful leading. For example, Herminia Ibarra and Otilia Obodaru cite a number of these skills as part of their 'Critical Components of Leadership', which include 'energizing', 'designing and aligning', and 'rewarding and feedback'.[33] The warmth and enthusiasm which Martinez tries to bring to her work (and which are very evident in interviews) are part of the crucial 'energizing' ability, with which a leader encourages and motivates others. Her rigorous approach to rehearsal, and to correcting mistakes, helps to align the musicians' playing to her idea of the music. Her insistence on adequate rehearsal time is another way that she 'designs and aligns', setting up structures which ensure that she achieves her goal of a successful performance.

I will discuss in more detail how Martinez fosters a sense of a team and of the overall goals that she is working towards in the section dedicated to 'Inspiration'. First, however, I will consider the challenges that she has faced, both those that might be experienced by any conductor, and those that are particularly an issue for women.

Tenacity

The first time I interviewed Martinez, she was in the middle of rehearsals for the week-long Festival of American Music at the Warehouse in Theed Street, near Waterloo (London). I was struck by how, as well as conducting almost every concert, she was concerned with so many details of the festival, from arranging complimentary tickets to making sure the lighting for her opera *Imoinda* enabled the cast to see her conducting. Lontano is an ensemble made up of freelance musicians who work for a range of groups, and decisions about who to engage for a particular concert, though sometimes delegated to musicians that she trusts, are also ultimately Martinez's responsibility.[34]

One of the main challenges, of course, is funding her projects. Although she has not always raised funding alone, for most of her projects, she has been the driving force. The Festival of American Music 2019 was funded by: The Amphion Foundation, The D'Oyly Carte Charitable Trust, The Alice M. Ditson Fund of Columbia University, The John S. Cohen Foundation, The Hinrichsen Foundation, The PRS Foundation, The RVW Trust, and The Royal Victoria Hall Foundation.[35] Each of these names corresponds to many hours of thought and form-filling. The musicians who work with Martinez are very much aware of this aspect of her work. Caroline Balding, the first violinist with Lontano for many years, described her admiration at the 'amazing' way that Martinez has kept the group going for so long, while retaining her enthusiasm and musical integrity. There is so much 'donkey-work' to do, Balding explained, beyond what happens in the concert hall or in the recording studio.

> It's so hard to get anything done these days, to raise the money . . . everybody's fighting over the last few coppers at the bottom of the pot. . . . She's a very, very hardworking person.[36]

Martinez herself considers that having moved from Cuba to America as a child of 11, as well as from America to England as a young woman, gave her 'a real sense of overcoming obstacles.'[37] She describes her own tenacity: 'if I believe something should be done, and it needs doing, I'll stick with it till it happens' (OdlM 2020). This determination fits well with the classic business text *Good to Great*, which describes the best kind of leadership as including 'ferocious resolve, an almost stoic ability to do whatever needs to be done.'[38]

Many writers on leadership emphasise the importance of resilience: the ability to bounce back from setbacks and deal with criticism, accepting that one will make mistakes. In *Dare to Lead*, Brené Brown describes it like this:

> If we don't have the skills to get back up, we may not risk falling. And if we're brave enough often enough, we are definitely going to fall. The research participants who have the highest levels of resilience can get back up after a fall, and they are more courageous and tenacious as a result of it.[39]

Martinez is philosophical about mistakes: 'I accept that everyone always makes mistakes. I make them all the time. . . . But I think that mistakes are really important because they help you to get better' (OdlM 2020). Similarly, she tries to take bad reviews in her stride, accepting that reviewing is a highly subjective business.[40]

> If they're good you keep them, if they're bad you let them go. But there are some reviewers who are good, and you should pay attention to them . . . If it sounds as if it comes from someone who doesn't know what they're talking about, just let it go.
> *(OdlM 2020)*

As a woman conductor who started working in the early 1980s, when women conductors were extremely rare, Martinez has faced an extra set of challenges. Although she always knew that she wanted to conduct,[41] Martinez is clear that initially she struggled to make her way, and that some of that struggle was because she was a woman. 'It was very uphill at one time, incredibly up-hill,' she said, giving an example from 'the early days that I started conducting orchestras':

> I remember a guy in the back of the cellos . . . who started shouting, 'I'm not going to be told what to do by a woman'. And it was a major . . . orchestra, I'm not going to say who it was, which orchestra. But I was surprised that they would let someone like that stay. Today that wouldn't happen at all.
> *(OdlM 2019)*

Martinez felt that 'in the early days, women weren't allowed to be firm and strong,' (OdlM 2020) and so the strong leadership that she has always tried to offer wasn't always appreciated. She is conscious of trying to strike a balance:

> As a woman on the podium . . . talking loudly, almost shouting, is not acceptable. You try to do it with a kind of charisma . . . . I will not flirt, that's ridiculous. But you have to have a sense of charisma and identity.
>
> (OdlM 2020)

The problem of talking like a leader without behaving unacceptably as a woman is well-established as a challenge for women in all forms of leadership. As Alice H. Eagly and Linda L. Carli have commented:

> Kim Campbell, who briefly served as the prime minister of Canada in 1993, described the tension that results: 'I don't have a traditional female way of speaking . . . I'm quite assertive. If I didn't speak the way I do, I wouldn't have been seen as a leader. But my way of speaking may have grated on people who were not used to hearing it from a woman. It was the right way for a leader to speak, but it wasn't the right way for a woman to speak. It goes against the type.'[42]

Some descriptions of Martinez's work in the 1990s also reflect this underlying unease with women's leadership; for example, in the patronising tone of this announcement, which appeared in *The Musical Times* in February 1994: 'Girls come out to play in next month's Women in Music festival at venues across London. Directed by conductor (conductoress?) Odaline de la Martinez.'[43]

Martinez is clear that the situation has improved in recent years, not least because there are now significantly more women in the orchestras that she conducts.[44] She feels that this has helped her style of communication to be accepted, in contrast to her earlier experience, when orchestras were almost all men.[45] It is interesting, however, that, as well as the importance she sees in being 'firm and strong', she also values a more cooperative approach, seeing what she does as 'sharing' and 'making music together' with the musicians she is directing (OdlM 2020).

The gradual increase in the number of women working in music has clearly helped Martinez, but so has her willingness to learn, both from her own mistakes and from the musicians she has encountered over the years. When I asked her who had helped her most in her career, she started with the composers whose works she loves, including J.S. Bach, George Crumb, Ethel Smyth, and then moved on to her teachers of piano, composition, and conducting in the USA and Britain.[46] Martinez seems not to have been adversely affected by the comparative lack of female mentors or role models. She is aware, however, of the importance of being willing to learn and be helped, as well as of resilience and tenacity. Asked what advice she would give to an aspiring female conductor, she replied: 'You'll find a lot of people along the way will help you. Keep getting your feet wet and getting your fingers burned . . . And then someone will help you move forward' (OdlM 2020).

Inspiration

Martinez's original aim in founding Lontano – to perform good music that needs and deserves to be heard – has continued to drive and inspire her work. As she puts it:

> When I was a student in Tulane University, my undergraduate school, someone who knew me quite a bit said, 'You're either going to be a missionary nun or a revolutionary.' . . . If I believe in something, I push it. I wasn't a missionary nun, but I'm on a mission.
>
> *(OdlM 2019)*

This sense of mission is a central component in descriptions of successful leadership. In their 'Critical Components of Leadership', Ibarra and Obodaru highlight qualities such as 'envisioning', 'empowering', and 'team-building', which are all about the ability to imagine a change for the better, and to find ways to get others to see and welcome that vision and then work together to achieve it.[47]

The musicians in Lontano are central to what Martinez has achieved. The ensemble started as a group of students at the RAM, and although inevitably many of the original players have been replaced over the years, there is a central core of about 30 musicians who are established members. She tries to encourage a sense of openness in rehearsal, where any member of the ensemble is welcome to ask questions, in contrast to many other orchestras, where questions are fed through the leader of each section (OdlM 2020). She also works hard to make the musicians feel appreciated:

> I give a lot of kudos to the leader, Caroline Balding . . .. She's a great leader – she knows how to speak to people diplomatically, much more diplomatically than me. I also encourage everyone to feel part of the team, and . . . tell them how much I value them.
>
> *(OdlM 2020)*

The sense of a team is also fostered by social occasions such as Christmas or summer parties and drinks after long days of recording. During the Coronavirus lockdown, when meeting was impossible, Martinez kept in touch by WhatsApp and email.

Martinez's vision of collaboration and support extends beyond Lontano to other musicians that she believes in. Pianist and composer Natalie Bleicher said:

> She's been very supportive to people, particularly women, and people from ethnic minorities, who tend to get overlooked still, unfortunately. She's dedicated a lot of her career to championing female composers, both dead and alive, and spotting them. Spotting people and believing in them.[48]

Martinez isn't ashamed to network to achieve her aims.

> Networking is really important – it's all about relationships. There has to be honesty on both sides . . . but you can still be friends. [And] perhaps in the process of that friendship, they begin to recognise your value.
>
> *(OdlM 2020)*

And this networking is also a way of keeping what she does 'outward facing', enabling her to, as Ibarra and Obodura describe it, 'test new ideas pragmatically against current resources . . . and work with others to figure out how to realize the desired future.'[49]

Her belief in the power and importance of good music has led Martinez to a number of initiatives beyond her work as a conductor. In 1992, she founded LORELT (Lontano Records Ltd), as a way of ensuring that valuable recordings did not disappear.

> I founded LORELT because I thought it was really important . . . [I kept seeing] living composers and contemporary composers being released on CD, and then finding that they were deleted . . . And I decided that I wanted a company that would never delete. And that would promote those that really needed to be heard.
>
> *(OdlM 2019)*

Through the Mornington Trust, Martinez has also organised workshops and concerts involving musicians from Lontano, schoolchildren from communities in South and East London, and musicians from Roma communities in the same areas. The two communities had initially been very mistrustful of each other, but the performances really helped to encourage understanding and combat prejudice and bad feelings (OdlM 2020).

Recently, Martinez had the opportunity to widen her sphere of influence in a different way. In January 2020, she co-curated a festival of music by women at the Juilliard School in New York. Focusing on composers of the twentieth century, it saw performances of music by 37 female composers from all over the world, including Romania (Myriam Marbé), Korea (Young-Ja Lee), Australia (Margaret Sutherland), and Russia (Sofia Gubaidulina), as well as the USA and Canada, and most Western European countries.[50]

While Lontano is a team that recognises Martinez as its leader, the orchestras that she has conducted elsewhere are already bonded as a group but need to be confident of the conductor's ability to lead. Martinez sees her enthusiasm and her belief in the music as the most important quality she brings to her work.[51] Nonetheless she recognises that this love for the repertoire she conducts can also make things harder when she encounters negative attitudes and prejudice. As she commented:

> An example is when I was doing [Ethel Smyth's] *The Wreckers* for the Proms. There was one particular singer, who was [a] very well known man, and . . . he started calling [the piece] 'Women's Institute Music' . . . He did it in front of the other musicians . . . it was so disrespectful to the composer.
>
> *(OdlM 2020)*

This belief in the music is clearly central to Martinez's success and to her identity, despite the difficulties it may sometimes cause. In writing on leadership, Herminia Ibarra, Robin Ely, and Deborah Kolb describe this as 'anchoring in purpose', which:

> enables women to redirect their attention towards shared goals and to consider what they need to be and what they need to learn in order to achieve their goals. Instead of defining themselves in relation to gender stereotypes . . . female leaders can focus on behaving in ways that advance the purposes for which they stand.[52]

Martinez confirmed this in the interviews:

> It's really funny because I never thought that I was a woman composing, or a woman conducting, or a woman putting on concerts; I was just a person. And it's the other people who look and see a woman, and that's where they either accept you or they don't.
>
> *(OdlM 2019)*

This is not only the case for women. In *Good to Great*, Jim Collins suggests that great leaders are 'incredibly ambitious – but their ambition is first and foremost for the institution, not themselves.'[53] In other words, successful leaders care about and believe in the thing that they are trying to create (a company, an ensemble, a concert series, a performance of a piece of music) rather than focusing on themselves and their career.

I asked Martinez whether she saw herself as ambitious, and her answer mirrored this exactly:

> I really believe in making a difference . . . and the better known you are, the more of a difference you can make . . . You want to be ambitious to be respected and better known, so people will actually pay attention to what you have to say . . . But always in the things you believe in. You have to really believe deeply in those things, otherwise it doesn't work.
>
> *(OdlM 2020)*

This confidence in the value of what she does stems ultimately from a faith that if good music is performed well, its worth will be recognised. Her success is evidence of her ability to recognise good music and do justice to it in performance. And above all, it demonstrates her commitment to the music she loves. That commitment is the foundation on which Martinez has built her leadership: the clarity of her communication, her tenacity in dealing with difficulties and setbacks, and her ability to inspire others with her vision. I asked Odaline de la Martinez how she would like to be remembered, and this was her answer:

> I really love music. I really love making music, whether it's writing it or conducting it or promoting it . . . If people say 'she really loved music' that's a very good thing to say.
>
> *(OdlM 2019)*

I hope she gets her wish.

Notes

1. With grateful thanks to: Nicola LeFanu (Composer), Natalie Murray Beale (Conductor), Natalie Bleicher (Piano and Composer), Andrew Sparling (Clarinet), Caroline Balding (Violin), Monika Pietras (RCM Library), Trevor Herbert and the Musicology Discussion Forum at the RCM, and of course Odaline de la Martinez.
2. No editor given, *On Women and Leadership HBR's 10 Must Reads* (Boston, MA: Harvard Business Review Press, 2019); Sheryl Sandberg with Nell Scovell, *Lean In: Women, Work and the Will to Lead* (London: Allen, 2015). Academic texts include Valerie Stead and Carole Elliott, *Women's Leadership* (Basingstoke: Palgrave Macmillan, 2009).
3. This was confirmed for me by the conductor Natalie Murray Beale in a private communication.

4. For example, Charles Barber's, "Conductors in Rehearsal," in *The Cambridge Companion to Conducting*, edited by José Antonio Bowen (Cambridge: Cambridge University Press, 2002), 17–27 touches only briefly on leadership issues such as making the players feel valued or how to deal with mistakes. Charles Seaman's, *Inside Conducting* (Woodbridge: Boydell and Brewer, 2013) engages rather more with these issues, discussing, in the chapter on 'Rehearsing' (pp. 50–59), the importance of respecting the musicians' own knowledge, and how and when to point out mistakes, but still only as a small part of general rehearsal technique.
5. Prom 31 1984 in Proms Archive, accessed May 2, 2023, www.bbc.co.uk/events/enrj5v.
6. Because of this book's focus on Women in Music Leadership, I won't be discussing Martinez's work as a composer in any detail, though it certainly merits attention.
7. These categories are consistent with the 'Critical Components of Leadership' highlighted in the Global Executive Leadership Inventory. The components are taken from 'The Global Executive Leadership Inventory [which] is a 360-degree feedback instrument developed at Insead's Global Leadership Center.' Drawing on interviews with bother senior executives and MBA students, it identifies a number of crucial abilities that successful leaders need to have. See Herminia Ibarra and Otilia Obodaru, "Women and the Vision Thing," in *On Women and Leadership HBR's 10 Must Reads* (Boston, MA: Harvard Business Review Press, 2019), 51–66, (pp. 56–57).
8. James Naughtie, Interview "Odaline de la Martinez," *BBC Music Magazine*, March 2019, 38–42, p. 41.
9. Anonymous, "Martinez, Odaline de la," in *International Who's Who in Classical Music* (London: Routledge, 2005), 561–62, p. 561.
10. Odaline de la Martinez, interview with Carola Frances Darwin (hereafter, CFD), 5 August 2020. (Subsequently OdlM 2020 in the text).
11. " 'I Haven't Looked Back Since' Interview with Odaline de la Martinez," *Kapralova Society Journal* 14, no. 2 (Fall 2016): 8–10, accessed September 1, 2020, www.kapralova.org/journal27.pdf, p. 8.
12. "Interview," *Kapralova Soc.*, p. 8.
13. She has conducted all the BBC orchestras, as well others in Britain, the USA, Canada, Colombia, Mexico, Brazil, Denmark, South Africa, Australia, and New Zealand. Further details at www.lontano.co.uk (Accessed 1 September 2020).
14. www.lontano.co.uk.
15. 'Martinez' in *Who's Who*, 561.
16. 'Martinez' in *Who's Who*, 561.
17. www.lontano.co.uk.
18. Including, recently, an honorary doctorate from Surrey University (2019), the Opera America Female Composer Award (2015), and Lukas Lifetime Achievement Award for Latin American Music (2019). Odaline de la Martinez, private communication, 19 August 2020.
19. 'I decided . . . that there were so many people who were being neglected who needed to be heard, particularly British and American composers.' Odaline de la Martinez, interview with CFD, 26 February 2019 (subsequently OdlM 2019 in text).
20. 'Dame Ethel Smyth . . . has been a real growing passion. She's now in my heart . . . together with Villa Lobos. . . . It took time, it took doing a lot of pieces over and over again, particularly the Serenade and some of the other pieces. In time, she's quite a voice, quite a personality.' OdlM 2019.
21. Silvina Milstein, https://composersedition.com/silvinamilstein/, Erika Fox, www.erikafox.co.uk. Anthony Gilbert, accessed September 1, 2020, http://anthonygilbert.net/worksc.php. (Accessed 1 September 2020).
22. Nicola LeFanu, interview with CFD, February 27, 2019.
23. 'an example of this: Ethel Smyth . . . she wrote 11 books and I've read all of them.' OdlM 2020.
24. OdlM 2020. She also mentioned that when composing, she first establishes the music's rhythm.
25. Nicola LeFanu, 2019.
26. Natalie Bleicher interview with CFD, February 27, 2019.
27. Andrew Sparling, interview with CFD, March 2, 2019.
28. Malcolm Miller, "Lipkin's Oboe Concerto," *Tempo* 176 (1991): 65–66, accessed September 1, 2020, www.jstor.org/stable/944659, p. 65.
29. Robert Anderson, *The Musical Times* 136, no. 1826 (1995): 203, accessed September 1, 2020, www.jstor.org/stable/1004184.
30. Paul Conway, "Arts Centre, Aberystwyth: Nicola LeFanu's 'Dream Hunter'." *Tempo* 66, no. 260 (2012): 59–60, accessed September 1, 2020, www.jstor.org/stable/23263091, p. 60.

31. Rian Evans, "Lontano/De La Martinez," *The Guardian*, March 10, 2010, accessed September 1, 2020, www.theguardian.com/music/2010/mar/10/lontano-de-la-martinez-review.
32. Nicola LeFanu 2019.
33. These components are taken from The Global Executive Leadership Inventory; see Note 5. Ibarra and Obodaru, "Women and the Vision Thing," 56.
34. Andrew Sparling described some of the issues that can arise in 'fixing' an ensemble, but asked me to keep the details confidential. Andrew Sparling 2019.
35. These funding bodies are listed on the programme for the Festival at accessed September 1, 2020, www.lorelt.co.uk/lontano/wp-content/uploads/2019/01/SeventhFestivalAmericanMusic_FINAL.pdf.
36. Caroline Balding, 2019.
37. "When I first came to England, the first year, I was in shock because everything was different. The light switches go the other way, the light bulbs go in differently." OdlM 2020.
38. Jim Collins, *Good to Great: Why Some Companies Make the Leap . . . and Others Don't* (London: Random House, 2001), 30.
39. Brené Brown, *Dare to Lead* (London: Vermilion, 2018), 243–44.
40. "If you're in London doing a concert and you have three reviewers, one will love you, one will hate you, one will be neutral." OdlM 2020.
41. "I've wanted to be a conductor since I can remember. I also recall being told that women didn't conduct orchestras – interestingly enough not by anyone in my family." 'Interview' *Kapralova Soc*, 8.
42. Alice H. Eagly and Linda L. Carli, "Women and the Labyrinth of Leadership," *On Women and Leadership*, 1–20: 8.
43. Anonymous, "News," *The Musical Times* 135, no. 1812 (February 1994), accessed September 1, 2020, www.jstor.org/stable/1002963, p. 71.
44. 'when I started working with orchestras, there were many fewer women. All the BBC orchestras had women, but all the principals were men. As women started to come into the orchestras, the whole dynamic changed.' OdlM 2020.
45. 'They were used to having a man up front, they were used to being told what to do in a certain way. For example, when I want to go from, say, rehearsal number 1, I say 'Right, shall we go from rehearsal 1? Shall we do this, shall we do that?' . . . but they were used to 'Right, rehearsal 1'. So, for them, those things were difficult.' OdlM 2020.
46. Dr Castro Silva and Dr John Baron, at Tulane University; Paul Patterson and Reginald Smith Brindle (composition) as well as Elsa Cross (piano) in England. As a conductor she particularly values what she learned from Jan Harrington at Indiana University, OdlM 2020.
47. Ibarra and Obadaru, "Women and the Vision Thing," 56–57.
48. Natalie Bleicher 2019.
49. Ibarra and Obodaru, "Women and the Vision Thing," 58.
50. www.juilliard.edu/news/144766/trailblazers-celebrating-women-composers-focus-2020. (Accessed 1 September 2020).
51. "You need to develop a really quick relationship [with] warmth, sense of humour, enthusiasm, [and] of course you really need to believe in the music." OdlM 2020.
52. Herminia Ibarra, Robin Ely, and Deborah Kolb, "Women Rising," *On Women and Leadership*, 39–50: 49.
53. Collins, *Good to Great*, 21.

Bibliography

Anderson, Robert. *The Musical Times* 136, no. 1826 (1995): 203. Accessed September 1, 2020. www.jstor.org/stable/1004184.

Anonymous. "News." *The Musical Times* 135, no. 1812 (1994): 71. Accessed September 1, 2020. www.jstor.org/stable/1002963.

Anonymous. "Martinez, Odaline de la." In *International Who's Who in Classical Music*, 561–62. London: Routledge, 2005.

Anonymous. "'I Haven't Looked Back Since' Interview with Odaline de la Martinez." *Kapralova Society Journal* 14, no. 2 (Fall 2016): 8–10. Accessed September 1, 2020. www.kapralova.org/journal27.pdf.

Anonymous. *On Women and Leadership HBR's 10 Must Reads*. Boston, MA: Harvard Business Review Press, 2019.
Barber, Charles F. "Conductors in Rehearsal." In *The Cambridge Companion to Conducting*, edited by José Antonio Bowen, 17–27. Cambridge: Cambridge University Press, 2002.
Brown, Brené. *Dare to Lead*. London: Vermilion, 2018.
Collins, Jim. *Good to Great: Why Some Companies Make the Leap . . . and Others Don't*. London: Random House, 2001.
Conway, Paul. "Arts Centre, Aberystwyth: Nicola LeFanu's 'Dream Hunter'." *Tempo* 66, no. 260 (2012): 59–60. Accessed September 1, 2020. www.jstor.org/stable/23263091.
Eagly, Alice H., and Linda L. Carli. "Women and the Labyrinth of Leadership." In *On Women and Leadership*, 1–20. Boston, MA: Harvard Business Review Press, 2019.
Evans, Rian. "Lontano/De La Martinez." *The Guardian*, March 10, 2010. Accessed September 1, 2020. www.theguardian.com/music/2010/mar/10/lontano-de-la-martinez-review.
Ibarra, Herminia, Robin Ely, and Deborah Kolb. "Women Rising." In *On Women and Leadership*, 39–50. Boston, MA: Harvard Business Review Press, 2019.
Ibarra, Herminia, and Otilia Obodaru. "Women and the Vision Thing." In *On Women and Leadership*, 51–66. Boston, MA: Harvard Business Review Press, 2019.
Miller, Malcolm. "Lipkin's Oboe Concerto." *Tempo* 176 (1991): 65–66. Accessed September 1, 2020. www.jstor.org/stable/944659.
Naughtie, James. "Interview 'Odaline de la Martinez'." *BBC Music Magazine*, March 2019, 38–42, 41.
Sandberg, Sheryl with Nell Scovell. *Lean In: Women, Work and the Will to Lead*. London: Allen 2015.
Seaman, Charles. *Inside Conducting*. Woodbridge: Boydell and Brewer, 2013.

Websites *(All Accessed September 1, 2020)*

www.bbc.co.uk/events/enrj5v
http://anthonygilbert.net/worksc.php
https://composersedition.com/silvinamilstein/
www.erikafox.co.uk
www.juilliard.edu/news/144766/trailblazers-celebrating-women-composers-focus-2020
www.lontano.co.uk
www.lorelt.co.uk/lontano/wp-content/uploads/2019/01/SeventhFestivalAmericanMusic_FINAL.pdf

PART III

Women's Practices in Music Education

Women's Practices in Music Education: An Introduction

Laura Hamer and Helen Julia Minors

Part III examines a broad range of examples concerning music education, revealing women's musical leadership in a range of case studies. Focused upon the UK, Ireland, and North America, the chapters consider approaches to music education which have developed notions of self-leadership and coaching to advance leadership, as well as examples of ensemble leadership and conducting, through to surveys of how gender is constructed within syllabi. Notions of representation are present across the section. Cases also explore assessment, group teaching, and choral leadership in terms of building a community.

In music education, women's leadership is rather public in that it is seen by our students and integrated into larger institutions, whether they be schools, colleges, or universities. The chapters here cover a range of leadership types across formal curriculum development and delivery, to extracurricular activities, to development courses for educational leaders within music education and wider into the health care sector (the sector within which Judith Francois, Chapter 17, works), using principals from musical leadership. The educator as performer, conductor, role model, and coach are ever present: the many hats a trained music educator holds are central to understanding how these women lead music education and teaching through their own musical practices.

This part of the book offers detailed case studies and approaches within music education. First, we start with two chapters that support the personal development of colleagues through encouraging self-development. In Chapter 17, Judith Francois illustrates how personal development approaches can build confidence and resilience alongside leadership skills. Self-leadership, in terms of controlling one's own actions in order to positively influence others in the workplace, can be developed though embodying rhythm. Francois tackles gender and leadership to explore women's experiences as well as opportunities to develop their own leadership skills. She shows how rhythm, pace, and timing are integral to developing one's role as leader to be effective, inclusive, and controlled. Following this, Jane Booth and Jane Cook offer four detailed coaching case studies to illustrate how professional coaching and their particular model and practice can support personal development. These real-life examples, anonymised for ethical reasons, set out four very different case studies which each represent feelings, emotions, barriers, and problems which resonate with other parts of the book.

The following examples all show practices within education whereby the authors are teachers/lecturers, as well as researchers. Chapters 19 and 20 take specific women leaders as their case study. The first, by Anne-Marie Beaumont, is autoethnographic in sharing her lived experience as a lecturer and programme leader within a UK Higher Education institution. She charts how she set up an Irish Ceílí Band within her music department and shows how her cultural heritage brought something additional to the musical experiences of the largely UK domicile students. She integrates dialogues with students to ensure the student perspective is present throughout her reflection on her practice. Then Margaret J. Flood offers a specific case study of Cathi Leibinger, who is currently an active musician and leader. Leibinger's own words are analysed to chart the lived experiences of a renowned musical leader. Moreover, Flood situates these experiences in the context of the lack of women's representation both in musical leadership and in the literature of music education. Both these chapters are powerful, as they are personal, lived experiences, strongly presenting the first person within the education context.

The next chapter surveys the place of women within music syllabi, setting the UK context in relation to curriculum and syllabus reviews within exam boards for high school education in particular. In Chapter 21, Abigail Bruce and Chamari Wedamulla draw out the changes, debates, and practices over the last decade within the UK and show advocacy work for change which has impacted reviewed and renewed curriculum, but also show what work remains to be done to ensure equitable representation of women, as composers, performers, and makers of music within our education systems. Their calls speak loudly to the advocacy work within Part VI.

The final four chapters each take a different part of music education: conducting, performance assessment, piano teaching, and choral practice. In Chapter 22, by Katherine Hanckel, the gender disparity within conducting, within education and the wider workplace, and within music history, is charted, providing data and evidence. If music education has gender disparity, then the result will also be disparity in the many professional roles. Hanckel gives the specific example of conductors in classical music. Chapter 23 tackles assessment calibration. Michelle Phillips shares her recent project in exploring how we calibrate marking to grade performance exams. She asks whether degree classification in one institution is and should mean the same as another, considering the UK context whereby there are conservatoires, music departments within universities, and private providers. Chapter 24 looks at group teaching in the context of piano tuition, written by three well-established educators with expertise in piano performance and piano tuition in the USA and UK. Cynthia Stephens-Himonides, Margaret Young, and Melanie Bowes share their long experience in the classroom and piano studio. Their personal experiences are central to illustrating how they have each developed their educational practice, which is student-centred. In Chapters 17 and 18, they draw on the benefits of having role models and mentors to support self-development. They engage with social capital development and the notion of disruption in finding alternative solutions and ways of doing things to avoid the replication of previous processes. Seeking new ways to do things ensures teachers are authentic and students receive tuition which is bespoke to their needs. And finally, in Chapter 25, Rebecca Berkley shares her long experience as choral leader and music educator across all levels of music education in the UK, to chart how she trains young, woman identifying, choral leaders. Using the case study of Universal Voices, a community choir of 7–12-year-olds run by the University of Reading, she illustrates the importance of integrating novice conductors on PGCE and MA Music education programmes, thereby integrating music education across primary- and high-school-aged children, alongside university students, in building a community of practice.

Many of the issues introduced within Part III – particularly the importance of mentors, role models, and ensuring women are represented across the music industry and then can be represented within the syllabus – act as drivers for issues within Part VI concerning advocacy, and issues present within the music industry, discussed in Part IV.

17
EMBODYING THE RHYTHM OF SELF IN LEADERSHIP

Judith Francois

Leadership is seen as an aspiration and necessary product of success, with many searching for the concepts that would best allow the intended qualities to thrive. For women, the search for the magic ingredient is no less earnest; however, they may also have other hurdles to jump. Evidence indicates that for women, gaining a leadership role presents its own challenges, and that managing the environment when you get there presents more of the same. For many, these can materialise in the form of inequality of opportunity, pay gap, and lack of respect, which can affect a woman's confidence and ultimately ability to maximise her skills. This, juxtaposed with the realities of intersectionality where, for example, components of race, gender, identity, and beliefs are also simultaneously at play, adds to this lived experience.

The solution to leadership is often encapsulated by the idea of using a strategy or methodology to achieve a task. This can lead to an external focus on action, and less attention to the person who is doing it. Changing this focus to an inside-out style, with understanding self as the primary goal in leadership, offers the opportunity to reframe this approach.

This notion of self-leadership builds from such a premise and sets the expectation that there is an onus on us to recognise the qualities that we hold within, and to be able to use them in a manner that demonstrates drive and the ability to manage self. Self-leadership is defined as 'a process by which individuals control their own behaviour, influencing and leading themselves by using specific sets of behavioural and cognitive strategies'.[1] Acknowledging this approach can involve considering sets of behaviours and personal responses to experiences, which comes with its own outcomes. This standpoint is indicative of not only our different perspectives but also requires consideration of our own repeated behaviours, patterns, and vibrations, which in themselves are representative of the leadership beat that can be produced.

The opportunity to listen to our own leadership beat in this milieu provides another way of understanding personal leadership rhythms, starting with an appreciation that:

> At the heart of each of us, whatever our imperfections, there exists a silent pulse of perfect rhythm, a complex of wave forms and resonances, which is absolutely individual and unique, and yet which connects us to everything in the universe.[2]

This chapter explores the concept of rhythm and the links to the theoretical perspectives of leadership and self-leadership. This includes examining how these patterns might influence behaviours, as well as considering how working and resonating with individual rhythms might help to resound more clearly with self and what that might mean in leadership situations.

The concept of leadership is one that is not easily defined but is intertwined with several other facets that help build this picture. One perspective is that leadership can be conceived as a method utilised by one person persuading other groups or individuals to achieve a common purpose.[3] The authors attest to this meaning that leadership has to be understood through exploring it as a process, influence, occurring in groups, and entailing the inclusion of common goals. A moveable feast, leadership is perceived as ever changing, responsive to the environment, those involved, and dependent on how power is agreed upon.[4] Perspectives encapsulated by understanding that the leadership environment is volatile, uncertain, complex, and ambiguous (VUCA), and that attention to each of the themes in VUCA is required in order to best appraise situations and avoid the misinterpretation of conditions.[5]

Others have captured the nature of the doing in leadership through four Critical Frames that incorporate the notion of depth analysis related to considering the type of emotional response, 'emancipatory analysis', concerned with the creation of actions that are beneficial for all. 'Looking awry' is the ability to perceive things in a different manner and thus start observations from a different viewpoint. Finally, 'network analysis' involves the ability to circumnavigate across organisational complexities and social interactions.[6]

Gender and Leadership

In terms of leadership, women are not frequently seen in positions of power, especially in business and politics. It is conceivable that they must override the challenge of essentialism, whereby the constructs of male and female expectations are culturally developed, and the resulting gendered response devised[7] must navigate an uneven playing field.

Capturing the 'why' of women's leadership experiences and opportunities is offered through the lens of a three-pronged exploration model of a leadership labyrinth. This rationalises a number of reasons for the under representation of women leaders and notes interrelated issues of **'Human Capital'**, which covers the areas of education, work life balance, work experience, and development options. **'Prejudice'** relates to perception and bias and **gender difference**, where the focus is on the style and effectiveness and stereotypes about women's ability to lead.[8]

It seems women may be more passive leaders in the work environment when undertaking task-focused work, but they are equally capable of undertaking task-related and problem-solving activities. Despite this, their success is not rated as highly as men and they are less likely to be liked.[9] This is a nod to the acknowledgement that personal bias has been socially constructed and the realisation of the need to appreciate how these perceptions intersect when interacting with others.[10] Such societal constructs are compounded by the knowledge that women's own beliefs hamper them in stepping into leadership positions.[11] Potentially, the opportunity to explore self and personal biases through the lens of the 'projections of self', where understanding is gleaned by examining perceptions of self in the *institution*, consideration of the *embodied and cultural self* – for example ethnicity, *personality* – including how this interrelates with others, *expertise* – the meaning people take from a role, along with *role power*.[12]

As well as the task-related behaviour described, women also appear to prefer a more collaborative approach in decision making and thus a leaning to democratic leadership,[13] along with a preference for a more transformational leadership approach, associated with idealised influence, motivation, intellectual stimulation, as well as focusing on needs of the team.[14] As a result, women are perceived as being more supportive than male counterparts.[15]

At the same time, though, there is a tendency for women to be perceived as more emotional than men. For example, a study by Fischbach, Lichtenthaler, and Horstmann[16] explored the responses to a series of emotions and to the terms *successful managers, men, women, male managers, women mangers, successful men managers*, and *successful women managers*. Male and female perceptions of emotions and women differed. Women believed specific emotions to be associated with successful managers. The researchers noted that when considering the question of women, respondents did not correlate women with perceived leadership qualities. Only when combined with the term 'successful manager' did similarities between men's and women's beliefs about leadership coincide.

In addition, the type of emotion in leadership, such as 'fear, shame, and sadness' were seen as less attributable to leadership behaviours, while there was agreement that successful managers and men displayed less emotion. This suggests that female leaders are being measured against the expectations of male counterparts and with expected responses that other women thought women should do.[17] These perspectives are a testimony to the creation of social constructs on the accepted behaviours for women.

There also remain challenges for women leaders from ethnic backgrounds, who may suffer additional bias relating to the social constructs as to whether they can be and are perceived as leaders, along with other actions that contribute to creating further discrimination. The notion of managing conformity holds special challenges for women from black and minority communities who have the additional elements of trying to conform with the expected leadership styles, as well as managing concerns about fairness and integrity.[18] In terms of leadership the constraints experienced do not automatically mean that success is impaired; in fact, some of the learning, like being part of different cultural groups, brings with it additional understanding that can help bring more creative problem solving, and the criticism of women's leadership may prove a spur in reaching their goals.[19]

There is a change towards incorporating more perceived feminine traits within leadership and thus a move away from the perceived masculine presentation of the same, providing a more balanced perspective of good leadership.[20] This gives an opportunity to concentrate on the outcomes of leadership, rather than pinhole behaviours to social construction of gender.

Followership

Although the who and what of leadership is bound up with a number of ideas relating to who a leader is and what a leader must do, the question of who is being led and how must also play a central feature. There are several established ideas as to the means of managing and motivating followers. These include the notion of trait theory, concerned with the identification of specific characteristics that a person is born with, and behavioural aspects, concerned with type of personal response and contingency approaches where action is dependent on the situation. More recently there is the idea of transformational leadership, deemed as enabling both the aspirations of the followers and that of the leader to better align, resulting in followers' increase in personal satisfaction and productivity.[21]

Additional suggestions are that followers' reactions to the leader are directly linked with their own beliefs about suitable responses; for example, whether they should hold a passive approach and defer to the leader or hold a co-production attitude and view themselves in partnership with the leader.[22] There are additional possibilities through behaviour modelling; for example, improving followers' ethical judgement by actively demonstrating and teaching skills in relation to the same.[23] This leads to the question of self-leadership and the role of self in leadership performance.

Self-Leadership

Self-leadership is concerned with the individual actions in directing and motivating self, which will have positive outcomes on personal efficacy.[24] It entails the use of flexible strategies to empower and to control personal behaviour and outcomes,[25] along with the use of behavioural and cognitive strategies as a means to leading and directing themselves.[26] Behaviour-focused approaches include natural rewards and the creation of positive thoughts.[27] Other strategies include the ability to plan personal goals, be self-critical, and set tasks to remediate any shortcomings of behaviour, as well as identification of desirable behaviours and working towards sustaining these, even when the task itself is not desirable.[28] This is an approach thought to provide the room to change unhelpful behaviour and introduce alternative positive patterns of thought.[29] Further strategies include notions of self-cueing, in which the use of objects, notes, or role models is considered a driver in completing tasks.[30,31] The inclusion of positive visualisations that help with achieving the intended actions is also useful.[32] Finally, there is self-talk, in which space is allowed for internal reconsideration of events and evaluative strategies in order to review any aspect of self that may be preventing motivation to complete the task,[33] and to ensure that conversations with self are framed in a positive manner.[34]

The focus on the leading self is also evident in the construct of authentic leadership,[35] which centres on this premise and is wholly based on achieving outcomes, using personal psychology as its basis (see Table 17.1). Some opinions indicate that authentic leadership and perception of integrity are coupled, being evidenced in transparency and the congruence between words and actions.[36]

The principal features of these self-leadership propositions lie with the understanding that there are some skills that individuals possess that enable leadership abilities to be maximised, thus suggesting that the ability to lead is set within a set of skills, where and how they are used and become central to growth. and in which self, in some way, must be both the protagonist and antagonist. Thus far, the focus has mainly been constructed on the basis of doing and thinking, but more embodied ideas offer less traditional viewpoints.

Embodied Leadership

Learning within the organisational setting can be understood through 'embodied acting' and investigative activities.[37] Equally, thinking broadly about leadership of self and using an embodied approach to learning in which both the mind and the body are given consideration allows for a more rounded approach. There are a number of ways to apply this approach, including mindfulness, breathing, and visualisation,[38] along with reflecting on habitual behaviour and using expressive art forms such as music, drama and poetry.

Table 17.1 Authentic Leadership Constructs

Authentic Leadership Constructs	Associated Behaviour
Self-awareness	A conscious examination of self
Relational Transparency	Concerned with building relationships that allow open and truthful conversations
Self-regulation	Focused on setting expected standards of behaviour for oneself
Balanced processing	Using and interpreting information gleaned about self in an unbiased way

The concept of an 'integral' perspective on leadership is also envisioned as a 'philosophy that envisions a holistic understanding of consciousness and human potential'.[39] Here the 'physical, emotional, mental, and psychic' are seen as a means to appreciate the differing levels of engagement, and has to be understood as not merely something to be taught but also experienced; it is this experience that provides the insight.[40] The notion of rhythm and leadership fits well into this discussion.

Rhythm

Rhythm is seen as a 'strong regular repeated pattern of movement 'and is a paradigm that can be examined within the concept of business, providing an opportunity to identify different rhythms and consider how to manage change within an organisation.[41] Ideas that accord with leadership development and the understanding of leadership rhythms are strategies for enabling engagement,[42] offering the opportunity to focus on what is happening in reality and not just what is noted on the surface, thus affording leaders insight to 'openings', or ways forward.[43]

The presentation of the rhythms is variable and can be understood as a cyclical response where the leader verifies followers' self-worth, resulting in followers working to match the espoused expectations and/or behaviours.[44]

Other perspectives explore the notion of sound and soundless work, 'active interaction' (for example, through meetings), and silence envisioned as individual engagement.[45] The authors suggest that the nature of our current world means that we have insufficient time to engage with silence. The need for silence is exemplified in other investigations focused on individual and group innovation strategies, noting that although individual and collaborative working both yielded results, groups exposed to intermittent collaborative engagement produced better solutions overall.[46] Surely this is an accolade for the need for space, but is possibly also aligned with the notion of understanding the pace of the work being undertaken.

Pace

Pace can include considering interactions and thinking about these both in terms of how relationships are built and sustained, along with how relaxed or spontaneous interactions are. Whether relationships are sustained is largely dependent on how well this balance is sustained, and whether such actions are seen as useful.[47] Despite such reservations, it seems that leaders have some important responsibilities in managing this equilibrium.

Firstly, role modelling by the leader is vital in fostering the right environment to produce a balanced pace between sound and silence.[48] Secondly, appreciating the power to change behaviour, whereby the follower will try to emulate the leader's behaviour, here the leader becomes a pace-maker. In this manner the leader becomes a 'zeitgeber', 'i.e. the major rhythm form which others' rhythms must follow'.[49] There is also acknowledgement that the opposite might be true, where the leader may follow the pace of the follower.

The leader must be aware of the dynamics of the team and the subsequent emerging rhythms. The illustration of group dynamics, forming storming, norming, and performing, provides this opportunity.

The forming stage is construed as getting to know each other; storming as the jostling for positions; norming is associated with agreeing upon certain activities and understanding relationships; in performing, everything is working well and the task can be the main focus.[50] Groups are thought to be working within any one of these sequences and can move between them, depending on the circumstances and development of the group. Coupled with the view of 'punctuated equilibrium', where groups focus on a task, they may stay in the same position until some sort of critical event moves them from this stance.[51]

Of course, the rhythm of leadership is also about working within the wider rhythm of the organisation, which also sets its own rules on norms, potentially producing sequences in the management of change, which could be seen through the regularity or irregularity of response, and termed as being 'focused, punctuated and temporarily switching'.[52]

It is important to remember, though, that this is all set within the organisation's own expectations of change, where the rhythm of change encapsulates both the length of time between change and how long the change and the more sustained outcomes achieved by those with more regular rhythms last.[53]

Yet in some respects, the behaviour in an organisation can be likened to a theatrical production in which an element of suspense is often present. The organisation must manage its own real-life suspense during this period of unknowing; for example, managing the uncertainty of organisational restructures.[54]

Other perspectives turn to consider the concept in terms of understanding the nature of organisational change, identifying 'radical change leadership rhythm' when there is drastic change. Here a directive management approach is required, as well as a 'developmental change leadership rhythm', benefiting from an incremental more exploratory approach.[55] Ultimately, it seems that an appreciation of organisational decision-making cannot be comprehended outside of the understanding of time.

Timing

The concept of time is socially constructed and will therefore have different implications for various settings and cultures.[56] Both time and rhythm have been described as important drivers, with time described as moving people through the past, present, and into the future, and rhythm attributed to guiding emotions.[57] In terms of understanding how individuals and organisations work within the concept of time, a 'temporal fit' is required, where both the organisational and individual perspectives are congruent.[58]

Translating the traditional language of leadership behaviour to a more rhythmic translation is offered through the analogy of dance. It is the difference between the waltz, offering a positivist perspective and ordered and correct interaction, compared to the constructivist chaotic and attention-seeking approach of a rave.[59]

A further typology drawing links between rhythm and leadership identified five styles of leadership and associated behaviours and rhythms,[60] comprising:

The flowing style, associated with a steady pace
Staccato style, conceived as dramatic with eruptions of energy
Chaos style, able to go with whatever direction the movement brings. Such individuals can live with uncertainty and can provide support and advice in times of calamity
Lyrical style is conceived as having a twirling energy with an adaptable style, and can encourage engagement of others
Stillness style, the illusion of no movement while in fact creating an understanding of 'inner and outer voices' and using this mindset to create opportunities for shared understanding

Exploring these symbolic responses may offer insight into the rhythmic self, as well as to understand the cocreated experience that may unfold. Building on this perspective, it's possible to revisit more traditional leadership behaviours and consider them in similar terms.

For example, take the analysis of four more traditional leadership styles: a democratic, autocratic, authoritarian, or the laissez-faire approach. These styles could be understood as having associated rhythms.

- Autocratic approach, where power is monopolised by an individual, has the potential to offer followers no movement and to feel unappreciated and coerced,[61] but on the other hand offer some psychological safety in providing a hierarchical framework.[62] In terms of rhythm of control, there are heightened expectations of delivery with the holder leading the beat.
- Laissez-faire, where the absence of any direction or response from the leader[63] manifests in an avoidant leadership style,[64] can lead to power being taken by team members and/or bullying.[65] In terms of the associated leadership rhythm, this may be discordant with no clear pattern, or with the rhythm being managed by someone other than the leader.
- Bureaucratic leadership is linked to a leader meeting hierarchical expectations and procedures.[66,67] In terms of its connection to leadership rhythm, it produces a persistent beat, potentially conducted by policies and the rate of procedural change. However, the focus on these areas constrains decision-making and ideas.
- The democratic leader is interested in involving team members in the decision-making process, allowing for creativity while ultimately the leader remains in charge.[68] Potentially a collaborative rhythm allowing individual and joint tempos to all take turns at being centre stage. the same authors warn that this collaborative approach can be replaced by uncertainty when decisions are less clear.

In practice, all rhythms or patterns of behaviour bring with them their own stories that are reliant on the circumstances, cultures, and environments.[69]

Entrainment

Entrainment is conceived as 'the process by which the powerful rhythmic vibrations of one object are projected upon another object with a similar frequency, thereby causing that object to vibrate in resonance with the first object'.[70] The speed and strength of entrainment is dependent on the circumstances of the entrainment experience.[71] The concept is described further in the integral entrainment matrix as consisting of Symmetrical Entrainment, associated with rhythms that entrain each other. Asymmetrical entertainment occurs when they do not, as well as whether they occur within a human system and therefore are conceived to be Inner entrainment, or between human systems and therefore outer.[72] An understanding of entrainment for leaders is important not only because it raises leaders' consciousness, but it can also afford them a better understanding of the rhythms occurring in their surroundings.[73]

This can help in assessing team dynamics. For example, the pull of entrainment for some groups in organisations means that once they have become used to performing at a slower rate they are unable to come out of a particular pattern, even when the deadlines have been brought forward.[74]

The psychological responses by individuals towards affinity and identity offered by entrainment provides an opportunity to consider this concept with relational behaviours.[75] The positive links between trust entrainment and predictability, where both follower and leader are dependent on some sort of mutual agreement, are beneficial in building these relationships. Indeed, the effectiveness of the leader is directly connected with how similar the patterns of behaviour and rhythms are between follower and leader.[76] Furthermore, the likelihood of this happening may be linked with the notion of ***synchrony preference***. This is seen as being related to individuals' 'willingness to adapt one's pace and rhythm within social interactions for the purpose of creating a sense of synchronicity and flow between interaction partners'.[77] The choice of whether synchronicity is more likely to occur includes circumstances where there is an affinity with the number of tasks that a person is happy to manage at one time. At the same time, dominant behaviour of overly hurried responses are negatively correlated with the possibility of obtaining synchronicity.[78]

Other behaviours on the temporal plane must also be considered in conjunction with these ideas, including chronemics, where the physical pace of walking, as well as interpretations of time and notions of promptness, are captured.[79] Or the rhythm of the voice creates another pattern through the *latency time* associated with the timing it takes to complete each syllable. This process is different depending on the language spoken.[80] Finally, the acknowledgement that even when we are still the body continues to pulse and that spending quiet time to explore our own vibrational patterns is important.[81]

Conclusion

Whatever action or behaviours are chosen, the leader must acknowledge that they have a preferred leadership style and appreciate that just like any entertainer, followers will gravitate to leaders who understand them; i.e. those with the same language, rhythm, and pace as themselves. This means that leaders need to be able to move through many different rhythms to remain connected. Without being able to recognise and use these elements, the possibility of leaders alienating themselves from followers becomes a real possibility. Consequently, a leader needs to have the ability to be able to look at such constructs and use them in order to build and add to the repertoire of leadership skills.

What is clear when discerning leadership skills is that how leadership is approached and acted on in a dynamic way within the context of the organisation, followers, and self are all critical factors. The issue for all of these lies in consideration of the rhythm of the approach taken.

Notes

1. Panja Andressen, Udo Konradt, and Christopher P. Neck, "The Relation Between Self-Leadership and Transformational Leadership: Competing Models and the Moderating Role of Virtuality," *Journal of Leadership & Organizational Studies* 19, no. 1 (2012): 68.
2. George Leonard, *The Silent Pulse* (Gibbs Smith, 2009).
3. Peter Northouse, *Leadership: Theory and Practice* (London: Sage Publication, 2010), 3.
4. Bridit Carroll, Jackie Ford, and Scott Taylor, eds., *Leadership: Contemporary Critical Perspectives* (London: Sage Publications Limited, 2015), X1X.
5. Nathan Bennett and G. James Lemoine, "What a Difference a Word Makes: Understanding Threats to Performance in a VUCA World," *Business Horizons* 57, no. 3 (2014): 312.
6. Simon Western, *Leadership: A Critical Text* (London: Sage Publications Limited, 2019).
7. Ibid.
8. Northouse, *Leadership*, 307–17.
9. Carol Watson and Hoffman Richard, "The Role of Task-Related Behavior in the Emergence of Leaders: The Dilemma of the Informed Woman," *Group & Organization Management* 29, no. 6 (2004): 659–85.
10. Western, *Leadership*, 92–93.
11. Alice Eagly and Jean L. Chin, "Diversity and Leadership in a Changing World," *American Psychologist* 65, no. 3 (2010): 218.
12. Western, *Leadership*, 93–94.

13. Watson, *Leadership*, 680.
14. Northouse, *Leadership*, 177.
15. Mats Alvesson, Martin Blom, and Stefan Sveningsson, *Reflexive Leadership: Organising in an Imperfect World* (London: Sage, 2016).
16. Andrea Fischbach, Phillip W. Lichtenthaler, and Nina Horstmann, "Leadership and Gender Stereotyping of Emotions," *Journal of Personnel Psychology* 14, no. 3 (2015): 153–62.
17. Fischbach, Lichtenthaler, and Horstmann, "Leadership," 160.
18. Eagly and Chin, "Diversity," 219.
19. Ibid.
20. Ibid., 221.
21. Carroll et al., *Leadership*, 73.
22. Melissa K. Carsten, Mary Uhl-Bien, and Lei Huang, "Leader Perceptions and Motivation as Outcomes of Followership Role Orientation and Behavior," *Leadership* 14, no. 6 (2018): 731–56.
23. Robert Steinbauer, Robert W. Renn, Robert R. Taylor, and Phil K. Njoroge, "Ethical Leadership and Followers' Moral Judgment: The Role of Followers' Perceived Accountability and Self-Leadership," *Journal of Business Ethics* 120, no. 3 (2014): 381–92.
24. Bercu Kör, "The Mediating Effects of Self-Leadership on Perceived Entrepreneurial Orientation and Innovative Work Behavior in the Banking Sector," *SpringerPlus* 5, no. 1 (2016): 1–15.
25. Jeffrey D. Houghton and Steven K. Yoho, "Toward a Contingency Model of Leadership and Psychological Empowerment: When Should Self-Leadership Be Encouraged?," *Journal of Leadership & Organizational Studies* 11, no. 4 (2005): 65–83.
26. Andressen et al., "The Relation Between Self-Leadership and Transformational Leadership," 68–82.
27. Houghton and Yoho, "Toward a Contingency Model," 65–83.
28. Kör, "The Mediating Effects."
29. Andressen et al., "The Relation Between Self-Leadership and Transformational Leadership."
30. Kör, "The Mediating Effects."
31. Jeffrey D. Houghton, Andrew Carnes, and Christopher N. Ellison, "A Cross-Cultural Examination of Self-Leadership: Testing for Measurement Invariance Across Four Cultures," *Journal of Leadership & Organizational* Studies 21, no. 4 (2014): 414–30, p. 415.
32. Ibid.
33. Kör, "The Mediating Effects."
34. Houghton and Yoho, "Toward a Contingency Model," 65–83.
35. William L. Gardner, Bruce J. Avolio, Fred Luthans, Douglas R. May, and Fred Walumbwa, "'Can You See the Real Me?' A Self-Based Model of Authentic Leader and Follower Development," *The Leadership Quarterly* 16, no. 3 (2005): 343–72.
36. Hannes Leroy, Michael E. Palanski, and Tony Simons, "Authentic Leadership and Behavioral Integrity as Drivers of Follower Commitment and Performance," *Journal of Business Ethics* 107, no. 3 (2012): 255–64.
37. Wendalin M. Küpers and David Pauleen, "Learning Wisdom: Embodied and Artful Approaches to Management Education," *Scandinavian Journal of Management* 31, no. 4 (2015): 493–500.
38. Küpers and Pauleen, "Learning Wisdom," 497.
39. Danny Sandra and Sharda Nandram, "Integral Leadership Through Entrainment: Synchronizing Consciousness," *Advances in Management* 6, no. 12 (2013): 17.
40. Ibid.
41. Kenneth W. Kerber and Anthony F. Buono, "The Rhythm of Change Leadership," *Organization Development Journal* 36, no. 3 (2018): 55–72.
42. Robert B. Denhardt and Janet V. Denhardt, *The Dance of Leadership: The Art of Leading in Business, Government, and Society* (London and New York: ME Sharpe, 2005).
43. Ibid, 46.
44. Allan C. Bluedorn and Kimberley S. Jaussi, "Leaders, Followers, and Time," *The Leadership Quarterly* 19, no. 6 (2008): 654–68.
45. Ethan Bernstein, Jesse Shore, and David Lazer, "Improving the Rhythm of Your Collaboration," *MIT Sloan Management Review* 61, no. 1 (2019): 29–36.
46. Ethan Bernstein, Jesse Shore, and Lazer, David, "How Intermittent Breaks in Interaction Improve Collective Intelligence," *Proceedings of the National Academy of Sciences* 115, no. 35 (2018): 8734–39.
47. Bluedorn and Jaussi, "Leaders, Followers, and Time," 660.

48. Bernstein et al., "How Intermittent Breaks in Interaction Improve Collective Intelligence."
49. Bluedorn and Jaussi, "Leaders, Followers, and Time," 658.
50. David Levi, *Group Dynamics for Teams* (London: Sage Publications, 2011), 40.
51. Bluedorn and Jaussi, "Leaders, Followers, and Time."
52. Patricia Klarner and Sebastian Raisch, "Move to the Beat – Rhythms of Change and Firm Performance," *Academy of Management Journal* 56, no. 1 (2013): 161.
53. Ibid., 174–77.
54. Rosabeth K. Moss, "Strategy as Improvisational Theater," *MIT Sloan Management Review* 43, no. 2 (2002): 76–81.
55. Kenneth W. Kerber and Anthony F. Buono, "The Rhythm of Change Leadership," *Organization Development Journal* 36, no. 3 (2018): 55–72.
56. Mary E. Zellmer-Bruhn, Christina B. Gibson, and Ramon J. Aldag, "Time Flies Like an Arrow: Tracing Antecedents and Consequences of Temporal Elements of Organizational Culture," in *The International Handbook of Organizational Culture and Climate* (2001) p. 17.
57. Denhardt and Denhardt, *The Dance of Leadership*.
58. Zellmer-Bruhn et al., "Time Flies Like an Arrow," 27.
59. Arja Ropo and Erika Sauer, "Dances of Leadership: Bridging Theory and Practice Through an Aesthetic Approach," *Journal of Management & Organization* 14, no. 5 (2008): 566.
60. Robin D. Johnson, *Dance of Leadership: Mastering the Art of Making a Difference Using Your Unique Style* (Tobin D Johnson, Self Publish, 2013).
61. Helga Hoel, Lars Glaso, Jorn Hetland, and Cary Cooper, "Leadership Styles as Predictors of Self-Reported and Observed Workplace Bullying," *British Journal of Management* 21, no. 2 (2010): 453–68.
62. Annabel H. De Hoogh et al., "Diabolical Dictators or Capable Commanders? An Investigation of the Differential Effects of Autocratic Leadership on Team Performance," *The Leadership Quarterly* 26, no. 5 (2015): 687–701.
63. Northouse, *Leadership*, 182.
64. Ibid., 198.
65. Hoel et al., "Leadership Styles as Predictors of Self-Reported and Observed Workplace Bullying," 457.
66. Mary Uhl-Bien and Russ Marion, "Complexity Leadership in Bureaucratic Forms of Organizing: A Meso Model," *The Leadership Quarterly* 20, no. 4 (2009): 631–50.
67. Tony Bush, "Emotional Leadership: A Viable Alternative to the Bureaucratic Model?', *Educational Management Administration & Leadership* 42, no. 2 (2014).
68. Fatma İnce, "The Effect of Democratic Leadership on Organizational Cynicism: A Study on Public Employees,' *İşletme Araştırmaları Dergisi* 10, no. 2 (2018): 245–53.
69. Mats Alvesson, Martin Blom, and Stefan Sveningsson, *Reflexive Leadership: Organising in an Imperfect World* (London: Sage, 2016), 31.
70. Mitchell L. Gaynor, *The Healing Power of Sound: Recovery from Life-Threatening Illness Using Sound, Voice, and Music* (Boulder, CO: Shambhala Publications, 2002).
71. Danny Sandra and Sharda Nandram, *Spiritual Leadership as a Driver of Organizational Entrainment* (Kidmore End: Academic Conferences International Limited, 2017), 444.
72. Sandra and Nandram, *Integral Leadership*, 19.
73. Ibid., 18.
74. Bluedorn and Jaussi, "Leaders, Followers, and Time," 7.
75. Bluedorn and Jaussi, "Leaders, Followers, and Time," 657.
76. Bluedorn and Jaussi, "Leaders, Followers, and Time," 663.
77. Sophie Leroy, Abbie J. Shipp, Sally Blount, and John-Gabriel Licht, "Synchrony Preference: Why Some People Go with the Flow and Some Don't," *Personnel Psychology* 68, no. 4 (2015): 761.
78. Leroy et al., "Synchrony Preference," 794.
79. Sylvia Bonaccio, Jane O'Reilly, Sharon O'Sullivan, and Francois Chiocchio, "Nonverbal Behavior and Communication in the Workplace: A Review and an Agenda for Research," *Journal of Management* 42, no. 5 (2016): 1044–74.
80. A. Tomatis, *The Conscious Ear: My Life of Transformation Through Listening* (Station Hill Press, 1991).
81. D. Campbell, *The Roar of Silence: Healing Powers of Breath, Tone and Music* (Quest Books, 1989), 20.

References

Alvesson, Mats, Martin Blom, and Stefan Sveningsson. *Reflexive Leadership: Organising in an Imperfect World*. London: Sage, 2016.

Andressen, Panja, Udo Konradt, and Chistropher P. Neck. "The Relation Between Self-Leadership and Transformational Leadership: Competing Models and the Moderating Role of Virtuality." *Journal of Leadership & Organizational Studies* 19, no. 1 (2012): 68–82.

Bennett, Nathan, and G. James Lemoine. "What a Difference a Word Makes: Understanding Threats to Performance in a VUCA World." *Business Horizons* 57, no. 3 (2014): 311–17.

Bernstein, Ethan, Jesse Shore, and David Lazer. "How Intermittent Breaks in Interaction Improve Collective Intelligence." *Proceedings of the National Academy of Sciences* 115, no. 35 (2018): 8734–39.

———. "Improving the Rhythm of Your Collaboration." *MIT Sloan Management Review* 61, no. 1 (2019): 29–36.

Bluedorn, Allan C., and Kimberley S. Jaussi. "Leaders, Followers, and Time." *The Leadership Quarterly* 19, no. 6 (2008): 654–68.

Bonaccio, Sylvia, Jane O'Reilly, Sharon L. O'Sullivan, and François Chiocchio. "Nonverbal Behavior and Communication in the Workplace: A Review and an Agenda for Research." *Journal of Management* 42, no. 5 (2016): 1044–74.

Bush, Tony. "Emotional Leadership: A Viable Alternative to the Bureaucratic Model?," *Educational Management Administration & Leadership* 42, no. 2 (2014).

Campbell, Don. *The Roar of Silence: Healing Powers of Breath, Tone and Music*. New York: Quest Books, 1989.

Carroll, Brigid, Jackie Ford, and Scott Taylor, eds. *Leadership: Contemporary Critical Perspectives*. London: Sage Publications Limited, 2015.

Carsten, Melissa K., Mary Uhl-Bien, and Lei Huang. "Leader Perceptions and Motivation as Outcomes of Followership Role Orientation and Behavior." *Leadership* 14, no. 6 (2018).

De Hoogh, Annabel H., Lindred L. Greer, and Deanne N. Hartog. "Diabolical Dictators or Capable Commanders? An Investigation of the Differential Effects of Autocratic Leadership on Team Performance." *The Leadership Quarterly* 26, no. 5 (2015): 687–701.

Denhardt, Robert B., and Janet V. Denhardt. *The Dance of Leadership: The Art of Leading in Business, Government, and Society*. London and New York: ME Sharpe, 2005.

Eagly, Alice H., and Jean L. Chin. "Diversity and Leadership in a Changing World." *American Psychologist* 65, no. 3 (2010).

Fischbach, Andrea, Phillip W. Lichtenthaler, and Nina Horstmann. "Leadership and Gender Stereotyping of Emotions." *Journal of Personnel Psychology* 14, no. 3 (2015): 153–62.

Gardner, William L., Bruce J. Avolio, Fred Luthans, Douglas R. May, and Fred Walumbwa. "'Can You See the Real Me?' A Self-Based Model of Authentic Leader and Follower Development." *The Leadership Quarterly* 16, no. 3 (2005).

Gaynor, Mitchell L. *The Healing Power of Sound: Recovery from Life-Threatening Illness Using Sound, Voice, and Music*. Boulder, CO: Shambhala Publications, 2002.

Hoel, Helga, Lars Glasø, Jørn Hetland, Cary L. Cooper, and Ståle Einarsen. "Leadership Styles as Predictors of Self-Reported and Observed Workplace Bullying." *British Journal of Management* 21, no. 2 (2010): 453–68.

Houghton, Jeffrey D., Andrew Carnes, and Christopher N. Ellison. "A Cross-Cultural Examination of Self-Leadership: Testing for Measurement Invariance Across Four Cultures." *Journal of Leadership & Organizational Studies* 21, no. 4 (2014).

Houghton, Jeffrey D., and Steven K. Yoho. "Toward a Contingency Model of Leadership and Psychological Empowerment: When Should Self-Leadership Be Encouraged?" *Journal of Leadership & Organizational Studies* 11, no. 4 (2005).

İnce, Fatma. "The Effect of Democratic Leadership on Organizational Cynicism: A Study on Public Employees." *İşletme Araştırmaları Dergisi* 10, no. 2 (2018): 245–53.

Johnson, Robin D. *Dance of Leadership: Mastering the Art of Making a Difference Using Your Unique Style*. Tobin D Johnson, Self Publish, 2013.

Kerber, Kenneth W., and Anthony F. Buono. "The Rhythm of Change Leadership." *Organization Development Journal* 36, no. 3 (2018): 55–72.

Klarner, Patricia, and Sebastian Raisch. "Move to the Beat – Rhythms of Change and Firm Performance." *Academy of Management Journal* 56, no. 1 (2013): 160–84.

Kör, Bercu. "The Mediating Effects of Self-Leadership on Perceived Entrepreneurial Orientation and Innovative Work Behavior in the Banking Sector." *SpringerPlus* 5, no. 1 (2016).

Küpers, Wendalin M., and David Pauleen. "Learning Wisdom: Embodied and Artful Approaches to Management Education." *Scandinavian Journal of Management* 31, no. 4 (2015): 493–500.

Leonard, George. *The Silent Pulse*. Layton: Gibbs Smith, 2009.

Leroy, Hannes, Michael E. Palanski, and Tony Simons. "Authentic Leadership and Behavioral Integrity as Drivers of Follower Commitment and Performance." *Journal of Business Ethics* 107, no. 3 (2012): 255–64.

Leroy, Sophie, Abbie J. Shipp, Sally Blount, and John G. Licht. "Synchrony Preference: Why Some People Go with the Flow and Some Don't." *Personnel Psychology* 68, no. 4 (2015): 759–809.

Levi, Daniel. *Group Dynamics for Teams*. London: Sage Publications, 2011.

Moss Rosabeth, K. "Strategy as Improvisational Theater." *MIT Sloan Management Review* 43, no. 2 (2002): 76–81.

Northouse, Peter G. *Leadership: Theory and Practice*. London: Sage Publication, 2010.

Ropo, Arja, and Erika Sauer. "Dances of Leadership: Bridging Theory and Practice Through an Aesthetic Approach." *Journal of Management & Organization* 14, no. 5 (2008): 560–72.

Sandra, Danny, and Sharda Nandram. "Integral Leadership Through Entrainment: Synchronizing Consciousness." *Advances in Management* 6, no. 12 (2013).

———. *Spiritual Leadership as a Driver of Organizational Entrainment*. Kidmore End: Academic Conferences International Limited, 2017.

Steinbauer, Robert, Robert W. Renn, Robert R. Taylor, and Phil K. Njoroge. "Ethical Leadership and Followers' Moral Judgment: The Role of Followers' Perceived Accountability and Self-Leadership." *Journal of Business Ethics* 120, no. 3 (2014): 381–92.

Tomatis, Alfred. *The Conscious Ear: My Life of Transformation Through Listening*. Barrytown, NY: Station Hill Press, 1991.

Uhl-Bien, Mary, and Russ Marion. "Complexity Leadership in Bureaucratic Forms of Organizing: A Meso Model." *The Leadership Quarterly* 20, no. 4 (2009): 631–50.

Watson, Carol, and L. Richard Hoffman. "The Role of Task-Related Behavior in the Emergence of Leaders: The Dilemma of the Informed Woman." *Group & Organization Management* 29, no. 6 (2004): 659–85.

Western, Simon. *Leadership: A Critical Text*. London: Sage Publications Limited, 2019.

Zellmer-Bruhn, Mary E., C.B. Gibson, and Ramon J. Aldag. "Time Flies Like an Arrow: Tracing Antecedents and Consequences of Temporal Elements of Organizational Culture." In *The International Handbook of Organizational Culture and Climate*, 22–52. Chichester: Wiley, 2001.

18
LEARNING TO COACH, COACHING TO LEAD

Jane Booth and Jane Cook

In a world that cries out for more leaders and for a new type of leadership, we believe that Coaching and/or Mentoring offers crucial tools that align well with women's natural sense of nurture and collaboration,[1] allowing for scaled professional development targeted to bring maximum impact for our organisations. This chapter examines the potential for key Coaching and Mentoring skills to extend the leadership toolkit and benefit women in leadership roles within the music profession, illustrated by four case studies. The authors, Jane Booth and Jane Cook both work for *Guildhall Ignite* at the Guildhall School of Music & Drama, London.[2]

Coaching and Mentoring began at the Guildhall School in 2012. Initially an internal project to develop the skills of Mentors in a world-leading Conservatoire, the work had a clear and deep impact on those taking part, and a desire grew to further hone the skills that the initial training had brought. *Guildhall Ignite* now offers its own professional coaching training programme internally and externally. *A Coaching Approach in and through the Performing Arts* is accredited by the European Mentoring and Coaching Council (EMCC) and supports professionals in a range of roles, including teachers, mentors, leaders, managers, and executives seeking to become executive coaches.

Our journey to date has involved projects with other Higher Education Institutions (Universities and Conservatoires in the UK and internationally), diverse performing arts organisations and venues, and the wider civic and corporate sector (see our website for client and partner details). The case studies included in this chapter blend our experiences of working with Women in Music at a range of International Higher Education and Organisational settings. With the exception of Case Study 4 (and with express consent), all individuals discussed have been anonymised. Whilst staying true to the themes that clients bring to their coaching sessions, we have blended multiple roles, sources, and scenarios in order to preserve the confidentiality we guarantee our clients. No one individual or institution is identifiable.

Context

In 'As Long as We Associate Leadership with Masculinity, Women Will Be Overlooked', Chamorro-Premuzic suggests that 'brash narcissistic male leaders'[3] continue to predominate our professional world. Writing in 2017, Sarah Babb stated that: 'In most cultures masculinity and leadership are closely linked: the ideal leader, like the ideal man, is decisive, assertive, and independent'.[4] If this is so, then understanding how we coach women to lead has never been more important. Recent studies of women in leadership positions have repeatedly noted distinctions in how women's leadership is perceived compared to the leadership styles of many men. On the one hand, there is enormous pressure on women leaders to show they can be as tough as their male peers. And on the other hand, those who seek to be collaborative and consultative are often dismissed as weak or soft, as Babb notes.

Coaching can certainly help women better navigate these tensions,[5] but we have found that being coached by even the most experienced executive coach may be complemented by other forms of learning and growing. The complex skills that women need are still only rarely modelled at senior leadership level. As Peter Hawkins points out, if we want cultural change in our organisations, then that change needs to be driven by the culture of tomorrow.[6] Such change will therefore ensure that we have a more diverse body of leaders at the leadership table, including more women, amongst other under-represented groups. How can we empower women not just to be effective leaders now, but to be recognised as effective leaders within the current (male-constructed) culture? We have found that teaching women to integrate a coaching approach into their leadership style can help significantly, particularly with some of the most complex areas of challenge for women.

It's Tough Being a Boss

In their leadership positions, women know that they are expected to 'set high standards, be in control . . . challenge hard if [employees] are underperforming'; and likewise 'be nice, give away your power . . . staff today won't tolerate being told what to do'.[7] At the same time, women are more likely than men to be criticised for not being 'firm' enough with their team or not expressing their views with conviction – being too 'soft.' For women, this apparent contradiction is doubly challenging: when they are competent and effective (as is expected of leaders), they are more likely than men to be criticised for being harsh and unlikeable; '[s]upervisors routinely give high-performing women some version of this message "You need to trim your sharp elbows."'[8]

Writing about the many very positive qualities of 'quiet leaders' – for instance, such qualities as measured and thoughtful, trusted, and empowering – Blaire Palmer claims that to be more successful, recognised, and valued in the workplace these leaders (both men and women, but more stereotypical of women's style of leadership) 'need help learning to have healthy arguments. They need to step out of the weeds,[9] create stronger boundaries and hold people to higher standards'.[10]

This is an issue that is often brought to the coaching room and to our coaching courses. We have found that teaching leaders robust coaching skills, directly linked to leadership roles, goes a long way in helping many women (and male leaders with a 'quieter' leadership style) to be both effective and have strong, positive relationships with their team, holding people to account, fostering engagement, being firm and fair, collaborative, and decisive. And women leaders criticised for being too harsh find using the coaching approach helps them be firm whilst also drawing on their listening and empathy skills to connect more authentically and effectively with their teams and harness engagement.

Learning to coach can help women use their emotional intelligence – often referred to as soft skills[11] – more effectively in the workplace. Our accredited foundation-level courses offer professionals in a range of roles (advisor, mentor, teacher; or leader, manager, principal performer, or executive) the opportunity to develop coaching skills to enhance their skillset for the roles they occupy. We refer to this as using a *coaching approach* in their work (participants will also learn about taking on the role of a coach working with a client in a range of settings). As a development tool, coaching skills can support many aspects of a line manager's work including managing performance. The essence of how to manage performance, a skill every boss needs to have, is not to rely on appraisal but to be able to build the kind of trust where honesty, mutual respect, and constant two-way feedback is at its core.[12] These qualities also exist at the heart of a coaching relationship, and at *Guildhall Ignite*, we differentiate between using a *coaching approach* and taking on the role of a coach for a range of reasons.

It is crucial to distinguish between the nature of the relationships:

- between a coach and client, and
- between line manager and staff member

A coach holds their client's agenda and desired outcomes front and centre in the work. Within an agreed contract, a coach champions their client, holds confidentiality, and supports the client's choices to explore a future that can offer the most fulfilment and satisfaction. The client brings their own issues to work through with the coach, a trusted thinking partner.

In a line management relationship, the line manager holds a very different role. Employed by the organisation to ensure that the work of that organisation is delivered to the highest possible standards, they will bring consideration to all members of the team or department, and pay due diligence to the efficient use of all resources. In using a *coaching approach*, a line manager normally owns the agenda of the conversation and must also ensure that choices taken serve the interests of the organisation. Should a line manager stray into the singular role of coach to their staff member, a conflict of interest would arise and then the work could become unethical. The subject matter of 1:1s between manager and staff members can include topics for discussion brought by both parties; they may also include, where appropriate, discussions on staff well-being. Through all of this, the responsibilities and power held by a line manager will impact their interactions. It is impossible for a line manager to guarantee confidentiality with a direct report if something arises that impacts the organisation. Lastly, challenges felt by a staff member will, at times, be linked to their working relationship with their line manager – the openness of a productive coaching session will rarely if ever happen within such a power relationship. Jenny Rogers provides further discussion on the benefits of using a *coaching approach* in the line manager role.[13]

At *Guildhall Ignite*, we do advocate strongly for managers to develop key coaching skills to work collaboratively and developmentally. Coaching skills will support the staff members to problem solve from multiple perspectives and to assess the potential impact of their actions on others. The specific skills include active listening, open questions, offering challenges, and reflection through conversation. Also needed is a structure to ensure rigour in seeking meaningful outcomes, actions, and a space for review. Using these skills collaboratively increases staff engagement and raises motivation.

OSCAR: A Framework for an Effective Coaching Conversation

An effective coaching style conversation requires skill and nuance. These facets are developed over many hours of practice and with regular expert feedback, supervision, and personal reflection. Structure and sequence can also greatly affect the impact of a coaching session.

Within the coaching field, a range of models offers flexibility and choice in how the individual approaches this aspect.[14] The theoretical model underpinning our Coaching and Mentoring training at *Guildhall Ignite* is a conversation structure known as OSCAR and this will be the focus of the following case studies (see Figure 18.1).[15] OSCAR offers benefits beyond the specific frame of Women and Leadership, and has been showcased by *Ignite*'s associate coaches at international conferences and events on a variety of topics.[16]

The fundamentals of OSCAR are:

O = Outcome. The work between client and coach begins *for real** with a statement about the desired outcome for the session and the issue(s) that the client is looking to change. She/they may be looking for greater clarity over the future direction of a project, seeking a solution to a technical problem, or she may want to find a way to support a colleague who is struggling without falling into the rescue role she has so often found herself in previously. The **Outcome** is the thing that she wants to be different, the shift, the change that will feel like progress is possible.

S = Situation. Where is our client right now? What is or has been happening? Who is involved? What is at stake? What seems to be the problem? Some version of one or more of these questions will emerge at this point in the conversation. During this stage of the conversation, the coach will support the client to see the issue from several angles, recalling the wider picture, broadening out the discussion as it were, to *put all the cards on the table*, have a look at them and maybe even take a walk around the table to see how the cards look from different perspectives. Important too are the feelings attached to the scenario or issue: what feelings is our client experiencing about the issue she has brought to the session?

(The conversation does at times move back and forth between the O and S parts of the model. It wouldn't be unusual for a client to reassess her desired outcome here. She may want or need to re-evaluate and refine the original issue or problem in light of the insights gained in the exchange with her coach so far . . .)

C = Choices and consequences. A conscious move can take place when the coach senses that a body of information has been gleaned by the client about their issue or dilemma. The conversation shifts to looking at the options available to the client. **Choices and consequences** offer a space to brainstorm and to open up the imagination to a range of possible next steps. Generating these options can be energising, exciting, fun, and revealing. With a range of possibilities, our client can evaluate each one and ask herself which seems the most (or least) attractive. What would the impact be of taking/pursuing each of the options?

A = Actions. The coach will now want to encourage/nudge/press/pin down their client to an action or set of actions she can commit to. **Actions** may be as simple as taking some time to think further about something that feels blurry or messy. **Actions** may include a plan for writing that letter, exploring options for further training, committing to having a difficult conversation they have been putting off, etc. The coach will be looking for evidence that the client's body language, quality of the voice, and attitude align with their spoken commitments. In this section, the coach may also check with the client on potential obstacles to success. Asking 'what might get in the way' of the desired outcome can be a surprisingly useful moment in the coaching conversation.

R = Review. How will the client know she is making progress? What signs indicate that her actions are bearing fruit? How and when does she want to be held to account for her work? When will she know she's ready to contemplate or prepare for the next phase of the work? Might she and her coach catch up on this issue?

This OSCAR framework can support deep learning for a leader helping to build clarity, confidence, self-awareness, and authenticity, supporting remarkable speed of change and growth possible for an individual willing to engage in this form of activity.

Figure 18.1 OSCAR

> *Framing the OSCAR conversation is a connection, a sense of trust, a feeling of safety. We call this connection Rapport. Rapport needs to be established between coach and client before the work of OSCAR can begin. Rapport needs to be present throughout the coaching, and present as the coach and client conclude the session.

Figure 18.1 (Continued)

What does this look like in the coaching room? The first three case studies here are representative of a broad range of potential situations in which Coaching helps to unlock that sophisticated degree of self-awareness crucial to success. In these three studies, all names have been changed, and several similar cases have been blended and roles generalised. We do this to be able to bring you genuine real-life examples whilst preserving the confidentiality we guarantee our clients. Ethical awareness and application are central to the work of a coach. The final case study draws on a masterclass we have used in international conferences to illuminate the detail of the OSCAR model in more depth through the creative medium of a single music lesson.

Case Study 1: Leading Meetings

Nadia is coaching Margaret,[17] who is newly appointed to a leadership role in an arts organisation. It's a planned development coaching session. Margaret initially said that everything was fine and there was nothing really to talk about. When pressed by Nadia, Margaret says it might be helpful to talk through ways of running meetings; sometimes she feels the team does not take her seriously enough.

Nadia asks Margaret what she wants from her in this discussion. 'Maybe to help me understand more what is going on here', she says (O). (O) represents the O from OSCAR that indicates we're looking to find the Outcome of the session. Nadia asks Margaret to tell her in more detail what is going on at the moment, asking for specific examples (S). She summarises regularly to help Margaret reflect on her experience. Margaret finds this helpful, realising that the issue is perhaps more serious than she had initially thought. There are times when her team are not following through on what she (Margaret) thought they had agreed upon in meetings. Nadia at this point asks permission to give Margaret feedback on what she has noticed in their coaching sessions (using our feedback protocol[18]). Nadia has noticed that Margaret often talks very quietly. She has also noticed that Margaret sometimes does not finish her sentences but lets them drift off. She adds that even in this session, Margaret is doing this (and gives some examples). What is the impact on Nadia? It feels as if Margaret is not always convinced herself in what she is saying. Nadia wonders if perhaps her team experiences this also.

Nadia asks Margaret what she thinks, and Margaret agrees that this could be what is happening. Margaret remembers that when being questioned on why they had not done something, her team said they had not realised that was what Margaret wanted them to do.

Nadia and Margaret then explore choices for Margaret in taking this forward (C). The conversation reveals one key thing getting in the way of Margaret being stronger in meetings is her anxiety that her team might think her 'arrogant' or 'full of herself', which has led to a self-consciousness in how she gives direction. Nadia (using our giving information-coaching-style protocol) is able to offer some practical suggestions for Margaret to develop her own authentic leadership style in meetings. This 'offer of suggestions' leaves Margaret in control of her choices and supports the development of confidence (avoiding over-dependency). Reflecting on the options given her, Margaret decides: (1) to observe other leaders in meetings, reflect on how they talk to their teams, and consider what she can learn from their styles (what things they do/say that might suit her own developing leadership style); (2) to prepare more thoroughly for meetings, including deciding in advance what she wants to ask of her team and then practising how she might go about presenting it.

Nadia and Margaret decided that they would keep in touch on this issue between their regular sessions, including Margaret using Nadia to do some role-play practice before particularly important meetings.

Case Study 2: Taking on a New Team

Many of the women we have taught in our Coaching training programme have described the coaching approach as feeling *natural*, like *coming home*. They can let go of the idea that they need to *get control* by *acting like men*. The OSCAR framework allows women to draw on the more 'feminine' skills of empathy, co-operation, tolerance, and adaptability[19] and to take the conversation forward in a commitment to action and review. With the confidence that comes from knowing these skills, used within a robust coaching approach, women leaders are enabled to communicate decisively, effectively, confidently, and to hold people to account.

For example, take Della, newly appointed Head of Department.[20] It was made very clear at the interview that one of her main tasks would be to bring more discipline to her new team. They had had several interim Heads, none of whom had tackled a culture where everyone went their own way. Before starting her coaching programme, Della decided she first needed to be firm. She used a series of emails to make her expectations clear, including everyone attending meetings and completing all departmental paperwork on time. There was an enormous backlash. People complained they had to attend too many irrelevant meetings at inconvenient times. The paperwork was condemned as over-complicated and mostly unnecessary. Some people stormed, shouted, and complained to their Principal. Others went to other departments with sob stories about their job being made impossible. Della quickly got a reputation for being a patronising bully. She was appalled and came to our coaching course anxious and doubtful of a way back. What particularly struck Della was what she learned about the importance of trust and respect: 'Remember, the most important thing in persuading anyone to rethink and change their behaviour is not facts, control or being "right" – it's a relationship of trust and respect'.[21]

Returning to her team, she put the listening and summarising skills she had learned on the course to good use in a series of one-to-one sessions with her colleagues. Della used the first part of OSCAR (Outcome and Situation) to structure the conversations and co-create agendas that were useful for her – and for her colleagues. She used questions around Choices and Consequences to really understand what the problems were with the meetings and paperwork. She was careful not to over-promise in terms of actions.

As a result of this careful listening, Della was able to agree to a plan of action with the team, incorporating a number of their suggestions whilst also moving the team culture forward in the way that was needed to bring greater consistency in approaches and behaviours across the team. Because she had listened to them, they were more able to listen to her. She did not have to compromise on what needed to be done. She just needed to connect what she needed to happen with where her team were, treating them so that they felt heard, respected, and valued.

Case Study 3: Reconsidering Choices

Alexia, newly appointed to Director level for a music charity, gets feedback that she is seen as 'distant' and 'stand-offish' by her colleagues. Exploring the (S) of OSCAR with her coach helps her to identify what is meant. Alexia has young children and so to manage both her personal and professional responsibilities she has taken to saving time in a variety of ways. This includes bringing her own coffee-making equipment, thus missing out on the chat in the coffee queue at the local café; she goes home when she finishes work, rather than go to the bar for drinks on a Friday evening as she used to in her previous roles; she is pragmatic between meetings, planning her travel efficiently so that she arrives just on time. All of this means she does not participate in the more casual outside-of-work activities that her male colleagues do.

Going more deeply into what is happening, Alexia realises that she doesn't really know any of her colleagues very well. She has never engaged in 'small talk' (not 'her thing' at the best of times) and feels irritated when anything comes up in a meeting that is not directly and immediately relevant to the topic under discussion.

The culture of the organisation that Alexia has joined is very traditionally 'male'. The other directors and trustees are all men and know each other well. Alexia explains to her coach that they talk loudly, make jokes that she does not get, and if she is honest, she is not sure she likes them. Her coach helps her to identify that she is feeling angry and frustrated. She is working hard, getting a lot of work done that badly needed doing – and rather than getting recognition for that, she feels she's being criticised for 'not being friendly enough'.

Using (S) from OSCAR, Alexia's coach helps her to explore what she is missing by not having the rapport and trust she was used to having with colleagues in her previous job. Alexia acknowledges that this is having an impact on the quality of her work, as she is missing some key information that seemed to be coming from the informal conversations, and that this can sometimes make her defensive – which might come across as 'distant'. She also acknowledges that she is missing the benefits of 'teamwork' that she'd enjoyed at work in the past – for example, sharing skills/experience in problem solving.

In brainstorming this situation with her coach, Alexia identified three possibilities for action (C):

1) Do nothing. Keep focussed on her own work and shrug off explicit or implicit criticism of her social contact with the team as largely irrelevant to her own goals.
2) Identify one or two people in her new teams that she feels she might build more rapport with (for example, a colleague who has just had his first baby), and begin to explore ways to have more informal conversations with them (perhaps before or after more formal meetings) and see what might come out of such contact.
3) Acknowledge that, like them or not, every member of the team is now relevant to her own success and well-being at work, and to identify something positive in each of them (instead of adding to her already-long list of things she does not like about them!).

Thinking about the consequences (C of OSCAR), Alexia was honest and said that at the moment she could not see either (2) or (3) working, as she felt it was unreasonable that she was having to adapt to their culture and find time in her busy schedule to 'hang out'. 'Even my colleague with the new baby doesn't have my responsibilities for having to get back to the childminder', she said; 'his wife does that, so if something comes up and times change he is much more flexible than I can be'. She also could not see herself joining in the loud laughter. Her resentment and difference in personal style would get in the way. However, she could also see that the consequences of (1) were unacceptable, as in the end she could see herself leaving the organisation.

Alexia's coach asked her to think of the wisest leader she'd ever worked with and imagine asking her views on the situation. Alexia laughed for the first time in the session, and said immediately, 'I know exactly who to choose and I know what she'd say, too. She'd say, "Get over yourself Alexia. Look to the long game."'

'What does looking to the long game mean?' asked the coach.

'It means it's OK for me to feel annoyed and resentful that the people I'm working with aren't as similar to me as I'd like, but that staying with that feeling is going to harm me far more than them. Also, if one of my values is about respecting diversity (which it is) perhaps this is an opportunity for me to look below the surface to the human beings underneath'. This insight enabled Alexia to reconsider options (2) and (3).

In the next session, 6 weeks later, Alexia was able to confirm that her new approach was already starting to make a difference to her work, to her relationships with colleagues, and to her sense of well-being at work. There were still many things that annoyed her, but she felt she was managing these better, and there were also things she could enjoy and feel more relaxed with. Her quieter, drier humour was finding a place in the organisation, which pleased her and was the starting point for the next session – exploring what kind of colleague and leader Alexia would like to be in this new world.

What was probably the most important achievement over 6 months of coaching for Alexia in this situation was enabling her to find a way to be her authentic self while finding a meaningful way to connect with her colleagues and the organisation as a whole. Her negative, angry feelings were valid but over time were stopping her from making progress as a leader. Drawing on her generosity of spirit allowed her to reach out initially to find a way to connect with her new male colleagues without having to become 'one of the boys'. Over time, the rapport and trust created by Alexia provided her with the insights she needed to be more persuasive in changing old ways of working such as beginning to reduce the long hours and manage meetings (including finishing times) more efficiently.

Case Study 4: The Clarinet Lesson

Instrumental and singing professors with Coaching Training at the Guildhall School have adopted the OSCAR model within their teaching strategies, applying it in one-to-one lessons. Taking this a step further into the realm of professional development, the authors of this chapter have devised an activity in which *Guildhall Ignite* Head Coach Jane Booth (also a professional clarinetist specialising in historical instrument performance) explores in a public masterclass the potential of OSCAR with a fellow professional clarinetist. The report that follows documents one such event.

Neyire Ashworth is a specialist in modern clarinet performance, and in the session with Jane she learnt to play a piece on the Historical (Classical) Clarinet, which required her to negotiate some of the complexities of historical performance practice, including radically different fingerings, different approaches to phrasing, instrument response, and articulation (compared to the modern instrument). In accepting this challenge, Neyire needed to let go of being an expert clarinetist in her usual field, placing herself in the situation of being a novice, facing many unknowns, and likely leading to her making mistakes. As the learner and coachee, Neyire placed herself in a very vulnerable position. This account is shared with Neyire's permission.

In the masterclass, Jane adopted a dual role. As a specialist clarinetist drawing on Executive Coaching skills, her task was to create a safe space for exploration and learning, to recognise Neyire as an expert in herself (her life experience, her expertise, and her self-knowledge), to facilitate Neyire's learning, and to support her progress by creating positive conditions for growth. Jane brought her specialist knowledge as a performer on historical clarinets to the session and was mindful of how and when to deploy it.

Neyire's stated desires for the session included ensuring that she really 'made music' on the unfamiliar instrument (she wanted to find a way to communicate to her audience through the instrument), and a desire to learn something about embellishment[22] in classical repertoire. Jane and Neyire worked on a short piece from the early 19th century for clarinet and bass by French composer Jean-Xavier Lefèvre, something Neyire had not explored before. She had played the instrument a couple of times previously, but the last time had been several months ago so there was some recapping to do to find all the notes and to make an attractive sound she could enjoy (S). Playing the music over several times helped embed the fingering patterns and helped Neyire get a sense of how to control sound on the unfamiliar instrument. She remembered that she also enjoyed playing slowly when practising and did that a couple of times (Jane keeping her company with a bass line). It was starting to feel like fun and Neyire was beginning to be more exploratory and playful – this was audible and visible for all to witness. And once comfortable,

> she wanted to explore the embellishment idea. Jane and Neyire looked at the music together and discovered a handful of techniques that composer Lefèvre had already used to decorate the music himself (C). Choosing two that she felt she could easily apply, Neyire began the piece again. The idea was to deploy one of the techniques at every opportunity without worrying about it being 'good' or 'right' – just having fun, whatever came from the experiment (A). Afterwards, Neyire could reflect on this and decide which were the most appropriate embellishments and where they might work best – further refining this over time (R).
>
> Although this run-through could have been chaotic, it was not. The music took on a playful, light spirit; Neyire's playing found more expression, personality, and interest than she had ever thought possible in this situation.
>
> The prime qualities evident in the session had included empathy, humility, honesty, and humour. A spirit of non-judgement and curiosity had created room for big shifts and positive change to take place in a very small space of time. Also evident had been Neyire's willingness to be *vulnerable* in this situation. What would have been different if vulnerability had not been present? Given Neyire's high level of expertise and her status as an international clarinetist, accepting to expose herself as a novice on the early clarinet before a critical audience had taken great courage and generosity. But how had that been for Neyire?

Neyire: It struck me how that style of working builds energy. It's a space for experimentation and we lose our fear of getting things wrong. It's partly to do with being vulnerable.

Jane: What does it mean to be vulnerable, Neyire?

Neyire: It's an openness, a receptiveness to everything around and a sensitivity to everything . . . that you're taking in and observing . . . so it's a great starting point for learning. With vulnerability, your defences are down . . . that's how I feel. So, you're in a space, ideally a safe space . . . And if your defences are down, you're not going to be resistant to [new] information, you're going to be curious, or receptive . . . Vulnerability could also mean that there is a hierarchical relationship; it doesn't have to be that but it does depend on how comfortable you are with your vulnerability; it can be a bit of a power relationship if one's not careful. 'Oh, that person knows everything and I know nothing' . . . you know.

Jane: And what is it that allows you not to move into that thinking space?

Neyire: Well, the other person, so you! You know, if I feel safe, then I feel this shared discovery is of mutual benefit to both of us. It creates a sense of mutual respect, and I can feel I have a lot to offer. So, it's not that I don't know anything, it's that we're building on all the things I do know.

Jane: And I'm reminded how important it is that the person I'm working with can bring the whole of themselves to the work, their knowledge and everything that they are. So what you seem to be saying is that by creating this environment, it helps you to feel safe and to be accepting of yourself.

Neyire: In fact, that's the crux of it really. You're looking to me for my answers and that's empowering and enabling within the vulnerability. I mean, it's a really interesting dance of all those things . . . it's like a circle dance, isn't it?

Jane: Have there been any lightbulb moments in the work we've done?

Neyire: Connecting to that expressive voice and the excitement of it, the delight. Looking forward to the possibility that I might really be able to find meaning in that whole era of music through ornamentation, freedom, and improvisation. I think those are big moments . . . OSCAR leads to higher-level thinking.

The positive transformational potential of the OSCAR model in this teaching context has been reinforced in feedback received following our conference presentations. Observers note that unspoken communications – including body language and, in this instance, the musical sounds produced during the lesson – have at least as powerful an impact on how people connect as the words they use, supporting effective, useful, and productive work together. Picking up on these nuances is vitally important whatever the coaching context. Among the most significant comments (including some from female leaders and managers) received are:

- Jane checked in and established prior learning so there was a clear starting point for the work. We noticed that this validated Neyire, acknowledging her experience and what she had to bring to the context at hand.
- Jane checked for motivation to make sure the work would align with Neyire's interests and therefore her positive energy for action and change.
- It was amazing that Neyire went from struggling with the notes to performing a piece with feeling and imagination!
- It was really incredible how the work they did was so relevant to executive coaching and how terrific it was to bring something so creative into the room.[23]

Conclusion

Executive Coaching has been recognized as a powerful leadership development tool across the corporate sector for half a century or more. Embedded in research, the disciplines of the coach are supported and framed through a commitment to ethical practice, regular CPD, and supervision. Working with a coach can bridge the gap between a woman's current performance and her future potential. Training to use a coaching approach can help a female leader maximise her impact across their team and organisation. It builds employee engagement, strengthens and deepens relationships, and holds people to account whilst allowing for empathy, authenticity, and individuality. The experience of *Guildhall Ignite*'s associate coaches has revealed the huge potential for targeted coaching *in and through the performing arts* to support individual and team performance within organisational and performance-based activities across Music and Drama contexts. As a teaching tool and beyond, a coaching approach recognizes the unique qualities each individual can bring and draws out creativity, strengthens problem-solving abilities, and embraces diversity.

The reader will see that the OSCAR tool has been adapted by *Guildhall Ignite* to a wide range of professional development situations, some of which are shared here. Being coached and using coaching skills with others makes a significant positive impact on the effectiveness of women leaders across performing and leadership roles in music: focusing the mind, deploying strategic thinking with confidence, creativity, authenticity, and expressivity. Ways of being that feel natural to women (desire for collaboration, openness, deep listening, shared leadership) can be honed within a personal leadership style when working with a coach for professional development. Training to coach supports a female leader to become even more versatile and robust with her skillset. Women find this allows them to bring the best of themselves whilst leaving space to honour, value, and include the contributions of others.

Notes

1. Leonardo Christov-Moore, Elizabeth A. Simpson, Gino Coudé, Kristina Grigaityte, Marco Iacoboni, and Pier Francesco Ferrari, "Empathy: Gender Effects in Brain and Behaviour," *Neuroscience & Biobehavioral Reviews* 46, no. 4 (2014): 604–27, accessed April 16, 2023, www.ncbi.nlm.nih.gov/pmc/articles/PMC5110041/.
2. See ignite.gsmd.ac.uk.
3. Tomas Chamorro-Premuzic, "As Long as We Associate Leadership with Masculinity, Women Will Be Overlooked," *Harvard Business Review*, March 2019, paragraph 2, accessed July 26, 2020, https://hbr.org/2019/03/as-long-as-we-associate-leadership-with-masculinity-women-will-be-overlooked.
4. Sarah Babb, "Women in Leadership – Is Gender Equity Still an Issue?," *University of Stellenbosch Business School Executive Development Blog*, May 18, 2017, paragraph 10, accessed July 26, 2020, https://usb-ed.com/blog/women-in-leadership-is-gender-equity-still-an-issue. See also Herminia Ibarra, Robin J. Ely, and Deborah M. Kolb, "Women Rising: The Unseen Barriers," *Harvard Business Review*, September 2013, accessed July 26, 2020, https://hbr.org/2013/09/women-rising-the-unseen-barriers.
5. See, for example, Averil Leimon, François Moscovici, and Helen Goodier, *Coaching Women to Lead* (London and New York: Routledge, 2011).
6. Peter Hawkins, *Creating a Coaching Culture: Developing a Coaching Strategy for Your Organization* (Maidenhead: McGraw Hill Open University, 2012), 114.
7. Jenny Rogers, with Karen Whittleworth and Andrew Gilbert, *Manager as Coach: The New Way to Get Results* (Maidenhead: McGraw Hill, 2012), 3.
8. Ibarra, Ely and Kolb, "Women Rising," paragraph 23; § "Create Safe Identity Workspaces."
9. *How to Get Out of the Weeds as a Leader*, December 7, 2021, accessed April 15, 2023, www.dameleadership.com/research-and-insights/get-out-of-the-weeds/.
10. Blaire Palmer, "Overlooked and Undervalued – Why 'Quiet Leadership' Could Be the Answer to Your Culture Problem," *HR Zone*, July 2019, paragraph 13; § "Re-thinking What Leadership Looks Like," accessed July 26, 2020, www.hrzone.com/lead/culture/overlooked-and-undervalued-why-quiet-leadership-could-be-the-answer-to-your-culture.
11. Denise Trudeau-Poskas, "Soft Skills Are 2020's Hard Skills – Here's How to Master Them," *Forbes*, January 29, 2020, accessed April 13, 2023, www.forbes.com/sites/forbescoachescouncil/2020/01/29/soft-skills-are-2020s-hard-skills-heres-how-to-master-them/.
12. Rogers, Whittleworth and Gilbert, *Manager as Coach*, 3–5.
13. Rogers, Whittleworth and Gilbert, *Manager as Coach*.
14. Jeremy Sutton, "12 Effective Coaching Models to Help Your Clients Grow," October 7, 2020, accessed April 15, 2023, https://positivepsychology.com/coaching-models/.
15. Andrew Gilbert and Karen Shuttleworth, *The OSCAR Coaching Model: Simplifying Workplace Coaching* (Monmouth: Worth Consulting Ltd, 2009).
16. Such conferences and events include: Norwegian Academy of Music, December 2015 and September 2016; 'Innovative Conservatoire' (ICON) Seminar Kallio-Kuninkala, Helsinki, March 2016; ICONgo, University of Music and Performing Arts Vienna, Austria, February 2017; ICON, Sibelius Academy, Kunkkula, April 2017; ICONgo, Queensland, Australia, May 2017; EMCC Global Provider Summit, London, November 2018; 25th Annual Mentoring, Coaching and Supervision Conference EMCC Dublin, April 2019; IWML February 2019; ICONgo, Teachers Seminar, Akosticum Netherlands, February 2020; Music & Drama Education Expo, London, UK, March 2020; ICONgo, Voksenåsen, Oslo, October 2022.
17. Nadia and Margaret represent a range of individuals from many different organisations who have appeared as clients in our consulting rooms.
18. Rogers, Whittleworth and Gilbert, *Manager as Coach*, 129.
19. Christov-Moore et al., "Empathy: Gender Effects in Brain and Behaviour."
20. Names and roles have been blended and conflated so as not to represent any one person, role, or institution. The issues are typical of those that arise in many comparable institutions.
21. Guildhall Ignite, *Foundation Course Handbook 2019* (London: Guildhall School of Music & Drama, 2019), 76.
22. Embellishment in classical music (and likewise in jazz) is a fundamental creative and compositional tool (frequently used improvisationally by players) whereby a single note (pitch) within a melody is

replaced by an aesthetically pleasing alternative sequence of notes (often moving quite rapidly) that conforms to the underpinning harmonic framework (chord sequence).
23. 25th Annual Mentoring, Coaching and Supervision Conference of the European Mentoring and Coaching Council, Dublin, April 2019.

Bibliography

Babb, Sarah. "Women in Leadership – Is Gender Equity Still an Issue?," University of Stellenbosch Business School Executive Development blog (18 May 2017), paragraph 10. Accessed July 26, 2020. https://usb-ed.com/blog/women-in-leadership-is-gender-equity-still-an-issue.

Chamorro-Premuzic, Tomas. "As Long as We Associate Leadership with Masculinity, Women Will Be Overlooked." *Harvard Business Review* (March 2019), paragraph 2. Accessed July 16, 2020. https://hbr.org/2019/03/as-long-as-we-associate-leadership-with-masculinity-women-will-be-overlooked.

Christov-Moore, Leonardo, Elizabeth A. Simpson, Gino Coudé, Kristina Grigaityte, Marco Iacoboni, and Pier Francesco Ferrari. "Empathy: Gender Effects in Brain and Behaviour." *Neuroscience & Biobehavioral Reviews* 46, no. 4 (2014): 604–27. Accessed April 16, 2023. www.ncbi.nlm.nih.gov/pmc/articles/PMC5110041/.

Dowd, Maureen. "Lady of the Rings: Jacinda Rules." *The New York Times*, September 8, 2018. Accessed July 26, 2020. www.nytimes.com/2018/09/08/opinion/sunday/jacinda-ardern-new-zealand-prime-minister.html.

Gilbert, Andrew, and Karen Shuttleworth. *The OSCAR Coaching Model: Simplifying Workplace Coaching*. Monmouth: Worth Consulting Ltd, 2009.

Guildhall Ignite. *Foundation Course Handbook 2019*. London: Guildhall School of Music & Drama, 2019.

Hawkins, Peter. *Creating a Coaching Culture: Developing a Coaching Strategy for Your Organization*. Maidenhead: McGraw Hill Open University, 2012.

How to Get Out of the Weeds as a Leader, December 7, 2021. Accessed April 15, 2023. www.dameleadership.com/research-and-insights/get-out-of-the-weeds/.

Ibarra, Herminia, Robin J. Ely, and Deborah M. Kolb. "Women Rising: The Unseen Barriers." *Harvard Business Review*, September 2013. Accessed July 26, 2020. https://hbr.org/2013/09/women-rising-the-unseen-barriers.

Leimon, Averil, François Moscovici, and Helen Goodier. *Coaching Women to Lead*. London and New York: Routledge, 2011.

Palmer, Blaire. "Overlooked and Undervalued – Why 'Quiet Leadership' Could Be the Answer to Your Culture Problem." *HR Zone*, July 2019, paragraph 13; § "Re-thinking What Leadership Looks Like." Accessed July 26, 2020. www.hrzone.com/lead/culture/overlooked-and-undervalued-why-quiet-leadership-could-be-the-answer-to-your-culture.

Rogers, Jenny, with Karen Whittleworth, and Andrew Gilbert. *Manager as Coach: The New Way to Get Results*. Maidenhead: McGraw Hill, 2012.

Sutton, Jeremy. "12 Effective Coaching Models to Help Your Clients Grow," October 7, 2020. Accessed April 15, 2023. https://positivepsychology.com/coaching-models/.

Trudeau-Poskas, Denise. "Soft Skills Are 2020's Hard Skills – Here's How to Master Them." *Forbes*, January 29, 2020. Accessed April 13, 2023. www.forbes.com/sites/forbescoachescouncil/2020/01/29/soft-skills-are-2020s-hard-skills-heres-how-to-master-them/.

19
THE WORK THAT (IRISH) WOMEN DO
Reframing Leadership in a British University Ceílí Band

Anne-Marie Beaumont

As my life has changed as a result of emigration and motherhood, the impact on my sense of self and identity has been significant. Like many other female, mid-career academics, I have found myself riddled with doubts about whether I am 'leadership material' and reflecting on what that is, or should look like, within a contemporary British University Music Department. This chapter, therefore, draws on autoethnographic tools in its approach to self-reflective narrative and will consider the impact of gender, culture and expressions of Irishness in my own musical leadership style. The late Seamus Heaney (1939–2013) discussed what it means to be Irish[1] and the impact of our artist/creator identity on the work that we do. In talking about the act of writing (creating), he referred to: the identification of the origin of an idea; the creation of new conditions in which that idea can take flight; and the transformation of that into something that is both new and renovated.[2] In my own work as leader and musical director of a Ceílí-type band in a Post-92 British University Music Department, I actively draw upon this notion of origin and cultural heritage; I have created a liminal and free space in the physical geography of my institution in order to disrupt and transform the typical settler colonial constructs of Western European art music to better reflect and enhance the student learning experience; by doing so, I have created a new or renewed sense of community. As a post-92 institution with mostly first-in-family university students, there was often a lack of cohesion and shared identity which made it difficult to progress in group work. As a course leader, it was important for me to create a place where shared ideas (musical, academic, intellectual) could flourish and took it upon myself to think about ways of improving active engagement for our student community. As an Irish woman, I decided to use music as a way of bringing together diverse students and implemented a Ceílí band.

This work explores my own intersectionality and the 'between' space that I occupy as a practitioner and academic as well as an Irish woman in a British institution. In our weekly rehearsals, my leadership of this ensemble has alternated between classical Western European conductor idioms and much less structured rehearsal techniques more typical of the seemingly 'casual' encounter of the Irish traditional music session.[3] This chapter considers the impact of issues such as cultural heritage, musical practice, gender expectations and diasporic experience on my leadership of the group and on my student participants. It explores the challenge of leading an ensemble as an Irish woman working in a British university from positions rooted in cultural geography, transnational studies, feminism, narrative enquiry and autoethnography. This work is autobiographical in its focus and does not intend to outline either a model of practice for other Irish women in Britain, nor to suggest new ways of working in British university music departments; it is, rather, an exploration of how the deployment of Irish traditional music and community-based leadership methods both disrupt and enhance the student experience within university ensemble practice. By adopting a culturally responsive, situated learning approach, we have managed to create a unique musical community within my institution. Evidence of its success lies within student reports of greater enjoyment of ensemble rehearsals and the development of a new common language and original terminologies. It demonstrates that through a process of resistance to standard university ensemble rehearsal models and the deployment of Irish traditional music in this instance, a stronger sense of community identity and student engagement can be created.

Gender and (Irish) Music in the Public Sphere

In this work, I acknowledge the very real and substantial privilege I enjoy as an educated, white, Irish cis woman within a university position. I lay claim, however, to an intersectional identity that I occupy as an Irish woman in a British institution, where I have frequently been reminded of my otherness in terms of heritage and educational differences.[4] The immigrant experience frequently involves what Brah refers to as strategies of 'accommodation, complicity, resistance, struggle, [and] transgression', and these effectively describe various stages of my academic career thus far.[5] As a mid-career academic, I have now arrived at the struggle and transgression stage and have started to contest the standard approaches to musical leadership within the university setting, displacing settler colonial dominance as a result.

Even with this clear white privilege, recent immigrants to the UK from Ireland continue to experience some discrimination, though this is far less direct than that suffered by previous generations. Our otherness within Britain is still audibly marked: like many other Irish people abroad, I have been frequently praised for the softness of my accent and implored to say or repeat phrases for the enjoyment of listeners.[6] The lingering unease arising from this sense of being a performer of Irishness[7] and quaint cultural gestures meant that, for many years, I was reluctant to employ my knowledge of traditional Irish music and its social, pedagogical and andragogical structures within the ensembles that I run at my institution, thereby actively perpetuating Brah's definition of accommodation and complicity. Bronwen Walters' work has reflected upon the construction of a male Irish ethnicity in Britain and has queried what it means in relation to Irish women, arguing that they have become invisible in a way, an aspect that I struggled with for many years within my own career.[8] Being particularly conscious of my Irishness and female gender in a predominantly male department further inhibited my desire to draw attention to myself and, when combined with an upbringing redolent with gender-normative expectations, also made me reticent about taking a much more overt leadership role within my department, especially in terms of musical direction. Starting the Hub Ceílí band (re)established my Irishness as I resisted the urge to accommodate and comply, but also my previously self-subjugated ability to direct a musical ensemble in an attempt to reconstruct my heritage and identity.

There is a perceived dichotomy between a standard orchestral rehearsal process and the image of the less formal, democratically agreed-upon playing that occurs in traditional music sessions. Within both spheres, however, schemes of power are enacted: the conductor stands at the front in Western European art music directing their ensemble, and higher-status male musicians lead the session.[9] Very few public sessions are led by female musicians in Irish music and, although there has been an increase in the number of professional female conductors in recent years, they still remain in the minority.[10] From the earliest days of the Irish Free State (1922–1937), which promoted the importance of moral values, women experienced decades of exclusion from public houses. As the locus of much traditional music performance within a state that 'served to consolidate religious doctrine through state-sponsored morality', Irish traditional music has established itself very clearly along gendered lines with power frequently being maintained by male musicians.[11] Helen O'Shea notes: 'In Irish pub sessions, men's employment as leaders gives male musicians the legitimacy and authority that women musicians lack . . . in general, women are not perceived as "leadership material" '.[12] The participation of women in Irish traditional music pub sessions has started to change in recent years, and evidence suggests that more women are participating in and forming their own sessions in various venues in Ireland and beyond. These sessions have continued to occur most often within the domestic sphere as public sessions remain dominated by male musicians, with female participants reporting accounts of exclusion and harassment by their male counterparts.[13] In describing the types of harassment experienced by the female musicians with whom she spoke, O'Shea's writing echoes the types of patriarchal critiques that exist within academia.[14] My work as leader of a Ceílí-type band therefore resists decades of patriarchal dominance of the performance sphere and has resulted in many hours of anxious introspection about whether or not I have 'done the right thing' in establishing an Irish music ensemble in a British university.

Resistance and the Post-92 University

The university at which I work recruits most of its undergraduate students from within a 40-mile radius of the institution. The region has historically faced very significant economic and educational challenges, which continue today through widespread unemployment and limited opportunities for young school-leavers.[15] Many students are the first in their family to attend a Higher Education institution: they are more likely to experience disadvantage, drop out of university and the resulting mental health impact of this perceived 'failure' can be profound.[16] These students also occupy intersectional identities as non-traditional university-goers and, as a result of my own experience, I have tried to relate to their experience of a higher education setting. The importance of establishing a sense of community for these students within the university setting is one reason why situated learning stemming from a community of practice[17] approach has been adopted within our department.[18] The learning strategy has been designed with our unique student body in mind: flexible practice has become an essential part of curriculum planning, and I have tried to adopt a culturally responsive approach within my own professional practice. Understanding how social positioning within ensembles (and the negative feelings generated by that) has impacted student self-perception has resulted in a change to the rehearsal process and the adoption of new work methods.[19]

Instrumental work within our music department had always consisted of standard university ensembles – string orchestra, wind band, choir, chamber choir and various jazz groups – which had as their goal the pursuit of excellence. While this remains an essential part of what we do as academics and music teachers,[20] standard ensembles might be considered an exclusive practice which potentially denies important opportunities for musical growth to a large portion of our student body. Several of our ensembles were only accessible to students via an audition process, which frequently advantaged those with previous access to a good-quality primary and secondary school music service education. This left many capable, proficient, largely self-taught musicians feeling disenfranchised from our collaborative music-making activities and particularly impacted those first-in-family students.[21]

Drawing upon my own intersectional identity and having a desire to disrupt standard Western European ensemble practices at our institution, I decided to deploy traditional Irish music and offered the Hub Ceílí Band as an additional university ensemble. As a music with a long history of suppression, both by a colonial power and later the united opposition of the State and Catholic Church, traditional Irish music represents a disruptive force.[22] I aimed to employ a community music approach to foster growth and learning within the department as a means of reaching out to students who might otherwise have been excluded. At its heart were three guiding principles: inclusion, self-determination and fun. This was an ensemble open to everyone, whatever their socio-cultural backgrounds or musical abilities. My ambition was to create a sense of community to support the development of excellence through the provision of a new ensemble. I was keen to ensure that the more holistic skills of the community musician were a central part of the music-making process, and I hoped that students would develop a sense of 'ownership' of their ensemble experienceeven though the music and repertoire performed was new to all of them. The provision of new musical materials created an equal opportunity for all students to learn together without the disadvantages posed by some of our other ensembles. I wanted to assist personal and group development of skills and confidence, and to help groups and individuals make musical statements that reflect their lives in exciting and innovative ways. Following a basic model established by the *grúpaí cheoil* (performance groups which bring together learners of Irish music in a fun and supportive environment), the early days of our band sought to establish trust based on the importance of play in a social rather than purely musical sense.[23]

Resisting the Standard Ensemble: Space and the Musical Encounter

As previously noted, Irish traditional music performance tends to occur in either the communal space of the public house or within the domestic sphere of the home, neither of which were entirely appropriate for weekly university ensemble rehearsals. In many parts of Ireland, however, local Comhaltas groups (non-profit groups set up for the promotion of Irish traditional movements) run *grúpaí cheoil* (traditional music groups) in halls and community centres. The decision was taken, therefore, to hold a rehearsal in our social atrium space, rather than an ensemble room. It is a wide open space with low-level couches, a few coffee tables and a vibrant atmosphere. As such, I hoped it would mimic the physical environment of the traditional session, and it occupies what might be considered a 'third space'.[24] It exists outside the formality of the ensemble rehearsal room in an informal space occupied by other performing arts students. The proximity of this atrium to the university campus library was also considered; all those entering and leaving the learning centre were drawn into the auditory event of the rehearsal, including students from other disciplines such as health, education and sport science in the shared experience. Discussing the importance of public space for the creation of community, Freie emphasises that public spaces emphasise the

> value of equality as all members of the community are allowed access to them . . . Genuine public spaces act as leveling [sic] devices and serve to expand the possibilities of interaction among participants, whereas formal associations tend toward limitation, restriction and exclusion . . . In effect, public spaces help provide the glue for genuine community.[25]

For students, this might better be considered a liminal space where their encounter did not require the formality of the typical rehearsal studio.[26]

The choice of a social space populated by other performing arts was intended to unsettle the participants and to create a new ensemble dynamic which removed the need for the formality of the large rehearsal room. By deconstructing the concept of the 'rehearsal space', it was hoped that a broader musical experience could be achieved that was akin to Small's concept of musicking which he defines as: 'an activity in which all those present are involved and for whose nature and quality, success or failure, everyone present bears some responsibility'.[27] Finding myself 'on display', however, was an equally unsettling experience for me. I was hoping to recreate some of the informality of the 'Session' experience rather than the conventional behaviour that comes from a typical orchestral rehearsal, although there was mixed success with this approach. One student reported that 'having heard the ensemble on the atrium in my first week of my first year at the university I was a bit wary of attending'.[28] Another said:

> Because it is an ensemble that, as a musician, I just wasn't used to, it wasn't easy to just come in and slot into place. There seems to be less of a hierarchy in this ensemble so, in turn, it's more accepting of ability and other things'.[29]

Students within the space encountered the music in a serendipitous fashion, and the lack of a formal threshold which they were required to cross to the rehearsal space was rather unsettling for them. The encounter itself created a tension within students, between the desire to encounter this new music and the fear of walking away from it. Equally off-putting for newcomers was the blurring of the relationship between audience and rehearsing musicians, which was quite different from their usual encounter where there is frequently a barrier, such as a raised stage, between the performer and public.[30] After initial unease, students reported welcoming the informality and spontaneity that characterised our band rehearsals, with one student reporting:

> Ceílí is a completely different ensemble to every other ensemble I am in . . . it's also nice to see people with varying instruments all together in one ensemble; no matter their instrument or ability, everyone is involved, and that's nice to have everyone together; and you never know what's coming next, especially when a boron [sic] is thrown at you![31]

Beyond the band, students achieved success in other ensembles as well and demonstrated an increased confidence in taking on leadership roles in extra-curricular activities, using the band as a model for reflective practice in classroom management, leadership and programme design in assessed work.

Resisting Expectation: Repertoire and the Rehearsal Process

Standard Western European rehearsal behaviours have been resisted within the band, and I frequently ask students to add ornamentation or harmonies at will. The purpose of this is to create more of a workshop scenario, allowing students to find their own voice within the repertoire and thereby achieving musical independence.[32] However, this caused difficulties for some students who particularly struggled with problem-based learning in an ensemble setting.[33] Students were much more accustomed to working in a standard band-type rehearsal with a conductor (a perceived expert; in most instances a man) at the front leading the process and working from detailed musical scores; the absence of these created a significant level of discomfiture.³⁴ One student reported that they had to adapt in ways which were not common for them:

> [A]s a cellist, the tunes were mainly given for the violins. I often got given the same piece of music in treble clef, which is difficult to transpose on the spot, especially quavers. I then got given the bass line, mainly semibreves, which I don't mind but I would have liked something more challenging.³⁵

The aural transmission of Irish music and the unique interpretation of it is a central element of its character, and such a negative response on the part of students may have been born from a position of fear when encountering the newness of this ensemble leadership approach.³⁶ One new student even claimed that they had been 'demoted' and was rather offended when asked to play a bodhrán when their main instrument was not needed. This student was an advanced instrumentalist who had considerable experience of playing and leading external ensembles. He openly struggled to adapt to the musicking that was taking place in the band and became quite verbal in his critique during the rehearsal process. I asked him to simply observe our rehearsal protocols for a couple of weeks, during which he saw the democratic principles of the band at work. Several students offered suggestions, led rehearsals and set aside their own instruments to explore additional timbres in arrangements, during which time the importance of rhythm and driving percussion was realised. This modelling of practice encouraged the student to step back into the ensemble, take up a bodhrán and become quite proficient at this instrument. Continuous exposure to the repertoire and to the nature of our rehearsal processes led to a much more positive response from students when questioned about their participation and enjoyment:

> To be honest I had no idea what I was expecting; having previously been a part of my school's 'Irish band' led by a choral conductor, I wasn't expecting much, a few jigs and reels a bit of fun really . . . I was taken by surprise when I was handling piles of music, yes, a few jigs and reels, but also some beautiful songs and melodies that on the surface look simple but once the ensemble began to play together and became comfortable with the ornamentation sound[ed] so lovely!³⁷

For me, it was important that the process should be discursive,³⁸ and our repertoire has subsequently broadened to include more folk tunes from the British Isles. As a result of increased membership (27 students at the time of writing) I have started to create more detailed, though still rather sketchy, charts and lead sheets. The haste at which they are created often means that they are riddled with errors, but students have become quite inventive in problem-solving and working out solutions to issues that arise during the rehearsal sessions. They no longer expect me, as the leader/conductor, to correct or resolve them. This highlights the fact that they regard me less as the 'maestro' or the 'teacher', in other words, 'checker, the "fixer of all problems, the "judge and jury of musical correctness"', and more as a partner within the ensemble.³⁹

Active engagement with the rehearsal process is something that I encourage, although new students joining our existing Ceílí community have occasionally questioned what they perceive to be the chaotic nature of rehearsals, interpreting this as 'poor leadership'. Such an attitude is often the result of a podium-centric approach to rehearsals experienced during the formative years of musical training, and it takes significant effort and trust to overcome this.⁴⁰ Students have started to ask for the opportunity to 'conduct' the band themselves as a means of gaining experience of working with and directing large ensembles, so I make space in every session for a student-led rehearsal. Students' ability to request leadership opportunities, and in so doing to challenge themselves, to critically identify errors, to discuss and share ideas, are clear signs that trust has been formed within the ensemble and that the community strength and identity is growing. An authentic relationship of facilitator and participant has developed which is quite different from the conductor/performer or senior/apprentice paradigm that characterises some of our more standard university ensembles and Irish traditional music.

Reframing Leadership as the Development of Community

Existing members have remained a firm fixture of weekly rehearsals and new students have also joined. Flautists have willingly and voluntarily switched to tin whistles instead of flutes for some of the tunes and the violinists have started to play in a 'fiddle' style with looser wrists and tighter bowing than they might ordinarily employ in their classical repertoire. Students have embraced playing the bodhrán, the Irish frame drum, instead of their main instruments, and several have developed great technique and facility with it. Others have also sung rebel tunes and songs in Irish, demonstrating an openness to an experience that had previously unsettled them.

Students now add ornaments where they feel they belong and interestingly have developed their own unique language to describe the different ornaments that they were using: a 'Shh-lump' replaces the term for a traditional 'cut' in Irish music or acciaccatura. This new lingua franca has replaced the traditional terms that were more familiar to me from my youth: the 'cuts', '*casadh*/turns' and 'rolls' have been replaced with nonsense words that are understood by the entire band. This is clear evidence that students are forming their own community with a shared expression and language, as well as that they are resisting the standard conventional linguistic norms inherited from the Western European classical idiom and are attempting to approach music from an entirely self-directed perspective.[41] This act of language invention signifies a developing ownership of the rehearsal process and is a small but noteworthy feature of the collective creation of a community identity within our band.

The experimentation in terms of rehearsal space, standard etiquette/behaviour and the freedom to invent, amend and impose personal interpretation in ensemble music has led to 'positive epiphanies' in the student learning process.[42] These can be observed in the following comments from students:

> I can tell my playing has improved and adapted to the style as I used to really struggle with mentally adding in ornamentation, and now I do it like it's second nature, so now I feel like I can engage with the music more.[43]

Student embodiment of a new musical style, and even more importantly, the transformation of it into their own unique style is evidence that a different type of musical learning is taking place.

> It's nice to add the ornamentation whenever I want to or where I feel necessary; especially now having three years of experience in the ensemble, I feel like I am getting to grips with all the technical language and where to include them.[44]

Conclusion: Distributed Leadership

Having begun this chapter with a reflection on my own confidence crisis, it seems appropriate to conclude by revisiting my concerns about whether or not I am 'leadership material'. Through a process of resistance to institutional norms and the gendered restrictions in which we work, the desire to suspend the prevailing hierarchies of settler colonial dominance through the deployment of repertoire from my own cultural heritage and an approach to excellence drawn from community music practice, I believe that I have positively impacted ensemble practices within my department. I have deliberately disrupted long-accepted paradigms of musical leadership, and the evidence suggests that this has greatly benefitted the student experience. In enabling students to make their own interpretative decisions within a British university music ensemble and challenging the prevailing inherited power strategies implicit in Western European art music approaches to leadership, I have observed the following changes in our department. Those who are first in their family to come to university, who have frequently been disadvantaged educationally, socially and economically, have increasingly demonstrated independent thinking, problem solving skills and growth in self-confidence within the band. They have formed their own community which uses a unique descriptive language, explored new repertoire and instrumental techniques and have developed collaborative working methods enacted through a democratic process of discussion and negotiation. My role in all of this has been to facilitate this growth mindset rather than to directly lead or intervene in its development; perhaps I am, after all, simply enacting gendered stereotype of a woman raising happy, healthy children in a De Valerian vision,[45] but I believe that my work is more valuable than that. In fact, there is a strong case to argue for the replacement of the word 'leader' with that of 'facilitator' in university music-making, and it is important that we encourage students and colleagues of all genders to value the work of facilitation as highly as we value the concept of leadership.

Notes

1. 'Irishness' is a complex conceit which is often presented as a binary opposition: 'Irish-English' or 'Anglo-Irish' in political concepts, for example, but for Heaney, 'Irishness' is much more inclusive as he outlines in his Quincunx. Seamus Heaney, "Frontiers of Writing," in *The Redress of Poetry* (London: Faber & Faber, 1996), 186–203. 'Irishness' is a concept that I have struggled with as part of my identity while living and working in the UK, and I will discuss this further at a later point in this chapter.
2. Seamus Heaney, "Varieties of Irishness: In the Element of His Genius," *Irish Pages: A Journal of Contemporary Writing* 9, no. 2 (2016): 9–20.
3. Heaney further explored what it is to be a writer, which he attributed to the idea of following a 'sixth sense and proceeding on the off-chance'. Much of the work described in this chapter emerges from that notion of having a hunch about musical leadership and testing it out in my leadership of a band. Seamus Heaney, "Varieties of Irishness: In the Element of His Genius," *Irish Pages: A Journal of Contemporary Writing* 9, no. 2 (2016): 9–20, particularly see p. 9 and p. 14.
4. In recent decades there have been many discussions of Irishness, gender and otherness within the context of Irish women emigrants. Some of these, rather uncomfortably for me, ally Irish otherness with that of BAME communities, who experience levels of discrimination that I have not. Space prohibits detailed discussion here, but some useful texts include: Bronwen Walter, "Whiteness and Diasporic Irishness: Nation, Gender and Class," *Journal of Ethnic and Migration Studies* 37, no. 9 (2011): 1295–312; Fiona Barber, "Territories of Difference: Irish Women Artists in Britain," *Third Text* 8, no. 27 (1994): 65–75; Suzanna Chan, " 'Kiss My Royal Irish Ass' Contesting Identity: Visual Culture, Gender, Whiteness and Diaspora," *Journal of Gender Studies* 15, no. 1 (2006): 1–17.
5. Avtar Brah, *Cartographies of Diaspora: Contesting Identities* (London: Routledge, 1996), 138.
6. My feelings on this matter are not unique; they are complicated by diasporic experience and what Alderson and Becket refer to as 'a concern with the creation and interaction of Irish and British identities and cultures'. David Alderson and Fiona Becket, "Introduction," in *Ireland in Proximity: History, Gender, Space*, edited by Scott Brewster, Virginia Crossman, Fiona Becket, and David Alderson (London: Routledge, 1999), 2.

7. This idea of 'Irishness' is often represented by jovial renditions from colleagues and students like 'top o' the morning to ya' and other such sayings. However, Irishness is problematic, as 'constructed Irishness' arises from nineteenth-century British colonialism, which Jennifer Nugent Duffy suggests has emerged from 'encounters with exclusion'. Jennifer Nugent Duffy, *Who's Your Paddy? Racial Expectations and the Struggle for Irish American Identity* (New York: NYU Press), 243.
   The embedded cultural indexical cues of the Irish President, Michael D. Higgins, have been described by Lorraine Leeson and others in "'A President for all of the Irish:' Performing Irishness in an Interpreted Inaugural Presidential Speech," *Interpreting and the Politics of Recognition* (London: Taylor & Francis, 2017), 37. Bronwen Walters refers to the social construction of a 'Bridget' to match that of the 'Paddy'. *Outsiders Inside: Whiteness, Place and Irish Women* (London: Taylor & Francis, 2000), 77.
8. Bronwen Walters (2000).
9. Fintan Vallely, *Companion to Irish Traditional Music* (Cork: Cork University Press, 2011), 611. Comhaltas Ceoltóirí Éireann, an organisation for the promotion of Irish music, song and dance was established in 1951 and is now one of the main educational institutions for Irish traditional music. It has over 400 branches worldwide, offering approximately 1000 classes per week. In these lessons, children and participants are frequently taught and a master/apprentice relationship can develop. See accessed August 15, 2020, https://comhaltas.ie/ and Edward O. Henry, "Institutions for the Promotion of Indigenous Music: The Case for Ireland's Comhaltas Ceoltóirí Éireann," *Ethnomusicology* 33, no. 1 (1989): 67–95.
10. The Royal Philharmonic Society estimates that approximately 5.5% of professional conductors in Britain are female. Accessed August 19, 2020, https://royalphilharmonicsociety.org.uk/performers/women-conductors#:~:text=Only%20one%20British%20orchestra%20has,That's%205.5%25. See also: Vick Bain, 'Diversity in the Music Industry,' accessed August 1, 2020, https://vbain.co.uk/research, which similarly recognises the barriers that exist for women entering roles in music business as performers or managers.
11. Alderson and Becket, "Introduction," 62.
12. Helen O'Shea, "'Good Man Mary!' Women Musicians and the Fraternity of Irish Traditional Music," *Journal of Gender Studies* 17, no. 1 (2008): 57.
13. O'Shea describes how women musicians in Galway both resist and comply with 'patriarchal control' in creating their own uniquely female pub sessions in order to avoid the harassment that they had experienced from male musicians before relocating their sessions to the private domestic space of their own homes. p. 60.
14. I have experienced such criticism within my own professional career, where comments about my gender, caring responsibilities and 'lower standards of professional expectation' have been offered by male colleagues. For other testimonies see also: Yolanda Flores Niemann, Gabriella Gutiérrez y Muhs and Carmen G. Gonzales, *Presumed Incompetent II: Race, Class, Power, and Resistance of Women in Academia* (Logan: Utah State University Press, 2020). Kirsti Cole and Holly Hassel, *Surviving Sexism in Academia: Strategies for Feminist Leadership* (London: Taylor & Frances, 2017). Estrella Montes-López and Tamar Groves, "Micro-machismo and Discrimination in Academia: The Violation of the Right to Equality in University," *Culture & History* 8, no. 1 (2019): 1–10.
15. Several concerns have been raised about children's education, employment and mental health in the region, and results from the last three years of measurement data highlights a significant divergence from the national average. Further detailed breakdown of a variety of socioeconomic and cultural data can be found on the following site. Accessed August 3, 2020, www.thrivingplacesindex.org/candidates/E08000031.
16. Olivia Groves and Sarah O'Shea, "Learning to Be a University Student: First in Family Students Negotiating Membership of the University Community," *International Journal of Educational Research* 98 (2019): 48–54.
17. Jean Lave and Etienne Wenger, *Situated Learning: Legitimate Peripheral Participation* (Cambridge: Cambridge University Press, 1991).
18. Sarah O'Shea, Josephine May, Cathy Stone, and Janine Delahunty, *First-in-Family Students, University Experience & Family Life* (London: Palgrave, Macmillan, 2017).
19. A.M. Villegas and T. Lucas, "Preparing Culturally Responsive Teachers: Rethinking the Curriculum," *Journal of Teacher Education* 53 (2002): 20–32. Involving detailed reflexive work and understanding my own cultural position as an immigrant to the UK has formed an important part of my work for many years, and I have particularly tried to apply this within a wider curriculum which

seeks to build on community stakeholders and offer students career pathways that allow them to function at the heart of their own communities. Carlos R. Abril and Nicole R. Robinson, "Comparing Situated and Simulated Learning Approaches to Developing Culturally Responsive Music Teachers," *International Journal of Music Education* 37, no. 3 (2019): 440–53.
20. This begs the question of what university music-making should be about; whilst much work has been undertaken to explore the impact of a pursuit of excellence approach within a Conservatoire setting, there is more that needs to be done in regard to university spaces. Is our role as university teachers to encourage students to be the best they can be on their instruments, or is it to enable them to broaden their experiences and develop leadership strategies for future employment? Sheena Roberts, "Encouragement, Effort, Expectation and Entitlement in the Pursuit of Excellence," *Canadian Music Educator/Musicien Educateur au Canada* 48, no. 3 (2007): 46. Arielle Bonneville-Roussy, Geneviève L. Lavigne, and Robert J. Vallerand, "When Passion Leads to Excellence: The Case of Musicians," *Psychology of Music* 39, no. 1 (2011): 123–38.
21. Conversations with many students in personal tutorials reflected a feeling that they simply were not 'good enough' to be at university as a result of their perceived rejection from our established ensembles. The excellence that I sought to achieve in these rehearsals, therefore, was about the social experience of the ensemble rather than to achieve intrinsic virtuosity in the students' playing. This is built upon the model outlined by Gillian Howell, Lee Higgins and Brydie-Leigh Bartleet in their chapter, "Community Music Practice: Intervention through Facilitation," in *The Oxford Handbook of Music Making and Leisure*, edited by Roger Mantle and Gareth Dylan Smith (Oxford: Oxford University Press, 2017), 601–18.
22. Several centuries of oppression, cultural resistance and nationalism are detailed in Rachel Fleming's "Resisting Cultural Standardization: Comhaltas Ceoltóirí Éireann and the Revitalization of Traditional Music in Ireland," *Journal of Folklore Research* 41, no. 2 (2004): 227–57. Steven R. Millar's thoughtful exploration of musical rebellion in the post-Good Friday Agreement era, although rooted in analysis of practice in Northern Ireland, is another source of valuable information. Steven R. Millar, *Sounding Dissent: Rebel Songs, Resistance, and Irish Republicanism* (Ann Arbor: University of Michigan Press, 2020), accessed July 15, 2020, https://hdl.handle.net/2027/fulcrum.70795965r.
23. Studies of participation in music ensembles highlight the importance of the social aspects of rehearsal as well as the notion of 'fun'. Recent studies include Allan Hewitt and Amanda Allan, "Advanced Youth Music Ensembles: Experiences of, and Reasons for, Participation," *International Journal of Music Education* 31, no. 3 (2014): 257–75.
24. Oldenberg describes these as informal gathering places for people outside family homes and work. Ray Oldenberg, *The Great Good Place* (New York: Paragon House, 1989). The late Míceál Ó'Súilleabháin develops this notion further and describes the location of the session in the public house as 'common ground . . . public space, egalitarian, equal [and] accessible' in Francis Morton, "Performing Ethnography: Irish Traditional Music Sessions and New Methodological Spaces," *Representando la etnografía: sesiones de música tradicional de Irlanda y nuevos espacios metodológicos* 6, no. 5 (2005): 666.
25. John F. Freie, *Counterfeit Community: The Exploitation of Our Longings for Connectedness* (Lanham, MD: Rowan and Littlefield, 1998), 59.
26. June Boyce-Tillman, "The Transformative Qualities of a Liminal Space Created by Musicking," *Philosophy of Music Education Review* 17, no. 2 (2009): 184–202. See also Terry Sefton, "Teaching for Creativity and Informal Learning in Liminal Spaces," *Act* 17, no. 3 (2018): 79–100.
27. Christopher Small, *Musicking: The Meanings of Performing and Listening* (Middletown, CT: Wesleyan University Press, 1998), 10.
28. Conversation with Student A (March 2019).
29. Conversation with Student B (March 2019).
30. Jasper Winn, "The Reel Stuff," *World of Hibernia* 5, no. 4 (2000): 135.
31. Email from a student (March 2019).
32. For first-in-family students, such as those within my ensemble, the promotion of growth-mindset is just as important as the achievement of virtuosic passages in their solo performance. This discursive workshop approach to learning helped students to overcome negative feelings of self-doubt and start to offer useful suggestions and contributions to the rehearsal process. Kari Adams, "Developing Growth Mindset in the Ensemble Rehearsal," *Music Educators Journal* 105, no. 4 (2019): 21–27.
33. The learning goals from this first session were for students to successfully play through a tune before the end of the rehearsal and to problem-solve by improving their transposition skills or create a

harmonic accompaniment appropriate to their instrument. This was achieved through an iterative process of examples and discussion as well as through the provision of a lead sheet. For further discussion of problem-based learning in ensembles see: Richard Laprise, "What's the Problem? Exploring the Potential of Problem-Based Learning in an Ensemble Setting," *Music Educators' Journal* 104, no. 4 (2018): 48–53. Weidner refers to this as a 'cognitive apprenticeship', whilst Turner refers to it as crowdsourcing. Brian N. Weidner, "Achieving Greater Musical Independence in Ensembles Through Cognitive Apprenticeship," *Music Educators Journal* 104, no. 3 (2018): 26–31; Cynthia Johnston Turner, "Another Perspective: Crowdsourcing Our Ensemble Rehearsals," *Music Educators Journal* 100, no. 2 (2013): 68–71.

34. It may be a result of imposter syndrome, my innate unease about adopting a leadership role or indeed about introducing Irish music to classically trained British and international students, but there are also sound andragogical reasons for refusing to adopt a classic conductor's role within a rehearsal process. John P. Graulty, "Don't Watch Me!," *Music Educators Journal* 96, no. 4 (2010): 53–56.
35. Conversation with Student C (March 2019).
36. Philip Bohlman describes how wonder and fear can co-exist within a new musical encounter, "Music and Culture: Historiographies of Disjuncture," in *The Cultural Study of Music: A Critical Introduction*, edited by Martin Clayton, Trevor Herbert, and Richard Middleton (London: Routledge, 2003), 46–47.
37. Conversation with Student D (March) 2019.
38. Ramona Wis refers to this as the conductor adopting a 'servant-leader' role, which allows the ensemble members to 'function as artists rather than artisans'. Ramona M. Wis, "The Conductor as Servant-Leader," *Music Educators Journal* 89, no. 2 (2002): 17. Douglas Orzolek further builds on this idea by exploring the notion of 'engaged followership' within ensemble rehearsals and argues that collaborative learning is an essential part of this process. Douglas C. Orzolek, "Effective and Engaged Followership: Assessing Student Participation in Ensembles," *Music Educators Journal* 106, no. 3 (2020): 47–53.
39. Graulty, 53.
40. Edward Lisk, *The Creative Director: Alternative Rehearsal Techniques* (Fort Lauderdale: Meredith Music Publications, 1991).
41. Joyce Thomas and Deana McDonagh, 'Shared Language: Towards More Effective Communication," *The Australasian Medical Journal* 6, no. 1 (2013): 46–54.
42. Domenico Dentoni, Stefano Pascucci, Kim Poldner, and William B. Gartner, "Learning 'Who We Are' by Doing: Processes of Co-Constructing Prosocial Identities in Community-Based Enterprises," *Journal of Business Venturing* 33, no. 5 (2018): 607.
43. Conversation with Student C (March 2019).
44. Student B (March 2019).
45. Michele Dowling, " 'The Ireland That I Would Have': De Valera & the Creation of an Irish National Image," *History Ireland* 5, no. 2 (1997): 37–41.

Bibliography

Abril, Carlos R., and Nicole R. Robinson. "Comparing Situated and Simulated Learning Approaches to Developing Culturally Responsive Music Teachers." *International Journal of Music Education* 37, no. 3 (2019): 440–53. https://doi.org/10.1177/0255761419842427.

Adams, Kari. "Developing Growth Mindset in the Ensemble Rehearsal." *Music Educators Journal* 105, no. 4 (2019): 21–27. https://doi.org/10.1177/0027432119849473.

Alderson, David, Fiona Becket, Scott Brewster, and Virginia Crossman. *Ireland in Proximity: History, Gender and Space*. London: Taylor & Francis Group, 1999. Accessed August 7, 2020. http://ebookcentral.proquest.com/lib/open/detail.action?docID=169012.

Barber, Fionna. "Territories of Difference: Irish Women Artists in Britain." *Third Text* 8, no. 27 (1994): 65–75. https://doi.org/10.1080/09528829408576489.

Bell, Cindy L. "Critical Listening in the Ensemble Rehearsal: A Community of Learners." *Music Educators Journal* 104, no. 3 (2018): 17–25. https://doi.org/10.1177/0027432117745951.

Bonneville-Roussy, Arielle, Geneviève L. Lavigne, and Robert J. Vallerand. "When Passion Leads to Excellence: The Case of Musicians." *Psychology of Music* 39, no. 1 (2011): 123–38. https://doi.org/10.1177/0305735609352441.

Boyce-Tillman, June. "The Transformative Qualities of a Liminal Space Created by Musicking." *Philosophy of Music Education Review* 17, no. 2 (2009): 184–202.
Brah, A. *Cartographies of Diaspora: Contesting Identities*. London: Routledge, 1996.
Bull, Anna. "Gendering the Middle Classes: The Construction of Conductors' Authority in Youth Classical Music Groups." *The Sociological Review* 64 (2016): 855–71. Accessed August 4, 2020. https://onlinelibrary-wiley-com.ezproxy.wlv.ac.uk/doi/full/10.1111/1467-954X.12426.
Burke, Penny Jane, Anna Bennett, Cathy Burgess, Kim Gray, and Erica Southgate. *Capability, Belonging and Equity in Higher Education: Developing Inclusive Approaches*. Callaghan: University of Newcastle, 2016.
Chan, Suzanna. "'Kiss My Royal Irish Ass.' Contesting Identity: Visual Culture, Gender, Whiteness and Diaspora." *Journal of Gender Studies* 15, no. 1 (2006): 1–17. https://doi.org/10.1080/09589230500486850.
Clayton, Martin. *The Cultural Study of Music: A Critical Introduction*. Milton: Routledge, Taylor & Francis Group, 2012. https://doi.org/10.4324/9780203149454.
Cole, Kirsti, and Holly Hassel. *Surviving Sexism in Academia: Strategies for Feminist Leadership*. Taylor & Francis, 2017. https://doi.org/10.4324/9781315523217.
Dentoni, Domenico, Stefano Pascucci, Kim Poldner, and William B. Gartner. "Learning 'Who We Are' by Doing: Processes of Co-Constructing Prosocial Identities in Community-Based Enterprises." *Journal of Business Venturing* 33, no. 5 (2018): 603–22. https://doi.org/10.1016/j.jbusvent.2017.12.010.
Dowling, Michele. "'The Ireland That I Would Have': De Valera & the Creation of an Irish National Image." *History Ireland* 5, no. 2 (1997): 37–41.
Duffy, Jennifer Nugent. "Conclusion: To Belong." In *Who's Your Paddy?, Racial Expectations and the Struggle for Irish American Identity*, 241–46. New York: New York University Press, 2014.
Fitzgerald, Mark, and John O'Flynn. *Music and Identity in Ireland and Beyond*. Farnham: Taylor & Francis Group, 2014.
Fleming, Rachel C. "Resisting Cultural Standardization: Comhaltas Ceoltóirí Éireann and the Revitalization of Traditional Music in Ireland." *Journal of Folklore Research* 41, no. 2/3 (2004): 227–57.
Freie, John F. *Counterfeit Community: The Exploitation of Our Longings for Connectedness*. Lanham, MD: Rowman & Littlefield Publishers, 1998.
Gilmartin, Mary. *Ireland and Migration in the Twenty-First Century, Ireland and Migration in the Twenty-First Century*. Manchester: Manchester University Press, 2015.
Graulty, John P. "Don't Watch Me!." *Music Educators Journal* 96, no. 4 (2010): 53–56. https://doi.org/10.1177/0027432110370565.
Groves, Olivia, and Sarah O'Shea. "Learning to 'Be' a University Student: First in Family Students Negotiating Membership of the University Community." *International Journal of Educational Research* 98 (2019): 48–54. https://doi.org/10.1016/j.ijer.2019.08.014.
Harrison, Scott, Jessica O'Bryan, and Don Lebler. "'Playing It Like a Professional': Approaches to Ensemble Direction in Tertiary Institutions." *International Journal of Music Education* 31, no. 2 (2013): 173–89. https://doi.org/10.1177/0255761413489791.
Heaney, Seamus. "Frontiers of Writing." In *The Redress of Poetry*, 186–203. London: Faber & Faber, 1996.
──── . "Varieties of Irishness: In the Element of His Genius." *Irish Pages: A Journal of Contemporary Writing* 9, no. 1 (2016): 9–20.
Henry, Edward O. "Institutions for the Promotion of Indigenous Music: The Case for Ireland's Comhaltas Ceoltoiri Eireann." *Ethnomusicology* 33, no. 1 (1989): 67–95. https://doi.org/10.2307/852170.
Hewitt, Allan, and Amanda Allan. "Advanced Youth Music Ensembles: Experiences of, and Reasons for, Participation." *International Journal of Music Education* 31, no. 3 (2014): 257–75.
Howell, Gillian, Lee Higgins, and Brydie-Leigh Bartleet. "Community Music Practice: Intervention Through Facilitation." In *The Oxford Handbook of Music Making and Leisure*, edited by Roger Mantle and Gareth Dylan Smith, 601–18. Oxford: Oxford University Press, 2017.
Koliba, Christopher, and Rebecca Gajda. "'Communities of Practice' as an Analytical Construct: Implications for Theory and Practice." *International Journal of Public Administration* 32, no. 2 (2009): 97–135. https://doi.org/10.1080/01900690802385192.
Laprise, Richard. "What's the Problem? Exploring the Potential of Problem-Based Learning in an Ensemble Setting." *Music Educators Journal* 104, no. 4 (2018): 48–53. https://doi.org/10.1177/0027432118754636.

Lave, Jean. *Situated Learning: Legitimate Peripheral Participation, Learning in Doing: Social, Cognitive, and Computational Perspectives*. Cambridge: Cambridge University Press, 1991.

MacPherson, D. A. J., and Mary J. Hickman. *Women and Irish Diaspora Identities: Theories, Concepts and New Perspectives*. Manchester: Manchester University Press, 2014.

May, Josephine, Cathy Stone, Janine Delahunty, and Sarah O'Shea. *First-in-Family Students, University Experience and Family Life: Motivations, Transitions and Participation*. London: Palgrave Macmillan, 2017.

McCann, Anthony. "All That Is Not Given Is Lost: Irish Traditional Music, Copyright, and Common Property." *Ethnomusicology* 45, no. 1 (2001): 89–106. https://doi.org/10.2307/852635.

Millar, Steven R. *Sounding Dissent: Rebel Songs, Resistance, and Irish Republicanism*. Ann Arbor: University of Michigan Press, 2020.

Montes-López, Estrella, and Tamar Groves. "Micro-Machismo and Discrimination in Academia: The Violation of the Right to Equality in University." *Culture & History Digital Journal* 8, no. 1 (2019). https://doi.org/10.3989/chdj.2019.010.

Morton, Frances. "Performing Ethnography: Irish Traditional Music Sessions and New Methodological Spaces." *Representando La Etnografía: Sesiones de Música Tradicional de Irlanda y Nuevos Espacios Metodológicos* 6, no. 5 (2005): 661–76. https://doi.org/10.1080/14649360500258294.

Niemann, Yolanda Flores, Gabriella Gutiérrez y Muhs, and Carmen G. Gonzalez. *Presumed Incompetent II: Race, Class, Power, and Resistance of Women in Academia*. Logan: Utah State University Press, 2020.

O'Shea, Helen. "'Good Man, Mary!' Women Musicians and the Fraternity of Irish Traditional Music." *Journal of Gender Studies* 17, no. 1 (2008): 55–70.

———. "The Musical Traditions of Northern Ireland and Its Diaspora: Community and Conflict. By David Cooper. Farnham: Ashgate, 2009. 186 Pp. ISBN 978-0754662303." *Popular Music* 29, no. 3 (2010): 493–95. https://doi.org/10.1017/S026114301000036X.

Roberts, Sheena. "Encouragement, Effort, Expectation and Entitlement in the Pursuit of Excellence." *Canadian Music Educator/Musicien Educateur Au Canada* 48, no. 3 (2007): 46.

Sefton, Terry. "ACT 17 (3): 79–100 – ACT." *Teaching for Creativity and Informal Learning in Liminal Spaces*. Accessed August 28, 2020. http://act.maydaygroup.org/volume-17-issue-3/act-17-3-79-100/.

Shieh, Eric. "Developing Leadership in the Ensemble Classroom." *Music Educators Journal* 94, no. 4 (2008): 46–51.

Small, Christopher. *Musicking: The Meanings of Performing and Listening*, 10. Middletown, CT: Wesleyan University Press, 1998.

Stone, Christopher, and Lorraine Leeson. *Interpreting and the Politics of Recognition*. London: Taylor & Francis Group, 2017.

Thomas, Joyce, and Deana McDonagh. "Shared Language: Towards More Effective Communication." *The Australasian Medical Journal* 6, no. 1 (2013): 46–54. https://doi.org/10.4066/AMJ.2013.1596.

Turner, Cynthia Johnston. "Another Perspective: Crowdsourcing Our Ensemble Rehearsals." *Music Educators Journal* 100, no. 2 (2013): 68–71. https://doi.org/10.1177/0027432113505839.

Vallely, Fintan. *Companion to Irish Traditional Music*. Cork: Cork University Press, 2010.

———. "Playing, Paying and Preying: Cultural Clash and Paradox in the Traditional Music Commonage." *Community Development Journal* 49, Suppl_1 (2014): 53–67. https://doi.org/10.1093/cdj/bsu018.

Walter, Bronwen. *Outsiders Inside: Whiteness, Place and Irish Women*. London: Taylor & Francis Group, 2000.

———. "Irish Women in the Diaspora: Exclusions and Inclusions." *Women's Studies International Forum* 27, no. 4 (2004): 369–84. https://doi.org/10.1016/j.wsif.2004.10.006.

———. "Whiteness and Diasporic Irishness: Nation, Gender and Class." *Journal of Ethnic & Migration Studies* 37, no. 9 (2011): 1295–312. https://doi.org/10.1080/1369183X.2011.623584.

Weidner, Brian N. "Achieving Greater Musical Independence in Ensembles through Cognitive Apprenticeship." *Music Educators Journal* 104, no. 3 (2018): 26–31. https://doi.org/10.1177/0027432117746217.

Winn, Jasper. "The Reel Stuff." *World of Hibernia* 5, no. 4 (2000): 134.

20
'IT'S NOT ABOUT ME!'
The Life and Leadership of Cathi Leibinger

Margaret J. Flood

Every December, thousands of band directors[1] travel to Chicago, Illinois to attend the longest-running conference of their profession, The Midwest Band and Orchestra Clinic. The conference is where band directors of all abilities can network and socialise. The attendees, however, are overwhelmingly male. Hartley and Sheldon found that in 2007, 85% of the wind band conductors at the conference were male; only 15% were female between 1998 and 2008.[2]

Not only are female band leaders underrepresented at the Midwest Clinic, but they are also absent in the research literature. As an example, one recent book about the life and career of prominent band directors, entitled *The Conductor's Legacy*, featured interviews by ten prolific wind band directors, all of whom are male.[3] Despite the book being the idea of Paula Crider, a retired band director from the University of Texas at Austin and one of the first female college band directors, she herself was not included. It is equally perplexing that her female contemporary, Mallory Thompson, was not included either.

It was not until the 1990s that music education historians encouraged research of female band directors and the music curriculum began to include women as specific examples.[4] Livingston researched how often women in music education were mentioned in five history books, finding only eleven women's names were mentioned five or more times out of 334 citations. She noted also that none of the authors offered a direct summary of the influence of women in music education.[5] Heller and Wilson request new interpretations of past subjects be made in order to understand the influence of marginalised populations, particularly of women and people of colour. Humphreys found that there was an inequitable representation of sex and individuals from various regions within the historical representation of music education in history books.[6] He believes the top-down hierarchal approach to documenting the history of music education could be why the ordinary histories of lesser-known music educators, women, and minorities continue to be overlooked. Because men historically held more prominent positions, particularly in band directing, they existed within the top realms of the hierarchy, thus resulting more published documentation of their careers. Bowman suggests researchers should identify women who may have been overlooked and rewrite histories to include them.[7] After these discrepancies were revealed, Lamb, Dolloff, and Howe emphatically pointed out the need for more research to disclose new and important facts about the history of women in music and in music education.[8]

Music education historian Jill Sullivan completed a biographical project on women band directors in the military during World War II, highlighting the moment when women band directors were able to perform and conduct the country's military bands for the first time.[9] This study was one of the first major historical compilations solely about women band directors.

Sullivan's research on women military band directors was the impetus for this current project exploring one significant female band director in Florida. Despite the historically rich band tradition of Florida, there is little published documentation on either its current or past female band director leadership. In 2013, the Florida Bandmasters' Association (FBA) launched its legacy project, consisting of interviews with some of the most influential retired band directors, yet only six of 72 are female.[10] What is also problematic is the lack of representation of primary and middle school band directors.

The purpose of this case study is to reveal how the professional and personal life experiences of Cathi Leibinger helped to shape and helped to shape and influence her career development as prominent female band director in the United States of America. Furthermore, it aims to illuminate her leadership contributions and influences on the American band profession. Cathi is a former president of FBA and is a middle school band director at the Ransom Everglades School, a private school in Miami. As an active professional, she has yet to be a part of the FBA Legacy Project; nevertheless, her experiences as a mid-career band director and state leader are worthy of attention. This reassessment of her professional contribution asserts her legacy and shares, in this volume on women's musical leadership, how she contributed to leading change in the American band scene at the local, state, and national levels.

A secondary purpose of this study is to explore the life of one female band director at various stages of development through a qualitative research process that emphasises using her own narrative. This is intended to give music professionals an opportunity to gain a better understanding of the success, influences, and characteristics of one of its female leaders and to develop a more inclusive and diverse history of the music education profession.

Women Band Directors in Florida

In 2001, the Music Educator's National Conference (now known as the National Association for Music Education or NAfME) published demographics showing an approximate 2:1 ratio of male to female band directors nationwide. As the teaching level increased into high school, the male to female ratio became 3:1.[11] Leimer's study found the ratio in Florida to be approximately the same and that band directors at all levels were heavily male-dominated. Although her study showed an increase in female band directors between 2001–2012, the ratio remained similar.

The state of Florida has a noteworthy history of band directing. Some of the most prolific band directors across the country either have taught in Florida or obtained degrees from a Florida institution of high education. When looking at the demographic of band directors, however, the hall of fame inductees, and past leadership roles in state organisations and institutions, there is hardly a female presence. According to the membership of the FBA, even the K-12 school systems show a predominantly male cohort of band directors at the middle school and high school levels.[12] Prior to Cathi's appointment, only three women have served as president of the FBA: Cynthia Berry, Paula Thornton, and Linda Mann. There has never been a woman band director to serve as executive director, which is the highest position of leadership and the only paid position within the organisation.[13]

Cathi Leibinger

In May of 2018, Cathi Leibinger became the fourth female president of the Florida Bandmasters' Association. She was voted president-elect in January of 2017 and will serve a total of six years: president-elect (two years), president (two years), and past-president (two years). She is a successful middle school band director who consistently receives the highest music performance assessment ratings.[14] Cathi is an avid clinician and adjudicator throughout the country and recently conducted an honours band in Germany. She has an array of experience as a band director in the public and private schools of Miami, serving as a mentor and colleague to many students, teachers, and professional musicians. I met Cathi a year prior to her appointment and was intrigued by her personality, steadfast professionalism, genuine warmth, and sincere interest in listening to what other people had to say.

Methodology

A feminist biographical narrative approach is used to capture Cathi's personal story, 'which engages in research from a unique perspective that provides depth, meaning and context to the participants' lived experiences in light of the larger cultural matrix in which they live'.[15] I used a qualitative research lens with an interest in how Cathi makes sense of events and her own behaviors, and how her understanding of these influence her interpretation and construction of her narrative.[16] I wanted Cathi to share her experiences through her own words with the desire to try and capture more of her personality and interactions within her own personal and professional environments. Selection of Cathi as the participant was convenient and purposive. Since we both live in Miami, semi-structured, face-to-face interviews were conducted at her home.[17] To analyse the data, I used a constant comparative approach, allowing me to develop concepts and themes from the data throughout the entire process of collection.[18]

The guiding questions were shared with Cathi prior to the interview and were as follows:

1. Who and what have influenced her personally and professionally?
2. What does she believe makes her a successful band director?
3. What have been the biggest professional and personal challenges along the way?
4. What personality traits does she hold that may have influenced her to become a well-respected person within the national band community?

As a current professional in a position of leadership, I knew she would be sensitive to the information she chose to share. She agreed with the suggested topics and questions. One two-and-a-half-hour interview was conducted and transcribed verbatim by me. Emails and text messages were exchanged for member checking purposes. Memo-ing also took place, noting non-verbal communication that took place during the interview, initial coding notes, personal biases, and my own reflections. A second analysis of the transcript used a constructivist approach and grounded theory techniques that utilised in-vivo coding using gerunds to describe what exactly was being said by Cathi using her own words.[19] Six general themes and several interrelated sub-themes emerged during the coding process.

Researcher Biases

As a band director and adjudicator, I also have extensive experience teaching in both public and private schools that mirrors Cathi's experiences. Furthermore, sometimes Cathi and

I work together professionally, thus changing our relationship. This may have reflected bias during the interview process and coding; however, I continued to memo and reflect on my interpretations in the event my biases may have influenced any of the information offered by Cathi herself. As such, Cathi is a mentor to me, a role model, a peer, a collaborator, and the topic of my research. Her voice speaks loudly to me literally, metaphorically, and figuratively.

Cathi's Narrative

Qualitative research methodologies can easily be influenced by the actions and thoughts of participants. Before I present my findings, it is important to note the change in the initial interview protocol. Due to the prior sharing of interview topics with Cathi, she was immediately prepared to speak. As we sat by her pool on a warm April day in 2018, she began to share with me her recent experiences observing band programs throughout Texas. I paused her so I could begin recording, as she had already begun to answer my questions. The semi-structured interview previously planned quickly changed to a conversational interview. I allowed this change, as the most important part of my research protocol was to allow her to tell her narrative the way she wanted it to be told. This will ensure her voice is given and presented as authentically as possible. Instead, I used the prepared questions as a checklist and guide.

The purpose of this interview study was to explore the professional and life experiences Cathi believes to have helped to influence and shape her career development. As she told her story, the overarching theme that emerged was related to her identity. Three main themes associated with her identity that manifested were mentoring, successes, and challenges. Several smaller yet equally important themes related to Cathi's personal life and her business background also appeared, which continued to interconnect throughout her narrative.

Identity

Although this project revolved around a female band director, Cathi only directly addressed her gender in relation to her identity at the beginning of our interview session, where she explained what she thought was the difference between male and female band directors:

> We were talking about characteristics of males and females, specifically in the band directing field, and how some of the band directors – the female band directors who have been successful that I have seen, like Linda Mann, like Paula Thornton, are more about helping others than they are about helping themselves. They are also more about helping bands in general than their own band. I think we are seeing more of that compassion/empathy side from the men as society is allowing them to express it. But I think that women in general might be more predisposed to that nurturing kind of tendency.

Many of the traits and examples Cathi used to describe herself tended to lie under the idea of a nurturing band director. She spoke extensively about caring for others and the profession itself. She continuously repeated throughout the interview that what she did as a band director, a mentor, and a leader within the field was not about her. She felt the information she learned from her experiences observing bands in Texas and as a staff member of the American Band College (ABC) were to be shared broadly.[20] These character traits of *selflessness* and *caring* continued to reveal themselves throughout our conversation, particularly when she spoke of her experiences as a mentor and mentee.

Another important characteristic Cathi shared was of *vulnerability*. She told me the story of her recent experience taking her students to FBA Music Performance Assessments (MPA), where the students did not perform as expected and received a lower rating than the band is used to getting.[21] She did what she never thought she would do and posted her students' results on Facebook, just to show her own vulnerability. She also posted on the way to the performance, 'Today's the day when we put our ego and professional reputation in the hands of 13-year-olds and hope that they don't drop kick it across the stage', already addressing the vulnerability that she and other band directors felt. Cathi further revealed that this year she was hoping to receive the Five-Year Superior Award from FBA. She told me that she has yet to receive it because in the fifth consecutive year, her band continued to fall short of a Superior rating.

Another trait related to vulnerability that Cathi speaks of is that of *ownership*. She speaks of how she has learned to acknowledge and 'own up' to her own drawbacks and tries to teach her students the same:

> If you drop something, OWN IT! Throw your hands in the air! I'll give you a rating, we'll move on with our lives. In fact, one time in a concert – sixth grade beginning band – percussionist drops his cymbals, and the little euphonium player throws his hands in the air. I was like – not really good timing, but that's ok. It was between numbers, so we could laugh it off. It was awesome. One time I'm in the cafeteria and I dropped an entire tray of cafeteria food, and I just saluted the Russian judges, got the applause, cleaned it up, and moved on. I think it's that vulnerability. Letting the kids see that sometimes we are just clumsy-ass fools. It's embarrassing, but you're not going to die. Shake it off, buttercup!

She strongly believes that having this conversation about ownership and vulnerability, not only with students but with other band directors, is an important part of being true to one's authentic self. Cathi's emphasis on *authenticity*, through her own definition of what she believed to be authentic, was closely related to her personal life stories. She was vulnerable, raw, and honest when speaking about how she learned to be true to herself as an individual and as a band director.

> I've done a lot of work on integrating all aspects of my personality – childhood trauma and all of that. We compartmentalise so much, and it keeps us from being our authentic selves. Without revealing too much, I did go through a therapy group. It was a support group for childhood trauma, and I learned a lot about accepting — integrating personality – those kinds of things. That was a big turning point for me as well in being able to live; you know, you don't have to talk about things that happened to you as a kid, but if you acknowledge it personally, it kind of opens your eyes to how you react to certain situations.

Cathi further explains the importance of being able to adapt oneself, yet also be able to integrate one's own personality to be authentic. She feels many people who are stuck between those two phases struggle with self-realisation, emotional maturity, and emotional intelligence, and that she sees it particularly in band directors. Not many band directors are willing to allow people to help show them their blind spots, so they never truly learn how to be authentic teachers. In closing of our interview session, Cathi returned to this theme by stating, 'It's about relationships and vulnerability – I keep going back to that word – and authenticity. That who you say you are, is who you really are'.

Mentoring

Cathi hopes that by being her authentic self, she can help others do the same. She strongly identified herself as a mentor, and that was expressed through her various relationships and aspects of organisational leadership. I could also feel her sometimes mentoring me as I revealed some of my own stories and experiences. From the moment we met, Cathy was talking about how she could help others and the profession as a whole. She recounted a moment in Texas:

> As we are seeing these ideas and as we are seeing these resources, I notice that the rest of the directors are talking and brainstorming out loud about how to incorporate that into their own rehearsal, and all I could think of was how do we present a clinic at FBA, or how do we present this information to our directors? How do we help the entire state figure this out? There was one time when Wendy looked at me — she goes, 'you're always thinking of other people', and I go, that's kind of my job right now. I'm taking over as president of the state. My job is not about me, it's about raising the level of the bands across the state.

Moreover, Cathi spoke of mentoring local band directors in Miami and how important it was to encourage new directors. Returning to the previously mentioned Facebook post regarding her band's ratings, she took it as an opportunity to reach out to other directors by posting this:

> I know what we need to do and we're going to move forward. I want those of you that are in that same boat to not give up. I don't want you to feel like you're a failure because everyone else is posting Superior ratings. Sometimes we have an off year. Sometimes we are working against odds we just can't overcome. Don't let that make you stop. We need you in the trenches – you['ve] got to keep going.

The responses from band directors of relief and gratitude for that post indicated how much colleagues perceived Cathi as a mentor. She knows MPA is not a matter of life or death and that others need to know that, too. She even goes on to quote one of her mentors, Tim Lautzenheiser, a world-renowned band director: 'Those who matter don't mind, those who mind don't matter'.

Outside of our formal interview and during our first dinner meeting, Cathi often spoke of many of her mentors from ABC, including Tim and Colonel Gabriel (see Figure 20.1).

Cathi has surrounded herself with many great mentors who also taught her how to mentor others. One of Cathi's roles at ABC is that of what she calls 'jump counsellor'. She recounts a story from one session:

> One time, there was a director from Michigan — I walk up to her while we are getting ready for a rehearsal and I'm like, 'Are you having a good time?!' and the look on her face was NO. 'What's the matter?' and she poured her heart out – she goes, 'I just don't think I can make it through this program'. I just said, 'you're going to be fine. You're just going to take it one step at a time. You are going to eat the elephant one bite at a time. We're going to be there every step of the way, and you're going to make it'. Then there was another student – somebody calls me and says, 'Cathi, somebody's in the car driving back to Portland; they're going home'. I was like 'aww, heck no! Nu-uh! Get her on the phone!' I was like, 'What are you doing?' She's like, 'I just can't make it through this program. I'm not going to make it'. I said, 'Turn the car around'. I said, 'Listen.

'It's Not About Me!'

Figure 20.1 Cathi Leibinger and her mentor, Colonel Arnold Gabriel. Courtesy of Cathi Leibinger.

You've paid all this money to be here. You've got two weeks of clinics and rehearsals. Whether you finish your projects or not, get back here for the clinics and rehearsals part of it. Don't throw the money away. At least do that part of it because you can't get your money back. There're no refunds at this point, so turn the car around, get back here and we'll figure this out'. And she ended up graduating three summers later. I take care of the jumpers. That's my job.

During her twenty years with ABC, she has mentored countless band directors, many of whom continue to lead successful careers. She stays connected with many of them, particularly the two mentioned in the narrative earlier. Cathi is also very particular about how she mentors people and how she speaks with others, which she believes makes her unique. She claims to never want to say 'you should' to a teacher, but rather make suggestions. Her perspective is that she is not in that teacher's classroom on a regular basis, and what worked for her may not necessarily work for others.

Aside from being a mentor, Cathi also identifies herself as a *connector*. From the moment we sat down to talk, she was eager to connect me with her colleagues from around the country, particularly other women band directors. One of the best examples Cathi gave had to do with her non-profit that launched during the summer of 2018, called Musician Mentor Network (MMN).[22] The organisation has been created to connect band programs with other musicians and professionals who can help them run their programs successfully and efficiently. MMN provides services from discounted lessons and clinics to fundraising and helping booster programs creatively raise money to meet the needs of their band. She wanted to set up band programs with mentors through the connections she created during her career. To kickstart the organisation, she fundraised through Facebook by crowdsourcing and asking all her friends to support her by donating fifty dollars on her fiftieth birthday. She then encouraged her friends to find nine other people to match those fifty dollars. When I asked Cathi if she considered herself a connector, she replied with no hesitation, 'that's COMPLETELY how

I operate'. Her goal with the organisation is for her 'people to sit alongside band programs and parents and get them up and running and operating in a more professional manner, and then gradually letting them go and be[ing] here as a resource'. She also connected with other band directors for their input and feedback about her non-profit and to make sure what she planned was what was needed in their schools.

Cathi's *relationships* with others were important to her as a connector and mentor. Many of her band colleagues are also close friends. In order to create a deeper connection, she makes sure they talk about all aspects of life. She recounts a recent reunion with an out-of-state colleague:

> I had lunch with a band director from Pennsylvania. He drove two hours to see me because he just wanted to catch up. We didn't talk band. We talked about each other. We talked about his wife. We talked about my non-profit. We talked about gun violence – it could've been any friendship, not just a band director friendship. I think that part of my ABC connection — and some of the band directors I've met online – we've created this relationship that's not about the band. Because we don't work in the same town, so there's no competition. There's no rivalry.

She also credits her rich social life outside of her profession, and her ability to have strong relationships with others, as something that has played an important role in being a successful mentor and connector. Cathi articulates perfectly what sets her apart from many others within her profession: 'I don't care if you're a good band director, I care if you're a good person'.

Successes

Cathi seemed to equate many of her successes to her previously listed identity traits; however, through her explanation of her non-profit, it appeared that her involvement with business opportunities and her current status as a master's student in business also played a significant role. She likened much of her success, ideas, and mentoring ability to 'the security of being in the job long enough to know [what matters]'. She also strongly believed that her successes came mainly from *intrinsic motivation*. Although *extrinsic motivation* motivated her students, such as getting Superiors at MPA or having another award plaque on the band room wall, she is not interested in the materialistic end of it. She claims to sometimes struggle with intrinsic versus extrinsic motivation, particularly when speaking about her experiences taking online classes. She told me of a moment last semester when her professor docked her grade because of a technical error on behalf of the online submission website:

> I went from a 95 to an estimated 78 because of a technical error and it PISSED me off. But then I was like, Cathi, you keep telling people you don't really care if you finish the degree and at this point, you don't even care if you finish the class. You've gotten the information you need, you could drop it, and be fine with it. I did the work, but at the end of the day, does it matter what grade I get in the class? IT DOESN'T! That's an internal motivation versus an external motivation.

Cathi gives credit to her direct sales and leadership training from her other job working for AdvoCare, even receiving praise from one of the top salespersons in her upline for her achievements. She learned how to network and learned a lot about integrity, which she quickly related back to remaining true to her authentic self. When speaking of her own business start-up, she describes her integrity and motivation as a drive that just 'has to happen'. This drive was also a theme that exposed itself when she spoke of the challenges she has faced.

Challenges

Many challenges Cathi spoke of were related to her own job or the band profession as a whole. When asking her about her position at the Ransom-Everglades School, Cathi speaks about the pros and cons of her job as well as her need to do more.

> It's small, it's never going to be the best band in the world; it's never going to be something people stop and take notice of, but it provides me a really good salary, really good benefits, and a pretty easy lifestyle. I work from 7:30 to 4 and I live nine blocks away. I keep saying I'll never find both salary and job satisfaction in the position I have now. It's a GREAT gig and I'll stay as long as they have me, I think. But there's a sense of frustration that I should be doing more. I kind of think too, though, that even if I had every single kid in that school in my band, I don't know that it would be good enough. Because it's not about me. I think that's really the thing. It's not about me, so it doesn't matter what my band does.

She continues by speaking about the scheduling challenges she faces within a private school whose focus is on STEM (Science Technology Engineering and Math) and inclusion of Spanish language as a core requirement, which forces students to choose between only one arts elective or a second academic class. This happened shortly after they added orchestra and drama to the arts program to compete with other private schools in the area, thus spreading thin an already small population of students. She does not know what her program enrolment will be like later on, which is why she is focusing on Music Mentor Network (MMN).

> I've got to start thinking of something else, so that if I have to go, or feel like I need to go, I have something in the works. Like a parallel. I've worked with direct sales companies, and they always say, if you really want to make this your job, you need to bring the boat up so that you can step over. Don't make that leap of faith when it comes to income. You have to kind of ease into a parallel stream and then just step over when you're ready.

Although Cathi spoke of some of her challenges, many times she chose to highlight challenges within the profession. One challenge that bothered her the most was that some successful band directors were just not good people.

> I would much rather have a mediocre band with a good person in front of it than a good band with an asshole, and I've seen both. Because a mediocre band with a good person in front of it is usually all about the kids and creating good people and creating lifelong musicians who are going to grow up, and they may not be musicians or band directors, but they're going to support the arts and they are going [to] make sure their kid is in band because it was a great experience for them. They are going [to] perpetuate the art form. There's one band director I know in particular who worked the kids just beyond death. As soon as they graduated from high school, they were done with it. They wanted nothing, NOTHING to do with it – they were a FANTASTIC band. I mean outstanding! Known nationwide! Not a nice person. I'd rather have a mediocre band with a good person. I'd rather have a good band with a good person.

These directors were often praised for the musical performances the band produced, but were not good overall leaders, mentors, or good people in general, which bothered Cathi. She spoke of meeting people like this at ABC:

> We get these people at ABC who, on their entrance exams, their exit exams, their projects, everything that they do – 100% over the top. You put them on a podium, and they can't lead. Nobody wants to follow them, and you just look at them and you go, their kids have to be so disconnected. It's a problem. And the problem is that they never should have gotten through undergrad. Nobody should have ever said, 'this is the job for you'. It's not happening in any profession. If you can afford it, and you can make the grades on paper, who are we to tell you not to follow your dreams?

Cathi also speaks of her frustration with another band director:

> She'll talk smack about everybody, but if there's a really good director on the horizon, she'll praise them, but then she'll insert herself into the narrative about how she did all these things to get them there. Why do you have to insert yourself into someone else's narrative? It's not about you.

Another challenge of the profession Cathi reveals is that she feels band directors do not get out enough to see other bands and listen to them, particularly middle school teachers who do not have the opportunity to travel like high school band directors often do during marching band season and state concert band MPA. She thinks band directors often become too comfortable. She believes:

> You need to get yourself out there. It's really easy to get comfortable if you are a big fish in a small pond. If your band is always getting Superiors and you're always one of the best bands at districts, it's really easy to get lazy and complacent – you know where the bar is, and you know that you can clear it in your sleep.

Cathi thinks many band directors need to make a better effort to attend the Midwest Clinic, or travel to Texas like she did to observe how other bands are successful, so that they can become inspired to be better.

Many of the challenges Cathi spoke of relate back to the overall concept of identity. As evident in many of her quotes, her ideas about mentoring, relationships, vulnerability, motivation, and authenticity continued to resurface throughout each major theme. There is no doubt Cathi has made significant contributions to the band directing profession and the field of music education. These contributions are shown through her mentoring and continued analysis of the successes and challenges, and her impending need to make the profession and its members even stronger and more successful.

Implications

I believe allowing Cathi to lead the interview sessions and share her narrative in her own way facilitated her in allowing or her own values and personality to shine through. Using this methodological approach gave a glimpse into one woman's journey towards a major leadership position within band directing. This type of methodological flexibility allowed her to complete telling her stories before speaking of another topic. Often, she would even alert me when she was done by saying, 'and that's all I have to say about that!' This gave her the agency to manage her discourse and protect her leadership position, and also make it clear that her job is not about her, despite the nature of this narrative project.

Cathi used her personality traits and values to talk about her unique journey. This framework became important because it supports the most recent studies on teacher effectiveness and teachers' traits and values.[23] Though many of these studies were done through observations and descriptive research, they were rarely approached through the method of a biographical narrative using the participant's own words.

Cathi continued to keep the conversation in a positive light. Even when speaking of challenges, she always returned to how to improve the profession. The conversational approach allowed for a more honest reveal of her point of view. Aspects of mentoring and authenticity proved to be most valuable to Cathi, as these themes continued to echo throughout each interview and follow-up conversation.

Research continues to show a large gap in literature and documentation of the presence of female band directors. I suggest music historians start to document the stories of female conductors in a positive light, and not continue to point out the lack of female directors or emphasise marginalisation. I encourage them to rather seek to bring to fruition the successes of those who have risen through the ranks by allowing women like Cathi to tell their own stories in order for us to understand their contributions to the field.

Notes

1. For the purpose of this chapter, the terms conductor and band director will be used interchangeably.
2. Deborah A. Sheldon and Linda A. Hartley, "What Color Is Your Baton, Girl? Gender and Ethnicity in Band Conducting," *Bulletin of the Council for Research in Music Education* 192 (2012): 39–52.
3. Paula A. Crider and Frank L. Battisti, *The Conductor's Legacy: Conductors on Conducting for Wind Band* (Chicago, IL: GIA Publications, 2010).
4. George N. Heller and Bruce D. Wilson, "Historical Research," in *Handbook of Research on Music Teaching and Learning*, edited by Richard J. Colwell and Carol Richardson (New York: Macmillan, 1992), 102; Sondra W. Howe, 'Reconstructing the History of Music Education from a Feminist Perspective," *Philosophy of Music Education Review* 6, no. 2 (1998): 96–106; Jere T. Humphreys, "Sex and Geographic Representation in Two Music Education History Books," *Bulletin of the Council for Research in Music Education* 131 (1997): 6–86.
5. Carolyn Livingston, "Women in Music Education in the United States: Names Mentioned in History Books," *Journal of Research in Music Education* 45, no. 1 (1997): 130–44.
6. Humphreys, "Sex and Geographic Representation."
7. Wayne D. Bowman, *Philosophical Perspectives on Music* (New York: Oxford University Press, 1998).
8. Roberta Lamb, Lori-Ann Dolloff, and Sondra Wieland Howe, "Feminist, Feminist Research, and Gender Research in Music Education: A Selective Review," in *The New Handbook of Research on Music Teaching and Learning*, edited by Richard Colwell and Carol Richardson (New York: Schirmer Books, 2002), 648–68.
9. Jill M. Sullivan, "A History of the Marine Corps Women's Reserve Band," *Journal of Band Research* 42, no. 1 (2006): 1–41; Jill M. Sullivan, *Bands of Sisters: U.S. Women's Military Bands During World War II* (Lanham, MD: Scarecrow Press, 2011); Jill M. Sullivan, "Women Music Teachers as Military Band Directors During World War II," *Journal of Historical Research in Music Education* 39, no.1 (2016): 78–105, https://doi.org/10.1177/153660616665625; Jill M. Sullivan, *Women's Bands in America: Performing Music and Gender* (Lanham, MD: Rowman & Littlefield, 2017).
10. Florida Bandmasters' Association, "Legacy Project," accessed April 5, 2019, https://fba.flmusiced.org/legacy-project.
11. Monica Crew Leimer, "Female Band Directors and Adjudicators in Florida," (Master's diss. Unpublished, The Florida State University, 2010), 1.
12. Ibid.

13. Florida Bandmasters' Association, "History of the Florida Bandmasters' Association," accessed April 5, 2019, https://fba.flmusiced.org/about/history/.
14. The Florida Bandmasters Association Concert Music Performance Assessments occur annually and they have four primary objectives: (1) To provide opportunities for students and directors to perform in an environment which provides critical evaluation of its performance by noted experts in the field of band performance, (2) To provide the opportunity for students and directors to perform for their peers in a formal concert setting, (3) To provide a performance opportunity which will serve as a motivational goal for students and directors, and (4) To provide an opportunity for students and directors to hear performances of their peers and learn from hearing those performances, and to provide a goal that is so compelling that the preparation for attaining that goal becomes the vehicle for continued growth and to demonstrate students' abilities to apply musical fundamentals and concepts in an ensemble performance setting. These objectives can be found on the FBA website: https://fba.flmusiced.org/mpa/mpa-results-and-programs/. Four judges, three for the on-stage performance and one in sight-reading, rate bands according to the following scale: Superior (highest rating), Excellent, Good, Fair, and Poor (lowest rating). FBA District 20 private school concert band MPA results can be retrieved from the reports published at https://floridaschoolmusic.org/reports/
15. Natalee Popadiuk, "The Feminist Biographical Method in Psychological Research," *The Qualitative Report* 9, no. 3 (2004): 395.
16. Joseph A. Maxwell, *Qualitative Research Design: An Interactive Approach* (Thousand Oaks, CA: Sage Publications, 2013), 30; Kathryn Anderson and Dana C. Jack, "Learning to Listen: Interview Techniques and Analyses," in *Women's Words: The Feminist Practice of Oral History*, edited by Sherma B. Gluck and Daphne Patai (New York: Routledge, 1991), 23.
17. Svend Brinkman and Steinar Kvale, *Interviews: Learning the Craft of Qualitative Research Interviewing*, 3rd ed. (Thousand Oaks, CA: Sage, 2015), 6.
18. Steven J. Taylor and Robert Bogdan, *Introduction to Qualitative Research Methods: A Guidebook and Resource*, 3rd ed. (New York: Wiley, 1998).
19. Kathy Charmaz, *Constructing Grounded Theory* (London: Sage Publications, 2014).
20. The American Band College is a master's degree program specifically for band directors who wish to keep their job yet work towards a graduate degree online and over the summer holidays. American Band College, "What Is ABC?," accessed April 7, 2019, http://bandworld.org/abc/american-band-college.htm.
21. The Florida Bandmasters' Associate Music Performance Assessments are concert band and solo and ensemble performance events sponsored by the state that take place once a year in each school district throughout the state of Florida. These events are adjudicated by trained, successful band directors who provide a rating and feedback to those who perform.
22. Musician Mentor Network, "About," accessed April 7, 2019, www.musicmentornetwork.org.
23. Steven N. Kelly, "High School Band Students' Perceptions of Effective Teaching," *Journal of Band Research* 42, no. 2 (2007): 57–70; Steven N. Kelly, "High School Instrumental Students' Perceptions of Effective Teaching Music Student Teaching Traits," *Journal of Music Teacher Education* 17, no. 2 (2008): 83–91, https://doi.org/10.1177/1057083708317648; Peter Miksza, Matthew Roeder, and Dana Biggs, "Surveying Colorado Band Directors' Opinions of Skills and Characteristics Important to Successful Music Teaching," *Journal of Research in Music Education* 57, no. 4 (2010): 364–81; Kimberly Van Weelden, "Relationship Between Perceptions of Conducting Effectiveness and Ensemble Performance," *Journal of Research in Music Education* 50 (2002): 165–76.

Bibliography

Anderson, Kathryn, and Dana C. Jack. "Learning to Listen: Interview Techniques and Analyses." In *Women's Words: The Feminist Practice of Oral History*, edited by Sherma B. Gluck and Daphne Patai, 23. New York: Routledge, 1991.

Bowman, Wayne D. *Philosophical Perspectives on Music*. New York: Oxford University Press, 1998.

Brinkmann, Svend, and Steinar Kvale. *InterViews: Learning the Craft of Qualitative Research Interviewing*. Thousand Oaks: Sage, 2015.

Charmaz, Kathy. *Constructing Grounded Theory*. London: Sage Publications, 2014.

Crider, Paula A., and Frank L. Battisti. *The Conductors Legacy: Conductors on Conducting for Wind Band*. Chicago: GIA Publications, 2010.

Heller, George N., and Bruce D. Wilson. "Historical Research." In *Handbook of Research on Music Teaching and Learning*, edited by Richard J. Colwell and Carol Richardson, 102. New York: Macmillan, 1992.

Howe, Sondra W. "Reconstructing the History of Music Education from a Feminist Perspective." *Philosophy of Music Education Review* 6, no. 2 (1998): 96–106.

_____. *Women Music Educators in the United States: A History*. Lanham, MD: Scarecrow Press, 2014.

Humphreys, Jere T. "Sex and Geographic Representation in Two Music Education History Books." *Bulletin of the Council for Research in Music Education* 131 (1997): 6–86.

Kelly, Steven N. "High School Band Students' Perceptions of Effective Teaching." *Journal of Band Research* 42, no. 2 (2007): 57–70.

_____. "High School Instrumental Students' Perceptions of Effective Teaching Music Student Teaching Traits." *Journal of Music Teacher Education* 17, no. 2 (2008): 83–91. https://doi.org/10.1177/1057083708317648.

Lamb, Roberta, Laurie-Ann Dolloff, and Sondra W. Howe. "Feminist, Feminist Research, and Gender Research in Music Education: A Selective Review." In *The New Handbook of Research on Music Teaching and Learning*, edited by Richard Colwell and Carol Richardson, 648–68. New York: Schirmer Books, 2002.

Leimer, Monica Crew. "Female Band Directors and Adjudicators in Florida." Master's diss. unpublished, The Florida State University, 2010.

Livingston, Carolyn. "Women in Music Education in the United States: Names Mentioned in History Books." *Journal of Research in Music Education* 45, no. 1 (1997): 130–44.

Maxwell, Joseph A. *Qualitative Research Design: An Interactive Approach*, 30. Thousand Oaks, CA: Sage Publications, 2013.

Miksza, M., Matthew Roeder, and Dana Biggs. "Surveying Colorado Band Directors' Opinions of Skills and Characteristics Important to Successful Music Teaching." *Journal of Research in Music Education* 57, no. 4 (2010): 364–81.

Popadiuk, Natalee. "The Feminist Biographical Method in Psychological Research." *The Qualitative Report* 9, no. 3 (2004): 395.

Sheldon, Deborah A., and Linda A. Hartley. "What Color Is Your Baton, Girl? Gender and Ethnicity in Band Conducting." *Bulletin of the Council for Research in Music Education* 192 (2012): 39–52.

Sullivan, Jill M. "A History of the Marine Corps Women's Reserve Band." *Journal of Band Research* 42, no. 1 (2006): 1–41.

_____. *Bands of Sisters: U.S. Women's Military Bands during World War II*. Lanham, MD: Scarecrow Press, 2011.

_____. "Women Music Teachers as Military Band Directors During World War II." *Journal of Historical Research in Music Education* 39, no. 1 (2016): 78–105. https://doi.org/10.1177/153660616665625.

_____. *Women's Bands in America: Performing Music and Gender*. Lanham, MD: Rowman & Littlefield, 2017.

Taylor, Steven J., and Robert Bogdan. *Introduction to Qualitative Research Methods: A Guidebook and Resource*, 3rd ed. New York: Wiley, 1998.

Van Weelden, Kimberly. "Relationship Between Perceptions of Conducting Effectiveness and Ensemble Performance." *Journal of Research in Music Education* 50 (2002): 165–76.

21
ADDRESSING CYCLIC GENDER CONSTRUCTS IN MUSIC AND MUSIC EDUCATION IN THE UK

Abigail Bruce and Chamari Wedamulla

Gender equality has made significant strides in the last 100 years. The 21st century represents an age of modern values that seek to empower the female voice and #EmbraceEquity (2023).[1] As a modern democratic society, we would expect both Britain's music industry and its music education to reflect and promote gender equality, supporting women to realise their musical aspirations. Nonetheless, the UK's musical institutions are heavily permeated by the Western classical historical canon, which remains largely male-dominated. What does this prevailing cultural influence mean for gender parity in music education within modern British society?

This chapter explores the roles and representations of women in music education and the music industries in the UK. A scrutiny of curriculum resources and the value of cultural industry, wherein music is firmly situated, illuminates a perpetuation of particular gender constructs. Subsequently, the first section of this chapter will discuss the embedded value systems maintaining implicit binary gender stereotypes that heavily determine the roles of women in music industry and music education. The second part of this chapter will assess some existing attempts to re-address this issue of gender disparity within music education and highlight opportunities for the UK's musical institutions to better reflect modern societal values and end notable cycles of gender constructs.

Women Versus AO1: The Western Classical Canon (1650–1910)

As highlighted in the 2022 National Plan for Music, access to a high-quality music education for all is a clear expectation at all levels and stages.[2] The national plan's vision, to 'enable all children and young people to learn to sing, play an instrument and create music together, and have the opportunity to progress their musical interests and talents, including professionally', is consistent across all Key Stages.[3] Within this, the curriculum is non-prescriptive of any particular composers or musicians, implicating that subject leaders have the capacity to ensure fair gender representation. Nonetheless, the works of the so-called 'great masters' have been long attributed to the historical canon of Western classical, male, white and European composers. This is evident in several popular teaching resources, beginning in primary school. For example, Charanga, one popular online resource for listening activities in primary school music, features Beethoven, Bach, Haydn, Mozart and Debussy on its main teacher-access page.[4] Classroom generalists, who typically teach in primary schools across all subjects as opposed to music specialists, are likely to depend on the direction of such resources. As such, the perception of 'great composers and musicians' is largely influenced by the male-dominated historical canon, thus establishing gender constructs in music from the early stages of school-based music education.

Thereafter, popular GCSE and A-Level exam boards both offer similarly white- and male-dominated suggested listening for their *compulsory* Classical Areas of Study.[5] Whilst works by female musicians are suggested for wider listening and feature in post-classical areas of study, the set pieces for *compulsory* classical study are **all** written by white, European, male composers. This denotes that, throughout each school stage, musical learners *must* listen to the music of men, whereas the music of women is optional. The implication is that the music of women composers is seen as 'secondary' to the music of their male counterparts and as a tokenistic gesture rather than genuine inclusivity and diversity, as women's music often comes under the optional area of syllabi and curricula.

Undoubtedly, the underrepresentation of female composers for classical study is attributable to the historical canon overall and is not necessarily easily avoidable. Simply, music written by male composers has been better preserved and passed on for generations than that of women. This is reflective of the role of women in society pre-mid-twentieth century, and by virtue, their role in music at the time, as noted by Clara Schumann:

> I once believed that I possessed creative talent, but I have given up this idea . . . a woman must not desire to compose – there has never yet been one able to do it. Should I expect to be the one?[6]

Nonetheless, archival research is increasingly uncovering 'lost' works of female composers of the classical period. For example, the DONNE Women in Music project develops short video clips with the aim of making women's music more accessible on an online platform.[7] Many featured women achieved significant musical feats, particularly within their contexts. One example is Chiquinha Gonzaga, a Brazilian composer, pianist and the first woman conductor in Brazil. Having composed over 2,000 pieces of work, including 70 operettas, Gonzaga's contextual background both exemplifies and challenges gender inequality in music. In terms of legacy, Gonzaga is acknowledged by one of DONNE's founders, Gabriella di Laccio, for influencing the Bossa Nova style and writing a popular Carnaval song.[8] Much Euro-American music of the 50s–60s features Bossa Nova-like rhythms, and pseudo-Latin American influences. Therefore, Gonzaga's music would naturally lend itself to a UK curriculum, as an example of a 'great' classical influence, as the curriculum stipulates.[9]

However, on the other hand, the DONNE Research report shows that of the 20,400 compositions scheduled by 111 orchestras across 31 countries, only 7.7% are the works of women.[10] The increasingly un-archived legacies of many female figures in music could be similarly celebrated in music education with the study of stylistic influences adopted in modern music. However, their continued absence in music education can be attributed to social and cultural parameters of set areas of study, consistent across exam boards. Why do such parameters for set-works in curriculum resources persist in a 21st century music education?

The Value of Cultural Tradition

While the current curriculum itself does not stipulate areas of study, there is a consistent delineation of Western Classical tradition, indicatively white, European male, across curriculum resources. This singulation of one style and culture for compulsory study risks perpetuating a sense of superiority in respect to both gender and culture, which does not reflect modern British values. As such, it is clear that certain male composers of the Western classical 'era' are deeply embedded in implicit cultural value systems. This represents a common traditional view: that engaging with the musical heritage of Western classical tradition is crucial to national identity, as well as fundamental to understanding music.

Such a traditionalist view of music education is cyclically entrenched by the UK's cultural industry and many corresponding initiatives. Government white papers published by the Department for Culture, Media and Sport emphatically define the role of music within the cultural industry as to promote the 'gift' of 'our heritage'.[11] This reflects the sociological theory that culture-as-industry manifests as the engagement, protection and promotion of *inherited* activity and product.[12] The distribution of Arts Council England's (ACE) budget, serving to support a national portfolio of 660 arts organisations, pertains to this notion. Whilst the national portfolio organisations represent a vast array of diverse musical activity, 7.3% (£24,347,337.1) was given to the Royal Opera House alone. 1.26% (2 x 0.63–£2,097,900) is awarded to the two London Orchestras. Acknowledging in November 2022 that its investments in certain regions have remained historically low, ACE's announcement of the new national portfolio of funded organisations for 2023–26 includes 'level up' areas that are outside of London as set out by the government white paper.[13] However, it is clear that funding is prioritised for those organisations that adhere to the value of inherited cultural activity and product, perpetuating the Western classical canon. As musical works by female composers will always be newly attributed to the Western classical narrative, will they nver be considered part of the UK's cultural heritage from a traditional perspective?

Generational Perspectives

The values illustrated by the cultural industry may have permeated implicit value systems, particularly of older generations. Indeed, responses in Pitts' 2012 research suggested that some parents sought to achieve a measure of cultural capital by engaging their children in classical music.[14] The values attributed to the historical narrative are, however, likely disconnected from the values held by the majority of today's youth. Whether conscious or not, the lack of female representation within the perpetually associative list of 'the greats' might create significant cognitive dissonance for a generation wherein binary gender 'norms' are less typically encultured. Can we truly expect young learners to engage with syllabi if the list of music considered fundamental to our national identity is so disjunct from modern societal values? As Jessy McCabe notes (see Chapter 26), the lack of representation does not provide role models or examples of composers and musicians who reflect modern society.

The recent inclusion of set works by female composers on the Edexcel A-Level music syllabus reflects the changing generational views on gender equality. The change emerged as a result of a successful targeted campaign led by student Jessy McCabe in 2015.[15] German Romantic composer Clara Schumann (1819–1896) is now listed in 'instrumental music', Rachel Portman (1960) in 'music for film', Kate Bush (1958) in 'popular music and jazz', Anoushka Shankar (1981) in 'fusions' and Kaija Saariaho (1952) in 'new directions'.[16] Additionally, there is a substantial increase in the featured works of female composers on their 'suggested wider listening' list, particularly of the classical period in question. It includes the works of: German composer and pianist Fanny Mendelssohn (1805–1847); French composer and pianist Cécile Chaminade (1857–1944); English composer and member of the women's suffrage movement, Dame Ethel Mary Smyth, 1858–1944; and American composer and pianist Amy Beach (1867–1944), acknowledged as the first American woman to publish a symphony.[17] From a musicological perspective, these women demonstrate both musical talent and counter-stereotypic contextual study in varied capacities. In line with the set criteria for listening and appraising, this inclusion of musical works was therefore both purposeful and considered, and an important distinction from a tokenistic gesture toward gender inclusion. Nevertheless, other exam specifications do not seem to have made such significant changes. Readdressing this issue of representation of women across curriculum resources is a crucial first step toward gender parity, as it can have a significant impact on the aspirations of young female musicians.

Role Models in Music

Role models are evolution's way of showing us which behaviours are desirable and those individuals can aspire to replicate. In social theory, effective role-modelling requires a basis of similarities to identify with, including gender.[18] Research suggests that adolescent females are significantly influenced by same-gender role models, particularly in relation to career choices.[19] Undoubtedly, there is a consistent representation of females in certain performative roles in music, rather than creative or innovative, particularly within current curriculum resources. Excluding Edexcel, each resource mentioned in this chapter features Adele in pop studies. Kylie Minogue, Taylor Swift, Bette Midler and Alicia Keys are amongst others.[20] Such a representation of women as chanteuse or pop-icon across the curriculum is indicative of a significantly outdated social-normative construct, echoing Copland's 1960s view: 'musical creativity runs counter to the nature of the feminine mind'.[21]

Certainly, the role of the woman as performer rather than leader or innovator also manifests within the cultural industry. A recent survey of the world's 20 greatest orchestras and instrumental groups, as ranked by the UK's Gramophone magazine, supports that men are more likely to hold senior positions in these organisations. Those considered 'top roles', such as associate principal and concertmaster, are currently held by 79% men and 21% women.[22] Maintaining this, whilst there appears to be a good balance of gender in players in the two London orchestras, the Symphony (LSO) and Philharmonia (LPO), both conductors are male.[23] Thus, the availability of same-gender role models might be restricted in certain areas, particularly women in creative leadership in classical domains.

Nevertheless, a lack of female representation within the music industry extends beyond the UK classical music domains. Currently, only 17% of PRS members in the UK are women, and across all regions there is a 70:30 male-female proportion in creative or leadership roles.[24] Despite an overall rise in conversation and agendas aiming to improve inclusion and diversity in music, the percentage of female participants in the music industry remains unbalanced. This is true of all roles but is particularly applicable to female songwriters and producers. For instance, only 17.1% of Billboard's Hot 100 artists in 2018 were female; a mere 12.3% listed were female songwriters and 2% were female producers from 2012–18.[25] Thus, role models for creative careers like composers and singer-songwriters, and leadership role models, like producers and conductors, are largely unavailable. As role modelling theories suggest, a lack of female role models in such positions implicitly perpetuates misperceptions of attainable career goals for young female aspiring musicians.[26] Thus, the cycle of gender constructs in music continues, despite the overall social shift toward equality.

Despite clear issues of underrepresentation of women in the curriculum and in the music industry, consistent statistics find that girls are more likely than boys to study music at KS4.[27] In 2018, Arts Professional indicated that GCSE music entries from girls as 56% and boys as 45%.[28] Supporting this trend, a 2018 YouGov poll found that girls aged 6–15 are more likely than boys to say they enjoy music as a subject (48% vs 34%).[29] Nonetheless, Ofsted's* 2015 statistics indicate a decline of female progression in KS5, with 76% of boys that continue musical study gaining a full A-level, compared to 71% of girls.[30] **

* Office for Standards in Education, Children's Services and Skills (Ofsted) is a non-ministerial department that inspects and regulates services providing education and skills for learners of all ages.
**In schools in England, each year matches up with the key stages and age of students as following: Ages 3–5 – Early years & reception; Ages 5 to 7 – Key Stage (KS1) (school years 1 & 2); Ages 7 to 11 – KS2 (school years 3 to 6); Ages 11 to 14 – KS3 (school years 7 to 9); Ages 14–16 – KS4 (school years 10 & 11 – students take the General Certificate of Secondary Education or GCSE exams); Ages 16–18 – KS5 (Qualifications include AS-Levels and A-Levels or NVQs or Diplomas).

Naturally, this would result in fewer women enrolling in higher education, particularly into courses related to composition, screen composition and music technology.[31] This pattern of gender in educational progression correlates with a lack of role models in these fields.

Differently, women have consistently made up a significantly larger proportion of teachers in the UK, where 75.5% identified as female in 2021.[32] This is not subject-specific, nor does it account for community arts leaders or peripatetic teachers. Nonetheless, it does suggest that musical learners are more likely to encounter a female teacher in their school-based music education, aged 5–16. These figures are not surprising given that, historically and presently, women working in the field of music have been most likely to be teachers and educators.[33] In fact, women were often confined to private or home teaching till the late 19th century. In this vein, a female teacher in the classroom context may be considered a leadership role, and it certainly indicates the progress made since the 1920s suffragette movement. On the other hand, as Howe posits, women in music education could be seen as 'extensions of activities in the home'.[34] This view reflects the generic gender associations of women as nurturers and caregivers, most suited to social, communal careers, particularly with children,[35] and it is easy to see the remnants of this view in today's workforce statistics.

On the other hand, men have always been more likely than women to teach music in colleges and universities.[36] A 2000 study carried out by Lisa Whistlecroft found that only 18% of lecturing staff across 83 institutions were female.[37] A more recent report commissioned by the EDIMS (Equality, Diversity & Inclusion in Music Studies) shows a notable difference in gender disparity among academic staff, where men are more likely to hold senior and professorial positions than women.[38] Does this relate to role modelling in social-normative career-model cycles? In correlation, women have been less likely to enrol in music courses in higher education. Moreover, in 1999, a study on gender and technology in UK higher education highlighted a construction of women as 'technologically incompetent' in that women had to work harder than men, or 'prove' themselves, for recognition in the technological fields.[39] It is perhaps unsurprising then that Whistlecroft's study also found a mere 18.5% of female lecturing staff across music technology and studio, electroacoustic and composition.[40] It is evident that invisible gender barriers still exist within institutions music in the 21st century, and that these appear to be related to implicit manifestations of perpetuated stereotypes.

Role Models in the Curriculum

Despite growing rejection of binary social constructions of gender, empirical studies maintain that gender stereotypes continue to implicitly shape personal expectations for both men and women.[41] Subsequently, they still largely influence perceptions of life-course options, and so the cyclic constructs of women in music and music education continues. As stereotypes are typically engendered by the time of adolescence, it is the responsibility of music education to challenge gender stereotypes.[42] This can be achieved by offering longitudinal exposure to a diverse scope of counter-normative representations of women in music across all key-stages. Such is proven to enhance role-model effects.[43]

It should be noted that there are *some* positive variances within typical gender representations in exam resources. For instance, AQA suggests Winifred Phillips under 'Topic Area 3: Film and computer gaming music 1990s to present' and Kate Rusby under 'Topic Area 4: Contemporary folk music of the British Isles'.[44] The former representation is particularly positive given that, statistically and stereotypically, technology is a male-dominated field. It is the responsibility of curriculum resource authors and regulators to ensure that their resources are more comprehensive and holistically considered regarding gender representation and intersectionally to all other forms including but not limited to identity, sexuality, ethnicity, race and faith.

Composer Kerry Andrew agrees that such an update is well overdue:

> At an all-girls school workshop I ran recently, the music teacher said that it was brilliant for the students to see, with their own eyes, a real-life professional female composer. At GCSE and A-Level, the classical composers studied in set-works are almost exclusively male. And white. Oh, and dead. It's glaringly obvious: if girls are presented with examples of successful female creators, in all genres, they might view composition as a viable profession for themselves.[45]

As Andrew implies, there is certainly a need to diversify curriculum resources with a fair representation of men and women in an array of musical roles and contexts. This is a feasible quest.

Whilst the 2015 Edexcel updates featuring a handful of female composers and singer-songwriters is a good start, there need to be examples of female leaders, creators and innovators, rather than chanteuse. Gonzaga, as previously mentioned, amongst a plethora of female singer-songwriters is one example of a classical female composer, whose stylistic features are evident in modern music and could act as alternative role models to young females. Tori Amos, for example, a creative singer-songwriter and skilled piano player from America, actively challenges an array of social 'norms' with poetic metaphors.[46] There could also be an inclusion of producers and conductors, such as Odaline de la Martinez, the first woman to conduct a BBC Proms (see Chapter 16). The representation of such 'counter-normative' women in the curriculum might compensate for the statistical under-representation of females in certain roles throughout history and in modern industry.

Beyond the general representation of music by women, however, the contextual study of female musicians and performers throughout history is a ubiquitous tool for critical discussions regarding gender, culture and influence. Madonna, as opposed to a highly sexualised 'pop-icon,' could provide a contextual study for female empowerment throughout the 80s. Certainly, androgynous figures, such as Annie Lennox and Pink, alongside the punk and new-wave icon Debbie Harry (or Blondie) could provide a starting point for critical discussion regarding social politics and gender. There is also scope to add more stylistic variances to the study of women in pop, exemplified by performers such as: Ella Fitzgerald, jazz; Aretha Franklin, soul; Billie Holiday, jazz; Patsy Cline, soul; Nina Simone, jazz; Dionne Warwick, soul. These examples are typically absent from music in schools, even though many of them were considered iconic or well-known in their time.

To truly achieve gender parity, the representation of men in curriculum resources should also be reconsidered. In contrast to over-representation of female performers in pop, it could be said that there is an under-representation of solo male performers in pop. David Bowie, George Michael, Prince, Stevie Wonder, Elvis, Bob Marley, Sam Smith and Ed Sheeran might all be considered worthy of mention, given their prominence in the pop industry. Many teachers of today's generation will likely be familiar with these examples, and as suggested listening is non-prescriptive, teachers should feel free to include a variety of composers and styles.[47] Therefore, the inclusion of more diverse examples of both men and women in music is both justified and feasible.

Organisational Outreach and Industry

To be most effective, gender representation in the curriculum should be practically consolidated with direct engagement with a breadth of real, living role models. Olsson and Martiny identified that the reinforcement of counter-stereotypic notions through direct community engagement and encouragement, as well as follow-up activities, had a clear effect on aspirations and behaviour.[48] In support of this, O'Neill's 2017 study of young people's musical learning ecologies maintains that engagement with musical activity in situated learning ecologies beyond the classroom is likely to be the most transformative overall.[49] Many schools maintain the importance of a breadth of exposures to cultural and creative experiences.[50] Additionally, the 2019 Music Commission Report (MCR), initiated by the ABRSM, found that a broader range of musical experiences had a positive impact on learners' progression. According to the findings, some suggestions of the report include more collaborative models between schools and relevant partners, new integrated approaches to music teaching and assessment, and parental involvement as a high priority in the musical progression of children and young people.[51] These have the aim of helping to reflect and emphasise the diversity and complexity of today's music sector.

There are a handful of youth-oriented organisational projects specifically aimed at positively encouraging gender-parity. These include but are not limited to: Youth Music UK funds, Girls Rock London (GRL!), Pan Intercultural Arts – Amies Freedom Choir, Brighter Sound – Both Sides Now, Girls Make Music by AudioActive and WeCreate by Generator, in partnership with music technology organisations, institutions and education hubs. These initiatives are aimed at encouraging girls and young women to write, record and perform music, improve self-confidence in music-making, and also provide guidance in early careers in music.[52] The MCR believes that music organisations, including conservatoires and the National Portfolio Organisations, have a vital role to play in 'inspiring young people by linking them to high quality performance and creative work'.[53] Nevertheless, many schools were found to work in isolation and therefore the potential for any such projects to align with and support the progression of musical learners is not being maximised.[54] There must be better communication between music educators and such organisations, to allow young female learners to engage with these projects and witness the availability of different roles in music.

Promisingly, there are also many existing projects and initiatives striving to achieve gender equality within the music industry. Help Musicians UK (HMUK) is a leading charity organisation that provides support for professional musicians of all genres.[55] In partnership with the international non-profit organisation Women in Music, HMUK launched two chapters, *Women in Music Great Britain* and *Women in Music Northern Ireland*, using dedicated membership forums. These chapters championed equality through networking via peer-to-peer discussions both online and at live events, aiming to spotlight women in sound engineering and production.[56] Additionally, Women Make Music, initiated by the PRS Foundation, promotes the development of female artists, bands, performers, songwriters and composers of all genres and backgrounds by providing funding opportunities and exposure for female musicians.[57] Key Change, another international initiative led by PRS and the Creative Europe programme, signed up to a 50:50 gender balance pledge by 2022 to encourage music festivals and conferences to empower more women in leading musical events and settings. This was initiated having identified just 20% or less of female representation amongst registered songwriters and composers across the participating countries.[58] Moreover, Women in Music, an initiative of the Association of Independent Music, hosts annual events for women in music from the creative industry, including live music, panels and keynotes, discussing the challenges of women working in a presently male-dominated sector and the lack of female artists on festival bills.[59] In supporting more women to engage and progress with different career routes, these commitments can undoubtedly improve gender parity in music. In turn, the availability of living female role models for young musical learners is diversified.

The array of programmes and projects for emerging female artists across the UK and EU appear to have been somewhat effective in balancing gender disparities in the industry. The recent results of the UK Music Diversity Report 2022 demonstrate a positive rise of the percentage of females (49.6% in 2020 to 52.9% in 2022) mirroring a 50:50 male-female balance in the UK music industry as a whole.[60] This is indeed a promising figure, but it does not necessarily implicate gender equality or an ethnically diverse workforce, as it shows a decrease of those working in music from a global majority background. Although the 2018 PRS Gender Pay Gap report indicates a slight improvement in bridging the equal pay gap, the 2022 Gender and Ethnicity Pay Gap report shows that the mean gender pay gap has increased in favour of men (10.6% in 2021 to 14.5% in 2022) contributing to larger gender pay gaps in parts of the industry.[61] Alongside the poor retention of females aged 35 and over in the industry, this indicates that factors such as unequal caring responsibilities and maternity discrimination might be discouraging women from taking leadership roles.[62] The report also found that although the ethnicity pay gap has been reduced, the proportion of ethnic communities working in lower-banded or lower-paid roles has not. Certainly, pressures regarding stereotypical expectations of women as carers, mothers and home-keepers have proven to impact young females' career aspirations.[63] Therefore, whilst many existing projects have been successful in advocating women's active role in the field as performers, artists and music-makers, more could be done by the industry to support female career progression, beginning in education.

Supporting Individual Progression

As a core pipeline for progression into industry, music education should empower young people to shape their own individual pathways as per the MCR's ambition.[64] Nevertheless, music-making activities currently have predetermined outcomes consistently based on a canonical brief and informed by areas of study, each with their own socio-cultural associations.[65] More experiential music-making activities offer the potential to both acknowledge and defy gender constructs through the exploration of self-concepts, with the creative use of sound as narrative or dialogue.[66]

Creative dialogues in musical collaboration have the potential to promote equality by enacting connectedness, tolerance, respect and empathy, as evidenced across a number of studies.[67] Thus, collaborative music-making, particularly when supported by community outreach, proves an opportunity to dissolve broad-reaching societal constructs. The MCR agrees that 'musical activities function as safe and enjoyable collaborative spaces where social barriers are broken down, emotions can be expressed, and confidence built'.[68] It is clear that the process of negotiating individual musical perspectives, enacted within a safe, collaborative social space and from a modern socio-cultural lens, is capable of such. Although such a social-constructivist type approach to music-making would require a fundamental shift in pedagogy, it could serve to promote a meaningful sense of individual and social agency,[69] thus defying social constructs attributed to any particular historical canon and re-aligning musical experiences with modern socio-cultural values.

Digital technologies are an underutilised resource that might further support young people in shaping their own pathways by facilitating both self-directed and tailored learning and collaboration.[70] The recent Youth Music Survey indicated that 39% of 1,001 children and young people surveyed in England, aged 7–17, Feb-March 2018, reported that they are already teaching themselves to some extent, particularly on digital platforms.[71] Differently, some schools and organisations, including TES' Creative School 2018 and HMUK, champion social platforms in support of collaborative project-work, particularly to share and showcase ideas, facilitating discussion and feedback.[72] Utilising such virtually collaborative platforms supports socio-constructivist learning approaches in music by diversifying the available opportunities for learners to engage with music. The growing list of low-cost and widely accessible digital resources allows young people to explore and apply musical skills in a wide range of areas. This would undoubtedly contribute to empowering young people to consider a broader range of progression pathways.

Additionally, schools, colleges and local universities might consider forming outreach partnerships between themselves to better support progression through educational transition stages. Such partnerships would afford mixed gender mentors that are closer in age; therefore, a mentors' achievements and behaviours represent attainable goals that can motivate younger students, as per role-model theory, affecting progression.[73] Regular, sequenced musical interaction between partner schools could connect phases of learning and support transitions, the current arrangements of which have been identified as generally weak in the MCR's recent consultation.[74] Perhaps, then, cross-transition-stage partnerships may also serve to address the decline of female applicants progressing in music in further and higher education.

Educational partnerships prove mutually beneficial in many ways and at all stages. The performances, tours, interactive workshops, and student-led talks that take place at Higher Education fairs, university open-days and subject taster-days could invite students to reassess their notions of the field by positively promoting a range of opportunities. Attending schools could justify any incurred expenses with budgets in place for the statutory delivery of career advice and guidance, which includes informed educational choices and pathways.[75] In addition to progression-based benefits, such events provide work for university students themselves. Moreover, outreach work in schools can be used as evidence to fulfil education or community-based assessments and modules, which many music degrees include. It may also count toward work experience for college and secondary students. Furthermore, cross-school outreach projects can be utilised as case study evidence for ArtsAward qualifications which are currently offered by many secondary school-based providers, including TES' Creative School 2018.[76] These opportunities, afforded by outreach, do not dictate any particular progression route, but rather encourage young musical learners to explore their own pathways.

Discussion and Conclusion

Recent years have seen some progressive changes in the music industry and music education that have begun to challenge certain gender constructs. Knowledge and representation of female composers initially buried in the classical music canon is improving, but few have an established place upon the male-dominated list of the 'greats'. There are abundant examples of female artists in various roles and contexts beyond solo-pop-performers, and similarly, of men in roles that defy embedded social constructs. The examples mentioned in this chapter are limited and many more could be explored, given that the curriculum and exam board study guides are non-prescriptive. However, those chosen reflect and demonstrate that there are musicians, composers and creators who are contemporary while defying gender norms. Present-day campaigns evidencing modern-generational views have led to the inclusion of female music composers in some exam boards programmes. Further considerations with respect to curriculum representation are vital, given that this provides implicit exposure to same-gender role models, pertinent to life-course perceptions.

Role models can be highly influential in providing direction and aspirations to pursue counter-stereotypic roles in music. Figures from industry surveys and reports indicate a slow but steady rise of female representation in the sector. Nevertheless, there is still a lack of female workers in senior and management positions.[77] It is also clear when examining certain musical and cultural settings that women's role in music is still largely maintained as performers rather than creators and innovators. Hence, whilst there is a 50:50 gender balance in the UK workforce overall, female workers are contained within some parts of the field, certainly restricting the availability of female role-models in said fields and thus emphasising cyclic gender constructs in music. Therefore, whilst some outreach programmes and projects offered across the UK are actively championing women in music, there does not yet seem to be alignment between the industry and education focussed on supporting individuals to shape their own pathways in musical progression. This proves a missed opportunity for gender parity.

More positively, this chapter has identified possible opportunities and innovative practices that seek to achieve parity in music education. These include mutually beneficial educational partnerships between all school-stages, which offer achievable and aspirational goals for progression, social-constructivist approaches that facilitate the individual voice and the practical inclusion of digital resources. The common foundations on which these possible solutions are built attempt to reflect and promote modern societal values, championing individuality over canonical music-making practices, replicating inherited cultural activity. Importantly, they all fulfil curriculum aims and requirements and can therefore be feasibly implemented. Based on these holistic requisites, as previously posited, teachers, educators, researchers and leaders in music might seize this time of change and uncertainty to explore and share their own ideas for music education. As it is the meso-structure of the classroom in which interactions between the learner and society take place, teachers, educators and administrators are in the best position to observe and facilitate the voices of independent learners. The dissolution of cyclic gender constructs and other invisible barriers in music and music education will evidently be an ongoing process. However, the prioritisation of the creative individual, in combination with new and existing industry initiatives, research, collaboration and outreach, as discussed, have the potential to eventuate normalised equality in musical engagement.

Notes

1. International Women's Day, "What's the IWD 2023 Campaign Theme?" 2023, accessed July 1, 2023, internationalwomensday.com.

2. Department for Education, "The Power of Music to Change Lives: A National Plan for Music Education," 2022, accessed February 10, 2023, www.gov.uk/government/publications/the-power-of-music-to-change-lives-a-national-plan-for-music-education.
3. Ibid, 5.
4. Charanga, "Musical School and the 2014 National Curriculum for Music," 2017, accessed November 23, 2018, https://charanga.com/site/musical-school/2014-national-curriculum-for-music/.
5. AQA, "Resource List: Study Pieces and Listening List," 2019, accessed April 12, 2019, www.aqa.org.uk/resources/music/gcse/music/teach/resource-list-study-pieces-and-listening-list; OCR, *GCSE (9–1) Specification Music*, Oxford and Cambridge: Cambridge Assessments, 2018, accessed April 4, 2019, www.ocr.org.uk/Images/219378-specification-accredited-gcse-music-j536.pdf, p. 45.
6. Mark Savage, "Five Forgotten Female Composers Will Be Celebrated on BBC Radio 3," 2017, accessed July 23, 2020, www.bbc.co.uk/news/entertainment-arts-38079139.
7. Drama Musica, "Donne Women in Music," 2018, accessed February 10, 2023, www.drama-musica.com/Donne.html#.
8. Gabriella Di Laccio, "Introducing Chiquina Gonzaga (1847–1935)," Presented at the International Women and/in Musical Leadership Conference, London, March 2019.
9. Department for Education, "National Curriculum in England: Music Programmes of Study," 2013, accessed April 12, 2019, www.gov.uk/government/publications/national-curriculum-in-england-music-programmes-of-study/national-curriculum-in-england-music-programmes-of-study.
10. DONNE, "Equality & Diversity in Global Repertoire," 2022, accessed February 15, 2023, https://donne-uk.org/wp-content/uploads/2021/03/Donne-Report-2022.pdf, p. 6.
11. Department for Culture, Media & Sport, "The Culture White Paper," 2016, accessed July 23, 2020, https://assets.publishing.service.gov.uk/government/uploads/system/uploads/attachment_data/file/510799/DCMS_Arts_and_Culture_White_Paper_Accessible_version.pdf, pp. 13, 14, 40.
12. Randall Everett Allsup, "Transformational Education and Critical Music Pedagogy: Examining the Link Between Culture and Learning," *Music Education Research* 5, no. 1 (2003): 11; Charles Hampden-Turner and Fons Trompenaars, *Riding the Waves of Culture: Understanding Cultural Diversity in Business* (London: Brealey, 2011), 21.
13. Arts Council England, "National Portfolio Organisations," 2017, accessed November 28, 2018, www.artscouncil.org.uk/our-investment-2015-18/national-portfolio-organisations; Department for Levelling Up, "Housing and Communities, Levelling Up the United Kingdom," February 2022, accessed February 15, 2023, https://assets.publishing.service.gov.uk/government/uploads/system/uploads/attachment_data/file/1052706/Levelling_Up_WP_HRES.pdf.
14. Stephanie Pitts, *Chances and Choices* (New York: Oxford University Press, 2012), 103.
15. Nadia Khomami, "A-Level Music to Include Female Composers After Student's Campaign," *The Guardian*, 2015, accessed July 23, 2020, www.theguardian.com/education/2015/dec/16/a-level-music-female-composers-students-campaign-jessy-mccabe-edexcel.
16. Edexcel, *A-Level Music* (London: Pearson Education Ltd., 2015), 6, 84.
17. Elizabeth Davis, "We Need to Tell You About Amy Beach, the First American Woman to Publish a Symphony," 2018, accessed April 12, 2019, www.classicfm.com/discover-music/amy-beach/.
18. Donald E. Gibson, "Role Models in Career Development: New Directions for Theory and Research," *Journal of Vocational Behaviour* 65, no. 1 (2004): 134–56.
19. Penelope Lockwood, "Someone Like Me Can Be Successful: Do College Students Need Same-Gender Role Models?" *Psychology of Women Quarterly* 30, no. 1 (2006): 36–46.
20. AQA, "Resource List: Study Pieces and Listening List," 2019, accessed April 12, 2019, www.aqa.org.uk/resources/music/gcse/music/teach/resource-list-study-pieces-and-listening-list; OCR, "GCSE (9–1) Specification Music," 2018, accessed April 4, 2019, www.ocr.org.uk/Images/219378-specification-accredited-gcse-music-j536.pdf, p. 46.
21. Copland, cited in Stephanie Cant, "Women Composers and the Music Curriculum," *British Journal of Music Education* 7, no. 1 (1990): 7.
22. Oliver Stanley and Amanda Shendruk, "Here's What the Stark Gender Disparity Among Top Orchestra Musicians Look Like," *Quartz at Work*, 2018, accessed July 23, 2020, https://qz.com/work/1393078/orchestras/.
23. London Philharmonic Orchestra, "Who's Who," 2019, accessed April 12, 2019, www.lpo.org.uk/about/musician-biographies/; London Symphony Orchestra, "Players," 2019, accessed April 12, 2019, https://lso.co.uk/orchestra/players.html.
24. Women in Music, "The Stats," 2019, accessed April 2, 2019, www.womeninmusic.org/stats.html.

25. Smith L. Stacy, Katherine Pieper, Marc Choueiti, Karla Hernandez, and Kevin Yao, "Inclusion in the Recording Studio?: Gender and Race/Ethnicity of Artists, Songwriters & Producers across 600 Popular Songs from 2012–2017," USC Annenberg School for Communication and Journalism. Annenberg Inclusion Initiative, 2018, accessed July 22, 2020, http://assets.uscannenberg.org/docs/inclusion-in-the-recording-studio.pdf.
26. Penelope Lockwood, "Someone Like Me Can Be Successful: Do College Students Need Same-Gender Role Models?," *Psychology of Women Quarterly* 30, no. 1 (2006): 36–46.
27. Rebecca Johnes, "Entries to Arts Subjects at KS4," Education Policy Institute, 2016, accessed April 12, 2019, https://epi.org.uk/wp-content/uploads/2018/01/EPI-Entries-to-arts-KS4-1.pdf, pp. 11, 44.
28. Jonathon Knott, "EBacc Blamed for Growing Gender Imbalance in GCSE Choices," 2018, accessed April 7, 2019, www.artsprofessional.co.uk/news/ebacc-blamed-growing-gender-imbalance-gcse-choices.
29. Matthew Smith, "Which School Subjects do Boys and Girls Enjoy More?" 2018, accessed April 12, 2019, https://yougov.co.uk/topics/education/articles-reports/2018/09/04/which-school-subjects-do-boys-and-girls-enjoy-morex.
30. Ofsted, "A-Level Subject Take-Up," 2015, accessed April 12, 2019, https://assets.publishing.service.gov.uk/government/uploads/system/uploads/attachment_data/file/426646/A_level_subject_take-up.pdf.
31. Lisa Whistlecroft, "Women in Music Technology in Higher Education in the UK," *The Canadian Electroacoustic Community*, 2000, accessed April 6, 2019, https://econtact.ca/3_3/WomenMusicTech.htm.
32. Department for Education, "School workforce in England," November 2021 and June 2022, accessed February 16, 2023, https://explore-education-statistics.service.gov.uk/find-statistics/school-workforce-in-england.
33. ABRSM, "Learning, Playing and Teaching in the UK in 2021," 2021, accessed January 31, 2023, https://gb.abrsm.org/media/66373/web_abrsm-making-music-uk-21.pdf.
34. Sondra Wieland Howe, "A Historical View of Women in Music Education Careers," *Philosophy of Music Education Review* 17, no. 2 (2009): 177.
35. Naomi Ellemers, "Gender Stereotypes," *Annual Review of Psychology* 69, no. 1 (2018): 275–98.
36. Howe, *A Historical View*, 177–78.
37. Whistlecroft, "Women in Music Technology."
38. Anna Bull, Diljeet Bhachu, Amy Blier-Carruthers, Alexander Bradley, and Seferin James, "Slow Train Coming? Equality, Diversity and Inclusion in UK Music Higher Education," *Equality, Diversity and Inclusion in Music Studies Network* (2022): 64, accessed February 15, 2023, https://edims.network/report/slowtraincoming/.
39. Flis Henwood, "Exceptional Women? Gender and Technology in UK Higher Education," *IEEE Technology and Society Magazine* 18, no. 4 (2000): 21–27.
40. Whistlecroft, "Women in Music Technology."
41. Ellemers, *Gender Stereotypes*.
42. Douglas Bourn, Frances Hunt, and Hassan Ahmed, *Childhood Development Stages and Learning on Global Issues* (London: UK Government, 2017), 7.
43. Maria Olsson and Sarah E. Martiny, "Does Exposure to Counterstereotypical Role Models Influence Girls' and Women's Gender Stereotypes and Career Choices? A Review of Social Psychological Research," *Frontiers in Psychology* 9, no. 2264 (2018): np.
44. AQA, *Resource*.
45. Kerry Andrew, "Why There Are So Few Female Composers," *The Guardian*, 2012, accessed April 5, 2019, www.theguardian.com/commentisfree/2012/feb/08/why-so-few-female-composers.
46. Lori Burns, "Musical Agency: Strategies of Containment and Resistance in 'Crucify'," in *Disruptive Divas: Feminism, Identity and Popular Music*, edited by Lori Burns and Melisse Lafrance (New York: Routledge, 2002), 73–95.
47. AQA, Resource; Edexcel, A-Level, 54, 63, 84; Edexcel, GCSE (9–1) Music, (2015), 34, 37; OCR, GCSE, 45.
48. Olsson and Martiny, *Exposure to Counterstereotpyical Role Models*.
49. Susan O'Neill, *Mapping Young People's Learning Ecologies* (New York: Oxford University Press, 2017), 134.
50. Royal Opera House Bridge, "The Creative School: Leading Cultural Learning," 2017, 5; Steve Cook and Vicci Harrocks, *The Arts: The Magic Key to Unlocking Student Potential*, Education Show (London: The Royal Opera House, 2019).

51. The Music Commission, *Retuning our Ambition for Music Learning*, 2019, 3–4 and 42–44.
52. Youth Music, "Music-Making Projects for Girls and Young Women: Addressing the Gender Balance in Music," accessed April 5, 2019, www.youthmusic.org.uk/music-making-projects-girls-and-young-women.
53. The Music Commission, *Retuning*, 44.
54. Ibid., 42–44.
55. Help Musicians UK, "Women in Music," 2017, accessed April 7, 2019, www.helpmusicians.org.uk/about-us/women-in-music.
56. Ibid.
57. PRS Foundation, "Women Make Music," 2023, accessed August 2, 2023, https://prsfoundation.com/funding-support/funding-music-creators/all-career-levels/women-make-music-2/.
58. PRS Foundation, "Key Change," 2019, accessed August 2, 2023, https://prsfoundation.com/partnerships/international-partnerships/keychange/?gclid=CjwKCAjw_aemBhBLEiwAT98FMrr6VQ_R1oBKSvGqAN3iEXJr2XG8EXr5VtbkmrNcHCTH4Xj9EA5cSxoCop0QAvD_BwE.
59. Association of Independent Music, "Women in Music," 2019, accessed April 8, 2019, www.musicindie.com/initiatives/women-in-music/.
60. UK Music, "Diversity Report," 2022.
61. PRS for Music, "Gender Pay Gap Report," 2018; PRS for Music, "Gender and Ethnicity Pay Gap Report," 2022.
62. UK Music, *Diversity Report*; PRS, *Gender Pay Gap Report*.
63. Howe, *A Historical View*, 165.
64. The Music Commission, *Retuning*, 52–53.
65. AQA, *GCSE Music*, 2019, 10, 23; Edexcel, *GCSE*, 4, 22, 23; OCR, *GCSE*, 8.
66. Susan Hallam, *Music Psychology in Education* (London: Institute of Education, 2009), 146; Hall and Thomson, "The Importance of Story," 103–11.
67. Hall and Thompson, "The Importance of Story," 110–16; Cook and Harrocks, *The Arts*; O'Neill, *Mapping*, 135–39.
68. The Music Commission, *Retuning*, 8.
69. Hallam, *Music Psychology*, 146; Hall and Thomson, *The Importance*, 103–11.
70. Royal Opera House Bridge, *The Creative*, 5.
71. The Music Commission, *Retuning*, 57.
72. Cook and Harrocks, *The Arts*; HMUK.
73. Lockwood, *Someone Like Me*.
74. The Music Commission, *Retuning*, 45; Cook and Harrocks, *The Arts*.
75. Department for Education, *Careers Guidance and Access for Education and Training Providers*, 2018.
76. Cook and Harrocks, *The Arts*; Royal Opera House, *The Creative*, 5; Trinity College London, *What Is Arts Award?*, 2019.
77. Bull, *Slow Train Coming?*

Bibliography

ABRSM. *Learning, Playing and Teaching in the UK in 2021*. London: ABRSM, 2021. Accessed January 31, 2023. https://gb.abrsm.org/media/66373/web_abrsm-making-music-uk-21.pdf.

Allsup, Randall Everett. "Transformational Education and Critical Music Pedagogy: Examining the Link Between Culture and Learning." *Music Education Research* 5, no. 1 (2003): 5–12.

Andrew, Kerry. "Why There Are So Few Female Composers." *The Guardian*, 2012. Accessed April 5, 2019. www.theguardian.com/commentisfree/2012/feb/08/why-so-few-female-composers.

AQA. "GCSE Music." 2019a. Accessed April 12, 2019. https://filestore.aqa.org.uk/resources/music/specifications/AQA-8271-SP-2016.PDF.

———. "Resource List: Study Pieces and Listening List." 2019b. Accessed April 12, 2019. www.aqa.org.uk/resources/music/gcse/music/teach/resource-list-study-pieces-and-listening-list.

Arts Council England. "National Portfolio Organisations." *Artscouncil.org.uk*, 2017. Accessed November 23, 2018. www.artscouncil.org.uk/our-investment-2015-18/national-portfolio-organisations.

———. "2023–26 Investment Programme Announcement." 2023. Accessed February 15, 2023. www.artscouncil.org.uk/.

Association of Independent Music. "Women in Music." 2019. Accessed April 8, 2019. www.musicindie.com/initiatives/women-in-music/.

Bourn, Douglas, Hunt Frances, and Ahmed Hassan. *Childhood Development Stages and Learning on Global Issues*. London: UK Government, 2017. Accessed March 29, 2019. https://assets.publishing.service.gov.uk/media/5a7447eeed915d0e8e398742/253_global_learning.pdf.

Bull, Anna, Diljeet Bhachu, Amy Blier-Carruthers, Alexander Bradley, and Seferin James. "Slow Train Coming? Equality, Diversity and Inclusion in UK Music Higher Education," 2022, Equality, Diversity and Inclusion in Music Studies Network. Accessed February 15, 2023. https://edims.network/report/slowtraincoming/.

Burns, Lori. "Musical Agency: Strategies of Containment and Resistance in 'Crucify'." In *Disruptive Divas: Feminism, Identity and Popular Music*, edited by Lori Burns and Melisse Lafrance, 73–95. New York: Routledge, 2002.

Cant, Stephanie. "Women Composers and the Music Curriculum." *British Journal of Music Education* 7, no. 1 (1990): 5–13.

Charanga. "Musical School and the 2014 National Curriculum for Music." 2017. Accessed November 23, 2018. https://charanga.com/site/musical-school/2014-national-curriculum-for-music/.

Cook, Steve, and Vicci Harrocks. "The Arts: The Magic Key to Unlocking Student Potential." Speech given at the Education Show, London, January 25, 2019.

Davis, Elizabeth. "We Need to Tell You About Amy Beach, the First American Woman to Publish a Symphony." 2018. Accessed April 12, 2019. www.classicfm.com/discover-music/amy-beach/.

Department for Culture, Media & Sport. "The Culture White Paper." 2016. Accessed July 23, 2020. https://assets.publishing.service.gov.uk/government/uploads/system/uploads/attachment_data/file/510799/DCMS_Arts_and_Culture_White_Paper_Accessible_version.pdf.

Department for Education. "National Curriculum in England: Computing Programmes of Study." 2013a. Accessed April 12, 2019. www.gov.uk/government/publications/national-curriculum-in-england-computing-programmes-of-study/national-curriculum-in-england-computing-programmes-of-study.

———. "National Curriculum in England: Music Programmes of Study." 2013b. Accessed April 12, 2019. www.gov.uk/government/publications/national-curriculum-in-england-music-programmes-of-study/national-curriculum-in-england-music-programmes-of-study.

———. "GCSE Music." 2015. Accessed April 12, 2019. www.gov.uk/government/publications/gcse-music.

———. "School Workforce in England." 2017. Accessed April 12, 2019. www.gov.uk/government/statistics/school-workforce-in-england-november-2017.

———. "Careers Guidance and Access for Education and Training Providers." 2018. Accessed April 12, 2019. www.gov.uk/government/publications/careers-guidance-provision-for-young-people-in-schools.

———. "School Workforce in England: November 2021." June 2022a. Accessed February 16, 2023. https://explore-education-statistics.service.gov.uk/find-statistics/school-workforce-in-england.

———. "The Power of Music to Change Lives: A National Plan for Music Education." June 2022b. Accessed February 10, 2023. www.gov.uk/government/publications/the-power-of-music-to-change-lives-a-national-plan-for-music-education.

Department for Levelling Up, Housing and Communities. "Levelling Up the United Kingdom." February 2022. Accessed February 15, 2023. https://assets.publishing.service.gov.uk/government/uploads/system/uploads/attachment_data/file/1052706/Levelling_Up_WP_HRES.pdf.

Di Laccio, Gabriella. "Introducing Chiquina Gonzaga (1847–1935)." Conference Paper given at the International Women and/in Musical Leadership Conference, London, March 7, 2019.

DONNE. "Equality & Diversity in Global Repertoire." 2022. Accessed February 15, 2023. https://donne-uk.org/wp-content/uploads/2021/03/Donne-Report-2022.pdf.

Drama Musica. "Donne Women in Music." 2018. Accessed February 10, 2023. www.drama-musica.com/Donne.html#.

Edexcel. "A-Level Music." 2015a. Accessed April 12, 2019. https://qualifications.pearson.com/content/dam/pdf/A%20Level/Music/2016/Specification%20and%20sample%20assessments/GCE-music-specification-A-Level-2015.pdf.

———. "GCSE (9–1) Music." 2015b. Accessed April 12, 2019. https://qualifications.pearson.com/content/dam/pdf/A%20Level/Music/2016/Specification%20and%20sample%20assessments/GCE-music-specification-A-Level-2015.pdf.

Ellemers, Naomi. "Gender Stereotypes." *Annual Review of Psychology* 69, no. 1 (2018): 275–98.

Gibson, Donald E. "Role Models in Career Development: New Directions for Theory and Research." *Journal of Vocational Behaviour* 65, no. 1 (2004): 134–56.

Hall, Christine, and Pat Thomson. "The Importance of Story." In *Inspiring School Change: Transforming Education through the Creative Arts*, 100–18. New York: Routledge, 2017.

Hallam, Susan. *Music Psychology in Education*. London: Institute of Education, 2009.

Hampden-Turner, Charles, and Fons Trompenaars. *Riding the Waves of Culture: Understanding Cultural Diversity in Business*. London: Brealey, 2011.

Help Musicians UK. "Women in Music." 2017. Accessed April 7, 2019. www.helpmusicians.org.uk/about-us/women-in-music.

Henwood, Flis. "Exceptional Women? Gender and Technology in UK Higher Education." *IEEE Technology and Society Magazine* 18, no. 4 (2000): 21–27.

Howe, Sondra Wieland. "A Historical View of Women in Music Education Careers." *Philosophy of Music Education Review* 17, no. 2 (2009): 162–83.

International Women's Day. "What's the IWD 2023 Campaign Theme?" Accessed February 10, 2023. www.internationalwomensday.com/About.

Johnes, Rebecca. "Entries to Arts Subjects at KS4." *Education Policy Institute*, 2016. Accessed April 12, 2019. https://epi.org.uk/wp-content/uploads/2018/01/EPI-Entries-to-arts-KS4-1.pdf.

Khomami, Nadia. "A-Level Music to Include Female Composers After Student's Campaign." *The Guardian*, 2015. Accessed July 23, 2020. www.theguardian.com/education/2015/dec/16/a-level-music-female-composers-students-campaign-jessy-mccabe-edexcel.

Knott, Johnathon. "EBacc Blamed for Growing Gender Imbalance in GCSE Choices." *Arts Professional*, 2018. Accessed April 7, 2019. www.artsprofessional.co.uk/news/ebacc-blamed-growing-gender-imbalance-gcse-choices.

Lang, Kirsty. "Leonardo da Vinci, Green Book, Sian Edwards, New Music Curriculum." *Podcast Audio*. Front Row, BBC4, January 31, 2019. Accessed April 12, 2019. www.bbc.co.uk/programmes/m00027yt.

Lockwood, Penelope. "Someone Like Me Can Be Successful: Do College Students Need Same-Gender Role Models?" *Psychology of Women Quarterly* 30, no. 1 (2006): 36–46.

London Philharmonic Orchestra. "Who's Who." 2019. Accessed April 12, 2019. www.lpo.org.uk/about/musician-biographies/.

London Symphony Orchestra. "Players." 2019. Accessed April 12, 2019. https://lso.co.uk/orchestra/players.html.

OCR. "GCSE (9–1) Specification Music." 2018. Accessed April 4, 2019. www.ocr.org.uk/Images/219378-specification-accredited-gcse-music-j536.pdf.

Ofsted. "A-Level Subject Take-Up." 2015. Accessed April 12, 2019. https://assets.publishing.service.gov.uk/government/uploads/system/uploads/attachment_data/file/426646/A_level_subject_take-up.pdf.

———. "An Investigation into how to Assess the Quality of Education through Curriculum Intent, Implementation and Impact." 2018a. Accessed April 10, 2019. www.gov.uk/government/publications/curriculum-research-assessing-intent-implementation-and-impac.

———. "School Inspection Handbook." 2018b. Accessed April 9, 2019. www.gov.uk/government/publications/school-inspection-handbook-from-september-2015.

Olsson, Maria, and Sarah E. Martiny. "Does Exposure to Counter stereotypical Role Models Influence Girls' and Women's Gender Stereotypes and Career Choices? A Review of Social Psychological Research." *Frontiers in Psychology* 9, no. 2264 (2018), np.

O'Neill, Susan. "Mapping Young People's Learning Ecologies." In *Handbook of Musical Identities*, 125–39. New York: Oxford University Press, 2017.

Philpott, Chris. "The Justification for Music in the Curriculum." In *Debates in Music Teaching*, 48–64. New York: Routledge, 2012.

Pitts, Stephanie. *Chances and Choices: Exploring the Impact of Music Education*. New York: Oxford University Press, 2012.

PRS for Music. "Gender Pay Gap Report." 2018. Accessed April 4, 2019. www.prsformusic.com/about-us/corporate-information.

PRS Foundation. "Key Change." 2019a. Accessed August 2, 2023. https://prsfoundation.com/partnerships/international-partnerships/keychange/?gclid=CjwKCAjw_aemBhBLEiwAT98FMrr6VQ_R1oBKSvGqAN3iEXJr2XG8EXr5VtbkmrNcHCTH4Xj9EA5cSxoCop0QAvD_BwE.

———. "Women Make Music." 2019b. Accessed April 8, 2019. https://prsfoundation.com/funding-support/funding-music-creators/all-career-levels/women-make-music-2/.

———. "Women Make Music." 2023. Accessed August 2, 2023. https://prsfoundation.com/funding-support/funding-music-creators/all-career-levels/women-make-music-2/.

Royal Opera House Bridge. "The Creative School: Leading Cultural Learning." 2017. Accessed April 11, 2019. www.roh.org.uk/learning/royal-opera-house-bridge/the-creative-school-leading-cultural-learning.

Savage, Mark. "Five Forgotten Female Composers Will Be Celebrated on BBC Radio 3." 2017. Accessed July 23, 2020. www.bbc.co.uk/news/entertainment-arts-38079139.

Smith, Matthew. "Which School Subjects Do Boys and Girls Enjoy More?" 2018. Accessed April 12, 2019. https://yougov.co.uk/topics/education/articles-reports/2018/09/04/which-school-subjects-do-boys-and-girls-enjoy-morex.

Smith, Stacy L., Marc Choueiti, and Katherine Pieper. "Inclusion in the Recording Studio?: Gender and Race/Ethnicity of Artists, Songwriters & Producers across 600 Popular Songs from 2012–2017." USC Annenberg School for Communication and Journalism. Annenberg Inclusion Initiative. 2018. Accessed July 22, 2020. http://assets.uscannenberg.org/docs/inclusion-in-the-recording-studio.pdf.

Stanley, Oliver, and Amanda Shendruk. "Here's What the Stark Gender Disparity Among Top Orchestra Musicians Look Like." *Quartz at Work*, 2018. Accessed July 23, 2020. https://qz.com/work/1393078/orchestras/.

Teaching Schools Council. "Women Leading in Education – Coaching Pledge and Resources." *TSCouncil*, 2016. Accessed April 12, 2019. https://tscouncil.org.uk/women-leading-in-education-coaching-pledge/.

The Music Commission. "Retuning our Ambition for Music Learning." 2019. Accessed April 11, 2019. www.musiccommission.org.uk/.

Trinity College London. "What Is ArtsAward?" 2019. Accessed April 12, 2019. www.artsaward.org.uk/site/?id=1346.

UK Government Legislation. "Education Act 2002." 2018. Accessed April 11, 2019. www.legislation.gov.uk/ukpga/2002/32/section/78.

UK Music. "Diversity: Music Industry Workforce 2018 Report." Accessed April 8, 2019. www.ukmusic.org/assets/general/UK_Music_Diversity_Report_2018.pdf.

Ward, Helen. "Ministers Want All Pupils to Read Music, But Where Are the Teachers?" *Times Education Supplement*, 2019. Accessed April 12, 2019. www.tes.com/news/ministers-want-all-pupils-read-music-where-are-teachers.

Whistlecroft, Lisa. "Women in Music Technology in Higher Education in the UK." *The Canadian Electroacoustic Community*, 2000. Accessed April 6, 2019. https://econtact.ca/3_3/WomenMusicTech.htm.

Women in Music. "The Stats." 2019. Accessed April 2, 2019. www.womeninmusic.org/stats.html.

Youth Music. "Music-Making Projects for Girls and Young Women: Addressing the Gender Balance in Music." Accessed April 5, 2019. www.youthmusic.org.uk/music-making-projects-girls-and-young-women.

22
PIPELINE TO THE PODIUM
Can Gender Differentiated Pedagogical Approaches Address the Underrepresentation of Women Conductors?

Katherine Hanckel

I never set out to become a feminist. It is in my studies to become a greater musician that feminism has found me. Women, inclusive of the woman musician, have faced limitations throughout the history of humanity and while the situation improves steadily, it is apparent that there still exists a great disparity between the genders. As McCarthy[1] points out, we are all beholden to our genders as a parameter that our cultures have placed upon us. As of 2016, women in professional occupations received less compensation at an estimated ratio compared to men of 78%, in managerial positions an estimated 75% and in other occupations an estimated 83%. The link between gender and pay is directly tied to the hiring of women in the first place because from the onset, women are prone to seek lower-tier or inferior jobs and often overwork where the gender pay gap is more pronounced. This marked difference in compensation has been documented throughout the history of music, in which women are particularly underrepresented in the fields of conducting and instrumental music education.[2] This is often due to a perceived toxicity of an environment which further promotes difficulties in leading a balanced life and stems from the still-active presence of century-old issues faced by women conductors, including a focus on the limitations and sexualisation of the female body, leadership and relationship styles, motherhood, education and available opportunities.

Several different feminist theories have looked for ways to explain the role of women within music. As these theories continue to evolve, some views of these challenges change. In music performance, second-wave feminist ideals would say that women should not give in to the pressure of this sexualisation in order to succeed in classical music. Third-wave feminism would emphasise that women can be good-looking and embrace their sexiness without any effects on judgement of their intellectual or musical capacities.[3] But can they? Is it possible to separate one's identity as a woman from other characteristics? Women conductors are faced with the contradictory dilemma that socially they must present their femininity through their body in how they dress as well as their postures and mannerisms, but on the conducting podium they must renounce it lest they further call attention to their 'Otherness' as a woman in the field of music. By its very nature, the defining of women by this 'Otherness' reduces them to an economy of the same and fails to value their individual musicianship and the differences between all women. Here we see that third-wave feminist theories may be at odds with the realities of the current situation.

Other feminist theories provide a different perspective. Rosi Braidotti's postmodern metaphor of the nomad, whose defining characteristics are metaphorical mobility and violence, explains the woman musician's experience, particularly that of the university band director. Women band directors exhibit mobility as they typically teach at smaller universities and colleges and are often outside the influence of their teachers. Mobility means they must be noticed in order to survive, through recordings, performances and publications, but this provides a certain level of risk in that they are noticed in turn for this level of difference. Women band directors exhibit nomadic violence in acts of resistance to the misogynist foundations of their profession.[4] The mere presence of a woman as a university band director on the podium undermines the foundation of the profession and goes against what has been previously perceived as the norm of the white male band director. This chapter contains an examination of how such conditions came to be by investigating gender disparity in education and the workforce throughout the history of music and music conductors, and specifically amongst orchestra conductors and college band directors.

Such examination reveals a common factor across all fields that can be a powerful force to promote equality: pedagogy. The training of women in the workforce provides their foundation for success. In other fields, such as engineering, there is a clear indication that women are underrepresented even though they show high marks for statistical success.[5] Why is that? What happens in pre-service and in-service women professionals to cause such a disparity? The current state of gender-differentiated pedagogy as applicable in the training of women conductors could provide a means of addressing their underrepresentation.

Throughout this chapter, there is much discussion about how women are perceived, portrayed and interpreted. For the sake of brevity, it is not always described by whom these actions are perpetrated. However, it is possible to infer that the acting agent in these cases is the combination of society as a whole, and more specifically, the field of music performers, educators and scholars.

Gender Disparity in Education and the Workforce

Historically, women have held limited opportunities in the workforce due to inherent gendered factors. World War II created a substantial, although short-lived, rise in female employment across all fields and led to greater lobbying for inclusion and equity.[6] Since then, limitations on the growth of female representation in the workforce include the proclivity for women to enter the workforce after a period of inactivity, often related to motherhood, and restricted job mobility. However, as their level of education and experiences rises, so too does their representation at higher-level jobs.[7] And yet, as of 2022, women are underrepresented in the field of music higher education, accounting for 39% of music programmes in the United Kingdom at the university level even though the wider student population is 57% female. This percentage increases slightly to 49% female at the master's level before dropping back to 39% female at the doctoral level. The pipeline is even more pronounced at the level of university staff, where only 35% are female.[8] The lack of women pursuing these higher degrees and being represented on university staff created a fundamental lack of role models for incoming generations. Why was it that women were not pursuing advanced degrees? Elpus[9] acknowledges that male students often underperform compared to their female classmates in traditional academic measures of schooling such as reading achievement, rigour of selected course, graduation rate and attendance. However, males overperform females in the economic and social outcomes of school in general. In fact, men are more likely to accomplish higher levels in general than women.[10] What happens during schooling that leads men to achieve at greater levels?

Gender Disparity Throughout Music History

The history of female musicians parallels the history of women throughout society in general. Women performers and teachers of music have faced difficulties throughout American history based on the idea that women are meant to be interpreters and not creators within society.[11] The church was the birthplace of Western Classical music and thus exerted much influence over the development of music, including discouraging upper-class women from playing instruments, something they found acceptable only for prostitutes. Early American society held the expectation that women were to be home-keepers who cared for children and did not encourage their development as musicians because it was inappropriate and too physically demanding.[12] Puritans and their values formed much of early American society and it was not until 1872 that female voices were commonly added to choirs under the advocation of Lowell Mason. Operas, requiring distinct female parts, liberated women performers.[13] Acceptance of female performers began with solitary instruments such as the piano and harp which did not require overt physical exertion or contortion of the body. Violin, and then eventually other string instruments, were gradually accepted for women, partially due to the enlightened teachings of Boston Conservatory founder Julius Eichberg. Women began playing other wind instruments as part of all-female ensembles or at vaudeville shows. At this time a woman could play any instrument so long as she looked attractive while doing it. Throughout this development, emphasis on the sexualisation of women persisted. Women musicians have been the subject to comments, both in official avenues such as newspaper reviews, and in person by their colleagues, regarding their attractiveness and sex appeal or lack thereof, and how this made it difficult for men to work with them or to appreciate their musical contributions. This bias and tendency are often still present today.

As public education institutions adopted music curricula, instrumental music became a specialty dominated by men due to their perceived ability to better play, and look better playing, all of the instruments of an orchestra.[14] Women are still more likely to teach young students in the classroom and the per cent of female band directors at the university level may have been declining in the last 30 years,[15] even though the ratios of graduation from conservatories and graduate schools of music remain roughly equal between women and men. Only about 30% to 50% of professional orchestral musicians are women, with only about 7% of all music directors being women.[16] This again points to some occurrence during schooling that leads to a disparity in achievement. This 'pipeline' issue starts as early as high school. A study of the participation rates of American high school males and females enrolled in choir, band and orchestra ensembles as outlined by their senior year high school transcripts using four-year increments from 1982 to 2009 found statistically significant differences. Overall, females represented 61.1% of music students. This number is greatly influenced by the high ratio of almost 70% female to 30% male in participation in choir. However, females also overrepresent in orchestra at 63.67% female to 36.33% male. In band, the ratio is much closer to an even division with females slightly outnumbering males in every year studied, except the last.[17] Why is it that females at the high school level account for a greater per cent of music enrolment, at the conservatory level a roughly equal per cent, and yet at the professional level a significantly lower per cent?

Gender Disparity Amongst Conductors

Very few women have held prominent positions as conductors and rarely achieved the same level of accord as they had as music teachers and performers, often due to the fundamental idea that women are meant to reflect and not create in a profession that is rooted in masculine traits and patriarchal ideology.[18] Once on the podium, women often face different criteria for assessment such that their worth must be greater than their male colleagues in order to justify their success. They are devalued and judged on their gender, reduced to and objectified by their bodies in both positive and negative fashions. Their Otherness has caused them to be the subject of affirmative action processes and tokenism. This can be an advantage due to the memorability of being different which brings added press, but also added pressure.[19] Women orchestra conductors and college band directors share a history rooted in their Otherness and face challenges that are similar, but also distinct, within their specific fields.

Orchestra Conductors

Women's exclusion from male-dominated professional orchestras led to the creation of all-female performing ensembles starting with the Fadette Women's Orchestra of Boston in 1888.[20] As women became more accepted members in orchestras, gender representation began to approach an equilibrium amongst male and female members. The same, however, is not true for representation amongst conductors.[21] This may be due to the leadership implications of the role of conductor. Orchestral conductors represent a powerful force highly correlated with gender stereotypes so that women must de-sexualise themselves in order to conform to the expectations of musicians and audiences. These expectations stem from glorification of the conductor, a relatively modern construct that embodies patriarchal views of leadership. Women are less likely to identify with this due to the ruthlessness and single-mindedness required, aspects which are thought of as unfeminine. Women often must retrain themselves to use more masculine authoritarian approaches for which there are few female role models. Many women conductors prefer to view leadership with collaborative sensitivity balanced with authority, an approach more modern orchestras are ready for.[22] Other unique challenges American women conductors face are the balance of private life, including the ego of their spouse, and the tradition of major orchestras importing conductors from Europe.[23] All of these relationships require a delicate balance.

College Band Directors

Gender is an interior social construct that is manifest in culturally appropriate behaviour and the perception of that behaviour. The culture of music historically has been considered a feminine activity due to its lack of economic contribution. This creates cultural tension for male musicians who fear the stigma of homosexuality; the resulting homophobia in turn leads to greater misogyny within the profession. Additionally, music performance creates an asymmetrical power relationship between the audience and the music, further classifying the musician as 'Other'. College bands are firmly founded in a military tradition which sought to distance themselves from the femininity, and therefore the inherent 'Otherness', of music. Due to this compounded 'Otherness' of music performance, and the idea that women's presence only reinforces its femininity, women in the role of college band conductors could only further lower the aesthetic value of music.[24] Historically, bands have an added degree of segregation in that marching bands either separated women and not by their choosing, as in turn-of-the-century orchestras, into ensembles of their own, or relegated them to baton twirling or flag waving as feminine alternatives to wind instruments.[25] The cultures of music performance and college band both systematically contribute to the low representation of women amongst all college band directors who, in addition their underrepresentation, have salaries and rank amongst faculty that are lower than those of their male counterparts.[26] This per cent is lower than that of only a few years prior that Gould[27] indicates when she claims that women only constitute just over 5%, but never more than 10% of all college band directors in the United States and therefore have had, and currently provide, a lack of visible role models. As discussed earlier, the lack of representation of women within doctoral programmes and as music faculty creates a deficit of these role models. In Gould's[28] study of women college band directors, participants provided strong responses that were both positive and negative when asked about their own position as role models, with the most important influencing factor being their students' expectations. What are these student expectations? Are women college band directors not confident in their abilities to serve as role models? Could that stem from their own lack of role models? How can women band directors become more comfortable in their position as role models? Is it possible that some of this discomfort may stem from the training they themselves received? These questions are worth exploring more deeply to address the current underrepresentation of women conductors as college band directors.

Gendered Differentiated Pedagogy

There are currently several programmes that specifically support the advancement of women conductors, including The Linda and Mitch Hart Institute for Women Conductors at The Dallas Opera, The League of American Orchestras Seminar for Women Conductors, The College Band Directors National Association Mike Moss Conducting Grant, The Royal Philharmonic Society Women Conductors Programme and The Taki Concordia Conducting Fellowship. However, these programmes are only beneficial to woman who have already decided to pursue a career in conducting. Clearly the pipeline indicates that at this point it is far too late to enact effective change. Instead, it is crucial to address not only the differences in available opportunities between genders, but also the effect of musical pedagogy as a whole.

The concept of gender differentiated pedagogy is not a new one. In an examination of the differences in musical learning by gender at the secondary level in Hong Kong, Ho[29] found several significant correlations between gender and learning. Several external factors, such as pedagogy of the music teacher, mass media influences and parental involvement were all highly influential in a gendered manner. Similarly, Ro and Knight[30] found statistically significant interactions by gender of the effect of learning outcomes of instructional approaches, curricular emphasis and co-curricular involvement of college-level engineering students. Men and women taking the same coursework may perceive a different level of achievement and different specific learning outcomes and, as it currently stands, the teaching of engineering courses favours those methods statistically preferred by men.

Music students are highly influenced by their teachers' perceptions of their abilities, something which has long had a gendered bias. Music in the school curriculum, and the fight for its inclusion, led to its de-feminisation and association with the objective and absolute elements of music.[31] Additionally, the essential discipline required to master the technical excellence that music demands is inherently at odds with the feminist approach which encourages students to have wider interests. Performance perfection is the goal and the product is the bottom line. Music as an art form creates a world outside the very hardship required to master it and rejects aspects of the common feminist identity.[32] The concept of this feminist identity is largely ignored in attempts to address the gender disparity within music education, which instead is almost exclusively focused on altering the curriculum to include more women composers, performers and conductors. However, does this method of curricular inclusion have an actual impact on the perceptions and learning outcomes of students when it does nothing to address the actual teaching and training of musicians? As indicated in feminist pedagogical literature, the lived experience of the student is not always paired with academic knowledge, something which female conducting pedagogues themselves are resistant to change.[33] This resistance to change may be linked to the idea that feminist researchers within music pedagogy feel isolated and are mindful of the risk associated with identifying themselves by their ideology.[34] Thus, even though the need for gendered differentiation within music education is abundantly clear, even educators who identify as feminists are not clear on the best practices for implementing the necessary changes.

Discussion

Gender is an inherently ingrained aspect of our identity, and something which is increasingly important in our roles as educators and musicians. The quest for self-discovery of our own identities is a relatively new construct of the modern world. We are all faced with a tripartite paradox of humanity in that we are at the same time 1) the same as all other humans, 2) the same as only some other humans and 3) unique in ourselves and the same as no other humans.[35] Gender is paramount in this quest, because it is both a biological and social construct of which we are still lacking sufficient research. How does our gender influence how we think and perceive the world and impact our view of knowledge? How does it affect the way in which we acquire knowledge and skills? What paths do we have to explore our own self-identity and reckon with our self-knowledge as it relates to the human condition?

In 1975 Susan Starr, a well-known pianist and pedagogue, noted that women often exhibited poor technique due to their own sense of self-identity.[36] Cheng[37] notes a similar concept in that the obstacles women conductors face are often due to cultural conditioning in which they are taught to be nonaggressive and to fit in within their surroundings, values that directly contradict the role of a conductor. Within the study of music, this conditioning begins as early as the process of instrument selection, which has clearly been linked to indicate gender association and bias.[38] It is clear that the concept of identity is a fundamental element in our role within our chosen professional field, and that gender is an inseparable part of that. How do we grapple with our own sense of identity getting in the way of our journey to use music as a means of self-realisation?

The first step is to distance women from their male counterparts and respect that there are innate differences in genders. Women have been compared to men throughout history, both as part of key studies on gender and more sinisterly as a means of marginalising and refusing to acknowledge their inherent value. Thus, it is necessary to acknowledge that there are several traits associated with feminine personality that actually are suited to our roles as educators and conductors. One such trait is the greater personal emphasis on collegiality and the importance of interpersonal collaboration and flexibility, approaches which in many ways women have been socially conditioned to follow.[39] These approaches to leadership have the potential to increase job satisfaction amongst orchestral musicians and are becoming more popular in all realms of business.[40] The effect of this can be seen in the increased representation of women conductors in middle-tier orchestra director positions. This representation within middle and not higher tiers again indicates that the lack of representation is a 'pipeline' issue. However, this 'pipeline' is inherently flawed; the opportunities available to young women do not match those of their male counterparts, which leads women to view pursuing a career in conducting as an 'uphill struggle'. It also implies that the system will fix itself and is in no need of critique.[41] As it stands, the lack of female conductors, particularly at elite levels, provides fewer networking and role model opportunities for women entering the field of music. This lack of role models to identify with presents a unique challenge for women entering the field of music conducting. We all base our identities off the discovery of ourselves in relation to other people, particularly those we want to emulate. Additionally, the lack of role models also presents a deficit of women who have experienced the training process required to become an elite conductor, and thus a deficit of opinionsabout the efficacy of this training.

Suggestions for Further Research

There is a clear understanding of the importance of identity and culture on pedagogy, yet there exists a lack of research addressing these factors on the learning preferences and outcomes of women musicians generally, and conductors in particular. The prominence of male conductors persists even though orchestras have undergone fluctuations and changes in their more than 400 years of existence. This may be due to the relatively smaller pool of women conductors available, a concept which inherently emphasises the segregated nature of the field and lack of role models. Increasing this pool of qualified candidates would help to provide role models and feedback on their journeys. However, this first requires qualified candidates. How can we address the training of women musicians and conductors to better help equip them for these fields, thereby increasing the sheer number of qualified women conductors?

A clear cause of the underrepresentation of women in the elite positions lies in the 'pipeline' from early music education through high school, conservatory study and in the field. Many factors account for the underrepresentation of women conductors, but relatively little research explores the effect of culture specifically, other than how the subordination of women as marginalised person devalues them and constitutes them as 'Other'.[42] Culture is consistently one of the most important factors influencing both pedagogical practices as well as our self-oncepts of identity. Educational theories and research provide for historical and cultural backgrounds that may influence how a person learns and how the differences in education environment can support or discourage certain interests, self-efficacies and self-concepts between men and women.[43] For example, boys are more likely to be influenced by the encouragements and feedback given to them by their teachers and are seen as more creative. While girls are also more likely to participate in music at the secondary level, they are less likely to pursue careers in music. Additionally, girls are more cooperative and have overall more positive attitudes in regards to music, but they are more likely to exhibit submissive behaviour in the presence of high-achieving male musicians. This is supported by the fact that women are more likely to respond to pressures in cultural media and environmental influences.[44] There is a need for further research into the recruitment of and professional training opportunities for women conductors, particularly for a gendered critique of the pedagogy process for teaching women conductors. One reason this may not exist already is that male colleagues might argue the resulting process could 'compromise musical integrity'.[45] In fact, many musicians believe that changing the system of pedagogy to include a feminist perspective threatens the musical world they already know and understand. Lamb[46] admits that she sees herself as the greatest resistance to challenging the current experience of the musical process. With a deficit of research on this matter, these assumptions go unchallenged by facts and are allowed to perpetuate the underrepresentation of women in conducting.

Summary

Diversity is an important aspect of the creative process and encompasses multiple representations of the human condition. For music to continue as an artistic representation of this condition, we need people of all backgrounds and types participating in its creation. Marginalisation of one group within the arts only further marginalises them in the eyes of humanity. We must address how women, defined in music by their marginalised status, their 'Otherness,' can find a greater voice. Common issues quieting women in their quest to pursue conducting include the difficulties of balancing work and home lives, disparity of salary compared to their male colleagues and a dearth of role models that could provide insight on how to manage those previous aspects. However, there is also a deeper, more subconscious, layer that can account for the underrepresentation of women in conducting. This layer is formed by the innate nature of our identity as women and the strengths and weaknesses that that entails. We have been culturally conditioned throughout the millennia of human history to look, act and think in a certain way that is at odds with our roles as conductors. This conditioning cannot change overnight, but is there something in the way we train young women musicians that could help them embrace their identity rather than fight it? Instead of hiding our femininity, we should harness it as a force of creation and expression of our understanding of the wonders and limitations of the universal human condition.

Notes

1. Marie McCarthy, "Gendered Discourse and the Construction of Identity: Toward a Liberated Pedagogy in Music Education," *Journal of Aesthetic Education* 33, no. 4 (1999): 109, https://doi.org/10.2307/3333724.
2. Gheorghe H. Popescu, "Gender, Work, and Wages: Patterns of Female Participation in the Labor Market," *Journal of Self-Governance and Management Economics* 4, no. 1 (2016): 128–34, https://doi.org/10.22381/jsme4120165.
3. Marcia J. Citron, "Feminist Waves and Classical Music: Pedagogy, Performance, Research," *Women and Music: A Journal of Gender and Culture* 8, no. 1 (2004): 47–60, https://doi.org/10.1353/wam.2004.0004.
4. Elizabeth S. Gould, "Nomadic Turns: Epistemology, Experience, and Women University Band Directors," *Philosophy of Music Education Review* 13, no. 2 (2005): 147–64, https://doi.org/10.1353/pme.2005.0034.
5. Hyun Kyoung Ro and David B. Knight, "Gender Differences in Learning Outcomes from the College Experiences of Engineering Students," *Journal of Engineering Education* 105, no. 3 (2016): 478–507, https://doi.org/10.1002/jee.20125.
6. Shelley M. Jagow, "Women Orchestral Conductors in America: The Struggle for Acceptance-An Historical View from the Nineteenth Century to the Present," *College Music Symposium* 38 (1998): 126–45.
7. Popescu, "Gender, Work, and Wages."
8. Anna Bull, Diljeet Bhachu, Amy Blier-Carruthers, Alexander Bradley, and Seferin James, "Slow Train Coming? Equality, Diversity and Inclusion in UK Music Higher Education," Equality, Diversity and Inclusion in Music Studies Network, accessed November 16, 2022, https://edims.network/report/slowtraincoming/
9. Kenneth Elpus, "National Estimates of Male and Female Enrolment in American High School Choirs, Bands and Orchestras," *Music Education Research* 17, no. 1 (2014): 88–102, https://doi.org/10.1080/14613808.2014.972923.
10. Wai-Chung Ho, "Gender Differences in Instrumental Learning among Secondary School Students in Hong Kong," *Gender and Education* 21, no. 4 (2009): 405–22, https://doi.org/10.1080/09540250802537596.
11. Hinely, "The Uphill Climb of Women in American Music."
12. Jagow, "Women Orchestral Conductors in America."
13. Hinely, "The Uphill Climb of Women in American Music."
14. B.A. Macleod, "Whence Comes the Lady Tympanist?' Gender and Instrumental Musicians in America, 1853-1990," *Journal of Social History* 27, no. 2 (1993): 291–308, https://doi.org/10.1353/jsh/27.2.291.
15. Gould, "Nomadic Turns."

16. Marietta Nien-Hwa Cheng, "Women Conductors: Has the Train Left the Station?," *Harmony: Forum of the Symphony Orchestra Institute* (April 6, 1998): 81–90, accessed August 2, 2023, http://web.esm.rochester.edu/poly/wp-content/uploads/2012/02/Women_Conductors_Cheng.pdf.
17. Elpus, "National Estimates of Male and Female Enrolment."
18. Macleod, "Whence Comes the Lady Tympanist?"
19. Brydie-Leigh Bartleet, "'You're a Woman and Our Orchestra Just Won't Have You': The Politics of Otherness in the Conducting Profession," *Hecate* 34, no. 1 (2008): 6–23, accessed August 2, 2023, www.researchgate.net/publication/37812474_You're_a_woman_and_our_orchestra_just_won't_have_you_the_politics_of_otherness_in_the_conducting_profession.
20. Jagow, "Women Orchestral Conductors in America."
21. Brydie-Leigh Bartleet, "Women Conductors on the Orchestral Podium: Pedagogical and Professional Implications," *College Music Symposium* 48 (2008): 31–51.
22. Brydie-Leigh Bartleet, "Female Conductors: The Incarnation of Power?" *Hecate* 29, no. 2 (2003): 228–34.
23. Cheng, "Women Conductors."
24. Elizabeth S. Gould, "Cultural Contexts of Exclusion: Women College Band Directors," *Research & Issues in Music Education* 1, no. 1 (2003): 1–18.
25. Macleod, "Whence Comes the Lady Tympanist?"
26. Gould, "Cultural Contexts of Exclusion."
27. Elizabeth S. Gould, "Identification and Application of the Concept of Role Model," *Update: Applications of Research in Music Education* 20, no. 1 (2001): 14–18, https://doi.org/10.1177/875512330102000104.
28. Ibid.
29. Ho, "Gender Differences in Instrumental Learning among Secondary School Students in Hong Kong."
30. Ro and Knight, "Gender Differences in Learning Outcomes from the College Experiences of Engineering Students."
31. McCarthy, "Gendered Discourse and the Construction of Identity."
32. Roberta Lamb, "Discords: Feminist Pedagogy in Music Education," *Theory into Practice* 35, no. 2 (1996): 124–31, https://doi.org/10.1080/00405849609543712.
33. Bartleet, "Women Conductors on the Orchestral Podium."
34. Lamb, "Discords: Feminist Pedagogy in Music Education."
35. McCarthy, "Gendered Discourse and the Construction of Identity."
36. Hinely, "The Uphill Climb of Women in American Music."
37. Cheng, "Women Conductors."
38. McCarthy, "Gendered Discourse and the Construction of Identity."
39. Bartleet, "Female Conductors."
40. Cheng, "Women Conductors."
41. Bartleet, "Women Conductors on the Orchestral Podium."
42. Gould, "Cultural Contexts of Exclusion."
43. Ro and Knight, "Gender Differences in Learning Outcomes from the College Experiences of Engineering Students."
44. Ho, "Gender Differences in Instrumental Learning among Secondary School Students in Hong Kong."
45. Bartleet, "Women Conductors on the Orchestral Podium."
46. Lamb, "Discords."

Bibliography

Alsop, Marin. "About TCCF." 2020. Accessed January 1, 2019. https://takiconcordia.org/about-tccf/.
Bartleet, Brydie-Leigh. "Female Conductors: The Incarnation of Power?" *Hecate* 29, no. 2 (2003): 228–34.
———. "Women Conductors on the Orchestral Podium: Pedagogical and Professional Implications." *College Music Symposium* 48 (2008a): 31–51.
———. "'You're a Woman and Our Orchestra Just Won't Have You': The Politics of Otherness in the Conducting Profession." *Hecate* 34, no. 1 (2008b): 6–23.

Bull, Anna, Diljeet Bhachu, Amy Blier-Carruthers, Alexander Bradley, and Seferin James. "Slow Train Coming? Equality, Diversity and Inclusion in UK Music Higher Education." *Equality, Diversity and Inclusion in Music Studies Network*. Accessed November 16, 2022. https://edims.network/report/slowtraincoming/.

Cheng, Marietta Nien-Hwa. "Women Conductors: Has the Train Left the Station?" *Harmony: Forum of the Symphony Orchestra Institute* 6 (April 1998): 81–90.

Citron, Marcia J. "Feminist Waves and Classical Music: Pedagogy, Performance, Research." *Women and Music: A Journal of Gender and Culture* 8, no. 1 (2004): 47–60. https://doi.org/10.1353/wam.2004.0004.

Elpus, Kenneth. "National Estimates of Male and Female Enrolment in American High School Choirs, Bands and Orchestras." *Music Education Research* 17, no. 1 (2014): 88–102. https://doi.org/10.1080/14613808.2014.972923.

Gould, Elizabeth S. "Identification and Application of the Concept of Role Model." *Update: Applications of Research in Music Education* 20, no. 1 (2001): 14–18. https://doi.org/10.1177/87551233010200104.

———. "Cultural Contexts of Exclusion: Women College Band Directors." *Research & Issues in Music Education* 1, no. 1 (2003): 1–18.

———. "Nomadic Turns: Epistemology, Experience, and Women University Band Directors." *Philosophy of Music Education Review* 13, no. 2 (2005): 147–64. https://doi.org/10.1353/pme.2005.0034.

Hinely, Mary Brown. "The Uphill Climb of Women in American Music: Performers and Teachers." *Music Educators Journal* 70, no. 8 (1984): 31–35. https://doi.org/10.2307/3400871.

Ho, Wai-Chung. "Gender Differences in Instrumental Learning among Secondary School Students in Hong Kong." *Gender and Education* 21, no. 4 (2009): 405–22. https://doi.org/10.1080/09540250802537596.

Jagow, Shelley M. "Women Orchestral Conductors in America: The Struggle for Acceptance – An Historical View from the Nineteenth Century to the Present." *College Music Symposium* 38 (1998): 126–45.

Lamb, Roberta. "Discords: Feminist Pedagogy in Music Education." *Theory into Practice* 35, no. 2 (1996): 124–31. https://doi.org/10.1080/00405849609543712.

Macleod, Beth Abelson. "'Whence Comes the Lady Tympanist?.' Gender and Instrumental Musicians in America, 1853–1990." *Journal of Social History* 27, no. 2 (1993): 291–308. https://doi.org/10.1353/jsh/27.2.291.

McCarthy, Marie. "Gendered Discourse and the Construction of Identity: Toward a Liberated Pedagogy in Music Education." *Journal of Aesthetic Education* 33, no. 4 (1999): 109. https://doi.org/10.2307/3333724.

MTD Research. "Gender Analysis of Music Teachers." 2016. Accessed January 1, 2019. https://mtdresearch.com/gender-analysis-of-music-teachers/.

Popescu, Gheorghe H. "Gender, Work, and Wages: Patterns of Female Participation in the Labor Market." *Journal of Self-Governance and Management Economics* 4, no. 1 (2016): 128–34. https://doi.org/10.22381/jsme4120165.

Ro, Hyun Kyoung, and David B. Knight. "Gender Differences in Learning Outcomes from the College Experiences of Engineering Students." *Journal of Engineering Education* 105, no. 3 (2016): 478–507. https://doi.org/10.1002/jee.20125.

23
WOMEN LEADING CHANGE IN ASSESSMENT CALIBRATION

Michelle Phillips

Introduction

The higher education sector in the UK and globally has undergone significant changes over recent years. In the UK, this industry has experienced changes in regulation; for example, by the Office for Students, and new metrics have been introduced to measure performance in relation to aspects such as teaching and assessment, research, and knowledge exchange, and scrutiny of the value of higher education has increased. In particular, there are specific conditions which must be met for institutions to retain degree awarding powers; for example, B3 conditions of the Office for Students in the UK lay out certain benchmarks for student retention (remaining on the course), continuation (moving through the course successfully), and progression (referring to the progression into employment).

One of the most recent areas of interest from the media, quality assurance institutions and those responsible for collating league tables in the field of higher education in the UK, in terms of their scrutiny of what value students gain from a university degree, is grade inflation (or 'academic/degree inflation'). This refers to the risk that the number of top degree classifications (considered in the UK to be first-class and upper second-class degrees) increase year on year. Academic standards have been a subject of significant interest in recent years, as grade inflation has become common in many areas of the higher education sector. In 2018, the *Times Higher Education* magazine reported that:

> In 1996–97, just over half of undergraduates received a 2:1 or a first; 20 years on, three-quarters do. Firsts in particular are arguably no longer the special category they once were. The 8 per cent of students who earned one in 1996–97 ballooned to 26 per cent by 2016–17. Meanwhile, the share ending up with a 2:2 or a third-class degree has almost halved.[1]

Moreover, only a month before the time of writing of this chapter, *Times Higher Education-* stated: 'Globally, the focus on accountability for quality and standards in high education has increased over the past two decades'.[2] They attribute this to:

> Global competition for the education dollar, pressure of governments to account for public spending in financially challenging times, and increased access to education across

the globe, spawned by the move to digital education and a focus on increased access for minority and disadvantaged groups.[3]

Higher-education institutions in the UK are under increasing pressure to demonstrate the standard and quality of the education and qualifications that they provide.

Questions of what a first-class degree today should represent, and whether this is the same as a first-class degree in the same subject from the same institution ten years ago, may be of interest, for example, to potential employers. The sector has begun to examine whether a first-class degree in the same subject from two different institutions *should* mean the same thing. Have two students achieved the same level of qualification, or should the awarding institution have a bearing on how a degree classification is interpreted? Finally, in the current metric-soaked world of higher education, if one institution – perhaps a music conservatoire – grants a higher proportion of first-class degrees one year than another institution, should this play a role in an applicant's decision regarding which institution they choose to study at?

All of these questions address notions of 'calibration' in degree standards and invite an investigation of whether a piece of work (or performance) submitted for assessment at one institution may (and should) receive the same mark as it would if submitted to another. Of course, there are many factors which may influence this, including marking criteria, type of institution (e.g., conservatoire vs university music department), and whether an examiner brings their own tacit knowledge to the awarding of the mark (and indeed whether it is ever possible *not* to do so). These factors and questions all formed the backdrop to the design of the Conservatoires UK calibration event discussed in this chapter.

At a time when the higher education sector, and arts and humanities subjects in particular, is under ever-increasing pressure in the UK to justify its role and value (not helped by the recent COVID-19 pandemic – at the time of writing, the Institute for Fiscal Studies estimates that losses in the university sector 'could come in at anywhere between £3 billion and £19 billion, or between 7.5% and nearly half of the sector's overall income in one year'[4] with 'music & arts institutions'[5] being amongst those 'most affected'[6] – and not helped either by the recent economic crisis in the UK in 2023). It is important that questions of assessment, degree standards and the value of a degree are asked and rigorously explored.

Leadership: MusicHE

As I write this chapter, I am also the chair of MusicHE, the subject association representing all degree-awarding institutions that offer music as a degree subject, whether they be conservatoires, university music departments (whether post 92 or Russell group institutions, for example), or private providers. I am an academic and a leader of degree programmes within a conservatoire and a leader at this national level. The work presented here impacts my own leadership and teaching practice; it feeds into my leadership of MusicHE and it informs my research into musical practices. I note this not to change the research, but to declare my insider status and bias.

Background

The 'Degree Standards Project' (DSP), overseen by the Office for Students and led by the Higher Education Academy (now Advance HE) aimed to explore 'sector-owned processes focusing on professional development for external examiners'.[7] One specific aim of this five-year project (2016–2021) was to: 'Explore approaches to the calibration of standards, presenting recommendations for future work in this area'.[8] Four subject associations (Conservatoires UK, the Royal Geographical Society, the Royal Society of Chemistry, and the Veterinary Schools Education Group, chosen at random from the degree subjects commonly studied at UK higher education institutions) engaged in a series of workshops over the first two years of the DSP to explore calibration of academic standards. A series of outputs followed to disseminate the findings of these workshops: an online 'toolkit' of resources around calibration for use by external examiners and those training external examiners, a report on the main findings from the calibration events, and an event during which leaders of the four events presented their observations and findings to 130 delegates at a one-day conference.

This calibration component of the degree standards project focussed on notions of assessment, and how marks which form part of a degree classification are arrived at, moderated, and checked by relevant quality assurance processes such as the external examiner system in the UK. Assessment processes have always been key in the way in which the product of higher education institutions – the degree – is arrived at, and they are therefore of central importance to an investigation of the value of a degree and questions around whether any change, or perception of change, in this value may occur over time.

Assessment of a music performance as part of a degree programme involves the evaluation of a student recital/gig in line with a pre-defined (usually institution-specific) set of marking criteria. Each marker brings to the process their own knowledge, skills, and experience, applied both in their own career to date and seen in their interaction with colleague examiners.[9] Important to bear in mind here is that a set of standardised guidelines intended to be used to determine a student's mark will be interpreted alongside this tacit knowledge that an assessor brings to the process of judging performance.[10] For this reason, assessment processes are not necessarily objective exercises during which any two examiners would arrive at the same final mark, and a degree of variability between two markers is to be expected.[11] Although research suggests that students accept that any two assessors will give different marks for the same piece of work, there is a sense of a range in which this is acceptable.[12]

Music in Higher Education

In comparison to other disciplines in higher education (for example, those in the other Advance HE calibration workshops: geography, chemistry, and veterinary science), assessment in the creative arts brings challenges around the extent to which risk, innovation and 'wow' factors are rewarded in marking processes. As Gordon states, 'media arts and other creative subject areas entail a number of skills and qualities that are going to require subtle assessment procedures'.[13] Creativity itself 'is not easily defined and therefore is difficult to assess',[14] and examiners of creativity may therefore be more likely to employ their tacit knowledge, or intuition, of the value of a piece of work (or a performance) than assessors in other disciplines.[15] Per Jacobs, 'assessment in aesthetic fields presents a myriad of challenges in the higher education environment',[16] and current debates around the value and relevance of subjective versus objective judgements are far from conclusive.[17] The broader context here is that creativity has been acknowledged as an important skill in university graduates in the UK,[18] and one which higher education establishments should nurture and seek to develop, regardless of their field of degree study.[19] This makes the assessment of creative outputs of university students all the more pertinent in the current educational climate.

Examiners are likely to have received training in various ways; for example, through their own institution, via external training courses, and as part of external examiner experiences and courses. Such training for examiners and external examiners is vital, and arguably training specifically tailored to the creative arts is also important: markers need to be able to balance their own subjective or aesthetic responses with their judgement of achievement in line with institutional marking criteria, whilst also not putting aside their own tacit knowledge from their experience in the discipline and sector. However, whilst there is an emerging field of research around assessment in fine art and design disciplines,[20] there is still little research around the assessment of music performance. Such research is important in light of this, as well as considering that a student's final recital or performance as part of their degree studies can account for as much as one-third of their final degree classification.

Calibration Workshop

As part of the Degree Standards Project, a jointly run event on calibration in music performance assessment was planned by Dr Michelle Phillips (then Deputy Head of Undergraduate Programmes, Royal Northern College of Music, 'RNCM') and Professor Sue Bloxham (Emeritus Professor of Academic Practice, University of Cumbria). The event was funded by Advance HE (then the Higher Education Academy), and run in association with Advance HE, RNCM and Conservatoires UK ('CUK').

The one-day 'Calibrating Academic Standards in Music Education' event took place at the RNCM (Manchester, UK) on 27th February 2018, and brought together 24 external examiners for music from a range of the UK university music departments and conservatoires. The event had the following aims and intended outcomes, which were sent to delegates in advance of their commitment to take part:

Aims

- To raise awareness in music external examiners of the different standards for judging performance across providers of music education and across different instruments
- To build greater consistency in the judgement of performance across providers of music education and across different instruments and ensemble types
- To debate issues in judgement of music performance
- To create the conditions for future calibration in the field of music higher education

Intended Outcomes

- Greater capability and confidence amongst the participating external examiners that they can draw on accepted standards of performance in their examining role
- Greater awareness amongst external examiners of the potential for differences in performance standards across providers and across different instruments and ensemble types
- Agreed key criteria for the assessment of recitals
- Exemplar recital videos accompanied by agreed judgements on performance for use in calibration workshops within and across music education providers
- Identification of other resources that might be made available to assist in the calibration of standards

The day-long workshop, designed and facilitated by Phillips and Bloxham, involved presentations from those leading the event, and experts with experience of examining and calibration.

The main part of the day was devoted to four assessment exercises, during which the delegates undertook the following activity:

1) Delegates listened to a short performance of one full piece of music (c. five minutes) by the student performer, in standard concert hall recital format (the event took place in a recital room, and the performers were instructed to behave and perform as they would in their end-of-year recital);
2) Delegates noted the mark they would give to the performance based on their knowledge and experience examining in the sector (no marking criteria were provided);
3) In small groups of four to five people, delegates discussed their marks and arrived at a consensus mark for their group (or 'assessment panel');
4) All 24 delegates discussed their group marks and attempted to arrive at a consensus mark as a cohort.

In addition to four iterations of this process, with different student performances in each (classical piano, popular music voice, classical French horn, and classical cello), delegates discussed a sample of marking criteria for performance assessment from a range of UK university music departments and conservatoires. Finally, delegates summarised the overall findings of the day in relation to what they considered to be key criteria in any set of marking guidelines.

Questionnaire Research

Delegates completed a pre- and post-event questionnaire which asked about their own experience as examiners and sought to measure any change in how prepared and confident they felt in their roles as assessors of music performance in higher education. The findings which will be discussed here are in relation to the following two questions included on the questionnaire:

1. How well prepared do you feel for marking musical performance? (1 = very well to 5 = not at all);
2. How confident are you in your capacity to make judgements about musical performance that are consistent with your peers in your own and other institutions? (1 = very confident to 5 = not at all confident).

Results and Outcomes

Table 23.1 summarises the marks arrived at by each group of 4–5 delegates for each of the four performances. As can be seen from this table, groups were mostly able to arrive at an agreed mark during discussion (or 'social moderation'), and most groups awarded a mark within the same classification boundary (e.g., pass, 2.2, 2.1 or 1st class degree).

The marks given to each performance by individual delegates, prior to discussion with other delegates, had the following standard deviations (marks were made in percentages, hence the figures here represent percentage points):

Performance 1 (classical piano): 8.58
Performance 2 (popular music voice): 6.56
Performance 3 (classical French horn): 7.10
Performance 4 (classical cello): 7.23

Table 23.1 The Percentage Marks Arrived at by Each Group of 4–5 Delegates for Each of the Four Performances.

Delegate group	Performance 1 (classical piano)	Performance 2 (popular music voice)	Performance 3 (classical French horn)	Performance 4 (classical cello)
1	72	52	38	75
2	68	63	43	64–85 (no agreement)
3	70	58	44	74
4	68–70	58	34	2.1/1st class*
5	66	62	40	78–80

Note: * This group stated the mark in degree classification terms, rather than as a percentage.

This range of between 6.56 and 8.58 percentage points of variation between markers might be compared to Sadler's notion of what a student sees as an acceptable range of tolerance between different markers.[21] In spite of this variation within individual marks, all groups were able to arrive at a consensus mark via discussion, and they were able to do this using tacit knowledge alone, without reference to any prescribed marking criteria. Also, notably, there was significantly less variation in marks awarded by each group of delegates (as per Table 23.1) than in individual marks alone (which were also collected as part of the event).

These data suggest that there is a high level of consistency in the judgement of performance across assessors of music performance and across different instruments and styles of music. Moreover, social moderation in this case decreased the level of variability amongst groups of marks (compared to the marks given by individuals, which differed from one another to a greater extent).

Delegate responses to the aforementioned questionnaire items (which were asked of all delegates before and after the event) are summarised in Table 23.2.

These results suggest that delegates felt more prepared for their roles as assessors of music performance and felt more confident in their capacity to make judgements following this one-day calibration event. The differences in these average pre- and post-event responses were statistically significant ($p < 0.05$).

Table 23.2 Delegate Responses to Two Questionnaire Items (which were asked of all delegates before and after the event).

Question	Average response pre-event	Average response post-event	Level of statistical significance (p value)
1. How well prepared do you feel for marking musical performance? (1 = very well, 5 = not at all)	2.06	1.58	0.046
2. How confident are you in your capacity to make judgements about musical performance that are consistent with your peers in your own and other institutions? (1 = very confident, 5 = not at all confident)	2.33	1.74	0.030

The event had multiple other benefits for participants. Discussions over the course of the day gave delegates a chance to interact with a wide cross-section of other examiners in the field of music performance, and thus may have increased their awareness of how their own judgements might relate to norms in the sector. Also, key criteria for assessing music performance did emerge from the group discussion at the end of the day. Categories important to any set of marking criteria specifically for the assessment of music performance which were proposed by delegates at the event included expression/understanding/interpretation, technical competence, and presentation/communication.

Feedback relating to the event was overwhelmingly positive. When asked 'How likely are you to discuss the knowledge you have gained from today with colleagues including those who work as external examiners? (1 = very likely to 5 = not at all likely)', attendees gave an average response of 1.37 (this was the highest response of all questions across the pre- and post-event questionnaires). One delegate commented that they were scheduled to report back to their entire department the following day, and one stated, 'I sit on many external panels and will share and use this experience'. This gives confidence that the experiences and findings of the day may have a broader reach than the delegates at this particular event alone. When asked if they felt that there would be value in repeating the event, 89% of delegates stated that they would like to see a repeat of the day. In terms of what a second event might cover, many commented that they would welcome an event which discussed composition assessment.

Conclusions

The aims and intended outcomes of the event (as stated earlier) were considered to have been met. This event demonstrated that workshops designed to explore calibration of degree standards by experienced examiners can increase perceived level of skill and confidence for examiners and may be deemed overwhelmingly positive and useful by delegates. Moreover, although individual marks for a music performance may vary between experienced examiners, groups of examiners from different higher education institutions are able to arrive at a consensus mark through social moderation, even in the absence of marking criteria, when examiners are required to rely to a greater extent on tacit knowledge. They are able to do this in relation to a range of styles of performance, and regardless of whether their examining experience has largely been gained at a music conservatoire or university music department.

The main findings in relation to the event were presented at the Advance HE one-day conference 'Protecting the value of HE qualifications in the UK: Degree classification and external examining' on 22nd May 2019 (King's College London), and material produced during the event was adapted and made available online by Advance HE in order to help with the training of external examiners for music in the future.

Notes

1. Simon Barker, "Is Grade Inflation a Worldwide Trend?," 2018, accessed August 30, 2020, www.timeshighereducation.com/features/grade-inflation-worldwide-trend.
2. Anna McKie, "OfS Plans New Regulations – Free Speech and Grade Inflation," 2020, accessed August 30, 2020, www.timeshighereducation.com/news/ofs-plans-new-regulations-free-speech-and-grade-inflation.
3. Ibid.
4. Elaine Drayton and Ben Waltmann, "Briefing Note – Will Universities Need a Bailout to Survive the COVID-19 Crisis?," 2020, accessed August 30, 2020, www.ifs.org.uk/publications/14919.
5. Ibid.

6. Ibid.
7. Advance HE, "The Degree Standards Project," accessed May 10, 2020, www.advance-he.ac.uk/degree-standards-project.
8. Ibid.
9. D. Royce Sadler, "Beyond Feedback: Developing Student Capability in Complex Appraisal," *Assessment & Evaluation in Higher Education* 35, no. 5 (2010): 535–50.
10. Sue Bloxham, Peter Boyd, and Susan Orr, "Mark My Words: The Role of Assessment Criteria in UK Higher Education Grading Practices," *Studies in Higher Education* 36, no. 6 (2011): 655–70.
11. Sue Bloxham, Birgit Den-Outer, Jane Hudson, and Margaret Price, "Let's Stop the Pretence of Consistent Marking: Exploring the Multiple Limitations of Assessment Criteria," *Assessment & Evaluation in Higher Education* 41, no. 3 (2016): 466–81.
12. Sadler, "Beyond Feedback."
13. Janey Gordon, 'The 'Wow' Factors: The Assessment of Practical Media and Creative Arts Subjects," *Art, Design & Communication in Higher Education* 3, no. 1 (2004): 61.
14. Janette Harris, "Developing a Language for Assessing Creativity: A Taxonomy to Support Student Learning and Assessment," *Investigations in University Teaching and Learning* 5, no. 1 (2008): 80.
15. Rob Cowdroy and Anthony William, "Assessing Creativity in the Creative Arts," *Art, Design & Communication in Higher Education* 5, no. 2 (2006): np.
16. Rachael Jacobs, "Curator and Critic: Role of the Assessor in Aesthetic Fields," *Higher Education Studies* 2, no. 4 (2012): 114.
17. See Jacobs, 2012 for a review.
18. Robyn Gibson, "The 'Art' of Creative Teaching: Implications for Higher Education," *Teaching in Higher Education* 15, no. 5 (2010): 607–13; Ian MacLaren, "The Contradictions of Policy and Practice: Creativity in Higher Education," *London Review of Education* 10, no. 2 (2012): 159–72; Margaret E. Madden, Marsha Baxter, Heather M. Beauchamp, and Kimberley Bouchard, "Rethinking STEM Education: An Interdisciplinary STEAM Curriculum," *Procedia Computer Science* 20 (2013): 541–46.
19. Veronica A. Segarra, Barbara Natalizio, Cibele V. Falkenberg, Stephanie Pulford, and Raquell M. Holmes, "STEAM: Using the Arts to Train Well-Rounded and Creative Scientists," *Journal of Microbiology & Biology Education* 19, no. 1 (2018): np.
20. See for example, Robert Harland and Phil Sawdon, "From Fail to First: Revising Assessment Criteria in Art and Design," *Art, Design & Communication in Higher Education* 10, no. 1 (2012): 67–88.
21. Sadler, "Beyond Feedback."

Bibliography

Advance HE. "The Degree Standards Project." Accessed May 10, 2020. www.advance-he.ac.uk/degree-standards-project.
Barker, Simon. "Is Grade Inflation a Worldwide Trend?" 2018. Accessed August 30, 2020. www.timeshighereducation.com/features/grade-inflation-worldwide-trend.
Bloxham, Sue, Peter Boyd, and Susan Orr. "Mark My Words: The Role of Assessment Criteria in UK Higher Education Grading Practices." *Studies in Higher Education* 36, no. 6 (2011): 655–70.
Bloxham, Sue, Birgit Den-Outer, Jane Hudson, and Margaret Price. "Let's Stop the Pretence of Consistent Marking: Exploring the Multiple Limitations of Assessment Criteria." *Assessment & Evaluation in Higher Education* 41, no. 3 (2016): 466–81.
Cowdroy, Rob, and Anthony William. "Assessing Creativity in the Creative Arts." *Art, Design & Communication in Higher Education* 5, no. 2 (2006): np.
Drayton, Elaine, and Ben Waltmann. "Briefing Note – Will Universities Need a Bailout to Survive the COVID-19 Crisis?" 2020. Accessed August 30, 2020. www.ifs.org.uk/publications/14919.
Gibson, Robyn. "The 'Art' of Creative Teaching: Implications for Higher Education." *Teaching in Higher Education* 15, no. 5 (2010): 607–13.
Gordon, Janey. "The 'Wow' Factors: The Assessment of Practical Media and Creative Arts Subjects." *Art, Design & Communication in Higher Education* 3, no. 1 (2004): 61.
Harland, Robert, and Phil Sawdon. "From Fail to First: Revising Assessment Criteria in Art and Design." *Art, Design & Communication in Higher Education* 10, no. 1 (2012): 67–88.

Harris, Janette. "Developing a Language for Assessing Creativity: A Taxonomy to Support Student Learning and Assessment." *Investigations in University Teaching and Learning* 5, no. 1 (2008): 80.

Jacobs, Rachael. "Curator and Critic: Role of the Assessor in Aesthetic Fields." *Higher Education Studies* 2, no. 4 (2012): 114.

MacLaren, Ian. "The Contradictions of Policy and Practice: Creativity in Higher Education." *London Review of Education* 10, no. 2 (2012): 159–72.

Madden, Margaret E., Marsha Baxter, Heather Beauchamp, Kimberley Bouchard, Derek Habermas, Mark Huff, and Gordon Plague. "Rethinking STEM Education: An Interdisciplinary STEAM Curriculum." *Procedia Computer Science* 20 (2013): 541–46.

McKie, Anna. "OfS Plans New Regulations – Free Speech and Grade Inflation." 2020. Accessed August 30, 2020. www.timeshighereducation.com/news/ofs-plans-new-regulations-free-speech-and-grade-inflation.

Sadler, D. Royce. "Beyond Feedback: Developing Student Capability in Complex Appraisal." *Assessment & Evaluation in Higher Education* 35, no. 5 (2010): 535–50.

Segarra, Veronica A., Barbara Natalizio, Cibele V. Falkenberg, Stephanie Pulford, and Raquelle Holmes. "STEAM: Using the Arts to Train Well-Rounded and Creative Scientists." *Journal of Microbiology & Biology Education* 19, no. 1 (2018): np.

24
INNOVATION AND LEADERSHIP IN GROUP TEACHING ACROSS THE LIFESPAN

Three Case Studies

Cynthia Stephens-Himonides, Margaret Young, and Melanie Bowes

This chapter examines the leadership of three women group piano teachers who have made an impact on group music teaching and learning through their pedagogies and leadership across their careers. We identified three group piano teachers who are deemed experts across the learning lifespan: childhood, early adult, senior adult. Through their retrospective narratives, these three case studies focussed on their musical experiences and training, role models and mentors, sources of support, entrance into the field of group teaching, support for other teachers, meaning of leadership, and self-perception of themselves as leaders in the field.

Learning an instrument or voice with the goal of an individual performance has typically relied heavily on the one-to-one (or master/apprentice) structure found firmly situated in pre-tertiary through conservatoire and university tuition. The relatively recent flourish of group instrumental instruction of individual performance skills has been found in the latter part of the 20th century.[1] Student motivation found in groups compared with the one-to-one setting, along with group teaching pedagogy and economy, gave momentum to the adoption of group keyboard teaching. Due to the recognised benefits of teaching piano in groups, the growth of piano classes at elementary and secondary school levels was rapid. The first college-level courses in the United States provided students with an opportunity to develop basic piano technique and learn standard piano literature.[2] These courses were popular because they were an efficient use of faculty members' time[3] and they provided students with an opportunity to meet with their teachers more often than did private piano instruction, thereby exposing them to more material and gaining additional practice of the tasks[4] introduced in classes.[5] In addition to pre-tertiary and tertiary teaching contexts, the more recent growth of piano learning in groups has been the uptake by amateur adult and third-generation, or senior adult, students.[6]

Although those who initiated and pioneered group learning of piano date early in the 19th century (UK) and 20th century (US), innovators and leaders in group teaching who have allowed the group piano's longevity despite the firm establishment of one-to-one instrumental teaching have yet to be investigated, particularly across the lifespan of music teaching and learning. As distinct from one-to-one teaching, group piano teaching relies on leading a group towards a shared learning aim; as such, it is a useful lens through which we can examine paths to leadership in teaching and learning while providing role models for future group teachers.

The implications of this study include furthering the skills and knowledge of teaching music in groups, as well as leadership skills in the field with the aim of providing effective and engaging music learning experiences across the lifespan.

Group Piano Teaching and Learning Context

Teaching and learning of piano in groups has taken many forms since the earliest records from Dublin, dating from 1815 and denoted by Richards, where he hypothesised that: 'The growth and development of piano class instruction were due to social demands, economical appeal, improved instructional procedures, and modified objectives'[7], and he concluded that through refinements over time, it can be seen that the following factors must be observed for group teaching to be effective.[8]

- A musically trained and experienced teacher who is adequately equipped with teaching materials and strategies;
- Appropriately sized group so that there are opportunities to listen and perform;
- Suitable time allotted for these opportunities as well as explore, contribute, and appraise within the lesson;
- A facility with appropriate equipment for the facilitation of musical expression across various levels of achievement.

Richards' summary of effective group teaching can be found in contemporary examples of group piano classes, but perhaps it is only relevant to certain class settings. Currently, group keyboard classes greatly vary in terms of size, instruments used (number of keyboards in the facility and technological capabilities of those keyboards), educational aims, and student outcomes. With variations in class size, pedagogy approach and aims, groupings, teacher profile, facilities, wider development in musicianship skills, and setting (whether it be the public school, private studio, or collegiate class), it is clear that the term 'group piano' is somewhat of an umbrella one, referring to many different scenarios where a group of students are together, with one teacher.

It is perhaps due to this multifarious reality of what group piano teaching has become that leadership, innovation, and direction have been sought and needed within this field. In order to learn how and why our three interviewed pedagogues can be seen to be those leaders, it is important to consider the context and development of the teaching and learning process within which they were working.

Johann Bernard Logier (1777–1848), who was a German composer and teacher (residing in Ireland), was seen as a key innovator of group piano curricula in the early 1800s, when he designed the harmony-focused Logierian System of Musical Education. His system was taught to groups of students, and classes were described as containing 'a recognized wide variance of level of attainment and background, ranging from the beginner to the more advanced pianist, all studying in the same class, and all generally playing simultaneously'.[9] Group piano has evolved since, and due to the introduction of electronic keyboards it became more widely available in the 1970s and 1980s. The advent of the keyboard laboratory, as described by Stephens-Himonides and Hilley,[10] led to the ability for students to play both out loud with each other (as they would have done when learning on acoustic pianos), and on their own with headphones, with their playing or practising not impacting the rest of the class. This created opportunities for more accessible settings, and meant the widening of multiple methods of teaching delivery and approaches.

Previous research does show that there are fewer opportunities for teacher education in group pedagogy.[11] Pike states that 'there are few meaningful formal opportunities for professional development of group-teaching skills or for observation of successful group-piano instruction available to teachers who wish to develop group-teaching skills'.[12] This and other studies have concluded that there is a wide disparity between approaches and success of teaching groups when it comes to those who are experienced and those who are not.[13]

The aims and objectives of group piano classes differ considerably depending upon the context of the class. Group classes for young children often focus on fundamentals of music theory and the development of rhythmic fluency through ensemble playing.[14] In most collegiate group classes, the aims are to develop functional piano and musicianship skills,[15] while in an adult class, the aim may be purely recreational and focused on enjoyment and wellbeing through learning familiar musical melodies.[16] The various approaches, aims, intended outcomes and experience of group teachers, alongside the limited opportunities for training, have led innovators, such as the three pedagogues interviewed in this chapter, to seek solutions and to share their findings with others who are experiencing the same frustrations and barriers as they themselves had felt. By providing for and sharing with others in their field, they have undertaken key leadership roles and paved the way for others to pursue careers and success in group piano teaching.

Methodology

For the purposes of this chapter on women leading in group keyboard teaching and learning, we decided to explore leadership in this field through examining leading experts' backgrounds, their beginnings of teaching in this context, and their perceptions of leadership in the field. Three expert teachers from the field of group teaching in each segment of the lifespan – children/youth, adult, and senior adult – were interviewed. Each of the three participants was from the US and identified as an expert in their area of group piano teaching, as evidenced by their experience of at least fifty years of teaching, leadership in music teaching organisations, publications (teaching methods and scholarly outputs), workshops, and recognition by their peers.

The expert teachers were contacted via email with the invitation to be interviewed based on their credentials in the field listed here and presented with the participant information sheet, along with fielding any questions about the project. Agreeing to participate in the interviews were Brenda Dillon (senior adult learning), Martha Hilley (adult learning), and Mayron Cole (children/youth learning). We briefly place their group teaching experiences in the context of which they participated in this study and their leadership roles.

Mayron Cole is the creator of the Mayron Cole Piano Method, which has been taught to thousands of students worldwide for over 30 years. She has been noted as a pioneer in teaching studio piano in groups using her method and has presented numerous piano teacher workshops on this method and group teaching. She has been a leader in advocating for group teaching in the independent piano studio for young beginning piano students. She has most recently released her method as free and accessible for all teachers and students.

Brenda Dillon, a longtime Project Director for the National Piano Foundation, serves as an advisory board member to the Frances Clark Center and consultant for Roland US. As a former college professor in Dallas, TX, she taught Recreational Music Making (RMM) classes at a senior center in a Dallas suburb. In addition to writing articles and developing RMM teaching and music materials, she does extensive teacher training throughout the US. She has been a leader in advancing group piano pedagogies for recreational piano learning and senior adult piano learning.

Martha Hilley's university group piano teaching spanned five decades whilst she actively presented workshops on group piano teacher training at conferences and seminars on the international, national, state, and local levels. Along with co-authoring group piano teaching texts *Piano for the Developing Musician* and *Piano for Pleasure*, she has been a leader in musicianship learning through group piano pedagogies. Also undertaken were university leadership roles, such as Director of Undergraduate Studies, and professional organisation roles, such as President of Music Teachers National Conference.

Interviews were conducted individually by one of the three researchers. The interviews were undertaken via online video conferencing due to the geographical distance between the researcher and teacher. The teachers consented to the interviews and the sharing of their responses. All interviews were audio recorded and transcribed by the researcher conducting the interview. We collated responses, analysed the responses using open coding to identify recurring themes, and finally discussed these to determine themes, presentation and organisation of the findings. Prior to analysis, the responses were summarised by the researchers and discussed for further clarification of the responses and compilation of the results.

The following questions were asked of each expert within the semi-structured interview:

- Please describe your musical training.
- Who were your major role models and sources of support?
- How did you get started in the group teaching context?
- How did you support other group keyboard teachers?
- What does leadership mean to you?
- At what point did you feel like you were perceived as a leader in group keyboard teaching?

Results: Musical Experiences and Training

Each of the three teachers began their formal music experiences by the age of seven, and all had relied on the local music teacher, whether they be a band director, their own mother, or local piano teacher. Their experiences varied with respect to a linear progression of learning and how they were taught. As Brenda states about one of her teachers: 'After he [previous teacher] left, my parents took me to the most wonderful piano teacher you could ever, ever have. She really was a musicianship teacher before we even had that term'. This was similar to Martha's formative music experiences in that she learned not only piano skills but also music theory and history, as well as opera. She states that she 'loved what I was doing'. While Mayron's early teachers left her working things out that she had not been taught, such as how to read music, and she was mostly taught by being given new pieces to take home and work out on her own, this suited her way of learning.

Another theme found in their formative backgrounds had to do with access to music lessons. As Brenda shares: 'There was no money for lessons, so my dad, who was the bus driver, asked the band director if he would teach me in return for eggs from our farm. That was my auspicious beginning'. Martha spoke of informal music experiences with her brother, cousins, and grandmother listening to an incredible record collection of symphonies and opera and writing their own stories and creating their operas with costumes, dancing, and singing involved. Another formative informal experience was when she was in church between her grandmother and great-aunt, listening to them sing harmonies. Mayron was inspired by her piano teacher to become a piano teacher as a young piano student, described in the next section.

Role Models and Mentors, or Other Sources of Support

Early piano teachers were mentioned as role models for Brenda and Mayron, with the latter remembering a quote from her teacher that changed her life when she was just ten years old:

> Mayron, you know so much about playing the piano . . . but when you die, you're going to take all that knowledge with you, unless you teach'. She says: 'That one

statement changed my life one hundred percent. I knew at that point, I had to teach what I knew.

However, all three teachers could pinpoint moments where others gave them opportunities, perhaps seeing their potential, and so set them on a trajectory for success. Martha mentions close friends and family, as well as the Head of Education at Wurlitzer at the time, and recalls how a former employee gave her a leave to attend a group piano symposium: 'He said "Martha, do you think I thought you were going to spend the rest of your life answering the phone?"'

Martha and Brenda spoke warmly of those more experienced teachers around them who mentored and guided them on how to teach groups. Brenda recalls: 'Those teachers were wonderful, they took me under their wing, and they started teaching how to be really effective'. However, Mayron reflected on how she was very much alone in her group-teaching endeavours. She learnt as she taught and did not have any mentors in that regard, only mentioning those who gave her the opportunity to reach a wide audience of teachers with her knowledge and experience.

Entrance into the Field of Group Teaching

During the time when all three teachers began teaching piano in groups, the training for such contexts was not existent. Brenda's invitation to her first position of group keyboard teacher came about because of her previous teaching experiences, and she learned on the job with support from local primary/secondary teachers. Martha's first experience in group piano teaching was as a graduate assistant during her master's course. Having no formal training in group teaching, she stated that she asked the students in these group piano classes lots of questions about what they wanted to learn on the piano. In describing her initial teaching experiences, she stated that she stayed at least two weeks ahead of students, as well as observing what she thought they needed. '[I] never worked so hard in my life' was her response when discussing her teaching experiences. Mayron was asked by the church music director opposite her house if she would take a group of six children to teach rhythm and pitch reading, so that they could better participate in the choir. After a year of teaching these students together, Mayron told them that they had done so well that they could each have private lessons with her for their second year of study. Their reaction was unexpectedly negative, claiming that they were happier staying as a group. This enthusiasm for group learning and this group of students in particular paved her way for innovation in group teaching.

These beginning experiences laid the groundwork for their passion and innovation in the group teaching context. After many years of experience in group teaching, Brenda became inspired by a workshop featuring Carl Brune and Barry Bittman, who introduced her to Recreational Music Making. She recalls: 'So when we came home from that conference, I thought I'm going to do this, and now is the time, it's a good time in my life to try it, so I decided to start a pilot project'. She eventually led thirteen different sections of these classes which removed barriers or challenges to teaching group classes for 55+ adults. She states that they 'did a lot of research at the time . . . And found a new strategy for enabling people who never before considered themselves musical . . . To discover the joy and wellness benefits of playing a musical instrument'.

Martha's pivotal decision during her postgraduate study to study her own group piano classes for her thesis led to her eventually becoming a group piano clinician for the Wurlitzer piano company leading to other group teaching opportunities within higher education. She reflected upon the role that the Wurlitzer Piano Company had on her and the group piano teaching and learning stating: 'So when I say Wurlitzer is responsible for my career? I mean, they were notoriously responsible for my career. Wurlitzer was innovating, not the university'.

Supporting Other Group Piano Teachers

Supporting others to teach effective group piano classes came as a result of either receiving support themselves, knowing how they benefited from it, or having had no support and wanting a different experience for new group piano teachers. Conventions and conferences have played a big role in giving these teachers a platform on which to offer their support, and to give training, not only themselves, but to facilitate training from other expert pedagogues.

In the early days of her group piano teaching at Dallas Community College, Brenda and her colleagues decided to form a Texas group piano association. She invited teachers from all over the state in a variety of teaching contexts, to provide education and support to teachers focusing on group piano. Brenda saw this as a means to expanding her own knowledge of group keyboard teaching because, as part of the work of the association, they asked nationally known presenters to give lectures and demonstrations on effective group keyboard teaching practices. Their quarterly meetings were so positive that they decided to expand and hold a National Group Piano Symposium (an event that would ultimately grow into the National Conference on Keyboard Pedagogy, which is a biannual conference that focuses on piano teaching and pedagogy).

Brenda served as a project director at the National Piano Foundation, where she helped support individual piano teaching projects, wrote columns for *Clavier Companion*, and ultimately was asked to chair a recreational music making conference track. She decided a few years ago that it was important for the next generation of piano teachers to take control of the Recreational Music Making track at the Music Teacher's National Association's National Conference. Seeing her experiences and education with famous pedagogues as a gift that she needed to share, Brenda felt that it was her duty to be a mentor to future pedagogues.

Martha states that group piano teachers needed to support each other, respecting each other's teaching goals and paths as group teachers. She supported other group teachers through the Texas Group Piano Association and the National Group Piano Association. Then through Roland and the advent of the digital piano, she worked with teachers in getting set up to teach in groups. She was also on a panel with three leading group piano teachers early in her career, leading to her work with Freeman Olson. Finally, Martha was a curriculum director of an international pedagogy conference as part of her numerous workshops for other group teachers. The numerous years of this support for other teachers lead her to contribute and lead on a national level as President of Music Teachers National Association.

Mayron realised that there was a need for her to share her expertise and experience when she was invited to attend the State of Texas Piano Convention to deliver a presentation on group piano, since she was one of a small number of teachers successfully teaching groups. As part of the convention, she had been given a booth to show the materials that she used for her group classes. She described how teachers were lining up to see her materials, but at this point they were not for sale; in fact, they were handwritten. This was what launched the sale of her group piano method, which included her books as well as training manuals. She has now made her materials available for free on her website, as part of her intent to continue supporting group piano teachers worldwide.

Leadership: Meaning and Perceptions

Both Brenda and Martha held formal leadership positions throughout their teaching careers. These roles existed both within higher education as well as national music teaching organisations and private foundations. Mayron did not serve as a formal leader within major music teaching organisations or within established institutions. These experiences shaped their views of leadership and what it means to be an effective leader in keyboard pedagogy. Martha spoke at length about the value she placed on the professional community, including her academic institution, and her development as part of her leadership roles. She said: 'You really know so much about where you are . . . what kinds of things you can do to help'. Brenda used her experiences within higher education to shape her beliefs about effective leadership:

> I watched [leaders], I watched their leadership skills and how they interacted and how they wanted everybody to succeed . . . I was fortunate because I didn't mind spending a lot of time helping organise things and helping get things started.

Mayron believed leaders were the risk-takers who were not afraid to be criticised or to be seen as renegades, but that leadership also meant compassion for 'teachers who want to learn'.

While none of these teachers actively sought out leadership positions, Brenda and Martha accepted leadership positions when they were asked to serve. Martha said: 'I'm one of the luckiest people I know. But you have to make sure that you're there when an opportunity comes'. Brenda said: 'For those of us who really don't mind hard work and who like to organise and don't mind putting things on paper that help the organisation, I think that's why in the past those things fell my way'. In a similar way, Mayron did not set out to write and share materials for use in group keyboard contexts. Instead, she found that it was an extension of pedagogical practices. Mayron was 'actually very proud. I just wanted to leave something good on this planet'.

All three teachers perceived their status as a leader when others began to recognise their contributions to the field. Mayron had never thought of herself as a leader, 'until one day it dawned on me that they're all doing what I am telling them to do, so I guess I'm the leader!' Martha felt she was a leader when she signed a textbook contract with her co-author Freeman Olson. The recognition of her work by a major publishing company 'kind of changed my life'. Brenda perceived herself as a leader when she was voted in as the presider of a national conference on group teaching. 'I was certain they were going to pick someone big . . . but they chose me . . . I kind of knew then'.

Responses from Brenda indicated she knew the limitations of her formal training, and she sought out new resources that would help her become a better teacher for her students. She desperately wanted to find joy in her teaching – and found opportunities to increase the enjoyment for both herself and her students. Her career seemed like a lesson in self-knowledge and finding opportunities that aligned with her personal and professional goals. Her style of leadership seems collaborative and is relationship-focused on her life and work. She is the consummate life-long learner: after her career in higher education and RMM, she recently began studying choral composing. She was never afraid to put herself out there – the RMM book series with Hal Leonard, for example. She had developed materials and decided to send them to someone and see what they had to say. The book was ultimately published with several complementary books added to the collection due to its popularity.

Martha's responses indicate signs of risk-taking and continually learning. Her early career decisions seemed based on her personal circumstances until she made that pivotal decision to take two risks. One was to write a thesis about her group piano students as a graduate assistant, which was not the norm, and two was to send it in draft form months later to the head of education in a major piano company (Wurlitzer). This led to a domino effect on her group teaching and leadership trajectory. She continually put herself out there to develop her pedagogies alongside supporting other group teachers. She took further risks with leadership roles outside of the music area within her institution. These roles led to more opportunities not only for her career but also for her students' learning experiences. The underlying philosophy behind her teaching and leadership choices seemed to emanate from a desire to help others.

Mayron had a distinct way of learning as a child, which was a result of her isolation and the time she had to focus on her piano studies. It was this that paved the way for her to innovate and create, not satisfied with the methods that were available to her. In this light she showed a real sense of entrepreneurship, plus a firm belief in her own thoughts and practice around piano learning. Group teaching was a tool to nurture strong musicianship skills, for students to grow up to be 'village musicians' who were able to accompany in church and play at local events. She felt strongly that there are too many piano teachers who learn to play as soloists and therefore lack the skills to be able to play with others. Her group piano mission was to develop these skills, and she had the determination to lead the way.

Discussion

Over the past several decades, researchers have explored the barriers and pathways encountered by women who engage in leadership skill development or leadership learning. While research into the efficacy of leadership styles is abundant, our analysis of the case study interviews led us to previous research exploring the lived experiences of women leaders. In 2012, Stead and Elliott's reflexive review of the literature surrounding women's leadership development resulted in the formation of a typology of strategies that were deemed essential to efficacious leadership learning.[17] Based on their review, they posit three strategies for women seeking leadership roles: self-positioning, developing social capital, and disrupting behaviours. We begin the discussion of our interviews within the framework of this typology.

Self-Positioning

The authors define self-positioning as envisaging, presenting and promoting oneself as a leader in relation to others, an organisation and to a broader external audience. This strategy can be evidenced through two categories: owning and learning. Ownership of one's ideas, identity, and leadership skills has been demonstrably effective in promoting leadership learning. The results indicated that these expert teachers practised ownership through their published materials. All three expert teachers developed and published materials that could be used regularly with their students. Similarly, these expert teachers continually sought new information about teaching, learning and leading, demonstrating a commitment to life-long learning.

Contrary to the ideas presented in Stead and Elliott,[18] these expert teachers sought to position themselves as leaders not as a career endeavour, but to help others succeed or to explore group keyboard teaching and learning contexts. None of the teachers we interviewed set out to become known as leaders; rather, they were recognised as leaders because of their dedication to group keyboard teaching and learning.

Developing Social Capital

Stead and Elliott define developing social capital as 'accessing and influencing through membership of formal and informal networks'[19]. The identification of mentors and role models is of particular importance to aspiring women leaders.[20] We found a variety of experiences related to mentorship with these expert teachers. Mayron remarked that she did it all herself and found that there were relatively few teachers who were engaging in similar teaching scenarios. As a result, she had very little to say about anyone serving as a mentor or a role model. Brenda and Martha both found that mentors played a critical role in their development as both teachers and leaders. Not only did they have role models with whom they regularly interacted, but they aspired to emulate famous group keyboard pedagogues who eventually became colleagues.

In comparing these teachers' experiences, the lack of institutional support was evident in Mayron's responses. Her group keyboard teaching was largely an individual enterprise whereas Brenda and Martha both worked within established tertiary institutions. All three expert teachers remarked on the importance of an early and influential role model. These teachers all studied piano with a teacher who not only fostered their musical development but also encouraged them to explore music and learning in a meaningful way.

Disruption

The third typology examined in Stead and Elliot[21] was disrupting, which they define as the disruption of 'existing norms and practices and creating alternative solutions'. They go on to define three methods by which women leaders can address common systemic barriers: becoming the radical, disrupting patterns of behaviour, and developing alternative pathways. The three teachers we interviewed represented each of those three categories. Mayron showed commitment through her narrative, stating:

> being the person out in front, taking the risks . . . [who is] not afraid to be criticised or to be seen as a renegade, to blaze a trail. A leader does what nobody else has done or is willing to do.

Martha emphasised the necessity of professional risk-taking and interacting with individuals beyond one's immediate network. Her interest in resisting common organisational procedures was evidenced by engaging with colleagues and organisational structures beyond music. Martha states:

> So as far as leadership positions go, in my 49 years in higher education, okay, I made a point. A really big point of getting outside of my building. I mean, not just outside of my classroom, but outside of my building. It is a mistake that I think so many people in higher ed make.

Our third teacher left a well-established career in higher education to pursue a new career as a leader in Recreational Music Making. Brenda spoke about how much she loved group teaching, but that RMM allowed her to focus on the aspects of the teaching and learning process she found most fulfilling. By exploring this new path, the scope of her reach and influence in music teaching and learning expanded. Using the framework of transformational learning, Andreas[22] argued that women leaders can overcome barriers in part by becoming fully engaged in the process of leadership learning and development. This embodiment can be found in the stories of our three interviewees as they all engaged in professional risk-taking and lifelong leadership learning.

In examining these three group piano teachers, it is clear that they embody many of the characteristics of effective female leaders. Women leaders often use empathy while building communion and consensus with the groups with whom they interact. Growe and Montgomery[23] determined that the 'female' leadership attributes of relationship-building, process over product and sharing are more effective than traditionally 'male' leadership approaches. In a reflective exploration of female leaders during the pandemic, Gedro et al stated:

> [Leadership is] about courage to experiment and to risk unpopularity. It's about compassion – leading with love and assuming others are doing their best. It's not about [the individual]; it's about ensuring staff have the resources, flexibility, and structure they need to find a way to facilitate individual power and control.[24]

As found in the results of these three case studies, each of the expert teachers had demonstrated these leadership attributes at points in their leadership careers, whether through risk-taking, compassion, or support for other group teachers.

The purpose of this study was to examine women leaders in group piano pedagogy across the lifespan through three case studies investigating their musical experiences and training, role models and mentors, sources of support, entrance into the field of group teaching, support for other teachers, meaning of leadership, and self-perception of themselves as leaders in the field. We found that each of these expert teachers had a commitment to lifelong learning, found ownership in publishing their teaching materials, had influential early role models, and took risks in various forms. A difference found was the lack of institutional support as a freelance teacher, which may affect access to mentorship. Further research could investigate how freelance music teachers locate and work with mentors throughout their careers. The diversity of these women's lived experiences demonstrates the various pathways women can take towards leadership skill development and the application of leadership styles to teaching and learning environments. Previous research has found that the efficacy of leadership styles or skills is demonstrably context-dependent.[25] While certain styles and skills are linked with particular environments (e.g. instructional leadership within a classroom), it is evident that adapting leadership skills to one's context is beneficial and valuable.[26] The ability to adapt one's leadership skills was beyond the scope of this project; however, future research could explore the effects of different leadership skills on group piano teaching and learning contexts.

The retrospectives of these three women group piano pedagogues demonstrated that they established themselves first as leaders within the context of their own teaching and learning, then within the larger field of group teaching, ultimately furthering the development of group piano pedagogy. As the co-authors are researchers and teachers in music teaching and learning, examining these women's paths to leadership in teaching and learning within and beyond the classroom context have provided us with effective practices of leadership learning and development, as well as lifelong learning. Their individual narratives shared collectively in this chapter have served as an informative (and inspirational) source for us, as well as the future innovators of music teaching and leadership.

Notes

1. Cynthia Stephens-Himonides and Martha Hilley, "Technology and Group Teaching," in *The Routledge Companion to Music, Technology, and Education*, edited by Andrew King, Evangelos Himonides, and S. Alex Ruthmann (London and New York: Routledge, 2016), 343–54; Margaret Young, "A National Survey of University-Level Group Piano Programs," *MTNA e-Journal* 7, no. 3 (2016): 13.
2. William Henry Richards, "Trends of Piano Class Instruction, 1815–1962" (DMA diss. unpublished, University of Missouri-Kansas City, 1962).
3. Barbara Locke, "The College Piano Class: Status and Practices of Group Piano Instruction at Selected Universities in Arkansas, Louisiana, Mississippi, Oklahoma, and Tennessee" (Doctoral diss. unpublished, The University of Southern Mississippi, 1987).

4. Ibid.
5. Diana Skroch, "A Descriptive and Interpretive Study of Class Piano Instruction in Four-Year Colleges and Universities Accredited by the National Association of Schools of Music with a Profile of the Class Piano Instructor" (Doctoral diss. unpublished, The University of Oklahoma, 1991).
6. Brenda Dillon, "Recreational Music Making," *American Music Teacher* 57 (2007): 21–23; Susan Hallam, Andrea Creech, and Maria Varvarigou, "Well-being and Music Leisure Activities Through the Lifespan," *The Oxford Handbook of Music Making and Leisure* (2017): 31–60; Pamela D. Pike, "Using Technology to Engage Third-Age (Retired) Leisure Learners: A Case Study of a Third-Age MIDI Piano Ensemble," *International Journal of Music Education* 29, no. 2 (2011): 116–23, 121.
7. Richards, "Trends," 1.
8. Ibid., 150.
9. Ibid., 8.
10. Stephens-Himonides and Hilley, "Technology," 322.
11. Young, "A National Survey."
12. Pamela D. Pike, "The Differences Between Novice and Expert Group-Piano Teaching Strategies: A Case Study and Comparison of Beginning Group Piano Classes," *International Journal of Music Education* 32, no. 2 (2014): 213.
13. Young, "A National Survey."
14. Yvonne Enoch, *Group Piano-Teaching* (New York: Oxford University Press, 1974); Christopher Fisher, *Teaching Piano in Groups* (New York: Oxford University Press, 2010).
15. Margaret Young, "The Use of Functional Piano Skills by Selected Professional Musicians and Its Implications for Group Piano Curricula" (Doctoral diss. unpublished, The University of Texas at Austin, 2010).
16. Brian Chung and Brenda Dillon, "Piano Teaching-Traditional or Recreational? What's the Difference?," *The American Music Teacher* 58, no. 2 (2008): 46.
17. Valerie Stead and Carole Elliott, "Women's Leadership Learning: A Reflexive Review of Representations and Leadership Teaching," *Management Learning* 44, no. 4 (2013): 373–94.
18. Stead and Elliot, "Women's Leadership."
19. Ibid., 378.
20. Anthony Thorpe, "Educational Leadership Development and Women: Insights from Critical Realism," *International Journal of Leadership in Education* 22, no. 2 (2019): 135–47.
21. Stead and Elliot, "Women's Leadership."
22. Sarah Andreas, "Exploration of Women's Leadership Development Challenges and Transformational Learning: A Positional Paper," *Advancing Women in Leadership Journal* 40, no. 1 (2021): 87–98.
23. Roslin Growe and Paula Montgomery, *Women and the Leadership Paradigm: Bridging the Gender Gap* (Columbus, OH: ERIC Clearinghouse, 1999).
24. Julie Gedro, Nicola Marae Allain, Desalyn De-Souza, Lynne Dodson, and Mary V. Mawn, "Flattening the Learning Curve of Leadership Development: Reflections of Five Women Higher Education Leaders During the Coronavirus Pandemic of 2020," *Human Resource Development International* 23, no. 4 (2020): 401.
25. Marcus Pietsch and Pierre Tulowitzki, "Disentangling School Leadership and Its Ties to Instructional Practices–An Empirical Comparison of Various Leadership Styles," *School Effectiveness and School Improvement* 28, no. 4 (2017): 629–49.
26. Wei Zheng, Olca Surgevil, and Ronit Kark, "Dancing on the Razor's Edge: How Top-Level Women Leaders Manage the Paradoxical Tensions Between Agency and Communion," *Sex Roles* 79 (2018): 633–50.

Bibliography

Andreas, Sarah. "Exploration of Women's Leadership Development Challenges and Transformational Learning: A Positional Paper." *Advancing Women in Leadership Journal* 40, no. 1 (2021): 87–98.
Chung, Brian, and Brenda Dillon. "Piano Teaching-Traditional or Recreational? What's the Difference?." *The American Music Teacher* 58, no. 2 (2008): 46.
Dillon, Brenda. "Recreational Music Making." *American Music Teacher* 57 (2007): 21–23.
Enoch, Yvonne. *Group Piano-Teaching*. Oxford: Oxford University Press, 1974.

Fisher, Christopher. *Teaching Piano in Groups*. Oxford: Oxford University Press, 2010.
Gedro, Julie, Nicola M. Allain, Desalyn De-Souza, Lynn Dodson, and Mary V. Mawn. "Flattening the Learning Curve of Leadership Development: Reflections of Five Women Higher Education Leaders During the Coronavirus Pandemic of 2020." *Human Resource Development International* 23, no. 4 (2020): 395–405.
Growe, Roslin, and Paula Montgomery. *Women and the Leadership Paradigm: Bridging the Gender Gap*. Columbus, OH: ERIC Clearinghouse, 1999.
Hallam, Susan, et al. "Well-Being and Music Leisure Activities Through the Lifespan." In *The Oxford Handbook of Music Making and Leisure*, edited by Roger Mantie and Gareth Dylan Smith, 31–60. Oxford: Oxford University Press, 2017.
Locke, Barbara A. "The College Piano Class: Status and Practices of Group Piano Instruction at Selected Universities in Arkansas, Louisiana, Mississippi, Oklahoma, and Tennessee." Doctoral diss. unpublished, The University of Southern Mississippi, 1987.
Pietsch, Marcus, and Pierre Tulowitzki. "Disentangling School Leadership and Its Ties to Instructional Practices–An Empirical Comparison of Various Leadership Styles." *School Effectiveness and School Improvement* 28, no. 4 (2017): 629–49.
Pike, Pamela D. "The Differences Between Novice and Expert Group-Piano Teaching Strategies: A Case Study and Comparison of Beginning Group Piano Classes." *International Journal of Music Education* 32, no. 2 (2014): 213–27.
———. 'Using Technology to Engage Third-Age (Retired) Leisure Learners: A Case Study of a Third-Age MIDI Piano Ensemble." *International Journal of Music Education* 29, no. 2 (2011): 116–23.
———. *Dynamic Group-Piano Teaching: Transforming Group Theory Into Teaching Practice*. London and New York: Routledge, 2017.
Richards, William H. "Trends of Piano Class Instruction, 1815–1962." Doctoral diss. unpublished, University of Missouri-Kansas City, 1962.
Skroch, Diana. "A Descriptive and Interpretive Study of Class Piano Instruction in Four-Year Colleges and Universities Accredited by the National Association of Schools of Music With a Profile of the Class Piano Instructor." Doctoral diss. unpublished, The University of Oklahoma, 1991.
Stead, Valerie, and Carole Elliott. "Women's Leadership Learning: A Reflexive Review of Representations and Leadership Teaching." *Management Learning* 44, no. 4 (2013): 373–94.
Stephens-Himonides, Cynthia, and Martha Hilley. "Technology and Group Teaching." In *The Routledge Companion to Music, Technology, and Education*, edited by Andrew King, Evangelos Himonides, and S. Alex Ruthmann, 343–54. London: Routledge, 2017.
Thorpe, Anthony. "Educational Leadership Development and Women: Insights from Critical Realism." *International Journal of Leadership in Education* 22, no. 2 (2019): 135–47.
Young, Margaret M. "The Use of Functional Piano Skills by Selected Professional Musicians and Its Implications for Group Piano Curricula." Doctoral diss. unpublished, The University of Texas at Austin, 2010.
———. 'A National Survey of University-Level Group Piano Programs." *MTNA e-Journal* 7, no. 3 (2016): 13.
Zheng, Wei, Olca Surgevil, and Ronit Kark. "Dancing on the Razor's Edge: How Top-Level Women Leaders Manage the Paradoxical Tensions Between Agency and Communion." *Sex Roles* 79, no. 11 (2018): 633–50.

25
TRAINING EARLY CAREER WOMEN TEACHERS IN CHORAL LEADERSHIP
Building a Community of Practice

Rebecca Berkley

The challenge of learning to conduct a choir is finding a choir that will let you practice on them. The further challenge of learning to conduct a children's choir is finding a sufficiently established group with a director who is willing to relinquish podium time to a novice conductor. Time given to training student conductors takes time away from concert preparation, and few school choir directors have the luxury of time to let trainee (pre-service) music teachers take over their choirs for their own training. Trainee teachers need to learn their craft as choral educators whilst they study so that they arrive in the workforce with a robust skill set. Providing trainee teachers with a strong model of effective choral education is, in my view, a cornerstone of teacher training in music education. To this end, I created a children's community choir called Universal Voices at the University of Reading, UK, specifically for our trainee teachers to learn how to run a choir by running a choir as part of their teacher training. As co-director of Postgraduate Taught Programmes in Education, and the leader of the Music Education specialism degrees at both undergraduate and postgraduate levels, I have the responsibility of making meaningful developments to the curriculum and opportunities for our trainee teachers. This endeavour has been integral to my leadership practices within higher music education and teacher training programmes.

Universal Voices is a community choir for children aged 7–12 at the Institute of Education, University of Reading. Established in March 2017, Universal Voices provides two things: a free, high-quality choral education to all children in the Reading area; and an opportunity for trainee music teachers to learn how to deliver an integrated choral education programme. Universal Voices is unique among UK Higher Education Institutions (HEIs), integrating foundation-level training for novice choral conductors into our teacher training programmes. Universal Voices is open to student volunteers on our Initial Teacher Education programmes, including BA Primary[1] Education with Qualified Teacher Status, and Primary Postgraduate Certificate of Education (PGCE) and Secondary Music PGCE, as well as Music Education students on the MA Education and Doctoral programmes.

This chapter presents a reflective discussion of my initial experiences, as programme leader and tutor, of using this children's choir as a learning environment for training women trainee teachers on an undergraduate teacher training degree as choral educators. Opportunities to work with the choir are open to all trainee music teachers, and the majority demographic are women. All trainee teachers represented here identify as women. The chapter opens with a review of the kinds of leadership activities that trainee teachers undertake with the choir. There follows an appraisal of the wider context of choral leadership education for primary music teachers, noting the early career opportunities for women music teachers and the challenge of there being a lack of consistent opportunity to work regularly with experienced practitioners in primary schools. The significance of the community of practice as a way of facilitating the development of professional knowledge among trainee teachers through trial-and-error learning is discussed. The chapter concludes with a discussion on the ways that a coaching approach to teaching choral education to women trainee teachers appears to support their learning.

Choral Education Training for Undergraduate Trainee Teachers

Scenario 1: Trainee Teachers Working with Universal Voices

Children gather in the rehearsal rooms where trainee teachers are waiting to meet them. The children are split into two groups according to age. Both groups start with singing games and warm-up exercises to ensure a creative singing focus to the start of choir rehearsals. The younger children sing playground songs, focusing on group line and circle games. The older children focus more on games that develop aural memory, diction and vocalise. The children then move into their solfa musicianship classes, where they work on the National Youth Choir of Scotland Musicianship scheme.[2] Each group is taught by a team of trainee teachers, with me acting as mentor and observer and co-teacher. The final part of the rehearsal is whole-choir singing, where the children work on current repertoire for performance. The trainee teachers sing with the children. Some may conduct the choir. We finish with a short plenary game, and trainee teachers dismiss the children to parents.

Trainee primary music teachers at the University of Reading work with Universal Voices. The choir gives these trainee teachers the opportunity to experience the roles and responsibilities of being a choral educator without having to take full responsibility for the choir's success. It is a supportive mechanism for the trainee teacher which they would not be able to achieve elsewhere, and they are unlikely to meet it in their placement schools. Trainee teachers work in flexible, self-selected teams, choosing from a variety of roles. They may be front-of-house managers, engaging with parents and dealing with child safeguarding. They can be teaching assistants facilitating effective behaviour management and providing targeted learning support. They can lead warm-ups and technical vocal coaching and conduct choir repertoire in rehearsal and performance. Most importantly, trainee teachers sing with the children and teach musicianship classes which use games and practical activities to teach aural memory, singing, rhythmic awareness, pitch recognition and notation reading. The joint planning and delivery of this these activities encourages trainee teachers to develop fluency and confidence in their own classroom musicianship skills.

The Value of a Community of Practice in Choral Education for Novice Primary Music Teachers

Joining a community of practice with more experienced colleagues is essential for teachers new to choral education pedagogy,[3] and the first priority was to establish this relationship among the trainee teachers who work with Universal Voices. There is a range of prior knowledge and experience of choral singing among trainee teachers, depending on their own schooling and opportunities to join choirs when they were younger. Some have never sung in a choir when they were at school and feel nervous about singing in front of children and their peers. Learning to teach a song and conduct is a significant challenge for them. Others identify as trained singers with extensive choral experience and feel more confident to lead singing, often having had some previous experience of vocal leadership. Novice teachers need to learn from more experienced teaching musicians how to create positive learning environments for singing to flourish in the primary school,[4] which demonstrate the long-term positive effect of modelling healthy singing and strong musicianship and aural training for children.[5] Our aspiration is that trainee teachers can take this professional knowledge out to their training placements and later to their professional appointments as qualified teachers. However, the shortage of qualified music teachers in primary schools in the UK mitigates against most trainee teachers being able to observe sustained good practice in choral education on school placement. Although many Music Hubs in the UK[6] fund additional support for singing in schools, including access to specialist visiting choral educators, effective choral education does not flourish in many primary schools, being more of a participatory activity than a core part of the music curriculum. In 2012, OFSTED reported that 'standards of singing were no better than satisfactory in two thirds of the primary schools inspected. Typically, these schools viewed singing more as a participatory activity rather than as a vehicle for promoting pupils' musical understanding'.[7] Many primary teachers express a strongly negative self-perception of their ability to sing and teaching singing and feel that leading high-quality choral education is out of their reach.[8] Singing is 'done' in many primary schools, but it is not a medium for sustained musical learning.

The lived experience of trainee and early career primary teachers working in choral education is not recorded in current research. Current scholarship focuses on the expert conductor's application of conducting technique and rehearsal strategies,[9] the characteristics of vocal physiology in children,[10] and cultural and social messages in choral education.[11] Much less is said about the early learning trajectories of novice music teachers as they test their emerging professional knowledge of choral pedagogy against teaching experience in their particular school, mobilising 'representations such as textbooks, lectures and technical instruments' into professional activities like teaching and conducting.[12] Scholarship needs to focus on the learning trajectories of trainee and novice teachers to understand how trainee teachers may develop sufficient autonomy as choral educators to be able to take this learning beyond their University studies and apply it to their own teaching in other schools, and thus replicate the community of practice elsewhere.

Women in Leadership in Music in Primary Schools

In UK primary schools, music teaching and extra-curricular music activity is led by the music co-ordinator, who devises and delivers a cohesive music education programme to all pupils in the school. Often, they are the only teacher of music in the school and are responsible for teaching across year groups. They may lead a team of other teachers in the school and bring in services such as whole-class instrumental teaching from the local music hub or private instrumental and singing teachers.[13] The music co-ordinator is an advocate for music in the school, and a role model for other teachers as a musician-teacher. Peer leadership skills are a necessity for a primary music co-ordinator as they lead and train other staff to teach music, addressing the significant challenge of how to support colleagues who lack music subject knowledge and confidence but still need to teach classroom music.[14] Preparing our students to take on this peer leadership early in their careers is a key focus of our training. Giving them confidence in their practical classroom musicianship skills is especially important. Working with Universal Voices gives trainee teachers the chance to explore their peer leadership skills among themselves as a 'soft' practice for later professional requirements as a music co-ordinator. These include empathy for peers as they try out their skills as novice music teachers, forming strong social bonds so peers feel motivated to try out their emerging musical skills and listening with sympathy and offering moral and practical support as peers express their emotional response to this new learning challenge.

Taking on this kind of leadership role requires significant resilience, imagination, and entrepreneurial acumen from the early career teacher. Experience on school placement shows that our trainee music teachers take an early role as the subject specialist in their classroom, sometimes supporting fellow trainee teachers and often also the class teacher who is mentoring them when on placement. Anecdotal evidence from our alumni suggests that those who chose to be a music co-ordinator progress to middle management sooner in their careers than in other subjects, because there are fewer qualified primary music co-ordinators in the workforce compared to other curriculum subjects. There is a shortage of teachers holding music qualifications at GCSE or practical Music Grade 5 or above achieved on an instrument.[15] Only 7% of primary teachers hold an undergraduate degree in music.[16] Not surprisingly, general classroom teachers who are not trained in music lack confidence when required to teach classroom music and lead extra-curricular music activities, which has a detrimental effect on quality music education being offered in the primary curriculum in the UK.[17] As the vast majority (85%) of primary teachers are women,[18] the early career woman teacher has an opportunity for leadership in music, but a significant challenge exists in that there are a limited number of qualified role models and mentors for them to work with in schools, and patchy and inadequate funding for in-service subject and further professional education.[19] A community of practice for choral education could supply the mentoring and sponsorship by experienced choral educators that these early career women teachers need to develop positive social capital in choral education training.[20] Even better would be for newly qualified music teachers to start their professional careers in primary schools with a robust training as effective choral educators and links established to a community of practice which will sustain them in further professional development, which is the longer-term goal of Universal Voices.

Universal Voices as a Professional Learning Environment

The core aim of Universal Voices is to provide trainee teachers both everyday and longitudinal experiences of the practical and educational challenges of delivering high-quality choral education to children aged 7–12. Reflection on practice to date suggests Universal Voices is particularly valuable as a community of practice for women trainee teachers taking their first steps in leadership when their learning is constructed from their own lived experiences of being trained. These trainee teachers are taught what to do by a more able and experienced tutor who encourages risk-taking and problem solving in a safe space. They develop agency as choral educators through reflection on their own practice and peer to peer learning, which can then be tested on in professional settings in schools.

In establishing Universal Voices as a community of practice for trainee music teachers, I was influenced by the concept of situated learning through legitimate peripheral participation,[21] where a learner moves to full engagement in the sociocultural practices of a community by practising as a master to a limited degree and with only partial responsibility for the whole activity over a period of time. Peer to peer learning facilitates trainee teachers' engagement with the sociocultural norms of their community of practice and promotes a learning curriculum which supports the learner's transformation into a practitioner 'whose changing knowledge, skill and discourse are part of a developing identity'.[22] I was also influenced by Fink-Jensen

(2019), who suggests professional knowledge in music teachers develops sequentially from T1, derived from everyday lived experience and prior tacit knowledge from previous experience, which she calls personal theories at the level of practice; this leads to T2, the practitioner's everyday operational theories, which are expressions of common-sense and commonplace teaching actions informed by professional conversations with colleagues. T3 theories exist at a meta-level and are built from wider and deeper consideration of normative practices and schools of thought in education and pedagogy.[23] As trainee teachers use a prescribed conducting and musicianship pedagogy in Universal Voices rehearsals, they are operating at T1 in choir sessions and further develop discourse relating to T2 through active, critical reflection on their practice. As they travel between T1 and T2, the trainee teacher becomes aware of how to access their own singing, musicianship and conducting skills and knowledge for teaching in rehearsals and performances with the children. Trainees come to understand how to influence the learning of the children by considering how to use their musicianship skills in their teaching and taking the content of the musicianship scheme of work, or choir repertoire and converting it into taught sessions to be delivered within a given time frame.

Giving teachers time for open and honest critical self-reflection (T2) on their emerging skills (T1) is particularly important so that learners can identify what they are doing to be successful, and determine how they might address any shortcomings.[24] Encouraging reflective practice supports trainee teachers' agency by investigating their decision making and encouraging self-evaluation of the feelings and actions taken as a result.[25] Regular group planning of teaching and conducting within choir rehearsals facilitates confidence among the trainee teachers, as they are risk-taking and problem solving together in a safe space.

Scenario 2: Team Teaching Musicianship Classes

Students P and Q are working in the study room planning their musicianship class. Their focus is teaching children to read rhythms comprising crotchets (using the rhythm sound ta), pairs of quavers (using the rhythm sounds ti-ti) and crotchet rests (using the rhythm sound z). The concept of rests has been prepared in previous sessions with games and rhythm work done aurally. P and Q debate how best to introduce the concept of how a rest is written down and sort through a pile of rhythm flashcards trying to determine the best order to present the written rhythms. Student R, who is in the year above and taught this musicianship class the previous year, chips into the discussion and offers to teach P and Q a clapping game that she used to present rests. The three students practice the clapping game, and Q records it on her phone, joking, 'I'll put that in the group chat!' In the musicianship class, P and Q teach the new song and associated rhythm card reading exercise with great success, and the children later ask that the whole choir learn it as a warm-up.

Trainees particularly benefit from taking charge of their own musicianship class, making autonomous decisions about assessing children's progress and inviting me to act as mentor and inspector to check in on the effect of the teaching they are doing. The peer mentoring that has spontaneously occurred among trainee teachers in different year groups on the undergraduate programme in the second and third year of the choir has greatly contributed to their shared understanding of what works with the children, and strengthened their resilience in taking on leadership roles. Some early anecdotal evidence suggests that T3 thinking emerges as trainee teachers replicate versions of Universal Voices in their school placements and in their first jobs as qualified teachers. Further investigation on the reproduction cycle of this community practice is needed to determine what kind of choral education training women trainee teachers would need to experience in university in order for their T2 and T3 thinking to be sufficiently established to transfer robustly to other school settings.

Supporting Trainee Teachers in Taking Leadership Decisions: A Coaching Approach

Reflecting that learners may have 'different interests, make diverse contributions to activity, and hold varied viewpoints' participating 'at multiple levels' in the community of practice,[26] I determined that trainee teachers should be given opportunities to engage with a rich variety of teaching, learning and organisational activities within choir rehearsals, to share their experiences and practice between other members of the group, and to be supported in formal and informal critique of their reactions to their learning through coaching conversations. To give life to the conversations among 'the ambient community of practice'.[27] I felt that there should be at least as many, and preferably more, informal interactions between peers as formal exchanges between me as the tutor with trainee teachers. Working in teams appears to enable women trainee teachers in take ownership of their learning by verbalising these problem solving and decision-making processes (a process also discussed in Chapter 17). It also avoids an excessively tutor-led approach to choral education, which could prevent the trainee teacher from becoming independent as a choral leader.

One area that the community of practice must support is the need for trial-and-error learning. By necessity, trainee teachers must find solutions to leadership challenges by making mistakes in public in rehearsals and performances, reflecting on these mistakes and trying an alternative set of actions to resolve the problem. Completing a task even to a limited degree is useful for trainee teachers to gain a perception of what the completed task looks and feels like, and to help them appraise honestly how the decisions they have made about their own actions and behaviours as teachers have influenced the outcomes they can see in the children's learning. A coaching approach to supporting women trainee teachers to work out for themselves the solution to the problem in hand has proved effective:

Scenario 3: Making Mistakes in Public

'I don't have performance confidence', says student Z. 'I have performance anxiety, and I struggle to perform in public. I've always had it'. As the concert date approaches, Z grows increasingly anxious about the piece she is to conduct. Her peers' encouragement about mistakes not mattering does not help her. She argues back that they can do it and she can't. At the dress rehearsal, Z's body language communicates anxiety. She stands defensively on the podium. Her posture is stooped with her hands low, and one foot rests on the top of the other rather than both planted firmly on the ground. The children mirror this and sing increasingly more quietly, fluffing their cues. The dress rehearsal does not go well, and Z grows tearful. In a plenary conversation, we discuss ways of dealing with performance anxiety. Z lists her favoured techniques of deep breathing and resolves to try these again, remarking that she wants to be successful, and wishes she was braver. Backstage, her peers sing for her so she can practice her cueing sequence, and they all model the high status walking we have practised in workshops. In performance, Z hits all her targets and achieves a creditable piece of conducting.

Not surprisingly, confidence and optimism improve with positive learning experiences, especially when coupled with chances to try out the new teaching behaviours that yield positive results from the children in the choir rehearsals.[28] The peer support Student Z experienced resulted in a marked increase in confidence following the experience described here. Having proved to herself that she was able to direct the children from first learning to complete performance in concert, she felt ready to try teaching more songs and asked to try a more challenging repertoire.

Women trainee teachers seem particularly keen to avoid exposing any perceived weakness in their skill set to the rest of the group. Any community of practice has work to do to challenge the mindset that their musical skill is a previously determined fixed entity, and so they cannot improve as conductors by working with the choir when their skills seem (to them) unformed and incomplete. Any previous negative experience in choral singing or music learning seems to cast a very long shadow, convincing trainee teachers that they cannot be successful now because of an earlier inability or mistake. The T1 theories[29] of women trainee teachers in this mindset are likely to be limited by a (wrong) belief that there are fundamental limits to their capabilities as singers and conductors because they had not already learned how to do these things in their previous learning at school. It seems particularly important for these trainee teachers to be able to regard the comforts and discomforts of trying out their new conducting skills alongside their peers who are progressing at different rates with calm equanimity, in order to accept that their individual progress is measured in their journey of self-awareness as a conductor and not judge their own quality by where they see themselves in a self-created league table of their peers. However, trainee teachers must still develop a critical mass of conducting skills and competencies to be successful and will have to take responsibility to learn techniques and actions that they find difficult to master. Again, a coaching approach enables trainee teachers to address areas of perceived weakness that they may be trying to avoid addressing by challenging defensive behaviour masking feelings of inadequacy.

Scenario 4: Avoiding Teaching the Difficult Bits

Student Y is rehearsing the final section of her song, which is a three-part quodlibet. In rehearsal, group 3 loses their way, and Y focuses on revising the words, which the children already know, and does not correct the rhythmic mistakes the children are making, which are the reason the choir loses their common sense of pulse. She runs the music again, and again group 3 goes wrong. Y gets a bit tetchy with the children, remarking: 'All you need to do is remember the words'. Later in a plenary conversation, Y comments that she feels she cannot conduct the end of the piece because she 'hates that bit' at the end. Further questioning reveals that she herself cannot sing this passage accurately because she has always 'been rubbish with rhythm'. Y accepts the suggestion that she is projecting her feelings about the music onto the children, and must master the rhythm if she is to lead the performance. She agrees to think of new ways of teaching part III. Her strategies include having the accompanist record the piano part onto her phone so that she can practice demonstrating the part III line until she is fluent, and practicing conducting the final passage in the mirror so her gestures are fluent and automatic and she no longer needs to look at the music. She returns the following week feeling more positive and leads a successful rehearsal. 'Still don't like the bit at the end though', she comments wryly.

As a trained singer who'd also taken additional conducting courses, Y had previously taken the lead in instructing fellow trainee teachers and had enjoyed being an expert among her peer group. Now Y felt vulnerable because, as an experienced choral singer, she knew what was going wrong and that it was her conducting that was causing the problem. At the same time, she was rejecting the solution as it touched on the sore spot of her perceived T1 prior tacit knowledge of being 'rubbish at rhythm' as a fixed entity. I used the peer support discussed earlier to listen and acknowledge her feelings, to gently facilitate her to challenge this view and enable her to take steps to address this aspect of her classroom musicianship. Y did not want a fellow student to help her, feeling that it would be a loss of prestige among her peers, but was prepared to work with me and the professional accompanist as trusted peers who would support her in this learning without making personal judgements. Giving trainee teachers agency to be conductors and teachers and walking with them as they do this among a supportive community of practice with their peers is key to achieving Universal Voices' goals of creating an opportunity for trainee music teachers to learn how to deliver an integrated choral education programme.

Conclusion – What Might Be the Reproduction Cycle of this Community of Learning?

Universal Voices is a unique project in a UK HEI as it offers a teaching placement for choral education within the university to trainee music teachers. The community of practice that is developing around Universal Voices emphasises team teaching, reflection on professional practice and encourages sharing of successes and challenges. It is a collaborative approach to leadership education, where tutor-led training links to trial-and-error learning and peer review to encourage trainee teachers' development of personal theories of professional knowledge.

Informal feedback from trainee teachers about this mode of learning has been consistently positive. Some evidence of choral leadership from women trainee teachers is emerging as they progress along their trajectories of professional knowledge, testing the choral pedagogy learned in university on school placement. What is not yet known is what the reproduction cycle of this community of practice might be, and what factors will assist trainee music teachers in consolidating this early training into their regular professional practice. I was obliged to suspend Universal Voices rehearsals during COVID lockdown, and the academic year 21–22 was focused on re-establishing the choir and re-starting the community of practice among students. Now that the choir is functioning again, my longer-term plan is to document the early stages of the leadership journey of women trainee teachers working as choral educators into their early careers as qualified teachers. I don't yet know how long it might take for a trainee teacher to progress from describing themselves as a 'newcomer' and then a proficient 'old-timer' as a choral director[30] who feels ready to replicate the learning they experienced when working with Universal Voices as a student at the University of Reading in their daily professional life. I do feel confident that this is an effective model for training the next generation of women choral leaders in primary schools and am keen to test my hypothesis with research.

Notes

1. In the UK, primary schools are for pupils aged 5–11 and secondary schools are for pupils aged 11–18.
2. Lucinda Geoghegan and Christopher Bell, *Go for Bronze* (Edinburgh: National Youth Choir of Scotland, 2004).
3. Alexandra Lamont, Alison Daubney, and Gary Spruce, "Singing in Primary Schools: Case Studies of Good Practice in Whole Class Vocal Tuition," *British Journal of Music Education* 29, no. 2 (2012): 251–68; Peter de Vries, "Music Without a Music Specialist: A Primary School Story," *International Journal of Music Education* 33, no. 2 (2015): 210–21.
4. Zoe Greenhalgh, *Music and Singing in the Early Years* (London: Routledge, 2018); Lamont, Daubney and Spruce, 251–68.
5. Albina Cuadrado and Gabriel Rusinek, "Singing and Vocal Instruction in Primary Schools: an Analysis from Six Case Studies in Spain," *British Journal of Music Education* 33, no. 1 (2016): 110.

6. In the UK, Music Hubs are groups of music organisations that co-ordinate to provide music services in schools. Each Music Hub must have a vocal strategy for a local area, which includes supporting the development of singing and choral education in the schools within the catchment area of that Music Hub. Arts Council England. *Music Education Hubs*, April 2019, accessed June 1, 2020, www.artscouncil.org.uk/music-education/music-education-hubs.
7. Office for Standards in Education. *Music in Schools: Wider Still, and Wider* (2012): 12, accessed June 1, 2020, www.gov.uk/government/publications/music-in-schools. This report collated evidence from 194 specialist music inspections and good practice visits in schools between 2008 and 2011.
8. Cuadrado and Rusinek (2016); Nicola Swain and Sally Bodkin-Allen, "Can't sing? Won't Sing? Asteraroa/New Zealand 'Tone-deaf' Early Childhood Teachers' Musical Beliefs," *British Journal of Music Education* 31, no. 3 (2014): 245–63; Sarah Hennessy, "Approaches to Increasing the Competence and Confidence of Student Teachers to Teach Music in Primary Schools," *International Journal of Primary, Elementary and Early Years Education* 45, no. 6 (2017): 689–700; Benjamin Thorn and Inga Brasche, "Musical Experience and Confidence of Pre-service Primary Teachers," *Australian Journal of Music Education* 2 (2015): 191–203.
9. Alan Gumm, "Choral Music Pedagogy: A Survey of How ACDA Members Rehearse and Conduct," *The Choral Journal* 56, no. 10 (2016): 85–93; Brenda Smith and Robert Sataloff, *Choral Pedagogy*, 3rd ed. (Plural Publishing Inc., 2013), https://ebookcentral.proquest.com; Janet Wyvill, "The Expert Australian Choral Conductor: Education or Experience? A Longitudinal Case Study Research Project Investigating Choral Conducting Expertise in Australia," *Australian Journal of Music Education* 3 (2015): 93–97.
10. James Daugherty, Jeremy Manternach, and Kathy Price, "Student Voice Use and Vocal Health During an All-state Choral Event," *Journal of Research in Music Education* 58, no. 4 (2011): 346–67; David M. Howard, Christopher Barlow, John Szymanski, and Graham F. Welch, "Vocal Production and Listener Perception of Trained English Cathedral Girl and Boy Choristers," *Bulletin of the Council for Research in Music Education* 147 (2001): 81–86; Desmond Sargeant and Graham Welch, "Age-related Changes in Long-term Average Spectra of Children's Voices," *Journal of Voice* 22, no. 6 (2008): 658–70; Graham Welch, "Singing and Vocal Development," in *The Child as Musician: A Handbook of Musical Development*, edited by Gary E. McPherson (Oxford: Oxford University Press, 2015), 81–86; Jenevora Williams, *Teaching Singing to Children and Young Adults* (Oxford: Compton Publishing, 2013).
11. Sarah J. Bartolome, *World Music Pedagogy: Choral Music Education*, Vol. 5 (London: Routledge, 2019); Nicholas McBride, "Critical Moments: Gay Male Choral Directors and the Taking Up of Gender Discourse," *Bulletin of the Council for Research in Music Education* 207–08 (2016): 63–79; Julia T. Shaw, "The Music I Was Meant to Sing: Adolescent Choral Students' Perceptions of Culturally Responsive Pedagogy," *Journal of Research in Music Education* 64, no. 1 (2016): 45–70; Jason M. Silveira, "Perspectives of a Transgender Music Education Student," *Journal of Research in Music Education* 66, no. 4 (2019): 428–48; Hyesoo Yoo, "Multicultural Choral Music Pedagogy Based on the Facets Model," *Music Educator's Journal* 104, no. 1 (2017): 34–39.
12. Jens-Christian Smeby, "The Significance of Professional Education," in *Professional Learning in the Knowledge Society*, edited by David W. Livingstone, David Guile, and Karen Jensen (Rotterdam: Sense Publishers, 2012), 52.
13. Nick Beach, Julie Evans, and Gary Spruce, *Making Music in the Primary School: Whole Class Instrumental and Vocal Teaching* (London: Routledge, 2011).
14. Michele Biasutti, Sarah Hennessy, and Ellen de Vugt-Jansen, "Confidence Development in Non-music Specialist Trainee Primary Teachers after an Intensive Programme," *British Journal of Music Education* 32, no. 2 (2015): 144; Pamela Burnard and Regina Murphy, *Teaching Music Creatively* (Abingdon: Routledge, 2017); Patrick Jones and Christine Robson, *Teaching Music in Primary Schools* (Exeter: Learning Matters, 2008)
15. General Certificate of School Education (GCSE) is the 16 plus school exam taken at the end of year 11 of schooling in the UK. Grade 5 practical music is an instrumental or vocal exam offered by one of the Music Exam Boards, such as the Associated Board of the Royal Schools of Music. These qualifications sit at level 2 of the UK National Framework for Qualifications Gov.uk. *What Qualification Levels Mean*, (n.d.), accessed June 1, 2020, www.gov.uk/what-different-qualification-levels-mean/compare-different-qualification-levels; and level 3 of the European Qualifications Framework Ec.europa.eu. *Learning Opportunities and Qualifications in Europe*, n.d., April 2019, accessed June 1, 2020, https://ec.europa.eu/ploteus/search/site?f%5B0%5D=im_field_entity_type%3A97.

16. Department for Education, *School Leadership 2010–2016: Characteristics and Trends*, 2018 (March 2019), accessed June 1, 2020, www.gov.uk/government/publications/school-leadership-2010-to-2016-characteristics-and-trends; – *Statistics on the size and charatacteristics of the schools' workforce in state-funded schools*. 2018 (March 2019), accessed June 1, 2020, www.gov.uk/government/collections/statistics-school-workforce.
17. All-Party Parliamentary Group for Music Education, the Incorporated Society of Musicians and the University of Sussex. *Music Education: State of the Nation*, edited by Alison Daubney and Gary Spruce, (January 2019), accessed June 1, 2020, www.ism.org/images/images/State-of-the-Nation-Music-Education-WEB.pdf; Biasutti, Hennessy and de Vugt-Jansen (2015); Hennessy (2015) "Approaches to Increasing the Competence and Confidence of Student Teachers to Teach Music in Primary Schools"; – "Overcoming the Red-feeling: The Development of Confidence to Teach Music in Primary School Amongst Student Teachers," *British Journal of Music Education* 17, no. 2 (2000): 183–96; Hilary Holden and Stuart Button, "The Teaching of Music in the Primary School by the Non-music Specialist," *British Journal of Music Education*, 23, no. 1 (2006): 23–38; Janet Mills, "The Generalist Primary Teacher of Music: A Problem of Confidence to Teach Music," *Bulletin Council for Research in Music Education* 6, no. 2 (1989): 125–38; Thorn and Brasche (2015).
18. Organisation for Economic Co-operation and Development. *Distribution of teachers by age and gender*. (2016), accessed June 1, 2020, https://stats.oecd.org/Index.aspx?datasetcode=EAG_PERS_SHARE_AGE.
19. Sarah Hennessy, "Closing the GaThe Generalist Teachers' Role in Music Education," in *European Perspectives on Music Education*, edited by Adri de Vugt and Isolde Mamlberg, Vol. 2 (Innsbruck: CPI Moravia Books, 2013); Incorporated Society of Musicians. *Consultation on the Future of Music Education*. (2018), accessed June 1, 2020, www.ism.org/images/images/Future-of-Music-Education-ISM-report-December-2018.pdf.
20. Jennifer L. Martin, *Women as Leaders in Education: Succeeding Despite Inequity, Discrimination, and Other Challenges* (Westport, CT: ABC-CLIO, LLC, 2011).
21. Jean Lave and Etienne Wenger, *Situated Learning: Legitimate Peripheral Participation* (New York: Cambridge University Press, 1991).
22. Lave and Wenger, *Situated Learning*, 122.
23. Kirsten Fink-Jensen, "Astonishing Practices: A Teaching Strategy in Music Teacher Education," in *Professional Knowledge in Music Teacher Education*, edited by Eva Georgii-Hemming, Pamela Burnard, and Sven-Erik Holgersen (London: Routledge, 2019), 143.
24. Biasutti, Hennessy and de Vugt-Jansen (2015); Richard Colwell, "Professional Development Residency Programme," *Quarterly Journal of Music Teaching and Learning* 7, no. 2–4 (1996/1997): 76–90; Lynne Rogers, Susan Hallam, Andrea Creech, and Costanza Preti, "Learning About What Constitutes Effective Training from a Pilot Programme to Improve Music Education in Primary Schools," *Music Education Research* 10, no. 4 (2008): 485–97; Deidre Russell-Bowie, "Mission Impossible or Possible Mission? Changing Confidence and Attitudes of Primary Preservice Music Education Students Using Kolb's Experiential Learning Theory," *Australian Journal of Music Education* 2 (2013): 46–63; Maria Varvarigou, Andrea Creech, and Susan Hallam, "Benefits of Continuing Professional Development (CPD) Programmes in Music for KS2 (Primary) Teachers Through the Example of the London Symphony Orchestra (LSO) On Track Programme," *Music Education Research* 14, no. 2 (2012): 149–69.
25. Catherine Beauchamp, "Reflection in Teacher Education: Issues Emerging from a Review of Current Literature," *Reflective Practice* 16, no. 1 (2014): 123–41; Donald Schön, *Educating the Reflective Practitioner: Toward a New Design for Teaching and Learning in the Professions* (San Francisco, CA: Jossey-Bass, 1987); – *The Reflective Practitioner* (New York: Basic Books, 1983).
26. Lave and Wenger, *Situated Learning*, 98
27. Ibid., 100.
28. Thorn and Brasche, Musical Experience, (2015)
29. Fink-Jensen, "Astonishing Practises," 143.
30. Lave and Wenger, *Situated Learning*, 57ff.

Bibliography

All-Party Parliamentary Group for Music Education, the Incorporated Society of Musicians and the University of Sussex. *Music Education: State of the Nation*, edited by Alison Daubney and Gary Spruce

(2019). Accessed June 1, 2020. www.ism.org/images/images/State-of-the-Nation-Music-Education-WEB.pdf.

Arts Council England. *Music Education Hubs*, April 2019. Accessed June 1, 2020. www.artscouncil.org.uk/music-education/music-education-hubs.

Bartolome, Sarah J. *World Music Pedagogy: Choral Music Education*, Vol. 5. London: Routledge, 2019.

Beach, Nick, Julie Evans, and Gary Spruce. *Making Music in the Primary School: Whole Class Instrumental and Vocal Teaching*. London: Routledge, 2011.

Beauchamp, Catherine. "Reflection in Teacher Education: Issues Emerging from a Review of Current Literature."*Reflective Practice* 16, no. 1 (2014): 123–41.

Biasutti, Michele, Sarah Hennessy, and Ellen de Vugt-Jansen. "Confidence Development in Non-Music Specialist Trainee Primary Teachers after an Intensive Programme."*British Journal of Music Education* 32, no. 2 (2015): 143–61.

Burnard, Pamela, and Regina Murphy. *Teaching Music Creatively*. Abingdon: Routledge, 2017.

Colwell, Richard. "Professional Development Residency Programme."*Quarterly Journal of Music Teaching and Learning* 7, no. 2–4 (1996/1997): 76–90.

Cuadrado, Albina, and Gabriel Rusinek. "Singing and Vocal Instruction in Primary Schools: An Analysis from Six Case Studies in Spain."*British Journal of Music Education* 33, no. 1 (2016): 101–15.

Daugherty, James, Jeremy Manternach, and Kathy Price. "Student Voice Use and Vocal Health During an All-State Choral Event."*Journal of Research in Music Education* 58, no. 4 (2011): 346–67.

Department for Education. *School Leadership 2010–2016: Characteristics and Trends* 2018, March 2019. Accessed June 1, 2020. www.gov.uk/government/publications/school-leadership-2010-to-2016-characteristics-and-trends.

———. *Statistics on the Size and Characteristics of the Schools' Workforce In State-Funded Schools 2018*, March 2019. Accessed June 1, 2020. www.gov.uk/government/collections/statistics-school-workforce.

de Vries, Peter. "Music Without a Music Specialist: A Primary School Story."*International Journal of Music Education* 33, no.2 (2015): 210–21.

Ec.europa.eu. *Learning Opportunities and Qualifications in Europe*, April 2019. Accessed June 1, 2020. https://ec.europa.eu/ploteus/search/site?f%5B0%5D=im_field_entity_type%3A97.

Fink-Jensen, Kirsten. "Astonishing Practices: A Teaching Strategy in Music Teacher Education." In *Professional Knowledge in Music Teacher Education*, edited by Eva Georgii-Hemming, Pamela Burnard, and Sven-Erik Holgersen, 139–55. London: Routledge, 2019.

Geoghegan, Lucinda, and Christopher Bell. *Go for Bronze*. Edinburgh: National Youth Choir of Scotland, 2004.

Gov.uk. (n.d.). *What Qualification Levels Mean*. Accessed June 1, 2020. www.gov.uk/what-different-qualification-levels-mean/compare-different-qualification-levels.

Greenhalgh, Zoe. *Music and Singing in the Early Years*. London: Routledge, 2018.

Gumm, Alan. "Choral Music Pedagogy: A Survey of How ACDA Members Rehearse and Conduct." *The Choral Journal* 56, no. 10 (2016): 85–93.

Hennessy, Sarah. 'Overcoming the Red-Feeling: The Development of Confidence to Teach Music in Primary School Amongst Student Teachers." *British Journal of Music Education* 17, no. 2 (2000): 183–96.

———. "Closing the Gap. The Generalist Teachers' Role in Music Education." In *European Perspectives on Music Education*, edited by Adri de Vugt and Isolde Mamlberg, Vol. 2. Innsbruck: CPI Moravia Books, 2013.

———. "Approaches to Increasing the Competence and Confidence of Student Teachers to Teach Music in Primary Schools." *International Journal of Primary, Elementary and Early Years Education* 45, no. 6 (2017): 689–700.

Holden, Hilary, and Stuart Button. "The Teaching of Music in the Primary School by the Non-Music Specialist." *British Journal of Music Education* 23, no. 1 (2006): 23–38.

Howard, David M., et al. "Vocal Production and Listener Perception of Trained English Cathedral Girl and Boy Choristers." *Bulletin of the Council for Research in Music Education* 147 (2001): 81–86.

Incorporated Society of Musicians. *Consultation on the Future of Music Education* (2018). www.ism.org/images/images/Future-of-Music-Education-ISM-report-December-2018.pdf.

Jones, Patrick, and Christine Robson. *Teaching Music in Primary Schools*. Exeter: Learning Matters, 2008.

Lamont, Alexandra, Alison Daubney, and Gary Spruce. "Singing in Primary Schools: Case Studies of Good Practice in Whole Class Vocal Tuition." *British Journal of Music Education* 29, no. 2 (2012): 251–68.
Lave, Jean, and Etienne Wenger. *Situated Learning: Legitimate Peripheral Participation*. New York: Cambridge University Press, 1991.
Martin, Jennifer L. *Women as Leaders in Education: Succeeding Despite Inequity, Discrimination, and Other Challenges*. Westport, CT: ABC-CLIO, LLC, 2011.
McBride, Nicholas. "Critical Moments: Gay Male Choral Directors and the Taking Up of Gender Discourse." *Bulletin of the Council for Research in Music Education* 207–8 (2016): 63–79.
Mills, Janet. "The Generalist Primary Teacher of Music: A Problem of Confidence to Teach Music." *Bulletin Council for Research in Music Education* 6, no. 2 (1989): 125–38.
Office for Standards in Education, *Music in Schools: Wider Still, and Wider* (2012). Accessed June 1, 2020. www.gov.uk/government/publications/music-in-schools.
Organisation for Economic Co-operation and Development. *Distribution of Teachers by Age and Gender*, 2016. Accessed June 1, 2020. https://stats.oecd.org/Index.aspx?datasetcode=EAG_PERS_SHARE_AGE.
Rogers, Lynne, et al. "Learning About What Constitutes Effective Training from a Pilot Programme to Improve Music Education in Primary Schools." *Music Education Research* 10, no. 4 (2008): 485–97.
Russell-Bowie, Deidre. "Mission Impossible or Possible Mission? Changing Confidence and Attitudes of Primary Preservice Music Education Students Using Kolb's Experiential Learning Theory." *Australian Journal of Music Education* 2 (2013): 46–63.
Sargeant, Desmond, and Graham Welch. "Age-Related Changes in Long-term Average Spectra of Children's Voices." *Journal of Voice* 22, no. 6 (2008): 658–70.
Schön, Donald. *The Reflective Practitioner*. New York: Basic Books, 1983.
———. *Educating the Reflective Practitioner: Toward a New Design for Teaching and Learning in the Professions*. San Francisco, CA: Jossey-Bass, 1987.
Shaw, Julia T. "The Music I Was Meant to Sing: Adolescent Choral Students' Perceptions of Culturally Responsive Pedagogy." *Journal of Research in Music Education* 64, no. 1 (2016): 45–70.
Silveira, Jason M. "Perspectives of a Transgender Music Education Student." *Journal of Research in Music Education* 66, no. 4 (2019): 428–48.
Smeby, Jens-Christian. "The Significance of Professional Education." In *Professional Learning in the Knowledge Society*, edited by David W. Livingstone, David Guile, and Karen Jensen, 49–68. Rotterdam: Sense Publishers, 2012.
Smith, Brenda, and Robert Sataloff, *Choral Pedagogy*, 3rd ed. San Diego: Plural Publishing Inc., 2013.
Swain, Nicola, and Sally Bodkin-Allen. "Can't Sing? Won't Sing? Asteraroa/New Zealand 'Tone-Deaf' Early Childhood Teachers' Musical Beliefs." *British Journal of Music Education* 31, no. 3 (2014): 245–63.
Thorn, Benjamin, and Inga Brasche. "Musical Experience and Confidence of Pre-Service Primary Teachers." *Australian Journal of Music Education* 2 (2015): 191–203.
Varvarigou, Maria, Andrea Creech, and Susan Hallam. "Benefits of Continuing Professional Development (CPD) Programmes in Music for KS2 (Primary) Teachers Through the Example of the London Symphony Orchestra (LSO) on Track Programme." *Music Education Research* 14, no. 2 (2012): 149–69.
Welch, Graham. "Singing and Vocal Development." In *The Child as Musician: A Handbook of Musical Development*, edited by Gary E. McPherson, 81–86. Oxford: Oxford University Press, 2015.
Williams, Jenevora. *Teaching Singing to Children and Young Adults*. Oxford: Compton Publishing, 2013.
Wyvill, Janet. "The Expert Australian Choral Conductor: Education or Experience? A Longitudinal Case Study Research Project Investigating Choral Conducting Expertise in Australia." *Australian Journal of Music Education* 3 (2015): 93–97.
Yoo, Hyesoo. "Multicultural Choral Music Pedagogy Based on the Facets Model." *Music Educator's Journal* 104, no. 1 (2017): 34–39.

PART IV

Performance and the Music Industries

Performance and the Music Industries: An Introduction

Laura Hamer and Helen Julia Minors

Part IV is distinct in the book as it offers fewer chapters, but each is on a different scale. The first two are co-authored sharing a multi-voiced experience in industry, and to give space for these voices and issues to be explored, these chapters are longer in length. The part also includes interviews with opera companies, overviews of programming festivals and artist profiles. As such, each chapter is longer (in some cases much longer), includes specific lived experiences, tables of details, figures to illustrate points, data and multiple cited voices to share the range of experiences in these industries. Examples are drawn from Italy, Paraguay, UK and USA.

The part examines a broad range of issues concerning women in the music industries, including issues of access, mentoring, maternity leave, language, the lack of diversity in ethnic representation, consumerism, programming, curricula advocacy, indigenous language and voices from those long in the music industries, all sharing a key issue: that of advocacy for change.

The music industries are perhaps the most public-facing issue in the book. We all hear music, experience it on TV and radio, hear it as we shop and socialise; we are all aware of social media, celebrity culture and hear about the music festivals and chart successes. But the lived experience of women working in the music industries is often unseen. The public see the shiny final events, which are polished, edited and broadcast/streamed/distributed. What are the experiences of women in these industries? This part tackles this question. Although it offers 6 chapters, they all are pitched in particular ways to share the voices of this experience with evidence, whether it be personal or data-led.

The first two chapters are co-authored in order to share that multi-voiced experience. Chapter 26 is led by the editors of this volume, but includes the voices of 7 other women who are leading change in the music industries within the UK. Through discussions led by some initial guiding questions (outlined in the chapter), these women share their experiences and thoughts on grassroots change, mentoring and coaching, maternity leave and support policies, language and advocacy. These 9 voices intersperse in a conversational chapter which is substantial in scale to allow for this rich experience of diversity in role, age, experience, background, ethnicity, faith and sexuality (among other things) to be given freely and shared

DOI: 10.4324/9781003024767-29

here. It is followed by Chapter 27, which is coauthored by Rebekah E. Moore and three of her graduates, Elizabeth Markow, Allison Gurland, and Shannon Pires, to chart their experience on placements and internships during their degree studies. Unique to this chapter is the advice and suggestions the three graduates give following their experience in the USA music industries, first as interns, now as colleagues continuing to work in those industries. Moore offers a reflection which calls for change in education to support the pipeline into industry.

The next two chapters give examples of specific issues in the music industries, which are relevant internationally though here they show specific case studies. In Chapter 28, Elizabeth Etches Jones gives specific data-led examples of opera companies, including interviews and precise activity examples, to chart executive decision making and opera culture situated within a need to balance innovation alongside consumerism. Etches Jones gives insightful insights into the work of Silent Opera, Opera Shack, Black Cat, PopUp Opera, Mahogany Opera Group and Swap'ra, among others, illustrating opera activity in the UK, beyond the larger national opera culture. Chapter 29, by Valentina Bertolani and Luisa Santacesaria, looks at Italian music programming, using data analysis to chart the context of Milan in 2019, pre-Covid19. As with the other chapter, the research is time-consuming and longitudinal, relying on at least the expanse of a full calendar year to collect data and experience before analysis.

To end this part, we include Jenni Roditi, author of an artist biography and reflection in Chapter 30. Roditi had one of the keynote addresses for the International Conference on Women in/and Musical Leadership in 2019, which developed into this volume. We felt it was important to share an example of lived experience which charts music education into music composition, performance improvisation into wellbeing, care and new innovations from the UK, outwards with performances, influences and experience much more widely. As such, like coauthored chapters, this requires space, figures to illustrate the activities and many references to the experience to reveal the lessons learnt, the changes undertaken and the advice this exceptional musician can share.

Chapters 26, 27, and 30 are autoethnographic. The 'I' is significant and is given freely to share the experience. As in all autoethnography, the experiences are shared with details of the culture and the context, and reflections are given with hindsight. All these voices continue to work within the music industries they are talking about here.

Many of the issues introduced within Part VI – particularly the importance of mentors, role models and ensuring women are represented across the music industry – are strongly shared with Part III, in relation to education innovations and issues present within Part VI exploring advocacy and activism. The overlap is intentional. The music industries' activities rely on a pipeline from education into the field, and the work that is done speaks to much wider, often global, audiences.

26
WOMEN'S MUSICAL LEADERSHIP IN MUSIC INDUSTRIES AND EDUCATION

Laura Hamer and Helen Julia Minors,
with Alice Farnham, Katy Hamilton, Emma Haughton,
Jessy McCabe, Sarah MacDonald, Davina Vencatasamy
and Eleanor Wilson

This chapter seeks to bring together a selection of variously experienced women musical leaders in dialogue with the explicit aim of discussing some of the crucial questions regarding the barriers affecting women in the music industries (in the broadest sense) and music education and the opportunities for development and support. Ultimately, we advocate for and give examples of the changes which need to be made to ensure wider access for women, retain women staff throughout their careers (not only at the intern and early career stages), and maintain progression opportunities within all sectors of the industry. This is a collectively voiced chapter, and the first of two in this part to ensure we share not only single case studies, but that we communicate experiences, debate issues, and offer suggestions, advice, and examples of the ways of making change happen.

Why are we doing this? The dialogue will, and does, bring out diverse experiences, at times contradictory opinions, and different resolutions to problematic situations, and as such it reveals that there are many ways of developing equality and equity in practice; that the right way is to make those changes, but how they are made is dependent upon the context and specific part of the industry. What is the point? By bringing these different experiences – encompassing teaching, creative direction, conducting, composing, work within music therapy, performing, criticism, and broadcasting – together, we hope to share solutions, advice, and to offer ideas for developing a sustained environment which is accessible to all, which is inclusive and diversity-friendly, aware, and active. It facilitates the voices of women across the generations, across sectors of the music industries and education and across genres/styles. But it shows a shared aim: for those women who have gained and maintained access and success in the industry, they/we wish to open the door, smash the glass ceiling, and remove the glass cliff[1] to enable others to follow. In essence, we share the call to advocacy which is further developed in Part VI. By creating a conversation chapter (one of a few in the book; see also Chapters 27, 45, and 46) within such a large volume of essays, we hope to show that the varied issues are relevant to a broad range of careers within the wider global music industry. We take a conversation from the UK to offer a shared cultural, contemporary experience. The collection of voices we present here represents diverse ages and career stages and years of experience (from colleagues in their early careers to senior leaders with over four decades in the industry), diverse races, faiths, sexualities, carers and non-carers, and different abilities (including neurodiversity). The unifying features are that we all identify as women working within at least one area of the music industry (though some of us work across several), and we were all based within the UK at the time of writing.

The approach we (Helen and Laura) have taken to developing this chapter has been to construct a structured set of questions which we put to all the participants in conversation. The conversations were recorded via MS Teams and then transcribed. Some conversations were held with Hamer and Minors and the individual (as in the case with Hamilton, McCabe, and Vencatasamy) and some were held in a larger online discussion (with Farnham, Haughton, MacDonald, and Wilson). As such, and as we will show here, there was opportunity to share advice and experiences in a responsive approach; in some instances, colleagues refer to each other in their discussions, showing the collective nature of the work, the aims, and the shared recognition that support of others is needed. It is important to note that the questions were presented as a stimulus but were not used to restrict the conversation. In what follows we present the voices of our participants in italics and accredit each by first name (as also done in Chapter 45). We do this to be authentic; colleagues speaking to each other in the UK usually use first names, whereas in citing published sources we have stuck to the tradition of using surnames. We accredit each voice for authenticity and to ensure experiences can be linked to their specific contextual experience. Moreover, this helps us, as researchers, in avoiding unnecessarily appropriating or modifying the discussion from our positionality. The varied positions we hold and experiences we have are what makes this conversation significant for this volume. The aim is to represent authentic lived experiences in an honest and open manner.[2] The 'I' of the insider is important here, as it is throughout the book where experiential and/or autoethnographic approaches have been taken.

First, we outline the nature of the questions we asked in Table 26.1; second, we offer an overview of the careers of our participants; and then we move into a multi-part discussion of the core issues, concerning: grass-roots leadership; mentoring and coaching with reference to all-women training; representation in the curriculum; programming key performance indicators (KPIs) of institutions and beyond; caring and support needs, with specific reference to maternity leave; and language and tone.

We began with some broad questions to spark debate, focusing on defining terms and teasing out the issues. In asking, 'What does leadership look like now?', we are trying to draw out the fact that leadership changes over time by necessity of the situation, but also due to our individual experience, confidence development, resilience, and changing status within work. Comparing this with a contextual look at 'What does musical leadership look like now?' encourages us to consider how leadership is changing around us and reminds us that leadership changes in government impact all aspects of the music industries and education due to policy and legislation changes. The only stable factor is change. As such, we look at some of the differences before exploring what musical leadership (in its broadest sense) could/might look like now and in the future.

As this book demonstrates throughout the range of topics and issues covered – and as defined in Chapter 1 – musical leadership has a wide range of definitions. But what does it mean for us personally?

> *I mean, leadership now I would say still looks very white and male overall, when you are thinking about politics. Especially at the moment, when you are thinking about people in power; who are the people that are informing and making decisions on our behalf?* (Ellie)
>
> *At the moment, it feels like the idea of leadership is beginning to broaden, so it was a very narrow thing. As more women and people from more diverse backgrounds*

Table 26.1 Initial Questions to Spark Debate

Introductory Questions:
1. What does leadership look like now?
2. What does musical leadership look like now?
3. What are the differences?
4. What could/should it (musical leadership) look like?

Broad Area/Topics for Discussion:
These questions and issues are intended as a starting point for debate. We hope that this will then evolve naturally into a conversation which draws upon our diverse perspectives:
1. How important is it for women to have other women as role models and mentors?
2. Women-only training: how important is this? Does it create a safe/safer space for women? Or does it reinforce barriers and boundaries, propagating gender stereotypes?
3. Female leadership: is this inherently different to male leadership? What is the evidence?
4. Should female leadership embrace (or celebrate) supposedly 'feminine' qualities/characteristics, e.g. nurturing, team-working?
5. Should KPI (Key Performance Indicators) be used to force the music industry to develop 50/50 representation, as seen at festivals?
6. If gender is pushed, are we ignoring other issues, such as race?
7. Music Education: what about syllabus content, assessment strategies, mentorship, etc.?

And Finally:
We would like to end the discussion by asking you all:
1. What are the most pertinent issues facing women in musical leadership today?

---

hopefully come into it, I think it is beginning very, very slowly to change, and I think until we kind of really acknowledge that leadership doesn't need to be a dictatorship . . . that's always going to be the issue. (Alice)

I wonder if there is a split . . . I had a think about this, and I wonder if there is a split between women and leadership within the education sector, and women and leadership in the broader professional sector? (Emma)

I think leadership, at the moment, is being shown by grassroots individuals [and collectives; see also Part VI] *who are making enormous changes, but then organisations, which are already in power, not necessarily recognising the significance of their actions in leading, to even the statements that they make about it.* (Jessy)

As Davina observed, the recent changes and rapid changes in government in the UK post the Covid19 lockdowns (notably with three UK prime ministers in post at different points throughout 2022, a new Scottish First Minister in 2023, and a new Welsh First Minister in 2024) have seen *immediate* and reactionary *leadership races* which have caused some major *shifts* in notions of what leadership looks like. Davina continues: *I think generally leadership is about being kind, and going to a goal, growth . . . a kind of emergence* (Davina). The context here for Davina shows that leadership needs to be both reactionary and proactive, but in addition, it needs a direction that is, in ideal terms, supportive of those following such leadership, and supportive of the overarching goals of each industry, sector, institution, activity, collective, and so on. We (Helen and Laura) have defined musical leadership:

as a concept which incorporates the roles musicians, in practice, take not only as conductors and musical directors, rather encompassing all leadership activity, all musicking activity, from project managing events, to leading workshops and lessons, to managing charities and networks, to leading change on the ground in small-scale projects; to leading instrumental ensembles, to leading sales and marketing, outreach work, to leading advocacy and activism activity.[3]

Essentially, by asking questions of leadership, linked to gender, we must ask ourselves: is women's leadership – or leadership by anyone identifying as a woman, non-binary, trans, gender expansive – inherently different to male leadership (arguably seen as 'traditional' leadership)? What is the evidence? And if we think, feel, and have evidence of a difference, should women's leadership embrace (or celebrate) supposedly 'feminine' qualities and characteristics, e.g. is a woman leader perceived as, acting as, and presenting as nurturing and team-working? Of course, these labels are restrictive and stereotypical, but what this conversation has revealed is the extent to which stereotypes have informed feedback women in leadership receive and are subjected to. There is *still this remnant that women should have the nurturing roles* (Sarah). Should KPIs (Key Performance Indicators) be used to force the music industries to develop 50/50 representation,[4] as seen with activism at some music festivals? If gender is pushed, are we ignoring other issues, such as race? Whatever we look to resolve, we must all reflect and enact change with an awareness of the intersectionality of our approach. To resolve one issue, we need to name it, but not at the expense of another. As such, music education should indeed diversify and decolonise its curriculum, ensure inclusive assessment strategies, and foster mentorship (see also Part III).

Our participants consist of seven women working within the music industries and/or education. Each has a mixture of roles within the industry and within the work they do as freelancers and as advocates. In their own words, they summarise their roles at the time of the recorded conversation. Jessy McCabe: *I am a SEND* [Special Educational Needs and Disabilities] *teacher*. Sarah MacDonald: *I am a choral conductor and composer and organist. I am Director of Music at Selwyn College, Cambridge and of the Girl Choristers at Ely Cathedral*. Alice Farnham: *I am a conductor, and I am the Artistic Director of Women Conductors with the Royal Philharmonic Society, Perth Symphony Orchestra Women on the Podium, and the Female Conductor programme in Dublin National Concert Hall from 2017–2022*. Katy Hamilton: *I am a researcher, a writer, and a musician*. Emma Haughton: *I am a fully funded Music PhD student, a freelance musician, and I conduct the Junior, Intermediate, and Senior Wind Orchestras at Sefton Music Service in North Liverpool. In the past I have led other Wind and Jazz ensembles in (less well resourced) high schools*. Davina Vencatasamy: *I am a music therapist, teacher, woman, mother. I am an EDI advocate and activist. I am also a researcher. I have been working in SEN and Mental Health settings with a wide range of client groups*. Eleanor (Ellie) Wilson: *I am General Manager of NMC Recordings* [since this recording, Ellie has moved upwards to be the Creative Director]. *If you don't know much about NMC, we are a registered charity that releases recordings by mainly living British and Irish composers and we have been going for thirty years. I have worked in the record industry since I left university, but I also have a sideline in other things. I also compose and I am a violinist*. What this shows is that although each has a defined role, e.g., director or teacher, there's much more going on in the professional lives of musicians. Each of us, the editors included, wear many hats, and each of us support advocacy activities and charity work by giving voluntary labour beyond that of our roles. As such, many of our comments come from a broad range of experiences within and beyond our employed and freelance roles.

Grass-Roots Leadership and Advocacy

If we could move to the next stage of our leadership development, we could move to an understanding of leadership as adaptive, supportive, faciliatory, and empathetic. Or, as Alice muses in the quote cited earlier, *until we kind of really acknowledge that leadership doesn't need to be a dictatorship* (Alice). Think of the possibilities. By leading from the ground up, in other words by people making changes in their areas without the need for a high-status decree or an invitation to make a change, the change is authentic and grown from a need and developed in collaboration, often in small local practices. Change takes time, as Ellie observes:

It just takes a long time, doesn't it . . . I mean, Alice, you would be in a better situation probably than me, but I am thinking about the recording industry . . . I know, looking at NMC's catalogue, we've probably got maybe three or five women conductors in the whole of our catalogue.[5] We have works by over 100 women composers on NMC. Representation is about 25% across the whole catalogue. Now you know we are a contemporary label and more likely possibly to have more women. I would be interested to see how that reflects across the industry? But I think until people can see those names on a daily basis when they are buying music, because it might be that they are not buying it because of the conductor, they are buying because of the composer that they want to hear or the orchestra or whatever. You know that kind of familiarity, you know it needs to be instilled in people's brains.

(Ellie)

Familiarity, recognition, and awareness that women can be and are active in all aspects of the music industry is something which is not widely known or discussed publicly. By making change in our respective roles, we lead change to help the next generations. Representation is key – the next generation needs to see themselves represented as role models. As Alice outlines:

I mean one of the things that I felt was important to do six years ago, and I still continue to do, is give it a push, give it a kick from the bottom up. Running these workshops and encouraging more women into [conducting]. There were a couple of things actually that Ellie said about it taking a long time . . . I completely agree with this, because I think it does take a really long time. But what was happening before that, well, from 1993 when I graduated to 2013, in those twenty years nothing had happened; nothing had really changed. So then I thought okay, it is no good just saying 'Oh, in time it will change'; we have to do something! That's very important. But then don't do it too quickly, and I have to be very careful about how I word this because . . . I think there have been some very good appointments of some fabulous conductors, but I think there has been a little bit of a knee-jerk reaction in the conducting world to appoint women when they are maybe not quite ready. And they make lots and lots of noise, the media gets very excited about it, so people think that there are women conductors all over the place because they get so much more attention than the men, which is not particularly fair on the men sometimes. But also, it feels knee-jerk . . . When you compare it to five, six years ago, how few women there were around, I don't think this journey should have only taken six years; I think it should take longer and it needs to be a much slower burn.

(Alice)

Essentially, the key issue here is that for change to be sustained and maintained, it needs time, investment, resources, and proper strategic planning. A knee-jerk reaction, as Alice outlines, might be momentary, or it might instil another barrier or a new imbalance. As others have also said, change will take more than time. Skolnik calls for a revolution but is very aware that: 'To change those institutions, there must be concurrent pressure both within and without'.[6]

The slow burn is necessary; meaningful change, which results in permanent change for the better, needs to be embedded into industry practice and be recognised for its benefits. To embed practice, it needs institutional policies and sometimes legislative policy at the national level (in other instances, both inside and outside an organisation, as Skolnik notes). Ticking a box one day is not helpful if that box is not valued beyond that day. Leadership does not reside only with those in higher positions of authority. All the authors of this chapter are musical leaders in different ways. As Katy expressed it:

Musical 'leaders' as I perceive them don't often, it occurs to me, have big badges and important titles. Simon Rattle is an exception: peer of the realm, eminent chief conductor of various very high-profile organisations, and spokesperson for the industry more broadly.[7] We might also mention John Gilhooly, director of the Wigmore Hall and Chairman of the Royal Philharmonic Society,[8] as a highly respected figure and one of the most influential people in UK arts administration.[9] But I think also of musicians like Nicola Benedetti[10] and all her fantastic education work; of Alice Farnham leading courses for women who would like to get into conducting, a field so traditionally male-dominated; of composers whose music reaches many people at professional and amateur levels (down to young children) like Cecilia MacDonald and Bob Chilcott; of founders of new and hugely important initiatives, like Chi-Chi Nwanoku and the Chineke! Foundation.[11] In the creative arts, I suppose leadership is much less confined by a managerial structure: if you can demonstrate success and skill in a given area, you can become (as in academia), the 'leader in your field'. And those leaders can make a real difference.

(Katy)

It seems though, that there are unwritten limits for certain sectors of the music industries. As Sarah put it: *you know, this far but not **this** far*. In diversifying leadership in the music industries, those currently with power and authority – and by default, with financial responsibility and control – must give up some of their power to share the leadership. As Davina reminds us, *power has been questioned. Different dynamics have been questioned*. The nature of power, who has it, and how it is distributed needs questioning. As we all develop as leaders we are on a journey; the goals might be set for us, by us, or with a team, but *people don't really know what styles [of leadership] they would like to emerge with* (Davina). As Davina makes clear here, it is important that we are adaptable to lead for diverse situations.

One could propose that if those in power do not see the need for change, they will never be incentivised to make any changes. Grass-roots changes – in other words, the main body of an organisation, from the floor up – can build expectations amongst music consumers, the ticket-purchasing population, those paying for streaming music, those who fund the activities of those in power. If we subscribe to Christopher Small's notion of musicking – i.e. that everyone is involved in doing music whatever their role, including the audience members – then we all can contribute to these grass-roots changes.[12] If there is an expectation from the consumer, then those in power will have no choice but to facilitate change. Hence, Alice's idea to *give it a kick from the bottom up* (Alice) is exactly what we all call for here. That where it is possible to support others, to act as a role model, ally, or mentor, or to call something out, we should stand up and do so. But there is also a need to be cautious, as being an ally is not something to impose, assert, or force; rather, it is important to be present when needed, asked, or invited to help.

Defining grass-roots activities is broad – essentially, we are referring throughout this volume to small-scale activities which individuals are doing regularly, such activities which can be brought together in collectives (Part VI), or be used in advocacy to make changes to, for example, curricula (Part III), or to set out our activities in new ways in community spaces, such as faith practices (Part V). We propose that each of us can make small changes. Small changes, done many times, grow to make larger changes. In the context of the music industries, smaller companies changing their representation by widening their reach of composers and performers is good work, while in education broadening the curriculum to be more inclusive of under-represented figures enables children to become aware of and see role models across all demographic criteria – also good work. Then in community practice, it becomes normalised to see a wider range of faces and hear a wider range of voices as people grow in confidence to participate. There is a problem, though: much activity which has been labelled as 'feminist' is often voluntary labour, and not all of it is necessarily feminist. We, collectively, work in the music sector and we are therefore fortunate to earn our living from making music in different ways.[13] So, we feel we should shoulder some responsibility to make change. But those making changes in small charities, in volunteering sectors, also need to be recognised and applauded.[14]

If new models of leadership are to be created, we are proposing that flatter structures might exist, even creating flipped hierarchies where leadership is adaptative according to the current needs, ground-up, from the bottom. This ensures all those in charge have experience of the skills within companies, in order to understand their teams. Leadership is not management! As Davina noted, in a formal employment structure: *there is this kind of idea that a flat hierarchy is the way . . . it needs to be in order to achieve equality*. But there are difficulties: *flat systems don't work. You need a power structure* (Davina). Without accountability and structure, there is no direction as a group in a unified manner. In order to ensure agency in individual team members and collective working, it is aspirational to share the leadership within teams, so that all can work towards a common goal. As Deborah L. Rhode notes: those in 'leadership positions should also reflect on what it is they are leading for'.[15] One such example proposed by Averil Leimon *et al* is the gig economy, where there is a flatter structure of management, with freelancers working across a wide range of venues. Of course, despite the 1.1 million workers this includes in the gig industry, it also relies heavily on freelancers, zero-hours contracts, and does not support long-term career progression and development or organisational employer-support programmes.[16] Those who are employed in the gig industry largely work alone, without a regular stable community in their field, due to the transient nature of the performing visitors.

Leadership needs to be distributed to ensure that more diverse voices can be at the metaphorical table, in board rooms, present in decision making. Katy proposes that *taking people by the hand and leading them* is a positive way to lead; it is leading by example. But we need more than this; indeed, as Rhode reminds us, '[w]omen need advocates', not only mentors, if our voices are to be heard when and where we are not present.[17] Katy is firm that the difference is *hierarchy*:

Creativity goes hand in hand with collaboration, and it may be precisely because you've gone (hierarchically speaking) 'sideways' somehow – by turning towards education, working with disadvantaged communities, looking to specialise in engagement with amateurs, collaborating with dancers or artists or poets – that you gain additional respect, popularity, or influence.

(Katy)

Our personal drivers for change are varied but all come back to ensuring that other women are represented and can be represented in our fields. Considering other ways of working is imperative. Mentorship can be an extremely effective method of facilitating support from the bottom up, and we explore this approach in the next section.

Mentorship

Those new to careers and those learning new ways of doing things all need support, training, mentoring, and guidance. The importance of support cannot be underestimated in making a change beyond the self, changing things to the point of removing a glass ceiling (or the glass cliff), to enable us collectively to lift others (and ourselves) up. European mentoring models propose ways in which individual growth can be facilitated by considering individual needs, individual concerns, and barriers in a way that helps the individual to explore the ways in which they can personally adapt and problem solve. Or as Clutterbuck puts it: 'The aim of mentoring is to build the capacity of the mentees to the point of self-reliance while accelerating the communication of ideas across the organisation'.[18] In other words, mentoring is good for everyone in an organisation.

There are many different models of mentoring, but European mentoring approaches refer to facilitating individuals, as opposed to the USA mentoring approach of picking someone who might already seem worthy of a push to the next level to guide them in following one's own footsteps.[19] Here, we are not talking about gatekeeping, but rather about sharing the keys. European mentoring is not selective at the point of one individual handing down knowledge to a chosen apprentice: rather, it asserts that we all have our own skills and supports self-facilitating. It is not only about giving advice, but also supplementary to that, and it differs in asking questions which enable the exploration of issues and finding possible solutions.[20] Importantly, we all feel that to encourage more people to engage with different musical practices, we need more diverse role models as well. A role model is someone who can practice and demonstrate a way of doing things, be a good example, and can be someone to trust and to ask help of. But a role model is not always self-nominated – often a role model is chosen by an individual. How do we feel about this issue – are we role models?

*I do consider myself as a role model now actually and I have done . . . I do some professional mentoring actually as well as teaching; so yes, I do. But actually **my** biggest role model is my teacher . . . he is a Russian man, 95 years old. So, you know he is still actually my greatest role model.*

(Alice)

As Alice notes here, we all have role models we have chosen from those who have supported and guided us. Ellie shared:

I am not sure I would feel confident enough to say I was a role model as such, but I am 100% a mentor, and that is because so many of our composers now that we are releasing are a lot younger. Many of them don't have publishers. Many of them have never even been to a recording studio before, so they have absolutely no idea where to start. I mean, I go into universities all the time talking to people about how you need to register for PRS. How you need to make money from your music. How you need to market your music and you have to be out there and you need to be doing it. And those are the things that I find

composers – actually, to tell you the truth, more often now even some of the more established composers – come to me and say, 'What am I meant to do here? Can you remind me?'
(Ellie)

Ellie's authentic response here shows a great understanding of her role in sharing best practices, in guiding from a position of success, but without self-congratulatory applause. Such openness to facilitate others without praise or reward is important to the mentoring process.

There is a responsibility in the sector to offer mentoring support, to give time to underrepresented voices, to be those much-needed role models, and to support those processes. In higher education in the UK, AdvanceHE runs two active training programmes which seek to diversify representation at leadership levels: Aurora, which aims 'to take positive action to address the under-representation of women in leadership positions in the sector',[21] and Diversifying Leadership, which 'is designed to support early career academics, professional services staff, Lecturers and Senior Lecturers from Black, Asian and minority ethnic backgrounds who are about to take their first steps into a leadership role'.[22] Whilst participants in the Aurora programme are allocated a mentor, within Diversifying Leadership, colleagues supporting the scheme are asked not specifically to mentor, but rather to sponsor. The role is different. In sponsoring a candidate, you can utilise mentoring approaches alongside actively opening the door to enable someone to shadow your work, to sit alongside you at the table, and to listen and even participate in the discussions.[23]

Passing power on and/or sharing power is needed, and we collectively see our roles as leaders in our fields to share that responsibility and to do what we can. There is a moral urgency. But we need to consider carefully: Do role models have to be other women? A role model can be most effective when we can see ourselves represented, but what we are looking for varies for each individual. It might be more important in some settings to see our faith, our ethnicity, our personality, rather than our gender. It is also important, though, that we can all see our ways of identifying within all levels of leadership. Role modelling has been shown in research to benefit individuals in various ways, but specifically to benefit those within the earlier stages of their education and careers.[24] As we choose our role models, we choose what we each want and need.

A mentor is very different to a role model and does not need to have the same characteristics as ourselves. It is more important that they understand the context and situation we are working within, to ask the questions which will help us grow our self-awareness and capacity to problem solve. In addition, allyship is vital. There is a role for men in supporting diversification in the music industries, and their allyship is vital here. In some cases, there are those who do not offer themselves as mentors or coaches in preference of modelling a more arguably masculine approach to management (as opposed to leadership). This though is where women can 'face a double bind',[25] as being confident and vocal in meetings can be read by some as being loud or aggressive; stereotypes have shown men doing the same can be seen as managers and strong leaders. As Rhode asserts: 'Men must be allies in the struggle'.[26] More has been written within business about the importance of male allies, noting that diversification of the boardroom is beneficial for all, because ultimately it is beneficial to the business.[27] There is also the issue of some women who have achieved senior and/or leadership positions pulling the ladder up behind them or modelling queen-bee syndrome.[28] The issue here is of a lack of support from other women; in other words, senior women supporting (or not) more junior women. If the individual has a beneficial experience, in the longer term it will impact positively on the institution, business, organisation, charity, and so on.

Embedding mentorship within the different sectors of the music industries would change the nature and practice of those industries. Each of us, as co-authors, have acted as mentors and/or set up mentoring schemes or other schemes to support wider access. (Many of the chapters throughout the volume in fact refer to mentoring in various contexts, notably in Parts

III, V, and VI.) Where we have been able to, we have personally made changes in our areas. But there are a range of opinions, as some offer women-only training (such as AdvanceHE's Aurora scheme, cited earlier), while others offer mixed training. Some who have been dismissive initially have changed their minds: if an initial mentoring scheme is women-only, might it give confidence and space for them to then engage in wider programmes? Some do not identify themselves as role models, of course, but are nominated as role models due to the impact of their work. Examples of women's collectives are included in Part VI, although, to state the obvious, the contribution and work does not have to be only led and done by women.

In ensuring role models, women need to be allowed access. Sarah's experience of musical leadership in a religious setting shows how women are usually given specific roles, which are seen to be less important and have less public status:

> *the orchestral conductor [for] the big evening Brahms series is a male conductor, but the afternoon matinee for the schools would be the female conductor. And in the cathedral world, where I am, the men are the directors of music, and the women – the few of us that there are – in most cases would be directors of the girls' choir.*
>
> (Sarah)

The accidental falling-into the role of mentor through the work she does is keenly felt: *I am certainly a mentor and a role model, but it was accidental rather than my decision* (Sarah).

Women-only training, such as Aurora (to name just one) has aims to offer a safe space where gendered experience can be shared and discussed. Alice has experience where in offering conducting workshops only to women, she has seen *women from more ethnically diverse backgrounds coming due to it being women-only* (Alice). Such spaces can be accessible, as they might be more culturally permissible. Women-only groups are a start to facilitating access, but beyond this, these women then need support to access mainstream activities, work, and opportunities.

We are essentially now referring to social capital. From education upwards, boys/men have experiences socially as children and beyond which women do not. Certain networks and relationships can be established which privilege boys (and this can be done unconsciously, working on cultural bias and historical assumptions). As we have different starting points, we each have different training needs. As such, we are beyond talking of equality; we are advocating for an equitable practice, which may mean some need more support or guidance than others to enable all to reach the same potential. This school of thought is why AdvanceHE has developed high-quality training for targeting specific people, notably women and those from underrepresented ethnic backgrounds (as discussed earlier).[29]

Sarah shared her experience running Organ Open Days for Girls at Cambridge with Anna Lapwood:

> *I think I would say that women-only training can be really useful at a particular age, and certainly my experience with Anna Lapwood running those organ Open Days for young teenage girls . . . If they are in a mainly male environment . . . I see . . . two or three girls sort of hide at the back. But one or two of them might say, 'Right, I will have a go', but generally speaking they will hide at the back and let the boys have a go at this, that, and the other. Whereas when we had a group of 40 young teenage girls, they were all, 'Can I try that? Can I try that?' and so at that age in particular, where they are sort of maybe just hitting into adolescence, it can be really useful at that stage.*
>
> (Sarah)

Anna Lapwood is Organist and Director of Music at Pembroke College, Cambridge, and a strong advocate for women at the organ. Through TikTok and YouTube, Lapwood has set up a hashtag to share her late-night rehearsals at the organ in the Royal Albert Hall. #playlikeagirl has seen huge success and has since led to Lapwood releasing her first album.[30]

The issue with training, especially in formal settings, is that if you feel different, you might not feel welcome, accepted, or included. *Where is the space for me?* (Helen) is a question *I have heard within performance settings*. Enforcing a binary can be equally negatively impactful, and we need to (and we do here in this volume) use 'woman' in its broadest definition. Certainly, *as a member of the Aurora Champion Advisory Group, I am very much aware and advocating for support of a broader definition beyond the binaries of the past* (Helen).[31] The work that we do and propose must not be done in isolation; each is one approach among many. Alice, in offering her short 1- to 3-day workshops, ensures she is helping provide access and is supplementing support to women's wider training needs. Katy, in considering gendered schooling, is aware that *all-girls' schools* impact girls differently: *then you don't have this idea that you can't do physics or maths*. As such, if we each commit to mentoring support, sponsorship, allyship, and grass-roots activity, we start to make the initial changes. Next, we need real representational changes in curriculum, programming, and more.

Representation: Curriculum, Programming, KPIs, and Beyond

We discussed the importance of having women represented within music curricula in all our interviews. Jessy's leadership within this area has already had enormous impact within the UK as, in 2015 – as a 17-year-old school pupil – she started a national petition to 'ensure the representation of women on the A-Level Music syllabus' after she realised that no women were included in the Edexcel syllabus she was studying after attending a 'gender equality and leadership programme for young women (Fearless Futures)' with her school.[32] Jessy's petition, which was hosted on the petition website Change.org, explained her motivation for setting it up and what she hoped to achieve:

> The current 2008 Edexcel A-Level Music syllabus has a total of 63 different set works from a variety of musical genres and eras. Yet not a single one of these set works was composed by a woman . . . I first thought this issue could be solved easily by contacting Edexcel directly and drawing their attention to their omission of women from the A-Level, as they advocate that students should 'engage in . . . appreciation of the diverse and dynamic heritage of music'.
>
> I thought the lack of women was simply a mistake, an oversight, as clearly their aim cannot be fulfilled without the representation of women. . . . the assertion by Edexcel's Head of Music that 'there would be very few female composers that could be included' simply isn't true . . . Surely, if BBC Radio 3 can play music composed by women for a whole day [an initiative broadcast on International Women's Day 2015], Edexcel could select at least one to be a part of the syllabus alongside the likes of Holborne, Haydn and Howlin' Wolf? This has got to change. How can we expect girls to aspire to be composers and musicians if they don't have the opportunity to learn of any role models?[33]

As Jessy recalled when we spoke to her, taking public action through starting an online petition was not her initial plan: *I had sent emails for six months to them about it and . . . you couldn't get past the student-facing support services; you couldn't get past people answering enquiries; because you are just a student, there is no other way around it.*

So she started her petition, which quickly garnered a lot of support on Twitter, accompanied by the hashtag #justonewoman. As Jessy remembered: *I didn't have Twitter before I started the petition; I got it two days after I started it and then that took off. So, yeah, it really did snowball from there.*

Off Twitter, the petition was also covered by several national newspapers.[34] The petition, which Jessy submitted to Mark Anderson, Managing Director of Pearson UK (the learning and publishing company who offered the Edexcel Music A-level which Jessy was studying at the time), collected 3,824 signatures and was successful.[35] Whether shamed by the publicity or genuinely moved to learn and change, Edexcel did revise their 2016 AS and A-level Music syllabuses to include music written by women, following consultation with a wide range of stakeholders with particular expertise in women's music (including Laura).

Intersectionality emerged again as a key issue when we discussed Jessy's advocacy for the inclusion of women's music on the A-level Music syllabus. She recalled that, when she finally achieved a meeting with Pearson:

One of the main things I remember from the meeting I had for that exam when I was seventeen was ... I almost didn't ask the question because I thought ... it was obvious, but literally at the end of the meeting I was about to sign up and I was like, 'Oh, just to double check, you will of course be bringing women from a variety of ethnic backgrounds on your syllabus?' and they were like, 'Oh! No, I think we are just going to look through a gender lens for now; you see we have some men from ethnic [minority] backgrounds' ... And I was like, 'Yes, but you don't have any women. You don't have any women from ethnic minority backgrounds', and at that point the chief executive jumped in and was like, 'Yes. Yes. We will do it'.

(Jessy)

Edexcel did include music by women from diverse ethnic backgrounds on their revised AS and A-level Music syllabuses.

Speaking with us, Jessy explained that: *I just did it because it seemed like a sensible thing to do.* She objected to the idea that curriculum change should be led by academics and stressed that: *I think we are massively undervaluing the teachers in schools or the children that they are working with to suggest that they can't do that, and that it needs to go through an institution first* (Jessy). Although women have been represented on Higher Education Music curricula since the noughties – albeit often siloed into specialist 'Women in Music' modules rather than integrated into the core syllabus – before Jessy's intervention, music by women was not commonly included at school level,[36] where so much of the important work of 'normalisation' happens. As Jessy commented, however, *younger years is really where ... more resources need to become available.*

Jessy's success at getting women included on the AS and A-level Music syllabus proves that one person can make a difference, and that you don't need to be in an official position of power to do it. As Helen responded, *we are back to the issue of grass-roots and that an individual can make a difference.* Grass-roots activism and one individual standing up to affect real change were ideas that recurred in our conversations with many of our other participants, and it is explored in greater depth throughout Part VI of the current volume, 'Advocacy: Collectives and Grass-Roots Activism'.

Ellie reflected that confidence (or the lack of it) can often be a big issue for women. For women composers, this can result in them being less likely to put themselves forward for funding: *It is a confidence thing. You have got to think how that then impacts things like funding applications. Look at PRSF Women Make Music. Before, when they looked at the statistics of who was applying for funding, the majority of them were men* (Ellie).

Sarah corroborated this impression by sharing that:

Selwyn Choir has made fifteen single-composer CDs over the past ten years; there isn't a single female composer represented. And that is not because I am going out of my way . . . the really, really top ones have Trinity Choir, so Cecilia McDowall doesn't need me to make a disc. Some of the younger generations don't have the confidence to send me their music and say, 'Look, I have got 70 minutes of music', and I have rejected several men who have said, 'Here's 70 minutes of music' and I say, 'Well, I am not going to do it; it is not very good'. I mean, I haven't even had that opportunity to reject 70 minutes of music by a female composer; they never come to me.

(Sarah)

In considering how best to achieve equal gender representation within music, we also asked all our participants for their views on how effective they felt the use of KPIs were, and whether they should be used to force the industry to develop 50/50 representation. Katy identified an important aspect of this:

I guess the crucial thing about problems like unbalanced gender representation is that they are systemic. So, the question to ask is: who or what could we usefully hold to account using devices such as KPIs? It may be easier to intervene in this way with some structures (such as music festivals via the Keychange scheme) than others. For example, if music colleges are roughly balanced in terms of male and female students, but certain sectors of the industry aren't, what's happening between graduation and employment?

(Katy)

On 50/50 representation quotas, Jessy commented that she thought that they should be used, but

I don't think they should be used alone because then you have the same issue with the reproduction cycle of . . . getting more of the same rather than actually the benefits: Advocating benefits and valuing the people that we get on board.

(Jessy)

An interesting point that also emerged during our discussion of KPIs and gender quotas was the danger of some women being pushed into roles before they were fully ready, ultimately doing them more harm than good as well as opening up potential criticism of 50/50 schemes or even of women holding such roles. As Alice cautioned earlier, it is important not to go too quickly, but to allow women time to develop and mature fully: *it needs to be a much slower burn* (Alice). In relation to this, Emma also observed that she felt that:

Perhaps some of them [the women conductors that Alice was referring to] *simply were not ready, or perhaps some were not right for the role. I think the KPI is fantastic, and it needs to exist, but . . . some female performers, for example, if they are not ready or they are not quite right for the role or the job, then they shouldn't be pushed to do it. So, I think there is a fine line. However, things like this need to be pushed because we are not yet at a level playing field where people just get booked due to fully objective standards and achievements. There is still an issue, and I think before that playing field is evened out this absolutely needs to exist, and we absolutely need to focus more on it.*

(Emma)

Ellie shared that she believed that such schemes do need to exist, going on to explain how recent discussions of gender quotas had prompted her to investigate what the gender representation within NMC's catalogue was, which led to her realising that about 90% of people sending in speculative proposals for recordings were men (chiming with the experience that Sarah shared). She had a positive story to share of how she had driven change towards greater gender equity:

What I did was I wrote to about eighty/ninety women composers that I knew, and I said, 'Look, I have just crunched the numbers and 90% of people that have been sending in on-spec proposals to us for recordings were men; why have you never applied to us before?' So many of them got back to me and they went, 'Oh, I didn't think I was ready. Didn't think you would be interested. It wasn't kind of what we thought NMC was about'. There were lots and lots of excuses and within two or three months I got a number of proposals in from women, and they went through exactly the same processes that we always do . . . We have an artistic panel: everyone has to listen to the music, make a decision and everything, and as a result a number of those ended up getting picked up and put into the release forward planning schedule, and then I have got a nice pool of releases I can pick from now and go, 'Right, actually in 2020 we can actually make a 50/50 splash' . . . And this year [2020], we have a 50/50 release schedule for the first time. So, it can happen.

(Ellie)

Ellie also stressed the importance of the outreach work that NMC do in normalising young people seeing women composers:

We are based in Bethnal Green, so we do a lot of work in inner London schools. And we get our composers, people like Errollyn Wallen, who look like the kids that they are teaching. It is so important, and they get taught composition and I just think that is just an incredible thing for a sort of eight- to ten-year-old to be getting. I mean, Errollyn is just amazing anyway . . . She is a great composer and musician, and I just think if you were a kid and she came in . . . she would be someone that you would remember probably when you are an adult and go, 'Do you remember when that composer came in?' and I am sure she would have an impact. So, we have been doing things like that because we have got those connections, but also . . . we've had contemporary composers write pieces for kids for violin, sort of Grade 2 to 6 level. So, you have got Tansy Davies, Mark Anthony Turnage, Colin Matthews, Daniel Kidane, Hannah Kendall . . . a mixture of people, men, women, also people of the Global Majority, and you just think . . . it gives kids an opportunity to realise they are playing music by living composers. Tick. They are not all dead and [they are] also people that look like them. I just think that that's something that needs to continue.

(Ellie)

Several of our participants concurred that contributing to the greater representation of women and other traditionally marginalised groups on music curricula, recording company catalogues, programmes, and broadcasts represents an important passing on of power: from those of us who have managed to obtain it (whether it be through official positions and authority and/or through educational, cultural, or economic capital) to others – particularly those younger than ourselves – and through doing so, to fundamentally change its nature. As Jessy expressed it: *[We must] redistribute the power that we have [been] given and not reproduce the kind of traditional cycles which have resulted in power remaining with individuals rather than being redistributed and diversifying the voices that are listened to.*

Caring and Support

Towards the end of each interview, we asked all participants: 'What are the most pertinent issues facing women in musical leadership today?' Caring responsibilities – whether this be for children, partners, elders, or other dependents – and taking time out from a career to take maternity leave emerged as key factors. Reflecting on a colleague who had recently gone on maternity leave, Ellie commented:

I wonder now whether she is going to be pushed behind because she is now going either to come back part time or she is going to decide that she wants to concentrate on being a mum for a few years, which is completely understandable. But I think more needs to be done in allowing women to have those choices and still get to the top.

(Ellie)

Despite legal protection for expectant mothers and those on maternity/shared parental/ paternity/adoption leave being in place in the UK, many women in these positions continue to face workplace discrimination.[37] Sarah reminded us that from an international perspective, less time is available for many women around the world in comparison to the UK: *in America, maternity leave is catastrophic* (Sarah).

In the UK, Statutory Maternity Leave is made up of 52 weeks. This consists of Ordinary Maternity Leave (during the first 26 weeks) and Additional Maternity Leave (during the second 26 weeks). Women are not obliged to take the full 52 weeks, though they are (legally) obliged to take two weeks' leave after their baby is born (or four if they work in a factory). Statutory Maternity Pay (SMP) is only available for 39 weeks, however. Of these, SMP is paid at 90% of the woman's average weekly earnings (before tax) for the first six weeks only and then at £156.66 or 90% of their average weekly earnings (whichever is lower) for the next 33 weeks.[38] Although many companies make up SMP with extra maternity pay, how much is available and for how long varies massively between different companies. For women who are self-employed – as many freelance musicians or private music teachers are – such additional financial support is not available, which makes taking Maternity Leave of any substantial length extremely challenging. Beyond any financial considerations, having to return to work very soon after giving birth also poses significant health and wellbeing dangers for mothers. For those who are freelancers, options open to musician mothers employed by a company on returning to work, such as flexible-working or home-working adjustments, are also not available.

Financial concerns do not end with Maternity Leave, as the cost of childcare in the UK is extortionate. Although working parents in the UK can be eligible for some free childcare hours per week for 3- and 4-year-olds (different schemes operate across each of the four devolved UK nations),[39] below this age full-time nursery places typically cost in excess of £1,000 per month. Given that much professional music-making and related professional activities (such as criticism) takes place at night or at other non-family-friendly times, becoming a parent poses multiple pragmatic and logistical challenges beyond the already significant financial considerations. The restraints and concerns of balancing a career in the music industry with caring are not exclusive to parents, as many of these also extend to those with other caring responsibilities, including elders and partners.[40]

The pandemic context was reflected in the interviews which took place during the UK lockdowns, as the combination of home-schooling/full-time childcare whilst also continuing to work from home – with everything often taking place in confined domestic spaces and the stress and uncertainty of the unfolding situation – made life extremely challenging for parents and carers. Multiple studies have demonstrated that mothers bore the brunt of the additional childcare and home-schooling responsibilities during the Covid-19-related lockdowns and were also more likely to suffer career setbacks or lose their jobs.[41]

Language and Tone

As part of the discussions outlined here, it became clear that language is a powerful device when it comes to expanding inclusivity to ensure wider representation is achieved and sustained. *Simple changes in language can make a huge difference. Like talking about Schumann, not Clara, if you're also going to talk about Wagner, not Richard* (Katy). Awareness of how we use language asserts an institutional and social culture. Language can be a barrier if it is highly gendered, elitist, and therefore potentially misrepresentative.

Language is a way to establish and propagate stereotypes, but it is also a way to tackle those limited perspectives. This was part of our discussion in which we moved to talking about specific challenging of gendered language. Male genitalia and male descriptors – especially 'ballsy' – have been used to represent strong, motivated, driven, and aspirational colleagues, the go-getters. Likewise, similar terms are highly negative, such as 'cock-up'. As a group, we tackled the term 'ballsy'. We became aware during the discussion that several of us had been referred to by this term. It was used in the discussion by the group, then critiqued, and then re-appropriated. Why? We needed to engage with our own enculturation with such language. Noting someone is 'ballsy' might be read as a positive attribute for a male colleague, while it can be seen as a negative comment to women. But some of us in leadership had seen it was starting to be appropriated and used positively for women by women too. Some of us, however, feel uncomfortable with this language.

How was 'ballsy' used in the conversation? It arose originally in discussions concerning *confidence . . . because I think I was a bit more ballsy, for want of a better phrase, when I was younger* (Emma). The discussion moved to highlight the importance of recognising confidence issues for both early-career women and for *a lot of teenagers; as Sarah said before, it is an awful age and there is just absolutely no confidence at all* (Emma). Such language can have negative import though, and we need to ensure we are *not being condescending* (Alice). There is a clear support network within women's training programmes which actively seeks to develop confidence. In the following comment, Emma refers to how she was inspired by Alice's training workshops to realise her own growth in confidence:

> And I am really eager to do conducting days with the girl's school that I teach woodwind in for two days a week. Alice's day was so inspiring, and I realised it is down to me as a conductor within the education sector to give these young girls a chance, and I think even at that age these experiences within a safe space [are] a completely different kettle of fish. I think confidence plays a big role and is key.
>
> (Emma)

Alice reflected on her experience of leading conducting workshops:

I did a webinar with one of my conductors that I did a workshop with, Olivia Clarke and Tom Service . . . We actually ended up talking a lot more about just conducting in general and leadership; it is quite interesting because . . . We talked about what is a conductor? And the mystery of this sort of leadership thing and this authority.

(Alice)

By workshopping these skills, questions were raised about leadership and the nature of the conductor's role in particular. The attributes of the role are reliant on *personalities, and I think that if we have more women conductors, we also attract more interesting male conductors as well* (Alice). Diversifying the field benefits all.

As Davina asserted, *We need inclusive language* (Davina). Language itself can set up a barrier to access, and regardless of intent, it can be offensive. Much work has been done in various settings to work on language, to ensure improvements are made in job advertisements, training, and in curricula.[42] In an effort to be inclusive, many institutions have created glossaries for key language; for example, York St John University has created a glossary to support trans awareness but is also redeveloping a wider inclusive glossary to inform the antiracist pedagogy.[43]

The musical context can be particular, for example, within conducting the use of language is *quite narrow . . . they say it has changed but I don't think it really has, this very narrow idea of what a conductor is, and what authority is, and what leadership is* (Alice). Ultimately, *I think, as Sarah was saying, it is down to personality . . . I mean, I think I am probably 'ballsy' . . . I think it is down to personality as much as a gender thing* (Alice).

We highlighted as researchers *that language is hugely gendered in society; depending on where you live and what experience you have had, it can be greater or lesser gendered* (Helen). We discussed some examples where gender and age were used in identifying people:

there was one article in The Spectator *. . . these weren't the words, but it was along the kind of lines of like 'Why are these seventeen-old girls asking for this kind of thing?' So, a lot of kind of like very much like complaining rather than advocating.*

(Jessy)

All the issues are intersectional: due to the context of the group varying in age – from a recent graduate up to senior colleagues, with varied lived experiences – the stereotypes associated with age were important to our positionalities.

Importantly, though, we were questioning our own use of language: *why would we want everyone to be ballsy?* (Jessy). A critical reflection requires us all to balance opinions and experiences to consider the best options for supporting change improvements.

If we are advocating to have more women as conductors . . . we want lots of different stances and different experiences and different ranges of leadership rather than a reproduction cycle, because then that becomes about numbers. Then we are not valuing the women who are becoming the conductors; we are just getting our quota figures up.

(Jessy)

Language remains central to managing and making change and to reflecting on our own experiences.

> *There's so much in a person's language; as I said before, it is just as soon as you look at something; we are so used to it we don't always question it.* [In discussing our activities] *nearly every one of us said something along the lines of being 'ballsy' or having [needing] masculine qualities* [and this came out simply by reassessing] *just the language we used.*
>
> (Ellie)

Experience perhaps changes perspective, the youngest of the group critically reflected on her own responses during our discussions: *Maybe it's naive of me, again another gender term, to think that you don't need to be 'ballsy' or you shouldn't have to be 'ballsy' to be a conductor. What do I know; I don't have experience of it!* (Jessy) Enculturation is a core issue here: those of us with the experience of hearing this language used for colleagues and for ourselves had adopted it, unconsciously to some extent. It is everyone's responsibility in the industry to consider language, to re-write procedural documents and policies, job descriptions, and so on, to ensure all use inclusive language. It is a learning journey, so we also need to be open to that development and change being on-going. How language impacts us is critical:

> *Let's say I was in that conversation and wasn't confident enough to bring up the fact that . . . like, this word is used. I would go away and be like, 'oh, well, I can't do conducting now because I am not 'ballsy' and 'I have no desire to be either', which has an enormous impact.*
>
> (Jessy)

We assert then, that language can act as a barrier to inclusion, language might formulate certain inaccurate assumptions, and therefore language can be actively exclusionary, even if it is used unconsciously.

Feminine language was also identified as related to, though different from, the masculinised language noted here. In reference to politics regarding how women are compared to their male colleagues, an example was given in relationship to recent prime ministers (within an international context): *I think it is really positive and really telling that people are less willing to use a lot of feminine language* (Emma). Gender-neutral language is one such goal the music industries need to focus on. Unless we can all use gendered language in a broader way:

> *I think at the end of the day, that in an ideal world these feminine adjectives or feminine language should just be able to be used broadly. Men can be nurturing, for example . . . it baffles me that these adjectives are still associated with the female discourse. . . . I guess it is how we perceive choices of language.*
>
> (Emma)

In response to these ideas, we discussed personal choices: that as a leader in a position of authority or power (of varying degrees) we should take the responsibility to lead by example. Alice reflected:

> *Yes, and it is difficult, the choice of language, isn't it, because there is feminine and masculine in many languages, not in English so much, but in French, German, and Russian,*

not Swedish, interestingly; you have feminine and masculine anyway for all the nouns, one or the other. . . . It is very hard to extricate a word. I don't know whether I think maybe we should embrace that rather than feel embarrassed by it and also say sometimes, 'Yeah, be more masculine at this moment'. I often say to my students they need to . . . if they need a bit of weight in the sound that they need to imagine they are a very overweight fifty-year-old man . . . to have that kind of ggrrhhhh! about them.

(Alice)

The point is not literal, but it is one whereby you can put yourself the in shoes of someone else by imagining their experiences and their positionality.

By associating ourselves with projects which focus on women, we do not wish to ignore other demographic qualities. But we are starting somewhere, from our lived experiences, to try to make change to improve things for everyone. How language can be inclusive, divisive, or exclusive is something we need to consider. Labelling projects themselves can cause pause for thought, as Sarah shared,

I was involved with the Multitude of Voyces anthologies about female composers which actually annoyed [a colleague] a little bit.[44] *. . . Actually, there's a huge amount more to diversity and you can't really call female composers, as a general rule, a downtrodden part of society.*

(Sarah)

The point here is valid to an extent, that one should not only focus on one area. *Diversity of all kinds is important . . . we can't win every single battle all at once* (Sarah).

What about transgender, non-binary, or gender expansive people? Within this volume, we actively use women to mean anyone who identifies as a woman, but how can language actively support everyone?

For people who don't identify as male or female, I think that [the use of broader language is] *actually going to help the development of all gender equality. Non-binary people want to be addressed with different pronouns and I think that is actually going to help us move away from a focus on gendered language. . . . So, I think it will be very interesting to see what happens in the future.*

(Emma)

From the perspective of a leading artistic creative director, Ellie really has worked with the impact of language in concrete terms. *The language changes so much, doesn't it. To a certain degree we are so dictated by what* [funding bodies] *use as a framework*. In other words, funding bodies request responses to specific questions, using acronyms such as BAME (Black, and Minorities Ethnicities) and gender identifiers, which can be limiting. BAME is a specific categorisation, but it is a limiting label and rather clusters a lot of diverse people together in the UK. *Because we are always trying to put people in boxes to categorise people because we need the stats for figures and for gauging things, but it is not always helpful to making change* (Ellie).

In considering the legitimacy of these changes and the efforts to seek and enable equality, we also need to share positive stories. We need and we are seeking *more women on boards* (Ellie), and we are *seeing more women from black and ethnic diverse backgrounds* (Ellie) submitting compositions. Everyone needs to see themselves represented in the industry to offer role models, and so we also need to reassess history to bring more diverse voices to the table. We might enable others to develop the confidence to make changes by seeing and witnessing other examples. Those with power, influence, and an employed position could use their status to support access actively by dropping the drawbridge to develop mentoring programmes and so on.

Conclusion

Change takes courage. So, we need those in leadership positions now to demonstrate how brave they are (Katy). In a book concerning women's musical leadership, this chapter has demonstrated some examples of what might be done, as well as revealing some lived challenges in the current UK music industries. Collectively, we advocate for more inclusive language and impose it through developing wider mentoring and coaching opportunities, encouraging grass-roots activities to develop and build from within an organisation, and to enable these activities and languages to feed into the new policies, activities, curricula, and KPIs.

Notes

1. The term 'glass cliff' was first used in 2005 by Michelle K. Ryan and Alexander Haslam to describe the phenomena that women tend to be most likely to be appointed to positions of leadership during times of crisis, i.e. when the danger of falling is greatest.
2. Six of the seven interviews took place during lockdown periods of the Covid-19 pandemic, and the last was held shortly after.
3. Laura Hamer and Helen Julia Minors, "Introducing WMLON: Women's Musical Leadership Online Network," in *Women's Leadership in Music: Modes, Legacies, Alliances*, edited by Iva Nenić and Linda Cimardi (Bielefeld: Transcript Verlag, 2023), 141.
4. The *Keychange Pledge and 50:50 Programming*, accessed August 8, 2023, https://britishmusiccollection.org.uk/article/keychange-pledge-and-5050-programming.
5. The composers catalogue can be found here, accessed August 8, 2023, www.nmcrec.co.uk/composers.
6. Jes Skolnik, "Beyond Representation: In Music And Media, Gender Equality Will Take A Revolution," *NPR* (2018), accessed August 8, 2023, www.npr.org/2018/08/07/634725840/beyond-representation-in-music-and-media-gender-equality-will-take-a-revolution.
7. Biography available here, accessed August 8, 2023, https://en.wikipedia.org/wiki/Simon_Rattle
8. Chairman, accessed August 8, 2023, https://royalphilharmonicsociety.org.uk/rps-today/who-we-are/chairman.
9. The pandemic has made Gilhooly much more prominent in the field as both a spokesperson within the classical music industry as well as due to the open online accessibility of the Wigmore Hall's approach to concerts and online streaming during lockdown. These strategic concert changes, utilising online streaming, gave Gilhooly much press attention for the work he was doing to maintain classical music in live settings
10. Nicola Benedetti, accessed August 8, 2023, www.nicolabenedetti.co.uk/.
11. Chineke! Foundation, accessed August 8, 2023, www.chineke.org/.
12. Christopher Small, *Musicking: The Meanings of Performing and Listening* (Middletown: Wesleyan University Press, 1998), 9.
13. See for example the recent Musician's Union report on pay brackets for musicians, accessed September 12, 2023, www.theguardian.com/music/2023/sep/11/nearly-half-of-working-uk-musicians-earn-less-than-14000-new-census-finds.
14. Within the Women's Musical Leadership Online Network, Music Industry panel workshop (16 June 2023), the delegates discussed the amount of volunteering, hidden labour, and personal cost for such activities. It was striking that every delegate and presenter in the room had self-funded some part of the change activity from their own pockets to make sure things improve, not for themselves but for the next generation. See accessed August 9, 2023, https://fass.open.ac.uk/research/projects/wmlon/events.

15. Deborah L. Rhode, *Women and Leadership* (Oxford: Oxford University Press, 2017), 135.
16. Averil Leimon, François Moscovici, and Helen Goodier, *Coaching Women to Lead: Changing the World from the Inside* (London and New York: Routledge, 2022), 14. As detailed, this economy is 2/3 male.
17. Rhode, *Women and Leadership*, 92.
18. David Clutterbuck, *Everyone Needs a Mentor: Fostering Talent at Work*, 3rd ed. (London: CIPD, 2001), 5.
19. Ibid.
20. Both editors of this volume are trained mentors and coaches who have also received mentoring in formal and informal settings and have offered formal mentoring on a number of schemes, including Aurora, the UK's leadership development programme targeting women run by AdvanceHE. See accessed August 9, 2023, www.advance-he.ac.uk/programmes-events/developing-leadership/aurora.
21. Aurora, AdvanceHE, accessed August 18, 2023, advance-he.ac.uk.
22. Diversifying Leadership, AdvanceHE, accessed August 9, 2023, www.advance-he.ac.uk/programmes-events/developing-leadership/diversifying-leadership#:~:text=The%20Diversifying%20Leadership%20programme%20is,steps%20into%20a%20leadership%20role.
23. As an active sponsor for the Diversifying Leadership programme, co-editor Helen has seen the personal benefits to the person she has recently been sponsoring, not only in terms of self-agency, but notably in terms of confidence development and resilience. A sponsor introduces, supports, and guides. It can be more direct than mentoring. Coaching, on the other hand, in comparison with sports, provides much more guidance and coaches through challenges, questions, and listening. Advice isn't a core part of any of these roles, but it can be drawn on in some circumstances. Advice is perhaps more the role of the leader or specific work manager.
24. Shahira Amin, "How Female Role Models Inspire and Empower Younger Generations," 2020, accessed August 9, 2023, https://twentythirty.com/article/how-female-role-models-inspire-and-empower-younger-generations?gclid=Cj0KCQjwldKmBhCCARIsAP-0rfzf57p0b8Sz07hoKTLwCLFglzktd-P4ACJY0LSZXKSyRAoxe8AFc1WAaAvkkEALw_wcB.
25. Rhode, *Women and Leadership*, 98.
26. Ibid., 34.
27. Grant Thornton, "The Role of Male Allies in Progressing Towards Gender Parity," 2022, accessed August 9, 2023, www.grantthornton.global/en/insights/articles/the-role-of-male-allies-in-progressing-towards-gender-parity/.
28. Queen Bee syndrome refers to women leaders who regard other women as a threat and prefer to be the only woman leader. See BBC News, "Queen Bees: Do Women Hinder the Progress of Other Women?," accessed August 25, 2023, www.bbc.co.uk/news/uk-41165076.
29. Aurora and Diversifying Leadership, AdvanceHE.
30. Anna Lapwood's TikTok can be found here, accessed August 9, 2023, www.tiktok.com/discover/anna-lapwood-organ.
31. See accessed August 9, 2023, https://advance-he.ac.uk/programmes-events/aurora/aurora-champion-advisory-group.
32. See Petition, "Ensure the Representation of Women on the A-Level Music Syllabus," accessed August 8, 2023, www.change.org/p/edexcel-ensure-the-representation-of-women-on-the-a-level-music-syllabus.
33. Ibid.
34. See, for example, Nadia Khomami, "Student Demands Female Composers on A-Level Music Syllabus," *The Guardian*, August 18, 2015), accessed September 9, 2022, www.theguardian.com/education/2015/aug/18/female-composers-a-level-music-syllabus-petition; and Paul Gallagher, "Jessy McCabe: Teenage Girl Launches Petition Calling for More Women to Be Represented in A-Level Music Exams," *The Independent*, August 19, 2015, accessed August 9, 2023, www.independent.co.uk/news/uk/crime/jessy-mccabe-teenage-girl-launches-petition-calling-for-more-women-to-be-represented-in-alevel-music-exams-10462293.html.
35. See Pearson | The world's learning company | UK, accessed August 8, 2023, https://www.pearson.co.uk/.
36. The WJEC (Welsh Joint Education Committee) is an important exception, as Grace Williams has long been studied in Wales.
37. Experiencing workplace discrimination around pregnancy and childcare issues is so widespread within the UK that Joeli Brearley established Pregnant Then Screwed as 'a charity dedicated to

ending the motherhood penalty, supporting tens of thousands of women each year, and successfully campaigning for change' on International Women's Day in 2015. See Home – Pregnant Then Screwed, accessed August 26, 2022, https://pregnantthenscrewed.com/.
38. See Maternity pay and leave: Overview, accessed August 26, 2022, www.gov.uk/maternity-pay-leave.
39. See 30 hours free childcare, accessed August 26, 2022, www.gov.uk/30-hours-free-childcare.
40. One example of a group supporting careers is Swap'ra, situated within the opera community, working with job and role shares to support families and carers. See accessed August 13, 2023, www.swap-ra.org/.
41. See, for example, Alison Andrew, Sarah Cattan, Monica Costa Dias, Christine Farquharson, Lucy Kraftman, Sonya Krutikova, Angus Phimister, and Almudena Sevilla, "How Are Mothers and Fathers Balancing Work and Family Under Lockdown?," *The UK Institute for Fiscal Studies*, May 27, 2020, accessed August 26, 2022, https://ifs.org.uk/publications/14860 and King's College London/Ipsos Mori, "Women Doing More Childcare Under Lockdown But Men More Likely to Feel Their Jobs Are Suffering," June 25, 2020, accessed August 26, 2022, www.kcl.ac.uk/news/women-doing-more-childcare-under-lockdown-but-men-more-likely-to-feel-their-jobs-are-suffering#:~:text=Women%20in%20the%20UK%20are,College%20London%20and%20Ipsos%20MORI.
42. Language has been a key point of discussion in the steering group of EDI Music Studies (EDIMS), accessed August 8, 2023, www.edimusicstudies.com/ and has arisen in every delegate discussion within the Women's Musical Leadership Online Network events, accessed August 9, 2023, https://fass.open.ac.uk/research/projects/wmlon/events.
43. Trans Glossary, accessed August 9, 2023, www.yorksj.ac.uk/policies-and-documents/trans-inclusive-framework/trans-glossary/.
44. Multitude of Voyces collate and publish anthologies of sacred music by women composers: Multitude of Voyces Registered Charity Number 1201139 – Sacred Music by Women Composers, accessed August 18, 2023, https://www.multitudeofvoyces.co.uk/.

Bibliography

30 Hours Free Childcare. Accessed August 26, 2022. www.gov.uk/30-hours-free-childcare.
Amin, Shahira. "How Female Role Models Inspire and Empower Younger Generations." 2020. Accessed August 9, 2023. https://twentythirty.com/article/how-female-role-models-inspire-and-empower-younger-generations?gclid=Cj0KCQjwldKmBhCCARIsAP-0rfzf57p0b8Sz07hoKTLwCLFglzktd-P4ACJY0LSZXKSyRAoxe8AFc1WAaAvkkEALw_wcB.
Andrew, Alison, et al. "How Are Mothers and Fathers Balancing Work and Family Under Lockdown?." *The UK Institute for Fiscal Studies*, May 27, 2020. How Are Mothers and Fathers Balancing Work and Family Under Lockdown? – Institute for Fiscal Studies – IFS. Accessed August 26, 2022. https://ifs.org.uk/publications/14860.
Anna Lapwood. Accessed August 9, 2023. www.tiktok.com/discover/anna-lapwood-organ.
Atonal. Accessed August 8, 2023. https://atonal.co.uk/about.
Aurora, AdvanceHE. Accessed August 9, 2023. See www.advance-he.ac.uk/programmes-events/developing-leadership/aurora.
Aurora Champion Advisory Group. Accessed August 9, 2023. https://advance-he.ac.uk/programmes-events/aurora/aurora-champion-advisory-group.
Bigo and Twigetti. Accessed August 8, 2023. https://bigoandtwigetti.co.uk/.
Chairman. Accessed August 8, 2023. https://royalphilharmonicsociety.org.uk/rps-today/who-we-are/chairman.
Chineke! Foundation. Accessed August 8, 2023. www.chineke.org/.
Clutterbuck, David. *Everyone Needs a Mentor: Fostering Talent at work*, 3rd ed. London: CIPD, 2001.
Diversifying Leadership, AdvanceHE. Accessed August 9, 2023. www.advance-he.ac.uk/programmes-events/developing-leadership/diversifying-leadership#:~:text=The%20Diversifying%20Leadership%20programme%20is,steps%20into%20a%20leadership%20role.
EDI Music Studies. Accessed August 8, 2023. www.edimusicstudies.com/.
Gallagher, Paul. "Jessy McCabe: Teenage Girl Launches Petition Calling for More Women to be Represented in A-Level Music Exams." *The Independent*, August 19, 2015. Jessy McCabe: Teenage Girl Launches Petition Calling for More Women to be Represented in A-Level Music Exams. Accessed

September 9, 2022. www.independent.co.uk/news/uk/crime/jessy-mccabe-teenage-girl-launches-petition-calling-for-more-women-to-be-represented-in-alevel-music-exams-10462293.html.

Hamer, Laura, and Helen Julia Minors. "Introducing WMLON: Women's Musical Leadership Online Network." In *Women's Leadership in Music: Modes, Legacies, Alliances*, edited by Iva Nenić and Linda Cimardi, 141–52. Bielefeld: Transcript Verlag, 2023.

Katy Hamilton. Accessed August 8, 2023. https://katyhamilton.co.uk/.

Katy Hamilton, Wigmore Hall. Accessed August 8, 2023. www.wigmore-hall.org.uk/artists/katy-hamilton.

Khomami, Nadine. "A-Level Music to Include Female Composers After Student's Campaign." *The Guardian*, December 16, 2025. Accessed August 8, 2023. www.theguardian.com/education/2015/dec/16/a-level-music-female-composers-students-campaign-jessy-mccabe-edexcel.

Khomami, Nadia. "Student Demands Female Composers on A-Level Music Syllabus." *The Guardian*, August 18, 2015. Accessed September 9, 2022. Student demands female composers on A-level music syllabus | Music | *The Guardian*.

King's College London/Ipsos Mori. "Women Doing More Childcare Under Lockdown But Men More Likely to Feel Their Jobs Are Suffering." June 25, 2020. Accessed August 26, 2022. www.kcl.ac.uk/news/women-doing-more-childcare-under-lockdown-but-men-more-likely-to-feel-their-jobs-are-suffering#:~:text=Women%20in%20the%20UK%20are,College%20London%20and%20Ipsos%20MORI.

Leimon, Averil, François Moscovici, and Helen Goodier. *Coaching Women to Lead: Changing the World from the Inside*. London and New York: Routledge, 2022.

Nicola Benedetti. Accessed August 8, 2023. www.nicolabenedetti.co.uk/.

NMC. Accessed August 8, 2023. www.nmcrec.co.uk/about-us/organisation/team.

Petition Ensure the Representation of Women on the A-Level Music Syllabus. Accessed August 8, 2023. www.change.org/p/edexcel-ensure-the-representation-of-women-on-the-a-level-music-syllabus.

Rhode, Deborah L. *Women and Leadership*. Oxford: Oxford University Press, 2017.

Sarah MacDonald. Accessed August 8, 2023. www.sel.cam.ac.uk/people/ms-sarah-macdonald.

———. Accessed August 8, 2023. www.elycathedral.org/people/sarah-macdonald.

Skolnik, Jes. "Beyond Representation: In Music and Media, Gender Equality Will Take a Revolution." *NPR*, 2018. Accessed August 8, 2023. www.npr.org/2018/08/07/634725840/beyond-representation-in-music-and-media-gender-equality-will-take-a-revolution.

Small, Christopher. *Musicking*. Middletown, CT: Wesleyan University Press, 1998.

The Female Conductor Programme. Accessed August 8, 2023. www.nch.ie/Online/default.asp?BOparam::WScontent::loadArticle::permalink=Female-Conductors-Programme&BOparam::WScontent::loadArticle::context_id=.

The Keychange Pledge and 50@50 Programming. Accessed August 8, 2023. https://britishmusiccollection.org.uk/article/keychange-pledge-and-5050-programming.

Thornton, Grant. "The Role of Male Allies in Progressing Towards Gender Parity." 2022. www.grantthornton.global/en/insights/articles/the-role-of-male-allies-in-progressing-towards-gender-parity/.

Trans Glossary. Accessed August 9, 2023. www.yorksj.ac.uk/policies-and-documents/trans-inclusive-framework/trans-glossary/.

Women Conductors. Accessed August 8, 2023. https://royalphilharmonicsociety.org.uk/performers/women-conductors.

Women's Musical Leadership Online Network. Accessed August 9, 2023. https://fass.open.ac.uk/research/projects/wmlon/events.

27
PREPARING WOMEN FOR MUSICAL LEADERSHIP
Student and Faculty Voices

Allison Gurland, Elizabeth Markow, Rebekah E. Moore, and Shannon Pires

This chapter considers educational opportunities in the university classroom and beyond to prepare future women leaders for diverse careers in music. Through personal testimonials, recent graduates of an American undergraduate music business programme advocate for the curricular transformations necessary for young women to envision their place as musical leaders; insist upon equal compensation, treatment, and opportunity; and foster equity and inclusion throughout their careers and across a broad spectrum of professional settings, from performing arts administration to the commercial music industry. Their former professor offers a reflection on their insights and the ongoing challenges of defining and achieving diverse representation and equity and inclusion in higher education. We have modelled this chapter after Parker and McDonald's contribution to *Movements in Organizational Communication Research: Current Issues and Future Directions*,[1] and we are indebted to their approach to critical reflexivity on difference, diversity, and inclusion for informing our concluding thoughts on intersectional leadership and the responsibilities of the privileged to institutionalise justice and equity in music.

Liz's Story

When I was a music industry major at Northeastern University, I was often surprised when 'she' or 'they' pronouns were used in the classroom to refer to producers or industry professionals. I could not easily imagine anyone but cis men, because I had rarely encountered examples of women, trans, or nonbinary people in these positions. My music industry coursework often reinforced the idea that men make the big creative decisions. Books like Fred Goodman's *The Mansion on the Hill* and various classroom case studies almost always conveyed men as creative geniuses. I almost always pictured a group of men in smoky meeting rooms, a man discovering and signing the breakout star, or a man *man*aging the desk in the studio recording, mixing, and mastering the next hit record.[2] Our predominantly male professors exclusively modelled male success, so it is unsurprising that students struggled to imagine that women could be just as successful in the music industries. As a result, those students who do not see themselves represented in these teaching moments may be discouraged to even seek out positions in creative leadership. The phenomenon is also intersectional: many students do not see their race or ethnicity, class, sexuality, disability, neurodiversity, or faith reflected in leadership, and this greatly affects their ability to imagine success for themselves. Teachers, mentors, employers, and fellow students all have an important part to play in informing how roles in creative leadership are imagined and reached.

So how do we break the cycle? How do we ensure that all students can imagine themselves in integral roles in the music industries? First, we must be proactive in acknowledging that gender discrimination and other forms of systemic marginalisation exist in music. We must talk about how and why industry leadership lacks gender diversity, in order to recognise our biases in favour of able-bodied men as the most capable and willing to take on the creative decision-making that shapes the popular music heard by millions or even billions of fans.

Once, during my record label internship in the spring of 2017, I was introduced to an older male tour manager of the headlining band while I was working the merchandise table for one of the artists signed to the label. In front of a room full of people he said to me, 'Oh, you're a fine-looking woman; you'll do great in the music industry'. I was humiliated and angry at this man and everyone in the room who did not say anything, including my male friend, a fellow intern and university peer. I was also angry at myself for not saying anything. Over the next few days, I rehearsed the conversation I would have with my internship supervisor about what had happened, how humiliated I felt, and how disappointed I was that I was not defended or supported in that moment. But by Monday, I convinced myself that this man did not mean any harm, and I worried that complaining might damage my college's relationship with the record label, or the label's relationship with that tour manager. I knew many women had endured much worse in the music industry, and I did not want to come across as weak or dramatic. That moment stuck with me for so long. I came to realise that I had no idea how to respond to someone objectifying me or suggesting that my looks, rather than my work ethic, were essential to my success. Of course, my friend and everyone else in the room that day were also unsure about how to speak up. While my peers and I were required to complete a semester-long internship preparation class, including a module addressing sexual harassment, misconduct, and assault in the workplace, we were never taught what to do about subtle forms of harassment, discrimination, or microaggressions. We did not know what to do when someone outside of the company we worked for did something that made us uncomfortable, or when someone questioned our qualifications or undermined women interns' work ethic but trusted in that of men.

My experiences during my internship, and my lack of preparedness to respond, led me to wonder if any of my classmates were having similar experiences. I spoke to other women in my classes at Northeastern University, as well as several at the neighbouring Berklee College of Music. Similarly, they all felt ill-prepared to handle situations like gender discrimination and sexual misconduct, and that our music business programmes and partnering companies for our internships – where we might one day work – should do better. Many students suggested that women's representation on faculty is critical to helping them feel included and more confident. One Northeastern University student responded: 'I feel more comfortable raising my hand and speaking out in classes with female professors, because I know what I say will be heard'.

In a study titled 'Students' Perceptions of their Classroom Participation and Instructor as a Function of Gender and Context', authors Crombie, Pyke, Silverthorn, Jones, and Piccinin found that both male and female students often credit female instructors with fostering a more comfortable and open learning environment.[3] But the representation of women is particularly important for female students to overcome what Hall and Sandler in their formative report called the 'chilly climate', described by Crombie et al. as the 'aggregated impact of a host of micro in-equities and forms of systemic discrimination that disadvantage women in academic environments'.[4]

Thankfully, higher education is doing marginally better than the commercial music industry when it comes to hiring more women. At Northeastern and Berklee, Boston's leading schools for music industry studies, women make up about one-third of the music business faculty, and gender gaps in faculty tenure and promotion are also narrowing: across the department, approximately 21% of female faculty hold tenured or tenure-track positions, compared to 28% of male faculty. Unfortunately, as in many other music or arts programs, the vast majority of music faculty (75%) hold non-tenure-eligible positions as teaching faculty, professors of the practice, or adjunct faculty: all positions with shorter contracts, smaller salaries, and, in the case of our adjuncts, no benefits. Alongside better representation, learning environments must prioritise advocacy for gender parity, fair labour practices, and anti-discrimination approaches in classrooms and on hiring committees. Simply hiring more women is not enough.

At one point during my interviews, a student from Berklee College of Music posed a question to me: 'Have you talked to any guys about this?' She had caught my assumption that gender issues are exclusively women's responsibility to handle and resolve. She described a classroom situation that suggests male students share this belief: whenever a discussion of gender was raised in her ethics class, all the men who were normally talkative and eager to participate would grow silent. She reasoned that they may have been uncomfortable or preferred to listen in order to learn. But perhaps, after years of formal education and conditioning to see men as the default norm, they assumed that gender does not impact them, and that any discussion of gender should be led by anyone other than men. Prior to these interviews, I also assumed that research on gender discrimination should focus on those experiencing discrimination. While it is important to centre the experiences of those who have suffered because of gender-based discrimination, it is equally important to insist students of all genders take part in the conversation, if we want to improve higher education and job preparedness for all students. Furthermore, existing preparatory training for interns and future professionals to 'handle' misconduct or gender discrimination, harassment, or assault in the workplace is incomprehensive. Professors should move beyond the textbooks and standard sexual harassment training to create an environment in which students are encouraged to ask questions about the full spectrum of gender discrimination they might witness or experience, from the chilly climate to discriminatory hiring. Programmes should include bystander intervention and allyship training for male faculty and students alike. Music business programmes should normalise open conversations about the internal dialogues that so many women are having regarding their gendered experiences in classrooms and professional settings. Instead of relegating this career training to one module in one course, professors should address equity and inclusion in *every* class and present students with diverse perspectives from a range of industry sectors. Through this strategy, gender equity and inclusion are embedded explicitly and assertively as a problem to be resolved in collaboration by all.

My Call to Action

Based on my own experiences and interviews with other students, I have outlined several recommendations I hope will be useful to professors hoping to better prepare all students for leadership in music:

1. *Encourage the tough conversations*. Talking about gender-based privilege or discrimination can be uncomfortable, but a problem must be named before it can be solved. Allow students to share and ask questions about the types of situations they might face, in a classroom environment in which they feel safe.
2. *Make men a part of these conversations*. Their contributions are needed, and may need to be compulsory, if gender inclusivity is to be attained. Let them know that they are not the enemy but are rather essential contributors to this important work.

3. *Self-reflect on your implicit biases.* Be aware of how you gender industry professionals in case studies and roleplay. Ensure that women, trans, and non-binary students can see themselves represented in important leadership positions so that they can envision and attain leadership positions in their own careers.
4. *Acknowledge intersectionality.* Collect as many perspectives as possible when talking about gender. Privilege and oppression are intersectional: BIPOC women, for example, likely experience both gendered and racialised discrimination.[5] The same holds true for disabled women, neurodiverse women, trans and nonbinary people, and all historically minoritised people.
5. *Leverage your own privilege.* As a white, cis-gender, straight-passing woman with access to higher education, I have been afforded many advantages and protected from many types of discrimination. Acknowledging that privilege is just the beginning of the work to achieve a more equitable music industry. Next steps include listening to people with experiences different than yours, lifting up the voices of those who might not have access to the same platform as you, stepping aside and letting others lead, speaking up for colleagues when you witness injustice, and creating safe space with your presence for everyone to exist as exactly as they are.
6. *Conduct a regular self-assessment:* Make yourself a personal checklist for self-reflection on your contributions to gender equity. You can start with the steps outlined here. Add more as you go. Update it continuously so that you can see your growth through this process.

Final Thoughts

I was very lucky to be part of a university programme composed of professors and students who wanted to listen and learn. My male friends showed me every day that they wanted me to feel comfortable and succeed as a student and music industry professional. My professors made important efforts to be more inclusive: they were receptive and responsive to feedback in class and were willing to pause for reflection if students had differing experiences based on their identities. I had incredible mentors at Northeastern, including Rebekah, co-author for this chapter. Doors were always open to have conversations about how professors could better support students, and professors were open to feedback about how we could feel more included in their classrooms.

I realise that this is not always the case, either in the university or in the music business, but if we normalise talking openly about gender, privilege, and oppression; work to prepare all students and future leaders to identify injustice and speak out against it; and encourage everyone to value diversity in music and equity for all who make it, then maybe we will be well on our way to doing better.

Allie's Story

When I walked onto Northeastern University's campus for my first-year orientation, I was shy, timid, and anxious. I watched the orientation leaders in awe. They were so outgoing and confident, and I could not imagine how I would get from my current state to theirs. But a few hours in, I found out that all the orientation leaders were second-year students. This fact blew my mind. With their level of confidence and familiarity, I assumed they were at least third-years – probably fourth-years. When I realised they were only a year older than I was, and that they went from being timid first-years to outgoing second-years in such a short time, I felt immense relief. I was able to see myself in their shoes and my potential as a successful college student. Role models were, and are, so important for me.

I experienced the same phenomenon as an intern at the Madison Square Garden Company in New York City. I worked in the Production Department, where I encountered a steep learning curve and had to take notes feverishly in order to learn the ropes. Learning production often felt like learning a new language. My supervisor, Chelsea, was an incredible mentor. After meetings, she would stay behind and teach me the production lingo I would need to know: When rigging lights or speakers, for example, a *dead hang* means that something is hung from a single point from the ceiling, and a *bridle* means it is hung from two points. The *baffle* is a drape that goes in front of the arena scoreboard to keep sound from bouncing off it during concerts. Chelsea invited me to shadow her throughout my internship; she constantly checked in and encouraged me to ask questions. I was so impressed by her confidence with the technical language and complicated software. Much like during my college orientation, I found myself thinking it would take forever for me to get to her level. And then once again my mind was blown when I found out that she was less than two years my senior. Chelsea led meetings with a commanding demeanour, delegated tasks professionally and efficiently to staff, contracted union workers, and was respected by those around her. Once I learned we were so close in age, I could imagine having my own successful career in production one day. Looking back, I am curious if Chelsea and the Northeastern orientation leaders also had supportive role models who helped them advance to the positions they hold now.

In addition to working on live event production in New York City, I was lucky to work in the Programming Department at The John F. Kennedy Center for the Performing Arts in Washington, DC. I was hired part-time after my internship ended and worked with the Kennedy Center for more than two years. There, I had another 'I know I can do this' moment: One day, my co-worker Bekah, who was scheduled to manage backstage, had to take over for a stage manager who was ill. As a result, I was placed in charge backstage during a sold-out performance featuring high-profile artists, and without Bekah's tutelage, because she was too busy stage managing to answer any questions. At first, I was nervous and wondered how I would possibly know what to do and when, in order to ensure a smooth production. But I took a deep breath and remembered I had been watching Bekah all day. Moreover, for months I had observed my amazing female co-workers manage events with composure and professionalism. At that moment, I was inspired to do the same. After the show, Bekah and the performers praised my performance under pressure. From then on, I had the confidence to continue to step up and take charge.

In addition to providing me with seminal role models and mentors, my internships taught me that a department's structure is key to equity and diversity in leadership. At The Kennedy Center, I worked in the Shared Services Programming Department, which manages programming as diverse as comedy, jazz, hip-hop, and classical music. The department employs a matrix management model, whereby each staff reports to two or more supervisors, fostering cross-departmental communication and encouraging cross-functional knowledge: keys to The Kennedy Center's creative and special programming success. In addition, it helps to flatten the structural hierarchy by prioritising shared leadership and input from staff at all levels. In *Arts Leadership in Contemporary Contexts*, author Jo Caust argues that shared leadership is key to increasing success among female leaders. She suggests that women in U.S. society tend to be oriented towards participatory work, and shared leadership depends upon mutual respect and collaborative skill-building.[6] Shared leadership can also help to deter abuses of power, a problem among both male and female leaders. By flattening the hierarchy, shared leadership allows several leaders to manage equally important responsibilities and maintain equal decision-making capacity.

Just as a management style is crucial to women's success in the live events industry, so is training and expertise in all departments. During my internships, I paid attention to the gender breakdown in programming and production: The Kennedy Center's Programming

Department was composed of ten women and three men, while the Production Department, though headed by a woman, was composed mostly of men. Programming is often considered to be the purview of women in performing arts administration, while production is usually managed by men. The Production Department at Madison Square Garden proved to be the exception: seven of the twelve employees were women. As an intern there, I learned the benefits of having diverse voices and points of view in production. It was refreshing to see co-workers who were supportive of each other and open to new ideas. Occasionally, outside promoters would express surprise or concern that a woman was running production for their show. But those women were excellent at their jobs, and those promoters never stayed doubtful for long.

Representation matters for women, but not all women are given equal opportunity in the live entertainment industry. Only two people of colour worked in my department at The Kennedy Center, and at Madison Square Garden, only one. As a white woman, I was able to find mentors who looked like me and had similar life experiences. One of the reasons Chelsea was a great role model was because I saw myself in her and saw who I could become if I followed in her path. All professionals deserve to benefit from positive mentorships so that they, too, can imagine themselves in leadership roles one day; but live entertainment has a long way to go to hire more BIPOC professionals in fulltime leadership roles.

My Call to Action

As a young woman who has studied, observed, and worked in the music industry for several years now, I have identified a few ways in which the live entertainment industries could invite a diversity of perspectives and experiences and benefit from the knowledge and expertise of women and all underrepresented groups:

1. *Hire more women in decision-making roles:* During the 2018 Women in Music Leadership Academy held in New York City, Julie Greenwald, Chairman and COO of Atlantic Records, said of the importance of women in Artist and Repertoire roles: 'If you have more women in A&R, you'll have more people actively looking for female producers and engineers and introducing them to all these young artists walking through the door'.[7] The same applies to live event production. While I have been lucky to be hired and trained by women, I have also witnessed the lack of gender and racial diversity in production leadership. If more women, especially women of colour, are given hiring power, then they will have the authority and inclination to hire more women of colour. There is also room for improvement in programming, as illustrated by the vast number of studies highlighting the dearth of female headliners at music festivals.[8] If more women are hired in programming positions in which they shape the types of shows and performers featured, then they can bring in more diverse artists. Then, hopefully, young women in the audience can see themselves onstage and be inspired to pursue their own music careers.
2. *Embrace shared and supportive leadership:* While in a departmental meeting at The Kennedy Center, I overheard one director say to another, 'I really admire the way you ran that show. It was amazing, and I definitely want to implement some of what you did into my shows. You're killing it!' This comment exemplifies one of the benefits of a matrix management system or other shared leadership model. It brings a group of leaders together in a room to learn from and encourage each other. Having multiple leaders in a department distributes power, responsibilities, and decision-making throughout a group. This can benefit the whole department, especially when the leaders are representative of the people they are leading.

3. *Implement mentorship programmes and bias awareness in hiring training:* Mentorship programmes are proven to be highly beneficial for mentors, mentees, and the company as a whole. According to a student-led Cornell University study that observed the effects of mentoring on diversity and employee retention and promotion: 'Mentoring has been proven to be more successful at promoting workplace diversity than diversity training programs alone'. In fact, mentoring programmes boosted minority representation at the management level from 9% to 24%.[9] The study also showed that these programmes improved retention rates among both women and minorities. Mentorship programmes are an effective way to improve diverse representation in the workplace. Much like gender or race bias in hiring decisions, however, mentor relationships are often formed between people who share similar identities. Companies must first commit to a diverse workforce, and then ensure inclusivity in their mentorship programmes. They might also encourage mixed-gender mentorship, so that more men in leadership roles can better understand their responsibilities to young women in their organisation and give those young women a better chance at becoming leaders, too. I have experienced this first-hand with Bobby, one of my co-workers at Madison Square Garden. He frequently went out of his way to explain things I did not yet understand and, like Chelsea, encouraged my many questions. He has also guided me through my post-graduation job search. I know that with the help and support Bobby and others have offered me, I will be a better mentor to young professionals in the future.

4. *Eliminate unpaid internships to increase access to professional development:* Internships are crucial to career advancement in music. Many of the full-time employees that I worked with during my internship had previously interned at the same organisations. If college internship coordinators prioritise placing more diverse interns in the music industry, then the music industry might reflect a more diverse workforce in the future. But for that to happen, internship programmes need to be more accessible. Currently, they disproportionately benefit students and young professionals who can afford to work for little or no pay. My internship at The Kennedy Center was unpaid, and at Madison Square Garden I barely received a living wage. As Elaine Swan notes in the *Handbook of Gendered Careers in Management*, 'internships reproduce financial, social, and cultural inequalities structured by class, gender, and race. Internships are difficult to access without certain kinds of cultural, economic, and social capital'.[10] All entertainment companies need to find a way to equitably compensate all interns. An internship in one's desired profession should not be a privilege: it should be treated as crucial to professional success and a requisite in higher education. Students who cannot afford to complete unpaid internships are unfairly disadvantaged and lack the opportunity to get a foot in the door with companies where they seek employment. If internship programmes are more accessible, then companies will benefit from increased diversity among their interns and, eventually, their full-time staff.

Final Thoughts

The world of live entertainment looks quite different after the total shutdown of live event programming due to COVID-19. I am no longer working at The Kennedy Center, and all but a handful of my Kennedy Center and Madison Square Garden co-workers have been laid off in recent months (at the time of writing). While the pandemic devastated the performing arts around the world, our extended intermission also presented an important opportunity for us all to re-examine our management practices and company culture so that, hopefully, as we come back together for live music again, we can commit to doing so in a diverse and supportive professional environment. I strongly believe that companies and organisations should make an effort to implement these changes and hire more women and people of colour in leadership roles. In that case, they too could witness the energy, passion, and work-ethic diverse leaders bring to the table.

Shannon's Story

One of my favourite movies growing up, *The Sisterhood of the Traveling Pants*, tells the story of four best friends who vow to send a pair of jeans to one another as a way of staying close during a summer apart. The film highlights the importance of female friendships and how four unique, powerful, smart women can lean on each other in the best and worst of times. The film also happens to pass the Bechdel Test, a measure of gender portrayal in works of fiction that has been adopted by critics to call attention to gender inequality in film.[11] Movies that pass this test include at least one scene in which two female characters have a conversation with each other about something other than a man. Its purpose is to increase awareness about women's objectification and lack of agency as a first step towards promoting change. While this is a bare minimum requirement for women's representation, a surprising number of films have failed this test. Films like *The Traveling Pants* model strong and supportive female relationships that were empowering to me when I was young, and which set a standard for the friendships I developed through college.

So, what is the Bechdel equivalent for the music industry? How often do we see two female executives talking about a female artist they have signed, or encounter a female producer in the recording studio? What would be the benefits of holding all creative industries to higher standards for gender inclusivity? What might it take for more women who have 'made it' to support women like me, at the beginning of their careers?

In 2018, I interned for a major record label in New York City. At first glance, the office seemed very welcoming for women: I spent seven months surrounded by a team of hard-working and passionate women. As I reflected on women's roles within the company, however, I realised that the majority were relegated to administrative capacities – roles that have historically been and continue to be filled mostly by women and which lack the decision-making power that men in management or executive positions wield. Even when women *are* able to secure executive positions, they often encounter the gender pay gap. Following the passage of a new law in the U.K., requiring all large companies to publicise their gender pay gaps, the British Headquarters of Sony Music Entertainment, Universal Music Group, and Warner Music Group revealed that women were paid 26.5% less than men on average. Female executives received 24.4% less in annual bonuses than their male counterparts at Universal, 50.1% less at Sony Music Entertainment, and 67.5% less at Warner Music Group.[12] The Artist and Repertoire Department at the company for which I interned included only one woman on staff. So, while a headcount might reveal a near-even gender split in a record company, an audit of who is responsible for making creative decisions, shaping the next generation of artists, and receiving equitable compensation reveals a scarcity of women with substantive creative power.

The lack of women's representation in the music business corresponds with poor representation on the most popular and critically acclaimed recorded music releases. The 2021 USC Annenberg Inclusion study examining gender, race, and ethnicity across 900 songs on the Billboard Year-End Hot 100 Chart and Grammy nominations across the top five categories between 2012 and 2020 found that only 2.6% of all producers, 12.6% of songwriters, and 21.6% of artists were women.[13] Further, over the Grammy's six decades of voting, only one woman, Linda Perry, was ever nominated for producer of the year in a non-classical category (2019). The report revealed what we might assume to be true: women remain sorely underrepresented in the commercial music industry. This is not because they do not create great music, as former Recording Academy President Neil Portnow would have us believe. During the 60th Annual Grammy Awards, in response to criticisms over the lack of women among the winners, he said:

> Women who have the creativity in their hearts and souls, who want to be musicians, who want to be engineers, producers, and want to be part of the industry on the executive level . . . [They need] to "step up".[14]

Several prominent recording artists promptly 'clapped back' via social media to remind him that women *are* creating great music, but they are rarely granted the same opportunities to succeed as men and are often overlooked by the voting members of The Recording Academy.

Despite some shortcomings, my record label internship was transformative. I felt appreciated and heard, and I got to learn more than I could have imagined from a group of women who continue to inspire me to this day. They also cared for, supported, and respected one another. They valued collaboration, highlighted each other's unique skill sets, and were always willing to lend a hand or lift each other up when needed. They fostered an environment and culture that made me feel comfortable enough to ask questions and share new ideas. As a result, I became a more confident and valuable colleague. Furthermore, the relationships I formed at the label and at other companies in the building led me to my current full-time position with a New York City music company.

In a 2019 study led by music producer and Berklee Professor Erin Barra, a total of 61% of women reported having a mentor, and of these, 92% felt that mentoring supported their career advancement.[15] While there was no significant difference in career outcomes between those with male or female mentors, many respondents noted that representation was important to them. One participant stated: 'Seeing representation of people like me (women) leading bands and being professional touring musicians really paved the way for what I do today. Seeing is believing. Representation matters'.[16] I relate to this statement. Seeing women represented in the music industry has always been empowering for me and has allowed me to imagine myself in their shoes. Amy Birnbaum, Senior Director of Artist and Public Relations and A&R at Round Hill Music, whom I interviewed about gender parity and the music industry, reinforced the importance of women mentors: 'I have a passion for mentoring and developing young women, and I think it's extremely important for young girls to know that they can be badass businesswoman!' She also noted that a leader should be a positive force and use their platform to uplift others: 'I always want to be a positive role model in the life of another person. I want to mentor students that are insatiably passionate, and specifically kids that may not have the same opportunities and educational resources as others'.

My Call to Action

1. *Pay interns:* Like Allie, I believe this must be a top priority. Despite the documented benefit of career mentorship, many women are unable to benefit because they cannot afford to work as unpaid interns, the standard model for on-the-job training for many U.S. college business programmes. Companies that *do* compensate interns often only pay minimum wage or slightly more, which will not come close to covering the costs of living in the music industry's U.S. epicentres in New York, Los Angeles, or Nashville. Making mentorship and internship programmes more accessible through fair compensation is a necessary step to creating a more diverse music industry. One organisation outside of higher education that is driving inclusivity and equality through accessible mentorship and career development for women is the U.S.

non-profit She Is the Music.[17] The organisation manages networking databases, mentorships, internships, and song-writing camps to increase the number of women working in music. I believe that this can be scaled to college and university music business programmes.

2. *Consider intersections of discrimination:* As a white cisgender woman with a college degree, I acknowledge that I benefit from several privileges. As we continue to work to create a more inclusive music industry, we must acknowledge our own privilege and use it to help amplify the voices of those who may not be afforded the same opportunity. Leaders who prioritise inclusion and want to increase diversity must remember that the intersection of gender, race, sexuality, education, class, and disability can further compound discrimination and exclusion. In a recent interview, Chrissy Nkemere, Global Chair of Diversity and Inclusion at Women in Music, said:

> Even as women, we fail to recognize that we have varying levels of privilege afforded to us depending on our race, sexual orientation, class, and more. Our differences make us stronger and more valuable as career people, as allies, and as mentors to young talent. The more we speak up and out, the better our chances are at eliminating this conversation altogether'.[18]

3. *Push for organisational change:* The women surveyed for the Annenberg Inclusion study and Berklee Women in Music report, as well as friends and colleagues I have interviewed, all concur that discrimination and harassment are two of the greatest challenges women face in today's music industry. As we become aware of our respective privileges and work to change our individual behaviours, we must also push for change at the organisational level by demanding formal training led by independent experts on gender bias and workplace discrimination. In addition to mandatory training on sexual harassment, training on the *value* of diversity and critical importance of inclusion should be mandatory. Safe spaces for learning and open dialogue are key to personal and organisational change. In my current role, most of my colleagues are women. Many artists who have entered our conference rooms have pointed out the rarity of this. I suspect this is possible at my current company because leaders invested in organisational transformation to improve the working environment for women and others who have been historically underrepresented, and to convert good ideas into action. We take part in monthly training sessions and global diversity dialogues with external facilitators, and our collective goals and recommendations are relayed by our task force to the company's leadership. The additional hiring of external ethics consultants to ensure safe spaces for employees to report cases of discrimination or harassment anonymously is also extremely important. People should not be afraid to lose their jobs after reporting mistreatment within the workplace.

Final Thoughts

When I think about my professional experiences, as well as those of my colleagues Allie and Liz, I realise that whether we are in a classroom, a performing arts institution, or a major record label, we have faced adversity because of our gender. But we have also benefitted greatly from strong female role models in leadership – from our professors to our department managers. We have been supported by them when we needed it the most. We have been made to feel welcome, respected, and capable of achieving anything we set our minds to. Through both our personal friendships and professional mentorships, we learn the value of sisterhood: it is the strength of collective belonging and collective action that will lead us toward true equality.

Rebekah's Reflection

I attended my first protest march at five years old, in the company of my feminist mother and my little brother. That day, we were marching for women's right to a safe and legal abortion. I never anticipated that nearly forty years later, our hard-won reproductive rights would be revoked, and I would be counselling young women in my classrooms on how to compel their congressional representatives to care about *their* right to life. In that span of four decades, I have marched with others in protest of many injustices, both those that impact me as a queer woman raised in rural poverty and saddled with student loan debt and those for which I bear some responsibility, as a white cis woman with a PhD and a tenure-track academic appointment in an intensely segregated city. During the Summer of 2020, while much of the world was still in lockdown due to the pandemic and the United States was reeling from more killings of unarmed Black men and women by police, I marched with friends and colleagues, all masked, in support of the Black Lives Matter movement. Within social movements, music and organised sound – call and response chants, drumming circles, marching bands, and collective singing – form the spiritually affirming soundscapes of protest. That summer, protesters chanted 'No justice, no peace! Prosecute the police!'; 'Say her name! Breonna Taylor!'; and 'Hands up! Don't shoot!'. Songs like Public Enemy's 'Fight the Power' (recorded and released 1989), Kendrick Lamar's 'Alright' (recorded 2014–2015, released 2015), and Beyoncé's 'Freedom' (recorded 2014, released 2016) blasted from amplifiers and car speakers as a reminder of the past and presence of protest within Black popular music.[19] It was through street protest, as much as my public school and college education that I learned about the injustices of sexist and racist oppression, the political power of protest, the collective effervescence catalysed by music and chant, and sadly, the inequities created by social constructions of race, gender, and ability that are often replicated in movement leadership.

In 2017, after a decade-long international career in the music industry and arts administration, I returned to the United States to stand before a traditional classroom of higher education as a music industry professor. In that classroom, I met many students who recognise the social and political power of popular music. I have served alongside them for a non-hierarchical Committee for Social Justice and Anti-Racism in Music, which seeks to align our department's programmes, policies, and practices with a social justice and anti-racist framework. Students are yearning for change within the music curriculum and their chosen professions: They want the equal opportunity, fair pay, and creative freedom that are so often discarded within the neoliberalist and monopolistic regimes of the global recording and live entertainment industries. Many of these thoughtful, inquisitive, and dauntless young people, including my co-authors here, remind me of the activists and organisers I have met marching for change. Allie, Liz, and Shannon demand that both higher education and the music business do better by women, and they have very good ideas on what that means.

Liz's contribution to this chapter draws on personal observations and interviews with students from music business programmes in the Boston area to: a) highlight the gendered inequities students expect to face as music professionals; and b) argue for changes to the curriculum and classroom dynamics to challenge systemic inequality. She argues that women's representation in classroom leadership is crucial. Women constitute a minority of music business faculty within Boston's most prestigious music programmes, yet students who have enrolled in woman-led courses and receive mentoring from female faculty report feeling better equipped to advance their careers. As Liz observes, an additive approach to achieve gender equity by hiring more women faculty or setting student enrolment and retention targets is not enough. Similarly, Sam de Boise argues in his study on gender inequalities in higher music education in the U.K. and Sweden: '[This approach] does not disrupt the classed, gendered and ethnic hierarchies on which institutional aesthetic priorities are based'.[20] Liz's call to action encourages educators to go further, and she also holds students accountable for warming the 'chilly climate' for women and other minoritised students. The college classroom environment is a critical setting to stimulate dialogue about gender bias, inspire students of all genders to imagine their responsibility to combatting discrimination as future leaders, and motivate a lifelong commitment to a more diverse and inclusive workforce.

De Boise's study finds that while women frequently equal or surpass the number of men accepted to music programmes in music performance, they are well outnumbered in music technology, production, and jazz performance.[21] Race, nationality, and class also factored into discrimination in the application and selection process.[22] My institution reflects an identical gender gap in these specialisations: women are a scant minority in the music technology major, advanced music production courses, and the instrumental sections of the rock and jazz ensembles – their numbers are predictably higher in the vocal sections. While women comprise the majority of enrolled students, their inequality remains a chronic challenge, in no small part exacerbated by a majority white male faculty and evidenced in student evaluations of courses and internships. This gender imbalance in music business education most assuredly correlates with the dearth of women in award-winning professional music production, as highlighted by the Annenberg Inclusion Study. Interestingly, female students are the majority within songwriting courses, suggesting that Shannon may be correct in inferring that the lack of women producing and writing for the Grammy victors has more to do with bias by the voting membership than a dearth of well-prepared female songwriters.

Based on recent research on gender inequities in the music business, observations during her record company internship, and an interview with a former supervisor, Shannon illuminates the pervasiveness of gender discrimination in the commercial music industry. As one strategy towards achieving gender equity, she argues for increasing women's representation across all record label leadership roles. Rather than being cordoned off into administration or marketing roles, women should be empowered to make the important creative decisions that impact talent development and the songs and records that make it to the market. Through mentorship and equal opportunity hiring, recording companies could reduce leadership's gender gap and increase the number of women appearing on performance charts and earning industry accolades. This would be very good for the recording business, as a more diverse workforce could translate to increased market share among diverse audiences, but one must tread carefully when making the 'business case for diversity'.[23] This motivating factor simply treats diverse bodies as company resources, rather than rightful participants in all facets of professional life. Rather than treating diversity as means to a profitable end, Parker and McDonald advocate for an 'intersectional leadership' among 'critically self-reflexive organizational members [who] develop the capacity to "see" inequitably derived difference and create innovative and adaptive ways of organizing for equity and inclusion'.[24] Thus, corporate diversity and inclusion strategies must reflect a commitment to social justice – an equal distribution of opportunity – and *not* only the company's bottom line.

In contrast to the majority male leadership of higher music education and the recording industry, the majority of performing arts professionals are women. Women rarely secure the highest positions of power within performing arts administration, however, and much like in the college classroom and on the hit record, they are often excluded from masculinised positions in staging and production. Allie shares her experiences as an intern as a rare exception. At the John F. Kennedy Center for the Performing Arts in Washington, D.C., many leadership positions across every department were held by women. Based on her personal experiences and interviews with former co-workers and supervisors, Allie outlines several changes performing arts organisations can implement to increase women's participation in crucial creative and operational decision-making and encourage young women's career advancement. Moreover, she advocates for the implementation of a collaborative management model similar to that employed at the Kennedy Center: it increases productivity, collective problem-solving, and cross-functional knowledge, as well as champions shared leadership among managers and junior team members. Echoing Liz and Shannon, Allie argues that mentorship is also crucial. Young women who are supported by successful and powerful women *and* men in their leadership development gain the skills and confidence necessary to rise to any leadership position they envision.

Closing Thoughts and Individual Commitments

As we reflect on this volume, many years in the making, we have been thinking deeply about the intersectionalities of oppression from which our privileges of race and education have largely protected us: the widespread and systemic anti-Black racism that crystallised in the wake of George Floyd's murder, the lack of access to safe and affordable healthcare that has been exacerbated by the pandemic, and the devastating and unequal impacts of economic crisis and climate crisis weigh heavily on us, and we wonder whether it is our place and time to lead conversations on equity and equality. This is an important time for the historically privileged to listen and reflect: to take up less space. At the same time, we all have a role to play in mobilising for equality: in musical leadership and the wider communities of which we are a part. To this end, we conclude by outlining the commitments we are each prepared to make; now, and for many years to come.

Liz will hold herself accountable to learning from the perspectives and experiences of BIPOC women, non-binary, and trans persons; uplift their perspectives; and speak up when their voices are ignored or silenced. Allie will commit to being a good mentor and role model to as many young people as possible. Her goal is to make it to a high leadership position and bring as many women up with her as she can. She believes that the pandemic and resultant shutdown of live entertainment present an opportunity for leaders in music to reflect on the future environments in which they will lead, identify the changes they want to make, and create a cooperative strategy to build new systems that support diversity, inclusion, and parity. Shannon wants to continue the work of advocacy in our industry by listening to and lifting up the voices of those who are disadvantaged by our current system. Rather than treating diversity and inclusion strategies as prescriptive, she is committed to thinking like an innovator about how to build new systems that work for everyone, in every professional environment she enters. In her music business classrooms, Rebekah will draw deliberately on the principles of anti-oppression that guide her activism and work as a volunteer for survivors of partner violence, articulated within social work as the 'moral, ethical and legal responsibility to challenge inequality and disadvantage' to build more equitable and inclusive courses and classrooms.[25] She is also inspired by efforts to decolonise the curriculum,[26] as well as criticisms that this work all too often leads to self-congratulatory tokenism, rather than a relational approach to systems of knowledge.[27]

In 2020, a year that profoundly changed how we think about our personal responsibilities for the health and wellbeing of others, both friends and strangers, we saw an opportunity to change how and why U.S. higher education institutions seek diversity, equity, and inclusion. When made true and actionable priorities, these equally important objectives create research and learning environments that welcome diverse perspectives and demand equal access to education and professional development. Collectively, we encourage institutions to be creative in handling their unique equity and diversity challenges, rather than seek out a one-size-fits-all approach. Each will need to develop interrelated strategies for advancing equity and inclusion in the curriculum. Reducing the gender gap in courses and programmes is a start, but holistic curricular assessments are also necessary in order to ensure course content reflects a breadth of backgrounds and perspectives. *Paid* internships with organisations committed to a diverse workforce, artist roster, and creative output enable students to bear witness to how these commitments are carried out in the professional environment.

We have a long way to go to create a diverse, equitable, and inclusive learning and professional environment in which women and all historically oppressed people have both agency and power to make and profit from music. That work begins in our classrooms, whether that classroom is in the streets, a recording studio, theatre, or university hall.

Notes

1. Patricia S. Parker and Jamie McDonald, "Difference, Diversity, and Inclusion," in *Movements in Organizational Communication Research* edited by Jamie McDonald and Rahul Mitra (London: Routledge, 2019), 135–54.
2. Fred Goodman, *The Mansion on the Hill: Dylan, Young, Geffen, Springsteen, and the Head-on Collision of Rock and Commerce* (New York: Vintage Books, 1997).
3. Gail Crombie, Sandra W. Pyke, Naida Silverthorn, Alison Jones, and Sergio Piccinin, "Students' Perceptions of Their Classroom Participation and Instructor as a Function of Gender and Context," *The Journal of Higher Education* 74 (2002): 51–76.
4. Roberta M. Hall and Bernice R. Sandler, *The Classroom Climate: A Chilly One for Women?* (Washington, DC: Association of American Colleges Project on the Status and Education of Women).
5. Black, Indigenous, and People of Colour.
6. Jo Caust, *Arts Leadership in Contemporary Contexts* (New York: Routledge, 2018), 40–41.
7. Cherie Hu, "Female Powerhouses Talk Diversity, Inclusion at American Express Women in Music Leadership Academy: Exclusive," *Billboard*, May 15, 2018, accessed November 8, 2020, www.billboard.com/articles/business/8448794/american-express-women-music-leadership-divesity.
8. A case in point in the City of Boston – while it was cancelled due to the pandemic, the 2020 Boston Calling Music Festival was slated to feature an all-male line-up.
9. Kaitlyn Conboy and Chris Kelly, "What Evidence Is There that Mentoring Works to Retain and Promote Employees, Especially Diverse Employees, within a Single Company?' (Cornell University, 2016) in Cornell University, ILR School site accessed November 8, 2020, http://digitalcommons.ilr.cornell.edu/student/116, 3.
10. Elaine Swan, "The Internship Class: Subjectivity and Inequalities – Gender, Race and Class," in *Handbook of Gendered Careers in Management: Getting In, Getting On, Getting Out*, edited by Adelina M. Broadbridge and Sandra L. Fielden (Cheltenham: Edward Elgar Publishing Limited, 2015), 40.
11. For a detailed description of the Bechdel Test and its applications, see Apoorv Agarwal, Jiehan Zheng, Shruti Kamath, Sriramkumar Balasubramanian, and Shirin Ann Dey, "Key Female Characters in Film Have More to Talk About Besides Men: Automating the Bechdel Test," in *Human Language Technologies: The 2015 Annual Conference of the North American Chapter of the ACL* (Denver, CO: Association of Computational Studies, 2015), 830–40, accessed November 8, 2020, www.aclweb.org/anthology/N15-1084.pdf.
12. Murray Stassen, "Revealed: What Major Labels are Paying Women Compared to Men in the UK," *Music Business Worldwide*, April 4, 2019, accessed November 8, 2020, www.musicbusinessworldwide.com/revealed-what-major-labels-are-paying-women-compared-to-men-in-the-uk/.
13. Stacy L. Smith, Katherine Pieper, Hannah Clark, Ariana Case, and Marc Choueiti, *Inclusion in the Recording Studio? Gender and Race/Ethnicity of Artists, Songwriters and Producers across 900 Popular Songs from 2012–2020* (Los Angeles: University of Southern California Annenberg Inclusion Initiative, 2019), accessed November 22, 2022, http://assets.uscannenberg.org/docs/aii-inclusion-recording-studio-20200117.pdf.

14. Michele Amabile Angermiller, "Grammys So Male? "Women Need to Step Up," says Recording Academy Present," *Variety*, January 28, 2018, accessed November 8, 2020, https://variety.com/2018/music/news/grammys-so-male-women-recording-academy-president-neil-portnow-1202679902/.
15. Becky Prior, Erin Barra, and Sharon Kramer, *Women in the U.S. Music Industry: Obstacles and Opportunities* (Boston, MA: Berklee Institute for Creative Entrepreneurship), accessed November 8, 2020, www.berklee.edu/sites/default/files/Women%20in%20the%20U.S.%20Music%20Industry%20Report.pdf, 22.
16. Ibid., 21.
17. See accessed November 8, 2020, https://sheisthemusic.org/.
18. Manon Jessua, "Women's Role and Place in Today's Music Industry," *MiDEM Music Industry Insights Blog*, March 4, 2020, accessed November 8, 2020, https://blog.midem.com/2020/03/women-s-role-and-place-in-todays-music-industry/.
19. In an article for *Medium*, Noriko Manabe has curated and transcribed several of the most popular Black Lives Matter protest chants, as well as several of the most frequently heard songs. See "Chants and Music from Black Lives Matter Protests, June 2020," *Medium*, June 7, 2020, accessed November 22, 2020, https://medium.com/@norikomanabe/chants-and-music-from-black-lives-matter-protests-june-2020-af854e4b31fb.
20. Sam de Boise, "Gender Inequalities and Higher Music Education: Comparing the UK and Sweden," *British Journal of Music Education* 35 (2018): 34.
21. Ibid., 29.
22. In fact, between 2011 and 2013, no UK conservatoire accepted a Black applicant of any gender. Ibid., 34.
23. Parker and McDonald, "Difference, Diversity, and Inclusion," 147.
24. Ibid., 148.
25. Beverley Burke and Philomena Harrison, "Anti-Oppressive Practice," in *Social Work: Themes, Issues, and Critical Debates*, edited by Robert Adams, Lena Dominelli, Malcolm Payne, and Jo Campling (London: Palgrave, 1998), 229, https://doi.org/10.1007/978-1-349-14400-6_19.
26. Elizabeth Charles, "Decolonizing the Curriculum," *Insights* 32 (2019): 1–7.
27. See Juliet Hess, "Decolonizing Music Education: Moving Beyond Tokenism," *International Journal of Music Education* 3, no. 33 (2015): 336–47.

Bibliography

Agarwal, Apoorv, et al. "Key Female Characters in Film Have More to Talk About Besides Men: Automating the Bechdel Test." In *Human Language Technologies: The 2015 Annual Conference of the North American Chapter of the ACL*, 830–40. Denver, CO: Association of Computational Studies, 2015. Accessed November 8, 2020. www.aclweb.org/anthology/N15-1084.pdf.

Angermiller, Michele Amabile. "Grammys So Male? "Women Need to Step Up", Says Recording Academy Present." *Variety*, January 28, 2018. Accessed November 8, 2020. https://variety.com/2018/music/news/grammys-so-male-women-recording-academy-president-neil-portnow-1202679902/.

Burke, Beverley, and Philomena Harrison. "Anti-Oppressive Practice." In *Social Work: Themes, Issues, and Critical Debates*, edited by Robert Adams et al., 229–39. London: Palgrave, 1998. Accessed November 27, 2020. https://doi.org/10.1007/978-1-349-14400-6_19.

Caust, Josephine. *Arts Leadership in Contemporary Contexts*. London: Routledge, 2018.

Charles, Elizabeth. "Decolonizing the Curriculum." *Insights* 32 (2019): 1–7.

Conboy, Kaitlyn, and Chris Kelly. "What Evidence Is There That Mentoring Works to Retain and Promote Employees, Especially Diverse Employees, Within a Single Company?." Cornell University (2016), in ILR School. Accessed November 8, 2020. http://digitalcommons.ilr.cornell.edu/student/116.

Crombie, Gail, Sandra W. Pyke, Naida Silverthorn, Alison Jones, and Sergio Piccinin. "Students' Perceptions of Their Classroom Participation and Instructor as a Function of Gender and Context." *The Journal of Higher Education* 74 (2002): 51–76.

de Boise, Sam. "Gender Inequalities and Higher Music Education: Comparing the UK and Sweden." *British Journal of Music Education* 35 (2018): 23–41.

Evlanova, Anastassia. *Top 5 Safest Countries in Asia Pacific for Women*. Singapore: ValueChampion Research, 2019. Accessed November 8, 2020. www.valuechampion.sg/top-5-safest-countries-asia-pacific-women.

Goodman, Fred. *The Mansion on the Hill: Dylan, Young, Geffen, Springsteen, and the Head-on Collision of Rock and Commerce*. New York: Vintage Books, 1997.

Hall, Roberta M., and Bernice R. Sandler. *The Classroom Climate: A Chilly One for Women?*. Washington, DC: Association of American Colleges Project on the Status and Education of Women, 1982.

Hess, Juliet. "Decolonizing Music Education: Moving Beyond Tokenism." *International Journal of Music Education* 3, no. 33 (2015): 336–47.

Hu, Cherie. "Female Powerhouses Talk Diversity, Inclusion at American Express Women in Music Leadership Academy: Exclusive." *Billboard*, May 15, 2018. Accessed November 9, 2020. www.billboard.com/articles/business/8448794/american-express-women-music-leadership-divesity.

Parker, Patricia S., and Jamie McDonald. "Difference, Diversity, and Inclusion." In *Movements in Organizational Communication* Research, edited by Jamie McDonald and Rahul Mitra, 135–54. London: Routledge, 2019.

Prior, Becky, Erin Barra, Sharon Kramer. *Women in the U.S. Music Industry: Obstacles and Opportunities*. Boston: Berklee Institute for Creative Entrepreneurship. Accessed November 8, 2020. www.berklee.edu/sites/default/files/Women%20in%20the%20U.S.%20Music%20Industry%20Report.pdf.

Smith, Stacy L., et al. *Inclusion in the Recording Studio? Gender and Race/Ethnicity of Artists, Songwriters and Producers across 900 Popular Songs from 2012–2020*. Los Angeles: University of Southern California Annenberg Inclusion Initiative, 2020. Accessed November 22, 2022. http://assets.u.scannenberg.org/docs/aii-inclusion-recording-studio-20200117.pdf.

Stassen, Murray. "Revealed: What Major Labels Are Paying Women Compared to Men in the UK."*Music Business Worldwide*, April 4, 2019. Accessed November 8, 2020. www.musicbusinessworldwide.com/revealed-what-major-labels-are-paying-women-compared-to-men-in-the-uk/.

Swan, Elaine. "The Internship Class: Subjectivity and Inequalities – Gender, Race and Class." In *Handbook of Gendered Careers in Management: Getting In, Getting On, Getting Out*, edited by Adelina M. Broadbridge and Sandra L. Fielden. Cheltenham: Edward Elgar Publishing Limited, 2015.

28
WOMEN LEADING OPERA IN THE UK
An Ethnographic Study of Innovation

Elizabeth Etches Jones

The opera industry, like all other areas of classical music, is constantly under scrutiny for its use of public funding, and its relevance to contemporary society has never been more questioned. Indeed, large-scale institutions (such as the Royal Opera House [ROH] and English National Opera [ENO]) have in recent years been forced to adapt their long-standing business models to incorporate outreach and education schemes both by the funding bodies that support them, such as the Arts Council England, and by the necessity to encourage new audiences to attend and become patrons as in the case of existing patrons. Innovation, both in terms of re-assessing the company-consumer relationship and in terms of creating new products that can sustain existing audiences and entice new punters, has never been more critical to the opera industry. Large national opera companies with significant budgets from state subsidies and donors have been able to instigate successful 'access' programmes whilst otherwise sustaining their traditional business models. The necessity to engage with the customer, regardless of organisational scale, is ever-pressing; as Robert Cannon writes: 'any house's policy is essentially determined by its understanding of its audience and how it wants to approach them'.[1] That is where smaller-scale opera companies have recently blossomed; since the early 2000s, small opera companies have developed products and experiences designed specifically for the twenty-first century. The advantages of the small-scale business model are considerable; close relationships with (often local) audiences, alongside significantly increased flexibility of model and flexibility of creative output, allow smaller companies to establish and cultivate new cultures of consumerism within the opera industry. The role of women in such endeavours is revolutionary, as a significant proportion of small- to medium-sized companies were founded by or are led by women who seek to innovate, particularly at a time when the future of the notoriously male-dominated opera industry and its place in society seem uncertain and in a constant state of flux.[2]

Methodology and Scope

This ethnographic study sought to explore the decision-making processes and leadership styles of women leading innovative opera companies (opera companies seeking to disrupt the industry through new ways of either administrating or presenting opera). Using semi-structured, informal interviews, it aimed to gain insights into the variety of ways that small- to medium-sized opera companies with female leaders developed their current business models and relationships with their consumers. Being a female executive in the opera industry is an unusual status, particularly in larger institutions, and this study also sought to highlight the extent to which being a woman in the opera industry affects the careers of those seeking to lead the industry in new directions.

An interview-based methodology was crucial to understanding and representing both the shared and differing experiences of those in leadership positions; a core set of identical questions for the participants enables points of comparison, and participant-specific questions, as well as open-ended questions, expanded the discussions in order to generate a more accurate picture of each participant's attitudes to the industry, their own work, and the future of opera.

The scope of this study is limited, primarily due to the timescale of the project (January to February 2019). Future expansion of the number and range of leaders and their leadership styles could yield still more insights and useful conclusions to add to those found in this study.

Table 28.1 details the participants of this study and their respective companies.

Representing a range of perspectives was essential to this study, which necessarily engaged with organisations of varying sizes and ages, diverse (and some shared) aims, as well as leaders at different stages of their careers and working in a variety of geographical locations across the UK and abroad (particularly in the case of Daisy Evans). Although the selected group does

Table 28.1 The Participants and Their Respective Organisations

Name	Role	Company	Years Active	Company's Unique Selling Point (USP)
Clementine Lovell	Founder	Pop-Up Opera	2011 – 2019	• Unusual productions of opera • Opera in accessible locations across the UK (e.g. pubs/clubs)
Ally Rosser	Executive Manager	Mahogany Opera Group	2003 – present	• Experimental opera; stretching the boundaries of opera and who it is for • Opera for children
Daisy Evans	Founder	Silent Opera	2011 – present	• Radically realising texts • Innovating with technology • Re-orchestrating operas
Emma Doherty	Artistic Director	The Opera Shack	2018 – present	• Story-led performances • Combining opera with spoken word narration • Immersive productions, used to empower communities through workshops
Julie Aherne	Company Director	Black Cat Opera	2013 – present	• Traditional operas performed to high standards for new audiences • Corporate and public settings, including festival and gala performances
Isabella Pitman	Founder, Chief Executive	National Student Opera Society (NSOS)	2018 – present	• Providing information resources (e.g. ticket schemes) for students • A community platform for student opera societies and enthusiasts • Co-ordinating events for students with partner opera organisations

not cover absolutely every innovative business led by women in the industry, it reflects some of the most vital and successful approaches to opera today.

Pop-Up Opera, for example, was a crucial organisation to include due to its sheer size and coverage of the UK, having performed in over 150 venues across the UK in the last 10 years, and being one of the few opera companies in the UK to be completely financially self-sustainable, without using government funding or charitable status for assistance. In many ways, Pop-Up Opera set a new precedent for experience-based opera in unusual locations, and Clementine Lovell created its unique brand by prioritising new audiences and accessibility.

Boasting an impressive career producing contemporary opera, Ally Rosser at Mahogany Opera Group demonstrates in her work how experimental opera and its emphasis on artistic innovation can be combined with commissioning new works for children in order to create a business that not only pushes the boundaries of opera, but that also encourages young people and new audiences to engage with the art form. Emma Doherty, at a relatively early stage in her career, has developed an opera company that uses opera as a tool for empowerment in the community and, alongside the local community work of The Opera Shack, has established her own directing career working in larger organisations.

Daisy Evans's professional career has been filled with technological and conceptual innovation; under her leadership, Silent Opera radically realises text, often with new orchestrations of 'traditional' works, and has performed across the world, supported by her considerable success and reputation as an independent director and 'auteur'. Julie Aherne at Black Cat Opera has created an opera company which thrives on festival and corporate performances aimed at those audiences perhaps less familiar with the standard opera repertoire, introducing new audiences to opera through public performances and through the company's corporate sponsor.

Each of these executives emphasised in their interviews that quality is a non-negotiable part of their business strategy, even in the cases where opera is being created with or for children. The quality of the product is therefore an essential selling point of such innovative organisations. Isabella Pitman of NSOS has created a resource and networking platform that encourages university opera societies and students to actively engage with opera companies, providing events with partner organisations as well as information for people who have limited experience attending opera, and encouraging nationwide dialogue through social media channels. The differing aims of these companies demonstrate the wealth of possibilities for the expansion of the opera industry outside of the large institutions. Whether government-subsidised or corporately funded, and regardless of geographical location, these companies each have specific USPs that define their brand, purpose, and audiences.

I undertook this research to highlight the work of women leading their smaller opera companies in generating revenue for the industry as a whole, as well as in developing new audiences and creating contemporary art. Whilst the responses from the participants at times indicate shortcomings in the larger institutions' working practices in the UK (such as lack of support structures for working parents and the precariousness of freelance opera work), this study has sought to shed light upon the decision-making practices and attitudes of women working in the industry and the challenges they face in doing so, rather than actively to criticise men working in opera. That being said, this study recognises that there are male-led organisations that innovate and men throughout the industry who encourage gender parity. I argue, however, that the proportion of innovative companies led by women and female teams is so significant that it merits a specific scholarly focus. In doing so, I aim to explore the following question: how does this section of the operatic workforce retain and develop its ideologies in an industry which favours the maintenance of the status quo?

The issue of bias was an essential methodological consideration when undertaking the interviews for this study. Personal experience and broader research projects have directed me to explore this area, but I have sought throughout this process to ask fair questions and to respond to information gained from the interviews without including my own experience. Having worked as a director, producer, and administrator in the opera industry, I have first-hand experience of many of the key issues facing women seeking a career in opera, as well as some of the ways in which both women and men can provide vital opportunities for those seeking to develop in the field, most notably through my three-year administration internship at New Chamber Opera. Whilst my personal experiences are not included in this study, they have served as a useful tool to contextualise many of the issues highlighted by some of the participants. It means I have a lived, somatic experience not only of the industry, but of leadership as a woman and as someone who has made decisions in relation to innovative practice while retaining quality.

Findings

After the interview process was completed, I sought to compare the participants' responses, and ten key common areas of discussion emerged. The majority of the participants shared approaches to these areas and concepts, and whilst there was some variation in the individuals' approaches to these ideas, the importance of each was agreed upon across the board. This section will present and explore these ideas in the context of recent scholarship on leadership and cultures of consumerism.

1. Innovation is Central to Operatic Success

Each of the participants described the ways in which they had to innovate in order to found or lead companies that stand out in the market. This is vital not only to their own career success, but also to the sustainability of the opera industry. Without innovation, be it technological or simply in terms of cultivating new attendance experiences, there is no likelihood of consumers developing or maintaining new or stronger connections to the industry. The opera industry is commonly perceived as stagnant and old-fashioned, yet this image is countered by every project run by each of these women: Daisy Evans incorporates cutting-edge technology to innovate, and Emma Doherty and Clementine Lovell innovate by bringing their operas into communities in accessible and unusual locations. Isabella Pitman is innovating by producing a tangible resource for the younger generation of operagoers, centralising systems and forging new networks, and Ally Rosser is one of the leading managers of experimental opera, encouraging artists to innovate creatively and push the boundaries of what opera can be and who it is for. Crucially, in most of these interviews, the term 'innovation' was brought up by the participants without prompt or question within the first five minutes, demonstrating not only the importance of discussing innovation in the opera industry, but also how central innovation is to these women's pioneering work. One of the crucial factors behind the decision to set up such organisations was the notion that each business needed to be flexible and adaptable to the innovative ideas of its executives. Alan Griffiths and Stuart Wall present five ways in which small companies survive, even in economic or industry crises, and these reflect the main reasons behind the participants' choices to establish and lead small- to medium-sized opera organisations:

- They can 'supply a small (niche) market either geographically or by producing a specialist item or service';
- They wish to 'provide a personal or more flexible service';

- Small companies allow leaders 'the opportunity to start their own business and to test their ideas in the marketplace';
- Small companies also allow the owners the 'decision not to grow' should they wish to avoid the risks of expanding a business;
- They wish to 'benefit from government support programmes directed towards helping the small firm survive and grow'.[3]

Despite the fact that each participant's idea of 'innovation' varied from artistic experimentation to business model-based innovation, 'flexibility' and 'adaptability' were key concepts mentioned or discussed at length by each of the participants, which is discussed further in the third section of this study's findings.

2. Traditional Organisational Structures in Opera Do Not Always Encourage Strong Female Leadership Teams

Creative and executive teams in opera have historically been (and often still are) male-dominated, placing barriers to those women seeking to reach the top ranks. Only in recent years has there been any sign of significant improvement in the large opera houses (defined in this study as having more than 100 employees), but this is often tokenistic and without significant internal cultural change. The example of Cressida Pollock at English National Opera remains vitally important; hired as their Chief Executive to save the company from financial ruin and further crisis in 2015, Pollock successfully led ENO to turn a corner and develop new ways of consumerism in the opera industry, and in doing so prevented the closure of a national cultural institution. Upon finishing her stint there, however, Pollock said in an interview that the criticism she received had felt cruel and over-personal, with her character and leadership style being referred to by many as 'formidable', 'tough', and 'steely'.[4] The perception of women in leadership positions has been the focus of a significant amount of scholarship over the years; for example, in a seminal study in 2000, Kristi M. Lewis found that anger from a male leader is often perceived as assertiveness, whereas anger from a female leader can be seen as instability or aggression.[5] The perpetuation of the male dominance of leadership teams in opera can be explained in part through theories such as role congruity theory, which suggests that men might be seen as more able to fulfil leadership positions in male-dominant organisations as a result of the 'masculine' nature of the work environment.[6] In 2004, Madeline Heilman, Aaron Wallen, Daniella Fuchs, and Melinda Tamkins showed that should a female leader perform equally to their male counterpart, they could be evaluated worse if the job was 'masculine' in nature.[7] Such scholarship contextualises the challenges facing those seeking roles typically assumed by men in the opera industry. Whilst such challenges are rife in the industry, it is important to note that there are men and women working towards gender parity in leadership teams in many of the UK's organisations. Regardless of the slower, broader movement towards employing women in executive positions, the women leading the opera companies in this study are paving the way for future female leaders in the industry by redefining leadership roles and their perceptions.

3. Finding the Best Team of Collaborators is Essential to Creating New and Interesting Productions

All participants said that their success as women in opera is not only due to their own skill and hard work, but also due to the (often mixed) teams which they have constructed to support their visions. Working in supportive, diverse, and respectful environments was one of the top concerns for each of the participants, with 100% saying that they actively choose the people they work with not only by gauging their talent and capability but also their ability to create positive working practices that are inclusive and fair, incorporating a significant amount of collaboration across specialisms and levels of seniority. In doing so, companies like Pop-Up Opera and Mahogany Opera Group have developed a remarkable reputation in the industry for their constructive and supportive working environments, which in turn has encouraged some of the most innovative and creative talent to work with them. By creating this reputation and supporting other women (alongside their male colleagues), opera companies can draw in the best talent and therefore create an even better product for their consumers. This approach creates resilience, due to its emphasis on learning from peers and supporting continuous development; this has been explored as part of organisational resilience studies by scholars such as Andrew Ishak and Elizabeth Williams, who argue that in order for a 'dynamic model of organisational resilience' to be implemented, organisations' processes must correspond to a 'growth mindset'.[8] Identity, whilst an important part of an organisation's 'brand', can be built around change and growth, allowing all aspects of the company (such as size, product, or methods of innovating) to be 'fluid and changeable' in order to survive in a dynamic way. In the opera industry, then, this can be applied to teams which develop products and strategies collaboratively. As the focus of many opera companies is the sustainability of the industry and their own organisation, the fluidity of products and structures to suit consumer demands and preferences can only be achieved dynamically through cultivating supportive and diverse teams, such as those found in the companies of this study's participants.

4. Business and Marketing Skills are Essential for Independent Success in Opera – Not Least Because It is a Competitive Environment, and Most People Cannot Afford to Rely on Their Artistic Skills Alone

When exploring their experience of opera, each participant was asked about the skills required to succeed when founding a 'different' type of opera company and running it day-to-day. Once again, the shared experience was striking; each of these women, when generating their own opportunities outside of the large opera institutions, has had to develop a strong business skillset, with networking, financial management, and marketing being the top three most mentioned skills. Many of the participants mentioned the fact that being a successful company founder, regardless of gender, requires much more than simply artistic vision or management capability; to be an innovative woman in opera, they have to be able to do everything, despite the often-experienced lack of administrative training before starting their careers. When starting an opera business, entrepreneurs voluntarily accept that opera is a risky industry due to its considerable expenses and fluctuating popularity. Yet it has been proven that women who set up organisations in order to take risks have a higher chance of success than those who engage in business for other reasons, as shown in the 2015 study by Andrea Rey-Martí, Ana Tur Porcar, and Alicia Mas-Tur which explores the motivations behind women entrepreneurs' endeavours and the success rates accompanying them.[9] To innovate in opera, and to break from traditional models of opera business, is in many ways the perfect opportunity for women with a broad skillset to succeed entrepreneurially.

5. Opera Should be a 'Transformative Experience' Rather than an Elitist Pastime. The Biggest Obstacle to Opera is its Association with Class Systems

Another idea that united these leaders was their individual experience of attending and consuming opera; the majority felt that their first experience (and some subsequent) were 'transformative' experiences, where the possibilities of stagecraft and the complexity of the art form were shown to them, and their interest had begun. All believed that the multi-faceted nature of the form enabled 'transformative experience' of some kind. This shared experience of opera united these women, who come from considerably different backgrounds (musical and non-musical), and was the driving force behind their approach to opera's stereotypes. Laurie Ann Paul provides a useful description of how such transformative experiences work on a personal level, which is directly reflected in the careers of these executives:

> Having a transformative experience teaches you something new, something that you could not have known before having the experience, while also changing you as a person. Such experiences are very important from a personal perspective, for transformative experiences can play a significant role in your life, involving options that, speaking metaphorically, function as crossroads in your path towards self-realization.[10]

In the case of this study's participants, social class was one of the crucial factors affecting the numbers of people who could access such transformative experiences through opera. Indeed, three of the participants chose to discuss the class associations of opera at length, with Daisy Evans providing a particularly pertinent example of class associations and opera even at the level of defining class. The example she suggested was originally published in an article in *The Telegraph*, which defined the 'elite' social class as follows:

> This is the wealthiest and most privileged group in the UK. They went to private school and elite universities and enjoy high cultural activities such as listening to classical music and going to the opera.[11]

In light of such associations and stereotypes of opera and its customers, all of the participants consulted in this study are working to re-define the genre of opera into an inclusive art form, but the challenge is significant. Isabella Pitman's work at NSOS is a good example of executives pro-actively making the consumer experience less exclusive, as she is developing ways to introduce people to opera and the process of consuming it. One example of this is NSO's commitment to informing those new to opera about the way ticketing schemes work for young people, and about how exclusive and popular performances at large opera houses, such as those with celebrity singers, generally require the purchase of 'friend' status in order to access early-release tickets due to the high demand.

6. Opera Does Not Lend Itself to Allowing Working Mothers to Work Flexibly and is Often not Supportive to Women Seeking a Balance of Parenting and a Career

Both Clementine Lovell and Ally Rosser raised the issue that opera and its working practices are not generally conducive to allowing equal opportunities between men and women on the grounds that compassionate rehearsal schedules, job-sharing, and childcare are rarely considerations in larger opera houses. Therefore, Pop-Up Opera and Mahogany Opera Group have made the active decision to support working mothers. Pop-Up Opera, for example, has allowed children into rehearsals and backstage where necessary and has supported job-sharing options where possible. Larger organisations are beginning to engage with this topic, largely thanks to the 'Swap'ra' movement.[12] The 'Swap'ra' movement was mentioned in three of the interviews for this study and constitutes an exciting and dynamic movement within the industry; founded by women, this group seeks to liaise with large opera institutions to establish better working practices for the women who work for them. By encouraging open discussion with male and female leaders in the industry, this group is enabling industry-wide change for women at every level of opera production and performance.

7. Developing Audience-Company Relationships is Essential

Whilst this seems like a common-sense approach to creating a sustainable business, it is surprising how opaque and irregular many opera companies' feedback loops with the customer are. Whilst all the major opera institutions engage in consumer feedback at some level, the results of this surveying and monitoring are rarely presented to the public, and never in their entirety. On the other hand, all the women in this study who run or have founded opera companies are tapped into their markets, regularly surveying them and tailoring their products to suit the needs and interests of their specific consumer demographics. This open and transparent company-consumer relationship is vital to the success of innovative companies and has resulted in both Silent Opera and The Opera Shack's impressive statistics on accessibility and encouraging younger and more diverse audiences. 50% of Silent Opera's audiences are under 30, and 60% have never seen an opera before. Similarly, 40% of The Opera Shack's audiences are new to opera, and 100% of their audiences so far have found their work to be completely accessible (these figures were provided by participants). Silent Opera publicises such statistics as part of its brand; by showing customers that their experience is important to the company and by asking for and reporting on feedback and data collected through online and in-person surveys, companies can develop a public image that is customer-focused, as well as generating a realistic and detailed picture of who their customers are, how they consume their products, and how they would like to see the business and its products develop or change in the future.

8. Understanding the 'Experience Economy' is Essential to Developing a Successful Opera Brand

We live in a time where a quality product alone does not guarantee financial success or repeat business. Increasingly, consumers demand great and unique experiences from the events they attend or places they go; often attributed to our social habits and desire to share good experiences for status or reputation reasons, this behaviour has developed into what many theorists term the 'experience economy'. Joseph Pine and James Gilmore provide a context for this economy in their article 'Welcome to the Experience Economy':

> [C]onsumers unquestionably desire experiences, and more and more businesses are responding by explicitly designing and promoting them. As services, like goods before them, increasingly become commoditized – think of long-distance telephone services sold solely on price – experiences have emerged as the next step in what we call the progression of economic value.[13]

Attending the opera is a social practice that fits well into that concept, with companies such as Glyndebourne and other country house operas relying on the 'experience' element of their product (namely the picnics and black-tie dress code) to attract new punters, and others offering an exclusive luxury experience involving champagne, dinner intervals, and the chance to see and be seen. These models, however, do not appeal to the broadest possible consumer demographic; that does not mean that they are unsuccessful in providing a certain experience, but the industry-wide drive to encourage attendance from a range of socio-economic backgrounds and locations means that London-centred luxury opera experiences only form a portion of the wider possibilities. Here, women are leading in multiple capacities; Silent Opera and The Opera Shack are driven by their interests in bringing unique experiences (such as opera in a pub or a cave) to places and groups of people who might ordinarily eschew the traditional institutionalised opera experience. Pop-Up Opera enabled country-wide accessible opera by bringing performances to relatable and everyday locations, as well as unique places that would attract customers looking for an even more unique experience. Mahogany Opera Group creates experimental 'experiences' as well as propelling a network of community and children's opera experiences for families to get involved in. Crucially in this case, there is crossover from the children's opera experience audiences to the experimental, something which one might not predict when looking at consumer habits in the opera industry.

9. New Productions and New Commissions are Central to Successful Working Practices and Should Include More Women at Senior Creative Levels

Today, it remains that for many female artistic directors and composers there are limited opportunities in the large opera institutions. This has led to a culture, particularly in the field of experimental opera, of innovative and creative women who are forced by lack of opportunity into working in more 'peripheral' or lower-profile projects. In the face of this challenge, remarkably productive groups have formed in both experimental opera and the outreach and charitable opera sectors, where unprecedented numbers of women are creating and developing opera and bringing it straight to the communities that want to consume it. Because of government subsidies and their requirements, larger companies are obliged to strive to achieve this on a large scale, but teams of women-majority creatives are demonstrating that creating new works specifically for the communities with which they are seeking to engage is the most productive way to develop and sustain new audiences, rather than simply fulfilling general criteria. Large companies, such as ENO and Opera Holland Park have, in recent seasons, actively sought to include more women at senior creative levels in their commissioning, but gender parity has yet to become an industry-wide expectation, remaining an achievement that is praised as exceptional rather than a standard. When the 2019/20 season at ENO was released, public support for its programme was profound; heralded by its Chief Executive Daniel Kramer as 'the rise of the feminine', more than half of this season was directed by female directors.[14] Such moves towards gender parity are essential to ensuring that new productions and new commissions appeal to twenty-first-century audiences. The participants in this study felt that female composers, librettists, and directors are under-represented and that this is a significant shortcoming of the industry.

10. Opera Is a Hierarchical Industry

Patriarchally led throughout its history, opera has yet to shed its hierarchical management systems. Throughout the interviews, it was universally acknowledged that a collaborative working environment is crucial to setting and achieving common goals, and for maintaining employee satisfaction and wellbeing. Larger institutions naturally have layers of seniority in their teams to manage the sizeable projects they undertake, but many participants felt that the relationships in the rehearsal rooms and between executive members still lack a broad sense of gender equality. Issues such as the undermining of women, or the necessity for them to work harder in order to be seen as driven or skilled in management and creative senior teams, were raised by multiple participants. Whilst there has certainly been some improvement, and there are certainly men who actively seek to deconstruct the destructive hierarchies found in traditional opera-making processes, my participants universally agreed that the playing field is very much uneven, and women have a lot to overcome before 'equality' can be found as an ethos in such hierarchies.

To explore the idea of the uneven playing field further, I asked each of my participants to suggest some advice for a young woman seeking to embark on a career in the industry, and this once again generated some clear parallels between participants' experiences and their views on how to negotiate the field. Some of their responses are listed here:

- Don't let the uneven playing field stop you
- Aim high
- Other women are vitally important
- Be confident enough to speak in meetings and put yourself forward
- Your voice is important – particularly in hierarchical organisations
- Contact women who can support you
- Women need to put themselves forward and not be shy
- Test your ideas (perhaps because of increased scrutiny of women's ideas)?
- Develop supportive teams and learn from other women
- Have an unrivalled passion for what you do
- Generate your own opportunities

Conclusions

The number of areas of shared experiences (including the reliance on supportive networks and on having a wide personal administrative and creative skill set) and ideas between the participants in this research was striking, despite the diversity of those interviewed. There were, however, areas such as corporate sponsorship, government subsidy, and the role of opera companies in the community that divided the participants, and this is evident not only in the content of the interviews, but also in their respective business models. These debates are occurring across the industry, and further exploration of each of these concepts on their own terms in the future will be a vital tool for understanding the mechanisms through which opera companies negotiate risky economic environments and shifting public opinions of opera and its role in society. Innovation, strong teams, and cultivating consumer-focused opera were the concepts that united the participants; whether innovating through technology, location, radical text realisations, resource management, or business models, these women have established a new culture of consumerism in the opera industry in which the experience economy reigns.

Recent shifts in larger organisations, including engagement with the Swap'ra movement and ENO's 2019 announcement, are a start. Such changes, influenced by changing expectations from those working within the industry, are causing all organisations to evaluate their practices and provide better working environments that encourage gender parity. A good reputation for fair and equal opportunities and a respectful organisational culture can lead to a superior brand, with audiences and professionals alike being drawn towards companies that are clearly reflecting more of the gender equality that is so regularly being called for in the industry. Self-reliance, resilience, flexibility, and a willingness to learn are all crucial skills that leaders in the opera industry depend upon, and an unrivalled passion for the art form was a focal point of each participant's career. Such devotion to the art form can be channelled constructively into countering stereotypes and developing products that are specifically tailored to provide customers with transformative experiences, with feedback loops providing essential information that can shape and ultimately increase the success of current and future endeavours. The organisations created by the women interviewed in this study, and the teams they have developed in their practice, will leave a legacy that will enable future female opera leaders to thrive.

Notes

1. Robert Cannon, "Opera," in *Cambridge Introductions to Music* (New York: Cambridge University Press, 2012), 383.
2. All information included in this article was accurate at the time of writing; this chapter serves as a snapshot of the work of companies and individuals consulted at the time of interviewing (January-February 2019).
3. Alan Griffiths and Stuart Wall, *Economics for Business and Management*, 3rd ed. (Harlow: Financial Times Prentice Hall, 2011), 139.
4. Giverny Masso, "Cressida Pollock: 'I Was Publicly Trashed Following My Appointment at ENO," *The Stage*, March 8, 2018, accessed August 28, 2020, www.thestage.co.uk/news/2018/cressida-pollock-publicly-trashed-following-appointment-eno/.
5. Kristi M. Lewis, "When Leaders Display Emotion: How Followers Respond to Negative Emotional Expression of Male and Female Leaders," *Journal of Organizational Behavior* 21, no. 2 (2000): 231–34.
6. Alice H. Eagly, "Role Congruity Theory of Prejudice toward Female Leaders," *Psychological Review* 109, no. 3 (2002): 573–99.
7. Madeline E. Heilman, Aaron S. Wallen, Daniella Fuchs, and Melinda M. Tamkins, "Penalties for Success: Reactions to Women Who Succeed at Male Gender-Typed Tasks," *Journal of Applied Psychology* 89, no. 3 (2004): 416–27.
8. Andrew W. Ishak and Elizabeth A. Williams, "A Dynamic Model of Organizational Resilience: Adaptive and Anchored Approaches," *Corporate Communications: An International Journal* 23, no. 2 (2018): 188.
9. Andrea Rey-Martí, Alicia Mas-Tur, and Ana Tur Porcar, "Linking Female Entrepreneurs' Motivation to Business Survival," *Journal of Business Research* 68, no. 4 (2015): 813.
10. Laurie A. Paul, *Transformative Experience* (Oxford: Oxford University Press, 2014), 17.
11. Helen Horton, "The Seven Social Classes of 21st Century Britain – Where Do You Fit in?," *The Telegraph*, December 7, 2015, accessed August 28, 2020, www.telegraph.co.uk/news/uknews/12037247/the-seven-social-classes-of-21st-century-britain-where-do-you-fit-in.html.
12. See: www.swap-ra.org
13. Joseph Pine and James Gilmore, "Welcome to the Experience Economy," *Harvard Business Review*, July–August 1998, 97.
14. Mark Brown, "More Than Half of New ENO 2019–20 Productions to be Directed by Women," *The Guardian*, April 3, 2019, accessed August 28, 2020, www.theguardian.com/music/2019/apr/03/new-eno-productions-directed-by-women-emma-rice.

Bibliography

Brown, Mark. "More Than Half of New ENO 2019–20 Productions to be Directed by Women." *The Guardian*, April 3, 2019. Accessed August 28, 2020. www.theguardian.com/music/2019/apr/03/new-eno-productions-directed-by-women-emma-rice.

Cannon, Robert. "Opera." In *Cambridge Introductions to Music*. New York: Cambridge University Press, 2012.

Eagly, Alice H. "Role Congruity Theory of Prejudice toward Female Leaders." *Psychological Review* 109, no. 3 (2002): 573–99.

Griffiths, Alan, and Stuart Wall. *Economics for Business and Management*, 3rd ed. Harlow: Financial Times Prentice Hall, 2011.

Heilmann, Madeline E., Aaron S. Wallen, Daniella Fuchs, and Melinda M. Tamkins. "Penalties for Success: Reactions to Women Who Succeed at Male Gender-Typed Tasks." *Journal of Applied Psychology* 89, no. 3 (2004): 416–27.
Helen Horton. "The Seven Social Classes of 21st Century Britain – Where Do You Fit in?." *The Telegraph*, December 7, 2015. Accessed August 28, 2020. www.telegraph.co.uk/news/uknews/12037247/the-seven-social-classes-of-21st-century-britain-where-do-you-fit-in.html.
Ishak, Andrew W., and Elizabeth A. Williams. "A Dynamic Model of Organizational Resilience: Adaptive and Anchored Approaches." *Corporate Communications: An International Journal* 23, no. 2 (2018): 180–96.
Lewis, Kristi M. "When Leaders Display Emotion: How Followers Respond to Negative Emotional Expression of Male and Female Leaders." *Journal of Organizational Behavior* 21, no. 2 (2000): 231–34.
Masso, Giverny. "Cressida Pollock: 'I Was Publicly Trashed Following My Appointment at ENO.'" *The Stage*, March 8, 2018. Accessed August 28, 2020. www.thestage.co.uk/news/2018/cressida-pollock-publicly-trashed-following-appointment-eno/.
Paul, Laurie A. *Transformative Experience*. Oxford: Oxford University Press, 2014.
Pine, Joseph, and James Gilmore. "Welcome to the Experience Economy." *Harvard Business Review*, July–August 1998, 97–105.
Rey-Martí, Andrea, Alicia Mas-Tur, and Ana Tur Porcar. "Linking Female Entrepreneurs' Motivation to Business Survival." *Journal of Business Research* 68, no. 4 (2015): 810–914.
Swap'ra. Accessed August 7, 2023. www.swap-ra.org.

29
DIVERSITY IN ITALIAN MUSIC PROGRAMMING

Symphonic and Chamber Music Programming in Milan[1]

Valentina Bertolani and Luisa Santacesaria[2]

Since the 1990s, music scholars have challenged the Western musical canon and its formation in order to draw attention to categories of individuals who were being systematically excluded from music history and narratives of music theory.[3] The topic is slowly reaching visibility within the public debate,[4] and some festivals are currently taking strong positions on gender equality. Notable examples are the 2019 editions of the Swiss Festival Archipel (renamed 'Archip-elles' and almost entirely dedicated to women composers and performers) and, in the pop music world, the Barcelona Primavera Sound Festival (titled 'The New Normal', featuring the same number of women and men artists). More and more data about music seasons and symphonic and lyric institutions focussed on the Western canon are being collected internationally, though rarely by the institutions themselves.[5] International campaigns such as the Keychange Initiative – led by the PRS Foundation and supported by the Creative Europe programme of the European Union – are raising awareness. This problematic yet meaningful initiative aims at encouraging international festivals to achieve gender balance in their programming.[6] However, these are exceptions. The concert world seems oblivious to the systemic exclusion of specific categories of artists.

Our contribution analyses the scene in Italy, particularly the 2018–2019 chamber and symphonic seasons in Milan. Within the Italian discourse, our work is one of the first scholarly contribution on diversity in music. For this reason, it cannot be compared to other data or studies on the Italian music scene; nevertheless, it must be seen in dialogue with a strong voice of intellectuals trying to map diversity (or lack thereof) in the cultural life of the country.[7]

Quantitative Data

For this chapter, we collected data about eight institutions in Milan, six of which are concert seasons and two are yearly festivals. We considered these institutions to be the most prominent in the area. All are publicly funded at the national and local levels.

The database used for this chapter is accessible online and includes names of the artists, whether they are performers (specifying their instrument), composers (specifying if living or deceased and period of musical activity) or conductors, their perceived gender identity and ethnic and racial background. A methodological note on data collection is present in our online report.[9]

Table 29.1 Institutions and Number of Events in the 2018–2019 Concert Season

Name of institution and foundation date	Number of events in the 2018–19 concert season	People interviewed + date of the interview
Società del Quartetto (1864)	22 (excluding off-seasons concerts)	Paolo Arcà (artistic director) and Dora Alberti (general secretary and audience relations) interviewed on 4 April 2019
I Pomeriggi Musicali (1945)	24	No interviews
MiTo Settembre Musica Festival (2007)	64 (excluding theatrical productions)	No interviews
Milano Musica Festival (1992)[8]	10 (excluding the event Secret Public)	Cecilia Balestra (artistic director) interviewed on 20 February 2019
Teatro alla Scala (1778)	8 (symphonic season only)	No interviews
Orchestra Sinfonica di Milano Giuseppe Verdi or laVerdi (1993)	32	Ruben Jais (artistic director) and Debora Saccinto (administration manager) interviewed on 20 February 2019
La Società dei Concerti, Foundation (1983)	28 (excluding museum series concerts, e.g. Music and tennis, music at the Museo Novecento, etc.)	No interviews
Serate Musicali, Cultural association (1992)	43 (excluding off-season concerts)	No interviews
	Total: 238 concerts	

Each country has different policies regarding data collection based on ethnic backgrounds and racial identity of its citizens. Italy does not have a clear framework to account for the ethnic diversity of its population. Indeed, ethnic diversity is often conflated with migration phenomena.[10] Similarly, the European Union uses a colour-blind attitude to data collection on demographics.[11] This idea that diversity comes from abroad (even from beyond Europe) is deeply rooted in the Italian mindset and emerges in what some artistic directors told us about ethnic diversity in their seasons.

As is standard with this type of research, we harvested publicly available data from websites of symphonic and chamber institutions rather than collect data through direct questionnaires sent to the artists involved in each season. This means we manually and subjectively assigned all categories that pertain to the individual identity of the artists. Thus, all data we have gathered are not voluntary submissions and identification from artists but assigned labels on our part, according to our own cultural background and sensibility. Harvesting data makes it difficult to work with identity categories such as gender and ethnic background, because we have to assign a value from an external standpoint, even though we fully support and acknowledge gender fluidity and self-identification. Nevertheless, with our quantitative data we exclusively want to draw attention to a discriminatory practice rather than describe the world in all its facets.

Given the oblivious nature of the discourse on diversity in Italy and the European Union and the lack of guidelines of best practices from the governments of reference and the methodology used to gather the data, we decided it was best to use binary categories as white/non white and women/men artists.

We would like to draw attention to some actions we put in place to limit the drawbacks of these choices. On the one hand, we decided to publish the dataset we created to be of service to the community at large. Yet, this shared database has no name associated with the categories we assigned. On the other hand, in the report published on our website,[12] we invite artists who participated in the seasons we study to volunteer their self-identification, thus helping us to move beyond harvested data and towards voluntary and reliable identity data. This way we will eventually represent diversity and identity in a more nuanced spectrum. We would like to note that this research was a labour of love. While carrying out this research, none of us was affiliated with a university or research institution. Thus, we did not have the infrastructure, funds or time to work with thousands of questionnaires.

Qualitative Data

In addition to quantitative data on diversity, we decided to collect qualitative data of three types: analysing online material (public funds received at various levels of government, economic sustainability,[13] number of employers, types of contracts) and submitted funding applications (which in Italy are accessible for funding at the national level through the Ministry of Culture). Moreover, between February and April 2019, we conducted semi-structured interviews articulated into five sections: 1. Management and budgeting; 2. Mission of the institution; 3. Data collection for their own purposes and grant requirements; 4. Views on public funding policies at the municipal, regional, national and European levels; 5. Discussion of artistic choices in general and regarding the 2018–2019 season specifically, with comments on the data we ourselves collected. Unfortunately, only three institutions participated in our interviews: Orchestra Sinfonica di Milano Giuseppe Verdi or laVerdi, the contemporary music festival Milano Musica, and the chamber music season Società del Quartetto.[14]

These three institutions are among the most important in Italy, and their choices influence the national musical scene. laVerdi is a symphony orchestra with its own concert season lasting from September to June, with approximately 10 concerts every month. The orchestra has had three main conductors: Riccardo Chailly (1999–2005), Zhang Xian (2009–2016), who was the first resident woman conductor in Italy, and Claus Peter Flor (2017 to the present). Since 2016, the artistic director has been Ruben Jais, who also works as an orchestra and choir conductor.

Milano Musica is a festival of contemporary music directed from its inception through 2012 by Luciana Pestalozza. The current artistic director is Cecilia Balestra. The festival normally takes place between October and November, featuring about 25 events between concerts, lectures and special events. Every year the festival honours a different contemporary composer: György Kurtág in 2018, Salvatore Sciarrino in 2017, Gérard Grisey in 2016. It is arguably the most important contemporary music festival in Italy. In its 26 years of activity, the festival has never honoured a woman composer or a non-white composer.

Società del Quartetto is a chamber music season; the subscription concerts, which take place at the Conservatory of Music 'G. Verdi', run from October to May. In addition to the subscription concerts, other concert series take place in different venues of the city. The musical programming includes composers from Baroque to early twentieth-century music.[15] Since 2007, the artistic director has been the composer Paolo Arcà.

Diversity in Italian Music Programming

Overview of Quantitative Data Results

Figure 29.1 is an overview of the quantitative data collected and shows a systemic discrimination against women as composers, conductors and soloists. It is not exclusively a matter of numbers: even the context in which minorities are presented often reinforces problematic narratives. For example, I Pomeriggi Musicali programmed only two women composers: Clara Schumann and Fanny Hensel (née Mendelssohn). However, the concert is titled 'The

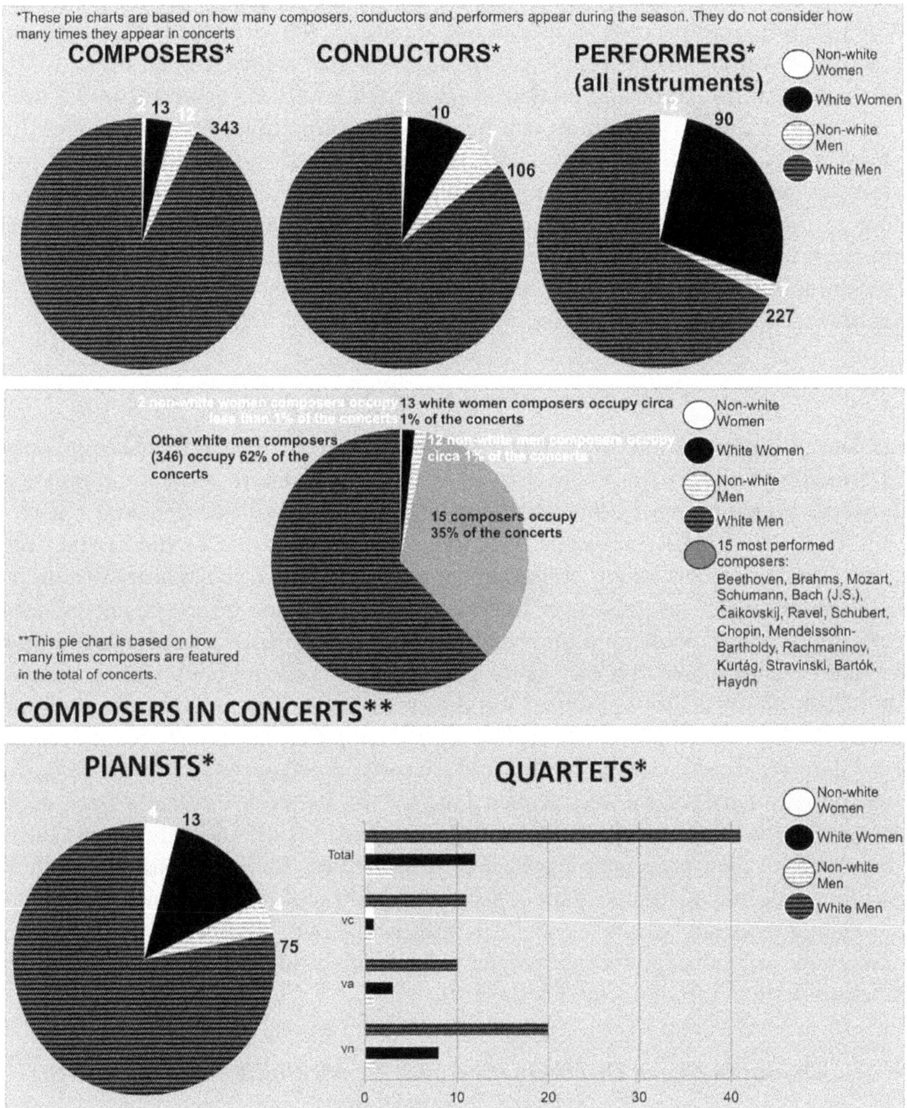

Figure 29.1 Overview of the quantitative data, seasons 2018–2019. For a full report visit: https://curatingdiversities.files.wordpress.com/2019/06/report-milan-june2019.pdf.

Mendelssohns and the Schumanns', and the music of Clara Schumann and Fanny Hensel was played along with that of their husband and brother, respectively. This presentation reinforces the idea of the 'domesticity' of women composers from the past.[16] In this case, including women composers reinforces, rather than disrupts, the gender narrative of traditional music histories.

When it comes to non-white musicians the discrimination is even more blatant. Only three out of eight institutions featured non-white composers and only one institution in Milan (MiTo) featured Black composers. Out of 238 concerts, there were only two non-white women in an authorial position: the Japanese Keiko Abe and the Congolese Pauline Mbuka Nsiala,[17] one of the members of the band Konono no.1 (both are featured by MiTo).[18] Sixty percent (9/15) of the non-white composers were presented in two concerts. One concert was performed by the Kronos Quartet, featuring transcriptions for string quartet of musics from The Who to improvisations of African traditional music;[19] the second was a programme proposed by pianist Antonio Ballista entitled 'Syncopations' that connected ragtime and early jazz authors to classical, romantic and modern composers. On the one hand, these two examples show the active role that performers can have in proposing diverse programming. Indeed, while most statistics focus on seasons and programming, exclusion is undeniably a problem of performers' proposed repertoires as well. On the other hand, the inclusion of composers of colour in these two concerts is achieved by pointing outside the realm of classical and contemporary music. These presentations reinforce the prejudice that there are no classical, romantic or modernist composers of colour.[20] This data confirms an anecdotal impression that the Milanese scene is highly imbalanced.

Overview of Qualitative Data Results

'Collect data' is a popular indication given in reports on how to achieve and improve equality and diversity. While we think that data collection is essential to show discrimination to a usually-sceptical elite of artistic directors, it represents merely a basic step, and it is far from being a solution to the discriminatory situation present nowadays; a situation that requires more intentional policies than just collecting data. In fact, behind the indication 'collect data' lies the assumption that professionals (such as curators, artistic directors, agents, teachers, educators and scholars) looking at the data will recognise the discrimination, question themselves about possible biases that they or their institutions hold and reinforce, and might even identify hidden discriminatory practices and therefore end – on their own – these discriminatory practices. We noticed this is not necessarily the case. Indeed, the responses to the showing of the data are those of denial (with justifications and excuses) and general defensiveness (and occasionally partial curiosity). Ruben Jais, Cecilia Balestra and Paolo Arcà explained these results by saying with conviction that artistic decisions are the only factors informing who they invite to their programming. Similarly, to the very homogeneous quantitative data we just presented, our qualitative data collection also showed a widespread and internalised attitude among professionals. We will focus mostly on two of these: 1. Understanding of 'discrimination' as a concept and its transferability among different types of discrimination; 2. Gender marking in job titles (or lack thereof).

1. Understanding of Discrimination and Transferability Among Different Types of Discrimination

All artistic directors convincingly voice a clear understanding and attention towards discrimination as a concept. In particular, laVerdi representatives even talked about discriminatory aspects we did not raise in our questionnaires (e.g. disability among performers). In all three institutions, we found a special attention towards economic and social discriminations and a commitment to be inclusive.

For example, Balestra noted:

> The event Secret Public was on the outskirts of Milan:[21] behind [the creation of] the sound boxes lies the idea of having 'antennae' . . . potential bridges between the Teatro alla Scala and the outskirts . . . It is very interesting to work on different social fabrics because, in my opinion, there is a possibility of a very happy integration.[22]

Similarly, Jais reported:

> We have always believed not only in our ability to produce a result of value, but also in the impact our activity has on the community and the social dimension. Here are all the activities we do for schools, hospitals, prisons . . . we created the first choir in the Opera and San Vittore prisons . . . we have collaborated with the San Raffaele and Niguarda hospitals.[23]

Jais also highlighted that for its thirtieth anniversary, laVerdi gifted to the city of Milan a series of free concerts on the outskirts and in socially and economically deprived areas.

In the online application for funds describing the three-year programming of the Fondazione La Società dei Concerti, there is a similar objective:

> With this part of the activity, we want to create the basis for a collaboration to bring classical music and professional musicians into areas of social, economic or personal distress. We organised a concert for the patients of the Sant'Anna Hospital in Como and two concerts for the guests of the Opera San Francesco for the poor of Milan.[24]

Società del Quartetto is also active on social and economic disadvantages. During the interview, Arcà noted that their seasonal programming is complemented by a series of off-season smaller concerts (which are not included in our data) which engage with different spaces around the cities, reaching out to a diverse audience. For example, they offer concerts for children and concerts at different times of the day, not only in the evening. Their season 'Giovani pianisti a Casa Verdi' [Young Pianists at Casa Verdi] offers performing opportunities to young performers studying at or newly graduated from the Milan Conservatory and the Municipal Music School. They also balance out invitations to established international performers (at the core of the mission of Società del Quartetto) with an attention to young and emerging performers, for which they schedule a special 'Astri nascenti' [Emerging stars] series.

A similar intention is identifiable in the online three-year funding application by I Pomeriggi Musicali, in which they explicitly take a stand against the elitism of music education in Italy (which is not included in public education, so its costs fall completely on family budgets). In collaboration with the Association Sconfinarte, I Pomeriggi Musicali also created 'I Piccoli Pomeriggi Musicali' [Pomeriggi Musicali for the little ones].[25]

Among the many different approaches, we can identify a common rationale behind the programmes. In particular: 1. all institutions identify discriminatory or disadvantaged positions based on social class and access to culture; 2. all institutions have a proactive attitude and put in place creative solutions to bridge the gap between the institution and the audience they want to include. (To this extent, it is worth noting that the Italian Ministry of Culture does not consider any free concert, unless organised in a place of worship or in a heritage location, as an evaluation parameter in their evaluation of institutional activity to assess how to distribute funding for the next year. This means that this outreach activity and free activities for the audience are done exclusively out of a deeply held belief in their importance, even though they will not bring extra points, so to speak, in the official evaluation of their activities.) 3. all institutions find value in being able to combine high-quality musical offerings with social inclusion and commitment to solving discrimination and underrepresentation. What is really interesting is that this identification of class and social discrimination, and the identification of the need for a proactive action to address it, is not automatically transferable to other forms of discrimination, disadvantage and/or underrepresentation, be them gender-, ethnic-, ability/disability-based, among others.

For example, turning to gender discrimination, on the one hand we noticed that there is generally an acknowledgement of general discrimination and inequality. Some examples of understanding of discrimination can be seen in sentences including: 'I still see [sexism] in the articles that come out in the newspapers: "ah, the woman director!" and this becomes the main fact, and it's wrong!'[26] (Jais) There might even be curiosity about the cause: 'I see that this year, Festival Archipel proposes a programme featuring only women composers: I was curious to go to discover composers I do not know'.[27] (Balestra) However, contrary to what happens in the case of class and social discrimination, there is no affirmative action or proactive action taken to balance the clearly unbalanced man/women, white/non-white situations. Indeed, a very outspoken position of not caring is chosen by every single institution we interviewed. Contrary to what happens in the case of class and social discrimination, the decisions are defended stressing the quality of the programming.

In the case of Milano Musica:

> I believe merit is what should count in the artistic field. I can be glad that there is a woman composer who wins a commission, but this remains on the emotional side that has nothing to do with [our] choices. The choice for me is to evaluate which artist/performer is closest to the work or to the composer we want to programme, or interests us more, considering the artistic line we would like to develop.[28]

Just before and immediately after showing the data, Balestra commented:

> [Data] will be of a prevailing male chauvinism. Of course, we are terrible about the [percentage of women] composers. I know it very well, we tell each other. However, our choice is based on the work, the score, the man author or woman author that seems most interesting.[29]

laVerdi:

> For us, being a woman or a man doesn't count. Instead, it's important that he/she has the ability to do the job.[30]

Similarly to Balestra, Jais continued:

> It's not that I invite a man pianist or a woman pianist because she is a woman or a man. I invite him/her because he/she knows how to perform that repertoire well.[31]

Società del Quartetto confirmed this way of thinking. Similarly to laVerdi and Milano Musica, the main concern with programming is quality and excellence. Moreover, like laVerdi and Milano Musica, Arcà states it is not his intention to directly address any gender inequalities (and possibly also any racial inequalities), as that in itself would be a discriminatory practice:

Precisely because of equality, I would never think of focussing my attention on gender.[32]

While social/class discrimination is met with a creative attitude bringing innovative and artistic solutions, gender or ethnic discrimination is met as a perceived limitation of choices that might endanger the quality of programming.

Toward the end of the twentieth century, meritocracy gained a positive connotation. Yet, many studies in recent years and in various high-achieving fields (from medical sciences to management) show how meritocracy can actually foster inequalities on the basis of gender and ethnicity. This phenomenon is called 'the paradox of meritocracy'.[33] This is also argued, in broader cultural terms, in Jo Littler's recent book *Against Meritocracy*. Littler links the myth of meritocracy to what she calls the 'egalitarian deficit.' The egalitarian deficit describes how non-white, non-rich, non-male etc. people are 'often doubly or trebly disadvantaged by neoliberal narratives of meritocracy whilst being particularly incited to climb [the social pyramid]';[34] in particular, in neoliberal meritocratic discourses, these individuals 'are simultaneously incited to address their lack of privilege themselves, individually, through cultural discourses of neoliberal meritocracy which deploy particular languages and accents of gender, race and class'.[35]

Simply put, artistic fields are highly professionalised and led by highly trained and educated individuals. Yet there is absolutely no proof that the quality of a season is linked to the number of white male composers, conductors or soloists presented in it or that addressing obvious discriminations would lead to lower quality in the programming.[36] We cannot believe that talent comes almost 0% of the time in the form of a non-white woman composer, and only 3% of the time in the form of a white woman composer or non-white man composer. Similarly, we do not believe that talent comes 1% of the time in the form of a non-white woman conductor and 6% of the time in the form of a white woman conductor or a non-white man conductor.

The data show structural biases rigging the system in favour of white male musicians.

Furthermore, these statistics would not be acceptable in any other field. For example, Milan is the home of several events to promote professional women in the workforce and in the STEM industry.[37] According to the UNESCO Institute for Statistics, in Italy in 2018 36% of employees in scientific research and development were women.[38] We agree these figures in STEM are not satisfactory. Consequently, we should not accept the statistics in the music sector as they are, either.

2. Language and Discrimination: Gender Marking in Job Titles (Or Lack Thereof)

We repeatedly encountered the idea that there are fewer women composers. And since in the artistic directors' mental image there are fewer women composers, they feel cornered in wondering who they should invite.

Ruben Jais:

> There are objectively a lot fewer women who choose to be composers. Whenever someone pitches projects to me, if they are from or about women composers, we take them into the same consideration.
> SANTACESARIA: But in percentage, [would you say that] fewer projects come from female composers?
> JAIS: Definitely fewer. I am stormed by male composers, old composers, young ones . . . women composers, instead, we had to look for them . . . so, it is more the fact that perhaps, similarly to the field of science there are fewer women inclined to choose a scientific career, perhaps there are fewer women within the music world inclined to choose a career as a composer. But objectively, I have no data . . . it is a perception based on my experience.[39]

Balestra's puzzlement is more explicit:

> I think I have no prejudices, either about women or about skin colour. However, objectively: who do we invite?[40]

These two quotes show a specific problem: Balestra's experience of puzzlement (who do we invite?) or Jais' instinctive perception of a dearth of women composers (a deeply rooted conviction presented initially as objective truth – 'objectively there are fewer women composers' – that is admittedly more of a gut feeling – 'it is a perception based on proposals I receive'). These two sentences show the inability of picturing clearly who women composers are. This is a problem we connect to the female lexicon used to describe musical professions.

Italian language has female and male genders for nouns, and this affects job descriptions.[41] This has been an extremely contentious problem. Not only is the plural (standard form: male plural) problematic; also, the feminine forms of traditionally male jobs tend to have a harder time entering the common language. This happened for example with 'mayor' (sindaco/sindaca), 'lawyer' (avvocato/avvocata), 'minister' (ministro/ministra). Notwithstanding the creation of reports and guidelines by linguists to make feminine forms (which are perfectly grammatical) widespread[42] and the political campaigns of high-profile Italian politicians, this is still a very uncomfortable transition in Italy.

Thus, the difficulty we encountered in our interviews in using the feminine forms of composer (*compositrice*), conductor (*direttrice*) and the title 'Maestro' ('Maestra') is not unusual. The latter case is the least used and the most complex one. While the word *maestro* means 'teacher' and it is used in this way, the title *Maestro* is also used to address those who have completed a conservatory education. *Maestra*, as the feminine form of *Maestro*, is seldom used as it can be associated with *maestra* (schoolteacher)[43] in a sexist combination: on the one side, the historically few women graduating from a conservatory and the other for employment one of the feminine jobs *par excellence*, i.e. the primary school teacher.

All institutions showed a problematic use of masculine/feminine job titles. Concerning the word *direttrice* [female conductor]: both laVerdi and MiTo (the only two institutions with women conductors) use non-female job descriptions. The same happens with artistic directors (f. *direttrice*, once again). On the website of Milano Musica, Balestra's role is described with the masculine *direttore artistico*. In other cases outside of Milan, some women do not use the masculine term but rather the general job description instead of the name for the role (i.e.: 'artistic direction' instead of 'artistic director').[44] It is meaningful to notice that this is still a practice in the field of music, as nowadays it happens very rarely that doctors, curators in the fine arts, professors etc. describe themselves using the masculine forms.[45] In our opinion, the lack of use of feminine forms for musical job descriptions goes hand in hand with the reinforcement of the idea that it is male professionals only who occupy those positions.

Final Reflections on Canon Formation and Solidification

Collecting quantitative data is very important, but it cannot be the only action. Our impression so far is that the very subtle and articulated discourse that we are increasingly producing in academia on canon construction and unbalanced historical narratives does not reach professionals in the music industry. However, we know that the programming choices of musical seasons and festivals substantially influence the reception of composers' work and consequently actively contribute to the formation of the canon.

Nevertheless, distinctions must be made. For example, the curatorial role of Jais and Arcà – whose concert seasons feature music from the seventeenth to the twenty-first centuries, with core programming around the eighteenth and nineteenth centuries – is different from that of Balestra, who curates a contemporary music festival. The programming choices of the three artistic directors have a different weight concerning the formation of the canon. The work of Jais and Arcà, in fact, is that of presenting the established musical canon with a critical eye and fresh ideas. Balestra instead manages the artistic choices of contemporary music: by programming works by composers not yet established, she is actually forming the new canon – an aspect she thoughtfully considers, as demonstrated in the interview. And it is in the curatorial choices that concern the new music that, we believe, reflection on gender and ethnic representation can lead to important results in the future, so that the new canons will be more inclusive and also more open and flexible.

Next Steps and Final Recommendations

This research focussed on the programming of publicly funded musical institutions and their artistic directors. However, these actors are operating within an ecosystem. We should scrutinise management agencies and press offices to be sure that the selections of who to manage and the communication and press releases do not feed into a mainstream narrative of systemic discrimination. Similarly, musical journalism and criticism should be scrutinised, and an investigation about gender and ethnic pay gaps among soloists is needed. Also, competition results and early-career commissions are crucial to develop a career. Thus, it is important to monitor whether juries are reinforcing stereotypes through their choices. Finally, soloists and artistic directors should be scrutinised about their programming choices.

Finally, here is a list of recommendations that are alternative to the ubiquitous and simplistic 'gather more data':

- Stop focusing exclusively on artistic directors and start considering the whole ecosystem of the industry.
- Request funding agencies (public or otherwise) and the institutions themselves to commission data collection to activate a form of internal analysis. Usually the work of data collection is a form of exploitative work where researchers are not paid for the service they are doing (such as in our case).
- Stop hiding behind the term 'merit' or 'talent' when data shows such blatant discrimination.
- Target the issue with specific policies with the conviction that this will not ruin the quality of the artistic offer. Everyone here is rooting for quality as well as inclusivity.

In conclusion, we would like to thank the artistic directors who participated in our interviews. Gathering quantitative data is nothing more than the starting point for a conversation. Without these conversations, the data are not finding their way to influence the decision making of curators to effect a positive change. Creating spaces for artistic directors to reflect is a first step towards action. We hope that these conversations will have an impact in future choices of these Milanese institutions and the funding agencies that support them.

Notes

1. This article has been submitted in April 2019, we received minor reviews and we re-submitted a final version in July 2020. We received minor formal and language edits in September 2022. Since our final version, important contributions to the field have been published, such as George Lewis, 'New Music Decolonization in Eight Difficult Steps', *Van Outernational*, 2020, https://www.van-outernational.com/lewis-en (accessed 22 October 2022). Furthermore, there have been some changes in the leadership of the institutions we mention (e.g., the Amici della Musica in Florence changed their artistic director). When we knew about these changes, we have provided an extra link through the Wayback Machine. For any problem, we advised to use the Wayback Machine on other links as well.
2. We wish to thank the artistic directors Ruben Jais, Cecilia Balestra, and Paolo Arcà, the administrator Debora Saccinto and general secretary Dora Alberti, who participated in our research and answered our questions. Their openness in discussing their choices advanced our research immeasurably.
3. Susan McClary, *Feminine Endings: Music, Gender, and Sexuality* (Minneapolis: University of Minnesota Press, 1991); Lawrence Kramer, *Music as Cultural Practice, 1800–1900* (Berkeley: University of California Press, 1990); *Queering the Pitch: The New Gay and Lesbian Musicology*, edited by Philip Brett, Elizabeth Wood, and Gary C. Thomas (New York: Routledge, 1994); the work of Marcia J. Citron, from *Gender and the Musical Canon* (Urbana: University of Illinois Press, 1993) to her own response fourteen years later 'Women and the Western Art Canon: Where Are We Now?,' *Notes* 64, no. 2 (2007): 209–15.
4. Susanna Eastburn, "Take Note – Why Do Women Composers Still Take Up Less Musical Space?," *The Guardian*, March 8, 2019, accessed April 16, 2020, www.theguardian.com/music/2019/mar/08/sound-and-music-female-composers-musicians-susanna-eastburn. Also see Mark Brown, "Female Composers Largely Ignored by Concert Line-Ups," *The Guardian*, June 13, 2018, accessed June 2, 2020, www.theguardian.com/music/2018/jun/13/female-composers-largely-ignored-by-concert-line-ups.
5. A.J. Gustar, *Statistics in Historical Musicology*, 2017, accessed April 16, 2020, www.musichistorystats.com/about; Institute for Composer Diversity, accessed June 2, 2020, www.composerdiversity.com/orchestra-seasons; Women's Philharmonic Advocacy, accessed June 2, 2020, https://wophil.org. A rare example of data and reflections collected by a symphonic institution are the posts collected on the "Story" page of the Baltimore Symphonic Orchestra website: e.g. Ricky O'Bannon, "The Orchestra Season by the Numbers: Database," accessed April 16, 2020, www.bsomusic.org/stories/the-orchestra-season-by-the-numbers-database.aspx.
6. The full list is available at accessed April 15, 2020, https://keychange.eu/blog/full-list-of-festivals-signed-up-to-keychange.
7. Women in the Italian art market, see, Silvia Simoncelli, *Donne Artiste in Italia. Presenza e Rappresentazione* (Milan: NABA, 2017); on publishing and women as authors, Sofia Biondoni, "Il posto delle donne nell'editoria," *InGenere. Dati, politiche, questioni di genere*, March 22, 2018, accessed June 2, 2020, www.ingenere.it/articoli/posto-donne-editoria; the hashtag #tuttimaschi [all men] and contributions by writer, intellectual and public speaker Michela Murgia, highlighting the lack of female journalists signing opinion pieces or stories on the front pages of national newspapers.
8. This festival offers concerts both in Milan and Turin. We based our data collection on the website page relative to Milan.
9. A full report and our database are available and downloadable under Creative Commons, accessed April 15, 2020, https://curatingdiversity.org/milano.
10. Lilla Farkas and European Commission. Directorate-General for Justice and Consumers, *Data Collection in the Field of Ethnicity: Analysis and Comparative Review of Equality Data Collection Practices in the European Union* (Luxembourg: Publications Office of the European Union, 2017), 23–24. See also the Italian National Institute of Statistics, "Indicatori demografici anno 2019,"

accessed June 2, 2020, www.istat.it/it/files//2020/02/Indicatori-demografici_2019.pdf, presenting again the parameter of migration as the only one hinting at diversity of population.
11. Farkas, *Data Collection*; also see, Ryan Heath, "Brussels is blind to diversity," *Politico*, March 12, 2018, accessed June 2, 2020, www.politico.eu/article/brussels-blind-to-diversity-whiteout-european-parliament/. The conflation population diversity/migration is also evident in the statistics available from Eurostat, the statistical office of the European Union, where one can browse statistics by diversity (age, gender and disability) or population (where once again only migration and migrant integration is mentioned); Eurostat, *Browse statistics by theme,* accessed April 22, 2020, https://ec.europa.eu/eurostat/data/browse-statistics-by-theme.
12. Accessed April 15, 2020, https://curatingdiversity.org/milano.
13. Every administration that receives public funds in Italy has to publish the funds received on their website. Some institutions are extremely forthcoming, such as laVerdi and Milano Musica, providing many data on the economic sustainability and their audience reach.
14. Similar difficulties are documented by the Guerrilla Girls, who asked 383 European Museum about the diversity of their artistic collection and less than a quarter answered. Cf. Guerrilla Girls, *Is it even worse in Europe?*, accessed June 2, 2020, www.whitechapelgallery.org/exhibitions/guerrilla-girls/.
15. For our inquiry, we considered only the subscription concerts.
16. Sarah Kirby, "The Only Thing "Womanish" Is the Composer': Music at Nineteenth-Century Exhibitions of Women's Work," *Music and Letters* 100, no. 3 (August 2019): 423–24.
17. This is a concert of transcriptions for violin quartets of various non-classical music. Konono no.1 is listed as author and one member is a woman of colour. So, we included this in the category of 'women authors of colour' even though the band is listed as the author.
18. The concert with music by Keiko Abe was scheduled on September 12 at the Conservatorio Giuseppe Verdi, Turin, and on September 13 at the Teatro Fontana, Milan, featuring Evelyn Glennie (percussion) and Philip Smith; the concert with Konono no.1's music was scheduled on September 6 at Conservatorio 'G. Verdi," Turin, and on September 7 at the Piccolo Teatro Grassi, Milan, featuring the Kronos Quartet.
19. Amanda Bayley, "Cross-Cultural Collaborations with the Kronos Quartet," in *Distributed Creativity: Collaboration and Improvisation in Contemporary Music*, edited by Eric F. Clarke and Mark Doffman (Oxford: Oxford University Press, 2017).
20. On the topic see the many works of the musicologist Eileen Southern, such as 'America's Black Composers of Classical Music," *Music Educators Journal* 62, no. 3 (1975): 46–59; Raoul Abdul, *Blacks in Classical Music: A Personal History* (New York: Dodd, Mead, 1978); John Gray, *Blacks in Classical Music: A Bibliographical Guide to Composers, Performers, and Ensembles* (New York: Greenwood Press, 1988); Earl Ofari Hutchinson, *It's Our Music Too: The Black Experience in Classical Music* (Los Angeles: Middle Passage Press, 2016). See also the 'Black Composer Series' originally published by Sony and recently reissued in a CD box: Thomas Jefferson Anderson, David Baker, Joseph Bologne de Saint-Georges, Samuel Coleridge-Taylor, Roque Cordero, José Maurício Nuñes García, Adolphus C. Hailstork, et al., "Black composer series 1974–1978," Sony Classical 06868, 2018, 10 CDs.
21. This was the opening event of Milano Musica 2018: two days featuring six containers, called 'sound boxes," hosting several concerts of about 15 minutes.
22. This and all following quotes have been translated by the authors. Original quote: 'Secret Public nelle periferie: dietro alle scatole sonore c'era l'idea di avere come delle "antenne", dei punti di potenziale ponte fra il Teatro alla Scala e le periferie . . .. Quindi, su tessuti sociali diversi è molto interessante lavorare perché, secondo me, c'è una possibilità di integrazione felicissima'.
23. Original quote: 'noi dalla nascita abbiamo sempre creduto non solo alla nostra capacità di produrre un risultato di valore ma anche dell'impatto che la nostra attività ha sul territorio e sul sociale. Ed ecco quindi che tutte le attività che noi facciamo per le scuole, negli ospedali, nelle carceri . . . noi abbiamo creato il primo coro nel carcere di Opera e di San Vittore . . . Abbiamo collaborato con il San Raffaele, con il Niguarda'.
24. Original quote: 'Con questa costola dell'attività si vuole gettare una base di collaborazione per portare la musica classica e i musicisti professionisti in ambiti di disagio sociale, economico o personale. Abbiamo organizzato un concerto per i degenti dell'Ospedale Sant'Anna di Como e due concerti a favore degli ospiti dell'Opera San Francesco per i poveri di Milano'.
25. The program of I Piccoli Pomeriggi Musicali 2019/2020. *I Piccoli Pomeriggi Musicali*, accessed April 16, 2020, www.ipiccolipomeriggi.it.
26. Original quote: 'capisco invece, lo vedo ancora [un atteggiamento sessista] negli articoli che escono sui giornali: 'ah la direttrice donna!' e diventa questo il fatto principale, è sbagliato!'

27. Original quote: 'Vedo che il Festival Archipel di quest'anno propone una programmazione di sole compositrici donne: ero curiosa di andare per scoprire compositrici che non conosco'.
28. Original quote: 'Credo che nell'ambito artistico valga il merito. Poi mi può far piacere che ci sia una compositrice che vince una commissione, ma questo rimane nel lato affettivo che non c'entra mai niente con le scelte. E la scelta per me è di valutazione di quale artista/interprete è più vicino all'opera o al compositore che vogliamo programmare, o quale compositore/compositrice ci interessa di più rispetto a una linea artistica che vogliamo sviluppare'.
29. Original quote: '[i dati] saranno dati di un maschilismo imperante. Certo, sui compositori siamo terribili. Lo so, lo so benissimo, ce lo diciamo. Dopodiché però la scelta è in funzione del pezzo, della partitura, dell'autore o autrice che ci sembra più interessante'.
30. Original quote: 'per noi che sia donna o uomo non conta. Conta invece saper fare il proprio mestiere'.
31. Original quote: 'non è che io invito un pianista o una pianista perchè è donna o uomo. Lo invito perché sa interpretare bene quel repertorio'.
32. Original quote: 'Proprio per un discorso di uguaglianza, non ho mai pensato di diversificare l'attenzione sul genere'.
33. Emilio J. Castilla and Stephen Benard, "The Paradox of Meritocracy in Organizations," *Administrative Science Quarterly* 55, no. 4 (2010): 543.
34. Jo Littler, *Against Meritocracy: Culture, Power and Myths of Mobility* (London: Routledge, 2017), 13.
35. Littler, *Against Meritocracy*, 70.
36. The idea of meritocracy used as a hidden bias has been presented also on the Baltimore Symphony Orchestra website by Ricky O'Bannon, *Can 'Excellence' Sometimes be an Excuse?*', accessed April 16, 2020, www.bsomusic.org/stories/can-excellence-sometimes-be-an-excuse/.
37. See the funding schemes to promote workforce equality to fight gender-based violence created by the regional governance *Regione Lombardia*, accessed April 16, 2020, www.regione.lombardia.it/wps/portal/istituzionale/HP/DettaglioBando/servizi-e-informazioni/enti-e-operatori/sistema-sociale-regionale/pari-opportunita/progettare-parita-2019; or the event STEMinthecity organized yearly by the city of Milan *Stem in the City*, accessed April 16, 2020, www.steminthecity.eu.
38. *Women in Science*, accessed April 16, 2020, http://uis.unesco.org/sites/default/files/documents/fs51-women-in-science-2018-en.pdf.
39. Original quote: 'ci sono oggettivamente molte meno donne compositrici per scelta. Tutte le volte che mi propongono dei progetti, se sono delle compositrici femminili le prendiamo in altrettanta considerazione. SANTACESARIA: Ma in percentuale arrivano meno progetti da compositrici . . .? JAIS: Molti, molti meno. Io ho l'assalto dai compositori, anziani, giovani . . . compositrici, le abbiamo cercate noi . . . per cui è più il fatto che forse come nel mondo della scienza ci sono meno donne inclini a scegliere la carriera scientifica, forse ci sono meno donne all'interno del mondo della musica inclini a scegliere la carriera di compositore. Però oggettivamente non ho dati alla mano . . . è una percezione in base a quello che mi viene proposto'.
40. Original quote: 'Credo di non aver pregiudizi, né riguardo alle donne né riguardo al colore della pelle. Però, oggettivamente: chi invitiamo?'
41. In English, gender marking of job titles is generally avoided and much less controversial. However, in Italy, as explained by sociolinguists such as Cecilia Robustelli, the use of the masculine gender usually hides sexist views.
42. Cecilia Robustelli, ed., *Linee guida per l'uso del genere nel linguaggio amministrativo* (Firenze: Regione Toscana, 2012), accessed April 16, 2020, www.cronacacomune.it/media/uploads/allegati/44/linee-guida-per-uso-del-genere-nel-linguaggio-amministrativo-robustelli.pdf.
43. Clementina Casula, *Diventare musicista: Indagine sociologica sui Conservatori di musica in Italia* (Mantova: Universitas Studiorum, 2018), 217.
44. See for example this organizational chart *Amici della Musica di Firenze*, accessed May 5, 2020, https://amicimusicafirenze.it/lorganigramma/, now accessible through the Wayback Machine here, http://web.archive.org/web/20200511104026/https://amicimusicafirenze.it/lorganigramma/ (screenshot from May 11, 2020).
45. See *Luigi Pecci Centre for Contemporary Art in Prato*, accessed May 5, 2020, www.centropecci.it/it/chi-siamo/team, now accessible through the Wayback Machine here: http://web.archive.org/web/20200810210841/www.centropecci.it/it/chi-siamo/team (screenshot from August 10, 2020)]. Here the team members are described with their feminine and masculine job terms. However, not all fine arts and visual arts museums in Italy do so: see *Museo del Novecento*, accessed May 5, 2020, www.museodelnovecento.org/it/il-museo. They use masculine terms for women directors.

Bibliography

Abdul, Raoul. *Blacks in Classical Music: A Personal History*. New York: Dodd, Mead, 1978.
Bayley, Amanda. "Cross-Cultural Collaborations with the Kronos Quartet." In *Distributed Creativity: Collaboration and Improvisation in Contemporary Music*, edited by Eric F. Clarke and Mark Doffman, 93–113. Oxford: Oxford University Press, 2017.
Bertolani, Valentina, and Luisa Santacesaria. "Report. Milan 2018-2019: Chamber and Symphonic Music." *Curating Diversity*, May 2019. Accessed July 2, 2020. https://curatingdiversities.files.wordpress.com/2019/06/report-milan-june2019.pdf.
Biondoni, Sofia. "Il posto delle donne nell'editoria." In *Genere. Dati, politiche, questioni di genere*, March 22, 2018. Accessed March 21, 2024. https://www.ingenere.it/articoli/posto-donne-editoria.
Brett, Philip, Elizabeth Wood, and Gary C. Thomas, eds. *Queering the Pitch: The New Gay and Lesbian Musicology*. New York: Routledge, 1994.
Brown, Mark. "Female Composers Largely Ignored by Concert Line-Ups." *The Guardian*, June 13, 2018. Accessed March 21, 2024. https://www.theguardian.com/music/2018/jun/13/female-composers-largely-ignored-by-concert-line-ups.
Castilla, Emilio J., and Stephen Benard. "The Paradox of Meritocracy in Organizations." *Administrative Science Quarterly* 55, no. 4 (December 2010): 543–76.
Casula, Clementina. *Diventare musicista. Indagine sociologica sui conservatori di musica in Italia*. Mantova: Universitas Studiorum, 2018.
Citron, Marcia J. *Gender and the Musical Canon*. Urbana: University of Illinois Press, 1993.
———. "Women and the Western Art Canon: Where Are We Now?." *Notes* 64, no. 2 (2007): 209–15.
Eastburn, Susanna. "Take Note – Why Do Women Composers Still Take Up Less Musical Space?." *The Guardian*, March 8, 2019. https://www.theguardian.com/music/2019/mar/08/sound-and-music-female-composers-musicians-susanna-eastburn.
Farkas, Lilla. *Data Collection in the Field of Ethnicity: Analysis and Comparative Review of Equality Data Collection Practices in the European Union*. European Commission, Directorate-General for Justice and Consumers, 2017. https://op.europa.eu/en/publication-detail/-/publication/1dcc2e44-4370-11ea-b81b-01aa75ed71a1/language-en.
Gray, John. *Blacks in Classical Music: A Bibliographical Guide to Composers, Performers, and Ensembles*. New York: Greenwood Press, 1988.
Heath, Ryan. "Brussels Is Blind to Diversity." *Politico*, March 12, 2018. Accessed July 2, 2020. www.politico.eu/article/brussels-blind-to-diversity-whiteout-european-parliament/.
Hutchinson, Earl Ofari. *It's Our Music Too: The Black Experience in Classical Music*. Los Angeles, CA: Middle Passage Press, 2016.
Kirby, Sarah. "The Only Thing "Womanish" Is the Composer': Music at Nineteenth-Century Exhibitions of Women's Work." *Music and Letters* 100, no. 3 (2019): 420–46.
Kramer, Lawrence. *Music as Cultural Practice, 1800–1900*. Berkeley: University of California Press, 1990.
Littler, Jo. *Against Meritocracy: Culture, Power and Myths of Mobility*. London: Routledge, 2017.
McClary, Susan. *Feminine Endings: Music, Gender, and Sexuality*. Minneapolis: University of Minnesota Press, 1991.
O'Bannon, Ricky. "Can "Excellence" Sometimes be an Excuse?." *Baltimore Symphony Orchestra*. Accessed July 2, 2020. www.bsomusic.org/stories/can-excellence-sometimes-be-an-excuse/.
———. "The Orchestra Season by the Numbers: Database." *Baltimore Symphony Orchestra*. Accessed July 2, 2020. www.bsomusic.org/stories/the-orchestra-season-by-the-numbers-database.aspx.
———. "By The Numbers: Orchestral Soloists." *Baltimore Symphony Orchestra*. Accessed July 2, 2020. www.bsomusic.org/stories/by-the-numbers-orchestral-soloists/.
Robustelli, Cecilia, ed. *Linee guida per l'uso del genere nel linguaggio amministrativo*. Firenze: Regione Toscana, 2012.
Simoncelli, Silvia. *Donne Artiste in Italia. Presenza e Rappresentazione*. Milan: NABA, 2017.
Southern, Eileen. "America's Black Composers of Classical Music." *Music Educators Journal* 62, no. 3 (1975): 46–59.

Sitography

All websites originally accessed April 16, 2020.

Institutions

Società del Quartetto. www.quartettomilano.it/stagione-2018-2019/.
LaVerdi. www.laverdi.org/it/categories/2018%20-%202019/stagione-sinfonica.
Milano Musica. www.milanomusica.org/it/sezione-festival/calendario.html.
MiTo. www.mitosettembremusica.it/programma/fufe/edizione-prossima.html.
Pomeriggi Musicali. http://ipomeriggi.it/events.php?ricerca=&dalm=10&dala=2018&alm=5&ala=2019.
Serate Musicali. www.seratemusicali.it/stagione-2016-2017/stagione-2018-2019/.
La Società dei concerti. www.soconcerti.it.
Teatro alla Scala. www.teatroallascala.org/it/stagione/2018-2019/concerti/concerto-stagione-sinfonica/index.html.

Other Websites

Baltimore Symphonic Orchestra. "Stories." www.bsomusic.org/stories/.
Centro per l'Arte Contemporanea Luigi Pecci. "Chi Siamo." www.centropecci.it/it/chi-siamo/team.
Guerrilla Girls. "Is It Even Worse in Europe?." www.whitechapelgallery.org/exhibitions/guerrilla-girls/.
Gustar, Andrew J. Statistics in Historical Musicology. July 10, 2017. www.musichistorystats.com/about/.
Institute for Composer Diversity. www.composerdiversity.com/orchestra-seasons.
Keychange. https://keychange.eu.
Italian National Institute of Statistics. "Indicatori demografici anno 2019." www.istat.it/it/files//2020/02/Indicatori-demografici_2019.pdf.
Museo del Novecento. "Il Museo." www.museodelnovecento.org/it/il-museo.
Regione Lombardia. "Progettare la parità." www.regione.lombardia.it/wps/portal/istituzionale/HP/DettaglioBando/servizi-e-informazioni/enti-e-operatori/sistema-sociale-regionale/pari-opportunita/progettare-parita-2019.
STEMinthecity. www.steminthecity.eu.
Unesco Institute for Statistics. "Women in Science," June 2018. http://uis.unesco.org/sites/default/files/documents/fs51-women-in-science-2018-en.pdf.
Women's Philharmonic Advocacy. https://wophil.org.

30
BEYOND MUSIC WORKSHOPS
A Composer and a Community

Jenni Roditi

In the spring of 1982, when I was twenty-one and a first-year[1] music composition student at the Guildhall School of Music, I suddenly had a very surprising experience. I was dealing with acute anxiety – due to a sudden split-up from a boyfriend – when something in me suddenly profoundly shifted. As the stress was building, I decided to go for a walk to try and steady myself. I got downstairs, left the building, and arrived on the pavement. There I asked myself a question: '*where are you going?*' I just couldn't answer the question. In the next moment a super-charged, benign, high-energy column of white light, coming from what felt like the heavens, shot through the crown of my head and filled me up from tip to toe. I was immersed in a column of bliss, love, and complete oneness with everything. I remained fixed to the spot and blinded by this light for an indeterminate amount of time. After some time, my sight slowly returned and I could see the world around me. Everything looked brand-new. I felt brand-new. The stress was completely gone! I felt a deep inner peace for the first time in my life.

I could dwell further on this experience, but I think it was an out-of-body, out-of-mind, peak experience[2] or temporary spiritual awakening,[3] revealing – shall we say – higher dimensions, and changing me from that moment on. Something tangible from the experience stayed in my system for about eighteen months, lessening gradually in an uneven fade-out. The first month was extraordinary, and then slowly I began to normalise back into everyday life, leaving the experience as a memory. That memory has not left me as a reference point in my life. I'm not free from anxiety as a result of what happened, but it gave me insight, hope, direction, and meaning. It has coloured my thinking, and that's why I find myself writing about it at the start of this chapter. That one-off experience became a background reality to everything for me.

In what follows, I critically reflect on how my work in music has been intuitively, almost unknowingly, directed by that experience. It is only now, looking back, that it occurs to me that this is the case. There has been a lifelong search for a wide and spacious middle way[4] between anxiety and awakening, composition and improvisation, performance and leadership, and music and silence. Studying Tai Chi, reading,[5] meditating, chanting, absorbing spiritual teachings, and of course, persistently at the heart of my creative activities, music, were all touched by that very unusual moment.

(1) This chapter is an opportunity to consider how my leadership work combines musicianship alongside a knowledge that the inner life is alive to transformational experience. I have offered professional compositions in concerts, music workshops in schools and a

conservatoire, adult voice workshops and training, one-to-one therapeutic voice sessions, and home concert-salons.

A creative drive and inner drama were always there for me. I was composing from the age of six and these energies moved me forward with some urgency. Music helped me through early life, – saved me even, from a sometimes frightening, and often tense and emotionally confusing childhood. I arrived at the age of 18 in spin of disorientations, perhaps the only thing holding me together being the music that I was able create. I became more conscious of the need to knuckle down and study composition when my dear friend, the late Katrin Cartlidge[6] told me in no uncertain terms "you're a composer, get on with it!" Katrin and I both wrote guitar songs as teenagers, and we also composed more adventurous pieces on the piano. We inspired each other a lot during the 1970's.

(2) When I was 19, having taken a year off after school, I started a performing arts degree (in music, theatre, and dance) at Middlesex Polytechnic. I felt sure by the end of the first year I'd taken a wrong step. With Katrin's words in my ears after and after submitting some scores, I was accepted on the Guildhall School's graduate course and I managed to get Camden council to transfer my full grant over for another three years (those were the days).

Free improvisation sessions at the Guildhall every Friday afternoon with Alfred Nieman,[7] helped me express and explore my rather unbounded instincts and I played piano in small ensembles that Alfred selected. He listed one-word themes on a whiteboard and each group had to choose a theme. After each piece the class discussed what they felt about their classmates' piece. The only rule was "no octaves!" Meanwhile, I was getting to grips with the challenges of producing written scores on handwritten transparencies with a fine ink pen. I was being trained by Guildhall composition teachers[8] in a 1980's contemporary classical language, but my singing, its depth of feeling, both alone and with Katrin, eventually pulled me back towards a more emotional and less abstract approach. It took me time to trust that, and for several years I splashed about trying to formulate music in a contemporary atonal language.[9] As a reviewer of my finals piece, *September Boxes* wrote, "a brittle, occasionally even brash, somewhat Varesian work . . ."[10] That style came to an end in 1989 when a strong need to explore my voice took over. (I write about this in detail below, and how this became my way into work "beyond music workshops").

I had composed a piece for the Gemini-Bhavan project[11] where Indian musicians collaborated with classical players, a Baylis programme[12] opera,[13] which was tugging between atonality and a modal language, an orchestral piece[14] which was my final fling of the paint on an atonal canvas, an album of guitar songs,[15] in which my voice really opened, and a playful music-theatre piece,[16] where I began to find the bones of a musical language of my own. These are some of my compositional explorations during that period. Keith Potter summed it up well in the opening remarks of his 1985 review: 'The young composer trying to make a personal statement of some kind against the pluralist backdrop I spoke of... is hardly to be envied these days'.[17]

(3) In 1990 I was approached by an eminent contemporary classical music producer. Looking back, I can see now why I might have been commissioned three times by Odaline de la Martinez[18] of Lontano.[19] I had let go of that abstract language which interested Ms Martinez as a conductor. Below you will read how my singing voice developed, while my composing (which I do not have space to write about) continued to draw from a feeling centre, using static and directional modal pitch fields, peppered with asymmetrical rhythms, and by 1997 'ardent lyricism'.[20]

I composed two full length chamber operas and a vocal overture for Lontano over a period of eleven years. The music (3 hours and 40 minutes in all) was all completed and staged in quite a few different concerts over that decade, in London, England, and even Zagreb, Croatia[21] by 2001.[22]

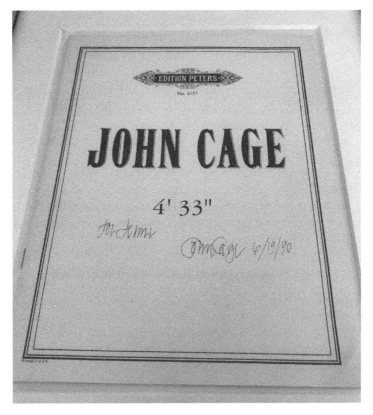

Figure 30.1 John Cage 4'33" score, given to Jenni and signed by the composer following her involvement in the Almeida Theatre schools workshops based around their production of Cage's Europeras 3 and 4 in 1990 (personal collection).

I was reaching for something after that '21-moment' as I call it. I wanted to be of use as a musician in a way that was open – and curious about bigger questions, and in experimental ways, like I had tasted in Alfred Nieman's sessions. My approach to composing was on the one hand studious, and on the other, alive to the echo chambers and kaleidoscopes of musical influences around me, while my gut said 'follow the inner thread'.

After graduating in 1985 I joined the composer-conductor Peter Wiegold in his Gemini music workshops. He often started his sessions by asking the children – what is music? The composer John Cage asked his audience something akin to this question, in his revolutionary piece 4'33" (1952), in which three movements are performed without a single note played. The piece questions 'what is music' and 'what is listening', as 4'33" of 'silence' brings you back to yourself (Figure 30.1 shows my copy of the score, signed by Cage). Who is listening? What is heard? The environment? The chatter in your head? What is musical? There may be no way to answer these kinds of questions definitively, but the piece opens a gap of existential doubt for some, and for others maybe a space in which to listen in new ways. By decoupling music *from* music, Cage's piece questions many divides: the divide between composer, performer, and audience comes to mind. It also reminds me of what happened when I decoupled *from* myself by asking that question: *'where are you going?'* I asked the question in the second person. There were two of me: *I* asked the question to the *You*. *She* never managed to reply because everything suddenly disappeared in a column of light. There was no I, no you, no she, no question, no answer. But there was love!

Five Case Studies

This chapter assesses my five main stages of leadership development seen in the following practices as composer, improviser, and performer: 1. Gemini Music Workshops, 2. Four Theatres of the Voice, 3. Voice Movement Therapy, 4. Vocal Tai Chi, 5. The Improvisers' Choir and The Open Choir for improvisers.

In preparing to write this chapter, I had a long conversation with my friend, composer-conductor Peter Wiegold.[23] An extract from that conversation appears in Stage 5, and longer examples from the whole conversation can be found online.[24] Peter has been a support and an influence on my work and we still continue our conversation, started in the summer of 1982 a few weeks after the 21 moment. Stage 1 touches on his pioneering work and how I became a part of it, in a kind of composer-workshop-performer apprenticeship.

Stage 1: 1984–1989: Gemini's Music Workshops

In the early eighties, as an undergraduate composer at the Guildhall, one contemporary music style that caught my attention was Extended Vocal Technique.[25] An early example of this is *Pierrot Lunaire* (1912), a melodrama by Arnold Schoenberg, which uses 'speech-song'.[26] I felt drawn to this theatre of the voice and began to explore my own singing in non-conventional ways. It opened the first of many vocal doors for me.

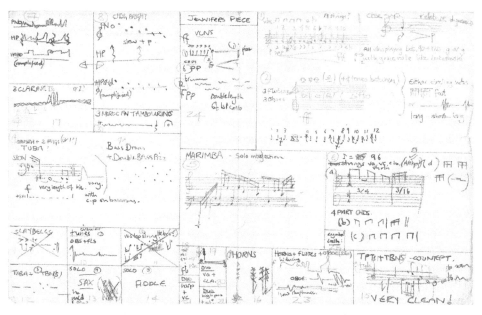

Figure 30.2 *September Boxes for Orchestra*, source material for my 1985 Guildhall School Symphony Orchestra finals undergraduate piece, taking a playful music workshop approach into composition: 'what does this size box and its position on the page suggest to you, musically? Sketch in some ideas.' A starting point posed to me by Peter Wiegold. From this I composed a notated orchestral score.

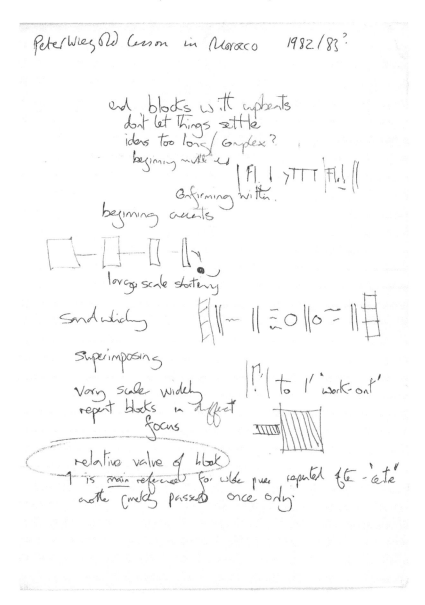

Figure 30.3 Composition lesson with Peter Wiegold, 1982/83, my notes.

In 1984, I started work as a composer, music-theatre artist,[27] and workshop leader with Peter Wiegold's ensemble Gemini. As well as performing and commissioning new works, Wiegold took classical players from Gemini into schools and universities, creating performances with these communities through music workshops. 'Gemini might be considered the musical equivalent of a theatre-in-education company', said one reviewer.[28] Gillian Moore,[29] surveying the contemporary music scene that was evolving to include music workshops, said that 'perhaps the idea came from breathing the air of the early 1970s with its politically driven, open-ended experimental forms, but the group [Gemini] soon began to put a strong emphasis on sharing the process of composing'.

Engaged by conversations I had had with Wiegold about cubism and juxtaposition as a musical form, I approached the end of my studies at Guildhall with a final orchestral piece, *September Boxes* (1985), drawing boxes on a page with different sizes and shapes, and then filling each with a music-graphic. I then translated and ordered these doodles into a full orchestral score. The piece was a scored version of the 'block form' that we were using in Gemini workshops. I remember one composer-teacher at the Guildhall not really liking my approach and telling me: 'Schoenberg composes, Messiaen juxtaposes!'. However, I went ahead and used this technique anyway.

A review of *September Boxes* said it was 'full of panache and also a fine sense of how to handle such drama in orchestral terms,'[30] but went on to opine that I was likely to 'move out of traditional concert hall composing... to develop further the side of... Gemini's work that Cardew[31] would have recognised as important'.[32] Gemini's music workshops were taken up by the Guildhall as the basis for a new post-graduate training, 'Performance and Communication Skills',[33] founded by Peter Renshaw[34] and Peter Wiegold in 1984. After my graduation, at the beginning of the new term in 1985, I was invited to join the teaching staff on this course. I was allocated half the undergraduate first-year students (about 60 people) as part of an expansion to the training. I ran five one-hour classes per week for four years. This was my first leadership role in an educational setting, leading a class, leading rehearsals, developing new group compositions, and facilitating improvisation for classical players. I was also leading on how to develop a new way of teaching performance by focussing on different ways to communicate. It was a pioneering leap for a conservatoire to include collective, empirical, and improvisational techniques more associated with theatre than classical music, and it was the beginning of a modernising, freeing-up approach in the training of classical musicians, which has continued since then at the Guildhall and expanded to other conservatories, too.

It was during one of my classes that I had an insight about leadership. I was well-versed in the Wiegold approach, with circle games, pulsed, timbral, modal, and free improvisation, and one-page scores,[35] but while reading *The Tao of Leadership*[36] and *The Inner Game of Music*,[37] I started to explore new approaches. I began to ask what my own leadership approach was. One day I lifted my hands off the usual workshop wheel and used an exercise from the *Inner Game of Music*. I don't have a record of what I did, but I remember that it threw the students back on themselves, and my notes say: '*Inner Game* had profound effect'.[38] I had stumbled upon something important.

I had explored leading group-compositions with one-page scores, with interlocking musical blocks, and with post-serialist note-spinning,[39] but these books were lifting my attention elsewhere, towards a mix of internal impulses and soft leadership that could meet the group and individual where they were at. I was discovering that leadership could be adaptive to the group. I also had to consider my own motivation as a teacher. I began to offer tasks that would weave between staying true to my own enquiry as an artist while attending to the needs of each member of the group and developing an empathy or third consciousness[40] between us.

Outside of my musical life, I had also discovered Tibetan Buddhism in 1985, meeting an authentic Tibetan *Rinpoche*[41] and his *sangha*[42] with whom I began chanting *pujas*.[43] This was my first experience of connecting voice to meditation.

Stage 2: 1989–1993: Four Theatres of the Voice

I took four courses in radically alternative ways to work with expressive voice, each with visionary approaches to singing: 1. Boris Moore's Roy Hart Theatre;[44] 2. Chloe Goodchild's Naked Voice;[45] 3. Gilles Petit's Indian Raga and Yoga;[46] and 4. Paul Newham's Voice Movement Therapy.[47]

All four courses took deep dives into specific ways of singing, moving, and thinking. Moore used Roy Hart Theatre methods combined with his precise attention to energised body work. Goodchild offered an approach to non-dual[48] consciousness in sound, using the Indian *sargam*[49] scale, mantras, improvisations with harmonium drone, and meditation. Petit taught classical Indian vocal raga in his 'Cosmic Theatre', which connected yoga poses with the *sargam* scale and his own French *chansons*. Newham's course was about voicework as a new form of therapy. All four were transformative experiences.

Chloe Goodchild's work opened up a profound inquiry into 'naked voice' and meditation, which she continues with her students to this day. She has an evolved spiritual presence which permeates her teaching and singing with grace and surrender. I often wept in her sessions as the atmosphere was so abundantly deep. She showed me how a build-up in energetic intentions could then saturate the voice before the first note was even sounded.

Gilles Petit's work transmitted an authentic and accessible approach for Westerners, like me, to get a good grasp of the basics of singing Indian raga. I felt my way around the ragas in his sessions for the first time. His deep attentiveness in approaching the sung note correctly, according to the Indian tradition as he understood it, was penetrating. The note needed both body and stillness, while losing attachment to the 'me' behind the sound: to simply let the note be itself. Getting out of the way through the presence of the sound itself might be one way to say it.

It was Newham's course that offered a qualification (a diploma from the Royal Society of Arts),[50] and this brought me quickly to the third stage of my professional development when he offered me his full roster of private clients. I started seeing about twelve people a week, over two days between 1993–1994 in a studio in Neal's Yard, Covent Garden. I moved the work to my new home in New Road, Crouch End in 1995 and continued to run 'therapeutic voicework' sessions for another 12 years.

Roy Hart Theatre

From 1989–1990[51] I attended a monthly, eight-weekend workshop in Paris[52] with Boris Moore of the Roy Hart Theatre.[53] (The Newham approach came from the same stable as Roy Hart. Newham had been studying with one of the Roy Hart Theatre founding members, Enrique Pardo).[54] I remember being entranced at seeing Boris Moore and members of the Roy Hart Theatre in his workshop improvising. It was so emotive and visceral. One particular memory was of their interpretation of the famous scene from Macbeth with the three witches, 'When shall we three meet again, in thunder, lightning or in rain?' Their vocal and physical embodiment went way beyond anything I'd seen before. By that point I'd seen enough Shakespeare to know it was *not* directed by a Royal Shakespeare Company director. This was wildly anarchic and vocally extreme in comparison. Each syllable from the text was a potential portal into elongated, expressionist, extreme vocal melodrama[55] and melisma combined with virtuosic body work. The power invoked was so vivid I could almost see smoke pouring from nostrils and flames licking around bodies. I sat, jaw dropped, pinned to the floor, spellbound.

From that course under Boris Moore's guidance, there was one moment I will never forget. In one session I was shaken by something that had happened in my home life and it triggered a regression in me. I was on the floor crawling forward on my belly in an imaginary tunnel. It was as if I was inside a void, perhaps moving through the birth canal. I only felt a sense of existence from the sound of my burbling voice on the next out breath. My psyche followed breath by breath, sound by sound, until the tunnel opened out and I was 'born'. It was a profoundly therapeutic vocal experience.

Stage 3: 1993–2005 – Voice Movement Therapy[56]

Forgive me if I don't have the words. Maybe I can sing it & you'll understand.
– Ella Fitzgerald[57]

After completing the inaugural Voice Movement Therapy course, in March 1993,[58] I became a certified 'therapeutic voice worker'.[59] Voice Movement Therapy landed me in a place where I could combine my skills and passion with an immediate practitioner pathway. In his 1998 book *Therapeutic Voicework*, Newham mentions me as the first person who verified to him that the work could be passed on.

> In the summer following the first series of short courses I became unable to work due to exhaustion and an exceptionally talented graduate from one of my training courses, Jenni Roditi, offered to take over my client practice. Jenni did this with extraordinary proficiency and skill and, in so doing, verified that the techniques were indeed solid enough to be passed on.[60]

In September 1992, I began the fourth step in these 'four theatres of the voice'. Paul Newham's book *The Singing Cure*[61] had just been published in January of that year, and it was a really exciting time. The therapeutically underlined synthesis of the unusual singing lessons of Alfred Wolfsohn[62] (the 'father' of the Roy Hart Theatre) and the radical theatre work of Roy Hart[63] were cross-fertilised by Newham with the therapeutic ideas of Carl Jung, Paul Moses,[64] and a number of others. Along with Newham's own inspired teaching and writing styles (notwithstanding some real challenges along the way) I felt this was something truly cutting-edge. I was happy to have found the work, and easily able to digest it and make it my own.

Alfred Wolfsohn's Life, Voice, and Singing Lessons

The 'four placements of the voice' is the model at the heart of Voice Movement Therapy, and it has a lineage of practitioners going back to originator Alfred Wolfsohn (1896–1962). Wolfsohn first taught this pioneering approach to the singing and sounding voice in Berlin following the First World War, from 1935–1943. Wolfsohn, a German Jew, fled Germany during the Second World War and settled in Golders Green, North London, where he continued his teaching. During the 1950s, Wolfsohn became unwell and he passed the work to his student, the South African actor Roy Hart, who had been studying with him since 1947.[65]

Alfred Wolfsohn had initially developed his four placements open model of the voice to heal himself from traumatic memories of the First World War. When war broke out in 1914, he was called up at age 19 to be a stretcher bearer in the trenches in Germany. It was a harrowing experience to hear wounded men crying out in agony and shells dropping all around. At one point he found himself facing a chilling choice: whether to risk his own life to save a friend who was wounded, or retreat to safety and save himself. He retreated. Later, he himself was wounded and left for dead on a pile of corpses. He somehow managed to get himself from there to safety in Holland. Author Mary Lowenthal Felstiner[66] has observed that Wolfsohn had later heard the voice of Hitler during WWII over loudspeakers many times, and after his experiences of WWI, he desired only one thing – to recreate a 'menschliche stimme' – a human voice to mend the fractures of the past.

To exorcise these shelled shocked and 'voice shocked' memories, and maybe 'survivor's guilt', haunting him after the war, as part of Wolfsohn's recovery in 1920s Germany, he began to voice out these aural hallucinations. One can imagine that he let out the entrapped shock inside him – voices he could still hear in his head of the soldiers on the battlefield 'in extremis', by expanding his voice, at whatever pitched height or depth he needed, to meet the memories, feelings, and sounds held within him. In so doing he managed to neutralise the inner nightmare by which he was afflicted, effectively curing himself of PTSD. At some point during this process, he named the division of the voice into four tessituras, and his view of how far the human voice could travel, no matter your gender, was transformed way beyond the classical model of SATB. By 1935 one imagines, having healed himself enough, he began sharing his work on the voice with others. He worked with students on scales and song interpretation, which involved men singing women's parts and vice versa, against the gender conventions. Sometimes he would converse for a long time with a student before the singing began. This work, and his deep understanding of the human condition, is described in a compelling biography by one of his closest students and a friend of his for many years, Sheila Braggins.[67]

I believe it was Wolfsohn who renamed the standard vocal tessituras, SATB, to that of a string quartet: violin, viola, cello, and double bass, representing the placements in the voice and, crucially, encouraging men and women to sing across all four ranges. This stretching of the voice to its extremes allowed the singer to reach more remote parts of themselves, often accessing unconscious material. His unusual singing lessons caught the attention of Peter Brook, Jerzy Grotowski, R. D. Laing, and Lionel Blue, among others, all of whom acknowledged his contribution to their work.[68]

Following the death of Alfred Wolfsohn in 1962, Roy Hart formed a theatre company to develop the applications of Wolfsohn's work in a new collective theatre approach to the voice. Importantly, Roy Hart performed the premiere of the composition 'Eight Songs for a Mad King' by Sir Peter Maxwell Davis in 1969, a music-theatre piece requiring Extended Vocal Technique.[69] The piece was performed by the Pierrot Players at the Queen Elizabeth Hall in London's South Bank Centre. I saw a memorable production of it in the 1990's at the Almeida theatre.

The Voice Map Metaphor

Newham's Therapeutic Voicework, originally called Voice Movement Therapy,[70] changed the Wolfsohn/Hart string quartet metaphor to (mainly) the woodwind family: from top to bottom: violin, flute, clarinet, saxophone. Newham said the woodwind family were closer to the vocal tract in the way they functioned. Woodwinds are blown instruments, not bowed, connecting breath to vocal sound. Sound passes from the lungs through the vocal folds which, in the case of the reeds of clarinet and saxophone, function similarly to the vocal folds. However, keeping the violin as the top placement was not congruent with this idea, which always bothered me.

In 1997, my colleague Bernadette O'Brien[71] and I were co-running 'Integral Voice' residential workshops. Bernadette, who had trained with Newham between 1993–1994 (in his second cohort of students), was also teaching the work to drama students at Rose Bruford College. She introduced the idea of imagining the sounds as if they were coming from the floors of a house. This helped the students to place and feel the sounds in their body. I liked this idea of working with the four floors of a vocal house and began to develop the idea and integrate it more fully into my work. Bernadette continued to use the Newham woodwind model as she says it is less evocative of states that may be associated with basements and attics, which for students may be too intense. I was happy to use the house model, as it always bothered me that the violin (not a woodwind instrument!) remained the top placement in Newham's model. The house also shifts the metaphor away from connotations of elitism associated with classical music, and I eagerly adopted this metaphor after having worked on it with Bernadette.

The Four Floors of the Vocal House are: **Attic**, a pinched, nasal sound, can be high or medium-low (violin); **Mezzanine**, a high to very high voice above the vocal break (viola/flute); **Ground**, a lower to quite high voice below the vocal break, (cello/clarinet); **Basement**, a wide-open throat, like when yawning, usually low, but can be used in Ground or Mezzanine (double bass/saxophone).

It is not only a simple vertical map of the voice, but a tangible way of shaping the vocal tract with a wide variety of timbres. Timbre is primary in the work. It is also a non-linear model, as a timbre-pitch in basement may sung above a timbre-pitch in attic. The metaphor provides guidelines that helps people navigate a way to colour-code their voice, from the narrowest, sharpest-sounding (attic) to the widest, broadest-sounding (basement) throat apertures. There are also more remote placements, the cellar – where the sound may be (metaphorically) dusty or dingy. Other vocal colours wash like the sea or crackle like fire across the folds. Oceanic whooshes, for example can be made both across the vocal folds or just in the mouth. The four floors may be blended, mixing say, mezzanine and attic and using other dials of modulation like breathy, steely, woody or crystaline. Most mysteriously perhaps, there is the great crossroads of the voice, known as 'the break' which can be surrendered to on many levels. The grainy, the wobbly, and the fracturing splinters of voice may all spark and shift the sounder's apprehension of their own process. Yet paradoxically, the break can also clear the voice and allow strong resonance to emerge. The break can produce powerful yodels, like gear-changes, leading right up to whistle notes above the attic, as a satellite dish on the roof! It is well-named 'the break,' as I have often heard people make important emotional breakthroughs using it. The palette is millions of colours rich. But how do these timbres 'unite with the thoughts and feelings'[72] of the client?

Linking Sound to Affect

Each vocal sound can be worked on technically and then at some point, any point, it might touch on an affect;[73] that is, live psychological material. Clues emerge as to which materials might be best to explore further. I follow the clues and help the singer touch into the arising, personally active material imaginatively, drawing out a relationship between the way their voice is moving and the unfolding inner narrative. The balance of working to achieve a technical win with a sound, over engaging with affect in the voice, needs to be assessed on a case-by-case basis.

What I took from Newham's training included verbal visualisations to graphically describe vocal sound, movement techniques like concave-convex posture work, massage strokes, breath work, aspects of a Jungian framework, and the placement model. Additionally, the emphasis on vocal timbre interested me as a composer, as within twentieth-century music timbre as a parameter had been elevated to the same level of importance as pitch and rhythm.[74] Bring these elements together with the wide and wild landscape of a voice through the four floors and you have a potent cocktail of elements working together in a cohesive way. For people who are willing to dive, or gently step, into a truth-seeking musical world of their own making it is, shall we say, sound.

The Voice Mirror

In my experience I have only offered Therapeutic Voicework to adults (it is not something that a young person below eighteen years of age could necessarily grasp[75]) and not often to classical singers. The practice seeks to meet peoples' voices from the gruffest to the most sublime, opening up a full vocal spectrum, mirroring the psyche and sounding out the whole person. One way to enter this process is to pick up on triggers, where the voice has an emotional charge or blocks where the voice sounds a bit dull. When introducing the voice map using tones, songs, or improvisation, I listen out for these triggers and blocks and invite them carefully into the session. Working through affect musically brings people to a place where they can begin to hear their voice and themselves afresh, often 'as if for the first time' as 'liberated voice'[76] begins to emerge through the processes that are undertaken.

As Margaret Pikes, one the Roy Hart Theatre founding teachers writes, "Wolfsohn and Hart were not interested in the mechanics of the vocal tract: the vocal folds, glottal flow, or resonating areas in the head. Their work was concerned with exploring and developing the *human*, as opposed to the *specialised*, voice."[77]

Two Sisters

One of the hardest client situations I have encountered (in the mid-1990s) was when two sisters (both in their late twenties) came to see me. They had just lost their mother and were in terrible shock and grief. Of course they didn't know, but I have a sister and our own mother had died only a few years before. It was hard to contain my own empathic response, but at that moment I was able to turn around what was live within myself in the service of their needs. Each new step that we took together created a sung emotional lifeline for them. I focussed in on vocal phrases they were hinting at and which I could encourage, asking them to develop 'micro-musical forms'[78] while remaining present to their shaky feelings. They were able to go inside their grief-laden voices and to sound out what was within them. I followed their intoning and our dialogue while encouraging their 'felt sense'.[79] They moved their focus downwards and inwards from verbal to non-verbal, from spoken to sounding. Their voices found some grounded strength and began to expand outwards, finally reaching a kind of mythic keening.

These two bereft daughters were invoking elements from a cultural act that in the modern, urban setting has largely been forgotten. This forgotten cultural act, weeping, wailing, and keening[80] in an improvised song-like form, used to be (and probably still is, in some parts of the world) a natural, healthy expression of loss, mostly sung by women in the Celtic and Gaelic traditions, and across various indigenous peoples of Asia, the Americas, Africa, and Australia, and can be known as the death wail.[81]

A grief song in the context of Vocal Tai Chi may not need to involve a death wail, but it will invite a personal encounter with your narrative of loss, in your own way, if you so choose, through your voice. It is a modulated journey, towards core feelings. In this gradated travel within, there may be a wide dynamic and pitch range, or it may be more stable and quieter, like a meditative journey with voice. A varying palette of vocal expressions may swirl on a sea of coursing emotion, sometimes in eddies, sometimes a giant wave or a sudden electric current. Or spontaneous mantras of contemplation may slowly lead to quiet revelation. In the most striking examples I have encountered, and there have been many, there can be a mixture of both these levels: a riding of the voice through its waves of emotion, while the sounding also moves within meditative awareness.

Each episode on this private journey can be interpreted with narrative content; regret, confusion, longing, searching, wistfulness, hurt, loneliness, as well as joy, love, and gratitude. A blended variety of emotional tones present themselves in between the shock, numbness, anger, and rage that are common initial reactions to a primary bereavement. A subtle process of meeting with the specific memory of the dearly departed filters through in the cracks of a breaking heart and the shaping of voice itself. This new, contemporary version of keening, which has always been a part of Vocal Tai Chi, helps the mourner piece together a new narrative for their lost relationship in its still-living, posthumous state. This may be sung-sounded with or without words. A particular phrase, text, or melody may catalyze the journey to help bring back the essence of the cherished lost one.

Especially in contemporary English life, it is more likely that, publicly, there is a different kind of cultural act. This might include the quiet sniveling into tissues, a biting of lips, a pursing of mouths, a grinding of teeth, a dark costume, a clenching of fists, and passive nodding acknowledgement to others, anything to stop the impact of deeper feelings spontaneously rising. Such a 'display of feeling' could be considered indulgent or bordering on hysterical within the English culture of 'stiff upper lips.

But this embodied form of mourning is anything but indulgent. It is the voice of life, quenching pain, in waves of intuitively formed vocal music. The loss is held inside the living energy of this self-generated song of sorrow. It arises from and is guided by the volition of the mourner. This gives them a sense of creative form and direction during a time when they are likely feeling, at times, out of control.

Crucially, what emerges beyond the outpouring in the ebbing of sorrowful flow is release and compassion for the loss. As the pain is made flesh, the psyche learns, right there and then, more about itself. Then, often without hesitation, the psyche gifts the singer/mourner back with some new flash of self-knowledge, grace, and peace. The subsiding torrent sinks back into a new reality and a fresh template of the narrative begins to settle in. The storm subdues after its time of high drama. The mantra moves into silence as the alignment deepens. The mourner feels rinsed-through, despite this fresh loss in their life. Something new seems possible after the airing of such mixed emotions, an improvised meditative song of keening. Natural closure, often with slower breathing, utterings of prayers and wishes, a soft weeping, and a vocal transparency – akin to love – follows. For now, complete.

Did this journey with the two sisters change their sense of what music itself actually is? I don't know. But there was wonder and disbelief at how the process had worked something through. These two-grieving children-adults-daughters had sung for their mother, and the effect was therapeutic, creative, and even ritualistic.

Just That Next Step

In this work, I hear people say: 'I never knew that sound was a part of me'. 'Is that *my* voice singing?' Voice is so central to all our identities. The work gives people a new sense of who they are as they perceive a new aspect of their voice sounding out. Music is reinventing them. To me as a composer, the sessions become an unfolding composition, the score being the person's life, held in their voice.

As needed, I sound with the singer, gently encouraging them to advance further, often without recourse to words. I listen to the grains and fragrances within the notes and the potential meaning and feeling they may carry. People are more or less musical within themselves; in terms of transformation, it doesn't need to be musically 'advanced,' but I am always encouraging new territory, 'just the next step'.

In our conversation about this work, Peter Wiegold spoke of a 'symphonic unfolding' of the session as an 'implicit musical journey' and linked that to the work that would later unfold in my choirs as well. One hour per session does create a precise arc of time, like a symphonic movement, so that by the end there is always a sense of arrival or pause. I follow the person and their vocal instrument, meeting needs and mixing musical and human interactions. When people reach an edge, they may need some permission to go there, which I gently and sometimes more urgently give them.

The Therapeutic Voicework private sessions ran for thirteen years, mainly as one-to-one sessions. As time went on, I became aware that something was missing: I was absent as an artist in my own right, and there was no audience. Stage Four was needed.

Stage 4: 2002 to Present: Silicon Quartz Crucibles, Raga, and Vocal Tai Chi[82]

I took some time to explore sound healing (2002–2004) through imbibing the utterly transformative sound world of silicon quartz crucibles, played by Native American/Czech musician and shaman Awa Hoshi.[83] She used a set of these crystal bowls in conjunction with healthy lifestyle diet, yoga and meditation. I needed to take care of some residual anxiety at this point, after some difficult years. I was lying on the floor in Sicily, in a flat opposite Mount Etna, listening to the intrinsic complexities and power of these quartz crucibles. I surrendered to the sonic mysteries in these wondrous vibrating crystal bowls. They were not all sweetness and light as a sound world. They were often oceanic, overwhelming, and bursting through my aural limits. There was no point resisting these tsunami waves of sound. All I could do was let them come in and be changed by them. I could physically feel their tree trunk-like mighty tones, criss-crossing from the left to the right side of my brain as if they were binding me back together in sonorous aural tree rings around my skull. These silicon crucibles, and the kindness of Awa Hoshi and her wonderful cook Myra, restored me and I was ready to return to the voice once more.

I was drawn back towards Indian classical vocal music,[84] and remembering my courses with Chloe Goodchild and Gillet Petit during the 1990s, I wanted to learn more about the raga – particularly the slow, introductory, non-rhythmic *alap*, which involves singing while in meditation, and in contrast, the fiery, fast *gamak* ornamentation. I participated in several rounds of study at the Asian Music Circuit Summer School,[85] learning a little of the *khyal*-style north Indian raga[86] and after so many years of free voice work, I enjoyed and probably needed the discipline of study again to deepen my vocal skills.

For three years before I launched Vocal Tai Chi in 2012, I was experimenting with improvised singing, drawing on the raga *alap gamak* and the *khyal* styles of singing which I studied between 2005 and 2009. A friend, Jazz Rasool, who was with me as I was practising, said one day, 'It looks like a vocal form of Tai Chi', as I was naturally moving my body as I sang during my *alap* practice. Thus began the emergence of my new practice.

The slow introductory raga *alap* is a very detailed form of vocal mirroring of psyche. The singer meditates vocally on the poetic and mythical qualities of the *rasa* – the flavour of the pitches in the mode and its tuning. There is myth, too, connected to prayers and stories for different times of the day and night. This microscopic enquiry into the scale, introducing each note, each slide, *shruti*,[87] and interval, reveals the singer's depth of devotion to each moment in this fine melodic line. It seemed to me the *alap* was about singing the very movement of the soul in a subtle dialogue between divine and earthly matters.

Vocal Tai Chi was named in 2009 (by my friend Jazz Rasool), but it sat on the back burner for two years (2010–2012) before I stepped out with it. I had done my Asian Music Circuit courses and I was experimenting with my own improvised versions of what I had learnt, and unconsciously adding my own movement style to this.

I had started learning Yang-style Tai Chi Chuan as a formal movement sequence in the early 1980s,[88] so it was natural for me to move with this style influencing me. Tai Chi is an ancient form of movement-meditation. It originated in China over two-thousand years ago. It was absorbed into all aspects of life: medicine, economics, philosophy, cooking, literature, calligraphy and most importantly, human relationships. Through mastering a sequence of movements, emphasising inner stillness with outer motion, Tai Chi is a profound approach to health. It is based on the principles of flow and balance between yin and yang, the receptive and the active poles of an invisible yet essential life-force energy known as Qi or Chi. Tai Chi weaves the yin and yang into a vibrant alignment which activates the Qi, harmonising a person's whole system into health. It is through these slow, disciplined yet relaxed movements, with conscious breathing, and a mental focus on both the minutiae and the magnitude of what is happening that Tai Chi has a positive effect on life itself.

Vocal Tai Chi as a title suggests a practice flowing slowly between the body and voice, but Tai Chi is also dynamic and interactive. Channelling Qi energy, masters of Tai Chi can activate intense involuntary shaking release work in their students. Tai Chi, for beginners, provides many safe harbours for the body and mind, especially if you are working with vocal risk-taking. I always bring these safe harbours – centred, connected to belly breath, and grounded through the feet – into sessions. It was perfect as a link to my previous work in Therapeutic Voicework and as a way to venture forth to the new stage. I set up Open Workshops that continue to this day.

The Loft[89]

Since 2004 I have been very lucky to live in a beautiful live-work space in Crouch End, London where much of my work has developed.

Figure 30.4 The Loft: Jenni talking to people gathered around at The Improvisers' Choir 'Land Mass' album launch (11 May 2019).

Source: Photo © Ronald Lovoie

I launched Vocal Tai Chi at the Loft in January 2012,[90] performing a solo-vocal improvisation concert. I produced some instrumental pre-recorded tracks that had modal centres and scales I could draw on.[91] It was a joyful coming-out occasion, and I sang freely with many influences.[92] I had found some artistic performance ground for myself.

Becoming Artist-Leader

As a leadership practice, Vocal Tai Chi offers workshops, one-to-ones, masterclasses, and since 2023 an apprenticeship.

At first, I tried without success to impart Vocal Tai Chi as my own freestyle, multi-genre singing language. It took me a moment to realise that what I was doing was too advanced, and people came because they wanted to find their *own* language, not learn mine. As Yehudi Menuhin said: 'Improvisation is the expression of the accumulated yearnings, dreams and wisdom of the soul', and each person has their own accumulations. People responded to the human aspect of what I was doing. Each person I worked with bypassed my advanced musical techniques, but what they saw in me was a vulnerability, intuition, and opening up to inner searching through the voice, and this is what they could use for themselves.

Here are some testimonials from the first Vocal Tai Chi workshops in 2012, which gives a sense from other voices of how this method makes one feel: 'It all made sublime sense. I learned to start to dare to apply my improvisation techniques I know from Drama to my voice' (Mandy Carr, Drama Therapist); 'The work is healing, deep, creative, expressive, spontaneous, and holistic. There is a vibrant synergy between all the elements, the performance, the material, and the audience. (Mohini Chatlani, Yoga Teacher); 'It feels like coming back to the beginning . . . The most important thing is connecting with other people, who are not necessarily singers, but that's irrelevant; we are making music together' (Mark Thomas, horn player, improviser, psychotherapist).

In order to meet people where they were (as had been first discovered in my early Guildhall teaching with the 'Inner Game of Music' exercise) and not bamboozle people with my developing artistic enquiry, I returned to the voice map metaphor (using the 'vocal house' version of it), which was accessible for all comers, accessible for all comers and I explored my personal vocal language when it was time for my own Vocal Tai Chi 'demonstration solo' in the workshop, to inspire and encourage others to stand alone and sing – and to give myself some space to live and breathe the music too. This practical solution provided a wide enough middle way for me to continue running sessions with the public, meet them where they were, *and* step into my vocal style as a vocal improviser.

The Vocal Tai Chi Workshop: Before Tea

After a spoken check-in round, the session starts. We stand in a circle, and I lead a voice, breath, and body warmup, integrating Tai Chi and mindful attention to actions. I then introduce the four floors of the vocal house,[93] or more advanced developments from there, depending on who is in the group. I add a tanpura (Indian drone) app or simple VTC backing track that makes the practice performative and focusses listening towards a modal centre[94] and simultaneously encourages connection with the inner felt sense. People work individually for a while, and then I suggest breaking the circle. People move into pairs or threes, and begin to interact vocally and physically as I suggest new enquiries, building on expression and experimentation. Inhibitions loosen and new vocal discoveries arise naturally, growing from my spontaneously felt instructions. As Louis Armstrong mused: 'What we play is life'.[95]

As may be apparent from this short description of the start of the workshop, I'm working with the group itself as the main source material. This is where Tai Chi is guiding the work strongly. The power of Tai Chi is perhaps summed up best by one phrase in the practice: 'yield and return'. 'Yield' lets the body and mind give way to the oncoming force (i.e. the specifics of what is alive in the group or, in martial art terms, your assailant) and 'return' is a follow-up from the yield, where you return to your centre, remaining rooted in yourself, with the earth current through your feet. Yielding is central to the Chinese feminine 'yin'[96] principle of receptivity which can be found in all people. I apply this feminine yin quality to my leadership (while not avoiding yang or masculine interventions when needed). I yield to the group and return to myself almost at the same time. From the group's perspective it may appear as if they have created the workshop for themselves. But it is receptive leadership, alongside the non-judgemental vocal challenges[97] that I set which, I hope, send a positive message of self-empowerment. I work with this feminine 'yin leadership' approach, which I discovered back in the 1980s when teaching at the Guildhall, after reading *The Tao of Leadership* by John Heider.

The Vocal Tai Chi Workshop: After Tea

After a tea break, the microphone is placed in the space and I sing to the group before the solos begin. I invite each member of the workshop to come up and sing their own Vocal Tai Chi solo on the mic. I am contextualising the work now as performance, but the audience are not strangers. They are bonded together for the afternoon as a workshop family. Performance, apart from anything else, is the act of being witnessed. This is humanising for all present. People sing their solo, aiming for some honesty, imagination, and to feel their music.

Standing Alone

The microphone is a symbolic icon of performance and can offer challenge as well as support. It interrupts the safety of the workshop circle as the singer stands alone in front of the group. Singers may find themselves welling up and shedding a tear and then singing through the tears. All present in the room naturally help hold the emotions and the soundings with the singer by simply being there. 'If I'm going to sing like someone else, then I don't need to sing at all', as Billie Holiday said.[98]

Free of the composed songs of others, people aim towards their own honest music. I coach these solos with interventions and with reference to the voice map as needed. As they progress, the improvised notes and sounds sung reflect the person back to themselves. Singing Vocal Tai Chi can be like hearing your life as a vocal metaphor or a meta-sounding. As the singer dives in, hidden parts that were unable to find a voice may come up and out. Yet there is nothing symbolic or meta about it: it is right here, more real than any symbol could ever be.

By working in this way, singers can find themselves in a new paradigm and often encounter personal edges beyond their comfort zone. I help the singer work through these. As the process continues, the backing track[99] sustains the musical space, and my job is to see what needs to be brought through in performance, technical, physical, psychological, and even sometimes spiritual terms. As edges are met, the soloist goes deeper, allowing new material to be voiced. The importance of the witnessing workshop-family-audience is needed in supporting the process, as the singer makes vocal discoveries and unearths the bones of a raw, authentic language. New music is heard, especially as edges are faced. Specific sonorities in the notes themselves are often the key to opening up this process. There may be a major vocal release, like a geyser shooting out hot water and steam, but it can also be a slow lifting of the veil.[100]

A Paradox

This spontaneous flow of the voice may take singers by surprise, especially if it is unusual for them to sing freely in front of others. There is a paradox: as resistances are encountered, opportunities arise for more of the voice to emerge. The sound may stumble, tighten, or harden; it may tremble, break, or disappear. There may be a dullness or some force. 'My voice' may be held as a concept, a fantasy, or an attachment. What does the singer do? It is a stopping point, even a breaking point, but it can also be a new starting point. Some parts of a more complete spectrum of the whole voice may only be found by crossing an unknown vocal bridge, where missing sounds are then found on the other side. As Philip Glass said: 'If you don't know what to do, there's actually a chance of doing something new. As long as you know what you're doing, nothing much of interest is going to happen'.[101]

Through its ancient wisdom and knowledge of the body and mind of breathing, moving, and staying in balance, Tai Chi offers a perfect grounding form. Vocal Tai Chi can then safely invite and honour the imperfections of being human, including unknown daemons, respectfully and honestly engaging with them. Then, incapacitated grief may rise as vibrant keening. Stuck anger can trumpet belly sounds of rage and courage. A quivering, distressed voice, for example, once encountered also spontaneously draws in self-insight, and perhaps love, to meet with this pain. As the pain hears her own voice, in unplanned trills, shakes, glissandi, and new melodic narratives, compassion can gently arise and soft pulsations of gratitude may also stir.

None of this could happen with advance planning from the students or the leader. Once the parameters are understood by all, there is a letting go and a meeting of what is without knowing the outcomes. It is crossing an unknown threshold. This can even become ceremonial as difficulties are met and relieved. New understandings arise for the soloist 'on the hot spot,' and the group senses transformation in the air. They may respond, clap, cheer, or cry with the soloist or rise to their feet to join in. An intuited dance-song, either initiated by me or the group, may end the workshop with an amplification, deepening, or quietening of the musical space.

'Right and wrong' have been redeemed within the first twenty minutes of the session, and there is no longer an excuse for self-resistance or self-judgement. After that, the singer only has their sound, their voice, their life in its present state. As John Cage said: 'The idea of a mistake is beside the point, for once anything happens, it authentically is'.[102] It may not all happen in one session, though a lot often does. Step by step, hidden layers of the voice, the person, and their music are uncovered. The process nearly always garners vivid, inspired, or intimate and vulnerable free-singing. Over time I began to feel it was a pity not more people were able to hear this new music and I began to wonder how I might bring that about.

Grief Tending[103]

Without setting out to put emphasis on supporting the grieving process, this is one of the areas that has often been of use to people. My original interest in developing Vocal Tai Chi was to explore my own spontaneous vocal language, connected to feeling states, and drawing on a variety of musical influences from different cultures that had impacted me as a composer. However, recognising my artistic research wasn't of that much interest to others; what drew people to the work was my ability to vocalise nuanced feeling states, not so much any particular experimental 'style' I might be personally developing. What became central was meeting people where they were in their lives. Teaching my fascination with ornamentation, for example, quickly went by the wayside in favour of using free-voice as a place of emotional sanctuary and daring to meet the unmet aspects of each person in an unselfconscious way.

Figure 30.5 Jenni conducting The Improvisers' Choir, at the first in a three-concert 'Club Vocalé' series held at the Earl Haig Hall, Crouch End, 26th September 2016.

Source: Photo © Steven Cropper

Figure 30.6 Jenni performing Vocal Tai Chi at Inspiral Lounge, Camden Town, London. April 2012.

Source: Photo © Katie Rose

Interestingly, and to my private delight, as these feeling states were opened up for people, they often contained unexpected vocal fissures, wobbles, and shakes: the very origination of what surely, in any given vocal culture over time, became formalised as ornamentation. These tiny vocal dips, swoops, lifts, and dives were originally sourced, I suggest, from a place of fragility, intensity, and unguarded feeling in the voice. What I had been particularly excited about musically for myself in Vocal Tai Chi turned out to be there anyway, with inexperienced singers, working unselfconsciously in their process. As a listener I found this to be so beautiful and real.

My two client case brief descriptions in this chapter both speak of work with grief-tending, but it is worth mentioning that this is only one lens through which to see the work. The practice can help work with discovery in many life-narrative contexts.

The second client example of grief-tending is when one female participant had just lost her brother. After her pre-tea group session, she stood shyly in front of the microphone for her solo spot. The backing track encouraged a musical starting point and spacious atmosphere. Her voice moved from within an unsettled silence, sounding rasping-out breaths, half-pitched tones, shakings, and soft voices from within the shadows of herself, to deeper in-breaths that slowly built up to her expelling stronger sounds. She found herself caught up in a rising energy, singing more strongly in vocalised, pitched, and musically shaped cries. She unbound her grief in expansive, climbing phases, beyond her control yet guided by a felt sense.[104] After several minutes, her burden of loss was relieved and her grief was filling up with darkly rich vocal timbres, full of melancholic love. She found her own power, way beyond her initial stuttering and overwhelm, and sent it out to the group, her brother, and beyond. Eventually, she returned to smaller expressions, soothing sequences, tiny unplanned trills, and then a gently settling melody. She was silent. Her awareness expanded into a deeper sense of self, and stillness descended. The group were clearly moved, and the feeling[105] in the room was palpable. Sometimes my role is simply to give space and permission, and I sit quietly in silence. Sometimes I am engaging with the person working in a detailed way. It depends on the situation.

Nature and Inner Nature

John Cage proposed that 'art should imitate nature in its manner of operation'.[106] In Vocal Tai Chi, I suggest that people are imitating their *inner* nature. This is a manner of creating that is as natural and wholesome as oxygen and is indeed imitating the inner nature of each person.

Though most people in the workshops do not know these performing artists, Vocal Tai Chi solos are often tangentially related to the sound worlds of innovative vocalists from various music scenes past and present – and in my view, these artists are almost impossible to pigeon-hole into genres: Maggie Nichols, Julie Tippetts, Elaine Mitchener, Martana Roberts, Cleveland Watkiss, Phil Minton, Randolph Mathews, Joan le Barbara, Shelley Hirsch, Cathy Berberian, and of course Meredith Monk. The starting points in VTC are simple but people travel far and wide vocally. They can come back to something as simple as a lullaby or a nursey rhyme, and then travel off somewhere new again.

Perhaps one should not compare Vocal Tai Chi solos sung by members of the public, often without a musical background, to that of professional artists, but they are somehow reminiscent, in places, to my ear. Vocal Tai Chi solos may not always adhere to perfect tunings or professional music standards, but I think when they don't, the singers make up for it by fully living inside their own sound worlds with every inch of what they have to give. There is a primordial quality, innocent and compelling in its own way.

Honest Music

I have seen that Vocal Tai Chi can unearth the honest free-songs of peoples' lives. These may be simple and reminiscent of a folk song, or complex and impressive, like some avant-garde jazz music. Wherever they sit on the genre spectrum, the work unlocks singers and so-called non-singers, unbinding them from the formalities of conventional song-form. Vocal Tai Chi may take people across an unknown vocal bridge and can become a rite of passage.[107]

Peter Wiegold said to me in our conversation[108] as part of my preparation to write this chapter: 'Vocal Tai Chi represents an advance on Therapeutic Voicework. It's more integrated, connected to a flowing musical outcome and now also integrates performance, which they are living, from within'.

The Main Workshop Elements

There are many Vocal Tai Chi elements, here are some of the main ones: 1. Embodiment and demonstration of the work by the facilitator; 2. Facilitated improvised voice work in groups and individually; 3. Basic Tai Chi grounding, centring, movement flow, stillness; 4. The four floors of the vocal house with micro, modular and macro musical processes, to expand knowledge and experience of the voice and to discover 'the voice in emotion' (JR).[109] 5. Formless forms – the tangible and intangible in balance; 6. Deep listening[110] to the environment around and within 7. Poly-vagal theory of safety and risk;[111] 8. VTC apprentices (2023) now finding their own approaches; 9. Massage, pressure points and light touch; 10. Participant-owned felt sense[112] enquiry;[113] 11. Underpinning drones and backing tracks;[114] 12. Singing in an unknown language;[115] 13. Triggers and blocks: supporting vocal-emotional edges; 14. Rites of passage and meeting thresholds; 15. Group discussion and experiential feedback; 16. The creative-witness role, where responses to the soloist may be created in poetry, prose, drawing or movement.

Stage 5: 2015 to the Present: The Improvisers' Choir

The integrative approach found in Vocal Tai Chi was to be taken further in Stage Five. I was itching to put the work in public concert form. One day I clocked that 'conduction'[116] might be the way to do that. I called auditions for creative professional singers and formed a conduction choir (see also the case studies on twentieth-century women conductors in Part II).

In May 2015, I auditioned twenty-five singers and selected ten of them. December 2015 marked the first performance[117] with The Improvisers' Choir (TIC) at the Vortex Jazz Club.

There was a sense of breakthrough afterwards, as none of us had done a performance like it before and the euphoria was unmistakable.[118] The singers were from multiple genres, and I conducted the improvisations with hand signals, shaping the music, drawing on key signs from Peter Wiegold and Martin Butler's *Notes Inégales*[119] band and adding additional ones.

Since then, special guests[120] have been invited to collaborate in some of the concerts, devising music with the choir around the guest's music and allowing them to find ways into the choir's music. As conductor, I integrate the guest, hold the overall space, shape 'symphonic' long lines, and aim to realise the 'implicit journey' of the whole across each piece and the complete concert.

In 2018, TIC recorded an album which became the soundtrack to a film by Sara Pozin, whose brief was to articulate in moving images the essence of the musical worlds of each piece. 'Land Mass' can be explored at the link[121] provided.

Figure 30.7 The Improvisers' Choir (TIC) with Jenni conducting. Koç University, Istanbul, Turkey. December 2016.

Source: Photo © Asena Kolaşın/Koç University Archive

Shape Shifting Over Thirty Years

Over the decades there has been a reframing of my role: I started as an ivory tower composer. I put my passion for voice aside for eight years (1981–1989) as I sweated over my piano studies and composing with clunky composition software. Then with a personal crisis in 1989, my experimental singing burst forth and I started the year-long course with Boris Moore from Roy Hart Theatre. Thirty years later, the schisms I always sensed as an artist between composer, performer, and artist-leader have slowly eased out, decade after decade. I have now gotten to the point where the roles seem almost inseparable; as, for example, in other recent collaborations (from 2018 to the present) with Adrian Lee[122] and Alistair Smith.[123] As colleagues we facilitate each other's creative and personal growth (such a pleasure) in dialogues and improvisations, perform live with a mix of improvisations and predetermined starting points, make remote audio-video recordings online, and also come together as artist-leaders to support others in workshops, gatherings, and concerts.

Allegorical Levels of Social Connection and Musical Practice

The only professional review, so far, for The Improvisers' Choir, in March 2019, called TIC's music 'a societal allegory'.[124] This speaks of a performance practice that points beyond music to its social implications. The allegorical quality in The Improvisers' Choir has several facets to explore. The choir are delivering publicly in an unusual social/musical set-up to bring about new music. They look unlike a conventional choir, who have their eyes in their scores, or an ensemble of instrumentalists sitting behind music stands. The singers stand in a semi-circle,

Jenni Roditi

without scores, looking directly at the conductor, the audience, and each other. It is a transparent situation, especially as the music is yet to be plucked from thin air.

Here is the full review comment: 'Jenni Roditi's vocal improvisation choir was poignantly reaffirming of the power of the individual voice, and the difference it can make as part of a collective, not least in the creative practice of collaborative music-making, but as a societal allegory'.[125] What is the 'social allegory' in this context? The conductor is the convener of the practice and takes on leadership responsibility. By holding the space and using an ear that draws on compositional as well as performance sensibility without the container of a score, the conductor is also reliant on the choir to spark the music into life. There is a high level of trust needed between all.

The conductor's role delineates a fine membrane between the singers and herself. This is a defining edge as well as a porous and flowing one, with influences moving to and fro across

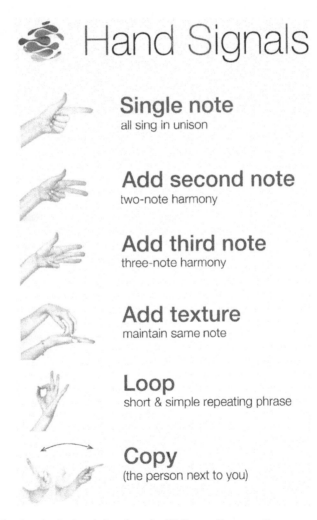

Figure 30.8   Conduction, basic signals handout for Wellcome Trust reading room public workshops on 22nd September 2018 and 28th February 2019, led by Jenni, with members of The Open Choir for Improvisers (TOCFI) present to support the public.

the membrane. As in an earlier reference to Vocal Tai Chi, where yin and yang are balancing life forces, this allegory symbolises leadership as a publicly observed exchange of spontaneous musical cooperation. The membrane sits at the point of equal, opposite, and interconnected force. The conductor is one point, and the singers are another. Yet, there is a third point that interconnects both – the music itself. Additionally, the audience, the room, and context of the event, and so on, all have an effect on what music might be made, in that moment.

The Improvisers' Choir works on the basis that a conduction role is very helpful for a musical overview. It also gives any conductor who may wish to explore this approach the chance to try out the art of sculpting spontaneous pieces, while allowing your own inner musical thread as part of a guiding journey for others.

As well as social cohesion and allegories within the music, being part of an improvising choir is to be part of a social community. The Improvisers' Choir has been a creative opportunity for each person to bring their vocal ideas to the group. Feedback from all the singers[126] suggests that they felt a sense of homecoming, as the music-making gave them a chance to offer their own original contributions.

Sister Choir

In 2016, I started TOCfi, The Open Choir for improvisers, a non-auditioned community choir using the same hand signals as in TIC. We ran weekly rehearsals and performed regularly for three years at the local Crouch End events and at the Loft, and sometimes with TIC and special guests. TOCfi singers, mainly graduates of Vocal Tai Chi were able to apply their new-found Vocal Tai Chi solo voices to the needs of a choir, get foregrounded solos, and now with live singers backing them, not a pre-recorded track.

Figure 30.9 Jenni with TIC, TOCFI, and special guest Cleveland Watkiss MBE at Earl Haig Hall, Crouch End, London. Concert on 25th November 2016.

Source: Image © David Godfrey

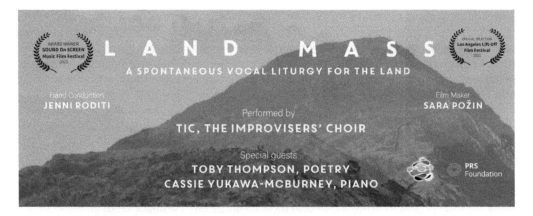

Figure 30.10 In 2019 TIC were funded by PRS Foundation, with generous matching funds from a private donor, to record an album. The result, completed in 2021, is a thirteen-track odyssey through the landscape of the choir's vocal reaches and enriched with visual interpretations of the journey, from the roots to the heavens.

Conduction and Circle Singing – Two Approaches to Group Improvised Singing[127]

For an up-to-date list of the TIC conduction signals, please see the website, detailed in the footnote.[128] A TIC piece calls on the choir to invent musical materials in the moment – drones, loops, group-chords, phrase harmonies, layering of textures and rhythms, and the conductor's hand signals represent each one of these, leaving the musical content to the choir themselves. When a TIC piece has found its feet, the conductor then signals for solos or duets to enhance the music. She may also shift the piece in several ways during the music, for example, using signals to indicate structural or pitch area changes drawing out an often-unpredictable morphing of the sound world. A TIC/TOCfi piece might also include a pre-suggested mood, a dramatic character, the weaving of texts and quotes,[129] or even a playful object, but the music will then either start from the signals themselves, or from either the conductor or someone in the choir energising the group by singing a spontaneous musical idea in the moment. (TIC came to a pause during Covid and has not started up again. I am considering offering 'conduction induction' workshops, – but with a better title (!) – for those interested in exploring this approach.)

Another approach to group improvised singing is Circle Songs[130] https://bobbymcferrin.com/circlesongs/) started by Bobby McFerrin[131] (www.thewellvocal.com). In circle songs the 'motor, interlock, counterpoint, and bass' (terms commonly used in the practice) are all invented musically by the singer-conductor who stands in the middle of the circle. She allocates her spontaneous ideas to different group-sections of the surrounding choir circle, who copy her. Once the piece has been built up, individuals from the circle are invited to step forward to solo and duet. She may also shift the piece by inviting another singer-conductor to come into the centre and take the music in a different direction. I saw this approach in action at the Omega Institute with Bobby McFerrin and his singer-conductor team, in the summer of 2015 over a weeklong residential course. Participants were also given a chance to learn how to lead this process themselves in smaller breakout afternoon workshop groups.

Vocal improvisation has many different outlets and communities around the world. 'Free vocal improvisation' has a long history going back to Dadaism or perhaps before. Raoul

Hausmann (1886–1971) created Dada nonsense sound-poster poems which used emotive speech based non-linguistic vowels and consonants in surreal monologues. Free vocal improvisation is described by leading vocalist Maggie Nichols as 'in our different rhythms together.' The approach of this music is hard to describe as it is free, yet there are characteristics that I expect have been defined by those who have delved deep into its approach. 'Freeness' might indeed be the best word for it, as presented in a (recently cut) BBC Radio 3 programme titled 'Freeness,' hosted by percussionist and arts researcher Corey Mwamba.

A new emerging practice, Collaborative Vocal Improvisation, is bringing new waves on the ocean of approaches to improvised vocal music. CVI was first named in 2021, as Guillermo Rozenthuler, a leading facilitator, writes – "each person (is) generating their own sounds and patterns spontaneously and in response to others, sometimes starting from an agreed prompt or idea, sometimes unfolding from the shared silence or from one person breaking into impromptu song." This community of practitioners was originally drawn together through the performances of pioneering vocalist Bobby McFerrin and a vocal improvisation model known as Vocal River, developed by his close artistic collaborator Rhiannon, (her full legal name). Over many years Rhiannon has devised a curriculum of improvised voicework that currently includes working with a performance process of collaborative voice-movement flow, inspired by the murmuration of starlings and 'group mind.'

Block Form Comes Full Circle

As in my student orchestral piece *September Boxes*, block-form is used with the TIC TOC choirs. Conduction[132] is an immediate version of that form, each signal shading or changing strata, creating traffic lights, left and right turns, and focus pulling. Distributed improvisation,[133] as it is also called can build a map of short-, medium-, and long-term musical outlines. With an improvised vocal orchestra, it is a very useful way to work with proportion, shape, orchestration, and many other components of composition.

'What Style is Your Music in?'

As for musical style, one comment offered by a TIC audience member struck me: 'Discovery of style as cultural and shared by community'. While the structure of the music is guided by the conducting, the style is definitely 'post-style style'[134] and it seems to me, what matters as much as style are the questions: who are the people involved? Which singers, special guests, producers, and audiences, and what are the events we make together? The combination of all these elements allows for the discovery of style, drawn from many places, gathered together through devising in rehearsals, and the conducting in the concert. While I do draw on my own tastes in directing the music, it is also about letting the style find its own way, as indeed the choirs and I are doing as performers.

Peter Wiegold was both excited and curious about the nature of TIC, and part of our 2019 conversation on the process is reproduced here to offer an insight into what we were reflecting on.

P.W. The thing about TIC (and TOCfi) is that you are now out front, conducting, leading directly. What was the first session with TIC like?

J.R. Tentative, stuttering. There were eight of us.

P.W. You're quite active when you do the signals. Your body is moving the whole time. The signalling is right at the heart of the flow of it, isn't it?

J.R. It's embedded.

P.W. And you go on journeys, six-, ten-, fifteen-minute journeys. So now finally, suddenly, you're a conductor. What are the challenges of conducting in that spontaneous way?

J.R. The main challenge is to wonder 'What's missing? What else will complete this episode?' Contrarily, 'What's clogging? What can I take out to reveal something new, specific?'

P.W. And it involves everyone completely listening. You haven't got scores, so any minute someone might be the butterfly in the Amazon, and tip it into a different direction. And your job is to be sensitive, ready for that.

J.R. Yes. It's a livewire situation.

P.W. I've seen several performances of TIC and at their best there's this incredible voyage that the music goes on. Unstoppable, like a big ship, shifting gears here, crossing an island there. I love that you seem to have, unlike the average improvising director, a real sense of a journeying-form that you're determined to take us on.

J.R. I think that's where I'm getting this interesting alchemy between composition and improvisation.

P.W. Yes, and it's live.

J.R. Yes.

P.W. The compositional mind is observing, 'This is too long' and 'This needs to go low when it's been high'.

J.R. All the time.

P.W. Yes, it feels like it's there. But there's another quality, almost a shamanic quality. There's a sense of it calling forth spirits and taking them on the journey. Are you aware of that?

J.R. Yes, I am. I soft pedal that, but from audience feedback[135] and my own experience, I know it's there.

In 2018, TIC won Nonclassical Battle of the Bands,[136] judged by several high-flyers in the business: Gabriel Prokofiev, Dominic McGonigal, and Alan Davey.[137] The project had come of age.

Boundaries

In a TIC pre-concert talk,[138] Helen Julia Minors, co-editor of this book, asked me in personal communication: 'when is it therapy and when is it art?' Psychotherapy requires confidentiality and happens behind closed doors. When therapy is involved in the arts there is potential for crossing over. In *making* something, it may be shared. But how does this question relate to my work?

In Vocal Tai Chi, workshop participants spend two hours together before improvising their solos. It is a private group (around eight people) and it is a safe space to lose control[139] if need be, for a moment, to weep or rage and fold that back into the music. There can be creative pain involved. A fluid relationship between the volition of the voice itself, a good technique, and creativity can ultimately take the improvisation into a high level of free vocal music. Behind the closed door of Vocal Tai Chi, art is there; so is therapy.

In The Improvisers' Choir performances (thirty to one hundred people in an audience), there are no signs of emotional distress from the singers, as might be the case in a Vocal Tai Chi workshop with less experienced singers, but there is a parallel vulnerability, similar to Vocal Tai Chi workshops, in terms of the risk-taking involved. Whether improvising in a closed workshop or within a vocal group in public, there is plenty of unpredictability. Singing from nothing, with no song or score, in public, in a small, exposed choir, is revealing work. No matter how experienced the singers are, there is a feeling of not knowing in the room as the performance starts. This brings edginess and electricity to the atmosphere in the audience.

Heroines and Heroes

It is not unlike Joseph Campbell's 'hero's journey,' although in the choirs' cases there are multiple heroines and heroes, living through it together, not just a single protagonist, as described by Campbell in his 1949 book on mythmaking, 'The Hero with a Thousand Faces':

> A hero ventures forth from the world of common day into a region of supernatural wonder: fabulous forces are there encountered, and a decisive victory is won: the hero comes back from this mysterious adventure with the power to bestow boons on his fellow man.[140]

The Improvisers' Choir is a focussed process, as individual musical inventions and intentions are balanced by the conductor and each member of the choir with the sensitivity of being together in an ensemble. As the sound worlds are built, 'fabulous forces' may well be met. As in Vocal Tai Chi, some creative pain may be involved. One audience member in a TIC performance reported sensing a 'quest of the soul' that she felt each singer pursuing. Rather like Miles Davis iconically saying: 'Don't play what's there, play what's not there', the music is 'open to receive'. Sometimes it loses its way or gets stuck, but that is part of encountering those 'fabulous forces'. If met well, the music finds a way to include the lostness, singing in the dark, welcoming the unknown. But it can be the place where some give up, thinking the improvisation has come to an end. But when the process is flowing well, or when the conductor senses a shift is needed, the unknown becomes a transition, a pull back and reveal, a yield and return, a turning point. Lost moments contain the seeds for new beginnings. You dig deeper, hear further, breathe slower – the music is asking for shift. It may be the very moment *not* to give up. That may be, in improvisational terms, a touching of the 'fabulous forces' that Campbell is referring to: there is still more to be discovered. Just having the courage to let the musical space clear, hear the room, wait, notice the details, maybe recognise a future point, liminal in the now, and start the new journey. It might feel lost to some, but to others it is a moment of alchemy.

Catharsis Is Therapeutic – the Audience

'Catharsis is the process of releasing, and thereby providing relief from, strong or repressed emotions'.[141] Aristotle proposed that the principle of tragic performance be 'purging, through pity and fear – catharsis'. This was an aesthetic principle in Classical Greece that was first understood by the dramatists of the time, to bring about a purging of the soul and self-realisation for the audience. Spiritual aspirations for a performance practice, no less.

In the context of improvising choirs, a vulnerability from singers in performance may well bring up pity (I prefer empathy) and fear (I prefer uncertainty) from audiences who may wonder – will the music get where it needs to go? Will they hang together as a choir? I direct the singers, but listeners may think: how does she conduct without a score? Without prepared music of any sort? Will the singers lose their way? That not knowing conveys an urgency which may draw an audience in. Through the journey of each piece, as in Vocal Tai Chi workshops, where individual edges are met, now in The Improvisers' Choir collective edges within the whole choir, are there to be met and moved through. That seems to have a strong effect on many listeners.

From audience feedback,[142] it seems that their experience is indeed cathartic, giving this practice what Campbell[143] called the 'power to bestow boons'.[144] That is not so surprising to me, as the work has come from the plural resources of my work as a composer, singer, and therapeutic voice worker.

Both in Vocal Tai Chi and in the Choirs projects, art and therapy seem to have coalesced, and through their combined chemistry a degree of awakening to a more vivid and holistic vocal consciousness[145] seems to be possible.

Here are some typical (anonymised) audience comments, which show a range of emotional and felt experiences: 'We're here, beauty, being new'; 'The forces rise, powerful. Are they for good or for harm? They cannot be resisted. We follow for better or worse'; including descriptions of it being 'Ceremonial'; or similes to life, 'Like a living organism being born'; 'Constructivism, search for order, dawn of society, ruling oneself, towards civilisation, desire to cooperate, productivity'; 'I find being-ness in the soundscapes, textures, rhythms'; 'Something from deep within'; 'Like a newborn being offered to the heavens'; 'I wanted to join in!'; 'I couldn't take my eyes off them'.

Conclusion

Benjamin Britten said in his famous Aspen lecture in 1964: 'I want my music to be of use to people, to please them and to enhance their lives'.[146] Gillian Moore, in referencing Britten's lecture describes the British composer scene thus: 'There is undoubtedly a vigorous, unbroken and still developing tradition of British composers before and after Britten deciding that they want to be more directly "of use"'.[147]

I've wanted to be of use. I have composed music all my life and my teaching, as described in this chapter, has run alongside it.[148] My leadership 'beyond music workshops', as a composer in a community, may not be within the educational framework that Gillian Moore refers to, but I have followed my own thread. I've wanted to work with adults, not children. I've needed to travel beyond music workshops, to open Pandora's Box and explore voice as music-theatre, opera, chanted, spontaneous, invoking, embodied, intuitive, unconscious, archetypal, therapeutic, transformative, meditative, communal, and ancestral. To explore voice from cultures other than my own upbringing, notably Indian, Sephardic, Flamenco, Balinese, and Bulgarian. Be it in my written scores, or in my leadership, in my operas, solo improvisations, in the solos I have coached, or the conduction choirs I've led, I was always looking for different ways into original vocal aliveness. I've looked for it in myself and encouraged it in others: a music-making that felt whole and connected to the real person.

I think of all my work as rooted in composing. The meaning of that word, composition, in today's plural world is not only the well-composed, fully notated new score, but also includes open and devised scores, cross arts, cross style collaborations, embedded artist-in-community projects, conduction, and much more. Some of these projects may only be recorded or filmed rather than existing as written scores; some may have a book of notes or digital files; and many will have passed by, unrecorded, on any level. Who knows how much music-making is documented only in ether? There, it may well be.

One way to consider this leadership practice is as applied composing. My skills are infused, and to some extent under the surface. There is space for others to contribute and be themselves while I guide, respond, and influence proceedings.

The original intention of taking the process of composing into schools in the first place, as I did with Gemini, was to demystify it. I have continued to hold to those values and to teach that as simply as we have always made up stories, drawing on our life experience, we can make up music, in a similar way.[149] In so doing, personal and collective narratives can come together in musical community. If we are going to create new allegories,[150] then drawing on who we are, where we find ourselves, is one place to start. Using simple, accessible 'formless forms'[151] that work well enough to contain *and* open up the human being is one way for these spontaneous songs and conduction pieces to come through. Sound makers can hear themselves and be heard. For those who wish to hear it, and for those in the ether who may sense it, this music is offered and not just through my efforts; others may wish to offer it too.[152]

After all, life may bring you to your knees and crack you open to a vast, all-inclusive light that is out of this world. Then you may have no choice but to help that memory come alive in this world, in your own way.

Here is some music to finish: a Facebook Live[153] vocal improvisation, accompanied by ten-string lyre, from July 2020. Lockdown number two was in full force, and I was suddenly ready to burst if I didn't sing. It draws on the energy of my Sephardic roots and is sung in an unknown language.[154]

Dedicated to my Mother, Averil Patricia Rodd. Born Hong Kong 14.02.1934. Died London, 26.07.1992. No matter what she sang, she danced. She knew joy in pervading darkness.

Acknowledgements

Grateful thanks for direct help with the chapter go to Peter Wiegold, Maria Lusitano, David Birk, Amy Corzine, Adrian Lee, Kate Allardyce, Peter Leanse. Grateful thanks for indirect help with the chapter go to Roland Denning, Wendell Henckel, Charlotte Preston, Patrick Tobin, Lora Wignal, John Sloboda, Orphy Robinson, Linda Rowe, Simon Minty, James Mills, Sholto Pridgeon, Maxwell Steer, Alistair Smith, Tara Jaff, Alex Cowan, and Alaena Adams. Biggest thanks to Helen Julia Minors and Laura Hamer.

Notes

1. Guildhall School of Music (1981–1985). First study composition, second study piano.
2. Peak experiences are 'a rare, exciting, oceanic, deeply moving, exhilarating, elevating experiences that generate an advanced form of perceiving reality and are even mystic and magical in their effect'. Abraham Maslow, *Religions, Values, and Peak Experiences* (London: Penguin Books Limited, 1964).
3. In the Western world, the concept of spiritual awakening has become synonymous with self-realisation: one's true nature or true self being regarded as a substantial essence, covered over by social conditioning.
4. The middle way is a path between two opposite paths. In Buddhism it is between asceticism and sensual indulgence. In the Hindu Vedas it is described as the three *Gunas: Sattva*: a middle point of open freedom and clarity between action, *Rajas*, and inaction, *Tamas*.
5. The first book that fell off a shelf into my hands during the first week of the experience mentioned was called *Zen, Dawn in the West*, by Roshi Phillip Kapleau (London: Anchor Press, 1979). The book describes Zen *Satori*, which is a 'seeing of one's true nature'. I recognised my experience as *satori* as I read the book.
6. Katrin Cartlidge (1961–2002) https://en.wikipedia.org/wiki/Katrin_Cartlidge

7. Alfred Nieman https://en.wikipedia.org/wiki/Alfred_Nieman I first met Alfred when I was 16. My music teacher at Parliament Hill Comprehensive School (sadly I forget his name), asked me to go and talk to him. Alfred lived in Hampstead, not far from my home. (I see from his Wikipedia entry that he was part of the National Association for Gifted Children.) I remember he said to me, "go to as many contemporary music concerts as you can! Drink them all in, good and bad!" I came away feeling like I'd just met an actual wizard.
8. Robert Saxton (for 3 years) and Oliver Knussen (a few sessions in year 3).
9. Interestingly, years later, in 2014, I returned to a somewhat densely atonal language in a piece titled 'Not This' (which seems like an amusing title now). It was a reference to an Indian expression, neti neti – 'not this, not that' which is a way to point towards non-dual thought.
10. Keith Potter, "When Taste Fights Opinion" *Classical Music*, April 13, 1985, 27.
11. 'Fruit Gathering' 1985, performed Albany Empire.
12. Bayliss programme, the education department at English National Opera.
13. 'Round Trip' 1986, performed Riverside Studios.
14. 'Six Coins in a Fountain' Schoenberg Symphony Orchestra, conductor, Richard Gonski. 1987, performed Conway Hall.
15. 'Devil and the Deep Blue' 1989, performed Chats Palace.
16. 'No Argument' 1990, performed Chat Palace.
17. Ibid. 5.
18. https://en.wikipedia.org/wiki/Odaline_de_la_Martinez
19. https://www.lontano.co.uk
20. Review of Spirit Child – The Prelude by Stephen Johnson, The Independent https://jenniti.substack.com/p/review-of-spirit-child-the-prelude
21. Inanna at the Music-Theatre Biennale, 1998, Zagreb, Croatia.
22. The Descent of Inanna (1992) performed ICA, (1994) The Place (1996) Chard, Devon (1998) Zagreb, Croatia. An example of the music, recorded in 2007 with Alexander Ingram, conductor is at https://youtube.com/playlist?list=PLNwfTiMEPhdeB_KMBtW4JOWz6ha0pwpKO&si=7KioZoWUj0kYqqDR and Spirit Child – the Prelude, (1997) performed St Johns Smith Square, (Ibid. 15), and Siddhartha – Spirit Child (2001) performed The Ocean, Hackney.
23. Personal Communications recorded with Peter Wiegold (September 24, 2019), the Loft, London.
24. Conversation with Peter Wiegold: more extracts, accessed August 8, 2023, https://theimproviserschoir.com/jenni-roditi-in-conversation-with-peter-wiegold-september-2019/.
25. Alternative to classical singing technique, used by twentieth-century composers including Berio, Maxwell Davies, Henze, Ligeti, Monk, Le Barbara, Stockhausen, Wishart.
26. Sprechgesang or sprechstimme in German, a mix of spoken and sung voice, similar to cabaret.
27. Wiegold's term – meaning a performer who crosses over music and theatre skills.
28. From a review of Gemini's work, Andrew Peggie, "Review," *Classical Music*, April 10, 1982.
29. Gillian Moore, "A Vigorous Unbroken Tradition': British Composers and the Community Since the Beginning of the Twentieth Century," in *Beyond Britten, The Composer and the Community*, edited by Peter Wiegold and Ghislaine Kenyon (London: Boydell and Brewer, 2015), 60.
30. Keith Potter, "When Taste Fights Opinion," *Classical Music*, April 13, 1985, 27.
31. Cornelius Cardew (1936–1981) was an English experimental composer and one of three founders of the Scratch Orchestra, accessed August 7, 2023, https://en.wikipedia.org/wiki/Scratch_Orchestra_(musical_ensemble).
32. Ibid.
33. Andrew Peggie, "Wiegold's Creative Programme in Schools," *Classical Music*, April 10, 1982: 'Briefly, it aims to make people aware of the value of sounds; in themselves, as signals, as patterns and as music. Furthermore it is concerned with people's responses to sounds, to each other in groups . . . through . . . body awareness and trust games, pulse and rhythm exercises, and collective improvisation . . . awareness, observation, experimentation, reflection and finally action – a process surely very close to the way we learn in real life'. The course eventually turned in a Department for Leadership at Guildhall, which ran until 2019.
34. Peter Renshaw, Head of Research and Development at the Guildhall School of Music in 1984, accessed August 7, 2023, https://en.wikipedia.org/wiki/Peter_Renshaw.

35. One-page score, or backbone score, fits onto one page of A4 and has one complete line of music, or outlined sections for an ensemble, and a blank music stave available for players to add their own ideas. Devised further in rehearsal.
36. John Heider, *The Tao of Leadership* (London: Humanics New Age, 1985).
37. Barry Green and Timothy Gallwey, *The Inner Game of Music* (London: Pan Books, 1987).
38. Roditi notes, Composer in the Community file, 1986–1990.
39. Using cells of pitches (e.g. rows of six notes) and applying 'the twelve-tone technique': original, inverted, retrograde, retrograde inversion.
40. See Richard Moss on his idea of 'falling in love with love' – or third consciousness, accessed August 7, 2023, https://richardmoss.com.
41. An honorific term used in the Tibetan language. It literally means 'precious one'.
42. Sangha – 'company' or 'community'.
43. Prayers.
44. One weekend a month for nine months, in Paris during 1989–1990.
45. A series of one-off workshops, Southwest England, during 1991–1992.
46. Various workshops and performances over ten years. London, Kefalonia, and Paris, 1992–2002
47. One week per month for six months, plus a final paper and case studies. September 1992-June 1993.
48. In spirituality, non-dual means 'not two' or 'one undivided without a second'.
49. A way of assigning syllables to pitches (solmisation) in Indian music.
50. The Dip VMT RSA qualification was voided after Paul Newham's Voice Movement Therapy trainings came to an end in 1999. Voice Movement Therapy was reincorporated in the USA. New trainings were led by Anne Brownell and Christine Isherwood who had trained in London with Newham and, in Isherwood's case, with me too.

    I now have a VMT-R (Registered) certificate from the Norma Canner Foundation of Voice Movement Therapy www.vmtusa.com/. The Foundation was set up by Anne Brownell to support the new trainings in Voice Movement Therapy. Their certificate was presented to me retroactively under a process called 'the grandfather clause', allowing those who trained with the founder of the work (Paul Newham) to receive retroactive equality with those who trained later, once the work had developed further, with the new trainers.

    Paul Newham's work was a synthesis of his encounters with Enrique Pardo and the Roy Hart Theatre, combined with a vision that the artistry and emotional power of the voice were ripe tools for therapeutic and even clinical applications. His journey developing Voice Movement Therapy halted as his past began to catch up with him and he withdrew from running more trainings in 1999. He disowned the words Voice Movement Therapy, as is apparent from his Wikipedia entry. He simply refers to 'music therapy' with several citations that point towards voicework as a form of therapy. His very unusual family background and considerable achievements as a writer and educator are described (by him, it appears) in great detail at accessed August 7, 2023, https://en.wikipedia.org/wiki/Paul_Newham.
51. Accessed August 7, 2023, https://paulnewham.com/.
52. 1989–1990.
53. Accessed August 7, 2023, https://roy-hart-theatre.com/.
54. Enrique Pardo, founding member of the Roy Hart Theatre and established Pan Theatre with Linda Wise, accessed August 7, 2023, www.pantheatre.com/gb/index.html.
55. Melodrama: a sensational dramatic piece with exaggerated characters intended to appeal to the emotions.
56. VMT moved to the USA in 1998/9 with new directors. The Norma Canner Foundation now supports the work.
57. Accessed August 7, 2023, www.ellafitzgerald.com/quotes/#/.
58. 1992–1993.
59. Without membership of the psychological associations UKCP or BACP, the term 'therapist' is not supported as a professional term, thus Voice Movement Therapy turned into Therapeutic Voicework in Paul Newham's journey and his later book. 'Therapeutic Voiceworker' became his title for the students who had worked with him.
60. Paul Newham, *Therapeutic Voicework, Principles and Practice for the Use of Singing as a Therapy* (London: Jessica Kingsley, 1998), np.
61. Paul Newham, *The Singing Cure* (London: Rider, 1993).

62. Biography of Wolfsohn, by Sheila Braggins, *The Mystery Behind the Voice,* Troubadour (2012), accessed August 7, 2023, www.troubador.co.uk/bookshop/media-the-arts/the-mystery-behind-the-voice-hb/. I had the privilege of sitting and talking with Sheila for many hours in her house in Finchley during the last years of her life. Sheila died in September 2014, age 86. This link https://iavmt.org/tribute-to-sheila-braggins/ includes a tribute that I wrote for her following her death. The link also includes photos of some members of the Voice Movement Therapy community at Sheila's funeral. That day, someone took photos of the stone laid at the Golders Green Crematorium for Alfred Wolfsohn – with the inscription 'Lerne Singen o Seele'. His stone is laid near to that of Sigmund Freud.
63. Roy Hart's voice on Spotify, accessed August 6, 2023, https://open.spotify.com/artist/4M7062ncx0 ls8Dr5OZBnaq?si=VaJSDpusS9W0kvu6QZaZog.
64. Paul Moses conducted research into the psychology of the human voice, seeking to show how personality traits, neuroses, and symptoms of mental disorders are evident in the vocal tone or pitch range, prosody, and timbre of a voice, independent of the speech content, accessed August 6, 2023, https://en.wikipedia.org/wiki/Paul_Moses.
65. After Wolfsohn died in 1962, Roy Hart took over his legacy and formed the Roy Hart Theatre, accessed August 6, 2023, https://roy-hart-theatre.com/.
66. Mary Lowenthal Felstiner, https://jwa.org/encyclopedia/author/felstiner-mary. Researcher and author on the life of the Jewish painter Charlotte Salomon. Her book is titled *To Paint Her Life: Charlotte Salomon in the Nazi Era* (Berkeley: University of California Press, 1997). Charlotte Salomon had a very close friendship with Alfred Wolfsohn in Germany. He influenced and guided her thinking and life before they had to leave (he to the UK, she to France) because of the Nazi regime. Salomon is remembered primarily for her series of autobiographical paintings made between 1941 and 1943 while in hiding in France. The pictures are deeply influenced by her relationship with Alfred Wolfsohn, titled *Leben? oder Theater?: Ein Singspiel* (Life? or Theatre?: A Song-Play). She was captured and deported by the Nazis and died, with her unborn child, in Auschwitz in 1943.
67. Ibid., 43.
68. Overview of Alfred Wolfsohn accessed August 6, 2023, https://en.wikipedia.org/wiki/Alfred_Wolfsohn.
69. *To Paint Her Life: Charlotte Salomon,* 7.
70. He renamed the work Therapeutic Voicework in 1998 when he published the following: Paul Newham, *Therapeutic Voicework, Principles and Practice for the Use of Singing as a Therapy.* He dropped the word 'therapy' because it meant further levels of psychological training would be needed for students to be eligible to join professional associations. Some of his students did go on to train as therapists and used voice as part of their therapy work; for example, Melanie Harrold and Bernadette O'Brien.
71. Bernadette O'Brien, "Psychotherapist and Embodied Voice Practitioner," accessed August 6, 2023, www.embodiedvoice.co.uk/.
72. Singing the Psyche – Uniting Thought and Feeling Through the Voice, Voice Movement Therapy in Practice, by Anne Brownell, Deirdre A Brownell, and Gina Holloway Mulder. Charles C Thomas, 2024.
73. Affect, in psychology, refers to the underlying experience of feeling, emotion or mood.
74. Some composers in the twentieth and twenty-first centuries who have put an emphasis on timbre: Ravel, Varese, Messiaen, Tristram Murial, Sofia Gubaidulina.
75. I have recently been asked to work with parents and children together which I have said I am interested to try.
76. Newham's term.
77. Owning Our Voices – Vocal Discovery in the Wolfsohn-Hart Tradition, by Margaret Pikes and Patrick Campbell. Routledge Voice Studies, 2021, 107.
78. Micro-musical forms: phrase patterns, timbres, dynamics, rhythms related *precisely* to the client's material. Carrying out a task-based micro-form instruction while inside a felt mood is central to the work. I also work with micro-characters (theatrical) and micro-movements (dance).
79. Eugene Gendlin: 'While a felt sense is partially emotional, Gendlin characterised the concept as a combination of emotion, awareness, intuitiveness, and embodiment," accessed August 20, 2022, www.goodtherapy.org/blog/psychpedia/felt-sense.
80. Keening (Irish: Caointeoireacht) is a traditional form of vocal lament for the dead in the Gaelic Celtic tradition, known to have taken place in Ireland and Scotland. Keening, which can be seen as a form of sean-nós singing, was performed in the Irish and Scottish Gaelic languages

(the Scottish equivalent of keening is known as a coronach). Keening was once an integral part of the formal Irish funeral ritual, but declined from the eighteenth century and became almost completely extinct by the middle of the twentieth century. Only a handful of authentic keening songs were recorded from traditional singers. It was typically sung by three women at the wake or graveside. It is difficult to find authentic spontaneous songs of keening that were documented, because the ritual was kept very private. Two performers that have recorded are Kitty Gallagher and Aine Minogue. Additional source, accessed August 20, 2022, https://dying.lovetoknow.com/death-cultures-around-world/keening-rituals-history-mourning.

81. https://en.wikipedia.org/wiki/Death_wail
82. accessed August 20, 2022, https://taichilife.com/about-tai-chi-qigong/.
83. Awa Hoshi, accessed August 20, 2022, http://crystalsoundinstitute.com.
84. Indian music was first taught to me by Viram Jasani at the Guildhall in 1985, accessed August 7, 2023, https://en.wikipedia.org/wiki/Viram_Jasani.
85. Asian Music Circuit founded by Viram Jasani, accessed August 7, 2023, www.amc.org.uk/index.html.
86. With the Pandits Rajan and Sajan Misra 1999–2005.
87. The smallest interval of pitch that the human ear can detect and a singer or musical instrument can produce.
88. Linda Hartley, my Tai Chi teacher.
89. Named in tribute to composer Meredith Monk and her New York loft, downtown Manhattan.
90. Pieces from the concert are on my *Blank Canvas* VTC album, accessed August 7, 2023, https://jenniroditi.bandcamp.com/album/vocal-tai-chi-solos-by-jenni.
91. I then used these in the workshops.
92. Often a blend of classical Indian, Sephardic, Extended Vocal Technique, the 'vocal house,' and *sprech-gesang*, among others.
93. If there are advanced people only, I will also introduce other vocal techniques.
94. Vocal Tai Chi, accessed August 6, 2023, https://jenniroditi.bandcamp.com/album/vocal-tai-chi-backing-tracks-for-your-own-solos.
95. Louis Armstrong, *In His Own Words: Selected Writings* (Oxford: Oxford University Press, 1999).
96. In Tai Chi 'yin and yang' are the two opposite yet interconnected forces of the universe: yin is receptive, yang is active.
97. People want and need to be challenged to move beyond their comfort zone. When they do, they feel they've achieved something new. In this way they create the workshop experience that they need, rising to the challenge that makes the difference.
98. Billie Holiday, accessed August 6, 2023, www.brainyquote.com/quotes/billie_holiday_384321#:~:text=Billie%20Holiday%20Quotes&text=If%20I'm%20going%20to%20sing%20like%20someone%20else%2C%20then,need%20to%20sing%20at%20all.
99. Backing tracks, accessed August 6, 2023, https://jenniroditi.bandcamp.com/album/vocal-tai-chi-backing-tracks-for-your-own-solos.
100. I have witnessed a few thousand of these solos alone as well, in the private sessions I have run since 1992.
101. Philip Glass, *Words Without Music: A Memoir* (London: Liveright, 2016), np.
102. John Cage, *Silence* (London: Calder and Boyers, 1969), 59.
103. https://grieftending.org/about-us/
104. Ibid., 56.
105. *The Field* by Lynne MacTaggart proposes 'a pocket of pulsating power' that connects everything in the universe, accessed August 7, 2023, https://lynnemctaggart.com/the-field-book/.
106. John Cage, cited by Nakai You, "How to imitate her nature of operation: Between what John Cage did and what he said he did," *Perspectives of New Music* 52, no. 3 (2014): 141–60.
107. Michael Meade explains the three stages of rites of passage: 'First, a phase of separation detaches us for the daily world and disrupts familiar patterns. The second step entails a period of undetermined duration involving uncertainty, ordeals and transitions. The third step involves reincorporation of community at a level of deeper understanding and greater unity'.
108. Ibid., 6.
109. Micro-musical forms: phrase patterns, timbres, dynamics, rhythms related *precisely* to the client's material. Carrying out a task-based micro-form instruction while inside a felt mood is central to the work. I also work with micro-characters (theatrical) and micro-movements (dance).

110. With a deep bow to Pauline Oliveros, *Deep listening* is 'an aesthetic based upon principles of improvisation . . . designed to inspire both trained and untrained performers to practice the art of listening and responding to environmental conditions in solo and ensemble situations'.
111. Our Ploy-Vagal World, How Safety and Trauma Change Us, by Steven W Porges https://amzn.eu/d/bVndz3X
112. Eugene Gendlin's felt-sense work: https://www.goodtherapy.org/blog/psychpedia/felt-sense
113. Ibid 56.
114. Backing tracks, https://jenniroditi.bandcamp.com/album/vocal-tai-chi-backing-tracks-for-your-own-solos
115. Detailed articulations (consonant/vowel combinations) and oral shaping of the voice to mirror internal musical impulses. Free-jazz improviser Maggie Nichols, who has used this for years, calls it *'speaking in tongues.'* Also known as 'creature language'.
116. 'Conduction is the process of guiding an ensemble of improvising musicians with hand cues and gestures, thereby forming only the contours of the music'. Butch Morris. Sun Ra, Frank Zappa, John Zorn, Phil Minton, and Peter Wiegold also work/ed with this approach, as does The London Improvisers' Orchestra.
117. Footage and good audio of the whole concert accessed August 6, 2023, https://youtu.be/OQlfOEDVN_4.
118. Ten-minute extract from the début concert accessed August 6, 2023, https://youtu.be/v2-ojDVtbXQ.
119. Accessed August 6, 2023, www.clubinegales.com/.
120. Ian Shaw, Cleveland Watkiss, Peter Wiegold, Toby Thompson, Cassie Yukawa McBurney.
121. Land Mass accessed August 6, 2023, http://theimproviserschoir.com/landmass.
122. Adrian Lee and Jenni Roditi collaborations accessed August 6, 2023, https://youtube.com/playlist?list=PLNwfTiMEPhdcJw0Z4JK90fiTSBa-07Jjk.
123. Alistair Smith and Jenni Roditi collaboration accessed August 6, 2023, https://youtube.com/playlist?list=PLNwfTiMEPhddRX0E5MVCFm3bjcPFCxYQ6.
124. Abigail Bruce, Ann Grindley, and Chamari Wedamulla, "Conference Report, Women In/and Musical Leadership," Newsletter of the *Royal Musical Association*, review of concert at Club Inégales (2019), np.
125. Ibid.
126. 'Social Dreaming' singers feedback from TIC and TOCfi, accessed August 6, 2023, https://theimproviserschoir.com/tic-singers-in-social-dreaming-experiment/ and https://theimproviserschoir.com/tic-singers-in-social-dreaming-experiment/.
127. ©Jenni Roditi with TIC and TOCfi. For a full list of signals, https://theimproviserschoir.com/the-signals/ Please request permission to use, accessed August 7, 2023, theimproviserschoir@gmail.com.
128. Accessed August 7, 2023, https://theimproviserschoir.com/the-signals/
129. Accessed August 7, 2023, https://bobbymcferrin.com/circlesongs/
130. One of the original exponents is Rhiannon, accessed August 7, 2023, www.rhiannonmusic.com/.
131. Exemplified in Istanbul concert, see accessed August 6, 2023, https://soundcloud.com/ticsingers/sets/tic-at-koc-university-istanbul.
132. Ibid., 90.
133. Also known as Soundpainting, accessed August 7, 2023, www.soundpainting.com/soundpainting.
134. Composer John Adams refer to his music as in a 'post-style style," which I've always enjoyed as his repost to the question – 'what style is your music in?'
135. See accessed August 6, 2023, https://theimproviserschoir.com/audience-feedback-from-tic-tocfi-concert-with-cleveland-watkiss-special-guest/.
136. For a blog on the performance see accessed August 7, 2023, https://theimproviserschoir.com/commentary-on-tic-at-nonclassical/.
137. Gabriel Prokofiev, founder of Nonclassical, Dominic McGonigal, composer, Alan Davey, Head of BBC Radio 3.
138. Part of this conference: http://fass.open.ac.uk/iwmlc. Concert (March 8, 2019), at Club Inégales. An in-depth audience survey from this concert with reflections from JR can be found here, accessed August 10, 2022, https://theimproviserschoir.com/audience-survey/.
139. There is a point beyond which 'losing control' requires a leader intervention. But touching in **for a split second** is sometimes just the thing that is needed.
140. Joseph Campbell, *The Hero with a Thousand Faces* (Princeton, NJ: Princeton University Press, 1949).

141. Oxford Reference accessed August 6, 2023, www.oxfordreference.com/display/10.1093/oi/authority.20110803095555720.
142. Audience feedback accessed August 7, 2023, https://theimproviserschoir.com/audience-feedback-from-tic-tocfi-concert-with-cleveland-watkiss-special-guest/; Audience Survey, accessed August 7, 2023, https://theimproviserschoir.com/audience-survey/.
143. Campbell, *The Hero with a Thousand Faces*, 97.
144. Michael Meade describes this as stage three of the rite of passage. Ibid, 69.
145. One of the singers in TIC, Veronica Chacon, commented in an email, "Singing is the very thing that makes me totally 'present' and 'awaken'. Singing with 'TICs,' under your lead, made me experience this phenomenon in a group! Collective Enlightenment!," April 7, 2019.
146. Peter Wiegold and Ghislaine Kenyon, eds., *Beyond Britten, the Composer and the Community* (London: Boydell and Brewer, 2015), 7.
147. Gillian Moore, "A Vigorous Unbroken Tradition': British Composers and the Community Since the Beginning of the Twentieth Century," in *Beyond Britten, The Composer and the Community*, Ibid., 45.
148. For catalogue of works see, accessed August 7, 2023, https://theimproviserschoir.com/catalogue-of-works/.
149. I honour excellence in music through the grade systems; it was just never my way.
150. As Bruce, Grindley, and Wedamulla, Newsletter, *Royal Musical Association* have observed in their review of The Improvisers' Choir.
151. Formless forms – the four floors of the vocal house, the signals.
152. Get in touch with the author about the next VTC apprenticeship and/or conduction induction courses.
153. See accessed August 20, 2022, www.facebook.com/jennivtc/videos/10157769775173877.
154. Using spontaneous nonsensical vowels and consonants to form new meaningless words that nevertheless articulate a felt sense of the vocal and musical moment.

Bibliography

Many websites are given for additional reading in the footnotes to offer biographies of names mentioned. Below includes the main references.

Adrian, Lee, and Jenni Roditi collaborations. Accessed August 6, 2023. https://youtube.com/playlist?list=PLNwfTiMEPhdcJw0Z4JK90fiTSBa-07Jjk.
Armstrong, Louis. *In His Own Words: Selected Writings* (Oxford: Oxford University Press, 1999).
Backing Tracks. Accessed August 6, 2023. https://jenniroditi.bandcamp.com/album/vocal-tai-chi-backing-tracks-for-your-own-solos.
Blank Canvas VTC Album. Accessed August 7, 2023. https://jenniroditi.bandcamp.com/album/vocal-tai-chi-solos-by-jenni.
Braggins, Sheila. *The Mystery Behind the Voice, Troubadour*, 2012. Accessed August 7, 2023. www.troubador.co.uk/bookshop/media-the-arts/the-mystery-behind-the-voice-hb/.
Bruce, Abigail, Ann Grindley, and Chamari Wedamulla. "Conference Report, Women in/and Musical Leadership." Newsletter of the Royal Musical Association, Review of Concert at Club Inégales, 2019, np.
Cage, John. *Silence*. London: Calder and Boyers, 1969.
Campbell, Joseph. *The Hero with a Thousand Faces*. Princeton, NJ: Princeton University Press, 1949.
Club Inégales. Accessed August 6, 2023. www.clubinegales.com/.
Felstiner, Mary Lowenthal. Accessed August 6, 2023. https://jwa.org/encyclopedia/author/felstiner-mary.
Gendlin, Eugene. "Felt-Sense." Accessed August 20, 2022. www.goodtherapy.org/blog/psychpedia/felt-sense.
Gillian Moore. "A Vigorous Unbroken Tradition': British Composers and the Community Since the Beginning of the Twentieth Century." In Beyond Britten, *The Composer and the Community*, edited by Peter Wiegold and Ghislaine Kenyon, 45–73. London: Boydell and Brewer, 2015.
Glass, Philip. *Words Without Music: A Memoir*. London: Liveright, 2016.
Green, Barry, and Timothy Gallwey. *The Inner Game of Music*. London: Pan Books, 1987.
Heider, John. *The Tao of Leadership*. London: Humanics New Age, 1985.

Hoshi, Awa. Accessed August 20, 2022. http://crystalsoundinstitute.com.
Kapleau, Roshi Phillip. *Zen, Dawn in the West*. London: Anchor Press, 1979.
Land Mass. Accessed August 6, 2023. http://theimproviserschoir.com/landmass.
Maslow, Abraham. *Religions, Values, and Peak Experiences* (London: Penguin Books Limited, 1964).
Newham, Paul. *Therapeutic Voicework, Principles and Practice for the Use of Singing as a Therapy*. London: Jessica Kingsley, 1998.
O'Brien, Bernadette. *Psychotherapist and Embodied Voice Practitioner*. Accessed August 6, 2023. www.embodiedvoice.co.uk/.
Peggie, Andrew. "Wiegold's Creative Programme in Schools." *Classical Music*, April 10, 1982.
Potter, Keith. "When Taste Fights Opinion." *Classical Music*, April 13, 1985, 27.
Roditi, Jenni. *The Signals*. Accessed August 7, 2023. https://theimproviserschoir.com/the-signals/.
Smith, Alistair, and Jenni Roditi Collaboration. Accessed August 6, 2023. https://youtube.com/playlist?list=PLNwfTiMEPhddRX0E5MVCFm3bjcPFCxYQ6.
The Best Advice Quincey Ever Got. Accessed August 7, 2023. https://youtu.be/DrnywDs1BMw.
The Improviser's Choir. Accessed August 8, 2023. https://theimproviserschoir.com.
Vocal Tai Chi. Accessed August 6, 2023. https://jenniroditi.bandcamp.com/album/vocal-tai-chi-backing-tracks-for-your-own-solos.
Wiegold, Peter, and Ghislaine Kenyon, eds. *Beyond Britten, The Composer and the Community*. London: Boydell and Brewer, 2015.
You, Nakai. "How to Imitate Her Nature of Operation: Between What John Cage Did and What He Said He Did." *Perspectives of New Music* 52, no. 3 (2014): 141–60.

PART V

Faith and Spirituality

Worship and Sacred Musical Practices: Faith and Spirituality: Worship and Sacred Musical Practices: An Introduction

Laura Hamer and Helen Julia Minors

Part V – 'Faith and Spirituality: Worship and Sacred Musical Practices' – examines women's musical leadership within religious and sacred practices. The part covers a range of different faiths, including Judaism, Christianity, Islam, and Buddhism. The possibility of women assuming leadership roles within faith contexts – whether musical or religious – has been keenly contested. The range of faiths covered within this part have widely divergent views on the permissibility of women leading worship, from The Salvation Army – which was one of the earliest Christian denominations to espouse gender equality – to Roman Catholicism and Islam, which do not allow women to lead worship.

Although a considerable amount of research exists on the rich tradition of Convent composition, especially that which flourished from the Middle Ages to the Early Modern period in Continental Europe,[1] and recent innovative initiatives such as *A Multitude of Voyces* have made a considerable amount of women's sacred music available to choirs in new performance editions, the studies presented in this part broaden both the geographic and the theological range of research. The chapters drawn together here – including studies of women's voices in Victorian Anglo-Jewish music, contemporary women Jewish cantors in the US devising music for new rituals, and women's roles leading and participating within *Shīʿah* rituals in Iraq – present considerations of women claiming spaces within religious music, devising and leading new rituals, and directing sacred musical education. The parts also draw together a number of case studies of women's sacred music, covering: the Roman Catholic compositions of Maruja Hinestrosa; the Buddhist popular music and music theatre of Imee Ooi; General Evangeline Booth's, Major Joy Webb's, and Dr Dorothy Gates' works written in service of The Salvation Army's ministry; and the inclusion of women's sacred compositions within Oxford Colleges. Theresa Parvin Steward's and Enya HL Doyle and Katherine Dienes-Williams' chapters, meanwhile, draw on Steward's and Dienes-Williams' own lived experiences leading music for worship. The chapters within this part draw on a range of methodological approaches covering archival, ethnographic, and autoethnographic research.

In Chapter 31, Danielle Padley surveys the diverse attitudes and practices concerning women's voices in Anglo-Jewish music which existed in Victorian Britain, paying particular attention to the (sometimes contested) introduction of female voices in congregational singing, their roles within music tuition, Jewish choral societies, and domestic worship, and concludes with a brief case study of the 'Sabbath classes' of Emily Marion Harris (1844–1900), which were tailored primarily towards poorer Jewish women and girls. Speaking in dialogue with Padley's study, in Chapter 32 Rachel Adelstein considers the creative roles of women cantors in present-day US synagogues leading congregational music, devising new (often Feminist) Jewish rituals in response to major life events experienced by their female congregants, and overviews the work of the Women Cantors' Network (WCN). Continuing the theme of women's religious compositions, in Chapter 33 Luis Gabriel Mesa Martínez presents a case study of Colombian composer Maruja Hinestrosa (1914–2002), which considers how she expressed her devout Roman Catholicism through her works, which frequently drew upon Latin American popular music genres.

In Chapter 34, Fung Ying Loo and Fung Chiat Loo provide a compelling study of Imee Ooi (b.1964), which considers how her popular music and music-theatre works exploring Buddhist themes display 'soft leadership' in the secularisation of popular contemporary Buddhist music. In Chapter 35, Ahmed Al-Badr presents an insightful investigation into women's roles leading and participating in *Shī'ah* rituals in Iraq, with a particular focus upon Karbala.[2] Continuing the theme of Muslim women's experiences of musical leadership, Theresa Parvin Steward explores her own experiences as a Muslim sacred musician working within a Baptist church in the US in Chapter 36.

The final three chapters of this part all explore aspects of women's musical leadership within Protestant Christian churches. In Chapter 37, Major John Martin focuses upon women's leadership in music ministry within The Salvation Army – one of the first religious denominations to embrace gender equality – through presenting three case studies based upon General Evangeline Booth (1865–1950), Major Joy Webb (1932–2023), and Dr Dorothy Gates (b.1966). In Chapter 38, Enya HL Doyle and Katherine Dienes-Williams explore women's musical leadership opportunities within the contemporary Church of England. Continuing the theme of women's inclusion within the Church of England, in Chapter 39 Caroline Lesemann-Elliott presents a study of gender representation in Anglican choral repertoire at a selection of colleges at the University of Oxford.

Notes

1. See, for example, Fiona Maddocks, *Hildegard von Bingen: The Woman of Her Age* (London: Faber and Faber, 2013) and Laurie Stras, *Women and Music in Sixteenth-Century Ferrara* (Cambridge: Cambridge University Press, 2018).
2. For a study of women's participation in *Shī'ah* rituals in Iran, see Talieh Wartner-Attarzadeh, "Female Leadership in Iranian-Arab Shi'a Rituals from Khorramshahr, South-Western Iran," in *Women's Leadership in Music: Modes, Legacies, Alliances*, edited by Iva Nenić and Linda Cimardi (Bielefeld: Transcript Verlag, 2023), 99–110.

31
LEADING THE WAY

Victorian Premonitions for the Female Voice in Anglo-Jewish Music

Danielle Padley

The title of this chapter is deliberately broad, allowing an exploration of the various sacred, secular, and in-between spaces in which the Jewish female voice played a significant musical role, whether through presence or absence, in Victorian Britain.[1] Perhaps somewhat predictably, there is less discussion of women as 'musical leaders' themselves than of the subtle shifts that paved the way for more obvious leadership roles for women in Anglo-Jewish musical practices later in the twentieth and twenty-first centuries.

An account of the female voice in Anglo-Jewish music is, to a degree, also an account of female displacement in Jewish worship, a topic which continues to be bound up in a multitude of religious obligations and personal preferences.[2] Likewise, discussions of the role of the female voice in Victorian Jewish worship are naturally discussions of music, given that the liturgy was almost entirely chanted or sung in most synagogues. Outside of worship, the growing popularity and accessibility of music across a number of spheres during this period – such as domestic circles, the concert hall, and the schoolroom – also changed the religious, social, and cultural expectations placed upon Jewish women.

This was a period of religious reform, both in the synagogue and the Anglican Church, the latter being influenced by such High Church groups as the Tractarians in Oxford and the Ecclesiological Society in Cambridge.[3] While by the end of the nineteenth century, only three so-called 'Reformed' synagogues had been established in Britain (in West London – discussed in some detail here, Manchester, and Bradford), catering for approximately one to two per cent of the Anglo-Jewish population, developing British social and cultural values affected the aesthetic principles upon which wider upper- and middle-class Jewish worship was based. The examples provided here illustrate changing perspectives and initiatives concerning the female voice during the period; they are, in the main, taken from a cross-section of opinion pieces, editorials, reviews, and advertisements printed in the leading Anglo-Jewish newspaper, the *Jewish Chronicle*.[4] First published in 1841, it represented an upper- and middle-class Anglo-Jewry whose views – and religious practices – were not always united. In fact, the narrative of the female voice in Anglo-Jewish worship is principally an upper- and middle-class one. The *Jewish Chronicle* rarely presented the views of the working classes – although it regularly reported on the various charities and institutions established to support the Anglo-Jewish poor, and as such they are given a voice in the final sections of this chapter. Despite this social bias, the collection of opinions given here is a small selection of a vast pool of varied and conflicting attitudes demonstrating the fragility, individuality, and humanity of Victorian Anglo-Jewish practice. Steeped in heritage and tradition, but also adapting to accommodate British values, one person's logical development was a challenge to another person's religious principles. The steps made in advancing the role of the female voice in Victorian Jewish music, whether religious or cultural, were thus fundamental to the soundscape of the Anglo-Jewish world.

'Not Too Prominently': Balancing Religious and Social Obligations

Victorian England was set up for male interaction in terms of political, financial, and religious authority. A campaign for Jewish emancipation which continued until the middle of the century principally benefited male members of the Jewish middle and upper classes, whose new privileges – the ability to attend Oxford and Cambridge universities, be appointed to senior political offices, and trade freely in the centre of London, to name a few – were of little relevance to the female (and poorer) Jewish population.[5] Synagogue worship was similarly entirely male-led. As cited in Jewish law, a *minyan* (quorum) of ten men was, and remains, a requirement for public Orthodox worship to proceed. Also of relevance is a Talmudic statement, *kol b'isha ervah*, commonly reduced to *kol isha*, and translated as 'the voice of a woman is nakedness'. In line with this statement, the Talmud stipulates that a woman's singing voice cannot be heard by men outside her own immediate family for fear of inspiring 'impure thoughts' and distracting men from their prayers and Jewish learning.[6] The degree to which this law relates to the sound of the female voice both within and outside of worship – during congregational singing, chanting prayers of mourning, in the home, as part of an ensemble, or during secular performance – has been debated and interpreted variously by rabbis across the millennia.[7]

Despite these religious obligations, there was a social expectation that in a religiously oriented Victorian Britain, families attended weekly faith services together. This extended to the Jewish community, whose upper- and middle-class communities particularly wished to demonstrate their observance of accepted British customs, which were largely dictated by the practices of the Church of England. To that end, both women and men attended synagogue, with women situated in an upstairs ladies' gallery, overlooking the prayers taking place in the sanctuary. Several articles in the *Jewish Chronicle* implied that, on multiple occasions, the former outnumbered the latter. This caused issues in some smaller congregations, where women were sometimes silenced due as much to the absence of men as to their presence. In 1904, a letter to the *Jewish Chronicle* described a visit to a tiny congregation in the middle of England, where the correspondent noted that:

> [T]he number of males above the age of thirteen was exactly ten, made up of nine men and a boy, and my visit to the town was hailed with delight, because one of the men had announced his intention of going away over the week-end, thus reducing the number of the congregation to nine – one below *Minyan*. Accordingly I went to prayers, but, alas! two men had gone away, leaving only eight men, one boy, and the twelve women. Consequently, there were no prayers, because such particular Jews would not hear of praying to God together unless there were at least ten males present. Now there occurred to me a little bit of calculation . . . one boy is more than twelve women.[8]

Letters written by and to the editors of the newspaper regularly outlined various views concerning the location and participation of women in the synagogue. It was often noted, for instance, that the capacity in most ladies' galleries was insufficient for the number of women in attendance, even in synagogues where a larger number of seats for women were available, suggesting that more women chose to come to services than were anticipated or catered for.⁹ Other complaints included the fact that the space was too hot, too cold, too drafty, or so obscured by a screen as to impact negatively on the ability to hear and follow the services; cue several other letters complaining about the 'idle chatter' descending from the ladies' gallery.¹⁰

It is easy to see why women began to be accused – by other women as well as men – of regarding the ladies' gallery as a place for social interaction rather than worship. Physically removed from the main event, neither a woman's presence nor her prayers were – religiously – of relevance to the service. One piece written by the *Jewish Chronicle*'s editors in 1872 demonstrated an astonishing lack of consideration for women who wished to attend prayers. Regarding the potential move of the Central Synagogue's male-voice choir to the ladies' gallery from their draughty position in the main sanctuary, not only did they note the 'impropriety' of this relocation, but they suggested that the gallery – and those who resided within it – formed no part of the Synagogue's attendant community:

> [I]t seems to us that a choir should always be a part of the congregation. It can only pray with the congregation, not for them . . . If the choir be banished to a loge in the ladies' gallery, it would necessarily cease to form part of what is understood as a 'congregation'.¹¹

While partly critical of the fact that the choir would be doubly removed, seated away from view, this opinion nonetheless acknowledges the separation apparently required – and actively constructed, in the form of a 'loge' – between male and female attendees, choir or otherwise. Another piece from the following year was also dismissive of the female congregation, indicating a preference for what was described nostalgically as an 'old fashioned' outlook, particularly regarding the notion that 'prayers should be prayed by a congregation of men and boys, but not too prominently by ladies'.¹²

Interestingly, this last opinion was framed within the context of a review of the services in Britain's first Reform Synagogue, the West London Synagogue of British Jews, which had a mixed choir from 1865.¹³ Numerous pieces in the *Jewish Chronicle* indicated that members of Orthodox synagogues regularly attended services at the West London Synagogue, suggesting that *kol isha* did not compel Orthodox male congregants to avoid situations in which female voices would be heard. Instead, their preferences – and prejudices – were a matter of taste and convention.

Choral Compromises: Attitudes Towards 'Singing Ladies'

The West London Synagogue, founded in 1840, had sparked considerable adversity amongst other, more Orthodox congregations in Britain, which deemed the Synagogue's largely aesthetic reforms to be subverting rabbinic authority.¹⁴ In reality, the Synagogue's adapted customs catalysed developments across other British synagogues, particularly regarding the standards of liturgical music. It could be hypothesised that a number of the more enlightened responses to the female voice in Anglo-Jewish worship included in this chapter would not have existed were it not for the advances made at the West London Synagogue.¹⁵

A series of reports and correspondence in the Synagogue's archives, starting in 1862, demonstrate that introducing female voices to the Synagogue's regular choir was no mean feat. The community's (Anglican) organist and choirmaster, Charles Garland Verrinder, fought with the Synagogue's wardens for three years following an initial report by the Musical Committee noting that 'the falling off in the number and capabilities of the boys' was causing the quality of the choir to be 'compromised'.[16] Ironically, the Synagogue had incorporated female singers into its choir for special occasions as far back as 1859, subsequently adopting a mixed choir for confirmations and even during High Holy Day services, the holiest days of the year.[17] The ministers of the Synagogue – David Woolf Marks and his deputy Albert Löwy – consented to the addition of women to the choir in February 1862, on the grounds that '[t]he participation of females in the service of the Choir on several successive occasions has met with the tacit concurrence both of the ministers and of the congregation'.[18] Marks' opening sermon in 1842 had also stated that he believed that women should 'participate . . . in the full discharge of every moral and religious obligation', a public statement which 'was an unheard of subject' for synagogues of the time.[19] The three years' struggle with the wardens therefore suggests that the deployment of female voices in the choir went beyond theological considerations. Logistics were put in place to protect the modesty of the female choristers: the choir was moved to a place in the synagogue where the women could be heard, but not seen; furthermore, the Synagogue's archives indicate women were not permitted, or did not feel comfortable, to sing in the choir upon getting married, as was the case for soprano Louisa Van Noorden in 1870.[20] Despite these apparent concerns for modesty and propriety, Verrinder was keen to promote the female voice as a medium for Jewish repertoire. During the early 1870s, he auditioned and hired some of the Jewish community's most able female choristers – many of whom went on to have prominent careers as soloists and teachers; he also ensured that his published scores acknowledged his support for the female voice. In his second volume of music for the Synagogue, published in 1870, all new repertoire was notated for 'contralto' rather than 'alto', the former being a term increasingly ascribed to female lower voices.[21]

Complaints concerning boy choristers were made by choirmasters and congregants alike at other British synagogues, including remarks that boy trebles had neither the musicality nor the vocal power to perform some of the more ambitious repertoire presented to them. However, few were willing to challenge religious or social expectations by either supporting or supplanting them with female voices. One piece from 1869 was explicit that:

> Sacred choirs should clearly consist of men and boys . . . Some persons carelessly assert that the difficulty we labour under in our ordinary choirs is the absence of female voices. This is simply a mistake.[22]

In 1874, Michael Henry wrote similarly regarding the necessary steps required to improve choral singing, none of which involved 'the objectionable intervention of singing ladies'.[23] By comparison, Henri de Solla, the Choirmaster at the Great Synagogue in Duke's Place, Aldgate (and previously a chorister at the West London Synagogue under Verrinder), wrote honestly about the realities of depending on boy choristers – even at the principal Ashkenazi synagogue in London – and the important musical role women could take in worship:

> I regret to state that the majority of these lads require a beadle as well as a choirmaster to enforce proper decorum in the synagogue. Were ladies' voices introduced this unseemly behaviour would be avoided, and the uncertainty attending the length of time a boy's voice may be *utilized* [sic] previous to his enforced dismissal be set aside.[24]

Despite some deep-seated and emotional responses, the usefulness and musicality of the female voice was generally acknowledged, particularly concerning plans to encourage congregational singing. However, a unified plan of action for adjoining them to the choir – or even the main congregation – was not forthcoming. One *Jewish Chronicle* editorial addressed the fact that – in most Orthodox congregations – female worshippers had entered a passive no-(wo)man's-land, neither removed from, nor invited into, the inner sanctum of worship:

> Clearly, the boagey [sic] which frightened the mediaeval Jew has not lost its power of terrifying even in this nineteenth century. The Israelite of Hyde Park and Maida Hill is at one with his forefathers of the Ghetto in the belief that openly to permit women to sing in the synagogue is to endanger the faith. In the cherishing of illusions the modern representative of Judaism actually surpasses his mediaeval prototype. He knows that nowadays ladies do sing in the synagogue; but he will not practically admit the fact either by recognising them as adjuncts to the choir or by shutting their mouths altogether.[25]

Another letter from 1896 acknowledged the improved standards of congregational singing through seating men, women, and children together in the main body of the synagogue, as H. Sylvester Samuel somewhat sardonically indicated was the case during a Chanukah service at the West London Synagogue:

> [A]s this innovation was tried last Sunday, and the sky did not fall, it might be tried on a Saturday without causing the collapse of Judaism.[26]

Concerns were not purely musical. Physical separation once again came into play, as did religious devotion. 'L. J. G.', likely Anglo-Jewish journalist Leopold Greenberg (later himself an editor of the *Jewish Chronicle*), wrote emotively about the spiritual contribution lost by having female congregants seated where their voices remained unheard:

> it has ever seemed to me hopeless to expect to look for an orderly, a devout, a solemn service, so long as that portion of the congregation, in which most naturally resides the bulk of the spirituality, is marked out for degradation, if not for insult, by being packed away in galleries, apparently allowed into the synagogue on sufferance. The aged mother praying to the Almighty by the side of her son, following his words and echoing them in her heart of hearts, how different a picture from the same mother of the same son pitched in different parts of a building where the voice of neither can be heard by the other ... And must they ... be separated as strangers to join only in the service end, the crush and throng of the synagogue lobby?[27]

The inconsistency of practices and musical quality across institutions meant that individual Orthodox synagogues took matters into their own hands. Bayswater Synagogue apparently found a solution to the problem of incorporating female singers: to have women sing from their seats in the ladies' gallery, 'and not be otherwise identified with the choir'.[28] In 1895, the Hampstead Synagogue sparked great debate by introducing both a mixed choir and an organ to its services.[29] While some welcomed the musical role women could play in religious services, others were more willing to accept their assistance were it to occur within environments better associated with female music-making activities: the home, the schoolroom, and the concert hall.

'The Priestess of the Home'

If religious principles and 'old-fashioned' values were the basis upon which a woman's role in the synagogue was decided, British cultural practices were responsible for their music-making opportunities outside it. In line with the growing popularity in Victorian Britain of choral societies, professional and amateur recitals, and music for religious instruction, Jewish women were coming to the fore as choristers, soloists, and music teachers. In the handful of large Jewish schools dotted up and down the country (principally in London, Birmingham, Liverpool, and Manchester, catering for the working classes), class singing teachers were often female, and the *Jewish Chronicle* was replete with advertisements for governesses and ladies able to instruct in theoretical and practical music, and of female singers offering tuition.[30] By the 1880s, several Jewish choral societies had been formed across the country, directed by well-known synagogue choirmasters and comprising male and female singers. The repertoire varied from one society to another, but often focused on famous sacred and secular works which were acceptable to Jewish performers; for instance, between 1891 and 1893 the Hebrew Choral Association in London performed the cantata *Israel in Adversity and in Deliverance* by Verrinder (of the West London Synagogue), Jewish-born composer Frederick Cowan's cantata *Rose Maiden*, and selections from Handel's oratorio *Judas Maccabeus*.[31] Choral society concerts also invariably involved solo turns for both male and female vocalists, many of whom became well-known within the Anglo-Jewish musical world and held solo recitals at prominent venues such as St James' Hall, the Beethoven Rooms, or Hanover Square.[32] Once again showing his support for women's voices, Verrinder published two concert pieces based on Hebrew liturgical texts (with English alternate lyrics), which stipulated that the solo parts could be taken by either tenor or soprano.[33] Another synagogue musician and rabbi, Francis L. Cohen, frequently presented lectures on the history of Jewish music, with vocal illustrations performed by his wife, Sarah.[34]

The increasing market for hymnals and psalters to aid Christian parlour worship and religious instruction inspired similar feelings about Jewish domestic practices. A lengthy editorial from 1869 unpicking and providing solutions for the lacklustre performance of music in synagogues (both chorally and within the congregation) asserted the appropriate place for women to make their contribution:

> Can we not render sacred choral singing a feature of the Jewish home? In Scotland, in Germany, and in many English families, this singing is a common domestic recreation . . . And who so fit to lead the children's voices at home as the priestess of the home – the Mother?[35]

The following year, the need for a standardised volume of music was noted for the newly formed United Synagogue, a body representing the majority of Orthodox communities in London. This plea included the following remarkable statement:

> If, however, the United Synagogues [sic] Vestry cannot undertake the duty, the best private channel to arrive at a successful issue would be a committee of Jewish ladies . . . while amongst every class of non-Jewish sects a due importance and reference is paid by the female portion to the chanting of sacred hymns, the Jewish ladies scarcely know the existence of Hebrew melodies. This is really a communal scandal; and the sooner a bright example be shown by one or more of our numerous lady-workers, the better it will prove for the refinement of the rising Anglo-Jewish generation.
>
> Why should there not be seen amongst the music rolls in Jewish drawing-rooms works treating on Hebrew sacred music, as well as other so-called sacred music? No doubt ladies accustomed to the unique compositions of the first masters would heave many a sigh if invited to patronise such a daring innovation as Hebrew sacred

music . . . let the effort be attempted in schools . . . No holier, no loftier calling can be undertaken by Jewish ladies, than assisting to instil into the breasts of our young a love for the manifold beauties of our ancient music.[36]

This piece highlighted – somewhat ironically, given the unclear position of women in the synagogue – the lack of knowledge amongst female congregants of Jewish sacred music. Aside from suggesting that female role models were required to instil devotional feeling and knowledge amongst other women, the emphasis continued to be on the suitability of women as teachers and guides for future generations of Jews. There was nonetheless a disconnect between the notion that women, as part of their domestic responsibility, were obliged and well positioned to lead future generations in the learning and performance of Jewish repertoire, and the practical aspects of Orthodox worship which dictated that their contribution to public worship was irrelevant and unvalued, easily replaced by that of those they had led.

A standardised volume of liturgical music did not appear until 1899, at which point it was compiled by a Choir Committee of male synagogue musicians – led by Francis Cohen – and published under the title *The Voice of Prayer and Praise: A Handbook of Synagogue Music for Congregational Singing*.[37] It is telling, however, that all collections of Jewish liturgical music published during the nineteenth century, including *The Voice of Prayer and Praise*, were printed in order that they could be performed with organ or piano accompaniment. With few exceptions, choirs performed almost all services *a capella*; moreover, until the very end of the century, most choristers were taught repertoire by ear.[38] The active prioritisation, in some instances, of keyboard accompaniment over harmonisations which could easily be sung demonstrated the intended purpose of these collections: as worship and performance aides for schools and 'the family circles'.[39]

The 'Jewish Priestess': Emily Harris' Sabbath Classes

In a chapter which has demonstrated the widely varied attitudes and practices concerning the female voice in Anglo-Jewish music, it feels appropriate to close with an example of leadership and empowerment which, rarely for this period, was an entirely female initiative.

In the late 1880s, author and teacher Emily Marion Harris (1844–1900) set up regular Saturday meetings – pointedly referred to in the *Jewish Chronicle* as 'Sabbath classes' – principally tailored towards women and girls of the poorer Jewish population. Harris' meetings took place in a classroom at the Westminster Jews' Free School on Hanway Street. While in keeping with the charitable activities of middle- and upper-class women and ladies' societies (both Jewish and non-Jewish) during this period, some were quick to criticise the venture, even suggesting that the congregation's attendance was the result of bribery in the form of 'two or three flowers and a few biscuits'; others, including Harris herself, indicated that the success was down to an egalitarian approach.[40] Writing about her Friday evening services, Harris explained:

Our routine consists in reading by turn the Sabbath evening prayers, those who understand Hebrew take their part in following the Holy language aloud, and their companions less skilled, or perhaps having sooner forgotten early instruction, adopt the easier English translation. Afterwards several chapters of the Bible in the same manner continue and conclude the religious portion of the evening.

> Boys have often joined us, having first attended the synagogue, then a little reciting and singing have blended with our efforts to be as happy as possible on the Friday night, the boys are sometimes the brothers of the girls; all under fifteen.[41]

Harris' account of her meetings highlights the juxtaposition between forms of worship which distanced and silenced women and those incorporating simple acts such as families sitting together, or taking turns to contribute to prayers and songs, which gave voice to all attendees regardless of status, experience, or gender. The caution indicated in Harris' correspondence is striking; while a rare example of a woman during this period who adopted a role as a spiritual (and musical) leader, she took great care to assert that 'this informal meeting in no way interferes with synagogue'. She closed with the concern that 'I trust that I am not intruding on a discussion that is the right of ministers'.[42] Other, male, contributors were more effusive in their descriptions of Harris' work; Oswald John Simon, a regular and outspoken *Jewish Chronicle* correspondent, referred to her as 'that most sympathetic Jewish priestess, Miss Emily Harris'. An admirer of high-quality worship music, Simon added: 'They have learnt to sing very well indeed'.[43]

A second series of services for women commenced in 1891 and were located, somewhat incongruously, at the Jewish Working Men's Club in Whitechapel; both examples illustrate the general feeling that services for and contributed to by women did not belong in a synagogue.[44] Interestingly, the *Jewish Chronicle*'s editors saw fault with the latter arrangement, proclaiming that 'Women's Services [sic] must be held in a synagogue . . . They must have the best we can give them – the largest synagogue, the most popular ministers, the finest choirs.'[45] It was later proposed that these services move to the galleries of the Great Synagogue and that 'the body of the Synagogue should remain empty'; however, as they would have been run by a male rabbi from the *bimah* (platform) in the sanctuary, it was deemed that 'to preach to empty benches would be absurd'.[46] Both of these statements demonstrate that, even in the absence of a male congregation, the contribution and placement of women remained fixed as distant, silent observers. To that end, Emily Harris' services were a rare form of religious and musical expression – led and performed by, and for the benefit of women.

Conclusion

In some ways, the role of the female voice in Victorian Anglo-Jewish music was predictable and follows a strikingly similar pattern to the role of women in Anglican religious and social life during the same period. The female contribution to parish choirs, in light of the growing popularity of surpliced male choristers introduced along with High Church practices, was almost entirely eradicated. Parallel discussions concerning the appropriateness of using female singers, their musical and vocal qualities, and their physical placement (should female choristers sing from their seats, or from the choir?) can be found in Victorian newspapers and periodicals, suggesting that such debates were far less about religion than they were about women.[47]

It is hard to identify a satisfying conclusion from the diversity of opinions and practices presented here, other than to say that this diversity, like a woven-together tapestry, left holes through which opportunities for women were suggested, initiated, and ultimately grew. Jewish women generally found their voices not in the synagogue, but in the more private and (ironically) more public spaces of the home, school, and the concert hall. However, their successes in these arenas were enough to convince some that the music of the synagogue would be far improved, musically and spiritually, by their vocal leadership.

Notes

1. The terms 'Anglo-Jewish' or 'Anglo-Jewry' have been used in existing historical accounts to describe both English and British Jews and Jewish practices. In the context of this chapter, they shall be used to refer to the widespread British Jewish community unless otherwise stated. In reality, however, much of the Jewish population in Britain during this period (around 30,000 people in 1850, closer to 100,000 by the first decade of the twentieth century) was based in England, with the majority of families residing in London.
2. For both historical and contemporary discussions see, for instance, Lindsay Taylor-Guthartz, *Challenge and Conformity: The Religious Lives of Orthodox Jewish Women* (Liverpool: The Littmann Library of Jewish Civilisation, 2021).
3. For further details of reform in the Anglican Church, and particularly its relevance to musical practices, see Steward J. Brown, Peter Nockles, and James Pereiro, eds., *The Oxford Handbook of the Oxford Movement* (Oxford: Oxford University Press, 2017), Bernarr Rainbow, *The Choral Revival in the Anglican Church, 1839–1872*, 2nd ed. (Woodbridge: Boydell Press, 2001), and Dale Adelman, *The Contribution of Cambridge Ecclesiologists to the Revival of Anglican Choral Worship, 1832–62* (Aldershot: Ashgate, 1997).
4. The *Jewish Chronicle* is still the principal medium of Jewish journalism in the United Kingdom. See David Cesarani, *The Jewish Chronicle and Anglo-Jewry, 1841–1991* (Cambridge: Cambridge University Press, 1994). In all following footnotes, citations from the *Jewish Chronicle* shall refer to the *JC*. Editorial pieces are cited by title only; citations of correspondence and external reports include details of the author, where known.
5. The Jewish emancipation narrative has been documented by numerous Anglo-Jewish historians; for a well-known early account, see Cecil Roth, *A History of the Jews in England* (Oxford: Clarendon Press, 1949). A more recent social history of Anglo-Jewry is Todd M. Endelman's *The Jews of Britain: 1656–2000* (Berkeley, Los Angeles, and London: University of California Press, 2002).
6. For details and a history of *kol isha*, see Saul J. Berman, "Kol 'Isha' [sic]," in *Rabbi Joseph H. Lookstein Memorial Volume*, edited by Leo Landman (New York: Ktav Publishing House, 1980), 45–66.
7. Gordon Dale, "Music and the Negotiation of Orthodox Jewish Gender Roles in Partnership 'Minyanim'," *Contemporary Jewry* 35, no. 1 (2015): 35–53 explores recent interpretations within communities which promote a more egalitarian form of Orthodox worship.
8. 'The Religious Status of Jewish Women," letter from 'R,' *JC* (July 1, 1904), 24.
9. Most synagogues had a considerably smaller seating capacity for women than men. As an extreme example, the small synagogue erected in Newport, South Wales, in 1870 included 'accommodation for about 100 persons on the ground floor, and about 10 in the ladies' gallery' ("Newport," *JC* [May 6, 1870], 4). A description of the consecration service at the Bayswater Synagogue indicated that '[t]he body of the synagogue was not quite full; but the ladies' gallery could not have contained a larger congregation without inconvenience to those present' ("Consecration of the Bayswater Synagogue," *JC* [August 7, 1863], 5). Another correspondent stated that, prior to alterations at the Hambro Synagogue, "the ladies' gallery was a dingy den, in which the lady worshippers were penned up like so many sheep' ('Judaism and the Daughters of Israel," letter from 'A Member of the United Synagogue," *JC* [October 5, 1877], 5).
10. 'An Appeal from the Ladies' Gallery," letter from 'Lady Worshippers at the Bayswater Synagogue' and editors' response, *JC* (October 14, 1870), 3–4. Following the High Holy Days, multiple communications from women complained about the ventilation of the ladies' galleries in the Bayswater and Central Synagogues; the former suffered from 'the absence of all ventilation," while the latter had 'too much'. Another series of correspondence concerned the Chief Rabbi's insistence that a grille be placed in front of the ladies' gallery in a number of synagogues (see 'Judaism and the Daughters of Israel," *JC*, 5–6). Another report described the various disturbances experienced by a female congregant surrounded by, for instance, "a lady [who] has been conscientiously seeking her place in the book for the last ten minutes," "two young girls whispering audibly, disturbing the thoughts of those near them," and her neighbour whose 'eyes rove round the synagogue, resting now on some dress which attracts her, now on some gay hat or cape, whenever the interest of the service wanes for her'. Far from criticising the women for their acts, the correspondent instead commented on the physical and spiritual distance for women in the synagogue which inspired it: 'one has the feeling that the majority of the worshippers are mere onlookers, that stead [sic] of "living"

in the service, it is all being done for them, by proxy as it were' ("The Spirit of Devotion," report written 'From the Ladies' Gallery," *JC* [18 September 1896], 9).
11. 'Synagogue Choirs," *JC* (November 15, 1872), 453.
12. 'Echoes of the Synagogue," *JC* (October 17, 1873), 476.
13. The full paragraph reads: 'The ladies and gentlemen, and the organ of West London Synagogue were, as usual, very melodious; but we still, being very old fashioned, adhere to the notion that prayers should be prayed by a congregation of men and boys, but not too prominently by ladies; and that the most magnificent organ is, as Mendelssohn Bartholdy believed, an impediment to sacred music. Certainly it is not (even though constructed by such admirable builders as Hunt [sic] and Davison, or played by such an admirable musician as Dr. Verrinder) a possible member of a Jewish congregation.'
14. For information on synagogue reform in Britain and the foundation of the West London Synagogue, see Anne J. Kershen and Jonathan A. Romain, *Tradition and Change: A History of Reform Judaism in Britain, 1840–1995* (London: Vallentine Mitchell, 1995); Philippa Bernard, *A Beacon of Light: The History of the West London Synagogue* (London: The West London Synagogue, 2013).
15. A second Reform community was founded in Manchester in 1858, and a third in Bradford in 1873. It is unclear whether Manchester's regular services incorporated a mixed choir, although one was used for its foundation service. See 'Manchester Congregation of British Jews," *JC* (April 9, 1858), 137.
16. Southampton, Anglo-Jewish Archives (AJA), MS 140 AJ 175 131/15, October 1863. For information on Verrinder's work as a performer, composer, and promoter of Anglo-Jewish music, see Danielle Padley, "From Lineage to Legacy: Charles Garland Verrinder and Victorian Anglo-Jewish Music" (Doctoral thesis, University of Cambridge, 2020).
17. "Reopening of the West London Synagogue of British Jews," *Morning Chronicle*, September 27, 1859, 5.
18. AJA, MS 140 AJ 175 131/15, February 1862.
19. David Woolf Marks, "Discourse Delivered at the Consecration of the 'West London Synagogue for British Jews," on Thursday, January 27th, 5602 [1842]," in *Sermons Preached on Various Occasions, at the West London Synagogue of British Jews. Series 1* (London: R. Groombridge and Sons, 1851), 1–26, 18.
20. MS 140 AJ 59 1/2, February 1870. Van Noorden wrote to the Wardens of the Synagogue resigning her position in light of her forthcoming marriage, "according to conditions of my engagement'. Already a well-known opera singer, it is unclear whether these were her conditions or those of the Synagogue. She continued to work as a singing teacher.
21. Padley, "From Lineage to Legacy," 135, 160–61.
22. 'Synagogue Singing," *JC* (December 17, 1869), 8–9, p. 9.
23. 'Synagogue Singing," *JC*, letter from Michael Henry (August 14, 1874), 321.
24. 'Music in the Synagogue," letter from Henri de Solla, *JC* (October 7, 1887), 6.
25. 'Synagogue Singing," *JC* (April 6, 1888), 8–9: 9.
26. 'An Object Lesson in Synagogue Services," letter from H. Sylvester Samuel, *JC* (December 4, 1896), 6.
27. 'Services for Women," letter from L. J. G., *JC* (February 13, 1891), 7.
28. 'Synagogue Choirs," letter from 'Harmony," *JC* (March 23, 1888), 7, and "Synagogue Singing" (April 6, 1888), 8.
29. Debates concerning these moves continued for over a month. See "A Protest from Hampstead," letter from "Gee," *JC* (June 7, 1895), 7; " 'Fair Play' at Hampstead," letter from David Solomon, *JC* (June 14, 1895), 10.
30. 'Jews' Free School," *JC* (June 17, 1870), 8–9, p. 8. A description of a charity dinner for the School (originally in Camden and now in Kenton, North London, maintaining its reputation as one of the UK's premiere Jewish schools) noted that: 'The National Anthem was given with good effect by a choir of the school children, who also sang several other compositions during the evening in a manner that bespoke the great care bestowed upon the singing class by the musical directress, Miss Martin.' Many smaller Jewish schools catering for 'young ladies' or 'young gentlemen' (in other words, the upper- and middle-classes) also offered music lessons to their pupils; see the notice from well-known poet and teacher Marion Hartog (née Moss) of her new Day and Boarding School, "Pestalozzian School," *JC* (December 19, 1851), 88. See also as an example of a Jewish governess indicating, among other skills, musical competency in an advertisement from "Mademoiselle," *JC* (February 15, 1884), 2.
31. 'Concerts for the Poor," *JC* (March 6, 1891), 16; (March 18, 1892), 16; (June 2, 1893), 7.

32. See, for example, "Musical Jottings," *JC* (June 3, 1870), 13, advertising a concert performed by Julia Sydney at the Hanover Square Rooms.
33. Danielle Padley, "Tracing Jewish Music Beyond the Synagogue: Charles Garland Verrinder's *Hear My Cry O God*," *Nineteenth-Century Music Review* 17, no. 2 (2020): 181–223, explores Verrinder's dual-language composition for performance outside the synagogue.
34. 'Literary Intelligence," *JC* (December 5, 1890), 16.
35. 'Synagogue Singing," *JC* (December 17, 1869), 9. This same article was cited for its opinion that choirs should remain male only; see Footnote 22.
36. 'A Jewish Standard Book of Sacred Music," letter from 'Moderator," *JC* (September 30, 1870), 9. Ladies' Committees were a common feature of Victorian Jewish life; they were involved in the day-to-day running of the synagogue and events within the Jewish community, from arranging flowers for special services to organising charity concerts, lectures, and other fundraising events.
37. Francis L. Cohen and David M. Davis, *Kol Rinnah V'Todah. The Voice of Prayer and Praise: A Handbook of Synagogue Music for Congregational Singing. Arranged and Edited for the United Synagogue with the Sanction of the Chief Rabbi* (London: Greenberg and Co., 1899). An earlier version of this volume was printed in 1887, but had little impact on standardising Anglo-Jewish liturgy across synagogues. See Danielle Padley, "From Ancient to Modern: Identifying Anglicanism in an Anglo-Jewish Hymnal," *Music and Letters*, 2022, gcac048, https://doi.org/10.1093/ml/gcac048.
38. 'Synagogue Singing," *JC* (August 13, 1875), 317; this piece criticised the fact that 'our synagogue choirs . . . are taught to sing by ear *only*' (italics as printed). This was still the case in 1899, when Cohen and Davis wrote that *The Voice of Prayer and Praise* aimed to provide 'more general instruction of choristers by note and not by ear'; Cohen and Davis, *The Voice of Prayer and Praise*, v–vi. A more detailed account of the role of Jewish liturgical publications in the domestic sphere is in Padley, "From Ancient to Modern'.
39. Cohen and Davis, *The Voice of Prayer and Praise*, viii. This volume also incorporated Tonic Sol-Fa notation for the two upper voice parts, in line with how music was taught in schools.
40. See "West Central Sabbath Class," letter "from a correspondent," *JC* (June 17, 1887), 9; 'The Sabbath Class at Hanway Street School," letter from Constance Flower, *JC* (November 2, 1888), 6; "Services for Women," letters from G. J. Emanuel and S. D., *JC* (February 6, 1891), 7, and letters from Claude G. Montefiore and L. J. G., (February 13, 1891), 7.
41. "Services for Women," letter from Emily Marion Harris, *JC* (February 20, 1891), 8–9, p. 9.
42. "Services for Women," *JC* (February 20, 1891).
43. "Services for Women," letter from Oswald John Simon, *JC* (January 23, 1891), 8.
44. "Supplementary Services," *JC* (November 6, 1891), 13–14, p. 13. It is unclear who ran these services, although the article suggests that they sprang out of more minor attempts at female participation in worship at the larger Orthodox London synagogues. It is stated that '[m]inisters will occasionally conduct the services, but as a rule the prayers will be read, and the sermons delivered by, ladies.'
45. "Supplementary Services," *JC* (November 6, 1891).
46. "The United Synagogue Election," report on proceedings, *JC* (May 13, 1892), 22.
47. For a more detailed study of female voices in Anglican worship, see Elizabeth Blackmore, "The 'Angelic Quire': Rethinking Female Voices in Anglican Sacred Music, c. 1889" (Master's thesis, Durham University, 2015).

Bibliography

Archival Sources

West London Synagogue Archives, Anglo-Jewish Archives, Hartley Library, Southampton University.

Secondary Sources

Berman, Saul J. "Kol 'Isha'." In *Rabbi Joseph H. Lookstein Memorial Volume*, edited by Leo Landman, 45–66 (New York: Ktav Publishing House, 1980).

Bernard, Philippa. *A Beacon of Light: The History of the West London Synagogue* (London: The West London Synagogue, 2013).

Blackmore, Elizabeth. "The 'Angelic Quire': Rethinking Female Voices in Anglican Sacred Music, c. 1889." Master's thesis, Durham University, 2015.

Cesarani, David. *The Jewish Chronicle and Anglo-Jewry, 1841–1991*. Cambridge: Cambridge University Press, 1994.

Cohen, Francis L., and David M. Davis. *Kol Rinnah V'Todah. The Voice of Prayer and Praise: A Handbook of Synagogue Music for Congregational Singing. Arranged and Edited for the United Synagogue with the Sanction of the Chief Rabbi*. London: Greenberg and Co., 1899.

Dale, Gordon. "Music and the Negotiation of Orthodox Jewish Gender Roles in Partnership 'Minyanim'." *Contemporary Jewry* 35, no. 1 (2015): 35–53.

Endelman, Todd M. *The Jews of Britain: 1656–2000*. Berkeley, Los Angeles, and London: University of California Press, 2002.

Kershen, Anne J., and Jonathan A. Romain. *Tradition and Change: A History of Reform Judaism in Britain, 1840–1995*. London: Vallentine Mitchell, 1995.

Marks, David Woolf. "Discourse delivered at the Consecration of the 'West London Synagogue for British Jews,' on Thursday, January 27th, 5602 [1842]." In *Sermons Preached on Various Occasions, at the West London Synagogue of British Jews. Series 1*, 1–26. London: R. Groombridge and Sons, 1851.

Padley, Danielle. "From Lineage to Legacy: Charles Garland Verrinder and Victorian Anglo-Jewish Music." Doctoral thesis, University of Cambridge, 2020.

———. "Tracing Jewish Music Beyond the Synagogue: Charles Garland Verrinder's *Hear My Cry O God*." *Nineteenth-Century Music Review* 17, no. 2 (2020): 181–223.

———. "From Ancient to Modern: Identifying Anglicanism in an Anglo-Jewish Hymnal." *Music & Letters* 104, no. 1 (February 2023): 31–58.

Roth, Cecil. *A History of the Jews in England*. Oxford: Clarendon Press, 1949.

Taylor-Guthartz, Lindsay. *Challenge and Conformity: The Religious Lives of Orthodox Jewish Women*. Liverpool: The Littmann Library of Jewish Civilisation, 2021.

32
SISTERS IN SONG
Women Cantors and Musical Creativity in Progressive Jewish Worship

Rachel Adelstein

Over the course of the Sabbath, progressive synagogues in the United States resound with music. Congregants sing prayers with joy and enthusiasm, sometimes led by a *hazzan*, or cantor, who may sing *a cappella* or play a guitar. A melody composed in Vienna in 1840 might give way to a tune written in San Francisco in 1969, which may in turn be followed by a melody composed only a year or two earlier by the cantor who leads it now. The liturgy blends the familiarity of ancient texts with a flexible approach to melody that engages and challenges the congregation in their prayer. This flow of liturgical creativity comes from the leadership of the cantor, the specialist who sets prayer to music.

The primary responsibility of the cantor is to represent Jewish congregations before the Divine and lead them in sung and chanted prayer. Ethnomusicologist Judah Cohen describes the cantor as 'a sacred vessel of Jewish music.'[1] Retired Ritual Director Debby Lewis of Chicago emphasises the relationship between the cantor and the congregation, describing the cantor as 'the one who takes people's prayers and lifts them up to God through song.'[2] Jewish law does not specify the gender of the prayer leader. However, a passage from the Talmud, the primary source of this law, asserts that *kol b'isha ervah*, or 'the voice of a woman is nakedness'. Medieval and Early Modern rabbis interpreted this to mean that a woman's singing voice could arouse men sexually, distracting them from prayer, and forbade women from singing in front of men in the synagogue and leading them in prayer. In addition, because women are exempt from the responsibility of daily prayer so that they can care for their children, rabbis asserted that women could not represent non-exempt men. From the thirteenth century CE, when the first separate seating areas or annexes for women appeared in German synagogues, into the early twentieth century,[3] learned women called *firzogerins*, or 'readers' in Yiddish, did lead services for women; however, these women did not lead prayer in the primary services attended by men.[4] Thus, until the middle of the twentieth century, almost all cantors were men.

The first woman to serve as the primary cantor for a synagogue was Julie Rosewald (1847–1906), who served Temple Emanu-El in San Francisco between 1884 and 1893.[5] However, it was largely during the 1970s and 1980s that the Reform, Conservative, and Reconstructionist movements admitted women to the role. During the same era, congregations also opened themselves to new, creative, and adaptive approaches to liturgy. Cantor Anita Hochman of New Jersey recalls that the congregation that hired her in 1981 viewed itself as being an unconventional place that 'preferred to think "outside the box" long before the phrase itself was coined', and hired a guitar-playing woman cantor as part of its flexible approach to ritual.[6] In the ensuing decades, women cantors have transformed progressive Jewish life in the United States with creative ritual innovation and a steady stream of newly composed prayer melodies and original liturgical songs.

Jewish Liturgical Flexibility

Within its predetermined structure, there is a surprising amount of space for creative interpretation within Jewish liturgy. The original text of the liturgy is in Hebrew; however, the progressive movements allow for varying amounts of translation into the local vernacular, and some prayers may be paraphrased or supplemented with new liturgical poetry, as in the American Reform prayerbook *Mishkan T'filah* (2007). A wide variety of musical styles are available for sounding prayer, ranging from relatively simple *nusach*, or traditional chant motives, and the artistic elaborations on these motives known as *hazzanut*, or the cantor's art, to folk melodies from different parts of the world and newer melodies composed for specific prayer texts. More traditional synagogues will not use instrumental accompaniment on the Sabbath and holidays.[7] However, beginning in the nineteenth century, some more liberal congregations introduced the organ, and in the 1970s, young cantors who had been inspired by songleaders at Jewish summer camps introduced the guitar into the synagogue.[8] Because girls and boys served as songleaders, many of the first women cantors brought guitars with them to their pulpits.

Within the relative flexibility of sounded ritual space, women cantors have room to explore a variety of ways to set prayer to music. Some women choose to sing traditional *hazzanut*. Although the style developed to favour men's voices by including a controlled vocal crack called a *krekhtz*,[9] women can and do learn the art. Cantor Jack Mendelson, a specialist in *hazzanut* who teaches at the Debbie Friedman School of Sacred Music in New York City, has developed particular techniques to teach women how to perform in this revered style. Mendelson's colleague, Cantor Mikhal Shiff Matter of Jerusalem, observes that Mendelson's techniques might help a female cantorial student to find 'a little more of a cantorial authenticity.'[10] However, because *hazzanut* is a style so strongly associated with a particular historical era in which women were not cantors, they are not expected to sing in this style, and their choice of whether or not to sing *hazzanut* is not judged as strictly as a man's choice would be. Some women have no interest in learning the style and believe it is old-fashioned and perhaps best suited to the male voice. Cantor Miriam Eskenasy of Indiana describes it as 'this interminable bellyaching that men do so well in traditional *hazzanut*. That, I love to listen to, but I just can't do it.'[11]

Many women cantors find their best means of expressing liturgical creativity in a more contemporary folk-rock musical style. The style gained popularity in Jewish summer camps, but it also recalls popular folk, rock, and pop from the 1960s, the era in which many of the first generation of women cantors came of age. Cantorial soloist Marian Neudel of Chicago noted a split between the sounds that Jewish Baby Boomers heard and the sounds that their parents preferred, observing, 'Sometimes I think my musical roots are much closer to Mahalia Jackson than to Yossele Rosenblatt.'[12] The folk-rock style is a sound that speaks to a more contemporary American experience than does the *hazzanut* of Eastern Europe, and thus it appeals both to American-born women cantors and their congregants. And because of its associations with summer camps, it represents a type of sounded liturgical space where women never had to compete with men but could claim their right to this sound from the beginning. Indeed, the primary name associated with this style is that of Debbie Friedman (1951–2011), a singer-songwriter whose folky, feminist meditations on Jewish liturgy have achieved the status of 'new traditional' synagogue music. Reform, Conservative, and Reconstructionist synagogues use her music openly. Even strictly Orthodox congregations that would not permit women's music otherwise have adopted Friedman's setting of the *Havdalah* (end of Sabbath) blessing.[13]

The wide range of liturgical music available to Jewish prayer leaders means that one of the most accessible ways for a woman cantor to exercise creativity in worship is simply to embrace a curatorial approach to music. Even within the relatively fixed narrative arc of an ordinary set of Sabbath services, there are numerous opportunities to choose between traditional and newer melodies, solo or congregational tunes, and music that emphasises particular emotional states that the ritual may evoke, including joy, meditation, romance, solemnity, majesty, and a range of others. Many of the women cantors I have consulted told me that part of their job was to ensure enough musical variety in services to sustain congregants' interest, while not overwhelming them with new material every week. Cantor Amy Zussman of Illinois told me:

> On a Friday night, I like to switch things up a little bit . . . So I might switch the *Shalom Rav* tonight and keep other things the same. And maybe I'll introduce a different *Mi Chamocha* but keep other things the same.[14]

Similarly, Rabbi Cantor Robin Sparr of Massachusetts observes that:

> My strength is that I have this spectacularly large repertoire. And, more importantly, I understand how to select from it in a way to create a service that is meaningful, that represents a variety of composers, that represents a variety of styles that offers every person in the sanctuary a moment of prayer.[15]

Zussman and Sparr's comments reveal the creative artistry that supports musical curatorship. It is not enough simply to string prayer melodies together; the cantor must also be attentive to her congregants' needs and tastes and challenge them enough to keep them engaged with the service.

Some cantors expand their curatorship and programme music thematically, scheduling different styles of services for each Sabbath of the month. Cantor Eskenasy described rotating between family-oriented music, formal music, and a more upbeat and relaxed style. She used this rotation as an educational opportunity for her congregation, saying, 'I like to teach a lot about Jewish music, so sometimes in the service, I would choose a piece from a different locale, or a different style.'[16] Cantor Deborah Martin of Wisconsin also curates services thematically, using a rare 'fifth Friday' to bring in new themes or musical styles to broaden her congregants' horizons and introduce them to music from other Jewish cultures beyond the heavily Eastern-European Ashkenazi background that informs much of progressive American Jewish life. In addition to fifth Friday-night services devoted to Sephardic Jewish music and Yiddish-language jazz, Martin has introduced explicitly feminist programming into the normal Sabbath services, open to all congregants. She described this as 'a service of Jewish women, not just music, but also writings', and selected women from her congregation to help her lead the liturgy. Like Eskenasy, Martin sees this kind of creative curatorship as educational, an opportunity to 'give people an idea that one way is not the only way.'[17] Within the flexible boundaries of written liturgy, women cantors have made a distinct space for themselves, their voices, and an eclectic approach to the sound of prayer.

Rachel Adelstein

Women Cantors as Creators

While the flexibility of Jewish liturgy does create ample space for the kind of creativity that comes from combining and varying pre-existing musical styles, this is certainly not the only expression of women cantors' musical creativity. Any cantor, male or female, might be expected to lead worship with this kind of creativity, and many do. However, for women, the need for liturgical creativity runs deeper, as women must actively create space for themselves in Jewish rituals in ways that men need not. Cantor Barbara Ostfeld observes that most Jewish liturgical texts omit women altogether, noting that women cantors 'sing words in which their ancestral mothers are transmuted into an afterthought, which are not meant for them to intone or even necessarily to heed.'[18] Lori Lefkovitz and Rona Shapiro, the founders of an online clearing-house for new Jewish rituals called Ritualwell.org, extend this idea to address the fact that, although in normative Jewish thinking, the body provides access to the spirit, almost all Jewish rituals centred on the body involved the male body only. Lefkovitz and Shapiro observe that the design of contemporary rituals often addresses this gendered imbalance, noting that 'Jewish women's spirituality can be characterized in part by its investment of spirit into the particularities of the *female* body.'[19] Although there is no mechanism for amending *halakhah*, the corpus of Jewish law, to include women, there is also no prohibition on developing new rituals that did not exist when *halakhah* was codified. Consequently, in their roles as leaders of prayer and ritual, many women cantors work not only to adapt existing rituals to include women, but also to devise new rituals to meet the particularly gendered needs of contemporary congregants.

The earliest modern feminist Jewish rituals appeared in the brief moment in the early 1970s when women had begun to take ownership of Jewish ritual, but their status as cantors was not yet official. The first of these rituals celebrated *Rosh Chodesh*, the festival of the New Moon. Traditional Jewish ritual marks the new moon with an extra blessing said during the Sabbath morning worship service. The eleventh-century rabbi and Talmud scholar Rashi (1040–1105) wrote that *Rosh Chodesh* should be a holiday of rest from work for women as a reward for the Israelite women's refusal to give their gold jewellery to help build the Golden Calf.[20] In 1972, encouraged by this rabbinic connection between women and *Rosh Chodesh*, women began to mark *Rosh Chodesh* specifically as a moment to affirm their role in Jewish culture.[21] For Passover in 1976, Esther Broner gathered several feminist Jewish friends, including Gloria Steinem, Phyllis Chesler, and Letty Cottin Pogrebin, to celebrate the first 'Feminist Seder'.[22] Since then, as women cantors have assumed ritual leadership in American congregations, they have followed and expanded upon these examples of creating rituals to acknowledge gender and women's presence in Judaism.

The creative challenge for such rituals is to make them meaningful and relevant to congregants living in the modern world while also maintaining a recognisable connection to millennia-old patterns of Jewish ritual and liturgical life. Sarah Ross locates the need for new, feminist Jewish rituals in the 1960s and 1970s when Jewish women in the United States 'turned from being objects, the suppressed, and the others and became subjects and (ritual) agents.' Further, she identifies a tension between the act of characterising a woman-oriented Jewish ritual as feminist in its distinction from official male-oriented ritual and the act of establishing connections to normative Jewish traditions in order to enhance the Jewishness of the ritual.[23] Women cantors often create these new rituals in response to particular requests from congregants seeking a Jewish way to acknowledge life events not addressed in normative Jewish ritual tradition. Such rituals might address physical events such as a pregnancy loss or the onset of menstruation, or an emotionally or socially significant event, such as healing from sexual assault or changing one's Hebrew name as part of gender transition.

Many women cantors devise these rituals by drawing on existing Jewish rituals that address one aspect of the problem at hand and connecting elements of these rituals together with a new feminist narrative. Cantor Dorothy Goldberg of Puerto Rico devised a name-changing service for women undergoing life-changing events such as divorce or widowhood that 'draws upon two ancient rituals: the changing of one's Hebrew name, and a woman's periodic immersion in the mikvah.'[24] Some women cantors also adapt the *mikvah*, the ritual bath in which Jewish women traditionally immerse themselves before marriage and after menstruation and childbirth, as both a source of communal solidarity in a female-only space and a source of healing from rape and abuse.[25] The Women Cantors' Network (hereafter WCN) often addresses questions about devising new rituals, both on its e-mail listserv and in its annual conferences. The 2010 WCN conference in Chicago featured both a workshop on how to devise wedding rituals for non-traditional (same-sex and interfaith) couples as well as one entitled 'Songs in the Key of Life Cycle', in which panellists discussed ways to use music to create meaningful new rituals for congregants. Similarly, at the 2014 conference in Washington, D.C., I offered a workshop on the anthropological foundations of ritual as a way to aid the practice of combining elements from extant rituals. Many of these new rituals can be found on Ritualwell.org, and new rituals and individual prayer texts appear in books published by both Jewish and general presses.[26] Cantors in need of a new ritual to help particular congregants or to address a situation affecting their entire congregation will often devise their own rituals but may also turn to published resources and to their colleagues for inspiration and prayer texts.

The act of devising new rituals can be a powerful experience both for the deviser and for the participants. One key measure of the success of a new ritual is the degree to which participants can recognise it as Jewish as well as useful. Lefkovitz and Shapiro use this balance as one criterion when deciding whether or not a new ritual should be posted at Ritualwell.org.[27] Cantor Ostfeld observes that, in expanding the corpus of Jewish ritual to encompass the needs of women, 'a woman cantor holds on to the very tradition that once excluded her, and in doing so, she transforms it.'[28] Congregants who ask women cantors to devise new rituals, and the women cantors who devise them, do not wish to abandon Jewish tradition altogether; rather, they wish to expand it. This is where the woman cantor may exercise her creativity in her role as ritual specialist; she employs her understanding of Jewish ritual and the needs of the moment to strike the perfect balance that resonates with tradition in innovative ways. Communities often ask for new rituals, because new rituals address congregants' spiritual needs in ways that normative ritual may not. Because these new rituals do not supersede normative liturgy but coexist with it, those congregants who need them welcome the addition, while congregants who do not need them usually tolerate the addition as long as it does not disrupt the practice of normative liturgy.

As important as new rituals may be to contemporary congregants, normative liturgy occupies the bulk of Jewish liturgical life. Here, too, many women cantors exercise their creative skills as composers. Although some women cantors are happy to lead worship according to classic melodies and the traditional *nusach* formulas described earlier,[29] others express a strong desire for liturgical music specifically composed for the female voice. Cantor Deborah Katchko-Gray explained to *Hadassah* magazine that women often need to transpose classic cantorial melodies composed for men's voices, and that when she published a volume of synagogue music composed by her grandfather, Cantor Adolph Katchko, she transposed his original music keys to better suit her soprano voice.[30] Consequently, when women cantors compose new melodies for familiar liturgical texts, they compose with female voices in mind and may often compose in slightly lower keys than those used in classic synagogue music. In an interview with Sarah Ross, Cantor Linda Hirschhorn suggests that composing specifically for women's voices is in and of itself a feminist act,[31] though not all women cantors would view their compositions this way; for many, composing music to suit their own female voices is simply a practical aspect of their creative practice.

In addition, much of the music by women cantors that I have seen is composed in distinctly contemporary styles that speak to women cantors' connections to modern Western forms of Jewish practice and the musical cultures in which they live. Women cantors compose liturgical music in Hebrew, English, and occasionally in other traditional Jewish languages such as Yiddish or Ladino. They draw stylistic inspiration from folk, rock, R&B, and rap, as well as classical choral harmony and world musical traditions, especially those from the Middle East. Because many women cantors work in synagogues that allow the use of instruments during worship, their compositions often include guitar chords or hand percussion as well as voice. Cantorial Soloist Susan Colin, one of three editors of *Kol Isha*, the Women Cantors' Network's 2019 songbook, described the editors' choice to set the book's contents as lead sheets, with melody, lyrics, and guitar chords, saying:

> At this point in congregational life, there's a lot of guitar stuff happening. That's pretty much the default . . . we wanted these to be simply presented, so that they would be easy to read and work with.[32]

The ubiquity of the guitar that Colin describes indicates the extent to which women cantors have taken ownership of contemporary styles of synagogue music, with which they have been working as long and as closely as men have.

Although not all of the women cantors with whom I have spoken identify specifically as feminists, there is a strong feminist approach to liturgy that runs through the music that women cantors compose. One of the earliest feminist interventions in Jewish liturgy was to alter the prayer *Avot*, an invocation of the three patriarchs, Abraham, Isaac, and Jacob, to include the matriarchs Sarah, Rebecca, Rachel, and Leah, as well.[33] Many congregations fit the extra names to the traditional chant melody either by drawing out a note to add the matriarch's name to her husband's or add the matriarchs in a group by repeating that section of the melody. However, in 1981, Cantor Sue Roemer composed a new melody for *Avot* that includes the names of the patriarchs and matriarchs naturally, without extending notes or repeating melodic passages, and also expressly addresses the Divine as 'God of our fathers', 'God of our mothers', and 'God of our parents'.[34] In this setting, the matriarchs assume a place in this moment of veneration that is uniquely theirs, and that is not borrowed from or conditional on the patriarchs. Roemer gives women a dedicated space in the liturgy, while still fitting the melody to the recognisable contours of the traditional chant.

Liturgical feminism is even more notable in songs that contain some lyrics in the vernacular. Some contemporary composers, male and female, who are setting the text of a relatively well-known prayer will combine the original Hebrew text with English lyrics; this practice helps Anglophone congregants who may not be especially skilled in Hebrew to grasp the meaning of the prayer. Others compose liturgical music that is largely an English meditation on a few lines from a prayer. In these cases, the English lyrics may or may not necessarily be a direct translation of the original Hebrew text. It is in the differences between the Hebrew and the translation or paraphrase of the English that the composer's commentary on the prayer may be located, and where a listener may encounter a feminist approach to liturgy.

Mayim Chayim, Living Waters composed in 2000 by Cantorial Soloist Tali Ann Katz of Florida, demonstrates such a meditation. Katz takes as her base text the phrase *mayim chayim*, which appears several times throughout the Hebrew Bible, and translates directly as 'living water'. In Jeremiah 2:13, which Katz cites as her source for this phrase, *mayim chayim* is a metaphor for the Divine, the source of life. Katz combines this reading of the phrase with a traditional association between water and femininity. Her first English verse speaks directly to the Divine, offering praises including 'source of joy', 'source of strength', 'source of hope', and 'source of peace'. In her second verse, Katz explicitly connects the *mayim chayim* with women: 'I hear our Mothers' call, *mayim chayim*./Breathe in the song they sing, *mayim chayim*.'[35] Katz composed this song to mark the moment when she entered the *mikvah* for the first time as an older woman, adapting this ritual to mark her choice to live a more consciously Jewish life.[36] In this adaptive ritual context, Katz's connection between a well-known Biblical phrase and her invocation of the feminine and of maternal connections establishes and highlights a female presence in the context of a male-dominated sacred text.

Some women cantors who compose channel their creative impulses into collaborative enterprises. Beyond the quasi-collaborative effort of composing music for a text drawn from liturgy or from a pre-existing poem, some women cantors work together with each other and with other songwriters to co-compose new liturgical music. Of the seventy-six non-commissioned songs published in *Kol Isha* (2019, to be discussed further), eight have collaborative credits for the music, the lyrics, or both. Rabbi Cantor Robbi Sherwin of Texas states that the role of the cantor is 'to help people envision their relationship with God through music.'[37] She puts this philosophy into practice by offering weekend-long workshops on group composition for synagogues. During these weekends, Sherwin selects one prayer text and leads participants through exercises in translating the Hebrew into English, analysing the meaning of the text, and drawing personal associations with aspects of the text. In addition to this intense collective textual study, participants offer suggestions for the characteristics of a new melody for this text. At the conclusion of the workshop, Sherwin combines these suggestions with lyrics reflecting the group's new understanding of the text to create a new, accessible song for the congregation.

While Sherwin's work represents an extreme form of inclusive compositional creativity, it falls within long-established patterns of women's compositional styles in Europe and North America. Musicologist Marcia J. Citron observes that women in the West are socialised as caretakers, encouraged to develop inclusive bonds, and 'to acquire knowledge and self-knowledge through interaction with others and for the benefit of the larger group.'[38] She suggests that this has influenced the way that women composers view the creative act of composition. Because cantors function as spiritual caretakers for their congregations, it is hardly surprising that women cantors might express something of this feminine social training in their creative work as well as in their spiritual work.

The Women Cantors' Network

The Women Cantors' Network (WCN) is a professional association that serves as a significant site of exchange and support for women in Jewish spiritual leadership. Founded in 1982 in Norwalk, Connecticut by Cantor Deborah Katchko-Gray, the WCN is a consciously non-hierarchical association that offers informal education, professional community, and creative opportunities to women, and a few men, who occupy positions of ritual leadership in Jewish communities.[39] Members need not be officially ordained by an accredited cantorial school, and their ranks include songleaders, rabbis, composers, and scholars as well as more traditional cantors. The WCN maintains an active e-mail listserv and hosts an annual conference.

This loose organisational structure accommodates a significant degree of creativity. The listserv provides a forum for members to discuss challenges they experience in their congregations and to devise solutions to those challenges. Topics of discussion range from questions about salary and contract negotiation to exchanging strategies for singing through the day-long fast on *Yom Kippur*.[40] The WCN also hosts an annual series of online presentations on the Zoom platform called 'Knosh 'n Knowledge', where members may offer lessons in ritual practice and musical performance. The annual conference provides opportunities for informal exchange of knowledge and learning through member-led workshops. Participants in the conference may share new music through the opening *kumsitz* (informal song-share), and at public and internal evening concerts. They may also attend workshops specifically devoted to addressing new situations and challenges that may arise within congregations. This professional structure gives collaborative support to spiritual leaders who might otherwise work in relative isolation as the only cantor in a given community. Peer support and knowledge exchange help members to find inspiration for creative approaches to liturgy, ritual, and composition as well as an appreciative audience for their creative efforts.

As mentioned earlier, in 2019, the WCN published a collection of compositions by members, called *Kol Isha*. The title translates as 'the voice of a woman', and refers to the Talmudic phrase *kol b'isha ervah*, discussed at the outset. Co-edited by Emily Howard Meyer, Anita Schubert, and Susan Colin, it is a collection of seventy-six compositions, including new melodies for popular prayers from the liturgy as well as original compositions on liturgical and spiritual themes. The volume also includes eight choral pieces commissioned by the WCN and a 'Welcome Song' attributed to 'Robbi Sherwin & Friends' composed as part of a workshop that Sherwin led in 2013, demonstrating for WCN members the group composition methods described earlier.

The initial idea for the songbook came from Cantor Deborah Katchko-Gray, who did not suggest a specific theme. The final product is a highly eclectic collection of contemporary liturgical and para-liturgical music. Co-editor Cantor Anita Schubert describes it as a

> celebration of the talents among the members of the Women Cantors' Network. It didn't have any purpose like, let's put out music for *Chanukah* or High Holidays or for life-cycle. It was, let's just get everyone's creativity into a book. And it becomes there for posterity.[41]

Co-editor Emily Howard Meyer observed that the songbook provided an opportunity for women who might otherwise have composed in obscurity to be published, and speculated that such an opportunity might have inspired more creativity:

> We all have this ability. We had a couple of people who had never written a song in their life, or they've only just written this one song. So even people who think that they're not creative have this creative outlet. And when given the opportunity to express it, they're there.[42]

In order to encourage this creativity, the editors accepted every submission that members sent to them, and even transcribed audio recordings from cantors who had never notated their compositions.

The contents of the songbook reveal the wide array of musical styles that women cantors employ to connect with congregants and address their personal and spiritual concerns. The book features choral music, folk-rock, lullaby, chant, and rap. Original lyrics sit side by side with ancient Hebrew liturgical texts. All three co-editors noted that the book offers musical selections for established public rituals such as the Sabbath and the High Holy Days, as well as for more private occasions, including a song that expresses the intensely personal experience of a stillbirth.

WCN member Charki Dunn's 2018 song 'What A Day' shows many of the characteristics of newly devised rituals described here. It is an intimate song, with a repetitive, rocking, almost chant-like melody. Its first-person lyrics show the perspective of a mother who learns of a pregnancy and then loses the baby. 'She is gone. I can't breathe. My heart is broke, she is gone, I can't breathe. What am I to do? Where am I to go?'[43] It addresses a life-changing event for which there is no extant ritual in the Jewish canon, but for which a congregant might turn to a spiritual leader such as a cantor seeking guidance. Stillbirths and miscarriages are also events closely associated with women and are often handled among a limited circle of family and associates. Co-editors Anita Schubert and Susan Colin both expressed deep gratitude for Dunn's submission. 'This was one of those ones that would not have a place anywhere else', Colin said. 'It's not something that will get used in my life very much. But there are moments that people will understand . . . I thought it was really brave of her to offer this.'[44] Schubert observed that a songbook celebrating the members of the WCN was an unusually appropriate place to publish this song. 'But that's the sort of thing: where else would it go? Who else would publish it? It's not the usual category.'[45]

The publication of *Kol Isha* positions the members of the WCN as sources of ritual creativity and innovation, rather than simply performers of preset and pre-arranged liturgy. In its celebration of women cantors' creativity, it places them within a larger historical tradition of Jewish musical engagement and conversation with liturgical texts. Susan Colin highlighted the importance of the title in emphasising female creativity, saying 'this, at its very core, is putting out there the role that women have in Jewish music and Jewish leadership.'[46] The WCN debuted this work at the 2019 conference in New Jersey. During the conference, the WCN offered a public concert in which members performed selections from the songbook. While past WCN concerts highlighted women cantors' voices and performance skills, the 2019 concert framed women cantors as liturgical innovators, accentuating their musical and spiritual creativity in the public arena.

Conclusion

By all measures, women cantors are now fully established in progressive Jewish spaces. Young women attend cantorial schools inspired by the women cantors who served their childhood synagogues, and very few members of progressive synagogues have never heard a woman leading prayer. Women have secure positions of ritual leadership and of institutional leadership as well, within cantorial seminaries and professional associations. With their position in Jewish religious life so firmly established, women cantors have opportunities to use their public platforms to support the creativity and innovation that they bring to Jewish liturgy and community life.

Innovation in Jewish ritual and liturgical music is a perpetual topic of contention between those scholars and practitioners who wish to preserve the music of the past and those who see the liturgy as a source of inspiration, following the Psalmist's exhortation to '*shiru l'Adonai shir chadash*', to sing a new song to the Divine. Yet as new compositions age, they acquire their own historical gravitas and cloak of tradition. Liturgical music composed in the 1960s and 1970s has become 'our traditional music' for many progressive congregations. One might well say that there is now a third layer of historicism in Jewish liturgical music. This 'new traditional' repertoire occupies a place in Jewish liturgical history following the cantorial standards of the early twentieth century and preceding the newest repertoire of the twenty-first century. The first generation of women cantors came of age in the era when the 'new traditional' repertoire was new, and they helped to create a significant space for flexibility and innovation in American synagogue music, reminding congregations that, as Cantor Deborah Martin observes, one way is not the only way.

Today, the daughters and granddaughters of the first women cantors, both metaphorical and increasingly literal, embrace the flexibility that their predecessors established. Contemporary women cantors approach tradition and liturgy with an inclusive eye. They welcome normative and traditional liturgy but are willing and able to innovate and create new rituals and new music as well. Their creative work in ritual and music addresses the needs of their congregants, helping them to understand the flexibility of tradition and adapt that tradition to contemporary circumstances. In this way, women cantors' creative and innovative ritual work helps progressive Jewish communities to embrace their Jewish heritage and expand their Jewish lives to meet the new challenges and demands of the twenty-first century.

Notes

1. Judah Cohen, *The Making of a Reform Jewish Cantor: Musical Authority, Cultural Investment* (Bloomington: Indiana University Press, 2009), 12.
2. Debby Lewis, interview by author (Chicago, IL, 2010).
3. Norma Baumel Joseph, "Meḥitza: Halakhic Decisions and Political Consequences," in *Daughters of the King: Women and the Synagogue*, edited by Susan Grossman and Rivka Haut (Philadelphia, PA: Jewish Publication Society, 1992), 117–34: 132.
4. Judah Cohen, "Professionalizing the Cantorate – and Masculinizing It? The Female Prayer Leader and Her Erasure from Jewish Musical Tradition," *The Musical Quarterly* 101, no. 4 (2018): 455–81, p. 460.
5. Judith Pinnolis, " 'Cantor Soprano' Julie Rosewald: The Musical Career of a Jewish American 'New Woman'," *American Jewish Archives Journal* 57, no. 2 (2010): 1–53, p. 1.
6. Anita Hochman, "My Cantorate," *Journal of Synagogue Music* 32 (2007): 33–35, p. 34.
7. There are many explanations for this tradition. The most well-known is that the lack of instrumental music is a sign of mourning for the destruction of the Second Temple in Jerusalem in 70 CE. Other reasons include considering the risk of breaking an instrument and having to repair it when work is forbidden on the Sabbath and a Talmudic warning against excessive noisemaking on the Sabbath.
8. Mark Goodman, "The Folk and Folk/Rock Movement of the Sixties and Its Influence on the Contemporary Jewish Worship Service," in *Perspectives on Jewish Music: Secular and Sacred*, edited by Jonathan L. Friedmann (Lanham, MD: Lexington Books, 2009), 41–56, p. 51.
9. Pamela Kordan Trimble, "*Kol Hazzanit* – Alternatives for Women Cantors to the Vocal Requirements and Expression of Traditional Hazzanut," *Journal of Synagogue Music* 32 (2007): 100–15, p. 112.
10. Mikhal Shiff Matter, interview by author (Jerusalem, Israel, 2011).
11. Miriam Eskenasy, interview by author (Chicago, IL, 2010).
12. Marian Neudel, interview by author (Chicago, IL, 2010).
13. Susan Colin, interview by author (online, Phoenix, AZ, 2020).
14. Amy Zussman, interview by author (Northfield, IL, 2010).
15. Robin Sparr, interview by author (Natick, MA, 2010).
16. Eskenasy, 2010.
17. Deborah Martin, interview by author (Madison, WI, 2010).

18. Barbara Ostfeld, "The Ascent of the Woman Cantor: Shir Hamaalot," in *New Jewish Feminism: Probing the Past, Forging the Future*, edited by Rabbi Elyse Goldstein (Woodstock, VT: Jewish Lights Publishing, 2009), 133–43, p. 138.
19. Lori Lefkovitz and Rona Shapiro, "Ritualwell.Org – Loading the Virtual Canon, or: The Politics and Aesthetics of Jewish Women's Spirituality," *Nashim: A Journal of Jewish Women's Studies & Gender Issues* 9 (2005): 101–25, p. 104.
20. Jody Myers, "Phasing In: Rosh Hodesh Ceremonies in American Jewish Life," in *Women Remaking American Judaism*, edited by Riv-Ellen Prell (Detroit, MI: Wayne State University Press, 2007), 231–56, pp. 233–34.
21. Myers, "Phasing In," 231.
22. Esther Broner, *The Telling: The Story of a Group of Jewish Women Who Journey to Spirituality Through Community and Ceremony* (New York: HarperCollins, 1993), 14. The Seder is the home ritual celebrating Passover, in which the story of the Exodus is re-told over a festive dinner, including symbolic foods, songs, liturgy, and narrative.
23. Sarah Ross, *A Season of Singing: Creating Feminist Jewish Music in the United States* (Waltham, MA: Brandeis University Press, 2016), 20.
24. Dorothy Goldberg, "A Woman Reborn: Name-Changing Service for Women Traveling a New Path in Life," *Journal of Synagogue Music* 32 (2007): 196–201, p. 196.
25. Pamela Nadell, "A Bright New Constellation: Feminism and American Judaism," in *The Columbia History of Jews and Judaism in America*, edited by Marc Lee Raphael (New York: Columbia University Press, 2008), 385–405, pp. 393–94.
26. Examples include Marcia Falk's *The Book of Blessings: New Jewish Prayers for Daily Life* (1996) and Rabbi Denise Eger's *Mishkah Ga'avah: Where Pride Dwells, A Celebration of LGBTQ Jewish Life and Ritual* (2020).
27. Lefkovitz and Shapiro, "Ritualwell.Org – Loading the Virtual Canon," 115.
28. Ostfeld, "The Ascent of the Woman Cantor," 139.
29. *Nusach* refers broadly to the short melodic motives that make up the musical modes of Jewish prayer. The traditional art of the *hazzan* is to improvise elaborate prayer melodies using the correct modes and motives as a base.
30. Joanne Lessner, "Sacred Music in a Female Key," *Hadassah*, 2018, accessed January 29, 2021, www.hadassahmagazine.org/2018/08/21/sacred-music-female-key/.
31. Ross, *A Season of Singing*, 179.
32. Colin, 2020.
33. It is unclear exactly when this custom began; however, it is likely to have started in consciously egalitarian synagogues in the 1970s. The Reform movement in the United States officially allowed the inclusion of the matriarchs in 1985. The Conservative movement allowed the inclusion in 1990. The matriarchs appear in the *Avot* prayer in prayerbooks published by those movements after those dates. Individual synagogues and individual prayer leaders may choose to include the matriarchs or not include them.
34. Sue Roemer, "Avot," in *Kol Isha: Songs and Settings of Prayers Composed by Members of the Women Cantors' Network*, edited by Susan Colin, Emily Howard Meyer, and Anita Schubert (Natick, MA: Women Cantors' Network, 2019), 30.
35. Tali Ann Katz, "Mayim Chayim, Living Waters," in *Kol Isha: Songs and Settings of Prayers Composed by Members of the Women Cantors' Network*, edited by Susan Colin, Emily Howard Meyer, and Anita Schubert (Natick, MA: Women Cantors' Network, 2019), 76.
36. Katz, personal communication with author.
37. Robbi Sherwin, interview by author (Austin, TX, 2011).
38. Marcia Citron, "Feminist Approaches to Musicology," in *Cecilia Reclaimed: Feminist Perspectives on Gender and Music*, edited by Susan Cook and Judy Tsou (Urbana: University of Illinois Press, 1994), 17–34, p. 24.
39. Deborah Katchko-Gray, interview by author (Ridgefield, CT, 2011).
40. *Yom Kippur*, the Day of Atonement, is the last day of the ten Days of Awe (beginning with *Rosh Hashana*) that make up the Jewish New Year. It is traditionally observed with a full day of liturgy, accompanied by a twenty-five hour fast lasting from sundown to sundown.
41. Anita Schubert, interview by author (online, Boynton Beach, FL, 2020).
42. Emily Howard Meyer, interview by author (online, Chevy Chase, MD, 2020).

43. Charki Dunn, "What a Day," in *Kol Isha: Songs and Settings of Prayers Composed by Members of the Women Cantors' Network*, edited by Susan Colin, Emily Howard Meyer, and Anita Schubert (Natick, MA: Women Cantors' Network, 2019), 126–27.
44. Colin, 2020.
45. Schubert, 2020.
46. Colin, 2020.

Bibliography

Broner, Esther. *The Telling: The Story of a Group of Jewish Women Who Journey to Spirituality Through Community and Ceremony*. New York: HarperCollins, 1993.

Citron, Marcia. "Feminist Approaches to Musicology." In *Cecilia Reclaimed: Feminist Perspectives on Gender and Music*, edited by Susan Cook and Judy Tsou, 17–34. Urbana: University of Illinois Press, 1994.

Cohen, Judah. *The Making of a Reform Jewish Cantor: Musical Authority, Cultural Investment*. Bloomington: Indiana University Press, 2009.

———. "Professionalizing the Cantorate – and Masculinizing It? The Female Prayer Leader and Her Erasure from Jewish Musical Tradition." *The Musical Quarterly* 101, no. 4 (2018): 455–81.

Colin, Susan, interview by author (online, Phoenix, AZ, 2020).

Dunn, Charki. "What A Day." In *Kol Isha: Songs and Settings of Prayers Composed by Members of the Women Cantors' Network*, edited by Susan Colin, Emily Howard Meyer, and Anita Schubert, 126–27. Natick, MA: Women Cantors' Network, 2019.

Eskenasy, Miriam, interview by author (Chicago, IL, 2010).

Goldberg, Dorothy. "A Woman Reborn: Name-Changing Service for Women Traveling a New Path in Life." *Journal of Synagogue Music* 32 (2007): 196–201.

Goodman, Mark. "The Folk and Folk/Rock Movement of the Sixties and Its Influence on the Contemporary Jewish Worship Service." In *Perspectives on Jewish Music: Secular and Sacred*, edited by Jonathan L. Friedmann, 41–56. Lanham, MD: Lexington Books, 2009.

Hochman, Anita. "My Cantorate." *Journal of Synagogue Music* 32 (2007): 33–35.

Howard Meyer, Emily, interview by author (online, Chevy Chase, MD, 2020).

Joseph, Norma Baumel. "*Meḥitza*: Halakhic Decisions and Political Consequences." In *Daughters of the King: Women and the Synagogue*, edited by Susan Grossman and Rivka Haut, 117–34. Philadelphia, PA: Jewish Publication Society, 1992.

Katchko-Gray, Deborah, interview by author (Ridgefield, CT, 2011).

Katz, Tali Ann. "Mayim Chayim, Living Waters." In *Kol Isha: Songs and Settings of Prayers Composed by Members of the Women Cantors' Network*, edited by Susan Colin, Emily Howard Meyer, and Anita Schubert. Natick, MA: Women Cantors' Network, 2019.

Lefkovitz, Lori, and Rona Shapiro. "Ritualwell.Org – Loading the Virtual Canon, or: The Politics and Aesthetics of Jewish Women's Spirituality." *Nashim: A Journal of Jewish Women's Studies & Gender Issues* 9 (2005): 101–25.

Lessner, Joanne. "Sacred Music in a Female Key." *Hadassah*, 2018. Accessed January 29, 2021. www.hadassahmagazine.org/2018/08/21/sacred-music-female-key/.

Lewis, Debby, interview by author (Chicago, IL, 2010).

Martin, Deborah, interview by author (Madison, WI, 2010).

Myers, Jody. "Phasing In: Rosh Hodesh Ceremonies in American Jewish Life." In *Women Remaking American Judaism*, edited by Riv-Ellen Prell, 231–56. Detroit, MI: Wayne State University Press, 2007.

Nadell, Pamela. "A Bright New Constellation: Feminism and American Judaism." In *The Columbia History of Jews and Judaism in America*, edited by Marc Lee Raphael, 385–405. New York: Columbia University Press, 2008.

Neudel, Marian, interview by author (Chicago, IL, 2010).

Ostfeld, Barbara. "The Ascent of the Woman Cantor: Shir Hamaalot." In *New Jewish Feminism: Probing the Past, Forging the Future*, edited by Rabbi Elyse Goldstein, 133–43. Woodstock, VT: Jewish Lights Publishing, 2009.

Pinnolis, Judith. "Cantor Soprano" Julie Rosewald: The Musical Career of a Jewish American "New Woman." *American Jewish Archives Journal* 57, no. 2 (2010): 1–53.

Roemer, Sue. "Avot." In *Kol Isha: Songs and Settings of Prayers Composed by Members of the Women Cantors' Network*, edited by Susan Colin, Emily Howard Meyer, and Anita Schubert. Natick, MA: Women Cantors' Network, 2019.

Ross, Sarah. *A Season of Singing: Creating Feminist Jewish Music in the United States*. Waltham, MA: Brandeis University Press, 2016.

Schubert, Anita, interview by author (online, Boynton Beach, FL, 2020).

Sherwin, Robbi, interview by author (Austin, TX, 2011).

Shiff Matter, Mikhal, interview by author (Jerusalem, Israel, 2011).

Sparr, Robin, interview by author (Natick, MA, 2010).

Trimble, Pamela Kordan. "*Kol Hazzanit* – Alternatives for Women Cantors to the Vocal Requirements and Expression of Traditional Hazzanut." *Journal of Synagogue Music* 32 (2007): 100–15.

Zussman, Amy, interview by author (Northfield, IL, 2010).

33
MARUJA HINESTROSA
Faith and Introspection in a Colombian Composer

Luis Gabriel Mesa Martínez

Maruja Hinestrosa was born in 1914 in Pasto, in southern Colombia. Despite the hostile climate towards women composers in her time and place, her trajectory stands out historically in the country for having overcome social prejudices to the point of solidifying a career as an artist, creator, and concert pianist. As a city that was significantly isolated from capital city Bogotá, Pasto represented an enormous challenge for those who desired to receive a professional musical education. The possibility of studying in the National Conservatory was distant, and local religious communities that offered some sort of artistic education were more frequently relied upon. This was the case for Hinestrosa, whose study of piano began in the Liceo de la Merced Maridíaz (a Franciscan nuns' school), thanks to the presence of a German nun, Sister Bautista, who brought with her teaching materials for this purpose.

For having been raised in a deeply conservative society, it is interesting to note that Hinestrosa's compositional work concentrates on musical expressions that articulate her Roman Catholic convictions within popular genres, some of which were heavily questioned by the moral canon of Colombian society. Hinestrosa's *boleros*, for example, became communication tools that allowed her to write music and lyrics that alluded to love, with occasional references to her Christian faith. At the same time, her stylistic versatility drove her to write more conventional works, as is the case in her version of *Ave Maria*,[1] dedicated to the Virgin of Las Lajas (one of the most emblematic shrines in Colombian religious architecture), or the secular vocal ballads that do not refrain from revealing her Roman Catholic beliefs. One example is her composition *We All Have a Cross to Bear* (c. 1960).

This chapter puts forth a reflection of the concepts of faith and introspection in the works of Maruja Hinestrosa (1914–2002), and in doing so uncovers the compositional language of a woman who broke the boundaries and social prejudices of her time and achieved an artistic legacy that deserves to be studied and disseminated. This research commenced in 2014, when the author's book and accompanying disc titled *Maruja Hinestrosa: la identidad nariñense a través de su piano* (*Maruja Hinestrosa: Nariño Identity Through Her Piano*) were published,[2] and it has continued through the circulation of academic articles, as well as his documentary film recently recognised as the 'Best Regional Short Form Film' at the 15th International Film Festival of Pasto (2019).[3]

In this new text, the author provides a deepening understanding of the musical world of Hinestrosa, offering a contribution to the musicological literature on the role of women composers within the context of Latin America. It is divided into three different sections, beginning with an approach to her music within the context of musical nationalism, followed by an examination of her Roman Catholic faith in a selection of vocal works, and ending with a reflection around the international impact of her earliest composition: *Cafetero* (1928–29).

Maruja Hinestrosa: A 'National' Composer

Little has been published about women and music in Colombia. However, the twenty-first century has opened interesting paths for the articulation between musicology and gender studies, not only among national scholars but also in dialogue with Latin American and Iberian research groups. The International Symposium *Mujeres en la música* (*Women in Music*) – held at the University of Costa Rica since 2017 – stands out as one of the main events in the region for this academic field, where local artists meet national and international scholars in a space that aims to provide a solid ground for discussion, but more importantly, in an emphatic attempt to make the work of women musicians more visible. Colombian composer Maruja Hinestrosa is one of those women, and for that reason, this chapter seeks to raise a global interest around her music, beyond the borders of the Spanish-speaking world.

Hinestrosa was born in Pasto (capital of the department of Nariño) on 16 November 1914. Being isolated from Bogotá, the city of Pasto was by no means a cradle of concert pianists, especially since the import of these instruments was directed to the big urban centres of the national territory. Nonetheless, the establishment in town of different religious schools brought an interesting spectrum of artistic possibilities, ranging from the choral training that was so important for Roman Catholic services to individual lessons on musical instruments.

Her son's collection of family archives, including interview recordings of Hinestrosa herself, was key to the reconstruction of data for this research.[4] In a personal communication with Lucía Pérez, for example, the composer recounted the specific circumstances under which she used to practice with the only available piano at the school. She also pointed out the nuns' bias towards the genre of music she was expected to play:

> They gave me permission to practice on the school's piano during recess, but no popular music! The nuns were its enemies. You could not play the slightest tune because it was the biggest sin. So, I would seize the opportunity whenever the nuns were not around.[5]

Hinestrosa's fascination with popular music is evident in most of her creative output, as dance forms and folk references served as inspiration for the vast majority of her compositions. Her use of Colombian Andean rhythms, such as *pasillo* and *bambuco*, denotes a keen interest in traditional and local practices very much in line with nineteenth-century styles, where piano music was one of many vehicles to communicate nationalistic ideals. It is challenging to define 'musical nationalism' as a common current for all Latin American countries, given the diverse notions of composers who certainly did not share the same approach around it. Carlos Chávez's *indigenismo* and his frequent use of Aztec musical instruments in México, for example, differed significantly from Manuel María Ponce's preference for the Spanish guitar in the same country (an instrument that has been territorialised all over Latin America as a symbol of local music, regardless of its colonial roots). Considering the emancipation movements since the early nineteenth century and the resulting divisions between privileged parts of society and marginalised communities (especially those of indigenous and African descent), the whole concept of 'nation' in the region needs to be addressed carefully.

Figure 33.1 Maruja Hinestrosa (c. 1930).
Source: Photo: Private collection of Jaime Rosero Hinestrosa (reproduced with permission).

For the purpose of analysing Hinestrosa's music, the term will be understood here as a construction of a musical discourse that often integrates elements of local relevance, such as folk dances, popular rhythms, and patriotic messages, without leaving aside the influences of European heritage (an inevitable outcome of colonial history). The piano, for that matter, constitutes a clear representation of Western legacy in this region, and it stands out as one of the instruments with a vast nationalistic repertoire, derived from Latin-American folk dances. Hinestrosa is definitely not an isolated case in this regard, for many other women on the continent felt identified with this particular approach in their compositions. That is the case of Colombian composer Rosa Echeverría, who also wrote *pasillos* for the piano such as *El Canal* (c.1860–80), or Teresa Carreño (1853–1917) in Venezuela, whose inclusion of *valse criollo* and *merengue* patterns shaped a significant side of her compositional style.[6] Another close reference along these lines is Brazilian composer Francisca 'Chiquinha' Gonzaga (1847–1935), whose strong connection with traditional music led her to propose a pianistic approach to Brazilian *tangos, choros, waltzes, polkas,* and *maxixes,* among other rhythms that are regarded as symbols of national identity.[7]

Back to Hinestrosa: her compositional catalogue reveals a deep knowledge of Latin American genres beyond the Colombian Andean dances mentioned here, probably a consequence of the circulation of foreign records in Pasto, where *tangos, boleros,* and *rancheras* seem to have shaped her own construction of a regional (and not only national) musical identity. Table 33.1 outlines a full list of works this author has identified so far, next to their corresponding musical genres.

The predominance of popular music in Table 33.1 implies that Hinestrosa did not follow the nuns' expectations throughout her career as a composer. One might even wonder if writing her own music was part of those expectations at all, as opposed to sticking to piano performance, bearing in mind that the conservative society of early twentieth-century Pasto did not encourage the training of women as creative artists. In the same interview mentioned earlier, Hinestrosa recalled the first time her mother introduced her to Julio Zarama,

Table 33.1 List of Maruja Hinestrosa's Compositions[8]

Genre	Titles
Pasillos	*Cafetero* (1928–29), *Picardía, Gloria, Cochise* (1969), *Serenata colombiana* (1944), *Destellos, Yagarí* (1959), *El periquete, Nuevo amanecer* (1987), and *Sarita mía* (2001).
Waltzes	*Las tres de la mañana* (1944), *Suite Valle de Atriz, La flor de la montaña,* and *Dulce sueño* (1928–29).
Boleros	*Ciegamente, Alma mía, Eco lejano* (c. 1940), *Navegando* (c. 1940), *Cruel amargura, Vuélveme a querer,* and *Angustia.*
Bambucos	*La molienda* (1943), *El Ingenio,* and *El guarangal.*
Tangos	*Amigo mío* (c. 1935), *Nos dan las doce* (c. 1935), *Reproche,* (c. 1935) and *Vacío* (c. 1935).
Ballads	*Pobre de mí, Madre mía,* and *Todos llevamos una cruz* (c. 1960).
Chilean *cueca*	*Arroyito pampero* (c. 1970).
Ecuadorian *sanjuanito*	*Yaguarcocha.*
Son Cubano	*Lamento africano* (1976).
Ranchera	*Mi viejo guardián 'El Galeras'.*
Fantasias	*Fantasía sobre aires colombianos* (c. 1950), and *Fantasía española* (c. 1950).
Sacred music	*Ave María.*
Other genres	*La nazarena, Bosquejos húngaros, Saudades, Ensueño, Bandera azul, Idilio,* and *El recuerdo.*

a renowned local musician who apparently wanted to dissuade her from pursuing a career in composition:

> He hit me on the head with my sheet of music and told my mum: 'put her to learn sewing, arithmetic, grammar . . . *that* she could make use of. Music is not meant for women, but only for us, men'.[9]

Such a hostile environment against women composers explains the lack of visibility for their works, not only in the common knowledge of Colombian mainstream culture, but even within the histories of music that have so far been published in the country. A remarkable exception came out in 2012 at Pontificia Universidad Javeriana, where two editors and nine different authors gathered to publish the first specialised book on Colombian women and music, titled *Mujeres en la música en Colombia: el género de los géneros*.[10] The first half of that title can be easily translated as 'Women in Music in Colombia', but the second half deserves special attention.

The word *género* in Spanish means both 'gender' and 'genre', which brings us to the importance of addressing the topic from a Hispanic perspective. As stated by Millán and Quintana in the book's foreword, the publication sought to provide updated grounds for academic discussion in Spanish; considering that most works related to musicology, gender, and sexuality up until then had been published in English. The well-known contributions of Susan McClary (1991), Marcia J. Citron (1993), or Lucy Green (1997), for example, were quoted as some of the references that provided a strong foundation for Spanish-speaking scholars to initiate their own production around the turn of the twenty-first century. Hence, the relevance of Hispanic publications such as Pilar Ramos's *Feminismo y música: Introducción crítica* (2003), Gemma Salas's *Música y músicas* (2009), and, two years after the Colombian compilation mentioned, Luis Gabriel Mesa Martínez's monograph titled *Maruja Hinestrosa: la identidad nariñense a través de su piano* (2014).

The latter was presented as a tribute to Maruja Hinestrosa 100 years after her birth. It offered an alternative approach in Colombian musicology, not only due to the specific focus on one woman composer, but also because it aimed to decentralise the history of national music and composers from the capital, Bogotá. The concept of 'identity' was central in the analysis of her works, raising the following questions:

1. Was musical nationalism a relevant discourse for a woman who was born and raised in Pasto, a city known for its historical dissociation with republican politics (since colonial times) and for its cultural proximity to Ecuador?
2. Was the predominance of international genres in her catalogue a sign of Latin American pride as opposed to a search for a 'national' sound?
3. If that search for identity was, instead, part of an individual and introspective process, what was the role of her Roman Catholic faith in a music trajectory where she clearly rebelled against the original expectations behind her Franciscan upbringing?

It seems clear that Sister Bautista wanted a more 'classical' path for Hinestrosa's training, but the scope of that label is problematic from a Latin American point of view. The assumption that 'classical' music only derives from Western European paradigms has long been accepted in Colombian society and educational institutions, including the pedagogical curriculum of the National Conservatory in Bogotá at the time of its foundation in 1910.[11] Official music academies were not established in Pasto until the late 1930s, so Hinestrosa's school years developed in a period of Colombian history when the National Conservatory was still the dominant archetype for the entire country.

Colombian violinist Guillermo Uribe Holguín (1880–1971) became the first head of that institution after spending three years at the Schola Cantorum in Paris, where he studied composition under the instruction of Vincent d'Indy. Holguín's controversial statements about popular music led to frequent debates amongst national composers, which is part of the reason he is often remembered as an exponent of Eurocentrism in the history of Colombian music education. As a composer, however, it may seem contradictory that many of his works alluded to Colombian dances and local references, such as his *Sinfonía 2 'Del terruño'* (*Symphony 2 'From the Homeland'*, 1924), even though he clearly prioritised the use of French compositional techniques as a way to convey European paradigms within the construction of new Colombian music. The following statement was published by Uribe Holguín himself in the *Conservatory Review*:

> There are those who believe we already have a national art. They are mistaken, for they are confusing 'national' art with 'popular' art ... As a result of bad taste, often a product of ignorance, that art spreads surprisingly fast.[12]

As expressed by Ricardo Miranda and Aurelio Tello in *La música en Latinoamérica*,[13] nationalism represented a decisive aesthetic current in the region's configuration of twentieth-century music. Hinestrosa's choices also reflected that interest, considering that 14 out of the 45 compositions listed in Table 33.1 were based on Andean Colombian traditions – namely 10 *pasillos*, three *bambucos* and, of course, her *Fantasía sobre aires colombianos* (*Fantasia on Colombian Dances*). A tribute ceremony for the composer in her later years (held at the Teatro Colón of Bogotá in 1992) included a heartfelt speech in which she expressed sincere admiration for rural musicians. Unlike Uribe Holguín's position, her words suggested passion and respect for popular music:

> It is, for me, a source of pride and satisfaction to be receiving this tribute tonight, dedicated to my work. In reality, I do not deserve it. I am one of many music lovers, just like everyone else in Nariño. I receive this with pleasure on behalf of all musicians and composers, known and also unknown. We must look at the peasants from the countryside. There are so many unknown composers among them. I receive this on their behalf.[14]

Such statements reveal an interesting side of Hinestrosa's ideas about musical identity, where her individuality and introspection played an important role in her rising above the common prejudices against rural music at that time. She also defied mainstream Colombian musical nationalism by writing compositions inspired by Mexican, Argentinian, Chilean, Peruvian, Cuban, and even the neighbouring Ecuadorian traditions (considering that these were often frowned upon in the minds of nationalist composers in Pasto). One example is her song for voice and piano titled *Yaguarcocha*, meaning '*Lake of Blood*' in *Quechua* (the local indigenous language spoken in most of the territories that once belonged to the Inca Empire), where she set aside any Roman Catholic references and decided to speak rather from an emic perspective.

According to Hinestrosa herself, she wrote this music in the city of Quito, a few hours after interacting directly with indigenous people in the Ecuadorian province of Imbabura.[15] Although not a direct exponent of indigenous music, Hinestrosa's lyrics for this song make frequent references to the mystical relationship between nature and the *Caranqui* people amid pentatonic scales and *sanjuanito* style patterns. In other words, her knowledge of Ecuadorian musical elements is noteworthy, for she achieved an idiomatic construction that was consistent with the neighbouring country's traditions and thus challenged strict nationalism in musical terms:

Music Example 33.1   Transcription of the first stanza of Maruja Hinestrosa's *Yaguarcocha*.[16]

Yaguarcocha

In the lake of Yaguarcocha
when the sun sets in the afternoon
laments are heard amidst the waves.
Voices that moan,
voices that cry,
longing for the greatness
of the defeated race
that tinged the waters with its blood.

Introspection and Faith in Hinestrosa's Roman Catholicism

As a composer and pianist, Hinestrosa is mostly remembered in Colombia for her instrumental recitals, but she set at least 25 of her piano works to lyrics, thus offering alternative versions for solo voice and piano accompaniment that unfortunately are rarely performed. In 1965, she recorded a long-play album with 12 of her compositions at Sonolux Studios in Medellín, in which she included a miscellaneous selection of piano solo pieces ranging from Colombian *pasillos* to more international genres like waltzes, *boleros*, and a Spanish *fantasia*. The absence of her *tangos* is worth mentioning, considering the popularity they had achieved since the 1940s through the phonographic production of the Victor record company. The latter featured celebrated artists from Latin America such as Luis Valente, an Argentine singer who collaborated with Terig Tucci and his Orchestra to record Hinestrosa's tango *Amigo mío* (*My Friend*) in New York City.

Beyond its original roots in Uruguay and Argentina, tango was territorialised in Colombia as a consequence of strong phonographic circulation in the 1930s. Additionally, the death of iconic singer Carlos Gardel in Medellín (due to a plane accident in 1935) reinforced a collective sense of fascination towards the voices of *tango* that made it to Colombia and left a legacy for the local audience. As expressed by ethnomusicologist Carolina Santamaría, those voices in Colombia were exclusively represented by men in spite of the admiration for women artists in the tango scene of Argentina: 'Tango-song's (*sic.*) topics, and social venues where those songs were performed, were part of an exclusively male social realm that offered no room for reputable women'.[17]

The fact that only male singers recorded Hinestrosa's *tangos* could also derive from that bias against the participation of women in this genre. In a probable attempt to avoid social prejudices, it may be inferred that she chose to be cautious, considering that the instrumental versions of those *tangos* were also excluded from her own phonographic album. However, even more striking was her decision to adapt the lyrics of her *tango Reproche* to a male gender identity. The following transcription shows the melody for the last *stanza* of the piece, as found on the original music manuscript that is currently part of her son's private collection. Notice the male gender in the Spanish word for 'alone' in the very last verse; *solo*, as opposed to the feminine *sola*:

Music Example 33.2   Maruja Hinestrosa, *Reproche*, Final Stanza.[18]

Reproach

And you left me at the edge of the road
like a pariah abandoned by destiny,
with the longing for your love,
alone, very alone with my sorrow.

It has been stated that Hinestrosa's Roman Catholic upbringing set the foundation for her musical career, yet the nuns' preference for classical European styles did not stop her from pursuing a different path, where Latin-American popular music represented a main source of inspiration. As a composer who also wrote the lyrics for all of her vocal works – except for her *Ave Maria*[19] and the waltz *Dulce sueño* (1928–29) – Hinestrosa seems to have found in poetry a way to reconcile her faith with the musical genres for which she was passionate. Her *bolero Eco lejano* (*Distant Echo*, c. 1940), for example, makes particular mention of an episode from her youth when, during a mass service, she felt mesmerised by the image of a devoted young man who was praying on his knees at the church of Saint John the Baptist in Pasto. According to her own testimony, the scene inspired her to write a romantic or idealised *bolero* inspired by the whispering sounds of his prayers:[20]

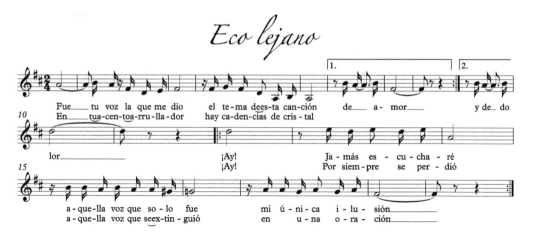

Music Example 33.3   Maruja Hinestrosa, *Eco lejano*.

Distant Echo

It was your voice that gave me
the theme for this love song.
In your irresistible accent
I hear cadences of crystal and of sorrow.
Oh! I will never hear that voice,
which was my only hope.
Oh! That voice was forever lost,
vanished inside a prayer.

Roman Catholic references are even more present in the lyrics of her ballads. In fact, the only recordings the author has identified so far feature the leading voice of Father Anselmo Caradonna, an Italian Capuchin priest who settled in Pasto in 1967, where he founded the Saint Francis of Assisi Institute.[21] The ballad *Todos llevamos una cruz* (*We All Have a Cross to Bear*), for example, begins with a clear hint of Christianity, even though the central theme of the song is, once again, an idealised notion of love, as suggested by the last two verses of the second stanza (see the translation following the music example):

Music Example 33.4   Maruja Hinestrosa, *Todos llevamos una cruz*.

We All Have a Cross to Bear

We all have a cross to bear along a Calvary,
we all feel the pain in our lives.
It is a commandment from the Lord to our fate.
His footsteps everyone will follow until the end.
And if only I could escape this martyrdom.
No. I would not want to see you ever again across my path.
And without you, my life without your love, I would feel immense joy and I would be happy,
but I was meant to love you so much, and this love will forever be my peace.

Along similar lines, the ballad *La madre mía* (*My Mother*) makes frequent allusions to Hinestrosa's Roman Catholicism, picturing the image of a daughter who longs for her mother as she remembers her childhood years with her: 'Your memory accompanies me in the vineyard of the Lord . . . I wish, dear mother, for the Lord to bless you under a new day's sun'.

Hinestrosa's setting of the *Ave Maria* is another composition that deserves special attention in relation to her faith.[22] It is a sacred piece for voice and piano that she dedicated to the Virgin of Las Lajas, certainly the most renowned architectural and religious symbol in the very south of Nariño. Unlike the other examples mentioned thus far, this work does not intend to articulate her faith and introspection through popular Latin-American music. On the contrary, it seems to fit into a category of Western art music, where the influence of European composers is evident, especially that of Franz Schubert, whose Lied *Ellens dritter Gesang* (1825) might have served as a direct reference.

The earliest references to the Sanctuary of Las Lajas date back to the eighteenth century, thanks to the chronicles of Juan de Santa Gertrudis (1759), a Spanish Franciscan friar who wrote about his travels through different regions of Colombia in a famous text known as *Maravillas de la naturaleza* (*Wonders of Nature*). Santa Gertrudis paid special attention to the cultural syncretism around this shrine, where indigenous people from the countryside of Nariño would often gather for Roman Catholic worship after hours or even days of pilgrimage. The temple represents a Marian apparition that, according to the local community, was first seen by an indigenous woman by the name of María Mueses in the eighteenth century. Her deaf daughter Rosa also witnessed the apparition and miraculously said to her mother: 'The *Mestiza* is calling me', hence the relevance of the sanctuary and its association with miraculous healing.[23] Hinestrosa's *Ave Maria* stands out as a tribute to the shrine, along the lines of other local composers like Luis Enrique Nieto (1898–1968), a close friend of hers who set the same Latin text to music in 1965 (the year the Second Ecumenical Council of the Vatican ended). However, references to this church are not limited to musical settings of the *Ave Maria*, for there are also many other composers in Nariño who dedicated a variety of sacred works to the Virgin of Las Lajas: Marceliano Márquez Díaz del Castillo (1864–1943), for example, wrote a hymn in her honour, while Teófilo Monedero (1895–1971) composed a whole symphony inspired by the shrine.[24]

The opening melodic contour of Hinestrosa's work resembles the beginning of the vocal line in Schubert's Lied, with subtle rhythmic differences. After a short piano introduction – written in sextuplet patterns in Schubert's case, but using a 6/8 time signature in Hinestrosa's – the singer introduces the first two words ('Ave Maria') with a lower neighbouring tone, followed by an ascending third skip and finally resolving downwards:

Figure 33.2 Sanctuary of Las Lajas. Roman Catholic Basilica church built on a cliff, overlooking the Guáitara River in the outskirts of Ipiales (Nariño).

Source: Photo: Fabio Martínez.

Music Example 33.5 Excerpt from Franz Schubert's *Ellens dritter Gesang*. Breitkopf & Härtel edition (1895).

Based on a poem by Walter Scott, *Ellens dritter Gesang* starts as an invocation to the Blessed Virgin Mary, followed by a text in German that Adam Storck translated from the English original.[25] Because of the opening words, the piece has been widely and mistakenly known as Schubert's *Ave Maria*, but despite its popularity as a musical setting to the traditional prayer, it was not initially intended as a sacred composition in Latin. Hinestrosa, by contrast, did choose the Roman Catholic Latin text and, unlike most of her works, she decided to leave aside any references to popular music, sticking to an arpeggiated piano accompaniment, under a delicate vocal line with a mostly syllabic treatment. Only one melismatic example is found over the word 'Iesus' ('Jesus'), where she uses a seven-note ornament as a cadential gesture (bars 26–27, see Music Example 33.7).

This syllabic approach was rather common in her vocal works, probably as an attempt to emphasise the importance of intelligibility. The original manuscript of the piece was found in the private collection of Jaime Rosero Hinestrosa, and it was first recorded for the accompanying disc to Mesa Martínez's book *Maruja Hinestrosa: la identidad nariñense a través de su piano* (2014). As part of the editing process – considering that the publication included 20 transcriptions of her works – this particular piece was not only examined by the author as a musicologist; it also drew upon the vocal guidance of Colombian soprano Carolina Plata.

Luis Gabriel Mesa Martínez

Ave María

Music Example 33.6   Excerpt from Maruja Hinestrosa's *Ave Maria*. Luis Gabriel Mesa Martínez's edition (2014).

Music Example 33.7   Bars 20–30 from Mesa Martínez's edition of Maruja Hinestrosa's *Ave Maria*.

Based on her singing experience, Plata suggested one slight modification between bars 21–22, where the term '*mulieribus*' (women) was originally treated as a four-syllable word, blending the sound of the vowels 'ie' as one unit, under the A-flat downbeat. Instead, Plata recommended not articulating that as a diphthong, but rather to separate the vowels (as can be seen in bar 22) in order to remain consistent with Latin prosody. This decision was also based on *The Correct Pronunciation of Latin According to Roman Usage*, where the *Ave Maria* text is used as an example for accurate syllable divisions. The source also suggests dividing the term '*mulieribus*' into five separate syllables (moo-lee-EH-ree-boos), confirming the stress on the 'e' sound alone.[26]

To sum up, Roman Catholic faith set a common ground for Hinestrosa's sacred and secular compositions, given her upbringing in a Franciscan school and the frequent references to Christianity in her interviews and songs, which suggest a strong sense of belonging to religious traditions. As a personal examination of her feelings, aspirations, and beliefs, vocal music represented a vehicle to project an introspective approach through her lyrics, supported by the romantic expressiveness of her accompaniment style. Not being a professional singer herself, the public circulation of her works often relied upon instrumental versions for solo piano (as can be appreciated in her 1965 album), but the finding of primary sources in Jaime Rosero Hinestrosa's collection was essential for this new understanding of her vocal repertoire.

Hinestrosa Beyond Borders

Having established a discussion around the national and religious ideas behind her music, it is important to recognise the international scope of her compositions that reached distant audiences beyond the Colombian borders, even if Hinestrosa's credit as a composer was not always acknowledged. Undoubtedly, the most recorded piece within her catalogue is *Cafetero* (*Coffee Picker*, 1928–29), an Andean *pasillo* that has been adapted to a wide variety of formats and for national festivals, as can be seen in the following table:

Table 33.2 Some National Recordings of Maruja Hinestrosa's *Cafetero*.[27]

Album Title	City	Record Company	Year of Release
The 'Shell' Album of Colombian Rhythms [10 LPs]	Bogotá	Shell	1957–1967
De mi terruño: Maruja Hinestrosa Piano Music [LP]	Medellín	Sonolux	1965
Jewels of Colombian Music, vol IX [LP]	Medellín	Sonolux	1985
To You, Colombia: Ten Years of the Hatoviejo Cotrafa Festival [CD]. Featuring Opus II Trío.	Medellín	Cotrafa	1996
From the Soul of Colombia [CD]	Medellín	Codiscos	1996
Symphonic Band of Nariño [CD]	Pasto	Fondo Mixto de Cultura de Nariño	1997
Music for the Peace of Colombia, vol II [CD].	Paipa	Bandas Ganadoras del Concurso Nacional de Paipa	1998
Colombian Concerts, vol II [CD]	Medellín	Entidad Universitaria Bellas Artes	1999
Entreverao, by Guafa Trío [CD]	Bogotá	Guafa Trío	2000

(*Continued*)

Table 33.2 (Continued)

Album Title	City	Record Company	Year of Release
The Best of Requinto Music, vol II [CD]	Bogotá	El Dorado	2001
XI 'Ruitoqueño' Festival of Colombian Music	Ruitoque	Festivalito Ruitoqueño	2001
The Sublime Music of Southern Colombia [CD]	Bogotá	Colmúsica	2002
Music Jewels of Colombian Song, nº 15 [CD]	Bogotá	Club Internacional Coleccionistas de Discos y Amigos de la Canción Popular	2003
Seresta II: Ancestral [CD]	Medellín	Guana Records	2002
'Mono Núñez' Festival, 2005 [CD]. Featuring: Gloria Belén Machado.	Cali	Funmúsica	2005
8º 'Cuyabrito de Oro' Festival [CD]	Armenia	Festival Nacional Infantil de Música Andina Colombiana Cuyabrito de Oro	2008
Maruja Hinestrosa: Nariño Identity Through Her Piano	Pasto	Little House Records	2014

Even beyond these Colombian albums, the composition has achieved international distribution since the first half of the twentieth century, thanks to a 78-rpm record from the Victor Company in New York, featuring Terig Tucci and his Colombian Typical Orchestra (catalogue nº 82176-A).[28] This could explain the presence of other songs based on the musical material of Hinestrosa's *Cafetero* in other Latin-American countries. This author's research provided evidence of the existence of a Costa Rican version with lyrics by Adán Guevara Centeno (1913–1980), over the same music she had originally written for this piano piece. The sources behind this new finding were examined as part of the author's fieldwork in San José and in the province of Guanacaste (2016), as a result of an academic collaboration between the University of Costa Rica and the Pontificia Universidad Javeriana (Colombia). The aim of the research was to understand the historical reasons behind the use of Hinestrosa's music in Central America, considering that Costa Ricans traditionally attributed the full credit of this composition to Adán Guevara, as opposed to the lyrics only.

An interview with Gerardo Duarte, Professor of Piano at the University of Costa Rica, brought to light interesting data related to the misconception around this piece's origin. His father, marimba player Ulpiano Duarte (1929–2015), was one of the musicians who used to collaborate with Adán Guevara. According to this testimony, Guevara never attributed the musical creation to himself, but the popularity of his vocal version in Costa Rica apparently perpetuated the idea that he was the original composer. What is most striking about this music correspondence is the fact that Guevara's version was titled *El hombre macho* (*The Macho Man*, c. 1953):

> I remember that my dad and Adán Guevara played and offered serenades together. Within their songs, *El hombre macho* always stood out as one of the most popular. I remember they both used to refer to the song as a Colombian *pasillo*, and I never heard Adán attributing the composition to himself. It was rather the people who constantly requested it as 'Adán's song', much in the line of other pieces that gain popularity due to their performers, more so than their composers.[29]

The earliest references to Hinestrosa's *Cafetero* date back to 1933 in Colombia, as can be corroborated in the 48th issue of *Ilustración nariñense*, a local journal where the piece was mentioned that year, as part of a composition contest. As for the Costa Rican version, the sources this author found during fieldwork dated back as far as 1953, which could suggest that Adán Guevara used the pre-existing instrumental material and then added lyrics to it.[30] By not giving credit to the composer (perhaps not deliberately), it should be noted that the original work of a woman was turned into a representation of patriarchal culture, as is evident in Guevara's lyrics:

The Macho Man (excerpt)

I am a real macho man
I bathe in my own sweat, while I work
I share my friendship with my mates
and for a woman I have love.

I am a gentleman
with my axe and my machete.
I work in the field and drive the cattle
and no other man can ever bring me down.

The fact that a piece originally written by a woman turned into a macho-themed popular song comes as a paradox, especially when feminine stereotypes have been historically used as an excuse to assume that women's compositions supposedly sound more delicate than men's. Hinestrosa's virtuosic decisions in the melodic phrases of *Cafetero*, as well as its rapid tempo when performed in its original version, are good examples of a demanding piano technique that is ironically absent in Guevara's song version (where the whole emphasis relies on the lyrics, while the tempo is significantly reduced for vocal articulation purposes).

On the other hand, this foreign adaptation of Hinestrosa's music in Costa Rica is not an isolated example of the piece's international relevance. *Cafetero* was also part of the national repertoire which a whole generation of Colombians identified with in the twentieth century, given the increasing recognition of Colombian coffee abroad (especially since the establishment of the National Federation of Coffee Growers in 1927). In fact, Hinestrosa deliberately named her first composition *Cafetero* when she premiered the piece in the 1930s, during a conference-opening event of this federation in the city of Pasto.[31] Years later, *Cafetero* was often reproduced on different radio stations from the coffee-growing regions of Colombia, and its popularity even reached and touched some of the local soldiers who were recruited to fight in the Korean War in the 1950s.[32] This is how the composer recalled an encounter with one of them during an interview with Lucía Pérez:

The military reservist who came here was eager to find out where the composer lived. They told him she was a woman, but nobody knew where she was or where she came from. When they confirmed that I was from Nariño, he came here and met me. What a joy that young man felt! And so did I. According to him, when they listened to this *pasillo*, they wielded the weapon and were not afraid to die, as they thought of Colombia.[33]

It is undeniable, in other words, that this composition crossed borders and disseminated a glimpse of Colombian music in distant parts of the world, despite the lack of recognition around Hinestrosa's name and artistic credit.

Conclusion

It is evident that Maruja Hinestrosa stood out as a woman who confronted social boundaries in Colombia in a permanent attempt to consolidate an artistic career. Moving on from the publication of the author's book in 2014, this research has examined her music from complementary perspectives, drawing attention to her role as a composer and pianist amid musical nationalism and gender discrimination in the country. This chapter, however, offers a deeper reflection around her Roman Catholic upbringing, as well as the significance of faith and introspection in her vocal works. Beyond her classical training and regardless of the Eurocentric discourses in the history of Colombian music education, it seems clear that Hinestrosa found an authentic voice as a result of her fascination with popular music and the messages conveyed in her own poetry.

New academic developments in musicology and ethnomusicology have unveiled the role of different women in the music of Colombia, including the compositions of Mercedes Párraga de Quijano (1825–54), Teresa Tanco Cordovez (1864–1945), and Josefina Acosta (b. 1897) in the capital city of Bogotá.[34] But Hinestrosa's case is not simply a matter of gender. It also highlights the necessity of reconsidering and hence rewriting a history that has concentrated, almost exclusively, on artistic production in major cities. Coming from an isolated region in the south of the country, Maruja Hinestrosa is here presented as an example of those voices that are rarely featured as musical exponents of international acclaim, but whose legacy must be brought to light as part of an effort to reroute conventional approaches in the history of music.

Notes

1. Date of composition unknown.
2. Luis Gabriel Mesa Martínez, *Maruja Hinestrosa: la identidad nariñense a través de su piano* (Pasto: Fondo Mixto de Cultura de Nariño, 2014).
3. Luis Gabriel Mesa Martínez (musicologist/producer) and Beltrán Maldonado, Luis Fernando (film director), *Maruja Hinestrosa: Fantasía sobre aires colombianos*. Documentary Film (Bogotá: Pontificia Universidad Javeriana, Centro Ático & Audioconcepto Estudios, 2019). The full documentary can be accessed online on the author's YouTube channel: www.youtube.com/watch?v=ikPhrSHGlpQ&t=2s
4. Most interviews, records, and music manuscripts were provided by Jaime Rosero Hinestrosa.
5. Interview between Lucía Pérez and Maruja Hinestrosa in the city of Pasto (2000). The recording of this conversation remains in the private collection of Jaime Rosero Hinestrosa. Unless otherwise specified, all translations from the original Spanish are by the author.
6. For further details about these features in Teresa Carreño's piano music, see: Juan Francisco Sans, "Teresa Carreño: una excepcional compositora venezolana del siglo XIX," *Revista de investigación* 34, no. 69 (Caracas: Universidad Central de Venezuela).
7. The 'Chiquinha Gonzaga' Digital Archive includes complete editions of her sheet music, which can be accessed at https://chiquinhagonzaga.com/acervo/.
8. Dates are unknown for those compositions that do not specify a chronological reference.
9. Lucía Pérez, personal communication/interview with Maruja Hinestrosa (2000).
10. Carmen Millán and Alejandra Quintana, eds., *Mujeres en la música en Colombia: el género de los géneros* (Bogotá: Pontificia Universidad Javeriana, 2012).
11. Ellie Anne Duque, "El estudio de la música: instituciones musicales," in *Historia de la música en Santafé y Bogotá 1538–1938*, edited by Egberto Bermúdez (Bogotá: Alcaldía Mayor de Bogotá, 2000), 139.
12. Guillermo Uribe Holguín, "Triunfaremos," *Revista del Conservatorio* 1, no. 3 (1911): 33–34.
13. Ricardo Miranda and Aurelio Tello, *La música en Latinoamérica* (México: Secretaría de Relaciones Exteriores, 2011), 145.
14. The full speech and part of the recital were broadcast on national television on March 27, 1993. One copy of the recording can be found at the Centre for Music Documentation of the National Library, Bogotá.

15. Information based on an interview to Maruja Hinestrosa by Patricia Gaviria, held in Pasto (undated). The original recording belongs to the composer's son, Jaime Rosero Hinestrosa.
16. All transcriptions were made by the author. This transcription is based on two phonographic archives belonging to Jaime Rosero Hinestrosa: one including the composer's solo piano performance and the other featuring her own voice, singing the lyrics *a cappella*.
17. Carolina Santamaría, "Tango's Reterritorialization in Medellín: Gardel's Myth and the Construction of a Tanguero Local Indentity," *Musical Quarterly* 92, no. 3–4 (2009): 195.
18. This and all following transcriptions of her music are based on original manuscripts and tape recordings belonging to the private collection of Jaime Rosero Hinestrosa (reproduced with permission).
19. Date of composition unknown.
20. Based on a personal communication between Maruja Hinestrosa and Cecilia Martínez, held in Pasto in 1987.
21. Based on the official website of the institute, accessed February 11, 2021, https://isfapasto.edu.co/fundador/.
22. Date of composition unknown.
23. Michael Taussig, *Shamanism, Colonialism and the Wild Man: A Study in Terror and Healing* (Chicago, IL: The University of Chicago Press, 1987), 204.
24. José Menandro Bastidas España, *Compositores nariñenses de la zona andina*, vol. 1 (Pasto: Universidad de Nariño, 2014), 108.
25. Yun Sun Song, "Liszt, Thalberg, Heller, and the Practice of Nineteenth-Century Song Arrangement" (Doctoral thesis, University of Cincinnati, 2011), 12.
26. Nicola Montani, ed., *The Correct Pronunciation of Latin According to Roman Usage* (Philadelphia: St. Gregory Guild, 1937), 44.
27. The album titles in this table have been translated from the Spanish originals.
28. The copy used for this research is also part of Jaime Rosero Hinestrosa's private collection.
29. Interview between Luis Gabriel Mesa Martínez and Gerardo Duarte, held in San José, Costa Rica (2016).
30. A comparative analysis between the two versions can be found in Mesa Martínez's article (in Spanish) 'From *Cafetero*, by Maruja Hinestrosa, to *Hombre Macho*, by Adán Guevara: Gender and Transnationalism Between Costa Rica and Colombia," *Cuadernos de música, artes visuales y artes escénicas* 13, no. 2 (Bogotá: Pontificia Universidad Javeriana, 2018): 123–45, https://doi.org/10.11144/javeriana.mavae13-2.dcdm.
31. More details about the importance of Hinestrosa's *Cafetero* as a national symbol can be found in: Luis Gabriel Mesa Martínez, "Del *Cafetero*, de Maruja Hinestrosa, al *Hombre macho*, de Adán Guevara: género y transnacionalidad entre Colombia y Costa Rica," *Cuadernos de música, artes visuales y artes escénicas* 13, no. 2 (Bogotá: Pontificia Universidad Javeriana, 2018): 123–45.
32. Colombia and Puerto Rico (the latter as part of the USA) were the only Latin American nations to send military units to the Korean War. The Colombian Battalion was the first from the country to serve in Asia in an attempt to build up relations between Colombia and the United States during Laureano Gómez's presidential period (1950–53).
33. Lucía Pérez, personal communication/interview with Maruja Hinestrosa (2000).
34. Beyond the capital, it is worth mentioning the recent findings around Rosa Echeverría, a nineteenth-century composer from Santa Marta (Caribbean region of Colombia). Although her lifetime dates have not been identified, some of her compositions have been digitised by a group of scholars who published the results of their research on the following website: www.coleccionistasdesonidos.com. Drs. Juana Monsalve, Daniel Castro Pantoja, Juan Fernando Velásquez, and Rondy Torres have worked as a team to bring these resources to light, as a contribution to musicological studies in Colombia, with a clear gender approach.

Bibliography

Bastidas España, José Menandro. *Compositores nariñenses de la zona andina*, Vol. 1. Pasto: Universidad de Nariño, 2014.

Bermúdez, Egberto. *Historia de la música en Santafé y Bogotá 1538–1938*. Bogotá: Alcaldía Mayor de Bogotá, 2000.

Citron, Marcia J. *Gender and the Musical Canon*. New York: Cambridge University Press, 1993.

De Santa Gertrudis, Fray Juan. *Maravillas de la naturaleza*, I-III. Bogota: Biblioteca Luis Ángel Arango, 1759 [1956].

Delgado, Rafael, ed. *Ilustración Nariñense*, IV Series, No. 48. Pasto: Imprenta del Departamento, 1993.
Duque, Ellie Anne. "El estudio de la música: instituciones musicales." In *Historia de la música en Santafé y Bogotá 1538–1938*, edited by Egberto Bermúdez, 125–48. Bogotá: Alcaldía Mayor de Bogotá, 2000.
Green, Lucy. *Music, Gender, Education*. New York: Cambridge University Press, 1997.
McClary, Susan. *Feminine Endings. Music, Gender and Sexuality*. Minneapolis: University of Minnesota Press, 1991.
Mesa Martínez, Luis Gabriel. *Maruja Hinestrosa: la identidad nariñense a través de su piano*. Pasto: Fondo Mixto de Cultura de Nariño, 2014.
_____. "Del *Cafetero*, de Maruja Hinestrosa, al *Hombre macho*, de Adán Guevara: género y transnacionalidad entre Colombia y Costa Rica." *Cuadernos de música, artes visuales y artes escénicas* 13, no. 2 (2018): 123–45. https://doi.org/10.11144/javeriana.mavae13-2.dcdm.
Millán, Carmen, and Alejandra Quintana, eds. *Mujeres en la música en Colombia: el género de los géneros*. Bogotá: Pontificia Universidad Javeriana, 2012.
Miranda, Ricardo, and Aurelio Tello. *La música en Latinoamérica*. México: Secretaría de Relaciones Exteriores, 2011.
Montani, Nicola, ed. *The Correct Pronunciation of Latin According to Roman Usage*. Philadelphia: St. Gregory Guild, 1937.
Ramos, Pilar. *Feminismo y música. Introducción crítica*. Madrid: Narcea, 2003.
Salas, Gemma. *Música y músicas*. Gijón: Consejería de Educación y Ciencia, 2009.
Sans, Juan Francisco. "Teresa Carreño: una excepcional compositora venezolana del siglo XIX." *Revista de investigación* 34, no. 69. (Caracas: Universidad Central de Venezuela). 2010.
Santamaría, Carolina. "Tango's Reterritorialization in Medellín: Gardel's Myth and the Construction of a Tanguero Local Identify." *Musical Quarterly* 92, no. 3–4 (2009): 177–209. https://doi.org/10.1093/musqtl/gdp018.
Schubert, Franz. *Ellens Dritter Gesang III*, Op. 56 n° 2. Leipzig: Breitkopf & Härtel, 1825 [1895].
Song, Yun Sun. "Liszt, Thalberg, Heller, and the Practice of Nineteenth-Century Song Arrangement." Doctoral thesis, University of Cincinnati, 2011.
Taussig, Michael. *Shamanism, Colonialism and the Wild Man: A Study in Terror and Healing*, 204. Chicago, IL: The University of Chicago Press, 1987.
Uribe Holguín, Guillermo. "Triunfaremos." *Revista del Conservatorio* 1, no. 3 (1911): 33–34.

Discography

Mesa Martínez, Luis Gabriel. *Maruja Hinestrosa: la identidad nariñense a través de su piano*. Compact Disc (Pasto: Fondo Mixto de Cultura de Nariño, 2014). https://open.spotify.com/album/3JClvXmqBxLsSaFaRYRZrm?si=MOe7ycmaQ0OOz9fx0prxqw.

Filmography

Mesa Martínez, Luis Gabriel (musicologist/producer) and Beltrán Maldonado, Luis Fernando (film director). *Maruja Hinestrosa: Fantasía sobre aires colombianos*. Documentary Film (Bogotá: Pontificia Universidad Javeriana, Centro Ático & Audioconcepto Estudios, 2019). www.youtube.com/watch?v=ikPhrSHGlpQ&t=2s.

Other Online Resources

Juana Monsalve, Daniel Castro, Juan Fernando Velásquez, and Rondy Torres. *Coleccionistas de sonidos. Siglo XIX: el álbum musical de Ana Cristina Echeverría* (2021) [Exposición digital]. www.coleccionistasdesonidos.com

34
UNDOING SANCTITY
Imee Ooi's Popular Contemporary Buddhist Music

Fung Ying Loo and Fung Chiat Loo

At a curtain call of a typical Buddhist live musical production in Kuala Lumpur, Malaysia, it is common to see Buddhist composer Imee Ooi (b.1964) appear onstage to thank her audience and patrons. She performs this act in a gentle, serene manner, with her palms together in front of her chest in the typical *Namaskara Mudra* hand gesture seen in a Buddhist greeting or prayer. Accordingly, this is always met with another wave of applause. Our experience of Ooi's Buddhist musical theatre productions began in the early 2000s. We watched the first Broadway-styled musical theatre based on a Buddhist theme, presented in a very different realm to the religious and musical endeavours to those we had experienced in the past. The presence of nuns and monks at a concert hall was unlike other concerts that we had attended, and an entire musical journey based on a religious theme crafted in a contemporary musical style left us with a different feeling of *dharma* appreciation.[1] Further research led us to understand its contemporaneousness as a form of religious cultivation in the Mahayana tradition that is very different from the Theravadin context which was taught to us by our parents.[2]

It has been two decades since Ooi – who founded IMM Music Works in 1997 – emerged as a familiar name among the Malaysian Buddhist community, as well as the virtual global Buddhist community. She has written and produced over fifty-five albums and seven musical theatre productions and was nominated and accepted as a Fellow of the United Kingdom's Royal Society of Arts in 2020. This chapter aims to discuss Ooi's 'soft leadership' in the secularisation of popular contemporary Buddhist music. Her works include songs and music based on Buddhist *dharma*, with lyrics mainly based on *sutra* (Buddhist scriptures) and *mantra* (short phrases for continuous repetition); moreover, she has written original books for musicals. We discuss her use of popular contemporary musical styles in her compositions consisting of Buddhist *dharma* intertwined with popular culture, reflecting what scholars Courtney Wilder and Jeremy Rehwaldt explain as a 'bidirectional relationship' in their study of contemporary Christian music.[3] In addition, Ooi's transmission of Buddhist *dharma* portrays a form of soft leadership, and her career in Buddhist music writing reflects the ancient Chinese philosophy of *wuwei* as will be discussed further. The Chinese word *wuwei*, translated as 'no action', is a philosophy of Daoism as stated by Lao Zi.[4] We found it intriguing to look at her devoted contemporary Buddhist music-writing journey, which shows elements of leadership characteristics that transcend those of the servant. It is a transformative and indirect type of leadership, thus relating to the concept of soft leadership.

Sound of Wisdom

It may not be a coincidence that Ooi's first name, Hui Yin (慧音), is translated as 'wisdom' and 'sound' in Chinese; hence, her world concert tour that began its journey in 2015 was titled *Sound of Wisdom: World Tour Dharma Concert* (淨世慧音). Upon her decision to carry out a journey in Buddhist music writing, Ooi adopted the English Romanisation of the Chinese dialect Hokkien pronunciation of *'Imm'* to subsequently name her production house IMM, thus following her English name Imee, which has the same sound as the Romanised Chinese 音 or *yin*. Teaching has always been a part of Ooi's life, as she started out in 1995 as a piano teacher and music lecturer at the Ocean Institute of Audio Technology in Malaysia. She has always been passionate about writing music, and has sent her works to local television drama productions and commercials. However, the fact that the Chinese popular music industry holds a minority market in the Malay-dominated country has created many challenges in pursuing a path in composition. Thus, Ooi did not initially pursue a career as a composer; she turned to education.

During an interview with BuddhaZine TV in 2016 as part of her *Sound of Wisdom* concert tour in Indonesia, the composer described her initial involvement with writing Buddhist music as 'unexpected'. Ooi met Ho Ling Huay, the artistic director of her Buddhist musical productions, when Ho was still a student at the Ocean Institute. Ho brought Ooi a particular chant and asked if she could write music based on it for dissemination purposes. Ooi, who grew up attending church with friends and relatives, had found gospel music to be especially beautiful, and she had always wondered about the absence of such music in her own religion. Therefore, she immediately agreed with Ho's suggestion.[5] This was her first step on her career path as a contemporary Buddhist music composer, with elements of influence from the Jesus People Movement from the West.

In the West, gospel music with lyrics based on the Trinity was originally rejected but then gained popularity during the 1920s.[6] Moreover, in the 1960s and 1970s, the Jesus People Movement – a transformation involving traditional Evangelical practices along with pop and rock music and hippie fashion, posters, and bumper stickers – immersed religion in the youth and popular cultures of the time.[7] By the 1970s, contemporary Christian music was developed into pop-rock, folk or country, pop music inspired by African American gospel music, and musicals.[8] In terms of the label of 'Buddhist music', the notion of singing-recitation (*changnian*) in *fanbai* (monastic chant) as 'music' was strongly rejected within the monastic tradition.[9] Notably, the absence of music from the Ten Precepts of Buddhism has been apparent. However, ethnomusicologist Paul Greene relates the 'music-like' characters experienced in Buddhist chanting as a 'sonic praxis' delivering 'pattern sounds'. More importantly, the chanting's contrasting pitches and rhythmic patterns, melodic contours, and sounds from the bells and gongs help in memorising the chants and facilitate group chanting.[10] Thus, music is a component in chanting; nevertheless, the function of the musical elements during chanting differs in terms of context and tradition. Furthermore, ethnomusicologist Chen Pi-Yen explains that the term 'music' is gradually becoming accepted within the Chinese Buddhist community. It brings *fanbai* and music with differing referential codes to the contemporary Buddhist community, with the former as a form of tradition with its liturgical function, and the latter related to modernity and society in the form of a song, usually in popular music style.

Apart from the discourse of chanting as 'music', the creation of a new Chinese Buddhist music movement did not begin with a significant link to popular culture. Chen explains that the Chinese contemporary Buddhist music movement began with Buddhist monk Hong Yi (1880–1942), who composed Chinese Buddhist devotional songs based on new lyrics with borrowed Western themes, such as from Beethoven or William Shakespeare plays. The devotional songs reflected Christian hymns and Western art songs of the Evangelical tradition.[11] In the Asian perception, Western music has long been seen as a symbol of modernity, with the adapted Western themes reflecting contemporary culture. Apart from chanting (*fanbai*) and devotional songs, the third type of commercial Chinese Buddhist music emerged during the 1980s. Originating in Taiwan, this style of music was marketed by recording companies as a commodity which included more popular musical styles, such as pop and rock. Yet some productions like Taiwan's electronic dance music *Rock Mantra* created controversy and were banned by some Buddhist associations.[12]

When Ooi started to write contemporary Buddhist music, her works presented a musical style that differs from that of Hong Yi's devotional songs, gospel music, or the commercial pop and rock Buddhist music that stemmed from the Jesus People Movement. Although Ooi embraced gospel music, her large collection of music based on the Buddhist *sutra*, *mantra*, and *dhāraṇī* (a longer form of *mantra*) in Sanskrit, Pali, and Tibetan does not reflect that, nor that of the easy listening Christian 'praise' and 'worship' music in a common language that features a pop and rock beat. Her early works that received instant recognition include the *Prajñāpāramitāhṛdaya Sūtram* (*Heart Sutra*) in Sanskrit and Chinese; *The Chant of Metta* in Pali; *Nīlakaṇṭha Dhāraṇī* in different languages including Sanskrit and Mandarin; and *Oṃ Oṃ Maṇi Padme Hūṃ* in Sanskrit – all of which still remain popular. A smaller number of works that are not influenced by chants are Mandarin devotional songs based on new lyrics, such as *Morning Prayer* (晨祷) and songs written for her musical theatre works.

The first impression of listening to Ooi's recomposed Buddhist chants recalls a revival of ambient music and Steven Halpern's new-age music of the 1970s and 1980s in the context of chanting. Whether it is the short six-syllable *mantra*, *Oṃ Maṇi Padme Hūṃ*, or the longer *Nīlakaṇṭha Dhāraṇī*, the music evokes a hypnotic and meditative ambience, as expressed by virtual communities on music-sharing channels. In the comment sections of her music posts, regular descriptions such as 'peace' and 'beautiful' and special compliments directed towards Ooi's voice are common entries. In an interview with local media, Ooi explained the reception of her music as 'people are keen to listen to this type of music because it is a healing medium, and they are able to use it for daily meditation, for yoga, and relaxation'.[13] Particularly noticeable was Ooi's own voice in her albums, one that reflects the composer's many years of writing, practising, and recording her own compositions, including the backup vocals. Her voice is also a light alto that exudes innocence and simplicity. The chants and songs are always nonchalantly performed by Ooi without any signs of conservatory training or virtuosic display, just pure heartfelt chanting as a Buddhist practitioner.

Dharma Mediated Through Contemporary Buddhist Music

In the last two decades, new composers and works of musical theatre – including singing activities and competitions based on devotional songs and commercial Buddhist music – have increased in Malaysia.[14] Much of this expansion was a result of Ooi's innovative role as she bridged music, popular culture, and Buddhist *dharma*. Ooi's concept in her compositions is an integration of nature, peace, and the principles of 'purity'. Her music reflects past popular Western culture that leads to an adaptive global familiarity and positive reception, and one that becomes a tool of 'soft power' under her leadership. When it comes to traditional leadership, most theories focus on leaders of organisations and direct leadership. The case of Ooi and her huge number of works dedicated to Buddhism may appear to some followers as relating to her leadership trait regarding the notion of the 'great man' or 'great woman' theory.

However, we find that to describe Ooi and her works – in the context of women, leadership, and religion – reveals an interesting complexity of leadership discourse that does not espouse one single theory.

The musical journey and interactions between Ooi and her followers reflect a contingent and complex spectrum of servant, transformative, indirect, and soft leadership. Moreover, there is an intersectionality of gender in the context of popular music and popular culture that further depicts her artistic position and her fans in the realm of Buddhism. As Ooi's leadership is mediated through contemporary Buddhist music, we see her music as a form of soft power, although the word 'power' may be antithetical within the Buddhist context. However, as Frank McGlynn and Arthur Tuden explain, 'power is immanent in human affairs' and studies in political science and anthropology conclude that power is a form of possession and one that causes changes in a social and cultural setting.[15] In Ooi's leadership, it is the soft power that we observed from her music which is apparent in her leadership in the transmission of Buddhist *dharma*; notably, it is what forms the complexity of her leadership patterns. Furthermore, this complexity draws on the fact that Ooi's popular contemporary Buddhist music is consumed by both physical and virtual Buddhist communities, revealing a bidirectional relationship between sacred and popular culture, from the level of *poiesis* to *esthesis*, by undoing sanctity and asceticism.

Ooi began with a typical servant leadership trait, defined by Greenleaf as one that 'begins with the natural feeling that one wants to serve, to serve first. Then conscious choice brings one to aspire to lead'.[16] When Ooi was first asked to transform a Buddhist chant into a contemporary song, it became her first *karmic fate* that evoked a journey to devote her life to contemporary Buddhist music writing. As an aspiring composer who met challenges to selling her music to the commercial industry, Ooi worked as a teacher until the first request to write a Buddhist chant came her way. Her path towards success as a contemporary Buddhist music composer reflects an unexpected leadership that reminds us of the ancient Chinese philosophy of *wuwei*, as Jack Barbalet explains:

> *Wuwei* as action cannot be described principally in terms of the actor's intentions or capacities but in terms of the thing acted upon and the processes to which it is subjected: synchronicity through action as *wuwei* replaces the notion of causality in power.[17]

The ancient Chinese philosophy from Lao Zi's *Daode jing* (400 BCE) is notably paradoxical with theories that stemmed from the basics of the *yin* and *yang* dichotomy, reflecting the causal relationship between the two oppositions where an extremity of *yin* (inactivity) will eventually lead to the beginning of *yang* (activity). Ooi's determination and effort in writing contemporary Buddhist music that eventually led to a full-time career today may be more precisely reflected in Herrlee Glessner Creel's description of a 'purposive *wuwei*' that depicts a more conscious way of effortless action in order to gain control and power.[18] Ooi did not force an intended profession nor an intention to lead but instead took a natural course to 'serve' following the requests from others to write and transform Buddhist chants as contemporary songs; thus she naturally excelled in musical composition.

Ooi's determination to devote her life to Buddhist music writing is a *karma* of her departure from the commercial music industry, one that can be likened to the traditional Chinese expression of leaving the 'red dust'.[19] In Chinese tradition, 'red dust' is a symbolic representation of the world of sensual pleasure, inextricably bound up with the pursuit of money, social hierarchy, and modernity that leads to a constant fluctuation between happiness and disappointment. The word first appeared in the Eastern Han Dynasty poet Ban Gu's (AD 32–92)

Western Capital Rhapsody in praise of the flourishing city of Chang'an. During our interview with the composer, there was a recurrent emphasis on the phrase 'to serve others' every time we discussed her productions and music-making experiences. To Ooi, her years of engagement in composing contemporary Buddhist music led her to a heightened level of motivation to help others, but not as one that solely furnished her own individual needs and cultivation. Her principles closely reflect the Mahayana tradition that opposes the self-cultivation theories of the Theravadins. Similarly, when it comes to her role as a producer and music director for her concerts and musicals, instead of being served, she believes in positioning herself as a role model and to serve her production crews with solutions to rectify problems while empowering them to succeed in their jobs.[20]

Along with direct human interaction, the large corpus of Ooi's works serve as a 'musical' version of the ancient practice of *chaojing* (抄经) or *sutra* copying. Unlike devotional songs or praise songs written with new lyrics, Ooi's works focuses on 'copies' of Buddhist chants repackaged in new music with new melodies. *Sutra* copying resembling sacred calligraphy began in China when the *Siddham* scripts were brought into the country.[21] A typical Mahayana tradition that considers new ideas for the aim of self-cultivation and as a tool to spread Buddhism, *sutra* copying transformed the orally transmitted religion into text form to reach out to many.[22] Tedious efforts in the ancient calligraphy of *sutra* copying are transformed in Ooi's arduous and painstaking efforts in composing, music programming, and recording of both solo and backup vocals, as the new contemporary songs are based on *sutra*, *dharani*, and *mantra*. Thus, Ooi re-transformed these chants back into an aural tradition in popular music style. The act of realising these works becomes Ooi's commitment 'to serve', serving the religious transmission of *dharma* to the world through media, and she has hitherto been in a never-ending pilgrimage of musically driven *nirvana* and commission of *dharma* transmission. More importantly, Ooi has committed to a regeneration of Mahayana practice and *sutra* copying via contemporary Buddhist music, and has been perpetually developing Hong Yi's contributions as a new musical practice of Buddhism.

Ooi has always had a propensity to serve and lives with a principle of simplicity that abides with that of the *dharma*. During an interview with Death Café, when Ooi was asked if she has a particular work ritual, such as a chant recitation or putting her phone away, the composer replied that there is none. However, she stressed the practicality of keeping her phone close in the case of an emergency involving family members or her fans. She recalled a past experience of receiving a text message requesting music to be sent to a dying grandparent.[23] Thus, the phenomenon of Ooi committing to requests to compose or to deliver Buddhist chants as music for her listeners or followers reflects what Sun describes as a paradoxical hierarchical relationship of 'servant' and 'leader' that differs to other forms of leadership, as the major focus of servant leadership is to serve the needs of others.[24]

Conversely, in the era of new media and commercial popular music, Ooi's principles as a contemporary Buddhist music composer reveal a thin line between the two contradictions that fluctuate between that of servant leadership and soft leadership.[25] We see that the latter has a concomitant indirect and transformational leadership trait – which we witnessed in Ooi's musical endeavour – that led to a major transformation of the contemporary Buddhist music genre mediated through social media platforms.[26] The relationship between her works and her community, which embraces chants in the form of contemporary Buddhist music as listeners or fans, reveals a contextual interpolation of religion and commercialised pop music. This includes morphed leadership traits from that of servant leadership, to indirect and transformative leadership, and finally to soft leadership, as what we believe is the best way to describe Ooi and her followers.

In the tradition of Buddhist chanting, there is an absence of notation due to the philosophy of Chinese Buddhism that believes that the mind is constantly changing,[27] reflecting principals from the *I Ching* and Taoism. However, it is not uncommon to find fixed-melody chants apart from free chants in the course of oral transmission and the former allowed uniformity among chanters.[28] Still, repetition is discouraged and thus a tune or melody that came from any individual contributes to each iteration of chants without a fixed melody. Despite this, the act of *sutra* copying regarding Ooi was transformed and mediated through contemporary popular 'songs' as fixed-melody chants and social media. Accordingly, the presence of a community of listeners realises this transformation. Specifically, transformation and an aim to establish contemporary Buddhist music as a mainstream musical genre has been Ooi's vision in her career path along with her religious practice. Francis J. Yammarino addressed the lack of studies on indirect leadership in transformative leadership that focus on the absence of physical proximity. Via 'leadership at a distance' through intermediaries such as mass media, apart from iconic leaders like Winston Churchill and Mahatma Gandhi,[29] the positive reception witnessed on the global social media platform of Ooi's alternative *sutra* copying approach in the form of popular music may be an ideal example of this leadership trait. Through music-sharing platforms, her listeners, who are mostly unknown to her, form a virtual community of Buddhist devotees and non-Buddhist ones who embrace her form of Buddhist chant recitation as contemporary Buddhist music or meditation music. It eventually has led to 'fandom' and depicts a synergy of transformational and indirect leadership.

Ooi's relationship with her listeners echoes the following three (out of four) leadership traits identified by Bernard M. Bass:[30] charisma, motivational inspiration, and intellectual stimulation, and substituting 'individualised consideration' with 'indirectness', as in the virtual space. Nevertheless, when Ooi was producing her live concert and musical theatre as part of a team effort, Bass's fourth trait, 'individualised attention', emerged. Productions of live performances included contemporary Buddhist music concerts such as her more recent *Sound of Wisdom* world tour and the Western-type musical theatre based on a Buddhist theme such as *Siddharta* (1999), *Above Full Moon* (2004), and *Princess Wen Cheng* (2008). During these productions, Ooi was engaged as a leader working with a team, which distanced her from her solitary composing in her studio. Ooi referred to these productions as *Fojiao Zhizuo* (Buddhist productions), but did not have a particular ritualistic approach in leading the team. Thus, she repeatedly emphasised acting as a 'role model' during our interview, and believes it was her role to provide them with solutions to problems:

> Being a leader does not mean one that is served by others [followers], but instead, it is the role of the leader to serve the others. More specifically, it is to help others succeed in the position they play. To me, I do not want to see the production team members eagerly await for the production to end as a form of relief, but to see them reluctant to leave the production because of what they embraced in that particular experience with a positive memory of well-being, that is the true value of a Buddhist production, this is important for a Buddhist production. The point here is not about giving instruction but to become a role model, and render help to those who meet obstacles that hinder task completion during the production.[31]

In terms of the perspective of leading a Buddhist production that is simultaneously a form of commodity that inevitably involves cost measures and risks of deficit, the optics show another facet of Ooi as a role model. A key component of her emphasis on the concept of a Buddhist production is the avoidance of exploiting others, and it remains as the backbone of her principle. Ooi stressed that it is more important to acknowledge and dismiss the idea of having a production if the confidence in the budget and the turnout is low. She asserts that a true Buddhist production should not engage with business tactics that victimise others for a return of personal profit. Ooi strongly believes that an act of selfishness to deal with one's failure to secure ticket sales is detrimental and defies positive energy. She was opposed to the cost of one's morale for the success of a production gained through bargaining tactics. She knew it was possible to exploit desperate performers in need of a performing platform to maintain their careers or ones who solely depend on donations and patronage.[32] She believes that the former costs one's morale in order to succeed with a production, while the latter is unjust, as the production team is not composed of nuns or monks who manage a Buddhist temple; instead it is one that incurs profit. Therefore, Ooi strongly enunciated that unjust remuneration defies the values of compassion within Buddhism.

Conversely, there are Ooi's live musical productions, along with her contemporary Buddhist music albums and singles published through social media music-sharing platforms and other online product sites. These works may reveal an interesting contextual ambivalence that fluctuates between that of religion and popular music as a commodity. Nevertheless, the consumption of Ooi's music and its practice that resulted in both stardom and fandom may reveal an antithetical relationship between her portrayal of the servant-leader in the act of musical *sutra* copying and the 'star personality' in what Simon Frith terms 'double enactment'.[33] We gathered that the traversing reflection of servant and the transformational and indirect leadership traits in Ooi conjointly engender what Rao calls 'soft leadership' and its '11 Cs'. As Rao explains, 'soft leadership involves use of integrative and participatory styles' where 'modern conditions' in the age of 'globalization, liberalization, privatization, and the rapid growth of technology have redefined the concept of leadership'.[34]

Firstly, Ooi's music is her soft power tool. The Buddhist chants that are void of the music manifested in Ooi's contemporary Buddhist musical style and as a form of 'fixed chant' in the context of 'popular song' have resulted in the positive reception among her listening community. The adopted popular culture in Ooi's contemporary Buddhist music and the acts of followers reciting chants in the form of a popular song emancipated from sanctity and asceticism led to its reception and adaptivity to modern lifestyles while maintaining the core teaching of *dharma*. The synergies between these map out how a bidirectional relationship between the sacred and popular forms of Buddhist chanting liberalise asceticism. Thus, Ooi's music becomes a type of soft power tool to exercise Buddhist *dharma* that recontextualises the copies of *sutra*, *mantra*, *dharani*, and *gatha* as popular songs among her community of listeners. Moreover, Ooi sees musical instruments as instruments of *dharma*. Accordingly, she called her piano *faqi*, which in Buddhism has a symbolic meaning that depends on the trends of Buddhist practice. For example, there are the large and smaller bells used in Chinese Mahayana Buddhist temples, which function as temporal signs to provide rhythmical demarcation and procedural direction in the ritual.[35] When Ooi transformed the chants into fixed-melody chants in the contemporary Buddhist music style and called her piano *faqi*, the notion of *faqi* becomes a transmission tool of *dharma* instead of just a symbolic representation.

Apart from the use of music as a tool, Ooi's gentle and timid characteristics as a woman composer and the stylistic formation of her simple musical style contribute to her soft power generation, which reflects a close relationship to the ancient philosophy of *Daoism*. The connotation of 'softness' in the notion of 'power' has been an intrinsic value mentioned in ancient Chinese philosophy, which can be found in Chapter 78 of Lao Zi's *Daodejing*: 'the weak can conquer the strong while the soft can conquer the hard' (*ruo zhi shengqiang, rou zhi shenggang*).[36] The philosophical intent has a paradoxical relationship where one can imagine the binary relationship between that of the soft and the hard, or the metaphorical concept of 'water' and 'feminine'.[37] Ooi and her contemporary Buddhist musical style ameliorate issues of male or female fetishisation and erotomania, with fantasies of heterosexual relationships commonly seen in the fandom of the popular music industry. Ooi, as a woman composer of a motherly appeal performing Buddhism via contemporary songs, breaks away from the stereotypical woman artist image in the popular music industry that embraces female sexuality as a form of power. Apart from the videos of her live performances, Ooi's music videos show an absence of the artist. Her live performances, in contrast, break free from the mainstream star image that comes from designed costumes, hairstyles, makeup, or an image that embraces female sexuality as a form of attraction. The composer has worn the same simple all-black outfit and shoulder-length straight hair with minimal makeup for years and has remained rather similar both in person and on stage. The intersectionality of 'female', 'softness', 'minimalism', and 'religion' generate to some extent her soft power.

The consumption of Ooi's contemporary Buddhist music, which has drawn a group of fans, reflects the outcome of her soft leadership. The transformation of chants as contemporary Buddhist songs has led to an unavoidable synergy of new hierarchical relationships between Ooi as a star with her listening community as fans or followers, and one that presents a different form of 'power balance' in the cohesion of popular culture, soft power, religion, and music. The achievement of stardom for Ooi came unexpectedly, as the condition of the local non-mainstream popular music industry and arts revealed a lack of authority and a market. Unlike many local musicians who have striven to develop a career as a composer or performer in the face of a lack of reception and market, Ooi's musical *sutra* copying has drawn a huge turnout, leading to a power hierarchy between her and her listeners as leader and followers, and as a star and her fans. In the course of power, Ooi evokes a different form of power, particularly a soft one that reflects what Joseph Nye describes as 'attractive power', an indispensable one in the generation of 'soft power'.[38] Mediating the transmission of *dharma* and chants via music as a tool through that of social media as a platform and live concert halls has created a new power balance and hierarchy that differs to that of the monasteries, *sangha*, and devotees. At the same time, Ooi's personal position as a mother and daughter and her emphasis on the need 'to serve' with her musical *sutra* copying have led her new musical works to retain the strongly feminine, 'servant', and 'indirect' characteristics of her soft leadership model.

Conclusion

Buddhist chants transformed into popular songs via musical *sutra* copying may at first seem to lie outside the purview of Buddhism from our own traditional Theravadin viewpoint. However, studying Ooi and her music, then utilising our own reflexivity, left us with a feeling of contemplation which resembled a new enactment of Buddhist *dharma*. Theorising contemporary Buddhist music in a Mahayana context, an in-depth contact with chants as popular songs, and a conversation with Ooi allowed us to cultivate a form of *dharma* transmission that led us to witness the efficacy of popular music and culture in the context of *dharma* transmission and Ooi's soft leadership. In terms of leadership and its concomitant power and hierarchy, the context of Buddhist chants as popular songs is normalised in the hands of Ooi, with the efficacy of her musical style as a tool of her soft power that reveals a positive outcome of *dharma* transmission. It is embraced by her fans and community as a new form of representation of the teaching of Siddhartha Gautama.

The interpolation of Buddhist *sutra* and *mantra* into a contemporary musical style that began from the notion of simplicity and *wuwei* reveals a form of soft power in Ooi. The reciprocal relationship between Ooi and her listeners forms a relational link that realises this form of soft power, including the formation of a new musical genre under a Buddhist theme. The phenomenon reflects a form of power that normalised Buddhist chants in popular music among a collective Mahayanian community, including non-Buddhists. As Max DePree describes, 'the signs of outstanding leadership appear primarily among the followers'.[39] Positioning Ooi's leadership amidst the ideas of servant and indirect leadership, through some of the spectrums of transformational and soft leadership, reveals the contingency in leadership that transcends the sanctity and asceticism of the practice of Buddhist chanting and *sutra* copying to a new paradigm. This is done with music that is mediated through a liminal space and closer to the hearts of her Buddhist collective community embracing popular culture.

Notes

1. In Buddhist tradition, *dharma* is the philosophical concept about universal truth taught by Siddhartha Gautama (c. 563 BCE/480 BCE – c. 483 BCE/400 BCE).
2. Although the Malaysian Buddhist community is primarily under the Mahayana influence, there are some smaller communities that follow the Theravada and Vajrayana traditions. The Theravada tradition spread from India and is practised primarily in Thailand, Cambodia, Laos, and Myanmar. It strongly focuses on an individual's effort in achieving enlightenment, especially through meditation, with the goal of becoming an *arhat* and achieving *nirvana*. In contrast, the Mahayana tradition spread to China, Japan, and Korea – as well as Malaysia – and its teachings can be integrated into normal life, where the final goal is not necessarily to become an *arhat*.
3. Courtney Wilder and Jeremy Rehwaldt, "What Makes Music Christian? Hipsters, Contemporary Christian Music and Secularization," in *Understanding Religion and Popular Culture*, edited by Terry Ray Clark and Dan W. Clanton (New York: Routledge, 2012), 157–71, p. 157.
4. Xiaogan Liu, "Daoism: Laozi and Zhuangzi," in *The Oxford Handbook of World Philosophy*, edited by Jay L. Garfield and William Edelglass (New York: Oxford University Press, 2011), 47–57, p. 50.
5. Veilaria Lee, "Interview with Imee Ooi," *BuddhaZine*, YouTube, May 28, 2016, accessed August 27, 2020, www.youtube.com/watch?v=PtWzthaOGUk.
6. Horace Clarence Boyer, "Contemporary Gospel Music," *The Black Perspective in Music* 7, no. 1 (1979): 5–58, p. 22.
7. Larry Eskridge, *God's Forever Family: The Jesus People Movement in America* (New York: Oxford University Press, 2013), 7.
8. David Stowe, *No Sympathy for the Devil: Christian Pop Music and the Transformation of American Evangelicalism* (Chapel Hill: University of North Carolina Press, 2011), 7.
9. Pi-Yen Chen, "Buddhist Chant, Devotional Song, and Commercial Popular Music: From Ritual to Rock Mantra," *Ethnomusicology* 49, no. 2 (2005): 266–86, p. 268.
10. Paul D. Greene, "Contemporary Buddhist Chanting and Music," in *The Oxford Handbook of Contemporary Buddhism*, edited by Michael K. Jerryson (New York: Oxford University Press, 2017), 565–75.
11. Chen, "Buddhist Chant, Devotional Song, and Commercial Popular Music," 272.
12. Chen, "Buddhist Chant, Devotional Song, and Commercial Popular Music," 281. The loud and rhythmic nature of rock music was perceived as blasphemous among conservative Buddhist communities and associations, as it contradicts the aim of achieving *śūnyatā* or emptiness, a realm of liberation. See Keping Wang, *Chinese Culture of Intelligence* (Singapore: Palgrave Macmillan, 2019), 157–62.
13. Anne Marie Chandy, "Imee Ooi Dreams of Creating an 'Olympics' Series for Dharma Music," *The Star Online*, March 15, 2019, accessed October 13, 2020, www.thestar.com.my/lifestyle/culture/2019/03/15/imee-ooi-concert-klpac-buddhist-sadhu-for-the-music-series (para. 25).
14. See Fung Chiat Loo, Fung Ying Loo, and Yoke Fee Lee, "Buddhist Hymn Competition in Malaysia: Music and Identity," in *Preserving Creativity in Music Practice*, edited by Gisa Jaehnichen and Julia

Chieng (Selangor: Universiti Putra Malaysia Press, 2011), 101–12; Fung Ying Loo, "Magic Mirror: The Musical," *Asian Theatre Journal* 30, no. 2 (2013): 538–44; Fung Ying Loo, Fung Chiat Loo, and Xiaohao Tee, "The Growing Phenomenon of Malaysian Musical Theatre Productions with a Buddhist Theme," *Procedia – Social and Behavioural Sciences Journal* 122 (2014): 473–76.
15. Frank McGlynn and Arthur Tuden, *Anthropological Approaches to Political Behaviour* (Pittsburgh: University of Pittsburgh Press, 1991), 3.
16. Robert Greenleaf, *The Servant as Leader* (Indianapolis, IN: Greenleaf Center, 1977), 13.
17. Jack Barbalet, "Laozi's Daodejing (6th Century BC)," in *The Oxford Handbook of Process Philosophy and Organization Studies*, edited by Jenny Helin, Tor Hernes, Daniel Hjorth, and Robin Holt (Oxford: Oxford University Press, 2014), 17–31, p. 29.
18. Herrlee Glessner Creel, *What Is Taoism? And Other Studies in Chinese Cultural History* (Chicago, IL: University of Chicago Press, 1970), 75.
19. See Luo Yuming, *A Concise History of Chinese Literature* (Leiden: Brill, 2011), 93.
20. Fung Ying Loo, "Interview with Imee Ooi," 15 November 2020, Kuala Lumpur.
21. The first record of *Siddham* script that appeared in China may be around 308 CE according to the information in the translated *Lalitavistara Sutra*. See Saroj Kumar Chaudhuri, "Siddham in China and Japan," *Sino-Platonic Papers* 88 (1998): 12.
22. John Stevens, *Sacred Calligraphy of the East* (Brattleboro, VT: Echo Point Books & Media, 2013), 6; Shen Hsueh-man, *Authentic Replicas: Buddhist Art in Medieval China* (Honolulu: University of Hawai'i Press, 2019), 35.
23. DJ May, Yiliang Hong, "Interview with Imee Ooi," Death Café, Facebook, September 18, 2020, accessed October 24, 2020, www.facebook.com/130028873696510/videos/3186976794693382/.
24. Peter Sun, "The Motivation to Serve as a Corner Stone of Servant Leadership," in *Practicing Servant Leadership Developments in Implementation*, edited by Dirk van Dierendonck and Kathleen Patterson (Cham: Palgrave Macmillan, 2018), 63–80, p. 64.
25. M.S. Rao, "Soft Leadership and Engaged Leadership," in *Engaged Leadership: Transforming through Future-Oriented Design Thinking*, edited by Joan Marques and Satinder Dhiman (Cham: Springer, 2018), 265–80, p. 217.
26. See Imee Ooi 黄慧音 www.facebook.com/imeeooi.immmusic/ and www.youtube.com/c/IMMPACARTS-imeeooi
27. Chen, 2005.
28. Reed Criddle, *Chanting the Medicine Buddha Sutra: A Musical Transcription and English Translation of the Medicien Buddha Service of the Liberation Rite of Water and Land at Fo Guang Shan Monastery* (Wisconsin: A-R Editions, 2020), 20.
29. Francis J. Yammarino, "Indirect Leadership: Transformational Leadership at a Distance," in *Improving Organizational Effectiveness through Transformational Leadership*, edited by Bernard M. Bass and Bruce J. Avolio (Thousand Oaks, CA: Sage Publications, 1994), 26–47, pp. 27–29.
30. Bernard M. Bass, *Leadership and Performance Beyond Expectations* (New York: Collier Macmillan Publishers, 1985).
31. "Interview with Imee Ooi," November 15, 2020, Kuala Lumpur.
32. Due to the lack of a market in the performing art industry in the country. See Fung Ying Loo and Jin Hin Yap, "Kuala Lumpur City Opera and Opera Revival in Malaysia: A Communal Approach to Undoing Hierarchy and Elitism," *International Review of the Aesthetics and Sociology of Music* 51, no. 2 (2020): 185–204, pp. 186–87.
33. Simon Frith, *Performing Rites: On the Value of Popular Music* (Cambridge, MA: Harvard University Press, 1996), 212.
34. M. S. Rao, "Soft Leadership: Make Others Feel More Important," *Leader to Leader* 64 (2012): 27–32, pp. 27–28, https://doi.org/10.1002/ltl.20019.
35. Chen, 2010, pp. 10–13.
36. Paul R. Gibson, *The Laozi, Daodejing* (Raleigh, NC: Score Books, 2015), 158.
37. Jack Barbalet and Qi Xiaoying, "The Paradox of Power: Conceptions of Power and the Relations of Reason and Emotion in European and Chinese Culture," in *Power and Emotion*, edited by Jonathan G. Heaney and Helena Flam (London: Routledge, 2015), 51–64, p. 58.
38. Joseph S. Nye, *Soft Power: The Means to Success in World Politics* (New York: Public Affairs, 2004), 6.
39. Max DePree, *Leadership Is an Art* (New York: Doubleday, 1989), 12.

Bibliography

Barbalet, Jack. "Laozi's Daodejing (6th Century BC)." In *The Oxford Handbook of Process Philosophy and Organization Studies*, edited by Jenny Helin, Tor Hernes, Daniel Hjorth, and Robin Holt, 17–31. Oxford: Oxford University Press, 2014.

———, and Xiaoying Qi. "The Paradox of Power: Conceptions of Power and the Relations of Reason and Emotion in European and Chinese Culture." In *Power and Emotion*, edited by Jonathan G. Heaney and Helena Flam, 51–64. London: Routledge, 2015.

Bass, Bernard M. *Leadership and Performance Beyond Expectations*. New York: Collier Macmillan Publishers, 1985.

Boyer, Horace Clarence. "Contemporary Gospel Music." *The Black Perspective in Music* 7, no. 1 (1979): 5–58.

Chandy, Anne Marie. "Imee Ooi Dreams of Creating an 'Olympics' Series for Dharma Music." *The Star Online*, March 15, 2019. Accessed October 13, 2020. www.thestar.com.my/lifestyle/culture/2019/03/15/imee-ooi-concert-klpac-buddhist-sadhu-for-the-music-series.

Chen, Pi-Yen. "Buddhist Chant, Devotional Song, and Commercial Popular Music: From Ritual to Rock Mantra." *Ethnomusicology* 49, no. 2 (2005): 266–86.

Creel, Herrlee Glessner. *What Is Taoism? And Other Studies in Chinese Cultural History*. Chicago: University of Chicago Press, 1970.

Criddle, Reed. *Chanting the Medicine Buddha Sutra: A Musical Transcription and English Translation of the Medicien Buddha Service of the Liberation Rite of Water and Land at Fo Guang Shan Monastery*. Wisconsin: A-R Editions, 2020.

DePree, Max. *Leadership Is an Art*. New York: Doubleday, 1989.

Eskridge, Larry. *God's Forever Family: The Jesus People Movement in America*. New York: Oxford University Press, 2013.

Frith, Simon. *Performing Rites: On the Value of Popular Music*. Cambridge, MA: Harvard University Press, 1996.

Greene, Paul D. "Contemporary Buddhist Chanting and Music." In *The Oxford Handbook of Contemporary Buddhism*, edited by Michael K. Jerryson, 65–575. New York: Oxford University Press, 2017.

Greenleaf, Robert. *The Servant as Leader*. Indianapolis, IN: Greenleaf Center, 1977.

Liu, Xiaogan. "Daoism: Laozi and Zhuangzi." In *The Oxford Handbook of World Philosophy*, edited by Jay L. Garfield and William Edelglass, 47–57. New York: Oxford University Press, 2011.

Loo, Fung Chiat, Fung Ying Loo, and Yoke Fee Lee. "Buddhist Hymn Competition in Malyaisa: Music and Identity." In *Preserving Creativity in Music Practice*, Gisa Jaehnichen and Julia Chieng, 101–12. Selangor: Universiti Putra Malaysia Press, 2011.

Loo, Fung Ying. "Magic Mirror: The Musical." *Asian Theatre Journal* 30, no. 2 (2013): 538–44.

———. "Interview with Imee Ooi." November 15, 2020, Kuala Lumpur.

———, and Jin Hin Yap. "Kuala Lumpur City Opera and Opera Revival in Malaysia: A Communal Approach to Undoing Hierarchy and Elitism." *International Review of the Aesthetics and Sociology of Music* 51, no. 2 (2020): 185–204.

Loo, Fung Ying, Fung Chiat Loo, and Xiaohao Tee. "The Growing Phenomenon of Malaysian Musical Theatre Productions with a Buddhist Theme." *Procedia – Social and Behavioural Sciences Journal* 122 (2014): 473–76.

Luo, Yuming. *A Concise History of Chinese Literature*. Leiden: Brill, 2011.

May, D. J., and Yiliang Hong. "Interview with Imee Ooi." *Death Café*, Facebook, September 18, 2020. Accessed October 24, 2020. www.facebook.com/130028873696510/videos/3186976794693382/.

McGlynn, Frank, and Arthur Tuden. *Anthropological Approaches to Political Behaviour*. Pittsburgh, PA: University of Pittsburgh Press, 1991.

Nye, Joseph S. *Soft Power: The Means to Success in World Politics*. New York: Public Affairs, 2004.

Rao, M. S. "Soft Leadership: Make Others Feel More Important." *Leader to Leader* 64 (2012): 27–32. https://doi.org/10.1002/ltl.20019.

Shen, Hsueh-Man. *Authentic Replicas: Buddhist Art in Medieval China*. Honolulu: University of Hawai'i Press, 2019.

Stevens, John. *Sacred Calligraphy of the East*. Brattleboro, VT: Echo Point Books & Media, 2013.

Stowe, David. *No Sympathy for the Devil: Christian Pop Music and the Transformation of American Evangelicalism*. Chapel Hill: University of North Carolina Press, 2011.

Sun, Peter. "The Motivation to Serve as a Corner Stone of Servant Leadership." In *Practicing Servant Leadership Developments in Implementation*, edited by Dirk van Dierendonck and Kathleen Patterson, 63–80. Cham: Palgrave MacMillan, 2018.
Veilaria Lee. "Interview with Imee Ooi." *BuddhaZine*, YouTube, May 28, 2016. Accessed August 27, 2020. www.youtube.com/watch?v=PtWzthaOGUk.
Wilder, Courtney, and Jeremy Rehwaldt. "What Makes Music Christian? Hipsters, Contemporary Christian Music and Secularization." In *Understanding Religion and Popular Culture*, edited by Terry Ray Clark and Dan W. Clanton, 157–71. New York: Routledge, 2012.
Yammarino, Francis J. "Indirect Leadership: Transformational Leadership at a Distance." In *Improving Organizational Effectiveness through Transformational Leadership*, edited by Bernard M. Bass and Bruce J. Avolio, 26–47. Thousand Oaks, CA: SAGE, 1994.

35
THE FEMALE ROLE IN SACRED MUSICAL PRACTICES IN *SHĪ'AH* RITUALS IN IRAQ

Ahmed Al-Badr

This chapter deals with the role of Iraqi women in the religious rituals and chants of Muslims who follow the *Shī'ah* sect in the city of Karbala in Central Iraq. The position of contemporary women is presented in these ceremonies from musical and religious approaches as innovators, performers, and leaders for the audience of female participants in rituals.

The process of religious leadership in Arab Islamic societies is restricted to men only, and women cannot lead the community religiously in any way. Singing is a prohibited act for women in Arab societies and especially in religious societies such as that in Karbala, where the fieldwork for this study took place. However, these restrictions were loosened in Iraq after 2003, which was after the *Shī'ah* gained greater freedom in practising their religious rituals. Said rituals were prevented from being practised for a long time due to restrictions imposed by the political regimes in Iraq, particularly in Karbala.[1] The opportunity arose for Iraqi women to challenge religious boundaries and break social restrictions to work in the fields of religion and music, which have been forbidden to women in Arabic and Islamic societies for several centuries. The women took the initiative to assume a social, artistic, and leadership role that combines music, poetry, and religious guidance within the religious rituals and chants of the *Shī'ah* sect in Iraq.

This chapter was completed based on three forms of sources: first, the fieldwork that I conducted during two religious' seasons in Karbala city throughout 2016 and 2017. The fieldwork included recording the activities of twenty rituals which were examined and analysed to obtain the musical/textual characteristics for this study. Additionally, multiple interviews were conducted with women who participated in religious rituals in Karbala. Second, I used a collection of various academic sources. The third was my continuous observation of the religious rituals of the *Shī'ah* for more than fifteen years.

The Emergence of the *Shī'ah* Doctrine in Islam and Its Rituals: Two Historic Moments, Two Prominent Characters, and Two Important Cities

Religious rituals among *Shī'ah* are closely related to the story of the killing of the martyr Hussein,[2] the grandson of the Prophet Muhammad, and to the events of the Battle of Karbala. This story is also one of the standard foundations of faith according to the *Shī'ah* creed, where the killing of Hussein is considered a form of self-sacrifice on his part for justice to prevail in society.[3] The details of the story of the martyrdom of Hussein and his relatives are the primary material for most of the religious rituals of the *Shīʿah*. In addition, this story and its characters are considered the fundamentals and religious basis for the *Shīʿah* who believe, according to Nakash, that Hussein's 'suffering is taken to be a source of salvation community through its own internalization and emulation suffering of the imam.'[4] Therefore, reviewing some historical facts of this story in brief is necessary to understand its role in the structure of *Shīʿah* rituals and ceremonies.

There are two important historical moments in Islamic history that were the main reasons behind the emergence of the *Shīʿah* sect in Islam. The first was in the year 632 CE, when the Prophet Muhammad passed away. The second was in the year 680 CE, when his grandson Hussein was killed. During the five-decade period between these two dates, a seed of discord grew among Muslims due to their disagreement over the person that should take over the rule of Muslims after the Prophet Muhammad.[5]

There was a group of Muslims who believed that Ali, the cousin of the Prophet Muhammad (and the husband of his daughter), was the first to receive the ruling after the death of Muhammad. However, Ali, one of the two most important characters among the *Shīʿah*, did not receive the caliphate of Muslims' position until twenty-four years after the death of Muhammad, and he was the fourth and last caliph during a period known as the rule of the *Rashidun* Caliphs.[6] After Ali's death in 661 CE, he was buried in Najaf, one of the two most important cities for the *Shīʿah*. Thereafter, Muʿāwiyah took over the caliphate until his death in 680 CE. He was then succeeded by his son, Yazid, who took over the caliphate, so that the Islamic rule was inherited for the first time starting a period of rule known as the Umayyad Caliphate (during 661–750 CE).[7] This was the real beginning of the emergence of the *Shīʿah* as a religious-political movement, demanding that the rule be in the house of the Prophet. Yazid faced opposition to the idea of inheriting power in Islam, especially from the people of Medina and the people of Iraq. Hussein, the second son of Ali, was one of the most prominent opponents in Medina to take over the caliphate in this way.[8]

During the first year of the Yazid's caliphate in Damascus, the matter had escalated as a large group of Muslims in the city of Kufa in Iraq sent letters of allegiance to Hussein asking him to come to Iraq, claiming that they would announce him as their caliphate. Based on that, Hussein, the second prominent character among the *Shīʿah*, travelled from Medina to Iraq with a large group of his family and relatives to take over the caliphate position there.[9] As soon as he reached Karbala, the second most important city for the *Shīʿah*, the story began, and the events and characters of this story form a very important core in the religious rituals and chants of the *Shīʿah* today.

Immediately after the arrival of Hussein, his family, and his supporters in Karbala, they were besieged by Yazid's army. They were denied water for three days before the day of the battle, in which Hussein and his army were killed. On the tenth day of the month of *Muḥarram* in 680 CE,[10] Hussein's army, consisting of seventy-two thirsty fighters, met with the army of Yazid, consisting of about four thousand fighters. Hussein was martyred and beheaded, and a large group of his relatives who accompanied him were killed in a short battle known as the Battle of Karbala. The surviving women and children were captured and sent with the head of Hussein to Yazid in Damascus. That day later became the date of the annual ritual which is now known as *ʿashura* (the tenth day).

This was a decisive battle as it clearly and continuously divided Muslims into two major branches, the *Shīʿah* and the *Sunnah*, as Hazleton has indicated.[11] The ideas, trends, beliefs, and rituals of this new *Shīʿah* religious sect took shape during the period that followed the Battle of Karbala and remain present to this day. Narrating the story of the killing of Hussein and his companions, describing the events of the battle, and dealing with the details of the conversations that took place between the characters of the story on both sides of the conflict constitute a fundamental axis in the rituals and chants of the *Shī'ah*, as Hamdar has explained.[12]

The Emergence of Religious Rituals Among the *Shī'ah*

There are three different opinions regarding the place and date of the first mourning council, but all of them agree that Zaynab, Hussein's sister, was the one who started the mourning of Hussein and his companions. Aghaie states that the mourning of Hussein started immediately, as his sister, relatives, and supporters mourned the tragedy.[13] Yet, Qutbuddin indicates that the first mourning was held by Zaynab, while she was being held captive in Damascus.[14] However, most *Shī'ah* of Iraq believe, as D'Souza reveals, that the mourning began in Karbala after Yazid released Zaynab and her relatives from captivity.[15] They brought Hussein's head back to Karbala and buried it with his body, and Zaynab began to narrate verses of poetry expressing her grief over the death of her brother. The people of the region met with them around the grave of Hussein and began to weep and wail. This was on the 20th of the month of *Ṣufer*,[16] the fortieth day after the killing of Hussein, which later became the date of the annual ritual known as the *Arbi'ineyeh* (the fortieth day). The *Shī'ah* unanimously agree that this visit to Hussein's grave is the inception of the annual rituals in the months of *Muḥarram* and *Ṣufer* every year. This ritual has been repeated annually from then until today, when every year in the month of *Muḥarram* inhabitants of Karbala and the surrounding area begin visiting the tomb of Hussein and staying in Karbala until the tenth day, *'ashura*. These people are known as *Alziwwār* (visitors);[17] they gather in meetings called *Majalis Al'aza'* (mourning councils) set up to commemorate the death of Hussein. These councils are open to visitors for fifty days, which is the period of reviving the rituals.

As for the methods of establishing the ritual and its performance, they have varied throughout history according to changing economic and political situations, as some regimes prohibited the *Shī'ah* rituals.[18] Through the annual practice of these rituals over fourteen centuries, whenever they have been allowed to be practised, a particular way of performing these rituals was formed. Specifically, this was within the mourning councils of men, as women were not allowed to hold their own mourning councils. Usually, women attend the men's council, but they sit separately in a place adjacent to the men's in order to facilitate the process of listening to sermons and the story of Hussein's martyrdom, which was delivered exclusively by a male preacher called *Almulleh*.[19] This situation lasted until 2003, when women began to establish their own mourning councils,[20] and from 2003 to the present day, *'ashura*, *Muḥarram*, and *Arbi'ineyeh* rituals have been performed and practised every year by women in Karbala. Before 2003, women's councils were held secretly among a limited number of women, because the political regime banned it. After 2003, women's councils became a socially acceptable matter and began to spread. These councils are now popular in most Iraqi communities, and women's councils are also widespread in countries such as Iran and Bahrain.[21] During these years, the form of the women's rituals developed and took its current final form. However, it turns out that there is only one ritual and it consists of five activities, but as it is repeated daily in different mourning councils, the word 'ritual' becomes pluralised. Four of the ritual's activities are *Khuṭbeh* (sermon), *Alleṭum Julusen* (slapping oneself while sitting), *Alna'i* (lamentation), and *Alleṭum wuqufen* (slapping oneself while standing), which are performed in the ritual during all fifty days of the mourning period. On the day of *'ashura* specifically (tenth of *Muḥarram*), the ritual is fully performed with its five activities, as the *Maqtel* (the killing story) activity is added to the rest of the other activities. The following is a review of the role of

Iraqi women in creating, performing, and leading *'ashura*, *Muḥarram*, and *Arbi'ineyeh* rituals among the female audience in Karbala.

Almullayeh

The *Almullayeh* is the woman who recites and reads a specific story or poem loudly.[22] She is the woman who leads the religious ritual in the mourning councils for women. There are two main attributes that must be available for the woman to be able to practise the *Almullayeh* function. The first is that she should be from a family with a good reputation. The second is that she should have the ability to sing properly and have a pleasing voice. The ability of the *Almullayeh* to read and write is an added advantage, though not essential as there are several *Mullayat* (plural of *Almullayeh*) who can compose and write the required texts for the ritual without relying on what is already in the field, which is usually imported from the material used in the mourning councils of men. There are also several *Mullayat* who can compose the required melodies for the rituals. *Almullayeh* as a function is limited to religious occasions only, especially on the *'ashura*, *Muḥarram*, and *Arbi'ineyeh* occasions. After performing the rituals, the *Almullayeh* usually returns to her normal social function as a housewife, employee, or private business owner.

The *Almullayeh* is usually accompanied by another woman who helps her in her work by directing the crowd in the slapping process and adjusting the rhythmic and kinetic accompaniment during the practice of the ritual. This woman is called *Almusa'ideh* (the assistant), and she usually stands to the left of the *Almullayeh*.

The Rituals of *Muḥarram*, *'Ashura*, and *Arbi'ineyeh* among the *Shī'ah*, and the Role of *Almullayeh* in Women's Mourning Councils

There are many religious occasions in the *Shī'ah* calendar, to the extent that there is at least one occasion every month.[23] Most of them are related to the birth or death anniversary of a member of the family of Hussein, but the *Shī'ah* practise specific rituals on three particular occasions: *Muḥarram* and *'ashura*, (the month and the day when Hussein was killed), and the *Arbi'ineyeh*, (the day of returning and burying his head).

The practice of these rituals begins in the month of *Muḥarram*. Men's mourning councils are held in mosques or in public squares, while women's are held in the house of a woman from the region who is able to meet the expenses of holding the council. The mourning council is held daily for fifty days, thirty in the month of *Muḥarram* and twenty in the next month, *Ṣufer*. Women's mourning councils are constantly held on a particular day of the month of *Muḥarram* in specific houses and families in Karbala. Consequently, people already know when a particular family will host the council annually; it is considered a sort of social prestige and religious connection for that family. After the tenth of *Muḥarram*, the councils are held intermittently and with an unspecified date throughout the remainder of the month of *Muḥarram* and the first nineteen days the month of *Ṣufer*. On the twentieth of *Ṣufer*, mourning councils must convene to practise the *Arbi'ineyeh* ritual. Figure 35.1 shows the period of holding the rituals during the months of *Muḥarram* and *Ṣufer*:

The women's mourning council is held in the guest hall, which is the largest room in Iraqi houses. If the number of attendees is more than the guest hall's capacity, the council will be held in the courtyard of the house (weather permitting). In both cases, women sit on the floor in rows facing one of the walls of the hall or the yard of the house, while the *Mullayeh* stands or sits on a stage or a high chair to deliver a religious sermon to the female audience and lead the process of practising the ritual.

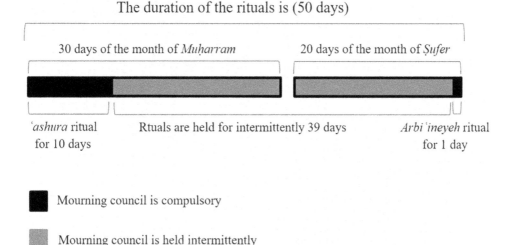

Figure 35.1 Period of holding rituals during the months of *Muḥarram* and *Ṣufer*.

The *Almullayeh* and women who participate in the rituals wear a *Hijab* (headscarf) to cover their hair during the rituals. In addition, a black cloak, which is called an *'abayeh*, should be worn on the head and covering the entire body; however, the *'abayeh* can be removed during the ritual for ease of movement. Under the cloak, the *Almullayeh* wears a black *Hashemi*,[24] with ornaments in the form of religious texts. In addition, the *Almullayeh* also puts a piece of black cloth over the *Hijab* called the *bwima*, which she wraps around the head. Usually, the *Bwima* is embroidered with a short religious phrase. Habitually, older women sit on the sides of the mourning council crying and slapping their thighs quietly, while younger women sit in front of them in order to participate in the rituals' activities.

Details of the Performance of the *Muḥarram*, *'Ashura*, and *Arbi'ineyeh* Rituals

Women often come to the mourning council before the *Almullayeh* arrives, and they often drink tea or eat before the council begins. As soon as the *Almullayeh* and her assistant arrive, women prepare for the start of the ritual which consists of five activities, as follows:

1. *Khuṭbeh* (sermon): a short sermon that lasts for approximately 5–7 minutes. It often includes religious content that discusses various sacred topics, such as the importance of prayer, the method of ablution, or commitment to the truth and following the path of morals. The sermon as an activity is the introductory part of the ritual, which is not repeated more than once and is usually delivered in the Iraqi colloquial dialect, *Ḥischeh*, in order to facilitate the process of communicating meanings to the women. After that, the second activity of the ritual begins.
2. *Alleṭum Julusen* (slapping oneself while sitting): takes place while everybody is sitting during the *Almullayeh*'s singing of a genre called *Leṭmeyeh* (a sad song combined with slapping). When twenty samples of this genre were examined and analysed, the tempo range was found to be between (crotchet/quarter note = 50) to (crotchet/quarter note = 110) and to fall in only two different time signatures (2/4) and (4/4). The results show that the *Leṭmeyeh* tempo depends on the age of the women who attend the ritual. For the elderly,

Figure 35.2 The *Almullayeh*, Umm Noor, wearing the *bwima* and the black *Hashemi* decorated with religious texts. All pictures in this chapter were captured from videos that were taken by my sister with the consent of the owner of the house and the attendees on the condition that all faces are covered.

the speed of singing would be slower; for younger women, it would be faster. That is why audiences can sometimes ask the *Almullayeh* for a faster or slower *Leṭmeyeh*. During the performance of the *Leṭmeyeh*, women begin to slap the right upper arm with the left hand and the left upper arm with the right hand simultaneously while sitting. Elderly women usually slap their thighs for ease. The slapping is usually timed with the strong beat in the bar. After the *Almullayeh* begins singing, her assistant begins the slapping first, accompanying the *Almullayeh*'s singing so that the women in the council become familiar with the melody,

The Female Role in Sacred Musical Practices in Shī'ah Rituals

rhythm, and the number of slaps in the bar through the self-slapping of the assistant. After two or three bars, women begin to slap together with the assistant in one unified rhythm, and the sound of slapping represents the rhythmic participation of the women, which regulates the process of rhythmic and spiritual interaction with the *Almullayeh*'s singing.

The melodic range of the *Leṭmeyeh* is between the minor third and the perfect fifth. It usually consists of one fixed melody that is repeated continuously, and what distinguishes it is the change of the poetic text within each repetition of the melody. In addition, in the majority of examples of the *Leṭmeyeh* genre, women sing with the *Almullayeh* together in a specific short part of the melody. Usually, the role of these short parts is to emphasise the tonic note of the melody. The slapping normally lasts five to seven minutes, then the women stop to rest for a few minutes. Music Example 35.1 shows a well-known *Leṭmeyeh* named *Itha terdoon* ('If you wish'), which reflects many of the musical characteristics that have been mentioned:

Music Example 35.1   Transcription of the *Itha terdoon* ('If you wish') *Leṭmeye*.

The text in this *Leṭmeyeh* is based on a dialogue between a sister and her brother (Zaynab and Hussein). Feminine *Leṭmeyat* (plural of *Leṭmeyeh*) are filled with an important role for women and children, and there are many references to family, mothers, sisters, and daughters. This is one of the important aspects that the *Almullayeh* has added to the ritual, as the *Leṭmeyat* in the councils of men do not address such ideas and avoid the inclusion of women in texts or stories of the rituals. The following is the arrangement of the text in *Itha terdoon* ('if you wish') *Leṭmeyeh*:

Sister: If you want to listen to my words	(*āh āh*)[25]
go back to the family, this is my intention and my goal.	
I cannot protect	(*āh āh*)
if I see the enemies, they will attack.	
Brother: We cannot go back, her brother answered	(*āh āh*)
your brothers know this calamity.	
Our family has been captivated after our death	(*āh āh*)
if I see the enemies, they will attack.	

The text does not follow any known Arabic poetic meter, as the lengths of syllables are arranged randomly, and their number is not equal in all the verses of the text.[26] However, during the performance, the *Almullayeh* controls syllables by lengthening the syllable wherever possible and necessary to compensate for the shortage in the number of syllables and to maintain the matching of the rhythmic pattern with the melody. By adopting this method, the melismatic style dominates the performance of this activity. This indicates that the one who wrote the text is unaware of poetic meter requirements. The text is fraught with emotions through the sister's request that her brother return to the family and that she is weak on her own and cannot defend herself, but the brother cannot return despite his knowledge of the family's fate after his death. The text was written in an easy, general, and local language that reflects the target audience as the general public and the *Almullayeh* as a folk artist.

3. *Alnaʿi* (lamentation): after a rest for a few minutes, the *Almullayeh* begins performing the activity known as the *Alnaʿi*. It is an improvisational performance of a poetic text written in the Iraqi local dialect. In addition, it is a melodic performance of the text within a range of four or five notes maximum that are sung in a conjunct melodic motion, devoid of any disjunct motion. Also, the melody tends to fall continuously towards the tonic note of the melodic contour. The *Alnaʿi* continues for about five minutes. It is considered a spiritual and religious break for the women of the mourning council before they start slapping again.

The text in the *Alnaʿi* addresses the situations of the women as wives, sisters, and daughters being confused when they were left alone after all the men were killed in the Battle of Karbala. The performance of the *Alnaʿi* is so sad that the women begin to cry upon hearing it, influenced by the sad meanings of the text and the performance of the *Almullayeh*. Moreover, women have confirmed that they feel great relief after the slapping and crying activity, and they return to their homes with a better psychological condition.

When the *Alnaʿi* ends, the *Almullayeh*, or sometimes the owner of the house, asks the women to prepare for the slapping again, and it may be done while seated as they did in the second activity or while standing, which is not unexpected. The *Alnaʿi* is one of the

Figure 35.3 *Almullayeh*, Umm Hawra, performing the *Alnaʿi*. She appears in the picture holding a notebook in her left hand while placing her right hand on her right cheek and closing her right ear so that she can hear herself clearly.

activities that may be repeated if there is time after the fourth activity, *Alleṭum wuqufen*, is concluded, by voluntary request of the women of the council.

The following is a well-known and very common *Alnaʿi*, which depicts Zaynab talking to her brother Hussein after his murder:

(*Āh*,	the son of my mother)
Sweet days	(Brother) with you, I spent sweet days
And they were short	(Brother) They did not continue and were short
If he died	(Brother) The house will be demolished if he died
Bid you farewell	(Brother) I came to bid you farewell
(Brother) *the separation*	I cannot bear your separation
(Brother) *forgotten*	You cannot be forgotten

One of the features of the *Alnaʿi* is that the *Almullayeh* adds different words or phrases that are not from the original text,[27] but she introduces them to establish the meaning and motivate the listeners. For example, as shown in the preceding text, the words in parentheses are new, such as *Ibn ummi* (son of my mother) and *Khuyeh* (brother).

The interesting thing about the way this *Alnaʿi* is performed is that it starts with the rhyme of the verse and then ends with it, shown as the underlined words. The *Almullayeh* sings it in this method to attract the attention of the listeners so that they focus on the meanings and discover the poetic relationship to the rhyme which, when repeated in its correct placement at the end of the verse, gives a form of linguistic comfort in understanding the text and anticipating it, as well as being more enticing for the listeners. It is a creative, textual, and musical characteristic that the *Almullayeh* has added to the improvisational performance of this genre.

The text here, as in the *Alleṭum Julusen* (slapping oneself while sitting), does not follow any known Arabic poetic meter. The lengths of syllables are arranged randomly and their number is not equal; however, this matter is not tangible when performing the *Alnaʿi*, as the discursive style and improvisational singing gives the *Almullayeh* the freedom to lengthen and shorten the syllables to serve the performance and gain the opportunity to add words that are not from the original text to support the melody and poetic ideas in the text. As a result, the melismatic style dictates the performance.

4. *Alleṭum wuqufen* (slapping oneself while standing): an activity that regularly follows the *Alnaʿi*, and it takes place inside the mourning council where women stand in the form of a circular ring called *halakat alleṭum* (slapping ring), while children, boys and girls under the age of six years old, and older women often sit on the sides of the room to allow space to form the ring. Children do not participate in the rituals, only watch and observe them. The following figure shows a bird's-eye view of the *Alleṭum wuqufen* activity.

The tempo of the melody in this activity is faster than the tempo of the slapping oneself while sitting activity, and this is what the nature of this activity calls for, as women begin to rotate within the ring they form while slapping different parts of their bodies. There is slapping on the right upper arm with the left hand and on the left upper arm with the right hand simultaneously. This type is the most common in all *Shīʿah* regions of Iraq.[28] However, slapping the chest is the kind that is used most commonly by the *Shīʿah* women of southern Iraq, and slapping on the face and/or forehead is the kind that is used by the *Shīʿah* women from the cities of Karbala and Najaf. Women from both cities inherited this way of slapping from their ancestors, who believed that they should be more remorseful than other women for not supporting Hussein on the day of *ʿashura* as they were the closest to the site of the Battle of Karbala. Consequently, slapping on the face and forehead is an expression of regret and sadness.

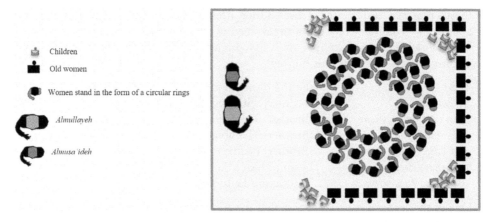

Figure 35.4 A bird's-eye view of the *Alleṭum wuqufen* activity.

The melody of the *Leṭmeyeh* in this activity consists of three or four melodies. Each melody is performed for a period ranging from one to two minutes during which the same melody is repeated continuously until the next melody arrives. The melodic range does not exceed the perfect fourth in this type of *Leṭmeyeh*; instead, most melodies are composed of two or three notes. The focus in this type of *Leṭmeyeh* is on the rhythm and movement more than on the melody. The nature of the melody and the way it is performed will be in a syllabic style so that the rhythm is obvious to the participants in the ritual, which facilitates the process of movement interaction with the *Leṭmeyeh*. The slapping in this activity falls on the strong beat of the bar. Three different time signatures dominated the melodies of the *Leṭmeyeh* in this activity: (2/4), 4/4, and (6/8). The following is the musical transcription of *dish imbellileh* ('I enter the shrine wet') *Leṭmeyeh*, which consists of four melodies (A, B, C, and D), each of which is performed by the *Almullayeh* with rhythmic singing and kinetic accompaniment by the women.

When the *Almullayeh* transfers to the next melody of the *Leṭmeyeh*, the women will remain silent to listen to the new melody, determine its tempo, and figure out when to start the rhythmic accompaniment by slapping and moving. This is done within moments, with the help of the assistant of the *Almullayeh*, so that the women do not lose the continuity of movement and slapping. The diversity of melodies, rhythms, and the manner of slapping in this ritual are factors of diversification that help women to endure the ritual and not feel bored or monotonous. Also, women always participate in singing in this activity, so they move in a circular motion, singing, slapping, and crying simultaneously. This activity of the ritual lasts between five to eight minutes and is rarely repeated. Usually, this activity is the last thing performed within the ritual of all the days of *Muḥarram* and *Ṣufer*, except for the tenth of *Muḥarram*, which contains five activities.

The following is a text of one verse for each of the four melodies of *dish imbellileh* ('I enter the shrine wet') *Leṭmeyeh*:

A: I enter the shrine wet (*waylah*)[29]
    and leave it dry (*waylah* it)
B: Let us offer condolences to Zahra'
    (Let us offer condolences to Zahra')

The Female Role in Sacred Musical Practices in Shī'ah Rituals

Music Example 35.2   Transcription of *dish imbellileh* ('I enter the shrine wet') *Leṭmeyeh*.

C: Oh Zahra', your son never has been forgotten
   Oh Zahra', your son (never has been forgotten)
D: They are my son and my nephew who died thirsty
   The Zahra' says help me (women)

Although the number of syllables is equal in all the verses of the four melodies, the lengths of syllables are arranged randomly, making the text unaffiliated with any known Arabic poetic meter. The text is fraught with emotion across a dialogue between women who wish to offer condolences to Zahra' (the nickname of Hussein's mother). In addition, the *Almullayeh* used the word 'women' in the final tune to give the *Alleṭum wuqufen* activity a feminine singularity that nurtures the collective bonding factor between the mourning women. Furthermore, one metaphorical image is used in the text of the first melody when the *Almullayeh* states that she would enter the shrine (of Hussein) wet, meaning full of sins, and leave it dry, meaning without sins. This is one of the main beliefs of *Shī'ah*: that by visiting the shrines of Hussein or his father Ali, all sins will be erased.

5. *Maqtel* (the killing story): this activity is performed only on *'ashura*, the tenth day of the month of *Muḥarram*, where the story of the killing of Hussein is narrated. During this

activity, the mourning council will be quiet and the audience does not play any role except crying while listening to the *Almullayeh* telling the story of the killing of Hussein and his relatives in the Battle of Karbala. The length of this activity is about twenty minutes if it is performed after the other four activities, as will be summarised. However, the story can also be told in detail, which can last up to two hours, but in this case the other four activities will not be performed on that day.

This activity is presented in the standard Arabic language and the *Almullayeh* adopts the recitative style in performing this activity. The script of the *maqtel* cannot be written by anyone, as all mourning councils should use the same printed and existing script.[30] Despite this, the *Almullayeh* inserts some phrases in the Iraqi colloquial dialect to clarify some details and emphasise some historical facts. She applies the *Alna'i* method of performance for these inserted phrases to arouse the emotion of the listeners and reduce the repetition of the recitative performance style. The following figure shows the standard structure of the ritual of its five activities:

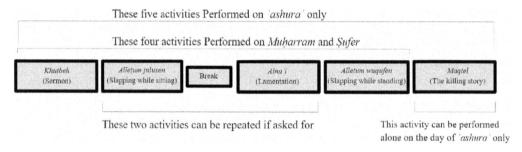

Figure 35.5 The standard structure of the *Muḥarram*, *'ashura*, and *Arbi'ineyeh* Rituals.

Conclusion

As explained in this chapter, we find that women play a vital role in the religious rituals of the *Shī'ah* in the Karbala province in Iraq through their role as creators of the text and melody, as performers of the *Leṭmeyeh* genre, and as leaders of the women's mourning council during the rituals. In addition, the *Almullayeh* was able to break the social and religious barriers that previously prevented women from singing, chanting, or interfering in religious affairs, and she combined these barriers and turned them into a tool that enabled her to change many social stereotypes that did not believe in the ability of women to participate in social, religious, and musical activities effectively.

We have detected the role and the solid connection between music, religion, and movement in most of the activities of the *Shī'ah* rituals. The position of the woman is also evident in this chapter through her role as an *Almullayeh*, by combining music and religion and creating countless *Leṭmeyat* that meet the listeners' religious needs. Further, the *Almullayeh* preserves the required religious themes and values and includes them in the text of her *Leṭmeyat*; she can compose a melody commensurate with the prestige of the ritual and to serve its different activities. Additionally, she is able to identify the slapping mechanism during the rituals in a way that serves the rhythmic accompaniment and responds to the women's spiritual need for the slapping factor as a form of self-flagellation. All these achievements contributed to the crystallisation of the *Leṭmeyat* as a religious musical genre on the one hand, and to finding a distinctive role for a woman as an innovator, performer, and leader within her socio-religious and musical career as *Almullayeh* on the other.

Notes

1. Syed Akbar Hyder, *Reliving Karbala: Martyrdom in South Asian Memory* (New York: Oxford University Press, 2008), 95.
2. The Iraqi community and some sources call him 'the Imam' or Imam Hussein.
3. Barak A. Salmoni and Paula Holmes-Eber, *Operational Culture for the Warfighter: Principles and Applications* (Washington, DC: Marine Corps University Press, 2008), 171.
4. Yitzhak Nakash, "An Attempt to Trace the Origin of the Rituals of 'Āshūrā'," *Die Welt des Islams* 33 (1993): 161–81, p. 162, www.jstor.com/stable/1570949.
5. Wilferd Madelung, *The Succession to Muḥammad: A Study of the Early Caliphate* (Cambridge: Cambridge University Press, 1997), 1.
6. Augustus Richard Norton, "Ritual, Blood, and Shiite Identity: Ashura in Nabatiyya, Lebanon," *TDR* 49 (2005): 140–55, p. 143, www.jstor.org/stable/4488690.
7. For more details, please see: Asma Afsaruddin, "Umayyad Dynasty," *Britannica*, 2013, accessed February 17, 2021, www.britannica.com/topic/Umayyad-dynasty-Islamic-history.
8. Peter J. Chelkowski, *Eternal Performance: Ta'ziyeh and Other Shiite Rituals* (New York: Seagull, 2010), 3.
9. Ibn El-Neil, *The Truth About Islam* (New York: Eloquent Books, 2008), 204.
10. *Muḥarram* is the first month in the Islamic annual calendar. *Muḥarram* means restricted, specifically the restriction of fighting and killing, as Arab tribes (before Islam) used to fight each other frequently. In this month, fighting is prohibited. The killing of Hussein and his followers in this month gave the event more importance among Muslims.
11. Lesley Hazleton, *After the Prophet: The Epic Story of the Shia-Sunni Split in Islam* (New York: Anchor Books, 2010), 206.
12. Abir Hamdar, "Jihad of Words: Gender and Contemporary Karbala Narratives," *The Yearbook of English Studies* 39 (2009): 48–100, p. 84, accessed February 17, 2021, www.jstor.org/stable/25679862.
13. Kamran Scot Aghaie, *The Women of Karbala: Ritual Performance and Symbolic Discourses in Modern Shi'i Islam* (Austin: University of Texas Press, 2005), 4.
14. Tahera Qutbuddin, "Zaynab Bint Ali," in *Encyclopedia of Religion*, 2nd ed. (Detroit: Macmillan Reference, 2005), 9937–39, p. 9938.
15. Diane D'Souza, *Partners of Zaynab: A Gendered Perspective of Shia Muslim Faith* (Columbia: University of South Carolina Press, 2014), 81.
16. *Ṣufer* is the second month in the Arabic and Islamic calendar. *Ṣufer* means to be empty or void. The origin of this name came from the life of Arabs before Islam, where most of the Arab tribes temporarily abandoned their settlements and went to invade weaker tribes, only to return afterwards.
17. They are called visitors as they visit the shrines of Ali and Hussein in Karbala and Najaf during this time.
18. 106–2 Joint Committee Print, *Annual Report on International Religious Freedom 2000* (United States Congress-Senate. Committee on Foreign Relations, 2001), 443.
19. The gentleman who recites and reads a specific story or poem loudly.
20. The Baath regime was overthrown and the *Shī'ah* took power in Iraq.
21. For a study of women's participation in *Shī'ah* rituals in Iran, see Talieh Wartner-Attarzadeh, "Female Leadership in Iranian-Arab Shi'a Rituals from Khorramshahr, South-Western Iran," in *Women's Leadership in Music: Modes, Legacies, Alliances*, edited by Iva Nenić and Linda Cimardi (Bielefeld: Transcript Verlag, 2023), 99–110.
22. *Almullayeh* is the feminine form of *Almulleh*. The source of the name comes from the Arabic standard word *Imla'*, which means 'recites and reads loudly'.
23. Toby Howarth, *The Twelve Shi'a as a Muslim Minority in India: Pulpit of Tears* (Oxon: Routledge, 2005), 46–49.
24. *Hashemi* is a garment made of very thin fabric with wide sleeves and sides.

25. The syllables in the parentheses are sung by the women who participate in the ritual. The syllables (āh āh) express the sadness and grief of the women who sing in the middle of the dialogue between the sister and her brother.
26. Arabic poetic meters are generally identified by the number and the order of long and short syllables in each poetic verse.
27. The text in the *Alna'i* activity has a variety of sources, such as being taken from a recording of a previous *Alna'i* activity or an extract from a published text. After 2003, many male and female poets began publishing poems that dealt with the story of the killing of Hussein from different angles.
28. These religious rituals are mainly held in Karbala at this time of the year. Women who cannot travel to Karbala hold local small councils in *Shī'ah* areas of Iraq, mainly in southern Iraq. Usually, these councils are brief and consist of two activities only, *Alleṭum Julusen* and the *Alna'i*.
29. The words and phrases given in parentheses are sung by women.
30. The original text was passed down through several generations, during which the text developed into the form used today. After 2003, the Ḥawza Al-'Imia Foundation, the highest religious authority for *Shī'ah* in Iraq, began printing these texts and distributing them free of charge.

Bibliography

106–2 Joint Committee Print. *Annual Report on International Religious Freedom 2000*. United States. Congress. Senate. Committee on Foreign Relations, 2001, 443.

Afsaruddin, Asma. "Umayyad Dynasty." *Britannica*, 2013. Accessed February 17, 2021. www.britannica.com/topic/Umayyad-dynasty-Islamic-history.

Aghaie, Kamran Scot. *The Women of Karbala: Ritual Performance and Symbolic Discourses in Modern Shi'i Islam*. Austin: University of Texas Press, 2005.

Beitler, Ruth Margolies, and Angelica R. Martinez. *Women's Roles in the Middle East and North Africa*. Santa Barbara, CA: Greenwood Press, 2010.

Chelkowski, Peter J. *Eternal Performance: Ta'ziyeh and Other Shiite Rituals*. New York: Seagull, 2010.

Cornell, Vincent J. *Voices of Islam: Voices of the Spirit*. Westport, CT: Greenwood Publishing Group, 2007.

D'Souza, Diane. *Partners of Zaynab: A Gendered Perspective of Shia Muslim Faith*. Columbia: University of South Carolina Press, 2014.

Efrati, Noga. *Women in Iraq: Past Meets Present*. New York: Columbia University Press, 2012.

El-Neil, Ibn. *The Truth About Islam*. New York: Eloquent Books, 2008.

Fuller, Graham E., and Rend Rahim Francke. *Arab Shi'a: The Forgotten Muslims*. New York: Palgrave Macmillan, 2001.

Hamdar, Abir. "Jihad of Words: Gender and Contemporary Karbala Narratives." *The Yearbook of English Studies* 39 (2009): 48–100. Accessed February 17, 2021. www.jstor.org/stable/25679862.

Hazleton, Lesley. *After the Prophet: The Epic Story of the Shia-Sunni Split in Islam*. New York: Anchor Books, 2010.

Howarth, Toby. *The Twelver Shi'a as a Muslim Minority in India: Pulpit of Tears*. Oxon: Routledge, 2005.

Hyder, Syed Akbar. *Reliving Karbala: Martyrdom in South Asian Memory*. New York: Oxford University Press, 2008.

Khosronejad, Pedram. *Women's Rituals and Ceremonies in Shiite Iran and Muslim Communities: Methodological and Theoretical Challenges*. Berlin: LIT Verlag Münster, 2015.

Madelung, Wilferd. *The Succession to Muhammad: A Study of the Early Caliphate*. Cambridge: Cambridge University Press, 1997.

Nakash, Yitzhak. "An Attempt to Trace the Origin of the Rituals of 'Āshūrā'." *Die Welt des Islams* 33 (1993): 161–81. www.jstor.com/stable/1570949.

Norton, Augustus Richard. "Ritual, Blood, and Shiite Identity: Ashura in Nabatiyya, Lebanon." *TDR* 49 (2005): 140–55. www.jstor.org/stable/4488690.

Qutbuddin, Tahera. *Encyclopedia of Religion*, 2nd ed. Detroit: Macmillan Reference, 2005.

Salmoni, Barak A., and Paula Holmes-Eber. *Operational Culture for the Warfighter: Principles and Applications*. Quantico, VA: Marine Corps University Press, 2008.

Wartner-Attarzadeh, Talieh. "Female Leadership in Iranian-Arab Shi'a Rituals from Khorramshahr, South-Western Iran." In *Women's Leadership in Music: Modes, Legacies, Alliances*, edited by Iva Nenić and Linda Cimardi, 99–110. Bielefeld: Transcript Verlag, 2023.

36
A MUSLIM IN A BAPTIST CHURCH
Discovering My Calling as a Sacred Musician

Theresa Parvin Steward

'You Don't Look like a Muslim'

For most of my life, I listened to other voices tell me what I should do or what I would be good at doing. There was little input from my own internal voice that mainly sought to please others: family, teachers, advisors, employers, and colleagues. I shied away from leadership roles and teamwork because I had trouble finding and sharing my own voice, especially when forced into the spotlight. In 2012, after relocating back to Richmond, Virginia, where my parents had eventually retired, and finishing a Ph.D. in Musicology at the University of Edinburgh, I was struggling to find fulfilling employment. I continued to have tunnel vision, thinking that the only position I could be satisfied in would be an academic one: what all my degrees had been leading me toward. By 2016, I had worked a number of part-time jobs as I continued to search for more sustainable academic employment. In the fall of 2016, I had a nearly full-time load as an adjunct lecturer. In addition to commuting four days per week to a university 120 km away, I was also teaching yoga and Pilates classes at two local gyms, teaching piano lessons privately and at a children's music academy, and was about to take on yet another part-time role as an Organist and Pianist for a local church, Grace Baptist Church. This new position, however, was no ordinary role for someone like me. And by 'someone like me', I mean for someone who is a Muslim woman.

Previously, I considered religion to be separate from everything else I did. My faith has always been a personal, private practice, one that I never had the opportunity to share with others outside of my family as I grew up in predominantly white American Christian communities. I have remained Muslim since birth, born to an Iranian Muslim mother and an English father who converted to Islam from Roman Catholicism upon marrying my mother in London, where she had emigrated in 1970. My mother, a devout Muslim who prays more than the prescribed five times a day, never forced religion upon me. Instead, she created an environment of love, care, and acceptance. We emigrated to the United States a couple of months shy of my sixth birthday, and after exploring the Southwest, Southern California, and driving up the West Coast, we settled in Bellingham, a small university town in Washington State, just south of the Canadian border. I would spend my formative years in Bellingham, where we did not have a local mosque, so religion became mainly a private practice with a few isolated visits to mosques outside of town. When I had questions about Islam, my father directed me to helpful books on the religion, Islam, and my mother shared with me her own personal experiences, subtly nurturing within me a strong sense of faith that continued to grow from a young age.

It felt odd, feeling like an outsider when most people did not know what made me 'different'. Being white-presenting and without a *hijab* (head covering), I never wore my Muslim identity on my sleeve. As a result, it was often assumed that I was likely raised as a Christian; so much so that I was often privy to hurtful or ignorant comments targeted towards my faith and my heritage by people who had no idea I was 'one of those'. I had many Christian friends who attended church every Sunday and spoke of Sunday school classes and the church summer camps they attended. It seemed like another world to me, and I sometimes wondered what it would be like if I could share my faith with others my own age. If I was asked about my faith and I responded truthfully, I was often met with blank or judgemental stares, and strange comments or questions in response: 'Well, my mother says if you're not Christian, you are going to hell', or 'So your mom is Muslim, but you're not really Muslim, right?' If I wanted to fit in and feel accepted, the only choice I had seemed to be to keep my faith separate from my interactions with others.

As an adult, I would often describe myself as a 'liberal Muslim' in order to help others understand how I fit into the mould of their expectations of a Muslim woman. This started to feel like I was justifying my beliefs and defending the 'type' of Muslim I 'appeared' to be. I have been told, 'You don't look like a Muslim', and my practices have been questioned: why I don't eat pork, but I do enjoy an occasional alcoholic beverage, or why I don't cover myself from head to toe. Most religions do not have a singular face or an image of conformity; diversity, especially in appearance, is well-acknowledged in Judaism and Christianity, for example. Islam, however, invokes a certain image in the minds of others, especially of Muslim women: darker-skinned, mysteriously veiled, and usually silent and subservient. It is an image that the world continues to work on dispelling as a universal truth. Rather than face the projected stereotypes while continually explaining myself, once again, it became easier not to talk about religion at all.

Throughout my life, I have always felt comfortable sitting in church. On Christmas Eves and Easter Sundays, my family and I sometimes went to mass. One would naturally assume it was at my father's request, as a former Roman Catholic who was raised in the church and its schools, but it was my mother who pressed us to go. I enjoyed these services as another way for me to be present with my faith and pray for all that I held dear in the world. My mother instilled within me a deep respect for all religious practices by showing me her acceptance and respect of them. Her parents had done the same for her. To them, it didn't matter if you prayed differently or attended a different kind of service in a different building; it was all worship of the same and holy God. Any time I would travel, especially within Europe, some of my first stops would be at churches: cathedrals, basilicas, small chapels, not only to admire the architecture, but also to light a candle and pray silently in an empty pew. In those sacred moments, I was reminded that no matter where I am in the world, God's presence is always there.

In 2016, when I met with Rev. Dr. Courtney Allen Crump, the Senior Pastor at Grace Baptist Church in Richmond, Virginia, I was hesitant to address my labelled difference in faith, which the Senior Pastor and the Church's Personnel Commission were unaware of at the time. Just before interviewing at Grace, I had applied for a position as a pianist at a local Southern Baptist church, ignorant of the difference between American Baptists and Southern Baptists. Despite a thorough auditioning process and the initial excitement of the Pastor and the Music Director, when I did not give a satisfactory or expected answer to the final interview question ('How were you raised as a Christian?'), I never heard from them again. So, as I was about to be hired at Grace, I requested another meeting with Rev. Dr. Crump to ask if there would be any issue or discomfort with my faith background. She barely batted an eye, and I'll never forget her response: 'Well, I'm just sorry you even had to ask that'.

Since then, my faith has never come into question at Grace. I have only felt acceptance and love from all. In fact, those who had a hard time reconciling my faith with my position in the church were mostly those outside of the church, even my own friends. Many just could not understand how I could be of one faith working in an institution of another. I often found myself explaining and justifying why I worked for a church, why my Sunday mornings were never free, and what it was like to be a part of the church's worship services. Some friends, mostly non-religious, asked, 'How does it feel to sit through a Christian service every week when you are not Christian?' One friend jokingly asked, 'Do you feel like a heathen on Sundays?' I tried to find the words to explain that I didn't really feel a difference between praying in church or praying at home, that I was fully aware of the differences in faith practices and beliefs, but it still didn't feel like a foreign faith to me. I felt connected to the community at Grace since we were all worshipping the same one God. Sadly, my answers never seemed quite enough for skeptics who implied, that they had already made up their mind as to how I should feel: an outsider, disconnected or even disenfranchised from the Church.

Some friends tried to paint the church as a Christian fundamentalist stereotype, assuming that it was a rigid, conservative place of rules and non-acceptance. They made jokes about how if you were anything but white and heterosexual, you probably were not welcome there, and they assumed that calling yourself a Christian meant you were judgemental and condemning in your views, and likely politically conservative. I could clearly see, even after one worship service, that this was not true at Grace Baptist Church. I tried not to let the comments of others bother me, but I felt hurt and frustrated. Once again, I found myself having to explain and defend religion; this time one that wasn't quite my own, but one that I felt I inherently understood; a faith community that welcomed me and so many others as children of one Holy God.

'If the Spirit of God Resides in the Breath, then Music . . . is a Manifestation of that Spirit'[1]

One year into my organist/pianist position at Grace I was fully aware that of all of the jobs I had held, I cherished my position at Grace the most. I was able to be even more active as a musician, I had freedom to choose which musical offerings to play each week, I collaborated weekly with a wonderful group of volunteer singers and sometimes with other church members who were also musicians, and I worked with an encouraging and supportive Minister of Music, Rev. Wanda Sauley Fennell. Being a church musician was different, of course, than my other performance roles. For one, I had to become better versed in hymnody and Christian sacred music. I already had much experience accompanying, so I quickly adapted to playing a supporting role for the choir and congregation, but I also had to become familiar with the preferences and peculiarities of how certain Baptist hymns are sung. My greatest challenge was becoming proficient at the organ, which required a different set of skills from what I was used to at the piano. What I realised only much later was that I was also becoming a very different kind of musician altogether: a sacred musician.

On the surface, adopting the role of sacred musician meant adapting to working within a different faith tradition. Rather than a challenge, this has been a welcome learning process. In Islam, music has no place in worship. One hears beautiful *azans* (calls to prayer) recited by *muezzins* (proclaimers who announce daily prayer times) from the minarets of mosques and stirring, hypnotic *tajweed*, or Qur'anic cantillation, in worship settings. Both sound musical to unfamiliar ears. But they are not, in fact, considered to be music at all. Worship services revolve solely around prayer and these holy recitative practices are considered forms of prayer and are culturally classified as *non-musiqa*, or non-music.

I did not associate music necessarily with faith; I was raised to enjoy music as a secular art form. I was trained and educated to perform and understand music as a series of notes and rhythms, to be beautiful and pleasing to the ear, and/or interesting to the mind. My parents worked hard to provide a musical education for me from the age of six, and I was privileged to have had wonderful music teachers and piano professors. However, through all my training, there was little mention in my education of what music could do for the soul. Curiously, it was listening to music that seemed to be emphasised as more of a soul-connecting practice rather than the actual performance of it.

Music was taught to me as an aesthetic form where musicality was emphasised, but not expanded upon in spiritual terms. This is ironic, given that so much of the canon of Western art music that is often required learning in music education revolves around religion. Many composers were compelled and driven by a greater force to write, and at times felt as though they had no other choice. Handel, upon completing his *Messiah*, remarked, 'Whether I was in my body or out of my body as I wrote it, I know not. God knows'.[2] Mozart revealed that before the debut of his 'Paris' Symphony No. 31 in D major, he 'prayed to God for His mercy that it might go well, dedicating all to His greater honour and glory'.[3] Both Beethoven and Brahms appealed to the Divine, the latter declaring, 'I feel vibrations that thrill all of me. These vibrations are of the Spirit illuminating the soul power within . . . I feel capable of drawing inspiration from above'.[4] Music has been often linked to the Divine: an example of Divine love, a manifestation of a Divine voice, described thus even by agnostic and non-Christian composers like Ralph Vaughan Williams and Gustav Mahler.[5] While I learned some of this sitting in a classroom taking music history courses, I did not learn about it while sitting at the piano, playing actual works that were so Divinely inspired. This education would only come into fruition much later during my work as a sacred musician.

Rev. Dr. Victoria Sirota eloquently writes about the role of the church musician in her book *Preaching to the Choir: Claiming the Role of Sacred Musician*.[6] I first encountered this book in the summer of 2019 while attending the American Guild of Organist's Mid-Atlantic Convention in Atlantic City, New Jersey. Rev. Dr. Sirota gave a workshop based on principles from her book, and I was captivated. I was nearly three years into my position at Grace and had not heard my role described in quite these terms: sacred musicians do not merely perform; being a sacred musician is a calling, and music a theology.[7] I was gradually learning, in Rev. Dr. Sirota's words, that 'The call of [the] sacred musician involves empowering the congregation to feel the divine presence, helping them to raise their voices in praise, and inspiring them with a taste of heaven.'[8]

Hymns come fully alive only with their texts, and there is not much in this world more moving than hearing a multitude of voices lift these texts in worship. As I accompany our choir and support our current Minister of Music, Rev. Chris Crowley, there are mini miracles that sometimes occur in worship. These are moments that Rev. Dr. Sirota describes as where 'heaven and earth meet, a liminal place,' when musical direction, accompaniment, choir, congregation, and space come into 'cosmic alignment'.[9] Such moments are nothing more than spiritually transcendent spaces in time where we can be connected to God. Playing an active part in these holy moments is indescribable and soul quenching. It sums up all that I neglected to grasp in my younger days of performance: the deep connection between music-making and spirituality.

As musicians, we are taught to strive for perfection, that technique is king, and virtuosity is what is often most impressive to an audience. We are trained to pay more attention to fingering and exact rhythms and much less to the spaces in between the notes; the moments that offer prayer, the moments that *are* prayer. As I began listening to those spaces between the notes, particularly when playing solo musical offerings, I began to develop a better understanding as to why I was in this role.

It is one thing for me to have a holy moment at the keys; I often do when I'm practising alone in an empty sanctuary. But to be witness to others experiencing something holy, seeing the smiles, the tears, hearing the spontaneous clapping upon completion, the quietly whispered and sometimes loudly exclaimed 'Amens' from the pews. When congregants began sharing with me afterwards their listening experiences, it opened my eyes. It began to change my view of performance and shape how I approach music in general, inside and outside the church.

Once, after a service, a congregant asked me if I was a seminarian. I assumed they were asking because Grace happens to have many members who are former seminarians. But they were asking because of what they felt in the music: 'When you play, it is transcendent; as if you can hear the Spirit in each note'. That was one of the greatest compliments I have heard and probably will ever hear. Now, I aim for this every time I sit at the keyboard with the hope that it is not a performance to observe from a distance, but an *experience* to be a part of, a spiritual journey through the notes, even if only for one soul sitting in the pews. As Episcopal priest Pittman McGehee notes, 'Spirituality is the deep human longing to experience the transcendent in our ordinary life'.[10] Call it escapism, soul-searching, a moment of bliss, or otherworldly, but for me, playing and sharing music means a journey closer to the Divine.

This is certainly not to say that every time I play is a transcendent experience. My humanity has shown many a time: when my nerves and self-doubt have had the better of me, when pages have fallen off the music stand, or two were accidentally turned at once, when I have loudly played a wrong chord, or hit the wrong piston or pedal on the organ, when I have inadvertently jumped ahead of the choir, and the list goes on. I continue to accept these learning moments that teach me humility and the power of being human. Sometimes I have an off day; there is some troubling event or thought that I can't shake from my mind, or I didn't sleep well the night before, and my anxiety is setting in. But I know these feelings are part of the shared human experience. Without them, I wouldn't be able to feel and share all the heartfelt emotions that go into my music-making, making it something more than just notes on a page.

Most of the time, however, these instances are triggered by overthinking. Sometimes it is holding on to a past moment – not forgiving myself for that wrong note I just played a few seconds ago – and then that doubt, that holding of guilt and shame, leads to yet another wrong note. A. Helwa writes, 'how can you experience forgiveness if you never make a mistake?' and continues on to describe how God, the All-Compassionate (*Ar-Rahman*), the Most Merciful (*Ar-Rahim*), forgives us constantly as an act of Divine love.[11] If God can forgive us daily, then surely I can forgive myself for a few wrong notes.

Too much overthinking and doubt can lead the ego to superimpose itself on to the performance. A. Helwa describes the ego as 'a veil that separates us from the oneness of God', inclined 'to be forgetful of the Divine'.[12] Once the ego is at work, the music becomes about me and not the greater work at hand. And so, every time I sit on the bench, I learn that an authentic expression and experience of the music flows more freely when I trust, feel, and breathe into it, when I can let go of the Self and fully embrace the Divine intention for performance: to play for God and to aid others in their worship of God.

'Make Room for One Another in Your Collective Life. Make Room and in Return God Will Make Room for You' (Qur'an 58:11)

In the spring of 2019, the position of Church Administrator at Grace became vacant, and I saw it as an opportunity for a healthy break from being stretched thin across multiple jobs and long commutes. So I took this new 'leap of faith' and left my academic position for the role of Church Administrator, in addition to my continued sacred music duties. My role continues to grow in ways I never expected. I have been accepted and appreciated by a supportive ministerial staff who, from the summer of 2019 until August 2021, happened also to be all-female. I have experienced and witnessed an extraordinary amount of respect and trust between staff members. This has encouraged creative leadership, which I have been embraced as a part of. When Rev. Dr. Crump or former Associate Pastor Rev. Suzanne Vinson referred to 'our ministries', I know they are being inclusive of me and what I offer, regardless of my faith background and lack of clerical title. I have learned to claim my own brand of 'ministry' as I care for others through the spiritual practices of the weekly tasks and responsibilities that hold much of what we do together and, of course, through music. These roles have grown far beyond the titles on paper of 'Church Administrator' or 'Organist' to a vital part of a team that cultivates a genuine bond between members of the church while inspiring deep connection between these worshipers and God. And as such, I am greatly fulfilled, more than I have ever been in my life.

Much of this fulfilment comes from a loving and caring congregation. A. Helwa writes, 'The first step of being Muslim is to profess your faith, but until you put your beliefs into action you don't actually possess faith.'[13] At Grace, all members of the congregation are seen as ministers to each other and to the world at large. And it is not just in name or word; these are compassionate human beings, faithful to God and to themselves. When one hurts, we all do. When one falls, we all help that person get back up. Grace is a place where love abounds and not just acceptance, but *encouragement* and *celebration* reign. Every person is encouraged to come as they are and to be true to themselves in the eyes of God, and that is something worthy of celebrating. This place, that has become my second home, has *encouraged* a young Muslim woman to participate in and contribute to worship planning and to take part in the essential running of its organisation without question. And this is *celebrated* alongside the countless gifts others have to offer at Grace.

The Effects of the COVID-19 Pandemic: Putting Beliefs into Action

March 2020 changed everything. Once it was no longer safe to gather in person, all worship services and church events became virtual offerings to watch and participate in from home. Since singing was affected greatly by the pandemic, my role as a sacred musician began to feel much more solitary. I recorded organ and piano accompaniments, and they were sent to the choir members who recorded their parts individually at home. The only sense of creating music together happened when listening to the final mixed product, but there was no live musical experience of this in a performance or auditory sense. As a live musician, the easy way would have been to retreat, to give up when music could not be heard live, when voices could not sing together in person, or to think that no recording was ever going to be as good as a live performance. But 'waiting it out' just didn't strike us as an option. Instead, the pandemic provided the perfect opportunity to live into our values at Grace.

Just as A. Helwa writes about 'putting beliefs into action' as a Muslim, Brené Brown writes about the importance of leading by, 'Living into our values . . . doing more than professing our values, practicing them.'[14] As soon as we closed our church doors, I felt a deep calling to provide musical solace for those around me. I needed to find a new way to connect with others through music. My days became filled with recording and sharing daily musical offerings on social media for our church community and beyond.[15] Over two hundred recordings later, I continued to share music for online worship and memorial services, birthdays, graduations, and virtual concerts. Sometimes, it was a hymn tune that helped us remember and honour significant days in the church calendar; other times, it was a 'heartsong' or a piece that provides peace or a burst of joy in crucial moments in our lives. More than ever, I became aware of how music, especially during challenging times, has the power to soothe, to heal, to comfort, to encourage, and to uplift.

The response to these musical offerings was often surprising. You never know who is listening. Sometimes it was members outside the church who found our Facebook page, other times it was someone I knew in my personal life outside of Grace, and sometimes it was friends of friends who were listening due to the power of sharing on social media. I have been connected to people that I've never met in person, but who listened regularly to these musical offerings. They shared their sentiments, their memories associated with the music; sometimes of a certain place in their lives, or a fond recollection from childhood, and often of a loved one who is no longer with them. This generosity in sharing these memories has been a great gift. It fuels me to make even more music. It feeds my soul.

It was strange only to be playing in front of a camera and not an audience. It also felt different to be in more of a solo role than a musically collaborative one. But although I was performing physically alone, I was playing for more people than I ever had until that point. I played more *for* people than I ever had before. Again, I was reminded that this calling is not about virtuosity or perfection; sometimes I offered the simplest of pieces. Especially during pandemic living, music was a source of consolation for many. If something significant happened in our external world, I allowed the music to reflect that. During the height of the Black Lives Matter protests in summer 2020, I recorded mostly arrangements of African American spirituals, always posting the original words that, when read amidst ongoing racism, conflict, and injustice, felt fresh and poignant once more. When our church suffered great losses of dear members in the period of a short time, our hearts were not yearning for joyous, celebratory preludes and postludes. We needed that balm of comforting music to help heal our grief-sick souls. Through this pandemic time, I have grown even closer to the heart of what it means to be a sacred musician. And it has been reaffirmed that, for me, music is no longer about performance, but about connection.

I continue to be reminded that the music I offer is not about me. On All Saints Sunday 2020, I played organ music from within the church sanctuary with the doors from the narthex open to the portico for those to hear outside as they lit candles in memory of their loved ones. This was not an opportunity to blast the organ at full tilt, and so choosing which registrations would work best yet could still be heard outside was a challenge. As I played hymns like 'Amazing Grace' and 'Be Thou My Vision', and pieces that were supposed to be comforting meditations, I thought how 'ugly' these hymns sounded to my ears from where I was playing; string stops too loud, overpowering principals and diapasons. I had no way to gauge the sound beyond the doors of the sanctuary. Afterwards, I didn't know how to feel; I just prayed that the music was at least clear enough to hear for those sitting socially distanced outside. A couple of days later, I received a phone call from a church member, who told me she had been in tears listening to the organ. She found the whole event very moving, and it was the music that reached her soul. I was humbled and extremely grateful. I checked in with my perfectionist ego and was again reminded that it didn't matter how 'ugly' it sounded to my ears; what mattered was how people felt hearing the organ play their favourite hymns for the first time in nearly eight months.

Easter 2021 provided another opportunity to share music, this time joyous and celebratory. When I blasted the loudest trumpets and horns and the brightest mixtures on the organ toward the wide-open doors, I reminded myself that it was not how deafeningly the organ blares through my ears that mattered; it mattered what it sounds like out there; that to those visiting the portico and listening, it was a reminder of the good news of the season. And in these extraordinary times, this was not just the usual celebration of resurrection but a recognition that once again, life as we know it would be changing, and we will eventually be resurrected from the pandemic. Music was there to comfort and uplift the soul and to provide much-needed hope.

In July 2021, worship services at Grace Baptist Church resumed in-person. It was a beautiful homecoming back into our building and a readjustment for all of us, particularly our staff, who had been working long hours 'behind the scenes'. For a period, we continued to collaborate on pre-recorded online services as well as in-person services, and I continued to provide online musical offerings once or twice a week. But I found that my energy was waning, and once we installed new equipment in our sanctuary to livestream our services, I gradually ceased recording. We found ourselves continually in times of transition with changes in our staff configuration and the instability of the ongoing COVID-19 pandemic, which continued to create shifts in how we gathered for worship. What has remained constant is how closely our staff works together in worship planning and thinking about congregational life as a whole; if anything, the pandemic brought us closer together in our shared leadership. At the same time, we also found ourselves exhausted and drained. Self-care became and continues to be a mantra that we remind ourselves to practice, so we can better take care of those in our community. In doing so, we are reminded of one of the significant lessons we learned during the height of 'lockdown': how to prioritise what is needed and how to let go of that which is not essential.

'No Religion Is an Island'[16]

It is natural to wonder whether being so strongly connected to the church would make me question my faith and at some point steer me towards considering a life in Christ. There are church members who address me as their 'sister in Christ,' sometimes unaware of my faith background. I am greatly honoured that these members, these friends, consider me as a sibling in faith. To live a life in Christ is not insignificant to me, nor lost on me. I know deep down that my heart belongs to Islam; there are fundamental beliefs that I cannot shed. But every day, I aim to walk in Christ's light and love; Jesus remains an important figure in my life, as are Abraham, Moses, the Prophet Muhammad (*Peace be upon him*), and all other prophets. How I practise my faith intersects with the work I do at the church; so much so that I consider worship services to be my time to worship. I pray alongside everyone else; I pray to God like everyone else. The work I do is an expression and extension of my strong Islamic faith.

The Qur'an states, 'There is no compulsion in religion' (Qur'an 2:256). So, rather than being compelled by my environment or by others to convert, my experience at Grace has educated me in the beauty of Christianity practised with love; and based on all religions of the book, love cannot be created by force but must be chosen of free will to experience and share. I do not need to convert to believe in the goodness of God and humanity. As rabbi and scholar Abraham Heschel once remarked in a lecture titled 'No Religion Is an Island': 'We are all involved with one another . . . religious isolationism is a myth.'[17] My spirituality and religion cannot exist in a vacuum, and I thank God it doesn't. Otherwise, I would not be where I am today.

On the holiest of Islamic days, my reverence is quieter because it is less visible; I don't have many to share it with. As I enter the holy season of Ramadan, I spend more time in my own spiritual practices. I read translations of the Qur'an, I pray and fast, and I reflect on how I can shape my life to better this world and honour Allah. And yet I am continually reminded of my connection to the faith community at Grace; for example, when Rev. Vinson sends me heartfelt Ramadan blessings or when I see other church members 'love' the Ramadan messages I post on Facebook and wish me 'Eid Mubarak' at the end of the holy month.

Rabbi Heschel remarked, 'our individual moments of faith are mere waves in the endless ocean of mankind's reaching out for God . . . where our souls are swept away by the awareness of the urgency of answering God's commandment'.[18] Because of this, I feel the connection between Ramadan and Lent, and I think of the experience of Ramadan as similar to the Lenten journey of a great Prophet who has preached peace and respect among all humans in their worship of the One God. Witnessing and experiencing an authentic and caring community of faith like Grace has only strengthened my own faith practices and inspired my personal understanding of and connection to God.

Towards the end of Ramadan in 2022, I was encouraged to speak for the first time on my faith background and experience in a church-wide Sunday School session. That day, my heart was overflowing. Church members responded with such support, love, and genuine interest and curiosity to learn more about another faith tradition and its practices. Following my presentation, I received notes and cards of appreciation, one of which will forever remain with me: a church member wrote that hearing me speak of my dedication made her 'want to be a better follower of Christ'. Months later, I let her know that this note still sat on my bookshelf at home where I could revisit her touching sentiments. To my surprise, she began to tell me about how she had begun incorporating a prayer mat into her prayer ritual. She explained that when I discussed the connection between the head and earth when prostrating in prayer, this spoke to her. In that moment in conversation with her, I felt not only seen, but I also felt connected; I no longer had to feel alone in my faith.

'This place where you are right now, God circled on a map for you.'
–Hafez, fourteenth-century Persian Sufi poet

Responding to the quote by Miles Davis: 'Man, sometimes it takes a long time to sound like yourself', musician and community activist Greg Jarrell writes, 'Sounding like yourself is not the sort of work done by yourself . . . It takes a whole community of friends and companions to help you learn who you are and what you have to say'.[19] I am thirty-nine at the time of writing this, and I can't find a better way to sum up how I have found my voice through my work. I struggled with finding it for so long because I had not found the right community to help me formulate it.

In January 2020, Rev. June Joplin, a pastor based in Mississauga, Ontario, was featured as an online guest preacher at Grace Baptist Church during what is considered by the Baptist Women in Ministry as the Martha Stearns Marshall month of preaching, which encourages women to speak from the pulpit, especially those who may have limited opportunities to do so. Rev. Joplin's sermon centred around these words from John 1:48: 'I saw you before you knew', and from Psalm 139:15–16: 'You saw me when no one else could see me.' She spoke of her coming out as a transgender woman, and despite being fired by her congregation as a result, she found great love in moments when she was 'seen' by her friends and loved ones. She concluded by expressing that being seen is not exclusive to LGBTQ+ communities. It is wonderful to be seen, no matter what our background may be. Her words resonated with me deeply, and no doubt, many others. Grace Baptist Church is the community that sees me. Once we feel seen, we can become more aware of how God invites us all into this Divine work of seeing. I not only feel free to let my light shine through my authentic Muslim self and the gifts I offer, but I am also more able to recognise the light in others. And when our lights intersect, beautiful things happen: God's work happens.

Never did I imagine that I would be working full-time in what is considered 'religious' employment, where there is no academic ranking, no glorified title, no big salary, no official prestigious awards, nothing like what my academic training supposedly, albeit unrealistically, prepared me for. But leadership means eschewing expectations, both those of others and ones that we hold of ourselves. Surprisingly I have discovered that all of my previous training seems to have led me to this very point. My musical training from a young age, my undergraduate studies in architectural design at the University of Virginia, my experience in office administration, my academic research and teaching skills, my training in mind/body practices, even the customer service jobs I held when I was younger, have all contributed to the way I lead in my current roles. Working for the church is a job unlike any other; one that requires commitment, self-discipline, collective responsibility, patience, compassionate care, navigating immeasurable loss and grief, and balancing self-care. And yet, I feel closer to God with every day of work. I feel closer to people around me. And I feel more like a leader now than I have in any other role in my life.

Leadership roles do not have to come with fancy titles or only be relegated to the loudest voices. I have learned, particularly through my work as a sacred musician, that leadership comes from how one expresses one's beliefs and allows one's work to be an extension of that. Much of my leadership comes from listening. As a sacred musician, I am always listening, and not just to music, but to others' needs, to the needs of a particular service, the needs of a family for a memorial or celebration, the needs of the current moment in our world. I have spoken loudly through music, saying much more than I could ever formulate into words.

Conclusion: Finding Belonging While Becoming Myself

Anna Quindlen writes, 'The thing that is really hard, and really amazing, is giving up on being perfect and beginning the work of becoming yourself'.[20] As a musician and an academic, one often wonders if one's good enough: good enough to compete with others, good enough to be successful, good enough to sustain a livelihood, good enough to be accepted by others. I was no exception, and I struggled when my music existed in isolation; the solitary nature of practising alone, the idea that classical music was a serious and elite art form, and the constant critiques, including the ever-present inner critic. Music was all about performance and a notion of perfection; anything less was failure. I became myself fully as a sacred musician when I realised the great power of my gifts that I had so blindly neglected; that even the simplest of tunes can impact someone so profoundly in that moment. A church member once told me, 'You need to be heard'. She didn't mean for fame or notoriety's sake, but because she could see, more clearly than I could at the time, that I had a gift that could reach and touch others. I know now that I have more gifts to share than I ever thought possible. More importantly, I have learned that music doesn't have to exist only for my pleasure or to satisfy my perfectionist tendencies; it can be a boundless spiritual tool and one that I can share with others.

My experience in a Christian environment has taught me how to reconcile my faith practices with my true passion of music after years of practising both in relative isolation from each other. This has allowed me to find a voice in musical leadership that manages to express both myself and my faith while fostering worshipful moments and spaces for a community to be one with their faith. I have discovered, as Rev. Dr. Sirota so aptly writes, 'that making music on sacred ground makes [me] happier than anything else on earth in the deepest place of [my] soul'.[21] This hasn't been due to my efforts alone; it is a testament to a church that leads with an open and authentic heart, one that *sees* others for who they are and the gifts they have to offer. In the words of Rev. Dr. Courtney Allen Crump, 'Grace is not a unicorn but a real life, embodied community of faith'. Undoubtedly, Grace Baptist Church is not the only faith community of its kind that exists, but it is a model of what every church, every institution, whether religious or not, can strive to be: one that welcomes and loves all who walks through its doors, and one that fully lives into its values. What began as just another part-time job blossomed into something so much more than I could have initially imagined. In turn, I continue to evolve, embracing my authentic, soul-searching self while letting go of expectations and assumptions of how I should be or should fit in. In the process, I have found a faith home. I, as a Muslim sacred musician, have found my community of faith, my family of faith, in a Baptist church.

Notes

1. Victoria Sirota, *Preaching to the Choir* (New York: Church Publishing Incorporated, 2006), 32.
2. Hal A. Lingerman, *The Healing Energies of Music* (Wheaton, IL: Quest Books, 1995), 239.
3. *Letters of Wolfgang Amadeus Mozart*, selected and edited by Hans Mersmann, translated from the German by H. M. Bozman (New York: Dover Publications, 1972), 107–08.
4. Patrick Cavanaugh, *The Spiritual Lives of the Great Composers* (Grand Rapids, MI: Zondervan Publishing House, 1996), 240.
5. Ibid.
6. Victoria Sirota, *Preaching to the Choir* (New York: Church Publishing Incorporated, 2006).
7. Sirota, *Preaching to the Choir*, 23.
8. Ibid., 18.
9. Ibid., 38.
10. As quoted in Brené Brown, *Dare to Lead* (New York: Random House, 2018), 197.
11. A. Helwa, *Secrets of Divine Love: A Spiritual Journey into the Heart of Islam* (Capistrano Beach, CA: Naulit Books, 2020), 33.
12. Ibid., 47.
13. Ibid., 121.
14. Brown, *Dare to Lead*, 186.
15. Grace Baptist Church, Facebook, www.facebook.com/gbcrichmond.
16. Abraham Heschel, "No Religion Is an Island,' in *Moral Grandeur and Spiritual Audacity*, edited by Susannah Heschel (New York: Farrar, Straus, Giroux, 1996).
17. Heschel, "No Religion Is an Island," 237.
18. Ibid., 239–40.
19. Greg Jarrell, *A Riff of Love: Notes on Community and Belonging* (Eugene, OR: Cascade Books, 2018), xiii.
20. Anna Quindlen, *Being Perfect* (New York: Random House, 2005), 15.
21. Sirota, *Preaching to the Choir*, 17.

Bibliography

Brown, Brené. *Dare to Lead*. New York: Random House, 2018.
Cavanaugh, Patrick. *The Spiritual Lives of the Great Composers*. Grand Rapids, MI: Zondervan Publishing House, 1996.
Helwa, A. *Secrets of Divine Love: A Spiritual Journey Into the Heart of Islam*. Capistrano Beach, CA: Naulit Books, 2020.
Heschel, Abraham Joshua. "No Religion Is An Island." In *Moral Grandeur and Spiritual Audacity*, edited by Susannah Heschel. New York: Farrar, Straus, Giroux, 1996.
Jarrell, Greg. *A Riff of Love: Notes on Community and Belonging*. Eugene, OR: Cascade Books, 2018.
Letters of Wolfgang Amadeus Mozart, selected and edited by Hans Mersmann, translated from the German by H. M. Bozman. New York: Dover Publications, 1972.
Lingerman, Hal A. *The Healing Energies of Music*. Wheaton, IL: Quest Books, 1995.
Quindlen, Anna. *Being Perfect*. New York: Random House, 2005.
Sirota, Victoria. *Preaching to the Choir: Claiming the Role of Sacred Musician*. New York: Church Publishing Incorporated, 2006.

37
POWER, POP, AND PERFORMANCE

Major John Martin

Founded in London by William and Catherine Booth in 1865,[1] The Salvation Army operates in 134 countries.[2] It is an Evangelical part of the Protestant Christian Church and an international charitable organisation structured in a quasi-military structure, with a worldwide membership of more than 1.5 million.[3] The Army has a specific set of beliefs, symbols, churchmanship, and ecclesiology,[4] and operates a non-sacramental worship structure, relying on the notion that Christian life is not governed by rituals. Internationally, the Army operates local worship centres, accommodation for the homeless and families, addiction-dependency programmes, emergency-disaster response, community services (youth, unemployed, counselling, charity shops), hospitals and clinics, schools, and education programmes. This leads to the Army being one of the most visible Christian agencies. Initially known as The Christian Mission, the name Salvation Army was adopted in 1878. Having been founded as the *East London Christian Mission* in 1865, the name *The Salvation Army* developed from an incident in May 1878. William Booth was dictating a letter to his secretary, George Scott Railton,[5] and said, 'We are a volunteer army'. Bramwell Booth, the eldest child, heard his father and said, 'Volunteer, I'm no volunteer, I'm a regular!' Railton was instructed to cross out the word 'volunteer' and substitute the word 'salvation'.[6]

The place of women and the use of music are potent reminders of both the Army's antecedents and their role in its mission.[7] The Army became one of the earliest religious organisations to embrace the ideal of gender egalitarianism. As Douglas Clarke notes, 'Amongst the most important *notae ecclesiae* of The Army would be:[8]

- Evangelism
- Christian living and discipleship
- Equality of opportunity between men and women.

The third *nota* has been an important characteristic of the Army since its formation.'[9] Much of the influence and importance of women in the Army is due to Catherine Booth, whose creativity, vibrancy, and determination demonstrated the value of women in ministry.

The Army's encouragement of women's public preaching and ministries contravened not only traditional theological standards for female silence and submission,[10] but also Victorian gender norms. When the Army commenced, the role of women in society was that of support, rather than leadership. Women played little part in the government and leadership of the nation's affairs; there were no women in Parliament and women did not even have the vote. Women had few rights, no place in the professions, and a minimal presence in church leadership. What was true in British society was also reflected in the life and ministry of the worldwide church in all denominations. Although the Bible Christian Church[11] and Primitive Methodists[12] allowed women to preach in non-Conformist denominations, in orthodox churches the idea of women clergy was unacceptable. However, from the beginning of the Army, the role of women – in an ecclesiastic function – was one of partnership, cooperation, and equality. Women were encouraged to do what their male counterparts did, especially with regards to ministerial roles, and William and Catherine Booth shared a conviction that women were integral to the ongoing mission of the Army.

As well as the place of women, the use of music is an integral part of the Army's mission and has always been a strong identifying component of its visible presence. In many ways, music is one of the most recognisable aspects of the Army. One attraction of Army meetings in its early days was the use of music hall tunes married to spiritual words.[13] In turn, these vernacular songs attracted many un-churched people into Booth's Mission Halls and since then, the Army has used music as a missional tool, developing resources, personnel, and repertoire in order to best represent its mission both to its own membership, and to those it seeks to reach. In every country in which the Army operates, music provides opportunities for engagement with local culture. Whilst its brass bands and choirs remain the most well-known expressions of its music-making worldwide, the Army seeks to embrace other musical styles and genres. For example, in local Army congregations throughout the world, musicians draw upon their own cultural backgrounds to create music styles to accompany worship. These include community choirs, jazz bands, ukulele bands, rock bands, timbrel playing, and rap groups.

Introduction to Case Studies

My three short case studies relate to women in leadership who have significantly influenced and contributed to the music and mission of the Army: General Evangeline Booth, O.F.,[14] (1865–1950), Major Joy Webb, O.F. (1932–2023), and Dr Dorothy Gates (1966–). Although they are from different generations, all have contributed to the canon of Army music and, I suggest, have made an indelible impression on Salvationists and others.

Power: General Evangeline Booth, O.F.[15] (1865–1950)

'In elite circles, she *was* The Salvation Army'.[16]

No one symbolised the possibilities for women's leadership in the Army more than Evangeline Booth, William and Catherine's seventh child. She rose quickly through the Army's ranks, eventually becoming head of the organisation in Canada from 1896 to 1904, Commander of the United States Salvation Army from 1904 to 1934, and then General of the International Salvation Army from 1934 to 1939,[17] serving at International Headquarters in London.

Eveline Cory Booth was born on Christmas Day 1865,[18] seventh of the eight children of William and Catherine Booth, who were leading the Christian Mission.[19] Like her siblings, she was raised within the new Christian movement and became accustomed to the language and beliefs of her parents, and the methodology and developing ecclesiology of The Christian

Figure 37.1 Evangeline Booth. By kind permission of The Salvation Army International Heritage Centre.

Mission. Together with her siblings, she was raised as a member of the fledgling mission operations and participated in the growth of the movement.

Like many children of Salvationist parents, Booth was surrounded by the musical instruments that were used as part of the mission, and she was able to develop her skills on the harp, concertina, and piano. When she was 21, after training at the Army's theological college, Booth became the Corps Officer (church leader) at Marylebone, Central London and then, at the age of 23, she was appointed by her father to be in charge of the work of the Army in Great Britain, in Canada from 1896–1904, and in 1904 to be the National Commander of the United States of America. William Booth appointed all his children to significant roles, and nepotism was charged against him when he placed so many members of his family in leadership positions.

Booth became an important figure in the United States. The Army was in an anomalous position among American religious groups in the early years of the twentieth century, most of which favoured either a social gospel of aid to the poor and needy, or a strict concentration on gospel preaching. Under Booth's leadership, the Army aimed to do both; it was theologically fundamentalist but at the same time socially oriented. The Army followed orthodox theology but the founders, William and Catherine, sought to preach the Christian gospel amongst the poorest of society. William Booth said, 'No one gets a blessing if they have cold feet, and nobody ever got saved while they had the toothache!'[20] Evangeline Booth followed the traits and ethos of her parents, becoming an advocate for the role of women in society in general, and the Army in particular. In 1930, she wrote:

> As a woman, standing in the front lines of service to humanity, it is with unbounded enthusiasm of gratitude that I hail down the dawn of this long-awaited day of opportunity. The forces of prejudice, of selfishness, of ignorance, which have attested the progress and curtailed the influence of womankind for centuries, are receding from the foreground of the future. The women's movement is spreading,[21] the exhilaration and invigoration of its spirit is in the very air we breathe.[22]

I suggest that Evangeline was commenting on the increasing role of women within the Army, as well as the political and social developments around the world, including the emergence of the Suffrage Movement in the UK.[23] Although the 1930s feminist movement was never as strong as it was in the 1920s, progress continued through the work of strong women leaders and progressive thinkers. In particular, first lady Eleanor Roosevelt championed feminism and expanded opportunities for women in the workforce. Furthermore, she advocated for children, social welfare, and racial equality.

By the 1930s, the Army had become a permanent fixture on the American religious, social, and political landscape, and as its head, Booth had the power to dictate policy, to make decisions regarding the Army's position in relation to the wider cultural changes taking place, and, as far as music was concerned, to influence where, how, and when music was performed and published. As a musician, she used music instinctively both as part of her ministry and for personal reflection. She began to compose music, seeking to use her experience as an officer to inspire her lyrics and melody. She used the power of the office of Commander and her charisma significantly to enable her music to have a life within the Army, insisting on commitment from those who worked with her. Her biographer, Margaret Troutt, recalls an account of her views on music and composition.[24] She writes:

> Her own compositions came to her as a result of her encounters with people. One day she visited a man serving a long sentence in Holloway Jail (London) who had once been a minister of religion. She wrote a song of hope and forgiveness as a result. She returned home late one evening in November after visiting a London slum. She could not banish the beautiful face and golden head of a fifteen-year-old mother bereaved of her baby. At one o'clock the following morning, Booth wrote one of her most decorated Army songs.[25]

It was during her time as National Commander of the United States that Booth began to demonstrate an increasing desire to compose songs, often during visits to her retreat cabin at Lake George in upstate New York. Troutt was a Cadet at the Salvation Army School for

Officers' Training College in Chicago when she first met Evangeline Booth. Throughout the years their paths crossed, she made a tremendous impact on her life.[26] Troutt recalls that every musician on her staff had to keep pencil and manuscript paper near the telephone. She records one specific occasion:

> One morning she awakened Muriel Creighton before five o'clock and asked her to come to the library to write a new melody. Over and over, she sang the melody for Creighton to transcribe until she was happy. Another member of staff, Richard Griffiths, was summoned to bring his cello.[27]

Commissioner Gosta Blomberg was her private secretary and was required to take a concertina and music when travelling. As he recalled:

> I often got a telephone call at three o'clock in the morning. Evangeline would sing a new tune she had composed while I wrote down the melody as fast as she sang it.[28] Then in the morning when I played it to her, she would either smile, recognising the tune, or frown, disowning it, saying 'This is not the song I composed! You must have dreamt it.'[29]

Booth was noted for her antipathy to those who objected to her autocratic style, and stories abound of clashes with musicians. Although she appreciated the role of musicians within the Army, one particular incident enshrined in Army folklore demonstrated that her authority was sacrosanct and her power was absolute. The Army arranged a series of Friday evening meetings at its headquarters in Manhattan. Music was played by a specially formed band, with Booth preaching. The band was conducted by Erik Leidzen,[30] a Swedish American Salvationist who was appointed by Booth to provide suitable music. During one of these special meetings, held on 26 May 1933, Booth, at the end of her preaching, spontaneously suggested that a song should be sung. Leidzen, highly-strung and always stiffly formal, informed the Commander that the band did not have the music and would not play it, as it would ruin what had preceded it. Perplexed, Booth turned to the band and commanded them to play. Leidzen intervened by laying his baton down, with the band following his lead by putting down their instruments. Booth summoned the solo cornet player – an Officer – to play the melody and the audience joined in. (As an Officer, the soloist would have been expected to obey the commands of Booth, rather than Leidzen). The next morning, Leidzen was dismissed from his role. In relating the story, McKinley writes:

> The incident, trivial in itself, caused confusion and resentment at the time among Salvationist musicians, who naturally admired Leidzen for his gifts. It illustrated the dangers to which leaders and Army musicians alike had become prey in the new era of professionalism when personalities and protocol seemed to replace service and zeal as the forces driving them to action.[31]

Booth knew how to use her popularity and power as a weapon to get her way. At the 1929 meeting of the High Council at Sunbury Court,[32] she was part of a large majority which favoured deposing her brother Bramwell as General and moving to a democratic method of electing leaders, thereby preventing the Army from becoming a hereditary monarchy of the Booths. She was nominated as a candidate but did not secure the votes to be elected General; but at the High Council of 1934, she was elected as the International Leader of the Army by her peers and, with it, the authority of the Office of General, thereby becoming the first woman to hold this position.³³

As was the case in the USA, and now as General living and working in London, Booth promoted her music and engaged the help of UK musicians in order for them to be arranged and published. Eric Ball was often summoned to her home to arrange them onto manuscript.³⁴ Troutt recalls one such incident:

> Ball comments, 'I played her songs and we would discuss them, criticizing, amending. "You do not like that chord do you, Ball?" "No, General, I don't", I replied. Smiling, her hand on my arm, she said, "But I want you to like it."'³⁵

Booth was part of a dynasty that formed and led the Army for 69 of its first 74 years. Her authority as a leader was typical of the autocratic nature of Army governance and churchmanship. She forged her own identity and used her personality and power to influence the musical output of the Army, including the publication of *Songs of the Evangel*, a book containing several of her vocal compositions (see Music Example 37.1).³⁶

As she did in New York, the now-General Booth had power to demand others assist her at a moment's notice, and that caused consternation with those who worked with her. Christine McMillian, who worked with Evangeline Booth as an administrator and who had the opportunity to observe her in all kinds of situations, comments:

> With all her egocentric proclivities, her maddening goings-on, she was charming, witty and alluring. She also had the style of a *prima donna*, immensely insecure, childlike, simple and almost naïve. She could be ruthlessly selfish, yet tender, compassionate and forgiving.³⁸

In emails and personal conversations with this author,³⁹ Salvationist musician, music historian, and editor Ron Holz told me a couple of stories to demonstrate this:⁴⁰

> As Billie Parkins put it once,⁴¹ if you got on her wrong side she would 'put you in the refrigerator'. If you worked with her, she was generous in many ways. Her musical talent as a singer and harpist was average, but she had a gift for melody. She used three

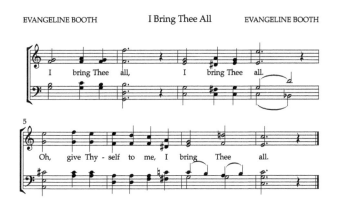

Music Example 37.1 Evangeline Booth, 'I Bring Thee All'.³⁷

talented men to arrange her *Songs of the Evangel* – Gosta Blomberg, Erik Leidzen, and Eric Ball – each had rough treatment along the way.[42]

Booth demonstrated that the office of National Commander and General gave her power to influence music as mission, and to enable her compositions to be published and used within an Army cohort. Her songs are still in use today.

Pop: Major Joy Webb, O. F (1932–2023)[43]

When the Joystrings walked through the doors of Abbey Road studios, they changed the face of religious music forever.[44]

The dichotomy between choosing which music was self-serving and which was mission-driven exercised the minds of music leaders within the UK during the 1960s, a time when change in social, sexual, and religious behaviour and musical expression revolutionised society. The 'Swinging Sixties' remains one of the defining decades of British life.[45] London had transformed from a bleak, conservative city, only just beginning to forget the troubles of the Second World War, into the capital of the world, full of freedom, hopes, and promise. By the 1960s, the first teenage generation free from conscription emerged in Britain. Young people were finally given a voice and freedom to do what they wanted, and they had more disposable income compared to previous generations, which they often liked to spend on records and attending concerts. The parents of the Sixties teenage generation had spent their youth fighting for their lives in the Second World War and wanted their own children to enjoy their youth and be able to have more fun and freedom. By the early 1960s, teenagers were already significantly different to those of a decade ago. One of the biggest defining aspects of the 1960s was music. Although rock and roll began influencing Britain in the 1950s, it was not until the early 1960s and the emergence of pop groups like The Beatles and The Kinks that music truly began its revolutionary changes. Young people began to stand up for their beliefs and their individuality. Within the Christian Church in general, and the Army in particular, the era presented opportunities for different musical expressions as it sought to present its music as mission.

Commissioner Frederick Coutts was elected General of the Army in November 1963,[46] and he expressed the hope that the Army might show a more modern approach in bringing the message of Christian faith to the 'man in the street'.[47] The idea attracted considerable media attention, and the press wanted photographs of the Salvationists in their 'pop' mode. However, the problem was that no such group or groups existed, although it was too good an opportunity to bypass since a great deal of publicity would be bestowed upon the Army.

Reporters and photographers were directed to the International Training College at Denmark Hill, where cadets studied to be Army officers. On the college staff was a young officer, Captain Joy Webb, a gifted pianist and vocalist, who also played the guitar. She was asked by the Training Principal to find some young women who had brought their guitars with them to the college and to gather a group together for a photographic session.[48] The girls were taken on a tour around Westminster to find a suitable backdrop for marketing purposes. In addition to the girl vocalists, three men joined, becoming regular members of the group.[49] Webb recalls these early days:

> *Time* magazine put us outside No. 10 Downing Street and featured us on their front cover. We were taken along to the Houses of Parliament and photographed at all angles with Big Ben in the background by other press photographers. This was followed by

Power, Pop, and Performance

Figure 37.2   The Joystrings on the Steps of St. Paul's Cathedral, London, 1964. By kind permission of The Salvation Army Heritage Centre.

a request from the visiting Canadian Broadcasting Corporation (the CBC) to hear the 'group' sing. At this point, two of the male cadets were asked to meet with me. Another college staff member was enlisted to play the string bass and a Salvationist colleague was invited to play the drums. I arranged a Salvation Army chorale selection for the group to present to the media and soon after, the group were invited to appear on the BBC *Tonight* programme.[50] Difficulty arose for presenter Cliff Michelmore to introduce the group of assembled Salvationists as they had no name. The idea of having a name had never occurred to the group or to anyone else.[51]

As they sang their songs that evening, a director of the EMI recording company was viewing the programme in his home.[52] He liked what he had seen and heard and initiated arrangements for the group to record. Webb and the cadets were brought into the studios to make a test recording. A single entitled 'It's an Open Secret' was released on 14 February 1964, with lyrics and music by Webb. The name on the single recording, appearing for the first time, was The Joystrings. Mr. Robert Dockerill, repertoire manager of EMI Abbey Road recording studios, and long-time friend of the Army, suggested that since the New Testament was full of the joy of being a Christian, the name Joystrings seemed appropriate. Webb became a national figure, and she was interviewed on Jimmy Young's *Saturday Special* radio show.[53] This was followed by the group taking part in recording at EMI's studios in London's West End on 24 February 1964 for the radio programme 'Friday Spectacular', broadcast from Radio Luxembourg.

The Joystrings' first public appearance was at Camberwell Salvation Army Hall, South London, where an estimated 60 percent of the audience were teenagers.[54] The Joystrings had become a 'pop' phenomenon, and their first single reinforced this fact by charting at number 32 in the UK. The public perception of the Army changed instantly with the onset of this brand of music, and the *News of the World*,[55] not generally noted for sympathetic reporting of religious matters, articulated what many people were observing. Its article headline for the edition dated 9th February 1964 exclaimed:

The biggest revolution in Britain's record business is timed to explode on Friday 14th. The group is "The Joystrings"; the song is "Open Secret". Its beat is wild enough to sweep half of the nation's winkle pickers on to the dance floor.[56]

This rather abrupt headline indicated the view from the paper that the Army were predicted to have a big impact upon the contemporary music scene.

The group became role models for a new generation of Salvationist musicians. Many formed their own local pop groups and, with evangelical zeal, sought to engage with the youth culture of their generation.

The recording of the group's first Christmas single, 'A Starry Night' (see Music Example 37.2) was released in 1964 and reached number 34 on the UK Singles Chart, later becoming a part of Christmas music for schools due to its success.[57]

Figure 37.3 The Joystrings, publicity photograph (1964). By kind permission of The Salvation Army Heritage Centre.

Music Example 37.2 The Joystrings, 'A Starry Night'.

During the five years of the group's existence, innumerable performances took place, including theatres, palaces, prisons, concert halls, schools, television studios, outdoor venues, recording studios, cathedrals, fundraising events, tours, photo shoots, factory canteens, holiday camps, clubs, and rallies. Webb was the leader of the group, but she also continued to compose music for Salvation Army vocal groups.[58]

Following her time as leader and songwriter of The Joystrings, Webb continued to work in her appointment as 'Officer for Modern Music', in the area of contemporary music and drama, resourcing Salvationists with new songs, scripts, musical vignettes, and training. For several years she led a group called Joy Folk, touring many parts of the world, and arranged various Army music events in the UK. She led the Sunbury Junior Singers, a group of young people who recorded many LPs. Six of her songs have been included in the recent edition of the Army Songbook,[59] and her most popular melodies have been arranged and featured in brass bands compositions, many of which have been recorded.[60]

Performance: Dr Dorothy Gates (b. 1966)[61]

Dorothy Gates was born and raised in Belfast, attending the Army at Belfast Dee Street (now Belfast Sydenham) until she moved to New York, USA to work for The Salvation Army Music Department as an Editor in the Music Department in New York. Gates received her Bachelor of Music degree in Composition and Trombone Performance from Queens University Belfast, Master of Music degree in Trombone Performance from the University of Michigan, and her PhD in Composition from the University of Salford. Her compositions include commissions from women, including *State of Mind*, a Suite for Symphonic Brass Choir for Monarch Brass (commissioned by the International Women's Brass Conference); *Imaginings*, Solo for French Horn & Piano (commissioned by Michelle Baker of the Metropolitan Opera Orchestra, New York); and *Servant of Peace*, Concerto for Trombone, with soloist Dr. Natalie Mannix (Professor, University North Texas) at the American Trombone Workshop in Arlington, Virginia in March 2018.

In recent years, some Salvationists have begun to express concern about whether the Army should change its identity, theology, and, especially, the way music is used in the context of mission.[62] The music of the Army in the nineteenth century was dominated by the use of brass bands, concertinas, organs, pianos, and guitars to accompany congregational singing and in order to help promote the organisation publicly. However, analysis regarding missional music has identified a need to abandon that which might be outdated in favour of adaptation and the adoption of repertoire more suited to a modern Christian movement. Alan Burns has examined Army identity and suggests that there are two categories of Salvationist, broadly speaking: the 'traditional conservative', who insists on adherence to inherited traditions and defends essential distinctives (such as traditional music and worship styles, flags, uniforms, orders, and regulations), and the 'radical liberals', who hold the view that tradition and traditionalism are

Figure 37.4 Dorothy Gates. By kind permission of The Salvation Army Heritage Centre Dorothy Gates.

preventing the Army from repositioning, reinventing, and rebranding itself as being fit-for-purpose in the twenty-first century.[63] Presently, the worldwide Salvation Army is grappling with a tension regarding what constitutes effective and appropriate music within the context of worship, mission, and culture. Throughout the Army world, music as mission is reliant on resources of personnel, local customs and culture, and available instrumentation. Whilst there are examples of indigenous expressions, and small music groups of varying types contributing to musical practices within the Army, it is still the case that the two largest musical groups are remnants of the early days of the movement: songster brigades (choirs)[64] and brass bands.[65]

The role of women composers, especially regarding brass band, is attracting interest and gaining momentum. However, whilst the major brass-brand contests still await a composition from a woman composer,[66] music from contemporary composers (not Salvationists) Judith Bingham, Liz Lane, and Lucy Pankhurst has been published recently. A study by the Tom Fleming Consultancy in 2016 on the role of women in music has suggested that:

> Women creators are often working in all-male environments. This can mean needing to work and push much harder to get their voices heard. Linked to this, the lack of strong female role models and recognition of what women do and have achieved in music-making in the past is a real issue in terms of shaping the ambitions and confidence of young women entering the industry.[67]

Publication outlets regarding the repertoire of music intended for the purpose of mission are based within Salvation Army Music Departments in Australia, Canada, USA, UK, and the Netherlands. Editorial processes include adherence to international guidelines regarding the suitability of music being considered for publication. Brass and choral composers within the Army have sought to understand the role of music as a component of mission practice and, within a Christian context, seek to facilitate worship or devotional thought in sacred and secular environments.

The publication of music within the Army is determined by a Music Council, a committee of Salvationists who meet bi-monthly to discuss and approve compositions for vocal and brass journals. One criterion is the inclusion of a musical reference to a hymn, thereby implicitly representing a Christian theme. Many composers use this requirement to elaborate and extend the melodic motif to provide a level of performance difficulty that challenges proficiency. Army composers have sought to provide meaningful repertoire within the changing language of worship, recognising that music is a 'vocabulary' irrespective of actual words, and the fact that the suitability of traditional concepts is becoming increasingly challenging. The balance between accepting musical challenges whilst conveying spiritual messages is one that is notoriously difficult to embrace.

Edward Foley has suggested that:

> the power of sound is based upon the presupposition that different senses provide different epistemic experiences. As a distinctive avenue to knowing, hearing enables the human imagination and thus the religious imagination to grasp and experience the transcendent in a unique and spiritually prized manner.[68]

Whilst Army music is often formulaic, pragmatic, and perfunctory, used to create atmosphere and response, other types embody a narrative of performance and entertainment. Amongst Army composers who seek to promote 'performance-based' music as mission, Gates provides a musical palette of compositions widely and critically accepted as being creative and innovative.[69] Within the history of Army brass composers, she is unique for being the only woman credited with having had substantial, complex, and demanding brass-band works published, and her reputation as a composer of original works embraces the wider brass-band cohort.[70] Contemporary Salvationists Chelsea Pascoe[71] and Rachel Ewing[72] are the only two other women composers for brass bands within the Army.

Gates believes in the power of art to enable one to see one's soul and even transform the world.[73] Noted for her consistency in producing works encompassing many genres, including brass band, solos, quartets, trombone features, and vocal music, her compositions have been performed in concert halls throughout the world, including Carnegie Hall, the Royal Albert Hall, Cadogan Hall, the O2 Arena, Queen Elizabeth Hall in London, and the Roy Thompson Hall in Toronto. In 2015, the New York Staff Band released a CD of Gates' music entitled *All Glorious*. She has also written for brass choir, brass/wind ensemble, solo instruments, chamber orchestra, and vocal groups within the Army. In 2011, she composed music (brass band and piano) for a silent movie that had been initially released in 1909 entitled *The Salvation Army Lass*.[74]

She is the Senior Music Producer for the Army's Eastern Territory in New York and has been the Composer-in-Residence for the New York Staff Band since 2002; the first woman composer/editor to be employed by the Army in this role. Recently, she has been the Senior Music Producer for the Army's Eastern Territory, and the Composer-in-Residence for the New York Staff Band (since 2002), the first woman composer/editor to be employed by the Army in this role. Together with her husband, Mark, they are now Lieutenants and lead the work of the Army at Staunton and West Augusta County, Virginia. Of her background, Gates writes:

> Since I was 13, I have been writing music. One of my earliest musical memories was taking John Lennon songs and turning them into trombone quartets that we could play in our trombone section in the Junior Band. I play trombone, as my father did; and piano, as my mother did. My love of music is only made greater by the fact that I can use it to express my faith. I think that is what connects music to an audience. They can sense what you are trying to get across to them, without words.

Gates explicitly uses her faith experience to influence her musical output. As a member of the New York Staff Band when it travelled to Cuba in 2016, she was inspired by how the Cuban Salvationists fully embraced Army culture. Of her visit there, Gates writes:

> Having lived under such a militaristic government for so long, one might think they [Salvationists in Cuba] would be hesitant to accept Army titles, ranks, or even uniforms. Instead, they accepted them and embraced them with pride and fervour. It was a beautiful thing to see, and it was a joy to perform our music for them. Part of me wanted to step away from my instrument and just be in the audience, among the Cuban Salvationists. I feel a kindred connection with the people who live in nations that are going through political difficulties. It is an understanding that is difficult to explain unless you have lived through it.

Much of Gates' 'performance' music is in the style of the Tone Poem. The Tone Poem, or Symphonic Poem, relates to a composition inspired by an extra-musical idea; for example, a story, landscape, picture or – in the case of the Army – a biblical theme. Musical compositions in this style require textual introductions in order for the listener to fully appreciate the attributes of the narrative. Nicholas Cook's assertion that 'the performance of music is crucial for it to be loved, understood, and consumed' resonates with the concept of the story-telling component of Gates's music,[75] especially her Tone Poems.[76]

Figure 37.5 Dorothy Gates conducting the Greater New York Youth Band, 19 March 2017 at The Salvation Army Montclair Citadel, NJ, USA. www.youtube.com/watch?v=VSyvIORTz0E. By kind permission of The Salvation Army Heritage Centre Dorothy Gates.

One of her most recent compositions, written in 2009 and entitled *Hope* (see Music Example 37.3), is a large-scale work for brass bands.[77] It is a three-movement work: 'Conflict', 'Despair', 'Hope' and is through-composed. This composition followed a series of world events in 2006, namely the invasion of Israel in Lebanon, the wars in Afghanistan and Iraq, the Darfur crises, and the on-going assault on Gaza and the West Bank. Gates writes:

> The sheer horror and despair I felt as I watched the images of seven little coffins being carried through the street led to two questions that continue to haunt me to this day: Why are some children born into horrific circumstances, and what is my response to this injustice as a Christian? Answering these questions took me on an odyssey of faith that I have tried to portray in music, through the sonority of the brass band. It hurt my soul so much that the only way I could express how I felt was through music. *Hope* has a Middle Eastern sound to it. Music takes over when words fail to describe the pain and the empathy felt in a person's heart.[78]

In order for Gates to discover Palestinian ethnic music and culture, she listened to film music, read books, and looked at images from the region. She incorporated the sounds of percussive instruments, the *doumbek* and the use of the *maqam*, and the system of melodic modes used in traditional Arabic music. Within the maelstrom of the sound palette, the songs 'A Little Star' and 'Jesus Loves the Little Children' were used, serving as reminders of Christian hope. Musical depictions of physical warfare were provided by percussion, chromatic scales, and crescendos from the whole band, before the recapitulation of the 'Hope' theme.

Conclusion

The role and place of women, and their leadership within music ministry, is embedded with a sense of pride within Salvation Army heritage, tradition, and ecclesiology. Throughout its

Music Example 37.3   Dorothy Gates, *Hope* (2009), bars 1–4.

Power, Pop, and Performance

Repiano B♭ Cornet

2nd B♭ Cornet

B♭ Flugelhorn

Solo E♭ Horn

1st E♭ Horn

2nd E♭ Horn

Music Example 37.3 (Continued)

Major John Martin

1st B♭ Baritone

2nd B♭ Baritone

1st B♭ Trombone

2nd B♭ Trombone

B♭ Euphonium

E♭ Bass

Music Example 37.3 (Continued)

Power, Pop, and Performance

Music Example 37.3 (Continued)

history, the Army has consistently and gratefully acknowledged the importance of the contribution made by women leaders, composers, and musicians, even though their actual musical output has been relatively small. The three subjects of these case studies – Evangeline Booth, Joy Webb, and Dorothy Gates – have contributed enormously to the repertoire and performance of the musical canon of the Army. Their impact on Army culture is noted as being of lasting significance; one which continues to illustrate the far-reaching parameters of power, generational influence, and contemporary compositions.

Notes

1. I will refer to The Salvation Army as 'the Army' throughout for sake of brevity.
2. *The Army Yearbook* (London: Salvation Books, 2020).
3. Ibid.
4. These include adherence to 11 doctrines of faith, known as the Articles of War, the use of militaristic metaphors and language, flags, and the wearing of distinctive uniform.
5. George Scott Railton was the first Commissioner (Senior Officer) in The Salvation Army. After working with William and Catherine Booth, he commenced the work of The Salvation Army in the United States of America (in 1880) and later in Canada (1881). He travelled widely overseas to support the work of the Army. Railton's son was the Reverend David Railton, a Church of England clergyman who conceived the idea of the Tomb of the Unknown Soldier.
6. Robert Sandall, *The History of The Salvation Army*, Vol. 1 (1865–1878) (London: Thomas Nelson and Sons Ltd, 1947), 229.
7. The International Mission Statement includes: 'Its mission is to preach the gospel of Jesus Christ and meet human needs in his name without discrimination'. The Salvation Army, International Headquarters, London, www.salvationarmy.org
8. A classic definition Protestant doctrine of the 'marks of the Church," proposed at the council in Constantinople in 381.
9. Douglas Clarke, "Female Ministry in the Army," *The Expository Times* 95 (May 1984): 232–35.
10. Evangeline's mother, Catherine Booth, Co-founder of The Salvation Army, contributed a book: *Female Ministry: Woman's Right to Preach the Gospel* (London, 1859). This formed the basis of the role of women within the Army. Although Catherine did not break new hermeneutical ground in her discussion of scriptural support for female ministry, she did provide opportunities for women to be ordained as Ministers of Religion. Booth indicates some important women as the biblical models for women in ministry in the Old Testament – Deborah, Huldah, and Miriam, as well as in the New Testament – Priscilla, Anna, Phoebe, Euodia, and Mary Magdalene.

11. The Bible Christian Church was a Methodist denomination founded by William O'Bryan, a Wesleyan Methodist local preacher, on 18 October 1815 in North Cornwall, England. The Bible Christians recognised the ministry of women, calling them 'Female Special Agents': *Chosen by God: The Female Itinerants of Early Primitive Methodism.* E. Dorothy Graham, https://etheses.bham.ac.uk/id/eprint.
12. Primitive Methodism was a major movement in English Methodism from about 1810 until the Methodist Union in 1932. They offered a simple and pure low worship style suited to the poor.
13. For example, the secular song, "Champagne Charlie is me name' was given sacred words, "Bless His name he sets me free!'
14. The 'Order of the Founder' is awarded specifically for Salvationists who have rendered distinguished service, such as would have specially commended itself to the Founder. Since its inauguration in 1917, over 200 Salvationists from around the world have received the award.
15. The citation for Evangeline Booth's O.F. reads: 'In recognition of twenty-five years' incomparable commend of Salvation Army forces in the United States of America; and of noble and generous services rendered in and for many lands." The Salvation Army International Headquarters (1930).
16. Sallie Chesham, *Born to Battle: The Salvation Army in America* (Chicago, IL: Rand McNally, 1965).
17. The General is elected by members of the High Council, a group of senior leaders from around the Army world who meet, when appropriate, for the sole purpose of choosing the International Leader.
18. She changed her name to Evangeline after being persuaded by Frances Willard, founder of the Women's Christian Temperance Union, to adopt the name as being more dignified and more befitting the commander of the Army in America.
19. The name was changed to The Salvation Army in 1878.
20. Robert Sandall, *The History of the Salvation Army: Volume One* (London: Thomas Nelson and Sons, 1947), 139.
21. Specifically, the role of women within the Army.
22. Evangeline Booth, *Woman* (London: Salvationist Publishing and Supplies, 1930), 7.
23. The Suffrage Movement in the USA commenced in Seneca Falls and enlisted women to campaign for the right of women to vote. Achieving this milestone took almost 100 years but, a law, passed by Congress on June 4, 1919 and ratified on 18 August 1920 – the 19th Amendment – granted women the right to vote.
24. Margaret Troutt, *The General was a Lady* (Nashville: A. J. Holman Co, 1980), 165–79.
25. The song 'The wounds of Christ' has been included in every edition of The Salvation Army Song Book.
26. Ibid, ix. Although Troutt and Booth did not work together, the author had access to official papers and interviewed many Army officers who did work with Booth.
27. Ibid., 169.
28. Although Booth was able to compose, she was not able to notate the melody and relied on others to do this for her.
29. Ibid., 170.
30. Following the confrontation with Booth, he joined the staff of the Goldman orchestra as a composer and arranger. There was a subsequent reconciliation between Booth and Leidzen.
31. Edward McKinley, *Marching to Glory: The History of the Salvation Army in the United States, 1880–1992* (Grand Rapids, MI: William B. Eerdmans Publishing Company, 1995), 216.
32. Sunbury Court is a conference centre that has been owned by The Salvation Army since 1925. Located at Sunbury-on-Thames, the 300-year-old mansion is the venue for important Army conferences and training courses.
33. General Eva Burrows (1986–1993) and General Linda Bond (2011–2013) have also been elected as International Leaders.
34. Captain Eric Ball was at the time a valued member of the Music Department at the British Territorial Headquarters in London.
35. Ibid., 178.
36. The book was the copyright of Booth, unlike the assignation to The Salvation Army of all other music.
37. *Songs of the Evangel*, 9.
38. Ibid., 239.
39. June and July 2020.

40. Ron Holz was until 2012 Professor of Music Literature and Instrumental Music at Asbury College, Kentucky, USA.
41. Major William Parkins was, at the time of Booth's tenure as National Commander, an officer who served at National Headquarters in New York.
42. Personal conversation, July 20, 2020.
43. Awarded the Order of the Founder in 2004. The citation said, "Throughout her officership, Major Joy Webb has demonstrated outstanding commitment to the creative and innovative use of music, poetry and drama in evangelism and worship, achieving unparalleled success in expressing the gospel in the popular idioms of the day while constantly reflecting the standards of the gospel in her personal life.' *The Salvation Army Year Book* (London: Shield Books, 2005).
44. Accessed April 17, 2020, www.crossrhythms.co.uk/articles/music/Joystrings.
45. 'The 'Swinging Sixties' is a colloquial term describing the youth movement and emphasising new and modern culture. London was its centre and the decade saw a flourishing in art, music, and fashion.
46. Frederick Coutts, a British Officer who was Territorial Commissioner for the UK at the time of his election as international leader.
47. www.45cat.com/biography/joy-strings
48. The Training Principal is the head of the Training College.
49. For further reference, see Sylvia Dalziel, *The Joystrings: The Story of The Salvation Army Pop Group* (London: Shield Books, 2013).
50. The BBC *Tonight* was a current affairs programme that was presented live every evening from 6 p.m. to 7 p.m. from February 1957 to June 1965. The programme covered topical matters, current affairs, and light-hearted items.
51. www.45cat.com/biography/joy-strings (last accessed May 14th, 2020).
52. EMI is a music recording company, founded in London in 1931.
53. This show was hosted by Jimmy Young, a BBC radio presenter.
54. Accessed July 11, 2020, www.45cat.com/biography/joy-strings.
55. *The News of the World* was a weekly national red top tabloid newspaper published every Sunday in the UK from 1843 to 2011.
56. Article in *The News of the World*, Sunday newspaper (February 9, 1964).
57. 'A Starry Night' is regularly performed by choirs and music groups around the world.
58. Vocal groups consisting of young people (Singing Company) and adults (Songster Brigade).
59. These include 'Noel," "I want to sing it," "Starry Night," "Lord, Your praises," "It is Jesus," and 'Share my Yoke'. *The Songbook of the Salvation Army* (London: The Salvation Army, International Headquarters, 2015).
60. Her popular song "Share My Yoke' has been arranged as a cornet solo and is used extensively in current brass band repertoire. Another song, 'Candle of the Lord', appears in 'Shine as the Light', a virtuosic brass band composition by Professor Peter Graham.
61. www.dorothygates.com.
62. Debates in SA press, Facebook pages, interest groups, anecdotal conversations.
63. Alan Burns, *Founding Vision for a Future Army: Spiritual Renewal and Mission in the Army* (London: Shield Books, 2013).
64. Although William Booth was reluctant to embrace choirs – he called them 'awkward, ugly and impossible to cast out' – he recanted and the first songster brigade was formed at Penge, South London.
65. The first use of brass instruments was in 1878 when four members of the Fry family in Salisbury, England played at the corps' open-air meeting.
66. The British Open, the National Brass Band Championships in the United Kingdom, and the European Championships are the most prized.
67. PRS Women Make Music Evaluation Report 2011–2016, www.prsfoundation.com.
68. Edward Foley, "Music and Spirituality – Introduction," *Religions* 6 (2015): 638–41.
69. Marie Speziale, Professor Emerita of Trumpet at Rice University said of Dorothy Gates' work *Hope*, "What an EXCITING piece! I must confess that it has been quite a long time since I've been this impressed with a piece for brass,' accessed August 2, 2020, www.midatlanticbrassbandfestival.com
70. Tredegar Band, conducted by Ian Porthouse, performed 'Hope' as part of their programme at the Royal Northern College of Music Brass Band Festival in Manchester, England on February 14, 2017.

71. Chelsea Pascoe is the Songster Leader at Belfast Sydenham. She is an active member of the Corps band and leads the Worship Team. Professionally, Pascoe is a music teacher at a leading grammar school in Northern Ireland.
72. Rachel Ewing is the music editor at The Salvation Army Territorial Headquarters in Toronto. She attends the North Toronto Community Church, where she is the bandmaster. Ewing is also the accompanist for the Canadian Staff Songsters.
73. Accessed August 12, 2020, www.dorothygates.com.
74. *The Salvation Army Lass* is a 1909 American silent short drama film directed by D. W. Griffith.
75. Nicholas Cook, *Beyond the Score: Music as Performance* (Oxford: Oxford University Press, 2013).
76. *The Glory of Jehovah (Exodus)*, 2019.
77. *Hope* for Brass Band published by Atiqa Music, 2009.
78. Taken from the Score notes.

Bibliography

Booth, Evangeline. *Woman*. London: Salvationist Publishing and Supplies Ltd, 1930.
Burns, Alan. *Founding Vision for a Future Army: Spiritual Renewal and Mission in The Army*. London: Shield Books, 2013.
Chesham, Sallie. *Born to Battle: The Salvation Army in America*. Chicago, IL: Rand McNally, 1965.
Clarke, Douglas. "Female Ministry in the Army." *The Expository Times* 95 (May 1984): 232–35.
Cook, Nicholas. *Beyond the Score: Music as Performance*. Oxford: Oxford University Press, 2013.
Foley, Edward. "Music and Spirituality – Introduction." *Religions* 6 (2015): 638–41.
Graham, E. Dorothy. "Chosen by God: The Female Itinerants of Early Primitive Methodism." PhD thesis, University of Birmingham, 1986.
McKinley, Edward. *Marching to Glory: The History of the Salvation Army in the United States, 1880–1992*. Grand Rapids, MI: William B. Eerdmans Publishing Company, 1995.
Sandall, Robert. *The History of the Salvation Army, Volume One (1865–1878)*. London: Thomas Nelson and Sons Ltd, 1947.
The Army Yearbook. London: Salvation Books, 2020.
The Joystrings: The Story of The Salvation Army Pop Group. London: Shield Books, 2013.
The Salvation Army Year Book. London: Shield Books, 2005.
Troutt, Margaret. *The General was a Lady*. Nashville: A. J. Holman Co, 1980.

38
'NO LADY NEED APPLY'
Women and Girls in Cathedral Musical Leadership

Enya HL Doyle and Katherine Dienes-Williams

On 8 April 1865, the *Musical Standard* carried an announcement by the vestry of Saint John Southwark inviting applications 'from Gentlemen desirous of becoming CANDIDATES for the office of ORGANIST. Ladies, and persons afflicted with blindness, will not be eligible.'[1] This was even though less than ten years earlier, a letter signed 'A Clergyman' asked readers of the *Musical World* in 1857 how it was that the announcements for parish organists appended the stipulation 'No lady need apply'. He cited the names of some of the most highly gifted organists of the time, among them Ann Mounsey Bartholomew, Elizabeth Mounsey, and Elizabeth Stirling, as evidence that women could play the organ and conduct choirs as well as their male colleagues. A Clergyman asked, 'Why should a really competent female be set aside (as is too often the case, to my own knowledge) for the sake of a less competent male, simply because she is female?'[2]

The questions raised today about women's capacity to lead music in churches in England and beyond eerily echo the correspondence cited by Judith Barger in her analysis of the appointment of women to parish church posts in the mid-nineteenth century.[3] Today, women's access to church and cathedral musical leadership positions remains as alive and contentious an issue as it was in centuries gone by. Indeed, fast-forward to 2020 – over one hundred and fifty years later – and Rachel Mahon became the fifth woman known to take up the Director of Music role at an Anglican cathedral in England; ten years after the appointments of Katherine Dienes-Williams (Guildford, 2008-present; co-author of this chapter) and Sarah Baldock (Chichester, 2008–2014). Thus, the representation of women in cathedral music leadership remains marginal. This dearth is demonstrative of the wider institutional issue of women's inclusion in church leadership and speaks to Christina Rees' reservations that 'It will not be enough to slot the women into the system and assume the result will be a renewed and transformed church'.[4]

Acknowledging the pervasiveness of the 'old boys' club' mentality in cathedral music-making in Britain in particular, this chapter seeks to provide a detailed reflection – currently lacking in modern scholarship – on the nature of leadership in Anglican cathedral music-making, and the ways women inhabit these roles in practice. The chapter will refer to qualitative data collected through interviews by the first author at ten cathedrals in 2017/2018. Broadly seeking to provide answers to two questions, this chapter explores how women and girls currently in leadership are included or excluded, as well as how the living out of these positions of leadership contributes to the norms and stereotypes which prevail about women in musical leadership and in turn impact upon the next generation seeking musical leadership in this space, especially those who will not grow up to be straight, white, cisgender men.

Leading Cathedral Music: A Short Introduction

Firstly, we want to ask: how does one best describe the role of cathedral organist, anyway? The title itself is open to many variations and interpretations; some are Director of Music, Master of the Music, *Rector Chori*, or *Informator Choristarum*.[5] The person inhabiting this role may have done so for decades or be new to the post. They inhabit the Roman Catholic cathedral or the respective cathedrals (in the UK) of the Churches of England, Scotland, Wales, and Northern Ireland. Some members of the Cathedral Organists' Association hold posts in collegiate churches with 'large' musical provision or collegiate foundations at Oxbridge Colleges. In most cases, the cathedral organist recruits, trains, and directs the choir in liturgical worship and rarely plays the organ. However, the person inhabiting the role may also frequently play voluntaries after services or give recitals. Posts are full-time or part-time. Some posts have separate directors for boy choristers and girl choristers. In the UK, as we write, the women inhabiting this role are the co-author of this chapter, Katherine Dienes-Williams, at Guildford Cathedral; Sarah Macdonald, who is a member of the Cathedral Organists' Association as she directs the girl choristers at Ely Cathedral (please see also Chapter 27); Dr. Elizabeth Anne Stratford at Arundel Roman Catholic Cathedral; Dr. Emma Gibbins at Newport Cathedral; Tansy Castledine at Peterborough Cathedral; and Rachel Mahon at Coventry Cathedral. Of this cohort, no fewer than three amongst the number came to the UK from Commonwealth nations with a church music tradition.

Women's inclusion as short-term members of cathedral choirs, particularly as Choral Scholars, is increasing. However, their positions in the choir, as more permanent features – in the same way as the Lay Clerks who often hold the position for decades – is less evident. We simply have not had enough of them over a long enough period to compare. Most of the women who have been given the opportunity to sing with a cathedral choir have been Choral Scholars who are there for one to three years or as deputy singers who only join the choir when others (almost exclusively men) cannot make the service. The hierarchy of adult singers means that Choral Scholars and deps naturally have less authority and power. Therefore, the lack of women making it into permanent Lay clerk positions impacts on the leadership within the choir both officially and unofficially.

In the context of musical leadership in the Church of England, history is vital, and so considering how the inclusion of female priests and bishops, which both came after the initial wave of introductions of girl choristers, affects leadership in cathedral music-making is vital. Perhaps unsurprisingly, the dearth of women's musical leadership in the Church is also inextricably linked to, and reflective of, the persistent resistance to women's entrance into the Episcopate (meaning that they are Bishops). The relative newness of the admission of women to this branch of church leadership within the Church of England (the first being inducted in 2015), we argue, has impacted how leadership has looked, sounded, and acted for almost the entirety of the Church's history. In January 2020, The Revd Canon Dr. Vicky Johnson joined the nine other women who hold the position of Precentor in a Church of England cathedral.[6] Alongside the twenty-four women bishops in the Church of England,[7] these women Precentors (representing a quarter of Anglican Cathedrals in England) and the 33% of all ordained priests who were women in 2020 have impacted increasing gender diversity in cathedral choirs by way of their leadership examples, not least due to their representation on decision-making panels.

Why So Many Men?

Credibility is a key facet of leadership more broadly conceived; people with minoritised aspects of their identity in leadership roles (including, but not exclusively, women) fight a particularly uphill battle in trying to convince others that they have the necessary 'authority' required to carry out their roles. One of the main intersections of authority in addition to class and gender, race/ethnicity, and disability/neurodiversity is that of age. The connection between authority and experience means that people are assumed to have more experience just by the nature of being (or appearing) older. Natural authority of elders and the connection between youth and naivety combine to suppress the advancement of younger leaders. Sam Friedman and Daniel Laurison have used Karen Ashcraft's theory of the 'glass slipper' to argue that feeling like you 'fit' in a particular job or institution has a tangible impact on the level of success you will have,[8] either getting the job or rising through the hierarchy thereafter.[9] With that in mind, a person's biases can seriously impact seriously another person's ability to carry out their role successfully even when they have all of the right skills and qualities. Donna Ladkin and Chellie Spiller acknowledge that, amongst other factors, 'women recognize the dominant masculine path to leadership in most organizations, and they know that conforming to this path often involves a high level of physical and emotional censoring and suppression'.[10] Ladkin's and Spiller's description of women navigating dominant masculine cultures is vital to understanding the barriers that women have to overcome in order to achieve the same positions as their male counterparts. What can be classified as authentic, valid, or effective leadership is intrinsically linked to a certain type of masculinity (categorised as authoritarian, lacking in vulnerability, following a strict hierarchy based on dominance and use of derogatory jokes and comments), so gaining credibility as a woman is difficult and worthy of discussion, and even more so for disabled (including neurodivergent) women, women from minoritised ethnic groups, and/or queer women.

In the context of cathedral music leadership in the Anglican church, there are also key attitudes which continue to pervade the Church's understanding of leadership – including essentialism[11] and complementarianism[12] – which affect the nature of diversity. We hold in our custody a tradition of so-called 'cathedral music' which is living, breathing, and inspiring. Acknowledging this, we also recognise that there is a small proportion of people identifying as female working in this profession, as mentioned at the beginning.

So, if notions of masculinity play into this discussion, so do understandings of femininity. The correlation between feminine, female, and womanly are in addition exacerbated by the persistent use of the antecedent 'woman' or 'female' before a job title, such as female conductor. By using the antecedent 'female' (or other labels which highlight race, ethnicity, class, disability, neurodiversity, or sexuality), there is an implication that these conductors are not the norm and that they inherently lead in a different (with different being synonymous for lesser) way. This idea has long since been considered in scholarship.[13]

Beyond an initial announcement, the persistence of the 'female x' title has ramifications for the authority, credibility, and authenticity of women's existence in these spaces. Often when a conductor who happens to be a woman is appointed to lead an orchestra or choir for the first time, they will be hailed the 'first female conductor'. The historic precedent which is being pointed out here is not necessarily problematic, although it draws attention to the patriarchal history of that choir or orchestra that it has taken until now to appoint a woman leader. In the context of leadership, Janet Brenneman noted the reluctance of her participants (in a study on female conductors) to self-identify as a 'woman' conductor. For example: she notes about Karen, one of the participants in her study:

> While Karen never offered a characterizing definition of a woman choral conductor, she had a tacit understanding that the definition is negative, and resisted the gender label. She recognised with some perceived reluctance that others label her according to her gender.[14]

Brenneman's observation of the reticence to be identified as a 'female-' or 'woman-' is telling of the ways that the antecedent is indicative of an implicit hierarchy in conducting.

The fact that the alto position is the only viable option for most women trying to get into cathedral music as a singer (because the treble lines are often still sung by boy trebles – although many Cathedrals do now have boy and girl choristers – and the tenor and bass parts by men) makes their appearance there somewhat on the back foot; the male countertenor is leader, and the rest of the back row in the choirs of Britain are also all male. Again, entering this male-dominated world, particularly if you have not been a chorister yourself, makes it harder for women to feel as though they belong and, even when given permanent positions, makes it difficult to imagine themselves as the leader, which in most cases is also connected to organ-playing as typically musical leaders in cathedrals are also required to be organists. This connects again to the entire culture of Anglican leadership generally and cathedral music-making specifically, as discussed earlier.

Are the barriers for women perceived or real? Everyone will have their own story to tell – but it must not obscure or detract from their actual talent and ability – in the best sense, their story will form part of it and enable it. Women are (usually, now) appointed to the post as part of a fair and equitable competitive process of shortlist, audition, and interview, although inclusive recruitment is and should be an ever-increasing concern for all institutions. There are many reasons why women have been unable to secure these permanent positions. The perceived authority of the countertenor voice and its ability to carry strongly across the cathedral is worthy of consideration, particularly in the context of gender and leadership. The persistence of countertenors in the back row of cathedral choirs has led to and solidified the perception that their voices make them natural leaders due to the opinion that countertenor voices ring out louder (which is preferable in bigger spaces). As a result of this purportedly physiological advantage, more precedence is given to the male countertenor over the female contralto in choral leadership. Michael Tippett wished to distinguish it from the alto sound.[15] G.M. Ardran and David Wulstan write about the perceived difference between the alto and countertenor voices as the terms were at that time prescribed to men. At that time (the 1960s), Ardran and Wulstan noted that 'refinements in tone-colour as distinguish one singer from another must be a question of natural ability and/or training the "placing" of the voice, that is, the control of resonance.'[16] The female alto voice appears to blend, and the countertenor voice appears to lead.

Similar to the views towards women playing the organ and conducting, the inclusion, or rather exclusion, of women and non-binary composers within service lists (see also Chapter 40) has been called into question. The second author has recently performed an organ recital of music written entirely by women, such as *folding, unfolding* by Pia Rose Scattergood (b. 1999), 'Tu es Petrus' from *Chorals Grégoriens* by Jeanne Demessieux (1921–1968), and 'Dance Tune' from *Six Pieces for Organ* by Erzébet Szönyi (1924–2019). Putting the programme together has been a fascinating journey for the author, reading about highly talented individuals who in some cases faded into obscurity, were denied access to higher institutions by their own families, who had to deal with taking on their families' financial difficulties, whose works were published with first name initials only.[17] Still, we tell the story. Little by little, we gather these stories together and we continue to be present. Reflecting on this, Katherine has observed that:

> I can acknowledge my own journey – it has, at times, been extraordinarily challenging, and I can acknowledge the prejudicial comments, tweets, conversations I have been party to – some utterly reprehensible. The 'milder' comments (!) include 'I love watching you conduct with that slit up the back of your skirt' and 'I'll have her keks (meaning trousers) off soon'. I can acknowledge too that on my journey, these comments have only made me more determined – more determined to make it different for the next generation. To offer a different story, a different experience, a positive, affirming, enabling, joyous career of making music. I see (and indeed teach) more and more young women inspired by the organ as an instrument, by choral direction, choral composition. These young women in turn need to see more and more women telling their story but as part of doing a job well – really well. Inspiring others to make music, creating outstanding performances and working hard to achieve their goals.

What About the Next Generation (and Their Parents)?

Preparing the next generation of cathedral leaders is one of the main jobs of both the ordained and lay leaders in the cathedral context.[18] Here, we will return to this discussion particularly as it pertains to leadership opportunities for choristers. One participant (D) reflected that at his cathedral they changed the system slightly as there were three senior girls, so there were two deputies, which is suggestive of the flexibility that is needed at times for the hierarchy. These two reflections reveal the individual approaches that can be taken in this regard at each cathedral. In fact, some cathedrals have disbanded head choristerships altogether owing to 'tiger-moms' (generally a derogatory term referencing mothers who are 'overbearing' and competitive on behalf of their child; we will return to this idea again in a moment) and a sense of competition which was unhealthy, but at least four of the cathedrals in this study still have head choristers, with Canterbury choosing to disband the position in 2019.[19]

Yet, it's true too that the intertwining of gender discrimination and musical leadership happens for children and young people involved in cathedral music-making as well. Participants involved in the first author's ethnographic research reflected on their experiences of having head choristers and the gendered ramifications of that hierarchy. In many ways, the positions of head choristers are not gendered in that both sets of choristers have their own leaders owing to being separate lines; there will be a Head boy chorister and Head girl chorister. This position was acknowledged by Participant A, who said: 'you're always relying on your older boys and girls to be the better leaders, the better readers. I think you have them anyway whether you give them a medal or not.' Likewise, Mackey contended that

> the two leaders in each group play a very important role; the director can call upon the head chorister to gather the other choristers, line them up, keep them quiet, or help a younger chorister find her place in the music.[20]

Participant O claimed that he was 'not entirely convinced that the benefits outweigh the disadvantages'. Some mentioned that the parents of the choristers have affected the decision not to have head choristers. In her thesis on girl choristers, Amanda Mackey understood York

Minster Director of Music Robert Sharpe's experience at Truro as having taught him to, as she describes it: 'distance himself from the practice of declaring any chorister better than any other, as it causes problems of competition and an unhealthy attitude amongst choristers and chorister parents alike.'[21] Participant H echoed this, noting their understanding that 'there's nobody at the pinnacle of the choir because you end up in a risky situation with parents, basically.' In 2002, the Dean and Chapter of Lincoln Cathedral were sued by chorister Pollyanna Molloy when she was not given the position of 'cope' (the equivalent of head choristers at Lincoln, for which appointed choristers are given a special cape). Her father, Michael, is quoted in an article in *The Telegraph* claiming: 'the choirmaster said that he refused to bow to parental pressure and had decided to award it to a girl a year younger, who had been in the choir for less time and was less musically advanced.'[22]

The thoughts of this chorister parent are indicative of the outside pressures on the leaders in the institution and begs the question of who really leads whom? The unofficial leadership opportunities which might indicate the answers to this question include the intentional spacing of the choristers and the distribution of solos. In addition to officially recognised leadership positions, the choral directors will space the choristers tactically. Graham Welch contends that 'novices are deliberately placed in between more skilled, older choristers'[23] often on the inside, sandwiched between two or more experienced choristers; information which an onlooker can gather because the probationers do not wear cassocks and the more experienced choristers often wear medals around their necks. Participant S, noting the situation at their cathedral, told the first author that there are two senior Choral Scholars, one of which stands on either side of the cathedral, as is the case for the boy choristers at that cathedral. In this way, the spacing of the entire choir is set to establish a hierarchy. Participant R noted in the year preceding the interview they had a boy chorister sing the solo in both services and claimed: 'interestingly, there was not a single word afterwards.' R did not go on to justify why this was interesting or why they thought that might have been the case. Given that there are two services, it is possible that there was no overlap in the congregation between the two services and therefore nobody noticed;[24] it may have been that there was a presumption that the solo was for boy treble due to the male as norm concept discussed in the first author's previous work, which outlines that 'the linguistics of power operating in accounts of the women and girls' "new" tradition ensures the hierarchy of male-as-norm, and women and girls are othered.'[25] Perhaps 'there was not a single word afterwards' because there was a belief that the boys were better than the girls on the whole or were more confident performing solos than their female counterparts.

Attitudes towards the girls (and boys) in terms of assumptions about confidence, quality, and skill will impact whether the girls feel able to lead. The so-called confidence gap between boys and girls (in which boys are more likely to give things a go and girls are more reserved or shy) is reportedly not always based on gender. One Director of Music reflected on their decision to give more solos to the boys at that specific cathedral due to their lack of confidence as a group at this time. Laura Guillen and others state that 'for women being competent is not always enough to appear confident', and the characteristics which the participants use to describe the girls and boys generally are indicative of this identified confidence-competence gap.[26] We argue that this is evident in cathedral music-making and results in girls being less likely to be given opportunities unless there is a gender-equal mandate or expectation (such as the common split of solo duties at cathedral Carol Services where a girl sings one service, and a boy sings the other). Some of the participants went so far as to note that at their cathedral the girls were 'better' than the boys. The views of the participants in this study are still in dichotomy with views from conservative campaigners that the girls do not have the 'quality' that is commonly associated with cathedral music. Connecting to tradition and voices, the boy choristers are the 'historic' kernel of cathedral music-making due to the perceived 'angelic' voices of young treble boys that has involved some characteristically anarchic assertions from campaigners for a 'traditional' cathedral choir. For instance, Peter Giles has claimed that 'Keeping the integrity of an art form is not normally a matter of gender, although this case is different. That which is intrinsic and that which is calculatedly mutational must be kept strictly separate.'[27] The use of 'calculated mutational' to describe the introduction of girls and women is particularly indicative of the general rhetoric of the group.[28]

These understandings in addition to other outside influences (e.g. money, school places, availability of adult singers) impact how leadership is understood and presented from within, how decisions are made and defended regarding the hierarchies of the singers. Related to discussions about the navigation of public perception by the Church of England more generally in terms of how it positions itself in line with the rest of the Anglican churches across the world, it is clear that the hierarchies not only have to be defended within the core cathedral community of musicians, but also to 'outsiders'; to chorister parents, for example, and to a wealth of other critics of the Anglican Church and its cathedrals who might perceive the Church of England as being 'out of touch'.[29]

Conclusion

We conclude that there are many systemic failings that have disallowed women's involvement in cathedral musical leadership throughout history. Today, we are failing to tell the story at every level of what it is really like on the inside of this profession, recognising that amongst our commonalities there is enormous variance of what we are required to do, what is appropriate, and who and what we manage in our respective work environments. Common perceptions of 'cathedral music' include those opinions asserted forthrightly via social media, often with reference to a 'nostalgia' for a bygone era, a questioning and/or commentary on performances, recordings, music lists, clergy, the Church, singers, organists, composers, and compositions. Many of these writers and commentators are 'without'; they do not work in the profession (although they may have done so many decades ago) or they are interested supporters of the continuity of music-making in cathedrals. Today's cathedral employees, as in other professional work environments, are subject to a social media policy, and/or a social media strategy; a strategy and policy which may or may not allow the story to be told.

We do, however, have a chance to tell the story, to tell with enthusiasm, passion, and energy as to why we love this profession, why we are inspired to help and assist this current generation and the next. We have to find those chances and seize them. Communication is a risk. We risk, in writing, in tweeting, in posting and commentating on our concerns and our negativity in failing to act; failing to concentrate and focus our minds on matters musical and practical which in turn enable music-making. We risk the over-publicity of a snapshot of something instantly accessible to the viewer or listener, but in reality unobtainable without years of practice, work, learning, and understanding. We risk the glamorisation and celebrity of a profession which can be anything but, a profession which is at its core about directing and playing music, and facilitating others to make that music, to learn it, to inhabit it, perform it, and offer it. We risk offering a dream, without acknowledging and supporting access to it and hard work to obtain it. The impact of not telling these stories has serious ramifications for women and girls who do not enter the cathedral world or the profession because they do not see it as a place for them. We must continue to create a legacy of inclusion and we will tell the story. Above all, we will endeavour to bring musicianship and joy in both learning and performance to those we work with. That is our task; that is our collective journey.

Notes

1. 'To Organists," *Musical Standard* 1 (April 8, 1865): 328.
2. A Clergyman, "No Lady Need Apply" [correspondence], *Musical World* 35 (August 29, 1857): 553.
3. Judith Barger, *Elizabeth Stirling and the Musical Life of Female Organists in Nineteenth-Century England* (London: Ashgate, 2007).
4. Christina Rees, *Voices of this Calling: Experiences of the First Generation of Women Priests* (Norwich: Canterbury Press, 2002), 28.
5. *Rector Chori* – Ruler of the choir – the term originates from a college of Vicars Choral who took the lead as singers, one or two of whom were known as *Rector Chori*, or 'Ruler of the Choir'. The term *Informator Choristarum* – a teacher of choristers – has been used to denote the post of Director of Music at Magdalen College Oxford since 1481.
6. A Precentor (Latin: *praecentor*) is a person who leads a congregation in its singing or (in a synagogue) prayers. In a cathedral, this is customarily a minor canon who administers the musical and worshipping life of a cathedral.
7. At the end of 2019, the position of Precentor is held by a woman at nine cathedrals in England: Bristol, Lincoln, Manchester, Newcastle, Peterborough, Portsmouth, Salisbury, Southwark, and Wakefield.
8. Karen Lee Ashcraft, "The Glass Slipper: 'Incorporating' Occupational Identity in Management Studies," *Academy of Management Review* 38, no. 1 (2013): 6–31.
9. Sam Friedman and Daniel Laurison, *The Class Ceiling: Why It Pays to be Privileged* (Bristol: Policy Press, 2019), 125–27.
10. Donna Ladkin and Chellie Spiller, *Authentic Leadership: Clashes, Convergences, and Coalescences* (Cheltenham: Edward Elgar Publishing, 2013), 248.
11. According to Elizabeth Grosz (1990, 334), essentialism 'refers to the existence of fixed characteristics, given attributes, and ahistorical functions for men and women which limit the possibilities of change and thus of social reorganization'.
12. Stanley Grenz and Denise Kjesbo note that for some conservative scholars complementarianism is a result of the idea that 'God created male and female equal but also designed the woman to complement the man by subordinating herself to his leadership' (1995, 18).
13. See L. L. Carli and A. H. Eagly (2017); C. De La Rey (2005); G. R. Goethals and C. L. Hoyt, (eds). (2017); J. M. Kouzes and B. Z. Posner (2017); E. A. Locke (1999).
14. Janet Brenneman, "On the Podium: Exploring the Gendered Self-Identity of Women Conductors," in *Personhood and Music Learning: Connecting Perspectives and Narratives*, edited by S.A. O'Neill, vol. 5. (Canadian Music Educators' Association, 2012), 126.
15. Trevor Beeson, *In Tuneful Accord* (London: SCM Press, 2009), 213.
16. G. M. Ardran and David Wulstan, "The Alto or Countertenor Voice," *Music & Letters* 48, no. 1 (1967): 19.
17. Barger, *Elizabeth Stirling*.
18. Some of the ways that the nomenclature of the choristers in particular maintains hierarchies which 'other' girls is discussed in Enya Doyle, "Let My Voice Be Heard: Barriers to Gender Diversity and Inclusion in Anglican Cathedral Music" (PhD thesis, Durham, 2020), 136–46.
19. It is unclear how many of the forty-two cathedrals still have head choristers because it is not actively publicised. So, we have instead taken the percentage of the cathedrals in this study as representative for the purposes of my argument.
20. Amanda Mackey, "New Voice: The Patterns and Provisions for Girl Choristers in the English Cathedral Choirs" (PhD thesis, Bangor University, 2015), 61.
21. Mackey, "New Voice," 81.
22. Jonathan Petre, "Girl Sues Cathedral for Choir Honour 'snub'," *The Telegraph*, September 10, 2002, accessed August 4, 2017, www.telegraph.co.uk/news/uknews/1406760/Girl-sues-cathedral-for-choir-honour-snub.html.
23. Graham Welch, "Singing and Vocal Development," in *The Child as Musician: A Handbook of Musical Development*, edited by Gary McPherson (New York: Oxford University Press, 2015), 450.
24. Generally, Carols from King's College, Cambridge sparks a conversation every year about the place of girl choristers in the English choral tradition amongst those who consider themselves musical aficionados and those who have very little interest in choirs beyond these annual services, www.theguardian.com/music/2018/dec/06/lesley-garrett-says-kings-college-choir-must-accept-girls

25. Enya Doyle, 138.
26. Laura Guillén, Margarita Mayo, and Natalia Karelaia, "The Competence-Confidence Gender Gap: Being Competent Is Not (Always) Enough for Women to Appear Confident," in *Academy of Management Annual Meeting,* Atlanta, GA. 2016, 19.
27. Peter Giles, *An Increasingly Fragile Musical Miracle* (The Campaign for the Traditional Cathedral Choir, n.d.), 7.
28. A systematic appraisal of how this rhetoric affects the inclusion and perception of girl choristers in cathedral music is discussed in length in Barrier Two of Enya Doyle (2020): 134–68.
29. http://cdnedge.bbc.co.uk/1/hi/uk/662277.stm#:~:text=The%20Church%20of%20England%20is%20seen%20as%20an,the%20Church%20understand%20the%20public%27s%20perception%20of%20itself.; Most believe Church of England is 'out of touch' with modern society – Digital Spy; https://inews.co.uk/news/synod-2023-church-england-rejects-same-sex-marriage-2136658

Bibliography

A Clergyman. "No Lady Need Apply" [correspondence]. *Musical World* 35 (August 29, 1857).

Ardran, G. M., and David Wulstan. "The Alto or Countertenor Voice." *Music & Letters* 48, no. 1 (1967): 19.

Ashcraft, Karen Lee. "The Glass Slipper: 'Incorporating' Occupational Identity in Management Studies." *Academy of Management Review* 38, no. 1 (2013): 6–31.

Author Unknown. "To Organists." *Musical Standard* 1 (April 8, 1865).

Barger, Judith. *Elizabeth Stirling and the Musical Life of Female Organists in Nineteenth-Century England*. London: Ashgate, 2007.

Beeson, Trevor. *In Tuneful Accord*. London: SCM Press, 2009.

Brenneman, Janet. "On the Podium: Exploring the Gendered Self-Identity of Women Conductors." In *Personhood and Music Learning: Connecting Perspectives and Narratives*, Vol. 5, edited by S. A. O'Neill. Canadian Music Educators' Association, 2012.

Doyle, Enya. "Let My Voice Be Heard: Barriers to Gender Diversity and Inclusion in Anglican Cathedral Music" (PhD thesis, Durham, 2020).

Friedman, Sam, and Daniel Laurison. *The Class Ceiling: Why It Pays to be Privileged* (Bristol: Policy Press, 2019).

Giles, Peter. "An Increasingly Fragile Musical Miracle" The Campaign for the Traditional Cathedral Choir, [online], n.d.

Guillén, Laura, Margarita Mayo, and Natalia Karelaia, "The Competence-Confidence Gender Gap: Being Competent Is Not (Always) Enough for Women to Appear Confident." *Academy of Management Annual Meeting*, Atlanta, GA, 2016.

Ladkin, Donna, and Chellie Spiller. *Authentic Leadership: Clashes, Convergences, and Coalescences*. Cheltenham: Edward Elgar Publishing, 2013.

Mackey, Amanda. "New Voice: The Patterns and Provisions for Girl Choristers in the English Cathedral Choirs" (PhD thesis, Bangor University, 2015).

Petre, Jonathan. "Girl Sues Cathedral for Choir Honour 'Snub'." *The Telegraph*, September 10, 2002. Accessed August 4, 2017. https://www.telegraph.co.uk/news/uknews/1406760/Girl-sues-cathedral-for-choir-honour-snub.html.

Rees, Christina. *Voices of This Calling: Experiences of the First Generation of Women Priests*. Norwich: Canterbury Press, 2002.

Welch, Graham. "Singing and Vocal Development." In *The Child as Musician: A Handbook of Musical Development*, edited by G. E. McPherson. New York: Oxford University Press, 2015.

39
UNSUITABLE FOR EVENSONG
Examining Exclusion and Diversity in the Repertoire of Oxford Collegiate Anglican Choirs

Caroline Lesemann-Elliott

This chapter discusses gender representation in Anglican choral repertoire based on a case study undertaken between 2017 and 2018 in Oxford. It features a quantitative analysis of music lists at eight Oxford collegiate chapel choirs and a qualitative analysis of interviews with those choirs' directors. The primary focus will be on how musical directors conceive of their role in developing and perpetuating Anglican musical culture, and how their conception relates to issues of gender equality in the Church of England.

Methodology

Oxford was selected as the location for this study for multiple reasons. Firstly, future leaders in the classical choral world (especially within the U.K.) regularly come from the collegiate choir backgrounds of the University of Oxford. Secondly, it was chosen for its place as a locus of wider theological and cultural upheavals that have a knock-on effect in the choral music world of England. Thirdly, it was chosen for its proximity and convenience of travel to London, a factor which binds the two cities' choral scenes together relatively closely. Lastly, it was chosen for its size: Oxford is a relatively compact city, with each college featuring a chapel choir no more than two kilometres apart. This impacts the social relationships between members of the choirs, including musical directors and organists. Given that it mainly falls to the musical director of a choir to decide what music is sung in services, a series of interviews was organised with musical directors at seven colleges and the main musical director of Oxford's Cathedral (Christ Church Cathedral).[1] These interviews were conducted in conjunction with a careful categorisation and analysis of the correlating choir's music list over the period of one year (either 2016–2017 or 2017–2018, depending on the resources available).[2]

The focus of this case study is designed to highlight larger issues of representation in Anglican choral music. Considering self-identifying women comprise around half the English population, their absence from the ranks of composers programmed is arguably a glaring example of the systematic exclusion of certain demographics from recognition in this field. There is significant need for further study with regards to race, sexuality, class, ethnicity, disability, and neurodiversity of composers represented on Anglican music lists.[3] This chapter is intended to be a precursor to further research on this topic based on an initial survey of an influential minority of Anglican choral institutions. Forthcoming research by Enya Doyle and Benjamin Liberatore will hopefully shed more light on issues of racism, nationalism, and patriarchy in Anglican music circles (see also Enya HL Doyle and Katherine Dienes-Williams' ' "No lady need apply": Women and Girls in Cathedral Musical Leadership, Chapter 38 within the present volume).

Women in Sacred Music: A Short Background

The lack of women composers programmed in Anglican choral music stems from deep-rooted beliefs around women and creativity. Rigorous academic research on historical women musicians and their practices stretches back as far as the 'New Musicology' movement in the 1980s and '90s.[4] The work of feminist musicologists since to uncover women composers has put the idea that 'women have never written music' under fire.[5] However, the field of historical English women's religious musical practice is, compared to that of their French and Italian counterparts, still underdeveloped, particularly with regards to English Protestant women.[6] While there is plenty written about women, religion, and music-making in Early Modern England,[7] performable editions of the music that they wrote is largely unattainable, especially when compared to the amount of music by their Italian counterparts, which has been made available recently by performing scholars within such ensembles as Musica Secreta (www.musicasecreta.org) and Cappella Artemisia (www.cappella-artemisia.com), as well as numerous contributors on the Choral Public Domain Library. This is not to say that no research has been done to acknowledge these contributions. Elizabeth Blackmore's research into the increasing importance of women in English parish church culture from the early eighteenth century onwards shows how this affected instrumentation choices, singing styles, and repertoire choices within choirs, as well as the production of new music.[8] David Shuker and Jane Schatkin Hettrick have also highlighted the amount of music that was composed for personal use by women organists, of which there were many throughout the eighteenth century (though mainly in parish churches).[9] Ian Bradley, June Haden Hobbs, and Alisa Clapp-Intyre have all discussed in depth the importance of women's hymn-writing and their role within music education as crucial to enforcing Victorian social values, particularly through Sunday schools.[10] English women have historically participated on a large scale in sacred musicking and continue to produce large amounts of music suitable for Anglican worship. However, music by women past and present fails to remain on Anglican music lists, and often fails to be sung at all in contemporary Anglican services.

The Oxford Sacred Choral Music Scene, 2016–2017: An Analysis of Music Lists

Each music list examined covered one liturgical year of services (between 2016 and 2017), with services primarily comprising Choral Evensong (a sung evening service) or Choral Eucharist (the celebration of Mass). Choral evensong generally comprises a choral setting of the versicles and responses, a setting of the Psalm for the day, the evening Canticles (a setting of the *Magnificat* either in English or Latin and the *Nunc Dimittis* either in English or Latin), and an Anthem. The Anthem setting is not restricted to specific texts, but can feature any devotional text – Biblical verses, liturgical texts, sacred poems, etc. – appropriate for the point in the liturgical year (i.e., Advent, Lent, feast days dedicated to certain saints, etc.). Choral Eucharist comprises a setting of the Mass Ordinary, a Eucharistic motet (sung during the distribution of the Eucharist), and a number of hymns, generally from the Common Praise hymnal. The

Eucharistic motet is, like the Anthem, somewhat flexible as it is not text-specific; it can feature any devotional text concerned with the Crucifixion and the partaking of Holy Communion (i.e., the consumption – albeit in Anglicanism, metaphorically – of Christ's flesh and blood). This study examined what music was sung for what purpose (i.e., to fulfil the requirement of Canticles, Mass settings, etc.). The key factors examined included the choir list the piece came from, the gender of the composer, the work featured, the number of times said work appeared, in what context said work appeared (i.e., evensong, eucharist, concert, etc.), the time period in which the composer worked, and their geographic location.

Seven out of 294 composers listed were clearly named as women, with their works comprising nine out of 843 total works listed; 41 works listed were by an unnamed composer. It is possible that some of these anonymous works may have been written by women. Three out of eight lists included no named women composers. The four choirs that featured named women composers had three or fewer. No music by non-binary composers was programmed. Each music list was overwhelmingly dominated by English composers (i.e., composers born and/or raised in English choral music circles).

Most works featured that were explicitly authored by women (i.e., not anonymous) were anthems, motets, or carols (generally for carol services). These are items on the order of service that are relatively short and have a set of rules for what can be programmed, with liturgical time of year being the only limit for texts selected, and even that limit is flexible. In theory, the flexibility of this genre would make it the perfect category to programme works by women composers, as the work does not have to satisfy a specific text requirement. The downside of programming anthems or motets by women, rather than other genres such as canticles, is that anthems tended to be reused less over the year, often appearing only once while a popular canticle setting might reappear several times. While this flexibility would allow a greater choice of works by women for inclusion in services, it is also more likely that those works might attain the status of a 'one-hit wonder'; that is, a singular piece performed only on a specific day of the liturgical year.

Settings of the Canticles and Responses are used just as often as anthems and motets, but are limited to a specific set of texts laid out in the Book of Common Prayer. These items are often repeated by choirs throughout the liturgical year due to the significantly smaller number of suitable works available to fulfil the canticle requirements of up to eight services per week. Yet even here several works are repeated far more than one might think necessary, and so the exclusion of settings by women is again hard to justify given their wide contemporary availability. Of the seven women composers who were included in the surveyed music lists, four were from the twenty-first century, two from the twentieth century, and one from the sixteenth century. Despite the interviewees' frequent assertions that women composers have become far more prominent in the last thirty years, women composers only comprised four out of 73 total composers featured from the same period. Just under two-thirds of featured composers active during the twenty-first century have an association with the Universities of Oxford or Cambridge (having either studied or worked there as musicians), with half of these composers being related to the University of Oxford specifically. In fact, the majority of composers programmed from the nineteenth century onwards are English, and the majority of these composers attended either Oxford or Cambridge. All Oxford-educated composers featured were male, while virtually all composers educated at Cambridge – barring Judith Weir, Master of the Queen's Music – were also male. One can infer from these statistics, and the preceding interviews, that the likelihood of a composer's work being programmed onto music lists at an Oxford collegiate choir dramatically increases if their name is known in the university's academic circles, especially if the composer attended the college of the choir.

Regarding programming, there are several discrepancies in terms of what directors believe about their programming methodology and what they actually do. For instance, Interviewee A said the following regarding music by women:

> The choir a few years ago did a concert entirely of women composers' music. Quite a number of those pieces have stayed in our repertoire . . . [that's] been very useful in terms of having the copies there, available, for the next tour or the next set of services.
>
> *[Interviewee A]*

However, in examining their music list, only two works are by a woman (and both by Cecilia McDowall, who is contracted with Oxford University Press). Therefore, it does not appear that this women-authored music has stayed on their list. Moreover, there is no guarantee that the works by Cecilia McDowall were featured in the concert discussed, as there is no record online of the concert's full repertoire. Interviewee E stated his love of contemporary music yet programmed only three contemporary composers, one of whom was himself, out of a total of 43, none of which were repeated over the year. Interviewee C stated that he was not aware of any works by historical women in currency, even though he was the only musical director to programme a pre-twentieth-century work by a woman.

A Paradoxical Tradition: Interviews with Musical Directors

The following analyses are based on interviews with musical directors from eight different chapel or Cathedral choirs at the University of Oxford. The participants were the only eight who responded as interested and available for an interview of all the chapel/Cathedral choirs of the University of Oxford contacted during the initial study. All participants were white and male; at the time of study (2017/2018), only one professional music director of an Oxford chapel choir was not a man, and there were no global majority music directors. Each interview was recorded and transcribed. It should be noted that the following quotes were selected as they concisely represented wider trends reflected across all the interviews. Some interviewees have elected to withdraw their quotes from this study, and therefore not all interviewees will be represented in selected quotes.

Answers to questions about the interviewees' backgrounds indicated a pattern of high-prestige education, generally attending fee-paying schools and/or Cathedral schools from a young age. These fee-paying schools included both independent private schools (i.e., fee-paying schools unregulated by a local state authority) and public schools in England.[11] When asked whether or not they had any experience in ensembles outside of the Church, or indeed outside of a choral context, most stated that their lives were mostly preoccupied with church music. The majority of interviewees attended all-male, fee-paying schools. The interviewees all had access to Cathedral music-making from a young age, either through experience as choristers or organists; again, generally in male-only institutions. In terms of higher education, all interviewees except one attended the Universities of Oxford or Cambridge for their undergraduate degree in music, and all held either a choral or organ scholarship, with six out of eight interviewees being first-study organists (the other two being first-study singers). Six out of eight stated that their first conducting experience occurred while they were at university, five of these as organ scholars. Most of the interviewees described 'side stepping' into the role of conducting with no initial formal training provided, either by being pressed into service by the musical director of the institution they were studying at or through their organ scholarship at said institution.

All interviewees stated that most women composers of whom they were aware were active in the twentieth and twenty-first centuries, and that they were only aware of choral music by women appropriate for the Anglican repertoire from the late twentieth and twenty-first centuries. The majority of women composers that were actually mentioned in the interviews were either instrumental composers or Hildegard von Bingen, with the number of names any interviewee could list remaining under four. Most interviewees named Judith Weir, but were unable to name more than one historical woman composer: generally, either Hildegard von Bingen or a composer from the twenty-first century, such as Judith Bingham. That all interviewees knew of Judith Weir is likely a result of her state-sanctioned post as Master of the Queen's Music, which is the most prestigious position a church composer can hold.

There were key differences in awareness between those musical directors who were first-study singers and those who are first-study organists. One of the two musical directors who was a first-study singer discussed the seventeenth-century madrigals of Francesca Caccini and Barbara Strozzi – which, while not suitable for performance in the context of Anglican worship, at least indicate an awareness of historical women composers in the Western tradition. This awareness could be the result of his work as a singing teacher; solo songs by Strozzi in particular are regularly recorded, with sheet music available in multiple anthologies and online resources, and have become popular in recital repertoire for young singers. This potentially reflects a lack of composer diversity in the repertoire organist musical directors were exposed to versus singer musical directors during their training (both in initial schooling and in higher education).

In addition to being largely unaware of music composed by women, multiple interviewees implied that what little music by women they were aware of was contemporary. They then proceeded to justify their lack of women composers on music lists by relying on stereotypes of contemporary music being difficult or inaccessible. For example:

> I certainly think [programming music by women] is important. For the most [sic], I think the question of feasibility is an interesting one . . . The large majority of music that has been written by women for the church has been done so in the late twentieth and twenty-first centuries as far as I'm aware, and for that reason it is written in a modern idiom largely. For that reason, it is on balance more difficult for my choir to pick up when because of my very limited rehearsal time I am required to lean very heavily onto the nineteenth-century canon of works that this choir has been singing for the last 40 years.
> [Interviewee B]

This justification reappeared throughout the series of interviews. In reality, much contemporary sacred choral music is perfectly accessible, particularly in modern carol and anthem anthologies (such as the *Oxford Flexible* series)[12] compiled to provide straightforward music for specific purposes. More importantly, while interviewees universally expressed a belief that women composers are presently flourishing in higher education institutions (particularly conservatoires), the overwhelming majority of contemporary composers they actually programmed were male. This is especially relevant considering that the data showed that they programmed music by twentieth- and twenty-first-century composers more than those of any other time period. Therefore, they were clearly willing to ask their choirs to sing music 'in a modern idiom' and yet refrained from programming modern women composers. It is worth noting briefly that directors also acknowledged in some cases that some of the singers in their choir had no experience singing in a church choir. This suggests that said singers would already be unfamiliar with most music they encountered in a church setting (even that which was considered 'standard' music in the Anglican choral canon), arguably making encounters with non-canonical music no more of a challenge than canonical music. More seasoned singers who might be more familiar with standard repertoire were often highlighted as more skilled, confident singers who guided their less-confident counterparts, which suggests they would likely be proficient enough musicians to learn new repertoire. It is worth noting that directors also noted that university-associated choirs are generally in a constant flux, with new singers with new abilities constantly changing the fabric of the choir and its educational background. It seems what the directors referred to is the concept of the choir as an institution rather than the choir itself. This conceptualisation deserves more attention and will hopefully be examined in future case studies.

All of the interviewees stated an explicit desire for the integration of more works by women into 'the repertoire'. However, they approached the matter with some detachment from their own role in developing this 'repertoire'. Yet simultaneously, interviewees seemed to be against the concept of doing music 'just because of who wrote it':

> Well, my view is that I choose the music that we're doing not because of who's written it but because it's good and that it serves our purpose, and if it's written by a woman, so much the better . . . inasmuch as we're dealing here with a tradition that has historically tended to exclude women, and so as a sign of social progress, it's good to be doing music that is by women to acknowledge the fact that we're within a progressive society, and we're looking for ways to reform traditions rather than to be stuck in them.
> [Interviewee E]

Here the interviewee appears to justify his music lists by stating they are compiled based on merit assessed by his own subjective criteria, as opposed to the gender of the composer, as otherwise he would have purposely ignored and excluded women composers. However, he simultaneously implies that this exclusion is negative, and appears to blame the lack of women composers on music lists as the result of previous music directors and historic institutional sexism that he himself bears no relation to. This is in spite of this same director later emphasising his close relation to his institution through his role as a music director. Furthermore, his ultimate stance on actively including women composers is unclear, as he implies that including individuals based on their gender is both a negative and positive action. Another similarly paradoxical statement can be found in the following exchange:

> Interviewer: Do you think 'positive discrimination' is something that's both worth doing and acceptable to do?[13]
> Interviewee G: Both. Very much worth doing and acceptable. I'd like there to be more awareness I suppose generally. I've always had a little bit of a problem with 'positive discrimination' . . . But it's a phrase that is used a lot. And everyone knows what you mean when you say it.
> Interviewer: I suppose one could argue that there's been positive discrimination the other way.
> Interviewee G: Well, that's a different conversation maybe.

Interviewee G declares his wariness of 'positive discrimination', but also that it is positive and acceptable. He implies that there is an assumption that when one uses the phrase 'positive discrimination', one is automatically speaking about including a marginalised group, rather than the universal default (though his position on this usage is unclear).

When these statements are compared with the following, some patterns become clear:

> Because I don't think anyone has been putting it out there, I think there's a tradition of not looking for it. [Interviewee G]

> [regarding sexism in Church music] I mean I think that's something that will inevitably change; the increasing number of girls' choirs in cathedrals and churches just means that there will be more experienced and trained women coming through into adult life who can compete on the same basis as men. [Interviewee E]
>
> So, it might take, for example, someone getting in touch with me and saying, 'I've edited these pieces by', well, whoever the composer is, 'would you consider doing them?' [Interviewee C]
>
> I think it's important, and I think it's the case that as more and more women composers succeed in getting pieces firmly entrenched in the repertoire, and a wide variety of style is available, [it] is apparent to choral directors internationally, because that's crucial for these composers, getting publishers and getting widely publicised. [Interviewee A]

The interviewees seem to distance themselves from the issue, using phrases such as 'there's a tradition of not looking for it' as opposed to 'we don't look for it', or framing change as an 'inevitable' external force, rather than highlighting what they themselves will do to affect this change. They suggest that others must undertake work – paid or unpaid – and provide editions before they will even consider using music by composers of marginalised demographics. The onus is placed on women composers to get their pieces 'firmly entrenched in the repertoire', even though musical directors ultimately establish and curate this 'repertoire'.

In discussing the interviewees' logic for programming repertoire, the issues that were raised repeatedly were practicality and liturgical propriety, with emphasis on the former. Practicality, in this context, meant what could be rehearsed to a performable standard within 45 minutes. For choirs with child choristers, there was also the issue of their ability. For choirs featuring few or no paid choral scholars, this issue was also relevant in that the directors expressed having fewer capable voices. Several interviewees discussed reliance on 'well-known' music (i.e. canonical Anglican repertoire)[14] for choirs with less-able singers as a method to save on rehearsal time.

Most interviewees emphasised their reliance on their own knowledge of appropriate works. At the same time, interviewees also highlighted their intentions to instil variety in their music lists, and saw their programming choices as an important aspect of their role as educators. This role, while perhaps not always explicit in the job description, was implicitly constructed throughout interviews by possessive language (i.e., directors talking about 'their' choirs), and more importantly by the sense of responsibility to impart information regarding 'the tradition':

> I think it's very important to keep a balance, especially in the collegiate environment where you're informing an approach, and just an awareness of the colossal amount of history actually that you need to do in music . . . so I do a fair amount of plainchant, polyphonic rep and try to make it clear that that's what grew out of that. [Interviewee F]
>
> I try to have a variety of different styles so that we range fairly widely across the full chronological span that is available to Anglican music, so from the sixteenth century to the present day, without too much of an emphasis on any one period. For evensong, there is perhaps a natural tendency for various reasons towards more recent music; a lot of the repertoire that typically choirs will sing for canticle settings will be more recent music. [Interviewee E]
>
> I try to keep a good level of variety within a term's music list.[15] There is music from the very established canon of Anglican repertoire, there . . . music that is written for the [Roman] Catholic church. [Interviewee C]

What this 'established canon' of Anglican choral music might be is a complex topic. It appears to be primarily constructed by musical directors based on their ideas of what the cultural history of Anglicanism entails, particularly regarding the early roots of Anglican church music and key points in English religious history (such as the Restoration of King Charles II, 1660). In terms of education and the 'established canon', there were routine references to an academically outdated concept of 'Counter-Reformation music', not only as representative of the Roman Catholic tradition, but as important to the historical education of the choir. Why this was so important to interviewees proved difficult to unpick in interviews, but it seems interviewees had a sense of the importance of insider-outsider paradigms when reflecting on programming decisions and constructed a paradigm of 'Anglican' versus 'not Anglican'. The result was the sense of Roman Catholic music as an 'other', therefore representing variety.

However, the extent to which Roman Catholic music constitutes variety within a tradition is debatable. Reference to Palestrina as an 'outsider' or as representative of an historical Roman Catholic 'tradition' appears regularly throughout interviews, even though works by Palestrina have been present on virtually all Anglican music lists around the country for decades. What is more telling is that the interviewees did not consider convent composers (such as Assandra, Aleotti, Cozzolani, Sessa, Vizzana, etc.) to be as important as their male counterparts (such as Victoria, Lassus, and Byrd) to Counter-Reformation repertoire. For example, Interviewee E describes how he chooses repertoire as follows:

> I also try to use earlier music, for example using canticle settings by sixteenth-century composers, Palestrina, composers from the [Roman] Catholic rather than the Anglican tradition, Palestrina, and his contemporaries.
>
> *[Interviewee E]*

However, when pressed on the lack of historical (rather than contemporary) women composers, he answered thus:

> A lot of the earlier music [by women] that I'm aware of perhaps relates more to the Catholic rite than to the Protestant one.
>
> *[Interviewee E]*

The implication is that Interviewee E does not see sixteenth-century Roman Catholic women composers as Palestrina's 'contemporaries', despite the fact that they wrote plenty of varied and programmable music and often in Roman school style. He therefore regularly programmes composers such as Victoria, Soriano, and Anerio as opposed to, say, Assandra, Aleotti, Leonarda, and Cozzolani, despite their liturgical and musical similarities. Interviewee E is happy to programme male Roman Catholic composers, but did not include female ones on the basis that their music was not written for the Protestant tradition.

While all the interviewees subscribe to the concept that music should be performed 'on its own merits' rather than because of the composer's identity, they also regularly indicated a belief that certain composers hold an objectively superior place to others, with no assessment of how they are assessing merit or superiority. They frequently reference specific composers as 'staples' of the Anglican repertoire:

> So we're going to do some Victoriana,[16] we're going to do some Gibbons, some Byrd . . . [to] try to educate them in the fact that just because on the surface it might not be the big bombastic shout our heads music . . . something like a Gibbons verse anthem

is a very beautiful thing, and if we can find our way through to that, and say this is it, the pinnacle of music-making at this time, this is the best music of its day, let's treat it like it's Bach . . . and try and get them to come at it like that.

[Interviewee G]

Interviewee G is not alone; each interviewee conveyed not only a sense of pride in the Anglican tradition, but a sense of obligation to it and by implication the works which it comprises. By using words like 'pinnacle', other interviewees gave subtle indications that they perceived works by certain composers – such as Bach and Byrd – as defining religious music during certain historical periods. By programming these composers extensively, the result was the exclusion of other aspects of historical religious music. The fact that these 'traditional' composers are entirely male shows an othering of music by women, an exclusion that contributes to wider perceptions around the role of women in Church music.

This othering has direct results on contemporary Church music. The composers commissioned by the interviewees were overwhelmingly male. The only woman commissioned was Judith Bingham, who was commissioned for a college's celebration of the anniversary of their first admission of women. A recording project saw Interviewee D commissioning works from four different women; however, these pieces did not reappear on the choir's music list during the year studied. The overall tendency of commissioning male composers is difficult to square with the interviewees' stated beliefs that there are more women choral composers active today than in the past. If they believe that women as composers are flourishing more today than previously and have a desire to programme more women's works on their music lists, then the question remains as to why they are not commissioning women as much as they commission men. Furthermore, interviewees have described instances of commissioning them mainly for situations in which the 'theme' of the event is a celebration of women, implying a continuing 'genderedness' of women composers, as opposed to the 'default' male composer.

Directors often wished to commission composers with a connection to their own college. In the cases of Interviewees A, C, and H, their associated colleges did not allow women until the late 1970s, meaning the ratio of women to men students has only just begun to approach parity. Musical directors also repeatedly noted a composer's 'background' (implied as institutional connections) as a reason for commissioning, or simply asking friends or acquaintances of theirs to write for their choirs:

We just sort of looked around at various composers who might fit the bill. In the end, we collectively decided that [unnamed well-known organist] would be the person to ask . . . and [they were] the favourite of the various composers we looked at as being somebody who could write something that the choir would be able to sing. [Interviewee E]

I asked [redacted], who is a friend of mine, who I knew would understand . . . I know his work, and so I knew that he would understand the necessity of writing carefully to that brief. He has the sort of background that would lead him to a suitable text.

[Interviewee C]

Women have only recently begun gaining access to Oxford chapel choirs, relative to the colleges' centuries-long histories. Christ Church Cathedral only allowed women to apply as lay clerks and choral scholars in 2018, and has now employed one female alto lay clerk and one female alto choral scholar. As of 2019, it admitted a girls' choir that sings once a week (comparably to the boy choristers, who sing six times per week). While colleges that do not admit women singers do accept women organ scholars, in 2019 only one Oxford collegiate choir

(Wadham College) had a full-time woman musical director or organist (Katherine Pardee), and only three chapel choirs across the university had women organ scholars.[17] If musical directors are only likely to commission their peers, there will naturally be more commissions offered to male composers than women.

Breaking the Cycle: Conclusions and Solutions

The quantitative analysis of the selected music lists clearly shows discrimination against women composers. How this discrimination comes about is the result of several interweaving patterns of thought. The qualitative analysis of interviews with the musical directors shows three core concepts:

1. The music directors are aware that sexist behaviour is bad, and as such they are consciously committed, at the very least, to not being perceived as sexist.
2. The music directors verbalised beliefs that 'the tradition' (i.e., Anglican liturgical music as it stands today) was an unequivocal good. However, when pressed on exactly why they believed this, they were unable to articulate their reasoning beyond specific pieces they liked or thought were objectively 'the pinnacle' of musicking.
3. Music directors believed themselves to be responsible for the training of choir members and held beliefs about what this entailed.

The latter two are closely linked insomuch as they create a cycle of perpetuating the same repertoire on music lists. In being the custodian of the choir's training, the music director thus becomes a custodian of 'the tradition' itself by contributing to its perpetuation. Equally because they believe the tradition is unequivocally good, and because they base the tradition on specific works allocated as objectively good, they continue to programme the same music in order to teach the choristers 'the tradition'. Therefore, rather than establishing 'the tradition' as a time in which individuals come together to make music for a specific purpose to a high standard (something musical directors clearly value), musical directors end up teaching choir members to become future gatekeepers of the tradition by ensuring they know all the standard repertoire and develop appropriate personal attachments to said repertoire. Thus, in order to justify the need to teach choir members the same music each year, music directors must justify this to themselves and rely on the idea that because it's within 'the tradition' it must be good.

This cycle means that when music directors are made aware of their own desire to reject sexism, the fact that they continue to uphold a tradition of male composers presents a distinct problem. Because of the ossified nature of the Anglican choral canon as it stands, a conscious choice to programme women is necessary for their integration. When approaching that choice, directors encounter a plethora of questions; from whom they should programme to where they can find the music to issues of suitability. At this point, judging by more recent research produced by the Oxford-based organisation One Equal Music on Anglican choral music (accessible via twitter, @oneequalmusic), music directors seem to give up altogether and return to the aforementioned cycle:

> All in all, we found data on 3459 pieces of music used in the liturgy. Of these, 70 were by women or non-binary composers . . . By way of comparison, William Byrd's music was sung 72 times in Michaelmas Term alone.[18]

Breaking the cycle requires two approaches. Firstly, directors need to make a commitment to accept new music much more regularly to begin with. This does not just mean contemporary music, but also historic music that may be unfamiliar or newly uncovered. If musical directors commit to, for example, 10–15% of music lists featuring new repertoire, and for the first few years that repertoire featuring only music by women, within a few years the music list will already be gender-balanced. This also spreads out the time and financial commitment necessary for this task. One series of resources already exists in the form of a series of anthologies produced by *A Multitude of Voyces* (published by Stainer and Bell),[19] which contain carefully vetted, high-quality, and accessible music designed for Anglican worship that spans history, all by women composers. However, these are designed to be a first step as these anthologies are not as diverse as they could be, remaining overwhelmingly white and homogenous as it pertains to gender, sexuality, and disability/neurodiversity. To build an Anglican choral tradition in which repertoire is regularly refreshed and injected with new music, singular copies and regular new music acquired from multiple different sources is necessary, which in turn requires larger investment by colleges into chapel/Cathedral music funds.

This is why creating numerical commitments for inclusion of women composers must be applied alongside a re-evaluation of what it means to be – and train – a choir member. Rather than the education of a choir member comprising learning set works of church music by canonic composers, the education must revolve around teaching musicians to sight-sing well, training aural skills, and developing a musicianship that enables them to perform a variety of musics, both as individual musicians and as an ensemble. It is essential that music directors encourage members of choirs to contribute to Anglican choral musicking beyond their singing and playing by inviting and appreciating repertoire suggestions, or indeed, by encouraging them to write and submit music themselves. This in turn is linked to the critical need for actively interrogating and acting on potentially discriminatory behaviour based on gender, sexuality, race, class, and disability/neurodiversity within Oxford's choral community. Even when singers from marginalised backgrounds manage to overcome the wide variety of barriers preventing their acquisition of a place within Oxford's chapel/Cathedral choirs, there are untold numbers of singers who have left this community due to experiences of racism, sexism, transphobia, classism, and other forms of discrimination. Active exclusion from engagement with the tradition is a significant reason for an overwhelmingly white, cis male-authored repertoire, and has yet to be fully addressed by leaders within the Oxford chapel/Cathedral choral community.

This approach lays the path for a future musical tradition that continues to develop, rather than one that relies entirely on what one individual perceives to be 'the tradition' that must be adhered to. This is particularly the case when such perceptions tend to originate from contemporary myths around the history of the Anglican church rather than the more convoluted, nuanced past that has been re-written to largely exclude women and global majority musicians. While there is much more that could be said on this topic, particularly when it comes to issues around accessibility and class associations of women and Church music, this chapter has shown the challenges women face as musical creatives in the Anglican church. While many interviewees have since expressed a desire for such actions to be included in this discussion, the numbers are still low. As of 2019, no Oxford collegiate chapel choir has achieved a gender-balanced music list.[20]

Notes

1. It is worth briefly noting that unlike most Anglican Cathedrals in England, Christ Church Cathedral functions both as the seat of the Bishop for the Diocese of Oxford and as a college chapel for Christ Church, Oxford (one of 44 colleges at Oxford University).

2. Music list spreadsheets can be made available upon request.
3. It is important to note that racial stereotypes in particular are still rampant in many Anglican institutions. Andrew Carwood, director of music at St Paul's Cathedral (London), for example, was quoted in the 2018 Church School Association report (3–4) as stating the following: 'I'd love to recruit more choristers from the black community, but many of them cannot easily work in the treble register because they are physically bigger than their contemporaries.' The Church School Association has since quietly deleted this comment, and uploaded a new version digitally. However, copies of the original remain held by Benjamin Liberatore.
4. Particularly useful is Marcia J. Citron's seminal work *Gender and the Musical Canon* (Urbana and Chicago: University of Illinois Press, 1993), as well as Christopher Wilkinson's discussions on 'master narratives' in U.S. undergraduate music history courses: Christopher Wilkinson, "A New Master Narrative of Western Musical History: An American Perspective," in *De-Canonizing Music History*, edited by Vesa Kurkela and Lauri Vakeva (Newcastle: Cambridge Scholars 2009).
5. Sylvia Glickman and Martha Furman Schleifer, *From Convent to Concert Hall: A Guide to Women Composers* (Westport, CT: Greenwood Press, 2003), 55–90; Robert L. Kendrick, *Celestial Sirens: Nuns and Their Music in Early Modern Milan* (Oxford: Oxford University Press, 1996); Craig Monson, "Disembodied Voices," in *The Crannied Wall: Women, Religion and the Arts in Early Modern Europe* (Ann Arbor: University of Michigan Press, 1992); Craig Monson, *Divas in the Convent: Nuns, Music, and Defiance in Seventeenth-Century Italy* (Chicago, IL and London: University of Chicago, 2012); Karin Pendle, *Women & Music: A History* (Bloomington: Indiana University Press 1991), 44–66.
6. Jane Flynn, "English Jesuit Missionaries, Music Education, and the Musical Participation of Women in Devotional Life in Recusant Households from ca. 1580 to ca. 1630," in *Beyond Boundaries: Rethinking Music Circulation in Early Modern England*, edited by Linda Austern, Candace Bailey and Amanda Eubanks Winkler (Bloomington: Indiana University Press, 2017) and Andrew Stefan Cichy, "'How Shall We Sing the Song of the Lord in a Strange Land?' English Catholic Music after the Reformation to 1700: A Study of Institutions in Continental Europe" (D. Phil thesis, University of Oxford, 2014), see in particular Chapters 2 and 3.
7. Amanda Eubanks Winkler, *O Let Us Howle Some Heavy Note: Music for Witches, the Melancholic, and the Mad on the Seventeenth-century English Stage* (Bloomington: Indiana University Press 2006); Linda Phyllis Austern, "'Alluring the Auditorie to Effeminacie': Music and the Idea of the Feminine in Early Modern England," *Music & Letters* 74, no. 3 (1993): 343–54; Linda Phyllis Austern, "'Sing Againe Syren': The Female Musician and Sexual Enchantment in Elizabethan Life and Literature," *Renaissance Quarterly* 42, no. 3 (1989): 420–48.
8. Elizabeth Blackmore, "The 'Angelic Quire': Rethinking Female Voices in Anglican Sacred Music, c. 1889" (Masters thesis, Durham University, 2015), 18–35.
9. Jane Schatkin Hettrick, "'She Drew an Angel Down: The Role of Women in the History of the Organ 300 B.C. to 1900 A.D," *The American Organist* 13, no. 3 (1979): 40–46; David Shuker, "More Than 'Distinguished Ornaments'? Women Organists in Late-Georgian England," *Organists' Review* 96, no. 1 (2010): 7–13.
10. Iain Bradley, *Abide with Me: The World of Victorian Hymns* (GIA Publications, 1997).
11. Public schools are somewhat difficult to define. They are generally understood as accepting anyone who could pay the fees, as opposed to town charter schools that serve only local residents who pay the fees. The Independent Schools Information Service defined public schools in 1981 as 'long-established, student-selective, fee-charging independent secondary schools'.
12. It is worth briefly noting that this series is still dominated by white cis-gender men, with only four pieces by global majority composers, and four pieces by women (all of whom are white).
13. This phrase was used in the context of wider cultural rhetoric around active inclusion of marginalised demographics.
14. See for example use of the motet *Justorum animae* by William Byrd (1543–1623) used by Interviewee C's choir four times in one year.
15. Oxford University works on a three-term system: Michaelmas (roughly early October to early December), Hilary (roughly late January to late March/early April), and Trinity term (roughly late April/early May to late June/early July).
16. This presumably refers to composers like John Stainer (1840–1901), Charles Villiers Stanford (1852–1924), and other such composers regularly programmed by interviewee G.

17. In 2019, the girls' choir at Christ Church Cathedral had a female music director – Helen Smee – who conducts one service per week. The organ scholars include Charlotte Courderoy, Charlotte Orr, and Sarah Hughes.
18. Anonymous, "Gender balance in the repertoire of Oxford Chapel Choirs: Overview for the year 2018/19," 2019, accessed April 20, 2020, https://oneequalmusic.wordpress.com/2019/06/21/gender-balance-in-the-repertoire-of-oxford-chapel-choirs-overview-for-the-year-2018-19/.
19. *Anthology of Sacred Music by Women Composers*, vols. 1–3 (Stainer and Bell).
20. Ibid.

Bibliography

Amanda Eubanks Winkler. *O Let Us Howle Some Heavy Note: Music for Witches, the Melancholic, and the Mad on the Seventeenth-century English Stage*. Bloomington: Indiana University Press, 2006.

Anonymous. "Gender Balance in the Repertoire of Oxford Chapel Choirs: Overview for the Year 2018/19." 2019. Accessed April 20, 2020. https://oneequalmusic.wordpress.com/2019/06/21/gender-balance-in-the-repertoire-of-oxford-chapel-choirs-overview-for-the-year-2018-19/.

Austern, Linda Phyllis. " 'Sing Againe Syren': The Female Musician and Sexual Enchantment in Elizabethan Life and Literature." *Renaissance Quarterly* 42, no. 3 (1989): 420–48.

———. " 'Alluring the Auditorie to Effeminacie': Music and the Idea of the Feminine in Early Modern England." *Music & Letters* 74, no. 3 (1993): 343–54.

———. "Nature, Culture, Myth, and the Musician in Early Modern England." *Journal of the American Musicological Society* 51, no. 1 (1998): 1–47.

Blackmore, Elizabeth. "The 'Angelic Quire': Rethinking Female Voices in Anglican Sacred Music, c. 1889" (MA thesis, Durham University, 2015).

Bradley, Iain. *Abide with Me: The World of Victorian Hymns*. London: GIA Publications, 1997.

Citron, Marica J. *Gender and the Musical Canon*. Urbana: University of Illinois Press, 1993.

Flynn, Jane. "English Jesuit Missionaries, Music Education, and the Musical Participation of Women in Devotional Life in Recusant Households from ca. 1580 to ca. 1630." In *Beyond Boundaries: Rethinking Music Circulation in Early Modern England*, edited by Linda Austern, Candace Bailey, and Amanda Eubanks Winkler, 28–41. Bloomington: Indiana University Press, 2017.

Glickman, Sylvia, and Martha Furman Schleifer. *From Convent to Concert Hall: A Guide to Women Composers*. Westport, CT: Greenwood Press, 2003, 55–90.

Kendrick, Robert L. *Celestial Sirens: Nuns and Their Music in Early Modern Milan*. Oxford and New York: Oxford University Press, 1996.

Lowen, Naomi. "Is Timid Programming Classical Music's Biggest Threat." *Conducting Business, New York Public Radio*, September 13, 2013. www.wqxr.org/story/317987-timid-programming-classical-musics-biggest-threat/.

Monson, Craig. "Disembodied Voices." In *The Crannied Wall: Women, Religion and the Arts in Early Modern Europe*, edited by Craig Monson. Ann Arbor: University of Michigan Press, 1992.

———. *Divas in the Convent: Nuns, Music, and Defiance in Seventeenth-Century Italy*. Chicago, IL: University of Chicago, 2012.

Pendle, Karin. *Women & Music: A History*. Bloomington: Indiana University Press 1991.

Schatkin Hettrick, Jane. "She Drew an Angel Down: The Role of Women in the History of the Organ 300 B.C. to 1900 A.D." *The American Organist* 13, no. 3 (1979): 39–45.

Shuker, David. "More Than 'Distinguished Ornaments'? Women Organists in Late-Georgian England." *Organists' Review* 96, no. 1 (2010): 7–13.

Stefan Cichy, Andrew. " 'How Shall We Sing the Song of the Lord in a Strange Land?' English Catholic Music after the Reformation to 1700: A Study of Institutions in Continental Europe" (D. Phil thesis, University of Oxford, 2014).

Wilkinson, Christopher. "A New Master Narrative of Western Musical History: An American Perspective." In *De-Canonizing Music History*, edited by Vesa Kurkela and Lauri Vakeva. New Castle: Cambridge Scholars, 2009.

PART VI

Advocacy

Advocacy: Collectives, and Grassroots Activism: An Introduction

Laura Hamer and Helen Julia Minors

Part VI presents 8 very different examples of advocacy, whereby women's collectives, charities, small companies, research-funded projects, and/or volunteering groups aim to make change and to make a long-standing difference through the work they do. The work itself varies from in the first chapters using history and data to show evidence of where change is needed, through to giving examples of historical advocacy which has been taken up by contemporary groups, through to in the next chapters establishing companies, collectives, and projects which have tangible change outcomes planned. Each chapter shows the context, reason, and rationale for the project/activity before charting what has been done, how it has been done, and what change has been made to date. They all share a central theme: the recognition that despite women's underrepresentation in the music industries, in the broadest sense, having been recognised for years, change has been excruciatingly slow – as such many of these advocacy roles and groups have also relied on activism and more grassroots work to actively assert and support change for the better, for all! As the chapters show, though, the work is not easy and for most it is voluntary labour which is rarely recognised outside of the group. Examples come from Europe (Austria, Germany, France, Ireland), Latin America (Argentina, Brazil, Costa Rica, Cuba, Mexico, Peru, Uruguay), the UK, and the USA.

Like chapters in Parts III and IV, Part VI also develops notions of self-leadership, coaching to advance leadership, as well as examples of group/collective work, though this is less theorised here and much more applied.

In advocacy work, through creating collectives and groups, women's leadership is assertively public. These women are using online platforms to share their stories, their calls, and their results as widely as possible. Some also work in academia, in the music industries, and perform, but their chapters here present the work they have done which goes beyond the day-job, beyond the means to live, into the heart and soul of their passion for generating more equitability in the music industries. To this end, many chapters are co-authored; where single-authored, writers make efforts to articulate the group nature of the work and reference other co-authored publications. It is vital that this work is seen and recognised to represent a wide range of voices. It cannot be a solo effort.

This part of the book offers, therefore, detailed case studies and approaches which call for your support, your help, your understanding, and shares ways of doing things that we hope might encourage others to join the struggle. First, we start with four chapters that give

DOI: 10.4324/9781003024767-45

specific, culturally focussed examples of advocacy work. In Chapter 40, Nicky Gluch presents a thought experiment in which she embodies a model of leadership using her experiences of mind:body duality, informed by Jewish-Spanish mysticism. This Kabbalistic enquiry encourages us to question the core issues of women's leadership in this setting. Chapter 41, co-written by jazz musicians, performers, and educators Tahira Clayton, Amanda Ekery, and Hannah Grantham, asserts the lack of representation of Black women in jazz, revealing discrimination in education and performance settings, showing how stereotypes have harmed access and put up unnecessary barriers. They set out a historical context of the performance sector, the recording sector, and education, giving strong examples of success against the odds. Notable examples include Mary Lou Williams and Maxine Sullivan, among others. The frustration felt and experienced by these women is at the forefront of the work. They advocate for role models and not only access, as access alone is shown to have a leaky pipeline of progression toward success (as also articulated in Parts III and IV). Briony Cox-Williams follows this in Chapter 42 with an example of the Salon, questioning the role of the audience, and actively adapting current practices with her recent project. The current example shows contemporary changes and experiments within a traditional Salon setting to modernise and diversify programming. In Chapter 43, Ananay Aguilar gives a copious overview of musicians' unions across Latin America, charting the challenges to access but importantly revealing what opportunities there are in the industries. The unions themselves have collected much data, and Aguilar analyses this data and women's experiences across a broad range of unions to bring a strong call that unions as collectives have powers to support change, and ultimately, that they have a responsibility to assert and support that change.

The following examples all show practices which relate to specific collective/groups. Helen Julia Minors, in Chapter 44, gives a survey of two projects: the first, Taking Race Live, funded within an educational setting to advocate and foster real change in removing the attainment gap; and then, as a result of the lessons learnt in the first project, she gives an overview of founding and co-chairing the EDI Music Studies Network UK (EDIMS). In both examples, co-leadership was used to share responsibility and labour and to peer mentor. Establishing new projects which are aimed at change is difficult, and like most in the section, this second example relies on volunteers from across the music industries to function and maintain its activity. Chapter 45, co-authored by Hilary Friend and Helen Julia Minors, charts the establishment, history, and work of Women's Revolutions per Minute (WRPM), which had been a small company set up to import and distribute music by women in a time when access to recordings on LP/CD was limited. Though initially set up as a company, its role to advocate and support women's representation in the industry was always a prime aim. The work and content of this company now reside in an archive at Goldsmiths, University of London. The chapter draws details on the contents of this publicly available archive. It is made clear that the work meant much to the co-authors, and in fact the advocacy nature of this company can be read within the resulting work of the preceding Chapter 44. Chapter 46 is co-authored by 6 women representing 2 organisations, Gender Relations in New Music (GRiNM) and Yorkshire Sound Wowen Network (YSWN). In this chapter, Stellan Veloce, Brandon Farnsworth, Rosanna Lovell, Heidi Johnson, Abi Bliss, and Eddie Dobson explore the founding context and history of both groups before case studies show how these collectives have fostered a sustained body of work that has had real impact. Some of the change made is revealed. It is important to note that both collectives continue and their references include their websites, where you can get involved and access more information. As with the previous examples, although these co-authors work within the music industries, doing a variety of roles, this work is largely voluntary and relies on lots of hours of hidden labour. The final chapter of the book, Chapter 47, authored by Laura Watson, presents the example of Sounding the Feminist (STF) and the work this collective has done with the National Concert Hall (NCH) of Ireland. Details are given from a number of policy and programming documents. The chapter crafts a story which is clearly a collaborative effort, again with voluntary time and energy given to make change in the programming, commissioning, and access for women composers to the NCH.

The chapters speak of different examples and spread their examples across more than 10 countries, but they speak as one in terms of: demanding equity in the music industries; seeking representation within all layers of the music industries including from education right up to the boardroom tables; they speak cyclically that ensuring role models are present at the top table enables those coming through to succeed and avoid a leaking pipeline; they each give historical context to show how the work was established in order to support others and to learn from this work; where possible they each give data, facts, and figures. Ultimately, though, each is both a collective and a personally experienced journey, which speaks not only from within research, from within autoethnography, from within practice, but from a place of struggle in battling to access, to sustain, to succeed, to enable, and to facilitate equity in the music industries. This volume is about celebrating women's musical leadership in all its forms, and to do that it is also about calling out the lack of representation in many areas still. This part gives evidence of the problem and attests how we each can play our part in making positive change. As Deborah L. Rhode has said, and as cited at the start of the book, we are aiming to do better, and we are doing better ourselves.[1] We share these examples to encourage everyone to join the journey to make a more equitable music industry globally.

Note

1. Deborah L. Rhode, *Women and Leadership* (Oxford: Oxford University Press, 2017).

40
POWER, CARE AND THE PARADOX OF LEADERSHIP
A Kabbalistic Enquiry

Nicky Gluch

Background

In January 2017, a workshop for female conductors was held at London's Southbank Centre. Open to the public, the event gave a platform to five notable young conductors and their teacher, Marin Alsop (then Associate Artist with Southbank and Music Director of Baltimore Symphony Orchestra). When articles appeared in *The Guardian* and *The Independent*, they unsurprisingly focused on the gender question. What surprised me, at least, were Alsop's and the participants' answers.

Asked about the hurdles that exist for female conductors, Alsop contended that the 'biggest challenge for women [is] how to deliver a gesture that elicits a powerful sound without any kind of apology, and without any kind of associated negative reaction from musicians'.[1] Natalia Raspopova, then Assistant Conductor of the Queensland Symphony Orchestra, took this point further when she added, '[g]enerally speaking, women need to think much more about projecting power – perhaps that's more natural to men'.[2]

I had myself encountered gender-based difficulties in my conducting training, which had commenced in 2015. I have a stark memory of a teacher describing one of my gestures as 'pink' and requesting that I 'man-it-up'. Through my attendance at international conducting workshops, I met and observed many developing conductors and noticed some trends among the female (minority) students. For example, some women struggled to comfortably inhabit the area in front of their chest and female students who made movements within a small range were often encouraged, in a gendered way, to be more expansive. (The conception is that women naturally take up less space than men, vis-á-vis the accusation of *man*spreading.) In thinking, however, that conducting is something one chooses to do, electing, literally, to stand on a dais, I had not considered that aspiring female conductors would struggle with power. It raised the question: what was meant by that word, power? If it is a gendered notion, and power is seen as the seat of a conductor's leadership, then there remains a gender disparity. But could this leadership not be considered in more nuanced terms?

Conducting and Leadership

This chapter presents a thought-experiment, which explores an embodied model of conducting leadership. It takes as its starting point, however, the perhaps-ironic notion that conducting is often seen as the embodiment *of* leadership. From as early as 1950, Peter Drucker used the analogy of the conductor/orchestra to analyse the relationship between workers involved in highly specialised tasks and a leader with an overall vision.[3] It was a model presumptive of a conductor having a natural authority, along the Weberian line of a:

> historically established belief in the legitimate status of those in power [where] obedience is owed to the *person* of the chief, or leader, and where both parties are thus bound by tradition and exhibit mutual loyalty in a complex pattern of duties and obligations.[4]

The irony predicates upon Bowen and Holden's observation that, as the dominance of the conductor increased in the nineteenth century, **two** types of conducting emerged. That of Mendelssohn and his disciples, which favoured technical transparency as the key to raising orchestral standards;[5] the Wagnerian school, on the other hand, was founded on principles of interpretation and charisma. Where Mendelssohn was kind, his rehearsal strategy described as commending what could be commended before 'with the greatest delicacy and firmness'[6] pointing out the flaws, Wagner was insistent. His belief that it was a conductor's duty to discover the 'poetic object' in music and to transmit that understanding to the 'layman'[7] encouraged a certain egoism and entitlement. With time, the Wagner school became dominant: this is in part because it was consistent with the zeitgeist of Austro-German Romanticism. (Previously, I have suggested that it was this ideology which nurtured the perception of the maestro as male.[8]) It may also, however, have prevailed because Wagner ridiculed the Mendelssohnian tradition in his book *On Conducting*, leaving his disciples with little choice but to dismiss it.

The conducting profession was thus shaped by an historic moment. This is problematic for two reasons: (1) because the more the notion of conductor as archetypal leader was affirmed (by Drucker et al.), the less one may have questioned what alternate models of conducting leadership were viable; and (2) because that historic moment has now passed, and so the Weberian notion of authority can no longer be presumed.

This second point is taken up by leadership theorist Barbara Kellerman. She identifies the contemporary leadership context as one of weakened leaders and strengthened followers and therefore criticises the leadership industry which perpetuates the idea that leadership is a guaranteed path to power, money, and achievement.[9] To Kellerman, a robust leadership system addresses the leader(s), the followers, and the context. The leadership industry, by implying that leadership can be learnt as skill in isolation, instead diminishes the consequence of followers and overlooks the importance of context.[10]

This presumes, at least, that leadership is being taught. In the context of conducting, however, a 2012 investigation by Nicholas Logie identified that though 'references to conductor leadership can be found in literature on management and studies into organizational leadership . . . issues of leadership appear to form only a tangential part of conductor training and development'.[11] Given Drucker's perception of conducting, this is unsurprising. If a conductor is perceived as an innate or natural leader, then leadership becomes a skill a young conductor is presumed to possess. Further, if the Weberian sense of a conductor's authority is presumed, that is, if obedience is owed to a conductor by way of tradition, then this would conversely explain why leadership skills may have been overlooked in conductor training.[12]

Wagner's characterisation of the conductor adds a layer to this traditional authority. As a charismatic leader, a Wagnerian conductor leads through the special trust they induce, their peculiar powers and unique qualities.[13] This capacity would further justify the appeal of conductors to the business world, such that they not only appear as archetypal leaders in management literature, but that they are consulted for their leadership insights. Peter Hanke is just one conductor who teaches principles of leadership to businesspeople. His workshops at the Saïd Business School are so successful (i.e. repeated) because of the allure of his ideas: namely that he can resolve any challenge or contradiction they seem to have encountered.

To elaborate, Hanke presents paradoxes of leadership which an artistic way of thinking is apparently able to reconcile. For example, he proposes to resolve the paradox between being inspiring and having control. 'Inspiration must push, challenge and sense the possibilities for change and transformation, and thus become an action, a way in which the manager can use himself as an instrument and not only as an observer'.[14] To Hanke, this form of leadership is demonstrated in the performing arts, where a theatre director guides an actor to represent a character who does things outside the actor's lived experience. By reframing this form of leadership as 'inspiration' rather than control, Hanke hopes to invite the leader to lead with greater courage that delimits their capacity, thereby delimiting the capacity of their followers.

Another of Hanke's tenets is to suggest that management and leadership are not the duality they are often perceived to be. Defining management as 'the firm and necessary operational side' and leadership as 'the airy, inspired moment of grandness',[15] Hanke believes that perceiving these as dichotomous limits the capacity for 'genuine, generous leadership' and rather that the concepts should be refined so that it is understood that a leader must draw on both parts.[16]

Whilst Hanke's ideas may be inspiring, Kellerman would criticise his approach for being highly leader-centric and giving little, if any, weight to context. Hanke's concept is to give business leaders the chance to conduct a choir through some simple choral pieces. As Hanke documents, after watching the leaders conduct he asks them some questions: what do you notice about how the musicians responded to your leadership; are you focusing on the details or the big picture; are you listening to all the singers or are you focusing on some 'favourites'?[17] The leaders answers the questions and, if willing, alter their gesture in line with what they think the questions require.

Hanke concludes that, whilst 'participants will not learn to master a conductor's professionalism during the short time . . . [some] are able to make [a piece] work perfectly and stimulate the singers in the same way as I could as a trained conductor'.[18] My concern with this conclusion is that it upholds both Drucker's notion of a conductor as natural leader and Weber's notion of traditional (in this case situational) authority. Without the score at hand, the business leaders are not conducting as we in the profession would understand it. Rather, they are being granted full situational power, gesturing towards a choir who are obliged to follow their actions regardless of musical sense.

The question this chapter asks is whether the merits of Hanke's paradox-resolving approach can be applied without affirming a leadership model based on charisma and traditional authority (often presumed to be a male characteristic). The problem with charismatic authority, as Donna Ladkin notes, is that it too perpetuates the preoccupation with the leader, thus diminishing the role of followers. To counter this, Ladkin proposes a consideration of aesthetic leadership which gives agency to followers, for it is they who make the aesthetic judgement about the person taking up the leadership role. It is this aesthetic which 'contributes to that almost immediate apprehension of what the person is like. It is the invisible yet very powerful bodily-informed, intuitive feeling we have about other people'.[19]

An appreciation of aesthetics, argues Ladkin, is part of considering the 'space' between leaders and followers. More significantly, it brings them into relation with one another. As she iterates, '[i]n taking seriously the "relational" dimension of leadership . . . it becomes apparent that a key way in which humans interrelate is through our bodily presence'.[20] This is an idea to which I now turn.

Conducting and the Body

Alan Radley conceives of embodiment as the notion that people are, as well as have, bodies.[21] Building on the work of Maurice Merleau-Ponty, Radley implicitly adopts Merleau-Ponty's notion that '[t]he body can symbolize existence because it realizes it and is its actuality'.[22] It is through the body that one experiences the world, and thus within an embodiment framework, cognition, or domains normally ascribed to the mind, becomes bodily, and the body, minded. The mind:body duality gives way to an interdependence which is most useful when considering a craft like conducting which, while undeniably intellectual, is essentially physical.

Returning to the notion that conducting was shaped by Romanticism, I have postulated that the conductor sits alongside the Goethean or Byronic hero, emotional, but undeniably male, white and heterosexual.[23] Emotional permittances changed in the twentieth century,[24] but in order to continue to assert a masculinity, conducting was, to borrow a term from Ben Spatz, *athleticised*.[25] The pinnacle of this is the establishment of conducting competitions, which turns conducting into a scoreable craft. These competitions physicalise conducting as the competitors are judged on their gestural technique (through video screening and early competition rounds) rather than on their capacity to rehearse and prepare an orchestra, which requires engagement with the social and psychological aspects of leadership.

The physicalising of conducting presents many obstacles. First, it places a primacy on gestural technique, presenting another reason why leadership skills may be overlooked. Considering that gesture is, in Carrie Noland's view, the nodal point where culture, neurobiology and embodied experience intersect, it could explain why the same gesture executed by a man or a woman resonates differently.[26] Athleticising conducting does not confront the historic perception of conductors as male and heterosexual, but rather may perpetuate the notion that there is an ideal conducting body. We know that women have been unsure as to whether they should dress like men when on the podium. What further limitations does physicalising conducting impose on homosexual male conductors, conductors of diverse genders or people of colour?

One attempt to combat the athletic has been to approach the somatic. In *What a Body Can Do*, Spatz refers to the diversity of somatics,[27] which includes amongst its practitioners F.M. Alexander, Marion Rosen, and Moshe Feldenkrais.[28] What unifies the field is a shared 'desire to regain an intimate connection with bodily processes: breath, movement impulses, balance and sensibility'.[29] Given that movement and breath are essential to music-making, it is unsurprising that workshops in Alexander Technique or the Feldenkrais method are offered to instrumentalists at the Conservatoire, though they are often framed as ways to enhance virtuosic technique and therefore as a support to the athletic realm.

Most conductors will similarly have a somatic practice they use to enhance their movement facility. At the end of Peter Hanke's workshop, he gave us instruction in tai chi, a technique he believes can improve the flow of conducting gestures. Other conductors have shared their breathing exercises. At the Australian Conducting Academy Summer School, each day of the weeklong programme begins with a yoga workshop.[30] Similarly, at the 2019 International Conducting Studies Conference, I spoke in a session which included talks on how ballet, a consideration of the Japanese aesthetic principle of *Ma*, or Laban technique could each be used to aid developing conductors expand their gestural repertory.[31]

Though somatics might intend to find ways to 'engage mind and body together',[32] of concern is whether these practices aid more than an awareness of the *physical* body. Most somatic practices are carried out individually, or in a non-interactive manner. Thus, it can be questioned whether somatics effectively addresses the notion of the 'body-subject':[33] the being, as well as having, a body. Radley expresses how when focus is placed on the physical, instrumental body there is a risk of marginalising 'the person in his or her aspect as a lived body'.[34] That is, somatic practices may enhance a woman's gestural capacity, but they will not elucidate why her gestures are read as less powerful than her male counterpart's.

If we presume that conducting technique is teachable to and therefore learnable by diverse physical bodies,[35] then we must accept that the gendered perception of conducting may have more to do with the body-subject than the body itself. If the answer is not, therefore, to converge on an ideal conducting body and gestural technique but rather to promote that a conductor's individuality is an asset to the profession, that it is their lived experience which aids interpretation, then the conductor as 'body-subject' must be addressed. Thus, from both the leadership and physical perspectives, conducting must be considered in line with Kellerman and Ladkin's views: by taking into account the leader, the followers, and the space in between.

The thought-experiment presented in the next section proposes a way of thinking about conducting that bridges the mind:body duality whilst addressing these aspects of leadership.

Conducting and Kabbalah

Like many musicians, my first exposure to music-making was in a sacred form. Unlike Richard Gill, however, who described his greatest school-boy music pleasure as singing Latin plainchant,[36] I grew up singing psalms in Hebrew. Many of the psalms start with an instruction to the conductor: *la-menatzeach*, a word which shares a root with *netzach*, one of the 10 dimensions in Kabbalah.

Though this may have encouraged my thought-experiment, it was not its origins. I learnt Kabbalah – Jewish mysticism codified in Mediaeval Spain – not in a religious context but rather at a secular university. In my course, Abraham Isaac Kook[37] was studied alongside George Steiner and Jacques Derrida as an example of a philosopher who contemplated the relationship between politics and religion. My interest in Kabbalah is thus as a way of contemplating being which has influenced people as diverse as Gottfried Leibniz, William Blake, Franz Kafka and Walter Benjamin.[38]

My consideration of Kabbalah as a lens through which to view conducting is motivated by the fact that the 10 Kabbalistic *sefirot*, dimensions of the spirit or psyche, are mapped onto the body.[39] This is not because the dimensions have a physical correlate, but because Kabbalah, in its own way, recognises the Merleau-Pontian idea (aforementioned) that '[t]he body can symbolize existence because it realizes it and is its actuality'.[40] Thus it is through experiencing the world, in being embodied, that one encounters the soul. The mind and body are not a duality but a continuum.

In relation to leadership, the first six *sefirot* are classified as intrapersonal and the last four as interpersonal. Thus, the Kabbalistic universe brings the other, followers, into consideration. Finally, these 10 dimensions are not unique to one type of person, and the dimensions, though gendered, are not gender limited. Understanding how these 10 dimensions can be harmonised in us, the individuals, is reliant upon the understanding that every individual possesses these same dimensions. Hence the hierarchy of leaders is mitigated, as is the notion that leadership is advantaged by being male.

In defining the *sefirot*, I look to two sources. Daniel C. Matt, a noted Kabbalah scholar and translator of the *Zohar*,[41] provides the sacred context, whilst Sanford L. Drob offers a secular application. Drob's interest in Kabbalah is motivated by what it reveals about the psyche. His article, 'The Sefirot: Kabbalistic Archetypes of Mind and Creation', was written when he was Director of Psychological Assessment at Bellevue Hospital, New York, and provides a psychoanalytic and philosophical reading of Kabbalistic tenets.[42]

When contemplating the three categories of the *sefirot*, intellectual, emotional, and quasi-physical, one might notice a similarity with Baruch Spinoza's three kinds of knowledge. The difference is simply in the order, for whilst Spinoza works up from imagination through reason to intuiting the infinite,[43] the *sefirot* inversely work down from the infinite, through reason towards existence.

I will briefly define these 10 dimensions before mapping them onto the body and viewing conducting leadership through this Kabbalistic lens.

Intrapersonal Sefirot

- The Intellectual *Sefirot*:

    The uppermost of the *sefirot*, just distinguishable from the infinite God element, is known as *Keter Elyon*, the supreme crown. As God is genderless, this element is deemed gender-neutral, implying that humans are driven by an essence above or beyond that which can be circumscribed by gender. This essence is best conceived as delight and will, an idea echoed by Freudian psychologists who claim that we are motivated by the pleasure principle.[44]

    Below *Keter Elyon* is the dimension of *Chochmah*, wisdom. It is a male element, the creative force that directs will. In Freudian terms, it is the foundation of the ego[45] and in Kabbalistic terms the cognitive dimension of the human psyche that connects the mind to the outside world. *Chochmah* is nothing, however, without its feminine counterpart *Binah*, understanding.

    As the uppermost female energy, *Binah* is perceived as the cosmic mother.[46] 'Impregnated' as she is by *Chochmah*, *Binah* is the womb in which the other dimensions develop. Essential to Kabbalah is the harmonising of opposites, and the role of *Binah* is to balance the desirous aspect of *Keter* with the intellectual aspect of *Chochmah*. 'Intellect is empty without interest and emotion, and emotion unfulfilled without thought',[47] writes Drob, and though *Binah* is defined as understanding, it might better be considered as the root of empathy.

- The Emotional Sefirot:

    The first of the emotional sefirot is *Chesed*, loving-kindness. It is through *Chesed* that God is said to have created the world and thus can be analogised with humanity's experience of spirituality.[48] *Chesed* is the dimension through which parents nurture their children and is the regard with which we should treat others, especially those less fortunate than ourselves.

    Chesed is opposed by *Gevurah*, power. *Gevurah* is the dimension of 'measure, limit and restraint'.[49] It sees loving-kindness metred out according to the capacity of the receiver and the receiver's merit. It allows us to execute judgement, and lead and direct as is appropriate.

    Balancing the forces of *Chesed* and *Gevurah* is *Tiferet*, or beauty. *Tiferet* allows humans to see that limitation can be to the benefit of an individual and indeed enhances, by tempering, the aspects of love and power within us all. More cosmically, *Tiferet*, as a male element, becomes the husband of *Shekhinah*.[50] As will be shown, if *Shekhinah* is considered existence, then what is suggested is that the goal of this existence is to achieve 'beauty'.

    These intrapersonal *sefirot* have the responsibility of harmonising forces within an individual. The lower *sefirot* expand and deepen these ideas to the interpersonal realm; that is, the interaction between the individual and society.

Interpersonal Sefirot

- The 'Physical' Sefirot:

  Netzach, *Hod*, and *Yesod*: endurance, splendour and foundation are the dimensions that broach the idea of a physical world. As the *sefirot* are meant to mirror God, they cannot be said to be truly spatial or corporeal, as the God form is not meant to be physically represented. Referring back to Spinoza, they are akin to his first level of knowledge, intimating, or imagining, reality.

  Netzach, endurance, introduces the idea that as humans it is our duty to consider the future, to build things of 'enduring value'.[51] Just as we should build our houses to last, so we should build a robust society and culture. Having children, the arts and religion all fall into the realm of *Netzach*.

  Hod, splendour, is about appreciating the physical world and finding the beauty in it, for we are its caretakers.

  Finally, *Yesod* is the foundation of the physical world. In a rather chicken-and-egg scenario, *Yesod* is fashioned by what it holds up, for it channels all that came before it to provide the building blocks for innovation. *Yesod* and *Chochmah* are said to mirror each other, for it is *Yesod* that brings to fruition the potential initiated by *Chochmah*.

  As *Chochmah* delivers the seed to *Binah*, so *Yesod* represents the (phallic) channel that delivers the seed of *Tiferet* to *Shekhinah*.[52] In the form of a *sefirah*, *Shekhinah* is termed *Malchut*, kingdom. It is the basest of the *sefirot* for it is, paradoxically, the most magisterial. A ruler, in biblical eyes, was to balance exaltedness with humility. *Keter* is the exalted ruler; that is why it is placed first. *Malchut*, on the other hand, is humble. That is why it must come last.

  Malchut is the dimension of existence. As the lower mother, *Malchut* is the womb in which the other dimensions mature and in which finite reality comes to be. The paradox of creation is that divine sovereignty is contingent on finite beings.[53] *Malchut* is analogised to be like time which itself has no form, but nothing can exist without it. In existing, we then give shape to time for if we are alive, so time must be passing.

Application: The Sefirot, the Body and Conducting

Keter, the supreme crown. For a conductor this is the intangible essence of music, the way in which art can communicate beyond the realm of the senses. What the conductor is trying to bring forth on the podium is simultaneously the essence of the piece and something singular. Like *Keter*, music should be informed by gender, but its essence is genderless, and it should be driven by delight and will. Its aim, and thus that of the conductor, should be to deliver pleasure (or stimulation) that far transcends reason.

Chochmah: wisdom. This is the creative intellect (aptly, the right brain) with which conductors approach music. From recognising all the constituent parts of a piece to how the notes form chords and how many bars make up a phrase, it is through *Chochmah* that a conductor turns this 'black dot' information into sound. *Chochmah* may be seen as the realm of interpretation, linking the dimension once again to the notion of ego. It is the personal mark, where *Keter* strives for something beyond the self.

To temper these two agencies exists the dimension of *Binah*, or understanding. It is through this element of reason (left brain) that conductors will be able to assess each situation, to determine what must please and what may be innovated depending on the piece and the audience. As mentioned, *Binah* can be considered as empathy. In contemporary models of

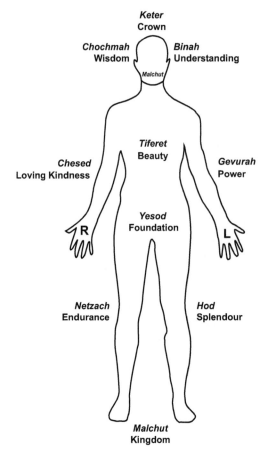

Figure 40.1 The *sefirot* mapped onto the human form.
Source: Illustration produced by the author.

leadership, we understand this notion as essential to good conductors. Though they prepare scores in isolation, conductors should be cognisant of, and concerned for, the musicians they will be working with. It is in this way that *Binah* can be seen to harmonise *Keter* and *Chochmah* and prepare a conductor for successfully transforming thought into action.

Below this intellectual realm come the *sefirot* of emotion. *Chesed*, loving-kindness, is the regard the conductor must have for the music. They must nurture it, see beyond its flaws and treat it as a parent would their child. In opposition to *Chesed* comes *Gevurah*, power. This is what permits a conductor to exercise artistic license over the piece. They have the power to shape it, to choose how long a note will be held, for example. Similarly, they are allowed to execute their judgement. They accept that a score approximates a sonic idea and so enhance, or temper, it as required.

Returning to the body map, *Chesed* is found to be the right arm and *Gevurah*, the left. In conducting, the right hand predominantly keeps time and the left hand is used more discriminately for shaping. I thus find it apt that *Gevurah*, the *sefirah* I claim is used to shape music, corresponds so perfectly with its physical conduit.

To harmonise the opposing factions of *Chesed* and *Gevurah*, comes the *sefirah* of *Tiferet*, beauty. To conductor Angel Gil-Ordóñez, beauty in music is the result of the perfect realisation of tension.⁵⁴ Music, in its intangibility, is the performance and reception of this tension. Conveyed in a way that moves or transfixes the listener, music becomes beautiful. As beauty was the goal of *Shekhinah's* existence, so the goal of the conductor should be to make the most 'beautiful' music they can. This means that they cannot hope the music will 'speak for itself'; they have to be prepared to make decisions to draw out the potential of a piece. On the flipside, they cannot be so finicky or harsh as to destroy the music in the process. With too firm a hand, too much power executed over the piece, the music will be stifled. *Tiferet* reveals to us the great paradox of leadership and, together with *Chesed* and *Gevurah*, exemplifies why leadership should not be gender limited.

To reiterate, *Chesed*, *Gevurah* and *Tiferet* are intrapersonal *sefirot*. They require one to bring into alignment dimensions within the self. The power, therefore, that a conductor has is over the music, rather than over the orchestra. It is in regard to the music, first, that a conductor must execute their judgement, and then these decisions must inform how they instruct an orchestra. Repositioned in this way, female conductors need not struggle with power *unless* they are afraid to make artistic decisions. In 2018, I observed a workshop for female conductors where the teachers repeatedly emphasised this idea. They stressed the need for the students to make decisions, for a conductor's confidence on the podium can only come through a confidence in their musical ideas. Through that confidence they are then empowered to lead.

Once the groundwork has been laid in the mind of the conductor by studying and considering the score in great detail, then they are ready to consider how to transmit that score to the orchestra. Bringing the conductor into relation with their 'society' are the lower three *sefirot*, *Netzach*, endurance, *Hod*, splendour, and *Yesod*, foundation. *Netzach* is the mind-set with which a conductor should approach their relationship with an orchestra. Endurance tells a conductor that they are trying to build a lasting relationship. Their manner must be honourable, firm but not overbearing, warm but not emotional. Musically, they must draw on *Binah*, considering the capacities of the particular ensemble and making musical decisions that respect the musicians and best realise their potential.

Hod, splendour. This is the energy a conductor should convey to the orchestra. They should inspire them to make beautiful music, to aim for excellence and reach artistic heights. *Hod* balances *Netzach*: as a conductor should be dependable, so too should they be dynamic. This is important both for the orchestral musicians in terms of having an energy to respond to and for the audience, for whom the conductor becomes performer.

Finally, to balance these dimensions comes *Yesod*, the foundation of the self and the channel of all preceding dimensions. In an orchestral setting, only the conductor has the full score. Their job, therefore, is to channel that score through their body in order to clarify and unify the individual parts in front of the orchestra. This unity is benefited by *Yesod's* element of attraction; in the body-map, *Yesod* not only delivers the seed of *Tiferet* but is the sex organs. The mystical allure, the fluidity to morph with the music and those they are in front of, is what permits a conductor to deliver their interpretation, bringing into fruition what began in their mind and what now must be delivered by others' bodies.

That deliverance is realised through *Malchut*. In the body map, *Malchut* is associated with the mouth. In its translation, *Malchut* is kingdom – the dominion where existence comes to be – and in the metaphysical analogy, *Malchut* is time. Thus, I posit that *Malchut* in conducting is the actual conducting. The 'making speak' of music that begins when the conductor gives their down beat may be conceived as the interrelation between time and being. If in *Malchut* creative potential is realised, so through the conductor is the composer's intention brought to life.

Conclusion

A running race begins with a starter's pistol; movement is initiated through sound. A conductor, inversely, has the privilege of initiating sound through movement. But they do not create sound. Their leadership is bodily and silent, uniting others' bodies to produce sound in concert. A conductor's leadership, thus, cannot be divorced from their gender as it similarly cannot be divorced from any other aspect of their physicality. Simultaneously, it should not be limited by these attributes. The conducting profession may have been shaped by an historic moment, but we can transcend the implicit physical assumptions by affirming conducting as a profession of leadership. This leadership is inherently relational and thus cannot be conductor-centric; the orchestra should be the focus and the reality of performing to an audience must be addressed. A Kabbalistic lens allows us to view conducting from these many angles. It is not posited as a solution but rather as a way of shedding light on ideas critical to our discourse and perhaps configuring them in a way just different enough to facilitate possibility.

Notes

1. "'This Is Not a Woman's Issue' – Tackling Conducting's Gender Problem," *Guardian*, February 6, 2017, accessed April 6, 2017, www.theguardian/music/2017/feb/06/this-is-not-a-womans-issue-tackling-conductings-gender-problem.
2. 'This is not a woman's issue'. Janet L. Borgerson supports this notion, writing that '[f]emale leaders may struggle with power, as power often is perceived to contrast with those practices and attitudes often traditionally associated with female characteristics and experience, demonstrated in caring work'. Taking up the Nietzschean idea that it is power which motivates human behaviour, Borgerson is not optimistic that simply understanding the tensions between power and care will improve the potential for female leaders. Rather, like Mary Beard, she believes that the system will have to change, with some people relinquishing power to make way for others. Janet L. Borgerson, *Caring and Power in Female Leadership: A Philosophical Approach* (Newcastle Upon Tyne: Cambridge Scholars, 2018), 126.
3. Nicholas Logie, "The Role of Leadership in Conducting Orchestras" (Unpublished doctoral diss., The Open University, 2012), 9.
4. Sonja M. Hunt, "The Role of Leadership in the Construction of Reality," in *Leadership: Multidisciplinary Perspectives*, edited by Barbara Kellerman (Englewood Cliffs, NJ: Prentice Hall, 1984), 161.
5. José Antonio Bowen and Raymond Holden, "The Central European Tradition," in *The Cambridge Companion to Conducting*, edited by José Antonio Bowen (Cambridge: Cambridge University Press, 2003), 114.
6. José Antonio Bowen, "The Rise of Conducting," in *The Cambridge Companion to Conducting*, edited by José Antonio Bowen (Cambridge: Cambridge University Press, 2003), 106.
7. Bowen, "The Rise of Conducting," 111.
8. Nicky Gluch, "Netzach: The Conductor in Kabbalah," *Devotion, Gender and the Body in European Religious Cultures 1100–1800: A Postgraduate Advanced Training Seminar (PATS) and Symposium* (August 18–19, 2017), Melbourne, Australia, accessed March 23, 2020, https://ucavt.goregister.com.au/rhasymposium2017/info/Abstracts.
9. Barbara Kellerman, *The End of Leadership* (New York: Harper Collins, 2012), 154.
10. Kellerman, *The End of Leadership*, 154.
11. Logie, "The Role of Leadership," i.
12. Max Weber, *On Charisma and Institution Building* (Chicago, IL: University of Chicago Press, 1968).
13. Hunt, "The Role of Leadership," 161.
14. Peter Hanke, *Extracts from Performance & Leadership* (unpublished translation of *Performance & Lederskab: Passionen Som Drivkraft* (Copenhagen: Børsens Forlag, 2018)), 58. It is presumed that the use of male pronouns is an old-fashioned simplification for the written mode, rather than a felt bias by the author.
15. Hanke, *Extracts from Performance & Leadership*, 39.

16. Ibid. This is an idea worth investigating, as the dichotomy is often presented in a gendered light. Janet L. Borgerson writes how 'organizations see female leadership styles as "management" and male leadership attributes as "leadership"'. Borgerson, *Caring and Power in Female & Leadership*, 22.
17. Hanke, *Extracts from Performance & Leadership*, 18.
18. Hanke, *Extracts from Performance & Leadership*, 19.
19. Donna Ladkin, *Rethinking Leadership: A New Look at Old Leadership Questions* (Cheltenham: Edward Elgar, 2010), 81.
20. Ladkin, *Rethinking Leadership*, 59.
21. Alan Radley, "The Elusory Body and Social Constructionist Theory," *Body & Society* 1, no. 2 (1995): 3.
22. Maurice Merleau-Ponty, *Phenomenology of Perception*, trans. Colin Smith (London: Routledge, 1962), 164.
23. Gluch, "Netzach: The conductor within Kabbalah'.
24. There are various theories as to why it became less acceptable for men to be outwardly emotional in the late Victorian and Edwardian eras. One idea is that the trial and imprisonment of Oscar Wilde led men to fear being associated with homosexuality. Another is that men saw a threat in the women's suffrage movement and sought to further differentiate their gender (consciously or otherwise). The First World War then called on men to be loyal citizens and be guarded by honour. They were 'hardened," as writes Michael Anesko. Michael Anesko, *Henry James and Queer Filiation: Hardened Bachelors of the Edwardian Era* (Cham: Palgrave Pivot, 2018).
25. Ben Spatz, *What a Body Can Do* (London: Routledge, 2015), 84.
26. Carrie Noland, *Agency and Embodiment: Performing Gestures/Producing Culture* (Cambridge, MA: Harvard University Press, 2009), 8.
27. A field of movement studies which encourages the practitioner to engage with their internal physical perceptions and experiences.
28. Spatz, *What a Body Can Do*, 97.
29. Ibid.
30. TSO, "Australian Conducting Academy Summer School," 2019, accessed September 19, 2019, www.tso.com.au/wp-content/uploads/2019/08/TSO_ACA_Booklet_WEB.pdf.
31. Sydney Conservatorium of Music, "International Conducting Studies Conference," 2019, accessed September 19, 2019, https://sydney.edu.au/content/dam/corporate/documents/sydney-conservatorium-of-music/research/ICSC%202019%20final%20schedule.pdf.
32. Spatz, *What a Body Can Do*, 97.
33. Radley, "The Elusory Body and Social Constructionist Theory," 5.
34. Ibid., 4.
35. Conducting is a profession which naturally accommodates those who are variably abled. One can conduct with affected lower-limbs and with vision impairments, and several prominent conductors have turned to the field when upper limb injuries required that they cease professional practice on their instrument.
36. Richard Gill, *Give Me Excess of It* (Sydney: Pan Macmillan, 2013), 31.
37. A twentieth-century century Kabbalist and first Ashkenazi Chief Rabbi of British Mandatory Palestine.
38. Daniel C. Matt, *The Essential Kabbalah: The Heart of Jewish Mysticism* (New York: Harper One, 1996), 17.
39. Key to Jewish theology is that God does not have a physical form. Thus, when the Bible says, "So God created man in His image, in the image of God He created him; male and female he created them' [Genesis 1:27] we consider this as being in God's *Divine* image rather than a bodily one. In Lurianic Kabbalah, this Divine image is anthropomorphised to give form to dimensions of the soul.
40. Merleau-Ponty, *Phenomenology of Perception*, 164.
41. The foundational Kabbalistic text, published by Moses de Léon in the thirteenth century.
42. Sanford L. Drob, "The Sefirot: Kabbalistic Archetypes of Mind and Creation," *Cross Currents* 47, no. 1 (1997): 5–29.
43. Internet Encyclopedia of Philosophy, "Benedict de Spinoza: Epistemology," accessed September 6, 2019, www.iep.utm.edu/spino-ep/#H3.
44. Drob, "The Sefirot: Kabbalistic Archetypes of Mind," 13.
45. Ibid., 15.

46. Ibid., 16.
47. Ibid., 17.
48. Ibid., 18.
49. Ibid.
50. Matt, *The Essential Kabbalah*, 9.
51. Drob, "The Sefirot," 21.
52. Matt, *The Essential Kabbalah*, 9.
53. Drob, "The sefirot," 22.
54. Personal correspondence, 2017, quoted with permission.

Bibliography

Borgerson, Janet L. *Caring and Power in Female Leadership: A Philosophical Approach*. Newcastle Upon Tyne: Cambridge Scholars, 2018.

Bowen, José Antonio. "The Rise of Conducting." In *The Cambridge Companion to Conducting*, edited by José Antonio Bowen, 114–33. Cambridge: Cambridge University Press, 2003.

_____, and Raymond Holden, "The Central European Tradition." In *The Cambridge Companion to Conducting*, edited by José Antonio Bowen, 114–33. Cambridge: Cambridge University Press, 2003a.

_____. 'The Central European Tradition." In *The Cambridge Companion to Conducting*, edited by Jose Antonio Bowen, 114–33. Cambridge: Cambridge University Press, 2003b.

Drob, Sanford L. "The Sefirot: Kabbalistic Archetypes of Mind and Creation." *Cross Currents* 47, no. 1 (1997): 5–29.

Gill, Richard. *Give Me Excess of It*. Sydney: Pan Macmillan, 2013.

Gluch, Nicky. "Netzach: The Conductor in Kabbalah." In *Devotion, Gender and the Body in European Religious Cultures 1100–1800: A Postgraduate Advanced Training Seminar (PATS) and Symposium*, August 18–19, 2017, Melbourne, Australia. Accessed March 23, 2020. https://ucavt.goregister.com.au/rhasymposium2017/info/Abstracts.

Hanke, Peter. *Extracts from Performance & Leadership* (Unpublished Translation of *Performance & Lederskab: Passionen Som Drivkraft*). Copenhagen: Børsens Forlag, 2018.

Hunt, Sonja M. "The Role of Leadership in the Construction of Reality." In *Leadership: Multidisciplinary Perspectives*, edited by Barbara Kellerman, 157–78. Englewood Cliffs, NJ: Prentice Hall, 1984.

Internet Encyclopedia of Philosophy. "Benedict de Spinoza: Epistemology." Accessed September 6, 2019. www.iep.utm.edu/spino-ep/#H3.

Kellerman, Barbara. *The End of Leadership*. New York: Harper Collins, 2012.

Ladkin, Donna. *Rethinking Leadership: A New Look at Old Leadership Questions*. Cheltenham: Edward Elgar, 2010.

Logie, Nicholas. "The Role of Leadership in Conducting Orchestras" (Unpublished doctoral thesis, Open University, 2012).

Matt, Daniel C. *The Essential Kabbalah: The Heart of Jewish Mysticism*. New York: Harper One, 1996.

Merleau-Ponty, Maurice. *Phenomenology of Perception*, trans. Colin Smith. London: Routledge, 1962.

Noland, Carrie. *Agency and Embodiment: Performing Gestures/Producing Culture*. Cambridge, MA: Harvard University Press, 2009.

Radley, Alan. "The Elusory Body and Social Constructionist Theory." *Body & Society* 1, no. 2 (1995): 3–23.

Spatz, Ben. *What a Body Can Do*. London: Routledge, 2015.

Sydney Conservatorium of Music. "International Conducting Studies Conference." 2019. Accessed September 19, 2019. https://sydney.edu.au/content/dam/corporate/documents/sydney-conservatorium-of-music/research/ICSC%202019%20final%20schedule.pdf.

"'This Is Not a Woman's Issue' – Tackling Conducting's Gender Problem." *The Guardian*, February 6, 2017. Accessed April 6, 2017. www.theguardian/music/2017/feb/06/this-is-not-a-womans-issue-tackling-conductings-gender-problem.

TSO. "Australian Conducting Academy Summer School." 2019. Accessed September 19, 2019. www.tso.com.au/wp-content/uploads/2019/08/TSO_ACA_Booklet_WEB.pdf.

Zander, Rosamund Stone, and Benjamin Zander. *The Art of Possibility: Transforming Professional and Personal Life*. London: Penguin Books, 2000.

41
TOPPLING SYSTEMIC EXCLUSION
Women's Roles in a Century of Jazz

Tahira Clayton, Amanda Ekery, and Hannah Grantham

Systemic exclusion of women in jazz education, music business, performance opportunities, the public eye, and history have all contributed to lower visibility and lower numbers of female leaders. In addition to analysing the past, this chapter will discuss how to directly create change through education, advocacy, and mentorship, in hopes of increasing opportunity and visibility of female leaders in jazz.

Like many widely disseminated canons, jazz's history is an imbalanced, diluted reflection of the diversity of the music's actual reality. As it is currently taught in many mainstream performance programmes in the United States, jazz's history is nearly or entirely devoid of female representation, outside of vocalists. It celebrates a long list of male musicians in a hubristic manner that avoids taking the time to critically look at their lives and careers. For most students, the entire history is presented only from a white male perspective, which frequently fails to capture the vast oral history present through the practice of signifying in jazz music.[1] This standard approach is a disservice to the Jazz Community. It erases the Black women who were deeply involved with the music from its earliest origins and the succeeding generations of women musicians who worked as composers, performers, managers, advocates, critics, scholars, historians, and mentors in the jazz community.

In the wake of seismic social justice movements such as #MeToo and Black Lives Matter, the jazz community has begun to reckon with its past. When the world came to a standstill as the 2020–2021 Coronavirus pandemic spread globally, the jazz community's racial and gender disparities were thrust further into the spotlight. Across the United States, music students past and present are speaking out against violence endured at the hands of professors and institutions meant to be places of learning.[2]

This period of reflection illustrates the effects of jazz's institutionalisation and emphasises the far-reaching impact gatekeepers have and continue to have on America's first classical music. For many in the community, this moment is a poignant reminder that the jazz community has grappled with misogyny and inclusion for a century and that the issue of misogyny intersects with conversations of racism, transphobia, homophobia, appropriation, and capitalist greed. In fact, women have spoken to these very issues for decades in their various roles as musicians, educators, and authors. As this chapter will demonstrate, incorporating women's work and words in jazz education will go a long way in furthering discussions of equity in jazz and analysing the structural discrimination that has shaped jazz.

Tahira Clayton, Amanda Ekery, and Hannah Grantham

A Brief History of Women in Jazz

Over the last century, women have contributed to jazz in a multitude of ways as musicians disseminating jazz culture around the world. In the pre-war years, American women travelled to Europe and beyond, as far as East Asia, performing on stages and the radio when they could not find steady work in the United States in an industry controlled by white men. While operating within an oppressive system that subjected them to immense scrutiny and violence, women emerged to create innovative music that resisted the limitations in place. Pursuing a career in music on their terms, women established their acts, scheduled their own tours, and spoke out about the demeaning situations the industry put them in at times.

Out of love for the music and a desire to build a life for themselves outside of the confines of jobs typically available to women at the time, women in the Jazz Age and beyond led illustrious careers that took them around the world. At home in the United States and abroad, American women pushed the music forward and positively challenged their peers musically. Their compositions and recordings brought jazz to new territories, crossing over into mainstream audiences and sacred spaces. A rich legacy of music produced by women like Melba Liston (1926–1999) and Una Mae Carlisle (1915–1956) reveals the intersectionality of women in jazz who played with musicians and influences from all around the world. Una Mae Carlisle recorded with musicians from across the African diaspora while living in Europe in the 1930s and excelled as a singer-songwriter before hosting her own nationally broadcasted radio show between the 1940s and 1950s. As a trombonist, composer, and arranger, Melba Liston was regarded as an ingenious composer who transcended genre, blending elements from bebop, Afrobeat, and soul music into her compositions. These women and others chipped away at segregation and racism through their performances and compositions. Their music spoke to the pain, the joy, the love, and the everyday life experiences of people of all classes and backgrounds.

Women in jazz influenced culture for generations and instilled a sense of humanity into jazz through their music and roles as mentors. Numerous women such as Maxine Sullivan (1911–1987) and Mary Lou Williams (1910–1981) used their experience and knowledge to help younger musicians and children. As a drug epidemic swept her Bronx community in the 1970s, Maxine Sullivan established a music programme for local students to learn about jazz and celebrate their community's history. Mary Lou Williams inspired countless musicians over the years from the piano bench in her Sugar Hill apartment and her office within the Mary Duke Biddle Music Building at Duke University. Through their positions as educators, these women shed light on Black music's long history and encouraged students by thoughtfully listening and providing constructive criticism. The histories they presented to students was inclusive, respectful, and mindful of the many influential musicians who went unrecorded or underacknowledged.

It has been documented for decades that women achieved many wonderful things as jazz musicians. Scholars like Sherri Tucker, Daphne Brooks, and Angela Davis have led this work by doing tremendous archival and oral history research published in books like *Swing Shift: "All-Girl" Bands of the 1940s*, *Liner Notes for the Revolution: The Intellectual Life of Black Feminist Sound*, and *Blues Legacies and Black Feminism*. These are among a body of works that have recovered women's careers in jazz and centred their exciting legacies. However, their successes came after overcoming the music industry's dismissive attitudes that failed to take their work seriously. The barriers that impeded women in the past parallel the practices that still prevent women from having equal opportunities. As this chapter will illustrate, women in jazz today, like their historical counterparts, are still advocating for safer working environments free from sexual harassment, equitable financial support for their work, opportunities to perform in a competitive field that relies on social connections, an end to a misogynistic jam culture, and a larger platform for women and people of colour to refigure masculinist narratives in jazz from positions of power.[3] Observing how these conversations have taken place over the last century exposes how systemic barriers were put in place to constrain women and other minority voices, and also provides insight into how the community can rebuild the art form from a place of collaboration and equity.

Obstacles experienced by women in jazz today may present somewhat differently than they did a century ago, but women still confront issues of working in unsafe environments. In the early twentieth century, jazz music was heard in barrelhouses, bars, and other venues trafficked mainly by working-class men. As Prohibition took hold across the nation, Black and tan clubs managed by organised crime leaders appeared in urban areas offering flashy jazz floorshows for white customers. These clubs presented a narrow view of jazz culture, substantially limited Black women's participation in jazz to singing or dancing, and excluded women who did not fit into the club owners' perceptions of beauty. Women who gained employment were thrust into stereotyped roles that reinforced rigid racial hierarchies within the United States and hypersexualised Black women in particular. Beyond the issues of gatekeeping and fetishising, women who worked in these clubs were in close proximity to violence and at times lost their livelihoods if they were caught in the crossfire of warring gangs. Many had family members or romantic partners escort them to and from their gigs to make sure they got home safely. Some women who boldly tried to make a play for a job often learned the extra duties for women in the band. As Abbie Lincoln recalled in later years to Amiri Baraka:

> So I decided I wanted to sing with Duke [Ellington]. He hadn't asked for a singer. But I just went up to see him and hit on him, telling him I wanted to sing with the band. Duke didn't say much; he just began to undress and walk toward the bedroom. Then he rolled the bed down, and I walked out of there . . . . I guess he was letting me know . . . up front . . . so I got right out of there.[4]

The women who braved the precarious circumstances of bars and clubs to immerse themselves in jazz culture were seen as separate from other women in domestic or traditional roles. Jazz women were known for their energetic freedom, embracing a lifestyle viewed by many at the time as outrageous or downright dangerous.[5] Therefore, to be an early woman in jazz was to go against the grain of widely held notions of acceptable woman-like behaviour, which limited their access to resources available to their male peers. Dependent on booking agents, managers, and club owners for work, women in jazz were frequently forced into positions that treated them as commodities and novelties. They were considered incapable of contributing meaningfully to the genre or the community. Due to their non-traditional lifestyles and lack of support, many women were left to navigate predatory environments on their own.

In addition to the onslaught of problems faced at their gigs, women also experienced oppressive misogyny from their male peers in jam sessions, also called cutting sessions. Held in late-night venues, jam sessions were and are predominantly male spaces intended for musical exploration and displays of musical mastery. As an integral part of jazz history, jam sessions served as incubators for young musicians to develop new jazz forms, such as bebop, and allowed musicians to network with one another. Lasting for hours on end, sessions featured musicians taking turns improvising and responding musically to one another in a competitive fashion. Women like pianist Mary Lou Williams and saxophonist Irma Young (dates unknown) participated in jam sessions out west in cities like Kansas City and Denver, where they demonstrated their skills and at times astounded their male peers. Williams grew tremendously from participating in jam sessions and used what she learned in these spaces to inform her compositions, playing style, and teaching later in her life. However, women also experienced silencing at jam sessions where men failed to take them seriously, heckled them as they played, or refused to invite them to a session.

Regardless of their status or fame, women in jazz struggled to gain exposure and make a steady living as musicians. As people across the United States and abroad purchased phonographs, recording music became a more lucrative option for musicians to increase their profits and audiences. In the blues-dominated soundscape that preceded jazz, Black musicians were not given as many opportunities to record as their white counterparts, and Black women were excluded from recording at all, especially as vocalists.[6] In 1920, following the devastating Red Summer of 1919, Mamie Smith became the first Black woman to record the blues in sessions led by composer Perry Bradford. Bradford had spent months pitching song ideas to disinterested recording companies who were sceptical of the commerciality of the blues and Black women musicians. However, the recordings were also deterred by threats of boycotts if any company recorded a Black woman. Overcoming the racism they encountered, Smith and Bradford successfully demonstrated the broad market for the blues by selling over a million copies of the seminal song 'Crazy Blues', which launched the race records industry. Lovie Austin and other women emerged in the young race records industry as bandleaders, arrangers, and composers building the foundations for later jazz recordings. However, as the blues recording boom faded, so did opportunities for women to record.

In an already-competitive industry that favoured white men and music that appealed to white consumers, women in jazz experienced immense challenges in getting recorded. Vocalists had it easier, but even they dealt with producers and contracts that curtailed their ability to control what music they performed. Women instrumentalists were overlooked for the most part, and unfortunately, many went unrecorded.[7] The crash of the recording industry during the Great Depression and the later recording bans of the 1940s exacerbated these problems, making it almost impossible for women to be recorded. In the days before the American Federation of Musicians' strikes of 1942 and 1947 led by James Petrillo, women like Ella Fitzgerald (1917–1996) and Una Mae Carlisle crammed in recordings that would get them through the duration of the strike,[8] but many women were not so lucky and found it increasingly difficult to get by financially.[9] In the post-war years and beyond, women continued to clash with gatekeepers who prioritised recording men and often denied women recording contracts. When women were recorded, their music was poorly marketed or underpromoted unless they did the work themselves. Overall, the dearth of recordings by early women instrumentalists contributes to the lack of knowledge about them and reinforces sexist ideas that women cannot play instruments and should only sing.

Like some of their male counterparts, women in jazz were also consistently misunderstood or derided by critics. Unpacking some of the problematic aspects of jazz history that erased women requires considering the positions of jazz critics who were predominantly well-educated, wealthy white men judging music based on their understandings of the world. Publications like *DownBeat* magazine, founded in 1934, have led the conversations of what good jazz is and who is considered successful for decades. The magazine has also been responsible for disseminating ideas that women do not belong in jazz by publishing articles like the anonymously published 1938 piece 'Why Women Musicians Are Inferior'.[10] In a scathing response to that article, Peggy Gilbert refutes its author's misogyny and vents the frustrations felt by many women in jazz. As she so eloquently states:

> It's your attitude we resent, because it expresses the attitude of all professional men musicians toward all women musicians. A woman has to be a thousand times more

talented, has to have a thousand times more initiative even to be recognized as the peer of the least successful man. Why? Because of the age-old prejudice against women, that time-worn idea that women are the weaker sex, that they are innately inferior to men.[11]

In her response, Peggy challenges men's practice of acknowledging a few 'exceptional' women, such as Mary Lou Williams, while refusing to work with other women. She also mentions the harsh criticism 'fired at women at all sides', which could be understood to reference the treatment women experienced from their male peers and the male critics who judged their music as inferior based on their gender.[12] This vitriol clearly impacted women's ability to work during their lifetimes. However, its more sinister legacy is felt in jazz history, which generally overlooks these conditions that excluded women from participating in the music.

In addition to the obstacles outlined here, Black women also faced racism that prevented them from thriving in an art form they helped create. Throughout jazz's history, Black women have been the community's innovators, advocates, caretakers, and historians, but they have felt added musical and societal pressures that have hindered their ability to succeed. The rigours of maintaining a music career have deterred musicians of any gender for generations. However, Black women working as musicians endured violence from their bandmates and audiences, racial discrimination that made touring risky, and community pressures to comply with respectability politics.

On top of the tensions they felt at times with their bandmates, Black women were also manipulated, censored, and taken advantage of by managers, collaborators, radio DJs, producers, and filmmakers. Vocalist Maxine Sullivan's interpretation of songs like 'Loch Lomond' in 1937 put her at the centre of arguments for freedom of expression after some took issue with swinging traditional music, which led radio directors to pull the song from rotation until being overruled by popular demand.[13] Along with other jazz women like Dolly Jones (1902–1975), Maxine also worked in films; they were cast in roles that reinforced stereotypes and projected images of Black women as the girl player[14] or the singing maid.[15] Mary Lou Williams and Una Mae Carlisle are two examples of composers whose music was co-opted by male colleagues with whom they collaborated. Carlisle notably sued violinist 'Stuff' Smith for $10,000 after he claimed to have written her nationwide hit 'Walking by the River'.[16] These examples collectively speak to the extra lengths Black women had to go to assert their genius and protect their work.

Foundations of Today's Jazz Culture

Prejudice, stereotyping, and discrimination shape the foundation of an environment in which women in jazz currently live. Today, jazz musicians function in two main environments: performance and education. Performance encompasses recording, touring, live performance, collaboration with other artists, and the business of selling and marketing music to audiences. Education encompasses youth programmes for students aged 5–18, higher education, professional development, and an enormous economic stream for organisations.

Main gatekeepers in performance and education environments are the decision makers about who is performing, which organisations are presenting, what is being presented as important, and who is teaching. As jazz has become institutionalised, the gatekeepers have perpetuated sexist stereotypes through their hiring, presenting of specific artists, and admission of learners. Due to the history of jazz music highlighting men's achievements, it is only natural that the gatekeepers see those achievements as the only history.

Women experience outright sexism and microaggressive sexism. Outright sexism includes getting paid less than a male colleague, while microaggressive sexism may be a male boss or peer referring to a woman as 'sweetie'. Microaggressive sexism may be more dangerous than those outright examples of sexism because microaggressions can cause a person to question their reality and judgement. A *New York Times* article from 1994 states:

> young women working in jazz are rarely as adept as men of the same age. And if they are, they have a special story that explains their growth, usually either a male mentor or a relationship with a man that gives them access to the jazz world.[17]

Microaggressions can hinder playing opportunities and in turn have economic ramifications on a woman's livelihood.

Jazz education has become institutionalised over the last 50 years. Musicians are being trained in higher education, teaching positions are a main source of income for professional musicians, and professional careers start in educational realms. Therefore, it is important to note that the jazz education environment is a major proponent of sexism, exclusion, and opportunity.

In the last decade, only seven girls have made Texas All-State Jazz Band, which is fewer than 2% of participants.[18] The Thelonious Monk Institute, now renamed the Herbie Hancock Institution of Jazz, has had six female graduates out of 77 since 1995. The University of North Texas' famed One O'Clock Lab Band has had zero female bandleaders since its inception in 1948. Of the 190 schools listed in Downbeat Magazine's 'Where to Study Jazz 2019', 10 schools have female deans/department chairs.[19]

In a survey of 628 college music majors, Kathleen McKeage reported:

> significantly more men participate in jazz programmes than women, that men spend more time than women do in jazz programmes before discontinuing participation in the idiom, and that there is a dramatic attrition rate for women between high school and college jazz participation.[20]

According to Dr. Ariel Alexander, most young females do not join or drop out of jazz education due to the masculine image of jazz, instrument stereotypes, and dominating and competitive settings. How are we addressing the masculine image of jazz in institutions? How are we fostering dominating and competitive settings through educational experiences? And more importantly, how are faculty, leadership, and curriculum at school affecting women's choices in jazz education, rather than why aren't women making the same choices as men?

Kathleen McKeage has commented that: 'Historically, women instrumentalists were not included in jazz pedagogy, as much of the training for musicians happened in nightclubs and performance venues that were predominantly male'.[21] However, as jazz education has become institutionalised, it is rare to find a working jazz musician who has not received training in higher education. Furthermore, there are after-school programmes, summer jazz camps, and educational competitions nationally and locally for middle and high school students that create a population of aspiring jazz musicians pursuing higher education. Now that jazz learning primarily takes place in academic settings, it is imperative to examine how jazz is being taught and by whom.

Some of the nation's top schools, which include the University of North Texas (UNT), Indiana University, The University of Miami's Frost School of Music, University of Southern California, and Juilliard, have abysmal female faculty and leadership ratios. A 2001 review conducted by The National Association for Music Education showed that 23% of faculty who identified jazz as their teaching area were women.[22]

Founded in 1947, the University of North Texas currently has two female faculty members out of 23, and there is a male dean and male One O'Clock Band Director. Indiana University's Jacobs School of Music has zero female faculty members out of 15 in the jazz department. Indiana's jazz chair is male, and the Guest Artist Program has brought in 20 artists, only two of whom were female. The University of Miami's Frost School of Music has one female faculty member who teaches voice out of 13 total faculty. Of their famous alumni listed on their website, nine are female (one instrumentalist, eight vocalists) out of a whopping 213. The University of Southern California only has two female faculty members, who both teach voice, out of 19 total faculty members. Lastly, at Julliard there are currently zero female faculty members in the jazz department out of 26.[23] Racial and ethnic disparities are another angle that should be examined in more focused studies. Unfortunately, this information is not usually publicly available on university webpages, but it could provide further statistical data to support analyses of how women of colour are involved with jazz higher education.

Additionally, some of these universities have undergone negative sexual harassment press similar to many universities in the last three years. In 2018, Kalia Vandever, a Julliard alumna, wrote an exposé detailing the sexism and harassment she experienced while being one of two female students in the jazz department, emphasising the lack of support she received from administration and faculty after reporting her experiences. Additionally, in 2016 a jazz faculty member was fired from UNT after sexually assaulting a student, and Miami underwent national publicity in 2010 for firing a faculty member who had several reports of sexual harassment and headlines that read: 'University of Miami Accuses Professor of Sexting, Mooning, and Harassing Students'.[24]

These numbers paint a stark picture of inequality. They show that top schools from different geographic regions around the United States continue to hire fewer female faculty members and even fewer female instrumental faculty members. Female students lack role models. Likewise, Black students lack role modelsas well. Consequently, sexism and harassment have become a norm in female students' experiences. Furthermore, faculty and administrators are expected to serve as role models for students, providing guidance and a love of the music. In a study done by McKeage, one female student reported quitting jazz because she was 'intimidated by students and professors' and felt uncomfortable in a jazz setting.[25] As Penn Barber notes: 'The lack of female role models in the field of jazz should serve as a detriment to females pursuing education in jazz'.[26]

Countless studies have shown the importance of having female role models and mentors for college female students. As Anthony Catanese has commented: 'The absence of women faculty sends a not-so-subtle message to students that women may not be welcome in the club and will probably have a significantly harder time trying to join'.[27] In a utopian education setting, gender of faculty members should not be a factor of success in students' learning. However, in male-dominated professions, having female mentors from the beginning of a student's education can show that someone of similar circumstance has succeeded and has overcome shared experiences.[28]

Beyond students' being able to see and learn from women who have overcome barriers, students' academic experience and ability to learn also improves. In a study that focused on woman experience with different gender mentors, 'female students experienced significant improvements in their levels of confidence regarding . . . comprehension . . . with the presence of a woman in a position of authority and expertise'.[29]

Curricular changes have greater impact on the student body at large, especially in required coursework. By having assignments such as transcribing female instrumentalists, playing music written by females, and discussing females throughout history, the Lils to the Louis

Armstrongs, if you will, all students become exposed to diversity in jazz and cultural norms can start to break down within the genre.

It is important to note that women in jazz education know that they are in a male-dominated sphere, which is often apparent from the population of their programmes and the make-up of the music community they live in. Even when females understand that success will be a challenge in a male-dominated field, success does not guarantee acceptance within that field. As McKeage asserts: 'Women must not only master their instrument but must negotiate a place within a traditionally male-dominated community'.[30]

Moving Forward

So, what can we do now to improve jazz education? Tracy McMullen, saxophonist and tenured faculty member at Bowdoin College, offers several suggestions. She states 'when students study jazz in colleges and universities, including conservatories, the curriculum should include Gender and Women's Studies courses. The deeply problematic history of race and gender in jazz demands this'.[31] What is not addressed to the entire student body is thus transmitted, which has implications beyond educational settings. Along these lines, musical assignments with female examples are imperative to expanding students' viewpoint of women's role in jazz music. By assigning a transcription by Vi Redd, playing a Carla Bley big band chart, and making efforts to present gender-diverse examples in classrooms, gender inclusiveness will become the norm.

From a faculty and leadership standpoint, there needs to be more hiring of females in jazz education. Guest artists need to have progressive mindsets, collaborate with females, and serve in furthering the mission of gender equity in higher education. Schools should also require trainings and seminars on how to teach appropriately and equitably, what language to use in the classroom to promote equality, and how to be an ally to students in and outside of school. Unconscious bias training should be mandatory, as it now is in many other sectors, notably in UK Higher Education institutions. As a collective jazz community, we also need to think about the vernacular we use. 'Killin, guys, sideman' are all slang words that exclude women and have aggressive underpinnings.[32]

Current extracurricular programmes that have been making big improvements to jazz education for females include El Paso Jazz Girls,[33] Chica Power, and Geri Allen's All-Female Residency. El Paso Jazz Girls is a cost-free Texas-wide organisation for females ages 11–18 to learn jazz fundamentals and create a support system. The programme invites participants on any instrument and vocalists to learn from an all-female faculty of professional musicians. Girls work together to compose their own music, learn about various topics like digital audio workstations, re-composition, and wellness, and perform and share their creations. El Paso Jazz Girls also serves as an ongoing resource for girls throughout the year as they participate in their school music programmes.

Chica Power is a similar programme in New Jersey for middle school females that is part of Jazz House Kids. The six-week programme started after staff noticed that only one or two females were in the top ensembles at Jazz House Kids. They believe that by having women teach, it breaks down barriers for learning, and students do not fear being talked down to, being seen as sexual prey, and can focus on receiving the information in a comfortable environment.

In 2014, the New Jersey Performing Arts Centre started the All-Female Residency, which was led by Guggenheim Fellow/piano legend Geri Allen (1957–2017). The Residency was one of the first of its kind, open to females ages 14–25, with a faculty of world-renowned professional musicians including Carmen Lundy, Ellen Rowe, Linda Oh, Ingrid Jensen, Marcus Belgrave, Stefon Harris, and Geri Allen. Ellen Rowe 'uses the word "powerful" to describe opportunities for women to perform jazz together in a supportive environment'.[34] The programme includes courses in improvisation, musicianship, jazz herstory (led by Columbia University professor and jazz historian Jasmine Griffin), and jazz theory. 'It's a rare opportunity to nurture a community and build confidence in young women of jazz who are embarking on careers in the industry or considering their options'.[35] Recognising the need for mentorship in a programme is integrated into all these programmes' curriculum.

In higher education, there are also academic programmes contributing to the movement of toppling systemic exclusion, like the Berklee Institute of Jazz and Gender Justice established in 2018 by drummer and activist Terri Lyne Carrington.[36] The programme, led by Carrington and Aja Burrell Wood, has re-developed curriculum, hosted concerts, and drawn upon intersectional feminist ideas rooted in social justice to transform the way jazz is heard and created. By establishing a safe and nurturing environment for people of all gender identities, the Institute is working to overturn the long-reigning jazz patriarchy and celebrate the jazz women who have long been at the forefront of musicking.

Performance-based activism continues to make strides for female players as well. We Have Voice, Sisters in Jazz, the Diva Jazz Orchestra, the Mary Lou Williams Women in Jazz Festival, the Washington Women in Jazz Festival, and the Women in Jazz Organization have been providing playing opportunities for women and communities of support.[37]

In all, the goal is to create a community of jazz that allows people to thrive and flourish, regardless of gender. Women in jazz are currently in need of more resources to sustain and thrive in the jazz community. Visibility, education, and increasing safety in working environments are crucial in order for woman in jazz to be seen as equal and contributing members to the culture and community and jazz. There is much work still to be done to address racial disparity and the acceptance of non-binary and transgender musicians in addition to the issues women still face in jazz. It is all intersectional, and by taking action in specific areas we can begin to rectify and rebuild a better jazz community for all.

Notes

1. Henry Louis Gates Jr., *The Signifying Monkey: A Theory of African-American Literary Criticism* (New York: Oxford University Press, 1989), 63–76.
2. *Orchestra is racist* @orchestraisracist, accessed October 1, 2021, www.instagram.com/orchestraisracist/.
3. Lisa Barg, "Taking Care of Music: Gender, Arranging, and Collaboration in the Weston-Liston Partnership," *Black Music Research Journal* 34 (Spring 2014): 99.
4. Amiri Barka, *Digging: The Afro-American Soul of American Classical Music* (Berkeley: University of California Press, 2009), 298.
5. Kelly Boyer Sagert, *Flappers: A Guide to American Subculture* (Santa Barbara: Greenwood Press, 2010), 11.
6. David A. Jasen and Gene Jones. *Spreadin' Rhythm Around: Black Popular Songwriters, 1880–1930* (London: Taylor & Francis, 2005), 258–62.
7. Sally Placksin, *American Women in Jazz: 1900 to the Present Their Words, Lives, and Music* (New York: Seaview Books, 1982), xiv.
8. "National Signs Una Mae Carlisle," *The Pittsburgh Courier*, December 20, 1947.
9. Tammy Kernodle, *Soul on Soul* (Boston, MA: Northeastern University Press, 2004), 91, 133–34.
10. Anonymous, "Why Women Musicians Are Inferior," *Downbeat Magazine* (1938).
11. Jeannie Gayle Pool, *Peggy Gilbert & Her All-Girl Band* (Lanham, MD: Scarecrow Press, Inc., 2008), 84.
12. Ibid., 85.

13. David Ware Stowe, *Swing Changes: Big-Band Jazz in New Deal America* (Cambridge, MA: Harvard University Press, 1994), 95.
14. *Swing*, directed by Oscar Micheaux (Micheaux Film, 1938).
15. *Going Places*, directed by Ray Enright (Warner Bros., 1938).
16. Ted Yates, "Una Mae Planning to Sue," *Atlanta Daily World*, May 26, 1941.
17. Peter Watrous, "Jazz View; Why Women Remain at the Back of the Bus," *The New York Times*, November 27, 1994.
18. *Texas Music Educators Association*, Audition Results, accessed February 27, 2022, www.tmea.org/all-state/audition-results/.
19. *Downbeat Magazine*, Where to Study Jazz, 2019, accessed February 27, 2022, www.downbeat.com/digitaledition/2018/DB1810_Education_Guide/_art/DB1810_Education_Guide.pdf.
20. Erin Flowers-Wehr, "Difference between Male and Female Students," Confidence, Anxiety, and Attitude towards Learning Jazz Improvisation," *Journal of Research in Music Education* 54 (2006): 338.
21. Kathleen McKeage, "Gender and Participation in High School and College Instrumental Jazz Ensembles," *Journal of Research in Music Education* 52 (2006): 344.
22. McKeage, "Gender and Participation," 344.
23. These statistics are reflective of numbers gathered in 2018.
24. Erik Maza, "University of Miami Accuses Professor of Sexting, Mooning, and Harassing Students," *Miami New Times*, June 1, 2010.
25. McKeage, "Gender and Participation," 352.
26. Douglas Penn Barber, *A Study of Jazz Band Participation by Gender in Secondary High School Instrumental Music Programs* (New Jersey: Rowan University, 1998), 9.
27. Anthony Catanese, "Faculty Role Models and Diversifying the Gender and Racial Mix of Undergraduate Economics Majors," *Journal of Economic Education* (1991): 276.
28. Penelope Lockwood, "Someone Like Me Can Be Successful: Do College Students Need Same-Gender Role Models?," *Psychology of Women Quarterly* 30 (2010): 37.
29. Sehoya Cotner, Cissy Ballen, D. Christopher Brooks, and Randy Moore, "Instructor Gender and Student Confidence in the Sciences: A Need for More Role Models?," *Journal of College Science Teaching* 40 (May 2011): 3.
30. McKeage, "Gender and Participation," 354.
31. Tracy McMullen, personal interview with the authors (8 January 2019).
32. Ibid.
33. El Paso Jazz Girls is founded and run by Amanda Ekery, co-author of this chapter. Learn more at www.epjazzgirls.com
34. 'NJPAC and Rutgers University partner for all-female jazz residency," *My Central Jersey* (June 23, 2016).
35. 'Regina Carter Appointed Artistic Director of NJPAC's All-Female Jazz Residency," *DownBeat*, June 14, 2018, accessed October 12, 2021, https://downbeat.com/news/detail/regina-carter-appointed-artistic-director-of-njpacs-all-female-jazz-residen.
36. *Berklee Jazz and Gender Institute*, accessed February 27, 2022, https://college.berklee.edu/jazz-gender-justice.
37. We Have Voice Collective, www.wehavevoice.org/; Sisters in Jazz, https://jazzednet.org/sisters-in-jazz/; Diva Jazz Orchestra, https://divajazz.com/; Mary Lou Williams Women in Jazz Festival, www.kennedy-center.org/whats-on/explore-by-genre/jazz/2021-2022/mary-lou-williams-jazz-festival/; Washington Women in Jazz Festival, accessed October 21, 2021, http://washingtonwomeninjazz.com/; Women in Jazz Organization, http://wearewijo.org/.

Bibliography

Barber, Douglas Penn. *A Study of Jazz Band Participation by Gender in Secondary High School Instrumental Music Programs*. Glassboro, NJ: Rowan University, 1998.

Barg, Lisa. "Taking Care of Music: Gender, Arranging, and Collaboration in the Weston-Liston Partnership." *Black Music Research Journal* 34 (Spring 2014): 97–119.

Burke, Patrick. "Oasis of Swing: The Onyx Club, Jazz, and White Masculinity in the Early 1930s." *American Music* 24 (Autumn 2006): 320–46.

Cameron, William Bruce. "Sociological Notes on the Jam Session." *Social Forces* 33 (December 1954): 177–82.

Catanese, Anthony. "Faculty Role Models and Diversifying the Gender and Racial Mix of Undergraduate Economics Majors." *Journal of Economic Education* (1991): 276–84.

Cotner, Sehoya, Cissy Ballen, D. Christopher Brooks, and Randy Moore. "Instructor Gender and Student Confidence in the Sciences: A Need for More Role Models?" *Journal of College Science Teaching* 40 (May 2011): 96–101.

Downbeat. "Regina Carter Appointed Artistic Director of NJPAC's All-Female Jazz Residency." *DownBeat*, June 14, 2018. Accessed October 21, 2021. https://downbeat.com/news/detail/regina-carter-appointed-artistic-director-of-njpacs-all-female-jazz-residen.

Flowers-Wehr, Erin. "Difference between Male and Female Students' Confidence, Anxiety, and Attitude towards Learning Jazz Improvisation." *Journal of Research in Music Education* 54 (2006): 337–49.

Gates, Henry Louis. *The Signifying Monkey: A Theory of African-American Literary Criticism*. New York: Oxford University Press, 1989.

Grantham, Hannah. "A Life Well-Sung: Maxine Sullivan (1911–1987)." *The Smithsonian National Museum of African American History and Culture*, July 19, 2019. Accessed October 21, 2021. https://nmaahc.si.edu/explore/stories/collection/life-well-sung.

Gussow, Adam. " 'Shoot Myself a Cop': Mamie Smith's 'Crazy Blues' as Social Text." *Callaloo* 25 (Winter 2002): 8–44.

Kernodle, Tammy. *Soul on Soul: The Life and Music of Mary Lou Williams*. Boston, MA: Northeastern University Press, 2004.

Lockwood, Penelope. "Someone Like Me Can Be Successful: Do College Students Need Same-Gender Role Models?" *Psychology of Women Quarterly* 30 (June 1, 2010): 36–46.

Maza, Erik. "University of Miami Accuses Professor of Sexting, Mooning, and Harassing Students." *Miami New Times*, June 1, 2010. https://www.miaminewtimes.com/news/university-of-miami-accuses-professor-of-sexting-mooning-and-harassing-students-6528355.

McKeage, Kathleen. "Gender and Participation in High School and College Instrumental Jazz Ensembles." *Journal of Research in Music Education* 52 (2006): 343–56.

"National Signs Una Mae Carlisle." *The Pittsburgh Courier*, December 20, 1947.

"NJPAC and Rutgers University Partner for All-Female Jazz Residency." *My Central Jersey*, June 23, 2016. https://eu.mycentraljersey.com/story/news/education/in-our-schools/2016/06/23/njpac-and-rutgers-university-partner-all-female-jazz-residency/85481008/.

Placksin, Sally. *American Women inn Jazz: 1900 to the Present Their Words, Lives, and Music*. New York: Seaview Books, 1982.

Pool, Jeannie Gayle. *Peggy Gilbert & Her All-Girl Band*. Lanham, MD: Scarecrow Press, Inc., 2008.

Sagert, Kelly Boyer. *Flappers: A Guide to American Subculture*. Santa Barbara: Greenwood Press, 2010.

Stowe, David Ware. *Swing Changes: Big-band Jazz in New Deal America*. Cambridge, MA: Harvard University Press, 1994.

Suisman, David. "Black Swan Rising." *Humanities* 31 (November/December 2010). Accessed October 21, 2021. www.neh.gov/humanities/2010/novemberdecember/feature/black-swan-rising.

Tucker, Sherrie. "Telling Performances: Jazz History Remembered and Remade by the Women in the Band." *Oral History Review* (1999): 67–84.

Watrous, Peter. "Jazz View; Why Women Remain at the Back of the Bus." *The New York Times*, November 27, 1994. https://www.nytimes.com/1994/11/27/arts/jazz-view-why-women-remain-at-the-back-of-the-bus.html.

Wilson, John S. "Women in Jazz, Past and Present." *New York Times*, June 11, 1978.

Yates, Ted. "Una Mae Planning to Sue." *Atlanta Daily World*, May 26, 1941.

42
MAPPING THE BOUNDARIES
Encountering Women's Creativity in the Salon

Briony Cox-Williams

This chapter explores the theoretical and practical underpinnings of a contemporary salon project. Salon Without Boundaries is a UK-based initiative set up by the current author with singer Pierrette Thomet, with a focus on women's creative work in both arts and sciences throughout history, offering both live events that encompass women's artistic and scientific cultural contributions, as well as an online resource library of primary sources, research, and first-hand accounts resulting from the cross-fertilisation of all these elements and disciplines. Prior to the launch of the salon project, the two founding members of the salon had already been working together for over twenty years, with the idea of the salon and its community at the centre of many musical events, acting as a driving force in the relationships between roles that included performer, teacher, scholar, and curator. Past events had often borne traits of a nineteenth-century European salon model through recognisable components such as smaller venues and audiences, and scale of repertoire, but also through less obvious elements such as audience interactions and concert programming. These events had become ever more explicitly salon-based over the years, culminating in a desire to find practical links between old and new salon strategies that could strengthen us as women practitioners in an art we saw as still mainly focused on male experience.

European musical salons of the nineteenth century offered an enormous breadth of types of experience to their participants, from the formal to the informal, from the superficial to the intense, from the culturally diverse to the musically specific. Within this range of experiences, there were many that offered women in particular a space for creativity, exploration, and daring, even a certain kind of danger. In the midst of a world of which Hedwig Dohm wrote in 1908, 'Keeping still – both outwardly and inwardly – was something desired by nature in the female child',[1] the women who ran their own salons often could be seen to be taking control of the ways in which they were *being noticed* – not in the sense of being the object of a gaze, male or otherwise,[2] but through their creative output, as multi-faceted creative beings who asked that their way of seeing the world be judged as valid. This was not just through musical performance and composition themselves but, crucially, through relationships developed with other participants, whether they were on 'stage' or acting as audience. It was these nineteenth-century relationships that eventually informed the twenty-first-century Salon Without Boundaries project, highlighting as they did essential aspects of concert practice and programming, especially around authority, responsibility, and emotional load.

DOI: 10.4324/9781003024767-48

Salon Models

In the extraordinary range of salon activity across the Continent, our particular interest settled on Berlin salons, built as many were on ideals of mutual education. In 1820, Rahel Varnhagen wrote:

> One would never find anywhere more women who receive guests, with the exception of Paris: more striving for knowledge and [a meaningful existence] would also be difficult to find.[3]

From Henriette Herz in the late eighteenth century, through Sara Levy, Fanny Hensel, and Fanny Lewald, to Felicie Bernstein and Aniela Fürstenberg in the 1890s, the members of these salons often saw art as a way of uniting people across class, sex, and religion, and of providing a freedom of expression and knowledge within a stifled society. There was a hunger for education, for the choices that education could offer. After all, in 1827 when Alexander Humboldt allowed women to attend his popular physical science lecture series given at the Berlin Singakademie, enormous numbers of women turned out for the events. Fanny Hensel wrote to Karl Klingemann that: 'Gentlemen may laugh as much as they like, but it is delightful that we too have the opportunity given us of listening to clever men'.[4] It is clear from Hensel's gently cynical tone that even in the face of a continuing contempt for the idea of higher education for women, there was a hunger for knowledge that overrode social strictures.

Indeed, Hensel was to prove central to our contemporary salon experience, drawn as we were to her *Sonntagsmusiken*, much as she herself would never have termed these as salons. Hensel's gatherings are well-known, but it is worth reiterating their evolution. The fortnightly events took place on Sundays between 11 a.m. and 2 p.m at 3 Leipziger Strasse, the Mendelssohn/Hensel residence. Similar musical gatherings directed by her parents Lea Salomon (1777–1842) and Abraham Mendelssohn (1776–1835) had been an integral part of Hensel's musical experience in the early 1820s, although these appear to have been centred on giving her brother Felix an entrance to German musical culture, and thus ceased when he left home. When Hensel resumed the events in 1831, she almost immediately recrafted them to her own design. No longer were these events in which musical friends of the Mendelssohn family played to and with each other, but much larger and more ambitious events in which a broad cross-section of Berlin musical culture, both local and visiting, mingled with an eclectic audience, many of whom were drawn from fields as disparate as science, philosophy, and politics, as well as the arts. Not only chamber music and song filled the programmes, but also choral and operatic repertoire, and even full orchestral works.[5]

One factor of Hensel's events that particularly drew our attention was the way that the core event concentrated on musical performance, with a cross-fertilisation of other idioms and other idea-centres coming from the relationship of the musicale to its participants' involvement in a wider community that grew out of their association here. This included such events as the already-mentioned science lectures given by Humboldt to both men and women at the Berlin SingAkademie, art exhibitions, and salons run by other women, all the way through to the casual get-togethers and passing discussions, both in person and written, that created the woven cloth in which more formalised events were nestled. It is clear from the writings of the time just how exciting these connections were, and how important they were for the growth of both society and culture at that time. What would our artistic and scientific heritage look like if, for example, the archeologist Karl Lepsius and mathematician Karl Jacobi had not sat in a room together, listening to Hensel playing Beethoven, while beside them Fanny's artist husband Wilhelm Hensel sketched the feminist writer Fanny Lewald?

In control of these events was of course Hensel herself, fulfilling her 'self-designated responsibilities as program director, composer, conductor, pianist, singer and "contractor"', as Sarah Rothenberg sums up comprehensively.[6] Her authority, both musical and otherwise, is clear. Yet Rothenberg goes on to suggest that 'the ultimate rewards and risks of such a situation are not a substitute for the lessons of the professional stage',[7] and here we might pause for thought. What are these lessons that must be learned from a 'public' exposure? Clara Wieck (1819–1896), writing to her fiancé Robert Schumann (1810–1856) from the salons of Berlin in the 1830s, is clear that there could be a kind of musical critique in the salon that was quite different to that engendered on the concert platform,[8] while Hensel herself points out the heightened attention caused by close proximity of performer and audience, when she writes to her brother of pianist Sigismond Thalberg's avoidance of the salon environment during his 1839 visit to Berlin:

> Unfortunately, I have heard though, that he does not play in salons, and one can learn only a little from a few concerts. One really needs to see these wizards play.[9]

While several sources both then and now have suggested that such language points to a comfort and ease that comes from 'playing to friends',[10] I would suggest that Hensel is implying that this physical closeness often proved to be a much more focused verification process than the 'public' concert platform, not least because of an awareness that it was not only the outcome that was being offered for scrutiny, but uniquely, the working-out process behind performance and composition alike. That this broader process was seen as being as much for audience consumption as the outcome seems clear in the documentation around the salons, the private correspondences and communications that were part and parcel of the salon experience, and which often point to a detailed and experienced analysis of what was on offer. Such writings assume a different kind of authority, not a lesser one, though history has of course tried to suggest otherwise.

Salon Without Boundaries: The Contemporary Salon

Of course, another important facet of the salon is its ability to allow room for the recognition of women's stories and expression. The half of humanity that has culturally inhabited the role of the silent symbol gains its own voice in the salon and speaks for itself, rather than through an observer. In setting up our own salon, we realised that possibly the most fundamental endeavour was to find opportunity to experience the sense of illumination and of continuous communication that could come from the highlighting of women's creative practice, not just in the arts but across all fields. Creatively and artistically, we wanted a place that would help change gendered cultural norms and enable us as artists to envisage ourselves not on the margins, but at the centre of a vibrant, culturally relevant, and socially empowering landscape shaped by the creativity of our own gender.

International communication was an intrinsic part of Salon culture, so we thought there was potential in the idea of an online Salon.[11] There are places on the web where one can find scores by female composers, see pictures painted by women, read their stories; there are also places that offer historical information on these, both directly and through biography. There are still further places that allow for discourse and investigation. What seemed to be missing is somewhere that combines all of these in one place, especially while offering the opportunity for everyone to join the debate, to have an opinion that matters. We wanted a place that would combine historical information and the output itself in one place, along with commentary, analysis, contextual exploration, and an awareness of the reality of women's lives away from the pianos and pens with which we express ourselves. But we also wanted a place to hear the music in person, so to speak, a place to meet other artists, to experiment, experience, discuss, and question. We therefore came to the conclusion that this needed a two-part Salon: the online element, and a live one, each of which would inflect the other, and neither of which would bear more creative authority.

We therefore wrote a mission statement that would encompass both sides of the salon. It is this statement that heads our website:
The mission of the Salon is to celebrate the contribution made to world culture by salons across the 19th and 20th centuries:

- by uncovering and showcasing the enormous wealth of artistic work by historical women;
- by interrogating historical and present-day gendered cultural practices;
- by opening metaphorical and actual doors to the pleasure and challenge of taking part in the discussion, debate and creativity of a true salon;
- and by creating its own space for contemporary creative work and performance by women and thus continuing the tradition of a salon culture that has transcended the boundaries of time and place: so that women from all parts of the globe and from all ages speak to each other, to each other's art, and to all of us regardless of time, place, status or gender.[12]

Bound up with this mission statement was our decision to make Fanny Hensel patron of the salon. Although Hensel is not an unfamiliar figure to many, it is worth a reminder of her wide sphere of creative output, from pianist to chorister, conductor, composer, writer, and of course *salonière* (although she herself never would have termed herself one, given the contemporary view that this term belonged more to the women in charge of the literary and political salons of Paris). And in the spirit of the salon, and the wider creative experience it celebrates, mention must be made of some of the other roles she filled – daughter, sister, mother, wife, social activist, organiser, educator, enabler, and lynchpin. All these roles inflected the creative voice we hear from her, and it is the unique combination she offers that led to our recognition of her as a woman who saw all those roles as equal, and of her musical spaces as places where, in Carolyn Heilbrun's words, 'women exchange stories, where they read and talk collectively of ambitions, possibilities and accomplishments'.[13]

In January 2018, we set up a placeholder website, explaining the historical beginnings of the salon and introducing ourselves. We added pages on women we felt were particularly influential for us, such as Hensel herself, Pauline von Decker, Jane Guest, Eliza and Sarah Flower, and Fanny Lewald. We then began to think about the 'live' elements of the project. At first, we thought we would offer two types of salons: contemporary and historical. There was so much material we wanted to share. We thought this might be a way of allowing the works to speak for themselves. We very quickly realised, however, that we were most interested in the dialogue between the new and old, and that dialogue was after all the central tenet of any good salon, particularly dialogue with our foremothers, the foremothers whose voices have so often been lost to the concert platform.

The programme for our inaugural event took shape quickly. We were touched and excited by the warm enthusiasm with which we were met when we asked women for their participation. We encountered the same enthusiasm from venues, who were fascinated with the concept.

Funding was forthcoming from the Royal Academy of Music and from Arts Council England. 'Mapping the Boundaries: Women, Creativity and the Natural World' took place at the 1901 Arts Club in London, on 14 November 2018. As well as our own performances of piano pieces and songs by Fanny Hensel (who we thought should have the first 'word') and her best friend, Pauline von Decker, there were contributions from Kate Heard, Senior Curator of Prints and Drawing at the Royal Collections Trust, on the scientific illustrator Maria Merian, and a joint contribution from the poet Elizabeth Lewis-Williams and composer Jenni Pinnock. Elizabeth read her cycle 'Met Obs', based on archival material from The British Antarctic Survey, in which her father took part; Jenni spoke about the currently ongoing process of setting these poems into a song-cycle. We performed two of the concept-sketches that Jenni had available.

In a way, the programme was the easy part. What took even more care and attention was the rethinking of our collaborative practice, both before the event, and during. After all, inclusion was a fundamental principle of salon culture, indeed a defining one, as Wilhelmy-Dollinger insists when she writes: 'Wherever this element of people without agenda, the free and tolerant was missing in a salon or died out, the salon quickly degenerated into a propaganda group or a sect'.[14] Wilhelmy-Dollinger also emphasises that 'every voice spoke for itself and was heard'.[15] This dedication to pluralistic communication meant that we had a heightened awareness of both the needs and creative wants of the performers, but also a sense that the audience bore both the freedom within and the responsibility for a type of participation that was probably new to all of us. Hensel's lament about Thalberg's absence from the salons is a lament for an ensuing inability to critique his playing. I would like to suggest however that Hensel is also speaking of a relationship with music-making that highlights a collaborative exchange between composer, performer, and audience, that rejects the monolithic and patriarchal authority of the composer as 'author' of 'the work'. The work thus does not reside in the notes, but in the process of communication. It is exactly this that we found ourselves most engaged with in our collaborations. Interestingly, this encompassed such practicalities as childcare, the ramifications of long-distance rehearsals and organisation, and the need, for both physical and social reasons, to offer refreshments to the audience on the night. In understanding how salons worked, we believed that these things were not peripheral to our music-making, but core to both interpretation and crafting of materials. Certainly, the apparently superficial aspect of providing food proved thought-provokingly fundamental to the salon experience. Simple refreshments were often offered in the original salons – a breaking of bread (quite literally at times, as nothing too elaborate was permitted, so that even less well-off women could take on the role of salonière without prompting comparison), with its social symbolism, brought together disparate groups to share their thoughts and comments on the evening's content. We had found the audience very willing but extremely uncertain of how to respond to an invitation to be part of the creative experience of the programme itself; the conversation in the interval and afterwards, which relaxed into the familiar environment of shared sustenance in the shape of fruit, cheese, and biscuits, and in which we as performers were participants rather than directors, allowed them to find their own creative authority within the listening experience and, perhaps even more importantly, to share that with us.

A second event took place in the Piano Gallery of the Royal Academy of Music in 2019. This was slightly more formal and looked at diaries in all their different forms as vehicles for women to find a voice to tell their own stories. This event allowed the primary material to speak for itself, finding relationships between women from different eras who were not even aware of each other's existence. Our question was: what happens if these women get to respond to each other? Content ranged from Hensel's *Das Jahr* piano cycle and Dominic Argento's setting of extracts from Virginia Woolf's diary (the first time creative output from a male artist had been included), to songs by Augusta Holmès, and a presentation on the science and mathematical riddles of the late eighteenth-century *Woman's Almanack*. Again, we invited input from the audience. We learned that the material itself is still unknown enough that the audience needed more context to understand their own response; they were still willing to speak to us fluently, away from the 'spotlight' of a formalised concert layout.

The Role of the Audience

This request for a change in audience response proved so integral to our definition of the salon experience that it warrants further analysis. Why was it considered so immediately challenging? Why did it have such an impact on our own engagement with our roles?

Historical audiences' behaviour has been carefully examined through many scholarly avenues, particularly those audiences of the burgeoning concert-going culture of the nineteenth century, which laid down the parameters of public musical life in Western classical music that are still to a large degree observed today.[16] In their 1998 book on audiences, Nicholas Abercrombie and Brian Longhurst examine audiences over the decades, from nineteenth-century spectators through to those of today, exploring how their changing nature has been driven by a changing delivery of content through evolving media. The authors divide types of audience into three – simple, mass, and diffused. The chart they offer in their book clearly lays out the main differences they see between these categories:

Table 42.1 Modes of Audience Experience, Abercrombie and Longhurst[17]

	Simple	*Mass*	*Diffused*
Communication	Direct	Mediated	Fused
Local/Global	Local	Global	Universal
Ceremony	High	Medium	Low
Public/private	Public	Private	Public and Private
Distance	High	Very High	Low
Attention	High	Variable	Civil Inattention

The authors argue that prior to recording technologies, all audiences fitted their definition of 'simple':

> There is a communication of some kind between a sender and a receiver, this communication is fairly direct, the context is spatially localised and, typically, takes place in a public space. There is a reasonably clear distinction between producers and consumers: producers perform and audiences appropriate the performance with a great deal of attention and involvement. Events involving simple audiences of this kind are exceptional, depend on a certain ceremonial quality, and demand relatively high levels of attention and involvement. . . . Performances to simple audiences are *noticed*.[18]

Certainly, many public concerts can be recognised within this scenario. They are indeed 'spatially localised'; the audience is separate from performers, not just physically but also in expertise; they require an extremely high level of attention (one that is often policed by members of the audience themselves); and ceremony is high, i.e., concert etiquette for both audience and musicians is complex and ritualised. It is also notable that the authors underline distance as an element of the 'simple' audience, a distance that for them is physical, social, and psychological, not just descriptive of the elevated stage at the front of the hall, but of a hierarchical difference between composer, performer, and audience. Even traditional concert costume underlines this difference.

Abercrombie and Longhurst turn their attention to the mass audience next: a category driven, they say, by the advent of early audio recording, radio, and television.[19] These methods of widespread dissemination meant that while performance could now be 'consumed' in private, there was still a sense of ceremony and a need for attentiveness. A notable change is that the distance is now 'very high' – performers are often invisible, with lifestyles that are unseen and unattainable by the masses.

It is the diffused audience, however, that interested us most as offering both definition and model of the salon audience experience we most wanted to recreate. Salons had audiences that consisted of both performers and non-performers, had a variable attention level depending on particular events, and had a deliberately low ceremonial aspect, even including what type of refreshment was considered appropriate. Intimacy, in many of its definitions, is descriptive of the salon. Under Abercrombie and Longhurst's terms, the salon thus occupies this category comfortably.

The authors see the diffused audience as a purely modern phenomenon, arising from a society in which:

> [t]he people, objects and events in the world cannot simply be taken for granted but have to be framed, looked at, gazed upon, registered and controlled. In turn, this suggests that the world is constituted as an event, as a performance; the objects, events and people which constitute the world are made to perform for those watching or gazing.[20]

They go on to describe this gaze as a 'possessive gaze'[21] that is the result of increasing capitalism – a description that is of course also immediately recognisable as relating to the traditional positioning of women as *created* or *created about*, rather than subjects of their own narratives. It is possible that the customary inhabiting of this performative position was a main reason for both the complexity and the success of the salons. After all, as Wilhelmy-Dollinger points out: 'One can with some justification describe the salons as a stage, a theatre, in which the actors and spectators were identical'.[22] In a way, women were giving a creative voice to the position they themselves had occupied for so long. Abercrombie and Longhurst's assumption that the diffused audience is a modern phenomenon and that it depends on modern media for its existence may also be the reason it has been difficult to define salon culture. It was a unique example of an ahistorical type of performer/audience interaction.

Salons were notable for their capacity to accommodate audiences and performers in different positions and roles. This was not only true of literary or political salons where all participants moved in and out of both roles several times within an evening, but also of musical salons in which participants could take on various degrees of active participation, again within the course of a single event. Such a fusion of roles is in part due, as Abercrombie and Longhurst point out, to a wider shared skill-pool of all participants.[23] In salons, audience-members as well as performers were likely to have active creative and performance experience, even if not specifically in music. This shared experience is also one of the factors reducing the distance between performers and audience. While the smaller physical distance created by the intimate spaces of a domestic setting was important, the shared experiences of the participants were absolutely fundamental to creating the unique environment of the salons. Not only were the participants at that moment part of a localised community; they were also part of a universal community. Universality is created both by the nature of creative response and by what Abercrombie and Longhurst call an 'imagined community' – a community created by a 'shared sentiment, history and purpose' that is as much a 'construction of identity' as a physical group of people.[24] The universal aspect of the salon community was assisted by the letters and diaries that were an integral part of the lives of women salon participants and that 'through letters continued, completed and broadened the here-and-now of the salon-conversation through the distance of time and space'.[25] Because the sense of shared community was so important, ceremony was usually low-key; in fact, Wilhelmy-Dollinger recognises rehearsal as part of the salon experience.²⁶ Hensel certainly appears to make little distinction in her writings between her attendance at rehearsals and at performances.

Interestingly, Abercrombie and Longhurst see the public/private issue, which has been so central to investigations into salon culture, as central to defining a diffused audience experience:

> The potential for erosion of the distinction between private and public inherent in diffused audiences' performances suggests a general characteristic of this audience form – the breaking of boundaries.²⁷

Breaking the boundaries between public and private has meant that salon culture has been notoriously difficult to place on this spectrum. To some degree, this has been due to the hierarchy of authority imposed, the assumption having often been that the private sphere has less agency, and that information concerning it is available to only a few. But authors Benn and Gaus, in exploring this issue, cast it in a different light when they assert that 'to insist that a piece of information is private is not necessarily to assert that no one but oneself should have access to it, but rather that the access should be under one's own control'.²⁸ Thus, to label certain aspects of salons as 'private' is not to limit them, but rather to recognise that control of them lay with the women who ran them. Salons, by being several times removed from an unambiguously public sphere, were a method of celebrating an uncensored creativity and of experimenting with an entire range of creative processes.

The Future of the Salon

Although world events have created a hiatus in proceedings at the time of writing, the salon remains committed to its combination of live and online events and material. A review of the opening event demonstrated that audiences are eager to recognise the boundless nature of what can be on offer in a salon environment:

> A memorable evening in a unique venue which replicated the salon entertainment of the 19th century and celebrated women's creativity past and present. The audience were entranced by the lieder of Fanny Hensel and Pauline von Decker, sung with control and passion. A biography of Maria Merian and her butterflies proved fascinating as she too was not widely celebrated in this country. The highlight of the evening for me was Elizabeth Lewis Williams' reading of her poetry on the Antarctic inspired by her father's journal. The ensuing discussion by the composer Jenni Pinnock explaining how she interpreted the poem was fascinating and informed the audience as to how mood, tone and space is transmitted through music. An impressive soiree devised by inspiring, intellectual women.²⁹

This is still very much a project in the making. We are applying for funding for our continuing events and for website production, to ensure that it can fulfil its multiple functions. We have many ideas in the pipeline for what comes next, particularly as the pandemic of 2020 has shown us more possibilities of connecting live and online events and resources in new ways, giving us fresh opportunities for global as well as historical reach, and ensuring that such considerations as venues and repertoire do not become barriers to musical communication. There is certainly no doubt that in the coming complex re-assessment of relationships and authority within the music-making world, the salon, with the paths to creativity and communication contained within it, has much to offer to musicians and audiences alike.

Notes

1. *German Feminist Writings*, edited by Patricia Herminghouse and Magda Mueller (New York: Bloomsbury, 2001), 42.
2. For a discussion on the male gaze see Laura Mulvey, "Visual Pleasure and Narrative Cinema," *Screen* 16, no. 3 (1975): 6–18.
3. Rahel Varnhagen's letter of 9 June 1820 to Wilhelmine and Henriette von Reden, *Gesammelte Werke*, edited by Konrad Feilchenfeld, Rahel E. Steiner, and Uwe Schweikert, 10 vols. (Munich: Mathes & Seitz, 1983), III, 22. Translation by Lorraine Byrne Bodley in "In Pursuit of a Single Flame: Fanny Hensel's 'Musical Salon'," in *Women and the Nineteenth-Century Lied*, edited by Aisling Kenny and Susan Wollenberg (Farnham: Ashgate Publishing, 2015), 46.
4. Sebastian Hensel, *The Mendelssohn Family (1729–1847) from Letters and Journals*, trans. Karl Klingemann (London: S. Low, Marston, Searle, & Rivington, 1884), vol. 1, 151–52. The original German can be found in Sebastian Hensel, *Die Familie Mendelssohn, 1729–1847* (Berlin, 1903), 173.
5. More detailed information can be extracted from Fanny Hensel's diary and letters. See Fanny Hensel, *Tagebücher* (Wiesbaden: Breitkopf & Härtel, 2002) and Marcia Citron, *The Letters of Fanny Hensel to Felix Mendelssohn* (Stuyvesant: Pendragon Press, 1987).
6. Sarah Rothenberg, "'Thus Far, But No Farther': Fanny Mendelssohn-Hensel's Unfinished Journey," *The Musical Quarterly* 77, no. 4 (1993): 698.
7. Ibid.
8. David Ferris, "Public Performance and Private Understanding: Clara Wieck's Concerts in Berlin," *Journal of the American Musicological Society* 59, no. 1 (2006): 400.
9. Marcia Citron, *The Letters of Fanny Hensel to Felix Mendelssohn*, trans. the current author (Stuyvesant: Pendragon Press, 1987), 549.
10. Ferris, "Public Performance and Private Understanding," 374.
11. It is telling just how far salon culture reached in the nineteenth century. This was partly through travelling musicians – a case in point is soprano Anna Bishop (1810–1884), the most travelled female singer of the century, who connected salons on different continents through her presence and her letters. See Charles Deal, *Travels of Anna Bishop in Mexico* (1849).
12. Briony Cox-Williams and Pierrette Thomet, "About the Salon Without Boundaries," 2018, accessed June 26, 2020, www.salonwithoutboundaries.com/about
13. Carolyn Heilbrun, *Writing a Woman's Life* (London: The Women's Press, 1989), 46.
14. 'Wo dieses Element des Zwanglosen und Freien und Toleranten in einem Salon fehlte oder abstarb, degenerierte er schnell zu einem Zweckverband oder zur Sekte'. Petra Wilhelmy-Dollinger, *Die Berliner Salons* (Berlin and New York: De Gruyter, 2000), 5.
15. 'Jede Stimme sprach für sich und würde gehört'. Ibid., 15.
16. See for example, William Weber, *The Great Transformation of Musical Taste: Concert Programming from Haydn to Brahms* (Cambridge: Cambridge University Press, 2008).
17. Nicholas Abercrombie and Brian Longhurst, *Audiences: A Sociological Theory of Performance and Imagination* (London: Sage, 1998), 44.
18. Ibid., 44.
19. Ibid., 57–58.
20. Ibid., 78.
21. Ibid., 82.
22. 'Man kann mit einigem Recht die Salons als eine Bühne bezeichnen, ein Theater, wo Schauspieler und Zuschauer identisch waren'. Wilhelmy-Dollinger, *Die Berliner Salons*, 15.
23. Abercrombie and Longhurst, *Audiences*, 75.
24. Ibid., 115 and 117.
25. 'sich brieflich das Hier und Jetzt des Salongesprächs auf räumliche und zeitliche Distanz fortsetzte, ergänzte und erweiterte'. Wilhelmy-Dollinger, *Die Berliner Salons*, 8.
26. Ibid., 152.
27. Abercrombie and Longhurst, *Audiences*, 76.

28. Stanley I. Benn and Gerald F. Gaus, eds., *Public and Private in Social Life* (New York: St Martin's Press, 1983), 8.
29. *The 1901 Arts Club*, accessed November 21, 2018, www.1901artsclub.com/guest-book.html.

Bibliography

Abercrombie, Nicholas, and Brian Longhurst. *Audiences: A Sociological Theory of Performance and Imagination*. London: Sage, 1998.

Benn, Stanley I., and Gerald F. Gaus, eds. *Public and Private in Social Life*. New York: St Martin's Press, 1983.

Bunzel, Anja, and Natasha Loges, eds. *Musical Salon Culture in the Long Nineteenth Century*. Woodbridge: The Boydell Press, 2019.

Citron, Marcia. *The Letters of Fanny Hensel to Felix Mendelssohn*. Stuyvesant: Pendragon Press, 1987.

Cox-Williams, Briony, and Pierrette Thomet. "About the Salon without Boundaries." 2018. Accessed August 3, 2023. www.salonwithoutboundaries.com/about.

Drewitz, Ingeborg. *Berliner Salons: Gesellschaft und Literatur zwischen Aufklärung und Industriezeitalter*. Berlin: Haude und Spener, 1984.

Ferris, David. "Public Performance and Private Understanding: Clara Wieck's Concerts in Berlin." *Journal of the American Musicological Society* 59, no. 1 (2006): 215–20.

Habermas, Jürgen. *The Structural Transformation of the Public Sphere: An Inquiry into a Category of Bourgeois Society*, trans. Thomas Burger and Frederick Lawrence. Cambridge: The MIT Press, 1989.

Heilbrun, Carolyn. *Writing a Woman's Life*. London: The Women's Press, 1989.

Hensel, Sebastian. *The Mendelssohn Family (1729–1847) From Letters and Journals*, trans. Karl Klingemann, 2 vols. London: S. Low, Marston, Searle, & Rivington, 1884.

_____. *Die Familie Mendelssohn, 1729–1847*, 2 vols. Leipzig: Insel-Verlag, 1903.

Herminghouse, Patricia, and Magda Mueller, eds. *German Feminist Writings*. New York: Bloomsbury, 2001.

Kenny, Aisling, and Susan Wollenberg, eds., *Women and the Nineteenth-Century Lied*. Farnham: Ashgate Publishing, 2015.

Mulvey, Laura. "Visual Pleasure and Narrative Cinema." *Screen* 16, no. 3 (1975): 6–18.

Plaskow, Judith. *Standing Again at Sinai: Judaism from a Feminist Perspective*. New York: Harper Collins, 1990.

Rothenberg, Sarah. "'Thus Far, But No Farther': Fanny Mendelssohn-Hensel's Unfinished Journey." *The Musical Quarterly* 77, no. 4 (1993): 689–708.

The 1901 Arts Club. Accessed August 3, 2023. www.1901artsclub.com/guest-book.html.

Weber, William. *The Great Transformation of Musical Taste: Concert Programming from Haydn to Brahms*. Cambridge: Cambridge University Press, 2008.

Wilhelmy-Dollinger, Petra. *Die Berliner Salons*. Berlin and New York: De Gruyter, 2000.

43
WOMEN'S LEADERSHIP WITHIN LATIN AMERICAN MUSICIANS' UNIONS
Opportunities and Challenges

Ananay Aguilar

In memory of Argentinian union leader María Laura Vigliecca (1969–2020)

Introduction

In mid-2018, I was asked to organise an event on gender equality for FIM, the French acronym of the International Federation of Musicians (Fédération Internationale des Musiciens). FIM is the association of musicians' unions around the world and, at the time, I was coordinating FIM's work in Latin America. FIM's General Secretary thought that the Swedish funder Union To Union, FIM's main sponsor for its Latin American projects, might make some additional funding available for an *ad hoc* capacity-building event.

FIM was founded in 1948 to represent performers in negotiations regarding neighbouring rights. It now has about 70 members in 60 countries, divided into three regional groups representing Europe, Africa, and Latin America. FIM's main objective is to protect and further the economic, social, and artistic interests of musicians represented by its member unions. It does this by supporting the organisation of musicians at national level and cooperation at international level; promoting national and international cultural policy; representing musicians or supporting representative organisations at collective agreements; and collecting evidence in support of the musical profession.

Gender equality was chosen as the main topic for this project for four main reasons. First, since its 19th Congress held in 2008, FIM had committed to encouraging and supporting activities conducive to achieving gender equality. In 2011, FIM and other social partners from the EU Audiovisual Sectoral Social Dialogue Committee adopted a Framework of Actions on Gender Equality to promote gender equality in the audiovisual sector throughout the EU. In its 21st Congress, held in 2016, FIM further committed to developing a coherent policy towards enhancing gender representation and participation within FIM's governing bodies (Motion 22). The first regional conference dedicated to gender equality was carried out in 2017 in Senegal, followed by another in the same year in Tanzania. Organising a regional gender equality conference in Latin America would continue FIM's efforts to bring the topic to the forefront of its activities and begin building a coherent policy. Second, when organising events, and despite always asking members to seek equal representation amongst speakers and participants, female representation was consistently low, reaching on average of only 30 per cent of women. This representation was nevertheless much higher than that amongst the unions' boards. FIM's governing body therefore felt that gender issues needed to be debated to both understand the issues and seek joint solutions. Third, Union To Union, FIM's funder of African and Latin American projects, had consistently demonstrated a commitment to gender equality by producing guidelines and reports on the topic, demanding gender equality at funded events and encouraging debate on the issue. FIM's governing body thought that Union To Union would be keen to fund a capacity-building event on gender equality. Finally, the time was ripe for such an event. The #MeToo campaign had reached the mainstream and a series of related campaigns were gaining media attention around the world. Union leaders would be keen to be seen supporting such an initiative.

One condition for the organisation of a gender equality event in Latin America was that it had to be a women-only event. Unsure about the rationale for this condition, I initially resisted it. I reasoned that in order to implement effective policies, gender issues needed to be debated with those in power. In Latin America, those were mostly men. However, literature suggests that women-only events could have a positive impact on women's careers, especially regarding promotion, pay, increased sense of connection, and overall outlook.[1] As I wrote the proposal, I began recognising the benefit of this condition: providing a space free of power-relations was more likely to encourage women to talk openly about workplace issues and career challenges. Once women opened up, it would be easier to support the creative design of strategies promoting gender equality.

The project objectives were threefold:

1) to increase the connection amongst women representatives of Latin American musicians' unions;
2) to expose the participants to a stimulating environment;
3) to make a realistic assessment of the music sector with an optimistic look into the future. This last objective involved two parts: a) making a realistic assessment and b) making sure that this assessment served to encourage positive action.

In addition, I proposed three deliverables:

1) strategies to continue encouraging a rise in female representation in leadership roles and in the membership;
2) strategies to monitor gender-based challenges in the musical sector;
3) a dedicated communication platform amongst the region for follow-up of the project's objectives.

Union To Union agreed to fund the project and gave me six weeks to organise the event. The event was held in Montevideo. It brought together 14 representatives from nine unions across Latin America and seven speakers, mostly from Uruguay and neighbouring countries. I was joined by one of FIM's Vice-Presidents, Déborah Cheyne, and a programme manager sent by the funder, Catarina Silveira. All in all, they represented 12 countries, with union leaders ranging in age from their early 20s to their 70s and encompassing a range of views about what feminism means and how it is expressed today.

The event lasted two and a half days. It started late on the first afternoon, featuring a panel of local and regional leaders, amongst them Carolina Cosse, Uruguay's Minister for Industry, Energy, and Mining, who was at the time contesting the leadership of the progressive party Frente Amplio for the Presidency in the 2019 presidential election.[2] The keynote was given by Sole Castro Lazaroff, an activist for gender equality. The second day was devoted to discussing relevant topics ranging from the differences between freelancing and full-time employment; developments in gender equality in the union sector, and case studies in different countries. Amongst the highlights were talks given by Patricia Roa of the International Labour Organisation; by Milagro Pau of the PIT-CNT (the local Trade Union Congress), and by independent singer-songwriters Mónica Navarro, Erika Büsch, and Rochy Ameneiro. The third and final day was assigned to designing strategies for the future. María Teresa Mira from Casa de la Mujer, an organisation dedicated to women's health, invited us to think through music industry stereotypes and strategies to combat them. After a productive day of planning for the future, the event closed with a keynote by Dr Lidia Heller, a leadership and motivation expert.

In what follows, I reflect on the different objectives and deliverables. I begin by describing the results from a questionnaire circulated to assess the situation in the local music sectors. I continue by reflecting on the impact of similar projects to then outlining the content of our own Declaration on Gender Equality in the Music Sector and its associated Plan of Action, designed to increase women's participation in music union work. I close the report with comments and feedback on the event itself and, crucially, with likely challenges faced by local unions for the implementation of initiatives on gender equality such as this.

Assessment of the Music Sector

In preparation for the event, I circulated a questionnaire to enquire about three main areas:[3] national laws encouraging gender equality, gender equality within national unions, and unions as organisers or participants in gender-related activities. Representatives of eight unions completed the questionnaire; these represented: SADEM of Argentina (Sindicato Argentino de Músicos, Argentinian Musicians' Union), SINDMUSI of Brazil (Sindicato dos Músicos Profissionais do Estado do Rio de Janeiro, Union of Professional Musicians of the State of Rio de Janeiro), UTM of Costa Rica (Unión de Trabajadores de la Música, Guild of Music Workers), UNEAC of Cuba (Unión de Escritores y Artistas de Cuba, Union of Writers and Artists of Cuba), SUTM of Mexico (Sindicato Único de Trabajadores de la Música, Union of Music Workers), SIMCCAP of Peru (Sindicato de Músicos, Compositores y Cantantes del Perú, Union of Musicians, Composers and Singers of Peru), and AUDEM (Asociación Uruguaya de Músicos, Uruguayan Association of Musicians) and FUDEM of Uruguay (Federación Uruguaya de Músicos, Uruguayan Federation of Musicians). In what follows, I present some of the results.

National Laws on Gender Equality and Women's Rights

Interestingly, among the respondents, Cuba appears to have the earliest legislative framework protecting gender equality. Article 44 of the Cuban Constitution of 1976[4] outlines the breadth of commitment to gender equality of the socialist state. It guarantees equality in opportunities for both men and women; the provision of childcare and care of the elderly to support the working family; support during pregnancy and first weeks of maternity, including temporary flexible or alternative working conditions for mothers during this period; and generally, any support necessary to warrant the principle of equality. I note that the latest reform of the Cuban Constitution, adopted in April 2019, sadly reduced the explicit support of the state, but added protection from gender-related violence.

Argentina appears to have the most comprehensive body of gender-related regulation, including on equality, payment, and opportunities. This stands to reason, as between 2003 and 2015 Argentina has had a progressive Peronista government led first by Kirchner and then, for two terms, his wife Fernández de Kirchner. Fernández was especially known for her work on human and women's rights. Neighbouring country Uruguay, with equally progressive governments since 2005 (Tabaré Vásquez and José Mujica), also has a broad framework for the protection of women's rights. My attention was especially drawn to the *National Strategy for Gender Equality* 2030 (2018), a government policy conducive to reaching significant gender equality milestones by 2030, following the lead from an earlier 4-year policy effort on gender. More generally, responses showed that legislation on gender equality and women's rights has been growing significantly in the last decade, with many long-overdue laws related to domestic violence, femicide, sexual violence, and maternity rights being adopted across the continent.

Gender Equality Within Local Unions

The main finding related to this section is that not all of the unions have detailed enough data to assess female membership accurately. Cuba, for instance, does have specific data for every governmental institution, including their two relevant unions. However, the UNEAC, with whom FIM has collaborated for practical reasons, is more akin to an independent national academy and accepts members only through invitation, so data was not readily available. In Brazil and Uruguay data is scarce, although the Uruguayan unions estimate that their female membership is of between 20 and 30 per cent. In Costa Rica, female membership is of 16 per cent, in Mexico 11 per cent, in Peru 13 per cent. If considering these three unions, female membership amounts to a very low 13.33 per cent; including the estimate of the Uruguayan unions reaches a still very low percentage of 16.25.

I expected the membership of the governing bodies to be easier to assess. However, UNEAC did not disclose any numbers, and neither did Brazil's SINDMUSI, which has suffered deep structural changes since the labour reform during Temer's government.[5] Data varies according to how inclusive the concept of the governing body was understood to be. While some unions, especially the smaller ones, took the term to denote the board, some others included the full administrative body. Amongst those who included only the board, female membership ranged from 0 per cent to 40 per cent (0 to 2 in 5). One union reported four women members out of a 28-strong governing body. Amongst all the respondents, the female proportion of the governing body was 22 per cent, which is higher than the female proportion of the union membership but still very low.

It is worth highlighting that the rate of women in the overall workforce is very high. In a study by the Pew Research Center, Janell Fetterolf claims that in many countries women account for more than 40 per cent of the labour force.[6] This is particularly the case in Latin America, where in most countries surveyed female labour was above 40 per cent, with Uruguay falling within the 45–49 per cent bracket. This compares with nearly 47 per cent both in the US and the EU.[7]

Comparative data about union membership across countries is more difficult to find and comes overwhelmingly from the US. According to the Institute for Women's Policy Research, of US wage and salary workers overall, 11.7 per cent of men and 10.5 per cent of women are members of unions.[8] Interestingly, the authors claim that women in unions earn more than non-unionised women, and that the gender-related pay gap is lower amongst unionised workers than the general population. While strictly speaking this may be the case, it is worth asking whether union membership is self-selected, with members generally in salaried work and more aware of their rights. Unfortunately, most musicians are freelance; salaried work in the music sector is the exception.

Regarding representation within union leaderships in the US, women representation in the largest unions ranges from 18 to 60 per cent.[9] An Argentinian report suggests that of 1,448 union leadership roles, only 80 are filled by women (5.5 per cent). In trade associations the situation is only marginally better, with 16.9 per cent of women in roles of leadership.[10] The authors claim that this reflects in-built codes of honour, unspoken agreements to preserve the *status quo*, and promotion processes historically designed by men based on traditional forms of mentor and sponsorship.

Unions as Organisers or Participants in Gender-Related Activities

Most unions surveyed engaged in activities to further female participation in the music sector. So, for instance, UNEAC of Cuba sponsors a women-only music festival, SIMCCAP of Peru run a Women's Committee for four years and until funding runs out, and FUDEM of Uruguay was at the time supporting a legislative proposal to create gender quotas for the public procurement of musical artists. SADEM of Argentina supported a similar legislative proposal and circulates amongst its members developments on any collective agreements that include gender equality and maternity support clauses.

The representative of UTM of Costa Rica, singer-songwriter Berenice Jiménez, actively participated in a series of women-run groups and initiatives independently of UTM. These included the organisation of the Costa Rican version of the international Sonora Festival, a festival of music by women composers; the participation in the International Symposium of Women in Music, and UNESCO-run discussion groups. She has also founded and participated in community-run groups such as Chicas al Frente (Girls at the Forefront), a discussion group on women's challenges in the workplace and public life, and Viajo Sola (Travel on my Own), a campaigning group to raise awareness of the difficulties faced by touring women. At the time of the event, Jiménez was not part of the board of the UTM; this changed on her return and counts as one of the event's achievements.

Unions or their representatives also campaign for wider women's rights. For instance, SUTM of Mexico organises events for its membership to talk about women's sexual and mental health. FUDEM of Uruguay has joined the public campaign against gender-related violence in relationships. SADEM of Argentina offers guidance for survivors of gender-related violence, organises and/or sponsors artistic interventions to create awareness and greater visibility of domestic violence, and promoted discussion about the 2018 legislative proposal on the voluntary termination of pregnancy. The representative of the Cuban UNEAC, Rochy Ameneiro, is also the leader of Todas Contracorriente (All Against the Current), a national campaign against gender-related violence. Ameneiro has used her prominent role as a singer-songwriter to tour the country with her campaign and promote her powerful campaign videos on TV and social media.

All in all, six of eight respondents (75 per cent) have engaged in some form of activity promoting gender equality and women's rights. This coincides with a report of UNI Global on gender equality, in which 78 per cent of the consulted unions promoted activities to organise more women and 72 per cent undertook activities that included gender equality as one of their topics.[11] This reflects a high degree of awareness of the need for greater gender equality in the region.

An Optimistic Look to the Future

I focused on a positive outlook because it is easy to lend too much attention to the daily setbacks whilst ignoring the large-scale achievements in gender equality over the last century. Esteban Ortiz-Ospina and Max Roser draw on a series of international studies to demonstrate that in most countries the gender gap has decreased in the last couple of decades; that gender-equal inheritance systems are now common across the world; and, more generally, that indices measuring overall gender inequality show increasing equality over the last century.[12] To be sure, their article also draws attention to current inequalities, such as the large gender pay gap; the under-representation of women in senior positions; the gap in ownership of land and productive assets; and the limited influence over household decisions. It also discusses some core challenges and its implications, such as the motherhood penalty on earning expectations. However, the article draws its strength from showing that, over time, gender inequalities have decreased and are likely to continue doing so.

I thus directed my attention to the question of how unions could depart from their current situation and foster greater gender equality through positive action. The greatest challenge here was not simply to create policies conducive to achieving greater equality but to think through how these could be implemented and individual targets monitored within the limited resources of most Latin American unions. We discussed other initiatives and drew some insight from them. Here, the work of UNI Global Union, the association of cross-sector unions from around the world, is exemplary.

UNI Global has several campaigns that are part of its Equal Opportunities section, including on gender-related violence (Breaking the Circle of Violence), on equal pay, and on women's health. The campaign most relevant for our purposes is the 40 for 40 campaign, which is part of the wider resolution to increase women's representation in the association. The campaign objective is to increase women's representation to 40 per cent by 2040 in all of UNI Global's decision-making structures and activities, as well as those of their member unions.[13] As part of its resolution to increase women's representation, UNI Global published guidelines on how to establish policies in union organisations, which is very much aligned with the process I describe here: determine the characteristics of the unions, define problem areas, seek solutions, and eventually, evaluate achievements.[14] This evaluation was published four years later in the report Equality in Union Culture, which outlines developments within its affiliate organisations since the implementation of the guidelines.

Figure 43.1 illustrates what practices unions around the world implemented during that period. Interestingly, all of the unions surveyed offered some form of training scheme directed at women. This is encouraging, yet this type of activity directed at women is also of limited impact: it risks perpetuating traditional structures by asking women to better adjust to them.[15] Luckily, 72 per cent of unions also organised activities on gender involving all genders. The practice perhaps most closely related to the 40 for 40 campaign was the establishment of quotas or positions reserved for women, which 44 per cent of unions implemented over the period.

100% Capacity-building and training for women
78% Organising more women
78% The establishment of an equality policy
72% Data breakdown by gender
72% Activities on gender equality for both genders
61% Specific internal structures
55% Communciation, information, and promotion of an equality culture
44% The establishment of quotas or positions reserved for women
44% Actions aimed at solving female members' specific problems
33% Amendments to the statutes of the union

The achievements linked to these initiatives are summarised in Figure 43.2. While it is clear that the different initiatives have achieved measurable cultural changes, the most successful development and most likely to achieve structural change is the increase of female participation both at decision-making position (66 per cent) and the organisation more generally (67 per cent).

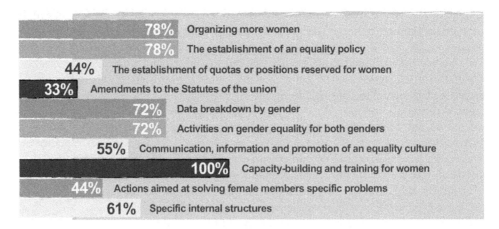

Figure 43.1 Practices that unions around the world implement to promote gender equality in their structure.

Figure 43.2 Achievements observed by those unions that have implemented some of the activities.

17% There was an increase in the understanding of gender issues among the members of the union
17% New networks and women collectives have been articulated at national and local levels
25% The constitutions and statutes that rule the organisation have been or will be modified in the near future
25% New internal structures to address the issue of equality have been created
33% There has been an evident growing recognition and respect for women
66% Female participation increased in the decision-making position
67% Female participation globally increased in the organisation

A Declaration on Gender Equality in the Music Sector

On the third and final day of the event, we focused on the deliverables; in particular, on designing strategies to increase female participation within the unions' leadership and membership. Based on insights from the previous day, we agreed that a set of targeted policies would provide a good starting point. However, I was particularly concerned about the likelihood of achieving proposed targets with the limited resources available to Latin American unions. Many Latin American unions depend on a government tax imposed on concerts involving artists from abroad. Income derived from this tax is often the main source of income for the unions. This is a source of great instability as income is dependent on sympathetic governments, regulatory stability, and a consistent union landscape, all of which are highly variable. Membership fees are not usually charged and when they are, they are mainly symbolic fees more akin to subscription fees. In this landscape, unions are often run by committed volunteers with low resources. A minority of the strongest unions have partnered with collective management organisations (which derive their income from licensing music to commercial users), and as a result their political independence is questionable.

In this scenario, I led the joint drafting of a policy document, the Declaration on Gender Equality in the Music Sector, which consists of four targeted policies: Article 1, to increase the number of women in the membership and governing body to 30 per cent and 40 per cent, respectively; Article 2, to census the membership (and resources allowing, relevant parts of the music sector as well) to account for differences in gender; Article 3, to promote and develop the inclusion of gender-related clauses in collective agreements; and Article 4, to periodically review the Declaration, commencing at FIM's 2020 Congress.[16] Crucially, and perhaps this was one of our greatest achievements, we attached to this document a set of guidelines, the Action Plan, on how these policies could be implemented considering the resources available.

Regarding Article 1, the quotas were set drawing on the survey and were perceived to be achievable. In the case of the quota for governing body, some boards already reach that proportion of women. More difficult would be attracting women to be members. We agreed to begin by identifying already-existing women's groups, such as those in which UTM representative Berenice Jiménez was active. Several representatives already knew and/or were part of women's groups and networks in their different home countries, so this would provide a start. Once identified, unions would offer these groups and networks some of the infrastructure available to them, such as a meeting space, access to dissemination channels, and a network of contacts. The idea was to attract women by association to an inclusive and supportive environment, rather than by imposition of the unions' ideals and interests, which by implication were shaped predominantly by men.

With regard to Article 2, participants felt that it was important to be able to visualise and monitor the details about the membership in order to raise awareness. Some unions still manage their membership data using paper files, so the data is not readily accessible for surveys of this kind. For several years, FIM has encouraged technological upgrades by offering a free digital platform and technical support to member unions. Uptake has been slow, so this initiative provided an opportunity to highlight the importance of moving with the times. Apart from processing affiliation and other data related to the unions' various services, participants also proposed the design of short questionnaires. Considering that response rates are often low, participants thought of making these a precondition to attendance at events or for access to services. Regarding census of the wider music sector, participants similarly thought about disseminating questionnaires linked to public events. More importantly, participants proposed mobilising their contacts at different organisations to get insights on relevant data.

Two other points in the action plan related to offering, first, a network of mutual support for women's initiatives and, second, training opportunities on gender-related issues. Regarding the first point, it was agreed that participants would stay in touch via WhatsApp, a free messaging service, and a group was created. It was encouraging to see that the keynotes also wanted to join and have since provided us with inspiring material about their activities and that of others. The WhatsApp group would serve not only to keep in touch, but also to monitor developments linked to the Declaration and to support each other on local campaigns. I also highlighted the importance of being able to demonstrate concrete developments to funders if we wanted to fund future events like this one. Finally, participants agreed that, in order to achieve the objectives of the Declaration, it was crucial that both members and union leaders received training on gender-related issues. Training should not only be aimed at raising awareness but also at the specific task of negotiating gender-related clauses in collective agreements (as in Article 3).

Representatives had four weeks to make their case for the adoption of the Declaration with the leadership of their respective unions ahead of FIM's next regional meeting held in Bogotá, Colombia. It was reassuring to find that the Declaration was adopted unanimously by the region's nine member unions. Since then, colleagues at United Nations, the International Labour Organisation, and the Mayor of Bogotá have circulated it amongst their teams and drawn on it for their gender-related work in the region.

Sense of Connection and Stimulating Environment

The adoption of the Declaration turned out to be a success, and so did the event itself. I circulated a brief questionnaire to evaluate the sense of connection between participants and find out whether they found the environment stimulating. Figure 43.3 shows the questions and answers. These demonstrate that in general terms, people felt satisfied with what they had learned and the network it offered. In particular, participants felt they wanted to learn more, which highlights the importance of keeping the debate open and offering tools for further development in the area.

A further sign that the participants valued their colleagues and the network provided was the creation of the WhatsApp group. Over a year on, the group is still active and regularly shares their various gender equality campaigns and activities. Two of the participants, from Cuba and Costa Rica, have already met to perform and campaign together and sent many pictures to the group.

Challenges Ahead

As reported, since the adoption of the Declaration, participant Berenice Jiménez was nominated to what used to be an all-male board, and so she is now one of the five-strong board of the UTM. In this new role, Jiménez has organised a workshop, presenting the experience and results from our event in Montevideo and comparing it with similar endeavours, such as the international KeyChange Manifesto launched by the UK Music industry's PRS Foundation.[17] Jiménez is now working on a proposal to create a Gender and Youth Committee with other union members and drawing on material presented at our event.

This is an encouraging start, which I hope will be followed by other initiatives. From FIM's perspective, no funding will be made available in the near future for a follow-up event. FIM's general policy remains that gender issues should always stay on the agenda, but women remain the minority both on the board, the executive committee, and at events. The case for greater gender equality needs to be made for the entire structure.

Tradition and prejudice are reportedly some of the greatest obstacles to gender-equality initiatives.[18] Tradition and prejudice are reflected in the invalidation of women's opinions or work through open dismissal or sexual harassment. As described earlier, tradition and prejudice are also embedded in organisational structures, with women or women-related activities

		Satisfaction	I wish to learn more
1	After the event, do you think you have a better understanding of the symptoms of gender inequality?	89%	95%
2	Do you think you have a better understanding of the value of existing institutional resources to address these symptoms?	71%	95%
3	Do you think you have a greater interest in gender equality issues?	96%	90%
4	Do you feel motivated to address gender inequality issues in your organisation?	95%	95%
5	Do you feel better prepared to address gender inequality issues in your organisation?	84%	95%
6	In general, how satisfied are you with this event on the following points?		
	a) I made connections with new and interesting colleagues.	97%	
	b) I was able to see new perspectives on familiar topics.	91%	
	c) Level of satisfaction with the event in general.	96%	

Figure 43.3 Responses to event feedback questionnaire.

receiving less mentor or sponsorship, being allocated fewer resources, and not being protected by specific policies and rights. In addition to these workplace obstacles, there are also inequalities at home, with women reporting an uneven load of family responsibilities as a barrier to greater participation in public life.

Creating a Declaration and Plan of Action, however well-meant, cannot be the end of the road. Quotas alone will not pave the way to equality if women do not feel empowered in the positions offered. Only multi-variable schemes that lead to women feeling like part of an organisation or workforce will succeed. Mobilising such schemes may feel overwhelming and be resource-intensive. Whilst this is recognised in the Declaration and Plan of Action, their implementation requires discipline and perseverance, not to mention time investment, from the various union leaders and their teams. For already-stretched teams fighting for basic labour rights such as a minimum living wage, gender issues might easily slip down the priority list.

This is not to say that traditional priority lists need not be challenged. Achieving gender equality requires deep structural change that will only be achieved one step at a time. With a small number of clear policy objectives and plenty of strategies to achieve these with existing resources, I hope to have collaboratively laid the foundations for moving a step closer towards a more gender-equal future in the Latin American music union sector.

Notes

1. Shawn Achor, "Do Women's Networking Events Move the Needle on Equality?' *Harvard Business Review* 13 (February 2018), accessed October 3, 2021, https://hbr.org/2018/02/do-womens-networking-events-move-the-needle-on-equality.
2. The party leadership was subsequently won by Daniel Martínez and Cosse moved on to be elected as a senator.
3. I circulated this voluntary questionnaire to find out about the state of gender equality in the national music sectors and their unions. The results were used to inform the project approach and to report to the funder, and were circulated to all of the contributors on completion.

4. Accessed August 3, 2023, http://pdba.georgetown.edu/Constitutions/Cuba/cuba1976.html.
5. In his controversial two-year government, Temer presented bills to promote outsourcing, freeze public spending on education and health, and increase the retirement age, which at the time triggered numerous strikes, stoppages, marches, and rallies. In particular, the labour reform sanctioned under Temer abolished the previously obligatory union tax. Unions are struggling to meet their demands, with many of them suffering redundancies and having to remove the benefits offered to their members. It has been claimed that the new regulations are in disagreement with the conventions of the International Labour Organisation. The new presidency of Bolsonaro is expected to further weaken the rights of minorities and the working class.
6. Fetterolf, Janell, "Women Make Up 40% or More of Workforce in Many Countries," *Pew Research Center* (Blog), April 7, 2017, accessed October 3, 2021, www.pewresearch.org/fact-tank/2017/03/07/in-many-countries-at-least-four-in-ten-in-the-labor-force-are-women/.
7. *Women's Bureau (WB) – Quick Facts on Women in the Labor Force in 2010*, U.S. Department of Labor, accessed June 26, 2019, www.dol.gov/wb/factsheets/qf-laborforce-10.htm.
8. *Institute for Women's Policy Research*, "Women in Unions," Status of Women in the States, accessed June 26, 2019, https://statusofwomendata.org/women-in-unions/.
9. Ibid.
10. Nélida Bonaccorsi and Marta Carrario, "Participación de la mujeres en el mundo sindical: un cambio cultural en el nuevo siglo" (2012): 16, 137.
11. UNI Equal Opportunities Department, "Equality in Union Culture: Booklet on Good Practices in Gender Equality in Union Organizations," 2012, accessed October 3, 2021, www.uniglobalunion.org/sites/default/files/attachments/pdf/GoodPracticesEN.pdf.
12. Esteban Ortiz-Ospina and Max Roser, "Economic Inequality by Gender," *Our World in Data*, March 21, 2018, accessed October 3, 2021, https://ourworldindata.org/economic-inequality-by-gender.
13. UNI Global Union, "Procedure for the Implementation of the 40% Rule," n.d., accessed October 3, 2021, www.uni40for40.org/contenidos/pdf/EN_40Percent_Rule.pdf.
14. Ibid.
15. Gemma Tracey, "Could Your Idea Improve Research Environments? Send Me Your Application," *LinkedIn*, March 18, 2019, accessed October 2, 2021, www.linkedin.com/pulse/could-your-idea-improve-research-environments-send-me-gemma-tracey/.
16. FIM-GLM, "Declaración sobre equidad de género en el sector musical sindical," November 29, 2018, accessed October 3, 2021, www.fim-musicians.org/wp-content/uploads/montevideo-declaration-action-plan-2018.pdf.
17. Accessed August 3, 2023, https://prsfoundation.com/2019/06/25/250-music-organisations-commit-to-keychange-50-50-pledge/.
18. Sue Ledwith, "GENDER and TRADE UNIONS: A Research Preliminary Report," 2011, accessed August 3, 2023, www.global-labour-university.org/fileadmin/GLU_research_projects/Gender_and_trade_unions/Summary_report_for_GLU_webpage_Mar_2011_1_.pdf; UNI Equal Opportunities Department, "Equality in Union Culture: Booklet on Good Practices in Gender Equality in Union Organizations"; Kate Phillips, "Achieving Gender Equality: A Trade Union Manual," *International Trade Union Confederation*, January 2008, accessed October 3, 2021, www.ituc-csi.org/IMG/pdf/manuel_ENGOK.pdf.

Bibliography

Achor, Shawn. "Do Women's Networking Events Move the Needle on Equality?," *Harvard Business Review*, February 13, 2018. Accessed August 3, 2023. https://hbr.org/2018/02/do-womens-networking-events-move-the-needle-on-equality.

Bonaccorsi, Nélida, and Marta Carrario. "Participación de la mujeres en el mundo sindical: un cambio cultural en el nuevo siglo." *La aljaba*. 2012, 16. http://www.scielo.org.ar/scielo.php?script=sci_arttext&pid=S1669-57042012000100007.

Fetterolf, Janell. "Women Make Up 40% or More of Workforce in Many Countries." *Pew Research Center* (Blog), April 7, 2017. Accessed August 3, 2023. www.pewresearch.org/fact-tank/2017/03/07/in-many-countries-at-least-four-in-ten-in-the-labor-force-are-women/.

FIM-GLM. "Declaración sobre equidad de género en el sector musical sindical," November 29, 2018. Accessed August 3, 2022. www.fim-musicians.org/wp-content/uploads/montevideo-declaration-action-plan-2018.pdf.

Ford, Liz. "Not One Single Country Set to Achieve Gender Equality by 2030 | Global Development." *The Guardian*, June 3, 2019. Accessed August 2, 2023. www.theguardian.com/global-development/2019/jun/03/not-one-single-country-set-to-achieve-gender-equality-by-2030.

Institute for Women's Policy Research. "Women in Unions." *Status of Women in the States*. Accessed June 26, 2019. https://statusofwomendata.org/women-in-unions/.

Lawrie, Eleanor, and Clara Guibourg. "Gender Pay Gap Grows at Hundreds of Firms," February 20, 2019. Accessed August 2, 2023. www.bbc.com/news/business-47252848.

Ledwith, Sue. "GENDER and TRADE UNIONS: A Research Preliminary Report." 2011. Accessed August 3, 2023. www.global-labour-university.org/fileadmin/GLU_research_projects/Gender_and_trade_unions/Summary_report_for_GLU_webpage_Mar_2011_1_.pdf.

Ortiz-Ospina, Esteban, and Max Roser. "Economic Inequality by Gender." *Our World in Data*, March 21, 2018. Accessed August 2, 2022. https://ourworldindata.org/economic-inequality-by-gender.

Phillips, Kate. "Achieving Gender Equality: A Trade Union Manual." *International Trade Union Confederation*, January 2008. Accessed August 2, 2022. www.ituc-csi.org/IMG/pdf/manuel_ENGOK.pdf.

Tracey, Gemma. "Could Your Idea Improve Research Environments? Send Me Your Application." *LinkedIn*, March 18, 2019. Accessed August 3, 2023. www.linkedin.com/pulse/could-your-idea-improve-research-environments-send-me-gemma-tracey/.

UNI Equal Opportunities Department. "Equality in Union Culture: Practical Guide to Establish Equality Policies in Union Organization." 2011. Accessed August 3, 2023. https://uniglobalunion.org/sites/default/files/imce/3-_booklet_on_equality_en.pdf.

———. "Equality in Union Culture: Booklet on Good Practices in Gender Equality in Union Organizations," 2012. Accessed August 3, 2023. www.uniglobalunion.org/sites/default/files/attachments/pdf/GoodPracticesEN.pdf.

UNI Global Union. "Procedure for the Implementation of the 40% Rule." n.d. Accessed August 3, 2023. www.uni40for40.org/contenidos/pdf/EN_40Percent_Rule.pdf.

"Women's Bureau (WB) – Quick Facts on Women in the Labor Force in 2010." *U.S. Department of Labor*. Accessed June 26, 2019. www.dol.gov/wb/factsheets/qf-laborforce-10.htm.

44
FROM 'WOMEN'S REVOLUTIONS PER MINUTE' THROUGH 'TAKING RACE LIVE' TO CO-FOUNDING 'EQUALITY, DIVERSITY AND INCLUSION IN MUSIC STUDIES NETWORK'

Supporting, Developing and Establishing Collaborative Networks for Change

Helen Julia Minors

Preamble: I, as Woman Musician-Educator

As a musician, educator, performer, broadcaster and musicologist my work has crossed many sectors and parts of the music industries. During the last two decades, I have become increasingly aware of the need to advocate for more diverse voices to be heard, facilitated and welcomed to the table that is leadership. This chapter offers a self-reflective perspective of my journey from my first steps in advocating for access to women's music to realising the need to support and speak with my students to advance equal opportunity for all in relation to race, ethnicity, faith, sexuality, disability as well as gender. An intersectional approach is the only approach to support sustained change.

I start this chapter by reflecting on my lessons learned by supporting the work of Women's Revolutions Per Minutes (2001–2003) during an internship. I then chart the questions, concerns and desired actions behind work done in collaboration as co-lead of Taking Race Live (2014–2019). I next explore how these experiential activities, working with others to support a beneficial activity-led approach to developing equality, diversity and inclusion, led to the founding of EDI Music Studies (2019 onwards). Although self-reflective to explore different forms of advocacy and networks, this is not a solo journey; my experiences are informed and supported by many collaborative voices, mentors, research partners, peers and colleagues. The journey is situated on my own formative experiences as a women brass player (trumpet/cornet), learning in a male-dominated area, from a working-class background, with good fortune of free instrumental lessons and supportive mentors in school/college and university. The mechanism of support I had access to was fed with the urge to pay it forward and to offer the same support in opening doors of opportunity for others. This journey is on-going and this book, co-edited with Laura Hamer, and its associated conferences and AHRC network, Women's Musical Leadership Online Network (January 2022– November 2023), is all part of this narrative.

My awareness of gender disparity began early, upon recognising that the brass bands I was taken to watch were all-male (at the time), and that few women musical leaders and even fewer women trumpeters were seen and heard on broadcast media (which has changed significantly in recent years). Early teacher compliments that I 'played like a boy' were meant with positivity, but these comments sat with me for a long time, urging me to learn and to change practices. Those feelings and urges were channelled by Prof. Margaret Lucy Wilkins during my time studying at the University of Huddersfield. She was ground-breaking at the time for running a final year module on Women's Music and supporting the contemporary music ensemble by providing scores and parts of music by women. Although pitched as a musicology module in which we explored historical composers in their socio-cultural context, the debates Wilkins led opened my mind to the possibilities that individuals can make change. I had the good fortune to perform some of Wilkins's music during the Huddersfield Contemporary Music Festival in 2001, and the experience of hearing the work introduced as being 'by a women composer' left me keen to hear more, and to move from this idea of the 'women composer' to wanting a time when we can simply say 'composer'. This led me to reassess how I chose repertoire to play and lately to curate and broadcast, actively searching for women composers. It expanded who and what I listened to.

It was an active choice to change my approach, whereby the realisation that the change I wanted to see and hoped for would need many hands in many areas of the industry. This realisation gave me the direction to continue asking questions and searching for new music (or new for me at the time). Wilkins became a role model (though I would not have used these words at the time), and she was active in developing mentorship with her students. I noted often in my student diary that we were often advised to 'broaden your network', and that 'women can support network building for each other', to 'keep sharing' and 'don't give up'. The idea of supporting others was not only words to Wilkins; she also embodied these sentiments in her practice. My first experience of actively being able to do something to support access to women's music came to me when in 2001 Wilkins put me in touch with Hilary Friend (see Chapter 45). From then, as an intern, I did some work with Women's Revolutions Per Minute [WRPM]. I had not heard of this organisation before; I did not know then what it meant to be an activist.

My musical journey moved me to a new mentor who not only gave me the opportunity to learn office skills, website editing skills and so on in a way that was meaningful for WRPM, but she also discussed with me politics, gender equality, societal change, sharing lived experience and history. I began reading more widely, learning from women's political speeches advocating for changes to women's voting rights, among other things. It was here I learned about feminism and advocacy and began to realise that gender alone was not the only issue to resolve to reach equality. These conversations often left me with more questions than answers and more frustrations about the inequalities in the world. But it gave me a critical grounding to my lifelong education that I banked and stored in order to utilise this learning when I was in a position to do so. I became adamant that I would integrate women into my teaching and performing, that I would somehow share this learning with the generation after me. It is perhaps no wonder that many years later my experience of positive and facilitating mentors (in the European sense of the word) led me to be trained and accredited as a mentor and coach myself (via SEDA). As Wilkins said often in her seminars and tutorials, 'listen first, think second, only then act'.[1] Both Wilkins and Friend were and are deep critical thinkers who understood that change was not a lightning bolt, but needed sustained work, effort and development over a period of time.

The work continues. My reason for sharing this experience is to encourage others that it is possible to make a difference and enact change, and to caution that sometimes this takes time (longer than we would like), but that a 'slow bake' (as I now refer to it in classes) can be what leads to a sustainable and developmental change in practice. The mission of DONNE, Women in Music, led by Gabriella Di Laccio, resonates with my thoughts and has become a guiding example of women leading sustained change. The mission of DONNE is

> a charitable foundation dedicated to achieving gender equality in the music industry. We are here to connect and empower anyone who identifies as a woman in order to create a more equitable music industry. Together we celebrate, advance, and amplify women in music so that they are seen, heard, and appreciated for their talent so they can leave a legacy of inspiration for future generations.[2]

Togetherness, working in collaboration, in dialogue, is vital in my own experiences.

Women's Revolutions Per Minute: Hearing Women's Voices

Why are women composers not heard in many concerts? Where are the CDs of women's music? Why do I not know of many women composers, and where can I go to explore their work? These were questions I enthusiastically, and naively, brought to Hilary Friend at WRPM on my first day. During my weekly visits to the archive, as we called the CD/work room, I would input CD details into the website and would listen to a wide range of music by women, which was all new to me. During the time with WRPM, Hilary encouraged my exploration and we set up a page on the website where I could start my list of women composers, adding short biographies, details and notes about their music, as a way to support access to the music and to sell the recordings; but for me, this also became a personal journey. I would add the name to the list with an entry only after I had heard everything in the collection that WRPM had on that composer. It was a slow process, which Hilary supported, and one that gave me a good awareness of a wide range of global music by women. Interestingly, the website is now stored in the WRPM archive held at Goldsmith's College, The University of London.[3] The internship was meant to support the office work of WRPM, notably inputting data and details to the website and sometimes helping with filing and administration, but the role became so much more for my learning. I learned skills in archiving, filing, broader skills in writing various communications, including press releases, and gained my first experience of dealing with customer queries by phone (before ordering online and then streaming became the norm). It was my first time also hearing about composers' experiences and their difficulties in getting their music heard.

WRPM's remit, discussed in Chapter 45, aligned to my own questions. The more I learned, the more I read (exploring the WRPM archive, now housed at Goldsmith's), the more my questions became concerns about the slowness of change and the need for more action. My first approach to change my own practice was to ensure I found, listened to and researched the women composers and musicians who were working contemporaneously to the male composers I was studying as part of my postgraduate training. I devoured everything I could find by Lily Boulanger, Germaine Tailleferre and then worked back in history to Cecile Chaminade and Louise Ferrenc. I added their music to my piano practice (largely because I could find more music by women for piano than I could for trumpet).

The conversations at WRPM tackled questions about where the women in the catalogue had been trained, who had supported them, who had encouraged them to pursue a career in music. The weaving stories of societal expectation of women, male mentors (often family members) and the battles these women had suffered personally to get their music played, heard and published. Various other organisations and publications were instrumental in this foundational learning: Women in Music, established in 1985, was then publishing a hard copy magazine with interviews with composers and performers. Now they have expanded with chapters across the globe.[4] Karin Pendle's seminal volume, *Women in Music: A History*, gave a cultural and historical overview of a selection of women composers and critically explored who their patrons were and who the performers were, exposing a matrix of women's musical networks throughout history.[5] There has been a plethora of new research since: Paula Wolfe has reassessed the role and presence of women in the studio in her volume *Women in the Studio: Creativity, Control and Gender in Popular Music Sound Production*.[6] The motivations behind the book stemmed from personal experiences and a desire to improve the situation for others. Bringing together women's research are two recent volumes: Rhiannon Mathias's *Routledge Handbook of Women's Work in Music*, which has developed from a series of conferences and workshops which have brought established and early-career musicians and researchers together,[7] and Laura Hamer's *Cambridge Companion to Women in Music since 1900*, which is significant as it spans genres, cultures and musical industries in exploring the many barriers faced by the pioneering women included in the volume.[8] All these volumes, and others, chart a significant change in some areas, but also reveal persistent barriers. DONNE, Women in Music's recent report of 111 international orchestras shows that only 7.7% of music performed and programmed for these orchestras was written by women.[9] As such, the conversation and work continue.

It took some years until I was ready to write and publish on any women musicians as I searched for new material and information. Following my doctoral research and initiation into academia, I ensured that my music history classes included music by women. I introduced music by women into my ensemble classes, and I included women songwriters alongside male songwriters in my popular music classes. It was not until I saw a call for score preface authors that I decided to write about Lili Boulanger, writing three prefaces for her Psalms (Psalm 24, 129 and 130), published by Musikproduktion Jürgen Höflich in Munich.[10] The delay for me was about confidence-building: it was this process made me aware of how important mentors were throughout a career, not only at the early stages. Having a mentor in my academic role, who was a female identifying senior researcher in the humanities, helped me see the importance of getting my voice out there. I realised I needed to be the mentor I would have wanted, and that I needed to seek new mentors at each stage of my own journey.

Mentorship: Women's Leadership

As noted by the University of Cambridge's 'Rising Women Leaders Programme': 'Research shows that diversity in senior leadership encourages innovation, improves decision-making, reduces corporate misconduct and improves financial returns.'[11] Seeing oneself reflected in positions in the workplace, in society and in your own communities offers role models, which can be encouraging and enlightening. Different perspectives enable a debate to broaden out to include a wider range of experiences. Having and being a mentor are valuable positions which co-create and share experiences, dialogues and ideas. It is a position of trust and respect. It should be a position of equity: despite the imbalance of experience (educational, industry or other), the people come together as people, not as manager and employee or teacher and student. Setting out a mentoring relationship as one of equals facilitates an open conversation which will not be limited to or reliant on judgements. When a mentoring role works well, the mentor facilitates the thought processes of the mentee by asking questions, by showing interest, by guiding the mentee to explore other options and new solutions. Clutterbuck outlines this faciliatory mentoring approach with reference to the ToGrow model, in that all the questions and discussions extend from the goals and the reality of the mentee's situation, leading to the options and the ways forward they will take.[12] It is not a role in which the mentor should impose ideas or actions, but rather support the mentee in finding their own path by facilitating their own confidence growth in their decision making. The process of questioning guides a mentee through a process of personal reflection, assessing a situation, the facts, their strengths and weaknesses, their power and control, their remit within the situation. As such, the mentoring relationship is all about the mentee. This observation was not familiar to me during my WRPM days or during my education, but it is a position I actively use now to facilitate my students and teams in co-working and collaborating on artistic and creative work.

This self-reflection is important as it guided my approach to establishing real action to facilitate change toward benefitting Equality, Diversity and Inclusion within the music curriculum. As Deborah L. Rhode has asserted: 'Women need advocates, not simply advisors'.[13] The point here is that one can be given all the advice in the world, but barriers can remain in the workplace if doors are not actively opened for everyone. If executive boards recruit junior colleagues who speak, look and sound like them, many voices are excluded.

Reflecting on setting up, developing and maintaining networks for change in the following case studies, I must consider to what extent I was not only collaborating with colleagues, students and musicians, but also to what extent the early frustrations that I felt excluded had encouraged me to speak to others to ask how they felt about the ways in which their voice might be heard. I had some hard questions I wanted to answer. And now, I was in a position to do something about it. Thanks to mentor support, advisors and advocates, I progressed in my academic career, becoming Associate Professor of Music, then Head of the Department of Music then School Head of Performing Arts. These positions leading degree programmes made me want to enact the type of change to facilitate access that I had considered during my teaching practice. In reflecting on how I was able to progress on my active journey I must acknowledge the importance of context: I was (for over 12 years) working within an institution, Kingston University, London, which had committed institutional key performance indicators to accessibility and to EDI. The institution had established a seminal 'inclusive curriculum framework',[14] in which students should be able to see themselves reflected in the curriculum. In other words, the reading, listening and source materials used to teach should represent a diverse range of voices and perspectives. Some have referred to such an approach as decolonising the curriculum.[15] It was rewarding to be working in such a time of positive change where the main goal was people-centred. Inclusion of all was an equitable aspiration. Making it a key performance indicator gave the work status in the institutional hierarchy to ensure all were aware and committed to the endeavour.

The training that supported the university drive for inclusion opened my eyes further to the intersections of voices, and not only to the inequalities and barriers faced by women but also those faced by staff and students who identified as Black and Asian Minority Ethnicities (often classed in data sets as BAME). Although it was now becoming possible to see data regarding student attainment divided by gender, ethnicity and age, the classification troubled me about the barriers this might be inadvertently setting up. The experience of my students was important to me, and after several conversations in class while sharing music written for dance, our conversations led to discussions of bodies in spaces. These student-led class discussions encouraged me to broaden my reading and my own learning and to share these in class. Nirmal Puwar's book *Space Invaders: Race, Gender and Bodies Out of Place* expanded my questions to include and to go beyond women's access, and to talk about access and equity for a much broader range of people.[16] 'Positions of leadership and authority are considered to be beyond their ontological status'.[17] As I was reading this book, I started conversations with colleagues in sociology about how we might do something specific to remove the attainment gap within our module; this was when I joined Taking Race Live. At the same time, I was vice chair and then elected chair of the subject association, MusicHE (formerly National Association for Music in Higher Education). I had access to heads of departments and leaders in academia to discuss my experiences and explore my questions further. This combination of collaborative work at institutional and national levels gave me a network of peer mentors to reflect with, to debate with and to learn from. I recognise now how privileged this position was. I had a voice at many tables and felt committed to making a positive difference. I was now exploring how to do that.

Taking Race Live: Kingston University

Taking Race Live was an all-woman-identifying team of academics from sociology, music, dance, media and drama. The network aimed to utilise experiences of race and identity (recognising an intersectional context) and to use those experiences through performances, to share experiences to promote learning, understanding and wider recognition that change was necessary. As we have written elsewhere, the project worked with student partners: each year of the project running (2014–2017), it recruited through competitive interviews a team of student partners who would co-lead the project, co-lead meetings and ultimately lead the creative content and curation of the annual symposium.[18]

The project was directed towards lived experience to encourage self-reflection, sharing and the value of that personal experience from a specific positionality – to reinforce that everyone's voice has value. As such, the linked modules all changed something of their practice. For me this meant a few things: I included a broader range of examples for analysis, but I also moved away from arrangement as a focus to improvisation. The module Aural and Analysis morphed into Aural, Analysis and Arrangement, and finally became Aural, Analysis and Improvisation. Why? I wanted the students' experience of music, performance and listening to guide their learning; in other words, I wanted to start from the students' contexts and cultures and invite them to explore new things from their own positions, rather than impose my own culture and canon on them.[19] I discuss elsewhere how student-led activities fostered a more co-creative collaborative structure, which integrated wider voices on as equal a footing as possible (considering we were working within an educational context).[20]

Nirmal Puwar's question guided the establishment of this project, with Sonja Sharma's leadership. Puwar asked: 'What happens when those embodied differently come to occupy spaces rarely occupied by them?'[21] What actions did I take because of this collaborative project? Beyond changing the module content and in fact rewriting the module through a module modification process within the university, I took the opportunity to speak with the trained student curriculum consultants who were sitting on all university validations, to speak through my proposed module changes and to hear their feedback. The feedback was vital for the things I did next: it was not just what was changed and needed to be changed that was important; my choice of language was equally important. I changed my online virtual learning site for the module to refer to 'we' and 'us' rather than 'students', and rewrote some of the exploratory questions to guide reading to refer to experiences, feelings and ideas, as well as to specific facts and issues. The ways in which the project developed shared with the university community, through pop-up events, that '[s]ocial spaces are not blank and open for anybody to occupy'.[22] We did dance and music performances in the foyers of the campuses. We did a pop-up interview with university community members asking about their culture, their food, their music. We took our project team discussions from within the classroom out into the corridors. Some of these activities can be seen on the project documentary.[23] The project received recognition with a Rose Award for Teaching, Learning and Assessment and Research (2016) and was a finalist for the Collaborative Award for Teaching Excellence, run by Advance HE (2017).[24] The feedback from these awards was useful to reflecting on what we had achieved but also what we might do next. The project had four full years of funding from the Office for Fair Access. Without the funding, the student partnership scheme, the events and the resources would not have been possible in the same way. But changing approaches to including personal experiences within curriculum design, to modifying language to being inclusive and to seeking student feedback on all aspects of the module design are always possible.

In this small project, we had achieved a lot, not least in removing the awarding gap in the associated modules (as outlined in our collaborative publication).[25] However, I was left with more questions and an awareness that I was making some changes within education, but not within the music industries that my students were heading into. As chair of MusicHE, I asked to speak to some leading figures in music, including exam board officials and various leading composers and performers in the wider industry. These conversations started in 2017 and were all about how we could make changes in supporting equity across the music industries. The 'slow burn' I mentioned earlier was true of this process. From a project spanning from 2014–2017, and from further conversation, EDI Music Studies was officially launched in January 2020.

Equality, Diversity and Inclusion Music Studies Network

Equality, Diversity and Inclusion in Music Studies Network UK is a collaborative network of musicians which developed from many supportive conversations, trial workshops and conferences. As Chair of MusicHE, I met with the then-Chair of the Royal Music Association, Simon McVeigh, and the Executive Director, Strategic Development lead of the ABRSM, Lincoln Abbott, along with Musical Director of both Academy Inégales, Club Inégales and the Third Orchestra, Peter Weigold.[26] Three meetings were held to discuss options and ideas of making changes that could support education, industry and community alike. With Simon McVeigh, and then his successor, Laudan Nooshin, we hosted a workshop at City University London in 2019, to discuss issues of EDI in the music industries. This was quickly followed by an open public conference at City University in January 2020, where EDI Music Studies was launched as a way for the network to continue the ideas, suggestions and calls for change we were hearing. Each of the organisations that had been present at the conference were invited to attend a first online meeting (this was developing during the Covid19 pandemic), and from there the now-large network has its own website and social media channels; it also has a steering committee and 13 working groups, each with their own active membership and group leads. Most groups are co-led. It was important to us that the network had co-chairs, as a single voice cannot represent the rich diversity of issues and experiences the group is trying to tackle. As many voices are better than one, we have always had 2 chairs, starting with myself and Laudan Nooshin. Now EDI Music Studies is being strongly led by Shrz Ee Tan and Amy Blier-Carruthers.

The instigation of the group was the clear collective need to make changes, not only in educational circles but more widely in the music industry. The approach to do this was to seek working groups to work on specific aspects, whether that be a resource page or a data collection exercise. EDIMS is a grassroots organisation. It does not live within a specific institution, nor is it a charity. It does not have a bank account. But to make the changes we wanted, we needed to get the data to speak powerfully, to reveal the anecdotal and lived experience of many. We sought donations to fund a researcher and data analyst and to find purchasing the HESA data to start the journey by charting the demographic context of current music degrees and departments. The report, *Slow Train Coming? Equality, Diversity and Inclusion in UK Higher Education*, was launched in November 2022.[27] As our joint co-chair preface notes, the report aims:

> to offer an overview and analysis of the current state of play in relation to EDI in Music Studies in the UK and to identify inequalities and barriers to music education, from student and staff perspectives, and what we might do as colleagues and communities to effect positive change.[28]

There are no real surprises in the report, but in analysing the data it shows the hard facts about the state of equality, diversity and inclusion within music in higher education, and it offers us as a network a basis to share case studies of how change might be enacted.

Reflections and Next Steps

In writting from a first-person perspective, I have changed my usual musicological writing style to reflect an autoethnographic description and reflection of a series of experiences. By doing so, I hope to show that as a women leader in higher education, there is a journey to leadership. It has shown me the need to advocate for women and other underrepresented groups, but more than that, not only to advocate but to try to lead positive change wherever possible. My journey from my early career experiences in Women's Revolutions Per Minute (explored in the following chapter) were foundational in enabling me to raise questions I had not even considered before. Moving from there into research, performing and teaching gave me an opportunity to share my questions with my students and audiences and to make some of the curriculum changes I had wanted. Projects like Taking Race Live and networks such as MusicHE and EDI Music Studies Network have given me and others a platform to advocate for change. I note that it has been important to making changes that my collaborators and I have had voices of leadership in education, at a national level and laterally at a grassroots national level. The different settings have been essential to enabling an intersectional dialogue to take place. Change in practice (such as in my teaching) and in process (now in a new role, having written a role description for a School level EDI lead and recruiting co-leads to the school management group to ensure EDI issues are considered in all we do) are important, but fundamentally, change when we encourage a new question enables recognition of an issue for the first time. Change of thought is the starting point for the change of practice which will inform industry.

Here, through sharing my 'insider' reflection as a women leader, I share a set of experiences which I hope will encourage others to self-reflect. I do this to show how the 'slow bake' of these changes is common and needed, as the change we make is not only to the curriculum, programmes and events we run, but is also a personal change where new insights are found along the way. A leader who accepts change and adapts is a leader who can facilitate all and can aspire to enable that positive personal change in their teams. I remain on my journey as an educational leader, now as a Head of School of Arts. I retain my early questions and aims. Through this volume, we are presenting a series of case studies and raising awareness; through the associated Arts and Humanities Research Council network grant, Women's Musical Leadership Online Project, we (as co-editors) are building a mentoring network for women in the music industry. We are doing things – together. I write this as it is powerful to me – the realisation that the changes I have been able to make have been done in collaboration with others. None of this has been an isolated activity. The journey continues – together.

Notes

1. Minors, personal tutorial notes (October 2000)
2. DONNE, "Women in Music," accessed December 28, 2022, https://donne-uk.org/.
3. *WRPM*, accessed December 28, 2022, www.wrpm.org.uk/.
4. *Women in Music*, accessed December 28, 2022, www.womeninmusic.org/.
5. Karin Pendle, *Women in Music: A History*, 2nd ed. (Bloomington: Indiana University Press, 2001).
6. Paula Wolfe, *Women in the Studio: Creativity, Control and Gender in Popular Music Sound Production* (London: Routledge, 2019).
7. Rhiannon Mathias, ed., *Routledge Handbook of Women's Work in Music* (London: Routledge, 2021).
8. Laura Hamer, ed., *Cambridge Companion to Women in Music Since 1900* (Cambridge: Cambridge University Press, 2021).
9. DONNE.
10. Helen Julia Minors (date), Psalm 130, Boulanger, Lili | Psalm 130 for voice & orchestra (musikmph. de), accessed December 28, 2022, https://repertoire-explorer.musikmph.de/en/product/boulanger-lili-2/; Psalm 129, Boulanger, Lili | Musical score, https://repertoire-explorer.musikmph.de/en/product/boulanger-lili-3/; and Psalm 24, Boulanger, Lili | Musical score, https://repertoire-explorer.musikmph.de/en/product/boulanger-lili-4/.
11. *Cambridge Rising Women Leaders Programme — Executive Education at CJBS*, accessed November 20, 2021, www.jbs.cam.ac.uk/executive-education/open-programmes/leadership/cambridge-rising-women-leaders-programme/.
12. David Clutterbuck, *Everyone Needs a Mentor*, 5th ed. (London: Kogan Page, 2019).
13. Deborah L. Rhode, *Women and Leadership* (New York and London: Oxford University Press, 2019), 33.
14. *Inclusive Curriculum Framework*, "Inclusive Curriculum Framework—Our Inclusive Curriculum—Equality, Diversity and Inclusion — Kingston University London," accessed December 28, 2022, www.kingston.ac.uk/aboutkingstonuniversity/equality-diversity-and-inclusion/our-inclusive-curriculum/inclusive-curriculum-framework/#:~:text=Kingston%20University%27s%20Inclusive%20Curriculum%20Framework%20defines%20our%20academic,the%20experience%2C%20skills%20and%20attainment%20of%20all%20students.
15. For example, the approach taken at Liverpool University, *Centre for Innovation in Education — University of Liverpool*, accessed November 20, 2022, www.liverpool.ac.uk/centre-for-innovation-in-education/resources/all-resources/decolonising-the-curriculum.html.
16. Nirmal Puwar, *Race, Space Invaders: Gender and Bodies Out of Place* (London: Berg Publishers, 2004).
17. Ibid., 22.
18. Sonya Sharma, Elena Catalano, Heidi Seetzen, Helen Julia Minors, and Sylvia Collins-Mayo, "Taking Race Live: Exploring Experiences of Race Through Interdisciplinary Collaboration in Higher Education," *London Review of Education* 17, no. 2 (2019): 193–205, https://doi.org/10.18546/LRE.17.2.07
19. Helen Julia Minors, 'Employability Skills within an Inclusive Undergraduate and Postgraduate Performance Curriculum in the UK', in *Teaching Music Performance in Higher Music Education: Explorng the Potential of Artistic Research*, edited by Helen Julia Minors, Stefan Östersjö, Gilvano Dalagna and Jorge Salgado Correia (OpenBook Publishing, 2024), 287–306.
20. Helen Julia Minors, Pamela Burnard, Charles Wiffen, Zaina Shihabi, and J. Simon van der Walt, "Mapping Trends and Framing Issues in Higher Music Education: Changing Minds/Changing Practices," *London Review of Education* 15, no. 3 (2017): 457–73.
21. Ibid., 141.
22. Ibid., 8.

23. *Taking Race Live Project, Documentary*, accessed December 28, 2022, www.youtube.com/watch?v=bAB-FnHcM9E.
24. "Kingston University—Taking Race Live Project," *Advance HE*, accessed December 20, 2022, www.advance-he.ac.uk/cate-team/kingston-university-taking-race-live-project.
25. Sharma et al., "Taking Race Live."
26. I lately curated the Women's Voices at Club Inégales series with Peter Weigold, as our conversations needed not only an educational testing ground but a live performative series to expand the work with public engagement. See Helen Julia Minors, "Club Inégales, Curation and Processes of Public Musicology," in *Routledge Companion to Applied Musicology*, edited by Chris Dromey (London: Routledge, 2023), 98–107.
27. Anna Bull, Diljeet Bhachu, Amy Blier-Carruthers, Alexander Bradley, and Seferin James, "Slow Train Coming? Equality, Diversity and Inclusion in UK Higher Education," *EDI Music Studies*, accessed December 28, 2022, https://edims.network/report/slowtraincoming/.
28. Ibid.

Bibliography

Bull, Anna, Diljeet Bhachu, Amy Blier-Carruthers, Alexander Bradley, and Seferin James. "Slow Train Coming? Equality, Diversity and Inclusion in UK Higher Education." *EDI Music Studies*. Accessed December 28, 2022. https://edims.network/report/slowtraincoming/.

"Cambridge Rising Women Leaders Programme – Executive Education at CJBS." Accessed November 20, 2021. www.jbs.cam.ac.uk/executive-education/open-programmes/leadership/cambridge-rising-women-leaders-programme/.

"Centre for Innovation in Education – University of Liverpool." Accessed November 20, 2022. www.liverpool.ac.uk/centre-for-innovation-in-education/resources/all-resources/decolonising-the-curriculum.html.

David Clutterbuck. *Everyone Needs a Mentor*, 5th ed. London: Kogan Page, 2019.

DONNE. "Women in Music." Accessed December 28, 2022. https://donne-uk.org/.

Hamer, Laura, ed. *Cambridge Companion to Women in Music Since 1900*. Cambridge: Cambridge University Press, 2021.

"Kingston University – Taking Race Live Project." *Advance HE*. Accessed December 20, 2022. www.advance-he.ac.uk/cate-team/kingston-university-taking-race-live-project.

Helen Julia Minors. "Club Inégales, Curation and Processes of Public Musicology." In *Routledge Companion to Applied Musicology*, edited by Chris Dromey, 98–107. London: Routledge, 2023, 98–107.

Helen Julia Minors, 'Employability Skills within an Inclusive Undergraduate and Postgraduate Performance Curriculum in the UK', in *Teaching Music Performance in Higher Music Education: Explorng the Potential of Artistic Research*, edited by Helen Julia Minors, Stefan Östersjö, Gilvano Dalagna and Jorge Salgado Correia (OpenBook Publishing, 2024), 287–306.

Minors, Helen Julia, Pamela Burnard, Charles Wiffen, Zaina Shihabi, and J. Simon van der Walt. "Mapping Trends and Framing Issues in Higher Music Education: Changing Minds/Changing Practices." *London Review of Education* 15, no. 3 (2017): 457–73.

Nirmal, Puwa. *Race, Space Invaders: Gender and Bodies Out of Place*. London: Berg Publishers, 2004.

Pendle, Karin. *Women in Music: A History*, 2nd ed. (Bloomington: Indiana University Press, 2001).

Rhiannon, Mathias, ed. *Routledge Handbook of Women's Work in Music*. London: Routledge, 2021.

Rhode, Deborah L. *Women and Leadership*. New York and London: Oxford University Press, 2019.

Sharma, Sonya, Elena Catalano, Heidi Seetzen, Helen Julia Minors, and Sylvia Collins-Mayo. "Taking Race Live: Exploring Experiences of Race Through Interdisciplinary Collaboration in Higher Education." *London Review of Education* 17, no. 2 (2019): 193–205. https://doi.org/10.18546/LRE.17.2.07

"Taking Race Live Project, Documentary." www.youtube.com/watch?v=bAB-FnHcM9E.

"Wolfe, Paula." *Women in the Studio: Creativity, Control and Gender in Popular Music Sound Production*. London: Routledge, 2019.

"Women and Leadership International." Accessed February 9, 2021. www.womenandleadership.org/.

"Women in Music." Accessed December 28, 2022. www.womeninmusic.org/.

"WRPM." www.wrpm.org.uk/ Accessed December 28, 2022).

45
WOMEN'S REVOLUTIONS PER MINUTE

Access to, Distribution, and Recognition of Music by Women

Hilary Friend and Helen Julia Minors

Women are still under-represented as musicians, whether they be composers, performers, technicians, producers, managers, or arts business creatives. Women's Revolutions Per Minute [WRPM] aimed to support the access to, the distribution of, and the recognition of music composed, produced, and performed by women. It began in 1977 as an independent music distribution company, then developed its advocacy work over the years by working in collaboration with other organisations, such as the Chard Festival of Music by Women and Raise Your Banners Community Choirs Festival. WRPM supported learning activities by distributing recordings to universities and offering placement work for students (all these activities are outlined in this chapter). Today, the work of WRPM is accessible via an archive currently hosted at Goldsmiths College, University of London.[1] The catalogue of this archive draws attention to some of the women who have faced the challenges that still exist with gender inequalities within the music industries. Notably it represents voices, names, and work by those who tried to make, and did make, a difference.[2] Collectively, **we** made something happen.

WRPM has a legacy worthy of documentation for three main reasons: at a time before online sales and global access to music, music lovers, collectors, and academics relied on both large and small distribution companies to access recordings. WRPM's role in the early days was vital to ensuring the presence and accessibility of music by women in the UK. For some, it was vital as an educational tool. Helen Julia Minors notes that:

> if it were not for WRPM, I would not have become aware of so many women composers during my studies and would not now be editing this book on Women in Musical Leadership or founding and co-chairing the EDI Music Studies Network UK.[3]

In what follows, we outline the history, activities, and role WRPM played in enabling and promoting access to music by women. Hilary (I) outlines the history and work of this distribution company and the archive development; we (Hilary and Helen) outline the legacy of the work and the potential for future advocacy utilising the archive; and in passing we hear from a few collaborators and the student intern (Helen) about their experiences of working, using, and engaging with WRPM.[4] We may now be in the digital globalised age where we can access music via many streaming platforms, but there remains a place for WRPM, not least to reassert the need for fair representation within streaming services, festivals, and the broader music industries.

The History of WRPM

In 2012, forty archive boxes arrived at the Special Collections Library, Goldsmiths University of London. Packed into those anonymous containers were the tangible products of years of work by women in WRPM, creative and challenging, enterprising and pioneering, intricate, detailed, and person-centred women. Much of their work, however, is only partly represented by the contents of those boxes and is much less tangible and often hidden. As such, it is vital that the history and aims of WRPM are documented to share how WRPM made possible the access to and promotion of music by women. This chapter describes some of the women's work spanning the years 1977 to 2017, reflects on the impact of this work, and highlights some key themes concerning access to this music, including the need for advocacy of this music, and the issue of a lived experience now archived for public access.

WRPM was an independent music record distribution and retail business trading from 1977 to 2005. After the first few years, it was a shop trading through direct sales at festivals and conferences, mail-order, and later online sales to promote music created by women by making it accessible and available. The in-person activity of sales at live events was a staple activity during the entire active period of WRPM: a face-to-face opportunity facilitated the development of many relationships which were otherwise impossible pre-internet distribution. As such, we claim that WRPM was a pioneer for equality and access to recorded women's music. Testament to this, WRPM operated as an intrinsic part of the Women's Liberation Movement. It brought together feminism and women's intellectualism into an active business, underpinned by an advocacy agenda. The style and aims of WRPM were in tune with that movement: it was grassroots activism, led by women on the ground who led marches, lobbied Parliament, and raised awareness through events and conferences.[5]

It is important in reflecting on WRPM's role to recognise that it has had three lives (three phases each affected by and impacting on its cultural era). In the first phase, WRPM was established in 1977 and run by two women until Caroline Hutton took it over and kept it going for twenty years from 1979–1999. The second phase follows to 2005 when Hilary (with Helen's contribution) expanded the catalogue and initiated a WRPM online presence. The third phase will be discussed later; it saw Hilary looking to the future after 2005 and managing the transition to a formally catalogued and maintained archive known as the WRPM Collection and Archive at Goldsmiths. A few years after the arrival of WRPM at Goldsmiths, I (Hilary) was appointed a Visiting Research Fellow to the Music Department there and contributed to the planning and development of WRPM at Goldsmiths and its use and future.

The third phase became visible with the arrival of those archival boxes, when the WRPM Collection and Archive was accepted as a part of Goldsmiths Special Collections.[6] The Collection of recordings is vast and has been catalogued: it contains just over twenty-five years of work, encompassing 1500 catalogue titles of music by women, many by women pioneer producers and independent labels and demonstrating the rich variety of forms that music by women takes. There are recordings on tape, vinyl, and CDs, along with some scores and books: there are 1553 recordings in total. Representing the changing eras, there is a mix of formats, consisting of 535 tapes, 335 vinyl LPs, and 683 CDs. The Archive of papers has been catalogued, but not every single paper is listed individually, due to the extent of the paperwork. The Archive contains a wide range of office documentation, including correspondence between WRPM and its collaborators, publicity materials, press articles, as well as all its accounts and tax returns, its employees, and other ephemera, all of which reveals the inner working of an alternative distribution company as a feminist – activist – enterprise. The catalogues of both Collection and Archive are available online.[7]

To clarify some wording, during the main period of WRPM trading (1979–2005), one of everything offered for sale in the catalogue (and later website) was kept back, not for sale, and always affectionately called *The Archive*. Helen remembers fondly that:

> part of my induction to working with WRPM in 2001 was to respect 'The Archive', notably that meant taking the opportunity to listen to it, to get to know it, and ultimately to respect it . . . it took me until 2003 to listen to everything that was at that time in *The Archive*.[8]

Both long-term women owners of WRPM shared a feminist agenda to promote and provide access to this music, and from the start these women had the aspiration that one day the music would be archived for future generations to access. Despite running a business for profit, both shared the values of the Women's Liberation Movement, and this has been passed down to the next generations. *The Archive* not only documents an era but enables actively listening to this music, now through the WRPM Collection.

The Archive 1979–2005 was a manifesto to ensure we retained one copy of every recording that featured in the sales catalogue for future generations. In so doing, the women involved in WRPM in those years recognised the value and significance of these hard copy recordings (many of which have yet to be digitised for online streaming or download).

This chapter will utilise the names of the materials as they are now labelled and catalogued within the WRPM collection at Goldsmiths. The recordings in its former *Archive* are the WRPM Collection, and the WRPM Archive is the associated papers. Both are open for public use for students, lecturers, researchers, and the general public.

I (Hilary) am an advocate of WRPM, which for me was a liberation. I (Helen) am also an advocate of WRPM, as for me it opened my research-eyes and my experience as a performer to music by women, and to wider issues of equality and diversity, which I have developed in my career since my student experience working for Hilary's leadership of WRPM. We recognise the WRPM Collection as a public site for future activism.

WRPM as a Music Distribution Business

In the WRPM Archive at Goldsmiths there is a small, folded leaflet: the programme of the Women's Festival held at the Drill Hall, London, in December 1977.[9] On the back is a note: 'How WRPM began'. WRPM's birthplace was a fertile mix of music, talks, discussions, comedy, song, film, dance, and drama, supported by the Arts Council of England and the left-wing Camden Council. On the 16th of December 1977, WRPM hosted a concert by two women musicians from the USA: Teresa Trull (b. 1954), who is a singer and songwriter from Durham, North Carolina specialising in folk, folk-rock, and country folk music, and Meg Christian (b. 1946), who is also a folk singer, songwriter, and guitarist, originally from Lynchburg, Virginia. Their music was produced by Olivia Records, a women's collective (much like the other women's collectives discussed in this part of the present volume) and independent record company set up in 1973 in Washington, DC, and later relocated to California.

To bring this music of American pioneering women's record companies over to the UK, it was necessary for WRPM to have a strategic approach to acquiring a range of recordings and targeting specific women's collectives. As such, sourcing music from women's record companies formed much of the early impetus for WRPM, particularly the music of lesbian singer-songwriters, which was not otherwise generally available in the UK despite this music being very successful in the USA. Embedded in the London festival was the Women's Liberation Music Workshop (WLMW): 'for women only, offering voice, acoustic and electric bass guitar, PA equipment, percussion, discussion'.[10] One of the workshop leaders was Tierl Thompson. She was a member of the Women's Arts Collective based in North London, which had been establishing a network of female musicians and a songbook project.[11] *Sisters in Song*, published in 1978, was a first for women in music to celebrate and promote themselves as creators of music.[12] Around the same time, Ova women's band set up Ova Music Studio (1984) with a focus on women owning the means of the production of their own music.[13]

Thompson and Nicole Freni[14] were the originators of WRPM. Shocked at the absence of music about the Women's Movement in exhibitions, they set about finding practical ways of raising awareness of music by women. They wanted to promote concerts by pioneering women musicians, and their aim was to import their records from the USA for distribution in the UK. They would buy enough of the American recordings at a low enough price to produce a sustaining profit from selling through outlets such as the then-flourishing independent music shops and radical book shops, as well as managing direct retail sales. Their practice was the start of WRPM: those initial aims, to make music accessible and to promote music by women from across the globe, was a consistent goal throughout 1977–2005.

This was a pioneering venture requiring many new skills and knowledge. In all the stages of its life cycle the mission of WRPM has been to provide access to women's music, and by doing so it has facilitated empowerment of those women. Moreover, it has offered a challenge to discrimination by offering a diverse and inclusive range of music. WRPM was always based on the hard and intensive work needed for such a challenge. Feminist values were at its core. There were many demands in establishing and maintaining the business and activism of WRPM:

- critical knowledge of the music industry, notably how it worked and what was missing;
- an understanding of what women wanted but could not find within the existing structures or offerings of the music industry;
- the determination to make something work and the ability to gather support for the enterprise, financial and personal;
- the ability to tolerate continuous financial anxiety, as the small-scale business was driven more by advocacy and activism than by financial goals – making money often came second to the values that underpinned the activities.[15]

For two years, Thompson and Freni made a start on their goals by promoting concerts by lesbian musicians and importing their music using the Women's Art Collective as their sales and business base. Their notebooks from 1978 in the WRPM Archive are vivid with the practical problems they had to solve – customs, tax, delays, percentages, cash flow.[16] They struggled to acquire imports and containers full of recordings from the USA on account when they were just starting out. Time-consuming detailed customer concerns such as defective records, tapes, and troublesome needles on vinyl record players also had to be continually addressed. This was an audacious enterprise and finances were shaky, as the Archive shows.[17] The core critical problem of WRPM began: how to stay true to the mission and at the same time survive financially.

In the wider context of radical feminism and social change of the late 1960s and 1970s, many women were pioneering change out of their own commitment, thereby offering their time and personal resources for free and in addition using their own finances to make a difference. The Women's Liberation Movement and social reforming legislation from the late 1960s onwards had already made an impact on the arts and publishing, where women had sought to publish and celebrate work by women. Virago Press and The Women's Press started in 1978. *Spare Rib* magazine challenged the stereotyping and exploitation of women from 1972 to 1993. Radical bookshops that took forward the changes were opening their doors, including Grassroots in Manchester and News from Nowhere in Liverpool.[18]

Silver Moon Bookshop in London, perhaps the closest in aims to WRPM, opened in 1984 and ran to 2001. Jane Cholmeley, co-owner of the bookshop, noted:

> Our aim has always been two-fold: to improve the condition of women in the world and to run a successful business. By highlighting women authors, we have helped to create a market for them; for example, many shops in non-metropolitan areas won't stock lesbian books at all.[19]

This was the philosophy and strategy that the WRPM pioneers were applying to music.

Caroline Hutton took over the WRPM project in 1979. Based in Birmingham, she was a young, active performing musician seriously involved with the Women's Movement. In her 2017 interview on BBC Radio 3, Music Matters, a feature designed to celebrate the forty-year anniversary, Hutton describes her early work with WRPM and its role in giving women, particularly lesbian women, an unrestricted voice in the context of the time.[20]

In her memoirs for Gay Liberation Birmingham, Hutton described how she travelled to the Michigan Women's Music Festival in 1977. There she met the women who were taking the first steps in creating WRPM. When Freni became ill, Hutton was urged by friends to keep the work going and, after consulting with other women music activists, decided to take it on. She too believed that trading was the way forward and developed the WRPM business with a sole trader structure. She used a printed catalogue for mail order,[21] but she also travelled around the country carrying all the recordings for sale on her back using public transport (as a non-driver) to festivals, conferences, and concerts to sell and promote women's music from a WRPM stall.[22]

In the same memoir, Hutton describes the ingenious way she managed to get stock in bulk delivered to the network of outlets that she was building up for WRPM all over the UK:

> I . . . discovered that Wholesome Trucking took wholefoods from London up to Manchester and Leeds and Liverpool via Birmingham, so there was a ready-made transport system for moving things around . . . I was in Birmingham, which was the centre, so this is networking, making coalitions where appropriate. So, I took on WRPM and expanded it a lot and ran it for 20 years and went from mainly serving radical bookshops to mainly running a mail order service.[23]

From the start, WRPM was a business, but a business underpinned by advocacy. At the core of the business was music by lesbian musicians within a range of musical styles and from a range of countries. The music, and WRPM, delivered a political message challenging the sexist music industry and promoting positive messages about women. From early on, the catalogue included the political songwriting of Peggy Seeger (b. 1935) and Frankie Armstrong (b. 1941), then it gradually expanded to embrace a wide range of classical composers, jazz, and world musics. The diverse content of the catalogue of music recordings is now one of the main resources for research in the WRPM Collection.[24] Most of the music was from independent record labels, but the music by these women was not getting enough exposure or distribution. Hutton built up a very long mailing list and maintained an extensive network of outlets, as well as taking the music personally to festivals, conferences, and concerts. Initially, she combined distribution and direct retail sales with promoting concerts and selling music on musicians' tours. As Hutton recalled,

> The Chris Williamson tour, Alex Dobkin, Holly Near, Sweet Honey in the Rock tour! Meg Christian, and Kay Gardener and Judy Small . . . [I]f the money and the stock-take added up at the end of the day it was very intense and great fun.[25]

In an interview in 1985, she clarified what she wanted to achieve, but the reference to finances is an indication of the continuing financial struggle that WRPM had from the beginning.

> WRPM's mission is to eradicate sexism in music: its aim is to provide positive images of women and to communicate how women are changing themselves and the world. How? WRPM is a womyn's music distribution business, which means that I supply records and cassettes to shops, to customers by mail order, and do some promotion for womyn's music. What? Womyn's music gives us a vision of how we can live our lives: to see and hear womyn being effective and proud of their work can be very inspiring. Music is a resource and helps us recharge our batteries to go on and face the next challenge, whatever form it takes.[26]

In the same interview, Hutton gave a frank picture of coming close to bankruptcy, but with persistent resilience and belief she developed a rescue plan: to target parts of the catalogue more precisely and to withdraw from promoting concerts. She succeeded in distributing music into mainstream stores, such as HMV and Virgin, and further widened the range of music in the catalogue. She investigated the potential for a WRPM record label and a magazine for women's music, although neither of these progressed due to lack of capital and a business partner.

In a later interview, Hutton revisited the strengths of the independent outlet compared to the mainstream. She rejoiced that some women were getting a toehold in the mainstream but pointed out that many preferred to remain independent to keep artistic control.[27] Over time, the role of distribution into larger stores diminished. Hutton thought this was partly a sign of her own success, and in early 1999 she decided to leave WRPM – not least because she needed to make a living. When she advertised for professional interest in taking over the business, my initial thought was that I did not want WRPM to close. WRPM had made a very big impact on me, and I knew anecdotally that it had also had a significant impact on many others. On re-launching WRPM under my (Hilary's) leadership, I constructed a questionnaire to formally gauge what the market wanted and how I could effectively function to balance the dual aims of this business with its aims to provide access to and to promote music by women. The responses articulated the impact of WRPM in ensuring access to a diverse range of music, to opening a channel to music which would not have otherwise been available in the UK, and to providing a community of likeminded individuals who would meet and see WRPM at festivals, conferences, and events.[28]

My first contact with WRPM was as a customer. I met Hutton at the stall at a concert in Manchester in 1986 by Sweet Honey in the Rock, the powerful African American women's *a cappella* group with its roots in the American Civil Rights movement. By becoming a WRPM customer, I not only received a catalogue of music including women classical composers previously unknown to me, but I also joined a community of women promoting music by women, activists, performers, and listeners interested in many different genres.

I went on to study Sweet Honey compositions, attend workshops with them, and experience their music of profound individual and collective artistry as activists and as composers. This was an indicator of an interest that I would find throughout my work with WRPM. The classical composers in the catalogue already included Hildegaard von Bingen (1098–1179), Barbara Strozzi (1619–1677), Maddalena Sirmen (1745–1818), Louise Farrenc (1804–1875), Fanny Hensel (1805–1847), Clara Schumann (1819–1896), Ethel Smyth (1858–1944), Lili Boulanger (1893–1918), Nadia Boulanger (1897–1979), Alma Mahler (1879–1964), Cécile Chaminade (1857–1944), Germaine Tailleferre (1892–1983), Priaulx Rainier (1903–1986), Elizabeth Maconchy (1907–1994), Grazyna Bacewitz (1909–1969), Minna Keal (1909–1999), June Boyce-Tilman (b. 1943), Chen Yi (b. 1957), Stevie Wishart (b. 1969), Lindsay Cooper (1951–2013), Nicola Lefanu (b. 1947), and Judith Weir (b. 1954), as well as many others on compilation CDs.

In 1999, I responded positively to Hutton's advertisement, as by then I had taken early retirement from Community Adult Education in Manchester and had realised that I wanted to do what I could to carry the WRPM message forward. Once I was approved at interview, Hutton and I completed a business transaction and outstanding stock was transferred, along with a comprehensive brief on the complexities of the accounts, arrangements with musicians, and long lists of customers, outlets, and supply chains.[29] I spent many hours absorbing and marshalling all the new information, listening to music that was new to me in the catalogue, and researching genres such as world musics and classical women composers that I felt were particularly important to expand. At the same time, I researched business structures, wrote a business plan,[30] and converted the sole trader business into a Company Limited by Guarantee with not-for-profit objectives.[31] Although this created onerous duties in formal accounting, I could now apply for some funding so long as it fitted WRPM objectives. I succeeded in getting some small financial support for initiating WRPM as an online business, by initiating a website, and a catalogue of CD sales online.[32]

The second life of WRPM was established, and the remit and breadth were outlined in the first catalogue of this period. The first WRPM catalogue sent to the mailing list was in March 2000. In it was an explanation of the changes to leadership, changes to business structure, and a clear list of pricing (which was more realistic in terms of financially balancing the business).[33] The catalogue also gave an overview of the ongoing work to launch the website. I started a redesign of the chapter mail-order catalogue by adding new titles, some of which had been suggested by respondents to the questionnaire I had conducted with existing customers. These titles included music by traditional singers and music for children, as well as other recordings. I had already started contacting suppliers and sourcing music to take to events, and I attended the London gathering of the International Alliance of Women in Music in July 1999. The very first concert I attended in my official WRPM role was held in London in aid of Medica Kosova in November 1999. It featured Holly Near, the Muse Choir from Cincinnati, and Moushumi Bhowmik. Before this concert, I had my first (but not my last) experience of the anxieties of importing music, when a large consignment from the main American supplier in North Carolina, Ladyslipper, vanished at UK Customs and the replacement arrived only just in time. In 2000, I traded at and participated in the Raise Your Banners Festival of Political Song in Sheffield, the Natural Voice Practitioners' Annual Conference with Frankie Armstrong in November, and the Women's Festival in Bradford in December. The following year, I took the WRPM stall to fifteen events, from Southampton Women in Music Day, run by COMA (then Contemporary Music for All), to Dundee

Women's Performing Arts Festival, which was coordinated by Dundee Repertory Theatre Community Network.

In the 2000 catalogue, an explanation of the business was given: 'WRPM is a one-woman, a computer and a front room sort of organisation, slowly expanding'.[34] That expansion started to take concrete shape in 2001. In partnership with Labrys Multimedia, a women's web design company, I set up a website for WRPM that complemented the printed catalogue, which had been completely redesigned with Andrassy Designs' community printshop. Instructed by Labrys at that time of online innovation, I learnt how to upload new items and update the website. I drew on my previous experience in organising and designing publicity, planning both the website and the printed catalogue so that they were extremely 'user-friendly'. I researched the technological innovations that could unlock sound archives and catalogues.

The website was not just a sales catalogue: the aim was for it to become a resource for networking, sharing contacts, sharing responses from customers, distributing information and research about women musicians and composers, and providing a platform to convey the aims of WRPM. I had a great deal of help from volunteers: in 2001–2003, during the summer and half terms, a student worked on placement: I (Helen) was that student. I spent the first summer inputting CD listings to the website and creating a historical list of women composers under the pseudonym Miss Music. I am now a Professor of Music and Head of the School of Arts at York St John University and co-editor of this present volume. I had been introduced to WRPM by composer and feminist musical advocate Margaret Lucy Wilkins, who had included recordings from WRPM in her final bachelor-year module on Women in Music, run at the University of Huddersfield (2000–2001). The placement was valuable experience for managing a website and archiving recordings, but of prime importance, as I reflect on my time with WRPM, was the twinning of a company strategy with the aims of a grassroots collective, ensuring access to and the promotion of women's music. Before online sales were the new normal, WRPM provided me with access to music I would not otherwise have heard.

WRPM at this time also benefitted from the extensive network of Women in Music (UK).[35] Their website and publications made sure to feature research about female composers, gathering information about their hidden or neglected work, along with suggestions for more reading and research. This proved to be extremely well supported by not only us (Hilary and Helen) but also by those organisations which collaborated with and supported WRPM. WRPM was actively trading online from 2001 to 2005. The website, in an archived but browsable form, can be accessed via the WRPM section of the Special Collections Goldsmiths website.[36] In the following year, I added a small number of audio clips of the permitted length while coming up against restrictions of streaming and copyright.

As the catalogue expanded, it was necessary to expand the online entries about the women composers to keep the details up to date and to start to develop this website as a resource. I (Helen) started some entries in 2001, and I (Hilary) maintained and increased the resource up until 2005. Women composers added to the online resource included: Chiara Cozzolani (1602–1678), Lucretia Vizzana (1590–1662), Francesca Caccini (1587–1640), Elisabeth Jacquet de la Guerre (1665–1729), Rebecca Clarke (1886–1979), Ruth Crawford Seeger (1901–1953), Sofia Gubaidulina (b. 1931), Grace Williams (1906–1977), Joan Trimble (1915–2000), Thea Musgrave (b. 1928), Pauline Oliveros (1932–2016), Annea Lockwood (b. 1939), Laurie Anderson (b. 1947), Joan Tower (b. 1938), Meredith Monk (b. 1942), Elena Radigue (b. 1932), Joan La Barbara (b. 1947), Kaija Saariaho (b. 1952), Sally Beamish (b. 1956), Deirdre Gribbin (b. 1967), and Roxanna Panufnik (b. 1968). The World Musics were also of particular interest; to expand the diversity of women musicians in *The Archive* and make it available for purchase, this section was expanded to over sixty women musicians.

I (Hilary) immersed myself in the micro-ways of running a micro-business by turning my front room into the WRPM Office, open to the public; conquering the credit card machine for increasingly insistent orders; covering the walls with terrifyingly risky boxes of stock; calculating profit margins; and minimising the costs of accounting. I (Helen) remember this front room fondly, as it was a treasure trove of music and Hilary was always happy for the music to be playing while we worked. This second life of WRPM maintained a network of 150 small suppliers, and I (Hilary) travelled the country to festivals and events as had my predecessor, Caroline. All the time I continued taking WRPM to events across the UK, visiting and talking to suppliers and musicians. As far as possible, WRPM used small distributors and negotiated sales arrangements with musicians directly.[37]

Over the years 1999 to 2005, the turnover of WRPM increased by 25% as the customer base widened. The website was crucial to this business success. The aim to ensure access to this music was a driving force for WRPM, notably in this second life. Ensuring that the music could be heard was crucial to encouraging sales: exploring unfamiliar music online is now common practice, but it was not so in 2001. Audio samples were put on the website, and extra space was created by the event stalls where visitors could sample the music with that (at the time) ageing bit of technology, a CD Walkman with headphones! WRPM brought music, musicians, and listeners closely together at pioneer festivals such as: the Chard Festival of Music by Women, (which ran from 1990 to 2003); the Chard Hotbed (2001–2002), which provided support and training for women musicians and composers, choral and political song festivals; Giving Voice Conferences in Wales (1999, 2002, 2004),[38] as well as smaller celebratory events organised by and for women.[39]

In handing over to me for the second life of WRPM, Hutton believed that my 'management experience' would help WRPM. In fact, my previous experience in controlling and deploying a large budget in a public service proved to be very different to running a small enterprise; even though my previous work had all been in a community setting with not-for-profit objectives. The work for WRPM, however, was not a one-way process, and it took forward my earlier work in Community Adult Education that was focused on a lifelong right to an open curriculum and negotiated relationships.

In an interview in 2000 for the Manchester-based feminist magazine *Eve's Back*,[40] I emphasised that running WRPM was: 'not just dispensing music over the counter'.[41] I heard musical histories from customers at the stall or as part of an apparently commercial transaction in person or over the phone. These personal conversations were significant; customers shared their own personal musical histories, often of discouragement and abuse from family members or at schools. An assumption that music was a male industry was commonplace. I heard histories of women finding empowerment through music and in some cases becoming active musicians themselves. They turned to WRPM for the role models and support: WRPM gave them evidence that women could be musicians and enabled them to hear a wider variety of music than would have otherwise been available.

WRPM worked to support women's individual musics and to support the recognition of women in music, both for me, for Helen as my student intern on placement, and for my customers. 'WRPM gave credence to what I had been taught in class at The University of Huddersfield by Margaret Lucy Wilkins and Rachel Cowgill: that advocacy and grassroots activism was still needed even as we started the twenty-first century'.[42] While I (Hilary) was encouraged to play instrumental music and sing early in my life, I had foregone, or rather been prevented from pursuing, longer-term serious music pathways. In and through WRPM, I found a very different musical life, and it inspired me to get a musical education for myself as I passed sixty. I became deeply interested in composition and political engagement, especially the work of Elizabeth Maconchy, analysis, and musicology. I am keenly aware of the absences and erasures of music by women, and I query the effect on women who have been largely listeners of music by men and only infrequently by women. This latter I still only rarely hear anything about.

WRPM as an Archive

While studying music from 2003 onwards and from 2006 at Morley College, I was horrified that in all my courses, while I was a student in both Adult and Higher Education, there was only one occasion when I was offered a piece by a woman to study. Consequently, one of the highlights of my WRPM years was delivering a large collection of recordings of music by women composers to the Brotherton Library at the University of Leeds. The collection had been ordered by Rachel Cowgill, then a lecturer in Music at the University Leeds and now Professor of Music at the University of York.

When I took the decision to close the trading side of WRPM in 2005 (for personal reasons), I reached out to find a possible successor. Times were financially precarious, however, and I had to consider what the next steps could be for WRPM as an *archive*. I was anxious that none of the work of WRPM, the music and the business, should in turn be obscured. The WRPM Collection of recordings that Hutton and I created had originally been held at Birmingham Public Music Library with the papers in the Public Archives. Despite their serious interest, those institutions had not been able to provide good access to the recordings, and I had become responsible for the welfare of both recordings and documents. I consulted as many relevant organisations, libraries, and archives as I could. Enquiries to the Women's Library in London (keen but unable to catalogue due to overload of work) and the British Sound Library (unable to keep the Collection together) did not have positive results.

I was not, however, prepared to leave WRPM and all it represented without listeners or users future-proofed. After moving to London in 2006 to pursue my music studies, I learnt that the Women's Art Library, an organisation with aims similar to WRPM, was housed at Goldsmiths University of London. It was part of a unique range of Special Collections, including the Daphne Oram Archive and the libraries of Peggy Seeger and Ewan MacColl. I approached Goldsmiths in 2010. As a dynamic university specialising in Social and Cultural Studies, I thought that it would be the right setting for the WRPM Collection, moving the informal *archive* into a properly catalogued Archive alongside the Women's Art Library. WRPM would have specialised curatorial and managerial support for its development while offering access to the general public, as well as students and researchers in many fields.

I embarked on a two-year period of negotiation spurred on by a very warm Goldsmiths' reception. Both Birmingham and Goldsmiths Libraries had to make detailed audits of the material, including condition, and had to be satisfied that the material was wanted and would be appropriately located.

Two key aspects of work were undertaken to develop WRPM at Goldsmiths. One was the longer-term preservation and protection of the Collection and Archive. Aims and objectives included: dedicating staff resources and funds to the securing of the assets; the improvement of the music cataloguing; full cataloguing of the papers; and the overall improvement of the online access to the catalogue and the website.

WRPM is already being used by many students and courses across the University and for a wide range of events. For example, the WRPM Collection has been used in research and course seminars, a series on feminist archiving, and new challenges to copyright. As WRPM Visiting Research Fellow I was able to be a direct resource for seminars and series, introducing recordings and other source material and in several cases learning through exchanges with students about their creation and use of music online and their experience of the music industry, new technologies, and creative enterprises. Significantly, a Wikimedia Day (2017) for improving the entries about women musicians was held within the Special Collections area, supported by staff both from the Women's Art Library and Special Collections. At this event contributors from Goldsmiths, Women in Music, and I, reunited with Helen, contributed to many articles by women (a key contributor to the event was Jessy McCabe; see Chapter 26). We were also able to draw on research done by Special Collections about the extent to which individual musicians had an online presence by that time.

The brilliant vinyl covers and the range of independent record labels and magazines provoke amazement and a kind of recognition, reminiscent of the reaction the WRPM stall could create for women who had never been able to see so much work by women on display before. As one customer referred to WRPM: 'It's like all the lights coming on at once'.[43] The BBC staff who visited WRPM in October 2018 also voiced a similar amazed recognition.

The second aspect of development of WRPM at Goldsmiths has been engagement and empowerment. Writing specifically about archives and engagement, Kate Eichhorn writes that 'there's a younger generation who no longer sees archives (public records) as a barrier but as a site for and a practice integral to cultural production and activism, sites of resistance'.[44] She identifies how in turn the work of earlier feminist generations has come to be rediscovered and honoured as part of reimagining and building the future when past work is made visible again after being previously obscured. In considering some case studies, Eichhorn refers to feminist archives coming out of the basements and the often-accidental, disorderly, and impenetrable nature of archives of feminist activism. She claims that there is often a sense in which 'feminism has been preparing itself for the archive all along'.[45]

WRPM does fit this account. WRPM certainly had lingered unused in a basement for several years, and it is true that what led indirectly up to my contact with WRPM was reading a tiny notice about an *a cappella* group looking for new members in Manchester. This was my accidental route to WRPM via Sweet Honey in the Rock. Yet Hutton had a sense of the importance of what she was building as she, and then I, kept 'one of everything' back from the sales table, despite the loss of income. And with the papers, she was very precise, keeping and labelling one of every letter she received with her replies. Some allies regretted the choice of a university base for WRPM as it moved the *archive* from a position of advocacy to a position of education. However, none of the community, or more specifically women-centred or sound-centred archive locations, had proved viable due to lack of space, staffing, resources, and listening facilities. As the history of WRPM shows, much of this grassroots work is self-funded and comes at the expense of the women themselves. At the time of writing, Feminist Archives North and South[46] and the Women's Liberation Archive[47] have taken up similar locations at Leeds and Bristol Universities to ensure sustainable futures for maintaining these valuable resources.

Displaying and introducing WRPM is ongoing, as is dealing with copyright issues. In 2017, funding was found in the Goldsmiths Music Department for Lisa Busby in Goldsmiths Popular Music Research Unit[48] to commission a short artist residency with feminist sound studies artist Holly Ingleton. In *Talking bout a Revolution*, Holly introduced several other sound artists to the Collection and invited them to activate it through shared listening and oral histories. A YouTube playlist emerged, and a performance score was created to trace and develop individual and collective pathways of resistance. In the words of Holly Ingleton and Lisa Busby:

> The WRPM Collection, housed alongside the Women's Art Library, offered a safe space to talk about struggles of marginalisation and survival within sound arts and

experimental musics while engaging with music and writing by those who have struggled before, for and with us.[49]

In a BBC Radio 3 programme in 2017, Peggy Seeger, one of the first musicians in the WRPM sales catalogue, said that it was WRPM that helped her to understand that there was a huge women's movement that she knew nothing about. Such was and is the process and impact of WRPM as we move towards more music created by women being heard and integrated into all aspects of programming, courses, and curriculum. There is still work to be done.

Notes

1. *WRPM Collection*, accessed August 3, 2022, www.gold.ac.uk/library/special-collections/wrpm collection/.
2. See WRPM sales catalogue, WRPM Collection, Ibid.
3. Personal communication, 2020.
4. Following best practice shared by many ethnomusicologists, including Bruno Nettle, *Theory and Methods in Ethnomusicology* (Free Press of Glencoe, 1964), we use pronouns carefully to demonstrate who is speaking in this chapter. Voice is important in autoethnographic work, so we carefully iterate whom 'I' refers to when there is a change of voice. Predominantly, 'I' refers to Hilary Friend unless otherwise stated.
5. Sisterhood and After Research Team, "Activism and the Women's Liberation Movement," 2013, accessed November 28, 2020, www.bl.uk/sisterhood/articles/activism-and-the-womens-liberation-movement.
6. WRPM Collection, accessed December 1, 2020, www.gold.ac.uk/library/special-collections/wrpmcollection/.
7. References to the WRPM Collection contents use the catalogue referencing system, as shown online. As such, short references will be used which denote WRPM, followed by the catalogue numbers. WRPM Collection, Catalogue, accessed December 1, 2020, www.calmview.eu/Goldsmiths/CalmView/Record.aspx?src=CalmView.Catalog&id=WRPM&pos=1.
8. Personal communication, 2020.
9. Women's Festival, Drill Hall, London (December 1977), in WRPM/11, *WRPM Collection*.
10. Ibid.
11. *The Women's Liberation Music Archive* can be accessed here: accessed December 1, 2020, https://womensliberationmusicarchive.co.uk/xyz/.
12. Women's Liberation Music Projects 1970s: Alison Rayner, Andrea Webb, Janie Grote, Nicole Freni, Terry Hunt, Tierl Thompson, "Sisters in Song," 1978, accessed December 1, 2020, https://womensliberationmusicarchive.co.uk/xyz/.
13. Kirsty Gillmore, "Ova Music Studio – Feminism and Female Music Production in 1970s London," accessed December 1, 2020, https://soundgirls.org/ova-music-studio-feminism-and-female-music-production-in-1970s-london/.
14. For more information see, *Nicolle Freni*, accessed December 1, 2020, http://nicollefreni.com/Home.html.
15. The accounts of WRPM are also held in the *WRPM Collection*; see WRPM/2; notable are the company accounts, WRPM/2/1 and the Grant Applications, WRPM/2/3.
16. The early grant applications can be seen at WRPM/2/3/1, and the handover notes from 1979 are also available, see WRPM/2/3/1.
17. Ibid.
18. For more details, see accessed November 30, 2020, www.newsfromnowhere.org.uk/.
19. Cholmeley, cited in Paton, Maureen, "Eclipse of Silver Moon," *The Guardian*, October 23, 2001, accessed December 1, 2020, www.theguardian.com/world/2001/oct/23/gender.uk2.
20. Tom Service, "Howard Skempton, Martyn Brabbins, Women's Revolutions Per Minute," BBC Radio 3, "Music Matters," October 28, 2017, accessed December 1, 2020, www.bbc.co.uk/programmes/b09bwvcy.
21. All these catalogues are available in *WRPM Collection*, see WRPM/6.
22. Caroline Hutton, 2008, personal communication.
23. Ibid.

24. See WRPM/17/CH and WRPM/17/HF.
25. Hutton, 2008.
26. Anon. 'Conversation with Caroline Hutton of WRPM," *Women for Life on Earth*, 10 (1985): no pagination.
27. The Green Party of the Music Business, *Powercut* 1 (1991/5), 24. See a copy in Articles and Mentions WRPM/10.
28. See Handover Records, WRPM/1/3, and Questionnaires, WRPM/2/6.
29. See WPRM/1/3.
30. See WRPM/1/2/7.
31. See WRPM/1/1/3.
32. See WRPM/3/2.
33. The catalogues all show the prices, and the financial accounts reveal the changes to financial management; see WRPM/6/1–57 and WRPM/2/1/1–22.
34. See WRPM/6/54.
35. Further details about the work of Women in Music (UK) can be found on the website, accessed December 1, 2020, www.womeninmusic.org.uk.
36. The archived WRPM website is available for viewing on the WRPM Collection located in the Special Collections & Archives at Goldsmiths, University of London. The website can be accessed directly at: accessed September 15, 2021, www.wrpm.org.uk.
37. See WRPM/8. In particular, see WRPM/8/1/1.
38. These events had specific themes, as follows: 1999 A Divinity of the Voice – Aberystwyth, Wales; 2002 The Voice Politic – Aberystwyth & Cardiff, Wales; 2004 Towards a Philosophy and Psychology of the Voice – Aberystwyth & Cardiff, Wales. See accessed December 1, 2020, https://thecpr.org.uk/archived-projects/.
39. See WRPM/8/2.
40. For more information on this publication see accessed November 30, 2020, https://thefword.org.uk/2001/08/eve's_back/. This journal ran until 2004.
41. Kay Bastin, "Interview with Hilary Friend, WRPM," *Eve's Back* (2001): no pagination.
42. Personal communication (November 2020).
43. Customer quote, anon., in WRPM Catalogue 2003, See WRPM/6/57.
44. Kate Eichhorn, *The Archival Turn to Feminism: Outrage in Order* (Philadelphia, PA: Temple University Press, 2013), 280.
45. Ibid.
46. *Feminist Archive North*, accessed December 1, 2020, https://feministarchivenorth.org.uk/.
47. Ibid., accessed December 1, 2020, https://specialcollections.blogs.bristol.ac.uk/2020/05/07/the-feminist-archive-south-and-womens-liberation-music-archive-at-special-collections/.
48. For more details see, accessed December 1, 2020, www.gold.ac.uk/pmru/.
49. Holly Ingleton and Lisa Busby, *The WRPM Game* (London, 2017), accessed December 1, 2020, https://avelospace.net/lee-ingleton/talks/challenging-rules-of-engagement/.

Bibliography

Anon. "Conversation with Caroline Hutton of WRPM." *Women for Life on Earth* 10 (1985): np.
Bastin, Kay. "Interview with Hilary Friend, WRPM." *Eve's Back* (2001): np.
Eichhorn, Kate. *The Archival Turn to Feminism: Outrage in Order*. Philadelphia, PA: Temple University Press, 2013.
Feminist Archive North. Accessed December 1, 2020. https://feministarchivenorth.org.uk/.
Feminist Archive South and Women's Liberation Music Archive. Accessed December 1, 2020. https://specialcollections.blogs.bristol.ac.uk/2020/05/07/the-feminist-archive-south-and-womens-liberation-music-archive-at-special-collections/.
Gillmore, Kirsty. "Ova Music Studio – Feminism and Female Music Production in 1970s London." Accessed December 1, 2020. https://soundgirls.org/ova-music-studio-feminism-and-female-music-production-in-1970s-london/.
Giving Voice Conferences, Wales. Accessed December 1, 2020. https://thecpr.org.uk/archived-projects/.
Hutton, Caroline. "The Green Party of the Music Business WRPM." *Powercut* 1 (1992): 24.
_____. Accessed December 6, 2020. https://gaybirminghamremembered.co.uk.

Ingleton, Holly, and Busby, Lisa. "The WRPM Game" 2017. Accessed December 1, 2020. https://avelospace.net/lee-ingleton/talks/challenging-rules-of-engagement/.

Nettl, Bruno. *Theory and Methods in Ethnomusicology*. New York: Free Press of Glencoe, 1964.

Paton, Maureen. "Eclipse of Silver Moon." *The Guardian*, October 23, 2001. Accessed December 1, 2020. www.theguardian.com/world/2001/oct/23/gender.uk2.

Raynor et al. "Sisters in Song." 1978. Accessed December 1, 2020. https://womensliberationmusicarchive.co.uk/xyz/.

Redfern, Catherine. "Eve's Back." Accessed November 30, 2020. https://thefword.org.uk/2001/08/eves_back/.

Service, Tom. "Howard Skempton, Martyn Brabbins, Women's Revolutions Per Minute." *BBC Radio 3*, "Music Matters," October 28, 2017. Accessed December 1, 2020. www.bbc.co.uk/programmes/b09bwvcy.

Sisterhood and After Research Team. "Activism and the Women's Liberation Movement." 2013. Accessed November 28, 2020. www.bl.uk/sisterhood/articles/activism-and-the-womens-liberation-movement.

The Women's Liberation. "Music Archive." Accessed December 1, 2020. https://womensliberationmusicarchive.co.uk/xyz/.

Women in Music (UK). Accessed December 1, 2020. www.womeninmusic.org.uk.

WRPM Catalogue. Accessed December 1, 2020. www.calmview.eu/Goldsmiths/CalmView/Record.aspx?src=CalmView.Catalog&id=WRPM&pos=1.

WRPM Collection. Accessed December 1, 2020. www.gold.ac.uk/library/special-collections/wrpmcollection/.

WRPM Website. Accessed December 1, 2020. www.wrpm.org.uk.

46
GENDER RELATIONS IN NEW MUSIC (GRiNM)* AND YORKSHIRE SOUND WOMEN NETWORK (YSWN)~

Case Studies in Activism and Organisation for Change

Stellan Veloce*, Brandon Farnsworth*, Rosanna Lovell*, Heidi Johnson~, Abi Bliss~, and Eddie Dobson~

Introduction

The idea of 'leadership' in activism for gender and diversity in music can be dangerous in that it oversimplifies a much more nuanced ecosystem comprising many grassroots collectives, networks, and formal organisations with diverse approaches, priorities, and values. This chapter offers responses from multiple voices within two organisations reacting to gender inequity in contemporary music and in music technology, respectively: 1. Gender Relations in New Music (GRiNM), who in detailing their projects and activism give an inside perspective to the systemic issues present in contemporary classical music; and 2. Yorkshire Sound Women Network (YSWN), who give an account of the organisation's creation and development into a non-profit community interest company, and questions around the related challenges, contradictions, and merits of this development and operation. The chapter is a collaboration between the two organisations, formed through discussion and exchange. The contributors include three different voices from both GRiNM and YSWN, just some from the many which (co)exist within the collectives. We hope that by detailing our experiences we can provide an insight into the potential forms of collective action and leadership.

Various publications quantify the situation of gender inequity, presenting data that has supported strategies for change. For example, female:pressure have been publishing surveys since 2013 'to address and quantify the deficit in equal opportunity and visibility for female artists in the electronic music scene' and showing that 'barely 10% of the artists listed in festival line-ups worldwide' were female.[1] The subsequent surveys in 2015 and 2017 have shown little change. The most recent USC Annenberg report shows that only 2.6% of producers are women.[2] Georgina Born and Kyle Devine's research shows how during a decade when applications to music technology degree courses in England (n38) increased by 1400%, 90% were from males.[3] Christina Scharff's research reveals disparaging statistics regarding university music departments and orchestras in Germany and the UK while also exploring the complex way in which various forms of discrimination persist for young female professional musicians.[4]

In 2016, following an extensive exploration of the Darmstadt Summer Course archive for the Historage initiative, Ashley Fure published *GRID: Gender Research in Darmstadt*.[5] The report quantified the gender gaps around the number of composers attending, those being commissioned or performed, and those receiving awards. It found that between 1946–2014, 4416 (92.968%) pieces by male composers were programmed, compared to only 334 (7.023%) by female composers, with the majority of these (312) programmed from 1984 onwards. Examining the number of female composition faculty (including visiting composers) shows the appointments of the first 7 female faculty members only in 1986, and an overall ongoing low percentage of female appointments despite an increase in number of faculty members appointed. Lastly, the report also presents the percentage of female participants from 1963–2014. This shows a steady 14% to 20% of participants being female until 1988, with the percentage increasing since then and reaching 44% in 2014.

Statistics made by GRiNM would confirm similar situations at other German New Music festivals: at the MaerzMusik festival, from 2010 to 2018, just 28% of pieces were by women,[6] transmasculine, or non-binary people, while at the Donaueschingen Musiktage between 2011 and 2017, it was only 18%.[7]

Overall, these reports reveal an alarming lack of diversity regarding gender identity, sexuality, ethnicity, and disability. It is important that data on these topics is not only presented in reports, but also considered carefully in how it impacts equality and accessibility.

Activisms for Change

Responses include the 2018 PRS Foundation's Keychange initiative,[8] SoundGirls' EQL Directory,[9] many conferences, and numerous positive interventions; for example, the University of Sydney's Composing Women programme.[10] But there is a long-established history of grassroots activism by women and non-binary, gender non-conforming people in music. Examples include collectives such as Discwoman[11], networks providing access to equipment and community, and non-profit businesses such as Women's Audio Mission,[12] which service local communities, young people, and early career professionals. Beats By Girlz[13] connects educators with facilities to deliver an education programme developed by Erin Barra, while SoundGirls.org[14] supports an international network providing education programmes. Other groups explore feminist foundations of digital inclusion and activism,[15] or prioritise music making and dissemination, releasing and promoting music/musicians online. Seraphine Collective in Detroit creates inclusive spaces for all marginalised people and uses their social and symbolic capital to pressure venues and festivals to do the same.

Within contemporary classical music (hereafter CCM) in Europe, we face a sector that remains male-dominated and Western-centric and which is not often called into question by artists or audiences. Discussing issues of gender equality and diversification often falls to small activist groups, rather than more established institutions. Older organisations such as Archiv Frau und Musik[16] in Frankfurt, which maintains an archive of works by women composers as well as organising various projects and events, continue to play an important role; however, the past decade has seen a groundswell of initiatives emerge in various countries that seem to emphasise an intersectional approach, and are just as focused on structural and artistic change as they are on the equal programming of composers other than white cis males. These collectives emerge out of local scenes to serve their specific contexts, addressing immediate concerns of those directly affected. These include Konstmusiksystrar[17] in Sweden, a support network for non-cis-male composers also engaged with forms of experimental programming, or Sounding the Feminists, who emerged in Ireland (see Chapter 47). At the Berlin University of the Arts, the student- and staff-initiated FEM*_MUSIC*_[18] has looked at feminist issues within the music department since 2016. Recent initiatives in education, such as the Association Européenne des Conservatoire (AEC)'s Gender and Diversity Working Group[19] (2017–2021) or the Art.School.Differences[20] research project in Switzerland (2014–2016), also take an intersectional approach, focusing on structural forms of exclusion rather than specific issues of gender discrimination.

The following case studies discuss how GRiNM and YSWN were formed in response to this *status quo*, followed by a summary of the issues we unpacked through this collaboration.

GRiNM

GRiNM is deliberately opaque. Although different individuals may speak or represent the group at particular events, we operate under our acronym. We feel this is an important aspect of the work as well as the potential of the group, in that it provides the possibility to speak out against significant, established institutions or individuals in the small, relationship-based cultural field of New Music. This deliberate obfuscation means that GRiNM can perhaps also be defined by what it is not: an association, a non-profit, a university research project, or a festival. Consequently, GRiNM is a strongly independent organisation, yet also one that has no funding. It succeeds on the strength of its nodes, volunteer labour, and on the willingness of the music community to support its goals.

The group was born in 2016 during the Darmstadt Summer Course for New Music. It originated as GRID, Gender Research in Darmstadt, a spontaneous group spurred into action following a panel organised by composer Ashley Fure discussing the breakdown of commissions by male and female composers over the course's history. As Fure writes in her initial presentation:

> Digging through the labyrinth of digitized material, the most pressing question that came to my mind wasn't what's *in* this archive, but what *isn't*? . . . What histories speak through the cracks and absences in the archive? An impossibly complex question, perhaps, but one I thought I'd start chipping away at through the lens of gender. . . . Our aim is not to impose an interpretation, but to carve out time for collective, focused engagement with the information.[21]

The 'digestion' of this information is the ongoing process of which GRiNM is a part. During that summer, a regular group held daily meetings in the Open Spaces, where participants can self-organise their own programmes during the course. Everybody, from all genders, showed great concern for the imbalances within the contemporary music scene, not only based on gender, but also on many other factors such as class or ethnic background.

Multiple guerrilla actions were organised by the group, from asking attending students, faculty, and artists to sign lifelong binding declarations in which they agreed to always promote gender equality while teaching, curating, and publishing, to sticking sheets with biographies of female composers that had been at Darmstadt onto rental bikes. A representative of GRID was subsequently invited to the official autumn feedback think tank. The group moved online and put together a document with a list of proposals for both short- and long-term change to help the institution improve.[22] The proposals were well received by the administrators and have since been partly implemented, such as changing the student demographics by splitting the 'first come, first served' policy into two (unfortunately gender binary) options: female/non-female, as well as reaching more gender diversity in the teaching faculty.

From 2017 on, GRID became GRiNM, persisting online and meeting occasionally in person in Berlin. Members felt the need to function as an umbrella network and stay open and decentralised to channel the diverse energies, geographically and politically, sparked by the events in Darmstadt. During this phase, GRiNM remained in conversation with various German New Music festivals: because CCM in Western Europe is sustained by established, state funded, yearly festivals, we have often focused on being active in these highly symbolic spaces. Such festivals often also serve the double role of both substantiating their communities and allowing them to re-evaluate their established norms. They are therefore an ideal space in which to intervene to change how the community functions. Being present as GRiNM, we aim to both bring attention to problematic issues around gender representation, cultural diversity, equality, and accessibility within New Music, and provide a platform for those affected or concerned with these issues to connect. By insisting on space for discussion at these events, we are attempting to gradually shift the frame of discourse of this community itself and trying to make such matters more widely accepted as the norm within this field.

GRiNM's first public meeting took place at the MaerzMusik Festival in Berlin in March 2017. It focused on brainstorming various ways people could take action, forming working groups and creating connections in order to sustain the group long-term. The group's next action took place at the Donaueschinger Musiktage in October 2017. The group's interventions included an advertisement in the printed programme. GRiNM also made a presentation to composition students and distributed stickers to passers-by reading '92.44% MEN' and '50/50?', hoping to provoke discussion about quotas and tangible actions that should be taken by festival programmers against gender discrimination.

At the MaerzMusik festival in 2018, GriNM launched its website GRiNM.org, which was designed to both present the group's statistics and activities and to allow for guests to submit posts. The group also organised another data-harvesting event to calculate statistics on female identified, transmasculine, and non-binary composers that have been commissioned over the festival's history.[23] In 2018, GRiNM was invited to participate in panels and give a workshop as part of the conference entitled 'Defragmentation: Curating Contemporary Music'. The group now consisted of an almost completely new group of active members. Working on a volunteer, unpaid basis, it largely depends on influxes of new volunteers to sustain its activities. Notably taking place at the first Darmstadt Summer Course since GRID's initial outcry, the event was the culmination of a research project organised by four major festivals, and was an attempt at establishing debates around 'gender & diversity, decolonization and technological change . . . as well as discussing curatorial practices' in the field of CCM.[24]

After the conference's opening speech, members of GRiNM stood up and read a statement criticising it as tokenistic, merely paying lip service to this slew of crucial issues and inviting delegates to join the group in a 'parainstitutional' discussion space in the form of a temporary tent set up in the front yard of the school building where the Summer Courses take place.[25] GRiNM symbolically used its speakers' fees to pay for this action. In addition to discussions and presentations in the tent, a guerrilla flyering action took place at the end of a concert, and a newly inaugurated Instagram page created by the group supported these actions online.

While the group's actions have mainly taken place in Germany, it has built connections to CCM practitioners all over Europe. Members of GRiNM have presented at several international music festivals and conferences, such as the Performance Studies Network Conference Oslo and the 2018 Sanatorium Dźwięku festival in Poland. In November 2019, GRiNM undertook its largest action to date, organising the GRiNM Network Conference 2019: Experiences with Gender and Diversity in New Music in Zurich. For the first time, rather than latching onto another event, the group asserted itself as the organiser. The idea was to bring together a wide range of people working in the fields of research, education, programming, and administration to share their experiences on the topic from different perspectives. The resulting conference worked to affirm the community of invited delegates dealing with diversity issues in their respective contexts and to challenge pre-existing ideas within the discourse around the diversification of people and practices in CCM. By gathering this community together, various faultlines became apparent, such as between supporting women, transmasculine, and non-binary artists in CCM directly, and an intersectional approach which also calls into question more fundamental aesthetic presumptions within CCM. This approach speaks to the reality that while festivals may be symbolically important events, they exist as the product of a far larger network of actors supporting them, including conservatories that train musicians and composers, ensembles specialising in this kind of musical practice, and professional composers working in this field, to name just a few. In this way, the GRiNM Network Conference continued the group's key activist gesture: its insistence on creating a space for these issues within contemporary music institutions, which unfortunately remain highly conservative, despite being recipients of significant government funding.

Reflecting on GRiNM

Despite aspiring to diversity, the group nevertheless reflects the field from which it originates, in that those involved are predominantly white, middle-class, and university-educated. While being international, including members from Australia, Canada, Denmark, Germany, Israel, Italy, Poland, the USA, and beyond, we all speak fluent English (the group's working language), and more specifically hold visas or passports that allow us to live and work in Berlin. So, while the group strives for openness and horizontal hierarchies, we are also aware that our point of departure is already one that is highly privileged. In light of this, GRiNM's focus is on asserting a space for historically disregarded voices, and on giving this space to others. We aspire to serve as allies for those who cannot be personally involved, either through geographic or other limitations, or those who cannot speak out due to institutional or political factors, among others. Our position is that these issues should concern everyone involved in the future of New Music practice. It should not be left to those who may already find themselves in marginalised positions to speak on these issues, often at the expense of speaking about their own creative practice.

The group counts among its members composers, researchers, curators, educators, journalists, and musicians, all of whom bring their own perspective and understanding to the group. The size of the group fluctuates, with some individuals engaging in specific events or actions that GRiNM organises while others are involved over longer periods of time. GRiNM's open structure means that anyone can join the group for as long as they want to or can, even if just to post a meme. During workshops we often receive many excellent suggestions for work that we could be doing, identifying festivals or institutions which need constructive criticism regarding equality and diversity. However, GRiNM considers itself more a platform or network where concerns, ideas, and knowledge can be exchanged, support can be offered, and connections can be established and shared.

The group focuses on its area of expertise, namely the design and framing of the specific actions that it undertakes in different institutions, in order to ensure their maximum impact. We often have an intimate, first-hand knowledge of the festivals and institutions in which we work. This allows for highly efficient operations, given that the group has zero resources of its own. In this way, the group is not a funded organisation which works to fulfil quotas or cultural policy, but rather a collective voice that dares to speak and act on issues we consider crucial and relevant. GRiNM can be provocative, annoying, inspiring, or welcoming, depending on who you are.

Yorkshire Sound Women Network

Organisation History

Yorkshire Sound Women Network began in July 2015 following a tweet inviting women interested or involved in music technology and audio to meet and share skills in music production. This was a response to concerns about a significant gender imbalance in music/audio production education and professions, and it was motivated by research on gender and engagement in music technology education which suggested that social context is of greater concern than access to technology in the music classroom.[26,27] This work suggested that girls lacked confidence in this area, with cultural norms associating technology and masculinity being significant factors in their decision to drop music technology as teenagers. The gender imbalance seemed to invite damaging assumptions: that women/girls are simply not interested in audio, feeding confirmation bias about gender and technology. This assumption is challenged in part by improved visibility of women who are established in the field, especially online.[28] By offering spaces for women it was possible to remove some of these concerns, lower the stakes, and increase opportunities to enjoy a less self-conscious practice with technology in music.

This first meeting was also motivated by Bourdieu's theoretical work on social fields, the inter-relationships of economic, social, and cultural capital, as well as social psychology research revealing the mediating influence of social interaction and place on collaborative learning and creativity.[29] In music technology, economic capital is important (as studio and equipment access facilitates learning), but social capital affords access to a community of peers and opportunities to talk. Social psychology research shows that talk is a key to higher mental development, learning, and creativity, so in terms of personal development, the connected musician is so much more likely to progress than more isolated peers.[30,31] From the outset, YSWN had potential to be a community creating opportunities for talk, collaboration, and personal development.

Sixteen women attended this initial meeting in Huddersfield, a group including sound system experts, a venue curator, a studio manager, a music technology academic, sound artists, and composers. We shared our backgrounds and our experiences of discrimination. Over the subsequent months we held meetings in Huddersfield, Sheffield, and Leeds, agreeing on the focus together, then sharing interests, our sound/music, equipment, and knowledge. These meetings also included discussion of feminism and collective organising as we explored our identity and structure as a group and our plans for the future. Early meetings included workshops on soldering a printed circuit board noise instrument, sound synthesis hardware, field recording, computer music production, and building piezo disk contact microphones. Another group called SONA was set up in Sheffield, serving women in that region and delivering a series of music technology workshops.

In December 2015, the AHRC Live Coding Research Network and the University of Huddersfield funded a YSWN live coding day delivered by Dr Shelly Knotts and Dr Joanne Armitage.[32] Within two hours of advertising, it was fully booked; this enabled us to challenge the assumption that women are not present because of lack of interest in audio.

The Huddersfield-based working group continued to meet, discussing the mission, beneficiaries, types of focus, and projects, while also sharing interests and diverse practices. In refining our aims and grappling with issues of purpose and sustainability, we explored how:

- to become sustainable and benefit people beyond those present in the room;
- not to exploit the labour of women delivering workshops or doing project management, promotion, and administration;
- not to benefit only white, able, middle-class women, without regard for the obstacles and obstructions faced by women of diverse ethnicities, with disabilities, of limited economic means, and those navigating several of these;
- to establish agreement on gender identity and inclusion.

In early meetings, many issues around gender and equity in music technology emerged; however, the group recognised that it would be beyond our capacity to tackle everything simultaneously, so we established our immediate priorities. We set up a bank account, which meant developing a constitution and adopting a basic committee structure with minuted meetings. The core group included members who would offer professional insight and guidance on our development, as we sought to maintain a democratic method for decision-making. YSWN's first successful Arts Council England application afforded business consultancy, website development, and a survey of community interests, which informed a business plan. Our working group of six (four white women and two women of colour) were asked to weigh up their priorities and hopes for YSWN, which were distilled into three strategic areas: education, community, and industry advocacy.

With support from the University of Huddersfield, YSWN employed a development manager, and the working group evaluated various operational structures (cooperative, collective, community interest company, and charity) before registering as a non-profit Community Interest Company. Our mission remains as seen on our website: 'to support a flourishing industry which welcomes, encourages and progresses the inclusion of women at all levels from studio floor to board room, and reflects the diversity of its participating communities'.[33]

Activities

Since becoming a Community Interest Company in May 2018, YSWN has focused on the three priority areas while growing and sustaining the organisation internally.

Education

YSWN has delivered two major music education initiatives supported by Youth Music: Go Compose (2018–2019) and WIRED (2018–2020). Both have offered participatory music and technology workshops for girls in Yorkshire and outreach workshops delivered in schools and community groups, while benefitting from partnerships with higher education institutions offering workshop space and specialist equipment. Go Compose saw over 50 girls participate across 19 days of workshop activities in Huddersfield including DJing, music production, audio electronics, and sound composition. WIRED set up two 12-week music technology clubs for 11- to 18-year-olds in Leeds and Doncaster and three further online courses across Yorkshire. Participants shared new aspirations following their involvement: 'I would love to become a sound engineer'; 'It's made me think about getting into DJing more seriously'; and

'I've decided to study music in the future'. Full information about all these projects can be found on the YSWN website.[34]

Community: Events and Workshops

YSWN groups have been established across Yorkshire. In 2019, the Amplify programme supported members of YSWN-affiliated groups in Calderdale, Huddersfield, and Sheffield to increase their music technology skills and develop artistically, while engaging new local participants and audiences. Groups proposed and delivered their own projects, which included beginner DJ workshops for adults, commissioning and supporting new music for performance, and an artist residency.

Building on an annual tradition of cross-region meetups and AGMs, three Level Up! events were organised for the YSWN community during 2019 – providing free training, music-making workshops, and career advice on areas including music production, sound for the moving image, and sound engineering. The events also encouraged attendees to meet and share ideas, leading to further informal networks and collaborations. Over 150 people registered for the events, and attendees said: 'I learned very useful tips and advice about breaking into the industry and having confidence within myself, and finally got a glimpse into the studio recording environment'; 'Just seeing so many females interested in music technology is something that I had never experienced before'.

Finally, a variety of activities and events have been organised independently by regional groups including Calderdale Sound Women Network, YSWN York, SONA, YSWN Huddersfield Makers, Leeds Sound Women, and Malta Sound Women Network. Each region has its own particular focus, and YSWN seeks to support this work.

Industry

YSWN commissioned and disseminated an industry-facing advocacy video and report, 'Volume Up!', which helped the organisation highlight gender inequality with key stakeholders in the audio industry. YSWN has also been represented at regional and national audio industry events such as SynthFest and Edinburgh Festival of Sound. Partnerships have been developed with organisations in the music industry, education, and cultural sectors, including YSWN becoming a Spotify EQL Partner to help inform their equity work.

YSWN has also set up three part-time paid traineeships for young women with music studios and venues in West Yorkshire: BASSment, Greenmount Studios, and Vibrations Studios. Through this, YSWN seeks to inform and change attitudes around positive action and meaningful industry support for women in audio. To develop this advocacy strand further, YSWN is working with a business coach to develop training and consultancy services for the music industry themed around workplace gender equity.

Organisational Development and Funding

YSWN has five Company Directors who have legal responsibility for the effective running of the organisation. Their role is to ensure that YSWN complies with its governing document, company law, and any other relevant legislation or regulations; that YSWN pursues the objects and priorities from its governing document and business plan; and to ensure its financial stability. Decisions are made at quarterly Working Group meetings involving Directors, paid staff, and Associates.

YSWN invested in staff to devolve the running of the organisation: recruiting a part-time development manager, coordinator, and bookkeeper and building a pool of 25 (to date) freelance YSWN Associates with a wide range of skills and expertise. Associates share the mission and values of YSWN and are contracted to deliver paid work on behalf of YSWN, such as facilitating education workshops, delivering gender inclusion training, or coordinating specific projects for which YSWN has sourced funding. Marketing and PR activities to date include launching a new website, growing a significant social media presence, and producing merchandise including stickers, lanyards, and pin badges. YSWN has secured investment totalling over £100k since May 2018 from a diverse range of income sources, including National Lottery funding, local authorities, trusts and foundations, corporate support, earned income, and individual donations.[35]

Issues of Institutional Critique

We have found several positive, and some potentially negative, consequences associated with YSWN's chosen route of becoming a formal company:

- **Accountability and transparency:** registering as a Community Interest Company (CIC) is a statement of intent that YSWN exists to benefit a specific community, on a not-for-profit basis, which is an organisational structure well aligned with YSWN's values. As a registered CIC, we have to demonstrate that we are consulting with and addressing the needs of this particular community through annual reporting to Companies House. YSWN also discloses its annual accounts so that we are financially transparent. We publish an annual review to share information about our activities publicly.
- **Funding:** Being a registered company opens up various funding opportunities to YSWN through grant-giving trusts and public monies. It gives funders reassurance that YSWN is a legally constituted organisation with clearly defined aims and priorities, satisfactory administrative and financial processes, and relevant policies and procedures, which in turn lessens the risk to funders' investments.

Negative aspects which may influence decisions around organisational structure include:

- **Responsibility:** Being a registered company does bring with it a responsibility to fulfil the company's statutory requirements and meet tax liabilities. Some may find this level of formality or responsibility burdensome, or may be unwilling to align themselves with what they perceive as commercial interests, seeing it as buying in to a patriarchal capitalist system. Such responsibilities may exclude certain, more disruptive, forms of activism.
- **Funding:** There can be a danger that activities become designed to fulfil funder priorities and requirements in order to secure monies, and this can compromise the organisation's mission. YSWN approaches this by a) ensuring we adhere to the priorities and activities agreed upon by the group in the business plan; and b) making sure funding applications are carefully researched so that they support YSWN's priority areas – not the other way around.
- **Hierarchical structures:** Being a registered company means that we have appointed Company Directors who have legal responsibility for the effective running of the organisation. This can pose issues for an organisation keen to be equitable and non-hierarchical. We have approached this by trying to recruit a diverse board of Directors who represent the community YSWN serves. We strive to develop a demarcation between the governance (voluntary directors) and operational (paid staff) aspects of the organisation so that Directors are not

unduly burdened with unpaid administrative work. Operationally, the organisation has adopted a flat, non-hierarchical structure.

Impact of YSWN: Further Questions

The question of who YSWN serves must be central in project development and accomplished through meaningful dialogue with sister organisations. While prioritising accessible venues and promoting inclusive practices, YSWN remains a largely homogenous organisation, particularly with respect to ethnicity, informing the stories, experiences, and wishes prioritised by the organisation. We aspire to be more representative of people of colour and welcome all opportunities to support and promote women and girls facing a full diversity of challenges, recognising that further work is needed in that area.

Closing Comments

In presenting the activities and goals of GRiNM and YSWN, we have offered two approaches to pursuing the goal of equity in gender diversity. GRiNM maintains a strongly independent grassroots movement, prioritising often-playful disruptions in contemporary music, while YSWN has pursued a structured non-profit approach, facilitating activities and events according to a business plan. Through collaborative authorship we observed similar challenges around organising, navigating diverse perspectives on voluntary labour, grassroots activism, and sustainability. This online cross-organisation collaboration led towards more in-depth discussion than could be presented here, beyond our story of disruption, reinvention, and exploration and closer to a shared self-consciousness about our homogeneity and desire to question who we are centring.

Considering the question of leadership in particular: based on this collaboration, we observe multiple examples of leadership and reject any specific or binary perspective. Leadership is seen where personal narratives of discrimination are amplified, resourcing the community with examples, and confidence in language that can be used when discussing ethnicity, gender, and disability. Organisations with significant economic and symbolic capital (i.e. PRS and Spotify) lead change through industry focused projects, helping people in the most visible positions of influence to show leadership. Leadership through networks, collectives, co-operatives, and non-profit enterprises builds economic and social capital directly amongst gender marginalised groups, inspiring new confidence for further activism. Here, responses to traditional patriarchal and discriminatory systems collectively renegotiate what structures they want or need, questioning the forms of leadership that best serve the community. Some, such as Women's Audio Mission, operate with a clear leader, but most follow collective organising. All responded to the challenges and negotiated priorities of a local community. Sometimes a horizontal internal structure (GRiNM) presents collective leadership, or a middle ground where a working group operates within a more hierarchically structured framework (YSWN). Both prioritise intersectionality, non-mainstream and more experimental practices, with a constant return to dialogue, value checking, and maintaining meaningful relationships with the communities we serve.

Rather than identifying as leaders, perhaps we are explorers, taking risks, experiencing the vulnerability of activism as a collective of collectives, facing online and face-to-face resistance, but steady in our belief that change requires the sum of our interventions. Practices of thinking, organising, and acting collectively centre heterogeneous ideas, opinions, and perspectives, which in turn foster a diversity of practice within the fields of music in which we operate. Perhaps this requires many forms of leadership.

Notes

1. female:pressure, *female pressure report 03* (2013), accessed October 3, 2021, https://femalepressure.files.wordpress.com/2013/03/fempressreport-03-2013.pdf.
2. Stacy L. Smith, Katherine Pieper, Hannah Clark, Ariana Case, and Marc Choueiti, "Inclusion in the Recording Studio? Gender and Race/Ethnicity of Artists, Songwriters & Producers across 800 Popular Songs from 2012–2019," 2020, accessed October 2, 2021, http://assets.uscannenberg.org/docs/aii-inclusion-recording-studio-20200117.pdf.
3. Georgina Born and Kyle Devine, "Music Technology, Gender, and Class: Digitization, Educational and Social Change in Britain," *Twentieth-Century Music* 12, no. 2 (2015): 135–72.
4. Christina Scharff, "Inequalities in the Classical Music Industry: The Role of Subjectivity in Constructions of the 'Ideal' Classical Musician," in *The Classical Music Industry*, edited by Chris Dromey and Julia Haferkom (New York: Routledge, 2018), 112–27.
5. Ashley Fure, "GRID: Gender Research in Darmstadt a 2016 HISTORAGE Project Funded by the Goethe Institute," 2016, accessed June 2, 2020, https://griddarmstadt.files.wordpress.com/2016/08/grid_gender_research_in_darmstadt.pdf.
6. This work is based on an intersectional feminism, and as part of that, references to women include 'all those who travel under the sign *women*'. Sara Ahmed, *Living a Feminist Life* (Durham, NC and London: Duke University Press, 2017), 14.
7. See accessed October 3, 2021, http://grinm.org/20171020%20-%20Donaueschinger%20Musiktage%20Statistics%20GRiNM.pdf.
8. PRS, *Keychange* (2017), accessed June 2, 2020, https://keychange.eu/blog/250-music-organisations-commit-to-keychange-50-50-pledge/.
9. SoundGirls, *Make it EQL* [n.d.], accessed June 2, 2020, https://makeiteql.com/.
10. University of Sydney, *Composing women. Nurturing Creativity in our Composition Students*, n.d., accessed June 2, 2020, www.sydney.edu.au/music/industry-and-community/community-engagement/composing-women.html.
11. Discwoman [n.d.], accessed February 18, 2022, www.discwoman.com/.
12. Women's Audio Mission [n.d.], accessed February 18, 2022, https://womensaudiomission.org/.
13. Beats By Girlz [n.d.], accessed February 18, 2022, www.beatsbygirlz.org/.
14. Soundgirls.org [n.d.], accessed February 18, 2022, https://soundgirls.org/
15. Annie Goh and Marie Thompson, "CargoCollective," n.d., accessed June 2, 2020, https://cargocollective.com/soniccyberfeminisms/about.
16. Archiv Frau und Musik [n.d.], accessed April 12, 2022, www.archiv-frau-musik.de/en/.
17. Konstmusiksystrar [n.d.], accessed April 12, 2022, www.konstmusiksystrar.se.
18. FEM*_MUSIC*_ [n.d.], accessed April 12, 2022, www.femmusic.eu/.
19. AEC-SMS (2017–2021) – Creative Europe Network [n.d.], accessed April 12, 2022, https://aec-music.eu/project/aec-sms-2017-2021-creative-europe-network/.
20. Art.School.Differences [n.d.], accessed April 12, 2022, https://blog.zhdk.ch/artschooldifferences/.
21. Fure, "GRID: Gender Research in Darmstadt," 1.
22. Gender Relations in Darmstadt [n.d.], accessed April 12, 2022, https://griddarmstadt.wordpress.com/.
23. GRiNM, "Maerzmusik Statistics," accessed August 4, 2020, www.grinm.org/20180321%20-%20Märzmusik%20Berlin%20Statistics%20GRiNM.pdf.
24. Darmstädter Ferienkurse [n.d.], accessed February 11, 2020, https://internationales-musikinstitut.de/en/ferienkurse/ueber/info/.
25. GriNM (2019), accessed June 2, 2020, https://grinm.org/.
26. Victoria Armstrong, *Technology and the Gendering of Music Education* (New York and London: Routledge, 2016).
27. Chris Comber, David J. Hargreaves, and Ann Colley, "Girls, Boys and Technology in Music Education," *British Journal of Music Education* 10, no. 2 (1993): 123–34.
28. *female:pressure* [n.d.], accessed June 2, 2020, www.femalepressure.net/.
29. Neil Mercer, *Words and Minds* (New York and London: Routledge, 2000); Karen Littleton, Neil Mercer, Lyn Dawes, Rupert Wegerif, Denise Rowe, and Claire Sams, "Talking and Thinking Together at Key Stage 1," *Early Years* 25 (2005): 167–82; Karen Littleton, Sylvia Rojas-Drummond, and Dorothy Miell, "Introduction to the Special Issue: 'Collaborative Creativity': Socio-Cultural Perspectives," *Thinking Skills and Creativity* 3, no. 3 (2008): 175–76; Vera John-Steiner, *Creative Collaboration* (New York and Oxford: Oxford University Press, 2000); Vera John-Steiner

and Teresa Meehan, "Creativity and Collaboration in Knowledge Construction," in *Vygotskian Perspectives on Literacy Research: Constructing Meaning Through Collaborative Inquiry*, edited by Carol D. Lee and Peter Smagorinsky (Cambridge: Cambridge University Press, 2000), 31–48; Holbrook Mahn and Vera John-Steiner, "The Gift of Confidence: A Vygotskian View of Emotions," in *Learning for Life in the 21st Century*, edited by Gordon Wells and Guy Claxton (Oxford: Blackwell Publishing Company, 2002), 46–58; Elizabeth Dobson, "Permission to Play: Fostering Enterprise Creativities in Music Technology Through Extracurricular Interdisciplinary Collaboration," in *Activating Diverse Musical Creativities: Teaching and Learning in Higher Music Education*, edited by Pamela Burnard and Elizabeth Haddon (London and New York: Bloomsbury, 2015), 75–96.
30. Neil Mercer, *Words and Minds* (New York and London: Routledge, 2000).
31. Mahn and John-Steiner, "The Gift of Confidence'.
32. Feminatronic [n.d.], accessed February 25, 2022, https://feminatronic.com/2015/11/20/event-introduction-to-live-coding-performance-with-shelly-knotts-and-joanne-armitage/.
33. Yorkshire Sound Women Network [n.d.], accessed February 25, 2022, https://yorkshiresoundwomen.com/about/.
34. Yorkshire Sound Women Network [n.d.], here accessed February 25, 2022, https://yorkshiresoundwomen.com/projects/.
35. Heidi Johnson, *Read YSWN's Annual Review* (2019), accessed June 2, 2020, https://yorkshiresoundwomen.com/news/read-yswns-annual-review/.

Bibliography

AEC-SMS (2017–2021). "Creative Europe Network." n.d. Accessed April 12, 2022. https://aec-music.eu/project/aec-sms-2017-2021-creative-europe-network/.
Ahmed, Sara. *Living a Feminist Life*. Durham, NC and London: Duke University Press, 2017.
Archiv Frau und Musik. n.d. Accessed April 12, 2022. www.archiv-frau-musik.de/en/.
Armstrong, Victoria. *Technology and the Gendering of Music Education*. [Place of publication not identified]: Routledge, 2016.
Art School Differences, [n.d.]. Accessed April 12, 2022. https://blog.zhdk.ch/artschooldifferences/.
Beats By Girlz [n.d.]. Accessed February 18, 2022. www.beatsbygirlz.org/.
Born, Georgina, and Kyle Devine, "Music Technology, Gender, and Class: Digitization, Educational and Social Change in Britain." *Twentieth-Century Music* 12, no. 2 (2015): 135–72.
Comber, Chris, David J. Hargreaves, and Ann Colley. "Girls, Boys and Technology in Music Education." *British Journal of Music Education* 10 (1993): 123–34. https://doi.org/10.1017/s0265051700001583.
Darmstädter Ferienkurse, [n.d.]. Accessed June 2, 2020. https://internationales-musikinstitut.de/en/ferienkurse/ueber/info/.
Discwoman [n.d.]. Accessed February 18, 2022. www.discwoman.com/.
Dobson, Elizabeth. "Permission to Play: Fostering Enterprise Creativities in Music Technology Through Extracurricular Interdisciplinary Collaboration." In *Activating Diverse Musical Creativities: Teaching and Learning in Higher Music Education*, edited by Pamela Burnard and Elizabeth Haddon, 75–96. London and New York: Bloomsbury, 2015.
FEM*_MUSIC*_ [n.d.]. Accessed April 12, 2022. www.femmusic.eu/.
female:pressure [n.d.]. Accessed June 2, 2020. www.femalepressure.net/.
female:pressure, "female pressure report 3." 2013. Accessed June 2, 2020. https://femalepressure.files.wordpress.com/2013/03/fempressreport-03-2013.pdf.
Feminatronic [n.d.]. Accessed February 25, 2022. https://feminatronic.com/2015/11/20/event-introduction-to-live-coding-performance-with-shelly-knotts-and-joanne-armitage/.
Fure, Ashley. "GRID: Gender Research in Darmstadt A 2016 HISTORAGE Project Funded by the Goethe Institute." 2016. Accessed June 2, 2020. https://griddarmstadt.files.wordpress.com/2016/08/grid_gender_research_in_darmstadt.pdf.
Gender Relations in Darmstadt. [n.d.]. Accessed April 12, 2022. https://griddarmstadt.wordpress.com/.
Goh, Annie, and Marie Thompson. [n.d.]. Accessed June 2, 2020. https://cargocollective.com/soniccyberfeminisms/about.
GRiNM. 2019. Accessed June 2, 2020. https://grinm.org/.
Johnson, Heidi. "Read YSWN's Annual Review." 2019. Accessed June 2, 2020. https://yorkshiresoundwomen.com/news/read-yswns-annual-review/.

John-Steiner, Vera. *Creative Collaboration* (New York: Oxford University Press, 2000).

———, and Teresa Meehan. "Creativity and Collaboration in Knowledge Construction." In *Vygotskian Perspectives on Literacy Research: Constructing Meaning Through Collaborative Inquiry*, 31–48. Cambridge: CUP, 2000.

Konstmusiksystrar [n.d.]. Accessed April 12, 2022. www.konstmusiksystrar.se.

Littleton, Karen, Neil Mercer, Lyn Dawes, Rupert Wegerif, Denise Rowe, and Claire Sams. "Talking and Thinking Together at Key Stage 1." *Early Years* 25 (2005): 167–82. https://doi.org/10.1080/09575140500128129.

Littleton, Karen, Sylvia Rojas-Drummond, and Dorothy Miell. "Introduction to the Special Issue: 'Collaborative Creativity: Socio-Cultural Perspectives'." *Thinking Skills and Creativity* 3 (2008): 175–76. https://doi.org/10.1016/j.tsc.2008.09.004.

Mahn, Holbrook, and Vera John-Steiner. "The Gift of Confidence: A Vygotskian View of Emotions." In *Learning for Life in the 21st Century*, edited by Gordon Wells and Guy Claxton, 46–58. Oxford: Blackwell Publishing Company, 2002.

Mercer, Neil. *Words and Minds*. London: Routledge, 2000.

PRS. "Keychange." 2017. Accessed June 2, 2020. https://keychange.eu/blog/250-music-organisations-commit-to-keychange-50-50-pledge/.

Scharff, Christina. "Inequalities in the Classical Music Industry: The Role of Subjectivity in Constructions of the 'Ideal' Classical Musician." In *The Classical Music Industry*, edited by Chris Dromey and Julia Haferkorn, 112–27. New York: Routledge, 2018.

Smith, Stacy L., Katherine Pieper, Hannah Clark, Ariana Case, and Marc Choueiti. "Inclusion in the Recording Studio? Gender and Race/Ethnicity of Artists, Songwriters & Producers Across 800 Popular Songs from 2012–2019." 2020. Accessed June 2, 2020. http://assets.uscannenberg.org/docs/aii-inclusion-recording-studio-20200117.pdf.

SoundGirls. "Make It EQL." n.d. Accessed June 2, 2020. https://makeiteql.com/.

Soundgirls.org [n.d.]. Accessed February 18, 2022. https://soundgirls.org/.

University of Sydney. "Composing Women. Nurturing Creativity in Our Composition Students." [n.d.]. Accessed June 2, 2020. www.sydney.edu.au/music/industry-and-community/community-engagement/composing-women.html.

Women's Audio Mission. [n.d.]. Accessed February 18, 2022. https://womensaudiomission.org/.

Yorkshire Sound Women Network. [n.d.]. Accessed February 25, 2022. https://yorkshiresoundwomen.com/projects/.

47

SOUNDING THE FEMINISTS

Campaigning for Institutional Change to Support Women in Music in Contemporary Ireland

Laura Watson

Introduction[1]

Sounding the Feminists (hereafter STF) is a volunteer collective which was established in 2017 to campaign for gender equality and increased representation of women in the music sector (including the educational system, cultural institutions, music industries, and communities) across the island of Ireland.[2] I write from a dual perspective: (1) as a musicologist who studies gender, particularly the systemic marginalisation of women's work in twentieth-century and contemporary Western musical culture; (2) as a cultural insider who is a feminist activist and one of five founding members of the STF Working Group. A similar dual positioning in a specifically gendered context has been extensively theorised by Sara Ahmed in *Living a Feminist Life*. In analysing what it means to operate as 'an academic as well as a diversity practitioner', she focuses on diversity practices within universities.[3] Ahmed's concept of the 'diversity worker' is applicable to many organisational settings. Here, I relocate that figure to another environment. I introduce the 'diversity worker' into institutions dedicated to upholding musical traditions, especially those relating to Western art music. I frame STF as 'diversity practitioners' who seek to integrate equality and diversity as standard considerations in Irish musical life. The STF Working Group believes that feminism must be intersectional and trans-inclusive, while acknowledging that many of us within the movement benefit from the social privileges that accompany white, middle-class, cis identities.

My discussion is motivated by the actions STF has implemented since 2017. In summary, these comprised (1) creating a mission statement; (2) forming partnerships which enabled us to steer research on gender issues in Ireland's contemporary music scene, commission new music by women, organise concerts to promote women composers, and host workshops to support women in the music industries; (3) consulting with public bodies. With this discursive approach, I borrow again from Ahmed's position on the relationality between diversity practice and theory; she argues that 'it is important to theorize from our own embodied work'.[4] As well as theorising the embodied work of STF, this chapter also has more fundamental goals. It is intended to document the origins and some key activities of STF thus far, to bear witness to feminist musical labour which otherwise might not be recorded. Reflecting the history of STF thus far, this labour is often referred to as 'campaigning', 'activism', 'advocacy', and so on.[5] Unconsciously, we appear to have shied away from 'leadership' as a descriptor. Nonetheless,

STF labour constitutes leadership because it has impelled music and arts organisations to adapt their policies and practices so that gender equality is on the agenda.

As a final introductory point, it is crucial to note the social landscape in which the STF movement emerged. It occurred at a unique moment in twenty-first-century Ireland, during a decade when the nation increasingly embraced progressive values. That radical shift was most visible in the passing of legislation for marriage equality and abortion rights. In anticipation of and alongside these developments, pockets of feminist-driven cultural and social activism flourished, creating space that supported collectives such as STF. My study therefore situates the ethos and efforts of STF in relation to a broader stream of political and cultural thought in contemporary Ireland.

Overview of STF's Mission and Public Actions

In mid-2017 the STF Working Group published a mission statement online:

> STF is an Irish-based, voluntary-led collective of composers, sound artists, performers, musicologists, critics, promoters, industry professionals, organisations, and individuals, committed to promoting and publicising the creative work of female musicians.
>
> STF recognises that contemporary attitudes, policies and practices towards music and gender are often built on institutions and traditions that resist change. In solidarity with groundbreaking sister movements such as Waking the Feminists[6], the STF Working Group was established in 2017. We aim to take positive action to improve the representation of women island-wide, who are working in many areas of the music sector. We seek to do so by working with partner groups on the following priority areas:
>
> - To address gender balance issues/intersectional feminism issues across music sectors;
> - To create new systems to promote gender fairness;
> - To build a community where issues of gender can be discussed;
> - To organise and audit areas of the Irish music sector in relation to gender balance;
> - To liaise with educational organisations and institutions throughout the country;
> - To liaise with other international groups such as Fair Play and Female: Pressure;
> - To encourage younger generations of musicians to become involved in these debates.[7]

The 2017 founding Working Group comprised three composers and two musicologists: Karen Power (Chair), Ann Cleare, Amanda Feery (composers); Jennifer O'Connor-Madsen and Laura Watson (musicologists). Over the years, various members stepped back, while a new member, educator Grace Tallon, temporarily stepped in. As of mid-2022, the Working Group consists of Power, Cleare, and Watson. As members' expertise is primarily in art music, STF has been mostly but not solely associated with this genre.[8]

The mission statement has informed STF actions. Starting in August 2017, Working Group members sought meetings with stakeholders such as national music and arts organisations. In parallel to initiating these consultations, we arranged a public meeting at the Irish Music Rights Organisation (IMRO) venue in Dublin city. Open to all concerned with gender inequalities in Ireland's music sector, this event on 13 September 2017 attracted a large gathering, while a livestream broadcast further expanded the audience reach.[9] The meeting was attended by representatives from flagship arts institutions (e.g. the National Concert Hall, Contemporary Music Centre, Irish Traditional Music Archive, IMRO); activists from other gender equality movements (e.g., Waking the Feminists); journalists; and individuals from a range of musical backgrounds (e.g. performers, including IMRO Chairperson and songwriter Eleanor McEvoy, students, independent artists, sound engineers, arts administrators, and instrumental teachers).[10] Lively debate ensued. Audience members spoke about gender bias across a spectrum of creative practices (classical performance, experimental composition, sound art, traditional and folk music, popular music) and adjacent industries (performance venues, media, archives, education). This discussion provided a forum to connect the STF Working Group, the public, and prominent figures from arts and media entities. It empowered the 'ordinary' individual (often a woman) to challenge the powerful decision-maker (often a man), thereby facilitating a type of dialogue that happens all too rarely. The meeting helped shape the agenda that the Working Group brought to its consultations in 2017–18 with stakeholder organisations.

By mid-2018, those conversations had solidified into several partnerships. STF's partner organisations now comprise: two Music Departments in higher education (at Maynooth University and Dundalk Institute of Technology); Irish National Opera (INO); Irish Baroque Orchestra (IBO); Quiet Music Ensemble; ConTempo Quartet; Music Network; and the Contemporary Music Centre (CMC).[11] As detailed here, the CMC collaboration has enabled STF to pursue research into gender inequality in the contemporary art music world. Further to these partnerships, the STF Working Group formed a five-year partnership initiative with Ireland's flagship music institution, the National Concert Hall (NCH). This was a striking development because a controversy associated with the NCH in 2016 had provided the catalyst for founding STF. The initiative was intended to run from 2018–23, but Covid-19 caused major disruption from mid-2020. Furthermore, Simon Taylor, the NCH CEO in situ at the outset of the partnership, retired in January 2021; he was replaced by Robert Read in February 2021. The combination of pandemic disruption and personnel change has had an impact on planned activities. Taylor had listened to criticism of the NCH at the September 2017 public meeting and engaged with STF to address the situation. Together, over the course of several meetings, the Working Group and NCH developed a medium-term, multifaceted strategy to address gender inequality in art music. This proposal was presented to state funders in early 2018. On 7 March 2018, the eve of International Women's Day, the NCH and STF announced a partnership initiative, supported by the Government's Creative Ireland programme.[12] With annual funding of €20,000 from Creative Ireland, a sum matched by the NCH, the amount promised was €200,000 over a five-year period. Intended to 'promote and commission work by female artists', this award represented a political and cultural intervention: perhaps the first explicit national investment in music by women. Speaking about the initiative, Josepha Madigan, Minister for Culture, stated: 'Ensuring equality across all areas of the arts requires not just fine words or putting in place good policies, it requires actions too.'[13] Simon Taylor explained that this initiative:

> sees the NCH embark on an ambitious curatorial and commissioning programme over the next five years in partnership with Sounding the Feminists. We are delighted to be working with Sounding the Feminists to develop and enhance opportunities for female composers and musicians in Ireland, across musical genres.[14]

Both Madigan and Taylor echoed two messages of the STF mission statement: action and collaboration – building communities, mentoring younger generations, fostering professional networks, and support for emerging composers.

Before exploring the NCH-STF schemes in detail, it is important to address contextual questions. Why did political will to support the STF movement emerge in 2018? What is the relationship between STF and other feminist cultural initiatives? How is it that a movement rooted in the world of art music, a niche interest in Ireland, attracted mainstream media attention? It is useful to analyse STF in the context of political discourses c. 2012–18.

Irish Social and Political Influences on STF

The STF movement began in 2016 as a spontaneous, unnamed, collective response to the normalisation of gender discrimination in the music profession in Ireland. The tipping point that provoked loud reaction, especially in art music, was the announcement of the NCH festival *Composing the Island: A Century of Music in Ireland 1916–2016*. The plans for *Composing the Island* magnified at a critical juncture the habitual marginalisation of women in music; for example, in the flagship Friday Night Season Concerts presented by the RTÉ National Symphony Orchestra at the National Concert Hall from 2004 to 2018, 78% of the composers performed were men and only 22% were women.[15] The 2010s were a period of political and social transformation in Ireland, delineated by the onset of recession in 2008 and the repeal of the Eight Amendment in 2018.[16] These years also saw the 2016 centenary of Ireland's Easter Rising – an occasion which generated sustained reflection on Irish history and identity and inspired a series of commemorative events, *Composing the Island* among them. Whereas 2016 was associated with the rise of populism in the UK and USA – the Brexit result and election of Donald Trump – Irish voters had recently endorsed progressive values (such as voting to legalise same-sex marriage) and would continue do so. This represented a radical shift for what was once a socially conservative and religious (predominantly Roman Catholic) country.

In May 2015, the electorate approved a referendum to permit same-sex marriage, thus enshrining marriage equality in law. Three years later, in an even more decisive ballot, voters supported the 'Repeal' referendum – the referendum to repeal the Eighth Amendment in the constitution, an amendment which had outlawed abortion in all circumstances. Within the space of three years, these referenda results transformed the legal status and healthcare rights of individuals who had previously been marginalised, silenced, and shamed. A distinctive quality of these referenda was not only the pro-LGBTQ+ and pro-choice outcomes, but also how these had been achieved. Central to both campaigns were grassroots foundations. Due to successive governments' trepidation about engaging with highly divisive social issues, it was up to the 'ordinary people' to lead, to mobilise local and online communities. These developments, especially the Repeal movement, are relevant to the STF narrative for two reasons: they demonstrated robust support for women's reproductive rights *and* that individuals without privileged access to corridors of power could drive radical change. Both developments created ripple effects empowering those who were striving for gender equality in other ways, including in music.

A significant factor in the Marriage Equality result was a high turnout, which included recent emigrants who had been persuaded to visit home at the time of the referendum for the sole purpose of voting (postal ballots are not available for Irish citizens abroad). The post-2008 economic downturn had caused a spike in emigration, particularly among younger generations. The #HomeToVote campaign ensured that this demographic nonetheless had a voice in the referendum. #HomeToVote exemplifies a grassroots development that empowered people who had been stranded on the peripheries of society to drive its change. #HomeToVote went viral again in 2018. Images of dozens of women in airports wearing 'Repeal' sweatshirts vividly illustrated the impact of online campaigns. As is discussed later, campaigners for gender equality in the arts around this time also used social-media hashtags as part of their strategy.

Without delving too much into the complex discourse surrounding abortion in Ireland, I briefly outline here a few developments from 2012 to 2018 that paved the way towards the Repeal referendum. Again, this narrative is relevant to STF as the movement emerged when a sustained campaign for women's reproductive rights gathered pace and eventually resulted in legislation giving women the right to choose. July 2012 saw the formation of the Abortion Rights Campaign (ARC), a volunteer-led movement which has campaigned for women's reproductive rights across the island of Ireland and organised events such as the annual March for Choice in Dublin city centre, which began in 2012. On 28 October 2012, Savita Halappanavar died of septic miscarriage in a Galway hospital. Upon realising that she was miscarrying, Halappanavar had requested a termination but, in accordance with Irish law at the time, she was denied this due to the presence of a foetal heartbeat. Consequently, she developed sepsis which proved fatal. Her death marked a turning point, leading to nationwide vigils, protests, and international media attention.[17]

In 2013, London-based Irish women formed the 'direct-action feminist performance group', Speaking of IMELDA, aimed at 'breaking down the barriers that prevent [Irish] women from speaking freely about abortion'.[18] A measure of their success is that this conversation migrated from the fringes to the mainstream, as Irish women recounted their abortion experiences. A prominent example included *Irish Times* columnist Róisín Ingle's account of travelling to England for a procedure.[19] Nearly four years after Halappanavar's death, in August 2016, the individuals behind the (now defunct) anonymous Twitter account @TwoWomenTravel live-tweeted the journey of a woman who required an abortion but was forced to travel to England as the procedure remained illegal in Ireland. By 2016, then, the debate about reproductive rights in Ireland was everywhere, from social media commentary to anonymous experiences documented live for public consumption to the publication in mainstream media of harrowing stories from women of all ages and circumstances. In April 2017, the government established a Citizens' Assembly to examine Ireland's abortion laws and the Eighth Amendment. The Citizen's Assembly recommended that abortion should not be regulated by the constitution and that the country should legislate for abortion. In September 2017, Taoiseach (Prime Minister) Leo Varadkar indicated the Government's intention to hold a referendum on repealing the Eighth Amendment in 2018. On 25 May 2018, 66.4% of the electorate who voted supported the proposal to repeal the Eighth Amendment. The repeal of the Eighth Amendment applied only to the Republic of Ireland. Northern Ireland is a separate legal jurisdiction (of the UK), where abortion services remain very restricted.[20]

Feminist Cultural Awakenings in Ireland, 2015–18

In parallel with and sometimes in direct support of pro-choice campaigns, a stream of feminist initiatives flooded Irish culture and media. Journalists, activists, and artists collaborated to imagine and promote a society that valued gender equality. As noted, this occurred when the 1916 commemorations were generating discussion about how the nation viewed itself and how it was regarded across the world. In this section, I review some key feminist cultural initiatives in 2015–18.

Anna Cosgrave founded the Repeal Project in 2016, 'with the intention of opening up a conversation around reproductive rights in Ireland'.[21] Project volunteers conceived various fundraising initiatives to aid Irish-based organisations that supported reproductive rights. The most memorable and effective strategy was the design and sale of a plain black jumper emblazoned with a white REPEAL logo. Cosgrave hoped women would purchase and wear these jumpers 'as statements of solidarity'; their popularity far exceeded her expectations.[22] In April 2017 the Repeal Project hosted an event at the Olympia Theatre, Dublin. Performers traversed genres and generations, from established Celtic folk singer Mary Black to contemporary Afro-folksoul artist Loah. Prominent activists such as Rory O'Neill, AKA drag queen Panti Bliss spoke too. Artists expressed solidarity with a cause which had hitherto been taboo in Ireland. In this respect, the contribution of Mary Black, who had established her career in the more conservative 1980s, is notable. The event was collective and gender-inclusive, featuring people of different ages and backgrounds, from various creative fields.

That ethos of collaboration and dialogue permeates another work inspired by the Repeal campaign. Weeks before the May 2018 referendum, journalist Úna Mullally published *Repeal the 8th*, a 'collection of stories, essays, poetry, art and photography emerging from, and inspired by, the movement for reproductive rights in Ireland'.[23] Mullally (who also spoke at the 2017 Olympia fundraiser) assembled a diverse group of artists and activists: they were predominantly but not exclusively women; they were mostly Irish-born or of Irish heritage, but they also included immigrant citizens. As with the Repeal concert, the voices here span the generations, from that of second-wave feminist icon Nell Cafferty to those of emerging writers. Mullally stresses the 'purposefully inconclusive' nature of the anthology and acknowledges its relation to 'a much larger canon'.[24] Underlining the importance of community and conversation in the struggle for gender rights, she states:

> The awakening of Irish generations is far more rapid now, as information is more accessible and connections can be made with others who are fighting similar battles. Both inspired and immersed in a new wave of feminism, as well as acutely aware of how progress made on women's rights continued to be reduced across the world, the movement for women's reproductive rights in Ireland has taken on an energy that is unstoppable.[25]

The 'rapid' awakening to which Mullaly refers is often facilitated by social media platforms. Such online communities enable democratic conversation and empower leaders to emerge from within. While Mullaly focuses on the movement for reproductive rights, the basic impulse she identifies, the urge to confront misogyny and gender discrimination, had already manifested in the arts world.

Late in 2015, Ireland's national theatre, the Abbey Theatre in Dublin, announced a forthcoming season in 2016 to commemorate the centenary of the Easter Rising. Titled *Waking the Nation*, the season was to feature ten new productions. To the dismay of women working in theatre, however, ninety percent of the new productions were written by men. Furthermore, only two women were named as directors across the season. Fiach Mac Conghail, then artistic director of the Abbey, initially dismissed criticism of women's exclusion from the season with a tweet. In response, theatre-maker Lian Bell and producer Maeve Stone deployed the hashtag #WakingtheFeminists (#WTF) to mobilise dissenting voices.[26] Bell and her colleagues subsequently organised a packed public meeting at the Abbey in November 2015, where dozens of women professionals in the field spoke about their experiences of discrimination. Waking the Feminists dedicated a year to an equality campaign which produced a seismic cultural shift.[27] They secured funding from the Arts Council to commission a gender audit into 'key creative roles in the top ten Arts Council-funded theatre organisations in the country over a ten-year period' (2006–15). The findings, published in *Gender Counts*, verified the existence of stark inequalities.[28] Prior to this, the backlash against *Waking the Nation* drove the Abbey Theatre to publish a Gender Equality Policy. Principles four and five of eight are excerpted here:

> 4. To achieve gender equality in all areas of the artistic programme over the next five years by presenting more work led by female theatre practitioners. Gender equality will be measured in five-year periods starting from 2017. There will be ongoing

flexibility within programming for a given year but over the course of each five-year period the artistic programme will achieve gender balance.
5. The Abbey Theatre commits to gender equality in the play commissioning process.[29]

The policy committed to supporting new and existing work by women, within a given timeframe. These principles plus the *Gender Counts* audit influenced STF.

Waking the Feminists focused on ameliorating professional conditions for women practitioners. STF shares this concern but also works to redress historical exclusion. Hence, the STF mission partly resonates with that of another Irish feminist project instigated in 2016: Herstory. Herstory tells 'the stories of modern, historic, and mythic women'.[30] STF stands in solidarity too with groups such as Mnásome (founded in 2017) and Fair Plé (founded in 2018). Mnásome, 'celebrating badass women in music',[31] focuses on the popular music industry; Fair Plé 'aims to achieve gender balance in the production, performance, promotion, and development of Irish traditional and folk music'.[32] While each tends to be aligned with a specific genre, representatives from these three collectives have collaborated, e.g., in a panel at the 2018 STF Symposium.

STF Origins in the Centenary Commemorations

In May 2016, six months after the #WakingtheFeminists protest, the National Concert Hall in Dublin announced its musical equivalent of *Waking the Nation*. *Composing the Island*, scheduled for September 2016, boasted '27 concerts of orchestral, choral, instrumental, song and chamber music by Irish composers written between 1916 and 2016'.[33] Yet, as observed by composers such as Jane Deasy, Jennifer Walshe, and Ann Cleare, an analysis of the festival programme revealed troubling gender disparities.[34] Cleare and her colleagues compiled statistics about the gender (im)balance as it pertained to categories such as composers, durations of performances, multiple performances of works, and gender representation across genres. The rarity of professional women composers in Ireland in the early twentieth century accounts for men's dominance in older repertoire, although Ina Boyle, Joan Trimble, and Rhoda Coghill were important exceptions to this trend and were represented at the festival with one work each. There was no justification for the marginalisation of women when programming contemporary, living composers. Membership records of relevant bodies indicate that women account for 25–30% of professional Irish composers.[35] Although a minority, *Composing the Island* disproportionately under-represented them. Across the board, only 19% of the works on the originally announced programme were by women; inequalities were more pronounced when data was scrutinised under the other categories mentioned.[36] Similar to how Waking the Feminists originated, it was social-media criticism by composer Siobhán Cleary that sparked a bigger reaction.[37] After initially deflecting Cleary's criticism, the organisers supplemented the festival with a piano recital by Isabelle O'Connell on 21 September 2016, which exclusively comprised repertoire by living women composers.[38] While this remedial action slightly improved the gender balance, it underlined that the marginalisation of works by women had become habitual.

Conversations about gender inequality in music did not die down. Instead, they shifted to a more formal setting – as evidenced by a meeting at the Contemporary Music Centre, Dublin in early 2017 where composers, performers, musicologists, teachers, and administrators voiced their concerns. Acknowledging the inspiration of Waking the Feminists, we agreed to take action under the banner 'Sounding the Feminists'. The term 'sounding' was chosen in preference to 'composing', which carries connotations of specific styles and genres. Attendees at a subsequent meeting in April 2017 elected those of us in the Working Group.

STF Leadership in Action

The most visible STF action was the partnership initiative with the NCH (2018–23). This comprises three strands: (1) annual chamber series; (2) commissioning scheme; (3) new programming. 2018–19 saw the first iteration of Strands (1) and (2). As I worked directly on Strand 1, that is the thematic focus of this section.

NCH-STF Chamber Series

Co-curated by STF Working Group representatives and Simon Taylor of the NCH, the Chamber Series ran in 2018–19 and 2019–20.[39] Each series constituted six concerts hosted by the NCH, usually in the venue's smaller spaces. Curating these series to fulfil the remit of promoting music by women was challenging. It provokes the question of whether such ventures should solely programme music by women *or* programme works by women and men as equals. In 2019–20 NCH and STF decided that the chamber series should exclusively feature music composed by women, whereas in 2018–19 the series had taken a more flexible approach to allow concerts that occasionally presented gender-balanced programmes (i.e., works composed by men as well as women). Why the different approach to the 2019–20 series? Firstly, we sought to programme more women, and this was a rare opportunity to curate a series exclusively comprising compositions by women. With STF better established, it felt safer to take such a 'risk'. This curatorial strategy prioritised *equity* above *equality*: i.e., it recognised that women composers begin at a disadvantage due to centuries of marginalisation and that this status means their work requires additional promotion before there is a chance of levelling the field. Both series were informed by a transhistorical and transnational ethos and featured diverse repertoire. Each spanned works from several centuries, representing composers from Ireland, Britain, Europe, Russia, the USA, and Asia. While both series were rooted in European traditions, they nonetheless demonstrated a heterogeneity of styles in which women have composed.

To present a series in which music by women forms a substantial part is to accept an extra burden of labour for curators and performers. This begins with acknowledging a problem (the absence of women on concert programmes) and continues with the strategising of solutions (such as establishing a women-only or gender-balanced compositional programme). Dialogue with sympathetic performers is essential, as the execution of such projects entails a balancing act between conceptual aspirations and practicalities. To give concerts of minority composers (whether marginalised on account of gender and/or other identity markers) one must overcome hurdles. These may be logistical, such as lack of access to published scores. They may also be cultural, such as limited familiarity with repertoires. Success is contingent upon performers' willingness and availability to engage in the additional labour of tracking down obscure scores and learning new material which may be of niche appeal. Organisations also have the task of coaxing uncertain audiences in the door.

Analysing two NCH-STF concerts, one each from the 2018–19 and 2019–20 series, sheds light on the kinds of programmes which may be produced by different governing principles (the women composers-only principle in 2019–20 and the more flexible gender-balanced principle occasionally evident in 2018–19). On 24 January 2019, pianist Una Hunt, violinist Gillian Williams, and flautist Miriam Kaczor performed a thematic programme of *Belle Epoque* French music. They played repertoire by Mélanie Bonis, Cécile Chaminade, Lili Boulanger, and Claude Debussy.[40] In a broad cultural sense, these composers share much common ground. All four were based in Paris. Bonis, Chaminade, and Debussy were close in age; Boulanger, born in 1893, was a generation younger but died in 1918, the same year as Debussy. This concert illustrated that conceptualising gender-balanced programming is an imprecise, subjective art. After all, three out of the four composers showcased were women – but Debussy, represented by *Syrinx* and the Violin Sonata, had a weightier presence than crude statistics would suggest. Not only is Debussy a canonic figure but his Violin Sonata commands a significant place in his œuvre as one of his last works, while *Syrinx* is central to the solo flute repertoire. A goal of this concert was to promote knowledge and understanding of works by women composers in late nineteenth-century and early twentieth-century France. To do so effectively, we as curators sought to contextualise the chosen figures historically and stylistically in relation to their peers, both women and men. That meant emphasising the musical training, aesthetic sensibilities, and social experiences which linked the four Parisian composers. In the pre-concert talk, I noted, for example, that Bonis and Debussy had studied in the same composition class at the Paris Conservatoire. Further mentioned was the fact that, decades later, Debussy and the much younger Boulanger composed their final scores while battling terminal illness and witnessing the destruction wreaked on France by the First World War.

A concert that exemplified the contrasting all-women 2019–20 series was Andrew Zolinsky's piano recital on 7 November 2019. His programme spanned composers from three centuries and as many continents: he played seventeenth-century Harpsichord Suites by Élisabeth Jacquet de La Guerre; repertoire by modernists Ruth Crawford Seeger and Betsy Jolas; and contemporary works by Katharine Norman, Judith Weir, Linda Catlin Smith, Deirdre McKay, and Unsuk Chin. Zolinsky's brief commentaries underlined artistic (rather than gendered) synergies between these composers. He observed, for example, that Baroque influences in the Weir, Norman, and Jolas scores echoed the opening Jacquet de La Guerre suites. Notably, too, Zolinsky's performances of the Crawford Seeger, Jolas, Norman, and Smith works marked their Irish premieres. That both series featured performances which counted as Irish premieres (even in the case of historical works) is indicative of women's under-representation in live settings.

In deciding whether to curate gender-balanced or all-women programmes, questions arise. Do all-women concerts continue the cycle of isolating these artists as 'women composers' rather than recognising them as 'composers'? Or does the concept of a gender-balanced programme deny some women an opportunity to be heard? How do living composers feel about the gendered presentation of their work? These questions are not easily resolved; nonetheless, it matters that we raise them. After all, to return to Ahmed's theories, 'diversity work is messy'.[41] While the work is 'messy', its rationale is not. Diversity practitioners 'aim to make thought about equality and diversity automatic' and 'must be persistent because this kind of thought is not automatic'.[42] What 'persistence' looks like in the Chamber Series strand is a willingness to experiment with possible programming strategies.

The gender-balanced approach, e.g., performing Bonis and Debussy in the same concert, can start a conversation about how equal promise and early education count for little in misogynistic societies which exclude women from public life. In 1883, Bonis's parents arranged a marriage for her to a much older widower. At twenty-five she became a stepmother to five children and would later bear three more; domestic obligation reined in her creative ambitions for a decade.[43] In contrast, her former classmate Debussy was free to focus on the Prix de Rome composition contest, which he won in 1884. When Lili Boulanger became the first woman awarded that honour in 1913, the competition had only been open to women for a decade. As with Bonis and Debussy, pairing Boulanger and Debussy in the concert hall offers an opportunity to reflect on the social conditions that inhibited women's careers. A 'balanced' approach to programming also orients the audience towards unfamiliar repertoire in a supportive way. To put it in rather binary terms, it maps the unknown figure (the comparatively obscure 'woman composer') in relation to a famous contemporary (the male 'great composer'). This can be useful in normalising the inclusion of works by women in concerts; it can foster expectations that equality and diversity should factor into planning.

When weighing the merits of strategies for increasing women's representation on concert programmes, institutions may be cognisant of wider cultural norms. In Ireland, the Abbey Theatre's post-Waking the Feminists commitment to achieving gender-balanced programming within five years offered a blueprint for other arts organisations. Such a solution may be commercially attractive and therefore more sustainable. Yet, a series solely dedicated to compositions by women has advantages too. Not unlike gender quotas for political parties, such a policy affords women greater access to the public sphere. The resulting diversity of musical styles which an audience may encounter in a single setting (as evidenced in the Zolinsky recital) testifies to a rich, centuries-long tradition of women working as composers. Building a series of such concerts powerfully amplifies this effect. Rationales exist for both gender-balanced and all-women music initiatives. Realistically, preference for one or the other may be influenced by commercial and cultural environments.

Commissioning Scheme

While the Chamber Series is effecting change, one issue which lies beyond its remit is the entrenched notion that large-scale works such as symphonies and operas are, as a rule, the manifestation of a masculine, canonic tradition. In truth, women have long composed major works for large forces. Nonetheless, prestigious institutions such as concert halls are still bastions of patriarchal (and white European) tradition.[44] As a step to counteracting this and with the aim of making a material difference to professional opportunities available to women, the NCH and STF established a Commissioning Scheme. Open to Irish or Irish-resident women composers (cis and trans women), the 2018–19 scheme comprised 'Emerging' and 'Established' categories. Claudia Schwabe and Jennifer Walshe, the respective winners in each category, had new works performed at the NCH. The gendered nature of the call did not deter applicants. The scheme was lauded as a model for other organisations to follow and its application process praised for 'present[ing] as few barriers as possible to anyone interested in applying'.[45]

Leadership Through Data Research, Policy Consultation, and Public Workshops

The *Gender Counts* audit commissioned by Waking the Feminists provided a blueprint for the STF Research Project. Conducted in partnership with the CMC, this project (like the Commissioning Scheme) addresses concerns about professional composition opportunities for women in Ireland. The central research questions are: (1) what was the gender balance in publicly funded composer opportunities on the island of Ireland between 1988 and 2018? (2) How much funding was received by composers during this time frame and what was the status of the work funded (with respect to its duration, scale, and platform)? Phase I, funded by the Arts Council, was completed in 2020 by Research Associate Ciara L. Murphy. Phase I was a scoping project to produce a research methodology for Phase II, conducted by Research Associate Michael Lydon in 2021–2. Upon completion of Phase II, STF made recommendations as to how publicly funded music organisations can enact policies to support gender equality.[46]

The STF Working Group has shown leadership through consultation with government bodies. In late 2018 and early 2019, Working Group representatives participated in a consultation process for the Arts Council of Ireland's new national policy on Equality, Human

Rights, and Diversity. Launched in 2019, the policy lauded STF as an organisation which had highlighted how 'women artists across a range of artistic disciplines continue to encounter serious impediments to advancing their careers'.[47]

Despite the STF Working Group's involvement with bodies such as the NCH, CMC, and Arts Council of Ireland, we remain conscious that STF originated as a grassroots movement by and for women who encounter common barriers to progressing their music careers. To address this, the Working Group partnered with IMRO in 2019 to run three free workshops open to cis women, trans women, and non-binary people. Participants included composers, performers, writers, and teachers at various career stages. Each workshop featured panelists from music, media, academia, and policy, sharing expertise on networking, grant applications, and pitching ideas to producers and editors. Since the 2017 public meeting, many women had expressed a desire to access practical advice which would aid professional development.

Conclusion

I mentioned in the introduction that the STF mission statement shies away from the term 'leadership'. After all, the goal of the movement is to effect change through dialogue and mutual support, with a Working Group elected to volunteer on behalf of the community. Yet, in retrospect, writing a few years later, it is apparent that the Working Group often acts in a leadership capacity. We have initiated actions such as those described here, which have transformed awareness of gender inequality in cultural institutions. These initiatives have improved the historical representation of women in live music settings and facilitated new professional opportunities for living composers and sound artists. STF representatives have contributed expertise to the formation of national policy in the arts. Explicitly naming these actions as 'leadership' (transcending 'activism', 'advocacy', and 'campaigning') seems a meaningful and potent gesture. Formal 'leadership' is traditionally synonymous with authority commanded by individuals who occupy the upper echelons of organisational hierarchies. Leadership, therefore, as an attribute associated with power, ownership, visibility, and exclusivity, is conventionally marked as masculine.

Systemic change, such as desired by the STF movement, cannot happen without leadership. But when the agents of change are primarily women whose work tends to be undervalued by the patriarchal establishment and therefore less visible, leadership looks different to masculinised norms. STF, like Waking the Feminists and the campaign for reproductive rights in the 2010s, emerged as a consequence of conversations and collaborations between social groups (primarily women) who felt disenfranchised. By operating as a collective and focusing on actions that responded to issues aired at public gatherings, STF has valued consensus. As outlined in the mission statement, the Working Group advocates leadership that supports dialogue, community building, and partnership. It has proved a positive development in many ways. Still, this is leadership which, as of 2024, still relies heavily on women's voluntary efforts. It has ironically exacted a cost in unpaid, gendered musical labour. The reality of these circumstances further exemplifies what Ahmed calls the 'messy work' of equality and diversity. Solutions are far from straightforward, but raising awareness is a start.

Notes

1. Thanks to all who have been in the Working Group of Sounding the Feminists, especially Karen Power and Ann Cleare. I am grateful for their feedback on an earlier draft. The views expressed here are my own.
2. *Sounding the Feminists*, 2017, accessed August 14, 2020, www.soundingthefeminists.com/.
3. Sara Ahmed, *Living a Feminist Life* (Durham, NC: Duke University Press, 2017), 93.

4. Ahmed, *Living a Feminist Life*, 102.
5. For discussion of what I theorise as gendered 'equality labour' in music and further commentary on STF, see Laura Watson, "Feminist Musical Activism in Ireland (2016–21) and Feminist Musicology," *Ethnomusicology Ireland* 8 (2023), www.ictm.ie/feminist-musical-activism-in-ireland-2016-21-and-feminist-musicology-laura-watson/.
6. Waking the Feminists is discussed later.
7. *Sounding the Feminists*, 2017, accessed August 14, 2020, www.soundingthefeminists.com/.
8. An example of STF work beyond art music is *Sounding the Feminists Symposium: Women in Popular & Traditional Music in Ireland*. This was co-organised with the Department of Creative Arts, Media, & Music at Dundalk Institute of Technology (November 23, 2018).
9. Sounding the Feminists, Public Meeting, IMRO, Dublin, September 13, 2017, accessed May 20, 2022, www.facebook.com/soundingthefeminists/videos/1320503941410216.
10. For coverage of the meeting, see Toner Quinn, "Sounding the Feminists Hold First Public Meeting," *Journal of Music* (September 25, 2017), accessed August 14, 2020, https://journalofmusic.com/news/sounding-feminists-hold-first-public-meeting.
11. STF "Our Partners," 2018, accessed August 14, 2020, www.soundingthefeminists.com/partners.php.
12. The National Concert Hall and the Department of Culture, Heritage, and the Gaeltacht published the same press release on their websites on March 7, 2018. See: accessed August 14, 2020, www.nch.ie/Online/default.asp?BOparam::WScontent::loadArticle::permalink=Newsroom-STF-NCH-Funding&BOparam::WScontent::loadArticle::context_id=; www.chg.gov.ie/department-of-culture-heritage-and-the-gaeltacht-and-creative-ireland-programme-to-co-fund-national-concert-hall-and-sounding-the-feminists-new-5-year-initiative-to-promote-creative-work-by-female-mu/.
13. Ibid.
14. Ibid.
15. Mark Fitzgerald, "Composing Equality," *Enclave Review*, ER16 (2018), accessed May 20, 2022, http://enclavereview.org/composing-equality/.
16. The Eighth Amendment was a clause added to the Irish Constitution in 1983 which acknowledged 'the right to life of the unborn' and outlawed abortion in all circumstances.
17. Kitty Holland and Paul Cullen, "Woman 'Denied a Termination' Dies in Hospital," *Irish Times*, November 14, 2012, accessed August 14, 2020, www.irishtimes.com/news/woman-denied-a-termination-dies-in-hospital-1.551412.
18. *Speaking of Imelda*, accessed August 14, 2020, www.speakingofimelda.org/.
19. Róisín Ingle, "Why I Need to Tell My Abortion Story," *Irish Times*, September 12, 2015, accessed August 14, 2020, www.irishtimes.com/life-and-style/people/r%C3%B3is%C3%ADn-ingle-why-i-need-to-tell-my-abortion-story-1.2348822?mode=sample&auth-failed=1&pw-origin=https%3A%2F%2Fwww.irishtimes.com%2Flife-and-style%2Fpeople%2Fr%25C3%25B3is%25C3%25ADn-ingle-why-i-need-to-tell-my-abortion-story-1.2348822.
20. For more on abortion services in Northern Ireland, see "Abortion in Northern Ireland: Recent Changes to the Legal Framework," April 27, 2022, https://commonslibrary.parliament.uk/research-briefings/cbp-8909/.
21. "Repeal: A Night in the Key of 8," accessed August 14, 2020, http://olympia.ie/whats-on/repeal-a-night-in-the-key-of-8/.
22. Anna Cosgrave, "Repeal Project," 2017, accessed August 14, 2020, www.her.ie/repeal/repeal-project-founder-anna-cosgrave-repeal-project-is-my-micro-contribution-to-a-movement-spanning-decades-308025.
23. *Repeal the 8th*, edited by Úna Mullally (London: Unbound, 2018). Kindle Edition.
24. Ibid.
25. Ibid.
26. Emer O'Toole, "Waking the Feminists: Re-imagining the Space of the National Theatre in the Era of the Celtic Phoenix," *Lit: Literature Interpretation Theory* 28, no. 2 (2017): 134–152.
27. Mary Moynihan, "How Waking the Feminists Set an Equality Agenda for Irish Theatre," November 22, 2018, accessed August 14, 2020, www.rte.ie/brainstorm/2018/1122/1012586-how-waking-the-feminists-set-an-equality-agenda-for-irish-theatre/.
28. Brenda Donohue et al., *Gender Counts: An Analysis of Gender in Irish Theatre, 2006–15*, June 2017, accessed August 14, 2020, www.artscouncil.ie/uploadedFiles/Main_Site/Content/About_Us/Gender_Counts_WakingTheFeminists_2017.pdf.

29. "Gender Equality Policy," August 30, 2016, accessed August 14, 2020, www.abbeytheatre.ie/gender-equality.
30. *Herstory*, accessed August 14, 2020, www.herstory.ie/home.
31. *Mnásome*, accessed August 14, 2020, https://mnasome.com/about/.
32. *Fair Plé*, accessed August 14, 2020, www.fairple.com/.
33. "Composing the Island: A Century of Music in Ireland," accessed May 20, 2022, https://orchestras.rte.ie/news-press/composing-the-island/.
34. Daragh Kelly, "Composing the Feminists," *TN2 Magazine* (25 September 2016). <www.tn2magazine.ie/composing-the-feminists/> [accessed 14 August 2020].
35. Adrian Smith, "How Sounding the Feminists Put Music and Gender in the Spotlight," *The Journal of Music*, April 11, 2019, accessed August 14, 2020, https://journalofmusic.com/focus/how-sounding-feminists-put-music-and-gender-spotlight.
36. Ibid.
37. Kelly, "Composing the Feminists'.
38. "Composing the Island: New Directions—Isabelle O'Connell, Piano," accessed May 20, 2022, www.journalofmusic.com/listing/04-09-16/composing-island-new-directions-isabelle-oconnell-piano.
39. Due to the Covid-19 pandemic, a 2020–21 series was not viable. For the 2018–19 series, see *NCH Chamber Music Programme, 2018–19*, August 17, 2018, accessed August 14, 2020, https://issuu.com/nationalconcerthall/docs/18_07_02_chamber_music_series_a5_v1. For the 2019–20 series, see *NCH Chamber Music Series, 2019–20*, accessed August 14, 2020, https://issuu.com/nationalconcerthall/docs/nch-chamber-music-programme-19-20?fr=sZmQ3ODcxNTk2.
40. A change in circumstances saw the programme altered from what was originally advertised.
41. Ahmed, *Living A Feminist Life*, 94.
42. Ibid., 96.
43. Christine Géliot, "Mel Bonis Biography," 2009, accessed August 14, 2020, www.mel-bonis.com/melboanglais.htm.
44. For data on the marginalisation of women in concert halls worldwide in 2020–21, see the Donne report *Equality and Diversity in Concert Halls: 100 Orchestras Worldwide* (July 2021), accessed May 20, 2022, https://donne-uk.org/wp-content/uploads/2021/03/Equality-Diversity-in-Concert-Halls_2020_2021.pdf.
45. Michael Dervan, "Keep It Simple: What the Arts Council Can Learn from Sounding the Feminists," *Irish Times*, October 31, 2018, accessed August 14, 2020, www.irishtimes.com/culture/music/keep-it-simple-what-the-arts-council-can-learn-from-sounding-the-feminists-1.3679666.
46. The Phase I report (authored by Ciara L. Murphy) and Phase II Proposal were published in a single document on March 1, 2022, accessed May 20, 2022, www.cmc.ie/news/03012022-1731/cmc-stf-publish-phase-i-scoping-project-report-dr-ciara-l-murphy-and-announce. The final Phase II report by Michael Lydon was published on November 8, 2023. See *Uneven Score*, accessed 25 April 2024, https://www.cmc.ie/sites/default/files/inline-media/cmc_uneven_score_report_v7.pdf.
47. *Arts Council Equality, Human Rights and Diversity Policy and Strategy*, 2, accessed August 14, 2020, www.artscouncil.ie/uploadedFiles/EHRD%20Policy%20English%20version%20Final.pdf.

Bibliography

Ahmed, Sara. *Living a Feminist Life*. Durham, NC: Duke University Press, 2017.
Barry, Aoife. "Abbey Theatre Admits Its 2016 Programme 'Does Not Represent Gender Equality'," November 9, 2015. Accessed August 14, 2020. www.thejournal.ie/abbey-theatre-gender-equality-2433534-Nov2015/.
Cosgrave, Anna. "Repeal Project," 2017. Accessed August 14, 2020. www.her.ie/repeal/repeal-project-founder-anna-cosgrave-repeal-project-is-my-micro-contribution-to-a-movement-spanning-decades-308025.
Dervan, Michael. "Keep It Simple: What the Arts Council Can Learn from Sounding the Feminists." *Irish Times*, October 31, 2018. Accessed August 14, 2020. www.irishtimes.com/culture/music/keep-it-simple-what-the-arts-council-can-learn-from-sounding-the-feminists-1.3679666.
Donohue, Brenda, Ciara O'Dowd, Tanya Dean, Ciara Murphy, Kathleen Cawley, and Kate Harris, "Gender Counts: An Analysis of Gender in Irish Theatre, 2006–15," June 2017. Accessed August 14,

2020. www.artscouncil.ie/uploadedFiles/Main_Site/Content/About_Us/Gender_Counts_WakingTheFeminists_2017.pdf.

Géliot, Christine. "Mel Bonis Biography," 2009. Accessed August 14, 2020. www.mel-bonis.com/melboanglais.htm.

Holland, Kitty, and Paul Cullen, "Woman 'Denied a Termination' Dies in Hospital." *Irish Times*, November 14, 2012. Accessed August 14, 2020. www.irishtimes.com/news/woman-denied-a-termination-dies-in-hospital-1.551412.

Ingle, Róisín. "Why I Need to Tell My Abortion Story." *Irish Times*, September 12, 2015. Accessed August 14, 2020. www.irishtimes.com/life-and-style/people/r%C3%B3is%C3%ADn-ingle-why-i-need-to-tell-my-abortion-story-1.2348822?mode=sample&auth-failed=1&pw-origin=https%3A%2F%2Fwww.irishtimes.com%2Flife-and-style%2Fpeople%2Fr%25C3%25B3is%25C3%25ADn-ingle-why-i-need-to-tell-my-abortion-story-1.2348822.

Kelly, Daragh. "Composing the Feminists." *TN2 Magazine*, September 25, 2016. Accessed August 14, 2020. www.tn2magazine.ie/composing-the-feminists/.

Moynihan, Mary. "How Waking the Feminists Set an Equality Agenda for Irish Theatre," November 22, 2018. Accessed August 14, 2020. www.rte.ie/brainstorm/2018/1122/1012586-how-waking-the-feminists-set-an-equality-agenda-for-irish-theatre/.

Mullally, Úna, ed. *Repeal the 8th*, Kindle ed. (London: Unbound, 2018).

Murphy, Ciara L. "Scoping Project Report: Sounding the Feminists Research Project, in Partnership with the Contemporary Music Centre, Ireland (Phase One)," March 2020. https://www.cmc.ie/sites/default/files/inline-media/stf_scoping_project_-_phase_i_final_report.pdf.

Quinn, Toner. "Sounding the Feminists Hold First Public Meeting." *Journal of Music*, September 25, 2017. Accessed August 14, 2020. https://journalofmusic.com/news/sounding-feminists-hold-first-public-meeting.

Smith, Adrian. "How Sounding the Feminists Put Music and Gender in the Spotlight." *The Journal of Music*, April 11, 2019. Accessed August 14, 2020. https://journalofmusic.com/focus/how-sounding-feminists-put-music-and-gender-spotlight.

Watson, Laura. "Feminist Musical Activism in Ireland (2016–21) and Feminist Musicology." *Ethnomusicology Ireland* 8 (2023). Accessed August 5, 2023. www.ictm.ie/feminist-musical-activism-in-ireland-2016-21-and-feminist-musicology-laura-watson/.

Websites

"Arts Council Equality, Human Rights and Diversity Policy and Strategy." 2. Accessed August 14, 2020. www.artscouncil.ie/uploadedFiles/EHRD%20Policy%20English%20version%20Final.pdf.

"Department of Culture, Heritage, and the Gaeltacht Press Release." March 7, 2018. Accessed August 14, 2020. www.chg.gov.ie/department-of-culture-heritage-and-the-gaeltacht-and-creative-ireland-programme-to-co-fund-national-concert-hall-and-sounding-the-feminists-new-5-year-initiative-to-promote-creative-work-by-female-mu/.

"Fair Plé." Accessed August 14, 2020. www.fairple.com/.

"Gender Equality Policy." August 30, 2016. Accessed August 14, 2020. www.abbeytheatre.ie/gender-equality.

"Herstory." Accessed August 14, 2020. www.herstory.ie/home.

"Mnásome." Accessed August 14, 2020. https://mnasome.com/about/.

"National Concert Hall Press Release." March 7, 2018. Accessed August 14, 2020. www.nch.ie/Online/default.asp?BOparam::WScontent::loadArticle::permalink=Newsroom-STF-NCH-Funding&BOparam::WScontent::loadArticle::context_id=.

"NCH Chamber Music Programme, 2018–19." August 17, 2018. Accessed August 14, 2020. https://issuu.com/nationalconcerthall/docs/18_07_02_chamber_music_series_a5_v1.

"NCH Chamber Music Series, 2019–20." Accessed August 14, 2020. https://issuu.com/nationalconcerthall/docs/nch-chamber-music-programme-19-20?fr=sZmQ3ODcxNTk2.

"Repeal: A Night in the Key of 8." Accessed August 14, 2020. http://olympia.ie/whats-on/repeal-a-night-in-the-key-of-8/.

"Sounding the Feminists." Accessed August 14, 2020. www.soundingthefeminists.com/.

"Speaking of IMELDA." Accessed August 14, 2020. www.speakingofimelda.org/.

INDEX

#EmbraceEquity 274
#HomeToVote 652
#justonewoman 346
#MeToo 579, 601
#playlikeagirl 345
#WakingtheFeminists 654–5

'abayeh 499
Abortion Rights Campaign (ARC) 653
accessibility 376, 381, 439, 560, 616, 622, 637, 639
Acosta Zavala, Kathy xvii, 13, 26–37
activism 3, 8, 13, 14, 33, 118, 334, 338, 346, 370, 564–5, 587, 623–4, 625, 630, 632, 636–7, 644, 645, 649–50, 659
Addio a Napoli (Pratten) 18
Adelstein, Rachel 438, 451–63
advocacy 3, 8, 13–14, 26–7, 220, 221, 333, 334, 335, 338, 339–42, 346, 360, 363–565, 370, 579, 612, 613, 622–3, 626, 630, 632, 642–3, 649, 659
Aguilar, Ananay xvii, 564, 600–11
Al-Badr, Ahmed xvii, 438, 495–508
Albert Palace, Battersea 16
Alhambra Music Hall 16
allyship 5, 343, 345, 360
Almullayeh 498–507
Almulleh 507n22
Alna'i 497, 502–3, 506, 508
Alvarez, Kira xvii, 126, 195–205
Alziwwār 497
American Band College (ABC) 264, 266–8, 270, 272n20
American Guild of Banjoists Mandolinists and Guitarists 28, 34n12, 37
American Guitar Society (AGS) 7, 26, 27, 29–32, 35n18

analysis: constructivist 263; data 334, 395; emancipatory 224; feminist 51; grounded theory 263; intersectional 58; interview 312, 316; leadership 229; musical 13, 93, 96, 100, 103–4, 176, 468, 530, 551–3, 617, 631; network 224; primary/secondary sources 52, 161, 592, 655; qualitative 550, 559; quantitative 550, 559; reception/reviews 38, 73, 595; representation 74; revisionist 67
Anglicanism 449n39, 552, 557
Anglican worship 449n49, 551, 560, 643
April, Elsie 7, 125, 141–50
Arab 204n36, 447n2, 495; Arabic 495, 506; Arabic music 533; Arabic poetry 501, 503, 505
Arbi'ineyeh 497–9, 506
archives 20, 32, 52, 74, 93, 154, 157, 183, 465, 651; International Harp Archives 167; West London Synagogue Archive 441–2; WRPM Archive 629, 631–2
Argentina 154–5, 167, 470–1, 563, 602–4
Arts and Humanities Research Council (AHRC) 620
Arts Council England (ACE) 276, 374, 593, 642
art song: Irish art song 14, 92, 95, 103; Western art song 485
'ashura 496, 497–9, 503, 505, 506
Asociación Uruguaya de Músicos, Uruguayan Association of Musicians (AUDEM) 602
Assessment (in education) 219, 280, 337, 371, 618; calibration 8, 220, 300–2, 303–6; community-based 282; composition 306; group 219; higher education 302–3; inclusive 338; performance 220, 265, 272n14, 272n21, 304; processes 302; self-assessment 361

Association Européenne des Conservatoire (AEC) 638
audiences 16, 40, 43, 47, 57, 67, 129, 130, 135–7, 155, 171, 174–6, 252, 293, 313, 334, 340, 363, 374–6, 383, 391–2, 403, 413, 415, 416, 422, 423, 425–8, 458, 471, 477, 483, 495, 498, 500, 502, 506, 512, 515, 524, 528, 532, 564, 575, 580, 582, 583, 619, 637, 643, 651; communicate to 243; critical 244; demand from 159; diplomats/dignitaries 202; diversification/reach 316, 369, 374, 381–2, 650, 656, 657–8; music-hall 185, 188; the role of 595–7; salons 68–9, 73, 590, 591, 592, 594, 597–8; taste 156; working-class 84, 89n44, 145
Australia 2, 41, 42, 214, 531, 570, 640
Austria 2, 52–6, 564
awards 207, 366, 518, 637; educational 617; honorary 93, 137–8

Baird, Kenneth 125, 127–40
Banjo World (periodical) 17
Baptist 8, 438, 471, 509–19
Barnby, Joseph 16
Baylis, Lilian 125, 127–40
Beeton, Mrs 20
Berkley, Rebecca 220, 321–32
Bernard, Andrès 170
Bertolani, Valentina 334, 386–400
Bliss, Abi 564, 636–48
Blumenthal, Jacob 16
Bone, Philip 18, 30
Booth, Evangeline 437, 520–427; 'I Bring Thee All' 525
Booth, Jane 219, 235–47
Boulanger, Lili 82, 614, 615, 628, 657
Boulanger, Nadia 66, 68, 70, 84, 125, 172, 176, 183, 189, 628; *Pièce pour orgue sur des airs populaires flamands* 84
boundaries 20, 28, 38, 108, 118, 207, 236, 337, 376, 377, 426–7, 453, 464, 480, 495, 590, 592–4, 597
Bowes, Melanie 220, 309–20
Branger, Jean-Christophe 126, 183–94
Brazil 2, 154, 155, 161, 167, 275, 467, 564, 602, 603
Bristol, Fifth Earl and First Marquess of 15
British Broadcasting Corporation (BBC) 6, 92, 93, 94, 149, 632; BBC Concert Orchestra 92; BBC Northern Ireland 207; BBC Orchestras 207; BBC Philharmonic 209; BBC Proms 136, 206, 279; BBC Radio 1, 6; BBC Radio 3, 345, 626, 633; BBC *Tonight* 527
British Theatre 131, 141, 142, 199
Bruce, Abigail 220, 274–89
Brunelli, Eva 172, 183
Buddhism 406, 437, 484–91

Cadi Sulumuna, Temina 126, 167–82
Cage, John 403, 417, 419; 4'33" 403
Calero-Carramolino, Elsa 13, 107–23
campaign/campaigning 13, 27, 31, 81, 276, 283, 386, 394, 440, 546, 547, 601, 604–5, 608, 649, 652–9
Cantors 437, 451–60
care 514
Carelli, Emma 7, 125, 126, 153–61
Cathedral 344, 510, 529, 550–1, 553, 556, 560; Anglican 541–7; Christ Church 558; Ely 338; St Paul's 527
Ceili bands 220, 248–51
Central Trust for the Redemption of Penalties by Work (CTRPW) 110
ceremonies 495, 496
challenges 8, 17, 39, 96, 130, 195, 200, 206–7, 210, 211, 223, 225, 237, 250, 263, 264, 269–71, 275, 279, 281, 290, 293, 302, 313, 324, 326, 328, 350, 354, 358, 367, 371, 376, 378, 402, 408, 416, 451, 458, 460, 484, 486, 531, 560, 564, 582–583, 600–9, 622, 631, 636, 645
chamber music 38–47
chamber music classes 168
chamber music concerts 84, 175, 388
chamber music performance 13
chamber music programming 386, 591, 655
Chaminade, Cécile 13, 14, 65–75, 84, 176, 277, 614, 628, 656
Chants 368, 484–5, 486–91, 495, 496, 497
Chappell, Arthur 16
Characteristic Fantasia (Francia) 18
Chevillard, Camille 172, 173
Clarke, Rebecca 629
Clarke, Sarah 13, 15–25
Clayton, Lady 18
Clayton, Tahira 564, 579–89
coaching 8, 145, 219, 235–47, 322, 326–7, 333, 336, 354, 416, 563
collectives 2, 8, 14, 337, 344, 346, 363–5, 606, 624, 636–7, 645, 650, 655; *see also* Gender Relations in New Music; Sounding the Feminist
Colombia 438, 464–80, 608
Colonne, Jules 172–3
Colonne, The Orchestre 82
community: American Jewish 201; Anglican 441; band 29, 263, 521; -based 249; Bronx 517; Buddhist 483–4, 487–91; building 219, 650, 659; cathedral 547, 560; Ceílí 253; choir 220, 321, 458, 521, 622; cultured 202; development 254–5; engagement 280–2; faith 511, 514, 516–19; interest company 642–5; jazz 579, 583, 586–7; Jewish 440, 441, 442, 459; leaders 278; learning 328; local 473; music 251, 638; Muslim 495–6; non-profit

636–7; opera 376, 382, 383, 388; practice 72, 118, 221, 250, 321–8, 341; professional 315, 457, 618, 642; run 604; salon 54, 590, 591, 596; services 520; spaces 341; student/university 248, 618, 630; theatre 142; workshops 401–29
conduction 420, 421–5, 428–9
conductors/conducting 53, 54, 69, 110, 125–6, 133, 137, 141, 185, 197, 200, 219–21, 248, 253, 337, 386, 389, 570–7; Alsop, Marin 1; Barbosa, Elena Romero 107; Bernstein, Leonard 198; Bickford, Zarh Myron 32; Chailly, Riccardo 388; Clavé, Aurea Rosa 107; Collingwood, Lawrance 131; Erdberg, Helen Victoria Rubin 125, 126, 183; Flor, Claus Peter 388; Ganz, Wilhelm 45; Golinkin, Mordechai 195; Kazanova 7, 125–6, 183–9; Macatsoris, Christofer 200; madame conductor 57; maestro 2; male 85, 277; Martinez, Odaline de la 125, 126, 206–15, 279; Norman, Ludwig 41; orchestral 126, 344; Rattle, Simon 340; Renié, Henriette 167–82, 183; role 2, 7; Schipek, Madame 16; training 321–8, 350–1; wind band 261; women 85, 107, 125, 250, 275, 290–7, 339, 351, 394, 420, 421–5, 428–9, 543–4, 567–9; Xian, Zhang 388; Zubeldía, Emiliana de 107; *see also* Leibinger, Cathi; MacDonald, Sarah
confidence 8, 176, 215, 219, 223, 238, 240, 245, 251, 254–5, 282, 303, 306, 322–7, 336, 341, 344, 346–7, 350, 353, 361–2, 370, 489, 531, 546, 575, 585, 587, 615–16, 641, 643, 645; self- 255, 280
Contemporary Music Centre (CMC) 650, 651, 655
Contemporary Music for All (COMA) 628
Cook, Jane 219, 235–89
Costa Rica 465, 478–9, 513, 602, 603, 604
Council for the Encouragement of Music and the Arts (CEMA) 134
Cox-Williams, Briony 564, 590–9
creative practice 422, 456, 592, 640, 651
creativity 302, 341, 366, 451, 452–5, 457–9, 520, 551, 590, 592, 597, 641
Cristofaro 18
Cuba (Cuban) 2, 126, 207, 208, 210, 469, 532, 563, 602, 603, 604, 608

Darwin, Carola 125, 126, 206–18
deep listening 245, 420
de Philippe, Edis 7, 125, 126, 195–202
dictatorship 108, 111, 112–13, 160, 337, 339
Dienes-Williams, Katherine 437, 438, 541–9, 551
Dilling, Mildred 169, 170, 174
dish imbellileh ('I enter the shrine wet') *Leṭmeyeh* 504
distribution 622–5, 627

diva 153–7, 160, 587
Dobson, Eddie 564, 636–48
Doyle, Enya H. L. 437, 438, 541–9
Dublin 92, 94, 96, 310, 338, 650, 653, 654, 655
Dubois, Théodore 168

early career 70–1, 93, 280, 315, 321–32, 335–6, 343, 349, 637
ecclesiology 520, 521, 533
EDI, equality diversity and inclusion 338, 618
EDIMS, Equality, Diversity and Inclusion Music Studies Network, UK 564, 612, 618–19, 622
education: higher education 1, 4, 220, 235, 250, 278, 282, 291, 300–6, 313–15, 317, 321, 617–19, 631, 642, 651; pupils 19, 323; re-education 109–11, 118
Egerton, Lady Beatrice 18
Egerton, Lord 18
Ekery, Amanda 564, 579–89
embodiment 254, 317, 407, 420, 568, 570
empowerment 65, 67, 279, 376, 416, 445, 625, 630, 632
England 2, 4, 13, 15, 38–47, 71, 94, 127, 135, 167, 211, 282, 438–40, 541, 547, 550, 551, 553, 593, 624, 636, 653
English National Opera (ENO) 125, 127, 137, 374, 378
Equity 335, 358, 362, 370, 565, 579, 615, 617, 618, 642, 656; *see also* gender, equity
Essex and Cammeyer (Publisher) 17
Etches Jones, Elizabeth 334, 374–85
Evans, Maude 19
Evensong 550, 551–2, 556
Evrard, Jane 172, 183, 189
exclusion (systemic) 14, 19, 250, 251, 293, 352, 367, 386, 390, 544, 550–62, 579–89, 638, 654, 655

Farnham, Alice 335–57
Farnsworth, Brandon 564, 636–48
fascism 108, 153, 154, 160
Federación Uruguaya de Músicos, Uruguayan Federation of Musicians (FUDEM) 602
female instrumentalists 85–6, 585
feminism 4, 5, 73, 79, 80, 83, 84, 109, 249, 290, 456, 468, 523, 601, 613, 623, 625, 632, 641, 649, 650, 654; Black feminism 580
Feminist musicology 3, 51, 68
fin-de-siècle 14, 65, 68, 79, 82, 83, 86, 101, 183
Finland 2, 167
Fisher, Henry 19
Flood, Margaret 220, 261–73
Florida Bandmasters' Association (FBA) 262–3
Fournier, Bertile 170
France 2, 7, 65–74, 79–86, 126, 167–8, 172, 173, 183, 184, 563, 657
Francia 18

Index

Francois, Judith 219, 223–34
francoism 108–12, 119
Fremantle, Elizabeth (Betsey) 15
Friend, Hilary xxix, 564, 613, 614, 622–35
Fuor di Parigi (Pratten) 16

Gabriel, Colonel Arnold 267
Gates, Dorothy 438, 439, 521, 530–7; *Hope* 533–7
gender: constructs 274–5, 277, 281, 283; disparity 96, 220, 274, 278, 291, 292–3, 294, 567, 613; equality 274, 276, 280–1, 353, 382, 383, 386, 437–8, 450, 600–9, 613, 614, 637, 638, 649, 650, 652–5, 658; equity 34, 125, 348, 360, 361, 368, 369, 586, 643; identity 386, 471, 637, 642; parity 141, 274, 277, 280, 281, 283, 360, 366, 376, 378, 382, 383
Gender Relations in New Music (GRiNM) 564, 636–42, 645
Gender Research in Darmstadt (GRID) 638
Germany 2, 8, 67, 108, 134, 174, 185, 196, 202, 263, 408, 444, 563, 637, 639, 640
Girls Rock London (GRL!) 280
Gluch, Nicky 564, 567–78
Golinkin, Mordechai 195–202
Gordon, Home 17
Granados, The 16
Grandjany, Marcel 168
Grantham, Hannah 564, 579–89
grass-roots 8, 14, 336, 339–46, 354
Grindley, Ann 14, 65–78
Guildhall School of Music 19, 235, 401
Guitar Societies 13, 26–34
Gurland, Allison 334, 358–73

Hallé, Charles 16, 40, 41
Hamer, Laura 1–12, 13–14, 69, 71, 74, 79–91, 125–6, 127–40, 219–21, 333–4, 335–57, 437–8, 563–5, 615
Hamilton, Katy 335–57
Hanckel, Katherine 220, 290–9
harp ensemble music: Quatuor de Harpes de Paris 170; Renié, Henriette 84, 125, 126, 167–82, 183
Haughton, Emma 335–57
Hawes, Fred 19
Help Musicians (HMUK) 280
Herliczka, Gertrud 172, 183
Hervey, Augusta 7, 13, 14, 15–25
Hervey, Cecilia, (Lady William), née Fremantle 15
Hervey, Lady Mary 16
higher education *see* education
Hijab 499, 510
Hinestrosa, Maruja 437, 438, 464–82; *Ave Maria* 476; *Boleros* 464, 467, 470, 471; *Cafetero* 477; *Eco lejano* 472; *Reproche* 471; *Todos llevamos una cruz* 472; *Yaguarcocha* 470
historical narratives 125, 141, 394
historiography 52, 66
Holmès, Augusta 176, 594
Howells, Herbert 92, 96, 97, 98, 100, 101, 103; 'Girl's Song' 93, 96, 97, 98, 100, 101
Hussein 495–8, 501, 503, 505, 506

Ibos, Jean 174
Ibos, Marie-Thérèse 174
Ickworth House 15
Il Gondolira (Pratten) 18
Imam 496
impresaria 203n2
improvisation 245, 334, 390, 401, 402, 404, 406, 411, 412–16, 420–23, 424–29, 502, 503, 587, 617; The Improvisers' Choir [TIC] 404, 414, 417, 420–27; 'Land Mass' 414, 420; Vocal Tai Chi 418–19, 420, 421, 423, 426, 427, 428; *see also* conduction
interfaith 455
intern 335, 359, 362, 363, 369, 622, 630
International Federation of Musicians [FIM] 600–1, 603, 607–8
International Guitar Research Archive (IGRA) 27, 32
Iraq 2, 437, 438, 495–508, 533
Ireland 2, 6, 8, 92–104, 207, 219, 249, 250, 251, 281, 310, 563, 565, 638, 649–59; National Concert Hall 338, 565, 650, 651, 652, 655
Irish Baroque Orchestra (IBO) 651
Irish Music Rights Organisation (IMRO) 650
Irish National Opera (INO) 651
Israel 2, 8, 195–202, 533, 640
Israel National Opera (INO) 126, 195–202
Israel Philharmonic Orchestra (IPO) 195
Italy 2, 18, 108, 154, 157, 158, 159–61, 167, 184, 333, 386–96, 640
Itha terdoon ('If you wish') Leṭmeye 501

Jewish: Anglo-Jewish 438, 439–46; Kabbalah 571–2; Liturgy 452, 453, 454, 456, 459; Worship 439, 441
Johnson, Heidi 564, 636–45
Johnson Quinn, Arianne 125–6, 141–50
Joystrings, The 526–30; 'A Starry Night' 529
Judaism 8, 437, 443, 454, 510

Karbala 438, 495–8, 502, 503, 506
'Kazanova et Ses Tziganes, La' 183
Kingston University xxix, 616, 617–18
Koivisto-Kaasik, Nuppu 14, 51–64
Kol Isha 440, 441, 456, 457, 458, 459

Ladies Choir 17
Ladies' Guitar and Mandoline Band 15–17

Index

Ladies' Orchestras 51–8
Ladies' String Band 17
La Presle, Jacques de 169
Latin America 113, 148, 275, 438, 465, 467, 468, 470, 563, 564, 600–11
leadership: choral 219, 321–8, 544; development 240; education 3, 619; ensemble leadership 219, 253; industry 359; management 4, 5, 8, 125, 322, 341, 362, 363, 569; musical 1–5, 8–9, 13–14, 125–6, 219–20, 248, 249, 255, 262, 334, 335–455, 358, 370, 428, 437–8, 518, 541–2, 545, 547, 551, 565, 613, 620, 622; women in 2, 235, 236, 323, 338, 343, 378, 521; women's leadership 3, 7, 9, 13, 67, 212, 220, 224, 225, 236, 316, 338, 438, 521, 563, 564, 600–11, 615
Le Dentu, Odette 170, 175
Leibinger, Cathi 220, 261–71
Lesemann-Elliott, Caroline 438, 550–62
Leslie, Henry 16
Lesprit-Maupin, Jacqueline 167, 170, 171, 173, 174
Leṭmeyeh 499–501, 504–6
Loo, Fung Chiat 438, 483–93
Loo, Fung Ying 438, 483–93
Lovell, Rosanna 564, 636–48
Lyon, Gustave 175

MacDonald, Sarah 335–57
Mahayana 483, 487, 489, 490
Majalis 497
Malaya 2
Malaysia 2, 483–94
Mandatory Palestine 195–6, 199
Maqtel 497, 505, 506
Markow, Elizabeth 334, 358–73
Martinez, Odaline de la 7, 125, 126, 206–18, 279
Martin, Major John 438, 520–40
Mascagni, Pietro 153, 154, 156, 157–9, 161
McCabe, Jessy 276, 335–57, 632
mentoring 5–7, 8, 333, 336, 342–5, 354, 364, 366, 368, 616, 620, 621, 656; peer 325; role models 5–7
Mesa Martinez, Luis Gabriel 438, 464–82
Mexico 2, 167, 196, 465, 563, 602, 603, 604
Milan 154, 158, 159, 161, 334, 386–400
Minors, Helen Julia 1–12, 13–14, 125–6, 219–21, 333–4, 335–57, 426, 429, 437–8, 563–5, 612–21, 622–35
Mocchi, Walter 153, 154–61
Montesquiou, Odette de 170
Moore, Rebekah E. 334, 358–73
mourning 412, 440, 497–9, 502, 503, 505, 506
Muʿāwiyah 496
Muḥarram 496–9, 504, 505–6

music: chamber 13, 38–45, 47, 84, 168–9, 174, 175, 386–400, 591, 655; choral 459, 550–60; classical 2, 3, 52, 84, 155, 195–6, 201, 202, 220, 276, 277, 283, 290, 292, 362, 374, 380, 391, 406, 409, 518, 579, 595, 636, 637; contemporary classical music 636, 637; jazz 27, 183, 184, 185, 250, 276, 280, 338, 362, 369, 390, 413, 420, 453, 521, 564, 579–89 626; new music 66, 209, 252, 395, 416, 421, 458, 487, 559–60, 564, 613, 636–41, 649; popular music (pop) 4, 6, 13, 17, 27, 276, 304–5, 359, 368, 437–8, 465, 467, 469, 475, 480, 484–91, 615, 632, 651, 655; sacred 8, 437–8, 444–5, 452, 495–508, 509–19, 551; symphonic 111
musical theatre 7, 141–50, 159, 483, 485, 488; see also British Theatre
Music Commission Report (MCR) 280
music education: access to 1; awarding gap 564, 617, 618; classroom musicianship 322, 323, 328; group tuition/teaching 8, 309–18; instrumental tuition 39; marking assessments 220, 300–6; pedagogy 282, 291, 294–5, 296, 309–10, 314, 318, 322, 323, 324, 328, 351, 584; recitals 303; see also education, higher education
music industries 333–4, 335–57, 358–9, 563–5, 612, 618, 622–3, 649
Music Mentor Network (MMN) 269
Music Teachers' National Association (MTNA) 27
Muslim 438, 495–6, 509–10, 514, 517, 519
Myers, Margaret 16, 17

Najaf 496, 503
National Association for Music Education (NAfME) 262, 584
National Student Opera Society (NSOS) 375
Newell, J. E. 19
New Music Company (NMC) 338–9, 348
'New Women'/'femmes nouvelles' ('New Woman'/'femme nouvelle') 18, 79, 82, 129
New Zealand 2, 42
nineteenth century 2, 5, 7, 13, 28, 38–9, 42, 43, 47, 54, 67–8, 71, 83, 85, 129, 184, 186, 439, 443, 445, 452, 465, 530, 541, 552, 568, 590, 595
Non-profit Organisation 281
Norman-Neruda, Wilma 7, 13, 38–47
Northern Ireland 92, 93, 94, 95, 207, 281, 542, 653
Norway 2

Office for Students (OfS) 300, 301
Ooi, Imee 437, 438, 483–93
Open University, The xxix
Opera: choruses 33; in English 131, 132, 135, 136; industry 8, 379, 382, 383; innovation 374–84; institutions 7, 379; repertoire 376
Oxford Collegiate Anglican Choirs 550–60

Index

Padley, Danielle 437, 438, 439–50
pandemic 9, 301, 318, 350, 364, 368, 370, 514–16, 579, 597, 618, 651
Paoletti, Matteo 126, 153–66
Paraguay 2, 333
Paris Conservatoire 41, 42, 82, 85, 168, 657
Parvin Steward, Theresa 437, 438, 509–19
patriarchal 8, 14, 51, 54, 57, 58, 66, 95, 160, 250, 293, 382, 479, 543, 594, 644, 645, 658, 659
pedagogy *see* music education
Performance Rights Society (PRS) 210, 277, 281, 342, 386, 424, 608, 637, 645; Keychange 637
Peru 2, 167, 469, 563, 602, 603, 604
Petite Caisse des Artistes (Little Fund for Artists) 126, 174
Phillips, Michelle 220, 300–8
Phoenix Green Amateur Mandoline and Guitar Ladies' Band 17
Pierné, Gabriel 84, 169, 170, 173
Pires, Shannon 334, 358–73
Poland 2, 639, 640
politics 3, 39, 47, 79, 86, 93, 107, 109, 153, 154, 156, 195–205, 224, 279, 336, 352, 468, 571, 583, 591, 613
Potpourri Espagnol (Zerega) 18
Powell, Bella 13, 38–50
power hierarchies 51, 57, 58
Pratten 18
Pratten, Catharina 16, 18, 19; *Bolero* 18
prejudice 38–50, 110, 214, 224, 390, 394, 441, 464, 469, 471, 523, 583, 608
prisons 391, 529; Franco's prisons 7, 13, 107–23
programming: concert programmes 167, 175, 176, 656, 658; festival programme 639, 655
Prophet Muhammad 495, 496, 516
protest 113, 159, 368, 515, 653, 655
Puccini, Giacomo 153, 154, 158–9, 161

Queen, The (newspaper) 17
Queen-bee syndrome 343
Queen Elizabeth Hall 409, 532
Queensland Symphony Orchestra 567
Queen's Music, Master of 552, 554
Queen Victoria 16, 65, 71
quotas 347, 348, 604, 605, 607, 609, 639, 641, 658

Raidió Teilifís Éireann (RTE) 93, 652
Rempp Verrey, Caroline 170
Renié, Henriette *see* conductors/conducting; harp ensemble music
Renié, Jean-Émile 168
repeal 155, 652, 653, 654
resistance 7, 13, 14, 51–2, 56–8, 108, 112, 113, 118, 249, 250–1, 254, 291, 295, 296, 417, 542, 632, 645

revisionist research 66, 67, 68
Roditi, Jenni 334, 401–36
role model 5–7, 8, 212, 220–1, 226, 276, 277–83, 291, 293–6, 309–13, 316–18, 324, 334, 337, 339, 341, 342–5, 354, 361–2, 367, 445, 528, 531, 564, 565, 585, 615, 630
Roussel, Albert 167
Rudd, Philip 16, 17

sacred musician 438, 509–19
Saint James's Hall 16
Saint-Saëns, Camille 167
salon culture *see* audiences, salons
sanctity 483–91
Santacesaria, Luisa 334, 386–400
Sassoon, Reuben 18
Schipek, Madame 16
Schubert, Franz 45, 86, 458, 459, 473, 475; *Ellens dritter Gesang* 473, 475
Scotland 2, 322, 444, 542
sect 495, 496
self-reflection 325, 361, 616, 617
Shannon, Orla 13, 14, 92–106
Shaw, George Bernard 43, 135
Shīʿah 437, 438, 495–508
Sindicato Argentino de Músicos, Argentinian Musicians' Union (SADEM) 602
Sindicato de Músicos, Compositores y Cantantes del Perú, Union of Musicians, Composers and Singers of Peru (SIMCCAP) 602
Sindicato dos Músicos Profissionais do Estado do Rio de Janeiro, Union of Professional Musicians of the State of Rio de Janeiro (SINDMUSI) 602
Sindicato Único de Trabajadores de la Música, Union of Music Workers (SUTM) 602
Slade, Miss 18
social media 333, 366, 376, 487, 488, 489, 490, 514, 515, 547, 604, 618, 644, 653, 654
Società Teatrale Internazionale (STIN) 153, 154, 155
soft leadership 406, 438, 483, 486, 487, 489, 491
soft power 202
Sounding the Feminist (STF) 565, 638, 649–62
Spain 2, 8, 13, 14, 18, 107–13, 184, 187, 571
Sparks, Paul 15, 16
spirituality 8, 437, 443, 454, 512, 513, 516, 572
Sri Lanka 2
Stafford House 17
Steinway Hall 18
Stephens-Himonides, Cynthia 220, 309–20
Strawberry Hill 20
Sullivan, Arthur 16
Sullivan, Maud 18, 19
Sullivan, Maxine 580, 583
Sullivan Prize 92
Sunnah 496

Sutherland, Duke of 17
Synagogues 159, 438, 439–44, 451–3, 456, 457
System of Redemption of Penalties by Work (SRPW) 110

Taking Race Live 564, 612, 617–19
teacher training 311, 321
Teatro Costanzi 126, 153, 158
Thomas, Charles 19
Tiri Tomba (Pratten) 16
trade unionism 80
Trimble, Joan 7, 13, 14, 92–106, 629, 655; 'Girl's Song' 97, 99, 100, 101, 102, 103
Troubadour, The (periodical) 19
twentieth century 3, 13, 14, 17, 26, 27, 29, 33, 39, 47, 66, 82, 93, 103, 125, 126, 127, 138, 148, 154, 161, 167, 172, 184, 214, 275, 393, 451, 460, 478, 479, 523, 552, 570, 581, 655

U.F.P.C. (Union des Femmes Professeurs et Compositeurs de Musique) 7, 13, 14, 79–86
underrepresentation of women 275, 278, 290, 291, 293, 294, 296, 297, 343, 392, 563
Unión de Escritores y Artistas de Cuba, Union of Writers and Artists of Cuba (UNEAC) 602
Unión de Trabajadores de la Música, Guild of Music Workers (UTM) 602
United Nations Educational, Scientific and Cultural Organization (UNESCO) 393, 604
Urso, Camilla 7, 13, 38–47
Uruguay 2, 470, 563, 601–4

Varennes, Françoise des 167, 170, 172–3, 174
Veloce, Stellan 564, 636–48
Vencatasamy, Davina 335–57
Victorian 13, 15, 16, 129, 143, 437, 439–46, 520, 551, 557
violence 51, 268, 291, 370, 579, 580, 581, 583, 603; gendered violence 51–8, 602, 604, 605
voice: faculty voice 358–73; liberated voice (see also improvisation); women's 437, 444, 456, 614

Waldegrave, Lady 20
Wales 2, 4, 18, 542, 630
Watson, Laura 565, 649–62
Wedamulla, Chamari 220, 274–89
Weigold, Peter 618
Whitfield, Sarah K. 126, 141–52
Widor, Charles-Marie 173
Wiener Damen-Capelle Maiglöckchen 51, 53
Wilson, Eleanor (Ellie) 335–57
women: Viennese Lady Orchestra 16; woman orchestras 85, 172; women composers 6, 13, 65–71, 82, 96, 104, 107, 142, 275, 294, 339, 346, 348, 386, 389–90, 392, 393–4, 457, 464, 468, 531, 532, 551, 552–60, 564, 604, 613, 614–15, 622, 628–9, 631, 637, 649, 655, 656, 657, 658; women conductors (see conductors); women musicians 3, 14, 42, 54, 57, 72, 73, 74, 79–86, 108, 126, 142, 168, 189, 250, 292, 296, 297, 465, 551, 579, 582, 615, 624, 625, 629, 630, 633; women music teachers 14, 79, 322; women's Choirs (see Ladies Choir)
Women Cantors' Network (WCN) 438, 455, 456, 457–9
Women's Liberation Music Workshop (WLMW) 625
Women's Revolutions Per Minute (WRPM) xxix, 564, 612–15, 619, 622–35
womyn 627
worship 8, 392, 437–8, 439–46, 451, 453–6, 473, 485, 510–19, 520–1, 531, 542, 551, 554, 560

Yazid 496, 497
Yorkshire Sound Women Network (YSWN) 636, 641–5
York St John University xxix, 624, 629
Young, Margaret 220, 309–20

Zaynab 497, 501, 503
Zerega 18
Zi, Lao 483, 486, 489

Milton Keynes UK
Ingram Content Group UK Ltd.
UKHW011556121224
451979UK00024B/112